The Family, Law and Society

Cases and Materials

The Family, Law and Society
Cases and Materials

Brenda M. Hoggett, MA (Cantab.)
of Gray's Inn, Barrister
Reader in Law, University of Manchester

David S. Pearl, MA, LLB, PhD (Cantab.)
of Gray's Inn, Barrister
Fellow and Director of Studies in Law
Fitzwilliam College, Cambridge
University Lecturer in Law

London
Butterworths
1983

England	Butterworth & Co. (Publishers) Ltd.,
	88 Kingsway, LONDON WC2B 6AB
Australia	Butterworths Pty Ltd., SYDNEY, MELBOURNE,
	BRISBANE, ADELAIDE and PERTH
Canada	Butterworth & Co. (Canada) Ltd., TORONTO
	Butterworth & Co. (Western Canada) Ltd., VANCOUVER
New Zealand	Butterworths of New Zealand Ltd., WELLINGTON
Singapore	Butterworth & Co. (Asia) Pte. Ltd., SINGAPORE
South Africa	Butterworth Publishers (Pty) Ltd., DURBAN
U.S.A.	Mason Publishing Co., ST. PAUL, Minnesota
	Butterworth Legal Publishers, SEATTLE,
	Washington; BOSTON, Massachusetts; and
	AUSTIN, Texas
	D and S Publishers, CLEARWATER, Florida

ISBN hc 0 406 59591 7
     sc 0 406 59590 9

Typeset by Colset Private Limited, Singapore.
Printed and bound in Great Britain
by Billing & Sons Limited, Worcester.

Preface

The aim of this book is to introduce the student of family law to a far wider range of material than is to be found in the statutes and law reports or even in a conventional law library. We believe that family law can no longer be studied through the conventional analysis of legal rules and principles alone, but must be placed in a broader context. During the past three decades, not only in this country but throughout the western world, the law has been abandoning the strict regulation of family relationships in favour of much greater, and usually discretionary powers of intervention should those relationships fail. Much of what the law is trying to do is highly controversial. We have therefore tried to select materials which will explain how the law came to be as it is, the context in which it operates, and what might be done to improve it. We have relied not only upon legal writings from this and other countries but also upon work in other disciplines, principally history, sociology and social administration.

The originator of the book was Stephen Cretney, sometime Fellow of Exeter College, Oxford and now a Law Commissioner. He withdrew from the project on his appointment to the Law Commission. We cannot pretend that he would have written the same book as we have done, but we hope that it has retained something of its origins, if only in that we have included many extracts from Law Commission publications both before and during his time. Many of our colleagues and friends have helped us in the preparation of the book, usually without knowing it, but we should particularly like to thank Kevin Gray, Larry Poos, Andrew Grubb and Jane Kenrick (none of whom, needless to say, is responsible for any errors which occur in the book). We had often heard stories of the wonders of the Butterworths staff, and we should like to express our considerable appreciation of them. Above all, however, we must thank our families, and particularly our children — Julia, Julian, Daniel and Marcus — for putting up with a great deal and contributing so much to their parents' understanding of a subject in which we are all involved.

We handed the manuscript to the publishers on 24 October 1982, but have been able to incorporate a number of recent developments at proof stage. Others, such as the consolidation of the matrimonial homes legislation and the numerous minor amendments to child care legislation contained in the Health and Social Services and Social Security Adjudications Bill, are still in the pipe-line. The text was written on the assumption that the remaining provisions of the Children Act 1975 relating to adoption would all have been implemented and replaced by the corresponding provisions of the Adoption Act 1976. We therefore refer to the provisions of the 1976 Act, although at present those which are in force are still contained in the 1975 Act. Subject to that, however, we have tried to state the law as at the date of this preface.

We have enjoyed writing this book and have learned a great deal in the process. We can only hope that those who read it will gain as much pleasure from it as we have done.

Brenda Hoggett, Manchester
David Pearl, Cambridge

24 March 1983

Contents

Table of statutes

References in this Table to Statutes are to Halsbury's Statutes of England (Third Edition) showing the volume and page at which the annotated text of the Act will be found. Page references printed in bold type indicate where the Act is set out in part or in full.

List of cases

Pages on which cases are principally treated are indicated by the use of bold figures.

Bibliography
[Asterisks indicate works from which extracts have been quoted.]

Chapter 1

* O. Aberle, U. Bronfenbrenner, E. Hess, O. Miller, D. Schneider and J. Spuhler, 'The Incest Taboo and the Mating Pattern of Animals' (1963) 65 American Anthropologist pp. 15, 16.
* M. Anderson, *Approaches to the History of the Western Family (1500–1914)* (1980) London and Basingstoke, Macmillan, pp. 40, 51, 69.
* M. Anderson (ed.), *Sociology of the Family* (1980) Harmondsworth, Penguin Books, p. 81.
* J. Beattie, *Other Cultures* (1964) London, Cohen and West, p. 125.
  L.K. Berkner, 'Peasant household organization and demographic change in Lower Saxony (1689–1766)' in R.D. Lee (ed.), *Population Patterns in the Past* (1977).
  A. Bradney, 'The Family in Family Law' (1979) 9 Family Law 244.
* Central Statistical Office, *Social Trends 12* (1982) London, HMSO, chart 2.12.
* F. Engels, *Origins of the Family, Private Property and the State* (1st edn., 1884) New York, Lawrence and Wishart, p. 244.
* R. Fletcher, *The Family and Marriage in Britain* (1966) Harmondsworth, Pelican Books, pp. 26–27, 128 (3rd edn., 1973).
* M.A. Glendon, *State, Law and Family* (1977) Amsterdam, North Holland, pp. 25, 26, 114.
* E.K. Gough, 'The Nayars and the Definition of Marriage' (1959) 89 Journal of the Royal Anthropological Institute pp. 23, 32.
* W.J. Goode, *World Revolution and Family Patterns* (1963) The Free Press, a Division of Macmillan Publishing Company, p. 41.
* C.C. Harris, *The Family: an introduction* (1979) London, Allen and Unwin, p. 49.
  J. Jackson, *The Formation and Annulment of Marriage* (2nd edn., 1969) London, Butterworths.
* T.E. James, 'The English Law of Marriage' in R.H. Graveson and F.R. Crane (eds.), *A Century of Family Law* (1957) London, Sweet and Maxwell, pp. 32–33.
* P. Laslett and R. Wall, *Household and Family in Past Time* (1972) Cambridge, Cambridge University Press, pp. 28–30, 63, 64.
* E.R. Leach, 'Polyandry, Inheritance, and the Definition of Marriage' (1955) Man, no. 199, p. 183.
* Law Commission, Report on *Nullity of Marriage*, Law Com. No. 33 (1970) London, HMSO, paras. 51–54.
* Law Commission, Report on *Solemnisation of Marriage*, Law Com. No. 53 (1973) London, HMSO, paras. 14–16.
  B. Malinowski, *The Sexual Life of Savages* (1929) (3rd edn., 1932) London, Routledge and Kegan Paul.
  A. MacFarlane, *Origins of English Individualism: the family, property and social transition* (1978) Oxford, Blackwell.
* K. Meselman, *Incest* (1979) New York, Jessey Bross, p. 24.
* L. Mair, *Marriage* (1971) Harmondsworth, Pelican Books; (1977) London, Scolar Press, p. 19.
* A. Oakley, *Housewife* (1974) London, Allen Lane; (1976) Harmondsworth, Pelican Books, pp. 236–237.
* A. Raeburn, 'Incest', *Cosmopolitan*, January 1980, p. 26.
* E. Shorter, *The Making of the Modern Family* (1975) New York, Basic Books; (1977) London, Fontana Books, p. 38.
* L. Stone, *The Family, Sex, and Marriage in England 1500–1800* (1977) London, Weidenfeld and Nicholson, pp. 26–27, 102–104.

L.A. Tilly, 'Individual lives and family strategies in the French Proletariat' (1979) Journal of Family History (IV).

C. Winberg, 'Population Growth and Proletarianization' in S. Akerman et al. (eds.), *Chance and Change* (Odense University Studies in History and Social Sciences, Vol. 52). (1978) Odense, Odense University Press.

R. Wall (ed.), *Family Forms in Historic Europe* (1983) London, Edward Arnold.

Chapter 2

S. Brownmiller, *Against our Will*, (1975) London, Secker and Warburg.

* Criminal Law Revision Committee, *11th Report* (Cmnd. 4991) (1972) London, HMSO, para. 147.

* Criminal Law Revision Committee, *Working Paper on Sexual Offences* (1980) London, HMSO, paras. 32 et seq.

J. de Montmorency, 'The changing status of a married woman' (1897) 13 LQR 187.

* Equal Opportunities Commission, *The Taxation of Husband and Wife: Response of the Equal Opportunities Commission to the Government Green Paper* (1981) Manchester, Equal Opportunities Commission, paras. 10 et seq.

* M.D.A. Freeman, 'But if you can't rape your wife, whom can you rape?' (1981) 15 Family Law Quarterly, 17–21.

* R. Graveson, 'The Background of the Century' in R.H. Graveson and F.R. Crane (eds.), *A Century of Family Law* (1957) London Sweet & Maxwell, pp. 2–3.

* Inland Revenue, *The Taxation of Husband and Wife* (Cmnd. 8093) (1980) London, HMSO, paras. 14 et seq. 31–41, 83–85.

J. McFadyen, 'Interspousal rape: the need for reform' in J.M. Eekelaar and S.N. Katz (eds.), *Family Violence: An International and Interdisciplinary Study* (1978) Toronto, Butterworths, p. 193.

S. Maidment, 'The law's response to marital violence: a comparison between England and the USA' in J.M. Eekelaar and S.N. Katz (eds.), *Family Violence: An International and Interdisciplinary Study* (1978) Toronto, Butterworths, p. 110.

A. Medea and K. Thompson, *Against Rape* (1974) London.

* C.A. Morrison, 'Tort' in R.H. Graveson and F.R. Crane (eds.), *A Century of Family Law* (1957) London, Sweet and Maxwell, pp. 91–93.

R.I. Parnas, 'Judicial response to intra-familial violence' (1970) 54 Minnesota Law Review 584.

* *Report of the Committee on One-Parent Families* (Chairman: The Hon. Sir Morris Finer) (Cmnd. 5629) (1974) London, HMSO, paras. 6.88–6.90.

O. Stone *Family Law* (1977) London, Macmillan.

* J. Temkin, 'Towards a modern law of rape' (1982) 45 MLR 405.

* *The Oregonian* (Rideout v Rideout), 20, 27 December 1978; 11 January 1979.

G.L. Williams, 'The Legal Unity of Husband and Wife' (1947) 10 MLR 16.

Chapter 3

M. Benston, 'The political economy of women's liberation' (1969) Monthly Review.

* E. Clive, 'Marriage: an unnecessary legal concept' in J.M. Eekelaar and S.N. Katz (eds.), *Marriage and Cohabitation in Contemporary Societies: Areas of Legal, Social and Ethical Change* (1980) Toronto, Butterworths, pp. 72–74.

L. Comer, *Wedlocked women* (1974) Leeds, Feminist Books.

* Council of Europe, European Commission of Human Rights, *Decision as to admissibility*, cases 9214/80, 9473–81, 9474/81 (1982).

W.B. Creighton, *Working women and the law* (1979) London, Mansell.

N. Dennis, F. Henriques and C. Slaughter, *Coal is our life* (1956) London, Eyre and Spottiswoode.

* Sir M. Finer and O.R. McGregor, 'The History of the Obligation to Maintain'. App. 5, *Report of the Committee on One-Parent Families* (Cmnd. 5629-I) (1974) London, HMSO, para. 36.

J. Gardiner, 'Women's domestic labour' (1975) New Left Review No. 89.

∗ H. Gavron, *The Captive Wife* (1966) London, Routledge and Kegan Paul, Harmondsworth, Penguin Books, pp. 90–94.

G. Gorer, *Sex and Marriage in England Today* (1971) London, Nelson.

A. Gray, *The Working Class Family as an Economic Unit* (1974) University of Edinburgh, Ph.D. Thesis.

∗ M.A. Glendon, *State, Law and Family* (1977) Amsterdam, North Holland, p. 75.

J. Harrison, 'Political economy of housework' (1974) C.S.E. Bulletin.

Inland Revenue, *The Taxation of Husband and Wife* (Cmnd. 8093) (1980) London, HMSO, tables 1–3.

J. Jephcott, N. Seear, and J. Smith, *Married Women Working* (1962) London, Allen and Unwin.

∗ A. Honoré, *The Quest for Security: Employees, Tenants, Wives* (1982) London, Stevens, p. 62.

∗ Law Commission, *Matrimonial Proceedings in Magistrates' Courts* Working Paper no. 53 (1973) London, HMSO, paras. 7–11, 24, 35, 37–43.

∗ Law Commission Report on *Matrimonial Proceedings in Magistrates' Courts*, Law Com No. 77 (1976) London, HMSO, paras. 1.12, 2.12–2.13, 2.17, 2.19–2.20, 2.60–2.61, 2.8.

H. Land, *Large Families in London* (1969) London, G. Bell & Sons.

W. Masters and V. Johnson, *Human Sexual Response* (1966) London, J. & A. Churchill Ltd.

∗ J.G. Miller, *Family Property and Financial Provision* (2nd edn., 1983) London, Sweet and Maxwell, p. 313.

P. Morton, *Women's work is never done* (1970) London, Leviathan.

∗ K. O'Donovan, 'Should all maintenance of spouses be abolished?' (1982) 45 MLR 431.

A. Oakley, *Subject women* (1980) Harmondsworth, Penguin Books.

∗ Office of Population Censuses and Surveys, *Family Formation Survey* (1979) London, HMSO.

∗ J. Pahl, 'Patterns of money management within marriage' (1980) 9 Journal of Social Policy 313, pp. 316–319.

S. Rowbotham, *Women's Consciousness, Man's World* (1973) Harmondsworth, Penguin Books.

∗ *Report of the Committee on One-Parent Families* (Chairman: The Hon Sir Morris Finer) (Cmnd. 5629) (1974) London, HMSO, paras. 4.386, 4.67–68.

∗ *Report of the Royal Commission on Marriage and Divorce* (Chairman: Lord Morton of Henryton) (Cmd. 9678) (1956) London, HMSO, paras. 1042–1046.

W. Secombe, 'The housewife and her labour under capitalism' (1974) New Left Review No. 83.

∗ J. Todd and L. Jones, *Matrimonial Property* (1972) London, HMSO, paras. 4.0–4.2.

E.P. Thompson, *The History of the Working Class* (1963) Harmondsworth, Penguin Books.

E.P. Thompson, *The Making of the English Working Class* (1968) Harmondsworth, Penguin Books.

∗ L. Tilly and J. Scott, *Woman, Work and Family* (1979) New York, Holt, Rinehart and Winston, pp. 21 et seq. 105, 123, 124.

∗ E. Wilson, *Women and the Welfare State* (1977) London, Tavistock, p. 176.

∗ L. Weitzman, 'Legal regulation of marriage: tradition and change.' (1974) 62 California Law Review 1169.

M. Young, 'Distribution of income within the family' (1952) 3 British Journal of Sociology 303.

∗ M. Young and P. Willmott *The Symmetrical Family* (1973) London, Routledge and Kegan Paul (1980) Harmondsworth, Penguin Books, pp. 28 et seq.

F. Zweig, *The Workers in the Affluent Society* (1961) London, Heineman.

Chapter 4

* Central Statistical Office, *Social Trends 12* (1982) London, HMSO, table 8,10.

* Central Statistical Office, *Social Trends 13* (1982) London, HMSO, table 8.1.

   M.D.A. Freeman, 'Towards a Rational Reconstruction of Family Property Law' [1972] Current Legal Problems 84.

   W. Friedman (ed.), *Matrimonial Property Law* (1955), University of Toronto. Comparative Law Series, 2, London, Stevens.

   K. Gray *Reallocation of Property on Divorce* (1977) London, Professional Books.

* O. Kahn-Freund, *Matrimonial Property: where do we go from here?* Joseph Unger Memorial Lecture, University of Birmingham, (1974) pp. 11, 20–21, 22, 23, 25, 46–47.

* Law Reform Commission of Canada, *Family Property*, Working Paper No. 8 (1975) Ottowa, Information Canada, pp. 9–10, 18, 19–22, 27.

* Law Commission, *Family Property Law*, Working Paper No. 42 (1971) London, paras. 0.12, 0.13, 0.15, 0.16, 0.25–0.29, 0.37–0.41.

* Law Commission, *First Report on Family Property: A New Approach* Law Com. No. 52 (1973) London, HMSO, paras. 21–24, 38, 41, 44, 47–59.

   Law Commission, *Second Report on Family Property: Family Provision on Death.* Law Com. No 61 (1974) London, HMSO.

* Law Commission, *Third Report on Family Property: The Matrimonial Home (Co-ownership and Occupation Rights) and Household Goods* Law Com. No. 86 (1978) London, HMSO, paras. 1.111–1.119 fn. 77.

* Law Commission, *Property Law: The implications of Williams and Glyn's Bank Ltd v Boland* Law Com. No. 115 (1982) London, HMSO, paras. 67, 72, 112, 114.

   H. Lesser, 'The acquisition of inter vivos matrimonial property rights in English law' (1973) 23 University of Toronto Law Journal 148.

* Sir Jocelyn Simon *With all my wordly goods* Holdsworth Club, Presidential Address, University of Birmingham (1964), pp. 1–4, 8–9, 10–13, 14–17, 100, 101, 102, 103.

* J. Todd and L. Jones, *Matrimonial Property* (1972) London, HMSO, p. 102.

Chapter 5

   R. Benedict, *Patterns of Culture* (1934) Boston, Houghton, Mifflin.

   E. Bergler, *Divorce Won't Help* (1948) New York, Harper.

* Central Statistical Office, *Social Trends 13* (1982) London, HMSO, chart 2.18. Source: Eurostat *Demographic Statistics 1980*.

   R. Chester, 'Divorce and Legal Aid: A False Hypothesis' (1972) 6 Sociology 205.

   R. Chester (ed.), *Divorce in Europe* (1978) Leiden, Martin Nijhoff.

   E. Clive, *The Divorce (Scotland) Act 1976* (1976) Edinburgh, Green.

* G. Davis, A. Macleod and M. Murch, 'Special Procedure in Divorce and the Solicitor's Role' (1982) 12 Family Law 39, pp. 39, 43–44.

   J. Dominian, 'Families in Divorce' in R.N. Rapoport, M.P. Fogarty and R. Rapoport (eds.), *Families in Britain* (1982) London, Routledge and Kegan Paul.

   E. Elston, J. Fuller and M. Murch, 'Judicial Hearings of Undefended Divorce Petitions' (1975) 38 MLR 609.

* Sir Morris Finer and O.R. McGregor, 'The History of the Obligation to Maintain' App. 5, *Report of the Committee on One-Parent Families* (Cmnd. 5629–1) (1974) London, HMSO, paras. 1, 2, 4, 5, 6, 13, 14, 17, 18, 30, 31, 34, 42, 43.

* C. Foote, R.J. Levy and F.E.A. Sander, *Cases and Materials on Family Law* (2nd edn., 1976) Boston, Little, Brown and Company, pp. 1073–1091.

* M.D.A. Freeman, 'Divorce without Legal Aid' (1976) 6 Family Law 255, pp. 257–259.

   P.A. Garlick, *Judicial Separation: Manchester Research.* (1982) University of Manchester.

   C. Gibson, 'The Effect of Legal Aid on Divorce in England and Wales, Part I: Before 1950' (1971) 1 Family Law 90.

C. Gibson and A. Beer, 'The Effect of Legal Aid on Divorce in England and Wales, Part II: Since 1950' (1971) 1 Family Law 122.

C. Gibson, 'The Association between Divorce and Social Class in England and Wales' (1974) 25 British Journal of Sociology 79.

C. Gibson, 'Divorce and the Recourse to Legal Aid' (1980) 43 MLR 609.

J. Haskey, 'The Proportion of Marriages ending in Divorce' (1982) 27 Population Trends 4.

J. Jackson, *Formation and Annulment of Marriage* (2nd edn., 1969) London, Butterworths.

H.H. Kay, 'A Family Court: The California Proposal' (1968) 56 California Law Review 1205, pp. 1218–1219.

∗ Law Commission, *Reform of the Grounds of Divorce — The Field of Choice* (Cmnd. 3123) (1966) London, HMSO, paras. 11, 15, 19, 52, 120.

∗ Law Commission, *Time Restrictions on Presentation of Divorce and Nullity Petitions*, Working Paper No. 76 (1980) London, HMSO, paras. 39, 40, 47, 48, 50, 52, 62, 64, 88.

∗ Law Commission, Report on *Time Restrictions on Presentation of Divorce and Nullity Petitions* (Law Com. No. 116) (1982) London, HMSO, paras. 2.14, 2.15, 2.27, 2.30, 2.31, 2.33.

∗ Law Society, Family Law Sub-Committee, *A Better Way Out: suggestions for the reform of the law of divorce and other forms of matrimonial relief; for the setting up of a Family Court; and for its procedure* (1979) London, the Law Society, paras. 33, 35–38, 40, 42, 44, 46–52, 58, 69, 70.

Law Society, Standing Committee on Family Law, *A Better Way Out Reviewed* (1982) London, the Law Society.

B.H. Lee, *Divorce Law Reform in England* (1974) London, Peter Owen.

∗ R. Leete, *Changing Patterns of Family Formation and Dissolution in England and Wales 1964–1976* OPCS Studies on Medical and Population Subjects No. 39 (1979) London, HMSO, tables 36, 38, figures 19, 20.

Lord Chancellor's Department, *Judicial Statistics — Annual Report 1980* (Cmnd. 8436) (1981) London, HMSO.

O.R. McGregor, *Divorce in England — A Centenary Study* (1957) London, Heinemann.

S. Maidment, *Judicial Separation — A Research Study* (1982) Oxford, Centre for Socio-Legal Studies.

B. Mortlock, *The Inside of Divorce* (1972) London, Constable.

Office of Population Censuses and Surveys, OPCS Monitors FM2 Series, Marriages 1980, FM2 82/2, Divorces 1980, FM2 82/1 (1982) London, OPCS.

F. Pollock and F.W. Maitland, *The History of English Law Before the Time of Edward I* (2nd edn., 1898) Cambridge, Cambridge University Press.

∗ Report of a Group appointed by the Archbishop of Canterbury (Chairman: The Rt. Rev. R.C. Mortimer, Lord Bishop of Exeter), *Putting Asunder — A Divorce Law for Contemporary Society* (1966) London, Society for Promoting Christian Knowledge, paras. 17, 18, 45(f), 55, 69.

∗ *Report of the California Governor's Commission on the Family* (1966), quoted in H.H. Kay, 'A Family Court: The California Proposal' (1968) 56 California Law Review 1205, pp. 1218–1219.

∗ *Report of the Committee on One-Parent Families* (Chairman: The Hon. Sir Morris Finer) (Cmnd. 5629) (1974) London, HMSO, paras. 4.29–4.32.

Report of the Royal Commission on Divorce (Chairman: Lord Gorell) (Cd. 6478) (1912) London, HMSO.

Report of the Royal Commission on Marriage and Divorce (Chairman: Lord Morton of Henryton) (Cmd. 9678) (1956) London, HMSO.

M. Rheinstein, *Marriage Stability, Divorce and the Law* (1972) Chicago, University of Chicago Press.

L. Rimmer, *Families in Focus* (1981) London, Study Commission on the Family.

∗ St. Mark, 'Gospel according to St. Mark' *Holy Bible* Authorised King James version, ch. 10.

Sir Jocelyn Simon, 'Recent Developments in the Matrimonial Law' Riddell lecture, 1970. Printed in *Rayden on Divorce* (11th edn., 1971) London, Butterworths.

Society of Conservative Lawyers, *The Future of Marriage — A Report by a Research Sub-Committee* (1981) London, Conservative Political Centre.

B. Thornes and J. Collard, *Who Divorces?* (1979) London, Routledge and Kegan Paul.

L. Tottie, 'The Elimination of Fault in Swedish Divorce Law' in J.M. Eekelaar and S.N. Katz (eds.), *Marriage and Cohabitation in Contemporary Societies: Areas of Legal, Social and Ethical Change* (1980) Toronto, Butterworths.

* United States' National Conference of Commissioners on Uniform State Laws, *Uniform Marriage and Divorce Act* (1970), s. 305.

W. Wadlington, 'Divorce Without Fault Without Perjury' (1966) 52 Virginia Law Review 32.

L. Weitzman and R.B. Dixon, 'The Transformation of Marriage through No-Fault Divorce — The Case of the United States' in J.M. Eekelaar and S.N. Katz (eds.), *Marriage and Cohabitation in Contemporary Societies: Areas of Legal, Social and Ethical Change* (1980) Toronto, Butterworths.

* J.M. Westcott, 'The Special Procedure — One Year Later — A Practitioner's View' (1978) 8 Family Law 209, pp. 212–213.

Chapter 6

M. Anderson, 'Family, Household and the Industrial Revolution' in M. Anderson (ed.), *Sociology of the Family* (1980) Harmondsworth, Penguin Books.

L. Baillyn, 'Career and family orientation of husband and wife' (1971) Human Relations 23, pp. 97 et seq.

J. Bernard, *The Future of the Family*, (1972) New York, World.

G. Brown and T. Harris, *Social Origins of Depression: A Study of Psychiatric Disorder in Women* (1978) London, Tavistock.

A. Campbell, P.E. Converse and N.L. Rodgers, *The Quality of American Life* (1976) New York, Russell Sage Foundation.

E. Chen and S. Cobb, 'Family Structures in relation to Health and Disease' (1960) 12 Journal of Chronic Diseases 544.

R. Fein, 'Men and Young Children' in J. Pleck and J. Sawyer (eds.), *Men and Masculinity* (1974) Englewood Cliffs, New Jersey, Prentice Hall.

* G. Douglas, 'The Clean Break on Divorce' (1981) 11 Family Law, pp. 42–43, 45, 48.

* Sir Morris Finer and O.R. McGregor, 'The History of the Obligation to Maintain', App. 5, *Report of the Committee on One-Parent Families* (Cmnd. 5629–I) (1974) London, HMSO, paras 26–27, 32–33, 35–38.

D. Gowler and K. Legge, 'Dual Worker Families' in R.N. Rapaport, M.P. Fogarty, and R. Rapaport (eds.), *Families in Britain* (1982) London, Routledge and Kegan Paul.

E. Granseth, 'Work sharing: a Norwegian experience' in R.N. Rapoport and R. Rapoport (eds.), *Working Couples* (1978) London, Routledge and Kegan Paul.

M. Greenberg and N. Morris, 'Engrossment: newborn's impact upon the father' (1974) 44 American Journal of Orthopsychiatry 520.

N. Guttentag and S. Salasin, *Women, Men and Mental Health* (1975) Paper presented to Aspen Conference on Women.

L. Hoffman and F. Nye, *Working Mothers* (2nd edn., 1978) New York Jossey-Bass.

P. Laslett, *The World We Have Lost* (2nd edn., 1971) London, Methuen.

J. Mortimore, *Dual-career families — a sociological perspective* (1977) Conference Papers, Minnisota.

P. Moss and I.P. Lewis, *Young children in the inner city* (1979) London, HMSO. (T. Coram Research Unit — Pre-school project)

A. Oakley, *The Sociology of Housework* (1974) London, Martin Robertson.

A. Oakley, 'Corventional Families' in R.N. Rapaport, M.P. Fogarty, P. Rapoport (eds.), *Families in Britain* (1982) London, Routledge and Kegan Paul.

S. Orden and M. Badburn, 'Dimensions of marriage happiness' (1968) 74 Journal of Sociology 715.

R.N. Rapoport, R. Rapoport and Z. Strelitz, *Fathers, Mothers and Others* (1977) London, Routledge and Kegan Paul.

R.N. Rapoport and R. Rapoport (eds.), *Working Couples* (1978) London Routledge and Kegan Paul.

R.N. Rapoport and R. Rapoport, 'The impact of work on the family' in P. Moss and N. Fonda (eds.), *Work and the Family* (1980) London, Temple Smith, pp. 172 et seq., 177.

R.N. Rapoport and R. Rapoport, 'Dual career families: progress and prospect' (1978) Marriage and Family Review.

C. Redican and G. Mitchell, *Male Parental Behaviour in Adult Rhesus Monkeys* (1972) Paper presented to Western Psychological Association, Portland, Oregon.

Report (Final) of the Royal Commission on Legal Services (Cmnd. 7648) (1979) London, HMSO, vol. 1, para. 13.64.

H. Ross and I. Sawhill, *Time of Transition: the Growth of Families headed by Women* (1975) Washington, Urban Institute.

R. Rutter, *Maternal Deprivation Reassessed* (1972) Harmondsworth, Penguin Books.

C.B. Rypma, 'Biological basis of the Paternal Response' (1979) The Family Co-ordinator.

K. Walker, (1979) Paper presented to the Annual Conference on Family Relations, Boston.

M. Weissman and E. Paykel, *The Depressed Woman* (1974) Chicago University of Chicago Press.

A. Wilensky, 'Women's work, economic growth, ideology and structure' (1968) 7 Industrial Relations 235.

Chapter 7

P. Bohannan, in P. Bohannan (ed.), *Divorce and After* (1970) Garden City New York, Doubleday, pp. 48–49.

R. Deech, 'The principles of maintenance' (1977) 7 Family Law 229, pp. 230–232.

R. Deech, 'Financial relief: the retreat from precedent and principle' (1982) 98 LQR 621.

J.M. Eekelaar and M. Maclean, *Financial arrangements on Divorce* (1982) Paper presented to the International Society of Family Law, Harvard University.

D. Freed and H. Foster 'Divorce in the fifty states: an overview as of August 1st 1979' (1979) 5 Family Law Reporter.

M.A. Glendon, *The New Family and the New Property* (1981) Toronto, Butterworths, pp. 52 et seq., 57–58

K. Gray, *Reallocation of Property on Divorce* (1977) London, Professional Books.

The Guardian, Letter dated 9 September 1982.

W.M. Harper, *Divorce and Your Money* (1979) London, Allen and Unwin.

Law Commission, *The Financial Consequences of Divorce: the Basic Policy: a Discussion Paper* (Cmnd. 8041) (1980) London, HMSO, paras. 24–28, 59, 66, 70, 73, 75, 77, 80, 84, 86.

M. Maclean and J.M. Eekelaar, *Children and Divorce: Economic Factors* (1983) Paper presented to the British Association for the Prevention and Study of Child Abuse and Neglect, Cambridge.

Law Commission, *The Financial Consequences of Divorce* (Law Com No. 112) (1982) London, HMSO, para, 17.

K. O'Donovan, 'The principle of maintenance: an alternative view.' (1978) 8 Family Law 180–184.

Report of the Committee on One-Parent Families, (Chairman: The Hon. Sir Morris Finer) (Cmnd. 5629) (1974) London, HMSO, table 5.1.

* The Scottish Law Commission, *Report on Aliment and Financial Provision* Scot. Law Com. 67 (1981) Edinburgh, HMSO, paras. 3.18–3.23, 3.62–3.68, 3.72–3.110.
* L. Weitzman and R. Dixon, 'The alimony myth: does no fault divorce make a difference?' (1980) 14 Family Law Quarterly 142, p. 151.

Chapter 8

A. Allott, *The Limits of Law* (1980) London, Butterworths.
* E.H. Butler, *Traditional Marriage and Emerging Alternatives* (1979) Harper and Row, London, p. 12.
* Central Statistical Office, *Social Trends 13* (1982) London, HMSO, tables 2.10, 2.11, p. 28.
* E.M. Clive, 'Marriage: an unnecessary legal concept' in J.M. Eekelaar and S.M. Katz (eds.), *Marriage and Cohabitation in Contemporary Societies: Areas of Legal, Social and Ethical Change* (1980) Toronto, Butterworths, pp. 72–73.
* S. Danielson, *Unmarried partners and their children: Scandinavian law in the making* Paper presented to the 11th colloquy on European law (July 1981) Messina; reprinted in (1983) 3 Oxford Journal of Legal Studies 59.
* R. Deech, 'The case against legal recognition of cohabitation' in J.M. Eekelaar and S.M. Katz (eds.), *Marriage and Cohabitation in Contemporary Societies: Areas of Legal, Social and Ethical Change* (1980) Toronto, Butterworths, pp. 309–310.
* C. Fernandez, 'Beyond Marvin: a proposal for quasi-spousal support' (1978) 30 Stanford Law Review 359.
M.D.A. Freeman and C.M. Lyon, *Cohabitation Without Marriage* (1983) Aldershot, Gower.
* M.A. Glendon, 'Withering away of marriage' (1976) 62 Virginia Law Review 663, p. 686.
* C. Harpum, 'Adjusting property rights between unmarried cohabitees' (1982) 2 Oxford Journal of Legal Studies 287.
M. King, *Cohabitation Handbook 2* (1975).
* International Association of Young Lawyers, Conference in Philadelphia (1980), an *Example of a Cohabitation Contract*.
* D. Meade, 'Consortium rights of the unmarried — time for a reappraisal' (1981) 12 Family Law Quarterly 213.
D. Oliver, 'The mistress in law' [1978] Current Legal Problems 81.
* D. Oliver, 'Why do people live together?' [1982] Journal of Social Welfare Law 215–217.
M.L. Parry, *Cohabitation* (1981) London, Sweet and Maxwell.
* L. Weitzman, *The Marriage Contract: Spouses, Lovers, and the Law* (1981) London, Collier MacMillan, p. 361.
* W. Weyrauch, 'Metamorphoses of marriage' (1980) 13 Family Law Quarterly 436.
A. Zuckerman, 'Formality and the family — reform and status quo' (1980) 96 LQR 248.

Chapter 9

D. Barber, *Unmarried Fathers* (1975) London, Hutchinson.
* Sir William Blackstone, *Commentaries on the Laws of England* (1st edn., 1765) Oxford, Clarendon Press, book 1, p. 447.
J. Brandon and J. Warner, 'A.I.D. and Adoption: Some Comparisons' (1977) 7 British Journal of Social Work 235.
C. Brinton, *French Revolutionary Legislation on Illegitimacy 1789–1804* (1936) Cambridge, Mass., Harvard University Press.
* Central Statistical Office, *Social Trends 12* (1982) London, HMSO, table 2.19.
* Central Statistical Office, *Social Trends 13* (1982) London, HMSO, chart 2.20.
* Ciba Foundation Symposium, No. 17 (new series), G.E.W. Wolstenholme and D.W.

Fitzsimmons (eds.), *Law and Ethics of A.I.D. and Embryo Transfer* (1973) Amsterdam, Associated Scientific Publishers, pp. 30–32, 37, 60, 62–63, 65–66, 73, 75, 91, 100–101.

* Council of Europe, *European Convention for the Protection of Human Rights and Fundamental Freedoms* (1950).

* Council of Europe, *European Convention on the Legal Status of Children born out of Wedlock* (1981).

E. Crellin, M.L. Kellmer Pringle and P. West, *Born Illegitimate: Social and Educational Implications* (1971) Windsor, National Foundation for Educational Research.

* K. Davis, 'Illegitimacy and the Social Structure' (1939) 45 American Journal of Sociology 215, pp. 215, 216, 219, 221, 223.

R. Deech, 'The Reform of Illegitimacy Law' (1980) 10 Family Law 101.

* B.E. Dodd, 'Blood Tests' (1977) 2 Court 18, pp. 18–20, 22.

B.E. Dodd, 'When Blood is Their Argument' (1980) 20 Medicine, Science and the Law 231.

B.E. Dodd and P.J. Lincoln, 'An Analysis of 1556 Cases of Doubtful Paternity Submitted for Blood Group Investigation' (1978) 18 Medicine, Science and the Law 185.

G. Douglas, 'Affiliation and the Single Woman' (1979) 95 LQR 197.

* H. Elisofon, 'A Historical and Comparative Study of Bastardy' (1973) 2 Anglo-American Law Review 306, pp. 318–319.

F. Engels, *The Origin of the Family, Private Property and the State* (1st edn., 1884) New York, Lawrence and Wishart.

* Sir Morris Finer and O.R. McGregor, 'The History of the Obligation to Maintain' App. 5, *Report of the Committee on One-Parent Families*. (Cmnd. 5629-I) (1974) London, HMSO, paras. 56, 57, 59–62, 64, 74, 75.

R. Fox, *Kinship and Marriage* (1967) Harmondsworth, Penguin Books.

C. Gibson, 'The Association between Divorce and Social Class in England and Wales' (1974) 25 British Journal of Sociology 79.

D. Gill, *Illegitimacy, Sexuality and the Status of Women* (1977) Oxford, Blackwell.

* M. Hayes, 'Law Commission Working Paper No. 74: Illegitimacy' (1980) 43 MLR 299, p. 299.

U.R.Q. Henriques, 'Bastardy and the New Poor Law' (1967) 37 Past and Present.

H.D. Krause, *Illegitimacy, Law and Social Policy* (1971) Indianapolis, Bobbs, Merrill.

* L. Lambert and J. Streather, *Children in Changing Families: A Study of Adoption and Illegitimacy* (1980) London and Basingstoke, Macmillan, pp. 55–57, 136, 140–142.

* P. Laslett, *The World We Have Lost* (2nd edn., 1971) London, Methuen, pp. 137, 140–141.

P. Laslett, *Family Life and Illicit Love in Earlier Generations* (1977) Cambridge, Cambridge University Press.

P. Laslett, K. Oosterven, and R.M. Smith (eds.), *Bastardy and Its Comparative History* (1980) London, Arnold.

* Law Commission, Report on *Blood Tests and the Proof of Paternity in Civil Proceedings*, Law Com. No. 16, (1968) London, HMSO.

* Law Commission, *Illegitimacy*, Working Paper No. 74 (1979) London, HMSO, paras. 2.10–2.12, 3.2–3.6, 3.8–3.9, 3.14–3.16, 9.12, 9.14, 9.17, 9.18, 9.23, 9.24, 9.27, 9.28, 9.33, 9.40, 9.47, 10.5, 10.6, 10.8, 10.9, 10.11, 10.17, 10.19, 10.20, 10.25, 10.26.

* Law Commission, Report on *Illegitimacy*, Law Com No. 118, (1982) London, HMSO, paras. 4.44, 4.45, 4.49, 4.50, 4.51, 10.6, 10.7, 10.8, 10.10, 10.11, 10.12, 14.10, 14.62, 14.63, 14.69, 14.74.

* Law Society, *Legal Aid Annual Reports* [1975–76] HC 12 (1976–77), [1976–77] HC 172 (1977–78), [1977–78] HC 5 (1979–80), [1978–79] HC 309 (1979–80), [1979–80] HC 160 (1980–81) London, HMSO.

* R. Leete, 'Adoption Trends and Illegitimate Births' (1978) 14 Population Trends 9, pp. 11, 13, 14, 15.

P. Lødrup, 'The Position of Children of Unmarried but Cohabiting Parents' in J.M. Eekelaar and S.N. Katz (eds.), *Marriage and Cohabitation in Contemporary Societies: Areas of Legal, Social and Ethical Change* (1980) Toronto, Butterworths.

* L. Mair, *Marriage* (1971) Harmondsworth, Pelican Books, pp. 11-14, 16.

* National Council for One Parent Families, *An Accident of Birth — A Response to the Law Commission's Working Paper on Illegitimacy* (1980) London, One Parent Families, pp. 2-4, 9, 11-12.

D. Parker, 'Legal Aspects of Artificial Insemination and Embryo Transfer' (1982) 12 Family Law 103.

* D. Pearce and S. Farid, 'Illegitimate Births: Changing Patterns' (1977) 9 Population Trends 20, figs. 1a and 1b.

G.R. Quaife, *Wanton Wenches and Wayward Wives* (1979) London, Croom Helm.

Report of the Advisory Group on the Law of Rape (Chairman: Mrs Justice Heilbron) (Cmnd. 6352) (1975) London, HMSO.

* *Report of the Committee on the Law of Succession in relation to Illegitimate Persons* (Chairman: Lord Justice Russell) (Cmnd. 3051) (1966) London, HMSO, para. 19.

Report of the Departmental Committee on Human Artificial Insemination (Chairman: The Earl of Feversham) (Cmnd. 1105) (1960) London, HMSO.

G. Rowntree, 'Some Aspects of Marriage Breakdown in the Last Thirty Years' (1964) 18 Population Studies 147.

* Scottish Law Commission, *Family Law — Illegitimacy*, Consultative Memorandum No. 53 (1982) Edinburgh, Scottish Law Commission, paras. 1.15, 1.16.

J. Seglow, M.L. Kellmer Pringle and P. Wedge, *Growing Up Adopted* (1972) London, National Foundation for Educational Research.

P. Tapp, 'The Social and Legal Position of Children of Unmarried Cohabiting Parents' in J.M. Eekelaar and S.N. Katz (eds.), *Marriage and Cohabitation in Contemporary Societies: Areas of Legal, Social and Ethical Change* (1980) Toronto, Butterworths.

B. Thornes and J. Collard, *Who Divorces?* (1979) London, Routledge and Kegan Paul.

* V. Wimperis, *The Unmarried Mother and Her Child* (1960) London, Allen and Unwin, pp. 126-127.

Chapter 10

B. Bettelheim, 'Fathers Shouldn't Try to Be Mothers' *Parents' Magazine*, October 1956, cited in J.A. Levine, *Who Will Raise the Children? New Options for Fathers (and Mothers)* (1976) Philadelphia, Lippincott.

* J. Bowlby, *Child Care and the Growth of Love* (2nd edn., 1965) Harmondsworth, Pelican Books, pp. 13-15.

* B. Brecht, *The Caucasian Chalk Circle* (Trans. by James and Tania Stern with W.H. Auden) (1963) London, Methuen, pp. 94-95.

* Central Statistical Office, *Social Trends 13* (1982) London, HMSO, chart 2.17.

G. Davis, A. MacLeod and M. Murch, *Judicial Appointments with Divorcing Parents* (1981) Department of Social Administration, University of Bristol.

G. Davis, A. MacLeod and M. Murch, 'Undefended Divorce: Should Section 41 of the Matrimonial Causes Act 1973 be Repealed?' (1983) 46 MLR 121.

M. Dodds, *A Study of the Practice of the Divorce Courts in relation to Children* (1981) University of Manchester, LL.M. Thesis.

* M. Dodds, 'Children and Divorce' [1983] Journal of Social Welfare Law (July).

J.M. Eekelaar, 'Children in Divorce: Some Further Data' (1982) 2 Oxford Journal of Legal Studies 62.

* J.M. Eekelaar and E. Clive with K. Clarke and S. Raikes, *Custody After Divorce:*

The Disposition of Custody in Divorce Cases in Great Britain (1977) Oxford, Centre for Socio-legal Studies, paras. 3.6, 6.1, 6.4, 6.5, 13.7, 13.23, 13.25–27, tables 8 and 34.

H. Foster and D. Freed, 'Life with Father' (1978) 11 Family Law Quarterly 321.

A. Freud, 'Child Observation and Prediction of Development' (1958) 13 The Psychoanalytic Study of the Child 92.

L. Fuller, *Interaction Between Law and Its Social Context* (1971) Class material for Sociology of Law, University of California, Berkeley.

* J. Goldstein, A. Freud and A.J. Solnit, *Beyond the Best Interests of the Child* (1973) London, Collier Macmillan, pp. 31–34, 40–41, 49–50, 51, 53, 62–63.

J.C. Hall, *Arrangements for the Care and Upbringing of Children* Published Working Paper No. 15 (1968) London, Law Commission.

* C. Itzin, *Splitting Up: Single Parent Liberation* (1980) London, Virago, pp. 130, 138.

* Justice, *Report on Parental Rights and Duties and Custody Suits* (1975) London, Stevens, paras. 89(h), 91, 92.

M. King, *Childhood, Welfare and Justice* (1981) London, Batsford Academic and Educational, p. 124.

R. Leete, 'One Parent Families: Numbers and Characteristics' (1978) 12 Population Trends 4.

J.A. Levine, *Who Will Raise the Children? New Options for Fathers (and Mothers)* (1976) Philadelphia, Lippincott.

N. Lowe, 'The Legal Status of Fathers — Past and Present' in L. McKee and M. O'Brien (eds.), *The Father Figure* (1982) London, Tavistock.

S. Maidment, 'A Study in Child Custody' (1976) 6 Family Law 195 and 236.

S. Maidment, *Child Custody: What Chance for Fathers?* Forward from Finer No. 7 (1981) London, One Parent Families.

A.H. Manchester and J.M. Whetton, 'Marital Conciliation in England and Wales' (1974) 23 ICLQ 339.

* R.H. Mnookin, 'Child Custody Adjudication: Judicial Functions in the Face of Indeterminacy' (1975) 39 Law and Contemporary Problems 226, pp. 249–255, 256–261, 286–287. © 1975 Duke University School of Law.

P. Morgan, *Child Care: Sense and Fable* (1975) London, Temple Smith.

* M. Murch, *Justice and Welfare in Divorce* (1980) London, Sweet and Maxwell, pp. 129–232, 157, 160–162, 194, 205–206, 212–217.

A. Platt, 'The Child Savers' in *The Invention of Delinquency* (1969) Chicago, Chicago Press.

Probation and Aftercare Service, *Specimen Welfare Officer's Report* (1981).

Report of the Committee of Inquiry into the Care and Supervision Provided in Relation to Maria Colwell (Chairman: T.G. Field-Fisher QC) (1974) London, HMSO.

Report of the Committee on Procedure in Matrimonial Causes (Chairman: Mr Justice Denning) (Cmd. 7024) (1947) London, HMSO.

* *Report of the Royal Commission on Marriage and Divorce* (Chairman: Lord Morton of Henryton) (Cmd. 9678) (1956) London, HMSO, paras. 366, 367, 371, 372, 376, 377.

* M. Richards, 'Post Divorce Arrangements for Children: A Psychological Perspective' [1982] Journal of Social Welfare Law 133, pp. 135–136.

M. Richards and M. Dyson, *Separation, Divorce and the Development of Children: A Review* (1982) Child Care and Development Group, University of Cambridge.

A. Roth, 'The Tender Years Presumption in Child Custody Disputes' (1976–77) 15 Journal of Family Law 423.

* M. Rutter, *Maternal Deprivation Reassessed* (1981) Harmondsworth, Penguin, pp. 124–125.

O.M. Stone, *The Child's Voice in the Court of Law* (1982) Toronto, Butterworths.

J.S. Wallerstein and J.B. Kelly, *Surviving the Breakup: How Children and Parents Cope with Divorce* (1980) London, Grant McIntyre.

* L.J. Weitzman and R.B. Dixon, 'Child Custody Awards: Legal Standards and Empirical Patterns for Child Custody, Support and Visitation after Divorce' (1979) 12 UC Davis Law Review 473, pp. 478–483.

Chapter 11

Association of Child Care Officers, *Adoption — The Way Ahead*, A.C.C.O. Monograph No. 3, London, Association of Child Care Officers (now British Association of Social Workers).

* J. Burgoyne and D. Clark, 'Reconstituted Families' in R.N. Rapoport, M.P. Fogarty and R. Rapoport (eds.), *Families in Britain* (1982) London, Routledge and Kegan Paul, pp. 299–301.

* Central Statistical Office, *Social Trends 13* (1982) London, HMSO, table 2.12, chart 2.23.

* Departmental Committee on the Adoption of Children (Chairman: Sir William Houghton), *Working Paper* (1970) London, HMSO, paras. 92–94.

M. Dodds, *A Study of the Practice of the Divorce Courts in relation to Children* (1971) University of Manchester, LL.M. Thesis.

J.W.B. Douglas, 'Broken Families and Child Behaviour' (1970) 4 Journal of the Royal College of Physicians 203.

J.M. Eekelaar, 'What Are Parental Rights?' (1973) 89 LQR 210.

* J.M. Eekelaar and E. Clive with K. Clarke and S. Raikes, *Custody After Divorce: The Disposition of Custody in Divorce Cases in Great Britain* (1977) Oxford, Centre for Socio-legal Studies, table 15.

E. Ferri, *Growing Up in a One-Parent Family* (1976) Windsor, N.F.E.R. Publishing.

F.F. Furstenberg, *Renegotiating Parenthood After Divorce and Remarriage* (1981) Paper presented at Biennial Meeting of the Society for Research in Child Development, Boston, USA.

V. George and P. Wilding, *Motherless Families* (1972) London, Routledge and Kegan Paul.

* J. Goldstein, A. Freud and A.J. Solnit, *Beyond the Best Interests of the Child* (1973) London, Collier Macmillan, p. 37.

W.J. Goode, *After Divorce* (1956) New York, Free Press.

N. Hart, *When Marriage Ends: A Study in Status Passage* (1976) London, Tavistock.

* A. Heath-Jones, 'Divorce and the Reluctant Father' (1980) 10 Family Law 75, p. 75.

M.E. Hetherington, 'Effects of Father's Absence on Personality Development in Adolescent Daughters' (1972) 1 Developmental Psychology 313.

* Justice, *Report on Parental Rights and Duties and Custody Suits* (1975) London, Stevens, p. 54.

H.F. Keshet and K.M. Rosenthal, *Father Presence: Four Types of Post-marital Separation Fathering Arrangements* (1978) Paper presented at N.I.M.H. Symposium on Mental Health Consequences of Divorce on Children, Washington D.C.

Law Commission, Report on *Matrimonial Proceedings in Magistrates' Courts*, Law Com. No. 77 (1976) London, HMSO.

* R. Leete and S. Anthony, 'Divorce and Remarriage: A Record Linkage Study' (1979) 16 Population Trends 5, p. 9.

* B. Maddox, *Step-parenting* (1980) London, Unwin Paperbacks, pp. 35–39.

* S. Maidment, 'Access Conditions in Custody Orders' (1975) 2 British Journal of Law and Society 182, pp. 185–187.

S. Maidment, 'Step-parent and Step-children: Legal Relationships in Serial Unions' in J.M. Eekelaar and S.N. Katz (eds.), *Marriage and Cohabitation in Contemporary Societies: Areas of Legal, Social and Ethical Change* (1980) Toronto, Butterworths.

S. Maidment, 'The Fragmentation of Parental Rights' [1981] Cambridge Law Journal 135.

D. Marsden, *Mothers Alone: Poverty and the Fatherless Family*, (1969) Harmondsworth, Penguin Books.

* J. Masson and D. Norbury, 'Step-parent Adoption' (1982) 6 Adoption and Fostering, no. 1, 7, p. 10.

* M. Murch, *Justice and Welfare in Divorce* (1980) London, Sweet and Maxwell, p. 93, table 16.

E. Newson and J. Newson, *Patterns of Infant Care in an Urban Community* (reprinted 1972) Harmondsworth, Penguin Books.

A. Oakley, *Becoming a Mother* (1979) Oxford, Martin Robertson.

M.L. Parry, 'The Custody Conundrum' (1982) 12 Family Law 213.

P.H. Pettitt, 'Parental Control and Guardianship' in R.H. Graveson and F.R. Crane (eds.), *A Century of Family Law* (1957) London, Sweet and Maxwell.

J. Priest, 'Step-parent Adoptions: What is the Law?' [1982] Journal of Social Welfare Law 285.

Report of the Committee on One-Parent Families (Chairman: The Hon. Sir Morris Finer) (Cmnd. 5629) (1974) London, HMSO.

* *Report of the Departmental Committee on the Adoption of Children* (Chairman: Sir William Houghton, later Judge F.A. Stockdale). Cmnd. 5107. London, HMSO (1972), para. 108.

* M. Richards, 'Post Divorce Arrangements for Children: A Psychological Perspective' [1982] Journal and Social Welfare Law 133, pp. 142–151.

M. Richards and M. Dyson, *Separation, Divorce and the Development of Children: A Review*. Child Care and Development Group, University of Cambridge (1982).

M. Roman and W. Haddad, *The Disposable Parent: The Case for Joint Custody* (1978) New York, Penguin Books.

G. Sanctuary and C, Whitehead, *Divorce — and After* (1970) Harmondsworth, Penguin Books.

H.R. Shaffer and P.E. Emerson, 'The Development of Social Attachments in Infancy' (1964) 29 Monograph Soc. Res. Child Development, no. 3, p. 1.

J. Tweedie, 'Give the Father Unlimited Access and Watch the Cookie Crumble' *The Guardian*, 27 September 1979.

* J.S. Wallerstein and J.B. Kelly, *Surviving the Breakup: How Children and Parents Cope with Divorce* (1980) London, Grant McIntyre, pp. 292–293.

A. Watson, 'Children of Armageddon: Problems of Custody Without Care' (1969) 21 Syracuse Law Review 55.

R.S. Weiss, *Marital Separation* (1975) New York, Basic Books.

R.S. Weiss, *Going It Alone: The Family Life and Social Situation of the Single Parent* (1979) New York, Basic Books.

Chapter 12

* M. Adcock, 'Social Work Dilemmas' in M. Adcock and R. White (eds.), *Terminating Parental Contact: An Exploration of the Issues relating to Children in Care* (1980) London, Association of British Adoption and Fostering Agencies (now British Agencies for Adoption and Fostering) pp. 16, 18–20.

M. Adcock and R. White, 'The Use of Section 3 Resolutions' (1982) 6 Adoption and Fostering, no. 3, p. 9.

M. Adcock, R. White and O. Rowlands, 'The Role of the Local Authority as Parent' (1982) 6 Adoption and Fostering, no. 4, p. 14.

M. Adcock, R. White and O. Rowlands, 'Section 3 Resolutions: Problems and Proposals' (1983) 7 Adoption and Fostering, no. 1, p. 48.

M. Adcock, R. White and O. Rowlands, *The Administrative Parent: A Study of the Assumption of Parental Rights and Duties* (1982) London, British Agencies for Adoption and Fostering.

* Lady Allen of Hurtwood, 'Whose Children? Wards of State or Charity' *The Times*, 15 July 1944.

* P. Ariès, *Centuries of Childhood* (1962) London, Jonathan Cape; reprinted in (1969) Peregrine Books, pp. 36–37.

A. Bainham, 'Wardship, Care and the Welfare Principle' (1982) 12 Family Law 236.

H.K. Bevan and M.L. Parry, *The Children Act 1975* (1978) London, Butterworths.

J. Bowlby, *Child Care and the Growth of Love* (1953; 2nd edn., 1965) Harmondsworth, Penguin Books.

* DHSS, Local Authority Circular LAC (76) 15, *Children Act 1975: Programme for Implementation in 1976/77, Annex A, Guidance on the 'Time Limit' provisions (sections 29, 30, 56, 57 and 58 (part)) which are planned to come into force on 26 November 1976,* para. 3 and leaflet no. 2.

* DHSS, *Personal Social Services, Local Authority Statistics, Children in Care of Local Authorities, Year Ending 31 March 1980, England,* London, DHSS, tables 4.02, 10.01, 19.03.

DHSS, *Social Services for Children in England and Wales 1979-1981,* HC 79 (1982-83) (1982) London, HMSO.

D. Fanshel and E. Shinn, *Children in Foster Care: A Longitudinal Investigation* (1978) New York, Columbia University Press.

T.B. Festinger, 'The Impact of the New York Court Review' (1976) 55 Child Welfare, no. 8.

V. George, *Foster Care: Theory and Practice* (1970) London, Routledge and Kegan Paul.

* J. Goldstein, A. Freud and A.J. Solnit, *Beyond the Best Interests of the Child* (1973) London, Collier Macmillan, pp. 71-80.

* J.S. Heywood, *Children in Care: The Development of the Service for the Deprived Child* (3rd edn., 1978) London, Routledge and Kegan Paul, pp. 7-10, 63-65, 92-93.

R. Holman, *Trading in Children: A Study of Private Fostering* (1973) London, Routledge and Kegan Paul.

* R. Holman, 'In Defence of Parents' *New Society,* 1 May 1975, pp. 268-269.

House of Commons Social Services Committee, *Children in Care, Minutes of Evidence,* HC 26-i and ii (1982-83) (1982) London, HMSO.

R. Jenkins, 'The Needs of Foster Parents' (1965) 11 Case Conference, no. 7, p. 211.

M. Jones, R. Neuman and A. Shyne, *A Second Chance for Families: Evaluation of a Program to Reduce Foster Care* (1976) Child Welfare League of America.

B. Kahan, *Growing Up in Care: Ten People Talking* (1979) Oxford, Basil Blackwell.

* S.N. Katz, 'Model Act to Free Children for Permanent Placement' in J.M. Eekelaar and S.N. Katz (eds.), *Family Violence: An International and Interdisciplinary Study* (1978) Toronto, Butterworths, ss. 1, 3 and 4.

* L. Lambert and J. Rowe, 'Children in Care and the Assumption of Parental Rights by Local Authorities' (1974) 78 Child Adoption 13, pp. 17, 18.

* National Council for One Parent Families, *Against Natural Justice: A Study of the Procedures Used by Local Authorities in Taking Parental Rights Resolutions over Children in Voluntary Care* (1982) London, One Parent Families, table 1, pp. 8-9, 24-25, 26.

* J. Packman, *The Child's Generation: Child Care Policy in Britain* (2nd edn., 1981) Oxford, Basil Blackwell, pp. 57-59, 64-65, 133-135, 137-138, 156-161, 195.

R. Parker, *Decision in Child Care: A Study of Prediction in Fostering* (1966) London, Allen and Unwin.

R. Parker (ed.), *Caring for Separated Children: Plans, Procedures and Priorities* Report of a Working Party Established by the National Children's Bureau, (1980) London, Macmillan.

* *Report by Sir Walter Monckton, KCMG, KCVO, MC, KC, on the circumstances which led to the boarding-out of Denis and Terence O'Neill at Bank Farm, Minsterley, and the steps taken to supervise their welfare* (Cmd. 6636) (1945) London, HMSO, paras. 2,3 and 54.

* *Report of the Care of Children Committee* (Chairman: Miss M. Curtis). (Cmd. 6922) (1946) London, HMSO, paras. 10, 138, 140, 144, 154, 171, 193, 370, 425 (ii), 427, 440, 441, 443, 461, 476, 478.

Report of the Committee on Children and Young Persons (Chairman: Viscount Ingleby) (Cmnd. 1191) (1960) London, HMSO.

Report of the Committee on Local Authority and Allied Personal Social Services (Chairman: F. Seebohm) (Cmnd. 3703) (1968) London, HMSO.

∗ *Report of the Departmental Committee on the Adoption of Children* (Chairman: Sir William Houghton, later Judge F.A. Stockdale) (Cmnd. 5107) (1972) London, HMSO, paras. 139, 148, 151, 152, 156, 157, app. D, para. 4.

∗ J. Rowe and L. Lambert, *Children Who Wait* (1973) London, Association of British Adoption Agencies (now British Agencies for Adoption and Fostering), pp. 36–39, 42–43, 47, app., table B4.

M. Rutter, *Maternal Deprivation Reassessed* (1972) Harmondsworth, Penguin Books.

M. Rutter and N. Madge, *Cycles of Disadvantage* (1976) London, Heinemann.

M. Shaw and K. Lebens, *Substitute Family Care — A Regional Study. 2: What Shall We Do with the Children?* (1978) London, Association of British Adoption and Fostering Agencies (now British Agencies for Adoption and Fostering) p. 20.

∗ E. Shorter, *The Making of the Modern Family* (1975) New York, Basic Books; (1977) London, Fontana Books, p. 203.

∗ J. Stroud, *The Shorn Lamb* (1960) London, Longman, pp. 242–243.

R. Thorpe, 'Mum and Mrs So and So' (1974) 4 Social Work Today, no. 22, p. 691.

G. Trasler, *In Place of Parents* (1960) London, Routledge and Kegan Paul.

∗ J. Tunnard, 'The Case for Family Involvement' in *Accountability in Child Care — Which Way Forward?* (1982) London, Family Rights Group, pp. 19–20.

G. Wagner, *Children of the Empire* (1981) London, Weidenfeld and Nicholson.

H. Wilson, 'Parenting in Poverty' (1974) 4 British Journal of Social Work 241.

Chapter 13

G. Adamson, *The Caretakers* (1973) Bristol, Bookstall Publications.

∗ J. Aldgate, 'Identification of Factors Influencing Children's Length of Stay in Care' in J. Triseliotis (ed.), *New Developments in Foster Care and Adoption* (1980) London, Routledge and Kegan Paul, p. 23.

∗ A. Bentovim, 'Psychiatric Issues' in M. Adcock and R. White (eds.), *Terminating Parental Contact: An Exploration of the Issues relating to Children in Care* (1980) London, Association of British Adoption and Fostering Agencies (now British Agencies for Adoption and Fostering), pp. 39–40.

J. Bowlby, *Attachment and Loss. Vol. 1: Attachment* (1971) Harmondsworth, Penguin Books.

∗ C. Day, 'Access to Birth Records: General Register Office Study' (1979) 3 Adoption and Fostering, no. 4, 17, pp. 27–28.

∗ D. Dudley, *Roman Society* (1975) Harmondsworth, Penguin Books, p. 190.

D. Fanshel and E.B. Shinn, *Children in Foster Care: A Longitudinal Study* (1978) New York, Columbia University Press.

V. George, *Foster Care: Theory and Practice* (1970) London, Routledge and Kegan Paul.

∗ J. Goldstein, A. Freud and A.J. Solnit, *Beyond the Best Interests of the Child* (1973) London, Collier Macmillan, pp. 39, 48, 49, 100, 101.

I. Goodacre, *Adoption Policy and Practice* (1966) London, Allen and Unwin.

E. Grey with R.M. Blunden, *A Survey of Adoption in Great Britain*, Home Office Research Studies No. 10 (1971) London, HMSO.

M. Hayes and C. Williams, 'Adoption of Babies, Agreeing and Freeing' (1982) 12 Family Law 233.

∗ J. Heywood, *Children in Care: The Development of the Service for the Deprived Child* (3rd edn., 1978) London, Routledge and Kegan Paul, pp. 150–151, 173–174.

R. Holman, *Trading in Children: A Study of Private Fostering* (1973) London, Routledge and Kegan Paul.

∗ R. Holman, 'The Place of Fostering in Social Work' (1975) 5 British Journal of Social Work 3, pp. 8–14.

* R. Holman, 'In Defence of Parents' *New Society*, 1 May 1975, pp. 268-269.

R. Jenkins, 'Long term Fostering' (1969) 15 Case Conference, no. 9, p. 349.

L. Lambert and J. Streather, *Children in Changing Familes* (1980) London, Macmillan.

News of the World, 10 October 1976.

* J. Packman, *The Child's Generation: Child Care Policy in Britain* (2nd edn., 1981) Oxford, Basil Blackwell, pp. 137-138.

* M.L. Kellmer Pringle, 'In Place of One's Own — A Look into the Future' in J. Seglow, M.L. Kellmer Pringle and P. Wedge, *Growing Up Adopted* (1972) Windsor, National Foundation for Educational Research, pp. 165, 170, 178.

* *Report (first) of the Child Adoption Committee* (Chairman: Mr Justice Tomlin) (Cmd. 2401) (1925) London, HMSO, paras. 4, 9, 11, 15, 18, 19, 28.

* *Report of the Committee of Inquiry into the Care and Supervision provided in relation to Maria Colwell* (Chairman: T.G. Field-Fisher QC) (1974) London, HMSO, paras. 10-12, 14-17, 19, 24, 28, 30, 36, 42, 59, 63, 315.

Report of the Committee on Child Adoption (Chairman: Sir Alfred Hopkinson KC) (Cmd. 1254) (1921) London, HMSO.

Report of the Departmental Committee on Adoption Societies and Agencies (Chairman: Miss Florence Horsbrugh MP) (Cmd. 5499) (1937) London, HMSO.

Report of the Departmental Committee on the Adoption of Children (Chairman: His Honour Sir Gerald Hurst QC) (Cmd. 9248) (1954) London, HMSO.

* *Report of the Departmental Committee on the Adoption of Children* (Chairman: Sir William Houghton, later Judge F.A. Stockdale) (Cmnd. 5107) (1972) London, HMSO, paras. 33-36, 38, 42, 82-88, 93-94, 97, 116, 120-122, 125-127, 144, 146, 164, 168-170, 221, 223-224, 237, 238, 244, 245, 252, 253, 301-303, 326, 327.

L. Ripple, 'A Follow-up Study of Adopted Children' (1968) 42 Social Service Review, no. 4, p. 479.

* J. Rowe, 'Fostering in the 1970s' (1977) Adoption and Fostering, no. 4, 15, pp. 15-17.

J. Rowe and L. Lambert, *Children Who Wait* (1973) London, Association of British Adoption Agencies (now British Agencies for Adoption and Fostering).

R. Ruddock (ed.), *Six Approaches to the Person* (1972) London, Routledge and Kegan Paul.

* J. Seglow, M.L. Kellmer Pringle and P. Wedge, *Growing Up Adopted* (1972) Windsor, National Foundation for Educational Research, pp. 9-10, 157-158, 165, 170, 178.

M. Shaw and K. Lebens, 'Children between Families' (1976) 84 Adoption and Fostering.

A.J. Solnit, letter to D. Fanshel, quoted in D. Fanshel and E.B. Shinn, *Children in Foster care: A Longitudinal Study* (1978) New York, Columbia University Press.

O. Stevenson, *Some-one Else's Child* (revised edn., 1977) London, Routledge and Kegan Paul.

R. Thorpe, 'Mum and Mrs So and So' (1974) 4 Social Work Today, no. 22, p. 691.

* R. Thorpe, 'The Experience of Children and Parents Living Apart' in J. Triseliotis (ed.), *New Developments in Foster Care and Adoption* (1980) London, Routledge and Kegan Paul, pp. 87-95.

* B. Tizard, *Adoption: A Second Chance* (1977) London, Open Books, pp. 1, 3-8, 206-209.

J. Triseliotis, *Evaluation of Adoption Policy and Practice* (1970) Edinburgh, Department of Social Administration, University of Edinburgh.

* J. Triseliotis, *In Search of Origins: The Experiences of Adopted People* (1973) London, Routledge and Kegan Paul, pp. 84, 85, 101.

* J. Triseliotis, 'Growing Up in Foster Care and After' in J. Triseliotis (ed.), *New Developments in Foster Care and Adoption* (1980) London, Routledge and Kegan Paul, pp. 134, 138, 139, 143, 147-148, 156-158.

E.A. Weinstein, *The Self Image of the Foster Child* (1960) New York, Russell Sage Foundation.

M. Wolins, 'Group Care — Friend or Foe?' (1969) 14 Social Work, no. 1.

S. Wolkind, *Children in Care: A Psychiatric Study* (1971) University of London, M.D. Thesis.

S. Wolkind and M. Rutter, 'Children Who Have Been in Care: An Epidemiological Study' (1973) 14 Journal of Child Psychology and Psychiatry, no. 2.

Chapter 14

L.J. Allen, 'Child Abuse: A Critical Review of the Research and the Theory' in J.P. Martin (ed.), *Violence and the Family* (1978) Chichester, Wiley.

D.L. Barker and S. Allen (eds.), *Dependence and Exploitation in Work and Marriage* (1976) London, Longman.

V. Binney, G. Harkell and J. Nixon (WAFE/DOE research team), *Leaving Violent Men: A Study of Refuges for Battered Women* (1981) London, Women's Aid Federation, England.

B. Birns, S. Barsden and W.H. Bridges, *Individual Differences in Temperamental Characteristics of Infants* (1969) Transactions of New York Academy of Sciences.

P.M. Bromley, *Family Law* (5th edn, 1976; now 6th edn., 1981) London, Butterworths.

V. Bullough, *The Subordinate Sex* (1974) Harmondsworth, Penguin Books.

B. Cade, 'Family Violence: An Interactional View' (1978) 9 Social Work Today, no. 26, p. 15.

J. Carter, 'Is Child Abuse a Crime?' in A.W. Franklin (ed.), *The Challenge of Child Abuse. Proceedings of a Conference Sponsored by the Royal Society of Medicine, 2-4 June 1976* (1977) London, Academic Press.

J. Carter (ed.), *The Maltreated Child* (1974) London, Priory Press.

J. Clifton, *It's Lonely but We're Coping: A Follow-up Study of Women Who Used a Refuge* (1980).

* J. Clifton, 'Factors Predisposing Family Members to Violence', in Social Work Services Group, Scottish Education Department, *Violence in the Family — Theory and Practice in Social Work* (1982) Edinburgh, HMSO, pp. 25-32.

J. Court, 'Characteristics of Parents and Children' in J. Carter (ed.), *The Maltreated Child* (1974) London, Priory Press.

L. Deltaglia, *Les Enfants Maltraités: Depistage et Interventions Sociales* (1976) Paris, Les Editions ESF.

* DHSS, *Memorandum on Non-Accidental Injury To Children* LASSL (74) 13, CMO (74) 8, 24 April 1074, paras. 3, 4, 14, 15, 16.

DHSS *Non-Accidental Injury to Children: Area Review Committees* LASSL (76) 2, CMO (76) 2, CNO (76) 3, February 1976 (amended by LASSL (76) 25, CMO (76) 27, CNO (76) 19, 9 November 1976).

* DHSS, *Child Abuse: Central Register Systems* LASSL (80) 4, HN (80) 20, August 1980, paras. 2.2, 3.2, 4.3-6, 4.10.

DHSS and Home Office, *Non-Accidental Injury to Children: The Police and Case Conferences* LASSL (76) 26, HC (76) 50, Home Office Circular 179/76, 18 November 1976.

DHSS, *Child Abuse: A Study of Inquiry Reports*, 1973-81, (1982) London, HMSO.

* R. Dingwall, J.M. Eekelaar and T. Murray, *Care or Control? Decision-Making in the Care of Children Thought to have been Abused or Neglected. A Summary of the Final Report* (1981) Oxford, Centre for Socio-legal Studies, pp. 30-31, 36-37, 37-38, 40-42.

R. Dobash and R. Dobash, 'Wives: the Appropriate Victims of Marital Violence' and (with C. Cavanagh and M. Wilson) 'Wife Beating: the Victims Speak' (1978) 2 Victimology.

R. Dobash and R. Dobash, *Violence Against Wives: A Case Against the Patriarchy* (1980) London, Open Books.

* M. Dow, 'Police Involvement' in M. Borland (ed.), *Violence in the Family* (1976) Manchester, Manchester University Press, pp. 132–133, 134–135.

* J.M. Eekelaar, R. Dingwall and T. Murray, 'Victims or Threats? Children in Care Proceedings' [1982] Journal of Social Welfare Law 67, pp. 71–78.

J.M. Eekelaar and S.N. Katz (eds.). *Family Violence: An International and Inter-disciplinary Study* (1978) Toronto, Butterworths.

M. Faulk, 'Men Who Assault Their Wives' (1974) 14 Medicine, Science and the Law 180.

L. Feldman, *Care Proceedings* (1978) London, Oyez.

S. Foulon, 'Reflexions sur L'Intervention Judiciaire en France' in A.W. Franklin (ed.), *Abstracts from the Second International Congress on Child Abuse and Neglect, London, 12–15 September 1978* (1978) Oxford, Pergamon Press.

* M.D.A. Freeman, *Violence in the Home* (1979) Farnborough, Saxon House (now Aldershot, Gower), pp. 45, 141–142.

M.D.A. Freeman, 'Child Welfare: Law and Control' in M. Partington and J. Jowell (eds.), *Welfare Law and Policy* (1979) London, Frances Pinter.

M.D.A. Freeman, 'Violence Against Women: Does the Legal System Provide Solutions or Itself Constitute the Problem?' (1980) 7 British Journal of Law and Society 215.

J.J. Gayford, 'Wife Battering: A Preliminary Survey of 100 Cases' (1975) British Medical Journal, no. 1, p. 194.

R. Gelles, *The Violent Home* (1972) Beverley Hills, Sage Publications.

D. Gil, 'Violence Against Children' in C. Lee (ed.), *Child Abuse: A Reader and Sourcebook* (1973) Milton Keynes, Open University Press.

T. Gill and A. Coote, *Battered Women: How to Use the Law* (1975) London, Cobden Trust.

* J. Goldstein, 'Psychoanalysis and a Jurisprudence of Child Placement with Special Emphasis on the Role of Legal Counsel for Children' (1978) 1 International Journal of Law and Psychiatry 109, p. 119.

* J. Goldstein, A. Freud and A.J. Solnit, *Before the Best Interests of the Child* (1980) London, Burnett Books, pp. 4–5. © 1979 The Free Press.

Judge J. Graham Hall and B. Mitchell, *Child Abuse: Procedure and Evidence in Juvenile Courts*, (1978) Chichester, Barry Rose.

N. Hart, *When Marriage Ends: A Study in Status Passage* (1976) London, Tavistock.

L. Hilgendorf, *Social Workers and Solicitors in Child Care Cases*, (1981) London, HMSO.

R. Holman and others, *Socially Deprived Families in Britain* (1970) London, National Council of Social Service.

Home Office, *The Child, the Family and the Young Offender* (Cmnd. 2742) (1965) London, HMSO.

Home Office, *Children in Trouble* (Cmnd. 3061) (1968) London, HMSO.

* House of Commons Select Committee on Violence in Marriage, *Report* HC 553 (1974–75) (1975) London, HMSO, paras. 10, 20, 21.

* House of Commons Select Committee on Violence in the Family, *Violence to Children. Vol. 1: Report (together with the Proceedings of the Committee)* HC 329-i (1976–77) (1977) London, HMSO, paras. 93, 95, 99, 101, 110, 114, 116, 117, 119, 173.

M. Jobling, 'Battered Wives: A Survey' (1974) 47 Social Service Quarterly 142.

* R.S. Kempe and C.H. Kempe, *Child Abuse* (1978) London, Fontana/Open Books, pp. 89–91, 129–130.

Law Commission, Report on *Matrimonial Proceedings in Magistrates' Courts*, Law Com. No. 77, (1976) London, HMSO.

* A. Lawson, 'Taking the Decision to Remove a Child from his Family' [1980] Journal of Social Welfare Law 141, pp. 146–147, 152–154, 157, 160–161.

* Legal Action Group Bulletin, 'Legal Aid for Parents At Last' [1982] L.A.G. Bulletin, August, pp. 1–2.

* Lord Chancellor's Advisory Committee on Legal Aid, 29th Report, in *Legal Aid*

Annual Reports [1978-79] HC 309 (1979-80) (1980) London, HMSO, paras. 40-43.

M. Lynch, 'Ill health and Child Abuse' *Lancet*, 16 August 1975, p. 317.

M. Lystad, 'Violence at Home: A Review of the Literature' (1975) 45 American Journal of Orthopsychiatry 328.

* S. Maidment, 'The Law's Response to Marital Violence in England and the U.S.A.' (1977) 26 ICLQ 403, pp. 416-420, 422-425, 443, 444.

* S. Maidment, 'Some Legal Problems Arising Out of the Reporting of Child Abuse' [1978] Current Legal Problems 149, pp. 150-151, 152-153, 170-171.

* S. Maidment, 'The Relevance of the Criminal Law to Domestic Violence' [1980] Journal of Social Welfare Law 26, pp. 29-31.

D. Marsden, 'Sociological Perspectives on Family Violence' in J.P. Martin (ed.), *Violence and the Family* (1978) Chichester, Wiley.

D. Marsden and D. Owens, 'The Jekyll and Hyde Marriages' *New Society*, 8 May 1975.

J.P. Martin (ed.), *Violence and the Family* (1978) Chichester, Wiley.

* J.S. Mill, *The Subjection of Women* (1869); reprinted in Everyman's Library (1929) London, Dent, pp. 232, 251-252, 253-254.

K. Millett, *Sexual Politics* (1969) London, Hart Davis.

National Society for the Prevention of Cruelty to Children, *At Risk: An Account of the Work of the Battered Child Research Department* (1975) London, Routledge and Kegan Paul.

J.E. O'Brien, 'Violence in Divorce Prone Families' (1971) 33 Journal of Marriage and the Family 692.

C. Ounsted and M.A. Lynch, 'Family Pathology as seen in England' in R.E. Helfer and C.H. Kempe (eds.), *Child Abuse and Neglect: The Family and the Community* (1976) Cambridge, Mass., Ballinger.

J. Packman, *The Child's Generation: Child Care Policy in Britain* (2nd edn., 1981) Oxford, Basil Blackwell.

M. Pagelow, *Battered Women — A New Perspective* (1977) Dublin, International Sociological Association.

J. Pahl, *A Refuge for Battered Women: A Study of the Role of a Women's Centre* (1978) London, HMSO.

J. Pahl, 'Police Response to Battered Women' [1982] Journal of Social Welfare Law 337.

R.I. Parnas, 'Judicial Response to Intra-family Violence' (1970) 54 Minnesota Law Review 585.

* R.I. Parnas, 'The Relevance of the Criminal Law to Inter-spousal Violence' in J.M. Eekelaar and S.N. Katz (eds.) *Family Violence: An International and Interdisciplinary Study* (1978) Toronto, Butterworths, pp. 188-191.

* E. Pizzey, *Scream Quietly or the Neighbours Will Hear* (1974) Harmondsworth, Penguin Books, pp. 98, 119-121.

* J. Renvoize, *Children in Danger* (1974) London, Routledge and Kegan Paul; (1975) Hardmondsworth, Penguin Books, pp. 20 and 24.

* *Report of the Committee of Inquiry into the Provision and Co-ordination of Services to the Family of John George Auckland* (Chairman: P.J.M. Kennedy QC) (1975) London, HMSO, paras. 19, 21, 45-47, 49, 54, 57, 58, 164, 181-183, 185, 194, 195, 206, 214, 215, 217, 224, 238, 241-243.

Report of the Committee on Children and Young Persons (Chairman: Viscount Ingleby) (Cmnd. 1191) (1960) London, HMSO.

* A. Samuels, 'Never Hit A Child' (1977) 7 Family Law 119, p. 121.

H.R. Schaffer and P.E. Emerson, 'Patterns of Response to Physical Contact in Early Human Development' (1964) 5 Journal of Child Psychology and Psychiatry 1.

P. Scott, 'Battered Wives' (1974) 125 British Journal of Psychiatry 433.

S.M. Smith, *The Battered Child Syndrome* (1975) London, Butterworths.

* C. Somerhausen, 'Reactions: Formal and Informal Social Control' in *Criminological Aspects of the Ill-treatment of Children in the Family* (1981) Strasbourg, Council of Europe, pp. 97-98.

Somerset Area Review Committee of Non-Accidental Injury to Children, *Wayne Brewer — Report of the Review Panel* (1977).

B. Steele and C. Pollock, 'A Psychiatric Study of Parents who abuse Infants and Small Children' in R. Helfer and C.H. Kempe (eds.), *The Battered Child* (1968) Chicago, Chicago University Press.

S. Steinmetz and S. Straus (eds.), *Violence in the Family* (1974) New York, Dodd, Mead.

A. Storr, *Human Aggression* (1974) Harmondsworth, Penguin Books.

H.I. Subin, *Criminal Justice in a Metropolitan Court: the Processing of Serious Criminal Cases in the District of Columbia Court of General Sessions* (1966) Washington, Office of Criminal Justice, US Department of Justice.

A. Weir, 'Battered Women: Some Perspectives and Problems' in M. Mayo (ed.), *Women in the Community* (1977) London, Routledge and Kegan Paul.

W.A. Westley, *Violence and the Police: a Sociological Study of Law, Custom and Morality* (1970) Cambridge, Mass., M.I.T. Press.

R. Whitehurst, 'Violence in Husband-Wife Interaction' in S. Steinmetz and M. Straus (eds.), *Violence in the Family* (1974) New York, Dodd, Mead.

E. Wilson, *The Existing Research into Battered Women* (1976) London, National Women's Aid Federation (now Women's Aid Federation, England).

M.E. Wolfgang and F. Ferracuti, *The Subculture of Violence: Towards an Integrated Theory in Criminology* (1967) London, Tavistock.

Chapter 15

* Anon., 'Mental Hospitalisation of Children and the Limits of Parental Authority' (1978) 88 Yale Law Journal 186, pp. 194–208.

B. Barry, *Political Argument* (1965) London, Routledge and Kegan Paul.

Beck, Glavis, Glover, Jenkins and Nardi, 'The Rights of Children: A Trust Model' (1978) 46 Fordham Law Review 669.

N. Berger, *Rights* (1974) Harmondsworth, Penguin Books.

* Sir William Blackstone, *Commentaries on the Laws of England* (1st edn., 1765) Oxford, Clarendon Press, book 1, pp. 434–435, 440–441.

J. Bowlby, *Attachment and Loss. Vol. 1: Attachment* (1965) London, Hogarth Press and Institute of Psycho-Analysis; (1971) Harmondsworth, Penguin Books.

J. Bowlby, *Attachment and Loss. Vol. 2: Separation — Anxiety and Anger* (1973) London, Hogarth Press and Institute of Psycho-Analysis; (1975) Harmondsworth, Penguin Books.

A.M. Clarke and A.C.B. Clarke, *Early Experience: Myth and Evidence* (1976) London, Open Books.

J.E. Coons and R.H. Mnookin, 'Toward a Theory of Children's Rights' in I.F.G. Baxter and M.A. Eberts (eds.), *The Child and the Courts* (1978) London, Sweet and Maxwell.

* Council of Europe, *European Convention for the Protection of Human Rights and Fundamental Freedoms* (1950), articles 8 and 9, protocol no. 1, article 2.

B.M. Dickens, 'The Modern Function and Limits of Parental Rights' (1981) 97 LQR 462.

* J.M. Eekelaar, R. Dingwall and T. Murray, 'Victims or Threats? Children in Care Proceedings' [1982] Journal of Social Welfare Law 68, pp. 68–69, 79–82.

R. Farson, *Birthrights* (1978) Harmondsworth, Penguin Books.

* M.D.A. Freeman, 'The Rights of Children in the International Year of the Child' [1980] Current Legal Problems 1, pp. 16–17, 20–21.

M.D.A. Freeman, 'Freedom and the Welfare State: Child-rearing, Parental Autonomy and State Intervention' [1983] Journal of Social Welfare Law 70.

M.D.A. Freeman, *The Rights and Wrongs of Children* (1983) London, Frances Pinter.

A. Freud and D. Burlingham, *Young Children in War Time: A Year's Work in a Residential Nursery* (1944) London, Allen and Unwin.

A. Freud and D. Burlingham, *Infants Without Families: The Case For and Against Residential Nurseries* (1944) London, Allen and Unwin.

J. Goldstein, A. Freud and A.J. Solnit, *Beyond the Best Interests of the Child* (1973) London, Collier Macmillan.

* J. Goldstein, A. Freud and A.J. Solnit, *Before the Best Interests of the Child* (1980) London, Burnett Books, pp. 8–10, 11–12, 16–17, 92, 93–94.

J. Holt, *Escape from Childhood* (1974) New York, Dutton.

J. Kagan, R.B. Kearsley and P.R. Zelazo, *Infancy: Its Place in Human Development* (1978) Cambridge, Mass., Harvard University Press.

R.B. Kearsley, P.R. Zelazo, J. Kagan and R. Hartman, 'Separation Protest in Day-Care and Home-Reared Infants' (1975) 55 Paediatrics 171.

I. Kennedy, 'The Karen Quinlan Case: Problems and Proposals' (1976) 2 Journal of Medical Ethics 3, p. 6.

N. Lowe and R. White, *Wards of Court* (1979) London, Butterworths.

N. MacCormick, 'Children's Rights: A Test Case for Theories of Right' (1976) 62 Archiv für Rechts und Sozialphilosophie 305.

J. Packman, *The Child's Generation: Child Care Policy in Britain* (2nd edn., 1981) Oxford, Basil Blackwell.

P.H. Pettitt, 'Parental Control and Guardianship' in R.H. Graveson and F.R. Crane (eds.), *A Century of Family Law* (1957) London, Sweet and Maxwell.

J. Piaget, *The Construction of Reality in the Child* (1937); translated by M. Cook (1955) London, Routledge and Kegan Paul.

J. Rawls, *A Theory of Justice* (1972) Cambridge, Mass., Harvard University Press.

C.M. Rogers and L.S. Wrightsman, 'Attitudes towards Children's Rights: Nurturance or Self-Determination' (1978) 34 Journal of Social Issues, no. 2, p. 59.

R.M. Rolfe and A.D. MacClintock, 'The Due Process Rights of Minors "Voluntarily Admitted" to Mental Institutions' (1976) 4 Journal of Psychiatry and Law 333.

M. Rutter, *Maternal Deprivation Reassessed* (1972) Harmondsworth, Penguin Books.

B. Tizard, *Adoption: A Second Chance* (1977) London, Open Books.

Chapter 16

* Sir William Beveridge, *Social Insurance and Allied Services* (Cmd. 6404) (1942) London, HMSO, para. 347.

DHSS/SBC, *Low Incomes* (1979) London, HMSO.

* J.M. Eekelaar, 'Public Law and Private Rights: the Finer Proposals' [1976] Public Law 64, pp. 70–77.

* Equal Opportunities Commission, *The Taxation of Husband and Wife: Response of the Equal Opportunities Commission to the Government Green Paper* (1981) Manchester, Equal Opportunities Commission, pp. 7–8.

F. Field, *Fair Shares for Families — the Need for a Family Impact Statement* (1981) London, Study Commission on the Family.

* V. George, *Social Security and Society* (1973) London, Routledge and Kegan Paul, pp. 124, 127.

P. Lewis, 'Cutting Poverty in Half' *One-Parent Times*, Spring 1979.

R. Lister, *Patching Up the Safety Net* (1977) London, Child Poverty Action Group.

R. Lister, *The No-Cost, No-Benefit Review* (1979) London, Child Poverty Action Group.

* R. Lister, 'Income Maintenance for Families with Children' in R.N. Rapoport, M.P. Fogarty and R. Rapoport (eds.), *Families in Britain* (1982) London, Routledge and Kegan Paul, pp. 432–434, 436–438, 442–445.

* National Council for One Parent Families, *Key Facts and Figures* (1983) London, One Parent Families.

Meade Committee, *The Structure and Reform of Direct Taxation* (1978) London, Institute of Fiscal Studies.

M. Phillips, 'Family Policy: the Long Years of Neglect' *New Society*, 8 June 1978.

D. Piachaud, *The Cost of a Child* (1979) London, Child Poverty Action Group.

C. Pond, *The Poverty Trap* (1978) Milton Keynes, Open University Press.

Report of the Committee on Family Policy (1972) Sweden.

* *Report of the Committee on One-Parent Families* (Chairman: The Hon. Sir Morris Finer) (Cmnd. 5629) (1974) London, HMSO, paras. 4.179–4.183, 4.193–4.207, 4.188–4.189, 5.104, 5.81–5.86.

Royal Commission on the Taxation of Profits and Income, *Second Report* (Cmd. 9105) (1954) London, HMSO.

Supplementary Benefits Commission, *Response of the Supplementary Benefits Commission to Social Assistance* (1979) London, HMSO.

J. Walley, *Social Security: Another British Failure?* (1972) London, Charles Knight.

M. Wynn, *Family Policy* (1972) Harmondsworth, Penguin Books.

Chapter 17

P.W. Alexander, 'The Follies of Divorce — A Therapeutic Approach' (1949) University of Illinois Law Forum 695.

N. Angell, 'The Family Court — One American Model' [1975] L.A.G. Bulletin 260.

V. Aubert, 'Competition and Dissensus: Two Types of Conflict Resolution' (1963) 7 Journal of Conflict Resolution 26.

V. Aubert, 'Courts and Conflict Resolution' (1967) 11 Journal of Conflict Resolution 40.

Sir George Baker, *Address to the Law Society's Annual Conference on 7 October 1977*; *Guardian Gazette*, 26 October 1977.

* L. Neville Brown, 'The Legal Background to the Family Court' [1966] British Journal of Criminology 139, pp. 139–142, 146–148, 149.

Brown and Bloomfield, *Legality and Community* (1979).

G. Davis, 'Conciliation or Litigation?' [1982] L.A.G. Bulletin, April, pp. 11–13.

G. Davis, 'Conciliation and the Professions' (1983) 13 Family Law 6.

G. Davis, 'Mediation in Divorce: A Theoretical Perspective' [1983] Journal of Social Welfare Law 131.

J.M. Eekelaar, *Family Law and Social Policy* (1978) London, Weidenfeld and Nicholson, p. 276.

J.M. Eekelaar and E. Clive with K. Clarke and S. Raikes, *Custody After Divorce: The Disposition of Custody in Divorce Cases in Great Britain* (1977) Oxford, Centre for Socio-legal Studies.

* D. Fraser, 'Divorce Avon Style — The Work of a Specialist Welfare Team' (1980) 11 Social Work Today 12, pp. 14–15.

* M.D.A. Freeman, 'Towards a More Humane System of Divorce: Murch and Participant Justice' (1981) 145 Justice of the Peace 173, pp. 173–174.

* C. Foote, R.J. Levy and F.E.A. Sander, *Cases and Materials on Family Law* (2nd edn., 1976) Boston, Little, Brown and Company, pp. 1092–1098.

Judge J. Graham Hall, 'Outline of a Proposal for a Family Court' (1977) 1 Family Law 6.

C.P. Harvey, 'On the State of the Divorce Market' (1953) 16 MLR 129.

Home Office, *The Child, the Family and the Young Offender* (Cmnd. 2742) 1965 London, HMSO.

* Home Office, *Marriage Matters. A Consultative Document by the Working Party on Marriage Guidance set up by the Home Office in consultation with the DHSS* (1979) London, HMSO, paras. 1.12, 1.15–1.17, 7.4, 7.5. 7.8 – 7.11.

R.M. Jackson, *The Machinery of Justice in England* (4th edn., 1964, 7th edn., 1977) Cambridge, Cambridge University Press.

Justice, *Report on Parental Rights and Duties and Custody Suits* (1975) London, Stevens.

Justice of the Peace, 'The New Domestic Court' (1979) 143 Justice of the Peace 570.

Justices' Clerks' Society, *Towards a Workable Family Court* (1976) London, Justices' Clerks' Society.

Law Commission, *Reform of the Grounds of Divorce — The Field of Choice.* (Cmnd. 3123) (1966) London, HMSO.

Law Commission, Report on *Matrimonial Proceedings in Magistrates' Courts*, Law Com. No. 77 (1976) London, HMSO.

* Law Reform Commission of Canada, *The Family Court*, Working Paper 1 (1974) Ottowa, Information Canada, pp. 7–8.

* Law Society, Family Law Sub-Committee, *A Better Way Out: suggestions for the reform of the law of divorce and other forms of matrimonial relief; for the setting-up of a family court; and for its procedure* (1979) London, the Law Society, paras. 142, 144, 145, 147, 148, 153, 154.

Law Society, Standing Committee on Family Law, *A Better Way Out Reviewed* (1982) London, the Law Society.

Law Society, Legal Aid Annual Reports [1979–80], HC 160 (1980–81) (1981) London, HMSO.

Lord Chancellor's Department, *Family Jurisdiction of the High Court and County Courts* Consultation Paper (1983) London, Lord Chancellor's Department.

O.R. McGregor, L. Blom-Cooper and C. Gibson, *Separated Spouses* (1970) London, Duckworth.

* R.H. Mnookin, 'Bargaining in the Shadow of the Law: The Case of Divorce' [1979] Current Legal Problems 65, pp. 65, 78–79, 96–99, 102.

G. Morgan, *Death Wishes?* (1979) Chichester, Wiley.

F.E. Mostyn, 'Has Divorce a Future?' [1975] L.A.G. Bulletin 285.

* M. Murch, *Justice and Welfare in Divorce* (1980) London, Sweet and Maxwell, pp. 223–224, 226–228, 241, 244–245, 251.

* L. Parkinson, 'Bristol Courts Family Conciliation Service' (1982) 12 Family Law 13, pp. 13–15.

L. Parkinson, 'Conciliation: Pros and Cons' (1983) 13 Family Law 22.

L. Parkinson, 'Conciliation: A New Approach to Family Conflict Resolution' (1983) 13 British Journal of Social Work 19.

L. Parkinson and J. Westcott, 'Bristol Courts Family Conciliation Service' *Law Society's Gazette*, 21 May 1980, p. 513.

* G.M. Parmiter, 'Bristol In-Court Conciliation Procedure' *Law Society's Gazette*, 25 February 1981, pp. 196–197.

R. Pound, *Interpretations of Legal History* (1923) Cambridge, Mass., Harvard University Press.

Report of the Committee on Children and Young Persons, Scotland (Chairman: Lord Kilbrandon) (Cmnd. 2306) (1964) Edinburgh, HMSO.

* *Report of the Committee on One-Parent Families* (Chairman: The Hon. Sir Morris Finer) (Cmnd. 5629) (1974) London, HMSO, paras. 4.282–3, 4.285–6, 4.288–9, 4.290, 4.298, 4,337, 4.347–9, 4.352–3, 4.355, 4.362–3, 4.404–5, 4.424.

Report of the Committee on Procedure in Matrimonial Causes (Chairman: Mr. Justice Denning) (Cmd. 7024) (1947) London, HMSO.

Report of the Royal Commission on Marriage and Divorce (Chairman: Lord Morton of Henryton) (Cmd. 9678) (1956) London, HMSO.

M. Rheinstein, 'The Law of Divorce and Marriage Stability' (1956) 9 Vanderbilt Law Review 633.

Society of Conservative Lawyers, *The Case for Family Courts* (1978) London, Conservative Political Centre.

* N. Tyndall, 'Helping Troubled Marriages: A Comment on the Work of the National Marriage Guidance Council' (1982) 12 Family Law 76, p. 76.

J.S. Wallerstein and J.B. Kelly, *Surviving the Breakup: How Children and Parents Cope with Divorce* (1980) London, Grant McIntyre.

C. Yates, 'Development of Conciliation in Divorce Proceedings' (1982) 132 New Law Journal 102.

Acknowledgments

Grateful acknowledgment is made to all the authors and publishers of the extract sources indicated in the Bibliography for their kind permission to reproduce material from their works; in particular, the following permissions are noted:

Adoption & Fostering (formerly *Child Adoption*): extracts are reprinted by kind permission of British Agencies for Adoption & Fostering; this quarterly journal is available from 11 Southwark Street, London, SE1 1RQ.

Family Law and the *Family Law Reports*: extracts are reprinted by kind permission of the publishers Jordan & Sons Ltd.

Family Law Quarterly: extracts are reprinted with the permission of Sanford N. Katz, Editor-in-Chief.

HMSO: extracts from Command papers and other parliamentary papers, Law Commission reports and working papers, OPCS reports and surveys, *Population Trends* and *Social Trends* are reproduced with the permission of the Controller of Her Majesty's Stationery Office.

S. Maidment, 'The Law's Response to Marital Violence in England and the U.S.A.' (1977) 26 ICLQ 403–444: extracts are reproduced by permission of the British Institute of International and Comparative Law, publishers of the *International and Comparative Law Quarterly*.

'Mental Hospitalisation of Children and the Limits of Parental Authority': extracts are reprinted by permission of The Yale Law Journal Company and Fred B. Rothman & Company from *The Yale Law Journal*, Vol. 88, pp. 186–216.

Extracts from the following are reprinted by permission of Penguin Books Ltd.:

J. Bowlby, *Child Care and the Growth of Love* (2nd edn., 1965, Pelican Books) — copyright © John Bowlby 1953, 1965 and (Pt III) Mary Salter Ainsworth 1965.

R. Fletcher, *The Family and Marriage in Britain* (3rd edn., 1973, Pelican Books) — copyright © Ronald Fletcher 1962, 1966, 1973.

L. Mair, *Marriage* (1971, Pelican Books) — copyright © Lucy Mair 1971.

A. Oakley, *Housewife* (1976, Pelican Books) — copyright © Ann Oakley 1974.

M. Rutter, *Maternal Deprivation Reassessed* (2nd edn., 1981, Penguin Education) — copyright © Michael Rutter 1972, 1981.

L. Tilly and J. Scott, *Women, Work and Family* — copyright © 1978 Holt, Rinehart and Winston: extracts are reprinted with the permission of Holt, Rinehart and Winston, CBS College Printing.

The Law Reports; *The Weekly Law Reports*: extracts are reprinted by kind permission of the Incorporated Council of Law Reporting for England and Wales.

Criminal Appeal Reports: extracts are reprinted by kind permission of Sweet & Maxwell Ltd.

Solicitors Journal: extracts are reprinted by kind permission of the publisher, Oyez Longman Publishing Ltd.

CHAPTER 1

The family and marriage

1 Definitions of 'household' and 'family'

Most people understand that the word *family* refers to a group of persons related to each other by blood and/or marriage. The introduction of an additional word, such as 'immediate', suggests that the members of the family probably live together within a single household, and (although to a variable extent) pool their resources for the common well-being of the unit. However, many important questions are immediately raised by this series of assumptions. Is it necessary for the members of the family to be related in the manner described? Is it a prerequisite that there be a single household? Why should members pool resources?

A *household* according to Stone, writing about the family in England from 1500-1800, consists of persons 'living under one roof'. Indeed, household and family were synonymous. In *The Family, Sex and Marriage* (1977), he says:

The core of any household is clearly the family, namely members related by blood or marriage, usually the conjugal pair and their unmarried children, but sometimes including grandparents, the married children, or occasionally kin relatives. But most households also included non-kin inmates, sojourners, boarders or lodgers, occupying rooms vacated by children or kin, as well as indentured apprentices and resident servants, employed either for domestic work about the house or as an additional resident labour force for the fields or the shop.

Laslett and Wall, in their major work published in 1972 entitled *Household and Family in Past Time*, define the two words 'household' and 'family' in the context of the historical demography which they collect and analyse:

It must be strongly stressed that in this vocabulary the word *family* does not denote a complete coresident domestic group, though it may appear as an abbreviated title. The word *household* particularly indicates the fact of shared location, kinship and activity. Hence all solitaries have to be taken to be households, for they are living with themselves, and this is the case when they have servants with them, since servants are taken as household members. . . .

The expression *simple family* is used to cover what is variously described as the *nuclear family*, the *elementary family* or (not very logically, since spouses are not physiologically connected), the *biological family*. It consists of a married couple, or a married couple with offspring, or of a widowed person with offspring. The concept is of the conjugal link as the structural principle, and conjugal linkage is nearly always patent in the lists of persons which we are using. For a simple family to appear then, it is necessary for at least two individuals connected by that link or arising from that link to be coresident: *conjugal family unit* (CFU) is a preciser term employed to describe all possible groups so structured.

No solitary can form a conjugal family unit and for such a group to subsist it is necessary for at least two immediate partners (spouses and/or offspring) to be present. More remotely connected persons, whose existence implies more than one conjugal link, do not constitute a conjugal family unit if they reside together with no one else except servants. Nor do brothers and sisters. Hence a widow with a child forms a conjugal family unit, but a widow with a grandchild does not, nor does an aunt with a nephew. Whenever a conjugal family unit is found on its own, it is always taken to be a household, just as solitaries are, and such a coresident domestic group is called a *simple family household*. The first mentioned person in the household of this and all other types is always taken to be head. . . .

An *extended family household* [or stem family] consists in a conjugal family unit with the addition of one or more relatives other than offspring, the whole group living together on its own or with servants. It is thus identical with the simple family household except for the additional item or items. If the resident relative is of a generation earlier than that of the head, say a married head's father, or a spouse's mother, or a widowed head's aunt, then the extension is said to be upwards.

Similarly the presence of a grandchild (without either parent) or a nephew or niece creates downward extension, and that of a brother, sister or cousin of the head or of his spouse, implies sideways or lateral extension. Some groups are extended vertically and laterally, and it should be noted that the presence of any kin or affine of the conjugal family unit creates extension however distant the relationship, though the relatives of a servant do not do so. It is particularly important that the whole phrase 'extended family household' be used for this category of domestic group, because the words 'extended family' by themselves have a highly significant but quite separate further meaning, which covers all relatives in habitual contact with a person, irrespective of whether they live with him.

Multiple family households comprise all forms of domestic group which include two or more conjugal family units connected by kinship or by marriage. Such units can be simple or extended, and can be disposed vertically and laterally. The disposition of a secondary unit, that is of a constituent unit which does not contain the head of the whole household, is said to be up if its conjugal link involves a generation earlier than that of the head, as for example when his father and mother live with him. Such a secondary unit can include offspring of the head's parents other than the head himself, that is his resident unmarried brothers or sisters, and the presence of such persons keeps this secondary unit in being if one or other of the head's parents dies. A secondary unit is disposed down if, for example, a head's married son lives with him along with his wife and perhaps offspring, with similar implications about siblings and widowhood. . . .

If conjugal family units within households of the multiple kind are all disposed laterally, as when married brothers and/or sisters live together, the overall arrangement is the one often referred to as the 'fraternal joint family' by social anthropologists. The expression 'joint family' is also widely used, however, to refer to all the forms of multiple family household.

It is necessary to consider another introductory matter, namely the difference between *familial experience* and *familial ideology*. There may be a correspondence between experience and ideology; however, it has been argued by Laslett and Wall that although the nuclear monogamous family has a claim to universality, it has never possessed a normative and ideological force:

There must be few behavioural institutions of which it can be said that ideology and experience are entirely congruent. No one would question that the English society of our day is correctly described as monogamous, because monogamous behaviour is nearly universal amongst a people whose belief in monogamy as a value is very widespread, and whose conduct is consistent with monogamy as the norm. It could be called the marital institution under which the English live, for no other distinct practice-with-belief exists alongside it as an alternative. Yet divorce is now quite frequent, scepticism about single spouse unions often encountered, and sexual intercourse outside marriage a commonplace. Indeed we know that children have been begotten illegitimately in appreciable numbers in England during the whole period for which figures can be recovered. . . .

Departure from the monogamous ideal of behaviour, amongst English people nowadays, and perhaps amongst their ancestors, has been particularly conspicuous within the élite, and rejection of the beliefs associated with monogamy especially common with the intellectuals, the makers of opinions and of norms. Monogamy as an institution, then, has been underwritten by a general correspondence of ideology and experience, but is consistent with an appreciable degree of disharmony between the two. We do not find ourselves enquiring how much they could diverge before a practice ceased to be *the* institution, and became one amongst others, *an* institution. We do not easily contemplate a situation where plural institutions, or highly variable behaviour, exist in one society at one time in such matters as sexual behaviour and marriage.

Yet if we turn to the question of how far any of the forms of the coresident domestic group, . . . could be called *the* institution, or *an* institution, of the societies where examples of them are found, this issue becomes inescapable. Glancing again at England as it is today, it seems safe enough to claim that the nuclear family, the simple family household, is *the* familial institution, and that again because experience of it, belief in it, willingness to obey its norms, are in fact all congruent with each other. The nuclear family, of course, complements the English institution of monogamy in a particular way. But it has, and has had for hundreds of years as far as we can yet see, a markedly better claim to universality in behaviour and experience than monogamous marriage with exclusively marital sexual intercourse. Yet the nuclear family never seems to have possessed the normative force, certainly not the ideological potential of monogamy, in England or indeed in Western culture.

The hiatus, therefore, between familial experience and familial ideology is of a somewhat different character than that which divides the two in the matter of monogamy. The intellectuals and opinion makers who deal in the ideology of our world, have a tendency to deplore the circumstance that the complex family household is not sufficiently established as a norm in our society. Extended and even multiple households exist amongst us, but not in anything like enough numbers to ensure that the widowed and the elderly unmarried have a family to live in, or our children the emotional advantage of the presence of the extended kin in the households where they grow up.

Laslett and Wall's definition of monogamy may be contrasted with following extract from Engels, *Origins of the Family, Private Property and the State* (1884):

Sex love in the relation of husband and wife is and can become the rule only among the oppressed classes, that is, at the present day, among the proletariat, no matter whether this relationship is officially sanctioned or not. But all the foundations of classical monogamy are removed. Here there is a complete absence of all property, for the safeguarding and inheritance of which monogamy and male domination were established. Therefore, there is no stimulus whatever here to assert male domination. . . .

Moreover, since large-scale industry has transferred the woman from the house to the labour market and the factory, and makes her, often enough, the bread winner of the family, the last remnants of male domination in the proletarian home have lost all foundation — except, perhaps, for some of that brutality towards women which became firmly rooted with the establishment of monogamy. Thus, the proletarian family is no longer monogamian in the strict sense, even in cases of the most passionate love and strictest faithfulness of the two parties, and despite all spiritual and worldly benedictions which may have been received. . . .

In short, proletarian marriage is monogamian in the etymological sense of the word, but by no means in the historical sense.

Questions

(i) Polygamy is permitted in some cultures; for example, according to the classical Islamic law a man is permitted four wives; the husband inherits a large slice of his wife's property, but she does have rights of ownership while she is alive and can inherit a share of the estate of her deceased father. Do you think that polygamy has anything to do with: (*a*) control of property and (*b*) male domination?

(ii) Section 8(3) of the Immigration Act 1971 states that the provisions introduced under the Act for immigration control over persons who are not British citizens shall not apply to any person so long as he is a member of a mission, or 'a person who is a member of the family and forms part of the household of such a member.' Advise the authorities whether the following are exempt from control: (*a*) the distant cousin of a Burmese diplomat who has been looked after by this diplomat and his wife after the death of the parents; (*b*) the fourth wife of a Yemeni diplomat who has been provided with separate accommodation by her husband in Yemen in accordance with the Islamic law; and (*c*) the young brother of an Indian diplomat who has equal rights with the diplomat in the joint property they have both inherited from their father?

(iii) Schedule 1, para. 3 of the Rent Act 1977 permits a statutory tenancy, in the absence of a surviving spouse, to devolve upon any person who was 'a member of the original tenant's family' and who was residing with the deceased at the time of, and for a period of six months immediately preceding, his death. Does this rule apply to the following: (*a*) a close friend of the original tenant, where both had for many years lived together in a platonic association; (*b*) the survivor of two old cronies who had shared a house; (*c*) a lady of 'independence' who had lived with the deceased for many years as his cohabitant but who had deliberatedly remained unmarried?

(iv) In *Carega Properties SA v Sharratt* [1979] All ER 1084, [1979] 1 WLR 928, the House of Lords emphasised that the relevant question under the Rent Act 1977 is whether the 'ordinary man' would regard the relationship in question as establishing 'a broadly recognisable familial nexus'. Historically, is this phrase restricted to a biological or marital connection? (See p. 274, below, for further discussion of this provision).

(v) In *M v M* (1981) 2 FLR 39, the Court of Appeal refused an application of a wife for a maintenance order against her husband in favour of a child of hers. The court decided that the husband had not treated the child as a child of the family (s. 52(1) of the Matrimonial Causes Act 1973). The parties were married in September 1970. They separated in April 1971. After the separation the wife became pregnant by another man. The wife did not want her family to know that the husband was not the father. The husband acquiesced in this state of affairs and allowed the wife's family to think the child was his.

Ormrod LJ: In my judgment the first question the learned judge had to ask himself was, 'Could there possibly be said to have been at any time during this child's life a family of which he could be treated as part?' In my judgment, the answer to that must be 'No'. These two parties, husband and wife, had been living apart in the full sense of the phrase ever since April 1971. There had been nothing whatsoever in their relationship which bore any relation to that of husband and wife. The learned judge himself put it that they were, if anything, friends, still on friendly terms. . . .

Here the husband has filed his petition (he has not got his decree yet) on the ground that the parties had been living apart in that sense for five years, and the one thing that emerges perfectly clearly from the fact of this case is that neither of them regarded the marriage as subsisting. Once you get to that stage, it seems to me wholly artificial to say that the family as a social unit continued to exist. It must, as a family, using the language in ordinary sense, come to an end when the parties regard their marriage as at an end. These two parties plainly regarded their marriage as at an end from April 1971 onwards. It is not necessary to go any further than that except to say that these two parties would not be treated as living together for any other purpose of the Matrimonial Causes Act. They would be separate individuals for the purposes of income tax, for example, and for affiliation proceedings.

They were living apart, held together only by the empty shell of this marriage which could have been dissolved at any time. . . .

My conclusions on the facts of this case are, firstly, that there was in fact at no time during this child's life a family. Therefore, it was not possible to treat the child as a child of this (non-existent) family; secondly on the question of 'treatment', it is a matter of fact to be judged by looking at and carefully considering what the husband in this case did and how he behaved towards the child. The difficulty in this case is that the husband, if he did anything, behaved towards this child not as if the child were a child of the family but as if, for certain purposes, the child was his own natural child. That is, he took part in the pretence without protesting. I do not think the evidence goes any further than that. The fact that he put the word 'Dad' on some Christmas cards and presents does not, in my judgment, amount to anything more than following the line he had taken up at the request of the wife, which was to cover up for her to all intents and purposes. He, as he said himself, was quite fond of the child as a child. He was kind to the boy and was quite pleased to see him on the rare occasions when he visited the mother. It goes no further than that.

Is 'child of the family' the same thing as 'child of the household'? (See *England v Secretary of State for Social Services* (1981) 3 FLR 222 where Woolf J held that the word 'household' in s. 1(1) of the Family Income Supplements Act 1970 had a wider meaning than 'living in the family's care at home' and payments of family income supplement could include children who were temporarily absent in the voluntary care of the local authority so long as ties with the parents and the home were sufficiently closely maintained.)

(vi) Does this mean that the legal meaning of family is different according to the functional context in which it is used? If so, should it be?

2 Approaches to the history of the family

In *Approaches to the History of the Western Family* (1980) Anderson distinguishes three approaches to family history: the demographic approach, the sentiments approach, and the household economic approach. These three schools of thought emphasise different aspects of the available source material. The extracts in this section have been selected to provide illustrations of the debate upon which family historians are currently engaged.

(a) THE DEMOGRAPHIC APPROACH

Peter Laslett and his co-workers at the Cambridge SSRC group for the History of Population and Social Structure are the major writers who adhere to this approach.

A particular matter which must be of considerable interest for the policy-makers of the present time is the historical evidence relating to the size of households, and whether this information has a bearing on the size, type and function of the family. It is to this question that the Laslett team has directed its gaze. Laslett suggests that the 'mean household size' (including servants in England) 'has remained more or less constant at about 4.75 from the sixteenth century right through the industrialisation period until the end of the nineteenth century when a steady decline set in to a figure of about three in contemporary censuses.' The work of the Group is based on 100 English communities at dates between 1574 and 1821. 70% of households are classed as two-generational and 24% as one generational. Only 6% contain relatives of three different generations and less than 1% of four generations. The major conclusion is that a nuclear familial form 'may have been one of the enduring and fundamental characteristics of the Western family system.' Indeed, Alan MacFarlane in *Origins of English Individualism* (1978) has argued that the nuclear family as a behavioural fact has existed in England since 1200.

However, recent research has tended to suggest that this view is a gross exaggeration and overgeneralisation. In Southern and Eastern Europe, households were of a more complex type (see Berkner, 1977). Indeed even in relation to England, Laslett's conclusions have been doubted, as Anderson (1980) explains:

If we imagine a household where land is transferred to a son on his marriage and the son subsequently has children of his own, then, if this occurs before his father's death, a three-generation family will appear in a census listing. A few years later, when the father has died, only a widow, married child and grandchildren will be left and the evidence for a stem household becomes ambiguous. On the widow's death, a nuclear household will result and the census listing will reveal no evidence of any extension at all. Nevertheless — and this is the crucial point — while no stem-family *household* is present, a stem-family *organisation* remains since, in due course, the same process will be repeated by the next generation. Indeed, even where no stem-family system is in operation the availability of data on ages frequently shows a marked life-cycle effect in household data which is not apparent in aggregate data.

What is at issue is the life cycle of the family: first, newly-married couple; second, nuclear family with children; third, extended family; and fourth, back again to nuclear family. Static listings of households conceal this pattern.

The conclusions of Laslett and other members of the group are also criticised by Edward Shorter, in *The Making of the Modern Family* (1975):

In earlier writings on the history of the family, sociologists acquired the bad habit of assuming that families before the Industrial Revolution were organized in clans or were at least highly 'extended'. Because any historian with even a passing familiarity with Europe's social history would realize at once the inaccuracy of that assumption, a revisionist reaction developed in the 1960s: the nuclear family was 'unearthed' time and again in history, to the accompaniment of loud shouts of discovery. As often happens to revisionists, these writers fell over backwards attempting to overturn the conventional wisdom; instead of merely correcting the sociologists' fantasies about clans and sprawling patriarchies, they tended to proclaim that at most times and places it was the conjugal family — mother, father, children, and servants — that had prevailed. The revisionists thus proceeded to create a little fantasy of their own; the nuclear family as a historical constant.

Now, many kinless families did exist; indeed, they often represented a majority of all households. But to get a sense of the typical experience of the average person, we must ask what kind of household a child would most likely have been socialized in: extended (stem), or nuclear? And there is a good chance that in better-off households as opposed to poorer ones, and in east Europe as opposed to west Europe, the average child was raised in a dwelling that contained many relatives besides his mother and father. . . .

Conjugal groups *minus* kin also turned up frequently enough in rural Europe. There were, for example, the pastoral regions of the Netherlands, where the grandparents seldom lived with the farmer and his wife. In Norwegian villages relatives co-resided with propertied peasants only about a fifth of the time, and the percentage was even lower among the cottagers. Across much of Lower Austria and in at least two well-documented villages in Salzburg province, three-generation households were unusual. . . .

Yet we must still consider the possibility that in such communities many households might, at some point in time, have contained several generations, but that death snatched away the grand-parents before the census-taker arrived. Thus in the census they appeared as single-family units, whereas they might actually have been, for a period of years, stem families.

However, in many other areas of western and central Europe, the stem family was common-place and the kinless family an anomaly. Frédéric Le Play, the nineteenth-century French sociologist, coined the term *famille souche* to denote families that passed on a given farm undivided from one generation to the next over long periods of time.

(b) THE ECONOMIC APPROACH

A question often asked is why a detailed knowledge of household composition should necessarily tell us much about familial behaviour? Indeed, there are many who see household composition as a by-product of more fundamental economic processes. There is a group of writers who seek to interpret the historical data relating both to households and to families in the context of the economic realities of the period and of the region. The major question is based around the value of the household as a means of production. Anderson summarises these writings for us, in the context of the family economy of the Western peasant, in *Approaches to the History of the Western Family* (1980):

This approach has taken as its central concept the often unconscious 'strategies' employed by family members to maintain a customary standard of living, both for themselves in the present and, under certain circumstances, for themselves and their descendants in the future. The types of strategies available are constrained in a number of ways: by the family's resource-generating potential (particularly its age/sex composition); by the mode of production in which the family is involved; by the income-generating relationships which are implied by that mode; by law, and custom regarding property acquisition (including inheritance); by the possibilities of access to alternative resource-generating activities (including wage-labour or domestic manufacturing) or resource-providing rights (including, for example, both customary rights to pasture animals on common land and social welfare provision); by the intervention of powerful groups external to the family (landlords, employers and others with power in the local community); by customs limiting the range of resource-generating options which individuals see as practically available at a point in time (for example, ideas over what is appropriate work for women). (Tilly, 1979).

For the Western peasant or yeoman farmer, the principal scarce resource was land, so family strategies were constrained by the conditions under which land could be obtained and by the labour inputs required to work it. The literature on continental Europe, on Ireland, and on some areas of England even in the early nineteenth century, portrays the dominant peasant/yeoman pattern as one where the family's subsistence needs could be met only through the continual application of the labour of all its members to productive tasks in agriculture or, to a greater or lesser extent, in certain craft or other domestically organised productive activities. Almost all production was intended either for family use or for local and known markets.

One of the central problems of the peasant family, from this perspective, was the need to ensure that enough labour was available to meet current and future needs while yet not having too many mouths to feed for the resource-generating capacity of the means of production (Winberg, 1978). On the one hand it was necessary to avoid childless marriages, which gave no security for old age (hence perhaps norms encouraging premarital intercourse to ensure marriage only to fertile girls). On the other hand too many children threatened current subsistence. This problem could, however, in some places be solved by one or more strategic responses. For example: one could acquire more productive resources as children grew . . . , one could expand non-agricultural activities and devote more effort to domestic craft production (but this was not always available) . . . , one could restrict family size by marriage to older women . . . , by some form of contraception (found in seventeenth-century England, eighteenth- and early-nineteenth-century Sweden and many other places) . . . or by some other strategy such as prolonging breast feeding. Finally, as in England, Scandinavia and elsewhere, poor households could regulate their numbers by sending 'surplus' children into service at an early age.

(c) THE SENTIMENTS APPROACH

There is another group of writers which is not prepared either to see household composition as a by-product of fundamental economic processes, or to deduce the historical development of the Western family from demographic sources. Shorter (1975) and Stone (1977) in particular have emphasised what has been termed 'the tale of sentiments.' Anderson illustrates the difference in the approach between Laslett, and the work of Shorter and Stone: 'The demographic approach started from a particular set of documents, by which their questions and conclusions have been constrained. The sentiments writers began with a set of questions about the ideas associated with family behaviour and were then faced with the problem of finding suitable source material to throw light on such ideas.'

The following extract is taken from Stone's chapter on family characteristics, in *The Family, Sex and Marriage* (1977):

In the sixteenth century, relations between spouses in rich families were often fairly remote. Living in big houses, each with his or her own bedroom and servants, husband and wife were primarily members of a functioning social universe of a large household and were rarely in private together. . . . Their marriage was usually arranged rather than consensual, in essence the outcome of an economic deal or a political alliance between two families. The transaction was sealed by the wedding and by the physical union of two individuals, while the emotional ties were left to develop at a later date. If they did not take place, and if the husband could find sexual alternatives through casual liaisons, the emotional outlet through marriage was largely non-existent for either husband or wife.

In any case, the expectations of felicity from marriage were pragmatically low, and there were many reasons why disappointment was minimal. The first is that the pair did not need to see very much of one another, either in elite circles, where they could go their own way, or among the plebs, where leisure activities were segregated, with the men resorting to the ale-house, and the women to each other's houses. . . .

The second reason why such a system was so readily accepted was the high adult mortality rates, which severely reduced the companionship element in marriage and increased its purely reproductive and nurturance functions. There was a less than fifty-fifty chance that the husband and wife would both remain alive more than a year or two after the departure from the home of the last child, so that friendship was hardly necessary. William Stout's comment on a marriage in 1699 could stand as an epitaph for many sixteenth- and seventeenth-century couples: 'they lived very disagreeably but had many children.'

Nor was the position very different amongst the lower classes in pre-eighteenth century France:

Eighteenth-century middle-class observers of social relations among the labouring classes, peasants and urban *petite bourgeoisie* in France could find no trace of affection in the marital relationship. Their observations may be biased by class and background, but if they are at all accurate, they must reflect a permanent feature of the traditional European society. All over France, 'If the horse and the wife fall sick at the same time, the . . . peasant rushes to the blacksmith to care for the animal, and leaves the task of healing his wife to nature.' If necessary, the wife could be replaced very cheaply, while the family economy depended on the health of the animal. This peasant pragmatism was confirmed by traditional proverbs, such as 'rich is the man whose wife is dead and horse alive.' The same lack of marital sentiment was evident in the towns. '*L'amitié*, that delicious sentiment, is scarcely known. There are in these little towns only marriages of convenience; nobody appreciates that true happiness consists in making others happy, who always reward us in kind.'

The bleak portrait is modified in a number of ways by Stone himself:

This rather pessimistic view of a society with little love and generally low and widely diffused affect needs to be modified if it is accurately to reflect the truth. Romantic love and sexual intrigue was certainly the subject of much poetry of the sixteenth and early seventeenth centuries, and of many of Shakespeare's plays. It was also a reality which existed in one very restricted social group: the one in which it had always existed since the twelfth century, that is the households of the prince and the great nobles. Here, and here alone, well-born young persons of both sexes were thrown together away from parental supervision and in a situation of considerable freedom as they performed their duties as courtiers, ladies and gentlemen in waiting, tutors and governesses to the children. They also had a great deal of leisure, and in the enclosed hot-house atmosphere of these great houses, love intrigues flourished as nowhere else.

The second modification of the pessimistic general description of affective relations concerns a far wider group, including many who were subjected to the loveless arranged marriage, which was normal among the propertied classes. It is clear from correspondence and wills that in a considerable number of cases, some degree of affection, or at least a good working partnership, developed after the marriage. In practice, as anthropologists have everywhere discovered, the arranged marriage works far less badly than those educated in a romantic culture would suppose, partly because the expectations of happiness from it are not set unrealistically high, and partly because it is a fact that sentiment can fairly easily adapt to social command. In any case, love is rarely blind, in the sense that it tends to be channelled along socially acceptable lines, towards persons of the other sex of similar background. This greatly increases the probability that an arranged marriage, provided it is not undertaken purely for mercenary considerations and that there is not too great a discrepancy in age, physical attractiveness or temperament, may well work out not too badly. This is especially the case where leisure is segregated, so that the pair are not thrown together too much, and where both have a multitude of outside interests and companions to divert them. In a 'low affect' society, a 'low affect' marriage is often perfectly satisfactory.

The final modification to be made to the bleak affective picture is that, owing to the high adult death rate and the late age of marriage, by no means all marriages among persons of property in the sixteenth century were arranged by the parents, since many of them were dead: marriages by choice certainly occurred, although freedom of choice was far more difficult to achieve for women other than widows.

Similar considerations are the basis of Shorter's work. Here he describes the change to 'domesticity', in *The Making of the Modern Family* (1975):

The 'companionate' marriage is customarily seen as the hallmark of contemporary family life, the husband and wife being friends rather than superordinate and subordinate, sharing tasks and affection. Perhaps that is correct. But the emotional cement of the modern family binds more than the husband and wife; it fixes the children, as well, into this sentimental unit. The notion of companionship doesn't necessarily say anything about the relationship between the couple and their children. Also, 'companionship' implies incorrectly that some form of intense romantic attachment continues to unite the couple. Both ideas are incomplete, and for that reason I prefer the expression 'domesticity' in demarcating the modern family from the traditional.

Domesticity, or the family's awareness of itself as a precious emotional unit that must be protected with privacy and isolation from outside intrusion, was the third spearhead of the great onrush of sentiment in modern times. Romantic love detached the couple from communal sexual supervision and turned them towards affection. Maternal love created a sentimental nest within which the modern family would ensconce itself, and it removed many women from involvement with community life. Domesticity, beyond that, sealed off the family as a whole from its traditional interaction with the surrounding world. The members of the family came to feel far more solidarity with one another than they did with their various age and sex peer groups.

(d) THE RELEVANCE OF THE HISTORY OF THE FAMILY?

Anderson asks the question whether family history can 'justify itself', in *Sociology of the Family* (now 1980):

. . . It can do so above all by drawing out the implications of these changes for the kind of family life which is possible today and, above all, by demonstrating that old moralities and old behaviours cannot meet new situations and that, accordingly, present problems require new and not obsolete solutions.

Perhaps the most significant, and certainly analytically the most difficult of these changes have been in the family's relation to production. The peasant household was the locus of production with head and spouse organizing production using the household's own labour and exploiting and co-ordinating the contribution of all household members. Each class of individual had a clearly prescribed role and each member was dependent on the activities of all the others. In this situation there is a high degree of role interdependence both between spouses and between generations. . . . Not merely was production a joint activity but almost all consumption was either shared or was undertaken in some way or other on behalf of the household.

By contrast, under our kind of capitalist system of production, work for the mass of the population becomes directed by others who select and reward labour on an individualistic basis. One or more household members leaves the domestic arena and each is remunerated by outsiders on a basis which normally takes no account of his or her family situation. The wage received is the personal property of the individual, is dependent on the individual's own level of activity and achievement, and is paid to the individual in private leaving him or her to negotiate with the rest of the family over how and to what extent the money is to be distributed in order to satisfy their wants.

The contrast between the jointness of income generation in the peasant family and its individualistic basis under capitalism was, to a considerable extent, concealed under early capitalist production by the continued participation of all except the youngest family members in income-generating activities. Even after legislation had removed children from full time factory employment there remained within local communities significant opportunities for children to add to family resources through cash or goods in kind obtained in return for odd jobs done outside school hours. In addition, the substantial levels of labour input required to process food and other materials for domestic consumption, together with the significant amount of domestic productive activity for both home production and for the market, allowed those who remained in the domestic arena to contribute significantly to family resource generation processes. Thus, in as far as the husband earned income outside the home on behalf of the family, the children (and particularly the male children) sought odd jobs on behalf of the family, and the wife (aided by the female children) produced domestically on behalf of the family, all resources being pooled together, the role interdependence remained and there was little analytical difference between this situation and the peasant system where the husband and male children worked in the outfield producing in part marketable products to pay the rent, while wife and female children worked in the infield and the home on the production and reproduction of labour power. Of course, because wages were the private property of the individual there was no guarantee that wages were in fact pooled — as the harrowing descriptions of the wives of nineteenth-century factory workers trying to extract their husbands from public houses on pay day testify. . . .

Models which assume that family-based decision making took place over how necessary income should be generated and over who should work in which sectors of production, have a clear empirical fit with data from most nineteenth- and early twentieth-century working-class communities.

However, developments of the last fifty years have moved most families significantly away from this position. Children have become almost totally dependent. They leave the home daily for education which is oriented far more to their individual futures than to their current family roles and subsequently enter the labour force to receive pay much of which is again retained for their own use even in the very few years that now typically remain between starting work and marriage. In this way children have almost totally ceased to be part of an interdependent resource-generating system. Similarly, in as far as both spouses enter the labour force and each receives a private reward for labour (and particularly as in many dual career families where outside workers come in to perform most of the domestic work, which anyway can now if desired require a much smaller labour input), the work of the spouses can no longer so easily be seen as a co-operative productive activity or even as involving a complementary division of labour where each performs different but interrelated tasks on behalf of the family unit. . . . The ties between family members thus become based not on an interdependence rooted in co-operative productive activity essential for survival, but on personal interdependence oriented towards the joint attainment of essentially intrinsic 'projects' of highly diverse kinds.

However, these aspirations are much more susceptible to change over time than are the basic survival objectives of pre-industrial European societies, and their interpersonal basis is much more fragile. . . . Thus it is not surprising that wherever we see communities moving from family groups based on property and co-operative production, so we also see a decline in parental involvement in mate selection and, usually, a fall in the age of marriage and a rise in marital instability.

These changes are further facilitated by the parallel changes in the roles of children in the family, which involve both a drastic reduction in the power of parents over their children and in their 'interests' in their children's future welfare. . . .

Viewed in a historical perspective, therefore, there is in the contemporary capitalist world a marked lack of structural support for familial bonds. In addition, demographic changes have increased the emphasis on intrinsic functions of marriage through the reduction in the period of the family life cycle which is devoted to the bearing and rearing of small children. Marriage at a younger age and an increase in life expectancy among adults have combined roughly to double the average duration of marriages unbroken by social dissolution; the median duration of such marriages is rapidly appoaching fifty years. At the same time, the fall in family size and the concentration of childbirth into the earlier years of marriage has led for the first time to a situation where the majority of the life span of marriages does not involve the bearing of and caring for, small children; far from being a brief interval in old age, the 'empty nest' situation, with all its attendant problems of role reallocation, is fast coming to comprise a majority of the marital cycle. Increased leisure has only come to extend still further the time and the energy available for interpersonal relationships between spouses and thus, by inference at least, to make more problematical a lack of success in them. . . .

Equally importantly, the other main prop to traditional family morality — close community supervision — has also been undermined and, indeed, in a comparative perspective, family behaviour has become the most private and personal of all areas of behaviour, almost totally free from external supervision and control.

Anderson concludes his review:

The study of the history of the Western family shows quite clearly that we cannot go back to a strict conformity to the family morality that we have inherited from the past without also — which is clearly impossible — reverting to the economic and social relations of the past. We are not peasants any more and thus cannot sustain a peasant morality. We have to develop new institutions and new behaviours to cope with new situations.

Questions

(i) What *exactly* can a lawyer learn from a knowledge of family history when he comes to interpret the statutory provisions where the words 'household', 'family', and 'child of the family' appear?

(ii) A. Bradney, in an article entitled 'The Family in Family Law' (1979), states: 'It seems clear that there is at least room for debate about the type of family, or types of family, which should be found in family law.' Do you agree with this view, and if so, which types would you have in mind?

3 The family as a social group

The historical strands — the nuclear unit, the rise of domesticity, the economic inter-relationship — are viewed, as we have seen, in different ways by the scholars who have looked at the evidence. Similarly, the modern family has been described by sociologists in many variations. Two extremes are Fletcher (1966) and Oakley (1974). The following extract is from Ronald Fletcher's *The Family and Marriage in Britain* (1966) and emphasises the sense of 'belonging' which is, for him, so important:

The family is, in fact, a community in itself: a small, relatively permanent group of people, related to each other in the most intimate way, bound together by the most personal aspects of life; who experience amongst themselves the whole range of human emotions; who have to strive continually to resolve those claims and counter-claims which stem from mutual but often conflicting needs; who experience continual responsibilities and obligations towards each other; who experience the sense of 'belonging' to each other in the most intimately felt sense of that word. The members of a family share the same name, the same collective reputation, the same home, the same intricate, peculiar tradition of their own making, the same neighbourhood. They share the same sources of pleasure, the same joys, the same sources of profound conflict. The same vagaries of fortune are encountered and overcome together. Degrees of agreement and degrees of violent disagreement are worked out amongst them. The same losses and the same griefs are shared. Hence the family is that group within which the most fundamental appreciation of human qualities and values takes place — 'for better for worse': the qualities of truth and honesty, of falsehood and deceit; of kindliness and sympathy, of indifference and cruelty; of cooperation and forbearance, of egotism and antagonism; of tolerance, justice, and impartiality, of bias, dogmatism, and obstinacy; of generous concern for the freedom and fulfilment of others, of the mean desire to dominate — whether in overt bullying or in psychologically more subtle ways. All those values, and all those discriminations and assessments of value, which are of the most fundamental importance for the formation of adult character are first experienced and exercised by children in the context of the family. Furthermore, these qualities are not 'taught' or 'learned' in any straightforward or altogether rational way; they are actually embodied in people and their behaviour.

Later, Fletcher offers a definition of the contemporary British family summarising the points developed in the book. He asserts that the modern British family is:

1. contracted or founded at an early age, and therefore of long duration,
2. consciously planned,
3. small in size,
4. to a great extent separately housed, and in an improved material environment,
5. economically self-responsible, self-providing, and therefore (*a*) relatively independent of wider kindred, and (*b*) living at a 'distance' from wider kindred, sometimes geographically, but also in terms of a diminished degree of close and intimate social life shared with them,
6. entered into and maintained on a completely voluntary basis by partners of equal status, and therefore entailing a marital relationship based upon mutuality of consideration,
7. democratically managed, in that husband and wife (and frequently children) discuss family affairs together when decisions have to be taken, and
8. centrally concerned with the care and upbringing of children — to such an extent that it is frequently called 'child-centred'.
    Finally, we might add:
9. that the importance of the modern family is widely recognized by government and by the whole range of social services, and is therefore aided in achieving health and stability by a wide range of public provisions.

When these points are considered, there can surely be little doubt that the characteristics of the family in contemporary Britain manifest considerable moral improvements upon the family types of the past. How, then, does it come about that the modern family is said to be in a condition of 'instability'? Why is it said that the family is 'declining in importance as a social institution'? On what grounds can it be argued that there is evidence of 'moral decline'?

Questions

(i) Do you agree with each of these nine points?

(ii) Is Fletcher correct in saying that the contemporary British family manifests a considerable 'moral improvement'?

(iii) What answers can you give to Fletcher's final three questions? (Remember that the book was published in 1966.)

Ann Oakley in her book *Housewife* (1974) presents a very different picture:

A greater equality may characterize the relationships between husband and wife in some areas — legal rights for instance — but mother and father roles, husband and wife roles, remain distinct, and — conspicuous of all — the allocation to women of the housewife role endures. Apparent changes, such as the increasing likelihood of a wife's employment, may not be changes at all, and we should not be taken in by surface appearances, nor by that pseudo-egalitarian phrase the 'dual-career' marriage. . . .

The capacity of the housewife's employment to affect fundamentally and permanently the structure of marital roles is undermined by the ideology of non-interchangeability, of role-segregation, subscribed to by the married couple — the ideology of gender differentiation which is basic to marriage as an institution.

Question

Ann Oakley is talking about marriage as an institution; and what is more, it is the nuclear arrangement which is the object of her scorn. But would an extended family household make the structure of personal relationships and sex differentiation any different?

4 The definition of marriage

We turn our attention to the definition of the conjugal unit or marriage. This is not as easy to describe as may at first appear. Harris (1979) expresses the problem in the following way: 'The inhabitants of Europe and America have an idea which they call marriage. People in other cultures have other ideas which are similar to, but not the same as, our ideas. Traditionally the argument has been about how dissimilar the ideas have to get to force us to stop describing their ideas as "marriage".' Leach (1955) argues that no definition can be found which applies to all institutions which ethnographers and anthropologists commonly refer to as marriage. Therefore he submits for consideration a definition based on a 'bundle of rights'. At least one part of the bundle must be present before the term 'marriage' can be used. The list, which according to Leach is not closed, is as follows:

A. To establish the legal father of a woman's children.
B. To establish a legal mother of a man's children.
C. To give the husband a monopoly in the wife's sexuality.
D. To give the wife a monopoly in the husband's sexuality.

E. To give the husband partial or monopolistic rights to the wife's domestic and other labor services.

F. To give the wife partial or monopolistic rights to the husband's labor services.

G. To give the husband partial or total rights over property belonging or potentially accruing to the wife.

H. To give the wife partial or total rights over property belonging or potentially accruing to the husband.

I. To establish a joint fund of property — a partnership — for the benefit of the children of the marriage.

J. To establish a socially significant 'relationship of affinity' between the husband and his wife's brothers.

In contrast with Leach, there are other scholars, of whom E. Kathleen Gough, in *The Nayars and the Definition of Marriage* (1959), is representative, who argue that 'the status of children born to various types of union (is) critical for decisions as to which of these unions constitute marriage.' As a tentative definition that would have cross-cultural validity, and will fit the unusual cases such as that of the Nayar,[1] Gough suggests: 'Marriage is a relationship established between a woman and one or more other persons which provides that a child born to the woman under circumstances not prohibited by the rules of the relationship, is accorded full birth-status rights common to normal members of his society or social stratum.'

A slightly different way of looking at the problem is suggested by Harris (1979). He says that the major question is to consider *tasks*. Thus it is irrelevant whether we 'strip the term marriage to a single criterion' or accept the 'bundle of rights' argument. The only significant question is the following: 'How do societies arrange for the orderly procreation and rearing of future generations and the transmission of material and cultural possessions?' Harris emphasises child rearing. We shall see later in Chapter 9, below, how judges in English courts have been preoccupied by similar considerations.

If nothing else, then, marriage is about the licence to beget children. There are therefore two questions which assume importance in legal terms. First, who is entitled to marry so as to produce these children? Second, how is such a relationship formalised?

Question

In *Corbett v Corbett (orse Ashley)* [1971] P 83, [1970] 2 All ER 33, Ormrod J said: 'on the other hand, sex is clearly an essential determinant of the relationship called marriage, because it is and always has been recognised as the union of man and woman. It is the institution on which the family is built, and which the capacity for natural heterosexual intercourse is an essential element.' Would the anthropologists agree?

Lucy Mair in her book on *Marriage* (1971) puts the point in this way, for the marriages in subsistence economies with which she is primarily concerned:

---

1. In a period before the British took control of India. Nayar women customarily had a small but not a fixed number of husbands. When a woman became pregnant, it was essential for one of those men to acknowledge probable paternity. The genitor, however, had no economic, social, legal or ritual rights in nor obligations to his children once he had paid the fees of their births. Their guardianship, care and discipline were entirely the concern of their matrilineal kinsfolk.

Marriage is primarily of importance as a knot in the network of kinship links that bind such a society together. It is the formally recognized means of recruiting new members to a line of descent, and it creates alliances between such lines. The making of marriages depends in part on the claims that men are entitled to make on one another's daughters; in part on the kind of alliance that men, seeking wives for themselves or their sons, believe will be advantageous; and to a small degree, and more in some societies than in others, on the individual preferences of a man and a woman. Marriage is a matter of serious concern to a much larger number of people than the spouses themselves. Hence it is hedged about with rules and ceremonies to a much greater extent than it is in those societies, which Radcliffe-Brown long ago reminded us are exceptional, that make an ideal of 'marriage for love'.

Question

We are no longer in a subsistence economy. Does this mean that marriage procedures and the rules about whom one may marry are no longer as important?

5 Restrictions and preferences on the choice of mate

Most societies have rules which restrict the range of choice of partners. These rules operate for the purposes of both sexual and marital relationships. Usually, these two categories coincide, but they do not always do so. The following extract from Beattie, *Other Cultures* (1964) provides an interesting description of the rules relating to exogamy and incest prohibition. The extract also describes examples where there is a preference for the selection of a specific category of kin. Prohibition and preference are closely linked. The rule that one must find one's marriage partner *outside* a defined group is called *exogamy* (or marrying outside); the rule that one must find her *within* a defined group is *endogamy* (marrying inside):

It is a common mistake to suppose that the incest prohibition rests simply on the idea of consanguineal propinquity. In many unilineally[2] organized societies all relatives on one's own side, however distant they are genealogically, may be prohibited as mates, while marriage with quite close relatives on the other side may be socially acceptable and even preferred. Sometimes these prohibitions and preferences are associated with very varying ideas about the parts played in conception and gestation by the father and the mother respectively. Some matrilineal peoples think that the father's role in conception is minimal, if it exists at all: it may be thought that he only 'opens the door', as it were, or at the most shapes the growing embryo through intercourse. The Trobriand Islanders of Melanesia are said to hold such a view. For many patrilineal peoples, on the other hand, the father is seen as the real *geniter* of his child; the mother is merely the receptacle in which it is contained and nourished until birth. But however conception be regarded, there are always some relatives outside the elementary family of spouses and children with whom sexual relations and marriage are prohibited.

How is this universal incest taboo to be explained? Earlier writers spoke of an instinctive and universal horror of incest, and of a 'natural' repugnance to the idea of cohabitation with near kin. But there is little or no evidence for the existence of such instinctive emotional attitudes as these. If there really were such an instinctive aversion it is hard to see how incest could ever occur, as in all societies it not infrequently does. The grounds for the taboo's universality lie elsewhere. They derive rather from the ubiquity of some kind of family or other group organization, and from the fact that certain of the social relationships which such organization implies are incompatible with the presence of sexual relations. . . . Thus there is no known society in which the father-daughter relationship could be assimilated to the husband-wife one; they serve entirely different social ends, and in every society they are regarded completely differently.

---

2. This means that descent is traced *either* through males *or* through females.

There is a further point. If the men of an elementary family were all competing for the sexual favours of the mother . . . or of a sister, the unity of the family group would evidently be destroyed. . . . By threatening to confuse social relationships which should be kept distinct they threaten the very social order itself, and with it the security and even the survival of the members of the society.

As well as prohibiting marriages between certain categories of kin, some societies permit, or even require, certain kinds of relatives to marry. Where people are obliged to marry into specific groups or categories of kin, as in some societies of south-east Asia and Indonesia, and among the Australian aborigines, we may speak of prescriptive marriage systems. Sometimes there is a reciprocal exchange of women between two groups (there may of course be several such reciprocating groups in the whole community), and everybody must marry into the appropriate group and not elsewhere. Such marriages are usually defined by reference to the kinship relation which unites the two groups concerned. Thus often marriage with a particular cross-cousin (commonly a man with his mother's brother's daughter, and so a woman with her father's sister's son) is prescribed. . . .

In societies in which social groups are formed on this basis, an important consequence of prescribed marriage of this type is the establishment of enduring relationships between the separate groups concerned, one group being bound to take, the other to receive, its women from the other. Where *all* marriages are prescribed in such ways, then the marriage system reflects the social organization of the society itself, and neither can be understood without reference to the other.

But in most societies there is no such obligation to choose a mate from a specific category of kin, though in some, including many African ones, marriage with certain categories of kin is socially approved, and may be practised to a greater or lesser extent. . . .

In many matrilineal societies, too, cross-cousin marriage is approved or permitted. The Ashanti of Ghana are an example. . . . Here also it may have important social implications. Thus an Ashanti . . . if he arranges for his daughter to marry his sister's son (who in a matrilineal society is his heir), provides that his daughter at least will have some share in the property he bequeaths. And if he obtains his sister's daughter as a wife for his son (who accordingly marries his father's sister's daughter), then his property and status, which by the rule of matrilineal inheritance pass to his brother (i.e. his sister's son), may in the next generation return to his grandson in the male line of descent. For his patrilineal grandson is also his sister's son's sister's son. This may sound obscure but it can easily be seen by anyone who likes to work it out with pencil and paper.

Question

Why do you think that English law, and other legal systems for that matter, are preoccupied with the prohibitions rather than the preferences for the selection of marriage (and sexual) partners?

Many scholars, from different disciplines, have grappled with the problem of why society does not tolerate incest, and why the taboo is almost universal. The following extract is from an article by O. Aberle, U. Bronfenbrenner, E. Hess, O. Miller, D. Schneider and J. Spuhler which appeared originally in the American Anthropologist (1963) under the title *The incest taboo and the mating patterns of animals*:

The incest taboo in any society consists of a set of prohibitions which outlaw heterosexual relationships between various categories of kinsmen. Almost always, it includes prohibitions on sexual relations between brother and sister, father and daughter, mother and son. Invariably, where any prohibitions are present, other, nonprimary relatives are tabooed as well. There are rare cases where the taboos seem to have been abandoned.

The authors describe a number of different theories:

1. *The inbreeding theory*. This theory asserts that the mating of close kin produces bad results, such as abnormal, enfeebled, or insufficiently numerous offspring. The incest taboo is therefore adaptive because it limits inbreeding, and arose on that account. . . .
2. *The socialization theory*. This theory asserts that the regulation and control of erotic impulses is an indispensable element in socialization — that it serves to maintain the growing child's motivation to accept the roles that he is taught. These roles include extrafamilial and societywide roles as well as those in the nuclear family. Since societies must be larger than a

single nuclear family to be viable, and since nonfamilial roles are different from family roles, these roles in the wider society must be learned by the child. In order for this learning to occur, the socializing agent must control but not directly gratify the child's erotic impulses. Therefore it is necessary that these impulses be frustrated and directed outside the nuclear family. The incest taboo does this.

3. *The family theory.* This theory asserts that unregulated sexual competition is disruptive for any group, that the family is a crucial group, and that the incest taboo is needed to maintain the family intact. The theory asserts that the incest taboo originated because it served this function. Freud, one of the proponents of this theory, made a vigorous effort to imagine the series of events which could have led from promiscuity and unregulated, lethal competition to the final promulgation of nuclear family taboos.

4. *The social and cultural system theory.* This theory asserts that, left to their own devices, human beings would prefer to mate within the family, but that the advantages of a wider group for mutual aid, collective economic security, internal peace, offense and defense, and of a wider group for the sharing of cultural innovations make family and suprafamily exogamy highly adaptive as a device for joining families or larger kinship groups. These advantages would be marked in any kinship-based society but were crucial in early human history. This is so because the first ordered human group to emerge was the family, and the incest taboo and exogamy permitted a society built on existing materials: these devices linked families by bonds developed within the family — the ties of parents and children and of siblings. Because of the strong tendency to mate within the family, the familial incest taboos were necessary to insure exogamy. . . .

5. *The indifference or revulsion theory.* According to this theory, the incest taboo is either a formal expression of the sexual indifference of kinsmen toward each other, or a formal expression of an instinctive horror of sexual relations among kinsmen. . . .

6. *The demographic theory.* This theory holds that for early man, the short life span, small number of offspring to reach maturity, spacing of those offspring, and random sex ratio made intrafamilial inbreeding a virtual demographic impossibility. Hence very early man bred out by necessity. Later, when technological improvements made for larger families and longer life, and intrafamilial mating became possible, the already existing pattern of familial exogamy was given normative backing through the creation of the familial incest taboo. This taboo sustained a practice advantageous from the point of view of group co-operation. . . .

The authors then discuss various criticisms that have been, or might be, directed at each of the six theories. We give here their views on the 'inbreeding' theory and the 'family' theory:

The inbreeding theory in its simplest form has been rejected for decades because it was thought to be wrong. In its pregenetic form the inbreeding theory asserted that inbreeding caused a weakening or deterioration of the stock. The facts of genetics provided a simple corrective to this notion. It was found that inbreeding could not produce 'deterioration' but could only bring to expression what was already present in the stock, . . . Therefore, it was argued, if deleterious recessives were present, they would appear with greater frequency as a result of inbreeding, but if advantageous recessives were present, they would also receive full expression. Thus the disadvantages of inbreeding were offset by the advantages. . . .

This simple corrective, however, does not stand up in the face of new information from the field of population genetics. . . . It has become clear that the ratio of deleterious and lethal recessive genes to selectively advantageous genes is very high indeed. This results from the random character of mutation. . . .

The family theory has certain empirical difficulties. It rests on the supposed acute conflict that would arise out of sexual rivalries between father and son over mother and sister, between mother and daughter over father and brother, between brothers over sisters, and sisters over brothers. Yet father and son, mother and daughter, brother and brother, sister and sister do in fact share sexual partners in a number of societies. With polyandry, father and son sometimes share the same wife (but not the son's mother), or brothers share the same wife (but not their sister). With polygyny, mother and daughter sometimes share the same husband (but not the daughter's father), or sisters share the same husband (but not their brother); there are a large number of instances of institutionalized sharing of sexual favors outside the marital bond, as well.

These objections to the family theory do not lead to the conclusion that the family could tolerate *unregulated* intrafamilial sexual relations. There is ample evidence that sexual competition is disruptive. But there would seem to be two solutions to the problem of maintaining order within the family, rather than one. The first solution is of course the interdiction of sexual relations except for the parents: the familial incest taboo. The second, however, is the institutionalization of sexual access in the family. This would define the time, place, and rate of access of each member of the family to every other. This institutionalization could not be a complete solution for all families. In some families there would be no male offspring, and in others no female. Cohabitation with the parent of opposite sex would temporarily solve this problem, but since children normally outlive their parents, the solution would be only temporary. Nevertheless, it would be possible to adopt this sort of institutionalization as the primary pattern, with secondary alternatives available. Thus societies with other preferential, or even prescribed, mating patterns, must ordinarily afford alternatives to these patterns, or redefine the groups suitable for prescribed alliances over time.

The family theory has one distinctive advantage. It is easy to see how human groups might evolve rules to deal with immediate and obvious potential sources of disruption of social life. If indeed jealousy threatened the integrity of the family, it is possible to conceive of the development of norms to cope with this. And the incest prohibitions of any society constitute a set of conscious norms.

Question

Do you think that the other four theories discussed by these authors are possible explanations?

Writing in 1979, Karin Meselman in *Incest* emphasises both the inbreeding biological explanation together with the social and the psychological factors:

Another well-established characteristic of the incest taboo is that the intensity of the prohibition varies markedly within the nuclear family. Almost universally, brother-sister incest is less severely taboo than father-daughter incest, while mother-son incest inspires the greatest horror. This differential cannot, of course, be explained by the harmful effects of inbreeding because all three of these unions would be equally likely to produce defective offspring on a purely genetic basis. In fact, the mother-son relationship would be the least likely to produce any offspring, since the mother would often be past the age of optimum fertility when her son reached puberty, yet this union is by far the most strongly condemned.

I suggest that, while the taboo on nuclear family incest probably had its origin in the advantages of avoidance of inbreeding, from the earliest times the incest taboo has been influenced by many other social conditions, taboos, and psychological factors that have nearly always been present in the nuclear family situation. Four such influences will be suggested here, but the list is not intended to be exhaustive, and readers can no doubt think of additional factors.

First, in humans and most other higher animals there is commonly a series of dominance relationships within any family or social grouping. Older, bigger individuals tend to be dominant over younger ones, and males are usually dominant over females within the same age grouping, due to the males' greater size and aggressiveness. Initiation of sexual relationships is importantly connected with the dominance hierarchy: Males are usually the initiators, and they tend to succeed with females who are less dominant than themselves. On the basis of these facts, one would expect that father-daughter and older brother-younger sister sexual relationships would be both more common and less socially reprehensible (since they do not violate social expectations about dominance) than mother-son or older sister-younger brother incest.

Societies commonly taboo sexual relationships involving adults and prepubertal individuals, particularly if the latter are very young. In our own culture, one has only to think of our stereotype of the 'child molester' to realize the strength of this prohibition in cases where the adult and child are not at all related. Within the nuclear family, then, one would certainly expect father-daughter and mother-son relationships to seem more loathesome than sibling incest, because they would be more likely to involve an adult and a child.

A related point is that, even when neither of the sexual partners is prepubertal, societies display an almost unanimous preference for sexual unions and marriages to occur between individuals of the same generation, possibly because same-age marriages enhance the likelihood that both partners will survive long enough to nurture and instruct their offspring. This preference suggests greater censure for parent-child incest, even when the 'child' is actually an adult.

A fourth and final factor to be discussed here is the special nature of dependency relationships involving nurturance of one individual by another. It has long been maintained . . . that the intense dependency relationship between a young child and its parents, especially the mother, is incompatible with overt sexuality and its concomitant courtship behaviors. Although there may well be distinctly erotic components in the parent-child relationship, theorists . . . are generally agreed that direct erotic expression would be extremely confusing for the child and might be expected to interfere with his or her emotional development. If the destructiveness of overt incest is greatest for the most intense dependency relationship, then we would expect mother-son incest to be the most intensely taboo and sibling incest to be the least.

The two previous extracts, by concentrating on the origins of the taboo, help us to understand *why* laws provide formal restraints to the inter-relationship of family members. Anna Raeburn's article on *Incest*, which was published in *Cosmopolitan* in 1980, provides a vivid account of what can happen today when an incestuous relationship occurs. She raises problems relating to treatment and prevention, which should be borne in mind in Chapter 14, below, when we deal with the general question of child abuse:

To those of us on the outside, incest seems incredible. Brothers are nice bumbling boys who live their own lives, or little horrors with occasional moments of vulnerability or wisdom. Fathers can be kind or cruel, close or distant, but sex is something they feel for mothers or others, not us. But if they do it is safely channelled into paternal pride in us as their offspring and is expressed as interest in our achievements and mutual affection in times of extreme happiness or grief.

I shall run the risk of being called chauvinist by some because I've never met a man who was his mother's lover, as a child or an adult, though I have met several situations in which the emotional set-up was well and truly established. Formal investigations indicate only between two and four per cent of cases involve mother and son or father and son. I've only met one man who spoke of an overt sexual relationship with his sister. He mentioned it briefly, I knew them both slightly, she did not confide in me and the feeling I had was that it all took place long ago. It had its time and its time was now gone.

A novel I picked up called *The Story of the Weasel* by Caroline Slaughter turned out to be the story of a love between a brother and sister at the turn of the century. The writer makes it very clear that a child's view of sexuality can be simpler and more to do with reassurances and comfort than the convolutions of a similar adult relationship. Although opinion on the subject of brother/sister incest varies widely, it is generally held to be nothing like as injurious as an incestuous relationship with a parent: the biggest danger is that it will be too ideal, too perfect, ever to be fully replaced by another, more acceptable attachment without a sense of loss.

When I was editing a problem page, I received a letter which was anonymous but which rang true in every detail. A woman wrote of her small daughter whose playmate was the little girl next door. When playing together, the neighbour's child had confided that her daddy 'did things' to her. The writer faced with this from her daughter, found an opportunity to ask the child herself and was convinced that she was being told the truth. 'The mother is away in hospital,' she wrote. 'What can I do?' In answering her, I spoke to a child psychiatrist and the police. Their advice was the same. The child's greatest chance of protection lay in her mother being told what was going on. Police and courts are a frightening experience for anybody let alone for a small child.

'In any case,' pointed out the police/press liaison man I spoke to, 'you're then placing the child in an even deeper quagmire of conflict. She's betraying her mother and father to each other and the family as a whole to outsiders. That's very hard for anyone to bear, harder for such a young child. If the case goes to court and the father defends himself, he may then reject his wife who took, as it were, the child's part and the mother may then make the child the object of her anger for the subsequent strains in the marriage. The child's best chance lies in the mother being able to protect her and reinforce the taboo.' On the one side this sounded like wise advice. On the other it sounded suspiciously like: least said, soonest mended, and I was profoundly grateful I didn't have the decision to make.

What shocked me was the response of the readers to the letter, easily the heaviest in my four years in the job. Some wrote to say they were upset and why had I published such a thing? But everybody else said I should involve the police, the police, the police, as if the forces of law and order could make right again what was obviously terribly and distressingly wrong.

Some time later a woman in her late twenties wrote directly to me and filled in a bit more of the shadowy emotional background. Her stepfather had begun to 'play' with her when she was about nine. Within herself she hated it but her body betrayed her. 'He knew how to touch me,' she wrote, still obviously in agony at the memory.

'It took me years to permit myself enjoyment with anyone else because I'd already involuntarily given my orgasm to him, though I felt he was the last person in the world who should have it.' But how can you fight against your body? And, anyway, doesn't this account begin to show how ambivalent the whole exchange must be? Some nine-year-old girls are very young and unformed intellectually or physically; for others some intimation of erotic undercurrents has already begun.

This same writer explained how she had escaped from her stepfather only when her mother divorced him, but although, on one level, this was of course a relief, on another she felt bereft, then guilty for such a feeling, and finally responsible, as if in some way her mother had known what was going on and therefore the divorce was *her* fault. Now years later, after a series of not very satisfactory relationships with men, she was settled with a man and had a daughter by him. And then her memories raised their ugly heads again. . . .

Obviously, the younger the child involved, the more the acts are forced upon her. With an older child the emotional cross currents in which she is caught are more and more destructive. Tom Hart has been Superintendent of a Regional Treatment and Assessment Centre in south London for many years. I had seen articles about him and read his last novel which is about a family in which father/daughter incest takes place, called *Don't Tell Your Mother*. It's an economic, effective story and it brings to light the extent of the mother's involvement in the whole thing as well, so I rang and asked if he would see me.

Tom Hart is grizzled and wise and tough and caring. His life's work has been with girls between the ages of fourteen and seventeen and he says he has never known a case of father/daughter incest where there was not a degree of collusion by the girl. 'Ninety per cent of the kids I see have a bad relationship with their fathers anyway,' he said. 'Many of these children have no conversation with their fathers between the age of twelve and sixteen. The child draws away naturally as she begins to grow up but the father feels rejected. He rejects her in turn and her feelings turn to anger. So mother has to be both mother and father of her adolescent daughter and, in turn, she incurs the child's rage for exercising Dad's role.'

All too many of us can relate to the feelings Tom Hart is talking about. But supposing your father didn't accept your growing up in this way and began to relate to you in another way — a sexual way? And suppose your mother had 'gone off' him? Or was out of the house a lot? Or wasn't very interested in you anyway? That would pave the way for him to manipulate your burgeoning sexual feelings into a relationship where he could maintain some form of contact with you and some kind of control.

By the same token, such a relationship would give you, the disgruntled adolescent who is always being told, 'We know more than you because we're older,' power over the grown-ups. For the father always demands secrecy from his filial lover and her threat to tell is, in turn, her trump card. But it's a trump card which misfires.

For how can the mother not know what is going on? The human mind has a horrifying capacity to choose what it will and will not believe. Very often it seems that the mother decides she does not *want* to know, for admitting such a thing throws her and her relationship with her husband into question. She prefers to turn a blind eye. Perhaps secretly she's pleased that she is relieved of the sexual burden. Or maybe she thinks, even more twistedly, that if her husband has to be unfaithful, she'd rather have it kept in the family.

Suppose the daughter tells anyway, not just her mother but someone outside the family? Then she has to face an intolerable burden of feelings, including guilt, anger, fear, bereavement (for her parents must be as lost to her) and hopelessness. What future has she now?

Tom Hart's reply to that was 'You must never forget the extraordinary resilience of children. They can survive and they do. More than that, their best chance is if they have saved some tears for themselves. If they will allow themselves to grieve for what has become of them, they can begin to heal.'

He added that opinions differed as to how damaging father/daughter incest was, but for his part he believed it scarred for life the physical and emotional life of the girl involved.

The woman who wrote to *Cosmopolitan* said, 'I've thought about what might have happened. Supposing I'd convinced somebody that I was endangered by my father's untoward interest in me. Then my sister and I would have been taken into care. Would this have made our lives any better than they were? And though my sister and I always regarded my mother as the angel of the family and my father as the devil, my mother effectively said that she couldn't do anything to help us, so without that as a first line of defence, we were completely powerless. Yet we've managed.'

My own feeling is that all we can do is to offer a hand when we see somebody stretch out for it. Nobody, bureaucracy or institution, can do very much for fear of making the situation worse. Only people can help people in this sort of tangled situation. And yet I confess that sounds a frighteningly frail gesture of hope against the confusion and misery of betrayal by the first man in your life.

6 Exogamy in English law

The English law is set out in Sch. 1 to the Marriage Act 1949. Prohibited degrees include relationships of the half-blood and through illegitimacy. Marriages between first cousins are permitted, but not those between uncle and niece. The Marriage (Enabling) Act 1960 changed the law, so that a man may now marry the sister, aunt or niece of his divorced wife; but he still may not marry the mother or daughter of his former wife, whether dead or divorced. Schedule 1 to the Marriage Act 1949 (as amended in 1960 and in 1975) lists the following prohibitions:

Male	*Female*
Mother	Father
Adoptive mother or former adoptive mother	Adoptive father or former adoptive father
Daughter	Son
Adoptive daughter or former adoptive daughter	Adoptive son or former adoptive son
Father's mother	Father's father
Mother's mother	Mother's father
Son's daughter	Son's son
Daughter's daughter	Daughter's son
Sister	Brother
Wife's mother	Husband's father
Wife's daughter	Husband's son
Father's wife	Mother's husband
Son's wife	Daughter's husband
Father's father's wife	Father's mother's husband
Mother's father's wife	Mother's mother's husband
Wife's father's mother	Husband's father's father
Wife's mother's mother	Husband's mother's father
Wife's son's daughter	Husband's son's son
Wife's daughter's daughter	Husband's daughter's son
Son's son's wife	Son's daughter's husband
Daughter's son's wife	Daughter's daughter's husband
Father's sister	Father's brother
Mother's sister	Mother's brother
Brother's daughter	Brother's son
Sister's daughter	Sister's son

Question

The criminal law prohibits only sexual intercourse between direct ascendants and descendants and brothers and sisters (Sexual Offences Act 1956, ss. 10 and 11): how would you account for the difference?

The Law Commission, in their *Report on Nullity of Marriage* (1970), saw no need to change the law:

51.   The prohibited degrees of relationship fall into two categories: consanguinity, *i.e.*, relationship by blood, and affinity, *i.e.*, relationship by marriage. The two categories must be examined separately when discussing whether the existing prohibitions should be modified.
52.   It seems safe to assume general acceptance of the view that a man should not marry his daughter, granddaughter, mother, grandmother or sister. It is in fact a criminal offence for a man knowingly to have sexual intercourse with such female relations (including those of the half-blood, or illegitimate), with the exception of his grandmother. The remaining prohibited degrees of consanguinity are, in the case of a man, his aunt and niece and in the case of a woman, her uncle and nephew. A man and his great-aunt and his great-niece, or a woman and her great-uncle and great-nephew, are not within the prohibited degrees. The question whether there should be any alteration in these existing prohibited degrees of consanguinity is partly biological and partly social and moral.

(a) In so far as the question is biological, the answer depends on an evaluation of scientific evidence. The marriage of uncle and niece, or nephew and aunt is permitted in some countries and by some religions and it may well be that there is no such biological objection to these marriages as to justify legal prohibition. They may well be no more objectionable biologically than the marriage of a man with his grandparent's sister or of a woman with her grandparent's brother, which is not within the prohibited degrees.

(b) Nevertheless, the question raises social and moral problems, the answer to which must depend on public opinion. Would public opinion tolerate or object to marriages between uncle and niece or nephew and aunt and, if it objects to such unions, does it wish to extend the prohibition to great-uncle and great-niece and great-nephew and great-aunt? Many people would no doubt instinctively hold the view that such marriages are unnatural and wrong, just as they would view with revulsion a marriage between brother and sister, even if there were no biological reasons against such a union. There are some matters of conviction on which men hold strong feelings of right and wrong though they cannot place their fingers on any particular reason for this conviction. It may be that such unions would be generally regarded as just as wrong as a marriage between adopter and adopted child — a union which is clearly considered objectionable although there cannot be any biological ground for this.

53. The prohibited degrees of affinity fall into two categories: those which prohibit a man from marrying his father's or grandfather's wife and his son's or grandson's wife and those which prohibit him from marrying his wife's mother, grandmother, daughter or granddaughter (and the equivalent male relations in the case of a woman). The historical objection to such unions was based on the ground that husband and wife were one, so that relationship by marriage are equivalent to relationship by blood. This reasoning is unlikely to appeal today and one must ask whether there exist social or moral reasons against such unions. As in the case of consanguinity, there are undoubtedly people who feel that such unions are morally wrong and should not be permitted. On the other hand, there are others who feel that such unions are no more objectionable than those permitted by the Marriage (Prohibited Degrees of Relationship) Acts 1907 to 1931 and the Marriage (Enabling) Act 1960.

54. The Morton Commission had as part of their terms of reference 'to consider whether any alteration should be made in the law prohibiting marriage with certain relations by kindred or affinity'. The Commission recommended that the then existing prohibition against a man marrying his divorced wife's sister, niece or aunt (or a woman marrying her divorced husband's brother, nephew or uncle) should be removed and this recommendation resulted in the passing of the Marriage (Enabling) Act 1960. In addition to this proposal there were 'a few witnesses' who proposed that all prohibitions on marriage with relations by affinity should be abolished. The Commission recommended that there should be no change in the law relating to the marriage of persons within the prohibited degrees of relationship other than that mentioned; this change was made by the 1960 Act. We know of no evidence that public opinion has changed since 1955 and now desires a revision of the existing prohibited degrees. The almost unanimous view of those who commented on our Working Paper No. 20 was that the law should remain as it is. We so recommend.

A number of proposals have been made to reform the law. One is to divide the degrees which are prohibited on the basis of consanguinity into two categories: the 'elementary' family (ascendants, descendants, brothers and sisters) and second, the 'outer' family. First cousins, at present outside the prohibited degrees, could be added to the list of members of the 'outer' family. Marriages between persons within the 'elementary' (or 'inner' family) would be barred. Reform within the 'outer family' (a marriage with one's aunt or niece) would be limited to permitting such marriages to take place once a court had granted leave. A court would consider such factors as the general public policy, the individual circumstances of the case, and any genetic hazards.

A second proposal for reform would be to abolish all prohibitions based on affinity, thereby completing the reforms which have occurred in English law during this century. This was done in Australia in 1975. A less radical solution would be to give the court discretion to exempt couples from the affinity prohibitions. This is the position under New Zealand law.

These arguments were aired in the House of Lords during the discussion of a Bill introduced in 1979 by Baroness Wootton of Abinger, designed to remove all prohibitions on marriages between persons related by affinity. As *Hansard* for 13 February 1979 reports:

Baroness Wootton of Abinger: My Lords, I beg to move that this Bill be now read a second time. The Bill does not, as the media would sometimes try to persuade your Lordships, herald a radical moral or social revolution. It attempts only to bring to its logical conclusion a development in our marriage laws which has been going on throughout the greater part of this century and, in a sense, for a good many centuries before, but in slow motion. In so doing, I hope that it will bring comfort and happiness to a number of distressed individuals, at practically no financial cost to the community and without any damage but rather with benefit to the institutions of marriage and the family.

The content of the Bill is contained entirely in the single sentence which gives it its title. It is a Bill which would enable any person to marry the former spouse of any of his relatives, or any relative of his former spouse.

As your Lordships are well aware, this list of what are known as the prohibited degrees goes back to the Old Testament and to the Book of *Leviticus*, where they are very eloquently set out. But they remained matters of ecclesiastical law only in this country until the time of Henry VIII, who after all had a good deal of practical experience of marriage. They were then incorporated into our Statute Law in an Act of 1540.

If I may now jump four centuries we come to the first important change that affects us and that was the Act of 1907 which allowed a man to marry his deceased wife's sister but gave no similar privilege to a woman to marry her deceased husband's brother. For that we had to wait another 14 years and when that change came it was not expressed in the same terms as the privilege conferred upon a man, because at that time men always married women but women never married men. The Act which therefore should have been the deceased husband's brother Act was the deceased brother's widow Act which, if we turn it round, comes to exactly the same thing if the marrying is done by the man and not by the woman.

Next, an Act of 1931 allowed marriage with the spouse of a deceased niece or nephew, aunt or uncle, and in 1949 a consolidating Act set out the whole marriage law with the prohibited degrees of both blood relations and affinities. As soon as that tidying up had been done it was immediately untidied because the Government proceeded to appoint the Morton Royal Commission on Marriage and Divorce, which considered the whole question of marriage, including such matters as property, nullity, the insanity of one partner and so forth. That Commission received evidence from the British Medical Association, pointing out that there could be no possible biological objection to marriage between any affinities since they were not blood related. . . . The Commission was much more concerned with the question of whether those privileges of marrying the relatives of former spouses should be extended to cases where the spouses had been divorced as well as to those cases where the marriage was ended by death. Eventually, after long and eloquent argument the Commission decided to recommend that relaxation and they reported, with three dissentients, in favour of it and it was subsequently embodied in the Marriage (Enabling) Act 1960. . . .

Lady Wootton turned to the problem of public opinion:

Of the scores of people to whom I have put the simple question: 'Do you think a man should be allowed to marry his step-daughter?' — people of all grades in life and of all kinds of political or religious persuasions — the vast majority, in fact all but about two or three, have replied with astonishment that such marriages were not already legal, adding such comments as: 'Why ever not? They are not blood related'.

Question

If the question is put to you, what would be your answer?

The Bishop of Southwark spoke in the same debate. He gave an example of a 'very human story' over which he had to advise:

The facts are as follows. I change the names, for obvious reasons. The people concerned live in my diocese and it would be wrong to disclose their identity. Mr and Mrs Jones have a child. The marriage is dissolved. Mr Jones disappears to another part of the world. The child goes into care. Mrs Jones marries Mr Smith. Then Mrs Smith — who was originally Mrs Jones — dies from cancer soon after the marriage. Mr Smith has had hardly any dealings whatsoever with

Miss Jones — that is to say, the daughter by the first marriage, for the girl is in the care of guardians.

Then, for educational reasons, Miss Jones, who is now 20; comes to live in the house of Mr Smith, who is 36. She is living there with another girl who is also educationally involved. During the course of time, the step-daughter — Miss Jones — becomes attached to Mr Smith, and *vice versa*. They fall in love. They go to the incumbent, who is an incumbent in my parish, who assumes that there is no reason at all why they should not be married. They go also to a lawyer who gives them the same advice. The marriage is announced. The matter is then referred to me. I consult my lawyers. I consult the Bishop of Exeter, the present Bishop of Birmingham and other lawyers, including the lawyers at Lamberth. From practically everyone I received nothing but sympathy — or, rather, Mr Smith received nothing but sympathy. But I was told that there was only one thing I could do and that was to say that such a marriage could not take place, not because it is criminal but because it is against the civil law, although I was told that it was not against the civil law for them to cohabit and to have children.

The young man, who is a practising member of the Church of England, and to whom religion means a great deal, is faced by a serious problem. Should he go to another country where he is entitled to marry his step-daughter or should he cohabit? For reasons I need not go into — chiefly financial, though — it was impossible for Mr Smith to go to another country and to marry Miss Jones. For that reason he remains in England, he cohabits and he has two children. These children are illegitimate and cannot be legitimised except possibly by adoption and if he should die first — and he is still a comparatively young man — the woman with whom he cohabits will get no widow's pension, either from the State or from his previous occupation.

One of the speakers in the House who made observations against the Bill was the Earl of Lauderdale. He said:

The case deployed this afternoon has been that affinity does not matter, although blood relationship does. I should like to suggest to your Lordships that Britain as a neurotic, violent society — increasingly neurotic, increasingly violent, increasingly lacking in respect for authority of any kind from any source — has derived those qualities in part, at any rate, from the dissipation of family life.

Question

Has he got a point?

The Bill was read a second time, and was discussed in Committee by the whole House. The Bishop of London moved an amendment:

Insert ('but if at the time on which the marriage of a man with any of the persons mentioned in subsection (2)(*a*) below, or of a woman with any of the persons mentioned in subsection (2)(*b*) below, is solemnized either of the parties to the marriage is under the age of 21, the marriage shall be void unless the Court has given its consent to the solemnization of the marriage.

In determining whether to give such consent the Court shall have regard to all the circumstances of the case, including the following matters, that is to say:

   (*a*) the degree of relationship between the parties to the proposed marriage;

   (*b*) the extent, if any, to which the dissolution of any previous marriage of either of those parties was caused by the conduct of the other;

   (*c*) the value to either of those parties of any financial benefit which that party will have the chance of acquiring if the proposed marriage takes place;

   (*d*) the interests of any children.

Questions

What difficulties, if any, are there in the Bishop's amendment?

In the result, the Bill fell on the dissolution of Parliament in April 1979. It was reintroduced, but was defeated on the second reading in June 1979.

What happens to Mr Smith and Miss Jones?

An Act to enable John Francis Dare and Gillian Loder Dare to be married to each other. [*27 May 1982*]

WHEREAS—

(1) On 18 December 1937 John Dare (then aged 22 years and a bachelor) married Gillian's mother (then aged 26 years and a spinster):

(2) There were two issue of that marriage and they are still living and aged 41 years and 36 years:

(3) John Dare and Gillian's mother lived together on terms of great affection until Gillian's mother died on 13 August 1951:

(4) No blood relationship exists between John Dare and Gillian Dare:

(5) Both John Dare and Gillian Dare are domiciled and resident in England:

(6) John Dare is now aged 66 years and Gillian Dare is now aged 49 years and, after Gillian's mother died, they formed the wish to be married to each other but a marriage between them would be void as falling within section 1 (1) of the Marriage Act 1949, in that they stand in the relationship of stepfather and stepdaugther:

(7) John Dare and Gillian Dare regard the legal impediment to their marriage as imposing hardship on them, and as serving no useful purpose of public policy, in the particular circumstances of their case:

(8) They accordingly desire that the impediment should be removed in their case:

(9) The object of this Act cannot be attained without the authority of Parliament:

Therefore John Dare and Gillian Dare most humbly pray that it may be enacted, and be it enacted, by the Queen's most Excellent Majesty, by and with the advice and consent of the Lords Spiritual and Temporal, and Commons, in this present Parliament assembled, and by the authority of the same, as follows:—

1. Notwithstanding anything contained in any enactment or any rule of law to the contrary, there shall be no impediment to a marriage between John Dare and Gillian Dare by reason of their relationship of stepfather and stepdaughter, and no marriage hereafter contracted between them shall be void by reason of that relationship.

2. In this Act (including the Preamble hereto)—

'John Dare' means John Francis Dare who was born the son of Charles Sandell and Elfrida Gallwey on 19 October 1915;

'Gillian Dare' means Gillian Loder Dare who was born the daughter of Eleanor Norah Iles on 20 September 1932;

'Gillian's mother' means Eleanor Norah Iles who was born the daughter of Francis William Iles and Norah Esme Iles on 11 February 1911.

3. This Act may be cited as the John Francis Dare and Gillian Loder Dare (Marriage Enabling) Act 1982.

Question

Have you any idea how much a private Act of Parliament costs?

Marriages which would be void under the present English law do take place elsewhere:

Catalano v Catalano
(1961) 148 Conn 288, 170 A 2d 726

Fred Catalano was married on 8 December 1951 in Italy to his niece, an Italian subject. Such a marriage was prohibited by article 87 of the Italian Civil Code, but since the parties obtained a legal dispensation for the marriage from the Italian authorities, the marriage was valid by Italian law. The couple lived as husband and wife in Hartford, Connecticut until the death of Fred in 1958. In this action for a widow's pension, the plaintiff claimed to be the lawful surviving spouse of the deceased.

Murphy J: To determine whether the marriage in the instant case is contrary to the public policy of this state, it is only necessary to consider that marriages between uncle and niece have been interdicted and declared void continuously since 1702 and that ever since then it has been a crime for such kindred to either marry or carnally know each other. At the time of the plaintiff's marriage in 1951, the penalty for incest was, and it has continued to be, imprisonment in the state prison for not more than ten years. Rev. 1949, §8551; General Statutes §52-223. This relatively high penalty clearly reflects the strong public policy of this state. We cannot completely disregard the import and intent of our statutory law and engage in judicial legislation. The marriage of the plaintiff and Fred Catalano, though valid in Italy under its laws, was not valid in Connecticut because it contravened the public policy of this state. . . .

Mellitz J dissented. He emphasised that Mrs Catalano 'was entirely innocent of any intent to evade the laws of Connecticut,' but even in a broader context, he was not prepared to accept that public policy compelled non-recognition:

We are dealing here with the marriage status of a woman who was validly married at the place of her domicil and who, so far as the record discloses, was entirely innocent of any intent to evade the laws of Connecticut. Mrs Catalano was a resident and domiciliary of Italy when her uncle came from America and married her in Italy. Although he returned to America soon after the marriage, she continued to reside in Italy for almost five years before she came to America and took up her residence in Connecticut, where she gave birth to a son. There is no suggestion anywhere in the record that at the time of the marriage she intended to come to America, that the parties had any intention of coming to live in Connecticut, or that the marriage was entered into in Italy for the purpose of evading the laws of Connecticut. If a marriage status resulting from a valid marriage, such as the one here, is to be destroyed, the issue bastardized, and the relations of the parties branded as illicit, it should follow only from an explicit enactment of the legislature, giving clear expression to a public policy which compels such harsh consequences to ensue from a marriage entered into under the circumstances disclosed here.

Cheni v Cheni
[1963] P 85, [1962] 3 All ER 873, [1963] 2 WLR 17, High Court, Family Division

The parties, who were uncle and niece, were married in Cairo in 1924 in accordance with Jewish rites. The intention of both was to enter into a monogamous union. According to expert evidence the marriage was valid by Jewish and Egyptian law and although potentially polygamous at its inception became irrevocably monogamous on the birth of a child of the marriage in 1926. The parties continued to live in Egypt until 1957 when they settled in England where they became domiciled. In 1961 the wife filed a petition praying that the marriage be declared null and void on the ground of consanguinity or, in the alternative, that the marriage be dissolved on the ground of the husband's cruelty. On the issue of nullity:

Sir Jocelyn Simon P: . . . Dr Gaon[3] told me that a marriage between uncle and niece is in accordance with general Jewish law. This was spelt out further by Professor James, Professor of the History of Religions at London University, and formerly a member of the Archbishop's Commission on Kindred and Affinity, 1937. In the Levitical Code marriage between aunt and nephew was prohibited, but not marriage between uncle and niece (see The Book of Leviticus, Ch. 18, verses 12-14). The distinction reflected the Jewish emphasis on the family as a primary unit of society, the aunt-nephew relationship reversing the natural order of authority, whereas in the uncle-niece relationship there is no confusion of authority. In Christianity up to the schism between the Eastern and Western Catholic Churches marriage was prohibited up to the relationship of first cousins, so that the relationship of uncle and niece, which was closer, invalidated a marriage. After 1064 the Western Church maintained its prohibition of marriages between uncle and niece and first cousins, but the impediment was capable under special circumstances of dispensation by the Pope. The uncle-niece impediment would be dispensed with only to avoid some greater evil, generally of a political nature. This is still much the situation in the Roman Catholic Church: the Revised Codex of 1918 shows that close consanguinous relationship in marriage is discouraged, though dispensable up to the first degree collaterally, i.e., the brother-sister relationship. The Reformation involved a general reaction against the papal system of dispensation. Luther dismissed the whole process and returned to the Levitical Code as the expression of God's will. The uncle-niece relationship is therefore permitted in

---

3. Dr Gaon, who gave evidence to the Court, was at that time the Chief Rabbi of the Sephardi Jewish Community in the United Kingdom.

many Lutheran churches, and the aunt-nephew relationship prohibited; though some Lutheran churches, such as those in this country and the United States, follow, as they are bound to, the law of the land. Calvin, on the other hand, did not accept the Levitical Code literally, but applied it by parity of reasoning. Uncle-niece and aunt-nephew stand in the same degree of blood relationship; the Levitical prohibition of aunt-nephew marriages was therefore applied to uncle-niece marriages. The Anglican communion in this respect followed the Calvinist line.

Mr Stirling accepts that this marriage was valid by the law of the parties' domicile, which is the proper law by which capacity to marry is to be tested. But, he says, there is an exception to this general rule, in that the courts of this country will not recognise the validity of a marriage which, even though valid by its proper law, is incestuous by the general consent of all Christendom, or, as he prefers to put it, by the general consent of civilised nations or by English public policy.

The President rejected Counsel's argument:

. . . The marriage in this case was in my judgment a valid one. I do not consider that a marriage which may be the subject of papal dispensation and will then be acknowledged as valid by all Roman Catholics, which without any such qualification is acceptable to all Lutherans, can reasonably be said to be contrary to the general consent of Christendom; . . . If the general consent of civilised nations were to be the test, I do not think that the matter can be resolved by, so to speak, taking a card-vote of the United Nations and disregarding the views of the many civilised countries by whose laws these marriages are permissible. As Mr Argyle observed, Egypt, where these people lived and where the marriage took place, is itself a civilised country. If domestic public policy were the test, it seems to me that the arguments on behalf of the husband, founded on such inferences as one can draw from the scope of the English criminal law, prevail. Moreover, they weigh with me when I come to apply what I believe to be the true test, namely, whether the marriage is so offensive to the conscience of the English court that it should refuse to recognise and give effect to the proper foreign law. In deciding that question the court will seek to exercise common sense, good manners and a reasonable tolerance. In my view it would be altogether too queasy a judicial conscience which would recoil from a marriage acceptable to many peoples of deep religious convictions, lofty ethical standards and high civilisation. Nor do I think that I am bound to consider such marriages merely as a generality. On the contrary, I must have regard to this particular marriage, which, valid by the religious law of the parties' common faith and by the municipal law of their common domicile, has stood unquestioned for 35 years. I must bear in mind that I am asked to declare unmarried the parents of a child who is unquestionably legitimate in the eyes of the law: *Re Bischoffsheim, Cassel v Grant* [1948] Ch 79, [1947] 2 All ER 830. In my judgment, injustice would be perpetrated and conscience would be affronted if the English court were not to recognise and give effect to the law of the domicile in this case.

Question

Are there any religious objections to Baroness Wootton's bill?

7 Age at marriage

W.J. Goode in *World Revolution and Family Patterns* (1963) describes the history of attitudes to the proper age to marry thus:

It seems likely that toward the end of the nineteenth century Western attitudes did alter toward a belief that very young girls should not marry. Prior to the twentieth century, marriages of girls aged 15–17 were not disapproved of providing that the man was sufficiently well-to-do. In the absence of sufficient data my hypothesis is that chronological maturity as a prerequisite for marriage was not an important focus of social attention in the West until about the turn of the century.

Let us consider this point. Prior to the French Revolution, the legal minimum age for marriage in France was 14 years for boys and 12 years for girls. These were also the legal minimum marriage ages accepted under both the older English law and Roman law. In most cases these minimum ages — the assumed ages of puberty for each sex — probably permitted parents to arrange the marriages of their children whenever it seemed suitable. Children of so young an age could not marry independently, and marriage in many Western nations without the consent of parents is even now forbidden to young people under 21 years of age. In the West, there has generally been a substantial difference between the legal minimum age for marriage and the minimum age at which young people might marry *without* parental consent. Since one youngster may be forbidden to marry because of parental refusal, and another of the same age may marry *with* parental consent, it is clear that Western laws concerning minimum ages at marriage were aimed at maintaining the power of the parent, *not* at enforcing a 'right' age at marriage. Over the past generation, a typical legal change has been to narrow the gap between the two age minimums by raising the age at marriage *with* parental consent, or establishing a lower age at marriage without consent.

Since marriage was not thought in the West to be properly based on free courtship until late in the nineteenth century, 'maturity' as measured by years was given no great weight. If a good match could be made for a girl of 15 or 16 years, her age was no barrier, and there were indeed many youthful marriages. Within noble or well-to-do rural families, a young couple could be married precisely because they did *not* have to support themselves or assume the responsibility of a profession.

In contrast to upper-class families, farming families in regions without free land did not ordinarily permit their children to marry until much later, when the parents were ready to relinquish control of the property, or had accumulated sufficient money to afford the marriage. Without land, marriage was not possible. And, of course, servants and apprentices might not marry at all, since their status was viewed as a semi-familial one, and they had no right to introduce a spouse into the family circle. However, a 'proper' age was not the question. Instead, it was whether there was adequate land or income available. Until the end of the nineteenth century the couple had either to wait for land or, if the productive unit was large enough, to become part of a larger kin group, taking part in its economic activities and sharing from the common store. Thus, age in itself was of little importance.

We must therefore conclude that in most parts of the West, until some time in the nineteenth century, marriage came relatively late for the bulk of the population, and the myth that marriages occurred extremely early as we go back in time comes from the fact that the many marriages at very young ages occurred among the most conspicuous classes. . . .

In the contemporary West, however, a 'proper' age (varying from country to country and from class to class — higher in the upper strata) has now come to be accepted, since, under the conjugal family system, a couple must be self-sufficient. The young couple cannot be extremely young, since they have to take care of themselves; on the other hand, they do not have to be very old, because they can be independent.

Here, we encounter an empirical puzzle. It seems likely that in the early period of England's industrialization, the age of marriage would not have changed greatly because, although they did work in the factories, for the most part children were given their jobs through relatives and often were supervised by their own male parents. They were not independent workers, and the traditions of the times dictated that they should give their pay to their parents. It was only when they obtained jobs on their own, without the intervention of parents or relatives, that they could make their own decision about choice of spouse or age at which to marry. However, the age at marriage did not change substantially until still later, i.e., in this century, and now seems to be tied at least in part to the independent participation of *females* in the labor force. The job becomes the young girl's 'dowry' in the unskilled and semiskilled white- and blue-collar strata, where, in fact, the highest proportion of women are to be found in the labor force.

The author continues by giving the figures of the median age at marriage for men and women (i.e. the age below which 50% of persons married in any one year):

Marriage Age for Spinsters and Bachelors and Number of Minors Married per Thousand Marriages in England and Wales, 1876–1956

	median age of marrying		*Number of minors (under 21 years of age) per thousand marriages*	
Year	*M*	*F*	*M*	*F*
1881–1885	25.9	24.4	73.0	215.0
1891–1895	26.6	25.0	56.2	182.6
1901–1905	26.9	25.4	48.3	153.1
1911–1915	27.5	25.8	39.2	136.6
1921–1925	27.5	25.6	48.2	149.2
1931–1935	27.4	25.5		
1941–1945	26.8	24.6	33.8	163.8
1951–1955	26.6	24.2	65.0	271.1
1956	26.2	23.7		

The median age at marriage increased during the 1970s following a drop in the 1960s. In 1979, the median age at marriage for men was 25.5 years and for women 23.0 years, compared with 23.7 years and 21.8 years respectively in 1970. We give below two charts taken from *Social Trends 12* (1982):

Age at marriage: by previous marital status

Great Britain

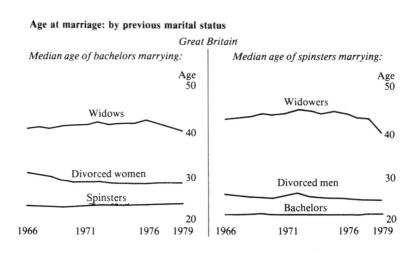

Source: Office of Population Censuses and Surveys;
General Register Office (Scotland)

Questions

(i) (*a*) Why do you think the median age dropped in the 1950s and 1960s? (*b*) Why do you think it increased in the 1970s? (*c*) What do you think will happen in the 1980s?
(ii) Bearing in mind the association between the age at marriage and divorce (page 150, below), should there be any changes in the law?
(iii) Should the minimum age of marriage be the same as the age of consent to sexual intercourse?

8   The formalities of marriage

As Lucy Mair explains in *Marriage* (1971):

There are some societies in which it is possible to get married almost without any formalities at all, and some in which a marriage without formality is a permitted alternative for people who cannot afford the formalities or do not attach importance to them. . . .
   There is a correlation between the amount of formality and display and the importance of the alliance that is being created. There are also in some societies — but these are different ones — ways of circumventing parental choice and forcing the consent of elders to a marriage agreed on by a young couple.

Informal Marriages

It is possible for a marriage to be created and announced in one breath by the simple fact that a couple are seen to be eating together. This is what happens in the Trobriand Islands in the Pacific, as they were described by Malinowski (in the *Sexual Life of Savages* (1929)) in the first ethnographic account to clothe formal statements of rules with the reality of actual behaviour. Since a marriage is concluded in such a simple way, a couple can marry in defiance of parental opposition. . . .

England is not the Trobriand Islands, although prior to the Council of Trent (1545–1563) all that was necessary to constitute a valid marriage according to the canon law was the free consent of the parties expressed in any way so as to provide evidence that they contemplated a permanent and lawful union. Even after the Council, 'informal' marriages were recognised by the ecclesiastical courts. Lord Hardwicke's Marriage Act of 1753 was designed primarily to prevent these informal and often clandestine marriages from being performed. A short description of the present English law is given by T.E. James, *The English Law of Marriage* in *A Century of Family Law* (1957):

From 1753 until 1836 the formalities required for a valid marriage had all to be in accordance with the rites of the Church of England.[4] After 1836 civil marriages were permitted. . . . There have been a large number of statutes modifying and extending the formal requirements; but now the matter is governed by the Marriage Act, 1949, which consolidated existing legislation and modified it to some extent.

Marriage according to the rites of the Church of England can be solemnised in four ways, that is, after due publication of banns,[5] by special licence,[6] by common licence[7] or by the certificate issued by a Superintendent Registrar without a licence. The resulting ceremonies, according to the rites of the Church of England, require the presence of at least two witnesses and of a clergyman in holy orders. . . .

The distinction between the superintendent registrar's certificate with and without a licence lies in the procedure to be followed which affects the time of residence and the display of the notice of marriage prior to the granting of the certificate.

Marriages by virtue of the superintendent registrar's certificate may be solemnised in the appropriate parish church or authorised chapel, if according to the rites of the Church of England; if they are in accordance with other rites, then in a registered building[8] or the office of the Superintendent Registrar, or according to the usages of the Society of Friends or of the Jews.

As a result of the Marriage (Registrar's General's Licence) Act 1970, there is power for the civil authorities to authorise a marriage to be solemnised at any convenient time or place. The Registrar General has to be satisfied, inter alia that one of the persons to be married is seriously ill and is not expected to recover.

---

4. Except for Quakers and Jews.

5. The banns must be published on three Sundays preceding the marriage. If the parties reside in the same parish, the banns must be published in the parish church. If they reside in separate parishes, then the banns must be published in both parishes. A clergyman is not obliged to publish banns unless the parties deliver or cause to be delivered seven days' notice in writing with their full names, place of residence and the period during which each has resided there.

6. These are special dispensations granted by the Archbishop of Canterbury enabling marriages to be solemnised according to the rites of the Church of England at any convenient time or place.

7. The common licence is issued under the authority of the bishop of the diocese. It can be granted only for the marriage in a church or chapel of an ecclesiastical district in which one of the parties has had his usual place of residence for 15 days immediately before the grant of the licence, or a parish church or chapel which is the usual place of worship of one or both of the parties.

8. This is defined as a 'separate building of public religious worship.'

The Law Commission's Report on *Solemnisation of Marriage* (1973) presents a powerful case for uniform civil preliminaries:

The need for compulsory civil preliminaries

14. We have said that the primary objectives of preliminaries are to ensure that 'there should be proper opportunity for the investigation of capacity (and, in the case of minors, parental consent) before the marriage, and that the investigation should be carried out, uniformly for parties to all marriages, by persons trained to perform this function,' and that 'there should be proper opportunity for those who may know of a lawful impediment to a marriage to declare it'. In fact it is difficult to imagine a system less calculated to achieve these objectives. It is not uniform. It does not ensure that there is always a proper opportunity for investigation or that the investigation is carried out by those who have been trained for that role. Nor does it ensure that those whose consents are required or who may know of impediments have an adequate opportunity of stopping the marriage. These strictures are least justified in the case of marriages after a superintendent registrar's certificate. There, at any rate, there is a three-week waiting period, an opportunity of investigation by trained personnel, and some information on which to base an investigation and a right to demand some further evidence. But, even there, there is no method whereby those who wish to object can be sure of doing so effectively. Potential objectors may in practice have no idea where the couple propose to marry. It is impracticable to search every marriage notice book in the country; and a search will be ineffective if the couple choose to marry in Church after ecclesiastical preliminaries. Nor will there be time to make searches if the couple have paid a little extra in order to cut down the waiting period from 21 days to one day. The outstanding absurdity of the present position is, perhaps, that the payment of an extra fee enables the major safeguard of a waiting period to be by-passed.

15. Although in the case of banns there is generally an equally long waiting period it is a less effective safeguard. . . . there is no legal requirement that the parties shall make an declaration about capacity, nor is there any legal duty upon the person to whom application is made for the publication of banns (who is not necessarily the incumbent himself) to satisfy himself on these matters although many clergymen do so. The historical justification for banns is, of course, that their publication will give adequate advance public notice of the couple's intention to marry which will enable anyone knowing of an impediment to come forward. In social conditions which prevailed in this country before the present century this may have been sound. To-day, with the growth and increased mobility of the population and the increase in urban living, it clearly is not. Unless the banns happen to be published in a church regularly attended by the parties and their friends and relations the chances of any impropriety coming to light are remote.

16. In our view, it is impossible adequately to reform the present system unless uniform civil preliminaries are made compulsory in the case of all marriages and unless the civil preliminaries are themselves reformed. Only then will it be possible to ensure that there is adequate investigation and to provide an effective system of raising objections. This is far from being a novel or revolutionary suggestion. When the Marriage Bill was introduced in 1836 it in fact provided for civil preliminaries to all marriages. The clauses which required this in the case of Church of England marriages were removed during the course of the Bill's passage in order to hasten the enactment of the Bill's major reforms. But the Government of the day then expressed the view that it would be necessary on a future occasion to carry the whole of the original plan into effect. Such preliminary enquiries as we have made suggest that the Church of England would not now oppose this rationalisation. It will not, of course, prevent the Church requiring publication of banns as an ecclesiastical preliminary to a Church wedding. All that we are proposing is that the publication of banns should cease to be a requirement of the civil law. This could, if desired by the Church, be coupled with the removal of the present obligation on incumbents to marry any of their parishioners (even though they have never set foot in the Church before), affording them the same freedom as ministers of the Roman Catholic and Free Churches to decide whether or not they will perform a particular marriage. Marriage by common licence would necessarily disappear. We would see no objection to the retention of the Archbishop's special licence but this would not be essential if the legislation were amended so that the Registrar General's licence could be used as a preliminary to a marriage according to the rites of the Church of England.

Questions

(i) Why do you think that these recommendations have not been the subject of any legislation? Were the Law Commission correct in their view that the Church authorities would not oppose universal preliminaries? (There is certainly some opinion in the Church, referred to in the Report, which feels that there would be a reduction of 'pastoral opportunities' and that 'universal civil preliminaries might lead to the eventual introduction of a compulsory civil ceremony.')

(ii) There are two other models different from the one which exists at present — whether it be modified or not by the Law Commission recommendations. One model would be to have universal civil procedures followed by a ceremony of marriage anywhere. Marriages would not be confined to Churches, places of public religious worship, or register offices. Another model, moving the other way, would be to impose compulsory civil ceremonies of marriage, which could be followed by religious blessings if the parties so desired. Do you favour either of these reforms?

Professor Mary Ann Glendon (1977) distinguishes compulsory pre-marital procedures from compulsory ceremonies necessary for the actual creation of a contract of marriage. As to the first, she states: 'the preliminaries required by modern States before a marriage can take place are revealing as indications of the degree to which the State is actively involved in regulation of marriage formation, as opposed to contenting itself with the promulgation of rules which describe ideal behaviour in the area but which have no real sanction.'

In commenting on the English law of marriage preliminaries, Glendon states that: 'the apparent complexity of the system. . . . masks the fact that the system as a whole exercises little control over the formation of marriage and that the English State takes little advantage of the occasion of marriage to promote any particular social policies.'

Question

What social policies do you think that the State should promote? In particular do you think that the State should impose longer waiting periods, greater publicity, compulsory counselling, compulsory medical tests, or evidence of financial or residential security? Or are all these impositions contrary to the basic freedom to marry?

CHAPTER 2

The legal structure of marriage

Blackstone's *Commentaries on the Laws of England* (1765):

. . . . By marriage, the husband and wife are one person in law: that is, the very being or legal existence of the woman is suspended during the marriage, or at least is incorporated and consolidated into that of the husband: under whose wing, protection, and *cover*, she performs every thing; and is therefore called in our law-french a *feme-covert, foemina viro co-operta*; is said to be *covert-baron*, or under the protection and influence of her husband, her *baron*, or lord; and her condition during her marriage is called her *coverture*. Upon this principle, of a union of person in husband and wife, depend almost all the legal rights, duties and disabilities, that either of them acquire by the marriage. . . .

Petruchio, in Shakespeare's *Taming of the Shrew* (1596):

> I will be master of what is mine own
> She is my goods, my chattels, she is my house
> My household stuff, my field, my barn
> My horse, my ox, my ass, my anything.

1 The common law

In this chapter, we discuss the legal rights and duties which accrue on marriage. Olive Stone (1977) refers to marriage as 'a series of complex and ever-changing relationships between two individuals of opposite sexes.' As we can see from the quotations above, the common law refused to acknowledge the legal existence of one member of this relationship and 'incorporated and consolidated' the wife's legal existence into that of her husband. In *A Century of Family Law* (1957), Professor Graveson sketched the legal position at common law in his introductory essay, *The Background of the Century*:

The English family in the years following Waterloo differed in many ways from the family of today. The husband was in a real sense the authoritarian head of the family, with very extensive powers over both person and property of his wife and children. But his right to inflict personal chastisement on his wife had greatly declined in importance since Blackstone had described it half a century before as one which the lower orders took seriously and cherished dearly. On marriage husband and wife became for many purposes one person in law, a doctrine of common law of great antiquity. In the words of a late nineteenth-century lawyer, 'The Creator took from Adam a rib and made it Eve; the common law of England endeavoured to reverse the process, to replace the rib and to remerge the personalities.' [de Montmorency (1897)] On marriage all the wife's personal chattels became the absolute property of the husband, while the husband could dispose of the wife's leasehold property during his life and enjoyed for his own benefit her freehold estate during her life. Subject to the institution by the Court of Chancery of what was known as the wife's separate estate in equity, the married woman, both physically and economically, was very much in the position of a chattel of her husband. But her position was not completely black. The doctrine of the legal identity of husband and wife was never applied to its extreme limit. In the words of de Montmorency, 'The English judges were too reasonable to be logical, if they could possibly help it.'

In criminal law a presumption existed that a wife who committed a felony (other than the most serious ones) had been coerced by her husband. Civilly the husband was liable for torts, such as slander, committed by his wife, while rules of evidence prevented husband and wife bearing witness against one another in all but the most exceptional circumstances. Each of these aspects of the nineteenth-century relationship of husband and wife . . . reflect the general position in the early nineteenth century when the relations of society were largely relations of status, that is, a legal position imposed by rules of general law by virtue of persons being in certain relationship with one another, such as husband and wife, parent and child, master and servant. The dominant character of these relationships was one of an often profitable guardianship to the person to whom the law gave control. But the idea of guardianship carried with it one of responsibility for the acts and defaults of what we may call the junior member of the relationship. Thus, while the husband obtained great economic advantages from marriage, he was liable to a great extent, both criminally and civilly, to suffer for the misdeeds of his wife, in a somewhat similar manner to that in which a master was and still is liable for the wrongful acts of his servant committed in the course of his employment.

The traditional organisation of society on a basis of status was undergoing a transformation in the early nineteenth century under the impact of the Industrial Revolution and the Napoleonic Wars. In an economic age of *laisser-faire* Bentham had propounded for almost half a century his dearest creed of the utmost freedom of contracting. As one aspect of this general demand for contractual freedom, he had advocated the introduction of judicial divorce, though not on a consensual pattern, despite the fact that he regarded marriage as a contract to which the principle of agreement should apply both in its formation and dissolution. In the century between 1761 and 1861 the population of England had increased threefold, with consequent changes in ways of life and modes of thought. Writing in 1861, Sir Henry Maine had said that the movement of progressive societies hitherto had been a movement from status to contract.

2 Making decisions — sexual relations

It is clear that so far as the law is concerned, one spouse no longer automatically predominates. However, the movement towards equality and joint responsibility has by no means been a simple process, and vestiges of the old common law approach survive to this day.

R v Clarence
(1888) 22 QBD 23, 58 LJMC 10, 59 LT 780, 53 JP 149, 37 WR 166, 5 TLR 61, 16 Cox CC 511, High Court

Mr Clarence had been convicted of an assault upon his wife occasioning 'actual bodily harm' and of unlawfully and maliciously inflicting upon her 'grievous bodily harm.' It appears that Mr Clarence, to his knowledge, was suffering from a form of gonorrhorea yet he nevertheless had marital intercourse with his wife without informing her of this fact. He infected her, and from this infection, it was claimed that his wife suffered grievous bodily harm. He was convicted, but he appealed successfully to the Queen's Bench Division against conviction. The case was considered by all of the thirteen judges: nine quashed the conviction and four dissented.

Hawkins J: . . . The wife *submits* to her husband's embraces because at the time of marriage she gave him an irrevocable right to her person. The intercourse which takes place between husband and wife after marriage is not by virtue of any special consent on her part, but is mere submission to an obligation imposed upon her by law. Consent is immaterial.

A. L. Smith, J: . . . At marriage the wife consents to the husband exercising the marital right. The consent then given is not confined to a husband when sound in body, for I suppose no one would assert that a husband was guilty of an offence because he exercised such right when afflicted with some complaint of which he was then ignorant. Until the consent given at marriage be revoked, how can it be said that the husband in exercising his marital right has assaulted his wife? In the present case at the time the incriminated act was committed, the consent given at marriage stood unrevoked. Then how is it an assault?

The utmost the Crown can say is that the wife would have withdrawn her consent if she had known what her husband knew, or, in other words, that the husband is guilty of a crime, viz., an assault because he did not inform the wife of what he then knew. In my judgment in this case, the consent given at marriage still existing and unrevoked, the prisoner has not assaulted his wife.

Question

Would Mrs Clarence have been guilty of the offence charged against Mr Clarence if she had been suffering from venereal disease, undisclosed to her husband?

In English law, a man cannot be found guilty of committing rape on his wife, unless there be a judicial separation, a separation order, a decree nisi of divorce or a non-molestation order. However, two American states, New Jersey and Oregon, have now totally abolished the marital exemption. Oregon was the scene of a fascinating case in 1978 which provided newspaper copy for many weeks: *Rideout v Rideout* (Or. Cir Ct. 5 Fam 2164). The following account is taken from issues of the *Oregonian* in December 1978 and January 1979:

Rideout was indicted Oct. 18 on a charge of first-degree rape, stemming from an Oct. 10 incident in which police say he raped and beat his 23-year-old wife, Greta.

At the time of the alleged incident, the Rideouts shared their Salem apartment. Since then, they have separated, and Mrs Rideout has filed for divorce.

In her testimony, which lasted almost two hours, Mrs Rideout said she and her husband had been arguing about sex and money the night before the Oct. 10 incident.

During that argument, she said, they discussed the fact that women in Oregon can charge their husbands with rape. Mrs Rideout said she learned of the 1977 statute about three weeks before the incident in her home.

Mrs Rideout testified that, on the afternoon of Oct. 10, she refused her husband's request to have sexual relations. She said her husband became very angry and told her ' "You are my wife and you should do what I want." '

Mrs Rideout said she attempted twice to run out of their apartment to escape her husband, but both times he followed her. On the second occasion, when Rideout caught up with her in a park near the apartment, Mrs Rideout said he took her by the arm and escorted her to the apartment, where he again demanded they have sex.

'He asked me, "Are you going to cooperate with me?" and I said no,' she said. She testified that he repeated that question twice, and when she answered negatively, he hit her on the left side of the face.

'I said to John, "Why are you picking on me?" and he said, "It's because I can't stand you, I can't stand you," ' she said. 'So I said, "Why don't you let me go?" And he said, "Because I love you, Greta." '

Mrs Rideout said she attempted to struggle and scream while her husband was forcing her to have intercourse with him. Finally, she testified, she decided to submit to his demands because she feared if he continued to hit her on the face, he would break her jaw.

At one point, Mrs Rideout said she saw the couple's two-year-old daughter, Jenny, watching the struggle. 'I heard Jenny scream, "Mommy, mommy." She was trying to get to me, she said,' adding that Jenny eventually left the apartment living room where the rape allegedly took place.

Mrs Rideout said that, when the assault was over, she hid in a neighbor's home, where she called the Salem Women's Crisis Center and the Salem police.

During his 45 minutes on the stand, Rideout said he hit his wife only after she had hit him a number of times during their Oct. 10 altercation. He said he struck her once, using more force than he had intended.

'She hit me first. She slapped me. I grabbed ahold of her arms and she slapped me again,' Rideout testified.

'Then I felt a pain . . . she had kneed me in the groin. I stepped back and then stepped forward and slapped her,' he continued. 'I stopped myself because I realized I was really angry. I had never hit my wife before intentionally. I said, 'Greta, I'm sorry, I didn't mean to do it." '

Rideout said he and his wife went into their bathroom to look at the injury to her face. He said she appeared to have some redness around one of her eyes. Rideout said he apologized to his wife, and then they had sex.

[Later] John Joseph Rideout was acquitted Wednesday of a charge that he raped his wife.
After deliberating for three hours, the Marlon County Circuit Court jury of eight women and four men delivered its unanimous verdict to Judge Richard Barber.

Pauline Speerstra, a member of the jury and a lawyer's wife, said jurors took 'four or five' votes before the final poll in which they unanimously found Rideout innocent. In the early votes, she said, a number of jurors remained undecided about the case.

Another juror, Joan Kay Lent, the wife of Oregon Supreme Court Justice Berkeley Lent, said the vote gradually turned for acquittal. 'We just weren't convinced (of Rideout's guilt) without a reasonable doubt.'

In an Editorial on January 11, 1979, the *Oregonian* reported:

Now that his trial is over, John Rideout, 21, reportedly is patching things up with his wife Greta, 23, who accused him of marital rape only to see him acquitted of the charge in Salem last month.

It may be that a San Diego, Calif., radio station we heard in Portland Wednesday morning was not far off base when it reported the reconciliation while it played violin music in the background.

'I think both me and Greta have changed tremendously, and I don't think we'd be together today if it weren't for the trial and the experience we went through,' he said.

'It made us see things average people in the world don't get to see. . . . It helped us grow and learn,' he said.

The arguments both for and against the marital rape exemption are summarised in the following extracts from an article by Michael Freeman, *But if you can't rape your wife, whom can you rape?* (1981).

In defense of the immunity
A number of justifications to be found in the literature will be considered briefly. Five main arguments have been put forward.

The first emphasizes the inappropriateness of using the criminal law in disputes between husbands and wives, a view that is not new: commentators on the problem of marital violence generally put it forward. Parnas (1970) used to do so; Susan Maidment still does. It is worth pondering her reasoning. She writes: 'Serious consideration must be given to whether prosecuting a husband for a criminal offence . . . will achieve anything in terms of improving the marital relationship, the mutual respect which the husband and wife should have for each other, or the husband's ability to understand and control his aggression.' (1978) She favors the family court mediation-oriented approach used in a number of American cities. But why should 'improving' marital relationships be the goal? Why, to quote police evidence to the British House of Commons Select Committee on Violence in Marriage, should 'every effort . . . *be made to re-unite the family*'. It is all very well to want the family to function properly, but when it has not done so, it may very well not be in the victim's best interests to use social work intervention to restore the status quo ante. [Some of these issues are referred to by us at pp. 535–547, below.]

Similar ideas have found their way to the marital rape debate. Thus, the South Australian report which produced legislation that has partially removed the marital rape exemption stated: 'It is only in exceptional circumstances that the criminal law should invade the bedroom . . . The wife who is subjected to force in the husband's pursuit of sexual intercourse needs, in the first instance, the protection of the family law . . . and not the protection of the criminal law.' (1976) Similarly, Joanna McFadyen (1978) by no means suggest[s] the application of the full force of the criminal law in every case. She advocates its use 'as a last resort on a continuum of resources focused on the increased well-being of the family unit and each of its members.' The significance of marital rape must not be underestimated. Rape is the most extreme example of legal sexism. It is, to quote Medea and Thompson, (1974) 'at one end of a continuum of male-agressive, female-passive patterns.' The McFadyen approach concentrates not on the well-being of the family unit but on the welfare of the husband and men everywhere. There is no reason why rape in marriage should be regarded differently from rape of a stranger. There may be a case for grading penalties but that would have to be based not on the fact of marriage but on that of previous sexual conduct. If the criminal law has no place in bedrooms a propos rape, why has it a place as regards assault, kidnapping, and theft? And why does the exemption not extend to those who cohabit? [The American Model Penal Code (Proposed Official Draft) (1962) did extend the exemption to 'persons living as man and wife' regardless of the legal status of their relationship.]

Freeman continues:

Second, immunity is sometimes justified on the basis of the difficulties of proving marital rape. There are, it is true, cases where it would be difficult to prove marital rape, as witnesses are unlikely to be found. But many crimes are difficult to prove, and no one has suggested removing them for that reason. This is particularly so in the case of rape, where lack of consent is the most difficult thing to prove. But this applies to all prosecutions for rape, particularly where the accused and victim have had a sexual relationship prior to the incident in question. Is it seriously being suggested that the only rapes that should be prosecuted are those where rapist and victim are complete strangers?

A third alleged rationale for the marital rape exemption is linked to the second, though it is arguably inconsistent with it. It asserts that the possibilities exist of a vindictive or unscrupulous wife bringing a malicious prosecution based on fabricated evidence, possibly for an ulterior purpose such as blackmailing her husband into making a favorable property settlement or custody arrangement. The vengeful-wife rationale is not convincing. If, as the second rationale argues, rape in marriage is difficult to prove, the threat of a rape prosecution would hardly be a potent weapon in a vindictive wife's hands. It is assumed that repeal of the immunity would 'open the floodgates to endless numbers of matrimonial complaints that wives have been raped,' a situation that has not materialized in jurisdictions that have done away with it. Though wives can now prosecute husbands for assault and sodomy, there is no evidence that they are doing this commonly and, in cases where they are, vengefully. Of course, the initiation of criminal proceedings is a potentially dangerous weapon that can be used by anyone against anyone else. Do we believe that women are more spiteful or more vengeful? If we do, we fail to appreciate the current context of rape trials or the stigma, trauma, and tribulation involved for the victim. Because women in rape trials often feel that they are on trial (Brownmiller, 1975), only a mentally unstable wife would be likely to initiate a prosecution except in the most serious circumstances.

A fourth line of defense stresses the possibility that a wife, having accused her husband of rape, will change her mind and reconcile with him. This weak argument was used when an attempt was made in Britain in 1976 to abolish the marital rape exemption. It is said that women who bring assault charges against their husbands change their minds next day, so that police time is wasted and little achieved. Whether that is so is debatable, but there are few calls for husbands to be immune from prosecution for assaulting wives. It may well be that prosecutions for marital rape should not take place where the spouses are subsequently reconciled. One must not forget that the state as the protector of married women generally has an interest in the prosecution over and above that of the victim (do prosecutions deter other husbands?), but it is difficult to argue from this that the act should not be a crime.

A fifth defense of the exemption states that a wife does not need the protection of the criminal law as she has alternative remedies in family law (as well as limited remedies in criminal law itself, such as prosecuting for assault). It is true that in England she can seek injunctions against molestation and exclude her husband from the matrimonial home; similar remedies exist in many American states. She may bring divorce proceedings against him. This defense overlooks a number of things. First, it is not all that easy for women, working-class women particularly, to leave their husbands, set up a home elsewhere, and bring divorce proceedings. That is one of the reasons why there is such an urgent need for extensive shelter provision. Second, there is no evidence that family law remedies offer sufficient protection. The English cases of *R v Clarke* [1949] 2 All ER 448; *R v Miller* [1954] 2 QB 282, [1954] 2 All ER 529; *R v O'Brien* [1974] 3 All ER 663; and *R v Steele* (1976) 65 Crim App Rep 22 are testimony to the inadequacy of these laws when a woman is faced with a determined husband. Third, the defense once again ignores the rationale of rape laws: rape is not just matrimonial misconduct. It may leave emotional and psychological scars or lead to the birth of a child. It is an offense of sufficient moment for women to be able to claim the protection of the criminal law.

The Criminal Law Revision Committee in its working paper on *Sexual Offences* (1980) considered whether there should be a change in the law in this area:

32. We referred these matters to the Policy Advisory Committee, who told us that in their opinion there was no longer sufficient ground to justify the husband's exemption, and that it should be removed. They did not see marital rape as a serious social problem, and shared our view that in practice these matters should be left where possible to the family courts.[1] They did not believe that there was any real danger that a change in the law would result in any substantial number of improperly motivated threats to bring charges of rape against husbands. However,

---

1. The Committee must here be referring to matrimonial proceedings in both magistrates' and divorce courts.

they regarded it as essential that a prosecution for rape by a husband on his wife should not be brought without the consent of the Director of Public Prosecutions.

33. Some of our members take the view that despite the apparent anomalies the law is better left unaltered. Their reasons are as follows. The relationship between husband and wife is probably the most complex with which the courts deal. Spouses have responsibilities towards one another and to any children there may be as well as having rights against each other. If a wife could invoke the law of rape in all circumstances in which the husband had forced her to have sexual intercourse without her consent, the consequences for any children could be grave, and for the wife too. In many, probably most, such cases a quarrel would be likely, followed a few days later by a reconciliation. But if an angry wife could call in the police, who would have a duty to investigate her complaint with all that follows when rape is alleged, some of us consider there might be little chance of a reconciliation. The type of questions which investigating police officers would have to ask would be likely to be greatly resented by husbands and their families. The family ties would be severed and the wife with children would have to cope with her emotional, social and financial problems as best she could; and possibly the children might resent what she had done to their father. Nearly all breakdowns of marriage cause problems. A breakdown brought about by a wife who had sought the protection of the criminal law of rape would be particularly painful.

34. Before the passing of the Divorce Reform Act 1969, the making of unreasonable sexual demands on a wife was always regarded as a form of cruelty entitling the wife to protection. Nowadays when a petition for divorce may be presented to the court on the ground that the marriage has broken down irretrievably, a factor to be considered is whether the husband has behaved in such a way that the petitioner cannot reasonably be expected to live with him (Matrimonial Causes Act 1973, section 1). A wife cannot reasonably be expected to live with a husband who forces her to have sexual intercourse with him when she does not want to do so. In addition, both in the High Court and in the County Court a wife can obtain an injunction against her husband restraining him from molesting her (Domestic Violence and Matrimonial Proceedings Act 1976, section 1). Magistrates' courts too have limited powers of giving protection (sections 16 to 18, Domestic Proceedings (Magistrates' Courts) Act 1978).

35. Even if wives cohabiting with their husbands were given the protection of the law of rape there would be many problems to be solved. First, there would be that of proof. Proof of rape is always difficult but would be particularly difficult when husband and wife had been cohabiting. Unless the wife could show marks of injury (and they would have to be relevant marks) or the husband (after being cautioned) made admissions to investigating police officers, the prosecution's case would nearly always rest solely on the wife's evidence. The difficulties which already exist in obtaining sufficient evidence in cases of rape would be of necessity greater in the case of the cohabiting husband and wife. Prosecutions in such cases would be unlikely, and the police would have had the time-wasting and distasteful task of investigating the wife's complaint.

36. Deciding when to prosecute is likely to be difficult also because of the time that may elapse between the occasion of the alleged rape and the complaint. This is a particularly likely problem, some of us consider, since a threat to reveal to the police an occasion of alleged rape could be used as a bargaining counter in negotiations for maintenance and the division of property on the breakdown of marriage.

37. Such are the reasons advanced by those of our members who wish to retain the present law. The majority of us, however, while recognising the difficulties involved, do not regard them as sufficient ground for leaving the law as it is. The present immunity of a husband does not rest on any sound basis of principle, and is in some quarters much resented. In the paragraphs that follow we set out the arguments which satisfy the majority of us that this immunity should now be abolished, and we make proposals which we believe will substantially meet the objections of the minority.

38. We have already said that as a statement of the subjection of the wife to the husband, [the] doctrine is totally out of accord with present-day attitudes, whatever may have been the justification for it in former times. In *R v Miller* [1954] 2 QB 282, [1954] 2 All ER 529 Lynskey J. undoubtedly narrowed the scope of the immunity by holding that a husband who raped his wife could be convicted of assault occasioning her actual bodily harm. The jury there found that the hysterical and nervous condition to which the wife had been reduced by the rape amounted to actual bodily harm; more commonly, it may be supposed, the evidence would be of physical injury.

39. It is difficult to explain why wives should be outside the protection of the law of rape when unmarried cohabitees are not. The explanation has been advanced that wives, unlike cohabitees, are protected in the family court. But there is no obvious reason why the protection given in the family court should disentitle the wife to the protection of the law of rape. . . .

40. Those who support [the present law] fear that if it were altered the police would have to make distasteful enquiries into the details of married life, and courts would be faced with issues

of fact that would be hard to determine. But these possibilities . . . already exist in the present law. . . . The fact is that the police are reluctant to bring criminal charges in these circumstances, since they think that such matters are better left to the remedies provided by the family court. There is no reason to suppose, therefore, that an abandonment of [the] rule would result in a great intrusion of the criminal law into family matters.

41. Lastly, there are technical as well as social reasons for acknowledging the simple principle that a wife is as much entitled to withhold consent to sexual intercourse as anyone else. The problem of constructing a provision on more restrictive lines would be formidable. . . . There is really no satisfactory way of listing the marital rapes that should be punishable as rape and not merely as some kind of assault. There would, too, we consider, be difficulty in drafting and applying a provision that would replace the present exceptions to the husband's immunity by a more general exception based on the termination of cohabitation.

42. How then should the law deal with marital rape? We have said above that to enact specifically that certain types of conduct should be rape would create insuperable problems of definition. However, if wives were to be treated in relation to rape in the same way as other women, that might lead to prosecutions which some would think were not desirable in the interest of the family or the public, although the police would probably only want to prosecute in the clearest cases. We are agreed that the only practical way in which control could be exercised is through a requirement for the consent of the Director of Public Prosecutions for prosecutions for marital rape. The Director has told us that if the law is changed such a provision would be essential, although he foresees difficulties in exercising his discretion in relation to these cases. In exercising his discretion in any crime he has two main concerns: whether there is sufficient evidence to warrant prosecution, and whether the public interest points to prosecution. He tells us that while he would be able to assess the evidence, it would be hard in many cases to exercise his usual function of judging the public interest served by prosecuting. We recognise that marital rape may well differ in this respect from other cases where the Director's consent is required, and we certainly would not recommend that the legislature should seek to spell out the factors which he should take into account in these cases. We anticipate, however, that with experience, as in other cases where his consent is required, the Director would be able to form a policy on prosecution for marital rape.

43. As we have said, we are divided on these matters. We should welcome comment on the problems that we have outlined and the proposals that we have made to meet them.

In *Towards a Modern Law of Rape* (1982), Jennifer Temkin criticises the reasons of the minority for favouring the retention of the marital rape exemption:

(1) The criminal law is not the best instrument for dealing with family matters.

There is concern lest the impetuous conduct of the wife in reporting the matter should impede reconciliation. It is considered that in the last resort it is to civil remedies that she should have recourse. But the assumption that reconciliation is a desirable goal in situations of this kind must be queried. There is no reason for the law to seek to encourage a woman to reconcile with a violent and sexually brutal man. Wives prepared to report marital rape to the police may well have husbands who fall into this category.

The dangers to which the minority refer currently exist under the present law. A husband who rapes his wife can be prosecuted for assault or an offence against the person if he uses force or injures her. Therefore a wife can, in most instances, invoke the criminal process at the moment with the same possibility of offending husband and children and hindering reconciliation. Moreover the present law applies to unmarried couples who also have families.

(2) Proof of the offence would be difficult to acquire.

It is of course true, that evidence will be difficult to acquire in cases of marital rape. It does not follow from this that marital rape should not be a crime. There are many crimes which are hard to prove but they remain nonetheless crimes. It is no easier for evidence to be obtained where a man is cohabiting with a woman, yet rape is a crime in these circumstances.

(3) There may be a time lag between the occasion of the alleged rape and the reporting of it to the police. This will exacerbate the problem of deciding whether or not to prosecute.

There is often a time lag between the commission of any rape and its reporting since the victim may have considerable misgivings about doing so. This is a factor which the police are used to taking into account and the D.P.P. should have no difficulty in weighing it in the balance along with many other factors.

In the light of the weakness of the minority argument, it is hard to resist the conclusion of the majority of the Committee and of the Policy Advisory Committee that the marital rape exemption should be abolished. The view taken here is that the principle of sexual choice ought not to cease to apply once the marriage vows are taken. A married woman should be as free as her unmarried counterpart to determine whether and when to have sexual intercourse. Abolition of the exemption has already taken place in many other countries. In September 1980, the Israeli Supreme Court held that a Jewish husband resident in Israel can be convicted of raping his wife and that the English common law rule should no longer apply. The words of Justice Bechor who gave the judgment of the court bear repetition: 'English common law holds that a woman must submit herself totally to her husband. This is an outrage to human conscience and reason in an enlightened country in our time.'

Questions

(i) Do you agree with Temkin and Freeman on the general point that the exemption should be abandoned?

(ii) If so, do you agree with the majority recommendation that a prosecution against a spouse should only be brought with the consent of the Director of Public Prosecutions? Why should not wives be treated in the same way as other raped women?

(iii) Do you think the *Rideout* case from Oregon is a typical example of what may happen if the marital rape exemption is abandoned?

(iv) Did that case bring the law into disrepute?

(v) If the marital rape exemption is abandoned in this country, and the facts of Rideout were to occur, would the Director of Public Prosecutions in your opinion be justified in bringing a prosecution?

Of course problems about sex are not usually of a type which would constitute rape:

Holborn v Holborn
[1947] 1 All ER 32, 176 LT 57, 111 JP 36, 63 TLR 87, 45 LGR 90, High Court, Probate Divorce and Admiralty Division

This was an appeal by the husband from a maintenance order on a summons by the wife on the ground of wilful neglect to provide reasonable maintenance. The question turned on whether the wife was justified in withdrawing from cohabitation. Under the old law, the husband could raise a defence if he could prove she left him without just cause.

Lord Merriman P: The case on which she mainly rested was this same sexual trouble. She says that the husband was 'after her day and night,' at all times and all seasons demanding sexual intercourse, sometimes even as much as five times in one night, and, having been refused, possibly because their tempers were frayed in this argument about money, he then made once more the revolting suggestion which had been made in Canada and had then proved to be the main cause of the earlier disruption of their married life. The wife says that it was for that reason she left home.

To justify the wife in withdrawing from cohabitation, as she did on May 5, by reason of misconduct on the part of the husband, there must be, in the words of the time honoured phrase which I have already used, some 'grave and weighty matter.' I am prepared — though the words were used in a very different context from the facts of the present case — to accept, as one of the paraphrases of that time-honoured phrase, some words used by Lord Merrivale P, in *Jackson v Jackson* on which counsel for the husband insisted. Lord Merrivale P, said ((1932) 146 LT 406 at p 407):

Is it right to say that the conditions imposed on the wife were unbearable for her or any other wife, conditions which it was not competent for a reasonable husband to set up? Were they such conditions that a reasonable wife, being so treated by an unreasonable husband, could not be expected to proceed with the conjugal life?

He was speaking there of difficulties arising through the presence of the husband's mother in the matrimonial home — very different facts from those of the present case — but they have this in common with the present situation, that there was nothing of a permanent or irrevocable character about the conduct which was being complained about. I must not be taken to say that those words are to be substituted for all other tests, but I am prepared to adopt them and adapt them to the circumstances of this case. If the wife's evidence is to be accepted, as it was by the justices, I think the conditions were such as to be unbearable by her, and that it was not competent for a reasonable husband to set them up. The conditions to which I have alluded had already once broken up the marriage and the husband knew perfectly well what effect they were likely to have and what effect such lack of consideration for her feelings was likely to have on this particular wife.

Question

If it had been the wife who had demanded intercourse five times a night and had made the 'revolting suggestion' do you think the judge would have concluded that the husband would have been justified in withdrawing from cohabitation? After you answer the question, consider the cases of *B(L) v B(R)*, below and *P(D) v P(J)* [1965] 2 All ER 456, [1965] 1 WLR 963. The facts of *P(D) v P(J)* are referred to in the concluding remarks of Davies LJ in *B(L) v B(R)*.

B(L) v B(R)
[1965] 3 All ER 263, [1965] 1 WLR 1413, 109 Sol Jo 831, Court of Appeal

The husband, then 27, and the wife, then 20, were married in April 1960. In spite of complaints by the wife of its effect on her health, the husband would not have sexual intercourse with his wife except at infrequent intervals of weeks or months. The wife said that the abstinence had a deleterious effect on her health and there was medical evidence that by October 1963 she was in a state of extreme nervous tension. Her petition for divorce based on the old ground of cruelty was dismissed. The wife appealed.

Davies LJ: . . . So here we have the picture of a man who obviously, on the evidence, was very under-sexed and completely disinclined to have sexual intercourse save at rare intervals. His young wife, one would assume, was of a normal disposition and was no doubt mentally and physically distressed and upset by the infrequency of the intercourse and with his indifference to and rejection of her overtures.

Counsel who appeared in this court for the wife has with great skill put every possible point that can be put on behalf of the wife. Substantially the argument put forward by counsel is this. He says, first, there is the undoubted fact that, owing to the husband's fault, intercourse took place between this young couple only very rarely. Secondly, he says that, as is proved by the evidence, the husband knew that this infrequency of intercourse was having an effect on his wife's health, for she told him so. Thirdly, he knew that it was wrong because he admitted to her, when they were discussing a return, that it was wrong. What precise weight one can attach to the word 'wrong' in this context I am not sure; he may have been merely apologising and saying that he would try to do better as, according to her evidence, he did during the next fortnight. Finally, linking up these points, counsel says that the husband's conduct here shows that he was pursuing a course of conduct with callous indifference to his wife's health. I appreciate the force of those arguments, but nevertheless I find it very difficult to come to the conclusion, with the best will in the world and with the utmost sympathy for the wife, that she has in the present case made out a case of cruelty. I cannot see that the evidence here would justify a finding that the husband was deliberately pursuing a callous course of conduct calculated to injure his wife's health.[2]

I consider that one does not get very much assistance from the decision of Stirling, J in another case, *P(D) v P(J)* [1965] 2 All 456, [1965] 1 WLR 963. The facts there were very different. There the husband was the petitioner. The wife never allowed him to have sexual intercourse at all; she was prepared only to engage in what the judge described as a degree of sexual love-play, but never allowed a completed act of intercourse. And it may very well be that to excite a husband in that way and then to stop him at the last moment might be a very serious and very cruel thing to do; but that is entirely different from the present case. This man did from

---

2. But see *Gollins v Gollins* [1964] AC 644, [1963] 3 All ER 966, where the House of Lords held that to be cruel, behaviour did not necessarily have to be aimed at the other spouse.

time to time have full and proper intercourse with his wife, though not as often as she wished. Although this husband, as I have said, was obviously very under-sexed, it would appear that from time to time he performed his duties in that regard with satisfaction to his wife, although his capacity or his desires in that respect were much less than hers. The real truth of this case is that the husband's appetite was less than that of his wife, and possibly his power also.

On these facts I cannot see that it would have been possible in this case for any judge to find a case of cruelty made out, and I would accordingly dismiss the appeal.

Questions

(i) Now consider the question posed on p. 40. Is the approach adopted by the three judges in these cases based on the fact that it will be easier for a court to be alarmed by allegations of exorbitant sexual demands — whether by the wife or by the husband — than by allegations that a partner's 'appetite and power' in sex is less than is usual?
(ii) Or is it that judges find it easier to condemn a woman for not having intercourse than a man?

Potter v Potter
(1975) 5 Fam Law 161, Court of Appeal

The parties were married in October, 1969. From the date of the marriage until some time in August, 1970, when the wife underwent an operation to cure a physical defect which had hitherto made her incapable of consummating the marriage, the husband had tried to have sexual intercourse with her on many occasions but without success, because she experienced great pain when penetration was attempted. Soon after the wife had returned home after undergoing surgery for her condition, the husband again attempted to consummate the marriage but this attempt also failed. The wife admitted that the cause of failure on this occasion was her emotional state following her operation and not any incapacity or unwillingness on the husband's part. Thereafter, the husband persistently refused to make another attempt to consummate the marriage although the wife wanted to have sexual relations with him and was now capable of intercourse — she claimed that she had sexual intercourse with another man on several occasions after December, 1973, and the medical inspector in the case formed the opinion that she was not a virgin and no longer suffered any impediment which would prevent the consummation of marriage. In August, 1973, the wife petitioned under s. 9(1)(*a*) of the Matrimonial Causes Act 1965, [now s. 12(*b*) of the Matrimonial Causes Act 1973] to have the marriage anulled on the ground of the husband's wilful refusal to consummate the marriage. (An alternative allegation that the non-consummation was due to the husband's incapacity was abandoned on the medical evidence adduced at the hearing of the suit).

The case came before His Honour Judge Solman in the Bromley County Court on May 22, 1974. He dismissed the petition on the ground that the husband's loss of sexual ardour for his wife which had followed upon the unsuccessful attempt at consummation soon after the wife's operation did not constitute a wilful refusal to consummate the marriage. In his view, 'wilful' must mean 'without reasonable cause', while loss of ardour for the wife was something which arose naturally and was not a deliberate act. The wife appealed against these findings.

Ormrod LJ said that the court had to decide what was meant by the phrase 'wilful refusal' in s. 9(1)(*a*) of the Matrimonial Causes Act 1965. Unfortunately, the note of evidence on which the court had to determine the appeal was brief and clearly incomplete. They were bound to assume that the Judge below had had material before him to make what was in effect a finding of fact that the husband's failure to consummate the marriage was due to his loss of ardour *quoad hanc* and not to wilful refusal. His Lordship referred to the opinion of Lord Jowitt, LC, in *Horton v. Horton* [1947] 2 All ER 871, at 874, that the words 'wilful refusal' connoted 'a settled and definite decision come to without just excuse', and that in determining whether there had been a 'wilful refusal' the court should have regard to the whole history of the marriage. Taking that as a description, if not a definition, of 'wilful refusal', his Lordship said that the wife had to show that the husband deliberately refused to have sexual intercourse without just excuse. If, as they were obliged to, they accepted as right the learned Judge's finding that the husband had lost his ardour in relation to his wife it was impossible to say that he had come to a deliberate decision to refuse to have sexual intercourse with her — loss of ardour was, in the words of the learned Judge, something which happened naturally and was not deliberate. They were enjoined by authority, his Lordship continued, to take account of the whole history of the marriage, and in so doing the inference they would make was that the relationship between the parties had been destroyed. His Lordship was therefore unable to differ from the finding of the learned Judge.

3 Making decisions — the choice of a home

The law governing the choice of the matrimonial home has developed since the second world war, not only in response to women's participation in the labour market, but also in response to a growing respect for their right to a voice in where they shall live. It is relevant, first, in divorce or other matrimonial cases in which it is alleged that one spouse has deserted the other; and secondly, in connection with the modern protection of rights of occupation in the matrimonial home. An example of the first is the following case:

Dunn v Dunn
[1949] P 98, [1948] 2 All ER 822, [1949] LJR 87, 65 TLR 570, 112 JP 436, 92 Sol Jo 633, 46 LGR 521, Court of Appeal

Denning LJ: In his able argument counsel for the husband put forward the proposition that the husband has the right to decide where the parties shall live, and that, if the wife refuses to join him, she is guilty of desertion unless she can prove that she had a just cause for her refusal.

If that were a proposition of law it would put a legal burden on the wife to justify her refusal, but it is not a proposition of law. . . . It is simply a proposition of ordinary good sense arising from the fact that the husband is usually the wage-earner and has to live near his work. It is not a proposition which applies in all cases. The decision where the home should be is a decision which affects both the parties and their children. It is their duty to decide it by agreement, by give and take, and not by the imposition of the will of one over the other. Each is entitled to an equal voice in the ordering of the affairs which are their common concern. Neither has a casting vote, though, to be sure, they should try so to arrange their affairs that they spend their time together as a family and not apart. If such an arrangement is frustrated by the unreasonableness of one or the other, and this leads to a separation between them, then the party who has produced the separation by reason of his or her unreasonable behaviour is guilty of desertion. The situations which may arise are so various that I think it unwise to attempt any more precise test than that of unreasonableness. Views as to unreasonableness may vary, and the decision is essentially one for the trial judge with which this court should not interfere unless the conclusion is one which could not reasonably be drawn. If a wife refuses to join her husband at a place when he is ready to receive her, that is, of course, a factor of great weight, but it is not necessarily decisive. Take this case. The judge has held that the wife's refusal was not unreasonable. She was living with the two children, aged 14 and 7, in the matrimonial home at Morpeth. She had never been away from Morpeth except for a few days in 1934. The husband wanted to uproot them for a stay in wartime at Immingham or Barrow. The stay was to be of uncertain duration and it might be for a few weeks or a few months. It was to be in rooms. The wife was deaf and had difficulty in making herself understood by strangers. A considerate husband would have recognised her difficulty and not have insisted on her coming. A considerate wife would have put up with the difficulties and gone. Neither was considerate. Neither was unreasonable. From his point of view he was not acting unreasonably; from her point of view she was not acting unreasonably. Each insisted on their own point of view, and hence the marriage came to an end. The decisive matter, to my mind, is that throughout the matrimonial home was at Morpeth and the wife was ready and willing to have him there on his leave whenever he could get there, and that is where the family were. Her refusal to go for a short stay elsewhere in the circumstances which I have mentioned, it seems to me, was not unreasonable. At all events, there was ample ground on which the learned judge could come to the conclusion which he reached, that it was not unreasonable on her part to fail to go and stay with him. Unless I could say that finding was unreasonable I do not think this court should interfere. I cannot say that, and, therefore, I think the appeal should be dismissed.

Question

In this case, Denning LJ held that neither spouse was being unreasonable, although equally neither party was considerate. Would another finding have been that *both* parties were unreasonable?

The second aspect of this question is the right to occupy the matrimonial home. At common law, each spouse had a personal right, as against the other spouse, to occupy a matrimonial home to which that other was entitled. But this gave no rights against third parties to whom the owning spouse might seek to dispose of his interest. The *Matrimonial Homes Act 1967* was passed to remedy this problem, but in the process it had also to provide a statutory definition of the rights of the parties inter se:

Protection against eviction, etc., from matrimonial home of spouse not entitled by virtue of estate, etc., to occupy it

1.—(1) Where one spouse is entitled to occupy a dwelling house by virtue of [a beneficial estate or interest] or contract or by virtue of any enactment giving him or her the right to remain in occupation, and the other spouse is not so entitled, then, subject to the provisions of this Act, the spouse not so entitled shall have the following rights (in this Act referred to as 'rights of occupation'): —

> (*a*) if in occupation, a right not to be evicted or excluded from the dwelling house or any part thereof by the other spouse except with the leave of the court given by an order under this section;
>
> (*b*) if not in occupation, a right with the leave of the court so given to enter into and occupy the dwelling house.

(2) So long as one spouse has rights of occupation, either of the spouses may apply to the court for an order declaring, enforcing, restricting or terminating those rights or [prohibiting, suspending or restricting] the exercise by either spouse of the right to occupy the dwelling house [or requiring either spouse to permit the exercise by the other of that right.]

(3) On an application for an order under this section the court may make such order as it thinks just and reasonable having regard to the conduct of the spouses in relation to each other and otherwise, to their respective needs and financial resources, to the needs of any children and to all the circumstances of the case, and, without prejudice to the generality of the foregoing provision, —

> (*a*) may except part of the dwelling house from a spouse's rights of occupation (and in particular a part used wholly or mainly for or in connection with the trade, business or profession of the other spouse);
>
> (*b*) may order a spouse occupying the dwelling house or any part thereof by virtue of this section to make periodical payments to the other in respect of the occupation;
>
> (*c*) may impose on either spouse obligations as to the repair and maintenance of the dwelling house or the discharge of any liabilities in respect of the dwelling house.

(4) Orders under this section may, in so far as they have a continuing effect, be limited so as to have effect for a period specified in the order or until further order.

(5) Where a spouse is entitled under this section to occupy a dwelling house or any part thereof, any payment or tender made or other thing done by that spouse in or towards satisfaction of any liability of the other spouse in respect of rent, rates, mortgage payments or other outgoings affecting the dwelling house shall, whether or not it is made or done in pursuance of an order under this section, be as good as if made or done by the other spouse; and a spouse's occupation by virtue of this section shall for purposes of [the Rent Act 1977 (other than Part V and sections 103 to 106)] be treated as possession by the other spouse and for purposes of Chapter II of Part I of the Housing Act 1980 be treated as occupation by the other spouse.

Where a spouse entitled under this section to occupy a dwelling house or any part thereof makes any payment in or towards satisfaction of any liability of the other spouse in respect of mortgage payments affecting the dwelling house, the person to whom the payment is made may treat it as having been made by that other spouse, but the fact that that person has treated any such payment as having been so made shall not affect any claim of the first-mentioned spouse against the other to an interest in the dwelling house by virtue of the payment.

[(5A) Where a spouse is entitled under this section to occupy a dwelling house or part thereof by reason of an interest of the other spouse under a trust, all the provisions of subsection (5) above shall apply in relation to the trustees as they apply in relation to the other spouse.]

(6) The jurisdiction conferred on the court by this section shall be exercisable by the High Court or by a county court, and shall be exercisable by a county court notwithstanding that by reason of the amount of the net annual value for rating of the dwelling house or otherwise the jurisdiction would not but for this subsection be exercisable by a county court.

(7) In this Act 'dwelling house' includes any building or part thereof which is occupied as a dwelling, and any yard, garden, garage or outhouse belonging to the dwelling house and occupied therewith.

(8) This Act shall not apply to a dwelling house which has at no time been a matrimonial home of the spouses in question; and a spouse's rights of occupation shall continue only so long as the marriage subsists and the other spouse is entitled as mentioned in subsection (1) above to occupy the dwelling house, except where provision is made by section 2 of this Act for those rights to be a charge on an estate or interest in the dwelling house.

[(9) It is hereby declared that a spouse who has an equitable interest in a dwelling house or in the proceeds of sale thereof, not being a spouse in whom is vested (whether solely or as a joint tenant) a legal estate in fee simple or a legal term of years absolute in the dwelling house, is to be treated for the purpose only of determining whether he or she has rights of occupation under this section as not being entitled to occupy the dwelling house by virtue of that interest.]

Effect of statutory rights of occupation as charge on dwelling house

2.—(1) Where, at any time during the subsistence of a marriage, one spouse is entitled to occupy a dwelling house by virtue of an estate or interest, then the other spouse's rights of occupation shall be a charge on that [a beneficial estate or interest], having the like priority as if it were an equitable interest created at whichever is the latest of the following dates, that is to say —

   (*a*) the date when the spouse so entitled acquires the estate or interest;

   (*b*) the date of the marriage; and

   (*c*) the commencement of this Act.

[(1A) If, at any time when a spouse's rights of occupation are a charge on an interest of the other spouse under a trust, there are, apart from either of the spouses, no persons, living or unborn, who are or could become beneficiaries under the trust, then those rights shall be a charge also on the estate or interest of the trustees for the other spouse, having the like priority as if it were an equitable interest created (under powers overriding the trusts) on the date when it arises.

In determining for purposes of this subsection whether there are any persons who are not, but could become, beneficiaries under the trust, there shall be disregarded any potential exercise of a general power of appointment exercisable by either or both of the spouses alone (whether or not the exercise of it requires the consent of another person).]

(2) Notwithstanding that a spouse's rights of occupation are a charge on an estate or interest in the dwelling house, those rights shall be brought to an end by —

   (*a*) the death of the other spouse, or

   (*b*) the termination (otherwise than by death) of the marriage,

unless in the event of a matrimonial dispute or estrangement the court sees fit to direct otherwise by an order made under section 1 above during the subsistence of the marriage.

(3) Where a spouse's rights of occupation are a charge on the estate or interest of the other spouse —

   (*a*) any order under section 1 above against the other spouse shall, except in so far as the contrary intention appears, have the like effect against persons deriving title under the other spouse and affected by the charge; and

   (*b*) subsections (2) to (5A) of section 1 above shall apply in relation to any person deriving title under the other spouse and affected by the charge as they apply in relation to the other spouse.

(4) Where a spouse's rights of occupation are a charge on an estate or interest in the dwelling house, and that estate or interest is surrendered so as to merge in some other estate or interest expectant thereon in such circumstances that but for the merger, the person taking the estate or interest of the other spouse would be bound by the charge, then the surrender shall have effect subject to the charge and the persons thereafter entitled to the other estate or interest shall, for so long as the estate or interest surrendered would have endured if not so surrendered be treated for all purposes of this Act as deriving title to the other estate or interest under the other spouse by virtue of the surrender.

(5) Where a spouse's rights of occupation are a charge on the estate or interest of the other spouse, and the other spouse —

   (*a*) is adjudged bankrupt or makes a conveyance or assignment of his or her property (including that estate or interest) to trustees for the benefit of his or her creditors generally; or

   (*b*) dies and his or her estate is insolvent;

then, notwithstanding that it is registered [under section 2 of the Land Charges Act 1972 or subsection 7 below], the charge shall be void against the trustee in bankruptcy, the trustees under the conveyance or assignment or the personal representatives of the deceased spouse, as the case may be.

[(6) At the end of section 10(1) of the Land Charges Act 1925 (which lists the classes of charges on, or obligations affecting, land which may be registered as land charges) there shall be added the following paragraph: —

   'Class F: A charge affecting any land by virtue of the Matrimonial Homes Act 1967';

and in the enactments mentioned in the Schedule to this Act there shall be made the consequential amendments provided for by that Schedule.]

(7) Where the title to the legal estate by virtue of which a spouse is entitled to occupy a dwelling house is registered under the Land Registration Act 1925 or any enactment replaced by that Act, registration of a land charge affecting the dwelling house by virtue of this Act shall be effected by registering a notice or caution under that Act, and a spouse's rights of occupation shall not be an overriding interest within the meaning of that Act affecting the dwelling house notwithstanding that the spouse is in actual occupation of the dwelling house.

(8) Where a spouse's rights of occupation are a charge on the estate or interest of the other spouse, and that estate or interest is the subject of a mortgage within the meaning of the Law of Property Act 1925, then if, after the date of creation of the mortgage, the charge is registered [under section 2 of the Land Charges Act 1972] the charge shall, for the purposes of section 94 of that Act (which regulates the rights of mortgagees to make further advances ranking in priority to subsequent mortgages), be deemed to be a mortgage subsequent in date to the first mentioned mortgage.

Section 1 of the 1967 Act provided a remedy which was not clearly available as between spouses who were jointly entitled to the matrimonial home. Accordingly, s. 4 of the *Domestic Violence and Matrimonial Proceedings Act* 1976 now provides:

Order restricting occupation of matrimonial home
4.—(1) Where each of two spouses is entitled, by virtue of a legal estate vested in them jointly, to occupy a dwelling-house in which they have or at any time have had a matrimonial home, either of them may apply to the court, with respect to the exercise during the subsistence of the marriage of the right to occupy the dwelling-house, for an order prohibiting, suspending or restricting its exercise by the other or requiring the other to permit its exercise by the applicant.

(2) In relation to orders under this section, section 1(3), (4) and (6) of the Matrimonial Homes Act 1967 (which relate to the considerations relevant to the contents of, and to the jurisdiction to make, orders under that section) shall apply as they apply in relation to orders under that section; and in this section 'dwelling-house' has the same meaning as in that Act.

(3) Where each of two spouses is entitled to occupy a dwelling-house by virtue of a contract, or by virtue of any enactment giving them the right to remain in occupation, this section shall apply as it applies where they are entitled by virtue of a legal estate vested in them jointly.

Section 1 of the Matrimonial Homes Act 1967 raises the question of how great a voice the non-owning spouse should have in the choice of a matrimonial home.   •

Wroth v Tyler
[1974] Ch 30, [1973] 1 All ER 897, [1973] 2 WLR 405, 117 Sol Jo 90, 25 P & CR 138, High Court, Chancery Division

The wife registered a charge under the Matrimonial Homes Act 1967 after her husband, who was the sole legal and beneficial owner of the house, had signed a contract for the sale of the house. The registration of the charge meant that the sale with vacant possession could not be completed, and the husband was thus held liable in damages. It is not immediately apparent from the facts of the case why the husband did not seek an order under s. 1(3) of the Matrimonial Homes Act 1967 for the wife's right of occupation to be terminated so as to allow the completion to go ahead. It certainly appears on the face of it that the wife had led both the husband and the prospective purchasers, a newly married couple, reasonably to believe that she was not actively dissenting from the wish of the husband to move from Kent, where they had previously lived, so as to set up home in a cottage in Norfolk. **Megarry J** commented on the facts in the following manner:

Let me add that I would certainly not regard proceedings under the Act by the defendant against his wife as being without prospect of success. As the evidence stands (and of course I have not heard the defendant's wife) there is at least a real prospect of success for the defendant. He does not in any way seek to deprive his wife of a home; the difference between them is a difference as to where the matrimonial home is to be. In that, the conduct of the wife towards the plaintiffs and the defendant must play a substantial part.

Megarry J was not prepared to order specific performance of the contract, for to do so would be to indirectly force the husband to take proceedings under the Matrimonial Homes Act 1967 against his wife. This was a decision which only he could take. Perhaps therefore, one should not feel too concerned about the fate of the husband — who had to pay damages amounting to £5,500 — for after all the remedy was in his own hands. Certainly, on the result of *Wroth v Tyler*, the wife had the 'casting vote.'

Questions

(i) A husband sells the matrimonial home of which he is the sole legal and beneficial owner and, with the proceeds of sale, purchases a house in which he instals his mistress. The entire transaction takes place whilst the wife is away looking after her aged mother. The wife had not registered a charge.
(*a*) Would a court assume jurisdiction and hear a wife's claim 'to enter into and occupy the dwelling house?'
(*b*) If the court does assume jurisdiction, what are her chances of success?
(*c*) Could the wife obtain an order to exclude the mistress?
(*d*) Could any order which the wife obtains include provisions restraining the husband from taking away the furniture?
(ii) On the above facts, if the wife had registered a charge, do you think this would have prevented (*a*) a sale and (*b*) the purchase by the husband of a new house and the wife's exclusion from that house?

The question which we are concerned with in the present chapter — making decisions about where to live — will of course be resolved from time to time by the decision of the courts. This is particularly true in the rented sector. Section 1(5) of the Matrimonial Homes Act 1967 is an important provision regarding rented property. If the tenancy is a protected or a statutory tenancy under the Rent Act 1977 (private tenancies) or a secure tenancy under the Housing Act 1980 (council tenancies) an occupying spouse may keep the tenancy of the other spouse 'alive', even though the latter spouse is not living in the accommodation. Schedule 2 to the Matrimonial Homes and Property Act 1981 now gives a spouse a right to seek transfer of a protected tenancy, a statutory tenancy or a secure tenancy.

Question

Does this mean that the tenant spouse cannot defeat the occupation rights of the wife by purporting to surrender the tenancy to the landlord?

Such 'secure' tenancies were originally confined to private tenancies. The *Report of the Committee on One-Parent Families (The Finer Report)* discussed this in 1974:

6.88 The reasons for the exclusion of council tenancies from the statutory protection appear to be that the landlord in these cases is a democratically elected public body which can be trusted to behave reasonably in dealing with its tenants, and which also may find itself in a position where its duty to the tenant conflicts with some other public duty, to resolve which it has to retain a free hand. . . .
6.90 . . . we can see no continuing good reason for depriving local authority or New Town tenants of the basic protection in security of tenure which the Rent Acts give to the tenants of private landlords. . . .
Our recommendation in principle is that security of tenure similar to the Rent Acts protection be extended to tenancies in the public sector. It should be noted that one effect would be always to interpose the court between an authority wanting possession and a tenant unwilling to go — a safeguard that we think would be of special value when the dispute with the authority was connected with or happened to coincide with some breakdown of marital relations within the home.

This recommendation was accepted, and council house tenancies are in most cases secure tenancies within the meaning given to that phrase under the Housing Act 1980 (see further Chapter 4, below). In particular the s. 1(5) protection applies to secure council tenancies. Further, if proceedings are brought against the tenant and as a result of those proceedings the tenancy is ended as against the tenant then in certain cases at least the spouse in occupation has the right to ask the court to adjourn the proceedings, postpone the date of possession, and stay or suspend execution of the order.

Question

The Finer Report (1974) stated that 'the protection which the wife and children may require when the family live in rented accommodation is protection in occupancy, which may be achieved irrespective of rights of ownership.' In the context of council housing, (a) do you think that it is appropriate that this protection should be exercised by the courts rather than by the local authorities, and if so, (b) why do you have this view? (For the courts' powers to transfer a tenancy, both private and council, after the termination of the marriage see Chapter 6, below.)

Barnett v Hassett
[1982] 1 All ER 80, [1981] 1 WLR 1385, 125 Sol Jo 376, High Court, Family Division

The parties, both married previously, married one another in February 1980. The wife owned a large and expensive house, 2 Spaniard's Close, as a result of the orders made in her favour at the end of her first marriage. The husband's previous house was sold in March 1980, and no doubt in anticipation of setting up the new combined families, he exchanged contracts for the purchase of a house and paid a deposit of £41,000. The exchange of contracts took place in November 1979. He moved into 2 Spaniard's Close in March 1980 and left it in July 1980. Clearly, the new marriage had not worked, and in May 1980, the husband informed the vendors of the house he intended to purchase that he could not complete. He forfeited the deposit. In December 1980, the husband applied to register a Class F land charge on 2 Spaniard's Close.

Wood J: . . . Before turning to the law I analyse the husband's case as follows: (i) he has rights under section 1(1)(*b*) of the Matrimonial Homes Act 1967 as a spouse not in occupation of the matrimonial home; (ii) he does not wish to occupy that home or any part of it; (iii) he does not now wish to prevent its sale (although I doubt whether that was his attitude until very recently); (iv) he wants to freeze part of the proceeds of sale — £60,000; (v) he therefore registered a Class F charge to force his wife to apply to this court to set it aside.

I turn to the Act of 1967 itself. It is unnecessary for me to review the history of the rights between husband and wife prior to the passing of this Act; suffice it to say that the provisions of the Act introduce new rights.

By section 1 the Act protects a spouse who has no rights to remain in the matrimonial home. . . . If not in occupation the right of a spouse is 'with the leave of the court so given to enter into and occupy the dwelling house': section 1(1)(*b*). The whole emphasis of the Act is to create and protect the right to occupation of a spouse not in occupation or a spouse already in occupation. This is made clear throughout the Act. The right to occupation must relate to a matrimonial home, and only continues during the existence of the marriage. A Class F charge is intended to protect that right.

One thing is abundantly clear, namely that this husband does not seek 'to enter into and occupy' the whole or any part of the matrimonial home. Is he entitled to ask the court to freeze any part of the proceeds of sale? I do not think so. . . . Section 3 of the Act seems to me to emphasise that any interest other than a right to occupy is to be excluded or disregarded. By that section a charge can only be registered on one matrimonial home at a time. If the intention of the Act had been to allow a spouse to place his or her hands upon proceeds of sale or to allow the prevention of such a sale then I would have thought that a charge on a matrimonial home not in occupation and when a sale was likely would be an obvious source for funds.

. . . in my judgment, the registration of this Class F charge in the circumstances of the present case was not a proper use of the process set up by the Act of 1967 and the charge will be set aside.

Question

What is the difference between *Wroth v Tyler* (see p. 45, above), and the behaviour of the wife in that case, and *Barnett v Hassett*, and the behaviour of the husband?

Megarry J in *Wroth v Tyler* called the statutory right of occupation 'a weapon of great power and flexibility:'

I can now say something about the nature of the charge and the mode of operation of the Act. First, for a spouse in occupation, the right seems to be a mere statutory right for the spouse not to be evicted. There appears to be nothing to stay the eviction of others. For example, if a wife is living in her husband's house with their children and her parents, her charge, even if registered, appears to give no protection against eviction to the children or parents. . . . Nor if the wife takes in lodgers does there seem to be anything to prevent the husband from evicting them. If, for example, the husband is himself living in the house, it would be remarkable if the Act gives the wife the right to insist upon having other occupants in the home against his will. The statutory right appears in essence to be a purely personal right for the wife not to be evicted; and it seems wholly inconsistent with the Act that this right should be assignable or otherwise disposable. I may add that there is nothing to require the wife to make any payment to the husband for her occupation, unless ordered by the court under section 1(3), though if she is in occupation against his will and by virtue of her statutory rights, it may be that she will be in rateable occupation.

Second, although the right given to an occupying wife by section 1(1) is merely a right not to be evicted or excluded 'by the other spouse,' and so at first sight does not appear to be effective against anyone except that other spouse, section 2(1) makes the right 'a charge' on the husband's estate or interest; and it is this, rather than the provisions for registration, which makes the right binding on successors in title. The operation of the provision for registration seems to be essentially negative; the right is a charge which, if not duly protected by registration, will become void against subsequent purchases, or fail to bind them. In this, the right seems not to differ from other registrable charges, such as general equitable charges or puisne mortgages. Yet there is this difference. For other charges, the expectation of the statute is plainly that they will all be protected by registration, whereas under the Act of 1967 there does not seem to be the same expectation.

Questions

(i) If statutory co-ownership is introduced (see p. 117, below), will the protection afforded under the Matrimonial Homes Act 1967 be of any value?

(ii) Does the wife's right of occupation give her the right to invite visitors to the home? (See *R v Thornley* (1980) 72 Cr App Rep 302.)

The Matrimonial Homes Act 1967 is confined to matrimonial homes, and only spouses obtain protection under its terms. Cohabitees are excluded. In Scotland the position is different. Section 18 of the *Matrimonial Homes (Family Protection) (Scotland) Act 1981* states:

'If a man and a woman are living with each other as if they were man and wife (a cohabiting couple) in a home which, apart from the provisions of this section —
    (a) one of them is entitled, or permitted by a third party to occupy; and
    (b) the other . . . is not so entitled to occupy,
the court may, on the application of the non-entitled partner, if it appears that the man and the woman are a cohabiting couple in the house, grant occupancy rights therein to the applicant for such period, not exceeding three months, as the court may specify.

Provided that the court may extend the said period for a further period or periods, no such period exceeding six months.'

If occupancy rights under this Act are granted, the 'non-entitled' partner has the right (*a*) if in occupation, not to be evicted and (*b*) if not in occupation, a right to enter into and occupy. Rights of third parties are not prejudiced.

Questions

(i) Do you favour similar amendments to the English law?
(ii) What problems would arise?

(See Chapter 8, below for a general discussion of the question of cohabitation.)

4 Making decisions — the birth of children

There is one particular matter on which the law does grant the casting vote to the wife, and this is the decision whether to abort a foetus or to give birth to the child already in the womb. This is of course a different question from the one relating to whether or not to have sexual relations, and whether to have those relations with or without contraceptives. There may be a remedy in the divorce court in those sad situations if it can be shown that refusal to have sexual intercourse is in the circumstances unreasonable (although see the cases at pp. 39–42, above). Likewise, if the court takes the view that it is unreasonable for one party to insist on contraceptives, then again a divorce petition would be likely to succeed. However, the law does not in these matters provide either party with a casting vote or a veto. So far as a possible abortion is concerned, however, the law clearly excludes the husband from any right to demand or to refuse such an operation for his wife:

Paton v British Pregnancy Advisory Service Trustees
[1979] 1 QB 276, [1978] 2 All ER 987, [1978] 3 WLR 687, 122 Sol Jo 744, High Court, Queen's Bench Division

The plaintiff, William Paton, was the husband of the second defendant, Joan Mary Paton. On May 8, 1978, the wife's general practitioner confirmed that she was pregnant. The wife thereafter applied for and obtained the necessary medical certificate entitling her to an abortion within the terms of the Abortion Act 1967. On May 16, 1978, the wife left the matrimonial home.

On May 17, 1978, the husband applied for an injunction to restrain the first defendants, the trustees of the British Pregnancy Advisory Service, and the wife from causing or permitting an abortion to be carried out on the wife. Sir George Baker P adjourned the case for one week to May 24, 1978, to enable all the parties to be represented. Also on May 17, the wife filed her petition for divorce.

The husband originally put his case on the basis that the wife had no proper legal grounds for seeking the termination of her pregnancy and that she was being spiteful, vindictive and utterly unreasonable in so doing. At the resumed hearing on May 24, it was accepted by all the parties that the provisions of the Abortion Act 1967 had been correctly complied with. The husband contended that he had the right to have a say in the destiny of the child he had conceived.

Sir George Baker P: By a specially endorsed writ the plaintiff, who is the husband of the second defendant, seeks an injunction in effect to restrain the first defendants, a charitable organisation, and particularly his wife, the second defendant, from causing or permitting an abortion to be carried out upon his wife without his consent.

Such action, of course, arouses great emotions, and vigorous opposing views as was recently pointed out in 1972 in the Supreme Court of the United States by Blackmun J in *Roe v Wade* (1973) 93 S Ct 705, 708–709. In the discussion of human affairs and especially of abortion, controversy can rage over the moral rights, duties, interests, standards and religious views of the parties. Moral values are in issue. I am, in fact, concerned with none of these matters. I am concerned, and concerned only, with the law of England as it applies to this claim. My task is to apply the law free of emotion or predilection.

Nobody suggests that there has ever been such a claim litigated before the courts in this country. Indeed, the only case of which I have ever heard was in Ontario. It was unreported because the husband's claim for an injunction was never tried.

In considering the law the first and basic principle is that there must be a legal right enforceable in law or in equity before the applicant can obtain an injunction from the court to restrain an infringement of that right. That has long been the law.

The law is that the court cannot and would not seek to enforce or restrain by injunction matrimonial obligations, if they be obligations, such as sexual intercourse or contraception (a non-molestation injunction given during the pendency of divorce proceedings could, of course, cover attempted intercourse). No court would ever grant an injunction to stop sterilisation or vasectomy. Personal family relationships in marriage cannot be enforced by the order of a court. An injunction in such circumstances was described by Judge Mager in *Jones v Smith* (1973) 278 So Rep 339 in the District Court of Appeal of Florida as 'ludicrous.'

I ask the question, 'If an injunction were ordered, what could be the remedy?' and I do not think I need say any more than that no judge could even consider sending a husband or wife to prison for breaking such an order. That, of itself, seems to me to cover the application here; this husband cannot by law stop his wife by injunction from having what is now accepted to be a lawful abortion within the terms of the Abortion Act 1967. . . .

The Abortion Act 1967 gives no right to a father to be consulted in respect of a termination of a pregnancy. True, it gives no right to the mother either, but obviously the mother is going to be right at the heart of the matter consulting with the doctors if they are to arrive at a decision in good faith, unless, of course, she is mentally incapacitated or physically incapacitated (unable to make any decision or give any help) as, for example, in consequence of an accident. The husband, therefore, in my view, has no legal right enforceable in law or in equity to stop his wife having this abortion or to stop the doctors from carrying out the abortion.

Missouri in the United States once had a spousal consent provision:

Section 3. No abortion shall be performed prior to the end of the first twelve weeks of pregnancy except:

(1) By a duly licensed, consenting physician in the exercise of his best clinical medical judgment.

(2) After the woman, prior to submitting to the abortion, certifies in writing her consent to the abortion and that her consent is informed and freely given and is not the result of coercion.

(3) With the written consent of the woman's spouse, unless the abortion is certified by a licensed physician to be necessary in order to preserve the life of the mother.

(4) With the written consent of one parent or person in loco parentis of the woman if the woman is unmarried and under the age of eighteen years, unless the abortion is certified by a licensed physician as necessary in order to preserve the life of the mother.

Planned Parenthood of Missouri v Danforth
(1976) 428 US 52, 49 L Ed 2d 788, 96 S Ct 2831, Supreme Court

The plaintiffs, a non-profit-making organisation which maintains a facility in Missouri for the performance of abortions, brought proceedings to obtain declaratory relief on the grounds, amongst others, that certain provisions of the Act deprived the organisation and its doctors and their patients of various constitutional rights; the right to privacy in the physician-patient relationship, the femal patients' right to determine whether to bear children and other constitutional rights.

The Supreme Court concluded that both s. 3(3) and 3(4) were unconstitutional: we report here their *opinion* relating to s. 3(3) (for a discussion of parental control over their children, see Chapter 15):

The appellees defend § 3(3) on the ground that it was enacted in the light of the General Assembly's 'perception of marriage as an institution,' Brief for Appellee Danforth 34, and that any major change in family status is a decision to be made jointly by the marriage partners. Reference is made to an abortion's possible effect on the woman's childbearing potential. It is said that marriage always has entailed some legislatively imposed limitations: reference is made to adultery and bigamy as criminal offenses; to Missouri's general requirement, Mo Rev Stat § 453.030.3 (1969), that for an adoption of a child born in wedlock the consent of both parents is necessary; to similar joint-consent requirements imposed by a number of States with respect to artificial insemination and the legitimacy of children so conceived; to the laws of two States requiring spousal consent for voluntary sterilization; and to the long-established requirement of spousal consent for the effective disposition of an interest in real property. It is argued that '[r]ecognizing that the consent of both parties is generally necessary . . . to begin a family, the legislature has determined that a change in the family structure set in motion by mutual consent should be terminated only by mutual consent,' Brief for Appellee Danforth 38, and that what the legislature did was to exercise its inherent policymaking power 'for what was believed to be in the best interests of all the people of Missouri.' Id., at 40.

The appellants, on the other hand, contend that § 3(3) obviously is designed to afford the husband the right unilaterally to prevent or veto an abortion, whether or not he is the father of the fetus, and that this not only violates *Roe* and *Doe* 410 US, 93 S Ct 705 but is also in conflict with other decided cases. See, e.g., *Poe v Gerstein*, 517 F2d 787, 794–796 (CA5 1975), appeal docketed, No. 75–713; *Wolfe v Schroering*, 388 F Supp, at 636–637; *Doe v Rampton*, 366 F Supp 189, 193 (Utah 1973). They also refer to the situation where the husband's consent cannot be obtained because he cannot be located. And they assert that § 3(3) is vague and overbroad.

In *Roe* and *Doe* we specifically reserved decision on the question whether a requirement for consent by the father of the fetus, by the spouse, or by the parents, or a parent, of an unmarried minor, may be constitutionally imposed. 410 US, at 165 n 67, 35 L Ed 2d 147, 93 S Ct 705. We now hold that the State may not constitutionally require the consent of the spouse, as is specified under § 3(3) of the Missouri Act, as a condition for abortion during the first 12 weeks of pregnancy. We thus agree with the dissenting judge in the present case, and with the courts whose decisions are cited above, that the State cannot 'delegate to a spouse a veto power which the state itself is absolutely and totally prohibited from exercising during the first trimester of pregnancy.' 392 F Supp, at 1375. Clearly, since the State cannot regulate or proscribe abortion during the first stage, when the physician and his patient make that decision, the State cannot delegate authority to any particular person, even the spouse, to prevent abortion during that same period.

We are not unaware of the deep and proper concern and interest that a devoted and protective husband has in his wife's pregnancy and in the growth and development of the fetus she is carrying. Neither has this Court failed to appreciate the importance of the marital relationship in our society. See, e.g., *Griswold v Connecticut*, 381 US 479, 486, 14 L Ed 2d 510, 85 S Ct 1678 (1965); *Maynard v Hill*, 125 US 190, 211, 31 L Ed 654, 8 S Ct 723 (1888). Moreover, we recognize that the decision whether to undergo or to forgo an abortion may have profound effects on the future of any marriage, effects that are both physical and mental, and possibly deleterious. Notwithstanding these factors, we cannot hold that the State has the constitutional authority to give the spouse unilaterally the ability to prohibit the wife from terminating her pregnancy, when the State itself lacks that right. See *Eisenstadt v Baird*, 405 US 438, 453, 31 L Ed 2d 349, 92 S Ct 1029 (1972).

It seems manifest that, ideally, the decision to terminate a pregnancy should be one concurred in by both the wife and her husband. No marriage may be viewed as harmonious or successful if the marriage partners are fundamentally divided on so important and vital an issue. But it is difficult to believe that the goal of fostering mutuality and trust in a marriage, and of strengthening the marital relationship and the marriage institution, will be achieved by giving the husband a veto power exercisable for any reason whatsoever or for no reason at all. Even if the State had the ability to delegate to the husband a power it itself could not exercise, it is not at all likely that such action would further, as the District Court majority phrased it, the 'interest of the state in protecting the mutuality of decisions vital to the marriage relationship.' 392 F Supp, at 1370.

We recognize, of course, that when a woman, with the approval of her physician but without the approval of her husband, decides to terminate her pregnancy, it could be said that she is acting unilaterally. The obvious fact is that when the wife and the husband disagree on this decision, the view of only one of the two marriage partners can prevail. Inasmuch as it is the woman who physically bears the child and who is the more directly and immediately affected by the pregnancy, as between the two, the balance weighs in her favor. Cf. *Roe v Wade*, 410 US, at 153, 35 L Ed 2d 147, 93 S Ct 705.

We conclude that § 3(3) of the Missouri Act is inconsistent with the standards enunciated in *Roe v Wade*, 410 US, at 164–165, 35 L Ed 2d 147, 93 S Ct 705, and is unconstitutional. It is therefore unnecessary for us to consider the appellants' additional challenges to § 3(3) based on vagueness and overbreadth.

Questions

(i) Are these two cases examples of the judiciary: (*a*) being reluctant to interfere in domestic relations; (*b*) championing the rights of women; or (*c*) suppressing the rights of men?

(ii) Can you think of any decisions taken by husband and wife in their marriage which the courts would actually force the parties to make jointly, by way of injunction if need be?

Jones v Smith
(1973) 59 Fl App 278, So 2d 339, District Court of Appeal of Florida

The case turned upon the constitutional provision relating to the right of privacy. The court decided that the decision to terminate a pregnancy is one that is purely personal to the mother and a matter between her and the attending physician. The court held further that 'any unreasonable governmental interference must yield to the mother's right of privacy.' The facts of the case are set out in the judgment.

Mager J: . . . This is an appeal from an order denying a claim for injunctive relief seeking to restrain the 'obtaining or aiding in the obtaining of an abortion'. Although pseudonyms are used the parties are real persons.

The primary question presented is whether a potential putative father has the right to restrain the natural mother from terminating a pregnancy resulting from their cohabitation. The appellant, who acknowledges that he is the father of the unborn child, is twenty-seven years old, was formerly married and is the father of a six-year-old daughter by such previous marriage. The appellee-mother is nineteen years old and unmarried and had been dating the appellant for approximately six months during which time the parties were frequently intimate. The appellant in seeking injunctive relief has indicated his desire to marry the appellee and to assume all the obligations financial and otherwise for the care and support of the unborn child; that, notwithstanding such affirmations, the appellee-mother, who has expressed her desire not to marry the appellant, has sought to terminate the pregnancy.

Although the appellant alleged in his complaint below 'that the mother's mental and physical health will not be endangered by bringing the child to term in allowing its natural birth' there is no allegation and proof that the proposed termination of pregnancy does not comply with Florida's newly enacted 'Termination of Pregnancy' law (Chapter 72–196, Laws of Florida, numbered as Section 458.22, Florida Statutes, F.S.A.). It is interesting to note a suggestion by the appellant that his own health would be affected if the pregnancy is terminated; testimony from a psychiatrist examining appellant suggested 'the possibility of him suffering depressing symptoms and depressive reactions in the future'.

The main thrust of the appellant's position is that as a potential putative father he has the 'right' to participate in the decision to terminate the pregnancy.

Because of the time factors involved and in particular the fact that the mother is reaching the end of the first trimester of pregnancy this court has granted an emergency hearing and has expedited its review.

The appellant contends that whatever right of privacy that the mother might have enjoyed, such right was 'waived' by virtue of her consent to and participation in the sex act. This argument is somewhat tenuous. The right of privacy of the mother with respect to a termination of pregnancy as delineated by the decisions of the United States Supreme Court is a right separate and apart from any act of conception. The determination of whether to carry the child the full term is not 'controlled' or 'waived' by virtue of the act of conception no more so than the fact that were the child conceived in the State of Florida would give the State the right to interfere with the termination of pregnancy during the first trimester. Moreover, whatever purported 'waiver' might have occurred as a result of the conception, the interest or 'right' of the natural father must remain subservient to 'the life or health of the female' (See F.S. Section 458.22(2)(*a*), F.S.A.).

Questions

(i) In the course of his judgment, Judge Mager asked the following question: 'Could a potential putative father (or for that matter a husband) seek an injunction to restrain the woman from using contraceptives or compel the woman to bear children?' What would be your answer to this question? Do you think there should be a different answer depending on whether the father is or is not married to the mother? (Judge Mager's answer is referred to in the judgment of Baker P in *Paton v British Pregnancy Advisory Service Trustees* [1979] QB 276, [1978] 2 All ER 987.)

(ii) If English law introduced a paternal veto, would it be contrary to Article 8 of the European Convention of Human Rights (set out on p. 573, below)?

5 The unity doctrine remaining today

(a) EVIDENCE

Shenton v Tyler
[1939] Ch 620, [1939] 1 All ER 827, 108 LJ Ch 256, 160 LT 314, 55 TLR 522, 83 Sol Jo 194, Court of Appeal

The appellant sought to administer to the respondent certain interrogatories designed to obtain from her admissions to the effect that a secret trust in favour of the appellant had been imposed upon the respondent (the widow) by her late husband before his death, and that the respondent had accepted the trust. The respondent objected to the interrogatories on the ground that she was not bound to answer questions relating to a communication made to her by her husband.

Sir Wilfrid Greene MR: . . . In considering the questions which fall for decision, it is necessary at the outset to distinguish four rules of evidence. The first is the rule which existed at common law, that neither a party nor the spouse of a party was a competent witness on behalf of that party. This rule related to the competence of the witness, and was not a rule of privilege. The second is the rule which existed at common law that a party was not a compellable witness against himself — I say compellable, although it may be that this was also a rule of competence and not of privilege, a question which for present purposes need not be discussed. The third rule is the rule that existed at common law that a spouse was not a competent witness against his or her spouse. I say competent advisedly since the English authorities appear to have excluded the evidence in such a case on the ground that the witness was incompetent, and not on that of privilege: see, for example, *Barker v Dixie* (1736) Lee *TEMP* Hard 264; *Davis v Dinwoody* (1792) 4 Term Rep 678. . . .

The reasons given for this third rule were various. For example, Lord Hardwicke, in *Barker v Dixie* said that this rule, and the rule forbidding one spouse to give evidence in favour of the other, existed in order 'to preserve the peace of families.' In Buller's Nisi Prius, 286 (cited arguendo in *Davis v Dinwoody*, the reason for the rule is said to lie in 'the legal policy of marriage'; while the rule forbidding one spouse to give evidence in favour of the other is said to exist 'because their interests are absolutely the same.' Lord Kenyon CJ in *Davis v Dinwoody* said that, quite apart from interest, the ground of both rules was the presumption of bias. Which of these and other reasons from time to time given is the least unsatisfactory (a question which has been much debated) I do not pause to inquire.

It is to be observed that this third rule only came into operation in the case where the other spouse was a party. Like the first rule, it was a rule affecting competence, and extended to the whole of the evidence which the witness might be able to give, whether it related to marital communications or not.

In stating the common law rules with which I have dealt, I have not referred to any of the recognized exceptions, since they are not relevant to the matter with which we have to deal. Of the three rules above mentioned, the first and third were apparently observed in Courts of equity as well as in Courts of common law. But the second rule was not observed in Courts of equity, since in those Courts it was from earliest times permissible to interrogate the opposite party.

The fourth rule, which is the rule now in question, is a rule not of competence or admissibility, but of privilege which protects marital communications as such. The question whether or not this privilege existed at common law, or is the creature of statute, lies at the heart of the present controversy. Whatever the true answer to it may be, the rule has nothing to do with the fact that one of the spouses may be a party to the proceedings. The privilege exists equally whether the witness or his or her spouse is or is not a party to the proceedings. Indeed, one of the reasons for the obscurity which surrounds the crucial question is that only in exceptional cases could evidence of a communication between husband and wife be admissible in proceedings to which neither was a party; and the result was that in the great majority of cases evidence of such communications was effectively excluded by the rules as to the competence of spouses already discussed. . . .

I pass over the Evidence Further Amendment Act 1869, and come to the Criminal Evidence Act 1898. That Act made a person charged with an offence and his or her wife or husband competent witnesses for the defence; and s. 1(*d*) provided that 'Nothing in this Act shall make a husband compellable to disclose any communication made to him by his wife during the marriage, or a wife compellable to disclose any communication made to her by her husband during the marriage.' It is natural to find this paragraph (unlike s. 3 of the Act of 1853) expressed in the form of a proviso. The effect of making the party charged and his or her wife or husband competent witnesses for the defence was to make them liable to cross-examination. The result would, or at any rate might, have been that the privilege given by s. 3 of the Act of 1853, although in language applicable to all cases, would have been held to have been taken away, and that the witness would have been compelled to answer in cross-examination questions relating to marital communications. The effect of para. (*d*) of s. 1 of the Act of 1898 is to preserve, in cases to which that section applies, the privilege conferred by s. 3 of the Act of 1853. . . .

If my view is right that the only rule that exists is that contained in s. 3 of the Act of 1853, it remains to consider whether, under that section, upon its true construction, the privilege continues to exist after the marriage has come to an end. In my opinion it does not. The section in terms relates only to husbands and wives; and no principle of construction known to me entitles me to read into the section a reference to widowers or widows or divorced persons.

Certain of the common law rules discussed by Sir Wilfred Greene MR (namely, that neither a party nor a spouse of that party was a competent witness on behalf of that party, and that a spouse was not a competent witness against his or her spouse) were altered by the legislative reforms of the nineteenth century. The Evidence Amendment Act 1853 allowed a husband or a wife of a party in a civil case to be a permissible witness for the party, and to give evidence on the other side. This Act was incidental to the Evidence Act 1851 which allowed the plaintiff and the defendant in civil proceedings to give evidence on their own behalf. A competent witness is normally obliged to give evidence at the instance of either party, thus in this sense husband and wife are compellable witnesses in civil actions. The 1851 Act excluded criminal matters, where the position is a little more complex. The wife is a competent, though not a compellable witness, for the Crown against the husband in specific matters under the Criminal Evidence Act 1898, the Sexual Offences Act 1956, s. 39, and the Theft Act 1968, s. 30. In certain matters regulated by the Evidence Act 1877 she is both competent and compellable. There is also one common law exception to the general rule of incompetence. As a witness for the accused, the accused spouse is competent but is not compellable.

The *Criminal Law Revision Committee* considered the present state of the law of evidence in their 11th Report (1972) and made a number of recommendations:
(i) The accused's spouse should be a competent witness for the prosecution in all cases in which they are not jointly charged, and compellable in cases of assaults or threats of violence of which he or she is the victim, or which are committed against a member of the accused's household under 16, together with sexual offences against such a person. (See p. 525, below, where *Hoskyn v Metropolitan Police Comr* [1979] AC 474, [1978] 2 All ER 136 is discussed.)

(ii) The accused's spouse should be a compellable witness for him in all cases in which they are not jointly charged.

(iii) The accused's spouse should be competent, without the accused's consent for a co-accused in all cases, and compellable where he or she would be compellable for the prosecution.

(iv) A divorced spouse should be competent and compellable as if he or she had never been married to the accused.

(v) There must be repeal of the privilege of communications between spouses in criminal actions. 'It would be undesirable that witnesses in criminal proceedings should enjoy greater privileges in these respects than witnesses in civil proceedings.'

The policy considerations which lay behind these recommendations are identified in the following extract from the *Report*:

147. How far the wife of the accused should be competent and compellable for the prosecution, for the accused and for a co-accused is in these days essentially a question of balancing the desirability that all available evidence which might conduce to the right verdict should be before the court against (i) the objection on social grounds to disturbing marital harmony more than is absolutely necessary and (ii) what many regard as the harshness of compelling a wife to give evidence against her husband. Older objections, even to competence, based on the theoretical unity of the spouses or on the interest of the accused's wife in the outcome of the proceedings, and in particular on the likelihood that his wife will be biased in favour of the accused, can have no place in the decisions as to the extent of competence and compellability nowadays. But the question of the right balance between the considerations of policy mentioned is one on which different opinions are inevitably — and sometimes strongly — held. The arguments relate mostly to compellability for the prosecution but, as will be seen, not entirely so. The argument for more compellability for the prosecution is the straightforward one that, if it is left to the wife to choose whether to give evidence against her husband, the result may be that a dangerous criminal will go free. The argument to the contrary is that, if the wife is not willing to give the evidence, the state should not expose her to the pitiful clash between the duty to aid the prosecution by giving evidence, however unwillingly, and the natural duty to protect her husband whatever the circumstances. It has been argued strongly in support of this view that the law ought to recognize that, as between spouses, conviction and punishment may have consequences of the most serious economic and social kind for their future and that neither of them should in any circumstances be compelled, against his or her will, to contribute to bringing this about. It is also pointed out that there is at least a considerable likelihood that the result of more compellability will be either perjury or contempt by silence. The particular provisions which we recommend are intended (in addition to simplifying the law) as a compromise between these views.

Questions

(i) Which of these arguments do you favour? Do you believe that the five recommendations of the Criminal Law Revision Committee represent a compromise between the two opposing views?

(ii) Is it any worse to make a wife testify against her husband, than it is to punish her for helping him to conceal his crime?

(iii) Why have these recommendations taken so long to be implemented (the *Hoskyn* case on p. 525, below, may help you)? [See the Police and Criminal Evidence Bill 1982, cl. 62.]

(b) TORT

Under the common law, as the husband and wife became 'one person in law' neither could sue the other and the wife could not be sued directly by a third party; all proceedings were brought against her husband. The common law position together with the amendments made to it by the legislation of the nineteenth century is summarised in the following extracts from C.A. Morrison's essay on *Tort*, in *A Century of Family Law* (1957):

At common law
(1) The wife still retained sufficient separate identity to be able to commit a tort or to have torts inflicted upon her. She might sue or be sued for these, but she had no procedural existence alone and her husband had to be joined with her in the action, and might thereupon become liable.
(2) The husband thus found himself under a liability for torts committed by his wife whether before or during marriage, but it was a joint liability with her. His liability might be justified on the legal ground that she had no procedural personality without him and he had to be joined as co-defendant; on the moral ground that he had her property, and that if his wife brought an action, he would acquire any damages she obtained.
(3) Husband and wife could not sue each other in tort.

As a result of statutory changes in the nineteenth century
In the second half of the nineteenth century there came a period of twelve years of reform by a series of Married Women's Property Acts which greatly altered the picture. The effects of the French and the Industrial Revolutions and perhaps the example of the Queen herself all aided in this feverish period of reform, which in little more than a decade changed the law of centuries. The 1870 [Married Women's Property] Act, designed primarily to protect the earnings of the married woman, did not affect the position in tort. The 1874 Act affected the position only of torts committed by the wife before marriage and reduced the husband's liability for these so that he was liable only to the extent of certain specified assets which he had acquired from or through his wife on marriage.

Judgment was to be a joint one to the extent to which the husband was liable and a separate one against the wife for the residue, if any. The main reform however came with the Act of 1882, which affected torts committed before or during marriage. This Act deprived the husband of all the interest he acquired by marriage in his wife's property and earnings, then, having recognised the married woman's capacity to acquire and dispose of property, it went on to regularise and protect that new position by altering the law in tort and contract. It was necessary that the separate property now recognised by statute should be protected against her husband and against outsiders. This meant, first, that against outsiders she needed the right to sue in her own name, for it would appear that she could not have compelled her husband to join with her to protect her property. This was achieved by dispensing with the need to join her husband in actions by or against her. It meant, secondly, that her property might need protection against even her husband. The Act recognised this by permitting an exception to the rule that husband and wife could not sue each other in tort. By section 12 the wife was given civil and criminal rights of action against her husband for the protection and security of her property. To these two main reforms was added a further which made the married woman herself liable to the extent of her separate property for her torts, whether committed before or during marriage, and liable to be sued alone for these torts. But she could be made bankrupt to the extent of her separate property only if she were carrying on a trade separately from her husband.

The doctrine of unity still prevailed in to the twentieth century. There were criticisms of this state of the law as early as 1930. In *Gottliffe v Edelston* [1930] 2 KB 378 McCardie J said: '. . . wives however wealthy of purse or independent of character, possess powers and privileges which are wholly denied to husbands. Husbands are placed under burdens from which wives are free. . . . Upon the husband there has fallen one injustice after another.'

Question

Would you criticise the common law in this way?

In 1935, five years after this judgment was delivered, the Law Reform (Married Women and Tortfeasors) Act abolished the rule which prevented wives from being sued by third parties. By s. 1, a married woman may sue or be sued in all respects as if she were a femme sole and is made subject to the law relating to bankruptcy and to the enforcement of judgments and orders. Section 3 provides that a husband shall not, by reason only of his being her husband, be liable in respect of any tort committed by his wife whether *before* or during the marriage. Finally, the Law Reform (Husband and Wife) Act 1962 abolished the common law prohibition preventing one party to the marriage from suing the other.

The common law fiction that husband and wife are in law one person was described by Oliver J in *Midland Bank v Green (No. 3)* [1979] Ch 496, [1979] 2 All ER 193; in the following way: 'It is a useful instrument for the furtherance of the policy of the law to protect the institution of marriage, but as an exposition in itself of the living law it is as real as the skeleton of the brontosaurus in a museum of natural history.' Oliver J was concerned in that case with the question of whether a husband and wife who agree with one another to injure a third person, and by their concerted action do injure him, are liable in damages for the tort of conspiracy. Oliver J's affirmative response to that question was the subject of an appeal.

Midland Bank Trust Co Ltd v Green (No 3)
[1981] 3 All ER 744, [1982] 2 WLR 1, 125 Sol Jo 554, Court of Appeal

Lord Denning MR: The point of principle raised by Mr Munby for the appellant is this. He says that the doctrine of unity between husband and wife is an established doctrine in English law. So well established that the doctrine and its ramifications are still part of our law today: and must still be applied by the courts except in so far as it has been altered by statute. One of the ramifications of the doctrine (that husband and wife are one) is that they cannot be guilty as conspirators together. So they cannot be made liable in damages for a conspiracy.

The authorities cited by Mr Munby show clearly enough that mediaeval lawyers held that husband and wife were one person in law: and that the husband was that one. It was a fiction then. It is a fiction now. It has been eroded by the judges who have created exception after exception to it. It has been cut down by statute after statute until little of it remains. It has been so much eroded and cut down in law, it has so long ceased to be true in fact, that I would reject Mr Munby's principle.

I would put it in this way. Nowadays, both in law and in fact, husband and wife are two persons, not one. They are partners — equal partners — in a joint enterprise, the enterprise of maintaining a home and bringing up children. Outside that joint enterprise they live their own lives and go their own ways — always, we hope, in consultation one with the other, in complete loyalty one with the other, each maintaining and deserving the trust and confidence of the other. They can and do own property jointly or severally or jointly and severally, with all the consequences that ownership entails. They can and do enter into contracts with others jointly or severally or jointly and severally, and can be made liable for breaches just as any other contractors can be. They can and do commit crimes jointly or severally and can be punished severally for them. They can and do commit wrongs jointly or severally and can be made liable jointly or severally just as any other wrong-doers. The severance in all respects is so complete that I would say that the doctrine of unity and its ramifications should be discarded altogether, except in so far as it is retained by judicial decision or by Act of Parliament.

I turn now to our particular case — conspiracy. So far as criminal conspiracy is concerned, a husband and wife cannot be found guilty of conspiring with one another. That is now statutory in section 2(2)(a) of the Criminal Law Act 1977. But they can be found guilty if the two of them jointly conspire with a third person.

Mr Munby says that the tort of conspiracy should be treated in the same way as the crime of conspiracy. He says that husband and wife cannot be made liable in tort for conspiracy with one another. But they can, he admits, be made liable if the two of them jointly conspire with a third person. For instance, he agrees that if the conspiracy charged in this case was between Walter (the husband) and Evelyne (the wife) and their other son Derek, and it was found that all three conspired together, all could be made liable in damages. But as the only conspiracy charged is against Walter and Evelyne alone, they cannot be made liable at all. That seems to me a most illogical and unreasonable state of the law, not to be accepted unless covered by authority, and there is none to cover it, no decision and really no statement of authority as far as I can discover. . . .

I see no good reason for applying the doctrine of unity to the modern tort of conspiracy. It is clear that in a like case father and son could be made liable in conspiracy; so mother and daughter; so man and mistress. Why then should not husband and wife be made liable? If the allegations against Walter and Evelyne are correct, they did a grievous wrong to Geoffrey. Together with their son Derek they deprived Geoffrey of his birth right, just as Jacob deprived Esau. Both are now dead, but their estates can be made liable in conspiracy, or at any rate Walter's estate which is the only one now before the court. It seems to me that Mrs Kemp [Walter's executrix] would be liable in full if the conspiracy were established which is alleged. And if she were held liable for the conspiracy and the damages which flow from it after giving any credit from the solicitors' action she would be liable for it, and then her only recourse would be against the lawyers who failed on her behalf to plead plene administravit, if she could prove that they were in any way at fault.

For these reasons I agree with the decision of Oliver J and would dismiss the appeals.

(c) PUBLIC LAW

Cardiff Corpn v Robinson
[1957] 1 QB 39, [1956] 3 All ER 56, [1956] 3 WLR 522, 120 JP 500, 100 Sol Jo
588, 49 R & IT 571, 1 RRC 83, 54 LGR 506, Divisional Court, Queen's Bench
Division

A husband lived with his wife and children in a house owned by his father. In
November 1954, after differences had arisen between the husband and the
wife, the husband left his wife and went to live elsewhere. The father raised
no objection to the wife and children remaining in the house. The husband
and wife agreed that the wife should remain in the house rent free and he
should pay her £6 per week by way of maintenance. He paid the rates to the
end of the financial year 31 March 1955, and then informed the Cardiff
Corporation that as he was no longer the occupier of the house his liability to
pay rates ceased. The Cardiff Corporation preferred a complaint against the
husband that being a person duly rated and assessed in their area by a general
rate in the sum of £19.1s.4d (the first installment of the 1955/6) rates, he had
not paid that sum. The Stipendiary Magistrate stated a case to the Divisional
Court.

Lord Goddard CJ: . . . The position is that, the respondent having left his wife and children, he
is under an obligation to maintain them and, among other things, to provide a roof over their
heads. He has done that by telling the wife that she may continue to occupy this house. Of
course, that would only be so long as his father allowed the wife and children to live there. It
seems to me obvious, therefore, that the husband has made this provision for his wife as part of
the obligation he is under to maintain her. Therefore, he is using this house, which his father has
allowed him to occupy, in the most beneficial way he can by housing his wife and children in
respect of whom he is liable to provide a home. It is agreed, and no one can deny, that if the
respondent goes out of the house and leaves his furniture in it, he is liable, so long as his
furniture is there, to pay the rates because there is a beneficial occupation. If he chooses to leave
the house and leave his wife and family there, why is it any different from leaving his furniture
there? He may come to an arrangement between himself and his wife under which his wife agrees
to pay the rates. That may be, but the local authority are not bound by any arrangement of that
sort. The only question here is: has the husband got a beneficial occupation? I think that he has,
because it enables him to provide for his wife and family who, if they had to provide a home for
themselves, would naturally require more money from him.

This case was followed in *R v Harrow Justices, ex p London Borough of
Harrow* (1983) Times, 7 February where Stephen Brown J held the husband
liable to pay the rates notwithstanding that he had given an undertaking to
leave the matrimonial home and that the wife was cohabiting with another
man. However, in *Routhan v Arun District Council* [1982] 2 QB 502, [1981]
3 All ER 752, the Court of Appeal decided that a former wife who was in
occupation of the house with her children was solely liable for the rates
because her right to remain there after the final dissolution of the marriage
was not a right conferred by the husband in discharge of his common law
obligations to maintain the children, but derived from the transfer of
property order. Lord Denning remarked anecdotally 'I remember well that
(the doctrine of unity) was invoked when I used to prosecute in the magistrates' courts. A wife was travelling on the railway with her husband's ticket.
When she put forward the excuse: "We are one in the eyes of the law," the
collector replied "But not in the eyes of the Southern Railway." But what
about the eyes of the income tax authorities? Income tax law aggregates their
resources and treats them as those of the husband. In 1980, the Government
published a Green Paper on *The Taxation of Husband and Wife*:

14. Since 1918 a married man has received an allowance higher than that given to a single
person, in recognition of the special legal and moral obligations he has to support his wife. Thus

the married man's allowance is essentially an allowance for two people, but it has always been less than twice the single allowance, since the expenses of two married people sharing one household are considered less than those of two single people maintaining separate households. . . . The current relationship of 1:1.56 is more or less in line with the 1:1.6 relationship established for social security purposes.

15. In addition to the married man's allowance, the husband whose wife goes out to work also gets the wife's earned income allowance. . . . This means that the married couple where the wife goes out to work get more allowances in total than two single people (2.56:2) and considerably more than the couple where she stays at home (2.56:1.56).

16. In addition to the main personal allowances — . . . . an individual's tax bill may be reduced by other reliefs and allowances, e.g. relief for mortgage interest payments. In the case of the married couple, the aggregation rule means . . . these reliefs and allowances have to be claimed by and given to the husband even where the expenditure giving rise to the allowance is incurred by the wife. . . .

Separate assessment
19. Ever since 1914 either husband or wife has been able to apply for separate assessment. This option does not reduce the total amount of tax which the couple pay, but it makes both husband and wife responsible for handling their individual tax affairs, and payment of their own share of the tax due. . . .

Wife's earning election
20. A couple may jointly elect to have the wife's earnings taxed separately as if she were a single person with no other income. . . . Although the wife's earnings election enables the wife to be treated as a single person so far as her earnings are concerned, receiving her own repayments and making good any underpayments on her earnings, any investment income she has continues to be treated as belonging to her husband for tax purposes. In addition he retains responsibility for completing returns of both his and his wife's total income.

There have been a number of recent changes in the administration of the tax system; nevertheless there is much criticism of the present system of taxation of married couples:

31. There are perhaps two major strands of criticism of the present system of taxing husband and wife. Both focus on the proposition that the married man's allowance in its present form is unsatisfactory. More specifically the first strand of criticism points to the different tax treatment of husband and wife. In other words, it sees discrimination *within* the family unit. The other strand of criticism, looking at the overall impact of taxation as *between* different types of family unit — single people, couples with only one earner, couples where both partners go out to work, one-parent families, etc — sees the current rules as favouring some types of family unit at the expense of others.

Discrimination within the family
32. The main focus of criticism here is the aggregation rule which deems the wife's income to belong to her husband for tax purposes and makes him responsible for all her tax affairs. This is seen as reducing the married woman to the status of her husband's 'chattel'. It has been criticized as a matter of principle, and there have been complaints about the practical effects. . . . Beyond this, however, a number of people feel particularly strongly about the issue of the married woman's privacy. Because a husband is liable for tax on his wife's investment income, it follows that he must get to know about any savings or investments she has. Criticism of our tax system as discriminating unfairly between husband and wife does not come exclusively from women: some men object to having to go through the process of obtaining details of their wife's income, dealing with all correspondence relating to it, and being liable for any tax due on it.

33. The second criticism focuses on the allowance for a married woman. People have taken issue with the fact that the wife's earned income allowance is given, not to the wife, but to the husband to set against her income and that, unlike all other personal allowances, it can be set against her earnings only and not against her investment income. In addition there has been criticism of the relative *size* of this allowance. The husband gets a higher tax allowance against his earnings than his working wife gets against hers, so that where two spouses are earning the same amount the wife takes home less than her husband. Allied to this are complaints about the way the couple's other allowances are usually allocated to the husband, thus further increasing his take home pay relative to that of his wife. This issue most often arises in respect of mortgage interest relief and is obviously a source of particular complaint where the wife is the one actually paying the mortgage interest.

Discrimination between family units
34. There are three main areas of criticism:
a. The favourable treatment where both partners work; this is criticised as excessively generous

both by comparison with the treatment of one-earner couples and by comparison with the treatment of single people.

b. The treatment of the one-earner couple. It is argued on the one hand that the allowance is inadequate where one spouse stays at home to look after dependent children, elderly relatives, etc, and on the other there is the point of view that there is no reason to give more than a single allowance where the spouse at home has no such responsibilities.

c. The treatment of married couples where each spouse has investment income.

These various criticisms are analysed in turn in the paragraphs below.

Two-earner couples

35. Since 1942 the couple where both husband and wife are earning has been able to enjoy total tax allowances around $2\frac{1}{2}$ times as large as a single person's allowance, whereas the couple where only the husband works get $1\frac{1}{2}$ times the single allowance. This feature of the tax system may be felt particularly by a couple who move from one category to another — eg where the wife gives up work to start a family. As long ago as 1954 the Royal Commission on the Taxation of Profits and Income concluded that the present arrangements were over-generous to two-earner couples because they gave them greater relief than two single earners. Their proposed solution was to restrict the wife's earned income allowance, but it is now commonly argued that it is the continued entitlement of the husband to a full married man's allowance, while his wife is enjoying the equivalent of a full single allowance, which creates the imbalance between two-earner couples and others.

One-earner couples

36. In recent years there have been suggestions that the married allowance for one-earner couples should be increased to the equivalent of the allowances given to two single persons. There seem to be two distinct (if inter-related) lines of thinking underlying this. On the one hand there is the body of opinion which considers it important to give every encouragement — fiscal and otherwise — for a mother to stay at home and look after her young children. On the other is the point of view that housework is just as much work as paid employment and the tax system should recognise it as such. At the same time, from another standpoint, it is sometimes said that the married man's allowance should not be given to one-earner families where the wife has no home responsibilities, on the grounds that in a society where it is common for wives with no home ties to work, it is wrong in principle for the tax system to give any relief for the wife who chooses instead to remain at home.

37. It is widely held that the present rules are very generous to couples where the wife is the breadwinner and the husband has no income. The couple get the same allowances as a working married couple (married allowance plus wife's earned income allowance), whereas only the married allowance is available where the husband is the breadwinner.

38. Finally, there is the criticism that, under the present rules, where husbands and wives both have investment income the tax bill can be higher than if they were two single people with the same total investment income split between them. This criticism is more frequently heard now that there are some $2\frac{1}{2}$ million wives with income-producing assets.

Conclusion

39. It is of course possible to meet each of these criticisms individually but there is no single 'solution' which would encompass answers to them all. It is only necessary to consider the two criticisms discussed in paragraph 36 to see some of the difficulties involved. The obvious answer to those who want more encouragement for family life in its traditional form would be to award the equivalent of two single allowances to all one-earner couples. But this would be objectionable to those who maintain that only families where the non-working spouse has specific home responsibilities should qualify for additional tax relief.

40. Moreover any 'solution' could well create as many problems as it would solve. For instance, a switch to independent taxation, under which husband and wife would each be treated as separate units, would certainly meet many of the criticisms outlined in the foregoing paragraphs. But a reform on these lines might not find favour with those married women who have no particular quarrel with the status quo. Independent taxation confers obligations as well as rights: every man and woman, married as well as single, would be responsible for filling in his or her own tax return, dealing direct with the tax authorities and paying his or her own tax bill. At present, in the case of a married couple, these obligations fall solely on the husband (subject to the rules for separate assessment under which the wife may choose to assume responsibility for her own share of the tax due). Moreover, . . ., mandatory independent taxation would mean a substantial shift in the relative tax bills paid by different types of family. In particular, couples where both spouses are working would, in relative terms, be worse off than at present.

41. It is clear, therefore, that any attempt to meet the criticisms of the current taxation of husband and wife must be a compromise between conflicting interests. . . . The present system itself represents just such a compromise. Moreover, even today, it is a compromise which seems to be broadly acceptable to many people.

The Green Paper proposes four models (or options): an extension of the present arrangement for independent and separate assessment; a fully transferable allowance; a partially transferable allowance; and a system of mandatory independent taxation. The views of the Government of the day as expressed in the Green Paper on the fourth option are clear from the following extract:

83. The preceding paragraphs have assumed that each spouse would be entitled only to a single allowance and that, where one was financially dependent upon the other, this would be recognised by transferability of the tax allowance or by a cash benefit (or by some combination of the two). It can however be argued that on top of the transferable tax allowance (or cash benefit) there should be an additional allowance or benefit, so that, if the basic tax allowance was fully transferable, the supporting spouse would get twice the single allowance and in addition an allowance (or benefit) in recognition of the dependent spouse's home responsibilities. This could be seen as extending the family's freedom of choice — eg for the wife to give up employment and stay at home to look after children or an elderly parent — and unlike a transferable tax allowance it would be in specific recognition of the circumstances that required her to stay at home. On the other hand, whereas independent taxation with a transferable allowance would remove what many people see as the bias in the present system in favour of a wife going out to work, an additional allowance for home responsibilities would introduce a new bias in favour of the wife staying at home in certain circumstances and against her going out to work; and it would produce a corresponding increase in the relative tax burden of working couples as compared with one-earner couples. Unless additional resources were available for such a new allowance (or benefit) its introduction would inevitably mean that the single allowance (and hence tax thresholds generally) would have to be held down to finance it. Furthermore, such a combination of allowances (and/or benefits) would be more complex than either a transferable tax allowance or a cash benefit on its own and could greatly increase the number of staff needed to run the system.

Conclusion
84. The main arguments for provision for the dependent spouse through cash benefit rather than tax allowance would seem to be that this would ensure that the benefit went direct to the supported spouse, and that it would be equally available for those whose incomes were below the tax threshold so that they could not benefit from a tax allowance. On the other hand:
a. **Distributional effect.** While the effects of providing for a financially dependent spouse through social security rather than through a tax allowance . . . do not point clearly towards or against a cash benefit, they indicate some of the difficulties inherent in a cash benefit approach. Replacing a tax allowance which varies with the taxpayer's marginal tax rate by a cash benefit, and thus effectively transferring income from one spouse to another, could have effects comparable with the switch from child tax allowance to child benefit [see Chapter 16, below]. But, whereas with child tax allowance it was not the claimant's own allowance which was at stake but only in effect an additional allowance for a dependent, with the abolition of the married allowance married men might be even more inclined to regard themselves as 'losers' particularly if their circumstances were such that the family did not stand to benefit from the additional social security provision available (e.g. if the couple were childless and the additional provision were made through child benefit). Furthermore, a transferable tax allowance would be more suitable than a cash benefit for the case where the supported spouse works part-time or for part of the year. With a cash benefit, there could be substantial problems in adjusting the level of the benefit to match such changes in income whereas with a transferable tax allowance the amount of the allowance available to the supporting spouse could move directly in line with the level of the other spouse's income.
b. **Form of the benefit.** But even greater problems arise when one considers the form which the benefit might take. . . . Although the Government would welcome comments on these and suggestions for other forms of benefit which might be more suitable, it seems unlikely that a satisfactory form of new benefit could be found. But, if one turns to the possibility of building upon existing benefits . . . it is apparent that, although it might be possible by a combination of benefits to achieve a coverage which could be broadly comparable with that of a transferable tax allowance, full coverage would not be attainable. . . . Child benefit, invalid care allowance and housewives' non-contributory invalidity pension might be extended in such a way as to cover categories a., b. and c. (dependent children, dependent relatives and incapacitated spouses). But they could not be extended to cover categories d. and e. (older spouses and the involuntarily unemployed). It would not be easy to defend the denial of provision for these cases on abolition of the married allowance; but it would be extremely difficult to provide for them through social security in a satisfactory way.

85. In the Government's view, the arguments against provision for a dependent spouse through the social security system, as set out in the preceding paragraphs, are very weighty.

The Equal Opportunities Commission's *Response to the Government Green Paper* (1981) is to continue to press for a revision of the tax system so as to tax all adults as individuals, keeping the personal allowance as at present, and using the revenue generated by the abolition of the married man's allowance to increase child benefit. (See p. 624, below, for a comment on this proposal so far as it relates to child benefit.) On practical grounds, the Commission concludes that any initial change can only be concerned with earned income:

After careful consideration, the Commission finds the options set out in the Green Paper unsatisfactory for the following reasons:

(*a*) the Green Paper, in its entirety, takes for granted that marital status as such, regardless of the circumstances of the couple and their needs, should be given special recognition in the tax system. Hence the continuance of the Married Man's Allowance (MMA) remains a basic feature of the options presented by the Green Paper, except where couples choose to have separate personal allowances. The Commission has already represented to successive Chancellors its view that the abolition of the MMA is the first condition of any effective reform, for the MMA embodies more than any other provision the outdated and objectionable assumption of dependency on which the present system is based;

(*b*) the first option presented, the option for independent taxation, . . . is essentially an extension of the present arrangement for separate assessment, by offering to each spouse what is called 'separate responsibility' for his/her own tax affairs. It will mean married couples are treated differently depending on the level and sources of their incomes, and the group which would stand to gain most would be those couples with a high joint income. Moreover, inspection of the specific elements of this option, such as the simplification of separate assessment . . . or the rewording of the aggregation rule . . ., reveals that the option involves superficial changes without altering either the underlying principle, which still remains that of aggregation, or its practical consequences. Finally, since the option is essentially a matter of choice by individual couples, it will be impossible to predict what proportion of couples will opt for the new system and what proportion opt to remain under the present system. Thus the possibility of deploying the revenue generated by abolishing the MMA for other purposes related to family responsibilities cannot even arise under this option;

(*c*) the second option, that of a fully transferable allowance, remains in essence joint taxation, as does the third option, that of a partially transferable allowance (which, moreover, introduces complications of its own). On the Inland Revenue's own reckoning both options would be costly in administrative terms, described as 'serious' in the case of the second option and 'substantial' in the case of the third option. . . . It is clear that the Revenue do not regard either option with any enthusiasm; nor does the Commission.

The most attractive of these three options is clearly the first, which the Green Paper claims would be 'relatively cheap, relatively inexpensive in terms of staff . . . and capable of early implementation.' But, in the Commission's view, these advantages have been achieved at the cost of avoiding any real reform of the fundamentally objectionable features of the present system.

11. We turn, therefore, to the fourth option, that of mandatory independent taxation. Here the Commission has concluded that the disadvantages of this approach have been substantially overstated in the Green Paper:

(*a*) independent taxation with non-transferable allowances would be disadvantageous to all married couples, except where the wife had substantial investment income of her own. But this is true only because none of the proposed forms of independent taxation provides for any method of distinguishing between married couples in which the wife has chosen voluntarily not to work and those in which the wife is unable to work because of the need to care for dependent children; the abolition of the MMA would generate revenue which could well be utilised to assist couples where the wife is unable to work because of the burden of dependency;

(*b*) the majority of childless couples where the wife was working would lose from most of the variations of independent taxation and gain from none. But this is only to be regarded as undesirable if it is assumed that the tax system has an obligation to reward the state of marriage as such, without regard to actual needs or responsibilities;

(*c*) the consequence that single persons generally would benefit from such a system is not inevitable; as the Green Paper notes, this outcome could be avoided if the yield from the changes went to increase child benefit . . .;

(*d*) the Commission has acknowledged all along, that one of the anomalies of the present system is that 'breadwinner' wives are more favourably treated, and in consistency it cannot argue for preferential treatment for them; consequently the fact that they would not stand to gain from a system of independent taxation is not regarded by the Commission as an objection to such a system but rather as a correction of an anomaly in the present system.

For these reasons, the Commission has chosen to concentrate on a closer examination of independent taxation as the fairest approach to reform.

12. In doing so, the Commission has started from three basic principles:

(*a*) that the present system is discriminatory on grounds of sex in its basic assumption (although some elements of individual taxation have been grafted on to the system in recent years), and that any serious attempt to reform it must start by treating the individual (rather than the married couple) as the basic tax unit; this involves the repeal of s. 37 of the ICTA;

(*b*) that individuals who do the same work are expected to receive the same reward, and they should be taxed in the like manner, ie, the taxation system should not introduce (or perpetuate) discrimination on grounds of sex when the system of payments and benefits is being reformed in order to eliminate discrimination on those grounds; and

(*c*) that individuals who have the same responsibilities and needs should be entitled to the same allowances, benefits and provisions.

In the Commission's view, this is the only approach consistent with the intention of the Sex Discrimination and Equal Pay Acts, which themselves are a manifestation of the merging social trends which the Commission described in some detail in its first public statement on the issue, *Income Tax and Sex Discrimination* (1978) (Ch. 6). Furthermore, the Commission favours this line of approach because it is convinced that a move to completely independent taxation will make it easier to move eventually to a system based on self-assessment which the Commission along with many other bodies believes to be preferable to the present system.

13. The most immediate consequence of this approach is to question the justification for continuing the Married Man's Allowance.

Questions

(i) Would some people object that the abolition of the married man's allowance and the use of the revenue to increase child benefit: (*a*) discriminates in favour of families with children; (*b*) discriminates in favour of high-income two worker families; and (*c*) does nothing to help the low paid — especially if only one works and there is only one child, or no child?

(ii) If a system of independent taxation is introduced, do you think that more people would decide that there is no point in getting married?

(iii) Do you think that the present system 'is a compromise which seems to be broadly acceptable to many people'? (See p. 60, above.)

(iv) Having read this chapter, is there such a thing as a 'legal structure of marriage' in the 1980s?

CHAPTER 3

Family economics — income

The economic arrangements of a husband and a wife do not exist in isolation. There is a need for a body of flexible rules within which the husband and wife are free to regulate their affairs. These rules exist in all marriages; whether they be created by the parties themselves, by the society and the culture within which they live, or imposed upon them by judicial or other external intervention. The concern of the lawyer in this area tends to be expressed most often in terms of finding sensible solutions to the re-allocation of the economic assets of the parties after the marriage has broken down and the parties are divorced or separated. However, no legal solution to this particular problem can reflect a logical and realistic re-adjustment of the tangled affairs unless there is a clear understanding of the economic expectations of the husband and the wife during the marriage. Thus, the question 'what happens to property after divorce?' is closely interlinked with the question 'what were the economic arrangements of the husband and the wife when they were married?' There are also two important ideological questions to be raised relating to support obligations of spouses for one another and the state involvement in the support of the family.

These chapters, therefore, are concerned both with marriage and with divorce; for a sensitive law on matrimonial property and support obligations must be aware of the possibility of divorce, and likewise a law on divorce re-allocation must be soundly based on the economic structure of the marriage as a going concern.

Professor Tony Honoré is fully aware of the link which we have just made between the dynamic and subsisting marriage and what has been described as the 'pathology of family law', when he categorises marriage ideologically into three distinct groups — as a partnership, as a contract, and thirdly as an arrangement by which a husband assumes the role of provider. The following extract is taken from *The Quest for Security: Employees, Tenants, Wives* (1982).

There are three main ways of viewing marriage. Some see it as a *partnership*. On a traditional view, it is a partnership, come what may, for life. In that case, after divorce the partnership notionally continues, and the wife is entitled to the support she would have received had the marriage not broken up, or at any rate to a standard of living which continues to be the equal of her husband's. That is, on paper, the point of view of English law. More often, marriage is now seen as an equal partnership which lasts, like other partnerships, until it is dissolved. On that view there must on divorce be a fair division of the profits of the partnership, including property acquired during the marriage. The division may go beyond property rights. Recently German law, by a bold innovation, has required spouses on divorce to divide up equally the expectancies of pension rights which they have acquired during marriage. These too are profits of the partnership.

Another conception of marriage is that of an *arrangement* (a collateral contract?) *by which a husband induces his wife to change her career*. Had it not been for the marriage she might, for example, have had good earning prospects. She gives these up to marry. On divorce she must now retrain, sometimes late in life, with diminished prospects. If so, her husband must compensate her by keeping her, during a transitional period, while she brings up the children, if she wants to, and redeploys. If, after a long time together, she has become emotionally attached to her status as a wife, her husband may also be required to compensate her for the wrench.

Yet another conception views marriage not as a contract but *as an arrangement by which a husband assumes the role of providing for his wife's needs and those of their children.* This idea, more ancient and deeply rooted in genetics than the contractual ones, makes the husband to some extent the wife's insurer. If she is in need, it is to him, rather than the state, that she turns in the first instance. It is he who must see to her subsistence, and perhaps more, in ill-health, old age or disablement. It is only in this framework of anticipated security that childbearing and childrearing can flourish. But how far does the husband's responsibility extend? How far, in modern conditions does that of the state or community? [italics added]

These three categories must be borne in mind when we consider the historical evidence.

1 The historical evidence

The economic process of change in the family has proceeded through three stages, as explained by M. Young and P. Wilmot in *The Symmetrical Family* (1973):

Even though there is so much in common between family life at each stage, and even though the boundaries between one stage and another are somewhat arbitrary, the rough-and-ready division seems to us useful, as does the generalization, even though it cannot any more than most generalizations do justice to all the evidence. In the first stage, the pre-industrial, the family was usually the unit of production. For the most part, men, women and children worked together in home and field. This type of economic partnership was, for working-class people, supplanted after a bitter struggle by the Stage 2 family, whose members were caught up in the new economy as individual wage-earners. The collective was undermined. Stage 2 was the stage of disruption. One historian has pointed the contrast in this way (E.P. Thompson 1963).

> Women became more dependent upon the employer or the labour market, and they looked back to a 'golden' period in which home earnings from spinning, poultry and the like, could be gained around their own door. In good times the domestic economy, like the peasant economy, supported a way of life centred upon the home, in which inner whims and compulsions were more obvious than external discipline. Each stage in industrial differentiation and specialisation struck also at the family economy, disturbing customary relations between man and wife, parents and children, and differentiating more sharply between 'work' and 'life'. It was to be a full hundred years before this differentiation was to bring returns, in the form of labour-saving devices, back into the working woman's home. Meanwhile, the family was roughly torn apart each morning by the factory bell.

The process affected most of the families of manual workers (and not all of these by any means). The trends were different in the middle class family, where the contrasts for both husbands and wives were somewhat less sharp than they had been in the past. But as working-class people were preponderant most families were probably 'torn apart' by the new economic system. In the third stage the unity of the family has been restored around its functions as the unit not of production but of consumption.

It is clearly not possible, since social history is unlike political or military history, to do more by way of dating than to indicate a rough manner when the successive waves of change started going through the social structure. The Stage 1 family lasted until the new industry overran it in a rolling advance which went on from the eighteenth well into the nineteenth century. The development of the new industry was uneven as between different parts of the country, coming much later to London than to the industrial north. It also outmoded the old techniques of production more slowly in some occupations than in others. But come it did, eventually, along with many other forms of employment which shared one vital feature, that the employees worked for wages. This led to the Stage 2 family. The third stage started earlier in the twentieth century and is still working its way downwards. At any one period there were, and still are, families representing all three stages. But as first one wave and then another has been set in motion, the proportions in Stage 2 increased in the nineteenth century and in Stage 3 in the twentieth.

The new kind of family has three main characteristics which differentiate it from the sort which prevailed in Stage 2. The first is that the couple, and their children, are very much centred on the home, especially when the children are young. They can be so much together, and share so much together, because they spend so much of their time together in the same space. Life has, to use another term, become more 'privatized'. . . . This trend has been supported by the form taken by technological change.

The second characteristic is that the extended family (consisting of relatives of several different degrees to some extent sharing a common life) counts for less and the immediate, or nuclear, family for more. We have not been able to discover much documentary evidence about kinship patterns in nineteenth century England. People certainly often lived with or near relatives, and we would expect, . . . that daughters more often maintained close links with their parents, and particularly with their mothers, than sons did with theirs. Extended families must have been used for mutual aid. But we doubt, . . ., whether they became so pervasive and so much the arena of women's lives until this century. Our belief is that since the second war, in particular, there has been a further change and that the nuclear family has become relatively more isolated in the working than in other classes.

The third and most vital characteristic is that inside the family of marriage the roles of the sexes have become less segregated.

Economic historians, Louise Tilly and Joan Scott, describe each of these three stages in *Women, Work and Family* (1979). They speak first of the family as the labour and consumption unit:

In both England and France, in city and country, people worked in small settings, which often overlapped with households. Productivity was low, the differentiation of tasks was limited. And many workers were needed. The demand for labor extended to women as well as men, to everyone but the youngest children and the infirm. Jobs were differentiated by age and by sex, as well as by training and skill. But, among the popular classes, some kind of work was expected of all able-bodied family members. . . . But whether or not they actually worked together, family members worked in the economic interest of the family. In peasant and artisan households, and in proletarian families, the household allocated the labor of family members. In all cases, decisions were made in the interest of the group, not the individual. This is reflected in wills and marriage contracts which spelled out the obligation of siblings or elderly parents who were housed and fed on the family property, now owned by the oldest son. They must work 'to the best of their ability' for 'the prosperity of the family' and 'for the interest of the designated heir.' Among property-owning families the land or the shop defined the tasks of family members and whether or not their labor was needed. People who controlled their means of production adjusted household composition to production needs. For the propertyless, the need for wages — the subsistence of the family itself — sent men, women, and children out to work. These people adjusted household composition to consumption needs. The bonds holding the proletarian family together, bonds of expediency and necessity, were often less permanent than the property interest (or the inheritable skill) which united peasants and craftsmen. The composition of propertied and propertyless households also differed. Nevertheless, the line between the propertied and propertyless was blurred on the question of commitment to work in the family interest.

One of the goals of work was to provide for the needs of family members. Both property owning and proletarian households were consumption units, though all rural households were far more self-sufficient than urban households. Rural families usually produced their own food, clothing, and tools, while urban families bought them at the market. These differences affected the work roles of family members. Women in urban families, for example, spent more time marketing and less time in home manufacture. And there were fewer domestic chores for children to assist with in the city. In the urban family, work was oriented more to the production of specific goods for sale, or it involved the sale of one's labor. For the peasant family, there were a multiplicity of tasks involved in working the land and running the household. The manner of satisfying consumption needs thus varied and so affected the kinds of work family members did.

When the number of household members exceeded the resources available to feed them, and when those resources could not be obtained, the family often adjusted its size. Non-kin left to work elsewhere when children were old enough to work. Then children migrated. Inheritance systems led non-heirs to move away in search of jobs, limited positions as artisans forced children out of the family craftshop, while the need for wages led the children of the propertyless many miles from home. People migrated from farm to farm, farm to village, village to town, and country to city in this period. Although much migration was local and rural in this period, some migrants moved to cities, and most of these tended to be young and single when they migrated. Indeed, in this period cities grew primarily by migration; for urban death rates were high and deaths often outnumbered births, a result largely of the crowded and unsanitary conditions that prevailed. Migrants came to the city from nearby regions.

In the second stage, the family wage economy, we enter a distributive period. As Kevin Gray (1977) says: 'In the distributive stage, production occurs outside the family, and the family merely distributes among the family members the economic product of the labour performed by the provider husband, the house-maker wife of course playing a vital role in this secondary process of distribution.'

Tilly and Scott emphasise that this distributive period (the 'family wage economy', as they call it) developed gradually during the mid-nineteenth century:

The family wage economy was an increasingly prevalent form of family organization. The wages of family members formed a common fund which paid for expenses and supported the group. . . .

The composition of the household no longer was dictated by a need for household laborers, as in the family economy, but by a need for cash. The balance among wage earners and consumers in the household determined family fortunes. . . .

When the children moved out to set up their own households, the parents were again on their own. The parents' wage-earning ability declined, sickness and other crises overtook them, and misery often ensued again. The need to balance wage-earners and consumers in the household underlay many of the decisions about women's work and domestic responsibilities in the family wage economy. . . .

Under the family wage economy married women performed several roles for their families. They often contributed wages to the family fund, they managed the household, and they bore and cared for children. With industrialization, however, the demands of wage labor increasingly conflicted with women's domestic activities. The terms of labor and the price paid for it were a function of employers' interest, which took little account of household needs under most circumstances. Industrial jobs required specialization and a full-time commitment to work, usually in a specific location away from home. While under the domestic mode of production women combined market-oriented activities and domestic work, the industrial mode of production precluded an easy reconciliation of married women's activities. The resolution of the conflict was for married women not to work unless family finances urgently required it, and then to try to find that work which conflicted least with their domestic responsibilities.

Figures on married women's employment from England and France reflect this clearly. Married women working in factories represented only a small proportion of all female factory operatives and an even smaller proportion of all married women in the labor forces of England and France. At its height, in the 1870s, over one-third of the British textile industry's women employees were married or widowed; but the inclusion of widows overstates the case, since, . . ., the position of a widow — the sole support of herself and her children — was not comparable to that of the married woman living with her husband. Moreover, even in the early factory towns, married women tended to become cotton pickers. Cleaning and beating the cotton with sticks was done by hand, not machine, and the pickers worked near but not in the mills. The work was performed intermittently and was not subject to factory discipline. . . .

In general, married women tended to be found in largest numbers in the least industrialized sectors of the labor force, in those areas where the least separation existed between home and workplace and where women could control the rhythm of their work.

The working-class wife and mother managed the family economy and supervised the family labor force. She created the affective community which bound family members to one another. Among wage-earning families the domestic responsibilities of the married woman increased as new kinds of family ties developed among family members. Married women continued to perform a variety of tasks in wage-earning families, but changing conditions of work and the changing organization of production altered their ability to easily reconcile these activities. The tasks of wife, mother, provider of food, and organizer of household affairs and of children's wage-earning activities consumed most of her time. Although she became a wage earner herself when necessary, direct involvement with production took far less of her time than had production for home consumption or for the market in the past.

Overall, the separation of home and work had some important effects on married women's activity. They were eliminated from participating in most of the more productive, better-paying jobs by employer and household preferences for single women as full-time workers. Nonetheless, they were not barred from becoming wage earners in the family interest. Many improvised work which could be reconciled with household responsibilities. Others took temporary low-paying unskilled jobs. Married women's patterns of work-force participation generally were irregular and episodic. Among urban families particularly, married women's time was important at home. They cared for larger households, were involved in buying and preparing food for their families, and organized the wage-earning activities of their children. Indeed, in these families the mother's domestic activity seems to have become increasingly important and valuable to the family.

Women no longer worked continuously throughout their lives, balancing their time between productive and domestic responsibilities as they had under the household mode of production. Instead they alternated different activities over the course of their lives. As daughters and young wives they spent most time earning wages. After children were born, home and family took more and more time, wage earning took less. The arrival of children interrupted employment often for long periods of time, since wage earning seriously disrupted a woman's ability to care for her children. Under the industrial mode of production women had increasing difficulty combining their productive and reproductive activities.

Question

The authors concentrate on working class families. Do you have the feeling that their comments might need modifying for the middle classes in the nineteenth century?

The authors describe how the consumer economy developed:

By the early twentieth century the higher wages of men particularly and the availability of cheap consumer goods raised the target income of working-class families. Necessities now included not only food and clothing, but also other items that once had been considered luxuries. What we have termed the family consumer economy then was a wage earning unit which increasingly emphasized family consumption needs.

The organization of the family consumer economy was not dramatically different from that of the family wage economy. The management of money and of family affairs in an increasingly complex urban environment did, however, require additional time and a certain expertise. As a result, the household division of labor tended to distinguish even more sharply than in the past between the roles of husband and wife and of daughters and wives. Husbands and unmarried children were family wage earners, while wives devoted most of their time to child care and household management. Wives continued, however, to work sporadically in order to earn wages to help raise the family's level of consumption.

Tilly and Scott inform us that women who worked chose to do so not simply from individualistic motives and certainly hardly ever for financial independence. Rather the prime motive was to improve the financial position of the family and to raise its standard of living. The mother's work was a supplement to her domestic responsibilities.

Question

Would it surprise you to be told that this view of a woman's reasons for working is now controversial?

2 The sociological evidence

In *Legal Regulation of Marriage: Tradition and Change* (1974), Lenore Weitzman writes:

The sociological data . . . are closely related to the economic data . . ., for in large part it is the changing position of women with respect to men in the larger society which has influenced and altered the position of the two sexes within the family. Thus the increased labor force participation of married women has probably been instrumental in causing a decline in the absolute authority of the husband, with a consequent growth in the wife's role in the family decision-making. With an expansion in women's roles, especially economic roles, outside the family, roles within the family have also become less strongly differentiated. Wives are assuming more responsibility for financial and domicile decisions, and husbands are assuming a greater share of the responsibility for housework and child care. In general, there is a strong trend toward egalitarian family patterns, those in which authority is shared and decisions are made jointly by the husband and the wife.

The spread in egalitarian family patterns may be briefly noted in several areas. First, there is an increase in the sharing of financial decisions within the family. As the wife's contribution to the total family budget assumes greater relative importance, financial responsibilities within the family are more equally shared. Decisions on family expenditures, savings, and the general 'struggle for financial security' are now made jointly or apportioned on a less sex-stereotyped basis. Second, the determination of the family domicile and the decision of when and where to move has become more of a family decision, with the needs and interests of the wife and children assuming a much greater importance than in the past. Although both of these trends represent a decline in the traditional authority of the husband, there is also a significant decline in the traditional authority of the wife as the husband assumes a more important role in household decisions and in household tasks. As noted above, the general trend toward more egalitarian decisionmaking in the family also varies by social class. While the working wife gains more power toward the lower socio-economic strata, there is a much greater acceptance of the ideology of egalitarianism toward the upper strata.

A third area in which there is a significant trend toward more egalitarian patterns is that of sexuality. The current sexual revolution has focused increased attention and emphasis on the wife's participation and satisfaction in sexual relations, and consequently on more mutual and egalitarian sexual relationships. Marital sex became more respectable for married women in the 1950's, though the husband was still seen as the initiator and orchestrator of marital sex. At that time a woman's own needs were secondary, but if she was a 'good and mature wife,' which meant, at that time, being able to have vaginal orgasms, she would be 'happy and satisfied.' In the late 1960's, however, with the publication of Masters and Johnson's research (1966) demonstrating the range of female sexual response, both men and women began to redefine female sexuality and women's sexual needs.

A fourth and closely related trend is in the increased sharing of responsibility for birth control. Knowledge and use of some form of contraception has become nearly universal in the United States today. By 1965, 97% of white and black couples in a national sample had used or expected to use contraception at some point in their married lives. The most recently introduced and most highly effective methods of contraception, the pill and the I.U.D., are the first to give women independent control over their reproductive decisions, and the first to allow couples a real choice about the number and timing of children. With technological advances in effective methods of female contraception, the decision of when to have children, as well as the decision of when to have sexual relations, may be increasingly decided by the husband and wife together.

Fifth, and most important, is an extended range of family roles which are now being shared or alternated between husbands and wives.

Questions

(i) Do you think that the extent to which husbands and wives share rather than segregate family activities in part depends on where they are in the socio-economic class structure? And if you do, why do you think this is the case?

(ii) Is Weitzman saying that industrialisation and changes in women's labour force participation are responsible for changes in family patterns?

The following extract is taken from Hannah Gavron's study of *The Captive Wife* (1966):

MIDDLE CLASS

The annual report of the National Food Survey of 1952 reported that the majority of wives understated their husbands' incomes by about 15%. In only one instance in this survey did a wife not know what her husband earned. 'I just don't know,' said a businessman's wife, 'the house was given us by his parents, he works with his father, so I've never really found out.' In every other case, all financial questions were quite open, although several wives admitted that they would be hard put to name an exact figure for their husband's income as 'perks' were involved, such as expenses, or a car on the company. Incomes varied from £5,000 — the highest — to £17 per week — the lowest.42% of the sample were living on incomes of less than £1,500 p.a.; 29% earned between £1,500 and £2,000 p.a.; 15% between £2,100 and £3,000 p.a.; 10% between £3,100 and £4,000, and 4% over £4,000.

54% of the wives drew a regular housekeeping allowance from their husbands' income which they tried to adhere to, although as a teacher's wife said, 'there are weeks when it just seems to go, and then I have to borrow money from Jim.' One wife said that she was really in charge of finances, and her husband simply took pocket money for himself from the bank, keeping the amount as small as possible. For the remaining 44% it was simply a case of drawing money when they needed it.

As far as the making of important financial decisions was concerned, there was complete unanimity among the wives that this was always a joint affair arrived at after joint discussion, and this was true even of the few wives who were anxious to indicate that their husbands 'still wore the pants'.

Division of labour within the home

21% of the couples simply shared the housework, and the husband did any household chore required, from ironing to washing nappies, from cleaning to cooking. In every case the wife remarked on how much more helpful her husband was than her father had been (indicating a change in patterns of family behaviour). All of these helpful husbands were also rated as helpful with their children, which reveals a great deal of role sharing among these families. It was also clear that the majority of these wives, though grateful for the help given, also regarded it as their due. 'I would certainly consider myself hard done by if he didn't share the running of the house with me,' said the actor's wife. A further 44% of the husbands had certain tasks which they always did as a matter of routine, such as bedmaking at weekends or washing up the evening meal. All these husbands were willing to do more if required, and were considered very helpful by their wives. In every case but one, this was thought to be an improvement on the behaviour of their fathers. 'My father was an exception,' said the wife of an articled clerk, 'he was at home a great deal so he just had to help.' These husbands were prepared to do more if asked. 'He used to help more,' said the store manager's wife, 'but now he's working so hard, I tend to leave him alone.' 'He's often very tired,' said the publican's wife, 'I don't really ask unless I'm desperate.' 'He would help more at weekends,' said the wife of a businessman, 'but now we employ domestic help, well I don't see the need for it.'

19% of husbands would wash up but nothing else. 'He's so unwilling to do anything,' a solicitor's wife said, 'that I just make a point about washing up, and leave it at that.' 'He looks pretty sour if I suggest anything other than drying dishes, so I don't,' said the bank clerk's wife. 'Maybe he would do more,' said a teacher's wife, 'but somehow I doubt it.' One wife was quite content. 'He dries the dishes, and helps with the children and that's all — but it's quite a lot!' The remainder, 17% of the husbands, would never help. 'My husband simply doesn't believe in doing housework,' said the optician's wife, 'but I do have help so I can't really complain.' 'He just won't ever do housework,' said the wife of a copywriter, 'but he makes up for it being a very good handyman, and mending things.' It was interesting to note that these wives tended to be slightly apologetic about their husbands' lack of helpfulness, not one of them felt it to be the man's right to be waited upon in his own home. The majority of these fathers were also not very participant with their children. There seemed to be no particular relationship between not helping and social background, not even with income, although those with full-time domestic help clearly had less need of their husband's assistance. The general overall impression is of a great deal of sharing of household tasks, which in 56% of cases was felt to be an improvement on the behaviour of the wife's father.

A factor which further emphasized the home consciousness of the husbands was the number who had been involved in the decoration of their home. 35% of couples had decorated their home together, and in a further 25% of cases this had been done by the husband alone.

It is possible to conclude that the wives whose husbands helped them took this as a matter of course, while those whose husbands did not felt called upon to give a reason for it. It is interesting to note that the wives did not take their husbands' help with the children nearly so much for granted, and constantly expressed their gratitude for their husbands' assistance.

WORKING CLASS

6% of the wives said they didn't know what their husbands earned, and the wife of a grocer's assistant was quite certain she did not want to know. 'Well it's not my business, is it?' she said. The rest, however, regarded it as their business, and with one exception, were quite happy to reveal the exact amount. The highest income was a minimum of £30 per week and 'often it's near £45,' said one wife whose husband ran a small newsagent's shop. Of the rest 10% earned over £20 per week, 31% earned between £15 10s. and £20 per week. 12% earned £10 or less, and the remainder, 33%, earned between £10 10s. and £15 per week. One wife whose husband was in prison was living on National Assistance.

Working-class wives were more inclined to regulate their housekeeping money, and 77% of the wives took a regular amount from their husband's pay packet each week, and tried to make do with it. The rest, 23%, just shared it out as needed. 'In fact I do very well out of it, because my husband takes virtually nothing,' said a postman's wife, 'but then of course I've had it if I run out!'

In 10% of families the husband was the one who made all the important financial decisions. 'I never understand money so I wouldn't be much help,' said the newsagent's wife. 'Money is not a woman's business,' said another. For the others, 90%, as with the middle-class families, financial decisions were always made jointly. 'We discuss everything,' said the wife of a skilled engineer, 'and we don't ever do anything we don't agree on.' 'We always talk it over first,' said a carpenter's wife, 'unless of course he's buying me something as a surprise!'

Division of labour within the home

54% of the working-class couples (as compared to 21% of middle class) simply shared the housework between them, with no division into man's work or woman's work. 25% of the husbands did regular tasks and would do more if asked, though many wives tended not to. 'We live in two rooms and I don't work,' said a window-cleaner's wife, 'well, it wouldn't be right to ask him to start cleaning when he's been working all day.' This was a common point made by those who 'didn't ask', that is that they could manage without their husband's help. 'If we had a house,' said the wife of a sheet-metal worker, 'well then it would be a different matter.' 12% of the husbands did the washing up as a matter of course. 8% did nothing, although it was not a matter of principle, but rather of just avoiding things. 'He'd wash up and grumble,' said a foreman's wife. 'He might even make a bed if I nagged, but he's not exactly what you'd call domesticated.' 'It's a question of time,' said a labourer's wife, 'he's never around at the times when I might really need help.'

As with the middle-class sample the majority of helpful husbands were helpful with the children too. In fact 31% of the working-class sample shared the running of the home, and the children completely. The majority of the working-class wives, 67%, noted that their husbands were more helpful than their own fathers had been. 'My father never did a thing,' said one, 'even though my Mum had five children on her hands.' Again this is evidence of the shift in family patterns over the previous generation.

As might be expected, more working-class husbands than middle-class decorated their homes. In fact only 8% of the husbands out of the total had *not* done their own decoration. 62% did it on their own, but 29% had the assistance of their wives. This home decoration tends to confirm the popularity of 'Do it yourself' among the working class. Willmott (1963) noted this at Dagenham. 'Everybody seems to be a handyman on this estate,' said one of his informants, and although the L.C.C. were committed to redecorating every five years the majority spent a lot of time improving their homes. Usually decorating the home involved painting and papering the walls with contemporary wall paper, building cupboards and book shelves, and putting down linoleum on the floor. Often the result was a transformation of small dark rooms into cheerful, bright-looking rooms whose basic discomforts had been well disguised.

In conclusion it can be said, that while both samples appeared to be very family-minded and home-centred, this was particularly true of the working class where the majority of fathers seemed as involved in the care of their home and family as did their wives.

Todd and Jones' survey of *Matrimonial Property* (1972) provides additional evidence of the general management of household affairs. It was carried out in early 1971 on behalf of the Law Commission:

4.1 Household duties involving regular expenditure

We wanted to have some picture of how the couple organised their roles with regard to handling their money, and we also wanted to lead up to asking the wife how interested she was in financial matters. In the first series of questions we asked the couple who usually bought the food, paid the gas or electricity bills, paid the rates, rent or mortgage and who, if there was any money left, dealt with the surplus. In these questions we were asking who carried out the tasks, not who provided the money for them.

Who usually dealt with:—	Buying food	Paying for gas or electricity	Paying rates, rent, mortgage	Dealing with any surplus
	%	%	%	%
Husband	3	38	45	20
Wife	89	49	45	36
Either or both	7	10	8	43
Other answer	1	3	2	1
	100	100	100	100
Base	(1877)	(1877)	(1877)	(1877)

In some cases someone other than one of the spouses carried out the duties, or there was some special method of payment, for example, payment by standing order. The wife was predominantly the person responsible for buying the food but in the other matters there was a fairly even split of responsibility between the couple. We examined in more detail whether the housing and earnings situation of the couple were associated with the sharing of responsibilities for paying bills for heating and lighting, and rates, rent or mortgage.

Who usually deals with:—	Paying for gas or electricity		Paying rates, rent, mortgage	
	Method of payment from husband's employment			
	cash	not cash	cash	not cash
	%	%	%	%
Husband	26	58	30	65
Wife	61	31	60	23
Either or both	9	10	7	10
Other answers	4	1	3	2
	100	100	100	100
Base	(1099)	(534)	(1099)	(534)

The method by which the husband is paid is closely associated with which spouse pays both types of bills, fuel and rates, rent or mortgage. Where the husband is paid in cash there is a much greater likelihood that the wife carries out these duties. Where the husband is not paid in cash it is most likely that he has responsibility for these bills.

We next examine whether these duties are associated at all with whether the matrimonial home is owned by the couple or not.

Who usually deals with:—	Paying for gas or electricity		Paying rates, rent, mortgage	
	Ownership of the matrimonial home			
	Couple do not own the home	Couple own the home	Couple do not own the home	Couple own the home
	%	%	%	%
Husband	27	49	29	59
Wife	58	40	61	30
Either or both	10	10	6	11
Other answers	5	1	4	—
	100	100	100	100
Base	(896)	(978)	(896)	(978)

The variation here is similar to that in the previous table. Where the couple own their own home the husband is more likely to take the responsibility for paying the bills for fuel and housing. Where the couple do not own their home these duties are more frequently carried out by the wife.

Thus the duties that the spouses carry out in relation to these particular household responsibilities are associated with other factors in their domestic situation.

4.2 Wife's interest in money matters
After the series of questions about household management we asked wives whether they liked to know about money matters or whether they preferred to leave such things to their husbands. We first classified separately those wives who said they received the whole pay packet and were obviously responsible themselves for domestic financial management.

Wife's interest in money matters

	%
Is given the whole pay packet	5
Likes to know about money matters	76
Prefers to leave such things to husband	19
	100
Base	(1877)

Giving the whole pay packet to the wife is often talked of as a regional phenomenon so we examined to what extent the 5% of wives in this position varied in the different economic planning regions.

Region	Proportion of wives who receive pay packet	Base
North	15%	(122)
East Midlands	8%	(142)
South West	8%	(152)
Wales	8%	(99)
Yorkshire and Humberside	5%	(199)
West Midlands	4%	(201)
East Anglia	3%	(62)
North West	3%	(275)
South East	2%	(391)
Greater London	2%	(234)
England and Wales	5%	(1877)

It is thus a way of life occurring most frequently in the North but also occurring more than average in the East Midlands, the South West and Wales.

Distribution of family income between its members is a difficult research field, and all the researchers quoted in this chapter comment upon the problems of working in this area. As Jan Pahl explains in *Patterns of Money Management within Marriage* (1980):

There is a considerable amount of scattered evidence on the subject, much of it historical, but attempts to draw together this empirical evidence and to discuss it in more general terms are few. As Young put it twenty-five years ago:

It is painfully obvious to the student of social policy that growing knowledge about the distribution of the national income between families has not so far been matched by a growth in knowledge about the distribution of the family income between its members . . . It has been taken for granted that some members of a family cannot be rich while others are poor.

That was written in 1952; in 1973 Young and Willmott were still saying much the same:

The evidence is not as good as we would like. The welfare state has certainly brought about some redistribution of income from men to women and children . . . about the disposal of earned income inside the family, the evidence is more circumstantial.

Many respondents are unable or unwilling to divulge details of incomes; both income and expenditure can vary greatly from week to week; there is a consistent tendency to underestimate spending on some items, such as tobacco and alcohol; it is difficult to decide in all cases who is actually in control of spending on different items; and it is impossible to take into account all the effects of the hidden economy — income from 'side jobs', presents of 'cheap' goods, gains from productive work on an allotment, at the sewing-machine, or on a neighbour's car.

A major problem area is the ignorance of many wives as to how much their husbands earn. Gorer, in his study, *Sex and Marriage in England Today* (1971), found that 'More than one wife in six who receive housekeeping allowances do not know what their husbands earn.' The report of the Hunt committee (1973), which was set up to consider families and their needs, does not contain information on the extent to which income was shared among members of the families whose circumstances it investigated; the report does, however, demonstrate the extent to which wives were ignorant of their husbands' incomes. While the percentage of single parents who refused to give information on income varied from 2% to 5%, the percentage of wives who refused to give information about their husbands' incomes varied from 11.8% in Halifax to 12.9% in Dundee and 26.2% in Dorset. It is likely that the difference between the refusal rate of the single parents and that of the wives reflects the difference between those who would not and those who could not give this information.

Much valuable evidence is to be found in the literature on community studies and in the work which has been done on family living standards; of the latter, the study by Land (1969) of large families in London and that by Gray (1974) of working-class families in Edinburgh are particularly useful. Because of the nature of the sources, there has been an overemphasis on patterns of income allocation among working-class families and a relative neglect of the patterns to be found in the middle class. I shall present a very simple, three-part typology of allocation systems, with a discussion of some of the variations most commonly found in each of the three systems.

The whole wage system
In this system the husband hands over the whole of his wage packet and the wife manages all their financial affairs, giving him a certain amount for his own personal pocket-money. This pattern has been documented, for example, by Kerr in Ship Street in Liverpool and by Humphreys in Dublin. Gorer (1966) showed that in his sample of 1,037 married women it was most common in the north west of England, where 23% of couples followed the whole wage system, and least common in the south east, where the proportion was only 6%. Land found that this pattern was particularly likely to be found among families living on social security. . . .

The allowance system
Under this system the husband gives his wife an 'allowance', which is sometimes called her 'wage' and which is related not so much to his actual income as to some norm of what would be an appropriate sum. If it bears a relation to his income it is to the average basic wage in the community. Dennis, Henriques and Slaughter, in their study of a coal-mining community, describe how the wife's 'wage' is kept low, at a level based on the minimum which a man is likely to earn, partly in order that the same amount can be handed over each week. If a man cannot hand over this amount he may 'borrow' from his wife and then 'pay her back' the following week. Most husbands contribute occasional sums for larger items of expenditure — furniture, clothes, a holiday and so on. Dennis, Henriques and Slaughter (1956) sum it up:

> The family's weekly wage is strictly divided into one part for the wife, with which she must maintain the household, and another part for the husband to spend as he will . . . This division of the wage between man and wife, and their duties and liberties in respect of the allotted shares, are aspects of the whole system of division between the accepted social roles of the sexes in Ashton. . . .

The pooling system
The third broad category in my typology has been described as 'the pooling of resources', 'the pool system', 'Share and share alike', or 'We keep the purse in the drawer and take money out when it is needed.' This pattern seems, not unexpectedly, to be more characteristic of couples where both husband and wife are earning. However, it has been shown, for example by Hunt, that the earnings of wives are usually used for the payment of household expenses, and so having an income of her own may not give a wife the same sort of economic independence as it does her husband. Jephcott (1962), in her study of women working in a biscuit factory, suggested that the power of married women *vis-à-vis* their husbands decreased when they acquired earnings of their own because this meant that their husbands kept more of their earnings for personal expenditure, while the women's earnings went mainly to pay for collective family expenditure.

Jan Pahl herself states that describing the different types of allocation system is only a first step. She asks a number of questions. What determines the pattern of allocation within any one household? What distinguishes the household with the whole wage system from that with the allowance system or the pooling system? Is there a significance for individual living standards of different patterns of financial allocation and responsibility? When and why do allocation systems change? Pahl hypothesises that there are links between the stage in the 'life cycle' and financial arrangements:

. . . I would suggest that the pooling system may be characteristic of the newly married couple who are both earning; this may change to the allowance system when the wife leaves paid employment to look after young children, and change again to a modified pooling system in the household with two earners or where teenage children may be contributing to the household economy; finally the pensioner household may adopt the whole wage system. On the other hand, is it possible that couples keep the same system throughout their married life, and that the prevalence of the whole wage system among older couples is an effect of generation rather than stage in the life cycle?

Questions

(i) Does this comment answer Pahl's first question?
(ii) What answers can you suggest to Pahl's other questions?

3 An ideological basis?

Mary Ann Glendon in *State, Law and Family: Family Law in Transition in the United States and Western Europe*, (1977) emphasises the difficulties which appear when this question is explored.

The prevailing ideologies of marriage have never been alike for all groups of any large population. In Western society, however, one ideology has been dominant and until modern times has found universal expression in the law. The family law of Western legal systems has traditionally embodied ideas of separate spheres of activity appropriate for women and men. It has carried the image of the woman as principal caretaker of the home and children, the man as principal provider, and of a family authority structure dominated by the husband and father. This should not be understood as meaning that the woman's *exclusive* task has been to care for home and children. In pre-industrial society, the wife was often a co-worker with the husband on the farm, in the craft and in the shop. The exclusively housewife-marriage seems to be a phenomenon of the 20th century. Already this period is beginning to appear to have been a brief interlude in history. Today, as more and more women engage in economic activity outside the home, housewife-marriage is only one of many current marriage patterns. Where housewife-marriage exists, it is now more apt to be a phase of a marriage than a description of the marriage from beginning to end.

Organized around a hierarchical model, with a clear division of roles between the sexes, traditional family law placed primary responsibility for support of the family on the male partner and vested authority in him to determine the place and mode of family life and to deal with all the family property, including that of the wife. Among the wealthy, property matters could to some extent be arranged so that the interests of the wife (and her family of origin) could be protected. The law paid little attention to the needs of the poor, even when large numbers of women began to be employed outside the home in the early 19th century in England, and later in France and Germany. The set of legal rules organized along these traditional lines persisted in England, France, the United States and Germany well into the 20th century, long after behavior of many married people had ceased to correspond to the image enshrined in the laws.

This model was constantly adjusted, beginning in the late 19th century and in the first half of the 20th century, but at last the center could not hold. Laws which might have been appropriate for the family production community, or for the housewife marriage when divorce was rare, no longer worked when many women's economic activity had been transferred to the marketplace and when divorce had become pandemic.

Although Glendon's point is a necessary reminder of the shift in emphasis of the women's economic activity, it is appropriate to recall that housework and child care continue to a great extent to be the responsibility of women. Elizabeth Wilson in *Women and the Welfare State* (1977) asks the question why:

Because more and more married women are going out to work, and because, although there has been a rise in the number of women who bear a child or children at some point in their lives maternity has become quantitatively less and less absorbing, the importance, drudgery, and significance of domestic work in the home has become more and more clear (Gardiner 1975). Why then is it retained? Why has it not been socialized when in the industrial sphere capitalism constantly seeks to transform and revolutionize its technology? The economic significance of domestic labour has been discussed for some years in the Women's Movement (e.g. Benston 1969; Morton 1970; Rowbotham 1973) and more recently the subject has been taken up by a number of socialists and Marxist economists (Harrison 1974; Secombe 1974). Whatever the precise nature of its relationship to surplus value it is clear that the domestic unpaid work of the housewife helps to keep costs down for the employer by making it possible for the worker to be cared for much more cheaply than would otherwise be possible. The socialized care of the worker — canteens, living accommodation, laundry — alone would be likely in this country to cost the capitalist more than the efforts of the housewife who takes pride in making do. Where it is cheaper for the workman to be separated from his family — as is the case in South Africa where black workers can be compelled to live in barracks — that is what happens. The strength of the working class has also much to do with the achievement of more tolerable living conditions.

There is a second reason for the retention of domestic work: the supportive emotional functions of the family. The intensity of the parental–child relationships within the family make for the vulnerability of the child and therefore the family is a highly functional ideological institution for the upbringing of children in such a manner that they conform, as adults, to authoritarian/submissive social relationships. Then there is the marriage relationship. It is pleasanter for workers to be married. The marriage relationship may have its problems, men may feel henpecked or hamstrung; the sexual relationship may have its inhibitions and disappointments, especially for the woman; yet State brothels could hardly provide an adequate substitute. . . .

A third reason for the retention of the unwaged housewife and her children as the dependants of the individual worker is that this arrangement reinforces the incentive of the father to work regularly and hard. The ability to support a family is early equated in the male child's mind as an essential part of his manhood. Much value is attached to virility and loss of his job can lead to the man losing also his sense of identity in his own and his wife's eyes. . . . The male role thus reinforces the work ethic quite directly.

Elizabeth Wilson's thesis is that even though women are now increasingly available to seek employment, there is an ideology which continues to define them narrowly as wives and mothers, responsible for the domestic work within the nuclear family.

Dear Madam,

I am sorry I have been unable to see you to collect your account which has run to _____ weeks and now stands at £ _____.

Settlement at your earliest convenience would be very much appreciated by

Your **Unigate** Salesman.

Question

Is this an example of Elizabeth Wilson's point?

There is a more invidious example. In March 1980 the Government changed the Immigration Rules. The new rules create a difference in treatment for the purposes of entry and residence between those who seek to enter as husbands or fiancés and those who seek to enter as wives or fiancées of people who are already settled in the United Kingdom. A male who is settled in the United Kingdom has the right to be joined by his wife or fiancée. A woman has the right to be joined by her husband or fiancé only if she is a citizen of the UK and Colonies, and if she or one of her parents was born in the United Kingdom. After considerable controversy, the rule was changed in March 1983.

The rule had been the subject of three specific complaints before the European Commission of Human Rights (1982) as in breach, inter alia, of Article 8 of the European Convention — the right to respect for family life (see p. 573, below). In the arguments on admissibility, the British Government submitted:

> . . . that this difference is justified to protect the labour market of the indigenous and settled population and to terminate primary immigration. As a category, husbands and fiancés provide the opportunity for the evasion and exploitation of immigration policy.
> Women are not necessarily bound to compete for employment and are unlikely to be bread winners. Women as bread winners are unusual,[1] for society still expects the man to go out to work and the woman to stay at home. This is a fact of life, a common pattern. The majority of women do not threaten the labour market particularly women from the Indian sub-continent. . . .

Questions

(i) Does this assertion confirm Elizabeth Wilson's thesis?

(ii) Do you find support in the above material for Lee Comer's complaint (1974) that 'women are the victims of the inequities of the family'?

(iii) If it does give support, should the law leave people free to arrange their lives thus, or should it encourage some different pattern?

(iv) If the latter, what and how?

4 Why do women seek employment?

Hannah Gavron (1966) conducted a survey during 1960 and 1961 amongst a sample of 48 middle class and 48 working class wives. She asked why they sought employment:

	M.C. %	W.C. %
Finance alone	6	15
Emotional and intellectual satisfaction alone	29	10
Financial, emotional and intellectual satisfaction	25	29
Emotional, intellectual satisfaction and 'automatic'	27	21
'Automatic'	4	8
Financial and 'automatic'	—	4
No desire to work	8	12

---

1. According to the Government's own figures there are probably between 150,000 and 200,000 breadwinner wives! (*The Taxation of Husband and Wife* (1980))

Finance was a more important factor in motivation amongst the working class sample but Gavron concludes from the figures that the attitudes of the working class women to employment were not very different from the middle class. Further evidence is available from the OPCS *Family Formation Survey* (1979):

Reason for working between first and second live births in four different time periods

Worked because:	1956–60	1961–65	1966–70	1971–5
Really needed the money	52	51	48	47
Wanted extra things	27	25	27	27
Liked it	16	19	20	22
Other reason	5	5	5	4

Source: Dunnell (1979) Table 6.5. Crown copyright.

Questions

(i) Ann Oakley, in *Subject Women* (1981), suggests that these surveys show that the 'public acceptability of selfish and work-centred reasons for employment may be growing.' Do you agree?

(ii) Do you think there is any correlation between the control and allocation of money described by Pahl and whether the wife has employment?

(iii) Gavron's sample was taken mainly from 'conventional housewife homes'. At p. 189, below, we discuss dual career families. Do you think that the answers would be any different amongst a sample of dual career families?

Three tables in *The Taxation of Husband and Wife* (1980) illustrate the place of women in the labour force:

Occupied/economically active population and activity rates: GB, 1921–1979

(All individuals over 16)

	1921	1931	1951	1961	1966	1971	1979 (Provisional)
Males and Females(mil.)	19.4	21.1	22.6	23.8	24.9	25.1	26.0
Activity rate %	58.1	60.7	59.6	60.5	62.1	61.2	62.1
of which:-							
Males (million)	13.7	14.8	15.6	16.1	16.0	15.9	15.8
Activity rate %	87.1	90.5	87.6	86.0	84.0	81.4	78.6
% of total	(70.5)	(70.2)	(69.2)	(67.5)	(64.3)	(63.4)	(60.8)
Females (million)	5.7	6.3	7.0	7.7	8.9	9.2	10.2
Activity rate %	32.3	34.2	34.7	37.4	42.2	42.7	46.9
% of total	(29.5)	(29.8)	(30.8)	(32.5)	(35.7)	(36.6)	(39.2)
of which:-							
Married Females (million)	0.7	1.0	2.7	3.9	5.1	5.8	6.7
Activity rate %	8.7	10.0	21.7	29.7	38.1	42.2	49.6
% active females	(12.9)	(15.2)	(38.2)	(50.2)	(57.1)	(63.1)	(65.7)
Unmarried Females (mil.)	5.0	5.3	4.3	3.9	3.8	3.4	3.5
Activity rate %	53.8	60.2	55.0	50.6	49.2	43.7	42.5
% active females	(87.1)	(84.8)	(61.8)	(49.8)	(42.9)	(36.9)	(34.3)

The first table shows how the participation of women in the work force in Great Britain has altered over the last 60 years. A telling observation from these figures is that, whereas in 1921 less than one in ten married women were working or looking for work, by 1971 nearly half of all married women were economically active.

The second table shows how economic activity varies with age. Those less likely to be working outside the home include married women in the 25 to 34 age group and in the 55 to 59 age group.

Provisional estimates of the number of economically active and inactive married women under 60, by age: GB, 1979

Thousands

Age	Economically active	Economically inactive
Under 20	66	63
20–24	560	412
25–34	1,618	1,524
35–44	1,827	895
45–54	1,698	892
55–59	700	645
Total	6,469	4,431

The third table confirms that it is family commitments which determine in very many cases whether or not a married woman is likely to be in paid employment (or seeking work). It is suggested in *The Taxation of Husband and Wife* that about 270,000 of the 1,355,000 economically inactive wives without dependent children live in households containing an elderly or disabled person.

Estimated number of economically inactive wives under pension age, by age and presence of dependent children: GB, 1978

Thousands

Age	With children	Without children	Total
Under 25	465	69	534
25–44	2,235	221	2,456
45–59	374	1,065	1,439
Total	3,074	1,355	4,429

Questions

(i) Would you expect a substantial proportion of economically active wives to belong to 'dual career' families?

(ii) W.B. Creighton (1979) says: 'women are still largely concentrated in the service and white-collar sectors, and in a small group of manufacturing industries, which include food, drink and tobacco, light engineering, and clothing and textiles.' Despite all the legislation, in 1979 the New Earnings Survey stated a woman's average hourly earnings to be 70% of a man's. There is also evidence to suggest that the majority of women in employment are in the absolute sense, 'low-paid'. Would you be surprised to discover that even amongst dual career families, the wife's income is substantially below the income of the husband?

5 Domestic arrangements and the law

Balfour v Balfour
[1919] 2 KB 571, [1918–19] All ER Rep 860, 88 LJKB 1054, 121 LT 346, 35 TLR 609, 63 Sol Jo 661, Court of Appeal

A husband agreed to give to his wife £30 per month whilst she was in England recuperating from an illness. He returned to Ceylon where he was employed. The Court of Appeal refused to enforce this agreement.

Atkin LJ: The defence to this action on the alleged contract is that the defendant, the husband, entered into no contract with his wife, and for the determination of that it is necessary to remember that there are agreements between parties which do not result in contracts within the meaning of that term in our law. The ordinary example is where two parties agree to take a walk together, or where there is an offer and an acceptance of hospitality. Nobody would suggest in ordinary circumstances that those agreements result in what we know as a contract, and one of the most usual forms of agreement which does not constitute a contract appears to me to be the arrangements which are made between husband and wife. It is quite common, and it is the natural and inevitable result of the relationship of husband and wife, that the two spouses should make arrangements between themselves — agreements such as are in dispute in this action — agreements for allowances, by which the husband agrees that he will pay to his wife a certain sum of money, per week, or per month, or per year, to cover either her own expenses or the necessary expenses of the household and of the children of the marriage, and in which the wife promises either expressly or impliedly to apply the allowance for the purpose for which it is given. To my mind those agreements, or many of them, do not result in contracts at all, and they do not result in contracts even though there may be what as between other parties would constitute consideration for the agreement. The consideration, as we know, may consist either in some right, interest, profit or benefit accruing to one party, or some forbearance, detriment, loss or responsibility given, suffered or undertaken by the other. That is a well-known definition, and it constantly happens, I think, that such arrangements made between husband and wife are arrangements in which there are mutual promises, or in which there is consideration in form within the definition that I have mentioned. Nevertheless they are not contracts, and they are not contracts because the parties did not intend that they should be attended by legal consequences. To my mind it would be of the worst possible example to hold that agreements such as this resulted in legal obligations which could be enforced in the Courts. It would mean this, that when the husband makes his wife a promise to give her an allowance of 30s. or £2 a week, whatever he can afford to give her, for the maintenance of the household and children, and she promises so to apply it, not only could she sue him for his failure in any week to supply the allowance, but he could sue her for non-performance of the obligation, express or implied, which she had undertaken upon her part. All I can say is that the small Courts of this country would have to be multiplied one hundredfold if these arrangements were held to result in legal obligations. They are not sued upon, not because the parties are reluctant to enforce their legal rights when the agreement is broken, but because the parties, in the inception of the arrangement, never intended that they should be sued upon. Agreements such as these are outside the realm of contracts altogether. The common law does not regulate the form of agreements between spouses. Their promises are not sealed with seals and sealing wax. The consideration that really obtains for them is that natural love and affection which counts for so little in these cold Courts. The terms may be repudiated, varied or renewed as performance proceeds or as disagreements develop, and the principles of the common law as to exoneration and discharge and accord and satisfaction are such as find no place in the domestic code. The parties themselves are advocates, judges, Courts, sheriff's officer and reporter. In respect of these promises each house is a domain into which the King's writ does not seek to run, and to which his officers do not seek to be admitted.

Questions

(i) The Crown's officers may not seek on their own initiative to be admitted into the house, but why make it difficult for the parties themselves to invite the judges, advocates and courts into the house?

(ii) Is the natural inequality in bargaining power of the spouses in housewife marriages an argument for or against making agreements for domestic financing enforceable?

(iii) Should spouses be free to make such agreements as they wish or should the law impose a preferred pattern?
(iv) If the latter, what pattern do you have in mind?

6 The duty to support

(a) AT COMMON LAW

Manby v Scott
(1663) 1 Keb 482, 1 Lev 4, 1 Mod Rep 124, 0 Bridg 229, 1 Sid 109, King's Bench Division

Hyde J: . . . In the beginning, when God created woman an helpmate for man, he said, 'They twain shall be one flesh'; and thereupon our law says, that husband and wife are but one person in law: presently after the Fall, the judgment of God upon woman was, 'Thy desire shall be to thy husband, for thy will shall be subject to thy husband, and he shall rule over thee' (Gen iii, 16). Hereupon our law put the wife *sub potestate viri.* . . .

[His wife] was bone of his bone, flesh of his flesh, and no man did ever hate his own flesh so far as not to preserve it.

Question

Has the duty of support at common law anything to do with the law relating to unity of property?

The details of the common law are described by Gareth Miller, in *Family Property and Financial Provision* (1974):

At common law a husband is under the duty to maintain his wife in accordance with his means, but there is no corresponding duty on a wife to maintain her husband. A husband will normally perform his duty by providing first, a suitable home where he and his wife will live together, and, secondly, necessaries such as food and clothing. It is unlikely that he will wish to undertake the management of the household himself, and instead he will generally provide his wife with an appropriate allowance. However, at common law a wife has never had the right to a separate allowance, but if she is living with her husband she is presumed to have his implied authority to pledge his credit for necessary household expenses.

This authority does not arise from the fact of marriage, but from the wife's usual position as housekeeper from which it can be inferred that the husband has held her out as his agent. It is open to a husband expressly to forbid his wife to pledge his credit and there need be no communication of this to any tradesman. However, if he has in the past held out his wife to a particular tradesman as having apparent authority, then it will be necessary to give an express warning to that tradesman. A husband may also rebut the presumption of implied authority by showing that she already had a sufficient allowance with which to purchase necessaries, or that she was already supplied with sufficient of the goods in respect of which a claim is made against him.

Generally a wife is not entitled to separate maintenance in a separate home unless she has a good reason for living apart from her husband. A husband's duty to maintain his wife is suspended while she is in desertion, but it revives on termination of the desertion. If she commits adultery which has not been connived at or condoned then her right to be maintained ceases altogether. Indeed, if the wife's conduct is such as to induce in the husband a reasonable (though of course mistaken) belief in her adultery, then he is not obliged to maintain her as long as he continues to have reasonable grounds for that belief.

A wife may, however, be living apart from her husband because he is in desertion or because she has been forced to do so by his misconduct. In such circumstances, in the absence of misconduct on her part, she is still entitled to be maintained. If a husband then failed to provide for his wife she was formerly entitled to pledge his credit for necessaries suitable to their joint style of living before the separation. The basis of this right was the so-called 'agency of necessity.' This could not be terminated by the husband forbidding his wife to pledge his credit or even by expressly forbidding tradesmen to give her credit. However, its value was limited because tradesmen were naturally reluctant to give credit if they were likely to become involved in a matrimonial dispute.

The wife's agency of necessity was abolished by section 41 of the Matrimonial Proceedings and Property Act 1970, but this leaves untouched the authority which she is presumed to have while running the husband's household, or any authority which she may have been held out by the husband as having.

The practical utility to a wife of the husband's common law obligation to maintain her has been limited owing to the difficulty of enforcement, but its influence has been, and continues to be, considerable. Although a wife will, wherever possible rely on one of the statutory remedies . . . the courts have constantly referred to the principles surrounding the common law obligation in interpreting the scope of these remedies. It has also played an important part in protecting the wife's occupation of the matrimonial home after a marriage has broken down but before it has been terminated by divorce. Once a marriage has been terminated by divorce then of course the husband's obligation is also terminated and financial provision thereafter is dependent entirely on statute.

Questions

(i) Mrs Splash buys a hat from Newstyle Ltd, instructing the assistant to send the account to her husband. In fact her husband told her the day before that if she wanted a new hat she would have to pay for it herself. Advise Newstyle Ltd as to their rights.

(ii) If there is anything left of the husband's common law duty to maintain, should it be expressly abolished by statute?

(b) MAINTENANCE AND 'HOUSEKEEPING'

The wife had, and usually still has the 'position of housekeeper' (Miller). But even after the Married Women's Property Act 1882 allowed the wife to keep anything she acquired by gift or purchase, money received for housekeeping remained the property of the husband. She simply had custody of it and any savings belonged to him. (See *Hoddinot v Hoddinot* [1949] 2 KB 406 at p. 84, below.) Further, the statutes under which she could apply for a maintenance order only permitted her to enforce any order after the parties had separated. This restriction was discussed in the *Report of the Royal Commission on Marriage and Divorce* (1956):

The husband's liability where the wife is cohabiting with her husband
1042. Some witnesses suggested that if a wife's only complaint against her husband is that of wilful neglect to provide reasonable maintenance for her or her children, she should be able to obtain an order which should be fully effective notwithstanding that she and her husband continue to live together as man and wife. They pointed out that a husband's neglect to provide for his wife may not be deliberate or malicious but may be due rather to thoughtlessness or improvidence and that the existence of an effective court order may then be sufficient to keep him up to the mark. As it is, however, the wife must leave her husband if she wishes to retain her order and thus marriages may be broken which might otherwise be saved; in fact, it may be said that the present law positively encourages the breaking up of the home where the sole or the main cause of the trouble is financial.

1043. Against this proposal it was argued that the existence of an effective order could only further exacerbate relations which were already strained, to the point where the final breakdown of the marriage would be inevitable. Moreover, it was said that the proposal would be impracticable. The amount of the order is based on what the wife requires to keep herself when living apart from her husband. If husband and wife were in fact living together then the husband could argue that he was being asked to pay too much since he was providing her with a home; on the other hand, she might say that she was not getting enough under the order since she was expected to make all the housekeeping expenses out of a sum intended for her own needs.

1044. Other witnesses were concerned more with the status of the wife in the home. It was said that a wife should not be dependent on the whim of her husband for the amount which he allows

her for housekeeping; every wife should have a right to a housekeeping allowance. Some of these witnesses proposed that the amount should be fixed by law as a certain proportion of the family income; others considered that the wife should be able to apply to the court for an order fixing the amount. These proposals we are unable to accept. The first would be clearly impracticable. The second would require the court in effect to determine the standard of living of the family.
1045. We are impressed, however, by the argument that the present law fails to make any provision for the case where the wife has constant difficulty in getting money from her husband but at the same time does not want to break up the home. We have been told that in fact quite often a wife who has obtained a maintenance order does not leave her husband and that the situation improves because he, not realising that her order is unenforceable, makes her regular payments. We therefore think that it would be desirable to allow a wife who has obtained a maintenance order solely on the ground of her husband's wilful neglect to provide reasonable maintenance for her (or for the children) to be able to enforce that order without leaving her husband.
1046. We have carefully considered the arguments advanced against the proposal but in our opinion their force has been exaggerated. If relations between husband and wife are already seriously strained, we think it unlikely that the fact that the wife has obtained a court order which is enforceable will make matters any worse. But where the situation has not gone so far we believe that in some cases at least there is reasonable hope that the making of an order may bring the husband to his senses. Moreover, the very fact that the court has power to make such an order may in itself have a salutary effect on those husbands who are apt to be careless of their financial responsibility for their families. We are encouraged in this view by evidence we received of experience in New Zealand, where there is no provision that a wife must leave her husband if she wishes to keep her order.
1047. As to the practical difficulty referred to in paragraph 1043, we feel confident that it is not insuperable. If the wife wishes to go on living with her husband we see no reason why the court, when assessing the amount of the order, should not take into account the fact that the husband is paying the rent. At the same time the court could point out to the husband that if he expects his wife to run his household he must pay her a sum over and above that specified in the order. If the wife subsequently left her husband she could apply for an increase in the amount of the order to meet the cost of providing accommodation for herself.

The opposing view is put by Lord Goddard CJ in *Wheatley v Wheatley* [1950] 1 KB 39, [1949] 2 All ER 428:

It would be undesirable for a married woman to go to a court and get an order against her husband, either with or without a separation clause, to maintain her, and at the same time to go on living in her husband's house. By so doing she would be getting a benefit twice over, because money received under a maintenance order is supposed to be to pay for the wife's board and lodging while she is living separately from her husband, and she would be getting lodging by still remaining with him. But, apart from that, it would seem most undesirable that spouses should be living in the same house under such circumstances. For myself I can conceive of nothing that is more likely to lead to assaults and general unhappiness and, very often, to actual attempts to eject the wife from the house by violence, than that a wife who has obtained an order against her husband, perhaps after a bitter contest before the justices, should go back and live in the same house with him.

Question

Why is the wife getting the money twice over?

The Law Commission in their Working Paper on Matrimonial Proceedings in Magistrates' Courts (1973) agreed with the Royal Commission. The Law Commission felt that there might be advantages if an order which is made on the ground of failure to provide reasonable maintenance (see p. 189, below) could be enforceable for the period of six months whilst the parties continued to live together. If the parties continued to live together for more than six months the order would become unenforceable. In their subsequent *Report* (1976), the Law Commission commented on the evidence submitted on this topic:

2.60 This tentative proposal by the Working Party, not unnaturally, aroused strong feelings amongst those commenting on the working paper. The feeling of the majority was that such a provision would be useful, but it was pointed out that there would be practical difficulties. How, for example, would payments be made under such an order? Would a husband who had failed to maintain his wife be required to send payments to the court each week for collection by his wife? Or would he be expected to make payments direct to her? Neither course would be free of difficulty. Another significant criticism of this proposal was that it might lead to a number of wives asking the court to 'fix the housekeeping'.

2.61 We have no doubt that cases occur in which the sole cause, or the real cause, of matrimonial difficulties is the husband's carelessness of his financial responsibilities. Where the parties are still living together in such cases, it seems to us to be wrong that the court should be unable to make an immediately enforceable financial order in favour of the wife. The result is that a wife who stays with her husband is worse off financially than she would be by leaving him. While the law is in such a state it may be argued that it is providing an inducement for the wife to leave her husband and is thus favouring the break down of the marriage instead of its repair. We, therefore, think that a maintenance order made in favour of a spouse while the parties are cohabiting should be enforceable notwithstanding the cohabitation.

The recommendation of the Law Commission is now contained in s. 25(1) of the *Domestic Proceedings and Magistrates' Courts Act 1978*:

25.—(1) Where —
   (*a*) periodical payments are required to be made to one of the parties to a marriage (whether for his own benefit or for the benefit of a child of the family) by an order made under section 2, 6 or 11(2) of this Act or by an interim maintenance order made under section 19 of this Act (otherwise than on an application under section 7 of this Act), or
   (*b*) the right to the actual custody of a child is given to one of the parties to a marriage by an order made under section 8(2) of this Act or by an interim custody order made under section 19 of this Act,
the order shall be enforceable notwithstanding that the parties to the marriage are living with each other at the date of the making of the order or that, although they are not living with each other at that date, they subsequently resume living with each other; but the order shall cease to have effect if after that date the parties continue to live with each other, or resume living with each other, for a continuous period exceeding six months.

Questions

(i) Is an order for maintenance of the wife and/or the children the same thing as an order for a housekeeping allowance?

(ii) When the wife obtains a maintenance order, whom should she spend it on?

At common law, any savings which the wife was able to accumulate from housekeeping allowances from the husband, and any property which she purchased out of such savings, belonged to the husband:

Hoddinot v Hoddinot
[1949] 2 KB 406, 65 TLR 266, 93 Sol Jo 286, Court of Appeal

A husband and wife regularly invested in football pools, in the husband's name, the savings on housekeeping moneys. Forecasting was the result of their joint effort. Their forecast won a prize of £138, 7s which was paid into the husband's bank account. Part of the money was used to purchase furniture in the home. The parties quarrelled and separated and the wife claimed the furniture or at least part of it.

Bucknill LJ: . . . I am not at all satisfied that she had got any legal interest in the housekeeping money as such. The money belonged to the husband, and I should have thought she held it in trust for him for keeping them both, and if the husband decides to take some of it away from the purchase of food and such things to invest it in football pools, it seems to me that the money still remained his, and that in the absence of any contract between them the proceeds or winnings on that housekeeping money also belong to him.

Questions

(i) If the wife holds the housekeeping money in trust for the husband, for keeping them both, might she not at least be entitled to retain sufficient of the money to maintain herself at their standard of living?

(ii) The husband decides the standard of living. What can a wife do about this if the standard of living is not appropriate to his means?

(iii) Husband and wife are both earning similar amounts. The wife does the household shopping one week and the husband does it the next week. In one week, when it is the wife's turn, she gives the husband her purse and asks him to do the shopping. There is more than enough in the purse. Will she be entitled to the change?

The *Married Women's Property Act 1964* now provides:

1. If any question arises as to the right of a husband or wife to money derived from any allowance made by the husband for the expenses of the matrimonial home or for similar purposes, or to any property acquired out of such money, the money or property shall, in the absence of any agreement between them to the contrary, be treated as belonging to the husband and the wife in equal shares.

Question

Has this provision made any difference to your answer to question (iii) above?

It seems that the legal position is little understood. For instance Todd and Jones (1972) asked the following two questions:

Whether knew [what] the legal position is with regard to savings from housekeeping		Husbands %	Wives %
	Yes	42	41
	No	58	59
		100	100
Base		(1877)	(1877)

We asked those who said they thought they knew the legal position what they thought it was.

Those who thought they knew the legal position		Husbands %	Wives %
Savings would belong to:	the wife	32	26
	the husband	44	54
	half to each	24	20
		100	100
Base		(787)	(777)

It will be observed that fewer than a quarter of those who thought that they knew the legal position in fact stated it correctly. Todd and Jones also asked the following question: 'If a husband gives his wife regular housekeeping money and she saves out of it, who do you think the savings should belong to; the wife, the husband, or half to each?' The answers were as follows:

Savings should belong to:	Husbands	Wives
	%	%
The wife	52	47
The husband	2	2
Half to each	46	51
	100	100
Base	(1877)	(1877)

Questions

(i) If a housekeeping allowance in part discharges the duty of support, why cannot a periodical payments order in part include a housekeeping allowance?
(ii) Or can it?

7 The enforcement of the duty of support

The history of the magistrates' matrimonial jurisdiction is not free from controversy. The Law Commission *Working Paper* (1973) describes the development in the following way:

7. The Matrimonial Causes Act 1857 established a secular court to hear and determine matrimonial causes. Named 'the Court for Divorce and Matrimonial Causes', it was empowered to dissolve marriages (a power previously exercisable only by Act of Parliament) and to grant judicial separation (a remedy previously available only in the ecclesiastical courts). The remedies provided in the 1857 Act (divorce, judicial separation, nullity and restitution of conjugal rights) dealt with breakdown of marriage but had little or no relevance save in the context of breakdown induced by grievous matrimonial offence, and the Act made no provision, except in one respect, for the exercise of any matrimonial jurisdiction by magistrates. The provision it did make was really directed towards a situation of irretrievable breakdown — the 'protection order' which magistrates were empowered to make to protect 'any money or property [a deserted wife] may acquire by her lawful industry' or otherwise against the claims of her husband and his creditors.
8. The 1857 Act was of very little value to anyone outside the propertied classes. The great majority of wives whom their husbands abandoned or maltreated had to make do with such relief as they could find in the poor law or the criminal law. The first help to the ill-treated woman was given by section 4 of the Matrimonial Causes Act 1878, which brought together the strands of the criminal and the poor law for her benefit. It provided that, if a husband was convicted summarily or otherwise of an aggravated assault upon his wife, the court or magistrate before whom he was convicted, if satisfied that the wife's future safety was in peril, should have power to order that she should no longer be bound to cohabit with her husband (such order to have the force and effect in all respects of [sic] a decree of judicial separation on the grounds of cruelty). The order might further provide for:
(i) the husband to pay the wife weekly maintenance, and
(ii) the legal custody of any children under 10 to be given to the wife.
9. The 1878 Act was followed by a wider ranging reform in 1886, when the Married Women (Maintenance in Case of Desertion) Act gave a more direct and economically useful remedy to wives. Under this Act if a married woman could establish that her husband was able to support her and his children but had refused or neglected to do so and had deserted her, a magistrates' court could award her maintenance of up to £2 a week. Powers under the 1878 Act were unaffected. The Summary Jurisdiction (Married Women) Act 1895 gave magistrates' courts their general matrimonial jurisdiction. It repealed section 4 of the 1878 Act and the whole of the 1886 Act, replacing their limited provisions by a general code of matrimonial relief available to married women (but not men) in courts of summary jurisdiction. In brief, the grounds upon which a wife could apply to a magistrates' court were that her husband had been convicted of violence to her, that her husband had deserted her, that her husband had been persistently cruel to her, or that her husband had wilfully neglected to provide reasonable maintenance for her and

her infant children. The magistrates could make a non-cohabitation order, order payment of maintenance of up to £2 a week, and grant the wife custody of a child under the age of 16. The wife's adultery, unless condoned, connived at or conduced to, was a bar to an order in her favour.

10. The 1895 Act was a major advance. While following the 1886 Act in allowing maintenance orders to be made without the court also having to make a non-cohabitation order, it empowered magistrates to order the payment of a weekly sum of money where the husband's only offence was 'wilful neglect to provide reasonable maintenance'. Thus, it constituted a code of matrimonial relief designed to deal with the situation where matrimonial breakdown had occurred but was not irretrievable, and to provide relief before it became irretrievable. This code remained the basis of the magistrates' law until 1960. The Licensing Act 1902 added habitual drunkenness by either spouse as a ground for an order. The Married Women (Maintenance) Act 1920 corrected the anomaly that no money could be ordered for the support of a child in the wife's custody by making possible an order for 10s a week. The Summary Jurisdiction (Separation and Maintenance) Act 1925 added to the grounds for an order, that the husband was guilty of persistent cruelty to the children, that he insisted on having sexual intercourse while knowingly suffering from a venereal disease, that he was forcing his wife to engage in prostitution, or that he was a drug addict. The Matrimonial Causes Act 1937 not only added to the grounds for an order that of adultery, but introduced the significant provision that a husband (as well as being able to apply for an order on the grounds of his wife's habitual drunkenness) could apply for an order if his wife committed adultery. The Matrimonial Proceedings (Magistrates' Courts) Act 1960 attempted to rationalise and modernise the law in the light of the recommendations of the Morton Commission on Marriage and Divorce (1956) and of the Arthian Davies Committee (1959). The major advance was that the Act made relief generally available to husbands as well as wives (though the husband had to prove impairment of earning capacity to obtain a money order) and gave power to make orders providing for the custody and support of children, even when the wife (or husband) failed to prove her (or his) ground of complaint.

11. Over the years Parliament has raised the limits of financial relief that the magistrates can order (there has never been a limit on the powers of the divorce court in this respect). An upper limit of £2 for a wife was fixed by the 1895 Act and of 10s for a child by the 1920 Act. These limits persisted until 1949, when the Married Women (Maintenance) Act substituted £5 as the wife's maximum weekly maintenance and 30s as the child's. The 1960 Act raised the limits to £7 10s a week for the spouse and to £2 10s for a child. Finally, the Maintenance Orders Act 1968, on the recommendation of the Departmental Committee on Statutory Maintenance Limits, abolished the upper limit for the maintenance of both spouse and child.

The Finer Committee on One-Parent Families (1974) suggested that the Law Commission was guilty of a 'seriously mistaken interpretation of history' in asserting that the magistrates' jurisdiction was designed to deal with situations where matrimonial breakdown had occurred but was not irretrievable. The view of the *Finer Report* is as follows:

36. The creation, . . . of a matrimonial jurisdiction to be exercised in the magistrates' courts was to have a profound and lasting effect on the arrangements, both substantive and procedural, which English law makes for regulating the consequences of matrimonial breakdown. All of the following characteristics were implanted into this part of our legal system. First, two separate jurisdictions, High Court and summary, existing side by side, but administering different and overlapping rules and remedies, came into being for the purpose of dealing with the same human predicament. Secondly, while the reforms of 1857 were designed to remove matrimonial disputes to the arbitrament of a superior and civil court of record, the jurisdiction created in 1878 was vested in inferior tribunals, given over to the criminal process, and universally known, because of their close association with the police, as 'police courts.' Thirdly, whereas the 1857 reformers regarded legal intervention into matrimony, maintenance and the custody of children as so delicate and important that the jurisdiction had to be entrusted to professional judges of the highest rank, the 1878 jurisdiction was to be exercised by a magistracy overwhelmingly lay in its composition. Finally, the concern for extending to a larger population the benefits which the 1857 reforms had afforded to the wealthy bore fruit in the creation of a secondary system designed for what were considered to be the special and cruder requirements of the poor.

The different treatment of the history led the two bodies to formulate different principles upon which the law and procedure should be based. The Law Commission's *Working Paper* suggested:

24. There is a clear contrast between the magistrates' jurisdiction and that exercised by the divorce court under the 1969 and 1970 Acts. The magistrates' jurisdiction is normally exercised at a stage earlier than irretrievable breakdown and is not concerned with change of status. Indeed, the marriage may only temporarily have run into difficulties. There is evidence that many orders made by the magistrates come to an end because the parties are reconciled. The role of the magistrates' court in dealing with those involved in matrimonial breakdown may perhaps be illustrated by comparing it with a casualty clearing station. All the casualties of marriage can be brought to the magistrates' court. Some are clearly mortal; they should go on to be laid to rest by proceedings in the divorce court; some are serious, being more likely than not to end in final breakdown; some however will respond to local treatment and may well recover completely; others are trivial, requiring no more than sympathetic handling and encouragement. It is the duty of those who work in a casualty clearing station to give attention and interim or substantive treatment to all, to do nothing which might turn a minor case into a major one, and to refrain from attempting to treat those whom they have not the competence or equipment to treat. So too the magistrates in their matrimonial jurisdictions. They must look to the possibility that no more may be needed than sympathy and the opportunity for reconciliation. But they must also have the means of treating the more serious casualties of marriage. Turning away from the language of metaphor, we suggest therefore that the role of the magistrates — the principle and objectives of their matrimonial jurisdiction — should be to enable them to intervene on the application of either party to a marriage:
(i)   to deal with family relations during a period of breakdown which is not necessarily permanent or irretrievable
      (*a*) by relieving the financial need which breakdown can bring to the parties,
      (*b*) by giving such protection to one or other of the parties as may be necessary, and
      (*c*) by providing for the welfare and support of the children; and
(ii) to preserve the marriage in existence, where possible.

The *Finer Report* refuted the 'casualty clearing station' approach:

4.383 We think the working party has allowed itself to be misled concerning the actual role of magistrates' courts in matrimonial breakdown by the attractions of a medico-military analogy. We have assembled compelling evidence to demonstrate that the very existence and persistence of the dual jurisdiction, and of the attitudes and institutions stemming from it, account for the presence in magistrates' courts of many very poor folk who possess neither knowledge nor expectation of any other legal cure for their marital ills. Nor is the analogy compelling when we find that two thirds of the casualties on the books in January 1966 were to be found there in July 1971, that nearly half of the discharges during this period had been patients for ten years or more at the time of their discharge, and that on 1 July 1971 there were some 58,000 magistrates' orders in force which were ten years old, or older. We doubt whether many clearing stations would find this a satisfactory work record.

The *Finer Report* argued strongly that the matrimonial jurisdiction of the magistrates' court used, as it is, by only one section of the community, serves to highlight the social divisions within the community. We discuss the argument advanced in favour of a family court in Chapter 17, below. The Finer Report is quite clear that 'a more general use of the magistrates' courts by all classes of the community' would be unrealistic. The thrust of the Report is contained in the following passage:

4.67 However, the most important feature of the contrast between the two systems is that they expose and give encouragement and effect to inconsistent public policies. The public policy of the latter part of the twentieth century is to promote the welfare of individuals and enhance respect for the law by disposing of dead marriages with decency and dignity, and a minimum of bitterness, distress and humiliation, and to do so in a manner that will encourage harmonious relations between the parties and their children in the future. This policy has been accepted by Church and State, has been legislated into the divorce law, and is implemented in the superior system of courts of law. The public policy of the latter part of the nineteenth century was to provide police court protection for the lower orders in their matrimonial troubles, and this, . . ., remains at the heart and sets the tone of the summary jurisdiction. There is evidence to suggest that one half of the complainants who obtain matrimonial orders in the summary courts never proceed to a divorce, but remain in a matrimonial limbo in which they are single in reality but married in law. In the five years 1968–1972 the number of matrimonial orders made by the magistrates averaged some 22,000 a year. On this footing, the summary jurisdiction embalms 11,000 dead marriages every year. But it could reasonably be held that the number of applications to the magistrates provides a more realistic measure of the number of collapsed marriages in this category than does the number of orders. Many women are refused orders because they have committed a matrimonial offence, even though their husbands have deserted them and no longer give them financial support (and, besides, may well themselves be guilty of a matrimonial offence at least as serious). On this view, the 11,000 cases above mentioned will be nearer 16,000 a year. It is notorious that a high proportion of the husbands and a lower proportion of the wives in this situation set up illicit unions and have illegitimate children.

4.68 We conclude that not merely do the two matrimonial jurisdictions co-exist as formerly, but one of them is founded on principles which have been rejected by the other. Even in the act of reforming itself, English matrimonial law has so far failed to escape from its habit of dispensing two brands of matrimonial justice, whose antinomy is now stronger than ever before.

Question

Now that the law applied by the magistrates' courts has been reformed along the lines advanced by the Law Commission in their report and working paper (see p. 94, below), is there much force left in the Finer Report's criticism?

The Law Commission's *Report* commented on the division of opinion between the working paper and the Finer Report in the following way:

1.12 We accept that there is evidence to show that very many of the casualties of marriage breakdown, once they have obtained a matrimonial order from the magistrates, do not seek any more permanent cure for their marital ills. Where reconciliation takes place, no further cure is required. Where there is no reconciliation, it is important that the parties should be aware of the availability of divorce and of legal aid to help them in divorcing. Effective arrangements are required to ensure that advice on such matters is readily available, but, provided it is, we think it realistic to expect that the function of the magistrates' courts in a dual system will to an increasing extent be that envisaged in our working paper. The reforms which we recommend in our present report will, we hope, contribute to the efficiency with which that function is performed.

Question

Do you think that this comment deals adequately with the points made by the Finer Report?

Under the 1960 Act, in order to obtain a matrimonial order in the magistrates' court, the applicant had to prove that the respondent had committed a matrimonial offence. The *Working Paper* fully accepted that the time had come for the obligation of each spouse to maintain the other to be recognised as the cornerstone to the new grounds. The obligation of support should be seen to be fully reciprocal. Given this general principle the *Working Paper* went on to consider the possible new grounds:

35. If the obligation to maintain were to be recognised in the general matrimonial law as fully reciprocal, in what circumstances should magistrates have power to order maintenance and what facts should they take into account in doing so? For the purpose of discussion we tentatively put forward the proposition that the principal ground upon which a court should have power to order maintenance should be failure by one of the parties to the marriage to provide such maintenance for the other party or for any children as is reasonable in all the circumstances. We recognise that such a formulation, which relies upon the concept of 'reasonable in all the circumstances', leaves a very wide discretion to the court. But we think this is a good starting point, particularly for the lay magistracy.

Questions

(i) Do you think it a good idea for the lay magistracy to have such a wide discretion?

(ii) Do you think it a good idea for anyone to have such a wide discretion?

The *Working Paper* continued:

37. If failure to provide reasonable maintenance were the principal ground on which magistrates could order maintenance, what additional grounds will be necessary? The existing law can be thought of as providing a remedy for two other basic situations:

　　(*a*) that where the parties are living together, the husband is supporting the wife but his conduct is intolerable and she wishes to leave him; and

　　(*b*) that where the parties are living apart but the husband is financially supporting the wife.

38. To take situation (*a*) first, at common law, as we have noted, two of the obligations of marriage are upon the husband to maintain the wife and upon each party to cohabit with the other. It is impossible, in our view, to formulate the policy relating to the enforceability of the obligation to maintain, whilst the marriage subsists, without having regard to the existence of the obligation to cohabit. To what extent then should the obligations to cohabit and maintain be regarded as separable, to what extent are they interlinked? To put the question in more practical terms, should the courts be able to intervene upon the application of either spouse if co-habitation has become intolerable, regardless of whether financial support for the applicant or members of the family has ceased? . . .

39. . . . The situation is not uncommon where a wife is compelled by necessity to continue to live with her husband even though his behaviour is such that she should not be expected to do so. He may be violent, dissolute or immoral. Unless the law allows the wife a remedy on some ground other than that her husband is not maintaining her, she will not be able to obtain the court's assistance to relieve her from her predicament by giving her some sort of financial independence. We think it right therefore that there should continue to be available a ground which will enable a wife in this position to escape from her husband and obtain financial relief if she needs it. We suggest this ground should be that the husband has behaved in such a way that the wife cannot reasonably be expected to live with him [see pp. 159–161, below. In *Bergin v Bergin* [1983] 1 WLR 279, the Family Division held that the justices must apply the same approach as that adopted by the Divorce Court under s. 1(2)(*b*) of the Matrimonial Causes Act 1973.] If such a ground were provided, it would follow that the principal defence available to a husband would be that he has not behaved in such a way. It would not be a complete answer to a wife's claim for maintenance on this ground that he was in fact maintaining her or that he had a home available for her which she was unwilling to share.

40. The question arises whether such a provision should be fully reciprocal. In other words, should a husband whose wife is violent, dissolute or immoral also be able to apply for an order? We have proposed . . . that the time has come when the law should recognise the duty of each spouse to support the other, leaving it to the court to determine in particular cases against whom an order should be made and for how much. It would follow that, if the law were to allow the wife a remedy on some ground other than that her husband is not maintaining her, such a remedy ought also to be available to her husband. In the vast majority of cases, the husband will be the principal wage-earner, and no question will arise of his needing to be maintained by his wife. Clearly, where the husband is able to maintain himself, he will have little to gain by approaching a magistrates' court for an order terminating his obligation to cohabit with his wife. But cases may arise from time to time in which the husband, for one reason or another, is unable to maintain himself. He may be temporarily unemployed or sick; he may be old and infirm; he may suffer from some mental or physical disability.[2] We therefore put forward for discussion the proposition that, in addition to the general maintenance ground we have suggested, it should be open to either party to a marriage (whether the parties are still living together or one of them has been driven to leave) to apply for a maintenance order on the ground that the respondent has behaved in such a way that the applicant cannot reasonably be expected to live with the respondent. . . .

42. We now turn to situation (*b*). If the parties have ceased to cohabit, it will often happen that a deserting husband will continue to maintain his wife. If he does not, then the failure to maintain

---

2. Or the parties may simply have arranged their lives in such a way that the wife is bread-winner?

ground is available to the wife; but if he does, on what ground could intervention by the courts be justified? Should the courts be able to intervene solely on the ground that the respondent refuses to live with the applicant, or, put in terms of the existing law, should desertion continue to be a ground for an order? One ground for intervention, we suggest, might be as a protection against the future. The wife in these circumstances might be thought to be justified in wanting an order as security against her husband's future failure to maintain her. We wonder, however, whether the effect of enabling the courts to intervene in this situation might not be simply to encourage unnecessary litigation. If there is genuine need for relief, for example because maintenance (though substantial) is irregularly paid, the court should be able to intervene on the ground that the husband is not maintaining, i.e. not providing reasonable maintenance. The same arguments apply a fortiori where there are any children of the marriage. Another possible justification for the court's intervention is that desertion can be difficult to prove and, as it remains a ground for establishing irretrievable breakdown and thus obtaining a divorce, it should be possible for the applicant to prove desertion as soon as it begins. But this alone may not be an adequate ground for an exercise of the magistrates' matrimonial law. The primary purpose of the existing desertion ground provided by section 1 of the 1960 Act is not to provide evidence for a later divorce, but to enable a deserted wife to obtain a maintenance order against her husband either to cover her immediate needs or as a safeguard for the future.

43. Nevertheless, our own inclination would be to preserve the existing position. We therefore provisionally propose that there should be a third ground on which it should be possible to apply to the court for an order: namely, that the respondent is in desertion. We should welcome views on this question.

Questions

(i) What arguments can you present against the retention of desertion as a ground?

(ii) Why is adultery not included?

(iii) Section 7(1) of the Domestic Proceedings and Magistrates' Courts Act 1978 states: 'Where the parties to a marriage have been living apart for a continuous period exceeding three months, neither party having deserted the other, and one of the parties has been making periodical payments for the benefit of the other party or of a child of the family, that other party may apply to a magistrates' court for an order under this section, and any application made under this subsection shall specify the aggregate amount of the payments so made during the period of three months immediately preceding the date of the making of the application.' In view of this, is there any reason to retain desertion as a ground?

The Working Paper stimulated a large number of comments. Some are reported by the Law Commission in their *Report* (1976):

2.8 The Working Party's analysis of the principles and objectives underlying the summary matrimonial jurisdiction was generally approved in the consultation — though some of those who commented had misgivings about the principle of equality as between husband and wife in the obligation to maintain. Opinions were, however, divided when it came to the three grounds of application for a matrimonial order proposed in substitution for the existing provisions in section 1 of the 1960 Act. The first two grounds, failure to provide reasonable maintenance and unreasonable behaviour, gave rise to little controversy. The Bar Council, however, thought that it would be sufficient to provide for an 'application for reasonable maintenance' without specifying the grounds on which the application might be made, and that if a ground of application was to be specified it should be limited to a failure to provide reasonable maintenance. Our own view is that it is right to give some guidance to the court by specifying the grounds on which an application may be made. We agree with the majority of those who commented on the working paper that both failure to provide reasonable maintenance and unreasonable behaviour should be grounds so specified.

2.9 On whether desertion should be retained as a separate ground opinion was more or less evenly divided. Those commentators who were opposed to the retention of desertion as a ground advanced a variety of reasons for their views. Some argued that desertion was simply a specific form of unreasonable behaviour, which, like adultery, would already be covered by the general ground. Others contended that desertion was a highly technical offence, difficult to prove and thus not appropriate to the magistrates' matrimonial jurisdiction.

2.10 Other commentators argued that the effect of including desertion as a ground would be to encourage applicants to institute proceedings to safeguard them against possible future failures to maintain. As for the argument that, since desertion remains a ground for establishing irretrievable breakdown and thus obtaining a divorce, it should be possible for the applicant to prove desertion as soon as it begins, it was asserted that magistrates' courts should not be used as a stepping stone to the divorce court since this would not be conducive to a conciliatory atmosphere.

2.11 We can see the force in all these arguments. We think, however, that the balance of advantage lies in retaining in the magistrates' matrimonial jurisdiction some means by which a wife who has been deserted can obtain a maintenance order soon after the desertion, whether or not her husband has ceased to maintain her. We do not think that a deserted wife for whom her husband is providing reasonable maintenance should be required to wait until that maintenance has ceased before making her application. We have therefore concluded that desertion should remain as a separate ground for a maintenance order.

2.12 We entertain no doubt whatever that the reformulated law should embody the general principle that each spouse has a duty to support the other. We think that the grounds on which each spouse may apply for an order against the other for maintenance during marriage should be identical, and that the guidelines to which the court is to have regard should be the same whether the application is made by the husband or the wife. It should then be for the court to determine whether an order should be made, and if so for how much, in the light of the particular circumstances of the case.

Questions

(i) What *is* the difference between wilful neglect to maintain and failure to provide reasonable maintenance?

(ii) Does the Law Commission answer the views of those such as the Bar Council who were unhappy about the retention of the 'conduct' grounds?

(iii) If so, is it a satisfactory answer?

(iv) Is desertion 'unreasonable behaviour'? (See further in Chapter 5, below)?

(v) Do you think that the acceptance of the general principle that *each* spouse has a duty to support the other advances the status of women?

On the relevance of a wife's adultery to her claim to support, the Law Commission reported that:

2.15 The Working Party considered at length the question whether, and if so to what extent, the courts, when considering the making of a maintenance order on one of the three grounds proposed in the working paper, should have regard to the conduct of the respective parties to the marriage. They concluded that, as regards adultery, it was not desirable and no longer acceptable to public opinion that the commission by the wife of a single act of adultery should be regarded as sufficient to disqualify her automatically from all financial relief. They could see no justification nowadays for a court's being bound to refuse to make a maintenance order in favour of an otherwise deserving wife because she has committed adultery; the more so since adultery is not a bar to an award of maintenance in divorce proceedings. . . .

These proposals were welcomed by all who commented on the working paper and we concur in them.

Question

Write a brief on behalf of an invented society — the Society for the Preservation of Standards in Marriage — designed to oppose the views of the Law Commission and the subsequent law.

On the role of conduct generally, the Law Commission continued:

2.17 On the wider question of what weight the courts should be enabled to give to the conduct of the parties, including adultery committed by either party, in deciding whether to make a maintenance order and, if so, for how much, the Working Party reached no firm conclusions. They noted, however, that so far as the divorce jurisdiction was concerned, these questions had been the subject of detailed examination by the Court of Appeal, which, in *Wachtel v Wachtel* [1973] Fam 72, [1973] 1 All ER 829 had been asked to determine, for the first time, after full argument, the principles that should be applied in the Family Division when granting ancillary relief following dissolution of a marriage.

This case is considered at p. 196, below. The Working Paper thought it relevant to consider how far the principles laid down by the Court of Appeal could be made to operate in the magistrates' matrimonial jurisdiction. The Law Commission invited comments in the *Working Paper* on four possible approaches:

(*a*) the obligation to maintain should be regarded as absolute and reciprocal and, thus, matrimonial conduct should not be taken into account in determining liability or quantum; or

(*b*) the conduct should be relevant in every case as regards liability, but should not be taken into account in determining the amount of an order; or

(*c*) conduct should be relevant, both as regards liability and quantum; or

(*d*) conduct should be relevant in every case, both as regards liability and quantum, but if the court decides to make an order, it should not reduce the amount it would have ordered below a sum sufficient to provide the applicant with the basic necessities of life.

The results of consultation

2.19 The general tenor of the consultation was to favour approach (*c*) (conduct should be relevant to both liability and quantum) though approach (*b*) (conduct should be relevant only to liability) also attracted considerable support. Approach (*a*) (conduct should be wholly irrelevant) was, in general, thought to be objectionable for the reason given in the working paper, namely, that it involves acceptance of the principle that a husband should always be required to maintain a wife who has misconducted herself, and should be required to do so however serious her misconduct may have been. It was generally agreed that such a principle would be inconsistent with accepted standards of morality and would not commend itself to public opinion. Approach (*d*) (conduct should be relevant to liability and quantum but should not reduce the amount below a sum sufficient to provide the basic necessities of life) attracted a little more support than approach (*a*).

2.20 The main area of disagreement amongst those commenting on the working paper centred on the question whether the magistrates should be able not only to refuse to make an order but also in appropriate cases to reduce the amount of maintenance they ordered by reason of the applicant's conduct. As noted above, the majority of commentators favoured approach (*c*) (conduct should be relevant to liability and quantum). The main reason given for preferring this approach was that it would offend the sense of justice of magistrates and litigants alike if the court's hands were tied in this matter, particularly having regard to the fact that it was futile to make a maintenance order which the husband considered unfair, since he might well prefer to go to prison rather than pay. It was recognised, however, that an approach which left the magistrates free by reason of any conduct which was not 'obvious and gross' to reduce the amount which they would otherwise have ordered would, to some extent, be at variance with the principles enunciated in *Wachtel v Wachtel*.

The Law Commission accepted approach (*c*). Thus,

[In] determining whether and if so how to exercise its powers to order financial provision the court should, to the extent to which it is just to do so, have regard to the conduct of the parties. Conduct may therefore, in a proper case, be relevant both to liability and to quantum. It seems to us that that principle, established as it has been by Parliament, must be accepted as equally applicable to cases where a magistrates' court is considering whether one party to a marriage should be ordered to make financial provision for the other while the marriage is still subsisting, and if so what provision should be ordered. We therefore think that in deciding whether to order such financial provision, and if so what provision to order, a magistrates' court should be required by statute to have regard to the conduct of the parties to the marriage to the extent to which it is just to do so. We further think that it should be made clear that the conduct to which the court is to have regard is limited to conduct which has relevance to the marriage.

Questions

(i) Do you think the Law Commission was right to propose principles based on the divorce jurisdiction?

(ii) What is conduct which has no relevance to the marriage? Is theft, or rape of a young girl, or shoplifting, conduct of that kind?

(iii) Does the acceptance of proposal (c) mean that conduct is or is not relevant to the question of whether the husband has failed to provide reasonable maintenance for the wife?

When considering factors other than conduct which courts should take into account in determining whether or not to make an order, and if so for what amount, the Working Party had recommended that the court should have regard to

> (a) the income, earning capacity, property and other financial resources of each of the parties; and
> (b) the financial needs, obligations and responsibilities of each of the parties.

The Law Commission's *Report* took the view that these two sets of factors were not adequate. They felt that the right course was to reproduce as far as possible the guidelines contained in s. 25 of the Matrimonial Causes Act 1973 (as to which see p. 195, below).

All these recommendations were implemented in the *Domestic Proceedings and Magistrates' Courts Act 1978*:

1. Either party to a marriage may apply to a magistrates' court for an order under section 2 of this Act on the ground that the other party to the marriage (in this Part of this Act referred to as 'the respondent') —

> (a) has failed to provide reasonable maintenance for the applicant; or
> (b) has failed to provide, or to make a proper contribution towards, reasonable maintenance for any child of the family; or
> (c) has behaved in such a way that the applicant cannot reasonably be expected to live with the respondent; or
> (d) has deserted the applicant.

2.—(1) Where on an application for an order under this section the applicant satisfies the court of any ground mentioned in section 1 of this Act, the court may, subject to the provisions of this Part of this Act, make any one or more of the following orders, that is to say —

> (a) an order that the respondent shall make to the applicant such periodical payments, and for such term, as may be specified in the order;
> (b) an order that the respondent shall pay to the applicant such lump sum as may be so specified;
> (c) an order that the respondent shall make to the applicant for the benefit of a child of the family to whom the application relates, or to such a child, such periodical payments, and for such term, as may be so specified;
> (d) an order that the respondent shall pay to the applicant for the benefit of a child of the family to whom the application relates, or to such a child, such lump sum as may be so specified.

(2) Without prejudice to the generality of subsection (1)(b) or (d) above, an order under this section for the payment of a lump sum may be made for the purpose of enabling any liability or expenses reasonably incurred in maintaining the applicant, or any child of the family to whom the application relates, before the making of the order to be met.

(3) The amount of any lump sum required to be paid by an order under this section shall not exceed £500 or such larger amount as the Secretary of State may from time to time by order fix for the purposes of this subsection. . . .

3.—(1) Where an application is made for an order under section 2 of this Act, the court, in deciding whether to exercise its powers under subsection (1)(*a*) or (*b*) of that section and, if so, in what manner, shall have regard to the following matters, that is to say —

    (*a*) the income, earning capacity, property and other financial resources which each of the parties to the marriage has or is likely to have in the foreseeable future;

    (*b*) the financial needs, obligations and responsibilities which each of the parties to the marriage has or is likely to have in the foreseeable future;

    (*c*) the standard of living enjoyed by the parties to the marriage before the occurrence of the conduct which is alleged as the ground of the application;

    (*d*) the age of each party to the marriage and the duration of the marriage;

    (*e*) any physical or mental disability of either of the parties to the marriage;

    (*f*) the contributions made by each of the parties to the welfare of the family, including any contribution made by looking after the home or caring for the family;

    (*g*) any other matter which in the circumstances of the case the court may consider relevant, including, so far as it is just to take it into account, the conduct of each of the parties in relation to the marriage.

Questions

(i) Since this Act has been passed, is there any thing left of the husband's common law duty to maintain?

(ii) Is an earning wife under any duty to provide housekeeping money (*a*) to a non-earning husband or (*b*) to an earning husband?

A recent case on the meaning of the Act is the following:

Robinson v Robinson
[1983] 2 WLR 146, Court of Appeal

The parties were married in 1976. The husband was a soldier and the wife ceased her employment after she married him. They lived in married quarters. In late 1980, the husband was posted to Belize, and the wife returned to her parents. When the husband returned from overseas duty in March 1981, the wife decided that she was not going back to him, although she did not tell him of her decision until August 1981. The wife applied for maintenance under s. 2 of the Domestic Proceedings and Magistrates' Courts Act 1978. The magistrates' found that the wife had deserted her husband and that this behaviour was 'gross and obvious'. The magistrates' court said 'the wife's desertion of her husband, he not having committed any misconduct, was a matter of the gravest importance in relation to this marriage and was a matter to be taken into account together with all the other matters set out in section 3 of the 1978 Act when deciding what financial provision order, if any, should be made in favour of the applicant.' The magistrates' court awarded her periodical payments of £15 per week, one-tenth of the joint income, for a period of five years from the date of the order. The wife appealed unsuccessfully to the Divisional Court and on further appeal to the Court of Appeal.

Waller LJ: The magistrates held that (the conduct of the wife) was 'gross and obvious miscon-duct' and in so doing were referring to the test applied by Lord Denning MR and Ormrod J (in *Wachtel v Wachtel* [1973] Fam 72, [1973] 1 All ER 827. The words 'gross and obvious miscon-duct' can be somewhat misleading, but as I understand it they were referring to the fact that this was an unusual case far removed from those where much blame could be put on both sides and it was a case where it would have been unjust to give the financial support which would normally be given. In answer to the question would it offend a reasonable man's sense of justice that this wife's conduct should be left out of account in deciding the financial provision which the husband should make, the magistrates were answering 'Yes it would' when they said: 'The wife's desertion of her husband, he not having committed any misconduct was a matter of the gravest importance in relation to the marriage . . .'. On the facts found the behaviour of the wife was quite capable of being within the terms I have outlined above. In my opinion it is quite impossible to interfere with the decision of the magistrates.

Slade LJ: . . . Section 3(1)(g) of the Domestic Proceedings and Magistrates' Courts Act 1978 by its terms expressly empowers and indeed obliges the court on an application for maintenance, such as that of the wife in the present case, to have regard to the conduct of each of the parties in relation to the marriage 'so far as it is just to take into account.'

If one were to disregard the line of authority beginning with *Wachtel v Wachtel* [1973] Fam 72, [1973] 1 All ER 829, I would have thought it difficult even to argue that the magistrates in the present case were clearly wrong in regarding it as 'just' to take into account the wife's conduct and having done so, substantially to reduce the amount of maintenance which they would other-wise have awarded to her. Among their primary findings of fact were findings that (i) the wife formed an intention to desert the husband in March 1981; (ii) her complaints about his conduct prior to that date were trivial and they were not the reason for, nor did they contribute to, her withdrawal from cohabitation; (iii) the disputes after April 1981 were caused by tension between the parties for which the prime reason was the wife's already formed intention to withdraw from cohabitation; (iv) the husband had not committed any misconduct.

Since the passing of the Act of 1978, it is plain that even a wife who has deserted her husband without just cause is still entitled to apply for maintenance under that Act. Nevertheless, on the basis of these facts as found by the magistrates, it was obviously a tenable view, which they in fact held, that justice required that the husband, who has been compelled to start a new life on his own through no fault or wish of his, should not have to pay as much maintenance to the wife as he would have had to pay her if misconduct on his part had been responsible for the break-up of the marriage.

. . . I do not think it can be said that the magistrates, . . . misdirected themselves on any point of principle. Nor, after considering all the facts of the case as found by them, am I satisfied that the exercise of their discretion was for any other reason clearly wrong.

Question

Could the husband in this case have been able to petition immediately and successfully for a divorce? (See p. 161, below.)

The Judicial Statistics for matrimonial and other civil proceedings in magistrates' courts suggest a dramatic drop in applications for 'married women maintenance orders' — from 28,004 in 1968 to 6851 in 1978. However, these figures do not correspond with the Law Society's statistics for legal aid certificates granted to complainants in magistrates' matrimonial cases, and it is thought that the latter will be the more reliable guide:

1969–70	39,214
1970–71	41,032
1971–72	43,175
1972–73	39,875
1973–74	36,782
1974–75	33,460
1975–76	31,903
1976–77	28,421
1977–78	25,719
1978–79	21,238
1979–80	21,809

[Source: Legal Aid Annual Reports]

Question

Which of the following do you consider the most likely explanation for the fall: (*a*) the reform of the law of divorce which came into force in 1971; (*b*) a fall in the number of married women needing support from their husbands; (*c*) the decision of the supplementary benefits authorities, following the

Finer Report (1974), no longer to advise married women who claimed benefit to take action against their husbands; or (*d*) some other reason or combination of reasons?

It is also possible for a spouse to apply to a divorce court for financial provision under s. 27 of the Matrimonial Causes Act 1973, on the ground of failure to provide reasonable maintenance for the applicant or a child of the family. The court may then award secured or unsecured periodical payments, and/or a lump sum of unlimited amount. Divorce courts have none of the unpleasant 'police court' connotations of the magistrates' jurisdiction, to which the Finer Committee took such strong exception, yet only 347 applications under s. 27 were made in 1980.

Questions

(i) Which of the following do you consider the most likely explanation for the rarity of applications: (*a*) that most would prefer to seek a divorce or judicial separation (see Chapter 5, below) instead; (*b*) that the legal aid fund would require a good reason for resorting to this remedy while a cheaper equivalent existed in the magistrates' court; or (*c*) some other reason?
(ii) Would it seem preferable to have all these remedies in the divorce court? (This question is discussed further in Chapter 17, below.)
(iii) Do the figures on maintenance applications support the views of the Law Commission or of the Finer Committee (see p. 86, above)?

8 Why not abolish maintenance during marriage?

This is a sub-heading in an article by Kathleen O'Donovan (1982). In this, she discusses the issues arising out of proposals to limit the continuing obligation to support a divorced wife (which are the subject matter of Chapter 7, below). She argues that in order to abandon the principle of maintenance for a former spouse, certain necessary material conditions must be present in society: namely, equality of partners in marriage, including financial equality; equal participation by both partners in wage earning activities; wages geared to persons as individuals and not as heads of families; treatment of persons as individuals and not as dependants by state agencies; and finally, provision for children by both parents, including financial support, child care, love, attention and stimulation. She develops her argument by saying that if these necessary material conditions for abolishing spousal maintenance on divorce are realised, then logically there should be a similar abolition within marriage: 'Each spouse in the ideal society would be an independent, economically self-sufficient, entity protected by the social security net in case of need. Consequently there would be no necessity for spousal financial support. The 'fundamentally repulsive' idea of dependent women would vanish.'

Eric Clive in *Marriage: An Unnecessary Legal Concept* (1980), is not prepared to wait for the coming of the ideal society:

It can be argued that real liberty and real equality require that wives be given maintenance and property rights against their husbands and that there are very good reasons for not extending these rights to unmarried cohabitees. The classical form of this argument is that husbands earn money and accumulate property while their wives do unpaid work looking after the home and the children. Therefore justice requires that the wives be given maintenance rights and claims against the husbands' income and property, at least on the breakdown of the marriage. There is obviously something suspect about this argument. It is a bit like saying that the remedy for slavery is to give the slaves rights to maintenance and rights to share in the master's property if he dies or goes out of business. . . . I am concerned only to point out that, while few family lawyers with any claims to liberal or egalitarian views would argue that a wife's domicile should automatically follow her husband's or that a wife should owe a duty of obedience to her husband, there are plenty who argue that a wife should have generous maintenance rights, succession rights and matrimonial property rights. We are obviously in a more difficult area here.

In a very theoretical sense, of course, marriage is obviously not a necessary legal concept in relation to finance and property. The state could base a private law right to maintenance on factual criteria such as the existence of dependent children or the length of dependent cohabitation or, more radically, it could provide a guaranteed maintenance allowance for all citizens who are not self-supporting, thus removing the need for any private law right of maintenance. It could decline to provide for any financial adjustment on divorce or could provide a form of adjustment equally appropriate to cases of cohabitation without marriage. It could ignore marriage completely in relation to the ownership and management of property during life, and could give succession rights, in so far as it resisted the temptation to confiscate for the common good, only to those who were factually, rather than legally, in a close relationship to the deceased. All these things would be legislatively possible, but it would be unsatisfactory to stop at this theoretical level. What has to be asked is whether the abolition of the legal concept of marriage would lead to such undesirable consequences in relation to finance and property as to be a practical impossibility.

The obligation of maintenance or support is often regarded as one of the fundamental effects of marriage. Its abolition would be viewed by many people with horror. Yet several factors have to be borne in mind in considering this question. First, most couples support each other willingly and gladly so long as their relationship continues. They would continue to do so if legal obligations based on marriage were removed. Second, maintenance claims are notoriously difficult to enforce once the relationship has broken down. Third, there is a close relationship between private maintenance and social security. It has been shown, for example, that in the United Kingdom most separated spouses are better off on supplementary benefit than on maintenance awarded by the courts. Fourth, there is a close relationship between private maintenance and patterns of employment. If both sexes have genuinely equal employment opportunities and if there are generous child minding allowances for the years devoted to bringing up dependent children, there is at the very least a much diminished need for a private law of maintenance. Fifth, there is an interesting relationship between private maintenance and tax policy. Let us assume that from the point of view of society it does not matter which set of dependants a wage earner supports so long as he or she takes a share in the cost of bringing up the next generation. If this is so, then the obvious way of dealing with those who do not share this burden is to tax them heavily. If a man walks out on his wife and young children and does not acquire a new family it may make more sense to extract his share of the social cost of dependency by taxation than by trying to recover maintenance specifically for his abandoned family. There would certainly be much less moral indignation about men 'getting off with it' by walking out on their dependants if they were walking into the rapacious arms of the tax collector. . . . In the light of these observations let us consider what would actually happen if the private law obligation of maintenance between spouses were abolished. . . . First of all, millions of happily married couples would continue to support each other as at present. Second, the many thousands of separated spouses who rely exclusively or mainly on supplementary benefit would continue to do so. Third, the many thousands of separated spouses who support themselves by working would continue to do so. Fourth, those in receipt of maintenance for children would continue to receive it. That would leave a comparatively small proportion of spouses (in practice almost entirely wives) worse off because they would no longer have a claim for maintenance. In the case of those without dependent children who had not lost anything by the marriage there would be no good reason for conferring a right to claim maintenance. In the case of those with dependent children or those who were otherwise in a worse position as a result of the marriage there would be a good reason for conferring a right to some sort of maintenance or financial provision *but the reason would be equally applicable to cohabitees in a similar position*. In short, the abolition of maintenance obligations between spouses would not be an unthinkable or undesirable proposition, (even if we accept the dependent position of many women in present circumstances), if maintenance or financial provision were awarded on the basis of dependent children and loss suffered as a result of cohabitation. And this would, to my mind, be a sensible basis. It would be unjustifiable to extend to cohabitees rights to maintenance and financial provision based on the idea of voluntary assumption of liability. Often this would be lacking. It would be perfectly justifiable to give them rights (unless they expressly contracted out) based on child-related dependency and other losses resulting from the relationship.

Questions

(i) Do you think that there is the political will to bring about O'Donovan's ideal society?

(ii) Would the proposal to abolish the reciprocal (in theory) duty of maintenance during marriage be supported: (*a*) by feminist groups, (*b*) by the Church of England, (*c*) by the CBI, or (*d*) by the TUC?

(iii) Does the sociological evidence presented earlier in this chapter support Clive's suggestion that most spouses support one another willingly?

CHAPTER 4

Matrimonial property

In the last chapter we concentrated on income. In this chapter, we turn our attention to a discussion of matrimonial property. For many families, until comparatively recently, only the former question had much relevance. However, there has always been a substantial group who have enjoyed the fortune of land, chattels, and stocks and shares. Rules have developed to regulate and administer this property during the marriage, and after the termination of the marriage by death. In contrast to the modern concern for what has been termed by the Finer Report as the 'pathology of the family', traditional property law has been concerned with a law 'which fortifies and regulates an institution central to society'. Property law is mainly about devolution rules within the kinship group.

In the last chapter, we also looked at the development of the consumer society, where families spend the money which is earned on food, shelter, clothes and luxuries. This economic shift has resulted in a need to apply matrimonial property law as traditionally conceived to new types of wealth. The 'new property' of the twentieth century is the property which can be earned and which is paid by employers in return for an individual's work, both as wages and as a deferred sum by way of a pension expectancy. Simultaneously with this change in the subject matter of property, there has been an expansion in the number of those who enjoy the new wealth. Major sections of the community now own luxury items and belong to pension schemes. Thus although matrimonial property law was developed in a different age by the land owners and the bourgoisie who in effect made their own laws by contracts, trusts, and wills, there has been a 'proletarisation' during the present century. The only restraint on this expansion is the ever present shadow of state involvement (interference?) through taxation, social security law, and death duties. These latter matters we shall return to in Chapter 16, below.

1 Historical background

The law which at present governs family property is based on the principle of separate property: 'each spouse may acquire and deal with his or her property as if he or she were single.' (Law Commission Working Paper on Family Property Law 1971.) But this was not always the case, as Sir Jocelyn Simon explains in *With all my Worldly Goods* (1964):

I invite you to accompany me to a village church where a wedding is in progress. The mellifluous cadences of the vicar's voice fall hypnotically on the ear — '. . . honourable estate . . . mutual society, help and comfort . . . comfort her, honour and keep her. . . .' Now he has reached the ceremony of the ring. The bridegroom bends a gaze of ineffable tenderness on his bride — '. . . with this ring . . . with my body . . . and with all my worldly goods I thee endow.' I hold my breath, aghast. Will the vicar rend his cassock? Will he sprinkle on his head ashes from the ancient coke stove? Will he hurl the bridegroom from the chancel steps with imprecation and anathema? For the man has committed the most horrible blasphemy. In that holy place, at this most solemn moment, actually invoking the names of the Deity, he has made a declaration which is utterly false. He is not endowing the bride with a penny, a stick, a clod. Nor does he intend ever to do so. And yet the service proceeds as if nothing untoward has happened. How does this come about?

The phrase originates in the ancient Use of Sarum, where it is almost unique in liturgy. It reflects a mediaeval custom, the endowment of the bride at the church door, dower *ad ostium ecclesiae* — itself a relic, I surmise, of a still more archaic usage, the payment of the brideprice negotiated between the families of bride and bridegroom.

Dower *ad ostium ecclesiae*, however, gave way to common law dower, where the law itself determined what interest the wife should have in her husband's property. That was a life estate after the death of her husband in one third of any land of which the husband had ever been solely seised at any time during the marriage for an estate of inheritance to which issue of the wife by the husband might possibly succeed.

But this was small compensation for the proprietary and personal rights that the wife lost at Common Law on her marriage.

In this country the feudal theory was, under the Norman kings, applied in all its rigour. The proper purpose of a tenement — and wealth at that time was largely to be measured in land — was the maintenance of a vassal in such a state that he could suitably perform his feudal services to his lord — not least military service. A married woman was considered to be generally incapable of performing the feudal services. Any freehold estate of which the wife was seised was therefore vested in the husband as well as the wife during coverture, and it was under his sole management and care. If there was any issue of the marriage born alive, the husband immediately gained an estate in the wife's freeholds corresponding to her dower in his lands, but extending to the whole estate, not merely to one third: this was significantly called the husband's estate by the courtesy of England. As soon as issue was born alive, he had therefore a life estate in his wife's land which he could charge to the full. Chattels being more evanescent than land, the Common Law took the simple course of letting the husband have them as his. Any goods, including money, in the wife's actual possession, came under his absolute ownership forthwith. Any property to which the wife might be entitled by bringing an action at law — her 'chose in action'; for example, any debt due to her — became the husband's if during coverture he recovered it or otherwise reduced it into possession. When leasehold interests began to be created, for the investment of money rather than for the enjoyment of land, the Common Law treated them largely as chattels: though they did not in theory become the husband's property, he might nevertheless sell them and take the proceeds as his own. During coverture the husband was entitled to the whole of the wife's income from any source, including her own earnings or the rent from her leasehold or freehold property. She could only bequeath her personal property with the consent of her husband; and such consent might be revoked by him at any time. On the wife dying intestate by virtue of this rule, all her personal property, including her leaseholds and her choses in action, passed to her husband. In such circumstances, it was a real triumph for 18th century self-satisfaction that Blackstone could write: 'Even the disabilities which the wife lies under are for the most part intended for her protection and benefit: so great a favourite is the female sex of the laws of England.' It could have been little less inconvenient to have been a favourite of Haroun-al-Raschid.

However, in mediaeval England, the wife did enjoy some limited rights. As Sir Jocelyn Simon says:

It is almost certain that in the 12th and 13th centuries our own law recognised, . . . a reserved portion of a man's chattels of which he might not dispose by will if he left wife or child. After payment of debts the estate was divided into 'wife's part', 'bairns' part', and 'dead's part' (the two former were also called 'the reasonable parts'). Only over the 'dead's part' was there freedom of disposition.

Why did they not lead the lawyers to adopt a system of Community of Goods similar to that of our continental neighbours? Why, indeed, did it not survive in England, as it has in Scotland to this day? I think there were two reasons. First, with the invention of the English system of heirship in land, the heir took the whole of the freehold estate, the widow only a life interest and only in a third. Furthermore, she did not automatically enter the land as of right at the death of her husband: she had to wait to be assigned her portion by the heir. In the field of devolution which remained firmly within the view of the common lawyers, the widow, therefore, looked like a pensioner of the heir rather than a partner of the ancestor.

Secondly, in the eyes of the mediaeval Church intestacy was almost a sin: the 'dead's part' must be suitably devoted to such pious uses (especially ecclesiastic benefaction) as would mitigate the transcendental pains and penalties which would otherwise be the reward for the deceased's terrestrial shortcomings. In order to make sure that nothing went wrong about this, the Church — in this country alone — secured jurisdiction over probate of wills. The common lawyers became intensely jealous. Moreover, the interference of the Church courts with morals made them highly unpopular with laymen too. Thus neither common lawyers nor laymen were in the least disposed to follow the Church courts or their law. So it came about that in Edward III's reign the Lords in Parliament expressly disapproved the custom of the 'reasonable part' of the personal estate reserved from disposition by will — it was an intolerable interference with freedom. Under such disapprobation the custom had died out in the province of Canterbury by the end of the 15th century. In the northern province it lasted until 1692, but was then abolished by Act of Parliament. The excuse was that a system of jointuring widows had been invented, and if they enjoyed both jointure and 'wife's part' there would be too little left for the younger children; so it was helpfully arranged that a testator could thenceforward leave his children with nothing at all.

It is well known that equity intervened. Simon puts it in the following way:

By the 17th century this state of things was no longer tolerable to wives of the upper class and their families. During the Middle Ages the influence of the Church and the cults of chivalry and courtly love had brought about a steady rise in the status of women. When in *The Way of the World* Millamant said, 'I may by degrees dwindle into a wife', she had plainly no intention of doing any such thing. But others besides the wife were interested in what happened to her property, not least her kinsfolk. They will wish to make suitable provision for her on her marriage, to ensure in particular that the children of the marriage, who will be their own blood relations, are properly advanced. But if there is no issue of the marriage the primary interest of the wife's kinsfolk is that the property which they have put into the marriage should return to them, rather than pass to the husband's family. This consideration was until quite modern times particularly potent among the ruling classes, where marriages were to be considered, at least partly, as political and economic alliances. But by the end of the Middle Ages a number of things had occurred which increased the relative value of personal as against real property, and thus eroded the interest of the kinsfolk as against that of the husband. First, the great contraction in population, which probably fell by one third during the 14th century, involved a considerable fall in the value of land to the upper classes: and 'in the long run the peasantry alone profited by the change from services in kind to services in money.' Secondly, as a result of the decline in the labour force, large portions of demesne land of manors which had previously been farmed directly by landowners were leased. As we have seen, leaseholds became classified as a species of chattel, so that the husband could sell them and pocket the proceeds, and would in any event take them on the death of the wife: only if the husband predeceased the wife without having sold them or given them away did she take them by survivorship so that they were capable of passing to her heirs. Thirdly, the rise of mercantilism to replace the largely agricultural society of the Middle Ages and the discovery of the wealth of the New World meant a further augmentation in the property which lay within the husband's field of claim as against that of the wife's kinsfolk — for example, the wife's choses in action, or her leasehold interests now treated as investments.

By this time, however, the Common Law was too far committed to the interest of the husband to be able to recognise the claims of the wife and her kinship group. It had lost the flexibility to provide new remedies for new needs as they arose. The Statute of Westminster II (1285) had restricted the Chancery's power of issuing new writs to cases similar to those covered by existing ones; and even these writs *in consimili casu* became stereotyped.

But if the Clerks in Chancery were powerless, the Chancellor himself was not. He was devising a system of Equity which would provide for the deficiencies of the Common Law. He could not — he did not attempt to — take its entrenched positions by direct assault; he would pivot on them and outflank them. His cherished weapon was the Trust. A woman about to enter matrimony, or her kinsfolk, could transfer property to a trustee: at Common Law it was in his ownership; but in Chancery he was bound to deal with it according to the terms of the trust — which could, simply, be according to the married woman's wishes. Or the trust could provide that, in the absence of any issue of the marriage to take a vested interest in the property, it should after the wife's death or that of her husband revert to her kinsfolk. Moreover, if the husband had recourse to the Court of Chancery, with its superior remedies, for the purpose of asserting his common law rights over the wife's property, that Court would as a condition of its aid compel the husband to settle on his wife and children part of any such property; and ultimately the wife herself or the children could initiate the claim. Over the wife's interest acquired in these two ways Equity at last gave her nearly all the rights of a single woman: she could give it away or sell it, or leave it by will to whoever she wished, or charge it with her contracts. A married woman could thus possess separate property over which her husband had no control whatever, and against which neither he nor his creditors had any claim. But in safeguarding in this peculiar way the interests of the married woman and of her kinship group, Equity took a further and decisive step away from any system of Community of Goods between married people.

Equity created a regime of separate property for married women. This regime was limited, however, to the investment property of the wealthy. Simon explains how the doctrines of equity were used in the late nineteenth century to deal with the needs of 'middle and lower middle classes':

First, the proponents of reform, led by John Stuart Mill, were principally interested in abrogating the subjection of women and in giving them equal political and civil rights with men. Men owned their own property, virtually untrammelled by any claims by their spouses. So women must be given similar rights. To entrench, say, the married woman's right to occupation of her husband's house would be to treat her as an unequal. Even Fitzjames Stephen, who controverted in this very field Mill's theory of equality, supported Mill's property proposals without pausing to consider whether there might not be some fairer régime for what he saw as the inevitable, the proper, role of the married woman. Secondly, Mill was at this time in the full tide of his individualism. Indeed, there was as yet no significant movement of thought orientated towards the foundation of society on small voluntary groupings, such as the family, of which the law of property should take specific cognizance. Thirdly, together with Mill there was a vociferous group of emancipated women writers, who were acutely conscious that the Common Law delivered over to their husbands the fruits of their professional activities, but who were understandably less concerned with the claims of all the housewives and mothers whose real needs were security in the matrimonial home and the right to participate in the proprietary benefits which their husbands enjoyed through their own economic self-abnegation. Fourthly, comparative jurisprudence was virtually unstudied at this time; and there was in any event a tendency to regard French political and social institutions with a well-bred distaste. Lastly, and most important, legal reform proceeds largely on the principle of inertia, not least in countries where the rule of precedent colours legal thinking. A movement once started continues of its own momentum. We have already seen the Common Law operate in that way in this very field. And now Parliament. Equity had permitted married women of the wealthier classes to own their separate property: how could it be denied to the generality of married women? So the Married Women's Property Acts did not attempt to remove married women's incapacities in any general way; still less in their interests to put restriction on the freedom of disposition of married men. Statute merely followed Equity in permitting married women to hold and handle and bind themselves with regard to any property which might come to them.

Questions

(i) Do you see similarities between the individualism of the nineteenth century and trends in the present generation designed to abolish the principle of maintenance in marriage (see p. 97, above)?

(ii) Modern feminists would regard chivalry and courtly love as the reverse of equalising the status of women. Why?

(iii) Do you think that a major reason why the Married Women's Property Acts were enacted could have been the tradesmen's difficulties in enforcing their debts?

2 Criticisms and survival of separation of property

Sir Jocelyn Simon made the following observation in his 1964 lecture:

But men can only earn their incomes and accumulate capital by virtue of the division of labour between themselves and their wives. The wife spends her youth and early middle age in bearing and rearing children and in tending the home; the husband is thus freed for his economic activities. Unless the wife plays her part the husband cannot play his. The cock bird can feather his nest precisely because he is not required to spend most of his time sitting on it.

In such a state of affairs a system of Separation of Goods between married people is singularly ill adapted to do justice. Community of Goods, or at the least community in acquisitions and accumulations, is far more appropriate. And as one leaves the sphere of those who enjoy investment property for that of those whose property largely consists of the home and its contents a régime of Separation is utterly remote from social needs.

The Law Reform Commission of Canada in a *Working Paper on Family Property* (1975) develop a similar theme:

Some basic defects in the law of separate property can be illustrated by examples of how the courts are required to apply that law. If during the course of a marriage the husband works and the wife stays home with the children, on divorce the wife will not have any share in any of the property purchased from the husband's earnings. The assumption behind this result seems to be that since she has been supported for part of her life — that is, she has not had to do any work for wages — then the law should not give her any share in property that was purchased out of wages. The law of separate property does not have any means for measuring, in terms of property rights, the value to her husband, her family and society of her work as a housekeeper or mother.

A married man is required by law to provide his wife and family with the necessaries of life: food, shelter, clothing. Since most employment occupies normal shopping hours, the task of making routine family purchases is usually undertaken by the wife, using money furnished by her husband. Everything she buys this way becomes her husband's property. . . . The law of separate property does not even go so far as to find that the spouses have a joint interest in savings from a household allowance.[1]

If both spouses work, the law of separate property has no effective ways to treat the family as an economic unit. Rather, the courts are obliged to trace the ownership of property to the spouse who was the source of the funds with which it was purchased. This becomes most harmful where the earnings of one spouse have been used to pay for property while the earnings of the other have been used for consumables such as holidays, food, children's clothing and so on. Because of the limitations . . . on credit available to married women, and the less certain continuity of married women's income, it is most often the husband's money that is used for charge account purchases, car payments, mortgage payments, and the like. It is legally immaterial to the question of who owns property that a wife's earnings have taken up enough of the slack in a family budget to allow a husband to be able to make payments on property.[2] The law does not look at the whole picture of the family finances in determining ownership, but only at whose money paid for each particular asset. This rule can work both ways, so that it is not always the wife who suffers the disadvantage. The point is not whether more wives or more husbands will take a loss in this situation, but rather that the spouse who produced sufficient additional income to allow the other to acquire property must take any loss at all.

The difficulties are taken up by the English Law Commission in 1971 in a *Working Paper on Family Property Law*:

0.12 It is said that equality of power, which separation of property achieves, does not of itself lead to equal opportunity to exercise that power; it ignores the fact that a married woman, especially if she has young children, does not in practice have the same opportunity as her husband or as an unmarried woman to acquire property; it takes no account of the fact that marriage is a form of partnership to which both spouses contribute, each in a different way, and that the contribution of each is equally important to the family welfare and to society.

The Law Commission give an example of how the principle works unfairly. This is what strict separation of property used to mean:

0.13 Mr Brown earns the family income. The home is in his name and he is responsible for the mortgage repayments and outgoings. Mrs Brown has given up her employment and earnings to attend to domestic affairs and to look after the family. She has no savings or private income, and cannot contribute in cash to the acquisition of property. If the marriage breaks down, the law regards the home, its contents, and any other property or savings acquired by Mr Brown in his name, as his sole property. Mrs Brown has a right to occupy the home and to be maintained, but she does not own the home or any other property acquired out of Mr Brown's earnings. On a decree of divorce, nullity or judicial separation she may apply to the court for property to be

---

1. See Married Women's Property Act 1964, p. 85, above.
2. See *Fribance v Fribance (No. 2)* [1957] 1 All ER 357, [1957] 1 WLR 384.

transferred to or settled on her [see Chapter 6, below]. If Mr Brown dies leaving a will which disinherits her (though this is relatively uncommon) she has a limited right of support, available only on application to a court and at its discretion: she has no right other than to ask for what is normally needed for her support. In short, she has no right of property in her dead husband's estate if he has made a will which disinherits her.

There are three reasons given for dissatisfaction with the principle of separation: (i) unfairness, (ii) uncertainty, particularly in relation to the matrimonial home, and (iii) that even when adjustments can be made, these adjustments depend on the discretion of the court after the termination of the marriage. As Sir Otto Kahn-Freund explains in *Matrimonial Property: Where do we go from here?* (1971):

0.15 Mr and Mrs Jones have been married for ten years and have three children. When they married they bought a house on mortgage. The deposit was paid partly from Mrs Jones' savings and partly from a loan from Mr Jones' employer. The mortgage instalments have usually been paid by Mr Jones. At the beginning Mrs Jones had a job; she went back to part-time work when the children were older. From her wages she paid a large part of the household expenses and bought some of the furniture. Occasionally she paid the mortgage instalments. A car and a washing machine were bought on hire-purchase in Mr Jones' name, but the instalments were sometimes paid by him and sometimes by her. Mr Jones has now left his wife and children and is living with another woman.

0.16 If, in the above situation, Mrs Jones asks what her property rights are so that she can make arrangements, she will receive no clear answer. In effect, the law will ask her what intentions she and her husband had about the allocation of their property, and to this she would only be able to reply that they had no clear intention.

Question

Which of the three reasons for dissatisfaction do you consider the strongest?

It is necessary to discuss the alleged uncertainty of the law in some detail. Lord Denning had attempted to introduce an element of discretion, both through his interpretation of the courts' powers under s. 17 of the Married Women's Property Act 1882 and through his approach to the ownership of 'family assets'. This may have made the law even more uncertain, but in his view it certainly made it more fair. In the event, the House of Lords, in *Pettitt v Pettitt* [1970] AC 777, [1969] 2 All ER 385 and *Gissing v Gissing* [1971] AC 886, [1970] 2 All ER 780 overruled his interpretation of s. 17 and emphasised that the interests of husband and wife in property must be determined in accordance with the ordinary rules of property law. A spouse who contributes to the cost of acquiring or improving a home which is legally owned by the other will be entitled to a beneficial interest, but the circumstances in which a trust will arise are notoriously difficult to predict.

Pettitt v Pettitt
[1970] AC 777, [1969] 2 All ER 385, [1969] 2 WLR 966, 113 Sol Jo 344, House of Lords

The case was concerned with work carried out by a husband upon a matrimonial home which was owned by his wife. The facts appear in the speech of Lord Reid.

Lord Reid: My Lords, the appellant was married in 1952. For about nine years she and her husband lived in a house which she had inherited. During that time her husband carried out a number of improvements, largely redecorating, on which he says he spent some £80. In 1961 this house was sold and she acquired another. After this had been paid for there was a surplus of a few hundred pounds and he used this money, apparently with the consent of the appellant, in paying for his car. The spouses lived for about four years in the new house. Then the appellant left her husband, alleging cruelty, and she obtained a divorce in 1967. The husband then left the house and raised the present proceedings. He said that during those four years he carried out a considerable number of improvements to the house and garden and estimated that in doing so he performed work and supplied material to a value of £723. He sought a declaration that he was beneficially interested in the proceeds of sale of the house in the sum of £1,000 and an order on the appellant to pay. Then an order was made that she should pay him £300. The Court of Appeal reluctantly dismissed her appeal, holding that they were bound by the decision in *Appleton v Appleton* [1965] 1 All ER 44, [1965] 1 WLR 25. They gave leave to appeal.

For the last twenty years the law regarding what are sometimes called family assets has been in an unsatisfactory state. There have been many cases showing acute differences of opinion in the Court of Appeal. Various questions have arisen, generally after the break-up of a marriage. Sometimes both spouses have contributed in money to the purchase of a house; sometimes the contribution of one spouse has been otherwise than money: sometimes one spouse owned the house and the other spent money or did work in improving it: and there have been a variety of other circumstances. . . .

Many of the cases have been brought by virtue of the provisions of section 17 of the Married Women's Property Act 1882. That is a long and complicated section: the relevant part is as follows:

'In any question between husband and wife as to the title to or possession of property, either party . . . may apply by summons or otherwise in a summary way to any judge of the High Court of Justice . . . and the judge . . . may make such order with respect to the property in dispute . . . as he thinks fit.'

The main dispute has been as to the meaning of the latter words authorising the judge (including a county judge and now a registrar) to make such order with respect to the property in dispute as he thinks fit. They are words normally used to confer a discretion on the court: where discretion is limited, the limitations are generally expressed: but here no limitation is expressed. So it has been said that here these words confer on the court an unfettered discretion to override existing rights in the property and to dispose of it in whatever manner the judge may think to be just and equitable in the whole circumstances of the case. On the other hand it has been said that these words do not entitle the court to disregard any existing property right, but merely confer a power to regulate possession or the exercise of property rights, or, more narrowly, merely confer a power to exercise in proceedings under section 17 any discretion with regard to the property in dispute which has already been conferred by some other enactment. And other intermediate views have also been expressed.

I would approach the question in this way. The meaning of the section cannot have altered since it was passed in 1882. At that time the certainty and security of rights of property were still generally regarded as of paramount importance and I find it incredible that any Parliament of that era could have intended to put a husband's property at the hazard of the unfettered discretion of a judge (including a county court judge) if the wife raised a dispute about it. Moreover, this discretion, if it exists, can only be exercised in proceedings under section 17: the same dispute could arise in other forms of action; and I find it even more incredible that it could have been intended that such a discretion should be given to a judge in summary proceedings but denied to the judge if the proceedings were of the ordinary character. So are the words so unequivocal that we are forced to give them a meaning which cannot have been intended? I do not think so. It is perfectly possible to construe the words as having a much more restricted meaning and in my judgment they should be so construed. I do not think that a judge has any more right to disregard property rights in section 17 proceedings than he has in any other form of proceedings. . . .

I would therefore refuse to consider whether property belonging to either spouse ought to be regarded as family property for that would be introducing a new conception into English law and not merely developing existing principles. There are systems of law which recognise joint family property or *communio bonorum*. I am not sure that those principles are very highly regarded in countries where they are in force, but in any case it would be going far beyond the functions of the court to attempt to give effect to them here.

Similar observations about matrimonial property were made by **Lord Morris:**

I cannot agree that section 17 empowers a court to take property from one spouse and allocate it to the other. But something may depend upon what is meant by 'family assets.' If what is referred to is an asset separately owned by someone who is a member of a family, then once the ownership is ascertained it cannot, under section 17, be changed. If what is referred to is property which, on the evidence, has been decided to be property which belongs beneficially to husband and wife jointly, I do not consider that section 17 enables a court to vary whatever the beneficial interests were ascertained to be. There would be room for the exercise of discretion in deciding a question as to whether a sale should be ordered at one time or another but there would be no discretion enabling a court to withdraw an ascertained property right from one spouse and to grant it to the other. Any power to do that must either be found in some existing provision in relation to matrimonial causes or must be given by some future legislation.

And by **Lord Hodson**:

The notion of family assets itself opens a new field involving change in the law of property whereby community of ownership between husband and wife would be assumed unless otherwise excluded. This is a matter of policy for Parliament, and I agree is outside the field of judicial interpretation of property law.

And by **Lord Upjohn**:

My Lords, we have in this country no doctrine of community of goods between spouses and yet by judicial decision were this doctrine of family assets to be accepted some such a doctrine would become part of the law of the land.

As a result of this case, Parliament enacted s. 37 of the *Matrimonial Proceedings and Property Act 1970*:

It is hereby declared that where a husband or wife contributes in money or money's worth to the improvement of real or personal property in which or in the proceeds of sale of which either or both of them has or have a beneficial interest, the husband or wife so contributing shall, if the contribution is of a substantial nature and subject to any agreement between them to the contrary express or implied, be treated as having then acquired by virtue of his or her contribution a share or an enlarged share, as the case may be, in that beneficial interest of such an extent as may have been then agreed or, in default of such agreement, as may seem in all the circumstances just to any court before which the question of the existence or extent of the beneficial interest of the husband or wife arises (whether in proceedings between them or in other proceedings).

Questions

(i) Mr Pettitt lost his case: would s. 37 have made any difference?
(ii) What interest would Mr Pettitt have acquired if he had spent his money on a new roof?

Gissing v Gissing
[1971] AC 886, [1970] 2 All ER 780, [1970] 3 WLR 255, 114 Sol Jo 350, HL, House of Lords

The facts are set out in the speech of **Lord Diplock**:

In the instant appeal the matrimonial home was purchased in 1951 for £2,695 and conveyed into the sole name of the husband. The parties had by then been married for some 16 years and both were in employment with the same firm, the husband earning £1,000 and the wife £500 per annum. The purchase price was raised as to £2,150 on mortgage repayable by instalments, as to £500 by a loan to the husband from his employers, and as to the balance of £45 and the legal charges was paid by the husband out of his own moneys. The wife made no direct contribution to the initial deposit or legal charges, nor to the repayment of the loan of £500 nor to the mortgage instalments. She continued earning at the rate of £500 per annum until the marriage broke down in 1961. During this period the husband's salary increased to £3,000 per annum. The husband repaid the loan of £500, and paid the mortgage instalments. He also paid the outgoings on the house, gave to his wife a housekeeping allowance of £8 to £10 a week out of which she paid the running expenses of the household and he paid for holidays. The only contribution which the wife made out of her earnings to the household expenses was that she paid for her own clothes and those of the son of the marriage and for some extras. No change in this arrangement was made when the house was acquired. Each spouse had a separate banking account, the wife's in the Post Office Savings Bank, and each made savings out of their respective earnings. There was no joint bank account and there were no joint savings. There was no express agreement at the time of the purchase or thereafter as to how the beneficial interest in the house should be held. The learned judge was prepared to accept that after the marriage had broken down the husband said to the wife: 'Don't worry about the house — it's yours'; but this has not been relied upon, at any rate in your Lordships' House, as an acknowledgment of a pre-existing agreement on which the wife had acted to her detriment so as to give rise to a resulting, implied or constructive trust, nor can it be relied upon as an express declaration of trust as it was oral only.

On what then is the wife's claim based? In 1951 when the house was purchased she spent about £190 on buying furniture and a cooker and refrigerator for it. She also paid about £30 for improving the lawn. As furniture and household durables are depreciating assets whereas houses have turned out to be appreciating assets it may be that she would have been wise to have devoted her savings to acquiring an interest in the freehold; but this may not have been so apparent in 1951 as it has now become. The court is not entitled to infer a common intention to this effect from the mere fact that she provided chattels for joint use in the new matrimonial home; and there is nothing else in the conduct of the parties at the time of the purchase or there-after which supports such an inference. There is no suggestion that the wife's efforts or her earnings made it possible for the husband to raise the initial loan or the mortgage or that her relieving her husband from the expense of buying clothing for herself and for their son was undertaken in order to enable him the better to meet the mortgage instalments or to repay the loan. The picture presented by the evidence is one of husband and wife retaining their separate proprietary interests in property whether real or personal purchased with their separate savings and is inconsistent with any common intention at the time of the purchase of the matrimonial home that the wife, who neither then nor thereafter contributed anything to its purchase price or assumed any liability for it, should nevertheless be entitled to a beneficial interest in it.

Earlier in his speech, Lord Diplock looked at the role of the agreement in the creation of an equitable interest in real property.

Any claim to a beneficial interest in land by a person, whether spouse or stranger, in whom the legal estate in the land is not vested must be based upon the proposition that the person in whom the legal estate is vested holds it as trustee upon trust to give effect to the beneficial interest of the claimant as cestui que trust. The legal principles applicable to the claim are those of the English law of trusts and in particular, in the kind of dispute between spouses that comes before the courts, the law relating to the creation and operation of 'resulting, implied or constructive trusts.' Where the trust is expressly declared in the instrument by which the legal estate is transferred to the trustee or by a written declaration of trust by the trustee, the court must give effect to it. But to constitute a valid declaration of trust by way of gift of a beneficial interest in land to a cestui que trust the declaration is required by section 53(1) of the Law of Property Act 1925, to be in writing. If it is not in writing it can only take effect as a resulting, implied or constructive trust to which that section has no application.

A resulting, implied or constructive trust — and it is unnecessary for present purposes to distinguish between these three classes of trust — is created by a transaction between the trustee and the cestui que trust in connection with the acquisition by the trustee of a legal estate in land, whenever the trustee has so conducted himself that it would be inequitable to allow him to deny to the cestui que trust a beneficial interest in the land acquired. And he will be held so to have conducted himself if by his words or conduct he has induced the cestui que trust to act to his own detriment in the reasonable belief that by so acting he was acquiring a beneficial interest in the land.

This is why it has been repeatedly said in the context of disputes between spouses as to their respective beneficial interests in the matrimonial home, that if at the time of its acquisition and transfer of the legal estate into the name of one or other of them an express agreement has been made between them as to the way in which the beneficial interest shall be held, the court will give effect to it — notwithstanding the absence of any written declaration of trust. Strictly speaking this states the principle too widely, for if the agreement did not provide for anything to be done by the spouse in whom the legal estate was not to be vested, it would be a merely voluntary declaration of trust and unenforceable for want of writing. But in the express oral agreements contemplated by these dicta it has been assumed sub silentio that they provide for the spouse in whom the legal estate in the matrimonial home is not vested to do something to facilitate its acquisition, by contributing to the purchase price or to the deposit or the mortgage instalments when it is purchased upon mortgage or to make some other material sacrifice by way of contribution to or economy in the general family expenditure. What the court gives effect to is the trust resulting or implied from the common intention expressed in the oral agreement between the spouses that if each acts in the manner provided for in the agreement the beneficial interests in the matrimonial home shall be held as they have agreed.

An express agreement between spouses as to their respective beneficial interests in land conveyed into the name of one of them obviates the need for showing that the conduct of the spouse into whose name the land was conveyed was intended to induce the other spouse to act to his or her detriment upon the faith of the promise of a specified beneficial interest in the land and that the other spouse so acted with the intention of acquiring that beneficial interest. The agreement itself discloses the common intention required to create a resulting, implied or constructive trust.

But parties to a transaction in connection with the acquisition of land may well have formed a common intention that the beneficial interest in the land shall be vested in them jointly without having used express words to communicate this intention to one another; or their recollections of the words used may be imperfect or conflicting by the time any dispute arises. In such a case — a common one where the parties are spouses whose marriage has broken down — it may be possible to infer their common intention from their conduct.

As in so many branches of English law in which legal rights and obligations depend upon the intentions of the parties to a transaction, the relevant intention of each party is the intention which was reasonably understood by the other party to be manifested by that party's words or conduct notwithstanding that he did not consciously formulate that intention in his own mind or even acted with some different intention which he did not communicate to the other party. On the other hand, he is not bound by any inference which the other party draws as to his intention unless that inference is one which can reasonably be drawn from his words or conduct. It is in this sense that in the branch of English law relating to constructive, implied or resulting trusts effect is given to the inferences as to the intentions of parties to a transaction which a reasonable man would draw from their words or conduct and not to any subjective intention or absence of intention which was not made manifest at the time of the transaction itself. It is for the court to determine what those inferences are.

In drawing such an inference, what spouses said and did which led up to the acquisition of a matrimonial home and what they said and did while the acquisition was being carried through is on a different footing from what they said and did after the acquisition was completed. Unless it is alleged that there was some subsequent fresh agreement, acted upon by the parties, to vary the original beneficial interests created when the matrimonial home was acquired, what they said and did after the acquisition was completed is relevant if it is explicable only upon the basis of their having manifested to one another at the time of the acquisition some particular common intention as to how the beneficial interests should be held. But it would in my view be unreasonably legalistic to treat the relevant transaction involved in the acquisition of a matrimonial home as restricted to the actual conveyance of the fee simple into the name of one or other spouse. Their common intention is more likely to have been concerned with the economic realities of the transaction than with the unfamiliar technicalities of the English law of legal and equitable interests in land. The economic reality which lies behind the conveyance of the fee simple to a purchaser in return for a purchase price the greater part of which is advanced to the purchaser upon a mortgage repayable by instalments over a number of years, is that the new freeholder is purchasing the matrimonial home upon credit and that the purchase price is represented by the instalments by which the mortgage is repaid in addition to the initial payment in cash. The conduct of the spouses in relation to the payment of the mortgage instalments may be no less relevant to their common intention as to the beneficial interests in a matrimonial home acquired in this way than their conduct in relation to the payment of the cash deposit.

It is this feature of the transaction by means of which most matrimonial homes have been acquired in recent years that makes difficult the task of the court in inferring from the conduct of the spouses a common intention as to how the beneficial interest in it should be held. Each case must depend upon its own facts but there are a number of factual situations which often recur in the cases.

Where a matrimonial home has been purchased outright without the aid of an advance on mortgage it is not difficult to ascertain what part, if any, of the purchase price has been provided by each spouse. If the land is conveyed into the name of a spouse who has not provided the whole of the purchase price, the sum contributed by the other spouse may be explicable as having been intended by both of them either as a gift or as a loan of money to the spouse to whom the land is conveyed or as consideration for a share in the beneficial interest in the land. In a dispute between living spouses the evidence will probably point to one of these explanations as being more probable than the others, but if the rest of the evidence is neutral the prima facie inference is that their common intention was that the contributing spouse should acquire a share in the beneficial interest in the land in the same proportion as the sum contributed bore to the total purchase price. This prima facie inference is more easily rebutted in favour of a gift where the land is conveyed into the name of the wife: but as I understand the speeches in *Pettitt v Pettitt* [1970] AC 777, [1969] 2 All ER 385 four of the members of your Lordships' House who were parties to that decision took the view that even if the 'presumption of advancement' as between husband and wife still survived today, it could seldom have any decisive part to play in disputes between living spouses in which some evidence would be available in addition to the mere fact that the husband had provided part of the purchase price of property conveyed into the name of the wife.

Similarly when a matrimonial home is not purchased outright but partly out of moneys advanced on mortgage repayable by instalments, and the land is conveyed into the name of the husband alone, the fact that the wife made a cash contribution to the deposit and legal charges not borrowed on mortgage gives rise, in the absence of evidence which makes some other explanation more probable, to the inference that their common intention was that she should share in the beneficial interest in the land conveyed. But it would not be reasonable to infer a common intention as to what her share should be without taking account also of the sources from which the mortgage instalments were provided. If the wife also makes a substantial direct contribution to the mortgage instalments out of her own earnings or unearned income this would be prima facie inconsistent with a common intention that her share in the beneficial interest should be determined by the proportion which her original cash contribution bore either to the total amount of the deposit and legal charges or to the full purchase price. The more likely inference is that her contributions to the mortgage instalments were intended by the spouses to have some effect upon her share.

Where there has been an initial contribution by the wife to the cash deposit and legal charges which points to a common intention at the time of the conveyance that she should have a beneficial interest in the land conveyed to her husband, it would be unrealistic to regard the wife's subsequent contributions to the mortgage instalments as without significance unless she pays them directly herself. It may be no more than a matter of convenience which spouse pays particular household accounts particularly when both are earning, and if the wife goes out to work and devotes part of her earnings or uses her private income to meet joint expenses of the household which would otherwise be met by the husband, so as to enable him to pay the mortgage instalments out of his moneys this would be consistent with and might be corroborative of an original common intention that she should share in the beneficial interest in the matrimonial home and that her payments of other household expenses were intended by both spouses to be treated as including a contribution by the wife to the purchase price of the matrimonial home.

Even where there has been no initial contribution by the wife to the cash deposit and legal charges but she makes a regular and substantial direct contribution to the mortgage instalments it may be reasonable to infer a common intention of the spouses from the outset that she should share in the beneficial interest or to infer a fresh agreement reached after the original conveyance that she should acquire a share. But it is unlikely that the mere fact that the wife made direct contributions to the mortgage instalments would be the only evidence available to assist the court in ascertaining the common intention of the spouses.

Where in any of the circumstances described above contributions, direct or indirect, have been made to the mortgage instalments by the spouse into whose name the matrimonial home has not been conveyed, and the court can infer from their conduct a common intention that the contributing spouse should be entitled to *some* beneficial interest in the matrimonial home, what effect is to be given to that intention if there is no evidence that they in fact reached any express agreement as to what the respective share of each spouse should be?

I take it to be clear that if the court is satisfied that it was the common intention of both spouses that the contributing wife should have a share in the beneficial interest and that her contributions were made upon this understanding, the court in the exercise of its equitable jurisdiction would not permit the husband in whom the legal estate was vested and who had accepted the benefit of the contributions to take the whole beneficial interest merely because at the time the wife made her contributions there had been no express agreement as to how her share in it was to be quantified.

In such a case the court must first do its best to discover from the conduct of the spouses whether any inference can reasonably be drawn as to the probable common understanding about the amount of the share of the contributing spouse upon which each must have acted in doing what each did, even though that understanding was never expressly stated by one spouse to the other or even consciously formulated in words by either of them independently. It is only if no such inference can be drawn that the court is driven to apply as a rule of law, and not as an inference of fact, the maxim 'equality is equity,' and to hold that the beneficial interest belongs to the spouses in equal shares.

The same result however may often be reached as an inference of fact. The instalments of a mortgage to a building society are generally repayable over a period of many years. During that period, as both must be aware, the ability of each spouse to contribute to the instalments out of their separate earnings is likely to alter, particularly in the case of the wife if any children are born of the marriage. If the contribution of the wife in the early part of the period of repayment is substantial but is not an identifiable and uniform proportion of each instalment, because her contributions are indirect or, if direct, are made irregularly, it may well be a reasonable inference that their common intention at the time of acquisition of the matrimonial home was that the beneficial interest should be held by them in equal shares and that each should contribute to the cost of its acquisition whatever amounts each could afford in the varying exigencies of family life to be expected during the period of repayment. In the social conditions of today this would be a natural enough common intention of a young couple who were both earning when the house was acquired but who contemplated having children whose birth and rearing in their infancy would necessarily affect the future earning capacity of the wife.

The relative size of their respective contributions to the instalments in the early part of the period of repayment, or later if a subsequent reduction in the wife's contribution is not to be accounted for by a reduction in her earnings due to motherhood or some other cause from which the husband benefits as well, may make it a more probable inference that the wife's share in the beneficial interest was intended to be in some proportion other than one-half. And there is nothing inherently improbable in their acting on the understanding that the wife should be entitled to a share which was not to be quantified immediately upon the acquisition of the home but should be left to be determined when the mortgage was repaid or the property disposed of, on the basis of what would be fair having regard to the total contributions, direct or indirect, which each spouse had made by that date. Where this was the most likely inference from their conduct it would be for the court to give effect to that common intention of the parties by determining what in all the circumstances was a fair share.

Difficult as they are to solve, however, these problems as to the amount of the share of a spouse in the beneficial interest in a matrimonial home where the legal estate is vested solely in the other spouse, only arise in cases where the court is satisfied by the words or conduct of the parties that it was their common intention that the beneficial interest was not to belong solely to the spouse in whom the legal estate was vested but was to be shared between them in some proportion or other.

Where the wife has made no initial contribution to the cash deposit and legal charges and no direct contribution to the mortgage instalments nor any adjustment to her contribution to other expenses of the household which it can be inferred was referable to the acquisition of the house, there is in the absence of evidence of an express agreement between the parties no material to justify the court in inferring that it was the common intention of the parties that she should have any beneficial interest in a matrimonial home conveyed into the sole name of the husband, merely because she continued to contribute out of her own earnings or private income to other expenses of the household. For such conduct is no less consistent with a common intention to share the day-to-day expenses of the household, while each spouse retains a separate interest in capital assets acquired with their own moneys or obtained by inheritance or gift. There is nothing here to rebut the prima facie inference that a purchaser of land who pays the purchase price and takes a conveyance and grants a mortgage in his own name intends to acquire the sole beneficial interest as well as the legal estate: and the difficult question of the quantum of the wife's share does not arise.

Lord Diplock concluded that he was unable to draw an inference that there was any common intention that the wife should have any beneficial interest in the matrimonial home.

Lord Dilhorne and Lord Morris were against indirect contributions entitling a spouse to some beneficial interest in the matrimonial home. Lord Reid and Lord Pearson would appear to permit a beneficial interest to be acquired through indirect contributions but do not elaborate this concept.

Thus, the separation of property principle survived the attempt by Lord Denning and others to sweep it away. However, Parliament stepped in to grant discretionary powers to courts to re-allocate property after the termination of marriage. Such discretionary powers can take into account non-financial contributions. These provisions, now contained in the Matrimonial Causes Act 1973, are looked at in detail in Chapter 6, below. Strict property law is still important — in cases of death, bankruptcy, and even management decisions which have to be taken during the marriage.

Re Holliday (a bankrupt), ex p the Trustee of the Bankrupt v The Bankrupt [1981] Ch 405, [1980] 3 All ER 385, [1981] 2 WLR 996, 125 Sol Jo 411, Court of Appeal

The husband and wife married in 1962 and had three children, all of whom were still under 15. In 1970, the husband and wife bought a house for the purpose of providing a matrimonial home. The house was conveyed to them on trust for sale as joint tenants. The marriage was dissolved in 1975, and on 3 March 1976 the wife gave notice of her intention to proceed with a property adjustment order. On the same day, the husband filed a bankruptcy petition in the county court, and was immediately adjudicated a bankrupt. The husband's trustee in bankruptcy took steps to realise the husband's interest in the house for the benefit of his creditors.

Buckley LJ: In these circumstances the wife finds herself saddled with the burden of providing a proper home for her children, which she would be incapable of doing out of her own resources, taking into account the value of her one half share of the equity in the Thorpe Bay property. That situation is attributable to the former conduct of the debtor in leaving the wife and family and going to make a new home for himself with another lady. This seems to me to afford the wife strong and justifiable grounds for saying that it really would be unfair to her, at this juncture and in these circumstances, to enforce the trust for sale. Of course, the creditors are entitled to payment as soon as the debtor is in a position to pay them. They are entitled to payment forthwith; they have an unassailable right to be paid out of the assets of the bankrupt. But in my view, when one of those assets is an undivided share in land in respect of which the debtor's right to an immediate sale is not an absolute right, that is an asset in the bankruptcy which is liable to be affected by the interest of any other party interested in that land, and if there are reasons which seem to the court to be good reasons for saying that the trust for sale of the land should not be immediately enforced, then that is an asset of the bankruptcy which is not immediately available because it cannot be immediately realised for the benefit of the creditors. Balancing the interest of the creditors and the interest of the wife, burdened, as I say, with the obligation to provide a home for the three children of the marriage, in my view the right attitude for the court to adopt is that the house should not be sold at the present juncture. Of course, in fact it cannot be sold without the concurrence of the wife or an order of the court; but in order to make the position clear, for my part I would be disposed to make an order to the effect that the house should not be sold without the consent of the wife or pursuant to an order of the court, before 1 July 1985, by which time the elder daughter will have passed her 17th birthday, and the boy, who is the eldest of the three children, will be older. By that stage the problems confronting the wife will be very different from the problems she has to deal with today.

Sir David Cairns: I agree with Buckley LJ that in all the circumstances here the voice of the wife, on behalf of herself and the children, should prevail to the extent that the sale of the house should be deferred for a substantial period. I reach that view because I am satisfied that it would at present be very difficult, if not impossible, for the wife to secure another suitable home for the family in or near Thorpe Bay; because it would be upsetting for the children's education if they had to move far away from their present schools, even if it were practicable, having regard to the wife's means, to find an alternative home at some more distant place; because it is highly unlikely that postponement of the payment of the debts would cause any great hardship to any of the creditors; and because none of the creditors thought fit themselves to present a bankruptcy petition and it is quite impossible to know whether any one of them would have done so if the debtor had not himself presented such a petition.

   Although there is apparently no previous reported case in which the interests of a debtor's family have been held to prevail over those of creditors in a bankruptcy, there have certainly been earlier cases in which family interests have been considered and set against those of the creditors: see *Re Turner* [1975] 1 All ER 5, [1974] 1 WLR 1556 where it was the wife's interest that was considered, and *Re Bailey* [1977] 2 All ER 26, [1977] 1 WLR 278 where it was the interests of a son of the family.

   In the earlier cases the trustee has succeeded, because no sufficiently substantial case of hardship of dependants was established. That is where, in my judgment, this case differs from the earlier ones. It may well be, however, that the hardship for the wife and children would be much less, or would have disappeared altogether, in five years' time or possibly even earlier. I therefore agree that it is appropriate that we should not at this stage defer sale for longer than five years or thereabouts, and that we should leave a loophole for earlier sale to be applied for if the circumstances change in such a way as to warrant it.

Question

(i) If Mrs Holliday had had no proprietary right in the home, what would have happened?
(ii) Why should creditors take second place to the family responsibilities of the debtor?

The law on matrimonial property has been considered by the Law Commission in a series of papers and reports culminating in a report published in August 1982. The separation of property principle has been subjected to minute scrutiny — yet it still survives.

3 The field of choice

There are three possible reforms: an extension of discretionary powers, community of property and deferred community of property. We consider each of these three proposals in turn.

(a) THE FIRST APPROACH: AN EXTENSION OF THE DISCRETIONARY POWERS OF THE COURT

In the *First Report on Family Property — A New Approach* (1973) the Law Commission acknowledge that there is a body of opinion that would oppose the introduction of any form of fixed property rights between husband and wife on the ground that this is unnecessary and in itself objectionable:

They believed that in so far as the existing law led to any injustice, the proper remedy was to allow the court to exercise its discretionary powers in matrimonial or family provision proceedings. It was claimed that all necessary reforms could be achieved by developing the traditional discretionary systems, which ensured great flexibility. The principal reasons for considering any form of fixed property rights undesirable were as follows:
(*a*) fixed property rights would cause more dissension and injustice than they would alleviate;
(*b*) the state should not interfere in the relations between spouses by imposing automatic rules regulating their property rights;
(*c*) fixed property rights would deter marriage and compel people to take advice before marrying.

Question

Is advice before marriage a good thing which should be encouraged?

By contrast, the *Canadian Law Reform Commission* (1975) put the alternative point of view:

Another drawback to a discretionary system lies in its lack of fixed legal rights. Even were equality to be stated as a general legislative policy, the essential nature of judicial discretion would leave the court free to make whatever sort of property disposition seemed to be appropriate in any given case. A married person would not have a *right* to equality, but only a *hope* to obtain it. If no concept of equality were contained in the law establishing a discretionary system, then it would be accurate to say that a married person would have no property rights at all at the time of divorce. Our concern here is not limited to the way things would work out in practice, since the courts would do their best to ensure that arbitrary dispossession did not occur. Rather, it includes the psychological advantage that accrues to a person who knows he or she has a positive right that is guaranteed and protected by law.

The same concern seems to have been felt by the great majority of those who put their view to the English Law Commission. The analysis of the findings of Todd and Jones' survey of *Matrimonial Property* (1972) confirms the view that the system of separation of property is often entered into with little thought to the legal consequences:

We asked those who had the home in only one person's name how they viewed the ownership of the home. In nine out of ten cases the spouses each thought of the home as belonging to both of them. Thus their attitude to the ownership of their home was not on the whole related to the arrangement of the legal title. This suggests that, rather than a specific choice being made, one spouse ownership was merely the result of the traditional pattern of ownership.

The Law Commission rejected a continuation of the present law, or the limited extension of the present system through the use of discretionary powers.

(b) THE SECOND APPROACH: COMMUNITY OF PROPERTY

The following extract is taken from the *Canadian Law Reform Commission* (1975):

The community property concept of marital property rights is based upon the assumption that marriage, among other things, is an economic partnership. As such, the partnership, or community, owns the respective talents and efforts of each of the spouses. Whatever is acquired as a result of their talents and efforts is shared by and belongs to both of them equally, as *community property*.

Community property regimes exist in Quebec, in many European countries and in eight of the United States. Quebec's community property regime, like the separate property regime in that province, is an option available to married persons who choose not to be governed by the basic regime providing for separate ownership of property during a marriage, with fixed sharing upon divorce.

The essential idea of community of property is very simple: the earnings, and property purchased with the earnings, of either spouse become community property in which each spouse has a present equal legal interest. Where the community is terminated — for example by divorce — the community property, after payment of community debts, is divided equally between the spouses. The community is also terminated by the death of a spouse, and in some jurisdictions, including Quebec, by an agreement between the spouses to switch to some other regime or to regulate their property relations by a contract. This simple formula conceals some rather complex rules. We can do no more in this paper than touch upon the general principles and a few of the major problem areas involved in community property systems without dealing with finer points in any great detail.

Under community regimes, there are three kinds of property: the separate property of the husband, the separate property of the wife, and community property. Typically, the property owned by either spouse before marriage is the separate property of that spouse, along with property acquired after marriage by a spouse by way of gift or inheritance. Separate property is not shared at the time of divorce, but rather is retained by the owner-spouse. All other property, however acquired, becomes community property, in which each spouse has a present interest as soon as it is purchased or obtained, and an equal share in its division upon divorce. In some jurisdictions, someone giving property to a married person must specify that the property is to be the separate property of the recipient. Otherwise it will be treated as a gift to both spouses, even though it is only given to one, and will become community property. In the Province of Quebec, some types of property owned before marriage become community property, but it is possible for persons giving such types of property to a single person to make the gift on the condition that it remain the separate property of the recipient should he or she thereafter marry under the regime of community property.

Under a community property regime, all property owned by either spouse at the time of a divorce is generally presumed in law to be community property unless it can be proved to be separate. In many marriages the spouses will not have adequate records of ownership or the source of funds used to acquire property. This produces the legal phenomenon of 'commingling' — that is, the separate property of each spouse eventually becomes mixed with that of the other spouse and with the community property, resulting in all the property being treated as sharable community property at the time of divorce. Commingling makes it impossible for the spouses to establish that certain items of property were owned before marriage, or otherwise fall into the classification of separate property.

Community property regimes, however, are enacted into law on the assumption that commingling is not what most people desire, and they therefore contain rather elaborate rules and formulae designed to deal with the fact that married persons will be using and enjoying the three different types of property created by the law of this regime — that is, the husband's separate property, the wife's separate property and the community property. These rules and formulae tend to make the essentially simple concept of community of property a rather complicated system in practice. For example, one typical rule is that property acquired after marriage in replacement of separate property does not become community property. This means that a spouse who wishes to replace or keep replacing property that was owned before marriage must keep an account and record of every transaction, so that at the time of divorce items purchased after marriage for which separate property status is claimed can be traced back to the original property owned before marriage, and can be shown to be replacements for such original property. If a person does not have adequate records, the replacement property will be presumed to belong to the community and shared between the spouses when the marriage is dissolved.

Even assuming that the separate property of a spouse can in fact be kept identifiable, it is necessary to have rules governing the situation where community funds are expended with respect to such property. If, for example, a husband owns a house as separate property and has it repaired, using community funds, the community property is entitled to reimbursement at the time of divorce to the extent of the value of the repairs. Or if he sells the house and buys another, using for the purchase some community funds plus proceeds of the sale, the rule might be that if more than fifty per cent of the price of the second house came from the first house, it remains separate property subject to an appropriate compensation to the community upon divorce. If more than fifty per cent of the price of the second house came from community funds, then it loses its character as separate property and becomes community property. In the latter case there would be a compensation paid from the community at the time of divorce to the husband's separate property equal to the amount realized on the sale of the first house. When it is recognized that most families only have available the earnings of one spouse, which belong to the community, and that many items of separate property over the course of a marriage would be maintained and repaired out of these earnings, or sold and 'traded up' for newer property using the proceeds of the sale of the separate property plus community funds, then some of the practical difficulties in accounting during the marriage and sorting out community and separate property at its termination become readily apparent.

In some community property jurisdictions, the income produced by a spouse's separate property (such as the profits from renting an apartment house owned separately by one spouse) becomes community property. In other jurisdictions, the rule is the other way, so that a spouse is entitled to keep such income separate so long, of course, as he is able to establish at the time of divorce that the source of the income was his separate property.

With respect to liability for indebtedness, some community property jurisdictions distinguish between debts contracted as community obligations, such as necessaries for any member of the family or the debts connected with the prosecution of a community business, and debts contracted with respect to the acquisition or disposition of separate property or the management of a separately owned business of one spouse. In other jurisdictions, the community property is liable for the debts of the husband but not the debts of his wife.

The *Canadian Law Reform Commission* views marriage as a partnership. Community strengthens the policy objectives of marriage:

This benefit not only makes a reality out of the concept of partnership, which we think strengthens the institution of marriage, but also carries with it the emotional and psychological benefits derived from the reality of present ownership for the spouse who is not gainfully employed outside the home.

Questions

(i) It could be said that individualism can be taken too far. Has not the ideal of partnership been taken too far by the Canadian Law Reform Commission?

(ii) Does community strengthen the policy objectives of marriages which do not fit into the partnership pattern?

(iii) Who manages the community property?

(v) Do you think community would produce more or less litigation than separation of property, and why?

(v) If occupation rights are ensured (see p. 43, above), does it really matter that there be no community of ownership?

(c) THE MATRIMONIAL HOME

The two areas which feature predominantly in Law Commission reports in England are the matrimonial home and household goods. We discuss each in turn. It is natural that discussions of community should centre around the home. The English Law Commission Working Paper, *Family Property Law* (1971) discussed the topic in detail, and formed the conclusion that a system of co-ownership should be introduced to meet many of the objections to the present law:

0.25 The matrimonial home is often the principal, if not the only, family asset. Where this is the case, if satisfactory provision could be made for sharing the home, the problem of matrimonial property would be largely solved. Under present rules, apart from any question of gift or agreement, ownership is decided on the basis of: (1) the documents of title, and (2) the financial contribution of each spouse. Part 1 of the Paper considers whether there should be alternative ways or additional considerations for determining ownership.

0.26 One possibility would be to allow the court to decide ownership of the home on discretionary grounds whenever a dispute arose between the spouses, taking into account various factors, including the contribution of each spouse to the family. The provisional conclusion is reached that, on balance, this would not be a worthwhile reform in view of the existing discretionary powers to award financial provision (which include powers to order a transfer or settlement of the property of either spouse) on a decree of divorce, nullity or judicial separation. Further, it would leave ownership uncertain in the absence of litigation.

0.27 Another possibility would be to introduce a presumption that the matrimonial home is owned by both spouses equally. Unless one of the spouses contested the matter, the presumption would apply. In the event of a contest equality would prevail unless.the presumption was rebutted. The chief problem under such a system would be to determine the circumstances in which the presumption should be rebutted. The choice may lie between narrow, and perhaps arbitrary, grounds and broad discretionary grounds which might result in considerable uncertainty.

0.28 A third possibility would be to go further than a presumption, which could be rebutted, and to provide that, subject to any agreement to the contrary, the beneficial interest in the matrimonial home should be shared equally by the spouses. We refer to this as the principle of co-ownership. The interests of the spouses would arise not from any financial contribution, nor from any contribution to the welfare of the family, nor from any other factors to be assessed by the court, but from the marriage relationship itself. There are advantages in this solution: it would in the absence of agreement to the contrary apply universally; it would acknowledge the partnership element in marriage by providing that the ownership of the principal family asset should be shared by the spouses; it would provide a large measure of security and certainty for a spouse in case of breakdown of marriage or on the death of the other spouse; and it would help to avoid protracted disputes and litigation.

0.29 The chief argument against the principle of co-ownership is that it could operate unfairly in individual cases. For example, a husband who paid for the house might find that, while he had to share ownership of it with his wife, he had no right to share *any* of her property. Since the sharing would operate only where spouses owned their home, the principle would not help [a wife] if [a husband] chose to invest his money and live in rented accommodation. An automatic rule might even induce him not to buy a home. Besides these objections there are certain practical problems to be overcome. One is to decide to what extent a spouse who is given an interest should be responsible for the liabilities in respect of the home which she may have no means of discharging unless she shares in assets other than the home. A second is to determine whether a spouse should be called upon to share a home which he or she may have owned absolutely before marriage. A third and serious problem is how to protect the interest of a spouse whose name is not on the legal title, while at the same time safe-guarding the interests of a purchaser or mortgagee. This, however, is essentially a matter of conveyancing machinery which should not be impossible to solve if it were decided to introduce the principle of co-ownership. The conclusion is reached that it would be practicable to introduce co-ownership, and that it would, on balance, have advantages over the present law. The Paper proposes that a new form of matrimonial home trust should apply whenever the beneficial interest in the home is shared between the spouses, in order that they should have a direct interest in the property.

In their *First Report on Family Property — A New Approach* (1973) the Law Commission emphasised the crucial distinction which exists in the present law between the position during marriage or on the death or bankruptcy of either party, and the position on divorce:

17. During marriage the efforts of a wife in caring for the family and the home give her no proprietary interest in the home. Unless she has made a financial contribution in circumstances entitling her to rely on the strict principles of trust law she cannot claim any proprietary interest in the home either during the marriage or on the death of her husband. However, if the marriage ends in divorce, the interests of the spouses in the home can be determined by having regard to their joint efforts in the marriage partnership in whatever form. In our view the difference between the rules applied to married couples and those applied on divorce can no longer be regarded as acceptable.

The Law Commission stated that the principle of co-ownership was widely supported:

21. It emerged clearly from the consultation that the principle of co-ownership of the matrimonial home is widely supported both as the best means of reforming the law relating to the home, and as the main principle of family property law. The great majority who supported

co-ownership included legal practitioners, academic lawyers, women's organisations and members of the public. Those who opposed co-ownership were those who were opposed to any form of fixed property rights, and they were relatively few in number.

22. Widespread approval of the principle of co-ownership of the matrimonial home was also revealed by the Social Survey [Todd and Jones, 1972]. Married couples were asked the following question:

'Some people say that the home and its contents should legally be jointly owned by the husband and wife irrespective of who paid for it. Do you agree or disagree with that?'

91% of husbands and 94% of wives who took part in the survey agreed with the proposition: the remainder disagreed. In the case of owner occupiers who had their home in the name of one spouse 87% of both husbands and wives said that they regarded the home as belonging to both of them.

23. The opinions expressed favouring the co-ownership principle are supported by a change in the pattern of ownership of the matrimonial home in recent years. The Social Survey analysed the pattern and found that 52% of couples owned their home; among the home owners 52% had their home in joint names. However, when the figures were broken down by the year of purchase of the home it was clear that a marked increase in the rate of joint ownership began in the middle 1960's and is continuing. The following table illustrates the position:

Year the present house was acquired	Proportion of owner-occupiers who owned the home jointly
1960–61	51%
1962–63	47%
1964–65	52%
1966–67	57%
1968–69	69%
1970–71	74%

In cases where the wife had made some financial contribution to the home the proportion of homes put into joint names was higher than in cases where there had been no such contribution. The rate of joint ownership was also very high in cases where the couple had owned more than one home.

24. The Survey considered the reasons for the trend towards joint ownership and concluded that —

'the factors associated with joint ownership of the matrimonial home were not those related to the couple themselves, such as the length of marriage and social class. Instead there were factors relating to the circumstances of purchase of the home; the year the present home was acquired; the number of times the couples had been through the process of buying a house and whether the wife had made any financial contribution to it'.

Having examined this evidence, the Law Commission arrived at the conclusion that, subject to the proviso that a husband and wife remain free to make any arrangements they choose, the principle of automatic co-ownership of the matrimonial home should be introduced.

We have seen that the case against the co-ownership principle rests on the following arguments:

(1) It is unnecessary to introduce any form of fixed principles since all necessary improvements can be effected through the discretionary powers of the court.

(2) The principle of co-ownership would be arbitrary and unfair in application. For example, in some marriages one party to a marriage would be required to share a home although there would be no obligation to share other property.

(3) There would be an unjustifiable interference in the property relations of spouses and in their freedom of choice.

Questions

(i) Do you see force in any of these arguments?

(ii) If you wished to do so, how would you counter them?

(iii) Why did the Law Commission leave it open to couples to make such arrangements as they chose?

(iv) Is not this the present position?

One of the problems of co-ownership by operation of law is that there are bound to be exceptions. In their *Third Report on Family Property* (1978), the Law Commission return to a consideration of the major exceptions which would be necessary if the principle were to be introduced. The first is in relation to an interest in property acquired on or before marriage. The Law Commission recommend that a home of this kind should be subject to statutory co-ownership unless the owner spouse takes positive action to exclude it. Such action can only be taken before the marriage:

1.113 We also recommend that it should affect only the particular home in question: it should not operate to exclude any subsequent home even if that home is purchased with the proceeds of sale of the first one. Finally, we emphasise that the owner spouse is to have this power of exclusion only when he holds a separate interest — an interest, that is, which is held by him otherwise than as a joint tenant or tenant in common *with the other spouse* (or, more accurately, with the person who is to become the other spouse).

There is some disagreement about whether an owning spouse should be allowed to make a 'secret reservation'. The majority of the Law Commissioners recommend that a reservation need not be communicated to a future spouse, but that there should be a written declaration, signed and attested by a witness to the effect that statutory co-ownership is not to apply. One Law Commissioner, Mr Marsh, considers, however:

that it would be potentially harmful to good matrimonial relations to allow one spouse by his own secret reservation to spring a surprise, perhaps after years of marriage, on the other spouse as to the ownership of the matrimonial home. He thinks therefore that a declaration should not have effect unless it has been communicated to the other spouse before marriage (which he emphasises does not necessarily mean that the other spouse consents).

Questions

(i) What arguments can you advance against the view that property acquired before marriage can be treated as community property?
(ii) Do you agree with Mr Marsh or with the other Commissioners about 'secret reservations'?
(iii) Or would you not permit any reservations at all?

Another exception canvassed in the *Working Paper* (1971) which had been the subject of considerable discussion related to homes acquired by one spouse from a third party by gift or inheritance during, or by gift in contemplation of, the marriage. The original view of the Law Commission was:

1.116 'If co-ownership were to apply automatically, the donor could not make an absolute gift to one spouse without asking the other spouse to agree to exclude co-ownership. It seems undesirable that a donor should have to ask for such an agreement. The result would probably be that the donor would either refrain from making the gift or resort to some other device (such as granting a life interest) to achieve his purpose.'
. . . We reached the provisional conclusion that homes of this kind should not be subject to co-ownership at all (though it was recognised that the donee spouse could always agree to share with the other spouse if he wished to do so).

However, in their *Third Report on Family Property* (1978), the Law Commission stated:

1.117. The weight of opinion expressed in consultation was against this conclusion. We see the force of the views expressed by those who disagreed. It can certainly be argued, for instance, that a spouse who acquires a home by gift is already fortunate enough, and that there is no reason to multiply his good fortune, and at the same time to prevent his spouse from participating in it, by excluding her from co-ownership. On the other hand we think the arguments advanced in the working paper are also sound.
1.118. We have therefore arrived once more at a compromise solution — namely, that co-

ownership *should* apply to a home of this kind *unless* the donor (a term which we use to include a testator or settlor) directs, in the instrument making the gift, that it shall not.

1.119. Our reasons for recommending this solution are much the same as our reasons for recommending a similar solution to the problem of homes owned by one spouse before the marriage. In this case, however, the solution was considered in the working paper and provisionally rejected on the ground that a declaration by the donor 'could appear invidious, and may be even more undesirable than an agreement to exclude.' Although the first part of this statement is obviously true — . . . we are no longer inclined to support the second part. We feel, moreover, that this solution, imperfect though it may be, is really the only one open to us. In view of our consultation and the further thought which we ourselves have given to the matter, we no longer feel able to recommend the automatic exclusion proposed in the working paper. But we do not feel it right to deny the donor any means whatever of bringing about an exclusion.

The third case where automatic co-ownership might be excluded is when there is an agreement between the spouses. The Law Commission recommended however that statutory co-ownership should only be excluded 'when the spouses have spelt out the beneficial holding which is to replace it.'

The appendix to book one of the *Third Report on Family Property* (1978) contains a Matrimonial Homes (Co-ownership) Bill. This Bill was introduced into the House of Lords as a private member's Bill by Lord Simon. It reached the second reading in that House on 12 February 1980. Lord Scarman, the former Chairman of the Law Commission, made the following speech:

. . . In married life the husband and wife should, unless they choose to organise their affairs in a different way, both of them own the matrimonial home. Of course the Bill operates as much in favour of a husband as it does of a wife, but let us not be deluded by that necessary feature of the Bill into thinking that this Bill is necessary for the protection of husbands. It certainly is not. This Bill is necessary as the law's safety net for the most vulnerable woman in our society, the devoted married woman while the marriage relationship is a living relationship and she has her family duties hard upon her. She is exceedingly vulnerable.

If of course, as so many women are, she is fortunate in her husband and her children there is no risk. There is of course no need for her protection by the law but if, like the girl on the flying trapeze, she takes a leap towards her partner and fails to get the appropriate support and grip as she flies through the air, then as she falls to the hard ground she needs the safety net of co-ownership for her support. At the moment our law does not provide that at all. She falls on the hard ground of legal ownership, separate property and nothing for her unless she has been well enough advised at the beginning of her matrimonial life to ensure that she agrees with her husband or fiancé joint ownership of the matrimonial home. So what this Bill is doing is providing a legal background of joint ownership of the matrimonial home if they have not agreed something else. This is a major reform which will be immensely important for the most vulnerable of all women in our society.

After dealing with a number of technical aspects of the Bill and the difficulties involved, Lord Scarman continued:

The other main criticism I have heard of the Bill is that it is unnecessary. Of course, it is unnecessary if men and women will always take legal advice when they are engaged in marriage, go to a solicitor and get joint ownership worked out and an agreement regulating their family property. But the importance of this Bill, as I have already indicated, is that it takes care of the feckless, the inadequate, the uneducated, the ignorant, the helpless woman; one can apply all those adjectives to an absolutely darling person of great virtue who needs help and protection, if you like, against her own inexperience in the wiles of the world. It is, therefore, not unnecessary, for the reason which I have developed.

Question

Do you not think that the 'darling person of great virtue who needs help and protection' would be the very person who would readily agree with the husband's wish that the property *not* be subject to co-ownership?

The Lord Chancellor, Lord Hailsham, made it clear that the Bill would not receive Government support. He alluded to two situations which concerned him:

The owner — let us call him Mr Hogg of 249A Anerley Road — marries Miss Smith and she thereupon becomes joint tenant because neither has objected to the operation of the general law. On the other hand, Mr Hogg does want the house to stay in his family; it is a family house. Mr Hogg unfortunately dies. Mrs Hogg, who was formerly Miss Smith, takes the lot, marries again outside the family and then dies. The first family loses the house. The second husband gets it if nobody does anything about it. Is that justice? For this purpose it does not matter whether you are a woman or a man; the story can be told the other way round.

Let us take another situation. Supposing the first marriage has children and that it has ended in divorce or death. The first marriage has children and nobody does anything about it. But there is a second marriage, and the second marriage results in children, too. As a result of the joint tenancy, the survivor of the first marriage gets the lot. And if he or she does nothing about it the survivor of the second marriage gets the lot and the children of the first marriage are altogether dispossessed. Is that social justice?

Question

Do you have an answer to Lord Hailsham's question?

Lord Simon answered the Lord Chancellor in the following way: 'It is as though he stood up and said, "I am passionately devoted to cheese and therefore I shall oppose anything that is put forward to prevent the quarrying of chalk".' The second approach, at least in relation to the matrimonial home, went into suspension with Lord Hailsham's speech. It was only resurrected when problems relating to third parties became crucial. The Law Commission re-examined the whole issue as a result of the decision of the House of Lords in the following case:

Williams and Glyn's Bank Ltd v Boland
[1981] AC 487, [1980] 2 All ER 408, [1980] 3 WLR 138, 124 Sol Jo 443, [1980] RVR 204, 40 P & CR 451, House of Lords

An account of the facts in this case appears in the Law Commission paper, *The Implications of Williams and Glyn's Bank Ltd v Boland* (1982):

3. In 1969 Michael Boland bought a house and went to live there with his wife and son. She had made a substantial contribution to the purchase price, but the title to the property was in the name of Michael Boland alone. In order to finance his business activities a loan, personally guaranteed by him, was obtained from Williams & Glyn's Bank, to whom he charged the house as security. The Bank made no enquiries about Mrs Boland's rights. The business failed, and the Bank brought proceedings for possession of the house, with a view to its sale with vacant possession and the recovery, from the proceeds, of so much of the loan as remained due.
4. The Bolands contested the Bank's claim for possession. Mrs Boland maintained that she had rights which prevailed against those of the Bank. She claimed that she was entitled to a property interest in the house by reason of her contribution to the purchase; that she occupied the house and was entitled to continue to occupy it; and that her rights constituted an 'overriding interest' which prevailed against the Bank. The Bank did not dispute that, as against her husband, Mrs Boland was entitled to a property interest in the house and to a right to occupy it. Rather, it maintained that her rights did not bind the Bank. The Bank succeeded before Templeman J at first instance, but his judgment was unanimously reversed by the Court of Appeal, whose decision was unanimously upheld by the House of Lords.

In the county court, the similar case of *Williams and Glyn's Bank Ltd v Brown* was also decided in favour of the Bank, and the appeals from the two decisions were heard together. We give below the most important extracts from Lord Wilberforce's speech in so far as it concerns the broader question of the rights of the wife in relation to the Bank:

Lord Wilberforce: The legal framework within which the appeals are to be decided can be summarised as follows.
    Under the Land Registration Act 1925, legal estates in land are the only interests in respect of which a proprietor can be registered. Other interests take effect in equity as 'minor interests,' which are overridden by a registered transfer. But the Act recognises also an intermediate, or

hybrid, class of what are called 'overriding interests': though these are not registered, legal dispositions take effect subject to them. The list of overriding interests is contained in section 70 and it includes such matters as easements, liabilities having their origin in tenure, land tax and title rentcharge, seignorial and manorial rights, leases for terms not exceeding 21 years, and finally, the relevant paragraph being section 70(1)(g):

'The rights of every person in actual occupation of the land or in receipt of the rents and profits thereof, save where enquiry is made of such person and the rights are not disclosed;. . .'

The first question is whether the wife is a 'person in actual occupation' and if so, whether her right as a tenant in common in equity is a right protected by this provision.

The other main element arises out of the Law of Property Act 1925. Since that Act, undivided shares in land can only take effect in equity, behind a trust for sale upon which the legal owner is to hold the land. Dispositions of the land, including mortgages, may be made under this trust and, provided that there are at least two trustees, or a trust corporation, 'overreach' the trusts. This means that the 'purchaser' takes free from them, whether or not he has notice of them, and that the trusts are enforceable against the proceeds of sale: see Law of Property Act 1925, section 2(2) and (3) which lists certain exceptions.

The second question is whether the wife's equitable interest under the trust for sale, if she is in occupation of the land, is capable of being an overriding interest, or whether, as is generally the rule as regards equitable interests it can only take effect as a 'minor interest.' In the latter event a registered transferee, including a legal mortgagee, would take free from it.

The system of land registration, as it exists in England, which long antedates the Land Registration Act 1925, is designed to simplify and to cheapen conveyancing. It is intended to replace the often complicated and voluminous title deeds of property by a single land certificate, on the strength of which land can be dealt with. In place of the lengthy and often technical investigation of title to which a purchaser was committed, all he has to do is to consult the register; from any burden not entered on the register, with one exception, he takes free. Above all, the system is designed to free the purchaser from the hazards of notice — real or constructive — which, in the case of unregistered land, involved him in enquiries, often quite elaborate, failing which he might be bound by equities. The Law of Property Act 1925 contains provisions limiting the effect of the doctrine of notice, but it still remains a potential source of danger to purchasers. By contrast, the only provisions in the Land Registration Act 1925 with regard to notice are provisions which enable a purchaser to take the estate free from equitable interests or equities whether he has notice or not. (See, for example, section 3(xv) s.v. 'minor interests'). The only kind of notice recognised is by entry on the register.

The exception just mentioned consists of 'overriding interests' listed in section 70. As to these, all registered land is stated to be deemed to be subject to such of them as may be subsisting in reference to the land, unless the contrary is expressed on the register. The land is so subject regardless of notice actual or constructive. In my opinion therefore, the law as to notice as it may affect purchasers of unregistered land, whether contained in decided cases, or in a statute (the Conveyancing Act 1882, section 3, Law of Property Act, section 199) has no application even by analogy to registered land. Whether a particular right is an overriding interest, and whether it affects a purchaser, is to be decided upon the terms of section 70, and other relevant provisions of the Land Registration Act 1925, and upon nothing else.

In relation to rights connected with occupation, it has been said that the purpose and effect of section 70(1)(g) of the Land Registration Act 1925 was to make applicable to registered land the same rule as previously had been held to apply to unregistered land: see per Lord Denning MR in *National Provincial Bank Ltd v Hastings Car Mart Ltd* [1964] Ch 665 at 689, and in this House [1965] AC 1175 at 1259.

I adhere to this, but I do not accept the argument which learned counsel for the appellant sought to draw from it. His submission was that, in applying section 70(1)(g), we should have regard to and limit the application of the paragraph in the light of the doctrine of notice. But this would run counter to the whole purpose of the Act. The purpose, in each system, is the same, namely, to safeguard the rights of persons in occupation, but the method used differs. In the case of unregistered land, the purchaser's obligation depends upon what he has notice of — notice actual or constructive. In the case of registered land, it is the fact of occupation that matters. If there is actual occupation, and the occupier has rights, the purchaser takes subject to them. If not, he does not. No further element is material.

I now deal with the first question. Were the wives here in 'actual occupation'? These words are ordinary words of plain English, and should, in my opinion, be interpreted as such.

After considering a number of old decisions, Lord Wilberforce continues:

There was physical presence, with all the rights that occupiers have, including the right to exclude all others except those having similar rights. The house was a matrimonial home, intended to be occupied, and in fact occupied by both spouses, both of whom have an interest in it: it would require some special doctrine of law to avoid the result that each is in occupation.

Three arguments were used for a contrary conclusion. First, it was said that if the vendor (I use this word to include a mortgagor) is in occupation, that is enough to prevent the application of the paragraph. This seems to be a proposition of general application, not limited to the case of husbands, and no doubt, if correct, would be very convenient for purchasers and intending mortgagees. But the presence of the vendor, with occupation, does not exclude the possibility of occupation of others. . . . Then it was suggested that the wife's occupation was nothing but the shadow of the husband's — a version I suppose of the doctrine of unity of husband and wife. This expression and the argument flowing from it was used by Templeman J in *Bird v Syme-Thomson* [1978] 3 All ER 1027, [1979] 1 WLR 440, a decision preceding and which he followed in the present case. The argument was also inherent in the judgment in *Caunce v Caunce* [1969] 1 All ER 722, [1969] 1 WLR 286 which influenced the decisions of Templeman J. It somewhat faded from the arguments in the present case and appears to me to be heavily obsolete. The appellant's main and final position became in the end this: that, to come within the paragraph, the occupation in question must be apparently inconsistent with the title of the vendor. This, it was suggested, would exclude the wife of a husband-vendor because her apparent occupation would be satisfactorily accounted for by his. But, apart from the rewriting of the paragraph which this would involve, the suggestion is unacceptable. Consistency, or inconsistency, involves the absence, or presence, of an independent right to occupy, though I must observe that 'inconsistency' in this context is an inappropriate word. But how can either quality be predicated of a wife, simply qua wife? A wife may, and everyone knows this, have rights of her own; particularly, many wives have a share in a matrimonial home. How can it be said that the presence of a wife in the house, as occupier, is consistent or inconsistent with the husband's rights and one knows what rights she has? And if she has rights, why, just because she is a wife (or in the converse case, just because an occupier is the husband), should these rights be denied protection under the paragraph? If one looks beyond the case of husband and wife, the difficulty of all these arguments stands out if one considers the case of a man living with a mistress, or of a man and a woman — or for that matter two persons of the same sex — living in a house in separate or partially shared rooms. Are these cases of apparently consistent occupation, so that the rights of the other person (other than the vendor) can be disregarded? The only solution which is consistent with the Act (section 70(1)(g)) and with common sense is to read the paragraph for what it says. Occupation, existing as a fact, may protect rights if the person in occupation has rights. On this part of the case I have no difficulty in concluding that a spouse, living in a house, has an actual occupation capable of conferring protection, as an overriding interest, upon rights of that spouse.

Lord Wilberforce goes on to consider whether such rights as a spouse has under a trust for sale are capable of recognition as overriding interests. He examines the structure of the Land Registration Act 1925, and reaches the conclusion that such rights are indeed capable of recognition. He then has a few words to say about general policy. He agrees with Templeman J at first instance to the extent that:

. . . Whereas the object of a land registration system is to reduce the risks to purchasers from anything not on the register, to extend (if it be an extension) the area of risk so as to include possible interests of spouses, and indeed, in theory, of other members of the family or even outside it, may add to the burdens of purchasers, and involve them in enquiries which in some cases may be troublesome.

But conceded, as it must be, that the Act, following established practice, gives protection to occupation, the extension of the risk area follows necessarily from the extension, beyond the paterfamilias, of rights of ownership, itself following from the diffusion of property and earning capacity. What is involved is a departure from an easy-going practice of dispensing with enquiries as to occupation beyond that of the vendor and accepting the risks of doing so. To substitute for this a practice of more careful enquiry as to the fact of occupation, and if necessary as to the rights of occupiers can not, in my view of the matter, be considered as unacceptable except at the price of overlooking the widespread development of shared interests of ownership. In the light of section 70 of the Act, I cannot believe that Parliament intended this, though it may be true that in 1925 it did not foresee the full extent of this development.

Lord Scarman: . . . But the importance of the House's decision is not to be judged solely by its impact on conveyancing or banking, practice. The Court of Appeal recognised the relevance, and stressed the importance, of the social implications of the case. While the technical task faced by the courts, and now facing the House, is the construction to be put upon a sub-clause in a subsection of a conveyancing statute, it is our duty, when tackling it, to give the provision, if we properly can, a meaning which will work for, rather than against, rights conferred by Parliament, or recognised by judicial decision as being necessary for the achievement of social justice. The courts may not, therefore, put aside, as irrelevant, the undoubted fact that if the two wives succeed, the protection of the beneficial interest which English law now recognises that a married woman has in the matrimonial home will be strengthened whereas, if they lose, this interest can be weakened, and even destroyed, by an unscrupulous husband. Nor must the courts flinch when assailed by arguments to the effect that the protection of her interest will create difficulties in banking or conveyancing practice. The difficulties are, I believe, exaggerated; but bankers, and solicitors, exist to provide the service which the public needs. They can — as they have successfully done in the past — adjust their practice, if it be socially required. Nevertheless, the judicial responsibility remains — to interpret the statute truly according to its tenor. The social background is, therefore, to be kept in mind but can be decisive only if the particular statutory provision under review is reasonably capable of the meaning conducive to the special purpose to which I have referred. If it is not, the remedy is to be found not by judicial distortion of the language used by Parliament but in amending legislation.

Fortunately, these appeals call for no judicial ingenuity — let alone distortion. The ordinary meaning of the words used by Parliament meets the needs of social justice.

Questions

(i) Surely not all married women have beneficial interests in the matrimonial home?

(ii) As a result of the *Boland* decision, it has been said that the cost of conveyancing has increased, and new sources of delay and complication have been created. Is this a reasonable price to pay for the additional protection accorded to those, especially married women, who have equitable interests in the family home?

(iii) If Mrs Boland had been asked to agree to the charge, in order to secure her husband's business and source of income, do you think that she would have done so?

(iv) Shortly after his marriage to Sarah in 1970, Frank bought a house for use as their matrimonial home. The house was conveyed to Frank alone. Sarah provided a small cash deposit for the purchase, and the balance of the purchase price was raised by a mortgage advance from the Wessex Building Society for the repayment of which Frank was solely responsible. Throughout the marriage Frank has paid the mortgage instalments out of his own bank account, but Sarah has often used her own cash resources to pay joint household bills. In 1974 Sarah received a legacy of £8,000 under her father's will and she spent this sum on the construction of a swimming pool in the back garden of the house. In 1977 Frank borrowed £50,000 in his own name from the Mercia Bank. The loan, which was secured on the matrimonial home, was intended to enable Frank to expand a business which he operated from rented premises in a nearby town. In March of this year Frank's business ran into difficulties and Frank has now been made bankrupt. Advise Sarah as to her rights (if any) in the matrimonial home.

The Law Commission *Report* (1982) commented on the protection afforded to wives as a result of the *Boland* decision in the following way:

67. In one sense *Boland* may be seen as a development of a well-established social trend towards the greater protection of the rights of wives. The appellate judges gave strong indications that there was a need to protect the interests of wives in the matrimonial home. [See for example Lord Scarman's judgment at p. 122] If a marriage breaks down, the court has in divorce and kindred proceedings wide powers over both spouses' property, which it will normally exercise so as to preserve for the wife not only her 'investment' in the matrimonial home but also her right to go on living there. If the husband dies intestate, the wife is entitled, in addition to an interest in residue, to a 'statutory legacy' sufficient (if the estate is sufficient) to cover the cost of an average house and to have the matrimonial home appropriated in satisfaction of that interest. If the husband's will or intestacy fails to make reasonable financial provision from the estate for his wife the court has wide powers to order that such provision should be made for her. The court also has extensive powers to set aside transactions intended to prevent or reduce financial provision being granted on divorce or death. Yet until *Boland* the fact that a wife had a share, even a majority share, in the home did not effectively prevent the husband from selling or mortgaging it without her consent, so as to defeat or jeopardise the interest which she had

acquired in the home, often by her own efforts. In our view this was a weakness in the wife's legal position which the decision in *Boland* has exposed and helped to repair.

The Law Commission think that the consistency of the *Boland* case with current social policy in favour of the protection of the wife in the matrimonial home is in contrast to its inconsistency with the policy of property law, which upholds the security of titles, the marketability of land and the simplification of conveyancing. The Law Commission itemise the problems as they see them:

72. The first problem is a *conveyancing problem*: how may a co-owner ensure that the co-ownership interest is protected against a purchaser and the purchaser ensure that he takes free of co-ownership interests of which he is unaware? The second problem is about the *effects of co-ownership*: in what circumstances should a co-owner be entitled to protect his enjoyment of the land against a purchaser? The third problem is a problem about *entitlement to co-ownership*: how, and in what circumstances, can the existence and extent of co-ownership be established with reasonable certainty? We shall find it convenient to deal with these problems separately; but we would stress that *Boland* seems to us to demand solutions to all three, not to any one or two of them.

They recommend that the first problem should be dealt with by the introduction of a requirement that co-ownership should be registered. As to the second problem, the consent of a married co-owner would be essential to the validity of dispositions of the matrimonial home. As regards the third problem, entitlement, the Law Commission return to a consideration of co-ownership which the Commission had discussed in the Working Paper, the first Report, and the third Report.

112. But *Boland* has added a new dimension. In the First and Third Reports the reforms we proposed were primarily designed to do justice between husband and wife and to eradicate the existing state of uncertainty as to their mutual interests. But we also mentioned the possibility that this uncertainty might spill over into conveyancing transactions. In our First Report, in referring to the uncertainty of the law, we said this —
'. . . if the house is in the name of one spouse, and the other has become entitled to a beneficial interest in it, there may be doubt in the event of a sale as to the respective rights of the beneficiary spouse and a third party purchaser.'
Boland has given these words a new significance. The case for equal co-ownership of the matrimonial home, as a clear and fair allocation of matrimonial property, remains in our view justifiable on its own merits, and has recently been supported in the Council of Europe;[3] but the state of the law as found in *Boland* provides an added reason for its introduction.

The Commission recommend the enactment of their own co-ownership Bill:

114. . . . We expect that two consequences of particular relevance to this report would follow from the enactment of the Bill.
    (i) An increasing number of married couples will provide expressly for equal co-ownership of their homes (e.g. by putting the house into their joint names), because enactment of the Bill will both reflect and encourage the growing tendency towards equal co-ownership and because, as we pointed out in the Third Report, express provision for equal co-ownership made by the parties is for several reasons more satisfactory than reliance on statutory co-ownership.
    (ii) The fact of statutory co-ownership will rapidly become common knowledge. This should substantially restrict the number of cases in which there is a failure to register a co-ownership interest when registration is necessary for the protection of the interest; and whereas a husband may be tempted to ignore the need to obtain his wife's consent to

---

3. Governments of member states are recommended to secure the rights of spouses to occupy the matrimonial home by appropriate legislation and 'to take into consideration the possibility of adopting systems of co-ownership . . . as one of the means of strengthening the right of occupation of the family home' (Recommendation R(81)(15) of the Committee of Ministers to Member States of the Council of Europe, adopted by the Committee of Ministers on 16 October 1981 as the 338th meeting of Ministers' Deputies).

a disposition where the existence or extent of her beneficial interest is uncertain, he will be less likely to ignore it when she has a statutory equal share in the home.

In our view, therefore, the Bill will do much to cure the present uncertainty regarding the existence and extent of co-ownership interests, not only directly by its provisions for statutory co-ownership but also indirectly by encouraging married couples themselves to provide expressly for equal co-ownership. Moreover, in those cases where statutory co-ownership will apply, the ownership of a half share in the matrimonial home will be a matter of such substance that the need to register the co-ownership interest for protection against purchasers is unlikely often to be overlooked.

Questions

(i) Do you think that Lord Hailsham will be satisfied?
(ii) The Law Commission proposed a system of registration of co-owners' rights. Do you think it fair to impose a registration system? And
(iii) Do you think that a system of registration of co-owners' rights is an improvement on the protection given by *Boland*?

The Law Commission propose that the co-ownership principle should be extended to the rented sector. The following table from *Social Trends 13* 1982 shows how important this sector is to the stock of dwellings in the UK.

Stock of dwellings: by tenure and change

	United Kingdom						Millions and thousands	
	1961 –70	1971 –75	1976	1977	1978	1979	1980	1981
Stock of dwellings — at end of period (millions)								
Owner-occupied	9.57	10.76	10.96	11.16	11.39	11.62	11.91	12.21
Rented from local authorities or new town corporations	5.85	6.40	6.56	6.70	6.79	6.84	6.82	6.76
Other tenures	3.77	3.19	3.09	3.01	2.93	2.86	2.80	2.72
Total	19.19	20.35	20.61	20.86	21.11	21.32	21.54	21.69

Relating the housing stock to the 'household type' and to the economic activity of the 'head of the household' will illustrate the important point that the rented sector accounts for substantial percentages of the households where there are 'one or two adults living with one or two children'. The table which follows on p. 126, showing household tenure and household type in 1980 is taken from *Social Trends 12* (1982):

In any event, local authorities increasingly use joint tenancy agreements in the case of husband and wife. If the tenancy is a joint one, the Housing Act 1980 provides that in general the tenancy is 'secure' so long as at least one of them occupies the dwelling house as his or her only or principal home (s. 28). The two major components of secure tenancies are the right of succession on the death of the first tenant and the security from eviction. Whether the tenancy is sole or joint, there is provision for only *one* succession on the death of the first tenant. Succession will be in favour, first of the tenant's spouse provided that that person 'occupied the dwelling house as his only or principal home at the time of the tenant's death,' or secondly, failing this, of any other member of the tenant's family who has resided with the tenant throughout the period of 12 months ending with the tenant's death. The other major element of the security of tenure conferred by the Housing Act 1980 relates to the circumstances in which possession of a dwelling house let on a secure tenancy may be recovered. A landlord cannot get possession from a secure tenant without a court order and the court cannot make such

	Great Britain					Percentages and numbers	
	Tenure					**All tenures**	
	Owner-occupiers		Tenants			Total sample size	
	Outright-owners	Mort-gagors	Local author-ity	Unfur-nished private*	Furnished private	(per-centages)	(numbers)
Household type							
1 adult aged under 60	16	23	28	14	19	100	870
2 adults, both aged under 60	16	48	23	9	4	100	1,533
1 or 2 adults, 1 or 2 children	6	53	32	7	1	100	2,484
1 or 2 adults, 3 or more children†	17	38	38	7	1	100	2,990
2 adults, 1 or both aged 60 or over	47	7	34	11	—	100	2,046
1 adult, aged 60 or over	37	1	44	18	1	100	1,742
Age of head of household							
under 25	2	31	29	13	.25	100	490
25 to 29	2	51	30	10	8	100	889
30 to 44	7	56	28	7	2	100	3,051
45 to 59	22	34	35	8	1	100	3,020
60 to 69	41	8	40	11	1	100	2,105
70 and over	43	1	39	16	—	100	2,110

* Includes those renting from a housing association, and those renting with job or business.
† Includes 3 or more adults with or without children.

an order except on the grounds specified in detail in Part 1 of Schedule 4 to the Housing Act 1980. These include non payment of rent, deterioration in the condition of the dwelling house, nuisance or annoyance and so on.

Questions

(i) It is often argued that joint tenancies have a psychological effect. However, where there is a joint tenancy, each partner is jointly and severally liable for the rent even if the arrears were due purely to the 'fault' of one of them. Is this too high a price to pay for the alleged psychological advantage of joint tenancies?

(ii) Why restrict rights of succession of a secure council tenancy to one?

(iii) If the husband dies in 1983 and the wife dies in 1984, what then happens to the children?

(iv) (*a*) Is the position of the children in (iii) the same under the scheme for succession to a Rent Act 1977 tenancy, and (*b*) if there is a difference, what justification if any is there for this difference? (Go and look at the Rent Act 1977, Sch. 1 Part 1.)

(v) The power of the local authority to transfer a tenancy agreement on its own initiative is no longer available in the case of secure tenancies. Do you think that this is an unfortunate restriction of the local authority's powers?

(vi) How, if at all, can a local authority remove a person's tenancy rights after serious domestic violence? (See further Chapter 14, below.)

(d) THE FAMILY ASSETS OTHER THAN THE MATRIMONIAL HOME

We return to the debate on co-ownership by examining other family assets, such as the household goods and the various investments of the family. Professor Sir Otto Kahn-Freund was a strong advocate of an introduction of 'community' in the family assets, and we quote the following extracts from his *Unger Memorial Lecture* (1971):

What I suggest is a general rule that such assets as form the matrimonial aggregate, — 'family assets', — should, in the absence of special circumstances, be shared by the spouses half and half. The special circumstances would have to be found by the court in the light of the facts of the case. It is here that the court should have a wide discretion, especially in assessing the significance in each case of various conflicting considerations. Some of the considerations enumerated in section 5 of the Matrimonial Proceedings and Property Act 1970 [now s. 25(1) of the Matrimonial Causes Act 1973; see Chapter 6, below] would be relevant, including above all, the value of pensions expectations which either spouse, — in most cases the wife, — stands to lose as a result of the termination of a marriage. Occasionally the court may also have to assess the value of the contributions made by either spouse to the welfare of the family, 'including any contribution made by looking after the home and caring for the family'. But this should only be done in exceptional cases, — and normally the value of the contributions should be deemed to be equal.

We have therefore arrived at the conclusion that husband and wife should be presumed to be entitled to one half each of an aggregate of assets and that a court should have the power to vary this rule in the light of the circumstances of individual cases.

But, of course, this leaves us with two fundamental problems: how should the assets which make up the aggregate be identified? And, equally important, is all this to affect the spouses themselves only, or also third parties?

Kahn-Freund answers his first question in the following manner;

I should identify the assets which are to constitute the aggregate not by reason of how, when, by whom and with whose resources they were acquired. My criterion of selection would not be their origin, but their purpose. My question would not be whether they have been acquired before or during the marriage, or acquired through work or thrift or through inheritance or gift. I should ask: what object are they intended to serve? Are they assets for investment, acquired and held for the income they produce or the profit they may yield on resale? Or are they household assets, family assets, which form the basis of the life of husband, wife and children?

Kahn-Freund rejects historical examples of 'family assets' which in his view 'belong to the dustheap of history'. There were three motivations in former times for introducing community schemes into continental Europe:

The first was to protect the wife who was assumed to be incapable of defending her property and of managing her affairs. The second was to protect the widow or the widower against the next of kin of the predeceasing spouse. The third was to provide capital for the husband's enterprise.

Kahn-Freund says of the first reason, 'to us the assumption that women are incapable of defending their property and are in need of tutelage looks absurd.' (But do you remember what Lord Scarman said in the House of Lords in February 1980, see p. 119, above?) Kahn-Freund continues:

An asset is a family asset if, at any given time it is by consent of the spouses, dedicated to the common use of the household family, irrespective of whether it was acquired before or after the marriage, or through the spouses' work or thrift or through inheritance or gift. It comprises the family home and its contents (furniture and equipment), but also a family car and other implements intended to be enjoyed by the family. It also includes such funds, however invested, as are, by the spouses' consent, at any given moment dedicated to future family expenditure, including expenditure for the benefit of a child of the family, or as have been saved by either spouse without the knowledge of the other and been dedicated by him for future family expenditure. In the absence of proof to the contrary any house or flat used as a matrimonial home is presumed to be a family asset, and so are all chattels in common use. No other asset belonging to either spouse is presumed to be a family asset.

The major problem relating to family assets is whether any principle of co-ownership should affect third parties. The Law Commission, possibly aware of this difficulty, state that in their view the primary consideration should be to devise a scheme which protects the 'occupation rights' of the spouses (see p. 44, above). In the first report, they say:

> . . . It is more important at this stage to protect the use and enjoyment of those goods than to change the ownership rules. The reason for this is that such goods usually have a rapidly diminishing realisable value; in most cases a spouse's share in the proceeds of sale of second-hand furniture would not go far towards the cost of its replacement (save in the case of antiques). Because of this a spouse's main concern is to retain the use and enjoyment of the goods and we propose that the spouse in occupation of the home should have this right. This would be essentially a support right supplementing the rights of occupation which are protected under the Matrimonial Homes Act 1967.

Todd and Jones (1972) produced the following information:

> We asked the wives whether they had contributed to the major items of matrimonial property and if so by what means. Among the couples who owned the home 79% of wives said they had contributed to it; among the couples who owned cars 57% said they have contributed to it; 85% of wives said they had contributed to the furniture and 76% said they had contributed to big items such as the cooker, refrigerator, washing machine etc. We suggested five possible means of contributing and asked each wife who had contributed which methods she had used. In terms of the home and contents over two thirds of those who had contributed said they did so from earnings during marriage, about a half said that their effort in the home had been a contribution, and a quarter to a third said that savings from before marriage had been used for the house or furniture.
> Thus a large proportion of wives felt that they have contributed to the matrimonial property, and a considerable number considered that their effort in the home had been a contribution.

Questions

(i) Does this constitute evidence in support of co-ownership for major household goods?

(ii) What do you do with those spouses who think that they have made no contribution? Would they be entitled to automatic co-ownership rights as well?

Co-ownership of household goods is not popular with the Law Commission. They reiterate their view against such a scheme in their Third Report (1978).

(e) THE THIRD APPROACH: DEFERRED COMMUNITY OF PROPERTY

A detailed description of deferred community appears in the Canadian Law Reform Commission's *Working Paper* (1975):

> Deferred sharing, or deferred community of property as it is sometimes called, is based on the idea that there should be separate ownership of property during marriage, and an equal distribution of property on divorce. Deferred sharing, therefore, lies somewhere between the extremes of separate property on the one hand and full community of property on the other. Deferred sharing regimes exist in Denmark, Sweden, Norway, Finland, West Germany and Holland. In Canada, Quebec adopted a deferred sharing regime in 1970 — the 'partnership of acquests' — as its basic family property law, applicable to all married persons who did not make a positive choice of community property or separate property. In addition, the Ontario Law Reform Commission, in the spring of 1974, made a formal and detailed proposal to the government of that province that legislation be enacted to create a deferred sharing system, known as the 'matrimonial property regime', to replace many fundamental aspects of the law of separate property in Ontario. Although there are some conceptual differences, its results are essentially similar to Quebec's partnership of acquests.
> The basic theory of the deferred sharing system is simple. In general terms, all property acquired by either spouse during marriage is to be shared equally when the marriage partnership is dissolved.

The possibility of a deferred community regime was raised in the English Law Commission working paper, and the Law Commission commented on the results of the consultation in the *First Report* (1973):

47. The proposals relating to such a system of 'deferred community' attracted far more interest and comment than did those relating to legal rights of inheritance. No clear view, however, emerged from the consultation. Some supported the principle of community with enthusiasm. Others opposed it forcefully. In between were those who were neutral or mildly interested and those who thought community would be unnecessary if co-ownership of the matrimonial home were introduced. On balance, the majority did not support deferred community. Some thought that community would give effect to the partnership element in marriage and create definite property rights without the need to depend upon the exercise of the court's discretion; it was seen as a natural extension of the principle of co-ownership of the home into a wider field. Others thought that community could be unfair if applied arbitrarily without regard to the circumstances and to conduct, that it would be a cause of dissension and that it would be inconsistent with the independence of the spouses.

49. Very few took the extreme view that fixed principles of deferred community should replace the present discretionary powers exercisable on divorce or in family provision proceedings. The vast majority thought that existing discretionary powers should be retained.

50. The Social Survey asked married couples what they thought would be a fair settlement in the following circumstances:

'A married couple with no children acquire during their marriage a house on mortgage, the furniture, a car and some savings — altogether worth about £3,000. Then by mutual agreement they decide to separate and some financial arrangement has to be made.'

The situation was considered on the basis that both spouses had been earning and on the basis that the husband had been working and the wife had been looking after the home. A range of solutions was offered for each situation.

51. Excluding those who said they 'did not know', the proportion of people who chose some form of sharing in each of the situations was over 90%. Predominantly (in at least 75% of cases) half-and-half sharing was preferred, and there was little difference in the views of husbands and wives:

'Changing the situation from one where both spouses were earning to only one spouse earning did not result in a large shift of opinion as to what would be a fair settlement in the event of a breakdown of marriage. Nine out of ten thought the possessions should be shared and three quarters thought the method of sharing should be half and half'.

52. The Survey stressed that they had expressly excluded from the situation factors which might have led to qualification, for example, whether there were any children or whether the separation was wanted by both spouses. Nevertheless, the results indicate that many people would consider that in principle some form of sharing at the end of marriage would be fair.

53. The principle of deferred community should be considered in the light of the conclusions we have already reached in this Report, namely that the principle of co-ownership of the home is a necessary measure which would be widely accepted as better achieving justice than the present law, and that a system of fixed legal rights of inheritance is neither necessary nor desirable. Assuming, for the moment, that the principle of co-ownership of the home will be implemented, is the further step of introducing a system of community needed in order to attain the proper balance of justice?

54. The Working Paper pointed out that anomalies could arise if a fixed principle of sharing were limited to just one asset. It would apply only where there was a matrimonial home. Further, the spouse who acquired an interest in the matrimonial home under the co-ownership principle might own other assets of similar or greater value which did not have to be shared. It was suggested that a wider principle of sharing might appear fairer. The results of the Social Survey throw some light on both these points. The Survey confirms that spouses who do not own their home seldom have assets of any substantial value. It also indicates that where a home is owned, it represents a substantial proportion of the total value of the spouses' assets. For the majority of home-owners, sharing the home would, in effect, be sharing the most substantial asset of the family. How far is deferred community necessary as a means of eliminating the anomalies in other cases?

59. *Our conclusion* is that if the principle of co-ownership of the matrimonial home were introduced into English law much of what is now regarded as unsatisfactory or unfair would be eliminated, and the marriage partnership would be recognised by family property law in this very important context. Having regard to our conclusions regarding co-ownership of the matrimonial home, to the broad interpretation by the court of its powers to order financial provision on divorce, and to our conclusion that the court should have similar powers in family provision proceedings, we do not consider that there is at present any need to introduce a system of deferred community.

Question

Would you say that a system of deferred sharing (the partnership of acquests) reflects a society which is striving towards increasing the role of women in the higher paid sectors of the employment market, better than does a system of co-ownership?

4 Rights of inheritance

(a) FIXED SHARE FOR THE SURVIVING SPOUSE?

The Law Commission *Working Paper* (1971) discussed a system of inheritance under which a surviving spouse would be entitled as of right to a fixed proportion of the estate of the deceased spouse whether he died intestate or testate and regardless of the terms of the will:

0.37 Such a system is to be distinguished from community of property and from the right to apply for family provision. Although theoretically it could co-exist with 'community', it would be a needless complication in a law which recognised and enforced a genuine community of property; accordingly we discuss it as an alternative or substitute for 'community'. It differs from the law of family provision in that an order for family provision is discretionary [see p. 132, below], and the amount of the order is assessed having regard to the means, needs and conduct of the applicant. A legal right of inheritance would be a property right in no way dependent upon the means, needs and conduct of the surviving spouse, all of which factors would be irrelevant. The system put forward for consideration is comparable with systems in certain other countries, including Scotland.
0.38. If any system of legal rights of inheritance were introduced, various questions would have to be answered. Chief of these is whether the system should replace the present law of family provision for a surviving spouse, or whether it should be in addition to that law. Provisionally we favour the latter view.
0.39. Other questions which arise are: —
    (*a*) what minimum amount or proportion of the estate should go, *as of right*, to the survivor,
    (*b*) whether a spouse should be able to waive a right of inheritance,
    (*c*) whether, and if so, how benefits received from the deceased during his life should be taken into account,
    (*d*) how to deal with dispositions made by the deceased with the intention of defeating rights of inheritance,
    (*e*) the relationship between rights of inheritance and the intestacy rules,
    (*f*) whether children should enjoy rights of inheritance.
0.40 We make a number of tentative suggestions as to the way in which these questions might be answered. For instance, we reach the provisional view that children should not have a legal right of inheritance; we suggest £2,000 or one-third of the estate (whichever is the greater) for the surviving spouse; and we indicate that it may be better not to complicate the law by seeking a solution within a system of rights of inheritance of the problems of benefits received or dispositions made during the lifetime of the deceased. The appropriate context in which to consider these problems may well be that of family provision, where the courts will continue to have a discretion to set aside dispositions and to make such financial orders as are considered necessary for the support of the survivor.
0.41. A legal right of inheritance would accrue to a spouse only on the death of the other: thus it could not touch their property rights while both were alive, and would not be available to a spouse on divorce, separation, or nullity (though its loss as a result of divorce, nullity or judicial separation would, like the loss of a pension right, be considered by the court awarding maintenance). These limitations are in contrast with a system of community of property, . . . which would operate during joint lives and would be available to the spouses, however their marriage ended. While 'community' has the advantage that its rights do not depend upon death, a system of rights of inheritance is less complicated and involves less interference with existing property law. In the great majority of cases — i.e. those in which a spouse makes adequate provision for his widow, or is content to leave the distribution of his estate to the rules governing an intestacy — there would be no need to invoke the law: a genuine disadvantage of 'community' is that it

presents all spouses with a complicated legal situation that more often than not requires legal advice to handle successfully.

Question

Would this raise problems similar to those of common law dower?

The Working Paper itself drew attention to a major disadvantage of fixed rights of inheritance:

4.71 A system of legal rights would be an imprecise way of protecting the survivor's interest in the family assets. It would take no account of the fact that the bulk of the family assets might already be vested in the survivor: the survivor's assets would be irrelevant unless derived from the deceased. It would not be limited to that part of the deceased's estate which could properly be regarded as family assets, and since it would operate only on death it would create a distinction between property rights on divorce and those on death.

Legal rights of inheritance are seldom of significance when a spouse dies intestate. Under the present law, the surviving spouse inherits personal chattels, the first £40,000 of the estate and a life interest in half of any residue where there are children; or the personal chattels, the first £85,000 plus half the balance where there are no children but other close relatives. In other cases, the surviving spouse inherits the whole estate.

Thus fixed shares are significant only when a testator fails to make adequate provision for a surviving spouse. In those circumstance, is it better for a fixed share or should there be legislation which enables a court to order provision to be taken out of the estate?

The *Working Paper* dealt with the issue as follows:

4.65 Both legal rights of inheritance and family provision law are designed to take care of the case where a deceased has accidentally or deliberately failed to make adequate provision for the surviving spouse. What is adequate would be decided in the case of legal rights by a fixed rule, and in the case of family provision by a court exercising its discretion in the light of all the circumstances. Legal rights would have the advantage of establishing a fixed standard capable of application without resort to the court: family provision enables the court to do justice in the light of the actual circumstances of the estate and the survivor.

The *First Report* noted the lack of support for the principle of legal rights of inheritance for a surviving spouse:

38. In the light of all the comments and views received we have considered again the principle of fixed legal rights of inheritance for a surviving spouse and its relation to family provision law. If one were starting from the position as it was in England before the introduction of family provision law [in 1939], it would be necessary to consider the best means of protecting the interests of the family of a deceased person and to weigh up the relative advantages and disadvantages of an automatic system of legal rights and a discretionary system of family provision operating through an application to the court. However, as the Working Paper suggested, and as the results of our consultation confirm, the issue now is whether it is necessary to supplement or reinforce family provision law by a system of legal rights.
39. Under family provision law the court can, in the exercise of its discretion, take into account the means and needs of all the parties concerned.

The Law Commission recommended substantial improvements to the family provision legislation. They rejected the introduction of a principle under which the surviving spouse would have a *legal* right to inherit part of the estate of the deceased spouse.

Questions

(i) The recommendations on co-ownership have not yet been implemented.

Do you think that fixed shares would be an alternative reform which is more acceptable politically?

(ii) Was one-third too much or too little?

(iii) The Law Commission also said in para. 44. 'The addition of a system of fixed legal rights of inheritance to the system of family provision law would, in our view, lead to uncertainty and confusion. Any advantage derived from the automatic operation of legal rights of inheritance would be offset by the disadvantage of rigidity and possible incompatibility with the new standards we propose for family provision law, and might even prejudice the survivor's interest in the estate.' Why not abandon family provision altogether and replace it with a fixed share?

(b) FAMILY PROVISION

Writing in 1974, Miller said that 'the aim of the present law of family provision is to ensure that reasonable provision is made for the *maintenance* of certain dependants of the deceased. It is not designed to enable members of the deceased's family to acquire a share in his estate without reference to their need for support, or in other words, dependency.'

The Law Commission at first advanced the belief that maintenance should remain as the governing factor. However, they subsequently had second thoughts and, so far as the wife is concerned, in their *First Report* recommended a change in objective:

41. At present, the aim, as expressed in the legislation, is to secure reasonable provision for the *maintenance* of the deceased's dependants, and this is clearly narrower in concept than the provision of a fair share (although in any particular case it may amount to much the same thing). 'Maintenance' is no longer the principal consideration in fixing the amount of financial provision for a spouse on divorce, and we have come to the conclusion that it would be anomalous to retain it as the main objective in determining family provision for a surviving spouse.

The recommendations of the Law Commission were enacted in the *Inheritance (Provision for Family and Dependants) Act 1975*:

1. Application for financial provision from deceased's estate
(1) Where after the commencement of this Act a person dies domiciled in England and Wales and is survived by any of the following persons: —
    (*a*) the wife or husband of the deceased;
    (*b*) a former wife or former husband of the deceased who has not remarried;
    (*c*) a child of the deceased;
    (*d*) any person (not being a child of the deceased) who, in the case of any marriage to which the deceased was at any time a party, was treated by the deceased as a child of the family in relation to that marriage;
    (*e*) any person (not being a person included in the foregoing paragraphs of this subsection) who immediately before the death of the deceased was being maintained, either wholly or partly, by the deceased;
that person may apply to the court for an order under section 2 of this Act on the ground that the disposition of the deceased's estate effected by his will or the law relating to intestacy, or the combination of his will and that law, is not such as to make reasonable financial provision for the applicant.
    (2) In this Act 'reasonable financial provision' —
    (*a*) in the case of an application made by virtue of subsection (1)(*a*) above by the husband or wife of the deceased (except where the marriage with the deceased was the subject of a decree of judicial separation and at the date of death the decree was in force and the separation was continuing), means such financial provision as it would be reasonable in all the circumstances of the case for a husband or wife to receive, whether or not that provision is required for his or her maintenance;
    (*b*) in the case of any other application made by virtue of subsection (1) above, means such financial provision as it would be reasonable in all the circumstances of the case for the applicant to receive for his maintenance.

(3) For the purposes of subsection (1)(*e*) above, a person shall be treated as being maintained by the deceased, either wholly or partly, as the case may be, if the deceased, otherwise than for full valuable consideration, was making a substantial contribution in money or money's worth towards the reasonable needs of that person.

2. Powers of court to make orders

(1) Subject to the provisions of this Act, where an application is made for an order under this section, the court may, if it is satisfied that the disposition of the deceased's estate effected by his will or the law relating to intestacy, or the combination of his will and that law, is not such as to make reasonable financial provision for the applicant, make any one or more of the following orders: —

    (*a*) an order for the making to the applicant out of the net estate of the deceased of such periodical payments and for such term as may be specified in the order;

    (*b*) an order for the payment to the applicant out of that estate of a lump sum of such amount as may be so specified;

    (*c*) an order for the transfer to the applicant of such property comprised in that estate as may be so specified;

    (*d*) an order for the settlement for the benefit of the applicant of such property comprised in that estate as may be so specified;

    (*e*) an order for the acquisition out of property comprised in that estate of such property as may be so specified and for the transfer of the property so acquired to the applicant or for the settlement thereof for his benefit;

    (*f*) an order varying any ante-nuptial or post-nuptial settlement (including such a settlement made by will) made on the parties to a marriage to which the deceased was one of the parties, the variation being for the benefit of the surviving party to that marriage, or any child of that marriage, or any person who was treated by the deceased as a child of the family in relation to that marriage.

(2) An order under subsection (1)(*a*) above providing for the making out of the net estate of the deceased of periodical payments may provide for —

    (*a*) payments of such amount as may be specified in the order,

    (*b*) payments equal to the whole of the income of the net estate or of such portion thereof as may be so specified,

    (*c*) payments equal to the whole of the income of such part of the net estate as the court may direct to be set aside or appropriated for the making out of the income thereof of payments under this section,

or may provide for the amount of the payments or any of them to be determined in any other way the court thinks fit.

(3) Where an order under subsection (1)(*a*) above provides for the making of payments of an amount specified in the order, the order may direct that such part of the net estate as may be so specified shall be set aside or appropriated for the making out of the income thereof those payments; but no larger part of the net estate shall be so set aside or appropriated than is sufficient, at the date of the order, to produce by the income thereof the amount required for the making of those payments.

(4) An order under this section may contain such consequential and supplemental provisions as the court thinks necessary or expedient for the purpose of giving effect to the order or for the purpose of securing that the order operates fairly as between one beneficiary of the estate of the deceased and another and may, in particular, but without prejudice to the generality of this subsection —

    (*a*) order any person who holds any property which forms part of the net estate of the deceased to make such payment or transfer such property as may be specified in the order;

    (*b*) vary the disposition of the deceased's estate effected by the will or the law relating to intestacy, or by both the will and the law relating to intestacy, in such manner as the court thinks fair and reasonable having regard to the provision of the order and all the circumstances of the case;

    (*c*) confer on the trustees of any property which is the subject of an order under this section such powers as appear to the court to be necessary or expedient.

3. Matters to which court is to have regard in exercising powers under s. 2

(1) Where an application is made for an order under section 2 of this Act, the court shall, in determining whether the disposition of the deceased's estate effected by his will or the law relating to intestacy, or the combination of his will and that law, is such as to make reasonable financial provision for the applicant and, if the court considers that reasonable financial provision has not been made, in determining whether and in what manner it shall exercise its powers under that section, have regard to the following matters, that is to say —

(*a*) the financial resources and financial needs which the applicant has or is likely to have in the foreseeable future;

(*b*) the financial resources and financial needs which any other applicant for an order under section 2 of this Act has or is likely to have in the foreseeable future;

(*c*) the financial resources and financial needs which any beneficiary of the estate of the deceased has or is likely to have in the foreseeable future;

(*d*) any obligations and responsibilities which the deceased had towards any applicant for an order under the said section 2 or towards any beneficiary of the estate of the deceased;

(*e*) the size and nature of the net estate of the deceased;

(*f*) any physical or mental disability of any applicant for an order under the said section 2 or any beneficiary of the estate of the deceased;

(*g*) any other matter, including the conduct of the applicant or any other person, which in the circumstances of the case the court may consider relevant.

(2) Without prejudice to the generality of paragraph (*g*) of subsection (1) above, where an application for an order under section 2 of this Act is made by virtue of section 1(1)(*a*) or 1(1)(*b*) of this Act, the court shall, in addition to the matters specifically mentioned in paragraphs (*a*) to (*f*) of that subsection, have regard to —

(*a*) the age of the applicant and the duration of the marriage;

(*b*) the contribution made by the applicant to the welfare of the family of the deceased, including any contribution made by looking after the home or caring for the family;

and, in the case of an application by the wife or husband of the deceased, the court shall also, unless at the date of death a decree of judicial separation was in force and the separation was continuing, have regard to the provision which the applicant might reasonably have expected to receive if on the day on which the deceased died the marriage, instead of being terminated by the death, had been terminated by a decree of divorce.

(3) Without prejudice to the generality of paragraph (*g*) of subsection (1) above, where an application for an order under section 2 of this Act is made by virtue of section 1(1)(*c*) or 1(1)(*d*) of this Act, the court shall, in addition to the matters specifically mentioned in paragraphs (*a*) to (*f*) of that subsection, have regard to the manner in which the applicant was being or in which he might be expected to be educated or trained, and where the application is made by virtue of section 1(1)(*d*) the court shall also have regard —

(*a*) to whether the deceased had assumed any responsibility for the applicant's maintenance and, if so, to the extent to which and the basis upon which the deceased assumed that responsibility and to the length of time for which the deceased discharged that responsibility;

(*b*) to whether in assuming and discharging that responsibility the deceased did so knowing that the applicant was not his own child;

(*c*) to the liability of any other person to maintain the applicant.

(4) Without prejudice to the generality of paragraph (*g*) of subsection (1) above, where an application for an order under section 2 of this Act is made by virtue of section 1(1)(*e*) of this Act, the court shall, in addition to the matters specifically mentioned in paragraphs (*a*) to (*f*) of that subsection, have regard to the extent to which and the basis upon which the deceased assumed responsibility for the maintenance of the applicant and to the length of time for which the deceased discharged that responsibility.

(5) In considering the matters to which the court is required to have regard under this section, the court shall take into account the facts as known to the court at the date of the hearing.

(6) In considering the financial resources of any person for the purposes of this section the court shall take into account his earning capacity and in considering the financial needs of any person for the purposes of this section the court shall take into account his financial obligations and responsibilities.

4. Time-limit for application

An application for an order under section 2 of this Act shall not, except with the permission of the court, be made after the end of the period of six months from the date on which representation with respect to the estate of the deceased is first taken out.

Questions

(i) Do you think that orders for periodical payments should cease on the remarriage of a *surviving* spouse?

(ii) Do you think that such orders should cease on the remarriage of a *former* spouse?

One of the few reported decisions on a widow's application is the following:

Re Besterman
(1981) 3 FLR 255, High Court, Chancery Division

Dr Theodore Besterman died in 1976 aged 71. Apparently, he believed he was the reincarnation of Voltaire, and he left most of his £1.3 million fortune to the Taylor Institute at Oxford University so that his life's work, the publishing of Voltaire manuscripts, could continue. He bequeathed to his wife chattels worth £790 and a life interest in war loan stock producing a gross income of £3,500. The widow applied under the 1975 Act for provision out of the estate of the deceased.

Judge Mervyn Davies: Mr Johnson [for the widow] submitted that the court was not concerned with any balancing operation between Mrs Besterman and the University. The only question was, he said, what sum is proper for the applicant. I accept that no balancing operation as such is to be conducted, but it seems to me that I may have regard to the fact that the interests of scholarship will be served if the charitable trusts created by the deceased's will are funded out of the deceased's estate in as ample a fashion as is possible consistent with proper provision being made for the applicant. That I may have regard to that fact appears from s. 3(1)(*g*), if not from s. 3(1)(*c*).

I go now to s. 3 and the matters therein directed to be taken into consideration. 'Financial resources' in s. 3(1)(*a*) requires account to be taken of earning capacity: see s. 3(6). I do not regard the applicant as having any earning capacity. In other respects the applicant's 'financial resources' are the items of jewellery already mentioned, and there is the £3,500 income arising under the will. Otherwise the applicant has very little. The applicant has no special 'financial needs' unless it be said that, having regard to her marriage over 18 years with her husband, her need is that some reasonable provision be made for her. . . .

Among the 'obligations and responsibilities' referred to in s. 3(1)(*d*), there was, in my view, a plain obligation and responsibility on the deceased to see that his wife, so far as the estate allows, may maintain herself on a scale of living having some semblance to the scale that was adopted during the marriage. As to s. 3(1)(*e*), I have already indicated in general terms the size and nature of the estate. If one puts on one side the books, manuscripts, etc., intended for the Voltaire Foundation, there are still left items of property, including investments worth £206,000, from which a substantial lump sum may be raised. Section 3(1)(*g*) permits me to take into account any matter which in the circumstances of the case I may consider relevant. I consider it relevant in the circumstances of this case to take into account the fact that the University and the Taylor Institute wish to take as full advantage as possible of the deceased's bequests and the fact that scholarship will be advanced by such bequests.

Proceeding to s. 3(2), I have of course in mind that the applicant is now 65 years old and that the marriage, although not a first marriage on either side, lasted for 18 years. As to s. 3(2)(*b*), I do not see that I can regard the applicant as having made any special contribution 'to the welfare of the family of the deceased'. At the same time I fully accept that Mrs Besterman played her part in contributing to the deceased's domestic arrangements and in making his home life happy.

Mr Johnson laid stress on the second part of s. 3(2). That shows that I must have regard to the provision which Mrs Besterman might reasonably have expected to receive had it been divorce and not death which terminated the marriage. . . . Mr Johnson submitted that from a divorce standpoint in 1976 an appropriate award would have been £350,000. He contended that the *Wachtel* third was a starting point or guide-line when assets of up to £1m. were available. From that foundation, Mr Johnson moved on to the 1975 Act. The applicant, it was said, would surely get as much as a divorced wife and it was right that she should get something more. On that footing, Mr Johnson said that £450,000 was the right sum to order. In putting forward that view, Mr Johnson said that he did not accept that under the 1975 Act any provision ought to be calculated on any annuity basis.

Mr Brodie for the University argued for a small sum. He drew attention to the fact that Mrs Besterman made no financial or working contribution to the marriage, and as well, that while the deceased may have accustomed the applicant to a lavish scale of living it was false to assess any order on that basis because it was evident that the deceased, in not attending to tax matters, had lived beyond his means. . . . I do not think that reasonable financial provision for Mrs Besterman within the Act requires the provision of so large a sum as Mr Johnson suggested. The effect of that would be to make provision for Mrs Besterman and as well to enable her to benefit those who come after her. The 1975 Act requires no more than that provision be made for the applicant alone. In such a case as this, where a large estate is concerned and both sides desire a once-and-for-all lump sum payment, the order made should ensure, if possible, that provision be made in a way that will interfere as little as possible with the deceased's testamentary dispositions. That means that in this case the applicant should be provided with a sum sufficient to enable her to purchase an appropriate annuity.

Mrs Besterman has already received £75,000 plus £31,000 from the estate. In my view, she should be paid a further £125,000 and her interest in the war loan worth £28,250 should be enlarged. Accordingly, in all, Mrs Besterman will receive from the estate £259,250.

The Court of Appeal (18 October 1982) was more generous to the widow, and the lump sum was increased to £378,000. In giving the judgment of the Court of Appeal, Oliver LJ referred to the fundamental flaw in the trial judge's calculation.

Oliver LJ: He should I think have looked at the position as a whole for the purpose of assessing what a reasonable provision would be in all the circumstances for the widow of a millionaire with no obligations to anyone else, and, indeed, a millionaire who had expressed himself as desirous of making very ample provision for her. What he did in fact, was to start from the position that particularly in the case of a large estate (and I am not quite clear why the size of the estate should be of particular relevance for this purpose) the court should start from the position that the provisions of the will must be upheld except to the extent that they are displaced by the obligation to maintain the widow during her lifetime. It was that which led him to adopt as the basis for his calculation the price of what he considered an adequate annuity and which led him to provide a figure which, for my part, I think was, in all the circumstances of this case, a good deal too low.

[He continued:] In my judgment, therefore, the learned judge misdirected himself and this is, therefore, a case in which it is open to this court to review the exercise of his discretion and to form its own conclusion.

What then is to be done? In the first place, I think that we must give much greater weight than did the learned judge to the provision which the plaintiff might have expected to get if the marriage had ended in divorce. What that is is a matter of speculation, but I would not seriously quarrel with Mr Johnson's suggestion that an overall sum of £350,000 could not be considered excessive. At the same time I do not think that I can accept that because the marriage did not terminate by divorce in fact, therefore and a fortiori, she must be entitled to more — Mr Johnson puts it (perhaps rather arbitrarily) at £100,000 more. As I have pointed out, however odd the result may be, the two Acts are not necessarily directed to achieving the same result and under this Act the overall criterion is what is reasonable.

I also think that the absence, which is inherent in a lump sum order, of an opportunity to return to the court does mean that, in assessing the lump sum, the court must take rather greater account than might otherwise be the case of contingencies and inflation. I accept Mr Jackson's submission that reasonable provision, in the case of a very large estate such as this and a wholly blameless widow who is incapable of supporting herself, should be such as to relieve her of anxiety for the future. I say 'in the case of a very large estate' not because there is any difference in principle but simply because the existence of a large estate makes that which is desirable also practically possible.

Question

Is this case an unjustifiable interference with the wishes of the testator?

The policy of the law, so far it applies to former spouses, is well explained by Ormrod LJ in the following case.

Re Fullard, Fullard v King
[1982] Fam 42, [1981] 2 All ER 796, [1981] 3 WLR 743, 125 Sol Jo 747, 11 Fam Law 116, Court of Appeal

The plaintiff was married to the deceased in 1938. They had two children. In 1976 the plaintiff petitioned for divorce and the decree was made absolute on 31 December 1976. At the time of the divorce, the plaintiff had £3,000 in savings plus an old age pension. The deceased had a similar amount. The matrimonial home, valued at £9,000 was in joint names. As part of the divorce settlement, the plaintiff paid the deceased £4,500 in cash and the house was transferred to the wife. The deceased went to share a house with the beneficiary. He died in January 1978. The plaintiff applied for reasonable provision from his estate. The judge dismissed her application and she appealed. Her appeal was dismissed.

Ormrod LJ: . . . The question is — and it is a simple question to my mind — is it unreasonable, or was it unreasonable, that this man made no financial provision by his will for his former wife? He thought he and the plaintiff had sorted out their financial claims as between each other when they reached the agreement about the house. It is right to say that if the plaintiff had been dissatisfied with that arrangement, she had her remedy. She could have applied to the court for an order and she might have succeeded in getting the whole of the house transferred to her without having to pay anything — or perhaps on payment of very much less. . . .

. . . It seems to me that the number of cases which, since the court acquired its wide powers under the Matrimonial Proceedings and Property Act 1970 to make property adjustments, can now get in within the umbrella of the Inheritance (Provision for Family and Dependants) Act 1975 post divorce must be comparatively few. In the course of argument I suggested one case where a periodical payments order has been going on for a long time and the husband is found to have a reasonable amount of capital in his estate. . . . Mr Reid [for the plaintiff] suggested that there was another possible situation — where a substantial capital fund was unlocked by the• death of the deceased, such as insurance or pension policies. Those are cases which could come within the Act of 1975. Apart from those, it seems to me there cannot be many cases which qualify.

Mr Reid rightly draws attention to the provisions of section 15 of the Act of 1975 which provides:

'On granting a decree of divorce, a decree of nullity of marriage or a decree of judicial separation or at any time thereafter, the court may, if the court considers it just to do so and the parties to the marriage agree, order that either party to the marriage shall not be entitled on the death of the other party for an order under section 2 of this Act.'

Certainly that provides a form of security against such applications as this.

On one view it might be said that the court, and legal advisers acting in these cases, might be well advised to remember section 15 and, if they can persuade the other side to agree, to write into an order the appropriate provision. I regard section 15 as a form of insuring against applications under the Inheritance (Provision for Family and Dependants) Act 1975 which some people may very reasonably wish to do having made financial provision of a capital nature for the former spouse. People obviously have other commitments — second wives (or husbands) and children and so on. I do not regard section 15 as materially affecting the question the court has to answer as the condition precedent to these applications. •

Question

Ormrod LJ referred to two situations where he felt that a successful application could be brought by a former spouse against the estate. Can you think of any others?

In *Re Fullard* [1982] Fam 42, [1981] 2 All ER 796 emphasis was placed on the importance of the post-divorce settlement. Ormrod LJ said, at the end of the judgment, '. . . the responsibility and obligations of a former husband for the maintenance of a former wife are to comply with such orders as the court has made or that the parties may have agreed between themselves. There are certainly no other legal obligations. In these days it might be quite difficult to say that he had a moral obligation — though there may be cases where it could be argued that he had.'

This *dictum* leads us into the discussion of the financial re-allocation and rearrangement after a divorce. This question has been raised on many occasions during this chapter, but always indirectly, and we have tried so far as possible to follow the rule that the property rights of the husband and the wife are rights which are capable of being ascertained without awaiting a divorce adjustment. Leaving divorce on one side has, however, to some extent been artificial, if only because many of the circumstances which create the difficulties only arise on marital breakdown. It is therefore to divorce itself that we now turn.

CHAPTER 5

Divorce

2. And the Pharisees came to him, and asked him, Is it lawful for a man to put away his wife? tempting him.
3. And he answered and said unto them, What did Moses command you?
4. And they said, Moses suffered to write a bill of divorcement, and to put her away.
5. And Jesus answered and said unto them, For the hardness of your heart he wrote you this precept.
6. But from the beginning of the creation God made them male and female.
7. For this cause shall a man leave his father and mother, and cleave to his wife.
8. And they twain shall be one flesh: so then they are no more twain, but one flesh.
9. What therefore God hath joined together, let not man put asunder.
10. And in the house his disciples asked him again of the same matter.
11. And he saith unto them, Whosoever shall put away his wife, and marry another, committeth adultery against her.
12. And if a woman shall put away her husband, and be married to another, she committeth adultery.

Thus the *Gospel according to St Mark*, in Chapter 10, lays the foundation for the Christian view of marriage and divorce which has influenced our law for so long. An almost identical account appears in St Matthew's Gospel (Chapter 19, verses 3 to 9), but with the significant addition of the words 'except it be for fornication' in his version of Mark's verse 11.

In this chapter, we shall first trace the history of our divorce law up until the major changes wrought by the Divorce Reform Act of 1969. Secondly, we shall consider the factual background and policy debate surrounding those changes. Thirdly, we shall outline how the law has developed since then. Fourthly, we shall look at the implications of recent procedural developments and fifthly at the rule prohibiting most petitions for divorce within three years of the marriage. Finally and in the light of these, we shall touch upon suggestions for 'a better way out.'

1 The history of English divorce law

A helpful summary of developments up until the second Royal Commission on Divorce (1912) appears in *The History of the Obligation to Maintain*, by Sir Morris Finer and Professor O.R. McGregor, which is Appendix 5 to the Report of the (Finer) Committee on One-Parent Families (1974):

The canon law of marriage
1. In medieval times most men, whether of high or low degree, married with the primary object of advancing their interests. For women, marriage was a protective institution. Monogamy did not require, or imply, that people should contract only one marriage in a lifetime, and remarriage was a frequent occurrence in all social groups thereby helping to fill the gaps among the married population which resulted from early deaths. Remarriage protected widows from the dangers of living alone in a violent society as well as feudal superiors from the risk that

unmarried dependants would fail in the full performance of services due from them. Moreover, the medieval laity were motivated by a desire 'to place the satisfaction of the flesh under the shelter of the sacrament'.

2. From the middle of the twelfth century until the Reformation, the law regulating marriage in England was the canon law of the church of Rome administered in courts christian. The canon law was framed in the belief that marriage is a permanent union of the natural order established by God in the creation, and consequently it affirmed that marriage made man and woman one flesh and partook of the nature of a sacrament signifying the unity betwixt Christ and his Church. Medieval christendom regarded marriage as an eternal triangle within which spouses established unbreakable bonds not only with each other but also with God. For this reason, the church maintained that marriage was indissoluble and that no earthly power, not even the Pope himself, could break the bond of a christian marriage. This theology was fortified by the conviction — born of much contemplation and, occasionally, some early experience of human sexuality — that sexual indulgence outside marriage involved mortal sin and created within marriage a formidable barrier to the achievement of spiritual purity. Thus the sacrament of marriage constituted also a defensive venereal citadel within which the generality of folk who lacked a vocation for virginity might find security. . . .

The canon law of nullity

4. In early English law, church and state recognised divorce *a vinculo matrimonii*. This was a divorce in the full sense. It dissolved the bond of marriage and left the parties free to marry again. The church of Rome, treating marriage as indissoluble, abolished divorce in this sense. Thereafter, the ecclesiastical courts granted in the case of a validly contracted marriage only a more limited form of relief. As against a spouse guilty of adultery, cruelty, heresy or apostasy, they might pass sentence of divorce *a mensa et thoro*. This had the effect of a modern judicial separation. It relieved the spouses of the obligation to live together — to share board and bed — but preserved intact the marriage tie.

5. Yet the practical realities of life in the middle ages demanded a method of legitimate avoidance of the rigours of the doctrine of indissolubility. The church provided such a method by developing an elaborate theory of nullity. It was argued that only a valid, consummated, christian marriage was indissoluble. If an impediment to the validity of a marriage had existed when it was contracted, then that marriage would be held by the ecclesiastical courts never to have taken place at all. Many impediments were soon established; the most important were the degrees of consanguinity and affinity within which marriage was prohibited. Before the Lateran Council of 1215, marriage was forbidden between persons to the seventh degree of blood relationship; afterwards, the prohibition was narrowed to the fourth degree, that is, to third cousins. To the impediments of blood were added those of affinity. Since sexual union made man and woman one flesh, it followed that all the blood kinswomen of a man's wife or even of his mistress, were themselves connected to him by affinity. To the impediments of sexual affinity the church then added yet another series created by the spiritual relationships of god-children. No wonder that Mr Joseph Jackson (1969) is moved to speak of the law of affinity as 'a mixture of mathematics and mysticism', and that Pollock and Maitland (1898) write of 'the incalculable harm done by a marriage law which was a maze of flighty fancies and misapplied logic'. . . . [See further in Chapter 1, above.]

The effect of the Reformation

6. By the time of the Reformation, many reformers were rejecting the canon law of marriage developed by the medieval church. They no longer regarded virginity as superior to marriage; they abandoned sacerdotal celibacy; they urged that marriage should be treated as a civil contract regulated by the state; and they favoured the dissolubility of marriage, although differing as to the grounds on which a divorce *a vinculo* ought to be granted. Nevertheless, the protestant doctrines of divorce, though much discussed in the second half of the sixteenth century, did not become part of the law of the land. On the contrary, by the beginning of the seventeenth century, the new church of England had affirmed its belief in the indissolubility of marriage mitigated only by divorce *a mensa et thoro*. The leading protestant country in Europe continued to maintain the jurisdiction of ecclesiastical courts over marriage and divorce, the formless and uncertain marriage contract, and the rigorous theory of indissolubility prevalent in medieval times. At the same time, it rejected the extravagances of the canon law of nullity. Thus, ironically enough, the principal effect of the Reformation on marriage in England was the sealing up of the loopholes and the rejection of the evasions and absurdities by which the medieval system had been made tolerable in practice. Yet whatever formal respect the rich and powerful accorded to christian theology, they were no more prepared than were their ancestors to tolerate the inconveniences inseparable from a system of rigidly indissoluble marriage. In seventeenth and eighteenth century England, these classes both sustained monogamous marriage and encouraged the accumulation of private property. It was natural, therefore, for

them to be more sensitive to the immediate damage which hasty and easily contracted marriages could inflict upon the orderly disposition of family property than to the remoter danger that sexual immorality might imperil their immortal souls. For these reasons, the state broke the exclusive familial jurisdiction of the ecclesiastical courts in two ways. First, it stepped in to regulate and formalise the procedure by which a valid marriage could be contracted. Secondly, it provided a machinery for the dissolution of valid marriages by Act of Parliament. . . .

Parliamentary divorce

13. As the ecclesiastical courts had no power to dissolve a valid marriage *a vinculo* and as the secular courts refused to invade the spiritual jurisdiction, only Parliament could break the indissoluble bond of marriage by intervening in particular cases through the procedure of sovereign legislation. The following Table shows the extent of its interference for this purpose by the passing of private Acts of divorce:

Period						Number	Percentage
Before 1714	...	...	...	...	...	10	3
1715–1759	...	...	...	...	...	24	8
1760–1779	...	...	...	...	...	46	14
1780–1799	...	...	...	...	...	53	17
1800–1819	...	...	...	...	...	49	15
1820–1839	...	...	...	...	...	59	19
1840–1856	...	...	...	...	...	76	24
Total	...	...	...	...	...	317	100

Source: Adapted from PP 1857, Session 2 (106–I), Volume XLII, page 117.

[The table] shows how rare parliamentary divorces were before the accession of George I and how their use increased steadily thereafter, so that one quarter of all the private Acts were passed in the twenty years before the system was abolished in 1857. Before the eighteenth century the main reason for Parliament's willingness to grant the privilege of marrying again was to continue the succession to peerages in the male line. When the Duke of Norfolk successfully petitioned the House of Lords for his divorce bill of 1700, he stated that his wife had 'made full proof of her adultery' and that he 'hath no issue, nor can have any probable expectation of posterity to succeed him in his honours, dignities, and estate, unless the said marriage be declared void by authority of Parliament. . . .' This soon ceased to be the only circumstance in which Parliament would intervene. Later Acts were passed in favour of professional men (including seventeen clergymen) and people engaged in business; indeed, such folk accounted for half the Acts passed between the middle of the eighteenth century and 1857. Nevertheless, all the promoters had one characteristic in common: they were very wealthy. They had to be, for the cost of a private Act and the related proceedings was formidable.

14. After the adoption of a series of Resolutions framed by Lord Chancellor Loughborough in 1798, the House of Lords imposed a standard procedure upon all applications. Before coming to Parliament a petitioner had first to obtain both a decree of divorce *a mensa et thoro* from the spiritual court, and an award of damages for criminal conversation against the wife's seducer in the secular court. The Resolutions further required that the petitioner should attend the House so that he might if necessary be examined as a witness, with reference both to collusion or connivance and also to another point which was always deemed of primary importance in judging divorce bills: whether at the time of the adultery he was living apart from his wife and had thereby contributed to her offence. . . .

17. This procedure, cumbersome, expensive and intricate as it was, could in practice be utilised only by aggrieved husbands. Only four wives were ever granted Acts and these were all passed in the nineteenth century. The first occurred in 1801. We quote Frederick Clifford's account of Mrs Addison's Act in full, both for its intrinsic interest and to show how, even at the close of the Age of Reason, the House of Lords could still be moved and bemused by arguments based upon the canonists' doctrine of the carnal affinities.

'Mr Addison had maintained a criminal intercourse with his wife's sister, a married woman. Her husband, Dr Campbell, obtained a verdict against him with £5,000 damages. Mrs Addison, after obtaining in the Ecclesiastical Court a divorce *a mensa et thoro*, applied to Parliament for a divorce *a vinculo*. Her husband did not appear. Lord Thurlow . . . made a powerful speech for the Bill. Every principle of justice, he said, would be violated by its rejection. But Lord Thurlow did not assert a woman's general right to the same legislative relief as was given to an injured husband. He found his chief defence of the Bill upon the old doctrine of the canonists, that commerce between the sexes creates affinity. In this case, he argued, if Mr Addison had previously had illicit intercourse with her sister, he could not have married his present wife, because such marriage would have been tainted by incest, and might have been pronounced void by an Ecclesiastical Court. A like result occurred by reason of this incestuous adultery. It made reconciliation legally impossible, for, by the affinity it had created, renewed cohabitation between Mr and Mrs Addison would become incestuous.'

Lord Thurlow's subtleties prevailed upon the Lord Chancellor, Lord Eldon, to withdraw his intended opposition to the establishment of this precedent. There is no record of any opposition in the House of Commons, and Mrs Addison obtained her Act. But Parliament held thereafter to the principle that adultery without more by the husband was not a sufficient ground for a wife to obtain an Act. Of the three other instances, in Mrs Turton's case in 1830 the adultery was incestuous; in Mrs Battersby's case in 1840 there was adultery aggravated by cruelty and followed by bigamy for which her husband was transported; and in Mrs Hall's case in 1850 there was also bigamy.

18. Two of the characteristics of the procedure of divorce by private Act of Parliament are now plain. It was so expensive that only the wealthy could avail themselves of it; and within the exclusive social sphere for which the procedure catered, it made a further discrimination between men and women. The discrimination which Parliament maintained between husbands and wives, in respect of the grounds on which it was prepared to dissolve a marriage, was justified in terms of the different effect of their adultery. As Lord Chancellor Cranworth explained to the House of Lords:

'A wife might, without any loss of caste, and possibly with reference to the interests of her children, or even of her husband, condone an act of adultery on the part of the husband but a husband could not condone a similar act on the part of a wife. No one would venture to suggest that a husband could possibly do so, and for this, among other reasons . . . that the adultery of the wife might be the means of palming spurious offspring upon the husband, while the adultery of the husband could have no such effect with regard to the wife.' [But see p. 283, below for a possible difference in attitude between the landed and commercial classes.]. . . .

The first Royal (Campbell) Commission on divorce

30. In 1850 a Royal Commission, under the chairmanship of Lord Campbell, was appointed 'to enquire into the present state of the law of divorce'. The commission was an explicit response to the dissatisfaction with the existing law we have been describing: 'the grave objection,' as Lord Chancellor Cranworth explained, 'that such complicated proceedings were too expensive for the pockets of any but the richest sufferers, and that relief was put beyond the reach of all but the wealthiest classes.' It followed, as Lord Campbell himself said, that the object of the commission was not in any way to alter the law, but only the procedure by which the law was carried into effect. The same points were made repeatedly in the debates on the Matrimonial Causes Act 1857, whereby the recommendations of the Campbell Report were given effect. Thus, the Act of 1857 did not, as is sometimes mistakenly thought, introduce divorce into England or discard a hitherto sacred principle of indissolubility of marriage. The Act (apart from some minor innovations) did no more than consolidate and transfer to a civil and more accessible court of law the jurisdictions that were already being respectively exercised by Parliament and the ecclesiastical courts. The only substantial change which it effected was to make more widely available matrimonial remedies which only the very few had until then enjoyed.

Question

Could it be that before 1857 only the very rich needed to divorce? What social changes in the years leading up to 1857 might have made it necessary for others to seek this remedy?

The Matrimonial Causes Act 1857

31. The principal provisions of the Act of 1857 were, accordingly, as follows. The matrimonial jurisdiction of the ecclesiastical courts was abolished, but re-created in a new court called 'the Court for Divorce and Matrimonial Causes'. In exercising the transferred jurisdiction, the divorce court was to proceed on the same principles as had guided the ecclesiastical courts. The remedy which those courts had formerly granted under the name of a decree of divorce *a mensa et thoro* was henceforth to be called a decree of judicial separation. The divorce court would also deal with petitions for the dissolution of marriage. A husband could present a petition for

divorce on the ground of his wife's adultery; a wife, on the ground of adultery aggravated by some other conduct (such as incestuous adultery, adultery coupled with cruelty or with desertion for two years or upwards) or on the ground of sodomy or bestiality. It is notable that Gladstone, while vigorously opposing the passage of the Act, was equally strong in contending that if it were passed at all it should not discriminate between the sexes:

'It is impossible to do a greater mischief than to begin now, in the middle of the nineteenth century, to undo with regard to womankind that which has already been done on their behalf, by slow degrees, in the preceding eighteen centuries, and to say that the husband shall be authorised to dismiss his wife on grounds for which the wife shall not be authorised to dismiss her husband. If there is one broad and palpable result of Christianity which we ought to regard as precious, it is that it has placed the seal of God Almighty upon the equality of man and woman with respect to everything that relates to these rights.' [See the extract from St Mark's Gospel at the beginning of this chapter.]. . . .

The number of divorces

34. The Act of 1857 opened the door to matrimonial relief for many whom the expense of the earlier procedures had excluded. In the four years following the passing of the Act 781 petitions for divorce and 248 petitions for judicial separation were filed in the new court. On the other hand, the Act, as these figures demonstrate, opened no floodgate. The highest number of decrees granted in any one year up to 1900 was 583 divorces (in the year 1897) and 57 decrees for judicial separation (in the year 1880). The new jurisdiction was wholly centralised in London, which acted as a deterrent to its employment by those who resided at a distance. Further, although the costs were not so wildly exorbitant as previously, they were still very considerable, and beyond the reach of people of ordinary means. It was not long before the criticisms which had preceded the Act regained currency. . . .

The Second Royal (Gorell) Commission on Divorce

42. In 1909, a Royal Commission was appointed, under the chairmanship of Lord Gorell 'to enquire into the present state of the law of England and the administration thereof in divorce and matrimonial causes and applications for separation orders, especially with regard to the position of the poorer classes in relation thereto.' By this time, while the High Court was dealing every year with some 800 petitions for divorce and judicial separation, the magistrates were dealing with some 15,000 applications for matrimonial orders. [This jurisdiction is discussed in Chapter 3, above.] In the ten years 1897–1906 the magistrates made more than 87,000 separation orders. Almost all of the magistrates' clientele were the poor, whose problems the terms of reference expressly recognised. Indeed, the themes and anxieties which had dominated the discussion in the preceding century, and which the intervening reforms had not laid to rest, continued to be strongly reflected in the evidence given to the commission: discrimination between the sexes; discrimination against the poor. The report of the Gorell Commission made a major, and still as yet unexhausted, contribution to its subject. It continues, more than sixty years after its publication, to impress by a quality of vision and humanity which may be illustrated by a passage which refers to the obligation:

'to recognise human needs, that divorce is not a disease but a remedy for a disease, that homes are not broken up by a court but by causes to which we have already sufficiently referred, and that the law should be such as would give relief where serious causes intervene, which are generally and properly recognised as leading to the break-up of married life. If a reasonable law, based upon human needs, be adopted, we think that the standard of morality will be raised and regard for the sanctity of marriage increased.'

43. As regards the law of divorce and its administration, the Gorell Report proposed, first, 'that the law should be amended so as to place the two sexes on an equal footing as regards the grounds on which divorce may be obtained'. . . . This recommendation was not followed until 1923. Next, the report proposed the broadening of the grounds on which either spouse might petition for divorce, by adding to adultery the offences of desertion for three years and upwards, cruelty, incurable insanity, habitual drunkenness and imprisonment under commuted death sentence. Extensions on these lines had to wait upon the Matrimonial Causes Act 1937. Thirdly, the Gorell Report recommended a decentralisation of procedure so that the High Court could sit and exercise divorce jurisdiction locally, for the benefit, in particular, of people of small means. It took another committee, in 1946, to produce any effective change in this respect.

The story since then is taken up in the main body of the *Finer Report*:

Lord Buckmaster's Act in 1923 had put husbands and wives on a footing of formal equality in respect of the grounds of divorce, by making it possible for each to petition against the other on the grounds of simple adultery. But it was not until the legal aid scheme of 1949 compensated wives for their lack of income or low earnings that they won practical equality of access to the court.[1]

The Third Royal (Morton) Commission on Marriage and Divorce

4.30 In 1951, Mrs Eirene White proposed, in a private member's bill, to permit divorce to spouses who had lived apart for seven years: that is to say, divorce which depended on the fact of separation over this period, and did not involve the proof, by one spouse against the other, of the commission of a matrimonial offence. Coming as it did, at the time when legal aid regarded as a social service was replacing help for the poor as a form of professional charity dispensed by lawyers, and the financial bar to the divorce courts was being lifted, Mrs White's bill was seen by its opponents as a measure to open the floodgates. Nevertheless, to the alarm of its opponents, and to the surprise of many of the supporters of the bill, it appeared as though the House might respond favourably. At this juncture, the government offered Mrs White a Greek gift in the shape of a Royal Commission. Mrs White accepted.

4.31 The Report of the Morton Commission in 1956, though divided, was decidedly against change. Reformers had urged that the doctrine of the matrimonial offence was out of step with people's actual behaviour and expectations in marriage, that the law was brought into contempt by the perjury thereby encouraged, and that the result was illicit unions and the birth of illegitimate children. The Church of England was the most influential opponent of change in the matrimonial law. It explained to the Royal Commission that the doctrine of the matrimonial offence was 'entirely in accord with the New Testament', asserted that divorce was 'a very dangerous threat to the family and to the conception of marriage as a lifelong obligation', and upheld its traditional view that, although much individual suffering and hardship might be relieved by making divorce easier to obtain, the damage to the social order must outweigh such benefits. . . . .

The pressure for reform

4.32 In 1956, it must have seemed that the Morton Commission and the Church of England had between them put the quietus on divorce law reform for many years to come. But the appearances were deceptive. The report proved to be little more than a ripple on the surface of a tide that was moving strongly in the other direction.

2 Divorce reform — the policy debate

The tide was moving strongly throughout the common law world — and we know of no better account of the many complex strands in the divorce debate than an imaginary conversation which appears in Foote, Levy and Sander's *Cases and Materials on Family Law* (1976). We have omitted those parts of the discussion which are relevant solely to the legal system in the United States of America, and supplied such information as exists on this side of the Atlantic to illustrate the earlier part of the argument on the vexed question of divorce 'rates.' These notes are collected at the end of the extract, on pp. 150–152, below.

A quadrilogue on divorce policy

The time is late evening on a warm night in midsummer. The place is a small cafe in Opatija looking out over the moonlit Adriatic. The participants — the Judge, the Professor, the Doctor, and the Bishop — are American delegates to the First International Interdisciplinary Congress on Family Stability and the Rights of Children. They have just emerged from a frustrating session at which they tried to follow a Yugoslav interpreter's simultaneous translation into English of an address in Polish on Polish family law as an expression of Socialist morality.

BISHOP: Well, whatever else one may think about communism behind the Iron Curtain, at least

---

1. This observation is based upon the respective proportions of husbands and wives who were subsequently legally aided (Gibson and Beer, 1971), but it should be recalled that part of the husband's common law duty to maintain his wife was to give security for her costs in litigation.

they are doing something about divorce. When you compare the way their divorce rate is going down with how ours shoots up —.

JUDGE: Ours is not 'shooting up.'

DOCTOR: I thought he said the Polish rate was rising.

BISHOP: No, it was down.

JUDGE: Professor, I noticed you switched to the French channel. Was that translation any better? Is divorce in Poland up or down?

PROFESSOR: The French was awful. I don't know. It doesn't make any difference anyway. Divorce rates prove nothing.

BISHOP: What do you mean, divorce rates prove nothing? It's humiliating to be here. Every time an American says anything about the sacredness of family life, these Europeans smile broadly because they know that we have the highest divorce rate in the world. . . .[2]

PROFESSOR: Bishop, until 1970 when Italy for the first time permitted divorce, the divorce rate in Italy was zero. Do you think that proves that prior to that time morality in Italian family life was so much better than ours, or haven't you seen any of Antonioni's movies lately?

JUDGE: The Bishop is right, though, that over the long haul our divorce rate has risen. I think there is cause for alarm. The divorce rate more than tripled between the Civil War and 1910, when it reached about one per thousand population. Then it rose to around 2.2 by 1960, stayed more or less level until 1967, and now has increased sharply again, attaining a level of 4.0 in 1972.

DOCTOR: That's per thousand total population?

JUDGE: Yes. And that ignores temporary fluctuations due to wars or depression.

DOCTOR: But those figures are misleading. Hasn't the proportion of adults who get married also risen since 1900?

PROFESSOR: Our statistics are inadequate, but apparently the higher marriage rate hasn't contributed very much to the increase in divorce. If you measure the number of divorces against a base of existing marriages, the results seem to be pretty much the same.[3]

BISHOP: I've heard it said that in the immediate postwar years there was one divorce for every four couples who got married.[4]

PROFESSOR: True, but that statistic seems totally meaningless to me. The two figures don't involve the same people. The most adequate statistic, of course, would be to follow a large sample of marriages through life. One could take a sample of marriages contracted, say, in 1955, and by following this sample find out how many persons were being divorced in each succeeding year. Then, after all persons in the sample had either been divorced or died, the true divorce rate could be established. . . .[5]

JUDGE: So nearly one in every four marriages is going to end in the divorce court.[6]

PROFESSOR: That's a frequently stated figure, but I don't think it is quite correct, if you limit it to first marriages. Persons who remarry after a divorce have a somewhat higher divorce rate,[7] so that if one counts first marriages alone it appears to be about one in five.

BISHOP: You fellows make it sound so urbane and lifeless with your figures. Do you realize the increasing moral instability and the rising numbers of children deprived of a normal home that lie behind this rise in divorce?

DOCTOR: But the proportion of children forced to grow up in a household that doesn't contain both his parents probably hasn't risen at all, Bishop. The death rate in 1900 for persons in the child-rearing stage of life — from the middle twenties to the middle thirties in age — was about eight per 1000 per year; now it's around one and a half. The decline in the proportion of child-rearing families broken by death more than compensates for the rise in families broken by divorce.

PROFESSOR: And of course this declining mortality is one of the many factors which have contributed to the rise in the divorce rate. Because many fewer spouses die young, more marriages are exposed to the risk of divorce. Many unhappy marriages which used to be terminated by death may now end up in the divorce court.

BISHOP: This is entirely irrelevant to the point I'm trying to make. A family broken by the death of one parent represents an inevitable tragedy, and death is morally neutral. A family broken by divorce, however, is not only a needless tragedy but an index of moral failure.

JUDGE: Is it the divorce which is the moral failure, Bishop, or is it the failure to make a go of marriage and establish a stable, secure home for the children?

BISHOP: Both represent the same failure.

DOCTOR: But they're not necessarily the same thing at all. The decree of divorce is merely the law's recognition of a failure which occurred months or years earlier when the family was in fact broken by separation. What I'd like to know is whether or not the underlying breakdown rate is going up. Are there really more separations today? We know that during the age of colonization in England, or when there was no divorce there, or when our own frontier still existed, it was commonplace for an unhappily married man just to disappear. His family would never see him again, and the chances were that he would establish a new family.

PROFESSOR: It still happens. We have what is sometimes called common law divorce. A couple separate, whether by agreement or by the desertion of one of them. One or both remarry, either formally or by starting a new household. Because they never appear on any divorce court records, we have no statistics on the incidence of this kind of breakdown — we never have had. But even in this day such poor man's divorce is probably far more frequent than we might guess. It would be interesting to take a random sample of people who hold themselves out as married and find out how many are in fact not legally married. I suspect you'd find a surprising proportion of illegality — bigamists, people previously married who've remarried after a patently invalid divorce or after no divorce, and so forth.

DOCTOR: Wouldn't you agree that this sort of thing was much more common a hundred or two hundred years ago than today? It was much easier to run away and start again then, and going to law was financially out of reach of a much larger proportion of the population.

PROFESSOR: It was more common, yes, but how much more we just don't know and we can never know.

DOCTOR: All that may have happened in the last 50 or 100 years is that changing customs, the increasing standard of living of the working classes, and things like the provision of legal aid for the poor have resulted in an increase merely in the proportion of breakdowns that are formally recorded by divorce. It would be quite possible, would it not, that the rate of family breakdown — and I'm not talking about death now, Bishop, but breakdown by separation — hasn't gone up at all?

PROFESSOR: It is possible, but not probable. If we could hold morality constant, I would expect the breakdown rate as well as the divorce rate to have risen substantially in the last 100 years.

JUDGE: I agree entirely. We keep forgetting the profound changes in our way of life. Imagine, for example, what the emancipation of women has meant to family life. Realistically, 100 years ago divorce was a privilege reserved for men alone. Especially if she was burdened with young children, a woman with an unhappy marriage had virtually no recourse but to endure it. There was heavy stigma against a divorcee; she had much less chance to remarry and to support herself. Now she can be relatively independent of her husband economically. If she wants to remarry, her chances are probably pretty good if she's still reasonably young [see Chapter 11]. Naturally some women are going to exercise their new equality by getting divorces.

PROFESSOR: I was thinking even more of the change in the family role brought about by the industrial revolution and all the trappings of modern urban life. In the old days, marriage used to be much more what it is today on an isolated farm — not only companionship and child-rearing, but also the basic economic unit providing livelihood, recreation, and often even education. To terminate your connection with the family then had much more drastic consequences. Psychologically and economically, family breakup is simply a lot easier today. All the brakes that used to hold the family together have been relaxed. Isn't one of the major causes for our sense of dissatisfaction with the way divorce law operates today a product of this change? Aren't we expecting entirely too much of law, as if it could step in and provide that stability which formerly was the product of economic and cultural forces?

DOCTOR: One more or less hidden aspect of this change which greatly concerns me is the role of the young mother in our new kind of family. It seems to me that we put young parents, especially the young mother, in an intolerable position. In the old family there were maiden aunts and grandparents to help with the children, and the wife was often her husband's partner in the economic sphere, especially on the farm. Her life may have been hard, but at least it had meaning. The modern wife is cut off from her husband's career, isolated in her little apartment or home from the relatives who could share the burdens of child care, educated as women have never been educated before, but then relegated to a role of house-cleaning and diaper-changing even more insignificant than that of her grandmother and great-grandmother.

BISHOP: I guess I'm just an old-fashioned conservative, but I'm mildly surprised to hear a psychiatrist characterize the role of a mother rearing children as insignificant.

DOCTOR: Bishop, you know what I mean. Of course it is critically important. All I'm saying is that our modern culture takes a young woman and throws her into this role without the help and reinforcement that the old-fashioned family used to provide.

BISHOP: Doesn't this just emphasize what I've been saying? If the moral stamina were there, the family would not disintegrate. I'll wager there isn't a woman in America who would willingly trade roles with her great-grandmother. Both she and her husband have it a lot easier today, and they know it. That they still can't make a go of it just points up the moral decline of our times.

PROFESSOR: I've recently had occasion to read a lot of colonial court records. For all their preoccupation with moral values, I saw little indication that the Puritans had any superiority over us on that score. Every third case was fornication or bastardy. Even if a couple got married, if their first child arrived in less than nine months, they were haled into court to be fined and censured. If a man came over from England leaving a wife and children behind, he would be ordered to go back to his family or take the consequences.

BISHOP: That strikes me as an admirable law.

DOCTOR: Come now, Bishop, you're kidding us.

BISHOP: I most certainly am not. The state has a strong interest in the stability of the family. Why shouldn't it take preventive measures? Why should a married man be permitted to abandon his wife and children in England and come to America to make trouble and probably break up another marriage besides his own? I think the colonists showed very good sense.

DOCTOR: Like most such laws, it probably wasn't enforced.

BISHOP: That's just the point. We've never given our legal structure half a chance. We've never really exploited — or indeed explored — the state's power to take effective preventive measures to discourage the break-up of families. I agree with the Doctor. We need to help the young mother in her difficult role and use law to reinforce family morality.

DOCTOR: I don't mean that kind of help! Are you really proposing that law can compel man and wife to live together? Do you think the state can turn love into a command performance?

BISHOP: I think the law can do a lot, yes. Take a typical situation today, a young man with his young wife and a couple of young children. They got married young; they weren't very mature about it; they acted precipitously. I'd do something about that, too, incidentally — tightening up our marriage laws would prevent a lot of divorces. But they were permitted to get married and now there are the usual frictions. Marriage has not turned out to be the bowl of honey they anticipated. Of course it never is, but they don't know that. The baby cries all night; the two-year-old has a cough and fever; the wife doesn't get enough sleep; she's shut up in the house all day; she feels neglected and frustrated. When the husband gets back from work, home is far from the Utopia he's imagined. The house is a mess, dinner isn't even started, his wife forgot to get the vermouth for the martinis, and at the first rebuff she has a crying jag.

DOCTOR: You paint an idyllic picture, Bishop. What are you leading up to, a divorce for incompatibility? [See p. 159, below.]

BISHOP: Now you've put your finger on it! If the depth of our moral bankruptcy can be epitomized by a single word in our divorce law, that's the one. Incompatibility, indeed! Of course they are incompatible. Every couple is. But a husband and wife with some maturity and some sense of responsibility for the innocent children they've brought into the world will do something about it. They will deliberately set out to strengthen their existing common interests and to develop new ones. Suppose the wife likes to bowl and the husband doesn't. Well, if he has any sense, he'll take his wife bowling once a week. Chances are he'll come to enjoy it too, and if he doesn't, she'll respond to his interest in her interests. It's a small thing to ask of him. In a petty matter he'll be demonstrating that love and marriage don't go together like a horse and carriage but are the product of give and take, self-sacrifice, and hard work.

PROFESSOR: That's a fine sermon, Bishop, but it strikes me as bad law. Of course in a world peopled by saints we wouldn't have these problems. But law must operate in this world, with immature people. You yourself stipulated that your hypothetical husband and wife were silly and immature.

BISHOP: But our law has a responsibility to help people develop the requisite maturity and responsibility. What happens now is that our divorce law encourages irresponsibility. Let's also suppose that our young husband meets an attractive young woman, and one thing leads to another. The new woman is always charming and attractive and never has irrational crying spells; indeed, under the circumstances, why should she? The husband draws from this contrast with his harried wife and tension-ridden home a distorted significance — that his wife doesn't understand him, whereas the other woman is sympathetic and builds up his ego. Our present divorce law literally invites this young fool to indulge his folly. It whispers to him, 'Go ahead. It's easy. Everyone else does it, why not you? You owe it to yourself to find happiness and self-fulfillment.'

PROFESSOR: But in this practical world, Bishop, what do you want? You can't have a legal action to compel the husband and wife to live together in misery while —

BISHOP: Not in misery, but to live together as they learn to love and respect and cherish one another.

JUDGE: Recently you typed yourself as a conservative, Bishop, but you're a wild-eyed radical if you really think that you can legislate that sort of thing. I happen to think the chances are high that the marriage you've described can be saved, and in my court we'd send them to the conciliation service for counseling. [See further, in Chapter 17.]

BISHOP: Would you prevent them from getting a divorce?

JUDGE: No, but we'd delay and counsel.

PROFESSOR: Bishop, what you're describing is the problem of your profession, not the law's. It isn't the compulsion of law which makes people moral or immoral, prone to divorce or resistant to it. The community's basic moral and sociocultural and religious values are what determine conduct, not what the law says [much of the evidence for the Professor's comments throughout comes from Rheinstein, 1972]. They are our only protections against further family breakdown.

BISHOP: Precisely. And the law can either strengthen these community values or it can subtly undermine them. . . . Imagine the effect on the young man in my story if, instead of offering him the prospect of easy divorce, the law were to say: 'Look here, young fellow. You can never get a divorce from your wife' — for certainly there is nothing in the situation I described which gives any moral basis for his getting a divorce — 'and if you try it and then try to marry your paramour, you'll go to jail for bigamy. If you try to live with her without marriage, you'll go to jail for adultery. And no matter what you do or where you go, we'll follow you and take from you the full measure of your obligation to support your wife and children and throw you in jail if you default.' You know as well as I do that any young man would think five times before he took a step which would have such drastic consequences. It would be enough to make him take stock and try harder to make a go of his marriage.

DOCTOR: If the law were ever really to do that, it would be a great day for the jail construction industry.

JUDGE: Bishop, it's a lovely dream, but it just won't work. It's impossible for the law to say that and really be able to carry out its threat. Juries wouldn't convict, judges wouldn't impose the prison sentences. Take just the question of support. You can send a man to jail today for non-support under existing law, but are you aware that it doesn't work out that way in practice? Any husband, if he really wants to, can and does evade most of his obligations.

BISHOP: I've heard that, and it bears out Dickens's observation about the law. A child could do better than you lawyers. . . . Everyone has to have a social security number; he has to reveal it to get a job; he has to put it on his income tax return. They have these big machines now by which they can trace these things electronically. We could find almost all defaulting husbands and throw them in jail — if the lawyers and judges wanted to uphold the law.

JUDGE: Suppose you find a defaulting divorced husband after a couple of years. By now he's 2000 miles away and has a new wife and baby. This time he appears to be making a success of his marriage. He's earning just enough to support them. If you make him do much for his prior family, what happens to the second family? They're innocent too, and they deserve some consideration. If you throw him in jail, neither family's supported and the state foots the bills for both. . . .

BISHOP: If that's the state's policy, I can only characterize it as short-sighted economy and misguided sentimentality. In the long run strict enforcement would save countless marriages and millions of tax dollars.

DOCTOR: Bishop, you men who know what's best for other people and want to ram it down their throats fascinate me —

BISHOP: Look who's talking!

DOCTOR: What's so horrendous about what your young man is doing? You said it was a silly marriage and that they're both unhappy. Let them separate if they want to. They'll both remarry, and we may substitute two at least tolerable families for one unhappy one.

BISHOP: It was a member of your own profession, Doctor, who wrote a book prophetically entitled 'Divorce Won't Help.' (Bergler, 1948)

DOCTOR: You amaze me! Did you read it?

BISHOP: Well, I skimmed it. I don't go in much for these theories that the reason why a man fights with his wife is because unconsciously he's getting even with his mother — or is it his father? Anyway, there's nothing very novel about the book's basic idea. Emerson said a long time ago that wherever a man goes, his shadow goes too, and that book proved what I've long suspected — that if you let a man out of one foolish marriage, he'll go out and make another just like it. You might as well stop him the first time, before he goes on creating family after family and wrecking each in turn.

DOCTOR: Bishop, tell me one thing. Would you prohibit all divorce?

BISHOP: I really think the Catholics are right. Theologically, I'm sure they are. Both Christ and Paul were very explicit, and my own church has become much too lax for my tastes. I suppose I would allow an innocent party to divorce and remarry in a very extreme situation like adultery.

PROFESSOR: You would approve, then, of those laws which used to prohibit the guilty party in an adultery divorce from remarrying the paramour during the lifetime of the innocent spouse? Or of statutes that prohibit a remarriage if either party 'has at any time failed to comply with an order to support lawful dependants,' unless the judge is satisfied that such person will be able adequately to meet his obligations?

BISHOP: Of course. I wouldn't allow the guilty party to remarry anyone. Nor would I permit an individual to assume new support obligations if he is unable to meet his existing ones.

DOCTOR: We are back again to forcing people to live together.

BISHOP: Not necessarily. Where there is cause, I would permit the parties to live apart, as where there is cruelty that really makes it unsafe for the wife to continue to reside in the same house with her husband. That would be what the church calls divorce *a mensa et thoro*, but there could be no remarriage. The law provides for that, does it not?

JUDGE: Yes, in many states, but unfortunately it's becoming obsolete and is now very little used.[8]

DOCTOR: Of what possible value is a procedure that recognizes that a marriage is finished but insists on retaining the empty shell?

PROFESSOR: It permits the wife to retain valuable inheritance and intestate rights for which alimony and property division upon absolute divorce is a very inadequate substitute.[9]

DOCTOR: It still sounds like a punitive device to me. It leaves the spouses with a choice of lifelong celibacy or an illicit union.

BISHOP: Unlike you, my dear Doctor, I do not feel a need to make divorce as attractive as possible.

JUDGE: It's interesting that the system which the Bishop advocates is approximately that which existed in New York prior to 1966, but it didn't seem to work as the Bishop envisioned. Once one takes account of all the evasive devices then utilized, the New York divorce rate appears to have exceeded the national average. . . .

BISHOP: And the reason a national divorce law wouldn't work is because you judges announce in advance that you won't enforce it. If you don't like a law, or if clients are willing to pay big fees, the motto of the legal profession seems to be evasion.

DOCTOR: I'd chalk that one up to the lawyers' credit. Our divorce law reminds me of a situation that the anthropologist Ruth Benedict (1934) described concerning the Kurnai tribe in Australia, which had such strict rules restricting marriage choices that usually a young man would find there wasn't a single girl whom he could lawfully marry. Dr Benedict pointed out that this didn't cause the Kurnai to reformulate their impossible marriage rules; instead, they institutionalized evasion. Those who wanted to get married would have to elope, and all the villagers would set out in pursuit, even though they too had been married in the same fashion. If the couple were caught before they reached a traditional place of refuge, they would be killed. But if they made it, they would then be accepted back into their tribe after the birth of a child. Isn't this the sort of thing the lawyer does with our divorce law? Despite some modest reform in recent years, we have, by and large, a silly law, out of step with psychological reality and with the wishes of many people, and yet the lawyer manages to make it work tolerably well.

BISHOP: Tolerably well?!

DOCTOR: By that I mean that almost anyone who really wants a divorce can get one. My experience with patients who have marital difficulties is that the law is entirely irrelevant to the resolution of the case. If they can progress to the point where married life reaches a tolerable level, they stay together whether or not they have grounds for divorce. If their treatment reveals that there is really nothing left on which to base a marriage, they get a divorce whether or not they have legal grounds. The law is at most an irritant, a sometimes expensive nuisance, but it is never determinative of the result. People want and get a divorce for their own reasons, which may or may not be sound, but the law has nothing to do with it.

PROFESSOR: There's a great deal in what the Doctor has just said, Bishop. The trouble with your position of strict enforcement seems to me very simple: it would be a practical possibility only if there were a virtually unanimous consensus that what you propose is right. We can enforce laws against murder and robbery and rape because virtually everyone agrees on the wrongness of such conduct. But we've seen over and over again that if a substantial proportion of the population believes that prohibited conduct is in fact right and another segment of the population doesn't care about strict enforcement, then you just can't make such a law work. This happened in the twenties with prohibition, and I think it is happening today with gambling and divorce.

BISHOP: I think we have just such a consensus. Most people agree that divorce is wrong. I'm shocked to hear you draw an analogy between taking a drink before dinner and divorcing your wife, as if people put those on the same plane.

PROFESSOR: But the ardent prohibitionists did just that, in part because they thought the one caused the other. I agree with you that probably most people think divorce is at least undesirable, that marriage should be for keeps. But that is a generality, and we start right off with perhaps a fifth of the population who did not apply that generality to their own lives.

BISHOP: Many of those may still feel what they did was wrong and despite their own conduct would support a strong law as the best thing for the community. In any event, your figure leaves four fifths, and that's a pretty strong majority.

JUDGE: The trouble is that people feel differently on the abstract question of what the divorce law should be than they do on whether divorce should be readily available to their relatives and friends who are trapped in unsatisfactory marital relationships. Suppose you see your own daughter in a desperately unhappy marriage. She made a mistake; you tried to stop her, but she went ahead anyway. Few people are going to take your position, Bishop, sitting back with a philosophic overview that tolerates the wreckage of a daughter's whole life so that her bad example can serve as a deterrent to future generations.

PROFESSOR: Bishop, if you will settle for a partial solution rather than total victory, I think we will find that there are at least some areas of agreement among the four of us. First, wouldn't we all agree that many divorces today represent cases much less aggravated than that of the Judge's hypothetical daughter — where the only alternative to divorce is lifelong misery? In many of the marriages that are terminated today the parties would have been better off if they had been kept together. In other words, at least some fraction of the existing divorce rate represents divorces that serve no real purpose either for the parties or society. Would you agree with that, Doctor?

DOCTOR: Yes.

PROFESSOR: The standard that ought to be applied, then, is one which would screen out these cases. I'm very much taken with the view of many of these Europeans — a view that is incidentally finding increasing acceptance also in the United States — that the proper test is not fault at all but a purely factual determination whether the marriage has irretrievably broken down [see p. 153, below].

DOCTOR: I would buy that.

BISHOP: That's no solution. That's worse than what we have now. All anyone would have to do would be to tell the judge that his marriage has broken down and he's free. That would encourage a change in the attitude towards marriage which would be disastrous for the nation. Before you know it, marriage would come to be regarded as nothing but a temporary institution and divorce would be normal.

PROFESSOR: No, no, Bishop, you misunderstand. This is not the same thing at all as divorce by mutual consent. The whole purpose is to prevent divorce for some trivial reason. But it would provide a dignified and blameless way out from a marriage where the breach is irreparable and due to a grave cause.

BISHOP: It is not the function of the state to make divorce blameless or dignified. If there is to be any divorce at all, it should be only to give relief where a wrong has been done.

PROFESSOR: But the existing grounds for divorce based on fault simply don't work, Bishop, and they invite the parties to scheme and manufacture causes of action. Moreover, these grounds are not really indicative of the true causes of the breakdown; they merely represent the symptoms. On the other hand, a fault system permits divorce where there is no reason why the marriage should not continue, as with an isolated act of adultery followed by repentance. The breakdown theory would cut through these fault fictions and permit divorce when, and only when, marriage has irretrievably broken down.

DOCTOR: I guess I was a little hasty in my agreement with you. The rabbit in the hat is that phrase, 'irretrievably broken down.' What would constitute an irretrievable breakdown?

PROFESSOR: Certainly adultery, or desertion, or cruelty.

DOCTOR: Aren't these just the same 'faults,' the same moral judgments we have today, with the difference that each judge can apply his own personal standard? If the Bishop here were a judge, grave cause woud exist only where there was adultery.

PROFESSOR: No, there's a great difference. We would not be concerned with who is guilty of what or whether both parties are guilty, or with condemnation of guilty parties. We could put an end to the disgusting spectacle of a ritualistic, name-calling public trial and permit the parties to bury their marriage with some sense of dignity. The judge would look at the total situation without regard to who was wrong, and if under all the circumstances it would be unreasonable to expect this marriage to continue, then that would constitute an irretrievable breakdown. . . .

DOCTOR: I can't see that under the breakdown theory giving the judge discretion to grant or deny divorce according to his estimate of the gravity of circumstances is any improvement over what we have today under the fault system. It seems to me a step backwards. Where divorces are granted on the basis of fault, at least the result is predictable.

PROFESSOR: Of course you could establish an objective standard for determining the gravity of the breakdown. Under the law which was in effect in Sweden until 1974, once the parties had separated, and lived apart for a period of a year, either party was entitled to a decree of divorce. But apparently some Swedes found this period too long, and utilized the fault grounds which had no waiting period. So since 1974, the period has been reduced to six months, and even that period is only mandated in a case where one party objects or where there is a child under 16.

DOCTOR: I concur. The only purpose of requiring any delay seems to me to be to make sure that the parties really want a divorce.

PROFESSOR: You don't want divorce to be immediately available upon sudden impulse?

DOCTOR: No. But I would think the period of delay should be quite short, a matter of months at most. Any longer waiting period seems to me to be moralistic.

PROFESSOR: About half the states in the United States presently grant divorce provided the parties have lived separate and apart for a requisite period.

DOCTOR: But to make them wait for what is often a period of years after the factual dissolution of their marriage is punishment plain and simple.

PROFESSOR: The purpose is not to punish but to make sure they really want it and to facilitate the opportunities for reconciliation. . . .

Question

We must, of course, be on the side of the professor — but which point of view appeals the most to you?

2. An English bishop might have been equally embarrassed, for the following chart appears in *Social Trends 13* (1982):

Divorce rates: international comparisons

Rate per 1,000 existing marriages

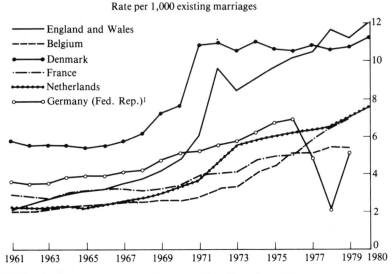

[1]1977 and subsequent years are not comparable with earlier years.
The First Law Reforming Marriage and Family Legislation came
into force on 1 July 1977.

Source: Demographic Statistics 1980, *(SOEC)*

3. You will have noticed that the chart which we give does relate divorces to existing marriages. As Dominian notes in his chapter in *Families in Britain* (1982), 'This increase is absolute and cannot be accounted for by an increase in population, marriages or longevity in life expectation.'
4. In England and Wales in 1980 there were 370,022 marriages and 148,301 decrees absolute of divorce (OPCS Monitors FM2 82/2 and 82/1 respectively).
5. Richard Leete (1979) has calculated the proportion (per thousand) of marriages in 1965 and 1970 which had ended in divorce by selected marriage durations:

Marital status Age at marriage	Year of marriage	No. of marriages (thousands)	Approximate duration of marriage				
			3	4	6	9	11
a) Males							
Bachelor							
All ages	1965	328.5	2	12	41	94	126
	1970	361.1	7	33	80		
Under 25	1965	210.1	2	15	50	113	150
	1970	254.2	8	38	92		
25–34	1965	99.2	2	8	27	65	89
	1970	90.9	6	23	55		
35 and over	1965	19.2	2	6	18	38	53
	1970	16.0	6	16	37		
Divorced							
All ages	1965	24.3	3	12	38	88	119
	1970	35.7	8	32	78		
Widower							
All ages	1965	18.3	2	5	14	29	37
	1970	18.7	5	15	30		

b) Females

Spinster							
All ages	1965	331.7	2	12	41	94	125
	1970	364.4	7	33	81		
Under 25	1965	275.7	2	14	46	104	139
	1970	310.6	8	36	88		
25–34	1965	42.6	2	6	21	48	67
	1970	43.3	5	17	42		
35 and over	1965	13.3	2	3	10	21	29
	1970	10.5	4	10	21		
Divorced							
All ages	1965	23.6	3	10	33	85	114
	1970	33.7	7	30	73		
Widow							
All ages	1965	15.8	2	6	17	36	46
	1970	17.4	6	17	33		

These figures are affected by the change in divorce law which came into force in 1971 and relate to marriages of relatively short duration. But Leete also calculated the proportions per thousand of people *born* in particular years who had divorced by selected ages. The figures below the straight line diagonal are projections:

England and Wales

Birth generation	Age (exact years)					
	25	30	35	40	45	50
a) Males						
1926	3	17	32	49	66	93
1931	3	14	34	58	94	125
1936	2	20	53	100	131	160
1941	4	36	98	153	194	224
1946	8	68	133	188	229	259
1950	16	84	149	204	245	275
1951	19	87	152	206	247	277
1952	21	88	153	207	248	278
b) Females						
1926	9	29	44	58	72	95
1931	8	24	43	64	95	120
1936	7	31	60	103	140	165
1941	12	50	108	136	194	219
1946	20	95	162	209	245	270
1950	34	111	176	223	259	284
1951	39	116	181	228	264	289
1952	43	119	184	231	267	292

(*Changing Patterns of Family Formation and Dissolution in England and Wales 1964–76*, 1979)

6. In *The Proportion of Marriages Ending in Divorce* (1982), John Haskey estimates that if current divorce rates were to continue at their present levels, one in three marriages in England and Wales would eventually end in divorce.

7. Leete's first table (above) does not necessarily support this, but the durations are too short for a clear picture to emerge.

8. Although rare in proportion to divorces, petitions for judicial separation have risen dramatically in recent years:

	Petitions			Grounds					
Year	Total Petitions	By Husbands	By Wives	Adultery	Behaviour	Desertion	2 years living apart	5 years living apart	Total Decrees
1971	211	10	201	63	111	3	—	1	38
1972	330	23	307	71	204	15	2	5	115
1973	430	20	410	85	284	8	2	5	190
1974	696	48	648	118	464	22	6	6	245
1975	936	52	884	124	717	59	4	3	323
1976	1,601	63	1,538	250	1,190	9	3	3	584
1977	1,980	137	1,843	298	1,507	12	9	3	761
1978	2,611	239	2,372	554	1,812	(Figures not			1,228
1979	3,650	322	3,328	686	2,741	available)			1,640
1980	5,423	482	4,941	895	4,274				2,560

Source: Civil Judicial Statistics

9. In England, a decree of judicial separation deprives a wife of rights of intestate succession (Matrimonial Causes Act 1973, s. 18(2)), but not of the status of widow for the purpose of state widow's benefits. Occupational pension schemes vary. Nevertheless, judicial separation is described by some solicitors as the 'older woman's remedy.' Other reasons for petitioning may be religious objections to divorce, the prohibition on divorcing within three years of the marriage, and the wish or need for ancillary relief or injunctions (research by Pamela Garlick, Manchester, and Susan Maidment, Keele, 1982). The fact that over half the petitions were grounded upon the respondent's behaviour, and that less than half proceeded to a decree, might point to the ancillary injunction as a prominent motive (for injunctions, see Chapter 14); but as more than half are presented within three years of the marriage, many may be replaced by divorce petitions.

The four disputants go on to discuss the law's attempts to promote reconciliation between the warring spouses and — as we shall see from the extracts reproduced in our final chapter — the judge suffers almost as severe a mauling as does the hapless bishop. For the moment, however, we must go on to trace how 'irretrievable breakdown of marriage' became the sole ground for divorce in English law. Foote, Levy and Sander themselves state that 'the acknowledged genesis of contemporary divorce reform in the Anglo-American world was the work of a group appointed by the Archbishop of Canterbury in the 1960s' (although this is a little unfair to earlier laws in New Zealand and Australia which had allowed no-fault divorce after a period of separation in certain circumstances). The Archbishop's group (under the chairmanship of the Rt. Rev. R.C. Mortimer, Lord Bishop of Exeter) published its report in 1966, under the title *Putting Asunder — A Divorce Law for Contemporary Society*. It drew three main conclusions.

First, as Jesus himself had accepted the Mosaic law for those whose 'hardness of heart' made them unable to understand the truth of Jesus' own teaching about life-long fidelity, and today's secular society was full of such people:

17. There is therefore nothing to forbid the Church's recognizing fully the validity of a secular divorce law within the secular sphere. It follows that it is right and proper for the Church to co-operate with the State, and for Christians to co-operate with secular humanists and others who are not Christians, in trying to make the divorce law as equitable and as little harmful to society as it can be made. Since ex hypothesi the State's matrimonial law is not meant to be a translation of the teaching of Jesus into legal terms, but [to] allow properly for that 'hardness of heart' of which Jesus himself took account, the standard by which it is to be judged is certainly not the Church's own canon law and pastoral discipline. . . .

18. The only Christian interests that need to be declared are the protection of the weak and the preservation and strengthening of those elements in the law which favour lasting marriage and stable family life; and these are ends which Christians are by no means alone in thinking socially important. . . .

Secondly, having considered the interpretation of the fault-based grounds; the shifts to which these put couples who were determined on divorce; and the inconsistency of having some fault and some (like incurable insanity and cases of cruelty for which the respondent could not morally be blamed) no-fault grounds:

45(*f*) . . . We are far from being convinced that the present provisions of the law witness to the sanctity of marriage, or uphold its public repute, in any observable way, or that they are irreplaceable as buttresses of morality, either in the narrower field of matrimonial and sexual relationships, or in the wider field which includes considerations of truth, the sacredness of oaths, and the integrity of professional practice. As a piece of social mechanism the present system has not only cut loose from its moral and juridical foundations: it is, quite simply, inept.

Thirdly, the courts should be empowered, after an enquiry into every case, to recognise in law the fact that a marriage had irretrievably broken down:

55. . . . As we see it, the primary and fundamental question would be: Does the evidence before the court reveal such failure in the matrimonial relationship, or such circumstances adverse to that relationship, that no reasonable probability remains of the spouses again living together as husband and wife for mutual comfort and support? That is in line with Lord Walker's definition of a broken marriage as 'one where the facts and circumstances affecting the lives of the parties adversely to one another are such as to make it improbable that an ordinary husband and wife would ever resume cohabitation' (Morton Report, 1956). The evidence falling to be considered by the court would be all the relevant facts in the history of the marriage, including those acts and circumstances which the existing law treats as grounds for divorce in themselves. The court would then dissolve the marriage if, and only if, having regard to the interests of society as well as of those immediately affected by its decision, it judged it wrong to maintain the legal existence of a relationship that was beyond all probability of existing again in fact.

In the light of what eventually happened, however, one further conclusion reached by the group should be stressed:

69. We may enumerate three principal objections to reducing the principle of breakdown to a verbally formulated 'ground' and introducing it into the existing law cheek by jowl with the 'grounds' defining matrimonial offences.

(a) The mutual incompatibility of the two principles would be glaringly obvious
The existing law is almost entirely based on the assumption that divorce ought to be seen as just relief for an innocent spouse against whom an offence has been committed by the other spouse. If then there were inserted into this law an additional clause enabling a guilty spouse to petition successfully against the will of an innocent, the whole context would proclaim the addition unjust. Conversely, if the legislature came to the conclusion that it was right and proper to grant divorce, on the petition of either party and without proof of any specific offence, when — and only when — a marriage was shown to have broken down irreparably, how could it justify retaining grounds which depended on the commission of specific offences, on which only injured parties might petition, and which required no evidence of breakdown at all? . . .

(b) The superficiality inseparable from verbally formulated 'grounds' would tend to render the principle of breakdown inoperative
One of our reasons for recommending the principle of breakdown is that it would enable the courts to get to grips with the realities of the matrimonial relationship instead of having to concentrate on superficialities. But if the principle were introduced into the law in the shape of yet another verbally formulated 'ground' (such as the Australian 'ground of separation'), the advantage hoped for would be lost. . . .

(c) The addition of a new 'ground' embodying the principle of breakdown would make divorce easier to get without really improving the law
As we have said, we have no reason to believe that the entire substitution of breakdown for the matrimonial offence would, in the long run, make divorce easier or increase the number of decrees granted to a significant extent; but quite obviously the mere addition of a 'ground of separation' would do both, since it would make divorce available where now it is not, while leaving undisturbed the opportunities now existing. . . .

Immediately following the publication of *Putting Asunder*, the Lord Chancellor referred the matter to the Law Commission. Their report, inaccurately entitled *Reform of the Grounds of Divorce — The Field of Choice*, was published only five months later. Their conclusions were summarised thus:

120. (1) The objectives of a good divorce law should include (*a*) the support of marriages which have a chance of survival, and (*b*) the decent burial with the minimum of embarrassment, humiliation and bitterness of those that are indubitably dead. . . .

(2) The provision of the present law whereby a divorce cannot normally be obtained within three years of the celebration of the marriage may help to achieve the first objective. . . . But the principle of matrimonial offence on which the present law is based does not wholly achieve either objective. . . .

(3) Four of the major problems requiring solution are: —
   (*a*) The need to encourage reconciliation. Something more might be achieved here; though little is to be expected from conciliation procedures after divorce proceedings have been instituted. . . .
   (*b*) The prevalence of stable illicit unions. As the law stands, many of these cannot be regularised nor the children legitimated. . . .
   (*c*) Injustice to the.economically weaker partner — normally the wife. . . .
   (*d*) The need adequately to protect the children of failed marriages. . . .

(4) The field of choice for reform is circumscribed by a number of practical considerations and public attitudes, which cannot be ignored if acceptable and practicable reforms are to be undertaken. . . .

(5) The proposals of the Archbishop's Group on Divorce made in *Putting Asunder*, though they are to be welcomed for their rejection of exclusive reliance on matrimonial offence, are procedurally impracticable. They propose that there should be but one comprehensive ground for divorce — breakdown of the marriage — the court being required to satisfy itself by means of a thorough inquest into the marriage that it has failed irretrievably. It would not be feasible, even if it were desirable, to undertake such an inquest in every divorce case because of the time this would take and the costs involved. . . .

(6) However, the following alternative proposals, if any of them were thought desirable, would be practicable in the sense that they could be implemented without insuperable legal difficulty and without necessarily conflicting with the critical factors referred to in (4): —
   (*a*) *Breakdown without Inquest* — a modification of the breakdown principal [sic] advocated in *Putting Asunder*, but dispensing in most cases with the elaborate inquest there suggested. The court would, on proof of a period of separation and in the absence of evidence to the contrary, assume that the marriage had broken down. If, however, this were to be the sole comprehensive ground of divorce, it would not be feasible to make the period of separation much more than six months. If, as seems likely, so short a period is not acceptable, breakdown cannot become the sole ground, but might still be introduced as an additional ground on the lines of proposal (*c*) below. . . .
   (*b*) *Divorce by Consent* — This would be practicable only as an additional, and not a sole comprehensive, ground. It would not be more than a palliative and would probably be unacceptable except in the case of marriages in which there are no dependent children. Even in the case of childless marriages, if consent were the sole criterion, it might lead to the dissolution of marriages that had not broken down irretrievably. . . .
   (*c*) *The Separation Ground* — This would involve introducing as a ground for divorce a period of separation irrespective of which party was at fault, thereby affording a place in the law for the application of the breakdown principle. But since the period would be substantially longer than six months, it would be practicable only as an addition to the existing grounds based on matrimonial offence. The most comprehensive form of this proposal would provide for two different periods of separation. After the expiration of the shorter period (two years is suggested) either party, subject to safeguards, could obtain a divorce if the other consented, or, perhaps, did not object. After the expiration of the longer period (five or seven years) either party, subject to further safeguards, could obtain a divorce even if the other party objected. . . .

(7) If any of these proposals were adopted, the following safeguards would appear to be necessary: —
   (*a*) The three year waiting period [see p. 179, below] should be retained. . . .
   (*b*) The court should have power to adjourn for a limited period to enable the possibilities of reconciliation to be explored. . . . [see Chapter 17].
   (*c*) The court should have a discretion to refuse a decree if attempts had been made by the petitioner wilfully to deceive it; but the present absolute and discretionary bars would be inapplicable to petitions on these new grounds. . . .
   (*d*) Additional safeguards would be needed to protect the respondent spouse and the children. These should include: —

(i) A procedure to ensure that the respondent's decision to consent to or not oppose a divorce, had been taken freely and with a full appreciation of the consequences. . . .

(ii) Retention, and possible improvement, of the provisions of the present law designed to ensure that satisfactory arrangements are made for the future of the children. . . .

(iii) Provisions protecting an innocent party from being divorced against his or her will unless equitable financial arrangements are made for him or her. . . .

(*e*) It is for consideration whether there should be a further discretionary bar based on protection of interests wider than those of the parties alone. If such a bar were introduced, it should be defined as precisely as possible so as to promote consistency in its exercise and to enable legal advisers to give firm advice to their clients. . . .

Question

In the light of this summary, do you agree that to title the report 'The Field of Choice' was 'inaccurate'?

The 'practical considerations and public attitudes' referred to in paragraph 120 (4) above are of interest now, nearly two decades later, when divorce law reform is once more under discussion:

52. (*a*) Public opinion would not accept any substantial increase in the difficulty of obtaining a divorce or of the time it takes, unless it could be shown that an appreciable number of marriages would be mended as a result.

(*b*) Experience shows that the chances of reconciliation between the parties have become almost negligible by the time that a petition for a divorce is filed.

(*c*) Whether a divorce is obtainable or not, husbands and wives in modern conditions will part if life becomes intolerable. The ease with which names can be changed under English law simplifies the establishment of a new and apparently regular 'marriage'; where the deception is not complete, the resulting children are the main sufferers because of the stigma that still attaches to the status of illegitimacy.

(*d*) Children are at least as vitally affected by their parents' divorce as are the parents themselves.

(*e*) Breakdown of a marriage usually precedes the matrimonial offence on which the divorce petition is based. Thus, an isolated act of adultery or isolated acts with different partners may be the grounds for divorce, but are likely to be the result of the breakdown of the marriage rather than its cause.

(*f*) Public opinion would be unlikely to support a proposal which had the effect of, say, doubling the amount spent on divorce proceedings; in so far as more Judges, more courts and more Legal Aid would impose a burden on public funds, it would be felt that the money could be better spent on other subjects, including, for example, marriage guidance and conciliation.

(*g*) Public opinion would be equally unlikely to support a great expansion of the Queen's Proctor's Office or the employment of additional public servants with the function of investigating the truth of the evidence given by parties to divorce proceedings. At the present time there is a shortage of trained welfare officers attached to the courts and no sudden addition to their numbers can be hoped for in the near future.

(*h*) Even where a marriage is childless, divorce granted automatically if the parties consent ('Post Office divorces') would not be acceptable; there must be an independent check if only to ensure that the economically weaker party really and freely consents to the divorce and to approve the financial arrangements worked out by the parties and their solicitors. The need for outside intervention is, of course, far greater where there are children.

Question

The Law Commission did not base these statements on any scientific opinion poll (although they were described as 'hard facts' in the Report) — how many of them, according to your impressions of the contemporary scene, would hold good today?

3 The law

The Divorce Reform Act 1969, by and large, translated the Law Commission's clear preferences into law. It came into force on 1 January 1971 and has since been consolidated with other relevant legislation in the *Matrimonial Causes Act 1973*:

1.—(1) Subject to section 3 below, a petition for divorce may be presented to the court by either party to a marriage on the ground that the marriage has broken down irretrievably.

(2) The court hearing a petition for divorce shall not hold the marriage to have broken down irretrievably unless the petitioner satisfies the court of one or more of the following facts, that is to say —

> (a) that the respondent has committed adultery and the petitioner finds it intolerable to live with the respondent;
>
> (b) that the respondent has behaved in such a way that the petitioner cannot reasonably be expected to live with the respondent;
>
> (c) that the respondent has deserted the petitioner for a continuous period of at least two years immediately preceding the presentation of the petition;
>
> (d) that the parties to the marriage have lived apart for a continuous period of at least two years immediately preceding the presentation of the petition (hereafter in this Act referred to as 'two years' separation') and the respondent consents to a decree being granted;
>
> (e) that the parties to the marriage have lived apart for a continuous period of at least five years immediately preceding the presentation of the petition (hereafter in this Act referred to as 'five years' separation').

(3) On a petition for divorce it shall be the duty of the court to inquire, so far as it reasonably can, into the facts alleged by the petitioner and into any facts alleged by the respondent.

(4) If the court is satisfied on the evidence of any such fact as is mentioned in subsection (2) above, then, unless it is satisfied on all the evidence that the marriage has not broken down irretrievably, it shall, subject to sections 3(3) and 5 below, grant a decree of divorce.

(5) Every decree of divorce shall in the first instance be a decree nisi and shall not be made absolute before the expiration of six months from its grant unless the High Court by general order from time to time fixes a shorter period,[10] or unless in any particular case the court in which the proceedings are for the time being pending from time to time by special order fixes a shorter period than the period otherwise applicable for the time being by virtue of this subsection.

2.—(1) One party to a marriage shall not be entitled to rely for the purposes of section 1(2)(a) above on adultery committed by the other if, after it became known to him that the other had committed that adultery, the parties have lived with each other for a period exceeding, or periods together exceeding, six months.

(2) Where the parties to a marriage have lived with each other after it became known to one party that the other had committed adultery, but subsection (1) above does not apply, in any proceedings for divorce in which the petitioner relies on that adultery the fact that the parties have lived with each other after that time shall be disregarded in determining for the purposes of section 1(2)(a) above whether the petitioner finds it intolerable to live with the respondent.

(3) Where in any proceedings for divorce the petitioner alleges that the respondent has behaved in such a way that the petitioner cannot reasonably be expected to live with him, but the parties to the marriage have lived with each other for a period or periods after the date of the occurrence of the final incident relied on by the petitioner and held by the court to support his allegation, that fact shall be disregarded in determining for the purposes of section 1(2)(b) above whether the petitioner cannot reasonably be expected to live with the respondent if the length of that period or of those periods together was six months or less.

(4) For the purposes of section 1(2)(c) above the court may treat a period of desertion as having continued at a time when the deserting party was incapable of continuing the necessary intention if the evidence before the court is such that, had that party not been so incapable, the court would have inferred that his desertion continued at that time.

(5) In considering for the purposes of section 1(2) above whether the period for which the respondent has deserted the petitioner or the period for which the parties to a marriage have lived apart has been continuous, no account shall be taken of any one period (not exceeding six months) or of any two or more periods (not exceeding six months in all) during which the parties resumed living with each other, but no period during which the parties lived with each other shall

---

10. The period is now fixed at six weeks.

count as part of the period of desertion or of the period for which the parties to the marriage lived apart, as the case may be.

(6) For the purposes of section 1(2)(*d*) and (*e*) above and this section a husband and wife shall be treated as living apart unless they are living with each other in the same household, and references in this section to the parties to a marriage living with each other shall be construed as references to their living with each other in the same household.

(7) Provision shall be made rules of court for the purpose of ensuring that where in pursuance of section 1(2)(*d*) above the petitioner alleges that the respondent consents to a decree being granted the respondent has been given such information as will enable him to understand the consequences to him of his consenting to a decree being granted and the steps which he must take to indicate that he consents to the grant of a decree.

5.—(1) The respondent to a petition for divorce in which the petitioner alleges five years' separation may oppose the grant of a decree on the ground that the dissolution of the marriage will result in grave financial or other hardship to him and that it would in all the circumstances be wrong to dissolve the marriage.

(2) Where the grant of a decree is opposed by virtue of this section, then —

(*a*) if the court finds that the petitioner is entitled to rely in support of his petition on the fact of five years' separation and makes no such finding as to any other fact mentioned in section 1(2) above, and

(*b*) if apart from this section the court would grant a decree on the petition,

the court shall consider all the circumstances, including the conduct of the parties to the marriage and the interests of those parties and of any children or other persons concerned, and if of opinion that the dissolution of the marriage will result in grave financial or other hardship to the respondent and that it would in all the circumstances be wrong to dissolve the marriage it shall dismiss the petition.

(a) THE 'FAULT-BASED' FACTS

At first sight, these provisions combine fault and no-fault 'grounds' for divorce in just the way so deplored by the Archbishop's group in *Putting Asunder*. In fact, however, as the following cases illustrate, the apparently fault-based 'grounds' are not always what they seem.

Cleary v Cleary
[1974] 1 All ER 498, [1974] 1 WLR 73, 117 Sol Jo 834, Court of Appeal

The wife left her husband and committed adultery. She then returned to her husband and they lived together for five or six weeks. She left again but did not repeat the adultery. She took proceedings unsuccessfully in a magistrates' court complaining of her husband's persistent cruelty and wilful neglect to maintain her. A few months later she petitioned for divorce on the basis of her husband's behaviour. The husband denied this and cross-prayed for divorce on the basis of her adultery. She withdrew her petition and the case proceeded undefended upon the husband's cross-prayer. The county court judge dismissed the suit and the husband appealed.

Lord Denning MR: . . . [On the words of section 1(2)(*a*)] a point of law arises on which there is a difference of opinion between the judges. The question is whether the two facts required by section [1(2)(*a*)] are severable and independent, or whether they are interconnected. In other words, is it sufficient for the husband to prove (*a*) that the wife has committed adultery and (*b*) that he finds it intolerable to live with her? Or has he to prove that (*a*) the wife has committed adultery and (*b*) that *in consequence thereof* he finds it intolerable to live with her? Are the words 'in consequence thereof' to be read into section [1(2)(*a*)]?

On the one hand, in *Goodrich v Goodrich* [1971] 2 All ER 1340, [1971] 1 WLR 1142, Lloyd-Jones J quoted from *Rayden on Divorce*, 11th ed. (1971), p. 175, where it was submitted that the two phrases are in the context independent of one another. The judge said: 'In my judgment that view is acceptable.' On the other hand, more recently in *Roper v Roper and Porter* [1972] 3 All ER 668, [1972] 1 WLR 1314, Faulks J took a different view. He said:

'I think that common sense tells you that where the finding that has got to be made is that the respondent has committed adultery, and the petitioner finds it intolerable to live with the respondent, it means, "*and in consequence* of the adultery the petitioner finds it intolerable to live with the respondent." '

So Faulks J would introduce the words 'in consequence thereof,' whereas Lloyd-Jones J would not. Which is the right view?

As a matter of interpretation, I think the two facts in section [1(2)(*a*)] are independent and should be so treated. Take this very case. The husband proves that the wife committed adultery and that he forgave her and took her back. That is one fact. He then proves that, after she comes back, she behaves in a way that makes it quite intolerable to live with her. She corresponds with the other man and goes out at night and finally leaves her husband, taking the children with her. That is another fact. It is in consequence of that second fact that he finds it intolerable — not in consequence of the previous adultery. On that evidence, it is quite plain that the marriage has broken down irretrievably. He complies with section [1(2)(*a*)] by proving (*a*) her adultery which was forgiven; and (*b*) her subsequent conduct (not adultery), which makes it intolerable to live with her.

I would say one word more. In *Rayden on Divorce*, 11th ed., p. 175, it is suggested (referring to an extra-judicial lecture by Sir Jocelyn Simon [Riddell Lecture 1970, see *Rayden*, pp. 3227, 3234]): 'It may even be his own adultery which leads him to find it intolerable to live with the respondent.' I cannot accept that suggestion. Suppose a wife committed adultery five years ago. The husband forgives her and takes her back. He then falls in love with another woman and commits adultery with her. He may say that he finds it intolerable to live with his wife, but that is palpably untrue. It was quite tolerable for five years: and it is not rendered intolerable by his love for another woman. That illustration shows that a judge in such cases as these should not accept the man's bare assertion that he finds it intolerable. He should inquire what conduct on the part of the wife has made it intolerable. It may be her previous adultery. It may be something else. But whatever it is, the judge must be satisfied that the husband finds it intolerable to live with her.

On the facts of this case I think the judge could and should have found on the evidence the two elements required, (1) the adultery of the wife and (2) the husband found it intolerable to live with her.

Appeal allowed.

Questions

(i) Husband and wife agree that they will live on the wife's earnings from prostitution; after some months of this the husband falls in love with a pure young virgin; he finds it intolerable to live with his wife; is he entitled to an immediate divorce?

(ii) The same husband leaves his wife to wait until he is free to marry his pure young virgin; is his wife entitled to an immediate divorce?

(iii) Do you find your answers to questions (i) and (ii) either (*a*) just, or (*b*) sensible?

(iv) If you are not happy with the answers to questions (i) and (ii), ought the result to be (*a*) that neither is entitled to an immediate divorce, or (*b*) that both are entitled to an immediate divorce?

(v) What difference, if any, would it have made to any of your answers if the husband's distaste for his wife had developed because she contracted a venereal disease in the course of her prostitution?

(vi) Does not the answer to Lord Denning's last example lie in s. 2(1)?

(vii) But if 'adultery' and 'intolerability' need have nothing to do with one another, why is s. 2(2) expressed as it is?[11]

(viii) In the magistrates' matrimonial jurisdiction (Chapter 3, above), adultery is only a ground for financial relief insofar as it falls within 'behaviour': what difference, if any, does this make?

---

11. A differently constituted Court of Appeal was troubled by this point in *Carr v Carr* [1974] 1 All ER 1193, [1974] 1 WLR 1534, but reluctantly accepted the *Cleary* interpretation of s. 1(2)(*a*).

Livingstone-Stallard v Livingstone-Stallard
[1974] Fam 47, [1974] 2 All ER 766, [1974] 3 WLR 302, 118 Sol Jo 462, 4 Fam
Law 150, High Court, Family Division

The husband and wife married in December 1969; they were then aged 56 and
24 respectively. Two months later, 'as the result of one of the few scenes of
violence which took place during the marriage,' the wife left. But in
September 1970 they were reunited. The marriage ended for practical
purposes in September 1972, when the wife left after the husband became
enraged in the course of an argument. The wife petitioned on the basis of her
husband's behaviour. Most of the incidents were 'trivial in themselves,' and
we quote only one of those described because of the significance attached to
it by the judge. It took place shortly after the wedding and before the first
parting.

Dunn J: . . . The wife also complained about another incident which was, perhaps, the most
illuminating incident so far as the husband's character was concerned. They had, naturally, had
some photographs taken at their wedding, and not very long afterwards the photographer came
round with the wedding album. The husband was out and the wife, exercising what one would
imagine was normal courtesy and hospitality, offered the photographer a glass of sherry which
he accepted and she had a glass of sherry too to keep him company. When the husband came
home he went to his cocktail cabinet, took out the sherry bottle and said, 'You have drunk half a
bottle of sherry. Don't you ever go to my cocktail cabinet again.' He asked her who she had been
drinking with and she told him what had happened. He forbade her to 'give refreshment to
trades people again.' He was naturally cross-examined about his attitude and it appeared to be
that if his wife took a glass of sherry with a tradesman — and he apparently classed the
photographer as a tradesman — then the glass of sherry might, as he put it, impair her faculties,
so that the tradesman might make some kind of indecent approach to her; and that was the
justification of his conduct on that occasion. To my mind, it is typical of the man. . . .
    I am quite satisfied that this marriage has broken down. The wife told me that in no circum-
stances would she continue to live with her husband, partly because he is so irresponsible with
Jason [their son] and takes so little interest in him. I cannot, of course, dissolve this marriage
unless I am satisfied that the husband has behaved in such a way that the wife cannot reasonably
be expected to live with him. That question is, to my mind, a question of fact, and one approach
to it is to suppose that the case is being tried by a judge and jury and to consider what the proper
direction to the jury would be, and then to put oneself in the position of a properly directed jury
in deciding the question of fact.
    Mr Reece, for the husband, has referred me to the cases — all of which have been so far
decided at first instance — *Ash v Ash* [1972] Fam 135, [1972] 1 All ER 582; *Pheasant v Pheasant*
[1972] Fam 202, [1972] 1 All ER 587; and *Katz v Katz* [1972] 3 All ER 219, [1972] 1 WLR 955 and
has submitted that incompatibility of temperament is not enough to entitle a petitioner to relief,
that the behaviour must be of sufficient gravity so that the court can say that it would, under the
old law, have granted a decree of divorce on the ground of constructive desertion. Mr Reece has
submitted that the best approach is to apply the test which was applied in the constructive
desertion cases, bearing in mind that the parties are married and that the conduct must be
sufficiently grave to justify a dissolution of the marriage; weighing the gravity of the conduct
against the marriage bond or, as Mr Reece put it, against the desirability of maintaining the
sanctity of marriage. I have in the past followed the reasoning of Ormrod J in *Pheasant v
Pheasant* [1972] Fam 202, [1972] 1 All ER 587 but, on reflection and with respect, I am not sure
how helpful it is to import notions of constructive desertion into the construction of the
Matrimonial Causes Act 1973. Nor, speaking for myself, do I think it helpful to analyse the
degree of gravity of conduct which is required to entitle a petitioner to relief under section
1(2)(*b*) of the Act. As Lord Denning MR has emphasised in another context (*Wachtel v Wachtel*
[1973] Fam 72, [1973] 1 All ER 829), the Act of 1973 is a reforming statute and section 1(2) is in
very simple language which is quite easy for a layman to understand. Coming back to my
analogy of a direction to a jury, I ask myself the question: Would any right-thinking person
come to the conclusion that this husband has behaved in such a way that this wife cannot reasonably be expected to live with him, taking into account the whole of the circumstances and the
characters and personalities of the parties? It is on that basis that I approach the evidence in this
case.
    The wife was young enough to be the husband's daughter and plainly considerable adjust-
ment was required on both sides. Mr Reece submitted that she had known him a long time and
that she knew exactly the kind of man that she was marrying; that the complaints which she
made are trivial; and that she cannot bring herself within section 1(2)(*b*) simply because the

character of her husband does not suit her. He further submitted that the reality of this case was that this young woman had simply got fed up and walked out, and walked out pretty soon too. I accept that the wife was a strong-minded young woman, but I am satisfied that she was anxious for the marriage to last and wished it to continue, that she wished to have children and bring them up and to have her own home, and that she did her best so far as she was able to adjust to her husband's character.

The husband was said, by Mr Reece, to be meticulous. I agree with Mr Beckman [for the wife] that more suitable adjectives would be self-opinionated, didactic and critical and I accept that the husband's approach was to educate the wife to conform entirely to his standards. He, in my judgment, patronised her continually and submitted her, as I have found, to continual petty criticisms and his general attitude is well exemplified by the incident of the sherry and the photographer whom he called 'the tradesman.' I accept that many of the incidents were, or might appear to be, trivial in themselves and that there is a paucity of specific incidents between September 1970 and November 1972. But taking the facts as I have found them in the round in relation to the husband's character, in my judgment, they amount to a situation in which this young wife was subjected to a constant atmosphere of criticism, disapproval and boorish behaviour on the part of her husband. Applying the test which I have formulated, I think that any right-thinking person would come to the conclusion that this husband had behaved in such a way that this wife could not reasonably be expected to live with him. There will accordingly be a decree nisi under section 1(2)(*b*) of the Matrimonial Causes Act 1973.

Questions

(i) The reasoning of Ormrod J in *Pheasant v Pheasant* [1972] Fam 202, [1972] 1 All ER 587, to which Dunn J refers, was this: 'Sub-para. (*b*) must have a sensible relationship with sub-para. (*c*). . . . Desertion means in law separation without consent and without just cause. In a suit based on sub-para. (*c*) a respondent therefore might, although it is not very likely, set up just cause by way of answer. . . . In the present case the husband, having left the wife, is undoubtedly in desertion unless he can establish just cause. On the evidence which he has given he could not begin to make out a case under the old law, and, even if the meaning of just cause is to be modified in the new law, he could only succeed if the concept of desertion has ceased to have any meaning. . . . The absurd result would be reached that a petitioner, unquestionably in desertion, would still be able to say that he could not reasonably be expected to live with his wife.' Is this reasoning convincing?

(ii) Ormrod J in *Pheasant v Pheasant* [1972] Fam 202, [1972] 1 All ER 587 then went on to say: 'The test to be applied under sub-para. (*b*) is closely similar to, but not necessarily identical with, that which was formerly used in relation to constructive desertion. I would not wish to see carried over into the new law all the technicalities which accumulated round the idea of constructive desertion but rather to use the broader approach indicated by Pearce J in *Lissack v Lissack* [1951] P 1, [1950] 2 All ER 233 and consider whether it is reasonable to expect this petitioner to put up with the behaviour of this respondent bearing in mind the characters and difficulties of each of them, trying to be fair to both of them, and expecting neither heroic virtue nor selfless abnegation from either.' Do you think that this test is likely to produce different results in practice from that put forward by Dunn J in *Livingstone-Stallard v Livingstone-Stallard*?

(iii) The most controversial part of Ormrod J's judgment in *Pheasant v Pheasant* [1972] Fam 202, [1972] 1 All ER 587 is the sentence immediately following that quoted in question (ii): 'It would be consistent with the spirit of the new legislation if this problem were now to be approached more from the point of view of breach of obligation than in terms of the now out-moded idea of the matrimonial offence.' Does the test quoted from *Lissack v Lissack* [1951] P 1, [1950] 2 All ER 233 necessarily involve any breach of obligation?

The reasoning of Ormrod J was followed in its entirety by Rees J in *Richards v Richards* [1972] 3 All ER 695, [1972] 1 WLR 1073 (in which a decree was denied even though the marriage had clearly irretrievably broken down), and as to the test adopted from *Lissack v Lissack* [1951] P 1, [1950] 2 All ER 233, but not as to the 'breach of obligation' idea, by Baker P in *Katz v Katz* [1972] 3 All ER 219, [1972] 1 WLR 955. But the test suggested in *Livingstone-Stallard v Livingstone-Stallard* [1974] Fam 47, [1974] 2 All ER 766 has been approved, expressly by Roskill LJ and indirectly by Cairns LJ, in the Court of Appeal in *O'Neill v O'Neill* [1975] 3 All ER 289, [1975] 1 WLR 1118. See also the Judicial Committee of the Privy Council in *Astwood v Astwood* (1981) 131 NLJ 990 where the importance of the parties' personalities was stressed. Nevertheless, there remains one problem which was demonstrated in:

Stringfellow v Stringfellow
[1976] 2 All ER 539, [1976] 1 WLR 645, 120 Sol Jo 183, 6 Fam Law 213, Court of Appeal

Ormrod LJ: . . . The allegations which are said to constitute behaviour within the limits of s. 1(2)(*b*) of the 1973 Act are simply these, that having been married since 1969, having had two children, and having been, I assume, reasonably happy together, the situation between them changed in January 1975 when the husband, to quote the words of the petition —
  'ceased to show any interest in keeping the said marriage alive and has failed and refused to show any affection towards the [wife]. (*b*) . . . has refused to have sexual intercourse with the [wife] and has rejected all approaches made by the [wife] saying that he was not in the mood or that he was feeling depressed. (*c*) [He] has regularly gone out in the evenings but has failed to take the [wife] out saying that he had no feelings for her. (*d*) [He] has told the [wife] that he could not stand her being near to him. (*e*) [He] is interested in sport and puts his sporting activities before the [wife] and the said children as a result whereof the said children have had no family life (*f*) [He] told the [wife] to go to her parents for a week so that he could sort out his feelings saying that he no longer loved the [wife] and that he wanted his freedom which he had lost by marrying her at the age of 19.'
The wife went to her parents, and returned after a week, but the husband insisted that he wished to part from her; and it is said, naturally enough, that his rejection of her upset her. And finally, on 23 March 1975, he left and has lived apart from her ever since.
  . . . What is the relationship between the two grounds (*b*) and (*c*) set out in s. 1(2) of the 1973 Act? (*c*) of course is desertion; and, if one reads (*b*) literally, it would be easy to conclude that no spouse could reasonably be expected to live with a spouse who had deserted him or her. In other words, ground (*b*) has to be given some meaning which is not quite its literal grammatical one if it is to co-exist with (*c*) because it is clear to me that if (*b*) is to be read literally there will not in fact be any case coming before the court on the ground of desertion because every deserted spouse could maintain that the deserter had behaved in such a way that he or she could not be expected to live with him. So it cannot mean that; it must mean something more than that; and, in my judgment, it means some conduct other than the desertion or the behaviour leading up to the desertion. It means something which justifies the court in finding that the marriage had irretrievably broken down before the period of two years had elapsed after the separation. So there must be some conduct on the part of the respondent spouse which goes beyond mere desertion or the steps leading up to mere desertion.
  This case on the evidence seems to me to be a classic case of desertion simpliciter, if I may put it that way. The whole married life came quickly to an end following a change in the husband which took place in January 1975. No complaint is made about his behaviour prior to that at all. In that month either he was ill or something happened to him which altered his attitude completely towards his wife. He did no more as far as I can see than indicate to her that his attitude had changed. His attitude having changed, he could not display affection to her, he could not have sexual intercourse with her, or would be very reluctant to do so, and inevitably during those weeks between January and his departure in March this relationship was breaking down. But I do not see any allegation in the petition which goes beyond describing the basic facts of a relationship between husband and wife which has for one reason or another broken down, and I cannot see any behaviour on this part outside the limits of that situation. So for my part I would certainly hold that the wife here failed to show that the husband had behaved in such a way that she could not reasonably be expected to live with him within ground (*b*). She certainly has a case on desertion, but under the Act in its present form she has to wait two years.

Questions

(i) Once again, in *Pheasant v Pheasant* [1972] Fam 202, [1972] 1 All ER 587, Ormrod J said that the wording in sub-para. (*b*) was 'ambiguous in several respects. It could be argued that "expected" is used in an anticipatory sense, meaning that the court should consider the conduct of the respondent and decide whether there is a reasonable prospect of the petitioner continuing to live with or return to the respondent. This construction would be consistent with the emphasis in the Act on irretrievability but it would require the court to make a decision at large about the future intentions and actions of the parties. It would also make the other four tests superfluous.' Is this reasoning convincing?

(ii) Would a jury think it reasonable to expect a wife to go on living with a husband who was no longer there to be lived with?

(iii) But what if the reason that the husband was not there was that he was suffering from an incurable disease with which the wife was no longer able to cope?

Thurlow v Thurlow
[1976] Fam 32, [1975] 2 All ER 979, [1975] 3 WLR 161, 119 Sol Jo 406, 5 Fam Law 188, High Court, Family Division

The wife suffered from epilepsy and a severe physical neurological disorder. From June 1969, her mental and physical condition gradually deteriorated. Her husband made a 'genuine, sustained and considerable effort' to cope with her at home, but was forced to give up, and since July 1972 she had required full-time institutional care and would continue to do so for the rest of her life. In 1974, the husband petitioned on the basis of her behaviour.

Rees J: . . . The husband's case therefore consists of allegations of both negative and of positive behaviour on the part of the wife. The negative behaviour alleged and proved is that between the middle of 1969 and 1 July 1972, she gradually became a bedridden invalid unable to perform the role of a wife in any respect whatsoever until she reached a state in which she became unfitted even to reside in an ordinary household at all and required to be removed to a hospital and there reside for the rest of her life. The positive behaviour alleged and proved is that during the same period she displayed bad temper and threw objects at her mother-in-law and caused damage by burning various household items such as towels, cushions and blankets. From time to time she escaped from the home and wandered about the streets causing alarm and stress to those trying to care for her.

I am satisfied that by July 1972 the marriage had irretrievably broken down and since the wife, tragically, is to spend the rest of her life as a patient in a hospital the husband cannot be expected to live with her. But the question remains as to whether the wife's behaviour has been such as to justify a finding by the court that it is unreasonable to expect him to do so. . . .

Questions of interpretation of the words in section 1(2)(*b*) of the Act of 1973 which arise from the facts in the instant case include the following: Does behaviour which is wholly or mainly negative in character fall within the ambit of the statute? Is behaviour which stems from mental illness and which may be involuntary, capable of constituting relevant behaviour?

I consider these questions separately. As to the distinction which has been made between 'positive' and 'negative' behaviour I can find nothing in the statute to suggest that either form is excluded. The sole test prescribed as to the nature of the behaviour is that it must be such as to justify a finding that the petitioner cannot reasonably be expected to live with the respondent. It may well be that in practice such a finding will more readily be made in cases where the behaviour relied upon is positive than those wherein it is negative. Spouses may often, but not always, be expected to tolerate more in the way of prolonged silences and total inactivity than of violent language or violent activity. I find myself in respectful agreement with the views expressed by Davies LJ in the Court of Appeal in *Gollins v Gollins* [1964] P 32 at 58:

'. . . I do not find the contrast between "positive" conduct and "negative" conduct either readily comprehensible or helpful, although these expressions are undoubtedly to be found in the decided cases. Almost any sort of conduct can at one and the same time be described both as positive and as negative. An omission in most cases is at the same time a commission.' . . .

I now turn to the question as to whether behaviour which stems from mental illness and which may be involuntary is capable of falling within the statute. . . .

. . . I propose to follow the principle stated by Lord Reid in *Williams v Williams* [1964] AC 698 at 723 and cited by Sir George Baker P in *Katz v Katz* [1972] 3 All ER 219 at 224:

'In my judgment, decree should be pronounced against such an abnormal person . . . simply because the facts are such that, after making all allowances for his disabilities and for the temperaments of both parties, it must be held that the character and gravity of his acts were such as to amount to cruelty.'

Sir George Baker P usefully suggested that this statement of principle may be adapted to meet the present law by substituting for the final words: '. . . the character and gravity of his behaviour was such that the petitioner cannot reasonably be expected to live with him.'

Accordingly the facts of each case must be considered and a decision made, having regard to all the circumstances, as to whether the particular petitioner can or cannot reasonably be expected to live with the particular respondent. If the behaviour stems from misfortune such as the onset of mental illness or from disease of the body, or from accidental physical injury, the court will take full account of all the obligations of the married state. These will include the normal duty to accept and to share the burdens imposed upon the family as a result of the mental or physical ill-health of one member. It will also consider the capacity of the petitioner to withstand the stresses imposed by the behaviour, the steps taken to cope with it, the length of time during which the petitioner has been called upon to bear it and the actual or potential effect upon his or her health. The court will then be required to make a judgment as to whether the petitioner can fairly be required to live with the respondent. The granting of the decree to the petitioner does not necessarily involve any blameworthiness on the part of the respondent, and, no doubt, in cases of misfortune the judge will make this clear in his judgment.

In the course of his most helpful submissions on behalf of the wife Mr Holroyd Pearce drew attention to some difficulties which he urged would arise if the law were such as to enable a decree to be granted in the instant case. It would mean, he said, that any spouse who was afflicted by a mental or physical illness or an accident so as to become a 'human vegetable' could be divorced under section 1(2)(*b*) of the Matrimonial Causes Act 1973. This was repugnant to the sense of justice of most people because it involved an implication of blameworthiness where none in truth existed and it was not what Parliament intended. The remedy was open to the petitioner in such cases to seek a decree of divorce on the ground of five years' separation under section 1(2)(*e*) of the Act of 1973 and if this were done no blame would be imputed to the respondent and also the special protection for the interests of the respondents provided by sections 5 and 10 of the Act of 1973 would be available whereas it would not if a decree were granted under section 1(2)(*b*). He cited two extreme examples to illustrate the point. One was the case of a spouse who was suddenly reduced to the state of a human vegetable as a result of a road traffic accident and was immediately removed to a hospital and there remained for life. The other was one in which supervening permanent impotency brought marital relations to an end.

There is no completely satisfactory answer to these submissions but what may properly be said is that the law as laid down in *Williams v Williams* [1964] AC 698, [1963] 2 All ER 994 does provide a remedy by divorce for a spouse who is the victim of the violence of an insane respondent spouse not responsible in law or fact for his or her actions and in no respect blameworthy. The basis for that decision is the need to afford protection to the petitioner against injury. So also in the insanity cases where the behaviour alleged is wholly negative and no violence in deed or word is involved but where continuing cohabitation has caused, or is likely to cause injury to health, it should be open to the court to provide a remedy by divorce. Before deciding to grant a divorce in such cases the court would require to be satisfied that the petitioner could not reasonably be expected to live with the respondent and would not be likely to do so in the case referred to by Mr Holroyd Pearce unless driven to it by grave considerations which would include actual or apprehended injury to the health of the petitioner or of the family as a whole. It is now common knowledge that health may be gravely affected by certain kinds of negative behaviour whether voluntary or not and if the granting of a decree under section 1(2)(*b*) is justified in order to protect the health of petitioners injured by violence so it should be in cases where the petitioner's health is adversely affected by negative behaviour. The safeguard provided for the interests of respondents is that it is the judge and not the petitioner who must decide whether the petitioner can reasonably be expected to live with the respondent; and that decision is subject to review upon appeal.

I do not propose to state any concluded view upon the case postulated in which a spouse is reduced to a human vegetable as the result of a road traffic accident and is removed at once to hospital to remain there for life . . .

In reaching the decision the judge will have regard to all the circumstances including the disabilities and temperaments of both parties, the causes of the behaviour and whether the causes were or were not known to the petitioner, the presence or absence of intention, the impact of it upon the petitioner and the family unit, its duration, and the prospects of cure or improvement in the future. If the judge decided that it would be unreasonable to expect the petitioner to live with the respondent then he must grant a decree of divorce unless he is satisfied that the marriage has not irretrievably broken down.

Approaching the facts in the instant case upon the basis of these conclusions I feel bound to decide that a decree nisi of divorce should be granted. This husband has conscientiously and courageously suffered the behaviour of the wife for substantial periods of time between 1969 and July 1972 until his powers of endurance were exhausted and his health was endangered. This behaviour stemmed from mental illness and disease and no blame of any kind can be nor is attributed to the wife.

Questions

(i) Is it possible for anyone nowadays to define the 'obligations of the married state'? How can a judge guess what a jury of 'right-thinking' people would think they were?

(ii) The Family Law Sub-Committee of the Law Society, in *A Better Way Out* (1979), stated that, in undefended cases, 'the evidence presents little difficulty — after several years of marriage, virtually any spouse can assemble a list of events which, taken out of context, can be presented as unreasonable behaviour [sic] sufficient on which to found a divorce petition.' Does this surprise you?

(iii) Why is the term 'unreasonable behaviour' a misnomer?

(iv) If you were drafting a petition based upon the other's behaviour would you be inclined to make it look as bad as possible (lest the court be tempted to probe more deeply) or as little as you think you can get away with (lest the respondent be goaded into defending either the petition itself or ancillary issues)?

(v) How little do you think you can get away with?

(b) THE 'NO-FAULT' FACTS

Santos v Santos
[1972] Fam 247, [1972] 2 All ER 246, [1972] 2 WLR 889, 116 Sol Jo 196, Court of Appeal

This was a wife's undefended petition on the basis of two years' separation and her husband's consent. The judge dismissed the petition because on three occasions since the separation the wife had stayed with her husband for a short while. These did not amount to more than six months and they had been apart for the requisite total of two years in all, but the judge's attention was not drawn to what is now s. 2(5) of the Matrimonial Causes Act 1973. The wife appealed and the Court of Appeal took the opportunity to consider a totally new point as to the meaning of 'living apart.' The Bench, Davies and Sachs LJJ and Ormrod J, were all family law specialists and the judgment was that of the whole court.

Sachs LJ: . . . The appeal first came before the court, differently constituted, on November 11, 1971. Then, after having heard the submissions of Mr Picard for the wife, it became apparent that it raised a very important issue as to the meaning of the words 'living apart' in section [1(2)(*d*)]. Does this relate simply and solely to physically not living under the same roof, or does it import an additional element which has been referred to in various terms — 'absence of consortium,' 'termination of consortium,' or an 'attitude of mind' — phrases intended to convey either the fact or realisation of the fact that there is absent something which is fundamental to the state of marriage. It was, accordingly, decided to refer the case to the Queen's Proctor for inquiry and such assistance as he considered that he could offer to the court. The appeal came on again for hearing on 16 December, when the Queen's Proctor was represented by Mr Ewbank, who presented to the court the result of a great amount of research in a most learned and interesting set of submissions for which we are much indebted. . . .

In the course of the argument before us reference was frequently made to the position of diplomats en poste in insalubrious foreign capitals, to those serving sentences in prison, to those in mental and other hospitals, and to prisoners of war — in the main, involuntary separations. None the less there are larger and no less important categories of separations which start voluntarily, such as business postings, voyages of exploration or recuperation trips when one party has been ill — all of which must also be looked at when endeavouring to determine what the legislature intended by the words 'living apart.'

As part of the fruits of that research already mentioned there was fully and fairly put before us material enabling us in relation to those words to examine a considerable range of parallel Commonwealth statutes and also decisions upon them reached in Australia, Canada and New Zealand. In addition, Mr Ewbank referred us to the comprehensive and helpful review by Professor Wadlington in the *Virginia Law Review*, vol. 52 (1966), p. 32, of the effect of comparable provisions in the legislation of a large number of individual states of the U.S.A. . . .

Their lordships then reviewed the Commonwealth authorities on comparable divorce legislation and the English authorities on similar expressions in English tax and criminal legislation.

The cogent volume of authority, to which we have been referred, makes it abundantly clear that the phrase 'living apart' when used in a statute concerned with matrimonial affairs normally imports something more than mere physical separation. This is something which obviously must be assumed to have been known to the legislature in 1969. It follows that its normal meaning must be attributed to it in the Act of 1969, unless one is led to a different conclusion either by the general scheme of the statute coupled with difficulties which would result from such an interpretation, or alternatively by some specific provision in that statute. . . .

Obviously this element is not one which necessarily involves mutual consent, for otherwise the new Act would not afford relief under head (*e*) in that area where it was most plainly intended to be available — where the 'innocent' party adheres to the marriage, refusing to recognise that in truth it has ended, often despite the fact that the 'guilty' one has been living with someone else for very many years. So it must be an element capable of being unilateral: and it must, in our judgment, involve at least a recognition that the marriage is in truth at an end — and has become a shell, to adopt a much-used metaphor.

If the element can be unilateral in the sense of depending on the attitude of mind of one spouse, must it be communicated to the other spouse before it becomes in law operative? That is a question that gave particular concern in the course of the argument. There is something unattractive in the idea that in effect time under head (*e*) can begin to run against a spouse without his or her knowledge. Examples discussed included men in prison, in hospital, or away on service whose wives, so far as they knew, were standing by them: they might, perhaps, thus be led to fail to take some step which they would later feel could just have saved the marriage. On the other hand, communication might well be impossible in cases where the physical separation was due to a breakdown in mental health on the part of the other spouse, or a prolonged coma such as can occasionally occur. Moreover, need for communication would tend to equate heads (*d*) and (*e*) with desertion — which comes under head (*c*) — something unlikely to be intended by the legislature. Moreover, bowing to the inevitable is not the same thing as intending it to happen.

In the end we have firmly concluded that communication by word or conduct is not a necessary ingredient of the additional element.

On the basis that an uncommunicated unilateral ending of recognition that a marriage is subsisting can mark the moment when 'living apart' commences, 'the principal problem becomes one of proof of the time when the breakdown occurred'. . . . Sometimes there will be evidence such as a letter, reduction or cessation of visits, or starting to live with another man. But cases may well arise where there is only the oral evidence of the wife on this point. One can only say that cases under heads (*d*) and (*e*) may often need careful examination by the first instance judge and that special caution may need to be taken. . . .

The difficulties arising from some of these problems at one stage led to hesitation as to whether after all 'living apart' in this particular Act might not refer merely to physical separation. But there are at any rate two cogent reasons against holding that the standard meaning does not apply. First, in any statute in which those words are used the same problems are normally inherent to a considerable degree — and it cannot be said that they have such a special impact in the Act of 1969 as to lead to the inference that the standard meaning is negatived. Secondly — perhaps more importantly — there are the injustices and absurdities that could result from holding that 'living apart' refers merely to physical separation; these, in our judgment, outweigh any hard cases or difficulties that can arise from the standard interpretations.

One category under head (*e*) is exemplified by the case of a long sentence prisoner whose wife has, with his encouragement, stood by him for five years — only for her to find that when he comes out he files a petition for divorce relying on ground (*e*). But the more usual categories relate to men who could unjustly find time running against them through absences on public service or on business in areas where; out of regard for the welfare of the wife or the children of the family, the former remains in this country: particularly hardly could this bear on men whose home leave did not for some years total the six months referred to in section [2(5)].

Turning from hardships under head (e) to absurdities under head (d), read in conjunction with section [2(5)] of the Act, it is plain that in cases arising under the latter head the spouses can spend up to 20% of their time together without interrupting the continuity of the separation (i.e. six months in two years and six months). Thus, if living apart means mere physical separation, a man who came home on leave for less than 20% of the two to two-and-a-half years immediately preceding the filing of the petition would be in a position to satisfy the court under head (d), even though he and his wife had been on excellent terms until they had a row on the last day of his last leave. As petitions under head (d) are normally undefended, there would be no evidence to rebut this presumption that the breakdown of the marriage was irretrievable and the decree would be granted. Unless — contrary to our view — the Act intended to permit divorce by consent simpliciter such a result would be absurd. On the contrary, the tenor of section [1(2)] is to ensure that under heads (c), (d) and (e) a breakdown is not to be held irretrievable unless and until a sufficiently long passage of time has shown this to be the case. . . .

The only specific provision of the Act upon which Mr Picard felt able to rely, if his general submissions failed, was section [2(6)] . . . [p. 157, above] . . . Those terms, he contended, should be interpreted as making it clear that no other element than physical separation could be taken into account under grounds (d) and (e).

It is unfortunately by no means plain what exactly the legislature had in mind when enacting this subsection — nor even what is its general objective. Three points on its phraseology are however to be noted. First, it does not use the word 'house,' which relates to something physical, but 'household,' which has an abstract meaning. Secondly, that the words 'living with each other in the same household' should be construed as a single phrase. Thirdly, it specifically refrains from using some simple language referring to physical separation which would achieve the result for which Mr Picard contended. On the contrary, use is again made of words with a well settled matrimonial meaning — 'living together,' a phrase which is simply the antithesis of living apart, and 'household,' a word which essentially refers to people held together by a particular kind of tie, even if temporarily separated and which has been the subject of numerous decisions in matrimonial as well as in other cases. Whatever the object of this subsection, the combination of the first and third points makes it plain that it does not produce the result which has been urged on behalf of the wife.

We are, however, inclined to think that its object is simply to ensure that the long drawn out conflict — so fully and comprehensively discussed in *Naylor v Naylor* [1962] P 253, [1961] 2 All ER 129 between on the one hand the series of cases exemplified by *Smith v Smith* [1940] P 49, [1939] 4 All ER 533 and the views expressed by Denning LJ in *Hopes v Hopes* [1949] P 227 at 236, and, on the other hand, the series started by *Evans v Evans* [1948] 1 KB 175, [1947] 2 All ER 656 should for the purposes of the Act of 1969 be conclusively resolved in favour of the former. Thus, the subsection makes it clear beyond further debate that when two spouses are living in the same house, then, as regards living apart, a line is to be drawn, in accordance with the views of Denning LJ, and they are to be held to be living apart if not living in the same household. If the subsection has some other meaning it will, incidentally, give rise to many problems, as for instance where husband and wife are in different arms of the services and there is for some time no matrimonial home. . . .

. . . Therefore 'living apart' referred to in grounds (d) and (e) is a state of affairs to establish which it is in the vast generality of cases arising under those heads necessary to prove something more than that the husband and wife are physically separated. For the purposes of that vast generality, it is sufficient to say that the relevant state of affairs does not exist whilst both parties recognise the marriage as subsisting. . . .

The case was therefore sent back for trial before a High Court judge.

Questions

(i) From the point of view of the innocent and loyal wife of the long sentence prisoner, why is it 'absurd and unjust' if he makes up his mind to divorce her just before he is released, but apparently not if he makes up his mind five years earlier and tells her nothing about it?

(ii) Is the real reason not that this is absurd and unjust to her, but that such a recent decision is not conclusive evidence that the breakdown is irretrievable?

(iii) Suppose a couple whose marriage is on the rocks have a trial separation but keep returning to one another for brief periods until they finally decide that it is all over: is that decision any less likely to be 'irretrievable' than that of a couple whose initial separation was 'for good' but who kept changing their minds? (The logic of *Santos* coupled with s. 2(5) would appear to be that the second couple get their divorce whereas the first couple do not.)

However, the notion that 'living with each other in the same household' is as much an abstraction as a physical reality can be very helpful to those couples who are still under the same roof:

Fuller (otherwise Penfold) v Fuller
[1973] 2 All ER 650, [1973] 1 WLR 730, 117 Sol Jo 224, Court of Appeal

Husband and wife separated in 1964, when the wife left the matrimonial home, taking their two daughters, and went to live with a Mr Penfold in the latter's home. She took the name of Mrs Penfold and they lived together as husband and wife. Four years later, Mr Fuller had a coronary thrombosis and was no longer able to live alone. He therefore 'went and became a lodger in the house' where his wife lived with Mr Penfold. The wife gave him food and he ate with others in the house. The wife also did the washing. He paid a weekly sum for board and lodging. After four years of this, the wife petitioned for divorce on the basis of five years' separation and the husband did not defend. The judge refused the decree and the wife appealed.

Lord Denning MR: . . . At the hearing the judge held that he had no jurisdiction to grant a divorce because he thought that when the husband came back to the house, he and his wife were not living apart. The judge referred to the cases under the old law, such as *Hopes v Hopes* [1949] P 227, [1948] 2 All ER 920; and also the cases under the new Act: *Mouncer v Mouncer* [1972] 1 All ER 289, [1972] 1 WLR 321 and *Santos v Santos* [1972] Fam 247, [1972] 2 All ER 246.

In *Santos v Santos* this court stressed the need, under the new Act, to consider the state of mind of the parties and, in particular, whether they treated the marriage as subsisting or not. Clearly they treated it in this case as at an end.

In this case we have to consider the physical relationship of the parties. From 1964 to 1968 the parties were undoubtedly living apart. The wife was living with the other man as the other man's wife in that household, and the husband was separate in his household. From 1968 to 1972 the husband came back to live in the same house but not as a husband. He was to all intents and purposes a lodger in the house. Section 2(5) says they are to be treated as living apart 'unless they are living with each other in the same household'. I think the words 'with each other' mean 'living with each other as husband and wife'. In this case the parties were not living with each other in that sense. The wife was living with Mr Penfold as his wife. The husband was living in the house as a lodger. It is impossible to say that husband and wife were or are living with each other in the same household. It is very different from *Mouncer v Mouncer* where the husband and wife were living with the children in the same household — as husband and wife normally do — but were not having sexual intercourse together. That is not sufficient to constitute 'living apart'. I do not doubt the correctness of that decision. But the present case is very different. I think the judge put too narrow and limited a construction on the Act. I would allow the appeal and pronounce the decree nisi of divorce.

Stamp LJ: I agree. I can only say that to my mind the words 'living with each other in the same household' in the context of the Act relating to matrimonial proceedings are not apt to describe the situation where the wife is indisputably living with another man in the same household and her husband is there as a paying guest in the circumstances Lord Denning MR has described. 'Living with each other' connotes to my mind something more than living in the same household: indeed the words 'with each other' would otherwise be redundant.

Questions

(i) Until this case, we had all thought that the operative concept was that of a common 'household' — were they sharing such things as meals and television, and was the wife still doing some things for her husband, even if they were not sharing a bed? — but does it now seem that the operative words are 'with each other'? Does that make the words 'in the same household' redundant?

(ii) If that be so, why should not withdrawal to a separate bedroom, together with the state of mind envisaged in *Santos v Santos* [1972] Fam 247, [1972] 2 All ER 246, be sufficient?

(iii) Why do the judges apparently think that it is more important when a wife stops cooking and washing for her husband than when she refuses to share a bed with him?

(iv) Suppose a woman comes to you and explains that she and her husband have had little do with one another for some time and would now like a divorce, although for convenience they are still living under the same roof: will you explain the law carefully to her before you seek further and better particulars of their circumstances?

(v) What questions would you then ask?

(vi) How do you think all this accords with the concern felt by the Archbishop of Canterbury's group for 'considerations of truth, the sacredness of oaths and the integrity of professional practice'?

The s. 5 defence has caused more difficulty than 'living apart':

Mathias v Mathias
[1972] Fam 287, [1972] 3 All ER 1, [1972] 3 WLR 201, 116 Sol Jo 394, Court of Appeal

The parties married in 1962 and had one daughter, now aged nine and a half. They separated in 1964. The wife had done very little work of any kind since then, believing it her duty to devote herself to the child. She lived on maintenance topped up with supplementary benefit. In 1971, the husband petitioned for divorce on the basis of five years' separation. The wife alleged that a decree would cause her grave financial hardship, through the possible reduction in her maintenance payments and eventual loss of widow's pensions. The judge granted a decree and the wife appealed.

Davies LJ: . . . when a wife, as in this case, is 'put away' under [s. 1(2)(*e*) of the 1973] Act, if I may use the expression, in the overwhelming number of cases there must be, I should have thought, some financial hardship. But on what we have before us in this case I am very far indeed from being satisfied that the hardship that this lady has suffered and will suffer could properly be called 'grave' financial hardship. And, of course, if there is not shown by her — and speaking for myself I have no doubt at all that the onus is on her to show — the probability of 'grave' financial hardship, then no question of refusing a decree can arise.

On the second part of the section, I would say, in the light of the history and of the factors that Karminski LJ has set out, that, so far from it being wrong to dissolve this marriage, I am absolutely satisfied that it would be wrong not to do so. The ages of the parties are about 35 and 32 respectively. We do not know the age of the husband's lady friend, but no doubt she is a young woman. All three of the parties, the husband, the wife and the lady, would, in the ordinary course of events, have many years to live; and in my view, unless there were strong reasons to the contrary, it would be ridiculous to keep alive this shell of a marriage and prevent perhaps all three of the parties settling down to a happier life in happier circumstances. The cohabitation lasted for some [1¾] years. They have been living apart now for some 7¾ years. I should have thought that the sooner that latter situation is put to an end the better. I agree, therefore, that the appeal should be dismissed.

Question

At first instance, Park J had said that in any subsequent proceedings for financial provision, he would want to know why the wife was not working: to what extent is it relevant that the financial hardship is 'self-inflicted'?

Le Marchant v Le Marchant
[1977] 3 All ER 610, [1977] 1 WLR 559, 121 Sol Jo 334, Court of Appeal

The husband was a post office employee and about to retire. He petitioned for divorce on the basis of five years' separation. The wife alleged that the possible loss of an index-linked widow's pension would cause her grave financial hardship. The judge granted a decree and the wife appealed.

Ormrod LJ: . . . It would be quite wrong to approach this kind of case on the footing that the wife is entitled to be compensated pound for pound for what she will lose in consequence of the divorce. She has to show, not that she will lose something by being divorced, but that she will suffer grave financial hardship, which is quite another matter altogether. It is quite plain that, prima facie, the loss of the pension, which is an index-linked pension, in the order of £1,300 a year at the moment, is quite obviously grave financial hardship in the circumstances of a case like this unless it can be in some way mitigated. The learned judge, however, did not approach the case in this way. He said that s. 5 had to be read with s. 10 of the 1973 Act. Section 10 is the section which provides, in sub-s (3), that before a decree nisi is made absolute in cases such as the present, the court is required at the request of the wife to investigate the financial position and not to make the decree absolute until it is satisfied either that the petitioning husband should not be required to make any financial provision for the wife or that the financial provision made by him is reasonable and fair or (and these are the words which cause the trouble) is 'the best that can be made in the circumstances'. So, as counsel for the wife says, s. 10 offers an elusive or, perhaps better, an unreliable protection to a wife placed in the position in which this wife is placed. The marriage would have been dissolved by the decree nisi, there would have been therefore a finding of fact that she has not suffered grave financial hardship in consequence of the decree and she would then have to do the best she could under s. 10.

It is also right to point out that there are many cases, and this is one, in which the powers of the court, extensive as they are under ss. 23 and 24 as well as s. 10, are not wide enough to enable the court to carry out by order various things which a petitioner husband can do voluntarily, even if compelled to do it voluntarily, so s. 10 is not an adequate substitute. The learned judge, in a sentence, took the view that if he could see from the husband's financial position that he would be able one way or the other to alleviate sufficiently the financial hardship falling on the wife as a result of the loss of her pension, that was good enough. In the view of this court, that is not right. The right way to approach this problem is Cumming-Bruce J's approach in *Parker v Parker* [1972] Fam. 116, [1972] 1 All ER 410, that is that the answer should set up a prima facie case of financial hardship, that the petition should be dismissed unless the petitioner can meet that answer in his reply by putting forward a proposal which is acceptable to the court as reasonable in all the circumstances and which is sufficient to remove the element of grave financial hardship which otherwise would lead to the dismissal of the petition. . . .

Now, at the last minute, and this is really one minute to midnight, counsel for the husband has at least made an offer. The offer is this. His client offers to transfer the matrimonial home or his interest in the matrimonial home to the wife forthwith. Secondly, he offers to pay her £5,000 when he receives the capital sum under his pension scheme (his position has clearly improved since the figures in the document P 1 were worked out) and in addition to that he proposes to take out a life insurance policy on his own life to provide on his death the sum of £5,000 which will be payable to the wife if she survives him and which she can then use as she thinks fit. That offer is without prejudice to any order for periodical payment which may be made hereafter by a registrar when the respective income positions have been investigated. . . .

The view which I have formed is that the present offer is a reasonable one in the sense that it will, if implemented, remove the element of grave financial hardship so far as the wife is concerned, and remove therefore the defence which she has to the present petition. . . .

I need only say that the decree absolute will not be made in this case until the matrimonial home has been transferred and the insurance policy has been taken out, and the lump sum paid over, to the satisfaction of the wife's advisers. In those circumstances, and in those circumstances only, would I be in favour of allowing a decree nisi to stand.

Rukat v Rukat
[1975] Fam 63, [1975] 1 All ER 343, [1975] 2 WLR 201, 119 Sol Jo 30, 4 Fam Law 81, Court of Appeal

The husband, a Pole, and the wife, a Sicilian, married in 1946. Both were Roman Catholics. They had not lived together since 1947, when the wife had visited Sicily with their daughter and the husband had written telling her not to return as he had fallen in love with another woman. Since then the wife had kept up the pretence that the marriage was still subsisting. In 1972, the husband petitioned for divorce on the basis of five years' separation. The wife alleged that this would cause her hardship on the grounds that: (i) the prospect of divorce was an anathema to her on religious and moral grounds because she was a Roman Catholic; (ii) because of the social structure of the area where she lived, divorce would cause serious repercussions for her and her child; and (iii) if a decree were pronounced she would not be accepted in her community in Sicily and would not be able to return to her home. The judge granted a decree and the wife appealed.

Lawton LJ: . . . One has to start, I think, by looking at the context in which the phrase 'grave financial or other hardship' occurs. The word 'hardship' is not a word of art. It follows that it must be construed by the courts in a common sense way, and the meaning which is put on the word 'hardship' should be such as would meet with the approval of ordinary sensible people. In my judgment, the ordinary sensible man would take the view that there are two aspects of 'hardship' — that which the sufferer from the hardship thinks he is suffering and that which a reasonable bystander with knowledge of all the facts would think he was suffering. That can be illustrated by a homely example. The rich gourmet who because of financial stringency has to drink vin ordinaire with his grouse may well think that he is suffering a hardship; but sensible people would say he was not.

If that approach is applied to this case, one gets this situation. The wife undoubtedly feels that she has suffered a hardship; and the learned judge, in the passages to which Megaw LJ has referred, found that she was feeling at the time of the judgment that she could not go back to Sicily. That, if it was genuine and deeply felt, would undoubtedly be a 'hardship' in one sense of that word. But one has to ask oneself the question whether sensible people, knowing all the facts, would think it was a hardship. On the evidence, I have come to the conclusion that they would not, and for this reason. The wife has been separated from her husband now since 1947. She returned in that year to Sicily. She has been living in Palermo with her mother and father. Her relatives have been around her; they must have appreciated that something had gone wrong with the marriage. I make all allowances for the undoubted fact that many male Sicilians leave their country to work elsewhere, and wives may be left alone for months and years on end. Nevertheless, 26 years is a very long time; and such evidence as there was before the learned judge was to the effect that it was almost inevitable that her family and those who knew her would have appreciated that there was something wrong. There would be some social stigma attached to that; she might be thought to have failed as a wife. But she has lived that down; and the fact that there had been a divorce in some foreign country would add very little to the stigma. . . .

Ormrod LJ: . . . The court has first to decide whether there was evidence on which it could properly come to the conclusion that the wife was suffering from grave financial or other hardship; and 'other hardship' in this context, in my judgment, agreeing with Megaw and Lawton LJ, must mean other *grave* hardship. If hardship is found, the court then has to look at the second limb and decide whether, in all the circumstances, looking at everybody's interests, balancing the respondent's hardship against the petitioner's interests in getting his or her freedom, it would be wrong to dissolve the marriage. . . .

In *Reiterbund v Reiterbund* [1974] 2 All ER 455, [1974] 1 WLR 788, Finer J held that the possible loss of a state widow's pension to a woman of 52 who would have to rely, as she was then relying, on supplementary benefit was *not* a grave financial hardship. He added this:

Finally, I would add a word on the second limb of the defence. It seems to me that the word 'wrong' must there be construed to mean 'unjust'. However, in determining whether in all the circumstances it would be wrong, or unjust, to dissolve the marriage, it seems to me that the court must be careful to avoid subverting the policy which led to the inclusion of s. 1(2)(e) as one of the facts establishing irretrievable breakdown by, so to speak, treating the para. (e) 'fact' as of a lower order than the other four. Irretrievable breakdown is now the sole ground for divorce, and it may be established through any one of the matters set out in s. 1(2), all of which carry equal weight in expressing the object of the legislation. It seems to me, therefore, that in considering the s. 5 defence, the court has to exclude from its consideration that a petition based on five years separation is brought by a 'guilty' husband (in the phraseology of the old law) against a non-consenting wife, for this would be tantamount to striking s. 1(2)(e) out of the Act altogether. (I might parenthetically point out that the Civil Judicial Statistics for 1972 [Table 10] show that of the 19,270 petitions for dissolution filed that year based on five years separation,

10,003 were by husbands and 9,267 by wives; so that the fear, to which s. 5 was largely a response, that the five years separation rule constituted, as it was said, a Casanova's charter, might with roughly equal ineptitude have been expressed by a reference to Messalina.) In the course of the argument I was referred to the bulk of the authorities so far decided on the construction and application of the s. 5 defence; I do not find any of them inconsistent with the view I have just expressed. The parties in this case are not young, but even if there were no prospect at all of the husband marrying again (and, as I said previously, there is at least a hint that he may) I do not consider that it would be wrong to dissolve this marriage. On the contrary, I think it is a case which is well within the policy embodied in the new law which aims, in all other than exceptional circumstances, to crush the empty shells of dead marriages.

Question

Can you describe a case, other than one such as *Le Marchant v Le Marchant* [1977] 3 All ER 610, [1977] 1 WLR 559, earlier, in which a divorce would cause grave hardship to the respondent *and* it would be wrong to dissolve the marriage?

(c) DOES FAULT MATTER?

Grenfell v Grenfell
[1978] Fam 128, [1978] 1 All ER 561, [1977] 3 WLR 738, 121 Sol Jo 814, 7 Fam Law 242, Court of Appeal

Husband and wife married in 1951 and separated in 1969. In 1974, shortly before they had been separated for five years, the wife petitioned for divorce on the basis of her husband's behaviour. The husband waited until the five years had elapsed and then filed an answer denying her allegations of behaviour and cross-praying on the basis of five years' separation. The wife filed a reply admitting separation but alleging that a divorce would cause her grave hardship, for the following reasons:

(1) She is of the Greek Orthodox faith. (2) As a practising Christian her conscience would be affronted if the marriage were to be dissolved otherwise than for grounds of substance whereby the true cause of the breakdown of the marriage will be determined by the court and a decree pronounced accordingly. (3) Further and alternatively the petitioner contends that the financial provisions set forth in the reply are inadequate in any event and that if implemented after a decree had been granted to the respondent the petitioner would suffer grave financial hardship.

The third reason was later abandoned. The registrar ordered, in effect, that the wife's reply should be struck out and that the case should proceed first on the prayer in the husband's answer. The wife appealed, first to the judge without success, and then to the Court of Appeal.

Ormrod LJ: . . . It is quite clear that the purpose of section 5 is to permit a party to a marriage to object to a decree being granted on the ground of five years' separation where dissolution of the marriage would result in grave financial or other hardship to that party. The only thing to be looked at is the dissolution of the marriage. The question is simply and solely: Will the dissolution of this marriage cause grave financial or other hardship? It has got nothing to do, in my judgment, with which of the parties initiates the proceedings, nor with the ground for the proceedings. The wife in this case, having herself asked for a decree of dissolution, cannot be heard to say that if her marriage is dissolved she will suffer grave financial or other hardship. It would be a plain case of blowing hot and cold, which, of course, is not a form of pleading which can be tolerated. Consequently, in my judgment, the registrar and the judge were entirely right to strike out the reply.

There is in fact no defence to the husband's prayer for a dissolution of marriage on the ground of five years' separation, in the light of the admissions made by the wife partly in the reply and partly in the petition.

I turn now to the second matter. The second point in this appeal is whether the wife should be permitted to go on with the allegations of behaviour in her petition in view of what has happened. It might be more accurate perhaps to put the question the other way round, in view of

Mr Ewbank's submission [for the wife], and ask whether the court has power to grant a decree on the husband's answer on the ground of five years' separation, all the necessary facts being admitted, and to refuse to hear the allegations of behaviour set out in the petition. I agree that it was a perfectly proper petition when it was filed, and I agree with the registrar that it would not be appropriate to strike it out under Order 18 on the ground that it was frivolous and vexatious. But it is necessary, I think, to draw attention to the wide powers the court has in its inherent jurisdiction to stay proceedings whenever it seems that it is appropriate to do so and the interests of justice as such require that course to be taken. . . .

To deal with this question which has arisen several times in the past, though I think this is the first time it has arisen in this court, it is necessary to remind ourselves what the Divorce Reform Act 1969 in fact did. There is one ground, and one ground only now, upon which the court has power to dissolve a marriage, and that is now set out in section 1 of the Act of 1973. The ground is that the marriage has broken down irretrievably. Parliament then went on in section 1(2) to prescribe five separate facts, one of which has to be established in order to prove that the marriage has broken down irretrievably. They are, of course, the well-known five. On proof of any one of those five — and Parliament plainly chose each of those five facts as being facts which would raise in any reasonable mind a presumption that the marriage had broken down — Parliament provided that the court should grant a decree of divorce unless it is satisfied on all the evidence that the marriage has not broken down irretrievably. In other words, on proof of any one of the five facts, there is a presumption, rebuttable, it is true, of irretrievable breakdown, and the onus is quite plainly on the party who is asserting that the marriage has not irretrievably broken down to satisfy the court by evidence that the presumption should be treated as rebutted. It is not, therefore, an adversary proceeding in any way comparable to the proceedings in other divisions of this court. Whichever side proves a fact under section 1(2), proves prima facie that the marriage has irretrievably broken down, and the court is not, in my judgment, concerned with anything else. . . .

On the pleadings in this case, as I have already said, once the reply was struck out, there was an admission by the wife that the marriage had irretrievably broken down and that the parties had been separated for five years. So that the court would be bound to grant a decree of divorce as soon as those matters were brought to the attention of the court. The wife would not be in a position to rebut the presumption of irretrievable breakdown and that would be that.

Mr Ewbank has sought to rely on section 1(3) of the Act of 1973, which provides:

'On a petition for divorce it shall be the duty of the court to inquire, so far as it reasonably can, into the facts alleged by the petitioner and into any facts alleged by the respondent.'

He says that that requires the court, imposes a statutory duty on the court, to conduct an inquiry into the facts alleged by the petitioner and by the respondent. The first comment to make on that is this: When the court is proceeding on the husband's prayer for a dissolution of marriage on the ground of five years' separation, he to all intents and purposes is the petitioner and the court's duty is to inquire into any relevant fact relating to his allegations. The wife, in her turn, is the effective respondent for the purposes of subsection (3), and it is the duty of the court to inquire into any relevant facts alleged by her. But, in the nature of things, on the facts in this case, there are no other relevant facts, other than the fact that the parties have been apart for five years and that the wife herself has asked for a decree and has herself admitted that the marriage has irretrievably broken down. There is nothing else to be inquired into.

There is no point, as I see it, in a case like this of conducting an inquiry into behaviour merely to satisfy feelings, however genuinely and sincerely held by one or other of the parties. To do so would be a waste of time of the court and, in any event, would be running, as I think, counter to the general policy or philosophy of the divorce legislation as it stands today. The purpose of Parliament was to ensure that where a marriage has irretrievably broken down, it should be dissolved as quickly and as painlessly as possible under the Act, and attempts to recriminate in the manner in which the wife in this case appears to wish to do should be, in my judgment, firmly discouraged. . . .

In those circumstances, I am quite satisfied that it would be entirely wrong to permit the wife to go on with her petition in this case, for the simple reason that facts sufficient to enable the court to grant a decree of dissolution are plain on the face of the pleadings.

Questions

(i) Do you think, from what you can gather from all these cases, that 'the general policy or philosophy of the divorce legislation as it stands today' is the same as it was in 1971?

(ii) What advice would you give to a couple who came to you wanting an immediate divorce?

(iii) What advice would you give to a wife who wanted a divorce as soon as possible from a husband who did not?
(iv) What advice would you give to the husband in question (iii)?
(v) Do you think that the answers you have given to questions (ii), (iii) and (iv): (*a*) reflect any credit upon the law; or (*b*) represent the reformers' original intentions?

Before we turn to procedure, two matters relating to the impact of the 'new' law deserve consideration. One is the extent to which the change in the law has contributed to the rising divorce rate. As the quadrilogue quoted earlier shows, this is a complex matter: but some evidence is provided by the following graph from Richard Leete's study of *Changing Patterns of Family Formation and Dissolution 1964–76* (1979).

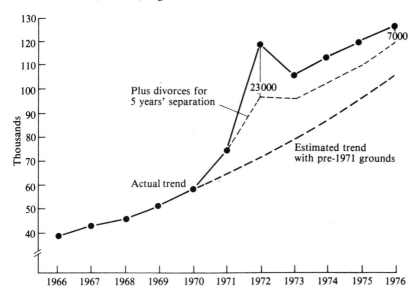

Divorces, 1966-76, England and Wales

The second point concerns the relative popularity of the five 'facts' upon which a divorce petition may be based and the relative frequency of petitions by husbands and by wives. Both are shown in the graph overleaf (p. 174), also from Leete (1979).

Dissolution by grounds, 1964-76, England and Wales

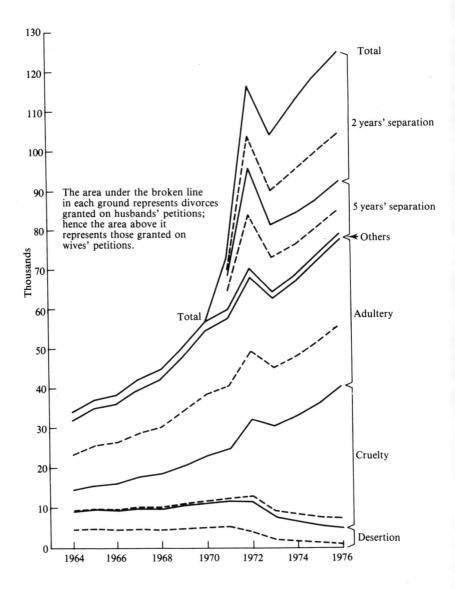

Questions

(i) Why do you suppose that the wife was the petitioner in 72% of the divorce petitions filed in 1980?

(ii) Why does that figure soar to 89% when the basis is 'behaviour' but fall to 59% when it is adultery?

(iii) Why are so few petitions based on desertion?

(iv) Why are so few based on five years' separation?

(v) Does the graph confirm or dispel fears that the five year 'fact' would become a 'Casanova's Charter'?

(vi) If in 1976 there were 7,000 more divorces than might have been expected from an extrapolation of the pre-1971 trend together with the five year cases, how would you account for the increase? (*a*) Is the general relaxation in the law allowing more already broken marriages to be legally dissolved; or (*b*) are more marriages breaking down than even the pre-1971 trends would suggest?

(vii) If you are inclined to favour explanation (*b*) in question (vi), does the increase of 7,000 (in a total of 126,000 in 1976) strike you as being large or small?

(viii) Carrying on from question (vii), what part, if any, might the change in the law have played in any increase in marriage breakdown?

Once upon a time, it was possible to point to the fact that (leaving aside the extra disruption caused by the two world wars) every leap in the divorce figures accompanied an extension in its accessibility to the less well-off, whether through the introduction of legal aid or the decentralisation of adjudication. It was thus possible to argue, as the Law Commission in 1966 did, that the rise 'may merely reflect the fact that a growing segment of society is coming to regard divorce as more respectable than other outcomes of a broken home.' Now that divorce is accessible to almost everyone, the continuing and steep rise must clearly be explained in other ways. Nevertheless, the simplicity and accessibility of the divorce procedure raises issues of a different kind, to which we must now turn.

4 The special procedure

One feature which has always militated against attempts to restrict divorce (whether on the lines suggested by the bishop in the quadrilogue or on those of the Archbishop's group in *Putting Asunder*) is the impossibility of forcing respondents to defend. By 1966, 93% of divorces were undefended, and the proportion is now a great deal higher: by 1977, the year in which 170,000 petitions were filed, the number of defended divorces disposed of was less than 3,000, and in 1980 it had dropped to just over 1,000. Originally, the law made valiant attempts to prevent this turning into 'divorce by consent': the Queen's Proctor was invented to ensure that the court was not deceived and both admissions of adultery and uncorroborated assertions of cruelty were treated with suspicion. Even today, the court has a duty 'to enquire, so far as it reasonably can, into the facts alleged . . .' (Matrimonial Causes Act 1973, s. 1(3)) and the cases contain warnings against being too ready to accept the petitioner's assertions at face value. But the country is clearly not prepared to make the huge investment in court and official time which would be involved in making a genuine investigation in every case: quite the reverse.

The following example from California, from the *Report of the Governor's Commission on the Family* (1966, see Kay, 1968) is close enough to the typical judicial hearing of an undefended divorce in England under the old law:

Attorney: Q: Mrs X, have you resided in the State of California for more than one year and in this county for more than 90 days prior to the commencement of this proceeding?
Plaintiff: A: Yes.
       Q: And during your marriage with Mr X, he has on many occasions been cold and indifferent to you?
       A: Yes.
       Q: And as a result of this conduct on the part of your husband, have you become seriously ill, nervous and upset?
       A: Yes.
       Q: And was this conduct on the part of your husband in any manner caused by anything you have done?
       A: No. . . .
(Optional)
       Q: And during the marriage, you at all times did your best to be a good wife to Mr X?
       A: Yes. . . .
(Following the questions relating to child custody and alimony, if appropriate, the remaining questions are addressed to the corroborating witness)
       Q: Mrs Y, you have known Mrs X, the plaintiff herein, for _____ years?
       A: I have.
       Q: And you have heard the testimony she has given here this morning?
       A: I have.
       Q. And to your personal knowledge is all of that testimony true?
       A: Yes, it is.
Attorney to Judge: Anything further, Your Honor?
Judge to Attorney: No, that will be sufficient. Plaintiff granted a divorce on the ground of defendant's extreme cruelty. . . .

The legal profession might defend such a proceeding on the grounds, first, that the judicial hearing ensured that they got the paperwork right, and second, that such a vital change in the parties' status required at least some solemnity. Others might question the enormous expenditure of both time and money involved: and the spur to doing so came from the observations of Elston, Fuller and Murch (1975), for these confirmed how short the hearings were, how little the judge enquired into the marriage, yet how many of the petitioners regarded it not only as a 'farce' but also as a nerve-wracking experience, and how let down they felt when the major issues of money, property or custody were 'adjourned to chambers.' Thus a 'special procedure' was invented for the very simplest cases in 1973 and extended to all undefended divorces in 1977: under this, the petitioner verifies the facts by an affidavit; the file is examined by a registrar; and if he is satisfied that the case for a divorce is proved, he issues a certificate; the case is then listed for the judge to pronounce the decree in open court; the judge has no discretion and the parties need not attend (although in practice, as we shall see in Chapter 10, those with children must attend a private appointment with the judge and this is often listed for the same day); only if the registrar refuses his certificate must the case go to a proper hearing before the judge. Defended divorces, on the other hand, are transferred from the divorce county courts into the High Court, where they are heard in the traditional way. At the same time, legal aid was withdrawn from undefended divorce proceedings, although it remains available for 'ancillary relief'.

The impact of this last provision has been studied by Gwynn Davis, Alison Macleod and Mervyn Murch as part of a wider investigation of the workings of the special procedure, recently reported in *Special Procedure in Divorce and the Solicitor's Role* (1982):

Background to the procedural changes

The measures in question were introduced primarily to save money. The proportion of people qualifying for legal aid declined after 1950 as the eligibility limits did not keep pace with inflation, but civil legal aid expenditure escalated rapidly during the 1970s. By 1976, divorce accounted for the bulk of the civil legal aid budget. This was due to a number of factors, including the rising divorce rate, the increasing proportion of women petitioners who were more likely to be legally aided, and the growing practice of financially assisted petitioners not applying for costs against the respondent. Research had shown that judicial hearings of undefended divorce petitions served little practical purpose. (Elston, Fuller and Murch, 1975) It was thought that their abolition, by removing the need for representation, would bring savings to the legal aid fund. It was also hoped that the changes would encourage more petitioners to prepare their own petitions, although this could still be done with a solicitor's help under the legal advice and assistance ('Green Form') scheme. This is limited to specified sums for petitioner and respondent, although solicitors can apply to the Area Legal Aid Committee for extensions. The services covered are also limited and do not normally include representation in court.

Although the primary legislation remained the same, when the changes were introduced they were thought to be significant for the following reasons:

    (i) formal responsibility for the conduct of the divorce in Green Form cases passed from the solicitor to the petitioner;

    (ii) it was thought that the changes might contribute to a greater use of alternative sources of legal help, such as citizens' advice bureaux and law centres; they might also bring more people into direct contact with county court staff and increase reliance on their informal advice;

    (iii) there was no longer to be a judicial hearing of the petition in open court;

    (iv) for the first time since the legal aid scheme was introduced it was being withdrawn from one area; and

    (v) since almost all divorces are now undefended, the above changes were likely to affect the majority of the divorcing population.

The Lord Chancellor's withdrawal of legal aid was challenged by The Law Society. They argued that:

    (i) the Green Form limits (then £45 for petitioners, £25 for respondents) would be inadequate to allow the necessary work to be done and would dilute the quality of service to clients;

    (ii) people would need representation at the new judicial appointments;

    (iii) the use of legal advice and assistance 'in tandem' with legal aid, with an unclear division of responsibility between solicitor and client, would be confusing and inefficient;

    (iv) the restrictions would mean a two-tier system, with one level of service for those who could afford to pay and another for those who could not.

The authors then describe their research and its results, which they summarise as follows:

1. The great majority of petitioner and respondent parents still consult solicitors. While technically they may be 'petitioners in person', this phrase is misleading, as practically all are advised by solicitors at some stage.

2. Although a quarter of our sample had sought information from CABs or legal advice centres, most had done so as a preliminary to seeking solicitors' advice.

3. Solicitors continue to deal with most of the paperwork associated with special procedure divorce. The complexity of the documentation and procedure encourages dependence on solicitors.

4. Some solicitors find it necessary to do work not covered by the Green Form.

5. Some of those interviewed told us that, at least in retrospect, they thought that their solicitor had not adequately explored the possibility of reconciliation. [See Chapter 17, below.]

6. The research identified a number of problems concerning the legal aid and advice schemes. These include:

    (*a*) people's uncertainty concerning whether or not they are eligible for help;

    (*b*) the distinction between the role of adviser under the Green Form scheme and representative under legal aid is not understood;

    (*c*) some people are deterred by worries about cost from seeking a lawyer's help as early as they might do otherwise;

    (*d*) some disturbing cases were encountered where it appeared that solicitors had not adequately informed their clients about their entitlement to legal aid.

    (*e*) some respondents are being advised not to defend the divorce because of cost and many feel aggrieved about this.

Conclusion

What impact has the extension of the special procedure and the withdrawal of legal aid had upon the provision of legal services for those who divorce? The changes relate primarily to people's entry into the legal system. They affect the mechanics of obtaining an undefended divorce but do not touch custody battles, disputes about finance or property, or contested divorces, all of which may be pursued under a full legal aid certificate as before.

Much of the policy debate between the Lord Chancellor's Legal Aid Advisory Committee and The Law Society about the withdrawal of legal aid from undefended divorce hinged on the question of what legal services were necessary in these cases. Many solicitors were unhappy with the limits. As we have seen, some provide their clients with extra services for which they do not get paid. This raises the question of whether the State should provide anything other than the minimum service necessary to meet the strictly legal requirements of the case.

We would argue that the divorce lawyer also has a responsibility to consider the social and emotional aspects, if only because these have a bearing on the legal issues. For example, clients may well use their lawyers as sounding-boards while working out problems such as access arrangements. On the particular point of the children's appointment we have come to the conclusion that the presence of a solicitor is not necessary.[12] But it is difficult to see how other aspects of the solicitor's service to his client may be objectively assessed. Some solicitors refuse to see their role as consisting entirely in the performance of a series of straightforward administrative tasks, although the Green Form scheme is designed to support little more than this:

> 'The special procedure has simplified the process but divorce is an emotional experience and people want support. Currently there is no system designed to do this. I'd say that three-quarters of my time is spent counselling.'

We may at present have the worst of both worlds: a system of legal advice and representation which does not allow solicitors to give adequate time to their divorcing clients and yet, through comparatively generous support for representation in ancillary matters, encourages a litigious approach.

Meanwhile, the hope that divorce under the Green Form would substantially reduce the cost to the legal aid fund of ancillary matters has not been realized. The number of legal aid certificates in matrimonial cases rose by 18% in 1980/81. The Law Society comment that the number of certificates in matrimonial proceedings has increased 'at a rate far in excess of the increase in the number of divorce petitions'. There has been no fall in the use of solicitors because there has been no fundamental change in divorce law or procedure. Overall the measures have made little impact on a system which is still largely adversarial in character and which, therefore, does not encourage genuine litigants in person.

A related point is made by J.M. Westcott in *The Special Procedure — One Year Later — A Practitioner's View* (1978):

The respondent who wants to defend

A new situation which has arisen, and which ought to be considered is that of the respondent who has received a petition to dissolve his marriage but who believes that the breakdown alleged in the Petition is not in fact irretrievable. He can no longer get legal aid to defend the petition purely on that ground though it has been established in the Court that it is a valid defence simply to argue that the breakdown is not irretrievable. . . .

What is still absent is an objective test by the Court. The acknowledgement of service should contain a question to the respondent 'Do you believe that the marriage has broken down irretrievably?' If the respondent were to answer 'No' then the Court should have power to call both parties before the registrar, so that, before the suit got any further, there was a real and objective enquiry into whether or not the breakdown was irretrievable.

We shall return to the question of reconciliation and conciliation — and the efforts currently being made in that direction by Westcott and others — in our final chapter. For the present, however, we should note the implications of these developments for the substantive law of divorce. In *Divorce Without Legal Aid* (1976), Freeman concluded that:

The introduction and extension of the 'special procedure' and the withdrawal of legal aid from divorce are more radical departures than was the introduction of irretrievable breakdown as the sole ground of divorce.

---

12. This is as a result of their observations of children's appointments, which were very similar to those of Dodds reported in Chapter 10.

His main reasons were these:

The actual effect of the Lord Chancellor's proposals on the *law* of divorce could also be profound. We do not yet have divorce on demand — at least in theory. In practice it may be argued that we have it anyway in the sense that the granting of a decree seems the inevitable consequence of filing a petition. The recent Bristol study of divorce county courts also suggests that curial investigation of the facts is somewhat perfunctory. (Elston, Fuller and Murch, 1975) Yet in theory to obtain a divorce certain conditions must be satisfied. The incompatibility of the 'special procedure' and satisfaction of these requirements is manifest. Thus, to take the fact in s. 1(2)(*d*) (where the 'special procedure' first applied), the courts have held that 'living apart' connotes a mental state as well as factual circumstance. (*Santos v Santos* [1972] Fam 247, [1972] 2 All ER 246, p. 164, above) This mental element must be a recognition at the outset of the two year period that the marriage is at an end. It may be unilaterally held and need not be communicated to the other party. But how is this mental element to be elicited in an undefended postal divorce? How can a Judge in rubber-stamping a decree satisfy himself that this condition has been met? That he cannot makes Sachs LJ's restrictions on the two-year separation ground all the more unreal.

This problem is more acute with the 'fault' grounds. The divorce law is based on breakdown but adultery and desertion remain justiciable issues. Desertion particularly is a complicated concept. But in the context of the 'special procedure' its various strictures must become a hollow form and nothing more. Similarly, the 'unreasonable behaviour' fact . . . will now become subject to the 'special procedure'. It replaced, of course, the old concept of cruelty, though it looks more like the concept of constructive desertion. For a time the courts appeared to put that construction on s. 1(2)(*b*): the inference was the behaviour complained about had to be 'grave and weighty'. Recent case law has moved away from this towards, one must say, something approaching an acceptance that incompatibility of the spouses is sufficient. This takes some reconciling with the 'desertion' fact in s. 1(2)(*c*). [See pp. 159-162, above.] What is to become of this dialectic when the 'special procedure' reigns supreme? We will have a text-book account of the rules which will gradually lag further and further behind the law in action, and ultimately, of course, we will have reform. . . .

· What is necessary is divorce law reform which rids us of our existing pretences and a procedure which admits that divorce has become an administrative rather than a judicial function. Once reforms like this are implemented the whole question of legal aid for divorce would become an irrelevancy. It may be that the Lord Chancellor's proposals will effect such changes by an indirect and circuitous route. But so long as the law and procedure remains tied to 'grounds' of divorce and a judicial framework the proposals are quite clearly unacceptable.

In 1978, 97% of all divorce decrees were granted under the 'special' procedure, and in both 1979 and 1980, the percentage had risen to 98. Of the remainder, it appears that roughly half were listed as defended causes, so that the percentage of undefended causes which are referred to the judge must be less than one-and-a-half. There may well, however, be geographical variations in this. The procedure raises technical problems, for example in the doctrine of estoppel and in the ways in which the respondent may seek to have the decree set aside, which are outside the scope of this book.

5 The three year rule

One attempt to stem the tide of divorce was first introduced as the quid pro quo for extending the grounds in 1937. It survives in the *Matrimonial Causes Act 1973* in the following form:

3.—(1) Subject to subsection (2) below, no petition for divorce shall be presented to the court before the expiration of the period of three years from the date of the marriage (hereafter in this section referred to as 'the specified period').

(2) A judge of the court may, on an application made to him, allow the presentation of a petition for divorce within the specified period on the ground that the case is one of exceptional hardship suffered by the petitioner or of exceptional depravity on the part of the respondent; but in determining the application the judge shall have regard to the interests of any child of the family and to the question whether there is reasonable probability of a reconciliation between the parties during the specified period.

(3) If it appears to the court, at the hearing of a petition for divorce presented in pursuance of leave granted under subsection (2) above, that the leave was obtained by the petitioner by any misrepresentation or concealment of the nature of the case, the court may —
  (*a*) dismiss the petition, without prejudice to any petition which may be brought after the expiration of the specified period upon the same facts, or substantially the same facts, as those proved in support of the dismissed petition; or
  (*b*) if it grants a decree, direct that no application to make the decree absolute shall be made during the specified period.
(4) Nothing in this section shall be deemed to prohibit the presentation of a petition based upon matters which occurred before the expiration of the specified period.

Retention was recommended both in *Putting Asunder* (1966):

In the body of our report we have recommended that the three-year restriction should remain. As regards the judge's discretion to allow exceptions to the rule, we believe that the appropriate relief for hardship or injury during the three years would be not divorce, but a separation order or decree of judicial separation, which would continue to be made on the basis of the matrimonial offence. For one thing, it is not desirable that persons who have been so unwise in their choice of partners as to be confronted with an 'intolerable situation' within three years of marriage should be enabled to marry again without an interval for reflection.

And in *The Field of Choice* (1966):

19. . . . This provision seems to have proved generally acceptable to public opinion and we know of no widespread agitation for its deletion. Its retention was advocated both by the Morton Commission and by the Archbishop's Group. In our opinion it is a useful safeguard against irresponsible or trial marriages and a valuable external buttress to the stability of marriages during the difficult early years. It therefore helps to achieve one of the main objectives of a good divorce law.

Those objectives, it will be recalled, were:

15. . . .
  (i) To buttress, rather than to undermine, the stability of marriage; and
  (ii) When, regrettably, a marriage has irretrievably broken down, to enable the empty legal shell to be destroyed with the maximum fairness, and the minimum bitterness, distress and humiliation.

Recently the Law Commission has been re-examining these assertions. In their Working Paper on *Time Restrictions on Presentation of Divorce and Nullity Petitions* (1980), the objections to the existence of any such ban are outlined:

47. Objections to the existence of any time restriction centre on the alleged inconsistency of such a restriction with the present policy of the divorce legislation. If it is the case that divorce should be available whenever a marriage has irretrievably broken down, why (it is said) should it matter whether the marriage has been in existence for three months or three years?. . .
48. . . . Critics usually claim that the existence of the restriction has little or no effect on the long term rate of marital dissolution and merely *postpones* divorces. This claim derives some support from a comparison of the English and Scottish divorce rates in respect of marriages dissolved by the end of the tenth year. . . . [see the graph opposite].
  This statistical comparison may well be thought to weaken the force of the argument that the three year restriction has a positive role in buttressing the institution of marriage.
50. If it be accepted that the main effect of the present restriction is to *delay* rather than prevent divorce, it would follow that the restriction only preserves, for an arbitrary period of time, the legal bond between some couples whose marriage has in fact irretrievably broken down. The restriction cannot compel them to live together, but it can and does prevent them from creating a new legally recognised relationship. This (it may be said) is tantamount to imposing a penalty for having made a mistaken choice of partner; and the penalty may in some cases be severe — for example, a wife deserted soon after marriage might wish to re-marry and have children; a wait of three years could make child-bearing difficult or dangerous for the mother and imperil the health of her child. . . .
52. Critics also claim that there is an inconsistency between the law of divorce and nullity. Breakdown in the early years of marriage is often brought about by failure to establish the

1977 Divorce decrees by duration of marriage expressed as cumulative percentage of marriages dissolved within ten years.

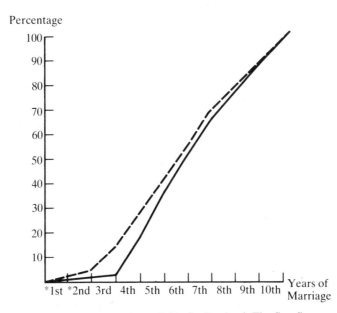

* Figures for these years are only available for Scotland. The first figure (a cumulative one) for England and Wales is for the 3rd year.

necessary minimum relationship physically and emotionally. If sexual incompatibility results in a total failure to consummate the marriage, nullity proceedings can be started immediately, but if there has been a single act of consummation nullity proceedings are not available, and divorce proceedings will (unless the court grants leave on the basis of exceptional hardship or depravity) have to be delayed until the three year period has expired.

Questions

(i) How many people do you think know about the ban anyway?
(ii) Even supposing that they did know and that it did persuade them to stay together for a little longer, what might happen while they did?

Nevertheless, the Commission could find two arguments against outright abolition:

62. There may, however, be one particular adverse consequence of the abolition of the restriction to which we feel we should draw attention. This is that the possibility of obtaining a divorce immediately after the wedding could increase the number of 'marriages of convenience', and perhaps facilitate the emergence of a class of 'professional bridegrooms' prepared, for a consideration, to contract marriages with persons wishing to acquire United Kingdom citizenship. We are not in a position to assess the magnitude of this risk but in any case it seems to us that measures to counteract it should (if appropriate) be taken in the context of nationality and immigration law. The risk of such abuses occurring should not, in our view, be allowed to govern the general policy of family law. . . .

64. If the present restriction were simply abolished undefended petitions, even those presented within a very short time after the date of the marriage, would be dealt with under the 'special procedure', so that a decree would be granted without any court hearing. This is an aspect of the matter which causes us considerable misgivings, since we consider it most important that the law should encourage spouses to explore any possibility of reconciliation, particularly if breakdown threatens in the 'difficult early years'. Allowing petitions to be dealt with under the special procedure would effectively prevent the court from considering whether the proceedings should be adjourned to enable attempts to be made to effect a reconciliation.

As to the working of the present exception:

39. . . . The Judicial Statistics show that applications for leave have greatly increased in recent years. In 1969 there were only 498 applications; in 1971 (the first year in which the Divorce Reform Act 1969 was in force) there were 530; in 1973 there were 786; and in 1978 the number had risen to 1,462. This increase is far greater than the proportionate increase in the number of divorce petitions: between 1973 and 1978 the proportionate increase in the number of applications for leave was 86%, whereas the proportionate increase in the number of divorce petitions was 41.2%.

40. The statistics also show that most applications for leave are successful. Thus in 1975, out of a total of 576 cases adjudicated upon, leave was refused in 31 cases (5.39%); the proportion of refusals in 1974 and 1973 respectively was 8.16% and 6.77%. Unfortunately publication of statistics relating to the refusal of leave was discontinued in 1975 but we understand from enquiries made in the Principal Registry of the Family Division and certain county courts that the proportion of refusals is probably in the region of 5%. These figures do not, of course, show that the restriction is ineffective in helping to prevent dissolutions within three years of the marriage since there will no doubt be cases where applicants are advised not to apply for leave because it is thought that leave will be refused.

C. v C.
[1980] Fam 23, [1979] 1 All ER 556, [1979] 2 WLR 95, 123 Sol Jo 33, Court of Appeal

The wife sought leave to petition within three years of the marriage on the grounds both of exceptional depravity and exceptional hardship. Before the marriage, the husband had led her to believe that he was heterosexual and that their marriage would be sexually normal. But it soon became clear that he was homosexual: he became impotent shortly after the honeymoon, showed less and less interest in his wife and more and more in a young male cousin, and left less than three months after the wedding. The full facts were not before the county court judge and he refused leave. The wife appealed.

Ormrod LJ: . . . Section 3 of the Act of 1973, and its predecessors, have troubled judges who have to apply their provisions ever since these were first introduced by section 1 of the Matrimonial Causes Act 1937. The principal difficulty lies in knowing what standards to use in assessing exceptional hardship and what is meant by the phrase 'exceptional depravity.' Both involve value judgments of an unusually subjective character, so much so that in the earlier cases in this court these appeals were treated as appeals from the exercise of a purely discretionary jurisdiction: *Winter v Winter* [1944] P 72 and *Fisher v Fisher* [1948] P 263. Later, in *Brewer v Brewer* [1964] 1 All ER 539, [1964] 1 WLR 403, it was held that exceptional hardship or exceptional depravity involved provisional findings of fact. The difficulty arises, partly, because all decisions at first instance are made in chambers and therefore cannot be reported, and, partly, because the reported cases in this court do not give much, if any, guidance on the standards to be applied. Moreover, standards in society in these matters are not stable and are subject to considerable changes over comparatively short periods of time.

Hardship is a concept with which judges are familiar in various contexts though it is often difficult to decide whether it can properly be called exceptional. A considerable degree of hardship is inevitable when a marriage breaks down in the first three years.

Exceptional depravity, on the other hand, is much more difficult. The word 'depravity' has fallen out of general use — it is not included in Fowler's Modern English Usage — so that it now conveys only a vague idea of very unpleasant conduct. In 1937 it may have carried to contemporary minds a much more specific meaning, but norms of behaviour, particularly in the sexual sense, have changed greatly in the last 40 years. It is unlikely that the meaning of 'depravity' and 'exceptional depravity' suggested by Denning LJ in *Bowman v Bowman* [1949] P 353 would find much support today.

In contrast, the change in the basis of divorce from the matrimonial offence to irretrievable breakdown with the expectation of relatively easy divorce may have increased the hardship involved in waiting for the specified period to elapse. . . .

In *Bowman v Bowman* [1949] P 353 at 355 and 356, Bucknill and Denning LJ both accepted that hardship arising from the conduct of the other spouse could be taken into account under the first limb of the proviso, whereas Romer LJ in *Hillier v Hillier and Latham* [1958] P 186 at 191 thought that exceptional hardship meant primarily hardship arising from the enforced delay. Willmer and Pearson LJ in *Brewer v Brewer* [1964] 1 All ER 539, [1964] 1 WLR 403 took the other view, relying on the use of the word 'suffered' in the past tense.

Be that as it may, it is now accepted that in dealing with these applications the judge may properly take into account hardship arising from the conduct of the other spouse, present hardship, and hardship arising from having to wait until the specified period has elapsed. In these circumstances it seems to be unnecessary in the great majority of these cases to rely on exceptional depravity with all its unpleasant overtones and difficulties. In practice, when it is alleged, the proposed petitioner often relies for proof of the element of exceptional depravity on the effect of the conduct on him or her.

This is precisely what occurred in this case. Miss Booth [for the wife] said at the outset of her argument that she did not intend to argue that the homosexual behaviour alleged against the husband could properly be said to amount to exceptional depravity. She did argue, however, that there were sufficient aggravating factors in the case to justify such a finding. All of these, in fact, impinged directly on the wife and we think provide much more convincing evidence of hardship than of depravity.

Question

Can you think of anything these days which is exceptionally depraved?

The Law Commission then considered various alternatives to the present rule, which they summarised in the form of a questionnaire thus:

A. *Should any change be made . . .?*
B. *If so, what form should the change take?*
   The possibilities canvassed in this paper are:
   (*a*) Outright abolition of the time restriction on the presentation of divorce petitions;
   (*b*) Retention of a time restriction, but allowing the court power to permit divorce within the restricted period in certain cases.
      If this solution is preferred it is necessary to decide: (i) what should the length of the restricted period be? and (ii) in what circumstances should the court have power to permit earlier divorce?
      (i) . . . We have suggested that a period of two years from the date of the marriage to the date of the petition might be appropriate. Would this be acceptable?
         If not, what other period would be preferable?
      (ii) . . . One of the options put forward is that the court should be empowered to grant a decree if, after a hearing before the judge at which the petitioner is available for examination, the court is satisfied not only that one or more of the 'facts' on the basis of which a divorce can be granted has been established, but also that the marriage has broken down irretrievably. Is this acceptable?
         Or is one of the other proposals considered in the working paper preferable? Those other proposals are:
      (i) The court would be given a discretion to grant a decree within the period. Guidelines might be laid down to govern the exercise of the discretion; but if so what should they be? *or*
      (ii) The court would be empowered to grant a decree within the period provided that the parties had gone through procedures designed conclusively to establish the absence of any prospects of reconciliation.
   (*c*) The final option considered in the working paper is the imposition of a bar on the presentation of divorce petitions within a period of either one or two years from the date of the marriage, with no discretion to permit earlier divorce.
      If this option is preferred, should the period be one year, two years, or some other period?
C. Is it agreed that the availability of divorce in the early years of marriage should not depend on whether or not the marriage is childless?
D. The final question is whether any proposal other than those discussed should be put forward?

Question

(i) How would you have answered this questionnaire?

The Law Commission's Report on *Time Restrictions on Presentation of Divorce and Nullity Petitions* was published in October 1982. On the underlying objective of the restriction, the Commission have this to say:

2.14 . . . It is perhaps a little simplistic to think of measuring the effectiveness of the restriction solely, for example, in terms of the number of marriages saved, as the underlying objective is more subtle: it is to shape an attitude of mind. . . .

2.15 In considering the effect on the public mind of having a restriction we were interested to note that the response to the Working Paper indicated that many people, quite independently of education, economic position and class, were ignorant of the present restriction, before they consulted their solicitors about divorce. Solicitors told us that clients to whom they had had to explain the existence of the restriction had expressed both surprise and incomprehension. It could, therefore, be argued that the restriction is unlikely to have any significant effect in furthering the policy of buttressing the stability of marriage; but as we pointed out in the Working Paper what is in issue is the effect of a *change* in the law. It is reasonable to suppose that the very making of a change would not only draw attention to the matter but would create, at least, an impression that divorce had been made either easier or more difficult. We should not like to contribute to an attitude of mind in which divorce comes to be regarded, not as the last resort, but as 'the obvious way out when things begin to go wrong'.

They thus conclude that some restriction is still desirable, although the present rule is unsatisfactory. They then consider and reject the various proposals put forward in paragraph B.(b) of their questionnaire, as being difficult to formulate in ways which would be understandable to litigants and easy for the courts to administer. On the suggested compulsory reconciliation investigation, they observe:

2.27 . . . We were impressed by the evidence of some commentators with experience of counselling young couples seeking divorce as to the poor prospects of success in a compulsory scheme. Strong opposition to compulsory reconciliation was voiced by others who described it as a gross and insensitive approach to what may be a highly charged situation. Further, as Lord Atkin pointed out during the passage of the Matrimonial Causes Act 1937, the worst cases that come before the court are often those where the marriage has not lasted very long: to *insist* on an attempt being made at reconciliation in such cases would be quite inappropriate.

Finally, therefore, they return to the absolute bar canvassed in paragraph B.(c) of the questionnaire:

2.30 In the Working Paper we said that the arguments in favour of the proposal that there should be an absolute bar on the presentation of divorce petitions within a stipulated period from the date of the marriage could be put in this way:

'The justification for a time restriction is one of public policy; it would devalue the institution of marriage to make divorce readily obtainable within days of the marriage. The present law is on this view based on a sound principle, but is objectionable because of the unsatisfactory nature of the exceptions whereby the court may allow a petition to be presented on proof of exceptional hardship or depravity. Although it would be possible to construct other exceptions, none of them is entirely satisfactory. The law would on this view be simpler and more comprehensible if it asserted the general policy by means of an absolute bar on divorce early in marriage.'

2.31 There was widespread support in the response to the Working Paper for the view that such a bar would have the obvious advantage of certainty and consistency, and would provide an adequate expression of public concern that the institution of marriage should not be devalued by precipitate divorce. It is, of course, true that such a bar may involve hardship. However, the response to the Working Paper reinforces us in our view that such hardship may, in many cases, be more apparent than real (provided that the period during which petitions may not be presented is comparatively short) particularly in view of the fact that, even where a marriage breaks down in the very early stages, the parties are eligible to apply for a wide range of legal remedies, by way of financial provision, protection and arrangements for custody of and access to children. Indeed the only relief which will not be available is the liberty to re-marry. Thus the number of cases involving actual hardship is likely to be minimal. . . .

2.33 We are, however, conscious that a considerable number of those who wrote to us favoured the total abolition of the restriction. We have sympathy with the logic of their arguments; yet we firmly believe in the public policy arguments recited above and the need to avoid the apparent scandal of divorce petitions being presented immediately after the marriage. We think that a one-year absolute bar is the least intrusive and most straightforward of restrictions which accords with many of the views which have been expressed to us and is, accordingly, likely to be the most generally acceptable.

Questions

(i) In family law generally, how would you weigh logic against the need 'to shape an attitude of mind'?

(ii) Is it relevant that research, by Garlick in Manchester and Maidment in Stoke on Trent and Stafford (1982; above, p. 152), indicated that between 50 and 52% of petitioners for judicial separation had been married for less than three years?

6 Further reform?

A great many criticisms of the present system have already been made, at least by implication, in what has gone before. The Law Commission was all set to embark upon a reconsideration of the ground for divorce when it was diverted by the urgent need to review the financial consequences (see further in Chapter 7). Opening shots had already been fired by the Family Law Sub-Committee of the Law Society in *A Better Way Out* (1979; see also 1982):

33. The first step towards a new system of family law is reform of the basis of divorce. There are two essential features of a reformed law on divorce:
    (*a*) the concept of the matrimonial offence must be eliminated, together with other elements which imply the existence of a contest;
    (*b*) though irretrievable breakdown itself should remain the sole ground for divorce, it should be proved by a clear, objective test. . . .

35. The adoption of the principle of breakdown based on separation was, we feel, a great step towards humane and realistic divorce law. The clearest evidence to the rest of the world that a marriage has failed or is in danger of doing so, is that the spouses have separated. It is also, we feel, the most reliable evidence to put before a court. There is no need to enquire into the history of the marriage or into elusive issues such as the feelings of either spouse about the other, except in some unusual cases in which the court may have to do so to ascertain the intention behind the separation. . . .

36. It may be recalled that a cause of resistance to the Parliamentary Bill which became the 1969 Act was that it enabled the so-called 'innocent' party to be divorced by the 'guilty' party. Attitudes have changed much even in the few years since that Act and the belief that there must be one spouse who is guilty and one who is innocent of bringing about the breakdown of a marriage is less widely held than it used to be. It is generally acknowledged that it is unusual to find a case in which the conclusion of an objective observer would not be that both spouses had contributed to a greater or lesser degree to the marriage's failure. The conduct of the apparently 'innocent' spouse can often turn out, on close investigation, to have been quite as destructive as that of the 'guilty' one though in less obvious ways.

37. However, there is still a tendency for spouses involved in divorce proceedings to seek to lay the blame on each other for the breakdown of the marriage, not only because of the resentment which they probably feel towards each other but also in an attempt to gain material advantage.

38. As we have said, the law should discourage conflict of this kind, but it is hard to see what more prolific a source of dispute there could be than to raise questions of conduct in matrimonial proceedings. Already troubled relationships are further embittered and the resolution of the real issues, practical and emotional, and constructive planning for the future, is made more difficult. . . .

40. The test of irretrievable breakdown of marriage as shown by separation for a specified period seems to us to satisfy the conditions we set out earlier (para. 33) for the ground for divorce. It should be adopted as the sole ground. . . .

42. The next question is what should be the minimum period of separation for the founding of a petition for divorce. . . .

44. . . . We do not think that there is now any justification for retaining different separation periods, depending on the respondent's consent or otherwise. The spouses' rights can be equally well protected by the courts whether the separation period is long or short. We do not believe that the possibility of reconciliation really survives for longer after separation when only one of two spouses wants a divorce. In any case, the minimum period of separation on which a petition can be based should be fixed at a length of time after which real prospects for reconciliation can no longer be said to exist. . . .

46. Two considerations which have influenced our thinking are: recent developments in other countries with comparable divorce laws; and practising solicitors' experience of their clients' attitudes to the present two year separation divorce.

47. Countries with divorce laws of this kind which have most recently introduced reforms are Sweden, Australia and the Federal Republic of Germany. In Sweden, Act No 645 of 1973 provides broadly that there is a 'right to divorce' if both spouses are agreed on divorce, though a six-month 'period for reflection' is required if they have custody of a child under 16. Where one spouse opposes the divorce, there is a similar right but only after the same six-month period for reflection whether there are children or not. In Australia, under the Family Law Act 1975, the sole ground for divorce is irretrievable breakdown of marriage shown by one year's separation. In other respects, the law is similar to ours. In Germany, the first Marriage Reform Act (1 Ehe. R.G.) of 1976 provides that a marriage may be dissolved if it has broken down, this being shown by the spouses having separated and it being unreasonable to expect cohabitation to be resumed. There is no absolute minimum separation period but if they have lived apart for less than one year, divorce cannot be pronounced unless continuation of the marriage would cause unacceptable hardship to the petitioner for reasons 'related to the person of the other spouse' (section 1565(2) BGB).

48. The second consideration is the ratio of unopposed divorce petitions based on two years' separation to those on other bases. If a petition is unopposed, it suggests that the spouses have agreed to divorce, though this does not always follow. If they have agreed, one would expect them to prefer a basis for the petition which does not impose on the petitioner an obligation to accuse the respondent spouse of misconduct, such as adultery or unreasonable behaviour. That being so, one would expect to find that most unopposed petitions were based on two years' separation. However, the divorce statistics show otherwise. . . .

49. The inference must be that the advantages of the relative amicability of the two years' separation divorce does not outweigh the disadvantages of this basis. We have little doubt that the explanation is that the period is too long. It is thought by solicitors with family law practices that many petitioners allege unreasonable behaviour or adultery simply to avoid a two-year wait.

50. A petition based on unreasonable behaviour or adultery can be filed as soon as the decision is taken, but the spouses may not by then have been separated for long or indeed at all. The advantage of immediacy is decisive. The evidence presents little difficulty — after several years of marriage, virtually any spouse can assemble a list of events which, taken out of context, can be presented as unreasonable behaviour sufficient on which to found a divorce petition (it must be remembered that we are discussing unopposed petitions); an act of adultery is still more easily proved. That is not to suggest that perjury is widespread in divorce proceedings. The facts described in most cases are genuine, but it is not true that they are the real reason for the breakdown of the marriage — they are more likely to be the consequence than the cause. Because two years is so long to have to wait before starting proceedings, it is common to resort to the exaggeration of commonplace behaviour — in reality perhaps no more than inconsiderate — into unreasonable behaviour, or to adultery, committed or admitted, as the pretext on which to base a petition which can be filed promptly.

51. Not only is this abuse undesirable of itself, but the system provides no discouragement to impetuous divorce. The abuse would be ended if the breakdown of marriage had to be proved by not less than one year's separation and this would also ensure that divorce proceedings were never begun without a period for reflection. It is therefore obvious that our proposal would not lead to 'easier' divorce; nothing is easier for spouses agreed on divorce than to construct a case sufficient for a divorce petition under the present law, though based on barely relevant facts. Once the spouses are committed to legal action by the filing of a petition, the chances of their giving serious thought to reconciliation much diminishes, however long the delay before the actual hearing. If they had to wait one year before being able to take such a step, it would ensure that they could never do so impetuously. Though a compulsory period for reflection might not save a great many marriages, it would be of value even if it saved a few, provided it was not so long as to cause hardship or resentment in others.

52. Our conclusion is therefore that irretrievable breakdown of marriage should be shown only by a period of separation of not less than one year immediately preceding the filing of a petition.

Two related procedural changes are suggested:

58. **Form of decree** — We have already expressed the view that the competitive or adversarial element should be removed as far as practicable from matrimonial proceedings. There should be no winner and no loser. We therefore recommend that the form of decree of divorce should be redesigned so as to eliminate any implication of its having been awarded to one spouse and against the other. It should simply record the dissolution of the marriage.

Joint petitions
69. We recommend that provision should be made to allow spouses to present joint petitions for divorce where they wish to do so.
70. We believe that this would eliminate a source of resentment in certain cases since the presentation of a petition by one party can be seen by the other as implying an element of accusation.

Questions

(i) Your client's marriage is desperately unhappy but her husband seems blissfully unaware of this. Your client cannot afford to leave the jointly owned matrimonial home and find somewhere else to live with their two young children, but her husband will not agree to sell it. If the Law Society proposals became law, would you advise her: (*a*) to grin and bear it; (*b*) to take action under the Married Women's Property Act 1882 to force a sale of the house; (*c*) to take action under the Domestic Violence and Matrimonial Proceedings Act 1976, s. 4 to try and get her husband to leave; or (*d*) to form a separate household under the same roof?
(ii) Which of those courses of action would seem least damaging to the children?
(iii) Would you answer any differently if the husband were a heavy drinker, given to violent argument, excessive sexual demands, and financial irresponsibility (the Law Society (1982) would not)?

One solution is that proposed in s. 305 of the *Uniform Marriage and Divorce Act* (UMDA) issued by the United States' National Conference of Commissioners on Uniform State Laws in 1970:

305. (*a*) If both parties by petition or otherwise have stated under oath or affirmation that the marriage is irretrievably broken, or one of the parties has so stated and the other has not denied it, the court, after hearing, shall make a finding whether the marriage is irretrievably broken.
 (*b*) If one of the parties has denied under oath or affirmation that the marriage is irretrievably broken, the court shall consider all relevant factors, including the circumstances that gave rise to the filing of the petition and the prospect of reconciliation, and shall
 (1) make a finding whether the marriage is irretrievably broken, or
 (2) continue the matter for further hearing not less than 30 or more than 60 days later, or as soon thereafter as the matter may be reached on the court's calendar and may suggest to the parties that they seek counseling. At the adjourned hearing, the court shall make a finding whether the marriage is irretrievably broken.

Questions

(i) Why not replace 'whether' with 'that'?
(ii) Would it be a revolutionary change to do as Mortlock (1972) suggests and do away with grounds in undefended divorces altogether?
(iii) But does not the readiness of each spouse to agree to a divorce depend at least in part on how the law will react if they do *not* agree? What then should be the grounds for a defended divorce?
(iv) Do we, as the Society of Conservative Lawyers in 1981 suggested, need a fourth Royal Commission?

CHAPTER 6

Finance and property after divorce

1 Introduction — the conventional and the dual worker families

We have seen in the previous chapters how traditional legal patterns of support and ownership have been the subject of major reassessments during the past few decades. In this and the next chapter, our concern is with divorce. We concentrate on the efforts by the courts to re-allocate the property of the parties and to make appropriate decisions on support for the parties and their children. We are concerned both with income and capital. Below the surface lies the vital question of the extent of the financial responsibility of the public towards the casualties of marriage breakdown. This question must remain unanswered at this stage, but will be dealt with in Chapter 16, below.

At the outset, we must remind ourselves of the different patterns of employed and domestic work within the family. We have already drawn attention in Chapter 3, above, to the existence of different economic arrangements in marriage. In broad terms we can identify the 'conventional housewife' family and the 'dual worker' family. It would be relevant in the context of the settlement on divorce to remind ourselves of the strains and the gains that can flow from these two patterns.

The following extract is from the work of Rhona and Robert Rapoport, *The impact of work on the family* (*Work and the Family*, edited by Peter Moss and Nickie Fonda (1980)). They deal with the research findings on both conventional pattern structures and dual career families.

The conventional pattern

Families who operate the conventional pattern, where husband/father is the exclusive breadwinner and wife/mother is the full-time housewife, have characteristic satisfactions and strains associated with them (Bernard, 1972; Young and Willmott, 1973; Rapoport et al., 1977; Campbell et al., 1976; Oakley, 1980).

The immediate impact on parents and children of these families is that fathers, being away from home most of the day most days, are much less involved in child care than are their wives. As Michael Rutter (1972) has put it, parenting in conventional families has come to mean mothering. Young and Willmott found that London fathers spent 7.1 hours daily at work or travelling to work, and 1.4 hours on household tasks which included DIY, helping their wives with washing up and so on, as well as interacting with children.

While we found in a survey of a London Borough that a high proportion of women who accept the housewife role express satisfaction, intensive interviews with these women uncover a number of characteristic dissatisfactions. Some of these are attributable to the role as well as to other conditions of their lives such as housing, neighbourhood, and so on. The greatest strains are felt by wives who have small children. They are at a point in the family life course which Wilensky (1968) has characterised as the 'life cycle squeeze'. Their husbands are out working full-time, or more in many cases, in order to be able to pay for the costs of establishing a home and providing for young children; and the wives are left to cope on their own. Wives who come through this period without being able to develop meaningful personal interests show, according to a Tavistock national stress study, a high degree of psychosomatic symptoms by the time they reach thirty-five (Irving and Hilgendorf, cited in Rapoport et al., 1977).

There seem to be two sources of housewife dissatisfaction in the early phase of family life and child-rearing: alienating characteristics of the housewife role which Ann Oakley (1974) has compared with a semi-skilled factory worker's job; and strains of near solo-parenting with little practical or emotional support from husbands. This is most acute in working-class families where, as Brown and Harris (1978) have recently demonstrated, the lack of a confidante is an important contributing factor to the onset of psychological depression. It has long been recognised that women generally suffer more than men from depression (Guttentag and Salasin, 1975), that communication difficulties contribute to depression (Weissman and Paykel, 1974) and that working-class wives feel less able to turn to their husbands to discuss problems than do middle-class wives.

The conventional pattern appears, on the whole, to be more satisfactory for husbands than for wives. But men have begun to question whether as fathers they may not be losing out on something important to them by their low participation in parenting. Biological analyses have now indicated that the human primate's hairlessness produces an animal which can enjoy tactile stimulation with children as well as with members of the opposite sex (Rypma, 1979). If given a chance to form a bonding relationship with their offspring, male monkeys, for example, will show similar protectiveness and involvement with the infants and similar signs of rage and grief when separated, as do females (Redican and Mitchell, 1972). This checks with findings in humans. Greenberg and Morris (1974) found in a study of thirty first fathers in three London maternity hospitals that they showed 'engrossment', bonding, absorption and preoccupation with the baby. The researchers interpreted this to mean that fathers have a potential for parental involvement that is not usually expressed in our culture but could be. Robert Fein (1974), in a similar study in the USA, indicates how fathers feel constrained from participating with their newborn children as much as they would like by the requirements of their jobs. Gronseth's (1978) study of work-sharing families in Norway, in which both fathers and mothers worked part-time so that they could share domestic tasks, indicates that many fathers derive particular pleasure from child-care experiences. Katherine Walker (1979), in two domestic time-budget studies, a decade apart, of American families, found that child care was the only area of domestic tasks in which fathers significantly increased their participation in domestic life. Whereas fathers in two-child families spent half an hour daily on non-physical care of their children in the 1960s, similarly placed fathers averaged a full hour in the late 1970s. (They also increased their share in 'meal preparation' and 'dishwashing', but it was 'not very dramatic . . . husbands' time doubled from 0.1 hour per day to 0.2 hour for food preparation . . . an increase of six minutes per day for an activity in which the wife used 1.5 hours if she was not employed and 1.2 hours if she was.')

Some studies also indicate the strain on men who are the family's sole breadwinner. It is suggested that this may be at the root of men's special vulnerability to heart diseases and ulcers. One American study by Chen and Cobb (1960) showed a correlation between the number of children a father had and his proneness to ulcer. The study did not, however, control for the wife's occupation, so it can only be taken to be suggestive.

(*Note*: Bear these findings in mind when you look at the court judgments which appear later in this chapter.)

The Rapoports are famous for their own work on 'dual career' families. In the same article, they identify some of the economic issues associated with this model of family and employment. The information in both extracts may well be relevant to the question of redistributing the family's existing wealth and potential wealth on divorce:

Dual-worker families
There have always been families in which both husbands and wives have worked regularly. Shopkeeping families like the baker's family described by Peter Laslett (1971) in *The World We Have Lost* persist to the present day; and shiftworking couples like those described by Michael Anderson (1973) for nineteenth-century Lancashire may actually be on the increase. There are many small businesses — pubs, inns, boarding schools, restaurants and the like — which rely on the team effort of a working couple.

But the modern pattern of dual-worker families, while somewhat similar to these long-standing patterns, is in many ways a new phenomenon. It arises through the increase in the number of married women choosing to work on a regular basis, and at the same time to have a family. As there are many motivations for the choice and many conditions under which it can operate, it is not surprising that there are various forms it can take. These affect the impact of the pattern on parents and children. We now have three generations of research on aspects of this pattern (Rapoport and Rapoport, 1978); with all the variations there are some generic issues that occur, and some characteristic ways of resolving them (Gowler and Legge, 1981).

Peter Moss has indicated some of the *economic* issues associated with the pattern. The consequences, if not the intentions, of operating the pattern are very different for those at the lower end of the social-class scale than for those higher up. At the lower end, it has the effect of keeping families above the poverty line. Higher up the scale, it enables families to increase their standard of living, taking holidays abroad, making home extensions or buying second homes and so on. It also has the effect of providing security against rapid downward mobility in the event of unemployment or career reversals of a breadwinner.

Another general feature of the pattern, also mentioned above, is that though there is a substantial basis in social values, particularly middle-class values, to support the pattern as an expression of an egalitarian orientation, the observed behaviour of husbands leads to the conclusion that this is often lip-service. Generally speaking, husbands do not replace the time by which their wives reduce household work. Sometimes, as Ann Oakley (1974) has shown, part of the husband's replacement takes the form of skimming off more enjoyable elements like playing with the children, leaving the wife with a more unremitting portion of drudgery. One writer on 'dual-career' families (Mortimer, 1977) noted that husbands in such families are often not aware of the discrepancy between what they say and what they do.

Nor is work outside the home a panacea, even when freely chosen. Weissman and Paykel (1974) noted that employed wives who are mismatched with their jobs are prone to depression in a way not dissimilar to 'captive housewives'. If a married woman, for example, takes a job for which she is over-qualified in order to escape the loneliness and boredom of being a housewife, she may come to feel that she has jumped from the frying pan into the fire, as regards the degree of personal stress she has to endure. This highlights the importance of 'fit' between person and role as an important intervening variable.

Just as there is a sub-group of conventional housewives who are reluctant in their role and would prefer to be at work, there is a sub-group of reluctant working wives. A recent study (Moss and Plewis, 1979) suggests that these women are more prevalent in the lower income groups, and that most of them would not like to stop work altogether but would rather work a little less in order to achieve a better balance between what a recent Russian study with similar findings called their functions as 'toilers, mothers, child-rearers and home-makers' (reported in *New Society*, 30 August 1979). Though this is a statistical tendency, reflecting the strains on women who have low income, ungratifying jobs and unsupportive husbands, it probably has wider validity.

However, for various reasons and in various ways, increasing proportions of families are adopting a dual-worker pattern. It is not, as some early commentators on research on dual-career families held, a freakish pattern tenable in peacetime only by a privileged minority. It is being chosen by increasing numbers of families because of its appeal to ordinary people — and its demonstrated feasibility. But, as with other patterns of work/family interrelationship, it has both gains and strains.

We are now able to define the issues with a fair degree of precision. Research on dual-worker families has now reached a state where it is possible to say that many of the early 'doomwatcher' hypotheses are 'unproven', and many of the 'advocacy' hypotheses can now be placed in perspective for further investigation. To illustrate this, there are two 'doomwatcher' hypotheses which can be examined:

    (*a*) that dual-worker marriages will produce marital conflict;

    (*b*) that dual-worker marriages will produce a poor environment for parenthood, leading to neglected 'latchkey' children who will swell the ranks of the delinquent, retarded and mentally disordered.

(*a*) *Impact on parents* Most of the reviews of literature that could help us to assess the hypothesis are inconclusive. Either they relate to overlapping but not identical populations (e.g. Hoffman and Nye's (1974) review of literature on working mothers; and Michael Rutter's (1972) review of literature on maternal deprivation); or they show no statistically significant relationship (which does not, of course, mean that there are never any negative consequences of the pattern). There are, however, some useful studies which contribute insight into the issues involved.

One American study by Orden and Bradburn (1968) of the National Opinion Research Center in Chicago suggests that marital happiness depends less on whether or not both partners work than on whether their choice was freely entered into. This work highlights the importance of the *meaning of work* (as well as the fact of working) as part of assessing work's impact on family life.

A study of British graduate couples by Lotte Bailyn (1971) indicates that while conventional families show a slightly higher proportion stating that their marriage is 'very happy', the proportions are not significantly less for working couples. Moreover, the latter are less likely to give stereotyped 'happiness' responses. But the subgroup which are markedly *low* on marital satisfaction are those in which the husband is extremely 'career-oriented' — i.e. seeks his major life satisfactions from his work and not at all from his family life (as distinct from men who place career first but also rate family as an important source of satisfaction). This circumstance occurs in conventional families, as well as dual-worker families.

Heather Ross and Isabel Sawhill (1975) of the Urban Research Institute in Washington note an association between the rising divorce rate and the rising rate of wives at work. They observe that the economic benefits of marriage are less decisive for wives who are independent earners, and that divorce has a different sub-cultural meaning among secular urban couples than in more conventional settings. The whole issue of the significance of divorce, and its occurrence at different points in the family and career cycles is involved here, but research to date provides more questions than answers.

On the other side of the coin is the body of literature from case studies of dual-worker families in which wives who hold satisfying jobs by choice express the view that they are more fulfilled; while husbands view them as more interesting marital partners. They emphasise the idea that both as spouses and parents, it is 'quality' rather than 'quantity' that counts, and that though the pattern is stressful they prefer it to the alternatives that they see for themselves, e.g. operating the conventional pattern and feeling bored and resentful.

Question

What do you think of the *second* hypothesis as a statement? Do *you* think it is unproven?

2 The historical background to the existing law

As we know, at common law the wife acquired the right to be supported by her husband for the whole of her life (see Chapter 3, above). Thus, when divorce was introduced into English law, it was thought to be only correct that the wife would have the right to apply to a court to obtain an order for support to substitute the voluntary payments to which she would have been entitled had the marriage continued.

Until recently, English law was dominated by a system of divorce based on the doctrine of the matrimonial offence. It necessarily followed that the court would attempt to make awards which kept an 'innocent' wife in the position in which she would have been had her husband properly discharged his marital obligations towards her. The Law Commission discussion paper entitled *The Financial Consequences of Divorce: the Basic Policy* (1980) reminds us of the following never to be forgotten words of Sir James Wilde (later Lord Penzance) in the Victorian case *Sidney v Sidney* (1865) 4 Sw & Tr 178, 34 LJPM & A 122:

. . . If, it was said, a man —
> can part with his wife at the door of the Divorce Court without any obligation to support her, and with full liberty to form a new connection, his triumph over the sacred permanence of marriage will have been complete. To him marriage will have been a mere temporary arrangement, conterminous with his inclinations, and void of all lasting tie or burden. To such a man the Court may truly say with propriety, 'According to your ability you must

still support the woman you have first chosen and then discarded. If you are relieved from your matrimonial vows it is for the protection of the woman you have injured, and not for your own sake. And so much of the duty of a husband as consists in the maintenance of his wife may be justly kept alive and enforced upon you in favour of her whom you have driven to relinquish your name and home.'

Further,

It is the foremost duty of this Court in dispensing the remedy of divorce to uphold the institution of marriage. The possibility of freedom begets the desire to be set free, and the great evil of a marriage dissolved is, that it loosens the bonds of so many others. The powers of this Court will be turned to good account if, while meting out justice to the parties, such order should be taken in the matter as to stay and quench this desire and repress this evil. Those for whom shame has no dread, honourable vows no tie, and violence to the weak no sense of degradation, may still be held in check by an appeal to their love of money; and I wish it to be understood that, so far as the powers conferred by the section go, no man should, in my judgment, be permitted to rid himself of his wife by ill-treatment, and at the same time escape the obligation of supporting her.

Question

Do you think that the knowledge that there is no escape from the financial ties and obligations of a marriage would operate in 1983 as a deterrent against divorce and a buttress to the institution of marriage?

What of a 'guilty' wife? Historically, a wife who had deserted her husband or committed adultery lost her common law right of maintenance. Although the position was ameliorated to a certain extent, the function of divorce was seen to be that of giving relief where a wrong had been done. This inevitably deprived many women of support after a divorce. And what is more, the courts were hardly aware of the significance of the material summarised earlier in Chapter 3. Domestic labour was never given any value whatsoever, except in so far as a right to be maintained can be seen as a reward.

Finer and McGregor describe the position in the following way in their *History of the Obligation to Maintain* (Appendix 5 to the Finer Report (1974)):

Alimony in the ecclesiastical courts
26. A right to maintenance in the strict sense — meaning a claim for the payment of money directly enforceable against the husband — was available to the wife only in the ecclesiastical courts, and even there was only ancillary to the power of these courts to pronounce a decree of divorce *a mensa et thoro*. Such a decree, if granted on its own, might have left the wife without the means of survival. The court would therefore at the same time pronounce a decree of alimony, under which the husband would be required to pay his wife an annual sum, calculated as a proportion of his income, or, if the wife had separate estate, a proportion of their joint incomes. It was common to award one third, sometimes less, sometimes — especially where the husband's property had come substantially from the wife — more. A decree of alimony could not be made separately from a decree of divorce *a mensa et thoro*, for which it followed that a wife who could not establish one of the offences on which such a decree could be granted could not be granted alimony either. Moreover, the means of enforcing an award of alimony were of more theoretical than practical utility. Alimony could not be sued for as a debt in the civil courts. Just as the common law courts refused to award maintenance on the grounds that this would have interfered with the ecclesiastical jurisdiction, so on the same grounds they refused to enforce the awards made in that jurisdiction. Before 1813, the only sanction for non-payment of alimony was excommunication or other ecclesiastical censure. Thereafter, a machinery for the imprisonment of the defaulting husband on a writ of *de contumace capiendo* became available, but there is little evidence to suggest that the threat of punishment here and now proved to be any more effective than the threat of punishment in the hereafter.

Maintenance after parliamentary divorce

27. A second species of maintenance attached to divorce by private Act of Parliament. The women who benefited from these awards of maintenance were very few in number. But the parliamentary practice is of cardinal historical importance because it established the principles that were adopted by the legislature as governing the right to maintenance when it established for the first time, in 1857, a system of divorce in the civil courts. The earliest Divorce Acts contained express provisions to ensure that the divorced wife should not be left in a state of destitution. Subsequently, a different practice prevailed:

'In the House of Commons there was a functionary called "The Ladies' Friend", an office generally filled by some member interested in the private business of Parliament, who undertook to see that any husband petitioning for divorce made a suitable provision for his wife. No clause to this effect was inserted in the Bill, lest it should be rejected in the other House, but, as a condition of obtaining relief, a husband was made to understand that, before the Bill passed through Committee, he must enter into a bond securing some moderate income to his wife.'

Two features of this practice call for special note. First, unlike the practice in the ecclesiastical court, which granted alimony only to an innocent wife, Parliament deliberately saw to it that a man could not use its process to rid himself of his wife, whatever her matrimonial misconduct might have been, without making some financial provision for her. Secondly, also in contrast with alimony, the provision which had to be made was not for the periodic payment of a sum of money. A husband seeking divorce by Act of Parliament had to make secured provision: that is to say, he had to make property available which, under the terms of an appropriate deed, was permanently set aside to secure whatever gross or annual amount he was to pay.

Finer and McGregor describe the beginning of the divorce court in 1857 (as to which see Chapter 5, above) and then continue:

Maintenance for wives under the new procedure

32. . . .The new divorce court could grant alimony ancillary to a decree of judicial separation on the same principles as alimony could previously attach to a decree of divorce *a mensa et thoro*. It could also in granting a decree of divorce dissolving the marriage, insist on the husband making financial provision for the wife of the kind which the Ladies' Friend, under the parliamentary divorce procedure, had previously secured for her benefit. In this connection, the Act provided that on any decree of dissolution of marriage the court might order the husband to secure to the wife such gross sum of money, or such annual sum of money for any term not exceeding her own life, as, having regard to her fortune (if any), to the ability of the husband, and to the conduct of the parties, the court should deem reasonable.

33. The use which the divorce court made of its powers of securing maintenance to the wife when dissolving her marriage took rather a curious course. Despite the fact that the distinctive feature of the parliamentary procedure which the court was supposed to have inherited was precisely that it guaranteed provision for the guilty (respondent) wife, the divorce court at first ruled that it would do this only in the rarest of cases. More than that, by 1861 (*Fisher v. Fisher* (1861) 2 Sw & Tr 410, 31 LJPM & A 1) Sir Cresswell Cresswell, the first Judge Ordinary of the court, was saying that a wife petitioner should be awarded less by way of maintenance on being granted a decree of divorce than she would have been granted by way of alimony had she sought a judicial separation, for this would tend towards the preservation of the sanctity of marriage. Four years later, this view of the law was rejected by the court, (*Sidney v Sidney* (1865) 4 Sw & Tr 178, 34 LJPM & A 122) which indicated in the same case that it would welcome a power, in dissolving a marriage, to make financial provision for the wife by way of an order for periodical payments, as well as by way of a secured sum. This power was granted by the Matrimonial Causes Act 1866, which provided that if a decree for dissolution of marriage were obtained against a husband who had no property on which the payment of a gross or annual sum could be secured, he might be ordered to pay such monthly or weekly amounts to his former wife, during their joint lives, as the court should think reasonable. By about the 1880s, the maintenance jurisdiction in divorce had come to be exercised to the following broad effect: the guilty wife, as under the old parliamentary practice, would have some modicum awarded to her; the innocent wife, as under the old ecclesiastical practice, would be granted a proportion, almost always one third, of the joint income, and, in addition, an amount in respect of any children committed to her custody.

37. In 1873, as part of the general re-organisation of the superior courts which then took place, the jurisdiction of the Court for Divorce and Matrimonial Causes, set up in 1857, was transferred to the High Court of Justice to be exercised in the Probate, Divorce and Admiralty Division of the High Court.

38. . . . the court began to state that the rule, borrowed from the ecclesiastical jurisdiction, of awarding one third of the joint income to the innocent wife was not a rule of thumb, and that in awarding maintenance it had to take into account all the circumstances of the particular case. Secondly, signs emerged of a recognition that the moral blame, if there was any, for the breakdown of a marriage might not be coincident with the finding of guilt in the divorce suit. It followed that an adulterous wife might in justice be entitled to a larger award than the sustenance which, following the former Parliamentary practice, the divorce court had conceded to her. As ultimately established, the rule was stated to be:

> 'Nowhere . . . is there to be found any warrant for the view that a wife who had committed adultery thereby automatically loses her right to maintenance regardless of the other circumstances of the case. . . . In practice a wife's adultery may or may not disqualify her from succeeding in her application for maintenance and may or may not reduce the amount allotted. At one end of the scale her adultery may indeed disqualify her altogether. It may do so, for example, where it broke up the marriage, where it is continuing and where she is being supported by her paramour. At the other end of the scale, her adultery will not disqualify her and have little, if any, influence on the amount.' (*Iverson v Iverson* [1967] P 134, [1966] 1 All ER 258)

Nevertheless, the discretionary nature of the jurisdiction gave ample opportunity to judges so inclined to take an idiosyncratic view on these matters. The passage from the judgment just quoted is immediately preceded by the words:

> 'At the hearing in July 1965, I was told by Counsel for the husband that those exercising jurisdiction in the district where this case originated, which was not Newcastle, took the view that a wife who had committed adultery is disqualified from obtaining maintenance after divorce. At the resumed hearing counsel for both parties repeated this statement. If that be the practice, it is wrong in law.'

The Divorce Reform Act 1969 altered completely the conceptual basis of divorce. Necessarily, the preconceptions inherent in the legal status of the husband and the wife, especially in relation to the doctrine of unity and the concept of lifelong support obligation unless the wife committed a matrimonial offence — all this could no longer form the underlying philosophy of a marriage. At the same time, there was awareness that in reality, certainly in conventional marriages and perhaps also in dual career marriages, a wife's performing the 'domestic chores' *was* a significant contribution in its own right towards the resultant value of the family assets. All this resulted in the enactment of the Matrimonial Proceedings and Property Act 1970 (now consolidated in the Matrimonial Causes Act 1973). This Act permits all financial orders to be made in favour of either husband and wife, enabling the court to rearrange *all* the couple's assets through periodical payments (secured and unsecured), lump sum payments and property adjustment orders.

The Act also sets out detailed guidelines designed to assist the court in the exercise of its powers. These guidelines are simply that; for the basic philosophy inherent in the Act is to permit a broad discretion within the framework of the legislative target. It is to this target that we must turn.

3 The principles of financial and property adjustment

Section 25 of the *Matrimonial Causes Act 1973* provides:

Matters to which court is to have regard in deciding how to exercise its powers under sections 23 and 24

25.   (1) It shall be the duty of the court in deciding whether to exercise its powers under section 23(1)(*a*), (*b*) or (*c*) or 24 above in relation to a party to the marriage and, if so, in what manner, to have regard to all the circumstances of the case including the following matters, that is to say —
    (*a*) the income, earning capacity, property and other financial resources which each of the parties to the marriage has or is likely to have in the foreseeable future;
    (*b*) the financial needs, obligations and responsibilities which each of the parties to the marriage has or is likely to have in the foreseeable future;
    (*c*) the standard of living enjoyed by the family before the breakdown of the marriage;
    (*d*) the age of each party to the marriage and the duration of the marriage;
    (*e*) any physical or mental disability of either of the parties to the marriage;
    (*f*) the contributions made by each of the parties to the welfare of the family, including any contribution made by looking after the home or caring for the family;
    (*g*) in the case of proceedings for divorce or nullity of marriage, the value to either of the parties to the marriage of any benefit (for example, a pension) which, by reason of the dissolution or annulment of the marriage, that party will lose the chance of acquiring;
and so to exercise those powers as to place the parties, so far as it is practicable and, having regard to their conduct, just to do so, in the financial position in which they would have been if the marriage had not broken down and each had properly discharged his or her financial obligations and responsibilities towards the other.
    (2) Without prejudice to subsection (3) below, it shall be the duty of the court in deciding whether to exercise its powers under section 23(1)(*d*), (*e*) or (*f*), (2) or (4) or 24 above in relation to a child of the family and, if so, in what manner, to have regard to all the circumstances of the case including the following matters, that is to say —
    (*a*) the financial needs of the child;
    (*b*) the income, earning capacity (if any), property and other financial resources of the child;
    (*c*) any physical or mental disability of the child;
    (*d*) the standard of living enjoyed by the family before the breakdown of the marriage;
    (*e*) the manner in which he was being and in which the parties to the marriage expected him to be educated or trained;
and so to exercise those powers as to place the child, so far as it is practicable and, having regard to the considerations mentioned in relation to the parties to the marriage in paragraph (*a*) and (*b*) of subsection (1) above, just to do so, in the financial position in which the child would have been if the marriage had not broken down and each of those parties had properly discharged his or her financial obligations and responsibilities towards him.
    (3) It shall be the duty of the court in deciding whether to exercise its powers under section 23(1) (*d*), (*e*) or (*f*), (2) or (4) or 24 above against a party to a marriage in favour of a child of the family who is not the child of that party and, if so, in what manner, to have regard (among the circumstances of the case) —
    (*a*) to whether that party had assumed any responsibility for the child's maintenance and, if so, to the extent to which, and the basis upon which, that party assumed such responsibility and to the length of time for which that party discharged such responsibility;
    (*b*) to whether in assuming and discharging such responsibility that party did so knowing that the child was not his or her own;
    (*c*) to the liability of any other person to maintain the child.

Questions

Read carefully the concluding words of s. 25(1):
(i)(*a*) Has the philosophy which resulted in the enactment of these words changed since 1971? (*b*) Has the underlying reality changed since 1971?
(ii) Were they even true in 1971? (refer back to Chapter 5 on divorce above).

Wachtel v Wachtel
[1973] Fam 72, [1973] 1 All ER 829, [1973] 2 WLR 366, 117 Sol Jo 124, Court of Appeal

This case is without doubt the most important decision on the subject of both financial provision and property allocation since the new legislation took effect. It has served as the starting point for judges, academics and the Law Commission and others in discussing the present law. The parties were granted cross-decrees of divorce, and the dispute between the parties over the financial consequences of the divorce was dealt with in subsequent ancillary proceedings. The judgment of the court appears below in full: the facts of the case are stated in the first few paragraphs.

Lord Denning MR read the judgment of the court. Mr and Mrs Wachtel were married on January 9, 1954. They were both then 28 years of age. They have two children, a son aged now 14, and a girl of 11. The husband is a dentist in good practice. On 31 March 1972, the wife left the home. On 21 July 1972, there was a divorce on the ground that the marriage had irretrievably broken down. In consequence many things have to be settled. The parties have made arrangements for the children. The son is with the father. He is a boarder at Epsom College, where his fees are paid by his grandfather. The daughter is with the mother. She goes to day-school. There remain the financial consequences. The parties have not agreed upon them. So they have to be settled by the courts.

On 3 October 1972, Ormrod J ordered the husband to pay to his wife (i) a lump sum of £10,000, or half the value of the former matrimonial home in Norbury, South London, whichever be the less: (ii) periodical payments of £1,500 per annum, less tax: and (iii) further payments of £500 per annum (£9.50 weekly), less tax, in respect of the eleven-year-old daughter.

The husband appeals to this court. The appeal raises issues of wide importance. This court is asked to determine, for the first time, after full argument, the principles which should be applied in the Family Division when granting ancillary relief pursuant to the powers conferred by the Matrimonial Proceedings and Property Act 1970 (in this judgment called the Act of 1970) following dissolution of marriage pursuant to the Divorce Reform Act 1969 (in this judgment called the Act of 1969). We were told by counsel both for the husband and for the wife that it was hoped that this court might feel able, to quote the phrase used in the argument, 'to lay down some guide lines' which would be of help in the future. There are divergencies of view and of practice between judge and registrars. Furthermore, counsel and solicitors are unable to advise their clients with a reasonable degree of certainty as to the likely outcome of any contested proceedings. It is very desirable to remove that uncertainty and to assist parties to come to agreement.

The parties separated on 31 March 1972. The husband's petition was filed on 18 April 1972, and alleged adultery by the wife with a doctor whose patient she was. By her answer dated 9 May 1972, the wife denied the adultery and cross-petitioned on the ground that her husband had behaved in such a way that she could not reasonably be expected to continue to live with him. Her answer was amended later to add two charges of adultery against the husband. The husband denied all the allegations against him. The co-respondent doctor also filed an answer denying the alleged adultery. These contested proceedings were heard before Ormrod J on five days between July 3 and 7 1972. The judge reserved his judgment at the conclusion of the hearing. He delivered the judgment on 21 July. He had, it seems, previously indicated to the parties that he was not satisfied that any relevant charge of adultery had been proved on either side, but he had given the husband leave to amend his petition so as to rely in the alternative upon section 2(1)(*b*) of the Act of 1969. [Now s. 1 (2)(*b*) of the Matrimonial Causes Act 1973.]

The judge granted cross decrees to both parties under section 2(1)(*b*) of the Act of 1969. He then proceeded to deal with the ancillary matters. He again reserved judgment, and delivered it after the long vacation, on 3 October 1972: . . . . It is against that second reserved judgment that the present appeal is brought.

The crucial finding of fact is that the responsibility for the breakdown of the marriage rested equally on both parties: . . . . The judge, having made that finding, determined that the only capital asset, namely, the matrimonial home, should be divided more or less equally between the parties. Since the evidence before the judge showed that the equity of the house in Norbury (after discharging the outstanding mortgage amounting to some £2,000) was about £20,000, he ordered the husband to pay to his wife a lump sum of £10,000 or half the net value of the house if and when sold, whichever was the less. So far as the periodical payment of £1,500 per annum is concerned, the judge appears to have worked on an earning capacity on the part of the husband of £4,000 to £5,000 gross taxable income. He appears not to have allowed anything for the wife's earning capacity, at least in terms of monetary value. On this basis the £1,500 represents about one-third of the judge's assessment of the husband's earning capacity. But if one adds to that figure of £1,500 the further sum of £500 gross which the judge ordered to be paid by the husband to the wife in respect of the eleven-year-old daughter, the total is £2,000 gross, considerably more than one-third of the figure which the judge took as the husband's earning capacity.

The husband's appeal was founded on the ground that in effect he had been ordered to pay his wife one-half of his capital, and about one-half of his income. Particular criticism was levelled in this respect at an important passage in the judge's judgment . . ., stating that Parliament had intended in the Act of 1970 'to bring about a shift of emphasis from the concept of "maintenance" . . . to one of re-distribution of assets and . . . "purchasing power." ' Mr Ewbank, for the husband, contended that the judge had but lightly concealed his view that the Act of 1970 had brought about a new concept of community of property so that it was just to give every wife — or at least almost every wife — half the value of the matrimonial home on the break-up of the marriage, and about half her husband's income. If that were right in the case of a wife held equally to blame with her husband for the breakdown of the marriage, what, he asked rhetorically, was the position of a wife who was wholly innocent of responsibility for such a breakdown? He further asked this: If as in the past, one-third of the combined available income of the parties had been regarded as proper maintenance for a blameless wife, with a reduction (we avoid the use of the word 'discount') in the case of a wife who was not free from blame, how could periodical payments totalling nearly one-half of the husband's earning capacity be justified in a case where the wife was found equally to blame with the husband for the breakdown?

Mr Ewbank also complained that the judge had really started from a presumption that equal division was right and had worked back from the starting point and, allowing nothing — or almost nothing — for 'conduct' had arrived at the determination we have stated. He contested the judge's view that it was right to disregard conduct where blame had been found to exist, especially as Parliament in section 5(1) of the Act of 1970 [now s. 25(1) of the Matrimonial Causes Act 1973] had enjoined the courts to have regard to the conduct of the parties. He also said that no, or no sufficient, account had been taken of the wife's earning capacity and that the £500 ordered to be paid for the child was in any event too high. He offered a lump sum of £4,000, together with a guarantee of any mortgage instalments which the wife might have to pay in connection with the acquisition of a new home for herself and the child. He urged this court in any event to reduce the £1,500 to £1,000; and the £500 to £300, or less.

Mr Gray, for the wife, supported the judgment on the broad ground that the long line of cases decided over the last century and more, which dealt with the issue of conduct, especially in relation to a guilty or blameworthy wife, were all decided when the foundation of the right to relief in matrimonial causes was the concept of a matrimonial offence. Now that concept had been swept away by the Act of 1969, the whole question of conduct in relation to ancillary relief required to be reconsidered, even though section 5(1) of the Act of 1970 preserved the obligation on the courts to have regard to 'conduct' in language not easily distinguishable from that of the earlier statutes from 1857 onwards. Although judges and former judges of the present Family Division of great experience have recently said that section 5(1) was only 'codifying' the preceding law and practice, Mr Gray contended that that was wrong and that the new provisions contained in section 5(1)(f) showed it to be wrong. Any approach to questions arising out of the Act of 1970 founded upon decisions before that Act and the Act of 1969 were passed was wrong, since the Act of 1970 ought not to be considered apart from the fundamental change wrought by the Act of 1969. Mr Gray particularly criticised the continued application of the so-called 'one third rule' under present day conditions, and drew attention to the fact (as is undoubtedly the case) that in *Ackerman v Ackerman* [1972] Fam 225, [1972] 2 All ER 420, where this court recently proceeded on the basis that that so-called rule was still applicable to cases arising under the Act of 1970, it had done so without the matters which have been argued on this appeal having been argued.

We will deal with these issues in order.

The conduct of the parties

When Parliament in 1857 introduced divorce by the courts of law, it based it on the doctrine of the matrimonial offence. This affected all that followed. If a person was the guilty party in a divorce suit, it went hard with him or her. It affected so many things. The custody of the children depended on it. So did the award of maintenance. To say nothing of the standing in society. So serious were the consequences that divorce suits were contested at great length and at much cost.

All that is altered. Parliament has decreed: 'If the marriage has broken down irretrievably, let there be a divorce.' It carries no stigma, but only sympathy. It is a misfortune which befalls both. No longer is one guilty and the other innocent. No longer are there long contested divorce suits. Nearly every case goes uncontested. The parties come to an agreement, if they can, on the things that matter so much to them. They divide up the furniture. They arrange the custody of the children, the financial provision for the wife, and the future of the matrimonial home. If they cannot agree, the matters are referred to a judge in chambers.

When the judge comes to decide these questions, what place has conduct in it? Parliament still says that the court has to have 'regard to their conduct': see section 5(1) of the Act of 1970. Does this mean that the judge in chambers is to hear their mutual recriminations and to go into their petty squabbles for days on end, as he used to do in the old days? Does it mean that, after a marriage has been dissolved, there is to be a post mortem to find out what killed it? We do not think so. In most cases both parties are to blame — or, as we would prefer to say — both parties have contributed to the breakdown.

It has been suggested that there should be a 'discount' or 'reduction' in what the wife is to receive because of her supposed misconduct, guilt or blame (whatever word is used). We cannot accept this argument. In the vast majority of cases it is repugnant to the principles underlying the new legislation, and in particular the Act of 1969. There will be many cases in which a wife (though once considered guilty or blameworthy) will have cared for the home and looked after the family for very many years. Is she to be deprived of the benefit otherwise to be accorded to her by section 5(1)(*f*) because she may share responsibility for the breakdown with her husband? There will no doubt be a residue of cases where the conduct of one of the parties is in the judge's words[1] 'both obvious and gross,' so much so that to order one party to support another whose conduct falls into this category is repugnant to anyone's sense of justice. In such a case the court remains free to decline to afford financial support or to reduce the support which it would otherwise have ordered. But, short of cases falling into this category, the court should not reduce its order for financial provision merely because of what was formerly regarded as guilt or blame. To do so would be to impose a fine for supposed misbehaviour in the course of an unhappy married life. Mr Ewbank disputed this and claimed that it was but justice that a wife should suffer for her supposed misbehaviour. We do not agree. Criminal justice often requires the imposition of financial and indeed custodial penalties. But in the financial adjustments consequent upon the dissolution of a marriage which has irretrievably broken down, the imposition of financial penalties ought seldom to find a place.

The family assets
The phrase 'family assets' is a convenient short way of expressing an important concept. It refers to those things which are acquired by one or other or both of the parties, with the intention that there should be continuing provision for them and their children during their joint lives, and used for the benefit of the family as a whole. It is a phrase, for want of a better, used by the Law Commission (see, e.g., Law Com. No. 25 (HMSO 1969), para. 50), and is well understood.

The family assets can be divided into two parts: (i) those which are of a capital nature, such as the matrimonial home and the furniture in it: (ii) those which are of a revenue-producing nature, such as the earning power of husband and wife. When the marriage comes to an end, the capital assets have to be divided; the earning power of each has to be allocated.

Until recently the courts had limited powers in regard to the capital assets. They could determine the property rights of the parties. They could vary any ante-nuptial or post-nuptial settlements. But they could not order a transfer of property from one to the other. They could not even award a lump sum until 1963. The way in which the courts made financial provision was by way of maintenance to the wife. This they often did by way of the 'one-third' rule.

Now under the Act of 1970 the court has power, after a divorce, to effect a transfer of the assets of the one to the other. It set out in section 5 various criteria. It was suggested that these were only codifying the existing law. Despite what has been said, we do not agree. The Act of 1970 is not in any sense a codifying statute. It is a reforming statute designed to facilitate the granting of ancillary relief in cases where marriages have been dissolved under the Act of 1969, an even greater measure of reform. It is true that in certain of the lettered sub-paragraphs of section 5(1) of the Act of 1970 one can find reflections of certain earlier well known judicial decisions. But this was not to ensure that earlier decisions on conduct should be slavishly followed against a different jurisdictional background. Rather it was to secure that the common sense principles embodied in the lettered sub-paragraphs, which found their origin in long standing judicial decisions, should continue to be applied where appropriate in the new situation. We regard the provisions of sections 2, 3, 4 and 5 of the Act of 1970 as designed to accord to the courts the widest possible powers in readjusting the financial position of the parties and to afford the courts the necessary machinery to that end, as for example is provided in section 4. It must not be overlooked in this connection that certain of the provisions of the Act of

---

1. Lord Denning MR here adopts the terminology of Ormrod J at first instance.

1970 are new: see for example section 7(2). Further, so far as we are aware, the principles clearly stated in section 5(1)(*f*) have nowhere previously found comparable statutory enactment.

The matrimonial home
The matrimonial home is usually the most important capital asset. Often the only one. This case is typical. When the parties married in 1954 they started in a flat. He was a dentist. She a receptionist. They both went out to work. They pooled such money as they had to get the flat and furniture and keep it going. Two years later, in 1956, they bought a house, no. 37 Pollards Hill North, Norbury, and moved in there. It has been their matrimonial home ever since. The purchase price in 1956 was £5,000. They did not put any money cash down, but bought it with a 100% mortgage. It was taken in the husband's name. The husband paid the mortgage instalments. The mortgage over the years has been reduced from £5,000 to £2,000. The house has increased in value from £5,000 to £22,000, or more.

After they moved into the house in 1956, the wife continued to go out to work until the son was born in 1958. She then stayed at home and looked after the children. But she helped her husband in various ways in his practice, such as by filling in the National Health forms, and helping as a receptionist from time to time. He put down a salary to her as part of his expenses against tax. This continued for all the years till 31 March 1972, when the wife left the house.

During the divorce proceedings the wife took out a summons under section 17 of the Act of 1882 claiming that, by reason of her financial contributions, she was entitled to one half of the equity in the house. Alternatively she claimed that, under section 4 of the Act of 1970, there should be a transfer to her of half the house or its value by way of a lump sum.

Before the Act of 1970 there might have been much debate as to whether the wife had made financial contributions of sufficient substance to entitle her to a share in the house. The judge said . . ., that it 'might have been an important issue.' We agree. But he went on to say that since the Act of 1970 it was 'of little importance' because the powers of transfer under section 4 enabled the court to do what was just having regard to all the circumstances. We agree. We feel sure that registrars and judges have been acting on this view: because, whereas previously we had several cases in our list each term under section 17 of the Married Women's Property Act 1882: now we have hardly any.

How is the court to exercise its discretion under the Act of 1970 in regard to the matrimonial home? We will lead up to the answer by tracing the way in which the law has developed. Twenty-five years ago, if the matrimonial home stood in the husband's name, it was taken to belong to him entirely, both in law and in equity. The wife did not get a proprietary interest in it simply because she helped him buy it or to pay the mortgage instalments. Any money that she gave him for these purposes would be regarded as gifts, or, at any rate, not recoverable by her: see *Balfour v Balfour* [1919] 2 KB 571, 88 LJKB 1054. But by a long line of cases, starting with *Re Rogers' Question* [1948] 1 All ER 328 and ending with *Hazell v Hazell* [1972] 1 All ER 923, [1972] 1 WLR 301, it has been held by this court that, if a wife contributes directly or indirectly, in money or money's worth, to the initial deposit or to the mortgage instalments, she gets an interest proportionate to her contribution. In some cases it is a half-share. In others less.

The court never succeeded, however, in getting a wife a share in the house by reason of her other contributions: other, that is, than her financial contributions. The injustice to her has often been pointed out. Seven members of the *Royal Commission on Marriage and Divorce* (Cmd. 9678) in 1956 presided over by Lord Morton of Henryton, said at p. 178:

> 'If, on marriage, she gives up her paid work in order to devote herself to caring for her husband and children, it is an unwarrantable hardship when in consequence she finds herself in the end with nothing she can call her own.'

In 1965 Sir Jocelyn Simon, when he was President, used a telling metaphor [see [1970] AC 777 at 811]: 'The cock can feather the nest because he does not have to spend most of his time sitting on it.' He went on to give reasons in an address which he gave to The Law Society (1965) 62 *Law Society Gazette*, 345:

> 'In the generality of marriages the wife bears and rears children and minds the home. She thereby frees her husband for his economic activities. Since it is her performance of her function which enables the husband to perform his, she is in justice entitled to share in its fruits.'

But the courts have never been able to do justice to her. In April 1969 in *Pettitt v Pettitt* [1970] AC 777 at 811, Lord Hodson said: 'I do not myself see how one can correct the imbalance which may be found to exist in property rights as between husband and wife without legislation.'

Section 5(1)(*f*)
Now we have legislation. In order to remedy the injustice Parliament has intervened. The Act of 1970 expressly says that, in considering whether to make a transfer of property, the court is to have regard, among other things, to:

'(*f*) the contributions made by each of the parties to the welfare of the family, including any contributions made by looking after the home or caring for the family.'

Mr Ewbank suggested that there was nothing new in these criteria in section 5(1)(*f*) . He referred us to *Porter v Porter* [1969] 1 WLR 1155 at 1160, where Sachs LJ said: 'The court must always take into account how long the marriage has lasted and to what extent the wife has rendered domestic services to the husband.' But in saying that, Sachs LJ was only anticipating the report of the Law Commission which was printed in the very week in which *Porter v Porter* was reported. In their *Report on Financial Provision in Matrimonial Proceedings* (Law Com No. 25) H. of C. (1968–69) No. 448, p. 34, para. 69 the Law Commission emphasised the importance of section 5(1)(*f*) and the change which it would make. They said:

'We recommend that in the exercise of the court's armoury of powers to order financial provision it should be directed to have regard to various criteria. Among these there is one of outstanding importance in regard to the adjustment of property rights as between the spouses. This is the extent to which each has contributed to the welfare of the family, including not only contributions in money or money's worth (as in the determination of rights to particular items of property) but also the contribution made (normally by the wife) in looking after the home and family. This should meet the strongest complaint made by married women, and recognised as legitimate by the Morton Commission in 1955, namely that the contribution which wives make towards the acquisition of the family assets by performing their domestic chores, thereby releasing their husbands for gainful employment, is at present wholly ignored in determining their rights. Under our proposal this contribution would be a factor which the court would be specifically directed to take into account.'

It has sometimes been suggested that we should not have regard to the reports of the Law Commission which lead to legislation. But we think we should. They are most helpful in showing the mischief which Parliament intended to remedy.

In the light thus thrown on the reason for subsection(1)(*f*), we may take it that Parliament recognised that the wife who looks after the home and family contributes as much to the family assets as the wife who goes out to work. The one contributes in kind. The other in money or money's worth. If the court comes to the conclusion that the home has been acquired and maintained by the joint efforts of both, then, when the marriage breaks down, it should be regarded as the joint property of both of them, no matter in whose name it stands. Just as the wife who makes substantial money contributions usually gets a share, so should the wife who looks after the home and cares for the family for 20 years or more.

The one-third rule

In awarding maintenance the Divorce courts followed the practice of the Ecclesiastical courts. They awarded an innocent wife a sum equal to one-third of their joint incomes. Out of it she had to provide for her own accommodation, her food and clothes, and other expenses. If she had any rights in the matrimonial home, or was allowed to be in occupation of it, that went in reduction of maintenance.

That one-third rule has been much criticised. In *Kershaw v Kershaw* [1966] P 13 at 17. Sir Jocelyn Simon P spoke of it as the 'discredited' 'one-third rule.' But it has retained its attraction for a very simple reason: those who have to assess maintenance must have some starting point. They cannot operate in a void. No better starting point has yet been suggested than the one-third rule. In *Ackerman v Ackerman* [1972] Fam 225 at 234, Phillimore LJ said: 'the proper course is to start again. I would begin with the "one-third rule" — bearing in mind that it is not a rule.'

There was, we think, much good sense in taking one third as a starting point. When a marriage breaks up, there will thenceforward be two households instead of one. The husband will have to go out to work all day and must get some woman to look after the house — either a wife, if he remarries, or a housekeeper, if he does not. He will also have to provide maintenance for the children. The wife will not usually have so much expense. She may go out to work herself, but she will not usually employ a housekeeper. She will do most of the housework herself, perhaps with some help. Or she may remarry, in which case her new husband will provide for her. In any case, when there are two households, the greater expense will, in most cases, fall on the husband than the wife. As a start has to be made somewhere, it seems to us that in the past it was quite fair to start with one third. Mr Gray criticised the application of the so-called 'one-third rule' on the ground that it no longer is applicable to present-day conditions, notwithstanding what was said in *Ackerman v Ackerman* [1972] Fam 225, [1972] 2 All ER 420. But this so-called rule is not a rule and must never be so regarded. In any calculation the court has to have a starting point. If it is not to be one third, should it be one half or one quarter? A starting point at one third of the combined resources of the parties is as good and rational a starting point as any other, remembering that the essence of the legislation is to secure flexibility to meet the justice of particular cases, and not rigidity, forcing particular cases to be fitted into some so-called principle within which they do not easily lie. There may be cases where more than one third is right. There are likely to be many others where less than one third is the only practicable solution. But one third as a flexible starting point is in general more likely to lead to the correct final result than a starting point of equality, or a quarter.

There is this, however, to be noted. Under the old dispensation, the wife, out of her one third, had to provide her own accommodation. If she was given the right to occupy the matrimonial home, that went to reduce the one third.

Under the new dispensation, she will get a share of the capital assets: and, with that share, she will be able to provide accommodation for herself, or, at any rate, the money to go some way towards it.

If we were only concerned with the capital assets of the family, and particularly with the matrimonial home, it would be tempting to divide them half and half, as the judge did. That would be fair enough if the wife afterwards went her own way, making no further demands on the husband. It would be simply a division of the assets of the partnership. That may come in the future. But at present few wives are content with a share of the capital assets. Most wives want their former husbands to make periodical payments as well to support them; because, after the divorce, he will be earning far more than she; and she can only keep up her standard of living with his help. He also has to make payments for the children out of his earnings, even if they are with her. In view of those calls on his future earnings, we do not think she can have both — half the capital assets, and half the earnings.

Under the new dispensation, she will usually get a share of each. In these days of rising house prices, she should certainly have a share in the capital assets which she has helped to create. The windfall should not all go to the husband. But we do not think it should be as much as one half, if she is also to get periodical payments for her maintenance and support. Giving it the best consideration we can, we think that the fairest way is to start with one third of each. If she has one third of the family assets as her own — and one third of the joint earnings — her past contributions are adequately recognised, and her future living standards assured so far as may be. She will certainly in this way be as well off as if the capital assets were divided equally — which is all that a partner is entitled to.

We would emphasise that this proposal is not a rule. It is only a starting point. It will serve in cases where the marriage has lasted for many years and the wife has been in the home bringing up the children. It may not be applicable when the marriage has lasted only a short time, or where there are no children and she can go out to work.

The lump sum provision

In every case the court should consider whether to order a lump sum to be paid by her husband to her. Before 1963 a wife, on a divorce, could not get a lump sum paid to her. All that she could get was weekly or monthly payments secured or unsecured. By section 5(1) of the Matrimonial Causes Act 1963, the court was empowered to make an order for the payment of a lump sum. This is now contained in section 2(1)(c) of the Act of 1970. This court has decided many cases about lump sums. They will be found usefully set out in Mr Joseph Jackson's chapter on the subject in his book on *Matrimonial Finance and Taxation* (1972), pp. 116 to 131. The circumstances are so various that few general principles can be stated. One thing is, however, obvious. No order should be made for a lump sum unless the husband has capital assets out of which to pay it — without crippling his earning power.

Another thing is this: when the husband has available capital assets sufficient for the purpose, the court should not hesitate to order a lump sum. The wife will then be able to invest it and use the income to live on. This will reduce any periodical payments, or make them unnecessary. It will also help to remove the bitterness which is so often attendant on periodical payments. Once made, the parties can regard the book as closed. The third thing is that, if a lump sum is awarded, it should be made outright. It should not be made subject to conditions except when there are children. Then it may be desirable to let it be the subject of a settlement. In case she remarries, the children will be assured of some part of the family assets which were built up for them.

But the question of a lump sum needs special consideration in relation to the matrimonial home. The house is in most cases the principal capital asset. Sometimes the only asset. It will usually have increased greatly in value since it was acquired. It is to be regarded as belonging in equity to both of them jointly. What is to be done with it? This is the most important question of all.

Take a case like the present when the wife leaves the home and the husband stays in it. On the breakdown of the marriage arrangements should be made whereby it is vested in him absolutely, free of any share in the wife, and he alone is liable for the mortgage instalments. But the wife should be compensated for the loss of her share by being awarded a lump sum. It should be a sum sufficient to enable her to get settled in a place of her own, such as by putting down a deposit on a flat or a house. It should not, however, be an excessive sum. It should be such as the husband can raise by a further mortgage on the house without crippling him.

Conversely, suppose the husband leaves the house and the wife stays in it. If she is likely to be there indefinitely, arrangements should be made whereby it is vested in her absolutely, free of any share in the husband: or, if there are children, settled on her and the children. This may mean that he will have to transfer the legal title to her. If there is a mortgage, some provision should be made for the mortgage instalments to be paid by the husband, or guaranteed by him. If this is done, there may be no necessity for a lump sum as well. Furthermore, seeing that she has the house, the periodic payments will be much less than they otherwise would be.

Remarriage
In making financial provision, ought the prospects of remarriage to be taken into account? The statute says in terms that periodical payments shall cease on remarriage: see section 7(2)(*a*), (*b*). But it says nothing about the prospects of remarriage. The question then arises: ought the provision for the wife to be reduced if she is likely to remarry?

So far as the capital assets are concerned, we see no reason for reducing her share. After all, she has earned it by her contribution in looking after the home and caring for the family. It should not be taken away from her by the prospect of remarriage. In *Buckley v John Allen and Ford (Oxford) Ltd* [1967] 2 QB 637 at 645, Phillimore J showed that it was a guessing game, which no judge was qualified to put his — or her — money on. His observations were disapproved by this court in *Goodburn v Thomas Cotton Ltd* [1968] 1 QB 845, [1968] 1 All ER 518. But they have been vindicated by Parliament.

So far as periodical payments are concerned, they are, of course, to be assessed without regard to the prospects of remarriage. If the wife does in fact remarry, they cease. If she goes to live with another man — without marrying him — they may be reviewed.

The present case
Coming now to the facts of the present case. The matrimonial home belongs in law to the husband. On the figures before the judge, its gross value was about £22,000; and, as already stated, the equity is worth about £20,000. Mr Gray sought to reopen these figures. We saw no justification for allowing him to do so, since these figures could have been challenged before the judge had it then been desired to do so. But we allowed Mr Gray to cross-appeal to argue that the judge, consistently with the principles which he sought to apply, should have ordered a lump-sum payment of £10,000, or half the net value of the house, whichever was the greater, and not, as the judge in fact ordered, whichever was the less.

So far as the husband's earning capacity is concerned, we venture to think that the judge's findings are self-contradictory; for, if the husband was spending at the rate of £4,000 to £5,000 per annum without incurring debts and was, in fact, at the same time making savings, his gross taxable income must have been considerably more than the £4,000 to £5,000 found by the judge. We propose to proceed on the basis of the husband's earning capacity (i.e. his gross taxable income) being not less than £6,000 per annum. This may well be too favourable to the husband who appears not to have disclosed part of his income as a dentist. We put the wife's potential earning capacity on part-time work as a dental nurse at £15 per week gross — say £750 per annum. The combined total earning capacity is thus £6,750 per annum gross, of which one third (if that be the right starting point) is £2,250. If one deducts the £750 from that latter figure of £2,250, the result is £1,500 — the same figure as the judge arrived at though he reached that figure by a different route.

The husband is presently living at the former matrimonial home. The son of the marriage, aged 14, is now at a boarding school at the grandfather's expense. The boy lives with his father in the holidays. The father has to clothe and maintain him in the holidays. Clearly this requires the father to maintain a home for the son. Both parties gave their ages as 46. Remarriage is thus a possibility, though not it seems an imminent probability. The wife undoubtedly contributed to the home for some 18 years and, so far as the evidence goes, was in every respect an excellent mother. This is clearly a case in which the wife has made a substantial contribution to the home, as, of course, the husband has out of his earnings.

Any lump sum ordered to be paid will, we are told, be raised by the husband by increasing the sum for which the house is mortgaged. To require him to pay a lump sum of £10,000 raised in this way might cost him around £900 per annum in interest; and, of course, he will have to repay the principal as well. If £900 is added to the total of £1,500, plus the £500 (i.e., £2,000), the result is the equivalent of an order for a periodical payment of almost half of what we have taken to be the husband's gross taxable income. We think an order for a periodical payment on this scale (omitting any consideration of a lump sum payment) would be too high, having regard to the wife's needs and to the husband's needs. But, even if the matter be approached by a different route, we still think the £10,000 figure is too high. The wife should be able to make a substantial deposit in order to purchase suitable accommodation (assuming she wishes to buy, and not to rent) with the aid of a considerably smaller sum; and, if the order for £1,500 as a periodical payment is upheld, there seems to us to be a margin within that figure beyond the requirements of ordinary living expenses out of which repayments of mortgage, principal and interest could be made. On the other hand, we think the husband's offer of £4,000 is too low in a period of notoriously inflationary house prices. The offer of a guarantee of the wife's mortgage repayments does not improve the wife's day-to-day position, though it might make the obtaining of mortgage facilities easier.

On the basis that the order for a periodical payment of £1,500 per annum is left untouched, we think the proper lump sum, taking every thing into account that the Act of 1970 requires, is £6,000, and we would vary the judge's order for £10,000 accordingly. We think the wife should have that sum, £6,000, free of any trust, or other terms.

We, therefore, see no reason to interfere with the order for £1,500 in favour of the wife on the basis of the figures we have just mentioned. But, with all respect to the judge, we think the figure of £500 for the child is considerably too high. We would substitute a figure of £300 per annum, which we would express as £6 per week so that the payment should be made gross of tax. We see no reason whatever on the facts of this case, as found by the judge, for making any reduction of any kind on the ground that the judge found the wife equally responsible with the husband for the breakdown of their marriage. To do so would be quite inconsistent with the principles which we think should be adopted in future in relation to conduct.

Looking at it broadly
In all these cases it is necessary at the end to view the situation broadly and see if the proposals meet the justice of the case. On our proposals here the wife gets £6,000 (nearly one third of the value of the matrimonial home). She gets it without any conditions at all. This seems to represent a fair assessment of her past contributions, when regard is had to the fact that she will get periodical payments as well. She also gets £1,500 a year by way of periodical payments, which is about one third of their joint incomes. She will also have the management of £300 a year for the daughter who is at a good school, and aged 11. These provisions are as much as the husband can reasonably be expected to make. It will mean that each will have to cut down their standard of living: but it is as much as can be done in the circumstances.

The appeal should be allowed to the extent indicated. The wife's cross-appeal will be dismissed.
Appeal allowed by varying lump sum payment of £10,000 to £6,000 and reducing payments in respect of daughter from £500 per annum to £300 per annum (£6 a week gross of tax).
Cross-appeal dismissed.
Husband to have costs of appeal not to be enforced without further order and leave to apply for costs to be paid out of legal aid fund.
Leave to appeal refused.

Questions

(i) Lord Denning MR gives two reasons for substituting one-third for the one-half approach used by the trial judge: does either of them convince you?
(ii) Would either reason have been valid if the wife had been working full time and: (*a*) earning as much as her husband, or (*b*) earning less than he did?

4. The one-third rule — as starting point?

At the end of the section in *Wachtel* on the one-third rule, Lord Denning MR himself said that the rule would not be applicable in a number of situations. The three major cases in which the rule has been least helpful are: (i) where there are substantial assets; (ii) where there are small resources; and (iii) in short marriages, especially when the wife has no children and can go back to work. We provide a few extracts from a selection of the large number of cases in this area, so that the reader can be given some idea of how the higher courts operate the principle. It must be remembered of course that the reported cases are taken from the High Court and the Court of Appeal. The approach of the county court registrars, who decide the great majority of cases, could well be somewhat different.

(a) SUBSTANTIAL ASSETS

O'D v O'D
[1976] Fam 83, [1975] 2 All ER 993, [1975] 3 WLR 308, 119 Sol Jo 560, Court of Appeal

This was an appeal by the husband against an order of Lane J on the ground that a lump sum award of £70,000 was much too high. The wife submitted that in all the circumstances the judge had got the answer 'just about right'. Orders for periodical payments of £1,000 per annum less tax for the wife, and £4,230 per annum less tax for the children were not disputed. The appeal was dismissed.

Ormrod LJ: The parties were married on 20 February 1960, when they were in their early twenties. Their three children were born as follows: a son on 5 July 1960, a daughter on 14 January 1962, and a son on 12 December 1965. The marriage lasted until March 1972, when, to the wife's surprise, the husband left her for another woman. Divorce proceedings followed and the marriage was dissolved by decree nisi on 16 November 1972; the decree absolute following in due course.

At the time of the marriage the wife was a ballet dancer with the Royal Ballet Company earning about £20 per week. The husband was employed in the building trade as a site foreman but, as the judge pointed out, this does not give a true picture of his position, because his father is a highly successful businessman in the building and property development sector, operating through a number of family companies. The husband was employed by one of these companies.

At the beginning of the marriage the husband and the wife lived in a small flat, and later in a larger one, although a house called Inglewood Cottage was built for them, but never in fact occupied as a matrimonial home.

In 1964 a hotel, which it will be convenient to refer to as the C hotel, came on the market. The husband and his mother bought the three-year lease for £3,000, each contributing one-half of the purchase price. In 1965 the mother died and her interest in this hotel passed to her husband. Before the lease expired the husband and his father bought the freehold for £20,000, and later an adjoining property. This, with later extensions, eventually produced a hotel with 130 bedrooms and a thriving business.

Lane J found that the wife had played an important part in building up this business from its very modest beginnings, working as receptionist, chamber-maid, cook, waitress, and clerk as required. The judge said that she 'certainly contributed substantially to its success.' The marriage broke down at the time when all the hard work of the husband and wife, and, indeed, both their parents, for the wife's parents also helped in the business, was coming to fruition. In consequence, the husband can now properly be described as a rich man.

This appeal, therefore, raises a number of difficult questions on the application of the greatly extended powers of the court to adjust the property rights of the spouses following a dissolution of the marriage.

In approaching a case like the present, the first stage should be to make as reliable an estimate as possible of the husband's current financial position and future prospects. . . .

Put very shortly, Mr Howlett's [the husband's accountant] estimate of the husband's present resources was the figure of £215,000, on the basis of a sale of all his assets and allowing for capital gains tax, although the tax would only be payable on any disposal which actually comes to be made. Obviously this is a notional figure and does little more than place the husband in approximately the right position on the scale of wealth. By far the largest item in this estimate is the husband's half share in the C hotel, including both the business and the freehold. The value placed upon this half share was £140,000 less capital gains tax of £13,000 if the whole share were to be disposed of. (The judge took the gross value at £186,000, but the difference is not enough to affect her ultimate conclusion.) In addition, he had shares in four family companies, one of which has assets worth approximately £500,000, and another very substantial assets. His shareholdings are, however, proportionally quite small, and have been valued on an asset basis, although he could only realise these interests with the co-operation of his family. On this basis his shares were valued at £90,000.

The husband also owned Inglewood Cottage, which was valued at £25,000. By the date of the hearing below the husband had mortgaged this property for £26,000, which he had given to the wife to buy a house for herself. This sum forms part of the £70,000 awarded by the judge. The husband appears to have chosen to borrow on Inglewood Cottage rather than to sell it for reasons of his own. It was available for sale as soon as the wife moved to her own house. Also to be borne in mind was the fact that the husband and the children are among the discretionary objects of a trust fund valued at £117,000, but presently invested in shares in the family companies which are not readily realisable. The wife herself was among the objects until she ceased to be a spouse.

The next stage is to consider the wife's position, not from the narrow point of 'need,' but to ascertain her reasonable requirements, bearing in mind that she will have to provide an appropriate home and background for herself and the children. Her first requirement is a house, and this has already been provided. The judge estimated that to run the house and a car and feed herself and the children and pay for all the incidentals would require about £2,750 per annum net of tax. She is earning £1,000 gross and has £100 family allowances.

Her next requirement, to comply with the terms of the concluding part of section 25, which requires the court to make such order as in all the circumstances is just, is a reasonable capital sum. In a case such as this it is probably better to regard this not so much as her share, but as one of the necessary factors in the attempt to put her in the position she would have been in had the marriage continued. The judge accepted her evidence that during the marriage her husband had said he would give her a share in the hotel, but had not in fact done so.

Having made these assessments, the judge decided on a figure of £70,000, including the house. In doing so she in fact applied the 'one-third rule' (though it might now be better to call it 'the one-third ratio') to the notional figure of £215,000, while fully recognising that it is not a rule. In cases on the scale of the present one this ratio may produce results which are, or may seem to be, too high, but inflation has already altered values very considerably, bringing many cases into the class in which the one-third rule would not have been accepted in the past. In our judgment, this figure of £70,000, or £44,000 apart from the house, is on the high side, but it is clear that Lane J took the view that the C hotel was likely to become an extremely profitable business in the near future, and that, although a minority shareholder in the family companies, the husband's interest in these companies was potentially very considerable, and, consequently, his resources in the wide sense were certainly not overvalued at £215,000 net of gains tax.

Mr Ewbank, for the husband, argued strenuously that to award such a lump sum would place the husband in an extremely difficult position. He submitted that it was wrong to make an order which would either force the husband to sell his business and so destroy his means of livelihood and that of his family, or compel him to borrow and so incur interest charges which would be crippling, and invited the court to rule accordingly. But it is unwise to make statements of general application in these cases. The danger of creating rigid rules of practice is too great. The statement, 'it is wrong to deprive a man of his sole capital asset,' was used, no doubt very appropriately in the particular circumstances, . . . but it is now being relied upon in argument in many cases as though it imposed a specific restriction on the exercise of the court's discretion.

The court must, of course, consider very carefully the effect on the husband of any order which it has in mind to make, because its purpose is to do justice to both parties, and the section specifically requires the court to have regard to what is 'practicable.' But in considering this aspect of the case the court is entitled to look at all the surrounding circumstances with a realistic eye. In many cases the difficulty of raising a large lump sum immediately may be very real, in which case arrangements for some form of deferred payment may be appropriate; in other cases, the husband might prefer to put forward alternative proposals to avoid having to raise a large cash sum; in others, the court may be able to find that there are ways and means of complying with the order. In the present case one of the family companies has recently sold a hotel for £500,000 and has bought the building next door to the C hotel. It appears still to have large liquid assets, so that the family are, or may be, in a position to invest some of these funds in the C hotel, thus freeing some of the husband's resources at present invested in it without prejudicing in any way his position as manager. It is legitimate, as Lane J did, to take such matters into account when considering the husband's submission that the lump sum should be reduced owing to his difficulties in realising part of his assets. Probably it will be found convenient in cases like this one to adopt the practice which in the past was used in cases where secured provision was ordered. The court would indicate the amount to be secured and then adjourn the application to give the husband an opportunity of putting forward proposals for compliance with the order and for the wife and her advisers to consider them. The court itself refrained from selecting the security unless the parties were unable to reach agreement upon the matter. So in a case like this the husband should be given every opportunity of putting forward a scheme which will enable the order to be complied with within generous time limits, and the court should refrain from devising ways and means itself once it is satisfied that the order it makes, or intends to make, is 'practicable.' Indeed, in some cases it may be found on further consideration that the most practicable way of dealing with the wife's position is to make one of the other orders provided for in section 24 in substitution, in whole or in part, for the lump sum order, the drawing up of which can be postponed until after discussions have taken place between the parties.

Mr Ewbank further submitted that all the wife's needs could be met by the provision of £30,000 (to include the house) and a periodical payments order of about £3,000 less tax. For reasons already indicated, we do not think in this case that a periodical payments order will be sufficient to place the wife in the position that the Act contemplates. Moreover, the court cannot overlook that as periodical payments cease on remarriage an order of this size must be a very strong disincentive, if not a prohibition, to remarriage to this comparatively young woman. She requires an adequate capital sum over and above the house.

Questions

(i) Ormrod LJ distinguished *Wachtel v Wachtel*. He said that *Wachtel* was essentially a case of two people starting their married life with little or nothing but their earning capacities, together founding a family, and building up by their joint efforts such capital as they were able to save. As the main capital asset was the matrimonial home, bought on mortgage and out of income, the *Wachtel v Wachtel* case represented, in Ormrod LJ's view, a true example of equal partnership.

Given Lord Denning MR's view on housework (see p. 200, above), and assuming that that is indeed what happened in the case of Mr and Mrs Wachtel, do you think that there *really* was an equal partnership in that case?

(ii) Ormrod LJ contrasted the *Wachtel* case with others: 'In other cases the situation is different. One or other, or perhaps both, spouses may bring into the marriage substantial capital assets, or may acquire such assets during the marriage by inheritance or by gift from members of their families.' He said that the use of phrases such as 'family assets' and the 'wife earning her share' cannot be applied to such situations without modification. It is necessary 'to go directly to the terms of section 25 for guidance.' But surely the legislature expect a judge to do this in all cases?

(iii) Or is Ormrod LJ acknowledging that the decision in *Wachtel v Wachtel* is tantamount to a doctrine of deferred community?

(iv) Do you think that the facts of *O'D v O'D* were (*a*) similar to that described by Ormrod LJ in question (ii) or (*b*) a *Wachtel* type partnership? or (*c*) somewhere between the two?

(v) Would it be better to adopt a classification based on the differing *expectations* described by Honoré at p. 64? These are: marriage as a partnership; marriage as an arrangement by which a husband induces his wife to change her career; and marriage as an arrangement by which a husband assumes the role of providing for his wife's needs and those of their children.

(vi) If the wife in *O'D v O'D* had argued that she was entitled to one half of the notional figure of £215,000, instead of the combination of income and capital awarded, would she have had any chance of success?

Ormrod LJ returned to a discussion of the one-third rule in *Potter v Potter* [1982] 1 WLR 1255. This case followed quickly on the heels of *Slater v Slater* (1982) Times, 26 March, when Sir John Arnold P (sitting in the Court of Appeal) had extolled the one-third principle in cases which fell between very large and very small sums of money available for re-allocation. Ormrod LJ was much more doubtful of the value of the principle, especially in a factual situation such as *Potter v Potter* where the only real matter for consideration was a division of capital assets:

Potter v Potter
[1982] 3 All ER 321, [1982] 1 WLR 1255, 126 Sol Jo 480, Court of Appeal

The parties were married in 1968 when the husband was 26 and the wife 22. The husband left the matrimonial home in 1974, and a decree of divorce was

ι

granted in 1979. There were no children, and neither of the parties had remarried. The husband owned his own photographic business. The wife worked throughout the marriage and continued in employment thereafter. The judge ordered the husband (i) to transfer his interest in the matrimonial home to the wife (not the subject of the appeal); and (ii) to make a lump sum payment of £23,900. In computing the lump sum the judge added together the capital assets of both parties, divided them by one-third, deducted the wife's assets and arrived at £30,000 as the appropriate figure; but since the marriage had only lasted six years, he reduced that sum and awarded the wife £23,900, which included a sum in respect of loss of pension rights. The husband appealed.

Ormrod LJ: The case to which the judge was referred, *Slater v Slater* (1982) Times, 26 March, is an example of the very understandable desire of judges to provide some kind of certainty in these cases if it is possible and the reason why the President in that case — which was . . . a periodical payments case — re-asserted the advantage of the one-third rule was simply that. As he pointed out, it was helpful to practitioners to have a clear understanding of what principles were likely to apply so that they could feel confident as to how to advise their clients, and he added 'that the issues would not be determined by caprice or judicial idiosyncrasy'.

The problem, when one comes to deal with capital, particularly in a case of this kind, is that one cannot use the one-third rule, . . . until the value of the assets of the parties have been ascertained. This is a highly speculative exercise in a great many cases, particularly where a small business is concerned. Applying the one-third rule to this case would mean that the amount to be paid by the husband would depend on valuations by accountants and here, in this case, the unfortunate judge had before him no less than four different valuations by four different accountants. The spread of the valuations ranged between £10,000 and £40,000 for the goodwill; so that it is wholly illusory to think that, by using the one-third rule in relation to capital, any certainty is achieved. It simply exchanges one uncertainty for another. And there are no indications as to which accountant is more likely to be right, because the whole thing is an imaginary exercise from beginning to end. When one adds the question of capital gains tax, one simply complicates the matter even further. I think it is very unwise, where capital is concerned, to try to work on a one-third basis. It is inevitable that there will be a high degree of uncertainty. We have said before that, however much that is to be regretted, there is no way of avoiding it of which I am aware, and I have never heard anyone suggest a way in which this uncertainty can be reduced. All one can do is to demonstrate, as far as one can, the ways in which the court should approach the problem and leave it to the parties to make the best assessment that they can. But for the concluding words of section 25, I would have no doubt that this case was not a case for a lump sum at all. The marriage, which has lasted for only six years and in which neither party have suffered any handicap so far as their careers or earnings are concerned, and where there are no children, is not one which in the ordinary way in these days should attract very much in the way of payment as between one spouse and the other after the marriage has broken down. However, that is not the principle we have to apply under the section and, in applying the concluding words of section 25, it is crucial to remember that the phrase is 'so far as is practicable' and, in most of the cases with which we have to deal in this court, it is that phrase which, in the end, proves decisive of the appeal. In this case the judge did not consider whether it was 'practicable' for the husband to raise £33,000, or what the consequences on the business would be, so that one does not know — except, from looking at the accounts, it was obviously going to be extremely difficult. The figure which . . . is clearly within his capacity because there is cash, or assets which may be rendered liquid and available, is £10,000.

Question

Ormrod LJ expressed considerable reservation about making any lump sum award at all in the present case. Dunn LJ had similar reservations. Why did they make an order?

(b) SMALL RESOURCES

Cann v Cann
[1977] 3 All ER 957, [1977] 1 WLR 938, 121 Sol Jo 528, 7 Fam Law, High
Court, Family Division

This was an application by the husband to vary an order made in the
magistrates' courts in 1960, when the parties were still married. They were
divorced in 1961. The couple were pensioners, the husband's total weekly
income was £23.46p and the wife's total weekly income was £13.30p. The
husband also had small savings amounting to £830 and he owned a motor car
valued at £250. The current amount of the order was £7.00 per week. The
husband's application to vary was unsuccessful and he appealed.

Hollings J: . . . Mr Jones [for the husband] submits that the one-third approach is right, and if
one applies the calculation it leaves £12.25 as the wife's as it were, entitlement. She has more
than that and therefore he submits that she should receive nothing and that any order should be
entirely nominal. The result for the husband, he says, would be that he would have £23.46,
expenses of £19.61, leaving £3.85 over for the husband. He submits that the gap suffered by his
wife should be filled by social security payments. As Sir George Baker P pointed out in the
course of Mr Jones' submission, that would only mean that the Department of Health and
Social Security would be entitled to, and probably would, take advantage of her entitlement to
claim against the husband in respect of social security payments because of the savings which he
has, and make that claim against his savings.

Hollings J rejected this approach:

Now clearly the husband's situation has altered for the worse since November 1974. He no
longer works, his income is reduced and is in the form of a pension. There was a discussion as to
the way in which any savings which the husband has should be taken into account, if they are to
be taken into account. So far as counsel are aware, and so far as I am aware, there is no authority
dealing with the question as to whether justices can take into account for the purposes of making
periodical payment orders, a description that stresses the income aspect, a capital sum owned by
the husband. Of course, one can take into account the interest or notional interest, that is
interest that could be earned in normal investment upon those savings; but there is no authority
to indicate whether the capital element can or should be taken into account. It might in future be
useful to explore the possibility of dealing with savings in the same way as damages are
calculated in personal injury actions, that is take the lump sum for its capital value and its
income producing value, take into account the respective ages of the parties — here I should say
the husband is 67 and the wife 70 — and applying the actuarial table find out what annuity could
be obtained from that sum, and apply a portion, if not the whole of that annuity, towards
supplementing the order. I do not think in investigating this case, that exercise is necessary. One
reason is that the sum of £830 has, sadly and regrettably, been seriously depleted by the
contribution which the husband had to make in respect of his legal aid for the purpose of this
appeal, a contribution of no less than £260 payable by 12 instalments of £21.70.

So far as the car is concerned, one knows the value of such an item is not always to be realised,
so the sum that is left in the hands of the husband is not, in my judgment, a substantial amount
of money for the exercise to which I have referred to be applied to it.

For myself I am satisfied that the one-third approach is quite inappropriate, in circumstances
of this kind where neither party is earning; then one has to look at each party's needs and see
what can best be done in all the circumstances. I have in mind particularly the words of the
statute under which the justices have jurisdiction. What was a reasonable sum in all the
circumstances of the case? Bearing that aspect in mind, I would hold that the justices were wrong
in not effecting some reduction, but by no means a reduction of the size contended for on behalf
of the husband. If one reduces the order made by the justices of £7 to the sum of £5, that is
reducing it by £2, the wife will have £18 and the husband will be left with £18.46 to cover
expenses of £19.61. That leaves him with £1.15 deficit. That deficit, I think, should properly be
financed out of interest from his savings, such as are left, or if necessary the interest plus capital.
In that way, the parties would, so far as it is possible in the circumstances of this case, be left with
a fair division of the respective pensions to which they are entitled. . . .

Perhaps Sir George Baker P exposed the real reason for the court's apparent
lack of concern for the husband's position, when he said in his judgement in
this case: 'Thirdly, it passes my comprehension how a man can spend three-

tenths of his capital sum in legal aid in trying to vary an order for his ex-wife.'

Question

What is the justification for the one-third rule when no distribution of capital is involved?

(c) SHORT MARRIAGES

In *Brady v Brady*, 27 February 1973, Divisional Court, the President, Sir George Baker P, said 'In these days of "Women's Lib" there is no reason why a wife whose marriage has not lasted long, and who has no child, should have a "bread ticket" for life.'

Questions

(i) Could a wife argue that a marriage was only short because the husband had ended it and thus deprived her of her opportunity of 'earning her right to share in the property and to proper and full periodical payments'? (See *Brett v Brett* [1969] 1 All ER 1007, [1969] 1 WLR 487).
(ii) Do you think that premarital cohabitation during which the wife has performed 'quasi-wifely' duties should be capable of lengthening what is otherwise thought to be a short marriage?
(iii) How short is short?

There have been a number of cases on the second of these three questions. The most recent is the following, in which the other cases are discussed:

Foley v Foley
[1981] Fam 160, [1981] 2 All ER 857, [1981] 3 WLR 284, 125 Sol Jo 442, Court of Appeal

The parties began to cohabit in 1962 when each was married to someone else. They had three children who were born in 1963, 1966, and 1969. They married in 1969, separated in 1974, and were divorced in 1977. The wife applied for financial provision for herself and the one child who was living with her. She had good employment and her earnings would enable her to maintain her style of life; she, also had realizable capital assets amounting to £10,000. The husband was not working and his future prospects were not very good; he owned a property (not the matrimonial home) worth £62,500 after capital gains tax. The wife agreed to her claim for periodical payments (for herself) being dismissed but she claimed a lump sum payment.

In assessing the amount of the lump sum payment the judge distinguished the period of the marriage and the period of cohabitation, indicating that in so far as s. 25(1)(*d*) of the Matrimonial Causes Act 1973 referred to the duration of the marriage he was not prepared to treat this as a marriage which had subsisted prior to 1969 but that as part of 'all the circumstances of the case' he took into account the wife's contribution to the family during the whole of the period they were living together. The judge was of opinion that the one-third calculation was not an appropriate starting point for computing the lump sum in this case. The one-third calculation would have given the wife £14,000. The judge awarded her £10,000. The wife appealed. The appeal was dismissed.

Eveleigh LJ: gives more information about the circumstances of the parties:

Eveleigh LJ: The husband had an unusual career with various occupations. He was described as a bullion dealer, a firearms dealer, a dealer in antiques. He and the wife lived well during the period of their cohabitation and the period of their marriage. At first they lived in a mews flat at 12 Pindock Mews, London, W 9. In 1972 they moved to a spacious flat in Ashworth Mansions, London, W 9. That was a rented flat and the wife now lived there. In 1959, before meeting his wife, Mr Foley bought a freehold property, 55 Upper Montague Street, London, W 1., for £5,250. He and his first wife converted the ground floor to a sandwich bar and they let it and it remains let. The top two floors were in a bad condition. They were let, however, on controlled tenancies. In the mid-1960s the second Mrs Foley [Mr Foley had been married before] who was, of course, not at that date married to Mr Foley, helped in this renovation of the upper floor of that property and Mr Foley spent some £4–5,000 on improvements. The wife (and I shall call her 'the wife' for the purposes of this judgment) helped in furnishing those flats and in the decoration and she collected the rents when they fell due.

Today, as the learned judge has found, the wife is an attractive woman, who dresses well. She is employed as a hairdresser in the Edgware Road at £75 a week and the learned judge estimated that she received tips of about £15 a week. She lives in the flat and she has the furniture. The learned judge made this finding, that the wife will be able to maintain the style of life that she has enjoyed over the last few years for some years to come. He assessed her capital at £10,000 and this was jewellery, paintings, a fur coat and some cash — her current realizable assets, as the learned judge called them. The two boys — because the daughter, it will be appreciated, was of responsible years — at first lived with the husband but in 1980 D went to live with the wife.

As to the husband, he was in arrears for maintenance to his first wife and the learned judge found that his free assets did not exceed his debts. . . .

As I have said, the learned judge [Balcombe J] came to the conclusion that the proper sum to award the wife was £10,000.

The wife now appeals and the first ground of her appeal is to the effect that the learned judge failed to take into account the period of cohabitation, that is to say, the period when the parties were living together before the marriage.

[However,] . . . In my view, the two periods, namely, cohabitation and marriage, are not the same. What weight will be given to matters that occurred during those periods will be for the learned judge to decide in the exercise of his discretion, but one cannot say that those two periods are the same. Ten years of cohabitation will not necessarily have the same effect as 10 years of marriage. During the period of cohabitation the parties were free to come and go as they pleased. This is not so where there is a marriage. In the great majority of cases public opinion would readily recognize a stronger claim founded upon years of marriage than upon years of cohabitation. On the other hand, in deciding these difficult financial problems there may be cases where the inability of the parties to sanctify and legitimize their relationship calls for a measure of sympathy which will enable the court to take what has happened during the period of cohabitation into account as a very weighty factor. *Kokosinski v Kokosinski* [1980] Fam 72, [1980] 1 All ER 1106 is one such case. *Campbell v Campbell* [1976] Fam 347, [1977] 1 All ER 1 is certainly not.

I do not regard Balcombe J as saying that the years of cohabitation are irrelevant. He simply says that they are not years of marriage within section 25(1)(*d*). That section requires the court to have regard to all the circumstances. Circumstances may be relevant for consideration in one case which would not be relevant in another, and the two cases, *Campbell v Campbell* and *Kokosinski v Kokosinski*, provide examples of this. But the matters specifically listed in s. 25 will always be relevant, because Parliament has said so. . . .

I therefore see no error in the approach of the learned judge to the problem and I cannot say that he wrongly exercised his discretion in this case, in so far, for the moment, as he considered what weight should be given to the years of cohabitation.

On the relevance of the one-third formula to the case, on which the Court of Appeal again supported the trial judge, Eveleigh LJ said;

. . . the second ground of appeal is that the learned judge should have started on the basis that one-third was the proper proportion for the wife. Mr Jackson [for the wife] argued that, starting from one-third, the wife, on the facts of this case, should actually have received more than the £14,000 which a 'one-third' calculation would have produced, and he referred the court to the authorities relating to the 'one-third' proportion. As I see it, one-third in many cases is a very useful starting point for the court in deciding what should be the final figure. It is a useful proportion to take and then adjust one way or another as the case demands. But it is in no way a rule of law, as I see it. It is an aid to the mental process when arriving at the appropriate figure and there are many cases where the 'one-third' figure would not enter the mind of the court, because it would be obvious from the start that the proportion would be nothing like that. For example, the young marriage that lasts but a day or two. It is an extreme case but it is not unknown in this court. So that I do not find it possible to criticize the learned judge because he in fact said that he did not regard the one-third as the starting point in this case.

One of the cases cited by Eveleigh LJ was the following:

Campbell v Campbell
[1976] Fam 347, [1977] 1 All ER 1, [1976] 3 WLR 572, 120 Sol Jo 116, 6 Fam
Law 214, High Court, Family Division

The question at issue was whether the three-and-a-half years of premarital
cohabitation should be taken into account.

Sir George Baker P: . . . Mr Sleeman [for the wife] attempts to persuade me that the 3½ years of
pre-marital cohabitation should be taken into account in assessing the length of the marriage.
The way he puts it is: 'She was for 3½ years performing wifely duties before marriage.' Now I
entirely reject that argument. Mrs Campbell was then a married woman with a large number of
children, most of them in care, living with a youngster. There is an increasing tendency, I have
found in cases in chambers, to regard and, indeed, to speak of the celebration of marriage as 'the
paper work'. The phrase used is: 'We were living together but we never got round to the paper
work'. Well that is, to my mind, an entirely misconceived outlook. It is the ceremony of
marriage and the sanctity of marriage which count; rights, duties and obligations begin on the
marriage and not before. It is a complete cheapening of the marriage relationship, which I
believe, and I am sure many share this belief, is essential to the well-being of our society as we
understand it, to suggest that pre-marital periods, particularly in the circumstances of this case,
should, as it were, by a doctrine of relation back of matrimony, be taken as a part of marriage to
count in favour of the wife performing, as it is put, 'wifely duties before marriage'. So I take this
as a marriage of 2 years and a month or two; after which it ended.

Questions

(i) Judgments such as these are based, to some extent at least, on an
ideological commitment to marriage. Do you think that such sentiments
actually help to enhance the status of marriage?
(ii) On the facts of *Foley v Foley*, do you think that the one-third formula
was rejected because, in the view of both the trial judge and the appellate
court, a five-year marriage is a 'short' marriage?
(iii) Is the rationale for the one-third rule the need to balance present shares
against future needs?
(iv) If it is, would legislating for automatic equal distribution of property
deprive us: (*a*) of the one-third approach to income distribution, or (*b*) the
rationale for *any* income distribution?
(v) It is noteworthy that in none of the recent judgments quoted has a judge
tried to explain why it is that a one-third formula allows the parties to remain
'so far as practicable' in the position 'in which they would have been if the
marriage had not broken down.' Did Lord Denning MR apply himself to this
question in *Wachtel v Wachtel*?
(vi) Do you think that the one-third formula is appropriate in cases where
the husband is applying for provision from his wife?
(vii) If not, why not?

Calderbank v Calderbank
[1976] Fam 93, [1975] 3 All ER 333, [1975] 3 WLR 586, 119 Sol Jo 490, 5 Fam
Law 190, Court of Appeal

This was an appeal from an order made by Heilbron J awarding an
ex-husband a lump sum of £10,000. Immediately before the breakdown of
the marriage, the husband and wife were living in a large house bought with
the wife's money. Their children were being educated at fee-paying schools
financed by the wife. The husband had suffered early in life from

poliomyelitis, and although he had made a recovery, he was to some extent physically weakened. At the time of the divorce he was not working except for an interest in a kennel business which the parties had started.

Scarman LJ: . . . . In the present case the judge came to the conclusion that the husband needed some capital to enable him to acquire, no doubt with the aid of a mortgage, a house suitable to his station in life and suitable for the accommodation of the three children when they came to stay with him.

Mr Hordern [for the wife] says that such a need if it exists is not one which under the section should be met by the wife. But there is no prohibition in the section on the court ordering the wife to meet that need if in the light of all the other circumstances to which I have referred it is reasonable that she should do so. And here when one stands back and looks at the broad outline of the married life one sees this picture: that over a period of 17 years this family, that is the husband, wife and the children, have looked to the wife's capital resources to finance them. The wife has done admirably by her family. She has made those resources available and the husband with her full consent has adapted his life style — working for a number of years at a business financed by the wife, living in a large and elegant house which the wife bought when she came into her family fortune and dependent upon her resources. So if one looks at the standard of life enjoyed by the family before the breakdown of the marriage, this is what it was — a high standard supported by the capital resources of the wife. Now upon divorce the judge has thought that about one eighth of those capital resources, that is to say £10,000 out of the sum of £78,000, should be made available to the husband so that, no longer able to live in the family house which by order of the court is now the property of the wife, he can at least have a home suitable to his way of life in which he can live and in which he can see his children. It is very difficult to fault the judge's conclusion except upon the theoretical or conceptual basis advanced by Mr Hordern that really this statute does not provide that a wife should make financial provision for her husband save in exceptional circumstances. Such a provision cannot be found in the relevant sections; on the contrary, they make fresh provision for regulating the financial arrangement between parties to a marriage which has broken down. It therefore becomes quite impossible in my judgment to fault the exercise of the discretion of the judge in making an order for a lump sum.

Cairns LJ: I entirely agree with the judgment Scarman LJ has delivered. In *Wachtel v Wachtel* [1973] Fam 72 at 95, it was held by this court in considering any periodical payment or any lump sum to be awarded to a wife after divorce the starting point should be that she should have one third of the joint income and one third of the joint assets. It was recognised that this was simply a fraction which might be considered appropriate in the ordinary case where the husband has been the earner of the whole or substantially the whole of the family income, where he will be making periodical payments to his wife and where he may be expected to have the greater call upon future earnings.

No such starting point is appropriate where it is the husband who is the applicant for a lump sum because there is no ordinary or usual case in which the wife is in the position to provide a lump sum for the husband. Every such case when it does occur is exceptional and the courts must simply decide on the basis of the criteria laid down in section 25(1) of the Matrimonial Causes Act 1973 what is the right sum to award. I see no reason to suppose that Heilbron J overlooked any of the matters set out in paragraphs (*a*) to (*f*) of that subsection, though it is true that she concentrated mainly on the needs of the husband. In so far as she decided that the husband had the need, if the former matrimonial home were sold, for a sum of money to enable him to obtain a new house I think that her finding is quite unassailable.

It is complained that the judge did not take sufficiently into account the husband's earning capacity or the expectation that he would not contribute to the maintenance of the children of the marriage or his occupation of Rudford House at the wife's expense for several years after the parting. The judge did refer to all these matters in the course of her judgment and I cannot see that it could be said that she gave insufficient weight to them. £10,000 is after all not a large proportion of £78,000.

The main attack on this judgment has been that the judge failed to consider whether the wife had an obligation to the husband to provide him with money for a new house. In so far as obligations and responsibilities are referred to in section 25(1)(*b*) I am of opinion (and it is accepted by Mr Hordern on behalf of the wife that this is the right interpretation) that the obligations and responsibilities there mentioned are obligations and responsibilities to persons other than the other spouse. But the overall consideration which is contained at the end of the subsection is in these words:

'. . . and so to exercise those powers' — that is powers to make financial provisions in one way or another — 'as to place the parties, so far as it is practicable and, having regard to their conduct, just to do so, in the financial position in which they would have been if the marriage had not broken down and each had properly discharged his or her financial obligations and responsibilities towards the other.'

If the judge did not direct her mind to this part of the subsection, and I would hesitate to hold that she did not although she did not refer to it expressly, I am quite satisfied that if she had done so she would not have and should not have awarded any smaller sum. I do not consider that in that passage the phrase 'obligations and responsibilities' means legally enforceable obligations and responsibilities. What fall to be considered in my view are the obligations and responsibilities which any reasonable spouse, living with the other spouse and living in the circumstances of a normal family life, would recognise as being owed to that other spouse.

In my judgment in all the circumstances of this case if the marriage had not broken down and each spouse had properly discharged his or her obligations and responsibilities to the other the financial position of the parties would have included a continuance of the situation of the husband living in a house for which he had not to pay. Since it is not now practicable that he should continue to live in that house I think it was quite right for the judge to award him such lump sum as would enable him to provide a suitable house for his needs. £10,000 could not be considered an excessive sum for that purpose. It will not, of course, provide him with so fine a house as Rudford House, and on the other hand the wife's financial position will be somewhat worsened inasmuch as her capital will be reduced by £10,000. But it is hardly ever practicable to avoid some worsening of the financial position of one or both parties to a marriage when the marriage is dissolved. I do not think that the object of section 25 in this case could have been better implemented than by the award the judge made and I therefore agree that the appeal should be dismissed.

Questions

(i) In this case, Scarman LJ said that the husband 'is not to be regarded as a layabout or as someone who has hung up his hat in the wife's house and made a decision there to live.' Should it have made a difference if the husband had been such a man?

(ii) Why did not the judge or the Court of Appeal even consider the one-third formula in this case?

5 Conduct

You will recall that Lord Denning MR, in *Wachtel v Wachtel* [1973] Fam 72, [1973] 1 All ER 829, p. 198, above, used the phrase 'obvious and gross' when describing that conduct which would justify the court in departing from the statutory objective in s. 25(1). Other judges have hardly improved upon this definition, although they have used slightly different language on occasions. For example, Sir George Baker P, in *W v W* [1976] Fam 107, [1975] 3 All ER 970, said that he would be entitled to take account of conduct in a case which would cause an ordinary mortal to throw up his hands and say 'surely that woman is not going to be given any money!'

The problem with a definition such as that is that 'ordinary mortals' *are* ordinary mortals, and might be tempted to throw up their hands in cases where the judges would consider that some financial provision was appropriate:

Harnett v Harnett
[1973] Fam 156, [1973] 2 All ER 593; [1973] 3 WLR 1, 117 Sol Jo 447, High Court, Family Division

Bagnall J deduced the following proposition from *Wachtel v Wachtel* [1973] Fam 72, [1973] 1 All ER 829:

It will not be just to have regard to conduct unless there is a very substantial disparity between the parties on that score. . . .

His lordship then described the final parting thus:

The final separation was sudden and tempestuous. For some eight months before June 1969, the wife (as she later admitted) had been having a ridiculous affair with a youth half her age to whom the parties had given occasional hospitality when he was a schoolboy and his parents were abroad, and who was then staying with them because his work was near. In the late evening of 27 June 1969, they were caught virtually in the act by the husband returning home unexpectedly early. He reacted understandably. He threw the boy out of the house and, after some violence, the wife also. She managed to return and stayed uneasily until 30 June 1969, when she left with the children and went to her parents. She never returned, and apart from the last five months of 1969, the children have been with her. Her association with the boy did not survive.

[However by] her answer in the suit the wife alleged cruelty including a number of incidents of physical violence as well as the incident (admitted by the husband) of 27 June 1969. . . .

In deciding the question of conduct I do not think it necessary to make findings on the specific allegations made by the wife. I think that before 1969 the marriage was foundering, and, if any serious crisis occurred, liable to break. This was due partly to misfortune in the husband's illness, mainly to the temperaments of the parties, partly even to the passage of time [the parties had been married for fifteen years]. The husband conceded that he was in part responsible for the breakdown. The wife clearly behaved foolishly and reprehensibly; I think that the need she sought to satisfy was solely physical, with no intention of destroying the marriage; she simply thought — if she thought at all — that she would not be found out. This behaviour was, in my view, susceptible of forgiveness by a reasonable and loving husband, who thought his marriage worth preserving and who wanted to maintain the unity of his family. . . . I am satisfied that the conduct of the wife fell far short of being gross and obvious, certainly in comparison with that of the husband, and probably also absolutely.

Questions

(i) What do you think that an 'ordinary mortal' would have thought of the wife's conduct in this case?

(ii) Is this, like *Wachtel* itself, another illustration of Vaisey J's favourite dictum that 'it takes three to commit adultery'?

Under the previous law, in which the court was deciding how much of the husband's income should be used to support his ex-wife, the tendency was, as Ormrod J observed in *Wachtel v Wachtel* [1973] Fam 72, [1973] 1 All ER 113 at first instance, to assume that 'financial provision for the wife should be discounted in proportion to her share of responsibility for the breakdown.' Thus she might only expect 100% provision for her maintenance if she had been 100% blameless; a finding that she was as much as one-quarter to blame for the breakdown might reduce her maintenance to 75% of what it would otherwise have been. However, as Ormrod J went on to remark, there was no statutory authority for this view of conduct in the Matrimonial Causes Act, and 'the analogy with contributory negligence is attractive but misleading.' As Lord Denning MR explained in the Court of Appeal (p. 198, above), once we accept the logic of equal participation in the enterprise of marriage, equal responsibility for the breakdown of the partnership should result in a roughly equal division of its accumulated assets.

Question

But does this reasoning apply where there are no assets to divide and periodical payments are the only issue?

As Ormrod J also observed in *Wachtel v Wachtel* [1973] Fam 72, [1973] 1 All ER 113, there is no reason to suppose that conduct which is relevant under s. 25(1) must be directly related to the breakdown of the marriage. For example, in *Jones v Jones* [1976] Fam 8, [1975] 2 All ER 12, the husband had made a violent attack upon his wife after the breakdown of their marriage, and this had reduced her capacity to earn her own living. As Orr LJ remarked:

> It was argued that conduct is to be considered as relevant only for the purpose of cutting down a claim by a wife to a share of matrimonial property and cannot be applied so as to increase it. I for myself cannot accept the validity of this contention. As was pointed out in argument, the question in cases of this kind involves conflicting claims to matrimonial property, and an increase of one involves inevitably a decrease of the other. Moreover, in my judgment, this was a case in which the conduct of the husband had been of such a gross kind that it would be offensive to a sense of justice that it would not be taken into account.

J (HD) v J (AM)
[1980] 1 All ER 156, [1980] 1 WLR 124, 10 Fam Law 82 High Court, Family Division

The husband and wife were divorced in 1969 and the husband ordered to make periodical payments to the wife. He remarried in 1972. Thereafter the ex-wife, partly because of psychiatric illness but also with the intention of harrassing the couple, 'conducted a sustained campaign of malice and persecution against them, subjecting them to a stream of letters and telephone calls, some of which were violently abusive. On one occasion she assaulted the ex-husband's second wife. On numerous occasions she was in breach of an injunction restraining her from molesting the couple. Her conduct also exacerbated a psychiatric illness from which the husband suffered. Eventually, the husband applied to have the periodical payments reduced to a nominal order because of her conduct. The wife cross-applied for an increase, arguing that conduct after the dissolution of the marriage, or after her right to periodical payments had been established, could not be taken into account.

Sheldon J: . . . I also reject counsel's second submission for the petitioner that, on an application to vary an order for periodical payments, the court cannot take into account a party's conduct after the dissolution of the marriage. In my judgment, indeed, not only is *Jones v Jones* [1976] Fam 8, [1975] 2 All ER 12, clear authority to the contrary, but to accede to such a proposition would be to ignore the provisions of section 31(7)[2] of the 1973 Act and to act contrary to plain justice and common sense. . . .

Clearly, in this context, any conduct which might be relevant to the extent that it effectively reduced the other party's means, income or ability to earn his living, where, to adopt the words of Sir George Baker P in *W v W* [1976] Fam 107, [1975] 3 All ER 970, 'it directly affects the [other party's] finances.' In that case, however, the learned President was concerned to exclude from consideration behaviour on the part of the wife which, after the dissolution of the marriage, was of 'no concern to her ex-husband.' . . .

In my judgment, indeed, any conduct by a party may be relevant in the present context which, whether or not it directly affects the other's finances, is such as to interfere with his or her life and standard of living and which is covered by the well-known passage in the judgment of Lord Denning MR in *Wachtel v Wachtel* [1973] Fam 72, [1973] 1 All ER 829, that is conduct which is 'both obvious and gross,' so much so that to order one party to support another whose conduct falls into this category is repugnant to anyone's sense of justice.

In the event, the judge decided to leave the order as it had been since 1972, but warned the ex-wife:

---

2. Section 31(7) of the Matrimonial Causes Act (1973) states that in exercising its powers to vary an order for financial relief 'the court shall have regard to all the circumstances of the case including any change in any of the matters to which the court was required to have regard when making the order to which the application relates'.

I would add also this by way of warning to the petitioner — that, in my opinion, if she were to persist in her harassment of the husband or his present family, the stage might well be reached at which a court would say that it would be repugnant to anyone's sense of justice that the husband should continue to maintain her at all.

Questions

(i) Suppose that a divorced wife who is in receipt of periodical payments from her ex-husband has an affair with another man: is that what Baker P meant by 'conduct which is of no concern to her ex-husband'?

(ii) If the answer to question (i) is 'yes,' suppose further that she becomes pregnant as a result of the affair and is obliged to give up her part-time job: how would you put her ex-husband's case in reply to her application for an increase in her periodical payments?

(iii) Suppose that the behaviour of the ex-wife in *J (HD) v J (AM)* had been entirely due to her psychiatric disorder: would this have made it any less 'obvious and gross' within the meaning attached to that concept by Sheldon J?

6 Remarriages

A particular aspect of the problems facing judges which has attracted considerable public controversy is the question of balancing the obligations of a husband who has remarried against his obligations to his former wife. In some cases, this question is seen as an aspect of conduct.

Blezard v Blezard
(1978) 9 Fam Law 249, Court of Appeal

Lawton LJ: This is a case, all too familiar, in which a man in his late 40s, who had been married for 25 years to a wife aged 51, left her with two children to look after for a younger woman in her mid-30s. It was his decision to leave and to set up home with and marry the younger woman. Through his counsel he submitted that, when a balance sheet was drawn up of the assets and liabilities of himself and his first wife and she was found to have more assets and less liabilities than he had, an adjustment should be made to enable him and his new wife to have a more comfortable and secure future. . . .

The idea has . . . got around amongst some lawyers, but not perhaps amongst right-thinking members of the public, that nowadays leaving one's spouse to set up home with another was a mere accident of life, which should be borne by the wife without fuss and which should not be taken into account when the court exercised its jurisdiction to rearrange the finances of the broken family . . . that was not the law. Such conduct may be of the greatest importance when the court came to make a property disposition order under s. 24 of the Matrimonial Causes Act 1973. His Lordship said 'may be' because each case must depend upon its own facts. When, as in this case, the husband's conduct had brought about his first wife's present situation and he had not alleged that she was responsible in any way for the breakdown of the marriage, his Lordship could see no reason why her living standards should be reduced to the same level as his. He decided to take another wife and the woman he married must have known that he had been married before and had left his first wife to marry her. The husband made the new conjugal bed and he should not be allowed now to say that it was uncomfortable to lie in. When this kind of situation arose in cases where the husband could not support two women, both may have to suffer, because any other result would be impracticable within the meaning of s. 25(1) of the 1973 Act. That was not this case. The first wife and the two children could be supported in something approaching the old standard of living. For these reasons, it seemed . . . that conduct was a material factor.

The other judge in *Blezard v Blezard*, Orr LJ, did not express himself in these terms. The question for him was whether the former matrimonial home, where the former wife was living with the daughter, should be sold in order to enable the husband to realise his only real asset. The younger girl was still 14 and the judge thought that her interests should be considered. He therefore ordered that the house should not be sold until the younger child had attained the age of 18.

Question

Do you approve of the views expressed by Lawton LJ in this case?

7 Shares versus needs?

H v H (Family Provision: Remarriage)
[1975] Fam 9, [1975] 1 All ER 367, [1975] 2 WLR 124, 118 Sol Jo 579, 5 Fam Law 17, High Court, Family Division

In this case both parties had remarried. The main question for decision was the effect of the wife's remarriage to a man of means, with a new home in their joint names, upon her claim for the former matrimonial home to be settled on her ex-husband and herself in equal shares, but in trust until the youngest child reached 18 or alternatively for a lump sum of £17,000. The children of the marriage, two girls and two boys, lived with the father in the former home.

Sir George Baker P: The wife does not suggest that she has any property rights in the sense of a legal interest, or a beneficial interest arising from a joint tenancy, under section 17 of the Married Women's Property Act 1882 or by virtue of improvements under section 37 of the Matrimonial Proceedings and Property Act 1970. Her case is that she has contributed to the welfare of the family, including looking after the home and caring for the family: see section 25(1)(*f*) of the Matrimonial Causes Act 1973; that in the 15 years of marriage she bore the four children, was a wife and mother, and in the early days washed, ironed, cooked for and looked after a paying guest; that with the husband she decorated a flat they had early in the marriage and part of a house they had in 1963; that she cleaned the stairs and bathroom of a tenanted house the husband owns; and that she gardened and supervised decoration and workmen. Under the new law such contributions can and must be adequately recognised on the division of the family assets, either as a moral claim, or as an accrued right, a beneficial interest, already in existence at the end of the marriage earned by her contribution: see per Lord Denning MR in *Wachtel v Wachtel* [1973] Fam 72 at 94.

Mr Jackson, for the wife, rightly points out that continuing financial provision orders (see section 28 of the Matrimonial Causes Act 1973) end on remarriage, but that a property adjustment order can be made after remarriage. The sole prohibition, contained in section 28(3) of the Matrimonial Causes Act 1973, is that a party to a remarriage shall not be entitled to apply for a financial provision order, and the courts have consistently held that that means 'make a new application.' An application which has already been made can be pursued: see *Jackson v Jackson* [1973] Fam 99, [1973] 2 All ER 395; *Marsden (JL) v Marsden (AM)* [1973] 2 All ER 851, [1973] 1 WLR 641 and *B v B* (1974) Times, 9 April, a decision of Latey J. This must, he submits, be because a proprietary right has already accrued as a result of the wife's contribution under section 25(1)(*f*) of the Act of 1973. She has earned that right and remarriage only affects that right by making it unenforceable if a claim, that is an application for its recognition, has not already been made. If such a claim has been made it would be imposing a penalty on the wife to hold, in the absence of a statutory provision, that her right ends with remarriage.

Mr Holroyd Pearce, for the husband, submits that this is a misconceived claim and that the wife has no entitlement in law or justice to such a claim because of, first, her remarriage to the second respondent and, secondly, an agreement made on 4 January 1973. I can dispose briefly of the agreement. . . .

The wife was concerned primarily about the children and I accept that she did not intend to give up any claim she might have in the house. The husband may have thought he was securing the house for the children but there is clearly no estoppel. In any event the agreement was reached before judgment was delivered in *Wachtel v Wachtel* [1973] Fam 72, [1973] 1 All ER 829 on 8 February 1973, and I doubt if legal advice at that time would have been able to accurately forecast the possibilities, I therefore disregard the agreement.

After referring to a few old decisions, and quoting from the judgment of Lord Denning MR in *Wachtel v Wachtel* (see p. 196, above), the judge said:

Lord Denning MR was careful to deal with the prospects, the likelihood, of remarriage. He said nothing of the fact of remarriage in relation to capital assets. It is said that the passage is obiter and its guidance is not binding upon me, but in a reserved judgment given in chambers on 27 March 1972, allowing an appeal by a wife against a lump sum award of £350,000 I had myself said:

> 'It would be strange, indeed repugnant, if, in the face of section 4 of the Law Reform (Miscellaneous Provisions) Act 1971, which prohibits the court from taking into account a widow's remarriage or prospects of remarriage in assessing damages in respect of the death of her husband, this court had to embark on an inquiry into this lady's prospects of remarriage before deciding upon the lump sum.'

In *Trippas v Trippas* [1973] Fam 134, [1973] 2 All ER 1 the wife was living with another man whom she might marry, but that did not affect her entitlement. The prospect, chance or hope of remarriage is, I think, irrelevant, but the fact of remarriage, which does not admit of speculation, is in my judgment, something which the court must consider in the course of carrying out its statutory duty under section 25 of the Act of 1973 'to have regard to all the circumstances of the case.' This accords with Bagnall J's view in *Jackson v Jackson* [1973] Fam 99 at 104, that the wife's intervening marriage is a factor to be weighed with all the others in a particular case, and with at least part of Latey J's conclusion in *S v S* (1973) Times, 11 December, reached after reviewing *Mesher v Mesher (1973)* [1980] 1 All ER 126. . . . *Hector v Hector* [1973] 3 All ER 1070, [1973] 1 WLR 1122 and *Chamberlain v Chamberlain* [1974] 1 All ER 33, [1973] 1 WLR 1557 that

> '. . . the following emerges as guidance . . . If the wife had remarried or was going to remarry her financial position on remarriage had to be considered. If it was guesswork whether she would or would not remarry, prospective remarriage should be ignored.'

To ignore remarriage entirely would be to ignore the financial needs of the parties in the foreseeable future: see section 25(1)(b) of the Matrimonial Causes Act 1973.

It seems to me that the real problem in any particular case is to decide how to translate a new marriage into money. How it is to be regarded and what part is it to play in the financial provision? Mr Jackson argues that a wife who remarries a poor man should get no more, and therefore a wife who remarries a rich man gets no less. I do not accept that submission. Remarriage to a poor man would reflect in her financial resources and financial needs, and would probably result in her receiving the full share of what she had earned. Equally, marriage to a wealthy man has a bearing on her financial needs and resources just as her own capital would be taken into account, for as Bagnall J said in *Harnett v Harnett* [1973] Fam 156, 164: 'Where the wife has some capital, that must be taken into account in determining what she should be given by the husband.' The Matrimonial Causes Act 1973, section 25(1), gives the court the widest possible power to achieve the statutory object, namely 'to place the parties, so far as it is practicable and, . . . just to do so, in the financial position in which they would have been if the marriage had not broken down . . .'

First, in my opinion, justice must be done in all cases not only in those in which conduct is relevant. That is a matter of construction. Then, it is not the wife alone who is to be placed in the same position but 'the parties.' Too often the husband's position tends now to be disregarded. In the present case I find that the husband, having remarried a lady of 29 with no income or assets and having to bring up and educate four young children, is near enough in the same financial position as he would have been if the marriage had not broken down.

I now turn to consider what that position is. The husband has a salary of £20,000 per annum and about £500 per annum from rents and dividends. The matrimonial home was bought by him in 1968 for £25,000 as the perfect home for the children. . . . The value has been taken for the purposes of this case as £65,000. The husband has two accounts with his bank one of which is designated 'House Purchase Account.' It is overdrawn to the limit of £20,000. Of this, £9,718 arose from house improvements and £6,516 from accumulated overdraft interest, of which, it is submitted for the wife, only a half should be charged against the house. His other account was overdrawn £20,358 in August 1973 (limit £20,000). Both accounts are secured by the title deeds of the matrimonial home. Only a part of the overdraft interest will in future be allowable against tax. The household effects are valued at £4,505 but half of this sum has already been paid to the wife.

The Judge then considered various other aspects of the husband's resources, and continued:

To summarise the husband's capital position, he can be treated broadly as having £35,000–£40,000.

Turning next to the second respondent [the second husband] he has an income of about £14,000 per annum gross which, after tax, will not be very greatly less than that of the husband. I do not think that it is necessary or desirable for me to go into his capital position in detail.

Suffice it to say that I have studied his lengthy affidavit in his own matrimonial proceedings and have regard to his oral evidence before me which I accept. I find that, as he said, he has capital, after allowing for capital gains tax, of approximately £50,000. There are some uncertainties. Mr Jackson and the wife were prepared to accept that the second respondent's capital position is roughly the same as the husband's. I find he is the better off; on any view his capital position is no worse.

Now the wife: the house where she lives with the second respondent was bought in January 1973 for a total of £65,000, of which £35,000 was for adjoining plots which, the second respondent hopes, are to be sold at a profit. The house and garden, which was put into their joint names, is therefore worth £30,000 plus £4,000 spent on it by the second respondent. The equity is probably about £14,000 although there is no very clear evidence. The wife is also a beneficiary under her grandfather's will subject to life interests. Her interest is valued at the present day at £2,250.

. . . She can fairly, I think, be treated as having notional capital of £7,000–£9,000.

In these circumstances, and with due regard to them all, I think, first, that it is unjust and impracticable to make the husband pay a lump sum. He cannot raise more money on the house, he has to pay for the four children and he has little other capital.

The wife needs no flat or house and I think most people would find it distasteful and unjust that a lump sum should be given to a wife for the probable benefit of the new family.

The Judge then made the following comment about the wife's claim:

But, the wife says, she has earned a share in the house and will accommodate her first family by allowing it to remain with them till the youngest is 18. She says that that share should be one-third of the house. If the concept of earning is to be applied to a domestic situation, then it should be applied with all its normal consequences. One is that if the job is left unfinished you do not earn as much. A builder agrees to build four houses. He goes off to a job which he prefers to do, leaving them in varying stages of completion. Leaving aside any question of special contractual terms, the best he could hope to receive is the value of work actually done, remembering also that the owner has to have the work completed. Is there any difference between four houses and four children? I think not. Any payment will in fact put her in a better financial position than if the marriage had continued and I would give her one-twelfth of the unencumbered value of the house (at present £65,000), her entitlement thereto to rank after the present charges for the bank overdrafts and not to be payable until the youngest child is 18.

Questions

(i) Is the comment about an 'unfinished' job a disguised way of making 'conduct' relevant?

(ii) In this case, the husband needed the house for the children, whereas the wife did not need the house for that purpose. Do you think that this fact affected the decision?

The parties in the above case were well-off by any standards. Most situations facing the courts, however, involve assets which are very limited indeed. In those circumstances, the court's obligation under the present law may well be in conflict with the desire to ensure that orders are not such as to produce intolerable burdens on the husband and his new wife (or possibly his new cohabitee). This must especially be the case if the wife has remarried. There is of course an underlying problem of the State's involvement in family support to which we turn in Chapter 16, below.

8 Housing

It will have been apparent from the earlier cases that the major matter which requires resolution on divorce is the reallocation of rights in the matrimonial home. There are a number of options available to the court. First, the court may decide to allow the husband to retain an interest in the matrimonial home even though the former wife remains in the home with the children. It is often considered appropriate for the sale of the home to be postponed until the youngest child has completed his or her education:

Mesher v Mesher and Hall
(1973) [1980] 1 All ER 126, Court of Appeal

The marriage took place in 1956 and the one child of the marriage (aged 9) lived with the mother. The house was in joint names. The judge ordered that the house be transferred to the wife, and the husband appealed.

Davies LJ: . . . Counsel for the husband submits that it would be quite wrong to deprive the husband of the substantial asset which his half-interest in the house represents . . ., one has to take a broad approach to the whole case. What is wanted here is to see that the wife and daughter, together no doubt in the near future with Mr Jones, [whom the wife intended to marry] should have a home in which to live rather than that she should have a large sum of available capital. With that end in view, I have come to the conclusion that counsel's submission for the husband is right. It would, in my judgment, be wrong to strip the husband entirely of any interest in the house. I would set aside the judge's order so far as concerns the house and substitute instead an order that the house is held by the parties in equal shares on trust for sale but that it is not to be sold until the child of the marriage reaches a specified age or with the leave of the court.

Harvey v Harvey
[1982] Fam 83, [1982] 1 All ER 693, [1982] 2 WLR 283, 126 Sol Jo 15, Court of Appeal

The parties were married in 1960. They had six children. The marriage broke down in 1979 and it was dissolved in May 1981. The judge made an order in the form used in *Mesher v Mesher*, namely that the home should be held in joint names of husband and wife on trust for sale in equal shares and that the sale of the property should be postponed until the youngest child attained 16 or completed her full-time education, whichever was later, when the wife should be at liberty to purchase the husband's share in the property at a valuation then made. The wife appealed.

Purchas J: . . . I am of the opinion that the wife is entitled to live in this house as long as she chooses so to do, . . . I do that on the basis that was adopted in *Martin v Martin* [1978] Fam 12, [1977] 3 All ER 762, that, had the marriage not broken down, that is precisely what she would have been entitled to do.
   I would vary the judge's order, first of all to say that the asset (the matrimonial home) be transferred into the joint names of the wife and the husband on trust for sale in the shares two-thirds to the wife and one-third to the husband; and further that such sale shall be postponed during the lifetime of the wife, or her remarriage, or voluntary removal from the premises, or her becoming dependent on another man. I have in mind that if she begins to cohabit with another man in the premises, then obviously that man ought to take over the responsibility of providing accommodation for her. Until one or other of those events occur, she should be entitled to continue to reside at these premises, but after the mortgage has been paid off, or the youngest child has reached the aged of 18, whichever is the latter, she should pay an occupation rent to be assessed by the registrar.

Ormrod LJ: I agree. This is another case which illustrates very aptly the proposition which has been stated many times in this court, that the effect of making a *Mesher v Mesher* order is simply to postpone the evil day to avoid facing the facts now.

Question

Are you attracted by this solution? In *Carson v Carson* [1983] 1 All ER 478, [1983] 1 WLR 285, Ormrod LJ said that the facts of that case, where the judge had made the type of order in *Mesher v Mesher*, where 'a very good example of the chickens coming home to roost.' What exactly does he mean?

In contrast, the court may decide not to postpone but rather to vest the title of the house in the name of the wife absolutely. In many of these cases the husband may be ordered to continue to pay the mortgage. Occasionally, the wife will be ordered to pay a lump sum to the husband; in effect to buy him out. The deciding factor in determining whether to postpone sale or to transfer ownership is often whether the court considers that the husband cannot or will not pay periodical payments. However, the court is bound to think hard before it deprives the husband of the only real capital asset he has.

Hanlon v Hanlon
[1978] 2 All ER 889, [1978] 1 WLR 592, 122 Sol Jo 62, Court of Appeal

The husband and wife married in 1957. They had two sons, both over 18, and two daughters, aged 14 and 12. The matrimonial home was in the sole name of the husband. During the 14 years of the marriage, the parties contributed equally in money and work to the family. The marriage was dissolved in 1974. The history of the litigation on ancillary orders appears in the judgment of Ormrod LJ:

The matter first came before the learned registrar in February 1976. That was a period when *Mesher v Mesher (1973)* [1980] 1 All ER 126 was being regarded as the 'bible' as far as this type of case is concerned. The consequence, as counsel for the wife has told us in the course of his submission, was that the wife's legal advisers took the view that the best she could hope for, on the facts of the case, was a *Mesher v Mesher* type of order, namely that she should remain in occupation of the matrimonial home until the youngest of the children was 17, or 18 as the case may be, whereupon it would be sold and the proceeds divided equally between herself and her husband. At the time when they were before the learned registrar both sides recognised that that type of order produced a number of unfortunate and undesirable results, with which I shall deal in more detail later.

In the result, the learned registrar decided that the best way of dealing with the matter in the interests of both parties was, in effect, to order an immediate sale of the property, but recognising that this would have the effect of destroying the family home for the wife and her four children, he suggested, and eventually ordered, that the wife should buy the husband out, buying him out on the footing that their beneficial interests in the house were equal; that meant in practice that the wife had to raise £5,000 to buy out the husband's interest. This suggestion apparently was put forward at a comparatively late stage, and the wife's advisers had not had an opportunity of going into it in detail particularly as to whether the wife could finance such an arrangement.

After the registrar's order, investigations were made and it became at once apparent, as everyone agrees now, that she could not possibly finance it. The reasons for that were, and it was even more obvious then than it might have been today, that in order to raise the further £5,000 she would have to pay off the existing mortgage of £3,600, making a total of something over £8,000 that she would have to raise on terms which, of course, were more onerous relatively, pound for pound, than the old mortgage; and also she had to carry out repairs.

So the wife applied for leave to appeal against the order out of time. Faulks J rejected her application and refused her leave; she came to this court; this court gave her leave of appeal and the matter went back to Rees J and hence back again to this court.

Ormrod LJ described the decision of Rees J in this way:

In the end, and I think it is not unfair to say almost in despair of solving the problem, the learned judge reverted to what he called 'the normal order'. By 'the normal order' he meant a *Mesher v Mesher* type of order, that is to say, the sale of the house to be postponed until the youngest child reached the age of 17 and the proceeds of sale divided equally. He had the case of *Martin v Martin* [1978] Fam 12, [1977] 3 All ER 762 in this court, and the judgment of Purchas J, cited to him, and no doubt he took account of it. There have been other cases in this court in which the court has drawn attention to the fact that *Mesher v Mesher* was not, in any sense of the word, a typical case. So the judge, in despair, made the *Mesher v Mesher* type of order.

It is as well to look and see what the results would be. The youngest child is 12, so we are talking about a postponement of sale for five years. In five years' time each of these parties will, we assume, receive £5,000 plus such inflationary increase as takes place in those five years. The Law Society, under the present regime which was not in force at the time of the registrar's order, will have a charge on each of those sums of £5,000 for the costs incurred by the respective parties. It is common ground, having regard to the scale of costs in this case, that inevitably neither of them can possibly in fact receive a sum in excess of the maximum fixed by the regulations, namely £2,500. That is the amount which is at present exempt from the Law Society's charge.

So the result of the learned judge's order is that in five years' time each of them will get £2,500, increased by whatever the inflationary increase is by then. (One hopes that, if inflation is severe, sooner rather than later the exemption figure will be raised.) But dealing with it in 1977 prices, they will each get £2,500 only.

It is common ground that that figure is inadequate to provide either of them with a home. Obviously the wife cannot provide a home for herself on that sum, let alone for any children who are still at home in five years' time. It is said that the husband equally, on his income, cannot possibly raise enough money to buy himself a flat if he is minded to. So the effect of the order will be, in the short term, to make the wife and such of the children who are still with her, homeless in five years' time, that is in 1982, while the husband, assuming that he is still in the police force, will have a perfectly safe house or flat, until he chooses to leave the force or has to leave the force. That is a situation which one cannot contemplate as being satisfactory in any sense of the word at all, and so we have to look at the matter again.

In looking at the matter again there is one other factor to be brought into account; that is that when these parties reach their retiring ages they will each receive a lump sum. There is a very considerable disparity between the lump sums that each will get. The husband can retire at any time between 1980 and 1985. At the earliest retirement he will get a lump sum of just over £4,000 at present rates; if he stays on until 1985 he will receive a lump sum of just under £7,000. The wife, on the contrary, cannot retire until 1988 when she will get a lump sum of just £3,000, which she can increase by another five years' work by the not very substantial sum of £600, giving her £3,600. So the husband, on retirement, will quite obviously be substantially better off than the wife.

I think it is right to say once again that the *Mesher v Mesher* type of order is not, in a great many cases, a satisfactory way of solving these cases. The facts in *Mesher v Mesher* were very different; in that case both parties had in fact remarried before the case came before the court, and the primary concern in the case was to preserve the home for the children.

In my judgment it is as well in this case to have another look at the history. Up to now everybody has been approaching the case on the footing that the interests of these two parties in this property were equal. That seems to me to be a doubtfully accurate assumption, or premise. Putting them as shortly as I can, the facts are these. Over 14 years of cohabitation these two parties no doubt contributed broadly equally to this family in terms of money, in terms of work and so on. From 1971 onwards, this is now for over five years, the wife has had the upbringing of these four children and has been working full-time as a community nurse. She has maintained the house as well as she could during those years, and on any view she has taken a considerable load off the shoulders of the husband over a period of five years, and she will continue to take a large load off his shoulders from now until the youngest child leaves home, which of course will not necessarily by any manner of means be in five years' time. A family like this will not simply dissolve completely on the 17th birthday of the youngest child. In fact, of course, she will be, as the mother of this family, maintaining the nucleus of the home effectively for a considerable number of years until the girls are married and settled on their own, and the boys are similarly married and settled on their own; that is what it really means in real life. So in my view she has made a very large contribution to this family. She has much less good prospects than the husband's so far as her future is concerned, because he will be able to retire when he is 58 and, like many police officers, will be able to take other employment, certainly for another seven years or maybe longer if he wishes. He is a completely free agent so far as his life is concerned; he is living to all intents and purposes a bachelor existence, at the moment contributing £7 per week, under the judge's order, for each of these two children. As I have said before, on any view £7 a week for girls, one of 14 and one of 12, is manifestly inadequate to cover the cost of feeding and clothing and all the other expenses which are unavoidable.

So the view I take of the case is that, as the cards have fallen, apart no doubt from his being unhappy at being on his own, in financial terms he has done a lot better than his wife, and is likely to go on doing a lot better than his wife.

We have to do the best we can to carry out the injunctions which Parliament has put on us by s. 25 of the Matrimonial Causes Act 1973. We have to take into account, and I shall for once recite some of them, income, earning capacity, and other financial resources which the parties to the marriage have, or are likely to have, in the foreseeable future. Correspondingly we have to take into account their financial needs, obligations and responsibilities, both now and in the future. We have to take account of the standard of living, age and physical and mental disability; none of those three very much matters. Then we have to take into account the contributions made by each of the parties to the welfare of the family, including any contribution made by looking after the home, or caring for the family; and at the end so to exercise those powers as to place the parties, so far as is practicable and, having regard to their conduct, just to do so, in the financial position in which they would have been if the marriage had not broken down and each had properly discharged his or her financial obligations or responsibilities to the other. 'Equality' is not to be found in that section, and for the reasons I have tried to outline briefly in this judgment, it is a very elusive concept.

The only other comment I would make about the background is that so far from this being contrary to anything that was said by this court in *Wachtel v Wachtel* the court, as appears clearly from the judgment of Lord Denning MR, contemplated that in a situation like this one of the ways of solving the problem would be to transfer the home to the wife and to relieve the husband, so far as it was possible or reasonable to do so, of the responsibility for making periodical payments. Of course, the court was not laying it down as law, or as a rule of practice or anything of the kind; it was set out there as one of the possible solutions, and one of the possible ways of meeting the requirements of s. 25 in this type of case, and in my judgment it is very much more likely to produce in many cases a fair and just result than the *Mesher v Mesher* type of order which, . . . was never intended to meet the kind of situation that we are now dealing with.

In those circumstances, the case for transferring this property to the wife, together with all the liabilities for its upkeep and for the mortgage, seems to me to be extremely strong.

Ormrod LJ reduced the order for periodical payments to a nominal sum.

In his judgment, Ormrod LJ referred to the problem of the Law Society charge. The comments were prophetic:

Hanlon v The Law Society
[1981] AC 124, [1980] 2 All ER 199, [1980] 2 WLR 756, 124 Sol Jo 360,
House of Lords

Mrs Hanlon wished to sell the house which had been transferred to her. It was worth £14,000 and was subject to a £4,000 mortgage. It was in need of repair and she wished to buy a smaller and no doubt more convenient house.

On the question whether the Law Society held a charge on the whole house pursuant to the legal aid regulations, the House of Lords held that this was indeed the case.

Lord Lowry: In the result I concur in dismissing the appeal and also join with your Lordships in expressing the hope that The Law Society will exercise the discretion which we all believe it has in relation to the charge on the appellant's home.

But the appeal has thrown into relief a problem which may be thought more difficult of solution than any of the questions which your Lordships have been called upon to answer. The object of legal aid is to provide the means of achieving justice through the courts which would otherwise be denied to persons of limited means. Yet the appellant, who has twice appealed successfully and who has ultimately been awarded the sole ownership of the matrimonial home, now emerges from litigation so costly, I might even say so ruinous, that if The Law Society decides, as it is quite entitled to do, to enforce its statutory charge, she will no longer have a house for herself and her children to live in.

Suggestions will, no doubt, be more appropriate on a legislative rather than a judicial occasion, but I might venture to put forward one idea. I do not, with respect, believe that the solution lies in making contributions on the instalment plan or in merely raising the threshold of liability to charge. Nor is it either reasonable or effective to try to frighten the parties into settling. Irresponsible advisers would not be deterred by a sanction directed only against their client and even highly responsible advisers (as in these proceedings) may advise an appeal (or more than one) in the hope (which may not be realised) of improving the lot of their client.

I am attracted by the Royal Commission's recommendation that the matrimonial home should once again be freed from any charge (Royal Commission on Legal Services, Final Report (1979) (Cmnd. 7648), vol. I, para. 13.64, p. 149). If this is done, I suggest that reform should be radical. For example, the registrar could be treated as an arbitrator whose decision on a section 23 and 24 application would be final subject to a case stated on a point of law. To give this method a chance of working the registrar would have to discuss his proposals with the parties before making up his order.

Questions

(i) Do you agree with Lord Lowry that the matrimonial home should be freed from the Law Society charge?
(ii) Do you think that the present system of the Law Society charge places a fetter on the discretion of the judges in legally aided cases?
(iii) What are the arguments for and against Lord Lowry's 'radical' solution of an arbitrator whose decision on ss. 23 and 24 applications should be final?
(iv) Are the arguments for his solution equally appropriate in the case of two non-legally aided litigants?
(v) Can you think of *any* way so to re-allocate the matrimonial home as to avoid the pitfalls of the *Hanlon v Hanlon* litigation?

We now consider the question of tenancies. Whereas orders of the court regulating the occupation of the home can be made under s. 1(3) of the Matrimonial Homes Act 1967 only during the marriage, there is jurisdiction to order the transfer of a tenancy from one spouse to the other in a case where the marriage is terminated by divorce or a decree of nullity (Matrimonial Homes Act 1967, s. 7). Prior to the Housing Act 1980, the jurisdiction under this provision was limited to protected or statutory tenancies under the Rent Act 1957, and even here such transfers could only be made between decree nisi and decree absolute. Council tenancies were excluded. However, s. 7 powers have now been extended to council tenancies (Matrimonial Homes and Property Act 1981). The court has the power to order the transfer, on granting a decree of divorce, nullity or judicial separation, or with leave of the court, at any time thereafter. The landlord's consent is not required, but it does have a right to be heard before an order is made.

Questions

(i) Do you think that this provision is an unnecessary interference in the powers and responsibilities of local authorities to determine housing priorities in their area?
(ii) Under s. 24(1)(*a*) of the Matrimonial Causes Act 1973, the court has a general power to order that one spouse shall transfer to the other, or to or for the benefit of a child of the family, 'such property as may be so specified.' Transfer of property orders may be made with respect to council tenancies. Can you think of any reason why an applicant should seek a transfer of property order under s. 24(1)(*a*) of the Matrimonial Causes Act 1973 rather than an order under s. 7 of the Matrimonial Homes Act 1967 with respect to a council tenancy?
(iii) Could *one* answer to question (ii) be that under s. 24(1)(*a*), the landlord has no express right to be heard?

In *Regan v Regan* [1977] 1 All ER 428, [1977] 1 WLR 84, Sir George Baker P decided that although the court has power under s. 24(1) to make a transfer of property order in respect of a council tenancy, the court should not do so if the order would not meet with favour by the local authority. Baker P said 'Housing is a matter for the local authority. It has always been so, and my own view is that it is unfortunate in many ways that the courts . . . may have to make orders . . . which put pressure on councils, or which may be rejected by councils.'

However, in a case under s. 1 of the Domestic Violence and Matrimonial Proceedings Act 1976 (see Chapter 14, below), *Spindlow v Spindlow* [1979] Ch 52, [1979] 1 All ER 169, where the parties were not married, Ormrod LJ said that the court has jurisdiction under that section to make an order the effect of which may be permanently to exclude one party from the house. In that case, the parties were joint tenants of a council house — but Ormrod LJ was not too concerned about local authority sensitivities. He said 'Parliament has . . . put onto the court the responsibility for making the decision, which was previously left with the housing authority.'

9 The developing philosophy of the clean break

Transferring title to the matrimonial home, rather than adopting the solution in *Mesher v Mesher*, fits into one trend which can be detected in recent court judgments, that is there should be a clean break. Likewise, lump sum awards as opposed to periodical payments fit into a similar emerging pattern. The doctrine of the clean break has emerged from the haze of the judicial involvement in this area as one major target which, within the framework of s. 25 of the Act, must be in the forefront of the judge's mind.

Minton v Minton
[1979] AC 593, [1979] 1 All ER 79, [1979] 2 WLR 31, 122 Sol Jo 843, House of Lords

In this case, the House of Lords collectively, and Lord Scarman in particular, stressed the requirement that the parties put the past behind them and begin a new life which is in no way overshadowed by a former relationship:

. . . There are two principles which inform the modern legislation. One is the public interest that spouses, to the extent that their means permit, should provide for themselves and their children. But the other — of equal importance — is the principle of 'the clean break.' The law now encourages spouses to avoid bitterness after family break-down and to settle their money and property problems. An object of the modern law is to encourage each to put the past behind them and to begin a new life which is not overshadowed by the relationship which has broken down. It would be inconsistent with this principle if the court could not make, as between the spouses, a genuinely final order unless it was prepared to dismiss the application. The present case is a good illustration. The court having made an order giving effect to a comprehensive settlement of all financial and property issues as between spouses, it would be a strange application of the principle of the clean break if, notwithstanding the order, the court could make a future order on a subsequent application made by the wife after the husband had complied with all his obligations.

Questions

(i) Is Lord Scarman being cruel to be kind?
(ii) Is the clean break approach consistent with the interests of the children?

The clean break and its limitations are discussed in *The Clean Break on Divorce* (1981) by Gillian Douglas:

It is proposed to examine the concept of the clean break in some detail, to decide whether this is a worthwhile development in the divorce law. First, the current law on the issue will be outlined, and it will be seen that there is some confusion as to whether a clean break can be imposed by the court without both parties' agreement. Secondly, divorce in its social context will be examined, and some cases will be highlighted which would seem to invite the clean break solution. Finally, some potential difficulties of the clean break will be explored.

After quoting from Lord Scarman's speech in *Minton v Minton*, Douglas continues:

Lord Scarman seems to have viewed the clean break in the context of the ancillary jurisdiction as meaning putting an end to the entanglement of the parties' financial affairs created by their marriage, so that they can each plan ahead for their separate futures, free of financial ties to each other. Such a definition inevitably seems to lead to the court deciding whether an order for periodical payments is to be made in favour of the wife, since this is the clearest example of a continuing financial tie. It is also the one that seems to cause the most controversy and bitterness, e.g. see the pressure group 'Campaign for Justice on Divorce'.

Yet the clean break may also be seen as a device for producing certainty in the parties' positions vis-à-vis each other, as in *Hanlon v Hanlon* [1978] 2 All ER 889, [1978] 1 WLR 592. There, the Court of Appeal varied a *Mesher* order[3] to one transferring the husband's interest in the matrimonial home to the wife, in return for reducing the order for periodical payments for the children to a nominal sum. Rather than postpone sale of the house indefinitely until further order, and then distribute the proceeds of sale in some proportion which 'would leave the wife in a state of perpetual uncertainty and neither party would know where ultimately they were going to be', Ormrod LJ, thought it 'far better that the parties' interests should be crystallized now, once and for all, so that the wife can know what she is going to do about the property and the husband can make up his mind about what he is going to do about rehousing.' This view has been echoed by Lord Denning in *Dunford v Dunford* [1980] 1 All ER 122, [1980] 1 WLR 5. However, it may be argued that the solution reached by the Court of Appeal in that case was not a clean break at all. The original *Mesher* order was varied to one transferring the husband's interest in the matrimonial home to the wife, but retaining a charge in his favour, enforceable when the house should be sold, and the order for periodical payments was struck out. There seems little difference between this type of order and the *Mesher* order, since the parties will still not receive their shares in the home, whether they be characterized as beneficial interest or charge, until some relatively undetermined date in the future. The essence then of the clean break as understood by the courts would seem to be that it means no continuing financial provision for the wife, and this indeed has been the point at issue in the cases.

It is important to note that Lord Scarman was talking of the parties' 'money and property problems'. Part of the confusion in the cases may stem from the apparent assumption that if the court orders a clean break, all further contact between the parties must and will cease, and that if this is not possible in the circumstances of the particular case, then the clean break is not an option. It will be argued that there is no reason why it should not be possible to achieve a clean break from dependence of the wife on the husband, even though there remain other links, such as their children, between them.

After discussing whether a clean break can be imposed by the courts without the parties' consent and arguing that this indeed should be possible she examines the three situations where a clean break would be desirable:

Low-income divorcees
Given the number of divorced women having to rely on supplementary benefits even though their ex-husbands are under a liability to help support them, it is suggested that it would be more sensible to refuse periodical payments where the parties are on low incomes, and to make a clean break instead. The judges have reiterated the principle that the husband should not get out of his obligation by throwing his wife onto the State, and this view has been propounded by Ormrod LJ, in a clean break case — *Moore v Moore* (1980) Times, 10 May. There, he said that a clean break was not applicable where the financial resources of the parties 'were insufficient', nor where one party was earning and the other could not earn (as here, where the wife had to look after the child of the marriage). The effect of a clean break in such cases, he thought, would mean people living on social security. He therefore ordered the husband to pay £10 per week to the wife and £8 per week for the child. But this means the wife will still have to resort to supplementary benefit. It may seem politically unrealistic to argue for State assumption of hitherto private liabilities, but it is submitted that the courts' attitude cannot be justified on either

---

3. See p. 220, above.

economic or social grounds. The figures show that the money recovered from liable relatives is a drop in the ocean as compared to that which is paid out in benefit. One must then add on the cost of collecting this money, and of the legal proceedings which determined the liability in the first place . . . periodical payments act merely as a reminder of former responsibilities, do little or nothing to relieve financial burdens, and are unnecessary sources of friction between the former spouses.

Short marriages

The short marriage with no children may seem even more suited to a clean break on divorce. The parties' financial affairs will be less interwoven, and it will *usually* be easier to restore the parties to their positions prior to the marriage (in contrast to the requirement of s. 25(1)) because they will not have altered their situations too drastically. Finally, there will be less attention paid to each party's contribution to the marriage, because less contribution will have been made. The matter then, should basically be one restoring the parties to their original positions. . . .

. . . It is unfortunately true that the average wage for women is well behind that for men, but unmarried women have to withstand this, and there is no reason why only divorced women should be compensated for inequality in society. Thus, where the wife is young and there are no children, [even] a rehabilitative period seems uncalled for.

Unreliable husbands

The courts do seem prepared to envisage a clean break where they doubt whether the husband will make regular periodical payments to his wife and children. In *Smith v Smith* [1970] 1 All ER 244, [1970] 1 WLR 155, Lord Denning MR transferred the husband's interest in the jointly owned home to the wife, whose husband had deserted her and now lived in New Zealand. His Lordship did this mainly as a recognition of the wife's efforts in keeping up the mortgage repayments since the husband had left, and bringing up their children, but he also stressed that it would be difficult for her to obtain any maintenance from the husband. He therefore ordered that no further applications from the wife for maintenance, secured provision or a lump sum be entertained; the wife agreeing to this course of action. In *Griffiths v Griffiths* [1974] 1 All ER 932, [1974] 1 WLR 1350, after a long and acrimonious divorce, the husband sought half the beneficial interest in the matrimonial home, saying that he needed this to set up a business in France. He was willing to make periodical payments to the wife secured on the capital. But Roskill LJ said that since the husband's earning position was doubtful (he had been unemployed for some time) and that it could prove awkward for the wife to enforce the payments in a French court, and 'having regard to the whole of the past unhappy history of this case it seems to me that the sooner there is a complete and final financial break between the parties the better for both and indeed for everybody else concerned' (p. 1360(*i*)). Again, the wife agreed. Recently, in *Doupis v Doupis* [1980] CA Transcript (80/136). Ormrod LJ transferred the matrimonial home to the wife, and relieved the husband of making any periodical payments for her or their child, because he might return to his home in Greece, or have to resort to supplementary benefit as he had done in the past. It is suggested that the use of the clean break could be extended to cover not just wives whose husbands are blatantly irresponsible or who have gone abroad, but those whose husbands have new commitments which suggest that they may prove to be erratic or resentful payers, because the court's main aim should be to safeguard the parties' positions in all circumstances.

Douglas concludes her article by considering the two situations where a clean break may *not* be desirable:

Children

Some Judges have expressed the view that the clean break is unsuitable where there are dependent children. In *Dipper v Dipper* [1981] Fam 31, [1980] 2 All ER 722 Roskill LJ pointed out that there was joint custody of the three children, and extensive access granted to the father, because the family was continuing to live under one roof, so that this was clearly not a clean break case. Similarly, in *Moore v Moore*, Ormrod LJ said that it was 'nonsense to talk about a clean break where there were young children. It could not apply as the parties had to co-operate because of the children'. It is unclear from the *Times* report of this case who had custody of the child of the marriage. Yet the clean break principle in the ancillary jurisdiction must be aimed at settling 'money and property problems', as Lord Scarman said in *Minton v Minton*, and it is surely possible to achieve a clean break from dependence of the wife on the husband in financial terms, even though other links, such as their children, remain. In any case, it is too sweeping to assume that there can *never* be a clean break if there are young children; indeed, in *Minton v Minton* there were four children in respect of whom the husband had to make periodical payments. It is to be hoped that the courts will not rigidly refuse to contemplate a clean break solution, simply because there are children involved, but will treat each case on its own facts in order to reach the best outcome, an approach advocated by Ormrod LJ in *Sharp v Sharp* (1981) 11 Fam Law 121.

The pressure to reach a settlement of some kind

It may be that procedural complications connected with divorce will prove more of an obstacle to the wider application of the clean break. There is considerable pressure on all who undertake legal proceedings to reach an outcome as soon as possible, because of the cost involved. The withdrawal of legal aid from undefended divorce petitions in 1977 as an attempt to recoup at least some of the estimated £22m then being spent by the Civil Legal Aid Fund on divorce, has been supplemented by further measures which may have the effect of forcing parties into what may be hasty and ill-informed decisions. The most notorious measure is the Law Society's charge on any money or property beyond the first £2,500 recovered or preserved in legally-aided proceedings under the M.C.A. 1973 or s. 17 Married Women's Property Act 1882. This has been brought into the forefront of public attention by the House of Lords decision in *Hanlon v Law Society* [1981] AC 124, [1980] 2 All ER 199. The husband having transferred the matrimonial home to the wife, she sought to sell the house and buy a smaller one so that she could better afford the mortgage instalments. It was held that the Law Society's charge extended to the costs of all the proceedings she had taken in connexion with her divorce and attached to the entire beneficial interest in the home. The only crumb of comfort for the wife was the ruling that the Law Society has a discretion to postpone enforcement of the charge or to transfer the charge to a replacement home.

After quoting from Lord Lowry's speech in *Hanlon v Law Society*, Douglas concludes:

This case highlights the danger of the clean break solution, which may put wives in a very difficult position in deciding how to settle. No charge attaches to periodical payments, in contrast to property, but such payments are taxable, they reduce entitlement to supplementary benefit, and they cease on remarriage. Seeking a lump sum is no solution, since this is money which attracts the charge, and the husband in any case may not be able to raise it. The charge is designed as an incentive to legally-aided parties to settle their problems as quickly as possible, as non-aided parties must do, but how is the wife to make up her mind? Lord Lowry cautioned that it is neither 'reasonable (n)or effective to try to frighten the parties into settling. Irresponsible advisers would not be deterred by a sanction directed only against their client and even highly responsible advisers (as in these proceedings) may advise an appeal (or more than one) in the hope (which may not be realised) of improving the lot of their client,' (p. 226c). The quality of the wife's legal advice becomes all the more crucial to her future; if she agrees to a clean break, there is no continuing jurisdiction in the court to vary the terms later — *Minton v Minton*, unless part of the agreement is yet to be implemented as in *Tilley v Tilley* (1979) 10 Fam Law 89, and the circumstances warrant the alteration. If the agreement contains periodical payments, there is jurisdiction under s. 31 to vary as in *Jessel v Jessel* [1979] 3 All ER 645, but the wife is at risk of the husband not paying. It is submitted that a clear policy by the courts in favour of the clean break as the best solution, for low-income divorcees at least, would help reduce the dilemma.

In *Hanlon v The Law Society* [1981] AC 124 at 127, CA, Lord Denning MR said:

The Family Court takes the rights and obligations of the parties all together — and puts the pieces into a mixed bag. Such pieces are the right to occupy the matrimonial home or have a share in it, the obligation to maintain the wife and children, and so forth. The court then takes out the pieces and hands them to the two parties — some to one party and some to the other — so that each can provide for the future with the pieces allotted to him or to her. The court hands them out without paying any too nice a regard to their legal or equitable rights but simply according to what is the fairest provision for the future — for mother and father and the children.

Question

Is this what Parliament has instructed judges to do?

CHAPTER 7

Finance after divorce — the call for reform

1 What do judges and registrars actually do?

Various arguments circulate at present with vociferous support from pressure groups. There is a poverty lobby active on behalf of single parents (Child Poverty Action Group, National Council for One Parent Families and others). The claims of this group are contested by the 'divided' parents represented by the Campaign for Justice in Divorce. This organisation is active in championing the claims of the earner, who is predominantly the former husband, who finds himself responsible for a second family whilst at the same time 'saddled' with the 'financial penalties' thrust upon him by the court at the time of the divorce to continue to support his first wife.

The debate suffers from a lack of hard evidence which can be used to support the claims of either group. However, some idea of what actually happens is beginning to emerge. Eekelaar and MacLean (1982) undertook to describe the present financial circumstances of a nationally representative .sample of those who have divorced in England and Wales since the introduction of no-fault divorce in 1971. They chose an 'omnibus survey' which approached a quota sample of 7,000 individuals in England and Wales in May 1981. The total list of respondents produced a total of 320 divorced men and 399 divorced women; from this they were given permission to approach 158 of the men and 217 of the women. As the researchers admit, 'the final sample size is small compared with large record based studies. But it contains detailed information which can only be obtained in a personal interview, and it is derived from a fully documented nationally representative sample of 7,000 individuals.'

Eekelaar and MacLean summarise their finding on maintenance payments as follows:

. . . (there were) very few payments made to support the wife alone (two men reported paying and two women reported receiving this form of maintenance). Payments for the wife and children were regularly paid by 28 men and received by 11 women for themselves and their children, and 55 for their children only. 23 of 28 men making payments reported paying out less than £100 in the previous twelve months. Twelve women reported receiving more than £1000 in the previous twelve months.

They conclude on the basis of their preliminary results that there is:

. . . no evidence that divorced women are 'living off' the resources of their former husbands. Even remarriage for them, does not remove them from the labour force, although it will frequently mean that full-time working will be substituted by part-time working.

This study was based on a small sample. The Scottish Law Commission commissioned a larger study from the Central Research Unit of the Scottish Office to assist them in the preparation of their Report. The Unit examined a sample of one in eight divorce actions decided in Scotland in 1980. The preliminary results were included in the Scottish Law Commission's *Report on Aliment and Financial Provision* (1981):

3.18 A periodical allowance was claimed in about 33% of all divorce actions but in only 16% of actions where no children were involved. In the cases examined there were no examples of claims by husbands. Figure 1 [below] shows the amounts claimed by wives. In 90% of actions where periodical allowance was claimed the amount per week claimed was less than £30, and in 47% it was between £10 and £20 per week. There were only a few cases where the amount claimed was £50 or more per week. The average amount of periodical allowance claimed was nearly £17 per week. The average amount claimed by pursuers without children was greater than that claimed by pursuers with children (£23 compared to £15 per week). This is perhaps not surprising. In many cases there is little enough money to provide for both aliment for children and periodical allowance for the person with care of them. To enable a complete picture to be obtained the study therefore also examined the amounts claimed as aliment for children.

Figure 1: Amounts of Periodical Allowance claimed

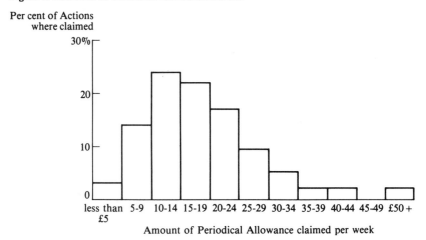

Amount of Periodical Allowance claimed per week

3.19 Aliment for children was claimed in 66% of all actions involving children and in 81% of such actions brought by wives. There were only one or two instances, in the cases examined, of aliment for children being claimed by husbands from wives. Figure 2 [opposite] shows the amount claimed per child per week and Figure 3 [opposite] shows the total amount claimed per week for all the children involved in a single divorce action. In 96% of cases where aliment was claimed the amount was under £20 per child per week. In 43% of cases the amount was between £5 and £9.99 per child per week and in 36% of cases the amount was between £10 and £14.99 per week. The average amount claimed per child per week was £8.50. In 91% of cases involving children the total amount of aliment claimed per case was less than £25 per week. The average amount was nearly £15 per week.

3.21 The amounts awarded did not differ substantially, over the whole sample, from the amounts claimed. An attempt was made by the researchers to identify cases where it seemed that the amounts awarded were unlikely to be paid. This involved noting cases where the where-abouts of the defender were unknown, where there had been a record of non-payment of aliment before the divorce, or where there were other indications that an award was unlikely to be paid. The process was necessarily subjective to some extent and the results must be treated with great caution, but it seemed questionable, on the basis of the limited information available in the documents, whether payment would be made in something like a third of the cases where aliment or a periodical allowance was awarded. It should not be inferred from this that payment would be made, or made regularly, in the remaining two thirds of the cases. Further research would be necessary to ascertain the actual extent of compliance with decrees for aliment and periodical allowance.

Figure 2: Amounts of aliment claimed: per child

Per cent of Actions
where claimed

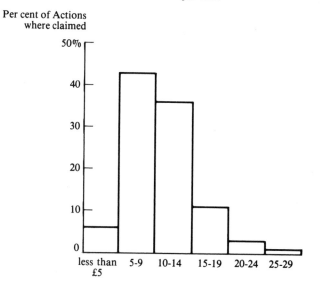

less than   5-9   10-14   15-19   20-24   25-29
£5

Figure 3: Amounts of aliment claimed: per case

Per cent of Actions
where claimed

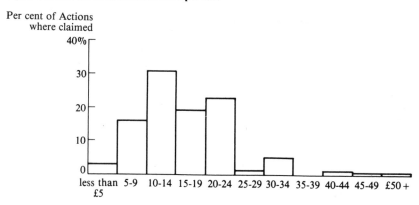

less than 5-9   10-14 15-19 20-24 25-29 30-34 35-39 40-44 45-49 £50 +
£5

3.22 The following tables show the extent to which pursuers and defenders in divorce actions were in employment or dependent on State benefits at the time of the divorce proceedings. The information was derived from the summons, affidavits or defences and is necessarily incomplete. In many cases, as we have seen, there is no claim for financial provision and no information on the parties' financial position, particularly that of the defender.

Table 2
Employment Status

Employment Status	Pursuer %	Defender %
In paid full-time employment	42.0	48.2
In paid part-time employment	14.6	1.7
Self-employed	1.7	4.0
Out of paid employment e.g. housewife, retired, unemployed	36.7	12.5
In prison	0	0.8
Not available	4.9	32.9

Table 3
Dependence on State Benefits

Dependency	Pursuer %	Defender %
Dependent on Benefits	29.7	7.7
Independent of Benefits	57.2	54.6
Information not available	13.2	37.7

3.23 More detailed information on all the above points will be available in the final research report. It is clear, however, that the scale of financial provision on divorce is less than is sometimes supposed. In about two thirds of all divorce actions there is no claim for periodical allowance and in about 90% there is no claim for a capital sum.[1] There are various possible reasons for the low incidence of claims for financial provision, including a lack of means on the part of both parties, the self-sufficiency of both parties, an intention to remarry, and the existence of voluntary arrangements. The nature of the research was such that it provides little information on parties' reasons for not claiming financial provision. It was noted, however, that in 8% of cases where there was no award of regular financial payments there was mention of informal financial arrangements.

It is important to remember that in Scottish law prior to 1964 no financial provision of any kind could be awarded to the 'guilty' spouse. For the purposes of financial provision the law regarded the guilty spouse as having died at the date of the decree, and the innocent spouse became entitled to claim legal rights — one-third of the husband's net moveable estate if there were children (one-half of this estate if there were no children), and the life rent of one-third of her husband's heritable estate. The only legal right available to an innocent husband was life rent of the whole of the wife's heritable estate. Claims in Scottish courts may still be affected by the fact that the law has changed relatively recently.

It is interesting to compare Table 3 of the *Scottish Law Commission Report* with a table produced in the *Report of the Committee on One-Parent Families* (*The Finer Report*) (1974) on the source of income of one parent families:

---

1. In only a few cases was there a claim for a capital sum and no claim for a periodical allowance. Overall, therefore, there was no claim for any financial provision in about 66% of cases.

Table 5.1
Main sources of income* of one-parent families at the end of 1971

Main source of income	Number of families (thousands)
Fatherless families other than widows' families:	
Earnings	140
Maintenance	50
Supplementary benefits	200
Other	10
All	400
Widows' families:	
Earnings	50
Widows' benefits	60
Other	10
All	120
Motherless families:	
Earnings	90
Supplementary benefits	10
All	100
Total number of one-parent families	620

* By 'main source' is meant the largest single source.
Note: Figures rounded to nearest 10,000.
Source: Family Expenditure Survey pooled data, 1969–1971; Department of Health and Social Security supplementary benefit statistics.

Question

Do these figures lend support (*a*) to allegations that divorced men (and their second wives) are greatly burdened by awards in favour of first wives; (*b*) to allegations that men may readily leave their first families in poverty; or (*c*) to any other conclusion?

The Campaign for Justice in Divorce believes that 'where the woman wishes (or is persuaded by her lawyer!) to use the power given to her by the courts, the usual outcome for the man is loss of home, contents, capital, if any, swallowed up by legal costs and the imposition of an unbreakable life long obligation to pay a third of his gross income (often more than half of his net income) to his former wife. There is no remission for good conduct attached to this punishment, his only hope is that she will die or remarry.' (Letter to the *Guardian*, 9 September 1982.)

Little research in this country has been carried out on attitudes to periodical payments. But an interesting survey, especially on the reasons acceptable as justification for alimony payments (periodical payments) was carried out in 1978 in Los Angeles County, California by Leonore Weitzman and Ruth Dixon, *The Alimony Myth: Does no fault divorce make a difference* (1980). The authors summarise the findings in the following manner:

Table 1
Attitudes Toward Alimony
From interviews with divorced men and women,
Los Angeles County, California, 1978

	PERCENTAGE WHO AGREE (Weighted Sample*)	
	Women (n = 111)†	Men (n = 112)
	(Percentage)	
A. A woman deserves alimony if she has helped her husband get ahead because they are really *partners* in his work	68	54
B. A woman does not deserve alimony if she had an *affair* and was unfaithful to her husband	23	40
C. A woman deserves alimony for at least a year or two so she can *adjust* to the divorce	31	21
D. A woman deserves alimony if she wants to go back to school or to be *retrained* so that she can get a good job to support herself	73	52
E. A woman deserves alimony if she's been married a long time and is *too old* to get a good job	87	66
F. A woman deserves alimony if she has young *children* and wants to stay home to care for them	67	63
G. A woman does not deserve alimony if she can go to work and support herself	65	85
H. A woman deserves alimony if her husband left her for another woman	29	39
I. A woman deserves alimony if she is *disabled* and can't support herself	94	87
J. A woman deserves alimony because when she got married her *husband promised to* support her for the rest of her life	9	3
K. A woman deserves alimony because her husband should *pay her back* for her years of work as a homemaker and/or mother	25	19
L. A woman deserves alimony because she can never recapture the years she has given to her marriage and the *opportunities* she *missed* to have a career of her own	20	4

* The interview sample was weighted to reflect the characteristics of the total divorcing population in Los Angles County.
†n refers to the number of cases (i.e., interviews) on which the percentages are based.

Questions

(i) How many of these 12 statements do you agree with, and how many do you disagree with?
(ii) Carry out a similar exercise amongst your colleagues.
(iii) The results may well be different. If they are, do you think that the differences result from the fact that the California research was confined to *divorced* men and women?
(iv) How many of these 12 statements do you think most English judges and registrars would agree with?

2 What is wrong with the present law?

The Law Commission, in their discussion paper *The financial consequences of divorce: the basic policy* (1980), summarise four specific complaints about the present law 'which are known to us:'

(a) Inconsistency with the modern law of divorce

24. A fundamental complaint is, we think, that the underlying principle of the law governing the financial consequences of divorce is inconsistent with the modern divorce law. The law (it is said) now permits either party to a marriage to insist on a divorce, possibly against the will of the other party, regardless of the fact that the other party may have honoured every conceivable marital commitment. Why (it is asked), if the status of marriage can be dissolved in this way, should the financial obligations of marriage nevertheless survive — particularly in cases where divorce has been forced on an unwilling partner, or where a wholly innocent partner is required to support one whose conduct has caused the breakdown? Instead (it is argued), divorce ought to provide a 'clean break' with the past in economic terms as well as in terms of status, and, so far as possible, encourage the parties to look to the future rather than to dwell in the past.

(b) Hardship for divorced husbands

25. We have been told that the continuing financial obligations imposed by divorce often cause severe economic hardship for those who are ordered to pay, normally of course the husband. It is not uncommon for a man to be ordered to pay as much as one-third of his gross income to his ex-wife until she either remarries or dies, and to be deprived of the matrimonial home (which may well represent his only capital asset) at least during the minority of the children. Unless she remarries this obligation to maintain an ex-wife can put divorced husbands under financial strain not only over a very long period of years but even into retirement. The obligation to maintain an ex-wife is particularly resented if the husband feels that it is his wife who is really responsible for the breakdown of the marriage; and such feelings are further exacerbated where he believes that his ex-wife has either chosen not to contribute toward her maintenance by working, or has elected to co-habit with another man, who might be in a position to support her but whom she has decided not to marry so as not to be deprived of her right to maintenance from her first husband. Finally it should be remembered that many more wives than husbands receive legal aid. The cost of legal proceedings therefore frequently weighs upon a husband as an additional financial burden and may even effectively prevent him from pursuing his case before the courts. For many husbands the effect of divorce may seem to involve not only the end of their marriage, but also the loss of home, children and money.

(c) Hardship for second families

26. The complaints which we have summarised so far apply primarily to husbands, whether or not they have taken advantage of the freedom to remarry conferred by divorce. However, particular resentment seems to be felt by men who have remarried after a divorce, and by their second wives. The burden of continuing to provide for a first wife can involve financial depriva- tion for a man who does not remarry, but the burden may well be acute if he remarries and has a second family. In such cases the impoverishment caused by the first wife's continuing claim upon her husband may well fall on all the members of his new family, and we have even been told of cases where husbands have had themselves sterilised because they feel that their continu- ing financial commitments to a former wife make it impossible for them to afford children in their second marriage. In particular the effect on a man's second wife is a frequent source of comment. It is claimed that she is invariably forced to accept a reduced standard of living by reason of the fact that part of her husband's income is being diverted to support his first wife; it is also claimed that a second wife may be forced, notwithstanding family commitments, to work, even although her husband's first wife, who possibly has no family commitments, chooses not to do so. Indeed some second wives have told us that they feel that they are being required personally to support their husband's first wife because the courts take a second wife's resources into account when assessing a husband's financial circumstances and his capacity to make periodical payments to a former spouse. Not surprisingly this feeling is a cause of particular bitterness where either the first wife has no children or has school-age children and does not herself work, or where she appears to enjoy a higher standard of living than the husband's present family. Even after a husband's death the existence of a former marriage can, we are told, threaten the financial security of a second family because under the Inheritance (Provision for Family and Dependants) Act 1975 a first wife can make a claim for reasonable financial provision out of her former husband's estate.[2] From the point of view of a husband's second family the freedom which he is given to remarry on divorce (which he might himself not then have wanted) might appear to be nothing more than a 'snare and a delusion'.

---

2. See *Re Fullard* [1982] Ch 42, [1981] 2 All ER 796, [1981] 3 WLR 743, (see p. 136, above).

(d) Hardship suffered by divorced wives

27. . . . There is no doubt that many divorced wives feel that the law still fails to make adequate provision for them. Not only is the starting point for assessing the provision to be made for a divorced wife only one-third (as opposed to one-half) of the parties' joint resources, but in practice divorced wives often face great difficulty in enforcing any order which the court has made. The law, it is true, requires that so far as practicable, the wife should be kept in the position she would have been in had the marriage not broken down, but, as the Finer Committee remarked in 1974, private law is not capable of providing the 'method of extracting more than a pint from a pint pot'. We have seen that economic realities often make it difficult for a husband to provide for his second family. The same economic factors also make it difficult for him to provide for his former wife. Obviously an income which has been adequate to support one family is often totally inadequate to support two. In these circumstances, where an order for periodical payments has been made against a husband or where he fails to comply with the terms of an order, the State, through the medium of the supplementary benefit scheme, already accepts a substantial burden of the support of divorced wives, albeit only at a subsistence level. Moreover first wives will often have recourse to supplementary benefit as a means of under-writing any orders made in their favour against their former husbands. Many such wives resent their dependency on what seems to them to be an inadequate level of State support and the drop in their living standards following the breakdown of the marriage, and this is particularly so where their husbands have remarried, and seem able to enjoy a high standard of living, . . . it is often suggested that wives in this position should avoid dependence on supplementary benefit by obtaining paid employment; but this may well be very difficult. They may have children to look after and, if they do, they may well experience difficulty in assimilating their working hours with the school hours and holidays of their children. Moreover some childless wives have told us that they find it hard to accept that their former husbands should now suggest that they obtain paid employment, when they may well only have stopped working because of the exigencies of their husband's career, or because of his attitude to his wife taking paid employment.

28. There is a further problem which is said increasingly to affect divorced women. Not only is difficulty often found in enforcing payments due under a court order, but in a period of high inflation the real value of an order is rapidly eroded. It is true that a wife who feels that circumstances have changed has a right to apply to the court for variation of a periodical payments order; but this is not a wholly satisfactory solution. First, it seems that in practice, even in times of high inflation, an application for variation is more likely to result in a decrease rather than an increase in the sum ordered to be paid. Secondly an application to the court will often serve to recall the distress of the original breakdown. One possible, and at first sight attractive, way of mitigating this problem might be to provide machinery for the indexation or inflation-proofing of periodical payments orders. However, there would be formidable technical and other difficulties in providing such machinery; and it might well be the case that indexation would exacerbate rather than reduce the problem. Often the root of the difficulty is simply that there 'is not enough money to go round'; and it is thus reasonable to suppose that any automatic up-lifting, taking effect without regard to the husband's means and commitments, would result in many more applications being made by husbands for reduction, and perhaps by even more refusals to pay. In either case, the volume of litigation would be increased and bitterness, distress and humiliation engendered.

An American anthropologist looks at it all in a slightly different perspective. The following short extract is taken from an essay by Professor Paul Bohannan in the collection edited by him, *Divorce and After* (1971):

Behind the idea of fair settlement of property at the time of divorce is the assumption that a man cannot earn money to support his family if he does not have the moral assistance and domestic services of his wife. The wife, if she works, does so in order to 'enhance' the family income (no matter how much she makes or what the 'psychic income' to her might be). Therefore, every salary dollar, every patent, every investment, is joint property.

In most states, the property settlement is not recorded in the public records of divorce, so precise information is lacking. However, in most settlements, the wife receives from one-third to one-half of the property. As one sits in a divorce court, however, one realizes that in many divorces the amount of property is so small as to need no settlement or even to cause any dispute. Judges regard settlement as the province of lawyers, and generally agree that the lawyers have not done their jobs if the matter comes to court.

Many wives voluntarily give up their rights to property at the time they become ex-wives. Some are quite irrational about it — 'I won't take anything from him!' Sometimes they think (perhaps quite justly) that they have no moral right to it. Others, of course, attempt to use the property settlement as a means of retaliation. The comment from one of my informants was, 'Boy, did I make that bastard pay.' It seems to me that irrational motives such as revenge or self-abnegation are more often in evidence than the facts of relative need, in spite of all that judges and lawyers can do.

Question

Is there anything wrong with revenge or self-abnegation? (Perhaps such feelings help a person to overcome the immense hurt of a broken relationship?)

One particular aspect of the debate is the question of whether married women are justified in looking primarily to their husbands for support if their marriages break down. After all, so the argument goes, emphasis is now placed on equality of opportunity for men and women, and it is indeed a fact that most women are employed outside the home for at least some period during their married lives. The argument has been most forcefully presented by Ruth Deech in a series of articles. We quote here from *The Principles of Maintenance* (1977):

For some time now there have been available to married women reliable contraception, education and full legal status. Legislation provides for equal opportunities and equal pay: 40% of the working force of employees are female, of whom two-thirds are married and 85% of married women have been in employment at some time during their marriage. But the concept of female dependency on the male continues to permeate the maintenance laws and in addition the comparatively recent state pensions and tax provisions are based on sexual stereotypes of the husband as provider and the wife as full-time housekeeper and child-rearer. This legal supposition of female dependency tends to deny freedom of choice to married and formerly married persons; it is widely considered degrading to women and it perpetuates the common law proprietary relationship of the husband and wife even after divorce. While they express the superiority of the male the maintenance laws are at the same time an irritant to the increasing number of divorced men who have always to be able to provide and who suffer the perpetual drain on their income represented by a former wife. Maintenance awards are emotionally charged with the desire on the part of the wife for retribution and by their nature unlikely to be readily enforceable because of the hostility surrounding their creation and the fact that the ex-husband is paying money without getting anything in return.

Legally speaking the most serious count against the present maintenance system is its effect on the breakdown principle in divorce. The breakdown law reflects a concept of marriage as a partnership of equals, as demonstrated by the five-year separation ground of divorce. But it is incompatible with a maintenance law which rests on a foundation of female dependency. This conflict is at the heart of criticisms of the divorce law. It gives rise to the hostility between the parties reflected in contested proceedings, many of which in truth concern the issue of maintenance; it is also responsible for this unpleasant nature of the 'grave financial hardship' cases and the meaning which has been given to the phrase 'having regard to their conduct' in section 25 of the Matrimonial Causes Act 1973.

Support of a wife after dissolution of marriage is logically and historically different from support during marriage. It originates in part in the alimony awarded to a wife in the days when the only 'divorce' was *a mensa et thoro*, which did not dissolve the marriage bond. The bond could only be dissolved by Parliament and when this exceptional and expensive favour was granted to a necessarily wealthy husband it was the custom to require him to set aside property for the support of his former wife. It was this power that Parliament gave to the Divorce Court in 1857 and very limited it was too: only to secured payments, and it was not granted to a guilty wife. [But cf. p. 193, above.] The provisions of the Matrimonial Causes Act 1973 Part II, apply to both sexes equally; but they furnish no new rationale to explain why one spouse should continue to support the other after divorce has terminated the marital relationship.

When commenting on s. 25(1)(c) of the Matrimonial Causes Act 1973, Deech says:

The standard of living enjoyed by the parties during the marriage. Even though the marriage is defunct, section 25(1)(c) lists this standard for consideration by the court in assessing maintenance and concludes by instructing the court to put the parties in the position they would have been in if the marriage had continued. Not only is this impracticable, as the husband is bound to suffer from having to pay out sums that he would not have had to find in the event of the continuation of the marriage, while the wife benefits correspondingly, it is also an admission that whilst the marriage is dissolved in law, it continues to affect the lives of the former spouses financially and therefore still provides for women a career alternative to an economically productive one. . . .

What relevance can there be to one's future life as a single person in the fact that one had benefitted from the lifestyle of the former spouse during a period when the marriage was in existence? The cynic might say that this factor only reinforces the tendency on the part of some to search for a spouse who can provide a lifelong meal ticket. . . .

Now that the Sex Discrimination Act 1975 and the Equal Pay Act 1970 have been passed there can no longer be any excuse for laws that treat women as lifelong dependants, although as long as the Sex Discrimination Act and the Equal Pay Act are not as effective as they should be, the woman's restricted career choice and lower earning power are factors that ought to be borne in mind. (One can hardly expect anti-discrimination legislation to be successful as long as other major areas of law assume that women can find support otherwise than by employment.) The economic position of married and single women is society is well known to be weak but it does not follow from this that the ex-husband, alone in the community, must atone for the deficiencies of the system.

She concludes by stating that maintenance should be rehabilitative and a temporary measure confined to spouses who are incapable of work because of infirmity or child care. Deech's view is shared by others, for example by Kevin Gray (1977) and by Harper (1979).

An alternative view, however, is presented by Katherine O'Donovan in *The Principles of Maintenance: An Alternative View* (1978):

Whilst it cannot be denied that laws based on sexual stereotypes are undesirable and ought to be eliminated what both Deech and Gray fail to see is that the current organisation of family life is premised on the assumption that one partner will sacrifice a cash income in order to rear children and manage the home. The dependence of the non-earning spouse on the wage-earner is inevitable under present family arrangements. This leads in turn to inequality of earning power of spouses. Without a major change in social and family structures the Deech or Gray proposals merely serve to perpetuate an already unfair situation and will not ensure equality.

The assumption of the role of housewife on marriage by the majority of women cannot be ignored. Over 90% women in Britain marry, and in 95% of marriages the husband is the chief economic support of the family. Although married women do work outside the home, composing one-third of the work force, there is a clear pattern of part-time work, shorter hours and lower earnings in work done by women by comparison with work done by men. One accepted explanation for this pattern is that duties in the home interfere with women's full participation in work; and the evidence is that, even where both partners to a marriage work, women retain the prime responsibility for home and children. Many married women give up work in order to raise a family. In so doing they forego the training and work experience which would enable them to earn more. They are also failing to provide for their future through insurance and pension contributions, as are those who work part-time, although to a lesser extent. No doubt women give up or reduce their employment cheerfully on behalf of their families, but whether they would continue to do so if denied the protection of the law is questionable. The argument can be made that the law affords little protection at present since maintenance is so difficult to enforce but this may be an argument for improving legal protection through, for instance, greater use of lump sum provision rather than for the abolition of maintenance . . . the law of maintenance contains a recognition of the sacrifice of a cash income by a spouse. This argument was best expressed by Latey J in *S v S* [1976] Fam 8, [1975] 2 All ER 19n, when he said:

'This wife like so many wives when there are children has come off worse as the result of the breakdown of the marriage. It is a sad fact of life that, where there are children, both husband and wife suffer on marriage breakdown, but it is the wife who usually suffers more. The husband continues with his career, goes on establishing himself, increasing his experience and qualification for employment — in a word, his security. With children to care for a wife usually cannot do this. She has not usually embarked on a continuous and progressing career while living with her husband caring for their child or children and running the home. If the marriage breaks down she can only start in any useful way after the children are off her hands and then she starts from scratch in middle life while the husband has started in youth.'

. . . .The idea of a family wage adequate to support a wife and children with the addition of child benefit has been built into wage structure since the nineteenth century. So the expectation of society is that a wife's work is covered by her husband's wages. On divorce, without maintenance, the housewife will have little or no income from wage-earning and no National

Insurance benefits to fall back on. If she does get a job, as already pointed out, her earning ability will be low.

Deech and Gray both propose that on divorce there should be a distribution of property acquired during marriage. Deech suggests that the Law Commission's proposals on co-ownership of the matrimonial home should be enacted. Gray proposes that an equal division of property take place. Both approaches involve recognition that the spouse who works at home is an equal partner in the marriage. But neither fully appreciate that without a regime of community of property true equality cannot be said to exist in matrimonial property law. . . .

For the majority of couples there will be a period in their marriage when their major asset, other than possible ownership of the matrimonial home, is the earning ability of the husband. This is why the law gives dependants a right of support after death, and not the fact that they are parasites — as suggested by Deech. . . .

Ruth Deech's argument is ultimately against marriage itself. If the spouse who undertakes housekeeping and child care should not consider marriage as (in part) an alternative career to one which is economically productive, then the answer is either not to marry, or to engage in paid work during marriage. But society does not seem ready for marriages in which both spouses work full-time. The present provision for nursery and pre-school facilities is inadequate. Children are prone to illness and are naturally dependent. Schools are not open for a full working day. And at present there is high unemployment. Participation in the workforce is not necessarily the answer, where there are young children; at least not without major changes in society, with the provision of communal laundries, cheap family restaurants, full-time nurseries etc. And male work attitudes would have to change to enable fathers to share equally in child care functions. It seems unlikely that this will happen. Deech argues that mothers with children should receive maintenance on divorce, and that it is only those who could earn who should be deprived. But withdrawal from the labour market at any time, current or past, affects earning ability, and it is fair that this diminution in earning ability be shared by both spouses.

Questions

(i) Is Deech against marriage, or simply against housewife marriage?
(ii) Are you?
(iii) If you are, would you first abolish housewife marriage or first abolish the housewife's right to support? (Refer back to Chapter 3 and pp. 188–191.)

O'Donovan concludes her article:

The notion that an equal division of property on divorce will wind up the (equal) matrimonial partnership and send the parties on their separate ways as independent individuals overlooks the fact that for nearly half of married couples their sole asset is wages and deferred wages in the form of pensions. The houseworker in such families would get nothing on divorce. This raises an important aspect of law which is dealt with only covertly by both Deech and Gray; that is the symbolic quality of law. At present the statement in the law of maintenance that the wage-earner must support the non-wage-earner is a statement of justice to the non-wage-earner. Admittedly — as the Finer Report makes clear — the law is unenforced and perhaps unenforceable. So the abolition of all but rehabilitative maintenance on divorce would be a recognition of reality. But there would be a new symbolic content of the legal rules. The statement would then be 'because of the equality of the sexes a divorced spouse must look to the state for support'. For those spouses in the community who do not own property and who divorce will this ensure equality?

The National Council for the Divorce and Separated would also oppose the argument advanced by Deech. An example of their thinking appears from a letter written by the Council's Vice President to the *Guardian*, 9 September 1982:

There is the effect upon the institution of marriage as we know it today. At present it is usually a matter of agreement between the partners that the family shall move about the country, or abroad, to further the prospects of the spouse with the higher, or with the potential for the higher, earning power, and that the children shall be cared for wherever they may be by the parent with the lower earnings.

In our present society there is an 80% chance that the partner with the lesser prospects of earning a high income will be the wife. It will be a foolish woman indeed who will give up her already slender prospects of a career, either to look after children or to move to follow her husband's job requirements, knowing that if marriage ends she will be expected to start again on the lowest rung of her promotion and pensions ladder and be deemed to be self-sufficient regardless of her husband's current financial position.

The effect upon future child-care patterns and upon the mobility of the work force would undoubtedly be slow to manifest itself but, as with so many social evolutions, would probably be irreversible.

Questions

(i) In general women earn less than their menfolk, but earlier (in Chapter 3 at p. 78) we also presented evidence that more and more work because they wish to do so, rather than because the money is needed: does either finding influence your view upon whether women should become self supporting after divorce?

(ii) Should an able-bodied house-husband be expected to support himself after divorce?

The discussion between Deech and O'Donovan is an argument about how women can advance in the labour market. (See p. 79, above.) The difference between them boils down to this: Deech thinks that matters will only improve when the ideological basis of a support-dominated maintenance law is abolished; O'Donovan believes that a support-dominated maintenance law can only be abolished after the infrastructure of employment laws, support services for child care, pension and social security laws, and taxation provisions have all been reorganised to permit a woman to survive without the need for support from her former provider.

Question

Which of these two views do you believe to be *politically* realistic?

3 Models for a law governing the financial consequences of divorce

In Part IV of their discussion paper, *The financial consequences of divorce: the basic policy* (1980), the Law Commission describe seven models which might form the basis of a law to govern the financial consequences of divorce. These are discussed as separate options, and more briefly in combination. It should be recalled that the Commission were dealing mainly with the parties' finances and only incidentally with reallocation of their property. We summarise below the major characteristics of each model:

59 Model 1: Retention of section 25 of the Matrimonial Causes Act 1973
. . . Whilst it is true that the failure of the Act to give any indication of the weight to be attached to any particular circumstance, or indeed to 'the circumstances' as a whole, can make it difficult for practitioners to advise clients on how a case is likely to be decided, it is claimed that any such disadvantage is more than outweighed by the advantage to be gained from the court having a discretion which can not only be adapted to the infinitely varied facts of each case (which can be foreseen neither by a judge nor by the legislature) but also to changing social circumstances. Moreover, in this view it is not only inevitable, but indeed desirable, that it should be left to case law to provide the coherent but evolving guidance on how to deal with such specific problems as

the difficulties arising from shortage of housing, the effects of the availability of supplementary benefit, pensions and other welfare benefits, and the policy to be adopted in relation to short marriages and the wife's earning capacity. . . .

66 Model 2: Repeal of the direction to the court in section 25 to seek to put the parties in the financial position in which they would have been had the marriage not broken down

. . . We consider the most fundamental issue raised by the present controversy over section 25 to be whether or not it is desirable to retain the principle of life-long support which that section seems to embody. It might therefore be argued that the simplest solution to the criticisms of the present law would be for Parliament to repeal the specific direction at the end of section 25(1), but otherwise to leave the section intact; the court would simply be directed to make whatever order it considered appropriate in the light of all the circumstances, including the circumstances listed in sub-sections (*a*) to (*g*) of section 25(1). This would enable the courts to adopt a flexible approach, taking into account not only all the relevant individual circumstances of the parties, but also changing economic factors such as the availability of housing and changing attitudes to the proper purpose of financial provision. . . .

70 Model 3: The relief of need

Under this model, the economically weaker party would be eligible to receive financial assistance from the economically stronger party if, and so long as, he or she could show that, taking into account his or her particular social and economic conditions, there is actual need of such assistance. The principle adopted would thus be one of individual self-reliance: after a marriage had broken down neither of the parties would have any automatic right to support, but rather only a qualified right insofar as it could be justified by special circumstances. In practice, the adoption of such a principle would entail placing an onus on the applicant to show that he was unable to support himself adequately. . . .

73 Model 4: Rehabilitation

. . . The concept of rehabilitative financial provision has been explained in a recent American case as:

'sums necessary to assist a divorced person in regaining a useful and constructive role in society through vocational or therapeutic training or retraining, and for the further purpose of preventing financial hardship on society or the individual during the rehabilitative process' *Mertz v Mertz* 287 So 2d 691 at 692.

The onus is therefore firmly placed on the spouse in receipt of a rehabilitative award to take steps to become self-sufficient, and in this respect we think that such an approach might often result in the wife having to accept a significantly lower standard of living after divorce than that which she enjoyed before. She would be given an opportunity to develop such skills as she possessed, but ultimately she would be expected to fend for herself. . . .

75 . . . The rehabilitative period might be limited by statute, to a maximum of two or three years or to the duration of some course of training, or it might lie in the discretion of the court. . . .

77 Model 5: The division of property — the 'clean break'

The essence of this model is the analogy of partnership. Where a partnership is dissolved, the partnership property is divided amongst the partners and that is the end of the matter. This, it is said, should also be the case where a marriage is dissolved. (Gray, 1977) The principle might be adopted in one of a number of forms. At the one extreme it would involve no continuing financial relationship between ex-spouses: their rights and duties inter se would be resolved at the time of the divorce by dividing the matrimonial property between them. Such division might involve using a fractional approach (e.g. both parties would be entitled to half of the property available for distribution) or it might reflect some other principle such as the 'rehabilitative' or 'needs' models suggested above. Alternatively, the division might be effected solely on the basis of the court's discretion in each individual case. However, other variations on the basic theme that the financial consequences of divorce ought to be resolved by means of a division of the matrimonial property might also be possible. Thus a law based on this model might provide, for instance, for a delay in the division where the matrimonial home is needed to accommodate a growing family, or for additional payments of maintenance on a rehabilitative or needs basis. . . .

80 Model 6: A mathematical approach

. . . On this approach the spouses' financial rights and duties inter se on divorce would be resolved by reference to fixed mathematical formulae which might then be adjusted to take into account particular factors such as the care of children or the length of the marriage. The result, it is said, would be two-fold. First, the parties and their legal advisers would in most cases be able to save time and money by negotiating a settlement in the knowledge that it accurately reflected current practice. Secondly, adjudicators would be able to decide cases in an entirely consistent fashion. . . .

84 Model 7: Restoration of the parties to the position in which they would have been had their marriage never taken place
On this view (e.g. Gray) the court should seek to achieve 'not the position which would have resulted if the marriage had continued, but the position which would have occurred if the marriage had never taken place at all'. The model is therefore a guiding principle, and might be carried into effect either by imposing an obligation to make periodical payments or by a once and for all division of the parties' capital (or a combination of both) which would be designed to compensate the financially weaker spouse for any loss incurred through marriage. . . .

86 A combination of models
. . . It might be argued however that many of the problems which could result if a particular model were to be adopted as the sole governing principle might be avoided if the law were to be based on a combination of these models. For instance, elements of the needs or rehabilitative approaches could be used to temper some of the difficulties that might arise if the division of property model were to be adopted by itself. Alternatively it would no doubt be possible, whilst maintaining the main structure of the existing law, to amend the guidelines at present contained in section 25, so as to direct the court's attention more specifically to certain matters, for example the possibility that a wife should be expected to rehabilitate herself after divorce.

4 Comparisons with other systems

It is arguable that the English law is so unique and idiosyncratic, that little would be gained by even a short glimpse at the solutions of others. Happily this view does not prevail to any large extent in this country, and the Law Commission is clearly aware of the legislation in the United States, in Europe and in Commonwealth countries. We give below an extract from Professor Mary Ann Glendon's book, *The New Family and the New Property* (1981) where she discusses spousal support laws and property division in the United States and certain European countries:

In the newer laws dealing with spousal support, there has been steady erosion of the older idea that each spouse, or at least the husband, has a continuing economic responsibility for the other after divorce, provided the other's 'fault' was not the cause of the divorce. The most recent laws reverse traditional expectations concerning post-divorce economic relations. In the new family law, after the property of the divorcing spouses is re-allocated between them, each is in principle responsible for himself or herself. . . . There is still considerable variety in the substantive law of alimony. In the United States, the approaches range from a few states which have clung to the traditional rule that support was available only to an 'innocent' wife against a 'guilty' husband, to Texas where permanent alimony cannot be given at all. In the middle are the growing majority of states where the courts have power, in varying degrees, to grant alimony as they deem 'equitable and just' under the circumstances of each case. In theory, after the 1979 U.S. Supreme Court decision in *Orr v Orr* 99 S.Cr 1102 (1979), [see *Calderbank v Calderbank* [1976] Fam 93, [1975] 3 All ER 333] holding that state laws providing alimony for wives but not husbands are unconstitutional, the 10 or 11 states which still had such laws could comply with the equal protection command of the Constitution either by denying alimony to both spouses or extending it on equal terms to both. It seems likely that these states will conform to one of the patterns of the states where maintenance was already available on a sex-neutral basis, rather than join Texas in ruling it out altogether.

A 1979 survey of the 50 states by Freed and Foster revealed that maintenance is increasingly being made independent of fault. In a few states, the conduct of the spouses is still one factor which the court may, in its discretion, take into consideration; and, in still fewer states, fault (sometimes only adultery) remains an automatic bar to maintenance. At the same time, however, a growing number of states are recognizing a new category of 'economic' misconduct (such as dissipation of family assets) as a factor that may be considered by the court.

It is now common for legislatures to provide the court with guidelines for their exercise of discretion in awarding spousal support. Such guidelines usually emphasize the need of the support debtor and the ability to pay of the support creditor. They tend to discourage permanent alimony. The most recent American statutes, like the new French, Swedish and West German laws, treat spousal support as in principle what it is in fact — an exceptional consequence of divorce. A typical set of guidelines for spousal maintenance is found in the Uniform Marriage and Divorce Act [UMDA $308]. It makes maintenance available only in specifically enumerated situations of need, and views it as essentially temporary and rehabilitative, aimed at making the recipient self-sufficient through entry or re-entry into the labour force as soon as possible after the divorce.

Thus, one trend makes alimony exceptional and temporary, and therefore would seem to limit its availability; while another might seem to widen its potential scope by making it independent of misconduct and available on the basis of need. However, since the 'need' test is always combined with an 'available resources' test, the sphere of application of such laws is, as a practical matter, severely restricted.

The *Uniform Marriage and Divorce Act* has been adopted in its entirety by only a handful of states. It has however been influential as a model:

Section 308. [Maintenance.] (*a*) In a proceeding for dissolution of marriage, [or] legal separation, . . . the court may grant a maintenance order for either spouse, only if it finds that the spouse seeking maintenance:
 (1) lacks sufficient property to provide for his reasonable needs; and
 (2) is unable to support himself through appropriate employment or is the custodian of a child whose condition or circumstances make it appropriate that the custodian not be required to seek employment outside the home.
Section 308: (*b*) The maintenance order shall be in amounts and for periods of time the court deems just, without regard to marital misconduct, and after considering all relevant factors including:
 (1) The financial resources of the party seeking maintenance, including marital property apportioned to him, his ability to meet his needs independently, and the extent to which a provision for support of a child living with the party includes a sum for that party as custodian;
 (2) the time necessary to acquire sufficient education or training to enable the party seeking maintenance to find appropriate employment;
 (3) the standard of living established during the marriage;
 (4) the duration of the marriage;
 (5) the age and the physical and emotional condition of the spouse seeking maintenance; and
 (6) the ability of the spouse from whom maintenance is sought to meet his needs while meeting those of the spouse seeking maintenance.

Section 72 of the *Australian Family Law Act 1975* bases itself on a very similar principle:

s. 72. A party to a marriage is liable to maintain the other party, to the extent that the first-mentioned party is reasonably able to do so, if, and only if, that other party is unable to support herself or himself adequately, whether by reason of having the care and control of a child of the marriage who has not attained the age of 18 years, or by reason of age or physical or mental incapacity for appropriate gainful employment or for any other adequate reason having regard to any relevant matter referred to in sub-section 75(2).

The relevant matters referred to in sub-s. 75(2) are:

 (*a*) the age and state of health of each of the parties;
 (*b*) the income, property and financial resources of each of the parties and the physical and mental capacity of each of them for appropriate gainful employment;
 (*c*) whether either party has the care or control of a child of the marriage who has not attained the age of 18 years;
 (*d*) the financial needs and obligations of each of the parties;
 (*e*) the responsibilities of either party to support any other person;
 (*f*) the eligibility of either party for a pension, allowance or benefit under any law of Australia or of a State or Territory or under any superannuation fund or scheme, or the rate of any such pension, allowance or benefit being paid to either party;
 (*g*) where the parties have separated or the marriage has been dissolved, a standard of living that in all the circumstances is reasonable;
 (*h*) the extent to which the payment of maintenance to the party whose maintenance is under consideration would increase the earning capacity of that party by enabling that

party to undertake a course of education or training or to establish himself or herself in a business or otherwise to obtain an adequate income;

(*i*) the extent to which the party whose maintenance is under consideration has contributed to the income, earning capacity, property and financial resources of the other party;

(*j*) the duration of the marriage and the extent to which it has affected the earning capacity of the party whose maintenance is under consideration;

(*k*) the need to protect the position of a woman who wishes only to continue her role as a wife and mother;

(*l*) if the party whose maintenance is under consideration is cohabiting with another person — the financial circumstances relating to the cohabitation;

(*m*) the terms of any order made or proposed to be made under section 79 in relation to the property of the parties; and

(*n*) any fact or circumstance which, in the opinion of the court, the justice of the case requires to be taken into account.

Question

Into which, if any, of the seven models, or combination of models, of the Law Commission do you consider the American Uniform Marriage and Divorce Act and the Australian Act to fall?

Returning to Glendon, she illustrates in *The New Family and the New Property*, how innovation in the field of marital property has taken a variety of forms:

. . . In most separate property systems, property redistribution regardless of the form in which title is held has replaced the mere unscrambling of title to assets. In many community property systems, on the other hand, the traditional technique of mandatory equal division has been modified, eliminated or supplemented by judicial discretion to award more than half of the community property to one spouse and even to reallocate property that was not part of the community. Various experiments along these lines are being tried in the different legal systems.

The development of new techniques for dealing with the economic aspects of divorce has accelerated with the recognition that the amount of money being transferred upon divorce now rivals, and perhaps exceeds, the amount passing by will or intestate succession. Two generalizations can be made about this process of legal adaptation to divorce as an ordinary method of marriage termination. In the first place, it has already produced a marked differentiation within most legal systems between the techniques used for dealing with property distribution upon divorce and those employed upon death. Second, the divergence among legal systems of matrimonial property is greatest in the divorce situation and least where the marriage is terminated by death.

She argues that functional comparisons have to be made according to whether the property question is raised in the context of, first, an ongoing marriage; second, divorce; third, testate or intestate succession; or fourth, third party interests. In the divorce situation Glendon states that various legal systems differ according to the extent and type of property available for enforced sharing upon divorce, the degree of discretion accorded to the judge, the role of private agreements, and the relevance of conduct. There is also always the fundamentally important question of the extent of public responsibility for the casualties of broken families:

Divergence among systems upon these issues did not fall along traditional community-separate property lines. Modernization of those systems of marital property law that once were characterized by a unified set of principles and techniques which governed property relations in the various situations that arose during marriage, and upon its termination by divorce, separation or death has resulted in the appearance of new techniques specifically tailored to each situation. Of course, the existence of special techniques for different marital property problems has long been characteristic of the Anglo-American separate property systems. In the formerly unified systems, such as the French and West German, it has become obvious that different interests are at stake depending on when and by whom the property issues are raised. When marriage is terminated by divorce, for example, the interests of the ex-wife, ex-husband, their existing dependants (and new families that either may enter) and the public welfare system may have to be considered. In the case of the intestate death of a spouse, the interests typically weighed are those of the surviving spouse and the blood relatives of the predeceasing spouse, with the former gaining everywhere in varying degrees.

Question

You will recall that the Law Commission (Chapter 4, above) considered that the courts should have power to treat death like divorce: do you consider that there are significant distinctions between the two?

5 The Law Commissions' recommendations

In December 1981, the English Law Commission published their report. Just a month earlier, the Scottish Law Commission had published their own report on *Aliment and Financial Provision*. The English Law Commission make the following recommendations in *The Financial Consequences of Divorce* (1981):

17. We have come to the conclusion that the duty now imposed by statute to seek to place the parties in the financial position in which they would have been if the marriage had not broken down is not a suitable criterion; and in our view it should be removed from the law.

The Report goes on to recommend that the guidelines in s. 25(1) should be revised to give greater emphasis: (*a*) to the provision of adequate financial support for children which should be an overriding priority, and (*b*) to the importance of each party doing everything possible to become self-sufficient. The latter should be formulated in terms of positive principle and weight should be given to the view that, in appropriate cases, periodical financial provision should be primarily concerned to secure a smooth transition from the status of marriage to the status of independence. One other specific recommendation is made, in relation to the problems associated with the so-called 'clean break'. There is some confusion at present as to whether a court has the power to dismiss a wife's claim for periodical payments without her consent. The Law Commission recommend that a judge should be granted this power, to be exercised in appropriate cases. Thus, of the models advanced in the discussion paper, the English report argues for the retention of a discretion-based framework. It has been suggested that 'in affording precedence to the interests of children', the Report does no more than build on existing English practice (Eekelaar (1982)). Equally, in cases where there are no children, the emphasis on self sufficiency and the clean break is nothing new in English law. The Report has also been criticised because it ignores the thrust of the argument which favours a division of assets on the basis of the principle of partnership. (See for example Eekelaar (1982).) However, the Law Commission have else-where pressed for a system of equal home co-ownership (see Chapter 4, above), and it is necessary to ask whether the doctrine of deferred sharing of family acquests would appease *both* the arguments supported by the National Council for the Divorced and Separated (and, for instance,

O'Donovan) and the Campaign for Justice in Divorce (and, for instance, Deech). A major criticism, however, is that the Report says little about the 'new property' — pension expectancy, life insurance policies and the like.

The approach and proposals of the Scottish Law Commission provide an interesting contrast to the English caution, in view of the different legal traditions in countries which are otherwise so closely linked. We close this chapter with a major extract from the Scottish Law Commission Report on *Aliment and Financial Provision* (1981):

Need for balance between principle and discretion

3.62 One of the main criticisms made of the present law on financial provision is that it leaves too much to the unfettered discretion of the court. We think that this criticism is justified. On the other hand we have no doubt that the courts must be left with considerable discretion to take account of the great variety of circumstances in cases which come before them. One of our main concerns in this Report has been to try to strike the right balance between principle and discretion. We take as our starting point the proposition that an order for financial provision should be made if, and only if, it is justified by an applicable principle. Some such starting point is essential if there is to be any underlying principle in the law. Immediately, however, an obvious difficulty arises. An applicable principle might, if it were unqualified, compel a court to make an order which would be unreasonable in the light of the parties' resources at the time of the divorce. One principle might, for example, be equal sharing of property acquired during the marriage and owned at the time of final separation. Application of this principle might require a husband to pay, say, half the value of the matrimonial home to the wife. But by the time of the divorce, which could be years after the sale of the home, the husband might not, through no fault of his own, have the means to make such a payment. Similar difficulties could arise if payment was sought from a wife in analogous circumstances. A law on financial provision on divorce would be open to serious criticism if it appeared to compel courts to make orders which seemed unreasonable in the light of the parties' actual economic position. For this reason we think that the courts should be directed to make an order for financial provision if, and only if, (*a*) the order is justified by an applicable principle, and (*b*) the order is reasonable having regard to the resources of the parties. This introduces at the outset a certain balance between principle and discretion. The balance can be maintained, and, in our view, should be maintained by the way in which the applicable principles are framed.

Identifying the applicable principles

3.63 In identifying the principles which should govern an award of financial provision on divorce we have applied the following criteria. First, the system must be such as could be justified to reasonable husbands and reasonable wives: it must be non-discriminatory as between men and women. Second, it must be capable of applying to many different types of marriage — whether long or short, with children or without children, with property or without property, whether housewife marriages or two-career marriages, whether entered into one year ago or forty years ago. Third, it must be capable of applying to cases where the marriage was ended because of the fault of the person applying for financial provision, or the fault of the other party, or the fault of both, or the fault of neither.

3.64 Applying these criteria, and taking into account all the submissions and comments made to us, we recommend:

> 31. The court should make an order for financial provision on divorce if, and only if,
> (*a*) the order is justified by one or more of the following principles:
> (i)   fair sharing of matrimonial property;
> (ii) fair recognition of contributions and disadvantages;
> (iii) fair sharing of the economic burden of child-care;
> (iv) fair provision for adjustment to independence; and
> (v)   relief of grave financial hardship
> and (*b*) the order is reasonable having regard to the resources of the parties. . . .

In the following pages we explain and develop each of the above principles.

FAIR SHARING OF MATRIMONIAL PROPERTY

A principle of quantification

3.65 When we refer to the principle of fair sharing of matrimonial property we are not talking about the division of specific items of property. How the value of a spouse's share would be satisfied would depend on the resources available at the time of the divorce. The court's powers would not be limited to matrimonial property (as defined) but would extend to all of the spouses' resources at the time of the divorce. The concept of matrimonial property would be relevant only as a means of arriving at a figure. . . . The basic idea is that it covers property acquired by the spouses, otherwise than by gift or inheritance, in the period between the marriage and their final separation.

The norm of equal sharing

3.66 It would be too vague to empower the courts to award simply a 'fair share' of matrimonial property. One of the major criticisms of the present law is that it provides no guidance on the amount of a capital sum which can be expected on divorce. It would, on the other hand, be too rigid to lay down a fixed rule of apportionment for all cases. We think that the best solution is to provide that matrimonial property should normally be divided equally between the parties but that the court should be able to depart from this norm of equal sharing in special circumstances. 3.67 We have opted for a norm of equal sharing for the following reasons. First, there is clear public support for this solution.[3]

. . . Our second reason for favouring a norm of equal sharing is that this solution was supported in submissions and comments made directly to us. Our third reason is that we felt unable to justify any system of sharing in fixed proportions which was not based fundamentally on the idea of equality. The way in which the title to property is held by spouses varies greatly from case to case and depends on a variety of factors which bear little or no relation to the way in which the spouses regard the property. It would be arbitrary and unfair to begin with the way in which the title is held and award the poorer spouse, say, such a sum as to give him or her a third of the 'joint' property. If the property was mainly in the husband's name the wife's share would be a third. If the property happened to be mainly in the wife's name the husband's share would be a third. We can see no justification for such a solution. It is sometimes suggested that the division of property on death provides an analogy. It is difficult to know, however, what division this analogy would suggest. In many cases the surviving spouse takes all the property — a solution which would hardly be appropriate on divorce. The old common law division into thirds — a third to the widow, a third to the children, and a third to the 'dead's part' (for heirs or legatees) — applied only to moveable property and is inappropriate on divorce, because divorce does not, and in our view should not, affect children's property rights. Where there were no children the surviving spouse took half of the moveable property. In our view the analogy with death is unhelpful. The situations on death and divorce are entirely different. On the dissolution of a marriage by death there is only one surviving spouse and there may or may not be other relatives or beneficiaries with competing claims. It has sometimes been argued that a wife should receive less than half of the capital on divorce because she also receives a share of her husband's income. This argument is based on certain assumptions which will often be unjustified, and it is inapplicable to the scheme we are proposing. We suggest later that the court should, where possible, adjust the parties' economic position by means of a capital sum or property transfer order, and should award a periodical allowance only where its other powers are insufficient. Moreover, under our proposals there would be no reason why a wife (or a husband) should not receive half of the matrimonial property *and* in certain cases a share of the joint income after divorce. A fair share of the assets accumulated during the marriage should not, for example, preclude income payments designed to provide partial compensation for the continuing burden of child-care. In short, we can see no good reason for giving either spouse, whether legal owner or not, whether wife or husband, less than half of the matrimonial property. The underlying idea is that of partnership in marriage and the only fair solution seems to us to be an equal division of the 'partnership' assets as the norm. We are confirmed in this conclusion by the fact that no system of matrimonial property of which we are aware provides for a division of such property in any fixed proportions other than equal shares.

3.68 Where there are special circumstances justifying a departure from equal sharing (and we give examples of such circumstances later) we think that the court should be directed to share the matrimonial property in such proportions as may be fair in those circumstances. It would be impossible to provide with precision for the infinite variety of special circumstances which may arise. We therefore recommend:

    32. (*a*) The principle of fair sharing of matrimonial property is that the net value of the matrimonial property should be shared equally or, if there are special circumstances justifying a departure from equal sharing, in such other proportions as may be fair in those circumstances. . . .

---

3. The Scottish Law Commission here refer to a survey carried out in 1979 (Manners and Rauta).

Definition of matrimonial property

3.72 . . . We . . . define matrimonial property essentially in terms of property acquired during the marriage; to take as the norm equal sharing of the value of such property; but to allow the court to depart from that norm if the property was not derived from the spouses' efforts or income during the marriage. This would provide a comparatively simple rule but would allow the court to take into account the fact, for example, that property was largely derived from premarital assets. In complicated cases the court could take a fairly broad axe. No solution to this problem is without disadvantages but, in our view, this solution has fewer disadvantages than any other . . . we recommend:

32. (b) Matrimonial property should be defined as any property belonging to either party or both parties at the date of final separation which was acquired (otherwise than from a third party by gift or succession) by him or them

    (i)   before the marriage for use by the parties as their joint residence or as furniture or equipment for their joint residence; or

    (ii) after the marriage.

Rights under life policies or pension schemes

3.77 . . . we are concerned with the value of rights on the break-up of the marriage rather than with what one spouse or the other might have received (by way of widow's pension for example) had the marriage continued. This is consistent with our whole approach to the question of financial provision on divorce, which is not to try to put the parties in the position in which they would have been had the marriage continued but rather to recognise that the marriage has not continued and make the necessary financial and property adjustments. One of these adjustments is, in our view, a sharing of savings made during the marriage, including savings made by means of life policies or retirement pension schemes. Our intention is that such savings should be taken into account if they have an economic value. To avoid argument about whether a spouse has a right or merely an interest under a pension scheme or similar arrangement the legislation should, we suggest, refer to rights or interests. We therefore recommend:

32. (c) Where either spouse has rights or interests under a life policy or occupational pension scheme or similar arrangement, the proportion of such rights or interests which relates to the period from the marriage until the date of final separation should be treated as matrimonial property. . . .

Special circumstances justifying departure from equal sharing

3.78 *Parties' agreement.* The parties may have agreed that a particular item of property should be treated as separate property or that property acquired during marriage should be shared otherwise than in equal proportions. In such circumstances it may be supposed that they would often settle the question of financial provision on divorce in accordance with their previous agreement without involving the court. If, however, one of them does apply for an order for financial provision their prior agreement should be regarded as a special circumstance which might justify a departure from equal sharing. We do not think the agreement should be conclusive. Circumstances may have changed radically since the agreement was entered into. It would be better, in our view, to preserve flexibility by enabling the court to take the agreement into account without requiring the court to be bound by it. The terms in which title to property was taken would not in themselves constitute an agreement.

3.79 *Source of funds or assets.* Property bought after the marriage may have been paid for out of funds owned by one party at the time of the marriage. It may represent merely a switching of investments. We think that this should justify a departure from equal sharing. Similarly we think that a departure from equal sharing could be justified if the source of the funds or assets used by a spouse to acquire property during the marriage was a gift from a third party (such as a spouse's parent). The underlying principle is the sharing of property acquired by the spouses' efforts or income during the marriage. Property acquired wholly or partially with funds or assets derived from other sources need not be shared equally. The possible combinations of circumstances which might arise are such that, as noted above, we prefer to deal with this question by giving the court a discretion rather than by laying down any rule. In practice few couples own substantial assets at the time of marriage.

3.80 *Destruction, etc, of property.* If one party has destroyed, dissipated or alienated matrimonial property that, we think, is a circumstance that the court should be able to take into account in deciding whether a departure from equal sharing is justified. We deal later with the effect of conduct generally in relation to financial provision on divorce. These particular types of conduct are, however, so closely related to the property that they can usefully be referred to separately in this context.

3.81 *The nature of the property and the use made of it.* Under the present law the court may take into account, in awarding a capital sum on divorce, the nature of the property and the use made of it. A spouse's capital may be tied up in a business, a farm, a pension scheme or a private company in such a way that it is not reasonable to expect it to be used as a source of money for payment of a capital sum on divorce. In the reported cases the point has been made that to force a defender to sell his business would often diminish the income available for a periodical allowance. Under our proposals, which express a preference for dealing with financial provision by means of a capital sum or property transfer, the emphasis would be rather different. The point would be not so much the diminution of a periodical allowance as the disproportionate hardship to the defender caused by a requirement for sale. Nevertheless we consider that the nature of the property and the use made of it and, in particular, the extent to which it is reasonable to expect it to be realised or divided or used as security should be circumstances which the court could, if it thought fit, take into account in departing from the principle of equal sharing. In appropriate cases the court could keep close to the principle of equal sharing, without causing undue hardship to the defender, by awarding a capital sum payable by instalments. In some cases, however, it would probably be necessary to recognise that an approximation to equal sharing was impracticable or inequitable in the circumstances.

3.82 Use of the matrimonial property as a family home is also a relevant factor. Under the present law on financial provision the courts, both in Scotland and in England, take into account the desirability of retaining a home for the children of the marriage. In certain cases we think that this consideration could justify a departure from the principle of equal sharing. This result seems to be supported by public opinion. In the survey of family property in Scotland informants were asked whether the law on family property should be affected if there were dependent children. 71% of men and 69% of women said that it should be affected. These informants were then asked in what ways the law should be affected. 81% said that the law should allocate more of the family property to the parent with the children than to the other parent.

3.83 There is a danger that the supposed needs of children (who, after all, often have to move house and suffer a drop in living standards even in unbroken families) could be used to justify results which would be unfair to one of the spouses. We think that any departure from the principle of equal sharing of matrimonial property should be kept to the minimum and that the courts should use the wide powers which will be available under our recommendations to achieve as fair a solution as is practicable. In some cases this may involve ordering an immediate counter-balancing payment of capital or transfer of property. In others it may involve an order for such a payment or transfer at a later date — say, when the children cease to be dependent. In others it may involve awarding less by way of a periodical allowance for child-care than would otherwise have been awarded.

3.86 We therefore recommend:

32. (*d*) Special circumstances which may justify a departure from the principle of equal sharing, if the court thinks fit, should include
   (i) the terms of any agreement between the parties on the ownership or division of any matrimonial property;
   (ii) the source of the funds or assets used to acquire the matrimonial property where those funds or assets were not derived from the parties' efforts or income during the marriage;
   (iii) any destruction, dissipation or alienation of matrimonial property by either party;
   (iv) the nature of the property, the use made of it (including use for business purposes or as a family home) and the extent to which it is reasonable to expect it to be realised or divided or used as security; and
   (v) the actual or prospective liability for any expenses of valuation or transfer of property in connection with the divorce. . . .

FAIR RECOGNITION OF CONTRIBUTIONS AND DISADVANTAGES

Purpose and scope

3.91 In many cases a spouse's contributions during the marriage will be recognised by his or her share of the matrimonial property. If both spouses have contributed to the welfare of the family, if both have enjoyed the same standard of living during the marriage and if both have earning potential on divorce which has not been affected by the marriage, then a fair sharing of any property built up during the marriage by their joint efforts or income will often produce a satisfactory result. In some cases, however, a share of the matrimonial property will not be a sufficient recognition of contributions made during the marriage. There may, for example, be no matrimonial property or it may be of small value. We think that it is essential, if justice is to be done, that there should be some further provision for the due recognition of contributions. Various situations have to be considered before it can be decided how this principle should be expressed.

3.92 The first is where the contributions of one spouse have contributed to an improvement in the other's economic position. A husband, for example, may have paid off a loan over a house owned by his wife before the marriage, or he may have worked for years extending and improving her house. Similarly a wife may have worked for years, unpaid, in a small business owned by her husband before the marriage and may have helped to build up its value. In all these cases one spouse has contributed to an increase in the capital of the other and we think it reasonable that the court should be able to award some financial provision on divorce in recognition of the contributions. The position is essentially the same where one of the spouses has contributed to an increase in the other's earning potential. A wife, for example, may have bought the husband into a partnership or franchise arrangement on such terms that there are minimal rights to capital but a valuable earning potential. A husband may have worked overtime to pay his wife's fees for some special course of further education or training. A wife may have helped her husband with his work on an unpaid basis (e.g. as a personal secretary or business manager) but because of the nature of his work (e.g. author, doctor, advocate, professional sportsman, entertainer) the result of her contributions may be an increase in his earning potential rather than in the capital value of a business. Again, there may be cases where one spouse's unpaid services as a housekeeper, hostess, domestic manager and child-minder could be shown to have contributed directly or indirectly to an improvement in the other spouse's economic position. It may be possible to prove, for example, that a wife's contributions of this nature have enabled her husband to work long hours furthering his career. In all these cases, where there is a demonstrable link between one spouse's contributions and an improvement in the other spouse's economic position, it seems to us that there is a strong case for enabling the contribution to be recognised where this is not already done by means of a share in matrimonial property.

3.93 The position becomes more difficult, however, if there is no link between the contributions and any improvement in the other spouse's economic position. Suppose, for example, that three men all started work in the same employment at the age of 20. The first married a wife who assumed the traditional housewife's role and did all the domestic work. The second married an idle woman and did most of the domestic work himself. The third remained unmarried and did all his own domestic work. All three lived in rented accommodation. None accumulated any savings. All advanced remorselessly up their salary scale. If the first man was divorced at the age of 40 it would certainly not be obvious that his wife's contributions over the years had contributed to any improvement in his economic position, although they may well have contributed to an increase in the time available to him for leisure activities. Should an industrious wife receive more than an idle wife in this case? Should the principle of fair recognition of contributions extend to contributions to the welfare of the family even if they have not improved the other spouse's economic position? One submission made to us was that such contributions were made voluntarily and should therefore be ignored. The same point could, however, be made about many contributions which have directly improved the other spouse's economic position. Another view put to us was that the law should take a hard line on the question of a housewife's contributions in order to encourage women to preserve their economic independence during marriage. In our view, however, it is not the function of financial provision on divorce to encourage people to adopt any particular life style during marriage. The law in our view ought to be neutral in this respect. We therefore reject these two arguments. We think, however, that there are other grounds for not recognising a claim based on contributions which have not resulted in any improvement in the other spouse's economic position. First, such contributions will often be evenly balanced. If, in the traditional type of marriage, a housewife could make a claim on the basis of contributions in work towards the welfare of the family, her husband could often do the same. One of the findings of the survey on family property in Scotland in 1979 was that 50% of married informants said that the contributions of the husband and the wife in unpaid work in the home were about the same. Moreover, if a wife could make a claim on the basis of her contributions in work, her husband could often make a claim on the basis of his contributions in money to the welfare of the family. In some cases (for example the lazy wife, the wife with domestic help) the husband would be able to make a claim on this basis for a payment out of the wife's separate property. We doubt whether this would be acceptable. Secondly, an attempt to work out which spouse had contributed more to the welfare of the family during the marriage would often involve an unproductive examination and investigation of conduct over many years. Thirdly, and more fundamentally, the purpose of financial provision on divorce is not, in our view, the punishment of bad conduct or the reward of good conduct. In our view its concern should be with the economic effects of marriage and divorce . . .

3.94 There is a further problem. One spouse may have sustained an economic disadvantage in the interests of the other party or of the family. The standard illustration is the well-qualified woman who married, say, 20 or 30 years ago and who gave up her own career prospects, perhaps with the encouragement or passive approval of her husband, in order to look after and bring up the family. There are other illustrations. A husband may have given up career prospects (for example the chance of a lucrative post abroad) in his wife's interests. An older woman may have given up a good position on marriage in order to look after her husband and may be unable to obtain employment again after divorce. One of the parties may have given up a tenancy in order to live with the other party on marriage. In all such cases there should in our view be the possibility of financial provision on divorce in recognition of the economic disadvantages sustained.

FAIR SHARING OF ECONOMIC BURDEN OF CHILD-CARE

3.106 We therefore recommend as follows: . . .
34.　　(*a*) The principle of fair sharing of the economic burden of child-care is that the economic burden of caring for a dependent child of the marriage after the divorce should be shared fairly between the parties to the marriage.
　　　(*b*) In applying this principle the court should have regard
　　　　(i) to any arrangements made or to be made for aliment for the child;
　　　　(ii) to any expense or loss of earning capacity caused by the need to care for the child;
　　　　(iii) to the age and health of the child, to the educational, financial and other circumstances of the child, to the availability and cost of suitable child-care facilities or services, to the needs and resources, actual and foreseeable, of the parties, including the need for suitable accommodation for any dependent child of the marriage, and to the other circumstances of the case.

FAIR PROVISION FOR ADJUSTMENT TO INDEPENDENCE

The principle
3.107 In many cases divorcing spouses will already be economically independent by the time of the divorce. In many cases an award of financial provision under one of the principles discussed above would be sufficient to provide for any necessary adjustment to post-divorce independence. In other cases, however, we think that a reasonable objective of an award of financial provision on divorce is to enable a spouse to adjust, over a relatively short period, to the cessation on divorce of any financial dependence on the other spouse. Depending on the circumstances, the purpose of the award might be to enable the payee to undertake a course of training or retraining, or to give the payee time to find suitable employment, or to enable the payee to adjust gradually to a lower standard of living. It would be essential to specify a maximum time over which the adjustment would have to be made because otherwise there would, in many cases, be no way of ensuring that a transitional provision did not become permanent life-long support. We think that a period of three years from the date of divorce would be an adequate maximum period, given that in most cases the final separation between the parties would be some considerable time before that. We considered whether an adjustment provision ought to be available for, say, three years after the termination of a period of child-care after divorce. We have concluded, however, that this would not be justified. The main purpose of a provision under this principle is to provide time to adjust. That time would be available where the spouse had a periodical allowance during a period of child care. To allow a periodical allowance for up to a maximum of sixteen years on the basis of child-care and then to follow this with a transitional provision for another three years would, we think, prolong dependence too long and would run counter to our general approach, which is to seek to terminate continuing financial links between the divorced parties except where a continuing link is clearly justified.

Factors to be taken into account
3.108 In addition to the usual factors such as the needs and resources of the parties, we think that it would be desirable to refer specifically, in relation to this principle, to the earning capacity of the payee, to the duration and extent of the payee's past dependency on the payer and to any intentions of the payee to undertake a course of education or training. We deal later with the relevance of conduct.
3.109 We therefore recommend as follows:
　35. (*a*) The principle of fair provision for adjustment to independence is that where one party to the marriage has been financially dependent on the other and the dependence has come to an end on divorce, the dependent party should receive such financial provision as is fair and reasonable to enable him to adjust, over a period of not more than three years from the date of divorce, to the cessation of that dependence.
　　　(*b*) In deciding what financial provision is fair and reasonable under this recommendation the court should have regard to the age, health and earning capacity of the applicant, to the duration and extent of the applicant's past dependency on the

payer, to any intention of the applicant to undertake a course of education or training, to the needs and resources, actual or foreseeable, of the parties, and to the other circumstances of the case. . . .

RELIEF OF GRAVE FINANCIAL HARDSHIP

Purpose and scope
3.110 It could be argued that the four principles which we have discussed so far are adequate to cover all cases where financial provision on divorce is justified. This would mean that if there was no matrimonial property, if there was no claim based on contributions or disadvantages, and if there were no dependent children, then a divorced spouse could be awarded at most a provision designed to ease his or her adjustment to independence over a period of not more than three years. Thereafter he or she would have no claim against the former spouse. While there is much to be said for this approach, we have rejected it. The four principles discussed already would not always ensure that a spouse who suffered severe financial hardship as a result of the marriage and the divorce could recover some financial provision in appropriate cases. A wife might, for example, have gone with her husband to some tropical country and might have contracted a disabling disease. Or she might have been permanently disabled as a result of injury in childbirth. We think that in such cases financial provision on divorce would be justified if it were reasonable having regard to the parties' resources. We have more doubt about whether a former spouse should ever be expected to relieve the hardship of the other if the hardship does not arise in any way from the marriage. If we were approaching the matter as one of pure principle we would be inclined to reject such a proposition as contrary to the idea that divorce ends the marriage. Financial provision on divorce is not, however, simply a matter of abstract principle. It is essential that any system should be acceptable to public opinion and it is clear from the comments we have received that many people would find it hard to accept a system which cut off, say, an elderly or disabled spouse with no more than a three-year allowance after divorce, no matter how wealthy the other party might be. We have concluded therefore that the law ought to provide, as a 'long-stop', for the case where one spouse would suffer grave financial hardship as a result of the divorce. In such a case the court should be able to award such financial provision as is fair and reasonable in the circumstances to relieve the hardship over such period as the court may determine. We do not intend this principle to be a gateway to support after divorce in all cases just as if the marriage had not been dissolved. We do not think, for example, that a man who suffers hardship on being made redundant at the age of 52 should have a claim for financial provision against a former wife whom he divorced thirty years before. We think that the general principle should be that after the divorce each party bears the risk of *supervening* hardship without recourse against the other. It should therefore be made clear in the legislation that it is only where the likelihood of grave financial hardship is established at the time of the divorce that a claim will arise under this principle. We recognise that if the principle is framed in this way there will be cases falling narrowly on the 'wrong' side of the line. The man or woman paralysed as a result of a road accident six months before the divorce would have a claim for financial provision. The man or woman who suffered a similar injury six months after the divorce would not. Similarly the spouse whose progressive disease was diagnosed before the divorce would have a claim but the spouse whose disease was first diagnosed after the divorce would not. We consider, however, that a line has to be drawn somewhere and that the right place to draw the line is the date when the legal relationship between the parties comes to an end. After that each should be free to make a new life without liability for future misfortunes which may befall the other.

Questions

(i) Does the approach of the Scottish Law Commission differ substantially from that of the English Law Commission?
(ii) If so, whose approach do you prefer?

The final paragraph raises the question of whether support for a former spouse should be a private or public responsibility when that person is incapable of supporting himself or herself owing to extreme disability arising during the marriage. The Scottish Law Commission suggest that it should be a private responsibility. Others such as Gray (1977) would suggest that the responsibility should fall onto the State. We said at the outset that the extent of public responsibility in financial terms towards the casualties of marriage breakdown lay below the surface throughout these two chapters. We turn to that topic, set in the wider context of state support for the family generally, in Chapter 16, below.

Martin Stevens MP introduced a Matrimonial Proceedings Bill into the House of Commons in the 1982/83 Session. It failed to get a second reading. The Bill contained, in the main, proposals put forward by the Law Commission Report. It proposed to discard the objective at placing the parties, as far as is practicable and having regard to their conduct just to do so, in the financial position in which they would have been had the marriage not broken down. The second major change was that the court, instead of being under a general duty to have regard to the conduct of the spouses, would be specifically required to take conduct into account if, in the court's opinion, it was such that it would be inequitable to disregard it. The remaining provisions required the court, in all applications for financial relief after divorce, to give first consideration to the welfare of any children of the family, and to consider whether it would be appropriate so to exercise its powers that the financial obligations of each party towards the other would be terminated as soon as just and reasonable.

Question

Are you pleased that the Bill was lost?

CHAPTER 8

Cohabitation

1 Underlying causes of non-marital cohabitation

Perhaps the major change which has occurred in the organisation of the family, both in the United States and in Western Europe, over the last few decades has been the fact that, whereas once cohabitation may have existed but was concealed, today various forms of relationships outside marriage are accepted by the wider community as perfectly appropriate behaviour. Until recently, it is certainly true to say that 'informal' arrangements have been confined to intellectual elites and the sub-cultures of the poor and racial and ethnic minorities for whom the structures of traditional marriage and divorce law have been to a large extent irrelevant. This is no longer the case.

Glendon, in *Withering Away of Marriage* (1976), reflects on some of the reasons for the acceptance by society of informal arrangements:

Today, however, informal marriage is increasingly common among other social groups and, perhaps more significant, increasingly accepted. These two facts interact. The more persons in a particular group 'live together,' the more such behaviour becomes accepted. The more acceptance this alternative to formal marriage gains, the more people employ it. Thus, informal marriage has become a recurring subject in popular songs and cartoons and was discussed in the 1972 federal government report on population. Cohabitation is favored among young people, among pensioners and others receiving benefits terminable or reducible upon formal marriage, and increasingly among other diverse social groups. It has been estimated that six to eight million people are involved in such arrangements and the writer of a legal handbook on cohabitation asserts that Bureau of the Census figures show that the number of couples living together without formal marriage increased by over 700% from 1960 to 1970. (King, 1975) . . .

Motivations to enter informal rather than legal marriage include economic advantages as in the case of many elderly people, inability to enter a legal marriage, unwillingness to be subject to the legal effects of marriage, desire for a 'trial marriage,' and lack of concern with the legal institution. This lack of concern is nothing new among groups accustomed to forming and dissolving informal unions without coming into contact with legal institutions. Among these groups legal marriage is but an aspect of the irrelevance of traditional American family law, law that is viewed as being property-oriented and organized around the ideals of a dominant social group. Lack of concern with marriage law has been growing, however, among many who definitely are not outside the mainstream of American life. Until recently these converts accepted unquestioningly the traditional structures of the enacted law, but they now find that on balance the enacted law offers no advantages over informal arrangements.

An interesting motivational study entitled *Unmarried Partners and their Children: Scandinavian Law in the Making* has been carried out by the Danish Social Research Institute to ascertain the motives either for marrying or for establishing unmarried cohabitation. (Danielson (1981 now 1983).) It was reported from this study that:

80% of the newly-weds had lived together before marriage, while among respondents who had been married for ten years or more only 22% had lived together before marriage. Among newly-weds, one-third had considered the possibility of (continued) unmarried cohabitation, while the long-time married couples in this respect registered only a small percentage.

The study also inquired if marriage offered any advantage. 61% of newly-weds said 'Yes', but 65% of the same group said 'Yes' also to the question if advantages were to be found in unmarried cohabition!

The researchers found that the 'trial marriage' accounted for a great many instances of unmarried cohabitation. Respondents in the Danish study who were cohabiting but unmarried were asked to give reasons why they had not married. The reasons given were as follows:

	Cohabiting unmarried persons %	Cohabiting divorced persons %
Will soon marry	4	5
Are considering marriage; want a trial period	36	36
Financial reasons	14	12
Will not be bound; need no written contract; no necessity	25	24
Other reasons	13	12
Don't know/not thought about it	8	8
No data available	—	3
Total	100	100
Number of respondents	109	134

Question

What do you think the 'other reasons' could be?

Butler *Traditional Marriage and Emerging Alternatives* (1979) stresses the interaction of what he calls 'personal growth' together with the major changes in the economic conditions of women as the two primary reasons which account for changes in the traditional pattern of a life long monogamous marriage:

The women's liberation movement has influenced sex roles in the family, spread equalitarianism in households, led to greater job opportunities, and influenced the growth of sexual equality; and it is having a substantial effect upon legal codes and enforcement.
  Similarly, personal growth and open communication have had an impact on traditional marriage and influenced emerging alternatives, and separately or together, these developments can cause the breakup of a traditional marriage. While these changes can occur in a family separately, they tend to cluster.

In contrast, Meade, in *Consortium rights of the unmarried — time for a reappraisal* (1981), tends towards the view that there are a large number of interrelated reasons why couples opt out of traditional marriage. They include the following:
  (1) a desire to avoid the sex-stereotyped allocation of roles associated with marriage
  (2) a belief that marriage is unnecessary or irrelevant if no children are involved
  (3) a reluctance to enter a supposedly permanent marriage
  (4) bohemian philosophy
  (5) a conscientious objection to state regulation of marriage
  (6) a desire to avoid the expense and trauma of a possible divorce
  (7) an insouciant outlook on legally sanctioned relationships
  (8) the desire for various forms of companionship
  (9) a trial period to test suitability for marriage

(10) the need to share expenses in the face of long-lasting inflation.

One reason left out of Meade's list which will be relevant in some cases is simply that the parties are *unable* to marry because previous legal ties have not yet been broken.

Questions

(i) Do you think any of the reasons given by Meade to be more important than any other?

(ii) Is there any relevance for the legal reformer in being told that 'trial marriages' account for most instances of cohabitation outside marriage?

(iii) If so, what is this relevance?

Supposed legal advantages or disadvantages of marriage as opposed to cohabitation play a very small part in decisions to cohabit. This point is made by Oliver in her survey of seven cohabiting couples, *Why do people live together?* (1982):

Although the couples interviewed had made very little reference to the legal aspects of marriage as influencing them in their decision to live together, and their failure to marry, it would nevertheless be of interest to lawyers to have some idea of what the attitude of cohabiting couples is to the legal aspects of marriage, and indeed to their own obligations, if any, to one another. On this point three couples stressed their sense of responsibility to one another: one couple had made mutual wills leaving everything to the other, another couple, of whom the man had children by his previous marriage, had agreed that the woman would leave all to the man ('all' meant the jointly-owned flat and contents) and the man would leave his share of the jointly-owned home and contents to the woman, and the rest of his estate to his ex-wife for the children. In the case of two of the couples there was a disagreement about support. The men were willing to support their partners should they become unemployed, while the women expressed extreme hostility to the idea of being supported. It may be that the desire to assert independence is a factor that influences some women to cohabit rather than to marry.

The cohabiting couples were asked in an open-ended question what differences they could think of between cohabitation on the one hand and marriage on the other. The couples seemed to be surprisingly unaware of the legal difference. Three respondents mentioned tax differences; eight mentioned that the children of unmarried couples are illegitimate, but, as will appear later, there was uncertainty about what this meant. Only two mentioned that there were support obligations between husband and wife and not between cohabiting persons. And four mentioned that the inheritance position is different for married couples from the position of unmarried couples. One mentioned that widows have pension rights while a surviving cohabitee would not. The respondents were then asked to say, specifically, whether they were aware, or not, of particular legal differences. All of the respondents said that they knew that the children of unmarried couples were illegitimate; but only eight knew that the father of an illegitimate child has no parental rights. Two spontaneously stated that they were under the impression that it was possible for an unmarried couple to adopt any children they might have and thus overcome the disadvantage of illegitimacy. Seven of them knew that there were support obligations between married couples but not between cohabiting couples. However, five believed there were support obligations between cohabitees. Ten knew that the court has power to transfer property on divorce. Six knew that there was no equivalent power on the breakdown of cohabitation, and the other six were surprised to hear that there was no equivalent power in respect of cohabitation. Eight of these respondents knew that a surviving cohabitee does not have rights on intestacy and two of the respondents thought that a surviving cohabitee did have rights on intestacy. Clearly a disturbing number of misconceptions about the law, were held by the respondents particularly relating to the position of illegitimate children, maintenance of cohabitees and the property rights of cohabitees. The married couple, who had both been through divorce, knew about all the legal differences between marriage and cohabitation, except that they believed property was split equally between the parties on divorce (and felt that this was fair).

Having established how much these couples knew (or thought they knew) about the differences between marriage and cohabitation, questions were then asked that were designed to discover their attitudes to these legal differences. A hypothetical situation was put to the couples. They were asked to imagine a husband and wife, married for five years, with two small children, who divorce. The respondents were asked whether the wife, if she had custody, should be supported, and whether a wife who does not have dependent children should be supported; and they were also asked what should happen to the matrimonial home. Thirteen of the fourteen respondents stated that the wife ought to be supported by the husband after divorce if she had the children living with her. The other respondent, a girl, felt that the wife should support herself and put the children in day nurseries, paid for out of her earnings and the husband's child-support payments. She was roundly scolded for this by her partner, who felt that an agreement to support was implicit in marriage and anyway the husband was under a moral obligation to support her until she was able to get a job, once the children were at school. This man also felt there was a similar moral support obligation between unmarried couples who had children. Four of the respondents felt that support obligations should continue if one spouse was disabled, and four felt that support should go to an innocent spouse. Nine respondents said that a rehabilitative award of support after divorce would be proper and one stated that there should be support after divorce of an unemployed spouse. The assumption all along was that it was the wife, not the husband, who would require support and they were not asked to consider specifically the possibility of the husband needing support. Ten of the respondents stated that a childless wife ought to work after divorce if possible, and some respondents were clearly under the false impression that a divorced wife is automatically entitled to lifelong support, and all felt that this was wrong. In practice, of course, awards to childless wives are by no means the rule, and it may be that a misunderstanding among some sections of the public about the support obligation makes marriage less popular than it might be. This is a point that would be worth exploring in any proper research project into cohabitation. Two respondents were of the view that the state ought to provide for parties who are unable to provide for themselves after divorce; but that particular question was not raised with most of the respondents. Three of the respondents to whom this question was put felt that state support should be given to a divorced wife only as a last resort. It is worth remembering here, of course, that all the respondents were middle class, all save one girl (who was strongly against support) were employed, and all but two were childless. It seemed from these responses that the respondents were broadly in agreement with the present legal *practice* regarding support after marriage. It was interesting also to note some evidence of the belief that guilt or innocence should be material factors in considering support.

The question was then put, what should happen to the matrimonial home if this hypothetical married couple were to separate? All respondents agreed that the parent with custody of the children should remain in the matrimonial home if there was nowhere else to go. Two felt that a disabled spouse should be entitled to remain in the home, and two felt that an innocent spouse should remain. Four stated that a spouse with nowhere else to go should be entitled to remain, and two mentioned that the parties' means would be a relevant consideration.

The couples were then questioned about their attitudes to the breakdown of a similar relationship, if the parties had not been married. Twelve of the respondents (including the married couple) stated that the man should be under a duty to support the woman if there were dependent children at home. One felt that there should also be a support obligation in the case of a disabled partner, and two, surprisingly, stated that there should be a support obligation towards an 'innocent' woman. Five stated that, if the cohabiting woman had been a housewife she should be entitled to rehabilitative support until she could obtain a job. Nine stated that in principle the obligations on separation of a cohabiting couple should be the same as those on the breakdown of marriage and two further respondents said that, if the couple had been together for four or five years then there should be similar obligations on breakdown whether of marriage or cohabitation. One man said that people should not be able to expect legal security without the commitment of marriage, and this man was one of the respondents who intended to marry once his divorce and that of his partner had come through. One respondent, the girl who had stated that a divorcing wife should place her children in a day nursery and go out to work, was very reluctant to erode the freedom of couples who live together, and treat the relationship like marriage, by imposing support obligations. She reluctantly conceded, when pressed by her partner, that there might be a moral obligation but she felt that any such obligation should not be legally enforceable. She stated that people ought to make contracts about these matters. This particular couple had not, in fact, made any arrangement that could, in the writer's view, be construed as a contract! But they had recently decided to marry within a year or so, having been together for four years.

Turning from the question of support of a cohabitee to the right to live in the home, all the respondents felt that a mother with custody of dependent children ought to be entitled to remain in the home if there was nowhere else for them to go. One felt that a disabled former cohabitee ought to be allowed to remain in the home, two felt that an 'innocent' cohabitee ought to be entitled to remain, and four stated that there should be a right to remain in the home if there was nowhere else to go. In this respect 10 of the respondents felt that cohabitation and marriage should have the same legal consequences, although there was some inconsistency here since six of the respondents stressed that cohabitation should be treated in the same way as marriage only if there were children; the hypothetical situation put to them had involved children, so their minds had been directed to couples with children.

2 Statistical data

The only statistical data giving any indication of the level of extra-marital cohabitation in Great Britain come from the general household survey. This is summarised in *Social Trends 13 1982*:

Cohabitation is more prevalent amongst widowed, divorced, or separated women than amongst single women (Table 2.10). Eighteen per cent of widowed, divorced, or separated women between the ages of 18 to 49 were cohabiting in 1980–1981 compared with only 9 per cent of single women. For women aged 18 to 24, the difference was even more marked (20 and 7 per cent respectively). Overall, 11 per cent of all non-married women aged 18 to 49 were cohabiting during 1980–1981.

Table 2.10 Proportion of women aged 18–49 cohabiting[1,2]: by age and marital status, 1980–1981

	Great Britain		Percentages and numbers
	Marital status		All single, widowed, divorced, or separated women
	Single	Divorced, divorced, or separated	
Age group			
18–24	7	20	8
25–49	11	17	15
All aged 18–49	9	18	11
Sample size (= 100%) (numbers)			
18–24	1,764	94	1,858
25–49	718	956	1,674
All aged 18–49	2,482	1,050	3,532

[1] Living with a man (other than husband) as his wife.
[2] See Appendix, Part 2: Cohabitation.
Source: General Household Survey, combined data for 1980 and 1981

Table 2.11 cover pre-marital cohabitation. It shows that 18 per cent of women under 50 who married in 1979 or 1980 (where the marriage was the first for both partners) had lived with their husband before the wedding. This compares with only 6 per cent who married in the early 1970s. Almost three in every five women under 50, whose marriage in 1979–1980 was the second or subsequent for at least one partner, had lived with their new husband before the wedding — more than twice the proportion who married in the 1960s.

Table 2.11 Proportion of women aged 16–49 in 1981 who had lived with their husband before their current or most recent marriage: by first or subsequent marriage, age at marriage, and year of marriage

Great Britain   Percentages and numbers

	Year of marriage					
	1960 –1964	1965 –1969	1970 –1974	1975 –1976	1977 –1978	1979 –1980
First marriage for both partners —						
age of woman at marriage						
(percentages)						
16–19	3	3	6	9	21	19
20–24	2	2	6	9	13	15
25–49	7	3	8		18	
All aged 16–49	3	2	6	10	16	18
Sample size (= 100%) (numbers)						
16–19	263	313	302	101	97	86
20–24	450	480	460	143	158	152
25–49	85	96	145		125	
All aged 16–49	798	889	907	281	304	277
Second or subsequent marriage for one						
or both partners						
All aged 16–49 *(percentages)*		26	43	71	51	58
Sample size (= 100%) (numbers)		120	214	97	129	122

Source: General Household Survey, 1981

Considerable research on unmarried couples has been carried out in Denmark. A summary of this is compiled by Svend Danielsen, *Unmarried partners and their children: Scandinavian Law in the Making* (1981 now 1983):

In 1973, at the request of the Danish Family Law Commission, the Danish Social Research Institute interviewed 2,000 persons aged between 18 and 50 years, including a group of 500 people who had been divorced in 1972 and a corresponding number of unmarried people. These interviews gave a first impression of the incidence of regular cohabitation. 27% of the unmarried respondents were living together with a male or female friend. Further, an unknown number of divorcé(e)s had settled down in cohabitation. The interviews also revealed that 65% of the instances of cohabitation had subsisted for less than two years, and that 20% had subsisted for more than three years.

During the last six years, Danmarks Statistik has studied developments at frequent intervals. Between 2,500 and 5,000 people aged over 16 years have been interviewed nationwide two or three times a year. They form a representative segment of the Danish population. Since 1974, questions relating to unmarried cohabitants have been included.

Figures illustrating the various forms of cohabitation are as follows: — In 1978–79 unmarried cohabitants made up 371,000 of a total population of 5,000,000. This means that 13% of all people living together were not married, and the rest were married. 23% of all unmarried people over 16 years of age; 35% of the divorced people; and 6% of widows and widowers were unmarried cohabitants. At the time of the first interviews in 1974, rather more than 200,000 people lived together outside marriage, or 8% of all cohabiting couples. The five-year period thus saw a substantial rise, viz. of 85%. It should be noted that the figures do not include married or legally separated people who lived together with some person other than their husband or wife.

All through the period of this study, the age composition has remained fairly unchanged, approximately 60% being 20–29 year olds, and 22–25% being older than 35. On the duration of cohabitation, the latest figures show that 22% had lived together less than 12 months; 19% one year; 15% two years; 15% three or four years; and 25% five years. No data were available for 4%. Of special interest is the group aged 35 or more; of these 53% had lived together for five years or longer.

18% of the interviewed couples had children of the union, and 10% children of other connections. The latter group included 2% that had children of both categories.

The most recent interviews took in also the degree or pattern of joint economy of partners. 75% of people who had cohabited for two years or more said that they had jointly bought furniture or a motorcar. 47% had signed the names of both partners on title deeds or tenancy agreements for their dwellings. 25% stated that either partner was a beneficiary of the other's will or life assurance policy, and when cohabitation had subsisted five years or more this figure was 31%. Actual cohabitation agreements directing how real property or other items of economic value should be distributed on termination of cohabitation or upon death were entered into only by 8%, — in the case of prolonged cohabitation (i.e. more than six years) by 13%.

Weitzman (1981) recites the US statistics: 'Starting from 1960 base-line data, the number of unmarried couples rose from 439,000 in 1960, to 523,000 in 1970, to 957,000 in 1977, to 1,137,000 in 1978. . . . It is likely that these figures substantially underreport the actual amount of unmarried cohabitation . . . the actual number of couples involved in a cohabitation relationship may be closer to 2 million.'

Questions

(i) Is it important for the lawyer to ask whether cohabitation is becoming: (*a*) institutionalised as an alternative to marriage; or (*b*) a new phase in a courtship process in which couples set up home before, rather than after, the 'paperwork'?
(ii) If you think it important, why do you think so?

3 Should any of the legal consequences of marriage be extended to unmarried cohabiting couples?

The Administration of Justice Act 1982 amends the Fatal Accidents Act 1976 and gives rights to claim under that Act to:

s. 1(3)(*b*) any person who —
   (i)   was living with the deceased in the same household immediately before the date of the death; and
   (ii) had been living with the deceased in the same household for at least two years before that date; and
   (iii) was living during the whole of that period as the husband or wife of the deceased;

In the House of Lords' debate on the Bill (*Hansard*, 4 May 1982) Lord Elwyn Jones said this:

We feel that, as there are in this country today hundreds of thousands of men and women living together over the years in a settled, permanent relationship as reputed spouses, in the event of the man — or possibly in some cases the woman — being deprived of the person on whom there was dependency, it would be proper that he or she should be embraced in the provisions of the Bill to deal with dependency when the person dependent has suffered loss through the negligence of a third party causing even the death of one of the reputed spouses concerned. I recall recollecting how, in our constituency surgeries, we came across that sort of tragic situation — of a sudden catastrophe happening — of, say, the husband being killed by a negligent driver with nothing left for the so-called common law wife.

Lord Elwyn-Jones, in this speech, adopts the philosophy of pretending that cohabitation is, in certain cases, like marriage, and attributes to it the traditional incidents of marriage. This has been the approach of the English courts. 'What in effect were cohabitation cases were disguised as cases involving presumptively legal marriages, estoppels, and implied agreements to pay·for services. . . .' (Glendon (1976).)

Cooke v Head
[1972] 2 All ER 38, [1972] 1 WLR 518, 116 Sol Jo 298, Court of Appeal

The plaintiff formed a relationship with the defendant, a married man, in 1962. In 1964, they decided to acquire land in order to build a bungalow for their use. It was their hope that the defendant would obtain a divorce from his wife. The conveyance was taken in the defendant's name, and he paid a deposit and raised a mortgage from a building society. The plaintiff helped in the construction of the bungalow. To adopt the words used by Lord Denning MR in his judgment: 'She used a sledge hammer to demolish some old buildings. She filled the wheelbarrow with rubble and hard core and wheeled it up the bank. She worked the cement mixer, which was out of order and difficult to work. She did painting and so forth. The plaintiff did much more than most women would do.' The bungalow was nearing completion when, in 1966, the couple separated. The defendant sold the bungalow, and the plaintiff issued a writ to determine the way in which the proceeds of sale were to be divided. The trial judge held that she should have one-twelfth of the proceeds. She appealed against that decision to the Court of Appeal:

Lord Denning MR: . . . I do not think it is right to approach this case by looking at the money contributions of each and dividing up the beneficial interest according to those contributions. The matter should be looked at more broadly, just as we do in husband and wife cases. We look to see what the equity is worth at the time when the parties separate. We assess the shares as at that time. If the property has been sold, we look at the amount which it has realised, and say how it is to be divided between them. Lord Diplock in *Gissing v Gissing* [1971] AC 886 at 909 intimated that it is quite legitimate to infer that:

'the wife should be entitled to a share which was not to be quantified immediately upon the acquisition of the home but should be left to be determined when the mortgage was repaid or the property disposed of.'

Likewise with a mistress.

The court decided that the plaintiff's share of the net proceeds of sale should be one-third.

Eves v Eves
[1975] 3 All ER 768, [1975] 1 WLR 1338, 119 Sol Jo 394, Court of Appeal

The plaintiff (referred to in the judgment of Lord Denning MR as 'Janet' because 'she has had four surnames already') met the defendant in 1968. The relationship lasted four and a half years and during this time she took his surname and had two children by him. He was a married man and they lived together initially in his house. In 1969, they moved to another house which was conveyed into the defendant's name. The house was paid for in part by the sale of the former house and in part by a mortgage raised by the defendant. As in *Cooke v Head*, the plaintiff put in a lot of initial work. Lord Denning MR said 'she stripped the wallpaper in the hall. She painted woodwork in the lounge and kitchen. She painted the kitchen cabinets. She painted the brickwork in the front of the house. She broke up the concrete in the front garden. She carried the pieces to a skip. She, with him, demolished a shed and put up a new shed. She prepared the front garden for turfing.' The couple separated in 1972, and she applied to the county court for a declaration of an interest in the house. On appeal to the Court of Appeal:

Lord Denning MR: . . . Although Janet did not make any financial contribution, it seems to me that this property was acquired and maintained both by their joint efforts with the intention that it should be used for their joint benefit until they were married and thereafter as long as the marriage continued. At any rate, Stuart Eves cannot be heard to say to the contrary. He told her that it was to be their home for them and their children. He gained her confidence by telling her that he intended to put it in their joint names (just as married couples often do) but that it was not possible until she was 21. The judge described this as a 'trick,' and said that it 'did not do him much credit as a man of honour.' The man never intended to put it in joint names but always determined to have it in his own name. It seems to me that he should be judged by what he told her — by what he led her to believe — and not by his own intent which he kept to himself. Lord Diplock made this clear in *Gissing v Gissing* [1971] AC 886 at 906.

It seems to me that this conduct by Mr Eves amounted to a recognition by him that, in all fairness, she was entitled to a share in the house, equivalent in some way to a declaration of trust; not for a particular share, but for such share as was fair in view of all she had done and was doing for him and the children and would thereafter do. By so doing he gained her confidence. She trusted him. She did not make any financial contribution but she contributed in many other ways. She did much work in the house and garden. She looked after him and cared for the children. It is clear that her contribution was such that if she had been a wife she could have had a good claim to have a share in it on a divorce: see *Wachtel v Wachtel* [1973] Fam 72 at 92–94.

The Court of Appeal decided that the defendant held the legal estate on trust for sale in the proportion one-quarter to the plaintiff and three-quarters to the defendant.

The above cases applied the doctrine of constructive or resulting trusts. The following case concerned the doctrine of estoppel.

Pascoe v Turner
[1979] 2 All ER 945, [1979] 1 WLR 431, 123 Sol Jo 164, 9 Fam Law 82, Court of Appeal

In 1961, the plaintiff met the defendant, a widow. In 1963, the defendant moved into the plaintiff's home, at first as his housekeeper. In 1964, the plaintiff and defendant began to 'live in every sense as man and wife'. In 1965, they moved to another house. The plaintiff paid the purchase price and he also paid for the contents. In 1973, the plaintiff moved out. The defendant stayed on in the house and, in reliance upon the plaintiff's declarations that he had given her the house and the contents, she spent money and herself did work on redecorations, improvements and repairs. In 1976, the plaintiff tried to evict the defendant from the house. It was the man's determination to get her out of the house which persuaded the Court of Appeal to conclude that a fee simple rather than a life licence was the right answer.

Cumming Bruce LJ: . . . The principle to be applied is that the court should consider all the circumstances and, the (defendant) having no perfected gift or licence other than a licence revocable at will, the court must decide what is the minimum equity to do justice to her having regard to the way in which she changed her position for the worse by reason of the acquiescence and encouragement of the legal owner. The defendant submits that the only appropriate way in which equity can here be satisfied is by perfecting the imperfect gift as was done in *Dillwyn v Llewelyn* (1862) 4 De GF & J 517.

This court appreciates that the moneys laid out by the defendant were much less than in some of the cases in the books. But the court has to look at all the circumstances. When the plaintiff left her she was, we were told, a widow in her middle fifties. During the period that she lived with the plaintiff her capital was reduced from £4,500 to £1,000. Save for her invalidity pension that was all that she had in the world. In reliance upon the plaintiff's declaration of gift, encouragement and acquiescence she arranged her affairs on the basis that the house and contents belonged to her. So relying, she devoted a quarter of her remaining capital and her personal effort upon the house and its fixtures. In addition she bought carpets, curtains and furniture for it, with the result that by the date of the trial she had only £300 left. Compared to her, on the evidence the plaintiff is a rich man. He might not regard an expenditure of a few hundred pounds as a very grave loss. But the court has to regard her change of position over the years 1973 to 1976.

We take the view that the equity cannot here be satisfied without granting a remedy which assures to the defendant security of tenure, quiet enjoyment, and freedom of action in respect of repairs and improvements without interference from the plaintiff. The history of the conduct of the plaintiff since 9 April 1976, in relation to these proceedings leads to an irresistible inference that he is determined to pursue his purpose of evicting her from the house by any legal means at his disposal with a ruthless disregard of the obligations binding upon conscience. The court must grant a remedy effective to protect her against the future manifestations of his ruthlessness. It was conceded that if she is granted a licence, such a licence cannot be registered as a land charge, so that she may find herself ousted by a purchaser for value without notice. If she has in the future to do further and more expensive repairs she may only be able to finance them by a loan, but as a licensee she cannot charge the house. The plaintiff as legal owner may well find excuses for entry in order to do what he may plausibly represent as necessary works and so contrive to derogate from her enjoyment of the licence in ways that make it difficult or impossible for the court to give her effective protection.

Weighing such considerations this court concludes that the equity to which the facts in this case give rise can only be satisfied by compelling the plaintiff to give effect to his promise and her expectations. He has so acted that he must now perfect the gift.

Bernard v Josephs
[1982] 3 All ER 162, [1982] 2 WLR 1053, 126 Sol Jo 361, Court of Appeal

The facts are given in the first paragraph of the judgment:

Lord Denning MR: This is all about a young lady, Maria Teresa Bernard, the plaintiff. In August 1973 it was her 21st birthday. On that very day she became engaged to be married. It was to Dion Emmanuel Josephs, the defendant. He was 30. Unknown to her he was already a married man, not yet divorced. They arranged to get a house and set up home together. It was 177, Dunstan's Road, SE 22. It was conveyed to them on 21 October 1974, in their joint names. It was a simple transfer by the vendor as beneficial owner 'to Dion Emmanuel Josephs and Maria Teresa Bernard,' without more, no declaration of trust, or anything.

The purchase price was £11,750. The whole of it was raised on mortgage from the Southwark Borough Council. They both signed the legal charge to secure it. They each paid some of the incidental expenses. She paid £200 of her own money. He paid £250 and £400 which he borrowed. They went into occupation and lived together as man and wife. The house was quite large. So they let off much of it to tenants. This helped greatly towards the mortgage instalments. Both went out to work. Their earnings enabled them to pay the rest of the outgoings and food, and so forth. Then after a year or two they quarrelled. She says that he was violent to her. So in July 1976 she left. He stayed on in the house. She applied for the house to be sold and for one-half of the proceeds. Meanwhile, in June 1975, he had got a divorce from his lawful wife. In April 1978 he married another woman. He took her to live with him in the house. They are childless.

The law
In our time the concept of marriage — I am sorry to say — is being eroded. Nowadays many couples live together as if they were husband and wife, but they are not married. They hope and expect that their relationship will be permanent. They acquire a house in their joint names. Most of the purchase price is obtained on mortgage in both their names. They are both responsible for payment of the instalments. Both go out to work. They pay the outgoings out of their joint resources. One paying for the food and housekeeping. The other paying the mortgage instalments. And so forth. Just as husband and wife do. But later on, for some reason or other, they fall out. They go their own separate ways. One or other leaves the house. The others stays behind in it. There is no need to divorce. They just separate. What is to happen to the house? Is it to be sold? If so, are the proceeds to be divided? And, if so, in what proportion? Or is one of them to be allowed to stay in it? If so, on what terms? If they had been husband and wife, our matrimonial property legislation would give the Family Division a very wide discretion to deal with all these problems. It is contained in sections 23 to 25 of the Matrimonial Causes Act 1973. But there is no such legislation for couples like these. . . .

In my opinion in ascertaining the respective shares, the courts should normally apply the same considerations to couples living together (as if married) as they do to couples who are truly married. The shares may be half-and-half, or any such other proportion as in the circumstances of the case appears to be fair and just.

Applied to this case
The judge assessed the shares in the house as half-and-half. He took it at the date of acquisition. But I think on the facts it would be the same — half-and-half — at the date of separation. Mr Josephs and his present wife have been in the house for over three years now. Miss Bernard has not been in it for five years. It would be unduly harsh to turn Mr Josephs and his wife out of this house — simply in order to provide funds for Miss Bernard. But, seeing that he has the use of her share, it would only be fair that he should pay an occupation rent in respect of it: see *Dennis v McDonald* [1982] Fam 63, [1982] 1 All ER 590. No doubt, however, he has been paying the whole of the mortgage instalments and this should be taken into account as well. It may relieve him of paying any occupation rent for her half-share.

The problem is to calculate the sum which Mr Josephs should pay to Miss Bernard to buy her out. This is to be done by taking the price obtainable for the house if it were sold now with vacant possession. Then deduct the sum payable to redeem the mortgage. Then deduct one-half of the amount paid by Mr Josephs since the separation for mortgage instalments (deducting, of course, the amount received from the tenants). He should only get credit for one-half, because he has had the benefit of her half-share. Then make any other special adjustments.

One of the problems in Lord Denning's approach is that some couples remain unmarried because they do not wish to make the commitment of marriage. As Griffiths LJ said, in his judgment in *Bernard v Josephs*, the task of the judge in cases under s. 17 of the Married Women's Property Act 1882 or, in the case of unmarried couples, under s. 30 of the Law of Property Act 1925:

. . . is to look at all the evidence placed before it and decide whether it indicates an intention by the parties that the beneficial ownership of the house should be held (in a case where the house is in joint names in law as here) in other than equal shares . . ., but the nature of the relationship between the parties is a very important factor when considering what inferences should be drawn from the way they have conducted their affairs. There are many reasons why a man and a woman may decide to live together without marrying, and one of them is that each values his independence and does not wish to make the commitment of marriage; in such a case it will be misleading to make the same assumptions and to draw the same inferences from their behaviour as in the case of a married couple. The judge must look most carefully at the nature of the relationship, and only if satisfied that it was intended to involve the same degree of commitment as marriage will it be legitimate to regard them as no different from a married couple. Parliament itself has recognised this and has made specific provision for it by providing in section 2(1) of the Law Reform (Miscellaneous Provision) Act 1970 that in the case of engaged couples where the agreement to marry is terminated:

'any rule of law relating to the rights of husbands and wives in relation to property in which either or both has or have a beneficial interest . . . shall apply.'

Questions

(i) Applying the principles you know from *Gissing v Gissing* [1971] AC 886, [1970] 2 All ER 780 (p. 107, above), if the litigants in each of these cases had been married, and the issues arose in the context, for instance, of the bankruptcy of the men, do you think that the women would have been entitled to the shares they were given?
(ii) If you do not think that this would have been the case, is it your view that Lord Denning MR was applying a disguised *Wachtel v Wachtel* [1973] Fam 72, [1973] 1 All ER 829 (p. 196, above), approach?

Deech, *The Case against Legal Recognition of Cohabitation* (1980) in general approves of these cases, whilst at the same time suspecting an underlying emphasis on 'dependence':

The . . . 'ordinary' legal principles that have been and should continue to be applied to cohabitants are those of property, of torts and of trusts. The traditional separate property approach is particularly suitable as it does not distinguish between married and unmarried persons, men and women. The trusts doctrine, which mitigates the alleged rigours of separate property, also achieves equality and has developed in recent years to reflect all types of contribution made to the acquisition and improvement of another's property. Trusts doctrines achieved a just outcome . . . in the English cases of *Cooke v Head* [1972] 2 All ER 38, [1972] 1 WLR 518, and *Eves v Eves* [1975] 3 All ER 768, [1975] 1 WLR 1338. The result of *Eves* was possibly over-generous and there is a recent tendency to use the doctrine of constructive trusts to achieve an equity based on female dependency and not on genuine contribution.
    The settlement of cohabitants' disputes by existing legal principles is fair and workable. The creation of special laws for cohabitants or the extension of marital laws to them retards the emancipation of women, degrades the relationship and is too expensive for society in general and men in particular. . . .

Deech opposes vehemently the extension of any acknowledgement of 'quasi-spousal' support to cohabitees. Fernandez, in *Beyond Marvin: A proposal for quasi-spousal support* (1978), takes a different view:

Inasmuch as the state is interested in the economic support of all its citizens, that interest extends to the needs of all unmarried cohabitants created by the breakup of their relationships. The economic need created by the termination of such a relationship can be fulfilled through public assistance or, as with legal marriage, through some form of spousal support. If quasi-spousal support is chosen, however, there are no structural grounds on which to categorize cohabitational relationships; various kinds of union will be equally in need of rehabilitative assistance upon breakup.

But despite the seeming desirability of quasi-spousal support for all unmarried cohabitants, the diversity of that group makes a blanket application satisfactory: A rule that imposes quasi-support obligations on all cohabiting parties infringes on personal freedom to opt out of marriage. In at least some circumstances, the decision of individuals to forego formal marriage in favor of cohabitation stems from a conscious effort to avoid the legal consequences of marriage, including spousal support. If the state imposes quasi-spousal support awards on the unmarried cohabitants without regard for the parties' reasons for entering or continuing the relationship, the effect may be to discourage those relationships and inhibit individual freedom of choice as to lifestyle.

To allow for extensive personal freedom to arrange lifestyles without forcing inequitable results on deserving parties, quasi-spousal support should be limited to those cohabitants who evidence genuine marriage-like expectations. Obviously, if the parties agree even tacitly that mutual exchange of benefits implies no future obligation, courts should award no quasi-spousal support. In relationships that are functionally equivalent to formal marriages, however, quasi-spousal support would be an appropriate remedy.

Questions

(i) Do you think that the difference of emphasis between Deech and Fernandez is similar to the argument between Deech and O'Donovan on support obligations generally? (see Chapter 7, above).
(ii) Did you side with Deech or O'Donovan on the previous occasion?
(iii) If you sided with O'Donovan in the general debate, are you inclined to switch to supporting Deech now?
(iv) If you are, why?

4 Cohabitation contracts — express and implied

Weyrauch, *Metamorphoses of Marriage* (1980) writes:

The legal device of contract is particularly useful for women from the middle classes and of high educational attainment who are self-assertive and competitive in their relations with men. It is less adequate for parties of the lower classes and those who, because of continued differential treatment of the sexes, lack equal bargaining power. The courts may then fall back on traditional conceptions of marriage as status and emphasize the conjugal obligations of the husband. If there is no marriage, the courts may surreptitiously apply public policy by reading into a supposedly implied contract provisions that never occurred to the parties. A host of legal theories, equitable in nature, may also affect the obligations of parties to quasi-marital relationships. Thus, the courts may develop remedies akin to those in modern contract law when dealing with terms that are manifestly unfair and oppressive, and may borrow the reasoning from commercial litigation when deciding marital and quasi-marital disputes. They may refuse to enforce unconscionable terms that have been found to exist between the parties, married or not, and imply a duty of good faith and fair dealing.

An example of an express *cohabitation contract* is this agreement drawn up by a firm of Philadelphia lawyers:

1. The parties desire to maintain their relationship as independent persons and to have their relationship be a natural consequence of their mutual love and affection without material or economic considerations. Each of the parties has, prior to the date hereof, achieved a measure of material independence and by the execution hereof, each party expresses his or her intention not to claim any interest whatsoever in the property accumulated by the other party prior or subsequent hereto, or in any of the income or appreciation derived therefrom except as expressly provided herein.

2. The parties intend and desire to hereby define and clarify their respective rights in the property of the other and in any jointly owned property they might accumulate after the date hereof and to avoid such interests, which, except for the operation of this agreement, they might otherwise acquire in the property of the other as a consequence of their relationship.

3. The parties desire that all property presently owned by either of them of whatsoever nature and wheresoever located and all income derived therefrom and all increases in the value thereof, shall be and remain their respective separate property. The parties agree that in no time during their relationship shall there be any transmutation of any of their separate property interests into jointly owned property, except by an express written agreement. The following events shall, under no circumstances, be evidence of any intention by either party of an agreement between the parties to transmute their separate property interests into jointly owned property or to transmute their separate income into joint income:

   (*a*) The filing of joint tax returns;
   (*b*) The designation of one party by the other as a beneficiary of his or her estate;
   (*c*) The co-mingling by one party of his or her separate funds or property with jointly owned funds or property or with the separate funds or property of the other party;
   (*d*) Any oral statement by either party;
   (*e*) Any written statement by either party other than the express written agreement of transmutation;
   (*f*) The payment from jointly held funds of any separate obligation, including but not limited to the payment of mortgage, interest or real property taxes on a separately owned residence or other separately owned real estate;
   (*g*) The joint occupation of a separately owned or leased residence.

4. Both parties to this Agreement have made to each other a full and complete disclosure of the nature, extent and probable value of all their property and estate. Attached hereto as Exhibit 'A' is a statement of the separate property of the parties as of the date hereof. It is understood that as a result of income from or increases in the value of their presently existing separate property, each party may acquire other and different separate property in the future.

5. Except as otherwise provided herein with regard to the income and appreciation of the parties' separate property, and except as the parties may otherwise agree in writing, property heretofore acquired by the parties or hereafter acquired by the parties, and the earnings themselves, shall remain separate property.

   Each of the parties covenants and agrees that all property now owned by either of the parties of whatsoever nature and wheresoever located and any property which he or she may hereafter acquire, whether real, personal or mixed, including but not limited to any earnings, salaries, commissions, or income resulting from his or her personal services, skills and efforts shall be and remain the sole and separate property of the party acquiring same and each party may dispose of said property as said party sees fit. . . .

8. In full settlement of any and all claims by either party to the property of the other of whatsoever nature and wheresoever located and any property which might be hereafter acquired, whether real, personal or mixed, including but not limited to any earnings, salaries, commissions, or income heretofore or hereafter earned, [A] agrees that upon separation or the acquiring of separate living quarters by the parties, [B] shall receive as follows:

   (*a*) Ten Thousand ($10,000.00) Dollars;
   (*b*) payment of the premiums for Blue Cross, Blue Shield for a period of one (1) year from the date of separation;
   (*c*) all right, title and interest to the property as set forth in Schedule 'B' attached hereto and made a part hereof.

9. This Agreement shall continue in force until it is modified by a writing executed by both parties.

10. This Agreement shall be construed under the laws of the Commonwealth of Pennsylvania.

11. The terms, provisions and conditions of this Agreement shall be binding upon any and all of the heirs, executors, administrators, successors or assigns of either of the respective parties hereto.

Question

Lord Wright in *Fender v St John Mildmay* [1938] AC 1, [1937] 3 All ER 402 said: 'the law will not enforce an immoral promise, such as a promise between a man and a woman to live together without being married or to pay a sum of money or to give some other consideration in return for an immoral association.' Scarman LJ in *Horrocks v Forray* [1976] 1 All ER 737, [1976] 1 WLR 230 said: 'When an illegitimate child has been born, there is certainly nothing contrary to public policy in the parents coming to an agreement, which they intend to be binding in law, for the maintenance of the child and the mother.' Do you think that a contract similar to the Philadelphia contract would be enforceable in English law?

Living Together Certificate

_____ and _____
commit themselves to one another as lovers, friends and housemates with the promise that kindness, good will and a sense of humour shall guide them through both the rainbows and rainstorms in the days ahead.
At _____

_____   _____
Signature   Signature

_____   _____
Date   Date

Question

The above is popular amongst a certain section of Californian society. Would the women in the cases cited earlier have been in a better or a worse position if they had signed documents similar to this one?

Marvin v Marvin
(1976) 134 Cal Reptr 815, Supreme Court, State of California

Michelle Marvin contended that in 1964, she and the defendant, the film actor Lee Marvin, entered into an oral agreement that: 'while the parties lived together they would combine their efforts and earnings and would share equally any and all property accumulated as a result of their efforts whether individual or combined.' Furthermore, she said that they had agreed to hold themselves out to the general public as husband and wife, and that she would 'further render her services as a companion, housekeeper and cook.' She gave up what she said was a lucrative career as an entertainer and a singer to devote herself full time to Lee Marvin. She alleged that she lived with the defendant for six years and fulfilled her obligations under the agreement. When the relationship broke up, the plaintiff sought a declaration of constructive trust upon one-half of the property acquired during the course of the relationship.

Tobriner J: We base our opinion on the principle that adults who voluntarily live together and engage in sexual relations are nonetheless as competent as any other persons to contract respecting their earnings and property rights. Of course, they cannot lawfully contract to pay for the performance of sexual services, for such a contract is, in essence, an agreement for prostitution and unlawful for that reason. But they may agree to pool their earnings and to hold all property acquired during the relationship in accord with the law governing community property; conversely they may agree that each partner's earnings and the property acquired from those earnings remains the separate property of the earning partner. So long as the agreement does not rest upon illicit meretricious consideration, the parties may order their economic affairs as they choose, and no policy precludes the courts from enforcing such agreements.

In the present instance, plaintiff alleges that the parties agreed to pool their earnings, that they contracted to share equally in all property acquired, and that defendant agreed to support plaintiff. The terms of the contract as alleged do not rest upon any unlawful consideration. We therefore conclude that the complaint furnishes a suitable basis upon which the trial court can render declaratory relief.

The court went on to add that, in the absence of an express agreement, the court may look to a variety of other remedies in order to protect the parties' lawful expectations:

> The courts may inquire into the conduct of the parties to determine whether that conduct demonstrates an implied contract or implied agreement of partnership or joint venture . . ., or some other tacit understanding between the parties. The courts may, when appropriate, employ principles of constructive trust . . . or resulting trust. . . . Finally, a nonmarital partner may recover in quantum meruit for the reasonable value of household services rendered. . . .

> We conclude that the judicial barriers that may stand in the way of a policy based upon the fulfillment of the reasonable expectations of the parties to a nonmarital relationship should be removed.

> The mores of the society have indeed changed so radically in regard to cohabitation that we cannot impose a standard based on alleged moral considerations that have apparently been so widely abandoned by so many. Lest we be misunderstood, however, we take this occasion to point out that the structure of society itself largely depends upon the institution of marriage, and nothing we have said in this opinion should be taken to derogate from that institution. The joining of the man and woman in marriage is at once the most socially productive and individually fulfilling relationship that one can enjoy in the course of a lifetime.

Question

Do you agree with the California court that recognition of contracts between unmarried couples does not derogate from the institution of marriage?

Deech (1980) is strongly in favour of the principle that cohabiting couples should not have 'special treatment or the questionable benefit of special laws':

> This is an argument for the application of contractual principles rather than fixed status in cohabitants' relationships, and the argument is, incidentally, equally relevant to spouses . . . but the judgment of Tobriner J unfortunately did not simply recognise the freedom of two individuals who happen to cohabit to make an express contract. He went on to hold that, in the absence of an express contract, the court should enquire into the conduct of the parties to see if it demonstrated an implied contract and that if there were no grounds for finding one, resort should be had to equitable principles such as *quantum meruit*, constructive or resulting trusts. This determination to apply what are in practice special family-based laws, or to force on the couple a legal framework when they have expressly rejected one and there is no express contract, is regrettable. How would a cohabiting couple know that unless they made a contract, the court would impose one on them, as seemed reasonable to the court? Given the context and lack of precedent, it would be difficult as well as arbitrary to find an implied contract for the sharing of property. . . .

> Constructive and resulting trusts are not objectionable in themselves, being ordinary principles of law. To establish a share by way of constructive trust, the female cohabitant needs to prove that she has been led to act to her detriment in the belief that the man intended that she should acquire an interest in the property and also that, as her part of the bargain, she contributed towards the acquisition of the property. It would be anomalous to find a constructive trust in favour of the female cohabitant, simply because she came to live with the owner, hardly a detriment. To avoid court-imposed solutions, the couple should be encouraged to make a contract, as in the Ontario Family Law Reform Act 1978, s. 52 of which provides that the

cohabiting couple may by agreement regulate their rights during or at the end of cohabitation or on death, in respect of the ownership of property, support, the training (but not the custody) of children and any other matter.

Should judges impose 'reasonable expectations' on the parties? Deech answers this question with a categorical *no*:

Given the desirability of regulation by freely made contract and the likelihood of its validity, why is it argued that courts should not automatically uphold a cohabitation contract made years earlier, because the parties' economic situation may have changed, because children are now involved, because circumstances generally have changed? It has also been argued that cohabitation contracts should be held void because there is not equality of bargaining power. That argument may easily be dismissed: it cannot be a general principle of contract law that women are not to be held to their bargains because of their weaker bargaining power or because they may become a burden on the State. The 'weakness' of the woman's position is a term much used. What does it mean when it is so applied? Fragile or comfortable? Weak in relation to a man's physical or intellect? Is the weakness self-induced or unavoidable?

It is agreed that the maintenance and custody of children should be a separate matter. One is left with the argument that changed circumstances justify the overturning of a freely made contract. This must be rejected as paternalistic and unjust to the party who enters the relationship and plans his future on the basis of the contract and in the belief that its provisions will govern. Moreover the bearing of children and changes in fortune of the parties can hardly be unexpected by cohabitants, especially not by those who make a contract. To apply such a doctrine to cohabitants, but to reject it in the case of other individuals' contracts where the more severe doctrine of frustration applies, is discriminatory.

Horrocks v Forray
[1976] 1 All ER 737, [1976] 1 WLR 230, 119 Sol Jo 866, 6 Fam Law 15, Court of Appeal

The executors under a will claimed possession of property which they alleged was owned by the testator (Mr Sanford). The action was defended by Mrs Forray, who stated that she had been the testator's mistress for 17 years, had a child by him, and had lived in the property in question from when it had been bought by the testator some 12 months prior to his death. Apparently, the widow had no knowledge of her former husband's activities.

Megaw LJ: . . . It may be that the bringing in of the conception of contract into situations of this sort does give rise to difficulties. It may be that some other approach to situations of this sort would be preferable. But that is not a matter for us. We have got to take the law as it is and to apply it as it stands. The law as it stands does involve that the defendant can only succeed in this case, on the submission now made on her behalf, if she shows that it is proper to infer the existence of a contract which permitted her to remain in this house for one or other of the three alternative periods which have been put forward and which I have already mentioned. And, of course, she has to establish that that is a contract which, properly viewed and in accordance with the terms which have to be applied, was one which continued to exist as a matter of law after the death of the late Mr Sanford.

Now, in order to establish a contract, whether it be express or implied by law, there has to be shown a meeting of the minds of the parties with a definition of the contractual terms reasonably clearly made out and with an intention to affect the legal relationship, that is, that the agreement that is made is one which is properly to be regarded as being enforceable by the court if one or the other fails to comply with it; and it still remains a part of the law of this country, though many people think that it is time that it was changed to some other criterion, that there must be consideration moving in order to establish a contract. All those elements, on the facts in *Tanner v Tanner* [1975] 3 All ER 776, [1975] 1 WLR 1346, and on the evidence accepted by the court, were present. Are they present in this case? The county court judge thought not, and therefore he held that there was no contract and, therefore, no contractual licence, ...

The basis of the assertion that there existed here a contractual licence is really this: that there was evidence that over a period of a good many years, beginning at any rate soon after the birth of the daughter, the late Mr Sanford had continuously provided accommodation for the defendant and her daughter. That accommodation had, I think we were told, involved about nine different addresses at one time or another. In addition to continuing to provide accommodation for the defendant, the late Mr Sanford had expended a very great deal of money, either by way of buying things for the defendant and her child or children, or by way of providing her with money with which she could herself buy things; and it is apparent that she was provided with what one could fairly describe as a reasonably luxurious existence. Her own evidence, as summarised by the judge in his judgment, was that the deceased had expended on her and her children something of the order of £4,000 or £5,000 a year. That was, as I understand it, in addition to the provision of accommodation. . . .

The fact that he had it in mind to seek to provide some security for the dependant in the event of his death certainly does not go anything like far enough to bring into existence what is necessary to show a binding contract of this nature. There was here, in my judgment, simply nothing on the evidence that would have entitled the judge to come to the conclusion that there was any such contractual licence. I say that without going on to consider what I think might well be an extremely difficult further barrier in the way of the defendant. Supposing that she had established something which otherwise could be regarded as being a contract, where is the consideration for that contract to be found? In *Tanner v Tanner* [1975] 3 All ER 776, [1975] 1 WLR 1346, the consideration was perfectly clear: the lady had given up her rent-controlled flat as a part of the bargain that she would move into the other accommodation. There is no such consideration here. However, I do not wish to decide this case, as far as I am concerned, on any question relating to absence of consideration. But I am satisfied that the judge was completely right in his view that the defendant had wholly failed to show the existence of a contractual licence. I would accordingly dismiss the appeal.

The Court of Appeal distinguished the following case:

Tanner v Tanner
[1975] 3 All ER 776, [1975] 1 WLR 1346, 119 Sol Jo 391, 5 Fam Law 193, Court of Appeal

The facts of this case are given in the judgment of Lord Denning MR:

In 1968 Mr Eric Tanner, the plaintiff, was a milkman during the day and a croupier at night. He had been married for many years. He had a daughter then aged 19 and a son aged 12. They lived together at 26 Achilles Road in West Hampstead. But, to use his own words, he got 'disgusted' with his marriage and went out and had 'a good time.' He went out with three women, he said, 'simultaneously,' meaning separately but during the same weeks or months. One of these women was an attractive Irish girl, Miss Josephine MacDermott, the defendant. She was a cook in a nursing home. She had a flat in 33 Steels Road, Hampstead, on the third floor. He visited her frequently. She became pregnant by him. She took his name and became known as Mrs Tanner. In November 1969 she gave birth to twin daughters. They decided it was best to get a house for her and the twin babies. They found one at 4 Theobalds Avenue, North Finchley. The plaintiff borrowed a sum on mortgage with a local authority. In applying for it, he filled in a form. He said that he was 45. His wife was 41. He had a son aged 14, a daughter age 20 and twin daughters of 6 months. That was a very misleading application, because he was not getting it for his wife and his older children. He wanted it for the defendant and the twin babies. By means of that misrepresentation the plaintiff got the house on mortgage. It was in his own name. The defendant and the baby twins moved in there. She brought a good deal of her furniture and spend £150 on furnishings for it. She moved into the ground floor. They let the first floor. She managed the lettings and collected the rent. Previously, whilst she was in her flat in Steels Road, Hampstead, the plaintiff had paid her £5 a week maintenance for the twins. But after she moved into Theobalds Avenue he paid her nothing for them or for her. She got a supplementary allowance under social security from the local authority.

This was an appeal by the defendant against the order of the county court for vacation of the premises.

Lord Denning MR: It is said that they were only licensees — bare licensees — under a licence revokable at will: and that the plaintiff was entitled in law to turn her and the twins out on a moment's notice. I cannot believe that this is the law. This man had a moral duty to provide for the babies of whom he was the father. I would go further. I think he had a legal duty towards them. Not only towards the babies. But also towards their mother. She was looking after them and bringing them up. In order to fulfil his duty towards the babies, he was under a duty to provide for the mother too. She had given up her flat where she was protected by the Rent Acts — at least in regard to rent and it may be in regard also to security of tenure. She had given it up at his instance so as to be able the better to bring up the children. It is impossible to suppose that in that situation she and the babies were bare licensees whom he could turn out at a moment's notice. . . . In all the circumstances it is to be implied that she had a licence — a contractual licence — to have accommodation in the house for herself and the children so long as they were of school age and the accommodation was reasonably required for her and the children. There was, it is true, no express contract to that effect, but the circumstances are such that the court should imply a contract by the plaintiff — or, if need be, impose the equivalent of a contract by him — whereby they were entitled to have the use of the house as their home until the girls had finished school. It may be that if circumstances changed — so that the accommodation was not reasonably required — the licence might be determinable. But it was not determinable in the circumstances in which he sought to determine it, namely, to turn the defendant out with the children and to bring in his new wife with her family. It was a contractual licence of the kind which is specifically enforceable on her behalf: and which the plaintiff can be restrained from breaking; and he could not sell the house over her head so as to get her out in that way.

Browne LJ: . . . I agree that there was here a licence by the plaintiff to the defendant for good consideration: it could not be revoked at will. What has troubled me is what the duration of this licence was to be. With some hesitation I agree with Lord Denning MR's view of what it was to be; that is, in substance it was a licence to the defendant to occupy accommodation in the house so long as the children were of school age and such accommodation was reasonably required for her and the twins, subject to any relevant change of circumstances, such as her remarriage.

There was no express contract in *Tanner v Tanner*. However, the court decided that it could infer the existence of a contractual licence because of the presence of consideration, namely the giving up of the flat and looking after their children.

Questions

(i) Is it consideration to look after the child of the relationship?

(ii) Zuckerman (1980) argues that the insistence of the Court of Appeal in *Horrocks v Forray* on a contract in its sharpest commercial form 'is a reflection of the lack of any other merit in the defendant's claim.' But would not the defendant have had a right to claim under the Inheritance (Provision for Family and Dependants) Act 1975, s. 1(1)(*e*) (see p. 277, below), and, if there had been enough money in the estate, at least a sporting chance of success?

(iii) In commenting on some of the analogous cases from Australia and Canada, Harpum, in *Adjusting Property Rights between Unmarried Cohabitees* (1982) states:

What is required is a broad statutory discretion (broader than that conferred by the Matrimonial Causes Act 1973 because the situations that exist are far more varied) to adjust the rights of cohabitees when they cease to live together. Already by statute, on the death of one cohabitee the other may have a claim against the estate of the deceased for reasonable financial provision, if the survivor was in some way economically dependent on the deceased: s. 1(1)(*e*) of the Inheritance (Provision for Family and Dependants) Act 1975. If on death, why not in life? The example of the 1975 Act could be followed and the trigger for the discretion could be a situation of total or partial economic dependence by one cohabitee on the other. The sooner such legislation is enacted the better.

(*a*) Do you approve of this approach, and (*b*) do you think Deech (see p. 268, above) would approve?

5 Legislative initiatives

Section 1(2) of the Domestic Violence and Matrimonial Proceedings Act 1976 (see Chapter 14, below) states that the rights under that Act to prevent molestation, enforce occupation of the common home, and exclude the other from the common home 'shall apply to a man and a woman who are living with each other in the same household as husband and wife as it applies to the parties to a marriage and any reference to the matrimonial home shall be construed accordingly.'

Davis v Johnson
[1979] AC 264, [1978] 1 All ER 1132, [1978] 2 WLR 553, 122 Sol Jo 178, House of Lords

The respondent, a young unmarried mother, who had the joint tenancy of the council flat with the appellant, the father of her child, left the home with the child because of his violent behaviour to her. She applied to the county court for injunctions to restrain him from molesting her or the child and to exclude him from the home. A deputy circuit judge granted the injunctions asked for. Subsequently, a division of the Court of Appeal in *B v B* [1978] Fam 26, [1979] 1 All ER 821 construed s. 1 of the Domestic Violence and Matrimonial Proceedings Act 1976 as procedural only. Following this decision and another case in the Court of Appeal, *Cantliff v Jenkins* [1978] Fam 47, [1978] 1 All ER 836, the judge in the county court in this case rescinded that part of the order of the deputy judge which excluded the appellant from the home: he went back to the flat; and the respondent and the child returned to an overcrowded home for battered wives.

On the respondent's appeal, the Court of Appeal (of five judges) by a majority declined to follow the earlier decisions and allowed the appeal. On the appellant's appeal, four of the five judges dismissed the appeal and construed s. 1(1)(c) and 1(2) of the Act as enabling a woman with no property or tenancy rights in the home to apply to the court to obtain an injunction to exclude her partner from the property for a limited period.

Lord Scarman: The availability of paragraphs (c) and (d) of subsection (1) to unmarried partners without any express restriction to those who have a property right in the house has an important bearing on the answer to the question which I consider to be crucial to a correct understanding of the scope of the section; i.e., what is the mischief for which Parliament has provided the remedies specified in subsection (1)? It suggests strongly that the remedies are intended to protect people, not property: for it is highly unlikely that Parliament could have intended by the sidewind of subsection (2) to have introduced radical changes into the law of property. Nor is it necessary so to construe the section. The personal rights of an unmarried woman living with a man in the same household are very real. She has his licence to be in the home, a right which in appropriate cases the courts can and will protect: see *Winter Garden Theatre (London) Ltd v Millennium Productions Ltd* [1948] AC 173, per Viscount Simon at 188–191; *Binions v Evans* [1972] Ch 359, per Lord Denning MR at 367 and *Tanner v Tanner* [1975] 3 All ER 776, [1975] 1 WLR 1346. She has also her fundamental right to the integrity and safety of her person. And the children living in the same household enjoy the same rights.

Bearing in mind the existence of these rights and the extent to which they are endangered in the event of family breakdown, I conclude that the mischief against which Parliament has legislated by section 1 of the Act may be described in these terms: — conduct by a family partner which puts at risk the security, or sense of security, of the other partner in the home. Physical violence, or the threat of it, is clearly within the mischief. But there is more to it than that. Homelessness can be as great a threat as physical violence to the security of a woman (or man) and her children. Eviction — actual, attempted or threatened — is, therefore, within the mischief: likewise, conduct which makes it impossible or intolerable, as in the present case, for the other partner, or the children, to remain at home.

Where, in my opinion, the seven Lords Justices fell into error, is in their inference that because the section is not intended to give unmarried family partners rights which they do not already enjoy under existing property law it cannot be construed as conferring upon the county court the power to restrict or suspend the right of possession of the partner who does have that right under the property law or to confer for a period a right of occupancy which overrides his right of possession. I find nothing illogical or surprising in Parliament legislating to over-ride a property right, if it be thought to be socially necessary. If in the result a partner with no property right who obtains an injunction under paragraph (c) or (d) thereby obtains for the period of the injunction a right of occupation, so be it. It is no more than the continuance by court order of a right which previously she had by consent: and it will endure only for so long as the county court thinks necessary. Moreover, the restriction or suspension for a time of property rights is a familiar aspect of much of our social legislation: the Rent Acts are a striking example. So far from being surprised, I would expect Parliament, when dealing with the mischief of domestic violence, to legislate in such a way that property rights would not be allowed to undermine or diminish the protection being afforded. Accordingly I am unmoved by the arguments which influenced the Court of Appeal in *B v B* [1978] Fam 26, [1978] 1 All ER 821 and *Cantliff v Jenkins* [1978] Fam 47, [1978] 1 All ER 836. Nor do I find it surprising that this jurisdiction was given to the county court but not the High Court. The relief has to be available immediately and cheaply from a local and easily accessible court. Nor am I dismayed by the point that the section, while doing no more for married women than strengthen remedies for existing rights, confers upon an unmarried woman protection in her home including a right of occupation which can for a period over-ride the property rights of her family partner.

For these reasons, my conclusion is that section 1 of the Act is concerned to protect not property but human life and limb. But, while the section is not intended to confer, and does not confer upon an unmarried woman property rights in the home, it does enable the county court to suspend or restrict her family partner's property right to possession and to preserve to her a right of occupancy (which owes its origin to her being in the home as his consort and with his consent) for as long as may be thought by the court to be necessary to secure the protection of herself and the children.

How, then does the section fit into the law? First, the purpose of the section is not to create rights but to strengthen remedies. Subsection (2) does, however, confer upon the unmarried woman with no property in the home a new right. Though enjoying no property right to possession of the family home, she can apply to the county court for an order restricting or suspending for a time her family partner's right to possession of the premises and conferring upon her a limited right of occupancy. In most cases the period of suspension or restriction of his right and of her occupancy will prove, I expect, to be brief. But in some cases this period may be a lengthy one. The continuance of the order will, however, be a matter for the discretion of the county court judge to be decided in the light of the circumstances of the particular case.

Secondly, the section is concerned to regulate relations between the two family partners. It does not, for instance, prevent the property owner from disposing of his property. It does not confer upon an unmarried woman any right of occupation of the family home comparable with that which a married woman has and can protect against all the world under the Matrimonial Homes Act 1967.

Thirdly, and most importantly, the grant of the order is in the discretion of the county court judge. It is for him to decide whether, and for how long, it is necessary for the protection of the applicant or her child. Normally he will make the order 'until further order,' each party having the right to apply to the court for its discharge or modification. The remedy is available to deal with an emergency; it is, as my noble and learned friend, Lord Salmon has said, a species of first aid. The order must be discontinued as soon as it is clear, upon the application of either or both family partners, that it is no longer needed.

For these reasons I would dismiss the appeal.

It will be recalled that in *Spindlow v Spindlow* [1979] Ch 52, [1979] 1 All ER 169 (see p. 225, above), the parties were joint tenants of a council home. There had been no violence in this case, and the court held that the discretion under the 1976 Act was to be exercised according to the same principles on which the High Court exercised the similar jurisdiction to eject a spouse from the matrimonial home, namely that the court should be primarily concerned with the welfare of the children and the provision of a home for them. (*Bassett v Bassett* [1975] Fam 76, [1975] 1 All ER 513.) No time limit was put on the exclusion in that case. Ormrod LJ made clear that he might not arrive at the same conclusion where the house is owned by one of the unmarried pair or one of the unmarried pair is a protected tenant of the property. *Spindlow v Spindlow* was decided before the Housing Act 1980 conferred rights of security on tenants of council accommodation (see p. 47, above), and the case must be read in the light of the position as it existed before that Act came into force.

Questions

(i) We know that there is jurisdiction to exclude one party to a marriage from a matrimonial home to which they are jointly entitled, under s. 4 of the Domestic Violence and Matrimonial Proceedings Act 1976. There is also power to transfer property rights (including council tenancies) after a divorce under s. 24 of the Matrimonial Causes Act 1973. Has the court similar powers in the case of unmarried couples? (Go and look at the Law of Property Act 1925, s. 30.)

(ii) What can an unmarried woman do when the man, with whom she has been living and who has been ousted by an order under s. 1 of the Domestic Violence and Matrimonial Proceedings Act 1976, stops paying the rent and purports to surrender his sole protected or secure tenancy to the landlord?

(iii) Would the following women, whose circumstances are described in the cases quoted earlier in this chapter, have protection under the Domestic Violence and Matrimonial and Proceedings Act 1976: (*a*) Janet Eves; (*b*) the defendant in *Pascoe v Turner*; (*c*) Maria Bernard *after* she had left; (*d*) Mrs Tanner; (*e*) Mrs Forray, after Mr Sanford's death?

An unmarried partner may qualify as a member of the family of a statutory tenant for the purpose of transmission of the tenancy on his death. Both the Housing Act 1980, s. 76(1) and the Rent Act 1977, Sch. 1, Part 1, para. 3 state that in the absence of a surviving spouse a statutory tenancy can devolve upon any person who 'was a member of the original tenant's family' and who was residing with the deceased at the time of and for a period of six months immediately preceding his death.

Watson v Lucas
[1980] 3 All ER 647, [1980] 1 WLR 1493, 124 Sol Jo 513, 40 P & CR 531, Court of Appeal

The defendant married in 1953 but his wife left him after a year. There was no divorce. In 1958, the defendant went to live with a widow, some 15 years his senior, in her flat, of which she was the protected tenant. The widow died in 1977. The plaintiff brought an action to recover possession of the flat.

Stephenson LJ: The ordinary man has to consider whether a man or a woman is a member of a family in the light of the facts, and whatever may have been held before *Dyson Holdings Ltd v Fox* [1976] QB 503, [1975] 3 All ER 1030, I do not think a judge, putting himself in the place of the ordinary man, can consider an association which has every outward appearance of marriage, except the false pretence of being married, as not constituting a family. If it looks like a marriage in the old and perhaps obsolete sense of a lifelong union, with nothing casual or temporary about it, it is a family until the House of Lords declares . . . that the case of *Dyson Holdings Ltd v Fox* was wrongly decided because the reasoning of the majority was wrong. The time has gone by when the courts can hold such a union not to be 'familial' simply because the parties to it do not pretend to be married in due form of law.

(*Note*: In *Dyson Holdings v Fox* [1976] QB 503, [1975] 3 All ER 1030 the court drew a distinction between the case where the relationship was stable, and where it was 'casual or intermittent.')

Helby v Rafferty
[1978] 3 All ER 1016, [1979] 1 WLR 13, 122 Sol Jo 418, 8 Fam Law 207, 37 P & CR 376, Court of Appeal

Miss Taylor was the tenant of a flat. Mr Rafferty moved into this flat and they then lived together until her death in 1977. For the last three years of her life, Miss Taylor was ill (she was an alcoholic) and Mr Rafferty looked after her. After her death, he continued to live in the flat. The landlord brought an action against him for possession. This was successful, and Mr Rafferty appealed.

Stamp LJ: The question accordingly turns on whether Mr Rafferty was at the date of Miss Taylor's death a member of Miss Taylor's family within the meaning of Sch 1, para 3.

Had the case fallen to be decided prior to *Dyson Holdings Ltd v Fox* [1976] QB 503, [1975] 1 All ER 1030, we would have been constrained to dismiss the appeal on the authority of *Gammans v Ekins* [1950] 2 KB 328, [1950] 2 All ER 140, a decision of this court which was subsequently applied by this court in *Ross v Collins* [1964] 1 All ER 861, [1964] 1 WLR 425.

The ordinary or natural meaning of the expression 'member of a family' would not, in my judgment, apply to a person in the position of Mr Rafferty. The way the matter was put in *Gammans v Ekins* by Asquith LJ who gave the first judgment in that case (a very short judgment) was this:

'The judge has not found which, and says that it makes no difference; but if their relations were platonic, I can see no principle on which it could be said that these two were members of the same family, which would not require the court to predicate the same of two old cronies of the same sex innocently sharing a flat. If, on the other hand, the relationship involves sexual relations, it seems to me anomalous that a person can acquire a 'status of irremovability' by living or having lived in sin, even if the liaison has not been a mere casual encounter but protracted in time and conclusive in character. But I would decide the case on a simpler view. To say of two people masquerading, as these two were, as husband and wife (there being no children to complicate the picture) that they were members of the same family, seems to be an abuse of the English language, and I would accordingly allow the appeal.'

I interpolate at that point to make it perfectly clear that there was no masquerading on the part of Mr Rafferty and Miss Taylor. There is no evidence that Miss Taylor ever called herself Mrs Rafferty. Jenkins LJ in that same case remarked that it would be extending the relevant section, which was then slightly different in wording, beyond all reason to hold that it applied when it was no more than a liaison between two elderly people who chose to pose as a married couple when they were not in fact.

However, the majority of the court in *Dyson Holdings Ltd v Fox* (that is to say James and Bridge LJJ), following the view expressed in *Brock v Wollams* [1949] 2 KB 388, that the word 'family' should be given its popular meaning, felt able to distinguish *Gammans v Ekins* [1947] 1 All ER 715 on the ground that during the period intervening between that decision and the relevant time in *Dyson Holdings Ltd v Fox* the popular meaning of 'family' had changed and by then comprised a situation where the two parties, man and woman, had been living together permanently and for a very long time, in that case some 40 years.

I confess that, apart from authority, I would have taken the view that the language of a statute by whatever process you apply to its construction, whether you construe it in its natural and ordinary meaning or whether you construe it in a popular way or whether you construe it in what has sometimes been called 'a legal way' (and I am not sure I understand what the difference is) cannot alter its meaning from time to time and that, in order to find out what Parliament intended by the statute, you must ascertain what the words of the statute meant when Parliament used those words. There is the further difficulty, as I see it, that the language of the relevant statutory provision has been repeated in successive Rent Acts with only a very slightly different arrangement of the words. As I rather indicated, I think, it appears to me that the difficulty of determining whether a particular meaning of the words in an Act of Parliament would be given to those words by popular vote or not would be of a different kind. Do you listen to the vociferous minority or do you imagine what the silent majority might have said at a particular time?. . . .In *Dyson Holdings Ltd v Fox*, the facts (which I take from the headnote) are these:

'The defendant lived with the tenant of a house as if she were his wife for 21 years until his death in 1961. They never married and had no children. After his death the defendant continued to live in the house for which she paid rent as if she were his widow until the plaintiffs, who owned the house, learned in 1973 that she was not in fact his widow. The plaintiffs accepted no further rent and brought proceedings for possession of the house against her as a trespasser. The defendant pleaded that at all times after the commencement of the tenancy and before the tenant's death she had resided with him as a member of his family and that she continued to occupy the house as her residence.'

As I have indicated, the Court of Appeal held that her claim was well-founded.

In the instant case the association between Mr Rafferty and Miss Taylor endured for five years and it only came to an end as a result of Miss Taylor's comparatively early death. I will refer to the facts of this case hereafter. If, however, one were to follow the dicta of Lord Denning MR in *Dyson Holdings Ltd v Fox*, it would hardly be possible to distinguish the facts of the instant case from those in *Dyson Holdings Ltd v Fox*. The only guidance to be found in the judgments of James and Bridge LJJ in *Dyson Holdings Ltd v Fox* as to the approach to be adopted when you define this kind of situation is this. First James LJ, referring to the relationship, says:

'. . . it is not restricted to blood relationships and those created by the marriage ceremony. It can include de facto as well as de jure relationships. The popular meaning of "family" in 1975 would, according to the answer of the ordinary man, include the appellant as a member of Mr Wright's family. That is not to say [and this is the important passage, I think, in his judgment] that every mistress should be so regarded. Relationships of a casual or intermittent character and those bearing indications of impermanence would not come within the popular concept of a family unit.'

It seems to me, if I may say so, to follow that in every case a judge has, in the view of James LJ, to decide whether the relationship was of such a casual or intermittent character as not to constitute the relationship required in order to satisfy the provision of the section.

Bridge LJ put the matter in a somewhat similar way. He said this:

'. . . It is, I think, not putting it too high to say that between 1950 and 1975 there has been a complete revolution in society's attitude to unmarried partnerships of the kind under consideration. Such unions are far commoner than they used to be. The social stigma that once attached to them has almost, if not entirely, disappeared. The inaccurate but expressive phrases "common law wife" and "common law husband" have come into general use to describe them. The ordinary man in 1975 would, in my opinion, certainly say that the parties to such a union [and here come, I think, the important words] provided it had the appropriate degree of apparent permanence and stability, were members of a single family whether they had children or not.'

I make the same comment on that passage as I made on the passage just quoted from the judgment of James LJ.

I conclude that *Dyson Holdings Ltd v Fox* established two propositions: first, that, notwithstanding *Gammans v Ekins*, a relationship between an unmarried man and an unmarried woman living together over a very long period can constitute the family relationship which is necessary in order to satisfy the section, and second, that on the facts in *Dyson Holdings Ltd v Fox* such a relationship was established. One has to ask: has the union such a degree of apparent permanence and stability that the ordinary man would say that the parties were, in the words of Bridge LJ, 'members of a single family'?

In my judgment, the judge in the court below, deriving such assistance as he could from *Dyson Holdings Ltd v Fox*, approached the question which he had to decide quite correctly. He summarised the facts which pointed in each direction and he concluded that there was not such a permanence and stability as to justify the view that each of the parties in the instant case was a member of the family of the other. . . .

The relevant facts in the instant case are these. Mr Rafferty, as I have said, took up residence about five years before Miss Taylor's death. They lived together, sharing a bed. They shared expenses, the life of each being bound up very closely with the life of the other. They went out together. They went about together. They went to shows together. They did shopping together. They went, I think, to the cinema together. As she got more ill, as unhappily she did, Mr Rafferty did all the things for her that a loving husband might be expected to do. He nursed her as a husband would have done. If it stopped there you might conclude that the situation was just such a one as the Court of Appeal in *Dyson Holdings Ltd v Fox* held satisfied the definition. But there was another side of the picture. In the first place, there was no charade. Miss Taylor did not call herself Mrs Rafferty. Nor was any attempt made, as I understand it, to throw dust in the eyes of friends as to the true nature of the relationship. Far from passing themselves off as husband and wife, when the time came for the mother to visit the flat, the parties did put up something in the nature of a charade in pretending that they were less intimate than was in fact the case.

The Court of Appeal took the view that Mr Rafferty had not been a member of Miss Taylor's family at the time of her death.

Questions

(i) Why should pretending to the woman's mother that there was less intimacy than in fact was the case be of any relevance to the *actual* situation?
(ii) Do you think that Miss Taylor would have succeeded had Mr Rafferty been the tenant and died?

(iii) Assuming the properties in question to have been secure tenancies in each of the five circumstances in question (iii) on p. 274, above, would those five women have been able to succeed to the tenancy had they lived there until the men died?

Under the *Inheritance (Provision for Family and Dependants) Act 1975*, s. 1(1)(*e*) a court may award reasonable maintenance to any person who 'immediately before the death of the deceased was being maintained, either wholly or partly, by the deceased.' It is important to remember, however, that the widow may apply under the same Act not only for maintenance, but for such 'financial provision as it would be reasonable in the circumstances of the case for a husband or wife to receive, whether or not that provision is required for his or her maintenance' (see Chapter 4, above). The unmarried partner is, therefore, in a much weaker position. She has no automatic rights on intestacy; and her rights under the 1975 Act are limited to the provision of maintenance. If the relationship was entirely *independent*, no rights at all under the 1975 Act will accrue. Likewise, it appears that no rights will accrue in a situation of 'mutual dependency'.

s. 1(3) For the purposes of subsection (1)(*e*) . . . a person shall be treated as being maintained by the deceased, either wholly or partly, as the case may be, if the deceased, otherwise than for full valuable consideration, was making a substantial contribution in money or money's worth towards the reasonable needs of that person.

Jelley v Illiffe
[1981] Fam 128, [1981] 2 All ER 29, [1981] 2 WLR 801, 125 Sol Jo 355, Court of Appeal

The facts of the case are fully set out in Stephenson LJ's judgment:

On 19 August 1979, the plaintiff, Thomas William Jelley, an old age pensioner, applied under the Inheritance (Provision for Family and Dependants) Act 1975, for reasonable financial provision to be made for his maintenance out of the estate of Mrs Florence Lilian May Illiffe, deceased, a widow, with whom the plaintiff had lived for eight years before her death.

The deceased was the widow of the plaintiff's wife's brother, who died in 1970. The plaintiff's wife died in 1968. In 1971 the plaintiff went to live with the deceased. . . . Her husband had left the house to her for her life and after her death to their three children, but by a deed of arrangement in 1970 they conveyed the freehold to her. It was clearly understood by them — and they said by the plaintiff also, though he denied it — that the house should go to the children after her death. And so it did. By her will made on 22 May 1972, of which the first defendant[1] and the plaintiff were executors and trustees, she left all her property, real and personal, to them upon trust to divide her residuary estate between her three children in equal shares. At her death on 8 April 1979, the house, valued at £16,000, constituted by far the greatest part of her estate, which was valued when probate was granted to the first defendant at £17,303.86 net.

The case took the form of an application for the proceedings to be struck out on the ground that there was no reasonable cause of action.

[The object of the Act] is surely to remedy, wherever reasonably possible, the injustice of one, who has been put by a deceased person in a position of dependency upon him, being deprived of any financial support, either by accident or by design of the deceased, after his death. To leave a dependant, to whom no legal or moral obligation is owed, unprovided for after death may not entitle the dependant to much, or indeed any, financial provision in all the circumstances, but he is not disentitled from applying for such provision if he can prove that the deceased by his conduct made him dependent upon the deceased for maintenance, whether intentionally or not.

Accordingly, I am of opinion that the court has to consider whether the deceased, otherwise than for valuable consideration (and irrespective of the existence of any contract), was in fact making a substantial contribution in money or money's worth towards the reasonable needs of the plaintiff, on a settled basis or arrangement which either was still in force immediately before

---

1. The deceased's son. The deceased had three children, one son and two daughters, who were the defendants to the action.

the deceased's death or would have lasted until her death but for the approach of death and the consequent inability of either party to continue to carry out the arrangement. To discover whether the deceased was making such a contribution the court has to balance what she was contributing against what he was contributing, and if there is any doubt about the balance tipping in favour of hers being the greater contribution, the matter must, in my opinion, go to trial. If, however, the balance is bound to come down in favour of his being the greater contribution, or if the contributions are clearly equal, there is no dependency of him on her, either because she depended on him or there was mutual dependency between them, and his application should be struck out now as bound to fail. Where what B does gives full valuable consideration for the substantial contribution A makes there is no dependency and B's claim under the Act should be struck out.

The court declared that there was a reasonable cause of action, and allowed the trial to proceed. Stephenson LJ, however, did express his doubts about the ultimate success of the plaintiff's case:

Here there are several indications that the plaintiff's case is likely to fail. He did a lot for the deceased, perhaps enough to equal what she did for him, including the provision of rent-free accommodation, so he may not have been on balance dependent on her. Then the house was her children's until they conveyed it to her and she remained under a moral obligation to leave it back to them on her death. He had a home with a daughter to go to.

Questions

(i) Can you think of a factual situation where the plaintiff would be successful in a claim under the Inheritance (Provision for Family and Dependants) Act 1975 s. 1(1)(*e*)?

(ii) Would any of the ladies mentioned in question (iii) on p. 274, above, have been successful if the gentlemen in those cases died?

(iii) Would any of the men succeed if the women died?

(iv) Does 'status' or 'contract' determine the rights which accrue under the Act?

Entitlement to or increases in social security contributory benefits for adult dependants is generally restricted to married partners. In contrast to entitlement, cohabitation with a man has the effect of depriving the woman of benefit, first in the social security area for benefits such as widow's allowance, widowed mother's allowance, the widow's pension, industrial injuries widow's benefit, and the child's special allowance. Secondly, cohabitation will deprive the claimant of entitlement to supplementary benefits.

In the latter case, the Supplementary Benefits Act 1976, Sch. 1, para 3(1) (as amended by the Social Security Act 1980) states: 'Where two persons are a married or unmarried couple, their requirements and resources shall be aggregated and treated (a) . . . as those of the man.'

R(G) 1/79, National Insurance Commissioner

This was a case where the issue was whether a widow's pension should be withdrawn on the ground that she was cohabiting. On 22 September 1975 the claimant's husband died and she was awarded widow's benefit in her married name from 23 September 1975. On 9 March 1976 she changed her surname by statutory declaration to the name of a man with whom she was living in the same house and with whom she had had a business relationship since 1963. Electoral rolls from 1970 onwards showed that she had used the man's surname since 1969. The National Insurance Local Tribunal found that she was cohabiting and the widow appealed. In upholding the decision of the Tribunal, the commissioner said:

9. As regards a sexual relationship, it is not necessary for the purposes of the proviso to section 26(3) of the Act[2] that there should have been or are sexual relations. The claimant denied that there was or had been any sexual relationship between her and Mr C. When the inspector first visited the claimant on 22 September 1976 he did so without previous warning and was shown that she and Mr C occupied separate bedrooms. Mr C attended the hearing before the local tribunal but it is not clear from the report of the proceedings whether or not he gave evidence. I accept that he denied that there was a sexual relationship and, in a written statement, dated 19 October 1976, he agreed with the claimant's version as to the history of their relationship. He did not appear at the hearing before me. Mr Rowland submitted that there was compelling evidence that there was no sexual relationship. There is some evidence that there was no sexual relationship, but the fact that the claimant had lived with Mr C in the same house for a number of years using his name as his wife would certainly be regarded as evidence of a sexual relationship in matrimonial proceedings. There is evidence from which a sexual relationship may be inferred were it necessary to make a finding on the matter.

10. As to their financial relationship, they were partners in business when the claimant was widowed. As I commented in Decision R(G) 5/68, household and financial arrangements are personal matters not easy to ascertain. Having regard to the evidence as a whole, I find that their business partnership probably extended to their living partnership and that resources were shared. Their general relationship certainly, in my opinion, possessed all the attributes of a woman having not only assumed the surname of the man but living with him as his wife. The local tribunal enquired into the circumstances very thoroughly, as appears from the report of their proceedings. The tribunal found that at the time when the claimant claimed widow's allowance she was carrying on a common home in the manner in which husbands and wives do.

Questions

(i) Why should contributory benefits not be paid for increased expenditure if there is evidence of actual dependency? (After all, dependant increases are paid for wives as an entitlement — and it does not follow that wives are necessarily dependent).

(ii) Is it odd that a widow's pension can be paid to a woman who has been separated from her husband for many years before his death, yet there is no pension entitlement for a cohabitant who may have been living with him for many years?

(iii) The *Finer Report* 1974 justifies the cohabitation rule in the law of supplementary benefits as follows: 'It cannot be right to treat unmarried women who have the support of a partner both as if they had no such support and better than if they were married.' Do you agree with this?

(iv) Should there be a different approach to the 'cohabitation rule' in cases of widow's benefits as opposed to supplementary benefits? (After all, has not her husband paid for her widow's pension with his contributions?)

(v) If you think that there should be a difference, why do you think this?

Clive, in *Marriage: An Unnecessary Legal Concept* (1980), stresses the growth of individualism and its implications for tax and social security:

Indeed if the object (of social security) is the relief of need it is not immediately obvious why the old widow or the old cohabitee should be preferred to the old spinster who has never cohabited with anyone, while if the object is the payment of benefits bought by contributions it is not immediately obvious why the contributor should not be allowed to nominate the beneficiary. On either view, marriage is irrelevant. It may be objected that while a man can have only one wife he may have several cohabitees and that the state could not afford to abandon the 'one man — one woman' system. Two answers may be ventured. First, a man may already have several wives

---

2. Social Security Act 1975.

successively in a contribution career. So nothing would change in that respect. The 'one man — one woman' system has already been abandoned. Secondly, if one man has several concurrent cohabitees then the chances are that some other man has none. Unless large numbers of cohabitees are drafted in from overseas it is unlikely that the pool of dependent women would be increased by abolishing marriage. There is, in any event, something fundamentally repulsive about this whole idea of dependent women. The long-term goal in this area should be the abolition of private dependency, by encouraging independence and treating poverty as an individual rather than a family phenomenon. Even before that goal is reached, however, it does not seem necessary to preserve the legal concept of marriage for the purposes of tax and social security laws.

Questions

(i) No doubt Deech (see p. 237, above) would agree with this statement. But do you?

(ii) Once again, how many of the women referred to in question (iii) on p. 274, above, would be deprived of supplementary benefits because of the cohabitation rule?

(iii) If you were asked to draft a clause to make provision for cohabitants would you define 'cohabitation': (*a*) by the reason that it was established; or (*b*) by whether there is dependence; or would you (*c*) refuse to define cohabitation until you were told what the legislation was about, and then try to define it accordingly?

CHAPTER 9

Legitimacy and illegitimacy

The bastard, like the prostitute, thief, and beggar, belongs to that motley crowd of disreputable social types which society has generally resented, always endured. He is a living symbol of social irregularity, and undeniable evidence of contramoral forces; in short, a problem — a problem as old and unsolved as human existence itself.

These are the opening words of Davis' seminal article on *Illegitimacy and the Social Structure* (1939), in which the sociologist seeks to discover the true nature of the illegitimacy 'problem' and what might be done to solve it. In the first section of this chapter, we shall consider how and why English law reached its present condition on the subject, using Davis' analysis as a guide. We shall then look at some of the recent factual data which may be relevant to the future direction of legal development, before considering the present law and the major issues which it raises. We shall continue with the current debate about reform, now gathering momentum in the wake of the Law Commission's Working Paper, published in 1979, and their Report, published in December 1982. Finally, in these days of genetic engineering, we must touch upon the vexed question of 'what is a parent?'

1 The how and why of English law

Davis identifies two approaches to the problem of illegitimacy — the 'social welfare' and the 'sociological.' The social welfare approach seeks to discover why individual women become unmarried mothers (or even why individual men become unmarried fathers) and then to cure their deviant tendencies. Nowadays, this attitude is associated with social workers, and with the welfare or therapeutic principles upon which their work has traditionally been based, but it is as much a development from the earlier deterrent attempts of Church and State as is the same approach to the prevention of crime.

Deterrence began in the medieval ecclesiastical courts, but the secular authorities took a hand once it appeared that failures in spiritual control were likely to cost the community money. The following example, and an explanation, are offered by Peter Laslett in *The World We Have Lost* (1971):

Anyone who committed or tried to commit a sexual act with anyone not his spouse, whether or not conception took place, ran the risk of a summons to the archdeacon's court — the lowest in the hierarchy of spiritual courts — a fine, and then penance in church at service time, or in the market place. If a person about whom a *fame of incontinency* had got abroad (that is a suspicion of a sexual escapade) ignored the summons or refused the punishment, then excommunication followed. This meant exile from the most important of all social activities, isolation within the community.

The lay courts and lay authority could be invoked for the more serious offences, and this often happened for the begetting of bastards. . . .

If the records of the church courts are filled with notices of sexual incontinence, those of the magistrates courts are studded with measures taken in punishment of unmarried mothers, and sometimes of unmarried fathers too, with provision for the upkeep of the child:

> 'Jane Sotworth of Wrightington, spinster, swears that Richard Garstange of Fazarkerley, husbandman, is the father of Alice, her bastard daughter. She is to have charge of the child for two years, provided she does not beg, and Richard is then to take charge until it is twelve years old. He shall give Jane a cow and 6s. in money. Both he and she shall this day be whipped in Ormeskirke.'

So ordered the Lancashire justices at the Ormskirk Sessions on Monday, 27 April 1601, though the language they used was Latin and lengthier. At Manchester, in 1604, they went so far as to require that Thomas Byrom, gentleman, should maintain a bastard he had begotten on a widow, and be whipped too. On 10 October 1604, he was whipped in Manchester market-place. . . .

The institutions of the old world must be looked upon in this way, as expedients to provide permanence in an environment which was all too impermanent and insecure. The respect due to the old and experienced, the reverence for the Church and its immense, impersonal antiquity, the spontaneous feeling that it was the family which gave a meaning to life because the family could and must endure, all these things helped to reconcile our ancestors with relentless, remorseless mortality and mischance. But they must not deceive the historian into supposing that the fixed and the ancient were the only reality: an unchanging, unchangeable social structure may well be essential to a swiftly changing population.

The legal warrant for Thomas Byrom's punishment is explained by Elisofon in *A Historical and Comparative Study of Bastardy* (1973):

The year 1576 was especially important in relation to rights of the bastard child; for this was the first time in English history that a duty of support was imposed upon the parents of an illegitimate child. The statute passed by Parliament read, in part:

> 'Concerning bastards begotten and born out of lawful matrimony (an offence against God's law and man's law), the said bastard being now left to be at the charge of the parish where they be born, to the great burden of the same parish, and in defrauding of the relief of the impotent and aged true poor of the same parish, and to the evil example and encouragement of lewd life; it is ordained and enacted that two justices of the peace, upon examination of the cause and circumstances, shall and may by their discretion take order as well for the *punishment of the mother and reputed father* of such bastard child, as also for the better relief of every such parish in part or in all, and shall make likewise by like discretion, take order for the keeping of every such bastard child, *by charging such mother or reputed father with payment of money weekly or other substentation for the relief of such child* and such ways as they think covenant. And if . . . the reputed mother and father shall not observe and perform the order, then the party making the default in not performing the order, be committed to the common gayle.' (emphasis added). . . .

The Act of 1576 was supplemented by another statute in 1609. It seems that while the statute of 1576 provided some relief to the parish's burden, it did not completely resolve the problem. Therefore, Parliament passed the Act of 1609, which provided for mandatory criminal sanctions against the mothers who had a bastard child which became chargeable to a parish. While the earlier act merely empowered a justice in his discretion to imprison the mother of the bastard child, this enactment mandatorily imposed a one year sentence on the mother of a bastard child which became chargeable to a parish.

Because of the duty of paying support, and the criminal sanctions imposed for having a bastard, numerous unwed mothers, in order to avoid these sanctions, began secretly murdering their illegitimate children and then would declare publicly the child had been born dead. To put an end to this practice, Parliament, in 1623, imposed the death penalty upon any mother who concealed the death of a child who would have been a bastard, unless the mother could prove with the aid of at least one witness that the infant was born dead.

Question

Which do you suppose was the most serious — the offence against God's law or burden of the parish?

The deterrent approach was thus carried on through the poor law. Its more recent history is taken up by Sir Morris Finer and Professor O.R. McGregor, in *A History of the Obligation to Maintain*, printed as an appendix to the Report of the Committee on One-Parent Families (1974). They begin with the report of the royal commissioners on the poor laws which led to the 'new' poor law of 1834:

56. In the case of such a mother, the report did not recommend any change in the methods of relief, but it urged the repeal of all legislation which punished or charged the putative father of a bastard who should become, the Commissioners said:

'what Providence appears to have ordained that it should be, a burthen on its mother, and, where she cannot maintain it, on her parents. The shame of the offence will not be destroyed by its being the means of income and marriage, and we trust that as soon as it has become both burthensome and disgraceful, it will become as rare as it is among those classes in this country who are above parish relief. . . . If we are right in believing the penalties inflicted by nature to be sufficient, it is needless to urge further objections to any legal punishment. . . . In affirming the inefficiency of human legislation to enforce the restraints placed on licentiousness by Providence, we have implied our belief that all punishment of the supposed father is useless.'

Behind this extreme statement of the providential foundations of the double standard of sexual morality lay the experience of abuses under the old bastardy laws. Under these, if a single woman declared herself pregnant and charged a man with being responsible, the overseers of the poor or any substantial householder could apply to any justice of the peace for a committal warrant. This would issue unless the accused man could give security to indemnify the parish or to enter into a recognisance to appear at Quarter Sessions and to perform any order which might there be made. The Commissioners thought that poor men were at the mercy of blackmail and perjury by unscrupulous women, and that the bastardy laws promoted social demoralisation.

57. The bastardy clauses of the Act of 1834 were in line with the opinions of the Poor Law Commissioners. . . .

However, not all sections of society took the same view of the problem:

59. With the dislike of Tories for the centralising tendency of Benthamite administrative reforms, went also a different view of sexual morality and obligation. The urban Victorians inherited a strict moral code. They got it from evangelical religious teachers who imposed it on the new middle class, the executive agents of their expanding industrial economy; and they planted it, as far as they could, on their lower orders. Their bookshelves carried the weight of such typical products of the evangelical outlook as Thomas Bowdler's *The Family Shakespeare, In which nothing is added to the Text; but those Words and Expressions are omitted which cannot with Propriety be read aloud in a Family*. These ten volumes reached a sixth edition in 1831, six years before the adolescent Victoria came under the influence of her first prime minister, a cultivated Whig who had been heard to respond to an evangelical sermon with the observation that 'things are coming to a pretty pass when religion is allowed to interfere with private life'. 'That d — d morality' which disturbed Lord Melbourne did not result from religious enthusiasm only. Differing provisions for the inheritance of family property were an important factor, too. The sexual waywardness of the territorial aristocracy did not endanger the integrity or succession of estates which were regulated by primogeniture and entail. Countless children of the mist played happily in Whig and Tory nurseries where they presented no threat to the property or interests of heirs. But middle class families handled their accumulating industrial wealth within a system of partible inheritance which demanded a more severe morality imposing higher standards upon women than upon men. An adulterous wife might be the means of planting a fraudulent claimant upon its property in the heart of her family; to avoid this ultimate catastrophe, middle class women were required to observe an inviolable rule of chastity. Just as the new poor law of 1834 represented a political triumph for philosophic radicalism by establishing an effective means of policing poverty, so it imposed middle class morality upon pauper women by seeking to police their sexual virtue.

60. Despite protests, the Poor Law Commissioners remained stout, for a time, in their insistence that to afford the mother of an illegitimate child a direct claim against the putative father for its maintenance would, by extending the rewards of matrimony to the unqualified and undeserving, tend to the destruction of the institution. In their sixth annual report in 1840, they printed with approval a report on the law of bastardy submitted to them by Sir Edmund Head, an Assistant Commissioner. We reproduce an extract which illustrates our earlier contention that the poor law contained within itself a special system of family law which applied exclusively to paupers and shows, also, the basis of the urban middle class fear of illegitimacy:

'. . . it is most characteristic of our legislation that questions of such moment as the *status* of illegitimate children, and rights and duties of their parents, should hardly be discussed at all, except in connection with Poor Laws. That the whole subject is one of extreme importance there can be no doubt. The framework of society in modern Europe rests on the institution of marriage. The church has dignified that rite with all its attributes of sanctity, and the state has endowed it with the most valuable civil privileges. In no country is respect for marriage more generally professed and more readily entertained than in England. . . . The recognition of a civil contract as the groundwork of matrimony in the Registration Bill was a great scandal to many persons. . . . We were told by many eminent members of the legislature that, to afford a woman who had once broken the marriage tie an opportunity of even seeing her children for a few minutes was an encroachment on the privileges of wives who had remained faithful, and in this way a direct encouragement to immorality. If this be so, what shall we say to the infringement of the exclusive privileges of the married state implied by conferring on the mother of a bastard that claim for its support from a definite father, which it is one great object of matrimony to secure? Does not the principle that anything short of marriage is sufficient to fix the paternity of the child involve in itself a direct attack on that institution?'

Against such arguments were set the findings of the Commissioners of Inquiry for South Wales who were appointed to investigate the Rebecca Riots. They reported in 1844 that the bastardy laws had:

'altogether failed of the effect which sanguine persons calculated they might produce on the caution or moral feelings of the weaker sex. (There was little prostitution in South Wales but) subsequent marriage — and that not a forced one — . . . almost invariably wiped out the light reproach which public opinion attached to a previous breach of chastity. (Now subsequent marriage was becoming rarer and women were exposed to) all the temptations of a life of vice (while) the man evades or defies the law, with a confidence and effrontery which has outraged the moral feeling of the people to a degree that can hardly be described.'

61. In the end, the Poor Law Commissioners gave ground and recommended in their tenth annual report that a mother should be given a civil action for maintenance against the putative father of her child. The Poor Law Amendment Act 1844 made a complete change by taking bastardy proceedings out of the hands of the poor law authorities and turning them into a civil matter between the parents. . . .

62. The Poor Law Amendment Act 1868 restored to the parish the power to recover from the putative father the cost of maintenance of a bastard child by providing that, where a woman who had obtained an order against the father of her child herself became a charge of the parish, the justices might order the payments to be made to the relieving officer. . . .

64. If the history of the legal rules which determine responsibility for the maintenance of bastards and their mothers is complicated, their treatment under the poor law was entirely straightforward. The mother was regarded as an able-bodied woman of demonstrated immorality, and relief was accordingly provided on a strictly deterrent basis in the workhouse. Mothers and babies were separated after the confinement and initial period of nursing. Most unmarried mothers could only use the workhouse as an immediate refuge during childbirth, after which they abandoned their children within it. Such unfortunates shared the fate of orphans and other deserted children who suffered deprivation as pauper children. But girls suffered worse than boys, because the workhouse served as a manufactory of prostitutes. Frances Power Cobbe's observation in 1865 remained true throughout the nineteenth century:

'The case of the girls is far worse than of the boys, as all the conditions of workhouse management fall with peculiar evil on their natures. . . . Among all the endless paradoxes of female treatment, one of the worst and most absurd is that which, while eternally proclaiming "home" to be the only sphere of a woman, systematically educates all female children of the State, without attempting to give them even an idea of what a home might be. . . .'

Workhouse children gained in the later decades of the nineteenth century from such advances in institutional care as cottage homes, sheltered homes and boarding out. But the need for change was only just beginning to be recognised in the early years of this century. The majority *Report of the Royal Commission on the Poor Laws and Relief of Distress* remarked in 1909 that:

'There is perhaps no more difficult problem in Poor Law administration than the treatment of unmarried mothers, and none in which discriminating methods might have greater results. The need for introducing a different system from the present has made itself universally felt amongst Poor Law workers, and there are certain points upon which our evidence is practically unanimous. . . . The fundamental mistake hitherto has lain in the tacit assumption that all unmarried mothers coming into the workhouse belong to the same class, and are to be dealt with on the same lines. It has become clear to us that in future we must distinguish between at least three classes: the feeble-minded or irresponsible, the young mothers who are responsible but have fallen for the first time, and the women who

have no desire to lead a respectable life . . . (and) who habitually make a convenience of the workhouse.'
. . .
74. One significant expression of the 'children's century' was the foundation in 1918 of the National Council for the Unmarried Mother and her Child. Lettice Fisher, the Council's first chairman, records that 'child welfare work went with a swing' in the immediate post-war search for a better life and that the council was not at first exclusively concerned with the unmarried mother and her child:

> 'The new Council was expected to work out schemes which could, if necessary, include not only unmarried mothers, but deserted or widowed mothers, and should aim at the provision of homes for expectant mothers, and small homes or foster-parents for such babies as could not be kept with their mothers.'

But the difficulty of raising money soon led to the abandonment of the original intention to care for all one-parent families, and the council had to restrict its work to the 'reform of the existing Bastardy and Affiliation Acts' and to securing 'the provision of adequate accommodation to meet the varying needs of mothers and babies throughout the country, with the special aim of keeping mother and child together'. The council stood for the public denial of the Victorian belief that the inferior status of bastardy, with its stigma for admittedly blameless children, was an essential buttress for the institution of monogamous marriage. Early successes were the Adoption and Legitimacy Acts 1926. . . .
75. The Adoption of Children Act 1926 made a momentous break with the law's age-long insistence upon a parent's inalienable rights over his child by enabling adopters to step into the shoes of the natural parents. Similarly, the Legitimacy Act 1926 brought into English law the *legitimatio per subsequens matrimonium* of Roman Law which the canon lawyers had unsuccessfully proposed when the Statute of Merton was debated in 1236. All that was achieved in 1926 was the concession of legitimation to the progeny of single persons who subsequently married. The Act did not apply to a child born of an adulterous union, that is, where either parent was married to someone else at the time of the birth. This limitation was imposed because, as the Home Office explained in an official memorandum:

> 'to allow children born in adultery to have the benefit . . . may remove a deterrent to adulterous intercourse, and may therefore be prejudicial to family life (which) in the interest of children generally is more important than the interest of a comparatively few illegitimate children.'

Children born of an adulterous union were not brought within the scope of legitimation until 1959. A decade later, the Family Law Reform Act 1969, enacting the main recommendations of the Committee on the Law of Succession in Relation to Illegitimate Persons, established near-equality of inheritance for all children. With this measure, English society has not completed but has come within the sight of completing a legal process achieved in countries which have altogether abolished the status of illegitimacy.

Questions

(i) Does the difference in patterns of inheritance between the landed aristocracy and the commercial bourgeoisie strike you as a plausible explanation for the difference in their attitudes to illegitimacy?
(ii) Does it strike you as odd that English law has already 'established near-equality of inheritance for all children,' even though there are still substantial differences between legitimate and illegitimate children in other areas of the law?

Davis' second, or 'sociological' approach to the problem of illegitimacy may help us to understand why English law has tackled the question of inheritance before it has dealt with the remaining disabilities of the child. Davis explains the approach thus:

Its central thesis is epigrammatically stated in Brinton's words (1936):

> 'Bastardy and marriage in this world are quite supplementary — you cannot have one without the other. In another world, you may indeed separate the two institutions and eliminate one of them, either by having marriage so perfect — in various senses — that no one will ever commit fornication or adultery, or by having fornication so perfect that no one will ever commit marriage. But these are definitely other worlds.'

. . . The gist of the theory is that the function of reproduction can be carried out in a socially useful manner only if it is performed in conformity with institutional patterns, because only by means of an institutional system can individuals be organized and taught to co-operate in the performance of this long-range function, and the function be integrated with other social functions. The reproductive or familial institutions constitute the social machinery in terms of which the creation of new members of society is supposed to take place. The birth of children in ways that do not fit into this machinery must necessarily receive the disapproval of society, else the institutional system itself, which depends upon favorable attitudes in individuals, would not be approved or sustained. . . .

People are not supposed to have illegitimate children, but when they do an emergency machinery is set into operation to give the child a status (though an inferior one) and to define the positions of the parents. In this way society continues. No one ever completely transcends the institutional boundaries. If he did, he would not be human. On the other hand, no one ever remains completely within the narrowest institutional boundaries. If he did, he would not be human. The fundamental explanation of nonconformity to the marital institutions is the same as the explanation of institutional nonconformity in general. . . .

The question as to why the child is punished for the sins of its parents is wrongly put. It assumes an explanation of what has yet to be explained. It should read: What is the status of the illegitimate child, and why is he given this status? Perhaps his status is partly explicable in terms of punishment, but not primarily. For one thing, the sociological identification of parent and child, which furnished the ancient raison d'être for punishing the offender in the person of his offspring, is present in illegitimacy only to a very limited degree. In the second place, illegitimacy is disapproved even in societies where premarital and extra-marital intercourse is sanctioned — in which case the motive cannot be a wish to punish the parents for illicit acts, because there are no illicit acts. The only way in which the punishment theory can make sense is in terms of procrastination and tangibility. Though illicit intercourse in our culture is disapproved officially, it is usually winked at or ignored in practice — by persons, indeed, who heartily disapprove of illegitimate children — partly because it is difficult to detect and control. The illegitimate child comes as a tangible and inescapable consequence of a clandestine act; it comes as a climax, a point at which public indignation can self-confidently boil over. The public attitude, thus born of procrastination, seems vindictive rather than preventive. But punishment for parental sin is not the sole motive for the treatment of illegitimate children and does not deserve the primacy generally given it. The inquiry must be pushed to a deeper level which will explain both the legal disabilities (concerning descent, inheritance, support, and domicile) and the social disabilities (concerning public opinion, folkways, and mores).

In other words, in order to understand the treatment meted out by society and the law towards those born outside marriage, we have to understand what marriage itself is designed to achieve. Lucy Mair, an anthropologist, discusses this in the first chapter of her book, *Marriage* (1971), intriguingly entitled, 'What is a husband for?' She first outlines Robin Fox's theory that in primitive societies, marriage is a mechanism for persuading father to stay at home in order to protect and support his children and their mother. She then examines some cultures in which, even though 'it is an ideal in all known societies that the begetting of children should be formally licensed in some way,' illegitimacy is common. She concludes:

If it were essential for the protection — in modern times rather for the economic support — of a woman with young children that the father of her children should be legally tied to her, these populations would not be able to survive. But they do. So we come back to the question, what is a husband for?

Husbands, considered as recognized fathers, are most important where they are the source of their children's social status and claims to inheritance. . . .

In the greater part of the world children take their status from the father; and even where the line of descent is traced through the mother it is usually no disadvantage to have a father of high status. There are societies. . . . that are divided into *patrilineal* or *agnatic lineages*, groups recruited by descent through males and recognizing common descent as far back as the members can trace their ancestry. A lineage has its patrimony, in land, cattle or capital, and as long as commercial activity is not much developed men depend on inheritance more than on acquisition; where there is commercial activity there is still nothing like inheritance to give you a good start in life. Men are always informally ranked by wealth, and where there is a formal ranking system it is legitimate descent that assigns places in it. Public office is often hereditary; so is the ability to approach nonhuman beings in ritual to secure their benevolence towards the society or some section of it. Because of the rules that define whom one may or may not marry, status by descent is significant when one is seeking a spouse.

The implications of this aspect of husbandhood and fatherhood are much wider than practical matters of economic support. . . .

A man is anxious to be the head of a numerous household when this provides him with a large working team; to be a member of a numerous lineage when this may be necessary for defence. He looks to his sons for support when he is old or sick. In societies organized in agnatic lineages religion is commonly focused on the cult of ancestors, and every man wishes to have descendants to make offerings to his spirit so that he will be commemorated in whatever is considered the appropriate way. In China up to the Communist revolution it was the first duty of a son to marry and produce a son to carry on the ancestor cult. The ancient Romans had very similar ideas. In lineage-based societies, and indeed in many others, marriage is an important way of forming alliances; this is one reason why men wish to become husbands as distinct from fathers.

In societies so organized, then, men wish to marry and women have no choice. Women do not have difficulty in inducing their consorts to marry them; but they are often penalized for entering into unlegalized unions, at any rate if these produce offspring.

Question

Engels (1884) described the development of such societies as the 'world historical defeat of the female sex . . . In order to make certain of the wife's fidelity and therefore of the paternity of her children, she is delivered over unconditionally into the power of her husband . . . [This type of marriage] is based on the supremacy of the man, the express purpose being to produce children of undisputed paternity; such paternity is demanded because these children are later to come into their father's property as his natural heirs.' In modern times, the reason given for the strength of the common law presumption that a child born to a married woman is her husband's child was that both woman and child would otherwise suffer the disabilities attached to adultery and illegitimacy. Is it at least possible that those disabilities were the *result*, not the cause, of that presumption?

The primacy of succession is reflected in the view of Sir William Blackstone, in his *Commentaries on the Laws of England* (1765):

The incapacity of a bastard consists principally in this, that he cannot be heir to any one, neither can he have heirs, but of his own body; for, being *nullius filius*, he is therefore of kin to nobody, and has no ancestor from whom any inheritable blood can be derived. A bastard was also, in strictness, incapable of holy orders; and, though that were dispensed with, yet he was utterly disqualified from holding any dignity in the church: but this doctrine seems now obsolete; and in all other respects, there is no distinction between a bastard and another man. And really any other distinction, but that of not inheriting, which civil policy renders necessary, would, with regard to the innocent offspring of his parents' crimes, be odious, unjust, and cruel to the last degree:

Thus, if inheritance has been the principal explanation for our laws of both marriage and legitimacy, it has little importance in the modern world. Nowadays, children are expected to get on by their own merit and not through the supposedly unfair advantage which inherited wealth and status can bring. The legitimate expectations which a child may have of his parents are spelled out by the Court of Appeal when allowing the appeal of a millionaire father against an order that, on divorce, he should settle £25,000 on each of his children:

Lord Lilford v Glyn
[1979] 1 All ER 441, [1978] 1 WLR 78, Court of Appeal

Orr LJ: . . . One finds in s. 25(2) of the 1973 [Matrimonial Causes] Act, which lays down the duty of the court in deciding whether to exercise its powers under (inter alia) s. 24(1)(*b*), that the court is so to exercise the power to order a settlement, like the other powers there referred to, as to place the child '. . . in the financial position in which the child would have been if the marriage had not broken down and each of the parties to the marriage had properly discharged his or her financial obligations and responsibilities towards him'. Whatever the precise meaning of that phrase a father, even the richest father, ought not to be regarded as under 'financial obligations or responsibilities' to provide funds for the purposes of such settlement as are envisaged in this case on children who are under no disability and whose maintenance and education are secure. We find support for this view in the following passages from the judgments of Scarman LJ in *Chamberlain v Chamberlain* [1974] 1 All ER 33, [1973] 1 WLR 1557, and of Bagnall J in *Harnett v Harnett* [1973] Fam 156, [1973] 2 All ER 593. In the first of these cases Scarman LJ said:

'Equally, I think the learned judge erred in this case in settling the house so that the beneficial interest at the end of the day became that of the children in equal shares. The order that the registrar made provided for the care and upbringing of the children in this house until they should finish full-time education. I think that that was an appropriate order. There are no circumstances in this case to suggest that any of these children had special circumstances that required them to make demands on their parents after the conclusion of their full-time education. The capital asset, the house, was acquired by the work and by the resources of their parents, and, provided their parents meet their responsibilities to their children as long as their children are dependent, this seems to me an asset that should revert then to the parents. Accordingly, I think that the learned judge was wrong to order a settlement and I think the learned registrar was right to divide this house in the way in which he did, beneficially between husband and wife, and to provide that at the end of the education of the children the house could be sold and the proceeds divided between the parents.'

In the second case Bagnall J said that —

'. . . in the vast majority of cases the financial position of a child of a subsisting marriage is simply to be afforded shelter, food and education, according to the means of his parents.'

For these reasons we think that Payne J was wrong in his approach to this issue but in any event, in our judgment, the order which he made was not justified in the circumstances of this case. There is not in this context, one rule for millionaires and another for less wealthy fathers, and in our judgment there was no means of judging whether the father, if the marriage had continued, would or would not have made a settlement in favour of the daughters. He might or he might not, and there was no reason to suppose that the first course was more likely than the other in view of the fact that he had already made a substantial settlement for the daughters in the form of the trust deed.

Such views may explain why the *Report of the Committee on the Law of Succession in relation to Illegitimate Persons* (the Russell Report of 1966) took a very simple line on the issue of intestate succession to both mother and father:

19. At the root of any suggestion for the improvement of the lot of bastards in relation to the laws of succession to property is, of course, the fact that in one sense they start level with legitimate children, in that no child is created of its own volition. Whatever may be said of the parents, the bastard is innocent of any wrongdoing. To allot to him an inferior, or indeed unrecognised, status in succession is to punish him for a wrong of which he was not guilty.

All children do not start level, however, if they have not had what the modern world thinks is due to every child — proper attention to his physical, emotional and intellectual needs throughout his childhood. Whatever may have been the position in primitive societies, modern society sees marriage as the framework within which both father and mother co-operate to bring up their children. The *Guardianship Act 1973* provides:

1.—(1) In relation to the custody or upbringing of a minor, and in relation to the administration of any property belonging to or held in trust for a minor or the application of income of any such property, a mother shall have the same rights and authority as the law allows to a father, and the rights and authority of mother and father shall be equal and be exercisable by either without the other.

Illegitimate children, however, are excluded from any such automatic relationship with both their parents. The question now is whether this is the best way in which the law can provide for their upbringing.

2 The factual background

The following graphs appear in D. Pearce and S. Farid, *Illegitimate Births: Changing Patterns* (1977). The first shows the fluctuation in actual numbers of illegitimate live births in England and Wales from 1850 to 1975:

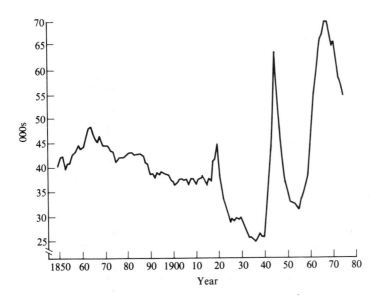

To some extent, however, illegitimate births rise and fall in time with the birth rate as a whole. More instructive, therefore, is the graph showing the ratio of illegitimate births to all live births occurring over the same period:

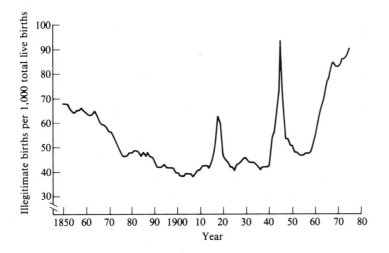

Questions

(i) Can a comparison of these graphs suggest anything to us about the reasons for having illegitimate children?
(ii) In particular, how would you account for the fact that, during the 1970s, while actual numbers fell, the proportion of illegitimate births began to rise again?

The trend is even more marked if we look at the figures for the years from 1975 to 1980, once again for England and Wales:

Year	Total live births 000s	Illegitimate live births	Rate per 000
1976	584.3	53,800	92
1977	569.3	55,400	97
1978	596.4	60,600	102
1979	638.0	69,500	109
1980	656.2	77,400	118

(Lest it be thought that matters are markedly different north of the border, it should be noted that the Scottish rate reached 111 in 1980 and 122 in 1981.) The underlying causes are obviously complicated, but some light may be cast upon them by other official figures. For example, an indication of the changing behaviour of different age groups between 1971 and 1981 is given by the following chart, which appeared in *Social Trends 13* (1982):

Births: by conception inside or outside marriage and age of mother

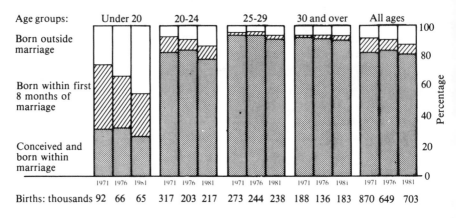

Great Britain

Births: thousands 92 66 65   317 203 217   273 244 238   188 136 183   870 649 703

Source: Office of Population Censuses and Surveys; General Register Office (Scotland)

The trend is once again emphasised if we remember that the top two portions of each column do not represent all extra-marital conceptions. A precise figure for all such conceptions is difficult to obtain, partly because official statistics cannot show us illegitimate conceptions by married women or before a second marriage, and partly because abortions take place usually some six months before births. Nevertheless, if one adds together (*a*) all illegitimate live births, (*b*) illegitimate still births, (*c*) abortions outside marriage, and (*d*) pre-maritally conceived live births, some impression can be gained. The following table gives the respective percentages of each in 1971 and 1980:

	(a)	(b)	(c)	(d)	Total no. of conceptions
1971	35.4	0.5	25.8	38.2	185,700
1980	36.9	0.4	39.2	23.5	188,300

Questions

(i) Why do you think that 'shot-gun marriages' are so clearly on the decline?
(ii) As such marriages have apparently been roughly twice as likely as others to break down (Rowntree, 1964; Gibson, 1974; Thornes and Collard, 1979), might this trend even be welcomed?
(iii) Given the *relatively* small increase in the total of births and abortions resulting from extra-marital conception, can we draw any conclusions from the *relatively* small increase in the percentage which result in illegitimate births? For example, could it indicate (*a*) that more women are now being left 'holding the baby'; or (*b*) that more women are quite happy to bear a child outside marriage?

Apart from undoubted improvements both in societal attitudes towards and in the economic circumstances of single mothers which have taken place in the last two decades, it is generally accepted that a large but variable proportion of illegitimate children are born into what used to be called 'stable illicit unions.' Around half of all illegitimate births are registered on the joint information of both parents (see p. 305, below as to the circumstances in which the father's name may be entered on the register). Furthermore, 'an exercise matching a sample of illegitimate births occurring during 1961 and 1971 with the mothers' census schedules showed that around one-quarter of illegitimate births occurred to women who described themselves on the census schedule as married. The fact that around one in six illegitimate births are subsequently legitimated is evidence that a sizeable proportion of such births are accepted' (Leete, 1978). There could, however, be other reasons for each of these findings. More convincing evidence comes from the National Child Development Study, which has followed the careers of *all* children born in this country in a single week in 1958. In *Children in Changing Families* (1980), Lydia Lambert and Jane Streather studied the data from the follow-up at the age of 11 (for an earlier follow-up at age 7, see Crellin, Kellmer Pringle and West, 1971). They wished to compare the development of those who had been born illegitimate and stayed with their mothers, with those who had been born illegitimate but adopted by strangers, and those who had been born legitimate. These are their findings on the children's 'family situation' (percentages within each birth status):

Legitimacy status	Natural parents	Step-parents	Adoptive parents	Mother alone	Father alone	Other situations
Illegitimate	41%	24%	0	20%	1%	14%
Adopted	0	0	93%	0	0	7%
Legitimate	91%	3%	*	4%	1%	1%

* Three legitimate children were adopted between 7 and 11, but another 15 were excluded from the study because they had been adopted before the follow-up at the age of 7.

. . . As expected, the majority (74%) of the 409 illegitimately born children were living in a two-parent family at age eleven. This number includes the children who had subsequently been adopted, but when they are excluded, the pattern is still clear. Out of the 294 illegitimate children who had not been adopted, 195 were living in two-parent families (65%). The proportion of illegitimate children living with both their natural parents at 11 (41%) was very similar to that at 7.

It is not possible to know whether this pattern is typical of the family situations of illegitimate children of this age in the general population. However, a study of 2511 children aged 9 to 14 years in Aberdeen found that at the time of interview 73% of the illegitimately born children were living in a two-parent situation of some kind and of these 34 per cent (25% overall) were living with their natural parents (Gill, 1977), figures which are very similar to our own.

In a later chapter, the authors comment:

When current theories about the family . . . have been matched against the reality of demographic facts, the discrepancy between the ideal of the conventional nuclear family and the actual diversity of family life has been obvious. While it is true that the majority of children continue to live with both their own parents, the rates of separation and divorce are such that increasing proportions of families are broken, for a time at least, and many are then reconstituted following remarriage. Gill (1977) has pointed out that the pathways of care for legitimate children are towards fatherlessness while those for illegitimate children are away from it. This pattern, and the resulting diversity of family life, is apparent when the parental-care situations at the age of 11 of the children in the present study are examined.

A more precise study of the fate of those born illegitimate was carried out by Richard Leete, in *Adoption Trends and Illegitimate Births 1951–1977* (1979). He calculated the numbers of children born illegitimate in a given year who had subsequently been adopted by a parent, adopted by strangers, legitimated or had died. The following brief extracts summarise his results:

The figures show that between 7 and 8% of the generations born in the 1950s and 1960s were, or can be expected to be adopted by age 16 by couples of whom one at least is a parent. . . .

The level of adoption of illegitimate children by non-parents is very much higher than that by parents. . . . some 20% of children born illegitimate between 1951 and 1968 were, or can be expected to be, adopted by non-parents by the time they become adults; . . . Since 1968 the rate of adoption in the first years of life has fallen greatly. Thus, just 9 per cent of children born illegitimate in 1974 had been adopted by age two, just half the proportion found for generations born during the early and mid 1960s. . . .

Among generations born in the mid and late 1960s it is likely that some 20% of illegitimate children will have been legitimated by age 16. For generations born during the 1970s there has been a sharp fall in the level of legitimation . . .

The main causes of attrition from illegitimacy have been non-parental adoptions and legitimations. Other things being equal, it follows that when the rate at which these events occur falls, as it has done since the late 1960s, increasing proportions of children born illegitimate can be expected to continue as such.

Fig. 3 Percentage of selected generations of illegitimate children alive and still illegitimate by given age, England and Wales

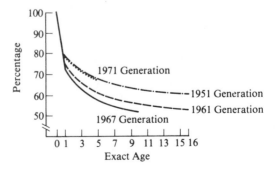

Questions

(i) Why do *you* think there has been a fall in *both* adoptions by strangers *and* legitimation?

(ii) Might it not have been expected that legitimation would increase following the Divorce Reform Act 1969?

(iii) Does the apparently increasing acceptance of illegitimacy, which these figures indicate, suggest to you that there is any need for law reform?

Lambert and Streather set out to answer the question 'does birth status matter?' The raw data showed that the illegitimate children who remained with their mothers were generally less likely to be living in favourable circumstances: their family situation has already been mentioned; in addition, 16% had been in local authority care at some time in their lives, compared with 3% of the legitimate; only 12% were in non-manual ('middle class') homes, compared with 34% of the legitimate and 60% of the adopted; many more of their mothers had 'come down in the world' from their social class of origin; 35% were receiving supplementary benefit or free school meals, compared with 13% of the legitimate and 4% of the adopted; they were also more likely to be over-crowded, less likely to have sole use of basic amenities, and less likely to be owner-occupiers, even when both parents were together. But when the authors studied the children's physical development and school attainment after making allowances for their family situation and environmental circumstances, a different picture emerged:

When no allowance was made for background circumstances, adopted children were, for example, reading better at 11, on average, than either legitimate children or illegitimate children. This achievement deserves to be commended, but when we looked at the reading scores of children who came from homes with similar environmental characteristics, illegitimate as well as legitimate children were reading just as well as the adopted. Conversely, where the home circumstances were less favourable, illegitimate children were not reading any worse than other children in such circumstances. The fact that illegitimate children were more likely than other children to be living in disadvantaged situations, rather than their birth status, was associated with their lower reading scores at 11. For most of the children the same was also true when maths ability was considered. The findings also showed that at the age of 11 children's physical growth was unlikely to be related to birth status.

When the children's social adjustment at 11 was considered within the context of their background circumstances, there continued to be a difference between illegitimate and legitimate children, and the apparently equivocal position of the adopted children tilted in the direction of the illegitimate. Although the adjustment of these two groups appeared similar, varying stress factors may have been at work in each group, even if, ultimately, they were all linked with birth status.

At the age of 7 the adopted children had already been showing signs of having more behaviour problems than legitimate children (Seglow et al, 1972). Between the ages of 7 and 11 all children are likely to have had periods of doubt and uncertainty about their origins and identity, and all but a handful of the adopted children knew for a fact that they were born to a different parents [sic] but probably did not know a great deal about them. By 1969, when these children were 11, the policy of greater openness in talking to adopted children about their origins was increasingly encouraged by professionals and the media. But, with the best will in the world, it is not an easy matter to put into practice, and may have added to, rather than diminished, the children's difficulties in adjustment. The finding, in other studies of adopted children, that there was an increase in problems around this age, followed by a later settling down, suggests that it may be a healthy sign that the adopted children in the NCDS were more troublesome in mid-childhood. It will be extremely interesting to study their adjustment at 16 to see what was happening during adolescence. Obviously teachers and parents would be right to show concern for difficulties in social adjustment at any age, but it may be the case that these are only an indication of possible maladjustment if they persist.

Illegitimate children who were not adopted were also more likely than legitimate children to have experienced difficulties in resolving uncertainties about their origins. Their mothers may have been more reluctant than adoptive parents to discuss the subject, and while some of the children were living with their own fathers, others may have been told even less about them than adopted children. However, the illegitimate children had been less well adjusted than legitimate children at the age of 7, which suggests that unless uncertainty about their origins was the contributory reason at both ages, other factors, such as the greater amount of change in their environmental circumstances, were also associated with their relatively poorer social adjustment at 11.

In conclusion

The general lack of association between children's physical development or their school attainment at the age of 11 and their birth status is a salutory reminder of the powerful influence of the environment for good or ill. Some children were fortunate and lived in an exceptionally favourable environment, and many of the adopted children were among this group. For other children, living in families with poor housing and low income, and experiencing the difficulties mainly associated with low social status were far more pressing and ever-present problems than whether their parents had been married when they were born.

Even if they were legitimately born, diversity in family life was becoming the experience of an increasing proportion of children, as their parents' marriages were broken or remade. The importance of birth status fades before a recognition of the practical needs of families for such things as adequate incomes and adequate housing if children are to grow up without disadvantage.

Illegitimacy and adoption are fascinating subjects, which deserve attention. Singling out such children and comparing them with legitimate children, in the way that has been done in this report, highlights their differences less than the needs shared by all children in changing families.

Questions

(i) Does not the association between illegitimacy and poorer environmental circumstances at least suggest something *to* the child's mother?
(ii) Could the greater tendency of the illegitimate children to show signs of stress, both at seven and at eleven, have anything to do with their birth status as such?

These findings relate, of course, to children born in 1958. Since then, major demographic changes have occurred which may have some bearing on the matters at issue. The table on p. 295 appeared in *Social Trends 12* (1982).

Question

Does the table opposite cause you to revise any of the impressions which you had gained earlier in this section?

3 Establishing fatherhood

Discussions of illegitimacy have always been bedevilled by the problems of proving paternity. It is easy to remember the first part of Lancelot's speech to Old Gobbo — 'It's a wise father, that knows his own child' — while forgetting the second — 'Truth will come to light; murder cannot be hid long, a man's son may; but in the end, truth will out.' The present advantages and disadvantages, not only for the child but also for his parents, of being born to a married woman, are amply illustrated by the four cases which follow overleaf:

Births: by birthplace of mother, 1971 and 1979

Great Britain

Percentages and thousands

	United Kingdom		Caribbean		India, Pakistan Bangladesh		Irish Republic		Other countries		All countries	
	1971	1979	1971	1979	1971	1979	1971	1979	1971	1979	1971	1979
Percentage of births which were:												
First within marriage	37	38	13	16	25	31	28	28	39	43	36	37
Second within marriage	31	33	13	16	25	28	26	29	31	32	31	32
Third or fourth within marriage	20	17	21	13	27	28	26	24	20	16	20	17
Fifth or later within marriage	4	2	17	4	21	13	9	5	4	2	5	2
Outside marriage	8	11	36	51	1	1	11	13	6	6	8	11
Total births (= 100%) (thousands)	773	620	13	7	22	28	23	10	39	41	870	706

Knowles v Knowles
[1962] P 161, [1962] 1 All ER 659, [1962] 2 WLR 742, 105 Sol Jo 1011, High
Court, Family Division

A decree nisi of divorce was granted to the husband on 22 May 1957 and
made absolute on 5 July 1957. The wife had a child on 19 April 1958. Her
doctor stated that he had examined her in October 1957 and thought that
conception was likely to have taken place in June. The wife's evidence was
consistent with conception in mid-June or in mid-July. For a birth on
19 April 1958, after a normal period of gestation of 270 to 280 days, conception would have taken place in the second week in July 1957. The wife applied
for maintenance for herself and the child and the husband denied paternity.

Wrangham J: There is undoubtedly a presumption . . . that a child born in wedlock to a married
woman is the child of her husband. That presumption applies not only to a child born during
wedlock but to a child clearly conceived during wedlock. That appears from such cases as *Re
Heath, Stacey v Bird* [1945] Ch 417, 115 LJ Ch 120 and *Re Overbury, Sheppard v Matthews*
[1955] Ch 122, [1954] 3 All ER 308 where what was being considered was the position of a child
which must, according to the laws of nature, have been conceived during wedlock but which had
been born after the death of the husband. The presumption that a child conceived during
wedlock is a legitimate child of the husband applies just as much whether that husband and wife
are living together in the ordinary way or whether they are separated by agreement, or by a deed,
or simply separated, or even if the wife has obtained from the magistrates an order for
maintenance, unless that order contains a non-cohabitation clause. That appears from *Bowen v
Norman* [1938] 1 KB 689, [1938] 2 All ER 776 and from *Ettenfield v Ettenfield* [1940] P 96,
[1940] 1 All ER 293. . . . The presumption ceases to operate if the parties are separated under an
order of the court such as, for example, a decree of judicial separation, which does away with
the duty of the spouses to live together. It seems to me that the basis of the presumption is that
the law contemplates spouses as fulfilling their marital duties to each other unless there has been
an actual order of the court dispensing with the performance of such marital duties. So long as
the law contemplates the spouses as performing their marital duties to each other, so long will it
contemplate that a married woman if she bears [a] child will be bearing it as a result of intercourse with her husband only.

Now, it does not seem to me (to take the steps one by one) that, for example, the presentation
of a petition for divorce can possibly be equivalent to a decree of judicial separation or a non-
cohabitation order by magistrates so as to dispense with the mutual marital duties of the
spouses, and, indeed, it appears to me to follow from such cases as *W v W (No 2)* [1954] P 486,
[1954] 2 All ER 829, and *Cohen v Cohen* [1940] AC 631, [1940] 2 All ER 331, that even after a
decree nisi has been pronounced the parties still owe to each other the marital duties which were
imposed on them by marriage. It has been repeatedly said that a decree nisi does not dissolve a
marriage, and if, as appears from the cases that I have cited, a spouse who has deserted the other
spouse remains under a duty to resume married life with that spouse even after a decree nisi has
been pronounced,[1] whether it be for nullity or divorce, it seems to me to be clear that the law
contemplates marital duties as still in existence, and, therefore, will treat the parties, from one
point of view, as fulfilling them. If this reasoning be correct, it seems that the presumption that a
child conceived during wedlock is legitimate continues to operate after the presentation of the
petition for divorce or nullity or after the pronunciation of a decree nisi either for nullity or for
divorce. . . .

Now that involves, of course, not merely a presumption as to the paternity, as to the person
with whom the wife had intercourse, but also a presumption as to the date of conception. I think
that if one has a presumption as to legitimacy it operates as to both, where both go to show
legitimacy. In the present case, to be legitimate the child has not merely to be conceived as the
result of intercourse between husband and wife but to have been conceived before the decree
absolute, and if there be a presumption of legitimacy at all it seems to me to be a presumption as
to both matters which in the present case constitute legitimacy; that is to say, I think that there is
a presumption that the child was conceived before the decree absolute and equally a
presumption that the child was a child of the husband. Of course, the presumptions as to both of
those facts are rebuttable by evidence.

Having reviewed the evidence, the judge could find nothing to rebut the
presumption, either as to the date of conception, or as to the identity of the
father, and ordered accordingly.

---

1. Although a husband may now be convicted of raping his wife after a decree nisi (*R v O'Brien*
[1974] 3 All ER 663).

Questions

(i) Why did the judge think it possible to use the presumption to determine *both* the likely date of conception *and* the likely father?

(ii) Does your answer to question (i) cast any doubt on the applicability of the presumption to conceptions which must have taken place *before* the marriage (where it is said to apply a fortiori, *Gardner v Gardner* (1877) 2 App Cas 723)?

(iii) Unencumbered by the judge's view of presumptions, which conception date would you consider more likely in this case?

The Ampthill Peerage Case
[1977] AC 547, [1976] 2 All ER 411, [1976] 2 WLR 777, 120 Sol Jo 367, House of Lords' Committee of Privileges

In 1921, Christobel, wife of the man who was later to become third baron Ampthill, gave birth to Geoffrey, who had been conceived by external fertilisation while his mother was still a virgin. Her husband petitioned for divorce, alleging that this was the result of Christobel's adultery. At the trial, the husband gave evidence that he had had no sexual intimacy of any kind with his wife at the probable date of conception and was granted a decree. On appeal, the House of Lords decided that evidence of non-access by a husband or a wife was inadmissible both in legitimacy proceedings and in divorce proceedings (*Russell v Russell* [1924] AC 687, 93 LJP 97: the rule was subsequently reversed in the Law Reform (Miscellaneous Provisions) Act 1949, s 7(1)). The divorce decree was rescinded. In 1925, the High Court made a decree under the then equivalent of s. 45 of the Matrimonial Causes Act 1973 declaring that Geoffrey was the legitimate child of Christobel and her husband. The marriage was eventually dissolved in 1937. In 1950, a son John was born of the third baron's third marriage. The third baron died in 1973 and both Geoffrey and John claimed to succeed him. Geoffrey relied upon the declaration, but John alleged that this was not binding, *inter alia*, because it had been procured by fraud. Blood samples were available from Christobel and the third baron, but not from Geoffrey.

Section 45 of the *Matrimonial Causes Act 1973*, although not in identical words, is to the same effect as the earlier legislation. Its material parts read:

45.—(1) Any person who is a British subject, or whose right to be deemed a British subject depends wholly or in part on his legitimacy or on the validity of any marriage, may, if he is domiciled in England and Wales or in Northern Ireland or claims any real or personal estate situate in England and Wales, apply by petition to the High Court for a decree declaring that he is the legitimate child of his parents, or that the marriage of his father and mother or of his grandfather and grandmother was a valid marriage or that his own marriage was a valid marriage.

(5) . . . on any application under the preceding provisions of this section the High Court or, as the case may be, the county court shall make such a decree as it thinks just, and the decree shall be binding on Her Majesty and all other persons whatsoever, so however that the decree shall not prejudice any person —

    (*a*) if it is subsequently proved to have been obtained by fraud or collusion; or

    (*b*) unless that person has been given notice of the application in the manner prescribed by rules of court or made a party to the proceedings or claims through a person so given notice or made a party.

Lord Wilberforce: . . . There can hardly be anything of greater concern to a person than his status as the legitimate child of his parents; denial of it, or doubts as to it, may affect his reputation, his standing in the world, his admission into a vocation, or a profession, or into social organisations, his succession to property, his succession to a title. It is vitally necessary that the law should provide a means for any doubts which may be raised to be resolved, and resolved at a time when witnesses and records are available. It is vitally necessary that any such doubts once disposed of should be resolved once for all . . .

Lord Simon of Glaisdale: . . . There is one status for which Parliament, in the wisdom of experience, has made special provision. This is the status of legitimacy. Status means the condition of belonging to a class in society to which the law ascribes peculiar rights and duties, capacities and incapacities. Such, for example, is the status of a married person or minor. Legitimacy is a status: it is the condition of belonging to a class in society the members of which are regarded as having been begotten in lawful matrimony by the men whom the law regards as their fathers. Motherhood, although also a legal relationship, is based on a fact, being proved demonstrably by parturition. Fatherhood, by contrast, is a presumption. A woman can have sexual intercourse with a number of men any of whom may be the father of her child; though it is true that modern serology can sometimes enable the presumption to be rebutted as regards some of these men. The status of legitimacy gives the child certain rights both against the man whom the law regards as his father and generally in society. Among the peculiar rights which a child is entitled to enjoy by virtue of the status of legitimacy is the right to succeed to a hereditary title of honour. If the hereditary title of honour is a peerage of the United Kingdom, the oldest legitimate son when of full age is entitled to be called to your Lordships' House on the death of the man whom the law regards as his father.

It was probably for two reasons that Parliament made special provision for judgment as to the status of legitimacy. First, no doubt, because, since fatherhood is not factually demonstrable by parturition, it is questionable; and it is generally in the interest of society that open questions should be finally closed. Second, no doubt, because since the legitimate child, by virtue of his legal relationship with the man whom the law regards as his father, is entitled to certain rights both as against the father and generally in society, it is desirable that the legal relationship between father and child should be decisively concluded.

His lordship then reviews the law and the evidence and concludes that the decree was not obtained by fraud or collusion, not least because, as the law stood in 1925, Geoffrey was entitled to the benefit of the presumption of legitimacy *even if* his mother had confessed to committing adultery at the relevant time. Finally:

. . . The law, in response to society's needs, enjoins that civil strife should be concluded by the final judgment of a court of law. To this there are well-recognised exceptions demanded by considerations of justice: where the judgment has been obtained by fraud, by collusion or by such a procedural irregularity as is liable to cause a failure of justice. John is seeking to add two further, unauthorised and undesirable, exceptions: first, where technological developments have furnished new modes of proof; and, secondly, where there has been a change in the law of evidence. Such further exceptions are undesirable, because if admitted there is no reason why there should be any end to litigation. The bitter waters would never ebb. . . .
Their lordships advised that Geoffrey had made out his claim to the barony.

Questions

(i) How many of the concerns suggested by Lord Wilberforce seem relevant to ordinary people today?

(ii) Both *Knowles v Knowles* and the *Ampthill Peerage Case* demonstrate the strength of the courts' traditional reluctance to bastardise a child, but we repeat an earlier question: were the disabilities attached to adultery and bastardy the *result*, rather than the cause, of the need to presume that the husband was father to his wife's children?

(iii) Is there any longer any need for such a presumption?

Re J.S. (A Minor)
[1981] Fam 22, [1980] 1 All ER 1061, [1980] 3 WLR 984, 124 Sol Jo 881, 10 Fam Law 121, Court of Appeal

An illegitimate child was born in September 1975. His mother had a 'continuous relationship' with a Mr R, but on two occasions, in November

1974 and January 1975, she had intercourse with the plaintiff. Since birth, the child had lived with his mother and Mr R as a normal family. The plaintiff became obsessed with the thought of the child, visited them until prevented by the mother, and sought a declaration in wardship proceedings that he was the child's father. Blood samples were taken from the plaintiff, the mother and the child, but refused by Mr R. The tests did not exclude the plaintiff from being the father. Heilbron J assumed that she had jurisdiction to grant the declaration sought, but refused it on the merits. The plaintiff appealed.

Ormrod LJ: . . . The court, of course, has from time to time to decide the issue of paternity in order to resolve some other issue between the parties, although it is rarely necessary to do so in wardship proceedings: *Re L* [1968] P 119, [1968] 1 All ER 20 was such a case. Biological parentage usually has little effect on the problems which the court normally handles in such proceedings.

There is certainly no statutory power to grant such a declaration, for there is no analogue to the powers now contained in the Matrimonial Causes Act 1973, s. 45, to grant by decree, declarations of legitimacy, legitimation, or the validity of marriage. The lack of any comparable procedure to determine the paternity of an illegitimate child may considerably reduce the practical efficacy of the policy of eliminating so far as possible the differences between the rights of legitimate and illegitimate children enacted by Parliament in Part II of the Family Law Reform Act 1969. The illegitimate child has one irremovable handicap; there is no presumption of paternity and it may be very difficult to prove.

There is, we think, no power to grant such a declaration under the wardship proceedings as such for, as we have already pointed out, it is not directly relevant to the issues normally dealt with in wardship proceedings.

If, therefore, there is power to grant such a declaration it will have to be found in the inherent jurisdiction of the court. But no authority for such a proposition was cited by counsel for the plaintiff, nor are we aware of any. On the contrary, for what it is worth, the only case which touches the point, *Aldrich v A-G* [1968] P 281, [1968] 1 All ER 345, a decision of Ormrod J at first instance, is against the plaintiff's contention. It is true that that case was concerned with a father who was trying to obtain a declaration that a deceased woman was his legitimate daughter but, in effect, what he was seeking was a declaration of paternity and, in our opinion, the reasoning in that case covers the present appeal.

We would, therefore, hold that the learned judge had no power to make a declaration of paternity and should have dismissed the summons of 19 May 1979. This conclusion accords with the view expressed by the Law Commission in their paper of 13th March 1979 entitled 'Family Law, Illegitimacy'. That, of course, disposes of this appeal but, since the matter was dealt with by the judge on the assumption that she had jurisdiction, and we have heard argument on the same assumption, we will deal briefly with some of the submissions which have been made.

The jurisdiction, if it exists, is admittedly discretionary, so the next question is whether the learned judge should have decided to exercise it in this case. In our view, she should have refused to do so for a number of reasons. In the first place, the declaration sought by the plaintiff is one of pure fact; it determines no legal rights except the right to apply under s. 14 of the Guardianship of Minors Act 1971, which is immaterial in this case because all forms of relief under that Act are available in the wardship proceedings. Such a declaration would be binding only inter partes; it would not affect the rights of persons not party to the present proceedings. In fact, the only purpose which it could serve would be to create an estoppel. Such a declaration is no more than a finding of fact formalised in an order of the court and made without reference to any specific legal issue between the parties. Its effect, therefore, is to prejudge such issues, and might adversely affect the interests of the child by, for example, precluding him from asserting in the future that he is the illegitimate son of Mr R.

In the instant case there is the further objection that to make an order declaring that A is the father of B, largely on serological evidence, is to transmute a mathematical probability into a forensic certainty when there is no necessity to do so. When it is necessary to give effect to statistical evidence of this kind in order to determine the rights of the parties, the court does so on the usual basis of deciding where the onus of proof lies and whether the party on whom it lies has sufficiently discharged it. The weight of the evidence may or may not be sufficient, depending on the issue which the court has to decide. But to make a formal declaration 'in the air' so to speak, is another thing altogether. It poses the question of the standard of proof. Counsel for the plaintiff argued strenuously that the learned judge should have been satisfied on 'the balance of probabilities' that Mr J was the father of the child, but what that much used phrase means in the context of a case like the present is by no means clear.

The concept of 'probability' in the legal sense is certainly different from the mathematical concept; indeed, it is rare to find a situation in which these two usages co-exist although, when they do, the mathematical probability has to be taken into the assessment of probability in the legal sense and given its appropriate weight. Nor is the word 'balance' much clearer. . . . In the criminal law the burden of proof is usually expressed in the formula 'The prosecution must satisfy you so that you are sure that the accused is guilty'. The civil burden might be formulated on analogous lines, 'the plaintiff (or the party on whom the burden rests) must satisfy the court that it is reasonably safe in all the circumstances of the case to act on the evidence before the court, bearing in mind the consequences which will follow'.

The learned judge, rightly in our opinion, adopted this test. In the course of her judgment she said: 'The degree of probability in an issue of paternity should, in my opinion, be commensurate with the transcending importance of that decision to the child.' We would express the proposition differently. In our judgment, if there is power to make a bare declaration that A is the father of B the court should not exercise its discretion to make such a declaration unless the evidence is conclusive or very nearly so. (We do not think that s 26 of the Family Law Reform Act 1969, which deals with the presumption of legitimacy and provides that it may be rebutted by evidence which shows that it is more probable than not that the person concerned is illegitimate, is in point in the present case where there is no presumption to rebut.)

. . . In wardship proceedings the interests of the child are paramount and all decisions must be taken in the light of those interests, although it may not be easy to evaluate them correctly. With hindsight it is now clear that it was unnecessary to consider the biological parentage of this child in order to reach a conclusion about access, which was the only live issue. The child is securely based in a two-parent family with the mother and Mr R, who fully accepts his role as de facto father, with the knowledge of the doubt of his being the biological father; the plaintiff is, to all intents and purposes, a stranger to the child. To allow the paternity issue to disturb this settled relationship was, in our view, an undoubted mistake and we find ourselves in full agreement with the mother's attitude. We can only regret that she allowed herself to be persuaded into providing samples of her own and the child's blood. Moreover, when it was known that Mr R was not prepared to provide a blood sample (which could only help Mr J to prove his case once the results of the other blood tests were known), it was clear that paternity could not be conclusively proved and that it could only be a matter of mathematical probabilities. . . .

In our judgment in wardship cases the court should proceed very carefully where a question as to paternity is raised. If it is to be raised there should be an order for the trial of the issue, but such an order itself should only be made if the court is satisfied that the determination of this issue will have a material bearing on some other issue that is to be tried, and that it is in the child's interest that this question should be investigated. Similarly, in wardship cases, orders under Part III of the Family Law Reform Act 1969 should only be made if it appears to be in the child's best interests that blood tests should be carried out and that the results are likely to be conclusive, ie that the other adults concerned are willing to provide blood samples. Had this practice been followed in the present case much stress and expense would have been eliminated.

Question

Was it indeed irrelevant to the access question that the plaintiff might possibly be the father of the child?

S v S, W v Official Solicitor
[1972] AC 24, [1970] 3 All ER 107, [1970] 3 WLR 366, 114 Sol Jo 635, House of Lords

Both were divorce cases in which the husband denied paternity of a child to whom the presumption of legitimacy applied. They arose before the Family Law Reform Act 1969 gave the courts power to direct that blood samples be taken from mother, child and any party alleged to be the child's father, in the course of any civil proceedings in which paternity is in issue. They were thus mainly concerned with whether the court had power to order that the child's blood be tested, but the speeches remain of interest upon the question of whether a court *should* now direct that blood tests be used.

Lord Reid: . . . The law as to the onus of proof is now set out in s 26 of the Family Law Reform Act 1969, as follows:

'Any presumption of law as to the legitimacy or illegitimacy of any person may in any civil proceedings be rebutted by evidence which shows that it is more probable than not that that person is illegitimate or legitimate, as the case may be, and it shall not be necessary to prove that fact beyond reasonable doubt in order to rebut the presumption.'

That means that the presumption of legitimacy now merely determines the onus of proof. Once evidence has been led it must be weighed without using the presumption as a make-weight in the scale for legitimacy. So even weak evidence against legitimacy must prevail if there is not other evidence to counterbalance it. The presumption will only come in at that stage in the very rare case of the evidence being so evenly balanced that the court is unable to reach a decision on it. I cannot recollect ever having seen or heard of a case of any kind where the court could not reach a decision on the evidence before it. . . .

I think that it was implicit in the argument of the Official Solicitor that to take a blood test is to imperil the child's status of legitimacy. But that must be on an assumption that if the case was decided without the blood test it would be held that the child is legitimate. Now that this depends simply on balance of probabilities it is very often impossible to forecast how the case will go. If one knew or suspected that on the other evidence the child would be held to be illegitimate then it would be in the child's interest to have a blood test because that would afford some chance that the decision would go the other way.

But that is only one reason why it is so difficult to assess the child's interest. On the one hand, it is said that with rare exceptions it is always in the child's interest to have a decision that it is legitimate. On the other hand, it is said that the value to a child of a finding of legitimacy is now much less than it used to be, and that it is generally better for the child that the truth should out than that the child should go through life with a lurking doubt as to the validity of a decision when evidence, which would very likely have disclosed the truth, has been suppressed.

. . . I accept the view that on average it is still a considerable disadvantage to be illegitimate. But I doubt whether, again on average this disadvantage would be greatly diminished by a decision in favour of legitimacy seen to have been based on inadequate evidence after refusal to allow a blood test. I think that the final abolition of the old strong presumption of legitimacy by s 26 of the 1969 Act shows that in the view of Parliament public policy no longer requires that special protection should be given by the law to the status of legitimacy. . . .

Lord Hodson: . . . In paternity cases such as those under consideration by your Lordships the court is not truly exercising the custodial jurisdiction in which the interests of the child are paramount but the duty of arbitrament between parties in which their interests are relevant and must be considered as well as the interests of the infant whose body it is sought to examine. Were it otherwise I think that the task of the court in deciding whether or not to order a blood test in the case of a child would in many, perhaps in most, cases be exceedingly difficult. Who is to say what is in the interests of the child and whether knowledge of true paternity would or would not favour his or her future prospects in life? How are these interests to be assessed? I find these questions especially difficult to answer in view of the fact that it must surely be in the best interests of the child in most cases that paternity doubts should be resolved on the best evidence, and, as in adoption, the child should be told the truth as soon as possible.

Questions

(i) Compare Lord Reid's remarks upon the standard of proof required for a married man to establish that he is *not* the father of his wife's child with those of Ormrod LJ in *Re JS* as to the standard of proof required to establish that a particular man *is* the father: can that difference be justified?

(ii) The Family Law Reform Act 1969 does not, of course, provide that blood may be forcibly taken from an unwilling man, but the court may draw such inferences as it sees fit from his failure to observe the direction to supply blood: why did the court not consider doing this in *Re JS*?

(iii) Are the arguments in favour of blood tests any less compelling when a man is trying to prove that he *is* the child's father than when he is trying to prove that he is not?

These cases raise the question of what a blood test can, and cannot, be expected to achieve. This is explained for the layperson by Dr Barbara Dodd in *Blood Tests* (1977):

. . . . Blood groups are suitable for the elucidation of problems of doubtful paternity because they appear in an individual in accordance with Mendelian laws of inheritance. The formation of blood group factors is controlled by genes which are present in the nuclei of most cells in the body. The genes pass from parent to child in the fertilized egg and it is important to realise that *each* parent contributes to their child a gene for a particular blood group.

If an individual has inherited the same gene from each parent he is said to be homozygous for that particular gene but if the gene he inherits from each parent is different then he is heterozygous. The consideration of a hypothetical blood group system may make the position clearer. Let us suppose there are two genes Y and Z controlling a particular blood group system. Three types of individual are possible, namely homozygous YY (each parent having contributed a Y gene), homozygous ZZ (each parent having contributed a Z gene) and heterozygous YZ (one parent having contributed Y and the other Z).

In the mating of a YY male with a YY female, all the children must receive Y from each parent and themselves be YY. The appearance of Z in a child, providing the mother-child relationship was not in doubt, would exclude the YY male from paternity. The mating of a YY male with a YZ female gives rise to children of two types. A Y gene from the father may pair with a Y gene from the mother to give a YY child, or Y from the father may pair with Z from the mother resulting in a heterozygous YZ child. The appearance of a ZZ child would indicate non-paternity since such a child must inherit Z from each parent and a YY father can only give Y to his offspring. Similarly when both parents are ZZ, only ZZ children can arise from the mating, but if both parents are YZ then children of all three types are possible. . . . In terms of actual blood groups, whichever of the many blood group systems are under consideration, the above principles apply in the interpretation of the results.

The chance of obtaining evidence which excludes from paternity a man wrongly named as being the father of a particular child

. . . The overall chance of excluding a non-father is about 90%. In other words, of 100 cases investigated in which the putative father has been wrongly accused, the full range of tests would be expected to exclude 90 of them from paternity. This figure requires emphasis. If a number of cases are submitted for a blood group investigation and none of them show an exclusion, then it is likely that in most of them the mother is naming the true father of the child, because if this were not so 9 out of 10 non-fathers would be expected to be excluded from paternity on blood group evidence.

The white cells have also been shown to possess substances peculiar to themselves by which they can be divided into many different types but as yet these white cell groups, for a number of technical reasons, do not regularly feature in cases of doubtful paternity in Britain. If they eventually do so, the overall chance of excluding a man, wrongly named as father of a child, will be raised to 97%.

The contribution of blood groups towards proof of paternity

The determination that one particular man and he only can be the father of a given child is at present impossible. Assistance towards giving a judgment can be obtained by calculating the chance an unrelated man from the general population has of possessing the required blood group genes for him to be a possible father for the particular child of a particular mother. If this chance is small enough to be significant (i.e. 1–2% or less) then the putative father who is one of this small number, being also known to the mother, is likely to be the true father of the child. The fact that the named man is known to the mother is an essential prerequisite! Even though but one man in a hundred is likely to be able to contribute the known paternal gene combination, there will be many such in the general male population!

To arrive at a figure for the frequency of men in the population whose blood groups would not exclude them from possible paternity in a given case, it has to be seen from the tests which blood group genes must be of paternal origin. Those present in the child and absent from the mother must obviously have been inherited from the father. Moreover, if the child is homozygous for a gene, for example if the child is ZZ (see above), then one of the two Z genes must be a paternal contribution. Sometimes it is not known whether a gene is maternal or paternal in origin.

The occurrence of less common or rare genes, absent from the mother but present in both putative father and child, is most helpful in pointing significantly to the putative father's paternity but if the results disclose a considerable number of genes in the child which must originate from the father, even if singly they are not uncommon, as a combination they may be possessed by few men in the general population. Thus it can be appreciated that not only does a wide range of blood group systems improve the chance of excluding a non-father from paternity but it also improves the chance of making a valuable contribution towards proof of paternity.

Such calculations can be made only for populations in which the frequencies of the various blood groups have already been derived from blood typing large numbers of individuals. It is important that the putative father's groups are related to the appropriate general population. Blood group frequencies vary in the different races of man. In Britain it is usually appropriate to refer to frequencies for Western Europeans but if, for example, non-white families are tested it may not be possible to make this kind of calculation. The calculation is invalidated if the named man's brother is a second possible father for the child.

. . . Most of the cases for which blood grouping is requested are either affiliation cases where one man is named, or divorce cases in which there is often the opportunity for testing more than one putative father.

There is something to be said for the Scandinavian practice of encouraging the mother to name all possible fathers of her child which is in contrast to the British habit of expecting but one named man in affiliation cases. In the latter situation only one putative father's blood is available for testing, and if the mother, who may genuinely not know which of two men is the true father of her child, selects the wrong man she has a high chance of finding him excluded by the evidence of the blood groups.

Since this was written, new tests have been introduced which increase the overall chance of exclusion to 93% (Dodd, 1980), and in Germany it may now be as high as 99.948%.

Questions

Another way of putting the probability calculation is to say that Mr X is, for example, 184 times more likely to be able to fertilise an ovum with the required sperm than he would be expected to be if he were unrelated to the child (Dodd and Lincoln, 1978). Scientists consider that these figures begin to be significant at the level of 100 times:

(i) Does this incline you to sympathise with Ormrod LJ's remarks about probability in *Re JS*?

(ii) Would such evidence persuade you to conclude: (*a*) that there was corroboration for a Miss B's allegation that Mr X was the father of her child? or (*b*) that Mr X was entitled to institute proceedings under the Guardianship of Minors Act 1971 for custody of, or access to, the child? or (*c*) that the grown-up child was entitled to a share in Mr X's intestate estate?

The only formal means at present available for establishing the paternity of an illegitimate child are affiliation proceedings and birth registration. Under s. 12 of the Civil Evidence Act 1968, a finding of paternity in the former, or the naming of the father in the latter, raises a rebuttable presumption in any subsequent civil proceedings. The standard of proof in affiliation proceedings is the balance of probabilities, although the remarks of Ormrod LJ in *Re JS* may also be applicable. In addition, s. 4(1) of the Affiliation Proceedings Act 1957 requires that any evidence given by the mother be corroborated in some 'material particular.' Judges have been reluctant to produce definitive lists of what may amount to corroboration, and have sometimes been diligent to construct it from the most unpromising material (see, for example, *Mash v Darley* [1914] 3 KB 1226, 83 LJKB 1740; *Moore v Hewitt* [1947] KB 831, [1947] 2 All ER 270; *Graham v Tupper* (1965) Times, 18 November; and *Simpson v Collinson* [1964] 2 QB 80, [1964] 1 All ER 262). But this is not always possible:

Cracknell v Smith
[1960] 3 All ER 569, [1960] 1 WLR 1239, 125 JP 46, 104 Sol Jo 956 Court of Appeal

The mother gave evidence that she met the defendant in December 1957 and had intercourse with him four times in January and February 1958 and once in March. She had an abnormal period in March, none in April and the baby was born in December. She also had intercourse with the defendant's brother in February 1958, but her subsequent February period was normal. The defendant did not give evidence but called his brother as a witness. The brother's evidence was '. . . thoroughly unsatisfactory. He spoke of frequent intercourse with the complainant and particularly to intercourse in March 1958, but he was clearly a very unsatisfactory witness and . . . the justices thought that he was a liar.' The justices made the order and the defendant appealed. (*Note*: the 'mother' referred to in the judgment is the complainant's, and not the child's, parent.)

Lord Parker CJ: . . . Two matters were said to amount to corroboration: first, that the mother's evidence was sufficient corroboration; secondly, that the silence of the appellant was a corroborative factor, the silence referred to being that he had not gone into the witness-box. The justices found that the respondent's evidence was sufficiently corroborated without saying by what. For my part, I am perfectly satisfied that the evidence of the mother was not sufficient corroboration or, perhaps more accurately, any corroboration; because the weight to be attached to the evidence is a matter for the justices. Quite apart from the fact that she was only speaking as to January and February 1958, and not as to March, I am quite clear that her evidence was mere evidence of opportunity. Mere evidence of opportunity and nothing more can be no evidence of corroboration. There are cases, of which *Moore v Hewitt* [1947]]KB 831, [1947] 2 All ER 270 is an example, and also *Harvey v Anning* (1902) 87 LT 687, in both of which there was something more than mere opportunity. In both cases there was evidence, unlike the present cases that the respondent was not being intimate with or associating with anybody else. Secondly, in *Harvey v Anning* there was, as an additional factor, the great difference in the social position of the parties, and in both cases there was real evidence of courtship and association together and not the very vague association spoken of by the mother.

It was then said, and this has been put forward as the main ground in this court, that the failure of the appellant to go into the witness-box, coupled with the fact that he called as a witness his brother who, as it turned out, was thought to be a liar, was of itself corroboration. For my part, I am perfectly clear that a respondent to a complaint of this sort is fully entitled not to go into the witness-box. If there is evidence against him, and some corroborative evidence, it may be that the justices are entitled to take into consideration the fact that he gave no evidence in considering the weight to be attached to the corroboration. But here, if I am right, there was no corroboration at all, and, in those circumstances, I am quite clear that the failure of the appellant to go into the witness-box cannot of itself afford corroboration. Nor, in my view, does the fact that he called his brother to give untrue evidence that this girl had been carrying on with him, the brother, and, indeed, with yet another brother at the material time. I do not think that that, again, can possibly amount to corroboration. . . .

Questions

(i) Must we assume that the magistrates' court disbelieved the defendant's brother because it believed the child's mother? Does this explain why the fact that the defendant called his brother to give untrue evidence could not be corroboration of her story?

(ii) Do *you* think it more likely than not that the defendant was the father of her child?

In their 1968 *Report on Blood Tests and the Proof of Paternity in Civil Proceedings*, the Law Commission quoted the view of the Scottish Law Commission that the corroboration requirement should be retained, 'for by the very nature of the case, caution has to be exercised in accepting the evidence of a woman raising an action of affiliation,' and themselves recommended that 'because of the danger of a perjured claim in this type of case . . . a man accused of paternity should not be denied the right to obtain blood tests.' In their 1979 working paper on *Illegitimacy*, however, the Law

Commission stated (in relation to proceedings for the maintenance of an illegitimate child):

9.47 . . . There are three reasons why we do not at present favour a formal requirement of corroboration. First, such a requirement can easily lead to a waste of time and money. Under the affiliation procedure, if the mother fails for lack of corroboration in the first instance, she is entitled to try again with better evidence: the first hearing is treated as having ended by her being non-suited, and the res judicata rule accordingly does not apply. Secondly, we do not think that a formal requirement is necessary in order to avoid injustice. A court will be aware of the risks attached to the acceptance of uncorroborated evidence, and this will affect the weight of evidence which is in practice required to discharge the burden of proof. Although civil cases are proved by preponderance of probability, the degree of probability depends on the subject matter, and we would expect courts to require paternity to be convincingly established. Thirdly, the formal requirement of corroboration may well have been justified in former times when it might have been difficult for the respondent to produce positive evidence to the contrary; but blood testing has changed the position. We therefore conclude that corroboration should be a relevant factor in evaluating the evidence to which it relates, but not a formal prerequisite. . . .

Questions

(i) Why exactly is perjury thought likely in these cases? Is it (*a*) because a lot of money might be involved; or (*b*) because the fact that a woman has sexual intercourse outside marriage makes her unreliable and untruthful as a witness; or (*c*) because affiliation complainants are invariably women and defendants invariably men; or (*d*) for any other reason?
(ii) If the answer to question (i) is (*a*), why is corroboration not required in any other civil litigation?
(iii) If the answer to question (i) is (*b*), why did the Report of the Advisory Group on the Law of Rape (Heilbron, 1975) feel able to reject the idea as an 'anachronism', whereas the Law Commission apparently did not?

The present position as to birth registration is explained in the Law Commission's working paper on *Illegitimacy*:

9.14 It is important to bear in mind that registration is essentially an administrative, and not a judicial, function, and that the registrar can accordingly act only on the basis of unchallenged evidence of paternity. We understand that on the registration of a birth the informant is asked to state the name of the child's father: the answer to that question is accepted unless it appears from the form of the answer itself or from the answers to other questions that the man named is not the mother's husband. If the informant cannot or will not state who the father is, the part of the register relating to the father will be left blank. It will also be left blank if the man is not the mother's husband, unless the registration or re-registration is made at the joint request of the mother and the man in question, or the mother declares that the man is the father and produces a statutory declaration made by him admitting his paternity (Births and Deaths Registration Act 1953, ss. 10 and 10A). The birth registration system has therefore a built-in procedure for acknowledging paternity in cases where no presumption can be derived from the mother's married status; and . . . this opportunity to register the father's name is taken in over half of all the cases in which illegitimate births are registered. Under the same provision a mother is entitled to require that a man's name be entered in the births register as the child's father if she produces an affiliation order made against him. The birth registration system thus permits a mother to insist on such an entry even against the man's will, and even if he disputes paternity.
9.17 The existing law thus discriminates against fathers. Even if an affiliation order has been made (or an order giving him custody or access under section 9(1) of the Guardianship of Minors Act 1971) the father of an illegitimate child can never have his paternity recorded without the agreement of the mother (and in certain cases the child), although, as we have explained, the mother can insist on the father's paternity being recorded. We do not believe that such discrimination is justifiable in principle.

Questions

(i) Was your stereotype of the illegitimate father a man who was anxious to avoid his responsibilities or a man who was anxious to assert his relationship in the face of the mother's determination to have nothing more to do with him?

(ii) Should the law on establishing paternity be the same in each of the cases mentioned in question (i)?

The Law Commission's working paper reveals an understandable pre-occupation with the rapist and other unmeritorious progenitors. It may be helpful to bear them in mind when considering the working paper's suggestions for improving the present law:

9.18 The following proposition now emerges. For birth registration purposes the registrar should be entitled to accept a paternity statement from either parent without the explicit consent of the other parent —
  (i)   where the registration reflects the application of the presumption of paternity based on marriage; or
  (ii) where paternity has been established by a court order.
This would constitute a change in the law only to the extent that it would allow a father to insist on his fatherhood appearing on the register (if necessary, by re-registration), where he has either obtained a declaration of parentage under the procedure dealt with below, or where an order giving him custody or access, or ordering him to pay maintenance, has been made. . . .

Formal methods of acknowledging paternity other than by court order
9.23 A considerable number of other jurisdictions, including New Zealand, most of the Australian states, Ontario, parts of the United States, and many civil law countries, have provided for acknowledgement of paternity otherwise than through the register of births. In New Zealand, for instance, an instrument of acknowledgment executed by the father and mother either as a deed or in the presence of a solicitor constitutes prima facie evidence of paternity. Such an instrument may be filed with the Registrar General.
9.24 We entirely agree that voluntary acceptance of paternal responsibilities is to be encouraged, but we suggest that the formal adoption of any such procedures here, by legislation, would be superfluous. The best solution, we think, would be to ensure that our registration system is sufficiently flexible to enable the evidence of paternity to be derived from the register. It would clearly not be helpful if the register and other instruments recognised by statute told different stories. An instrument recording an agreement between parties as to a child's paternity would still have evidential value; but in our view it should not be given any special status.

Court orders
9.27 . . . Our suggestion is that whenever a maintenance, custody, access or other similar order is made in proceedings in which the paternity of the child has been found or admitted, such finding or admission should, if either of the parties so wishes, appear on the face of the order. . . .
9.28 It should be repeated here that an incidental finding of paternity would only be recorded in the manner indicated above where the court goes on to make an order for maintenance, custody, access or the like. For example, if a man applies to the court for access to a child, and an order is refused on the merits despite the court being satisfied that he is the child's father, his application should simply be dismissed. It is only the existence of immediate rights or obligations in relation to a child which would justify the proposition that an application to the registrar of births may be made unilaterally. Furthermore, any reference to a finding of paternity in a case where no substantive order is made would be tantamount to the making of a declaration of paternity, and (as we argue later) we do not think that persons other than the child in question should have unrestricted access to the courts for such a purpose. . . .

Declaration of parentage
. . .
9.33 We think that there is a strong case for introducing a procedure for obtaining a declaration of parentage. There may be cases where it is important to establish parentage, but inappropriate to apply for any other relief, such as maintenance, custody or access under the Guardianship of Minors Acts or otherwise. We have two particular instances in mind. First, future entitlement to

property may turn on the issue. It is, we think, insufficient to say that the question could always be determined at the date of distribution, since by then the best evidence may no longer be available. It has to be remembered that blood test evidence is most satisfactory only when the child, his mother, and all likely fathers can be tested. Hence the sooner a test is carried out the better, in order to minimise the risk of the evidence becoming unobtainable by reason of the death or disappearance of relevant persons. In any event, questions of parentage cannot in all cases be determined solely by blood testing, and it may be important to have those concerned available to give evidence. Secondly the child, or indeed those claiming to be his parents, may think it emotionally important to have the issue judicially determined. The right to know the facts about one's origins is increasingly recognised, and it would be unsatisfactory if the law provided only artificial means (such as an application for a nominal award of maintenance) for doing so. . . .

9.40 It is clear that a child should be able to obtain a declaration that a named person is his father (or mother). Should the alleged parent, or any other person, be able to obtain a declaration of parentage? We think that there are cases in which it would be right to allow such applications. First, those claiming to be parents may have a proprietary or emotional claim to have the matter resolved just as much as the child himself. Secondly, a grandparent or other person may think it important in the child's interest that the matter be cleared up, even though the child's mother, for example, is unwilling to permit it. However, we have to accept that applications by parents and others might not be in the child's interests — for instance, where there is real doubt about parentage which the court is unlikely to be able to resolve, and the trial of the issue could only disturb a settled relationship. Hence we suggest that, in addition to the child, any other person should be able to seek a declaration that the child is the child of a named person or persons if, but only if, he can satisfy the court that it is appropriate, having regard to the welfare of the child, that the issue be tried.

Earlier in the working paper, the Commission considered but rejected one further possibility:

9.12 In some Commonwealth jurisdictions — for example Tasmania, New South Wales and Ontario, but not New Zealand or Queensland — cohabitation is treated in the same way as marriage, as prima facie evidence of paternity. Needless to say, only cohabitation as defined by statute counts for this purpose, the definitions ranging from the arbitrary (for example twelve months, as in Tasmania) to the vague ('a relationship of some permanence', as in Ontario). We incline to the view that this complication should not be introduced into the law. The value of a 'prima facie evidence rule' lies in its general applicability without further evidence. . . . But cohabitation (or rather, cohabitation 'as husband and wife', for only such cohabitation can be relevant) is by no means self-proving, especially if there are further statutory definitions going to the durability of the relationship.

The National Council for One Parent Families (as the National Council for the Unmarried Mother and her Child has now become) published a response to the Law Commission's working paper, entitled *An Accident of Birth* (1980). This accepts the point about cohabitation, but suggests that a cohabiting couple should be able to make a *joint* declaration of parentage, to be registered at the 'municipal offices.' The proposal that 'an incidental finding of paternity' in court proceedings should not be recorded or registered unless accompanied by a court order (para. 9.28, above) is regarded as 'a deliberate restriction on a child's right to know the identity of his or her father.' The matter should not be 'left with the court and the danger of an ambiguous judgment about the father's merit.' On the other hand, One Parent Families supports the proposal that any person other than the child who wishes to apply for a declaration of parentage should first have to satisfy the court that it is in the child's interests to have the issue tried (para. 9.40, above), although 'we recognise the contradiction with our previous recommendation. This might lead to a person taking court proceedings which may be certain to fail, purely for the reason of getting the father's name on the Birth Certificate. . . . However, having accepted the principle that a child's right to know the facts about his or her origin should be protected, we can see no alternative . . .'.

Questions

(i) How easy is it to judge what will be in the child's best interests? Suppose, for example, that Miss B has been brutally raped by Mr X, who is a very rich man, and a child Y results. Will it be in the best interests of Y to declare or register Mr X as his father, when X seeks and is denied an order for access while Y is a baby, if, 20 years later, Mr X is killed in a road accident having made no will?

(ii) Would your answer to question (i) differ if X had been prosecuted for rape and (*a*) convicted, or (*b*) acquitted after a defence alleging consent, or (*c*) acquitted after a defence alleging mistaken identity?

(iii) If you are sympathetic to the One Parent Families view, how far would you take it? In Finland, for example, while it is not a criminal offence for a mother to refuse to disclose the father's name, she is denied welfare benefits instead: a very high percentage of the children are thus enabled to know their origins, but what would the British libertarian say?

The Law Commission's eventual recommendations in their Report on *Illegitimacy* (1982) showed no disposition to go further than those of their working paper in recognising the child's 'right to know' at the expense of other considerations. On several matters, they followed the working paper quite closely:

14.10 There should no longer be any rule of law requiring corroborative evidence that the putative father is the natural father of a non-marital child [in proceedings for financial provision, as to which see the following two sections of this chapter] . . .

14.62 The present rule under the Civil Evidence Act 1968 whereby an adjudication of paternity made in the course of affiliation proceedings constitutes prima facie evidence of paternity should be re-enacted so as to apply to all proceedings brought under the Guardianship of Minors Acts and to proceedings brought by public bodies [also discussed in the following sections]. . . .

14.63 Consideration should be given to providing by rules that wherever, in court proceedings, it is found or admitted that a man is the father of a child and a financial provision, custody, access or other similar order is made, the finding or admission should appear on the face of the order [whether or not either party has requested it]. . . .

14.69 Where any order has been made giving the father any parental rights and duties, or requiring him to make financial provision for a non-marital child, both parents [it is clear from the discussion and draft Bill, however, that this is a slip for 'either parent'] should be entitled to register or re-register the birth . . . so as to have the father's name entered in the births register. . . .

14.74 It should be possible . . . for the father to be able to register or re-register the child's birth on production of a declaration by him in the prescribed form acknowledging his paternity, together with a statutory declaration by the mother stating that he is the father. . . .

It was *not* recommended that there should be any presumption of paternity other than through marriage, or any further procedure for voluntary acknowledgement, or any compulsory paternity proceedings, or obligation upon the mother to disclose the identity of her child's father. This caution may in part be explained by the Commission's reservations about introducing a procedure for court declarations of paternity, for which they had earlier thought there to be a 'strong case':

10.6 It is now necessary to record the anxiety which we have felt about the consequences of introducing a declaration procedure. First, there is the potential which proceedings for a declaration of parentage might have for disruption, not least by putting at risk the established relationships of the child whose parentage is at issue. Secondly, there is a problem relating to proof of parentage in particular where entitlement to British citizenship may be a consequence. . . .

10.7 . . . The arguments which we put forward in the Working Paper . . . do not, it may be said, take account of the potential use of such proceedings by the deluded or obsessed, or even for blackmailing or vindictive purposes. The distress and harm caused by the proceedings — perhaps merely the institution of proceedings — could greatly exceed any good which could be achieved for the claimant even if he succeeded. . . .

10.8 . . . Not infrequently, where no dispute arises [during childhood], a secure and contented childhood is provided for non-marital children by some family arrangement which ignores or conceals the true parentage. A claim to a declaration, pursued by a child when adult, could be intrusive or disturbing to the alleged parents and to their separate families. . . .

10.10 . . . There must . . . be some concern lest the court should regard itself as bound to grant a declaration merely because *some* evidence tending to establish paternity had been led and not contradicted. . . .

10.11 The problem of finding a satisfactory standard of proof in declaration proceedings is exacerbated by the fact that . . . the English court normally determines issues by adversarial means, that is on the basis of evidence which the parties choose to put before it. In a paternity dispute where, for example, financial provision is sought for the child, the applicant's assertion as to paternity is likely to be challenged by the respondent if the assertion is false. There is in such a case a 'proper contradictor', to test the applicant's evidence. There would often be no such contradictor in proceedings for a declaration of parentage.

10.12 . . . The risk of a false case being put forward and not contradicted is likely to be greater in cases where the successful applicant will gain a considerable advantage, at no cost to any other individual. . . . The risk is probably likely to be greatest in claims to British citizenship. . . .

Hence the Commission conclude that, although there should be a declaration procedure, only the child himself should be able to apply, and only where he was born in England or Wales. He should be required to state the effect of a declaration upon his citizenship and the declaration should only bind the Crown where the Attorney General is a party to the proceedings. The court should have power to call for blood tests from *any* party of its own motion, and to dismiss the application if these are not forthcoming. The court should make a declaration only if parentage is proved to its satisfaction.

Questions

(i) Does the case of *Re JS* (p. 298, above) incline you to support the limitation of proceedings to the child himself?

(ii) Is there any ground, other than that of practicability, for distinguishing the right of the illegitimate child to know who his father was from the right of the adopted child to know who his mother was (see Chapter 13)?

(iii) Does the failure of the matrimonial offence doctrine to prevent collusive divorces by consent (see Chapter 5) lend support to the Commission's fears about paternity declarations?

(iv) *Is* there any reason other than a desire for British citizenship which would lead a person to seek a declaration knowing (*a*) that the evidence was false, or (*b*) that it was very weak?

(v) Why is citizenship such a problem in this context but not, it would appear, in the context of sham marriages (see p. 182)?

(vi) What is there to prevent one judge being 'satisfied' on the balance of probabilities and another insisting, as the Court of Appeal suggested in *Re JS*, on evidence which is 'conclusive or very nearly so'?

(vii) Past worries were for innocent men wrongly *accused* of paternity, but now the worry is that men will wrongly *claim* it: why is there so much concern about a question of fact no more difficult than many with which the courts are faced every day (and with nothing approaching the objective assistance which blood tests can often provide)?

4 The legal effects

The remaining differences between legitimacy and illegitimacy are summarised thus in the Law Commission's working paper on *Illegitimacy* (1979):

Discrimination directly affecting the illegitimate child
2.10 It may be that the biggest discrimination suffered by a person born out of wedlock is the legal characterisation of him as 'illegitimate': we deal with the perpetuation of this label in Part III of this paper. The main practical areas in which there is legal discrimination are:
  (i) the maintenance of an illegitimate child is subject to the restrictions affecting the jurisdiction of the magistrates' courts: no lump sum exceeding £500 can be awarded and financial provision cannot be secured;
  (ii) although an illegitimate child can now inherit on the intestacy of either of his parents, he cannot take on the death intestate of any remoter ascendant or any collateral relation. In effect, therefore, he is treated as having no grandparents, brothers or sisters;
  (iii) despite recent reforms, an illegitimate child cannot succeed as heir to an entailed interest or succeed to a title of honour; and
  (iv) an illegitimate child if born outside the United Kingdom is not entitled as of right to United Kingdom citizenship even if both his parents are United Kingdom citizens.[2]

Discrimination affecting the father of an illegitimate child
2.11 From a strictly legal point of view, the father of an illegitimate child is today probably at a greater disadvantage than the child himself; and while many fathers may take little or no interest in their children born out of wedlock, other fathers who have lived with the mothers for perhaps many years are clearly affected by the discrimination. This discrimination takes a number of different forms:
  (i) the father has no automatic rights of guardianship, custody or access, even where an affiliation order has been made against him. Any such rights are obtainable by him only by court order or, if the mother has died, under the mother's will. The basic principle is set out in section 85(7) of the Children Act 1975: 'Except as otherwise provided by or under any enactment, while the mother of an illegitimate child is living she has the parental rights and duties exclusively'.
  (ii) Even if the father is awarded custody, he (unlike the father of a legitimate child) cannot obtain maintenance for the child from the mother, whatever her means.
  (iii) The father's agreement to the child's adoption is not required unless he has already been granted custody or has become the child's guardian by court order or by appointment under the mother's will. His position is therefore different from that of the mother, and of both parents of a legitimate child, whose agreement is required.
  (iv) The father's consent to a change of the child's name is not required unless he has become the legal guardian of the child by court order or under the mother's will.
  (v) The father's consent to the marriage of the child during the child's minority is not required unless he has been granted custody of the child or has become the child's guardian under the mother's will.
  (vi) There is no legal procedure by which the father can establish his paternity without the consent of the child's mother.

Procedural discrimination
2.12 There are, in addition, a number of procedural matters which point to the illegitimate child as 'different':
  (i) Maintenance for an illegitimate child involves the institution by the mother of a special form of proceedings (affiliation proceedings) which many people regard as involving a stigma.
  (ii) The mother cannot obtain maintenance for the child unless she is a 'single woman' at the date of the application for maintenance, or was so at the date of the child's birth. The phrase 'single woman' includes not only an unmarried woman (spinster, widow or divorcee) but also a married woman who is living apart from her husband and who has lost the right at common law to be maintained by him.

---

2. Under the British Nationality Act 1981, an illegitimate child may claim citizenship through his mother but not through his father.

(iii) Only the magistrates' court has jurisdiction in affiliation proceedings, whereas the High Court, the county court and the magistrates' court all have jurisdiction in cases where maintenance is sought for legitimate children.

(iv) Subject to certain exceptions, an application for maintenance by way of affiliation proceedings must be made within three years of the child's birth. There is no such time limit as respects legitimate children.

(v) There is a special rule of evidence applicable to affiliation proceedings: if the mother gives evidence, her evidence must be corroborated.

(vi) There is a special form of appeal from a magistrates' court in affiliation proceedings.

Questions

(i) Why, do you suppose, did the Law Commission choose the word 'discrimination' instead of, for example, 'distinction'?

(ii) Should the lack of an automatic relationship with the father be classified as 'discrimination affecting the father' or 'discrimination affecting the child' or both?

(iii) Before we look at certain aspects of the law in more detail, which, if any, of the items on the list seem to you to be most in need of change?

(a) SUPPORT FOR ILLEGITIMATE CHILDREN

Illegitimate children are expressly excluded from the power of the High Court to order parents to pay maintenance for wards of court, and from the power of magistrates' and county courts and the High Court to order parents to pay maintenance in custody proceedings under the Guardianship of Minors Act 1971 (Family Law Reform Act 1969, s. 6; 1971 Act, ss. 9, 10, 11 and 14). There is no other provision specifically aimed at parents, although either parent and that parent's spouse (usually, of course, the mother and her husband) might be ordered to make provision in the course of matrimonial proceedings between them, if the child has become a 'child of the family' (Domestic Proceedings and Magistrates' Courts Act 1978, ss. 1, 2, 11 and 88(1); Matrimonial Causes Act 1973, ss. 22 to 25 and 52(1)). Thus the only way in which the natural father can be obliged to make provision is by affiliation proceedings. The origin of these has been explained in the first section of this chapter and some of their procedural deficiencies are outlined in the Law Commission's list. As between mother and father, the court's jurisdiction and powers are contained in the following sections of the *Affiliation Proceedings Act 1957* (the only other bodies which may initiate proceedings are local authorities who provide the child with care and supplementary benefit authorities who provide support):

1. A single woman who is with child or who has been delivered of an illegitimate child may apply by complaint to a justice of the peace for a summons to be served on the man alleged by her to be the father of the child.

4. (1) On the hearing of a complaint under section 1 of this Act the court may adjudge the defendant to be the putative father of the child, but shall not do so, in a case where evidence is given by the mother, unless her evidence is corroborated in some material particular by other evidence to the court's satisfaction.

(2) Where the court has adjudged the defendant to be the putative father of the child it may also if it thinks fit in all circumstances of the case, proceed to make against him an order (referred to in this Act as 'an affiliation order') containing one or both of the following provisions —

(*a*) provision for the making by him of such periodical payments for the maintenance and education of the child, and for such term, as may be specified in the order;

(*b*) provision for the payment by him of such lump sum as may be so specified.

(3) In deciding whether to exercise its powers under subsection (2) of this section, and, if so, in what manner, the court shall, among the circumstances of the case, have regard to the following matters, that is to say —

    (*a*) the income, earning capacity, property and other financial resources which the mother of the child and the person adjudged to be the putative father of the child have or are likely to have in the foreseeable future;

    (*b*) the financial needs, obligations and responsibilities which the mother and that person have or are likely to have in the foreseeable future;

    (*c*) the financial needs of the child;

    (*d*) the income, earning capacity (if any), property and other financial resources of the child;

    (*e*) any physical or mental disability of the child.

(4) Without prejudice to the generality of subsection (2)(*b*) of this section, an affiliation order may provide for the payment of a lump sum to be made for the purpose of enabling liabilities or expenses reasonably incurred before the making of the order to be met, being liabilities or expenses incurred in connection with the birth of the child or in maintaining the child or, if the child has died before the making of the order, being the child's funeral expenses.

(5) The amount of any lump sum required to be paid by an affiliation order shall not exceed £500 or such larger amount as the Secretary of State may from time to time by order fix for the purposes of this subsection.

Any order made by the Secretary of State under this subsection shall be made by statutory instrument and shall be subject to annulment in pursuance of a resolution of either House of Parliament.

Questions

(i) 'Single woman' has been so defined by the courts that only a married woman who is still living with her husband is *likely* to be excluded (see para. 2.12(ii) on p. 310, above), but is there any good reason for depriving her child of the possibility of support from the natural father?

(ii) It is disputed whether a married woman who is living apart from her husband but has not lost her common law right to be maintained by him (see p. 81, above) is a 'single woman' for this purpose (see Douglas, 1979): if she is not, and her husband has not treated the child as a child of their family, from whom can she claim maintenance for the child?

(iii) It is easy to see how the situation has arisen, but is there any good reason for giving the courts much more substantial powers against step-fathers than they have against natural fathers?

(iv) Why are affiliation proceedings the only form of family litigation (apart from care proceedings, discussed in Chapter 14) in which an appeal lies to the Crown Court?

The Civil Judicial Statistics suggest a dramatic decline in applications for affiliation orders — from 8,718 in 1969 to 1,923 in 1978. A more reliable estimate, however, can be gained from the Law Society's figures for legal aid certificates granted to prospective complainants:

1975–76	7888
1976–77	6646
1977–78	6126
1978–79	6316
1979–80	7493

Source: Legal Aid Annual Reports

Question

Compare these with the figures for illegitimate births given on p. 290, above: how would you account for the fact that so few mothers of illegitimate children take the fathers to court?

Haroutunian v Jennings
(1977) 1 FLR 62, 8 Fam Law 210, 121 Sol Jo 663, High Court, Family Division

The father appealed by way of case stated against the amount of an affiliation order made against him. The facts appear in the judgment of the President.

Sir George Baker P: This is a case stated by the justices for the County of Greater Manchester who on 3 December of last year heard a complaint by the respondent to the case, she being the mother of a child Zachary born on 3 July 1976. The appellant was the father. That was admitted by the appellant and the justices then made an order for the maintenance of the child, an affiliation order, of £20 a week and ordered the father to pay the costs.

In the case itself there are set out the income of the parties and the contentions, namely that because of the father's income, and on his evidence, he could afford to pay a substantial amount; and by the father that he could not afford to pay any substantial amount. In the case the magistrates said, 'We did not believe the evidence given us by the father revealed his true financial position. We consider that he enjoyed a very high, even luxurious standard of living.' And as part of his expenditure was given as 'cigars at £6 a week' and he owned shares in an Armenian restaurant which owned the freehold of an hotel, the lease of a restaurant, the lease of two semi-detached houses, the lease of premises at Kensington and had other income, no challenge is made about that finding. They then ordered £20 a week as being well within his means and a proper amount for the upkeep of the child, and they said in terms: 'It was not our intention that this amount should be disguised maintenance of the mother.'

The question for the opinion of the Court is whether the justices gave themselves the proper directions and applied the proper considerations and whether they came to the proper conclusion.

The mother had been an airline hostess, but as the child was very young she had no employment and was looking after the child, her income being social security payments of £23 a week and family allowance of £3.50 giving her a total of £26.50 with expenditure on rent of £8, and her estimated expenditure on the child out of that money being £9 a week. We are told that today as a single householder she has £12.70 under the Supplementary Benefits Act 1976 and a rent supplement of £8 making £20.70 altogether with a benefit for the child of £3.60, a total of £24.30.

Shortly, the novel argument put forward by Mr Cadwallader on behalf of the appellant is not as I indicated that he cannot afford to pay, but that this is not in truth a sum awarded for the maintenance of the child. Whatever the magistrates may have expressed as being their intention, they were in fact producing a sum which was for the maintenance of the mother. . . .

But the argument which is put to us is this, that the mother receiving as she does a sum of £12.70 for herself as supplementary benefit, at least some of the £8 rent allowance must be attributed to the child and the £20 a week must in the circumstances be partly for the mother's maintenance and not for the maintenance of the child. That argument is further founded on a provision in the Supplementary Benefits Act of 1976 in the first Schedule, para. 3, subpara. (2) under the heading, '*Aggregation of requirements and resources*'.

'Where a person has to provide for the requirements of another person who is a member of the same household, not being a person falling within sub-paragraph (1) above' (which refers to spouses and the persons cohabiting as man and wife)

(*a*) the requirements of that other person may, and if he has not attained the age of 16 shall, be aggregated with, and treated as, those of the first-mentioned person. . . .'.

From that it is said that the more there is for the child by so much is the mother's amount reduced, because the child and mother are aggregated and the aggregation is £24.30 a week. Anything that comes in for the child from another source is simply taken off that total figure by the Commission. That seems to be supported by a passage in the Supplementary Benefits Handbook which was revised in February of this year at p. 20, para. 2: '*Maintenance payments.* Maintenance payments whether voluntary or under court orders for wives and children including illegitimate children are also counted in full as weekly income.' This lady has, we are told for reasons which are obvious, signed over to the Supplementary Benefits Commission any sums that she receives in respect of this child so she can draw her benefit and she is not dependent on payment being made regularly. The £20 simply goes to the Supplementary Benefits Commission.[3]

. . . The argument put forward seems to me to be fallacious, and it is fallacious because it is bringing in to a conception of maintenance for the child (and indeed it is founded on this), the sum which would be given as supplementary benefit for the child to be maintained at subsistence level. Now there is nothing of course in the Affiliation Act which says anything about subsistence level or anything about a minimum figure. The question is what do the magistrates think in their discretion is a proper figure for the maintenance and education of the child.

When Mr Cadwallader had to accept that something more than £3.60 a week might well be justified and indeed that something would not be limited to 50% or any percentage of the rent supplement of £8, it seems to me that his argument falls to the ground. What the magistrates have to look at is what is a reasonable figure having regard to the father's means for the maintenance of this child. The maintenance must be not only for food, clothing, heat, light and housing and so on but for care for a young child. And the fact that the money goes to the child and may eventually find its way into the pocket of the mother paying her for caring for the child seems to me to be something which the father cannot pray in aid to bring down the amount of the order. It can be tested in this way. If the mother was incapacitated by illness the maintenance of the child would necessitate a payment to someone, or to some organisation, for looking after the child as well as the child's housing, heat, light and food and clothing. It has long been accepted in fixing maintenance in this Division that the mother may well be forced and rightly forced to give up employment or not to take employment in order to look after a child. It seems to me perfectly proper that that should be reflected in a maintenance order for the child. Mr Cadwallader in the end was driven to conceding that some allowance must be made for the mother, and that seems to me then to leave the matter entirely within the discretion of the magistrates who can have regard to the fact that the father is a rich man. After all there is long historical precedent for accepting that a rich man will pay more than a poor man for the maintenance of his child, legitimate or illegitimate.

Balcombe J: I agree. It seems to me that the difficulty with which Mr Cadwallader was faced was exposed when he was forced to concede that had the magistrates ordered a sum of £50 per week which would have been far beyond the subsistence level payable by the Supplementary Benefits Commission, he could not have put forward the argument that he has sought to do. Further, the basic conception to which my Lord has adverted, that the maintenance of an infant child should include a sum towards providing the child with a roof over its head and, if its age is such that it requires it, the care of an adult, is reflected in the cases under the Fatal Accidents Act. I refer in particular to the recent case in the Court of Appeal of *Hay v Hughes* [1975] 1 QB 790 and to a short passage from the judgment of Buckley LJ at p. 811. The case was a case where the parents of two boys had been killed in a motor accident, and the question was what amount should be payable to them for their loss under the Fatal Accidents Act.

Buckley LJ said: 'They have lost parental love. They have lost the joys of a happy home. These losses cannot be assessed in monetary terms and so cannot support a claim for damages. They have lost the financial support of their father, the breadwinner of the family and with it they have lost the family home which he provided and maintained for them including the furnishings and ancillaries such as the family motor car and the provision of all those things which he provided for them to maintain them in the style in which that home was conducted. These losses can be evaluated in financial terms and accordingly can support a claim for damages. Although damages cannot be recovered for the loss of their mother's love, they.can be recovered for the loss of those services capable of being valued [in] terms of money which she would have rendered to them as their mother had she survived.' It seems to me that if it is possible to provide by way of financial compensation by way of damages for the loss of a mother's love and care, so equally can that be provided for by way of maintenance during a mother's lifetime. There is no reason why the maintenance for a child under the Affiliation Proceedings Act of 1957 should not include a proper sum towards the services rendered by the mother to that child.

I therefore agree that there was nothing in principle wrong about the justices' decision and see no reason to disagree with the figure which they reached which was a matter for their discretion.

---

3. The functions of the Supplementary Benefits Commission have since been taken over by the Department of Health and Social Security.

Questions

(i) If the father was such a rich man and the mother's needs could be taken into account, why did the court order a sum which was less than subsistence level?

(ii) What figure would you have ordered?

(iii) Compare the facts of this case with those of the cases in Chapter 6: can you estimate what level of income and capital provision might have been ordered for mother and child if the father and mother had been married to one another?

(iv) Assuming that there is a difference between your answers to questions (ii) and (iii) above, do you consider the difference to be justified in principle?

(v) Compare the cases of *Tanner v Tanner* [1975] 3 All ER 776, [1975] 1 WLR 1346 and p. 270, above, and *Lord Lilford v Glyn* [1979] 1 All ER 441, [1978] 1 WLR 78 and p. 287, above: if the courts were given power to award unlimited lump sums and make property adjustment orders in favour of illegitimate children, would they use them?

(vi) If the procedural and substantive differences between affiliation and other maintenance proceedings for children were removed, do you think that a large proportion of mothers would then use them?

Some suggestions in answer to the last question were made by Virginia Wimperis in her overview of *The Unmarried Mother and her Child* (1960):

In some cases, of course, the father is not known: even the woman herself may be in doubt when several men have been involved, or the relationship may have been so unpremeditated that she never learns the man's name. In *Midboro* the social records claimed that 93% of the fathers were 'known' (that is, something — their age, profession, marital status — was recorded in the case-papers) and only three of the two hundred and seventy-eight mothers disclaimed all knowledge of the man's identity. But some may not have liked to admit their own doubts, and these vague claims could not all necessarily be substantiated in a magistrates' court. Even if the man *is* the child's father there may often be no corroborative evidence — letters, witnesses — and on this, under the present law, the courts insist. So a number of women could not have brought a case.

This, however, is far from explaining why so many men have no affiliation orders brought against them. A much larger part of the explanation is that a considerable percentage of men — perhaps more than 50% — do in fact support their illegitimate children without the necessity for an order. We have seen that in *Midboro* 39% of the couples were living in stable cohabitation; and 7% unstably, the mother receiving irregular or uncertain support from the father. Again, many men agree, verbally or in writing, to send the mother regular weekly or monthly contributions for the child's maintenance. The sum may be large or small, but if it is guaranteed in a proper document (which may be drawn up with the help of a lawyer or social worker and duly stamped) it can be enforced through the county court if the man defaults, . . .

Meanwhile there is a further group of fathers who should be remembered: those who are never asked to contribute because the mother has decided from the beginning to have the child adopted, action she can take without consulting the man if he is not contributing to its support. If she is a married woman living with her husband, she may think it unwise to keep the child; if she is very young, her parents may bring pressure upon her to part with it; or again she may be among those who feel that a child needs a complete home and secure childhood and will be happier if it is adopted; others are unable to face the social difficulties that an unmarried mother must face.

As soon as an adoption order is made, the natural parents cease to have any further financial responsibility, so a woman who plans to place her child in infancy is unlikely to apply to the courts for an affiliation order against the father. It is, however, hard to say in how many cases the man's failure or inability to support the child decides the woman to have it adopted.

Questions

(i) How many fathers of illegitimate children are likely to be able to support both mother and child at a level which will raise them above dependence upon supplementary benefit?

(ii) Do affiliation proceedings seem to you to be so designed as to encourage the father to take a fatherly interest in his child?

(b) THE ILLEGITIMATE FATHER

Unless a court orders otherwise, the mother has sole parental rights and duties until her death (Children Act 1975, s. 85(7)). But in addition to the possibility of making the child a ward of court, the father has since 1959 been able to apply under what is now s. 9 of the Guardianship of Minors Act 1971 for custody of, or access to, his child. Unless and until he is given such custody, however, his agreement to the child's adoption is not required (Adoption Act 1976, ss. 16(1) and 72(1): *Re M (An Infant)* [1955] 2 QB 479, [1955] 2 All ER 911). The combined effect of these provisions is illustrated in the following cases:

S v O (Illegitimate Child: Access)
(1977) 3 FLR 15, 8 Fam Law 11, High Court, Family Division

The mother and father, then both in their teens, had an association which lasted some time. Their son was born in January 1976. Before and up to the birth, the mother was in a home, and after the birth the child was fostered for a short while. The father had only seen his son three times, and explained this by the rows which had accompanied his break-up with the mother. In March 1977, he applied to a magistrates' court for access and this was granted. The mother appealed.

Baker P: . . . It is not unusual for illegitimate mothers, when they have had a row, or rows, with the father and the association has broken up, to try to keep the father out of the child's life. The matter was not debated in the course of the case but it is worth remembering that so often in these cases, if there is no access, either because of an order or because the [father] has not, for some reason or other, availed himself of the possibility of seeing the child, and after a year or two the mother marries or forms a permanent association, questions of adoption arise. If she does marry, and an adoption application is made, the natural biological father is in a hopeless position because the mother is able to say: 'Well, he has not seen the child for so many years, and has not done anything about trying to develop, or even keep, a relationship.' It may be that this mother has not thought as far ahead, but the fact is that this is a little boy who has not father-figure at the present time and the question that the magistrates I think had to ask themselves — and did ask themselves — was: 'Is it for the boy's welfare, is it in his interests, that the natural biological father should be seeing the child?' — in other words that he should have a father or father-figure, there being no other.

The way the magistrates dealt with this in their reasons is as follows, and I shall quote various passages.

'The father' [they said] 'desired to bring a father's influence into the child's life; the mother, to close an unhappy chapter and to make a new life for the child. Had the child been legitimate then there could have been little dispute as to the father's rights. Because he was not so, the father's rights were virtually non-existent. Such rights as he had were to be looked at in the light of the child's welfare. Basing our decision on that approach we concluded that access was in the child's interest and we granted the order.'

They could, of course, have expanded the law on this matter, but basically I think they were absolutely right to look at the question in the light of the child's welfare. They found, in particular, that the father wished to get to know his son and to do all that he could for him. Their conclusion was that it was in the child's interest to know his father. Then follows a sentence which has been the subject of considerable criticism by Mrs Knightly [for the mother]:

'If in the course of the years access diminished and disillusionment set in, then so be it.'

Now, for my part, I think that there the magistrates were merely saying no more than: 'We don't know what the future may hold. There is of course the possibility that this won't work.' There is always that possibility in any case, and if it does not work, well, that is that. But it does not seem to me that the inclusion of that sentence in their reasons is to indicate that there is something detrimental, clearly detrimental to the child in allowing this man to have access. They continued:

'We accepted that while the law has recognized that the putative father has rights it has seldom seen fit to endorse these, and we would expect such an order for access to be a rarity.'

I do not altogether agree with that. In this court, in recent times, we have had many cases concerning access, and even custody, by the putative, illegitimate, father.

The law has developed considerably over the last 20 years. Cases like *S v H* (1968) Times, 12 June and *Re G (An Infant)* [1956] 2 All ER 876, turned on their own facts and findings and exercises of discretion. Lord Evershed, in the case of *Re G (An Infant)* (above), having reviewed the situation of an illegitimate child (incidentally it is a term which I try to avoid myself nowadays and I am very glad to see, for example, that in Jamaica the term has been absolutely abolished by statute passed last year, and it is no longer to be used), continued at p. 879:

'That being so, I think that the view which the courts generally take in regard to the interests of a child of lawful wedlock, that is to say, that it is in the child's interests to know both parents, is not at any rate by any means necessarily applicable in the case of an illegitimate child. For I think that that general view proceeds on the premise that the parents mentioned are the child's lawful parents.'

First, notice the word 'necessarily', and, secondly there are now the provisions of s. 14 of the Guardianship of Minors Act 1971, applying s. 9 of that Act, which specifically enable orders to be made in respect of illegitimate parents.

As has been said many times in this court, and in a decision by a full Divisional Court of this Division, *M v M (Child: Access)* [1973] 2 All ER 81, that access is a right of the child. In that case it was held that no court should deprive a child of access [to] either parent unless it was wholly satisfied that it was in the interests of the child that access should cease, and that was a conclusion at which the court should be extremely slow to arrive.

I, for my part, take the view that that applies equally to illegitimate parents. Children, whether born in wedlock or not, need fathers. If there is a father then he should have the opportunity of developing the relationship. Nothing that has been said in this case and nothing in the evidence satisfies me that there would be any detrimental effect upon this child, either at present or necessarily in future if access is given.

The magistrates went on to say, having dealt with the concepts which have changed:

'When there is a father who is willing and able to act as such within the limits of an illegitimate relationship, and at the same time that father gives evidence of being responsible and conscientious within the moral code that governs both parents, then we do not think the child should be robbed of that influence. Accordingly, being each of us agreed on this decision, we granted a right of reasonable access.'

In the end, of course, this was a decision in the discretion of the magistrates. Have they wrongfully exercised this discretion? Did they act contrary to the law in coming to the conclusion that they did? I think the exercise of their discretion cannot possibly be faulted. . . .

(*Note*: this does not of course mean that every application will succeed: see *M v J (Illegitimate Child: Access)* (1977) 3 FLR 19 and *B v A (Illegitimate Children: Access)* (1981) 3 FLR 27. Access after divorce, including the case of *M v M* referred to above, is discussed in Chapter 11, below.

Questions

(i) Does this case mean that the law on access is now the same for legitimate and illegitimate children?

(ii) Upon whom does the burden lie of proving which solution will be most in accordance with the first and paramount consideration of the child's welfare?

(iii) Would your decision in this case have been different, (*a*) on the facts as they were, or (*b*) if the mother had married another man during 1976?

(iv) Suppose that the father exercises access for three or four years and then the mother marries: what do you think should happen then?

Re E (P) (An Infant)
[1969] 1 All ER 323, [1968] 1 WLR 1913, 133 JP 137, 112 Sol Jo 821, Court of Appeal

An illegitimate boy was born in October 1965. In February 1966 the justices awarded the father access for two hours a week and made an affiliation order. The mother refused to marry the father and married another man in August 1967. In 1968 she and her husband applied to adopt. The father applied for custody in order to oppose the adoption and retain access. The adoption was granted and the father appealed.

Harman LJ: . . . The objection is a curious one. It is not because of the unsuitability of the adoption in itself; it is because the father wishes to maintain his connection with the child. He says that it is better for the child that it should remain under the stigma of bastardy because there will be compensations in the fact that he will keep in touch and will, as he says, later on send the boy to a grammar school if he is bright enough. The mother not unnaturally objects. She says — or it is said on her behalf; she is still an infant[4] and represented by her husband — that this child is being brought up in the house as one of the family and his position ought to be regularised as soon as possible, and that the best thing for him is to make a clean cut; and the judge has so found.

I for my part do not feel any hesitation in saying that I think that the judge was right. It is quite true that the father has shown himself a devoted father — so far as he can; two hours a week — and wishes to maintain himself in the picture. But I cannot think that in so doing he is considering the real advantages of the child. What he is doing is to forward his own pleasure. He has the pleasure at present of paternity without the trouble of bringing the child up. Two hours a week on Sunday morning is an agreeable interlude in his life, and that he wishes should continue. It does not seem to him to matter that the child will remain a bastard. The effect of the Adoption Act 1958, is to remove that stigma, so far as it can be removed, and to give children in that unfortunate position a fresh start in life without the slur attaching to their origin. I cannot help thinking that so solid an advantage certainly ought not to be thrown away in order that the father may have the pleasure of seeing the child and dandling him on his knee two hours a week on Sunday morning before he goes off to play football.

It is said that the judge paid insufficient attention to the evidence of a psychiatrist. I wish to say as little as I can about that. The psychiatrist, as usual, only saw one side; he never saw the mother or her husband, and he, as he says, 'acted on his brief'. I cannot think that his opinions, under those circumstances, ought to have weighed very heavily with the judge — indeed, I think they did not — and I for one endorse that point of view. This is a question of fact — what is the best for the child? It is best for the child that he should be adopted and become so far as possible a respectable member of society, and I would, therefore, dismiss both appeals, for if the adoption is made, the question of custody or access for the father must fail with it because he will necessarily lose any standing in the matter whatever and the child will, as in all adoption cases, be deprived of his real father. Counsel for the father says that that is very shocking; but it is the inevitable result of all adoptions. I for one think that the advantages much outweigh any disadvantages that there may be, and I would, therefore, dismiss these appeals.

Questions

(i) How, if at all, are the arguments in favour of a child having access to both natural parents (as to which see not only *S v O* earlier, but also sections (1) and (2) in Chapter 11 and section (1) in Chapter 13) affected by the marriage of the parent with whom the child is living?

---

4. She was about 20: this was before the age of majority was reduced from 21 to 18 by the Family Law Reform Act 1969.

(ii) How, if at all, are the arguments against adoption by parents and step-parents after divorce (as to which see section (4) of Chapter 11) affected in cases where the facts are identical save that the natural parents never married?

(iii) Is there another way of removing the 'stigma of bastardy'?

Re J (A Minor) (Adoption Order: Conditions)
[1973] Fam 106, [1973] 2 All ER 410, [1973] 2 WLR 782, 117 Sol Jo 372, High Court, Family Division

An adoption application by the mother and step-father of an illegitimate boy of six was countered by a wardship application by his natural father, who sought reasonable access. The case was eventually compromised on the following terms:

> 'It is in pursuance of the said Act ordered that the applicant be authorised to adopt the said minor upon the conditions set out in the Second Schedule hereto.'
> Schedule 2 reads as follows:
> '1. The Official Solicitor may at his sole and absolute discretion (*a*) arrange visits from time to time to be made by a member of his staff or other suitable person to the home or school of the minor; (*b*) Give such information as he thinks fit concerning the health, education and welfare of the minor to his natural father, (*c*) Supervise any future access by the minor to his natural father.
> '2. The adopters and the survivor of them shall consult and pay due regard to the advice of the Official Solicitor as to (*a*) the future education of the minor; (*b*) the nature and extent of any communication between the minor and his natural father; (*c*) the resumption and continuance of access by the natural father to the minor.'

In approving this settlement, Rees J rehearsed the arguments put forward by each side:

> The case on behalf of the father was that summarised earlier in this judgment, namely that because of his racial characteristics which J shares he has a special contribution to make in the future upbringing of J. The father puts himself forward as a devoted and loving parent who has established a lasting relationship with J during the three years before the separation and the contact with him since. Some evidence of his interest in the boy is that the father had made J a devisee by his will of a large house and land in the country and a beneficiary under a substantial discretionary trust. In all these respects J has been treated on a basis of equality with the father's legitimate children. The father's claim that the welfare of J is likely to be best served by an immediate resumption of access is supported by the evidence of three consultant physicians, all of whom have read the affidavit evidence but none of whom has interviewed J or the adopters, although one had two interviews with the father. Two of these consultants further considered that adoption would not solve the problems facing J. Several witnesses deposed to the father's devotion to J and to his suitability to maintain contact with him.
> The case for the adopters is that continued contact between J and his father is not in the best interests of J for two main reasons. The first is that the father's mode of life and moral character render him wholly unfit to have contact with, and to exercise influence over, J. A massive attack is made on the father in respect of his conduct in openly supporting mistresses (including, of course, the mother, among others). This part of the adopters' case finds considerable confirmation in the admissions made in his affidavits by the father, although he strongly puts in issue a good deal of the case which is made against him. It is also alleged against the father that he is a ruthless and dominating person and that these characteristics tell against contact with a very young child. The second reason advanced on behalf of the adopters is that the evidence in their possession establishes that J was seriously and adversely affected by the access to his father between January 1970 and October 1971. This evidence asserts that J showed a number of signs of stress immediately following each period of access followed by more or less lasting symptoms of insecurity and tension. The father's evidence is to the effect that such signs were at no time apparent to him nor to others during any occasion of access. There is the usual conflict between the parties, at present unresolved, whether signs of stress did follow occasions of access and, if so, what the cause was. On the latter point there is a difference of opinion between the consultants deposing on behalf of the father and the consultant appointed by order of the court.
> As I have indicated, no criticism of any kind has been made of the adopters in relation to their capacity as parents or of their affection or ability to provide an excellent home, education and

guidance for J. There can be no doubt but that the mother's husband is willing and able to provide for all the needs of J, financially and otherwise, as if he were his natural son. . . .

In summary form, the recommendations of the Official Solicitor may be stated in this way. He was of opinion that an adoption order would be in the best interests of J. In reaching that conclusion he took full account of the difficulties involved in an adoption order in the present case where the child has a firm recollection of his natural father which will never be erased from his mind, especially where there has been regular contact between the child and the natural father until the child was almost five years of age. He was also of opinion that some suitable arrangements should be made so that contact can be re-established between J and his natural father when J has developed a sufficient degree of maturity to make that course desirable in his best interests. The Official Solicitor relies on the opinion of the consultant physician appointed by the court that this stage might be reached in about five or six years from now when J becomes 11 or 12 years of age. The Official Solicitor recognises the manifold difficulties which arise in a case wherein it is contemplated, notwithstanding that an adoption order is made, that at some time in the future it may be in the best interests of the child that contact with his known natural father should be resumed.

After reviewing the adoption legislation and the authorities, including *Re B (MF)(An Infant)* [1972] 1 All ER 898, [1972] 1 WLR 102 (p. 501, below), the judge concluded:

The conclusion which I draw from the terms of the 1958 Act and from the authority cited above is that the general rule which forbids contact between an adopted child and his natural parents may be disregarded in an exceptional case where a court is satisfied that by so doing the welfare of the child may be best promoted. I have no doubt that the instant case is an exceptional one and also that there are very strong grounds existing at present to support the view that at the right time and in the right manner contact between J and his father is likely to be for J's real and lasting benefit.

Questions

(i) Were the 'exceptional' circumstances in this case (*a*) that the father was very rich; (*b*) that the father was Jewish and wanted to give his son a barmitzvah; or (*c*) that the father had established a relationship which he was genuinely anxious to maintain in some way?

(ii) Would the decision have been the same if the child had been a girl?

(iii) If this case suggests an acceptable compromise between the child's 'right to know' his origins and the advantages of adoption, is there any reason to reserve it for 'exceptional' cases?

(iv) How many of the arguments in favour of access in this case would have applied with equal force had the child been placed for adoption with strangers?

Re Adoption Application 41/61 (No 2)
[1964] Ch 48 [1963] 2 All ER 1082, [1963] 3 WLR 357, 127 JP 440, 107 Sol Jo 573, 61 LGR 470, High Court, Chancery Division

An illegitimate boy was born in September 1961. On 12 October his father applied to a magistrates' court for custody, but on 27 October the child was placed with prospective adopters at his mother's instigation. An adoption application was made to the High Court in November, but in May 1962 it was adjourned by Wilberforce J ([1962] 2 All ER 833, [1962] 1 WLR 866), so that the father could bring custody proceedings in the High Court, which could then be determined at the same time. This procedure was confirmed by a majority of the Court of Appeal in July 1962 ([1963] Ch 315, [1962] 3 All ER 553). The combined hearing of the two applications took place in May 1963.

Wilberforce J: . . . Whether in equity or in statutory proceedings, the putative father has access to the courts and the right to put forward his plans on their objective merits: his position as putative father may enable him to urge recognition, in the child's interests, of the ties of blood and natural affection, but it does no more for him than that. . . . Of course, the proposals of the mother must be considered in an analagous way. . . .

The mother's case is this, and she is supported in it by the Official Solicitor as guardian ad litem of the infant: the best thing for the child would have been to be brought up by its united parents. This has not been possible. The next best thing, in her view, is for it to be brought up by suitable people who can take the place of its two parents. I cannot go into the details of the proposed adoption, but this much can be said, that the child has been taken into a suitable home, with adopters who have everything in their favour: the right age, position in life, material prospects and suitability as parents. These facts do not rest on conjecture but on the evidence of eighteen months' actual care. The adopters' intention to adopt also a girl is a further point in favour of the adoption. There are risks in everything but this seems as hopeful an adoption as one could wish to find. The father's proposition is that he should have custody. At the present time and for about a year he will be a medical student, supported by a grant and an allowance. After that he expects to get a house appointment which would involve living in. Over this period of about two years the proposal is that the child should live with his parents. They have a house of their own, a floor of which would be at his disposal. They are comfortably off and would be able to employ help. They are willing to settle £2000 on the child. After, say, two years, the father should be making a good income and capable of setting up his own establishment. . . .

The adoption order was granted

Questions

(i) Compare the opening words of this extract with the position of legitimate parents as stated in *J v C* [1970] AC 668, [1969] 1 All ER 788 (pp. 474–480, below): are they the same?

(ii) Would a legitimate father be able to reclaim his child from foster parents in these circumstances?

Re C (MA)(An Infant)
[1966] 1 All ER 838, [1966] 1 WLR 646, 130 JP 217, 110 Sol Jo 309, 64 LGR 280, Court of Appeal

An illegitimate son was born in July 1964 to a 23-year-old mother and a 47-year-old father. While pregnant the mother decided not to marry the father. When the child was two months old, he was placed with prospective adopters, where he remained. The father became reconciled with his wife and they wished to bring up the boy together. The mother, however, denied the father all contact with the child. Adoption proceedings were begun in the county court. The father applied to the High Court for custody. The county court proceedings were then stayed and the adopters applied to the High Court. Both applications came before Ungoed-Thomas J in December 1965, when the child was 17 months old. The judge awarded custody to the father and the adopters appealed.

Russell LJ: . . . It is, I think, plain that in weighing up the pro's and contra's the judge did attach a great deal of weight to the personality and character of the father's wife, and to the importance of the natural link with the father in the circumstances of this case. I say this because numerically there are several other matters weighing the scales in favour of leaving the boy where he is. I instance the risk point; the relative ages of the proposed adopters and of the father and his wife; the probability of a youthful brother or sister for the boy (by adoption if not by natural birth) if he stays where he is; the stability prognosis of the two marriages, as to which I will say something later; the mother's wish that the boy should be brought up in the Roman Catholic faith; the possibility, if adopted, that the boy will never realise his illegitimacy, and the certainty that with the father he must do so at some time. I am not, however, persuaded that, regarding the welfare of the infant as the paramount consideration, the judge has in weighing all these matters decided wrongly. I myself do attach great weight to the blood tie. If a father (as distinct from a stranger in blood) can bring up his own son as his own son, so much the better for both of them, whether or not by the accident of events the legitimate relationship exists. (Here indeed there was an accident of events, for the child was conceived with the intention of marriage with the mother, and only the mother's change of heart or conscience prevented the link being legitimate.) As to knowledge of his illegitimacy, the circumstances which reveal that will reveal also the determination of his father to be his father; the determination that he should not be a boy with an unknown and perhaps abandoning father, which is a factor which can have bad effects on an adopted child, though usually only if the adoption has not been a success. In this connexion it was also argued that he would find out that his mother was prepared to abandon him to strangers; but this may be softened by telling him the reasons which she herself gives, that she thought it better for him that he should be brought up by two people than by one.

On the question of the prognosis of the stability of the two marriages, that of the proposed adopters is undoubtedly very good, for reasons which I need not set out. It is said that the prognosis for the stability of the father's marriage is not good having regard to his matrimonial history, and that a risk of breakdown, with ill-effects to the child, exists. In making that prognosis, however, it is of the first importance to consider the circumstances in which the father's marriage has been reconstituted. When I consider the single-mindedness with which the father has pursued the aim of securing to himself (with the aid of his wife) the upbringing of his son, and the impact made on the judge by the personality of the wife, the conclusion that I reach is that if the child is given to the custody of the father, that will act as a cement to the marriage which at least over-sets a prognosis founded on the father's matrimonial history. The situation is wholly different from that which those who are experienced in adoptions view with misgiving, namely, when two spouses hope by adoption of a stranger child to patch up a crumbling marriage. I would weigh this point of relative stability of marriage very lightly in the scales.

Harman LJ took it for granted that a natural father and step-mother, even if illegitimate, were preferable to adoptive parents (compare his views in *Re E (P)(An Infant)* [1969] 1 All ER 323, [1968] 1 WLR 1913, p. 318, above), although he did express some doubt about the passage of time. Willmer LJ, however, dissented, partly because of the age of the father and his wife and of his doubts about the stability of their marriage, but mainly because his interpretation of the medical evidence was that the risks of uprooting the child from the prospective adopters were far greater than the 'rather shadowy and conjectural advantages possibly to be derived from being brought up by his natural father and his exceedingly competent wife.' The medical evidence on the comparative value of the 'blood tie' as against the risks of disturbing the status quo was thus of vital importance. The fullest account of that evidence appears in the judgment of Russell LJ:

The written statement of Dr Soddy I divide into seven aspects. (i) The established relationship with the adopting mother is good, and the parental care excellent. (ii) The boy is perfectly normal. (iii) As a general proposition a change of mother after the age of six months is attended by a risk of lasting adverse effects, even if the substituted or second mother's care is adequate; this risk progressively increases when the change happens after six months, with a high level between twelve and thirty months, when the risk level begins to decline. (iv) (I read this as an aspect of adverse effect) Change between nine and eighteen months is attended with a particularly serious risk of long or even permanent impairment of the child's capacity to form relationships. (v) There is the additional danger that the disturbance in any particular case caused by the change may lead to demonstrations of rejection of the second mother, and the latter, unless unusually patient and loving may react to such demonstrations, leading to a vicious circle. (vi) The proposed second mother (the father's wife) may be to some extent not best situated to cope with the situation and to offset the risk, owing to her age, to the many years since she mothered a small child, and to the fact that, not being the natural mother, she can have no instinctual pull towards the child. (vii) A change would be to take an unjustifiable risk with the child's future.

Dr Soddy's oral evidence is at some points confusing, partly I think because of technical misunderstandings in question and answer. There was much discussion about instinctual ties, and it was submitted for the appellants that Dr Soddy did not give any evidence that the fact that a man is the biological or natural parent is to be expected to contribute something to the welfare and personality of a child brought up by him as his child which is not to be expected of a man who is not the biological or natural parent. I cannot agree. It is quite clear that the instinctual tie, to which reference was so freely made, is the pull which draws the actual parent to the child because it is known by him to be the child of the parent's body, and if it was irrelevant to the welfare of the child brought up by the natural parent I cannot imagine why it was ever brought in. At one point Dr Soddy's evidence was this:

'Q. — Do you attach any importance to the instinctual relationship, to the relationship between the child and the biological father? A. — Yes, indeed. Q. — And that, of course, is a crucial matter in this case? A. — Yes.'

He then said that the instinctual relationship between biological father and child became 'distinctly important' (which must mean to the child) at about eighteen months. Later on there is confusion between question and answer, to which my lord has already referred, which I think is cleared up shortly afterwards. The confusion is caused by a failure to appreciate that an infant has no instinctual tie or pull towards his parent; that tie or pull derives from communication. At this point appears the following statement by Dr Soddy:

'Unless there is communication between the two (i.e. the natural mother and child) the mother's instinctive factor can have no effect on the child.'

This indicates that the special instinctive factor of a natural mother *has* an effect on the child, if there is communication. This is made clear in the succeeding questions and answers:

'Q. — But assuming access in the case of the non-biological mother and the biological mother, would the instinctive one-way working of the biological relationship from the mother to the child (but not, as you said, vice versa), affect the upbringing or development of the child? Is that an important factor in the development of the child? A. — It is an important factor provided it is there at certain key periods. Q. — Which are they? A. — This is the nub of the whole issue. As far as the mother is concerned it is the period before six months which is vital, which is important in terms of instinct. As far as the father is concerned it does not seem to be. We might put it up a year. Q. — From a year? A. — To about eighteen months. We might raise the age to around eighteen months. Q. — From a year to eighteen months? A. — From eighteen months, around eighteen months. Q. — To when, in the case of a boy? A. — To two and a half or three.'

In the light of that expert evidence I think that it must be said that the boy in this case will lose an important factor in the development of his personality if he is not brought up by his natural father.

I turn next to the ultimate scope of Dr Soddy's evidence on the risk to the child's personality of a change from the proposed adopters to the father and his wife. He perfectly correctly agreed that for the full assessment of this risk in the particular case his data were incomplete, since he had no knowledge, on which he could place reliance, of the father and the wife; though, as indicated above, he attached importance to the instinctual tie of the natural father to the child. The quantitive degree of risk cannot be estimated by psychiatrists, because there are no means of telling how many cases there are in which a child has survived a crucial change of mothering without lasting adverse effects; such cases would naturally not come to the notice of the experts, and there is no occasion to study their case histories; their number is wholly unknown. He agreed that in cases of disturbed personality (I hope that that is not a misused technical phrase) a change of mother, if it has occurred, may be only one of the contributing factors. This I take to mean that in observed cases of disturbed personality the change of mother might not have had any lasting adverse effect but for its combination with other predisposing factors. Here Dr Soddy's evidence is that there does not appear to be any other observable predisposing factor, for he says that the boy is a perfectly normal child. In relation to the assessment of the risk, Dr Soddy accepted that the temperament and character of the transferee mother (here the father's wife) were 'crucial', were 'extremely relevant to the decision to be made about this child', and that in assessing the likely effect of a change of mothering to the father's wife her temperament and character were a 'highly relevant factor'. As stated, Dr Soddy had indicated what he considered to be certain prima facie possible disadvantages in the position of the father's wife; and on reading part of her evidence he speculated whether she had not an underlying motive in her desire to mother her husband's bastard, I think that of gratitude to him for the past and anxiety to reconstitute the marriage; but he said that he did not care to base any judgment on that foundation. Finally under this head Dr Soddy was asked, in connexion with the character of the father's wife and her situation:

'Q. — Would they reduce the effect of the risk of which you have spoken? A. — Under certain circumstances, yes. Q. — Would you expect them to be capable of completely nullifying effects? A. — It is a speculative question. I should doubt it, but I can only answer speculatively.'

And generally speaking on the question of risk, Dr Soddy said:

'There is an element of risk that depends on the combination of the particular circumstances in the case.'

Questions

(i) Is the risk one which you would have taken in this case?

(ii) Does this case strike you as: (*a*) an undesirable resurrection of old-fashioned ideas about the ties of blood; (*b*) a pioneering recognition of the claims of unmarried fathers; or (*c*) a straightforward application of the principle that the welfare of the child is the first and paramount consideration in any proceedings in which his custody or upbringing are in issue?

(iii) If you were a social worker in an adoption society with which an unmarried mother had placed her child for adoption and the father indicated that he wished to apply to the court for custody, would you: (*a*) place the child with suitable adopters straightaway, having ascertained that they would have the emotional strength needed for a court battle; or (*b*) wait for the outcome of custody proceedings before arranging a permanent placement?

(iv) Rewrite the facts of both *Re Adoption Application 41/61* and of *Re C (MA)* as they might have occurred had the father's consent to an adoption order been necessary: would the outcome in that event have been better for either child than what actually happened?

(v) Do you consider that any of the above five cases give reason to believe that the law is in need of change?

5 Reforming the law

In *Illegitimacy: Law and Social Policy* (1971), Harry D Krause reports upon a survey of American public opinion carried out in 1968. 20% thought that fathers and mothers of illegitimate children should be punished by the criminal law for bringing them into the world (this ranged from 29% in the south to 15% in the north west), but 70% did not (the opinions of the remaining 10% were either unknown or non-existent). Similarly, 20% thought that the discrimination imposed by the law upon the illegitimate child was an effective way to discourage sexual intercourse between unmarried persons, but 80% either did not or their opinions were unknown or non-existent. It seems unlikely, therefore, that there would be much public support for a return to the 'deterrent' approach. On the other hand, 96% of the Americans surveyed thought that the law should *not* disadvantage the illegitimate child for the misdeed of his parents and only 3% disagreed.

The Law Commission working paper on *Illegitimacy* (1979) surveys the basic question of discrimination in this way:

3.2 . . . It is not now easy to put convincing arguments in favour of discrimination, because such arguments would logically justify a return to the strict common law position, and it is difficult to believe that there would be any substantial support for turning the clock back in this way. Nevertheless, arguments in favour of preserving the principle of discrimination may still be used by those who are prepared reluctantly to accept, as an accomplished fact, the changes which have already been made towards improving the legal status of the illegitimate child, but think that no further reform should be made. We therefore briefly summarise the arguments in favour of discrimination. They are three in number though they are perhaps not altogether distinct.

3.3 First, it is said that the legal distinction between 'legitimacy' and 'illegitimacy' reflects social realities. This was certainly true at one time. The birth of an illegitimate child was regarded as bringing disgrace not only on the mother but also on her immediate family. The child could no more expect to be recognised as a member of the family and be received into the family home than he could expect to inherit family property. He was not a real member of the family group.

However, although there may still be cases where the illegitimate child is in this position, the evidence suggests that a significant and increasing proportion of all illegitimate children born each year are recognised by both their parents, at least if the parents have a relationship of some stability. . . .

3.4 Secondly, it is said that the distinction serves to uphold moral standards and also to support the institution of marriage. In relation to the preservation of moral standards, it is difficult to say how far the fear of producing illegitimate children influenced sexual behaviour in the past; since the risk of an unwanted pregnancy can now usually be avoided by contraceptive measures it seems improbable that such fears still influence sexual behaviour to any substantial extent. Support for the institution of marriage is of course of great importance, especially in the present context, because a married relationship between parents should in principle be more stable than an unmarried one, so creating a better environment for the child's upbringing. However, many marriages are not stable, and statistically it seems that marriages entered into primarily for the purpose of ensuring that an expected child is not born illegitimate are especially at risk. In a large proportion of marriages where the girl is under 20 she is also pregnant; and the failure rate of marriages where the girl married young is statistically high. We therefore find it difficult to accept that the institution of marriage is truly supported by a state of the law in which the conception of a child may encourage young couples to enter precipitately into marriages which may have little chance of success.

3.5 The third argument in favour of preserving discriminatory treatment asserts that the legal relationship between the child's parents should be relevant in determining the child's legal status: that as the legal relationship of marriage results in legitimate status for the child, so a relationship which does not accord with the norm should not result in normal status for the child. On this view it is regarded as significant not only that a legitimate child is the issue of a legally recognised union, the incidents of which are fixed by law and which can only be dissolved by formal proceedings but also that marriage, at least in its inception, is intended to be permanent. The relationship of an illegitimate child's parents, on the other hand, is not in general legally recognised and may never have been intended to be more than transient. However this argument is based on the premise that a child's status ought to be affected by that of his parents. This is the proposition which we do not accept; it is, after all, the child's status, and the nature of the relationship between his parents need not and should not affect this.

3.6 In general, where a child is involved, the law is that his welfare is the first and paramount consideration, transcending even the consideration of doing justice between his parents or between his parents and outsiders. We do not think that the arguments mentioned above in favour of discrimination are sufficiently strong to justify a refusal, as a matter of law, to apply the same welfare principle to children simply on the ground that they have been born out of wedlock. In particular, we see no justification for preserving the status quo. . . .

Two further reasons for reform are put forward in the Scottish Law Commission's *Consultative Memorandum on Illegitimacy* (1982):

1.15 Reform would be in line with this country's treaty obligations. The United Kingdom has ratified the European Convention on *the Legal Status of Children born out of Wedlock*. The preamble to this Convention notes that in a great number of member States of the Council of Europe efforts have been, or are being, made to improve the legal status of children born out of wedlock by reducing the differences between their legal status and that of children born in wedlock which are to their legal or social disadvantage. It records that the signatory States believe that the situation of children born out of wedlock should be improved and that the formulation of certain common rules concerning their legal status would assist this objective. The Convention then binds each Contracting Party to ensure the conformity of its law with the provisions of the Convention. A State is, however, allowed to make not more than three reservations. The present law of Scotland [and England] does not conform to two provisions of the Convention and the United Kingdom accordingly reserved the right not to apply, or not to apply fully, those provisions in relation to Scotland.[5] The policy of the Convention is to allow 'progressive stages for those States which consider themselves unable to adopt immediately' all of its rules and reservations are valid for only five years at a time. It is clear that the general

---

5. The provisions in question are: — Art. 6(2) 'Where a legal obligation to maintain a child born in wedlock falls on certain members of the family of the father or mother, this obligation shall also apply for the benefit of a child born out of wedlock.'
Art. 9 'A child born out of wedlock shall have the same right of succession in the estate of its father and its mother and of a member of its father's or mother's family, as if it had been born in wedlock.'

policy of the Convention is the reduction of legal discrimination against illegitimate children and that the United Kingdom's position would be more in accord with that policy if the reservations were unnecessary.

1.16 The United Kingdom is also a party to the *European Convention on Human Rights*. This Convention, by Article 8, provides that 'everyone has the right to respect for his private and family life, his home and his correspondence' subject to interference only on grounds of public interest. It has been held in the case of *Marckx v Kingdom of Belgium* that the provisions of Belgian law prohibiting an illegitimate child from inheriting from his close maternal relatives on their intestacy contravened Article 8 and that these different inheritance rights of legitimate and illegitimate children lacked objective and reasonable justification. In Scots law, as in Belgian law, an illegitimate child has no such inheritance rights, so that changes are necessary to prevent the continuing breach of Article 8 by the United Kingdom.

Having concluded that there was no justification for retaining the status quo, the English Law Commission go on to discuss two possible models for reform in their working paper (1979):

(b) First model for reform: abolition of adverse legal consequences of illegitimacy

3.8 In this model the concepts of legitimacy and illegitimacy are preserved, but further steps are taken to remove by statute certain of the practical and procedural consequences of illegitimacy: in particular, all consequences which are adverse to the child. Thus, affiliation proceedings would be abolished and the illegitimate child would be given a legal right, under the Guardianship of Minors Acts 1971 and 1973, to support from both his parents; he would be capable of succeeding on the intestacy of ascendant and collateral relatives as if he had been born legitimate, and so on.

3.9 The particular reforms for inclusion within such a scheme could be selective; and the model has what some may regard as the advantage of not necessarily involving the automatic removal of all discrimination against the father of an illegitimate child. . . .

(c) Second model for reform: abolition of the status of illegitimacy

3.14 This model involves the total disappearance of the concept of 'legitimacy' as well as of 'illegitimacy', for the one cannot exist without the other. It goes beyond the mere assimilation of the legal positions of children born in and out of wedlock, since that solution, which has been considered above, would still preserve the caste labels which help artificially to preserve the social stigma now attached to illegitimacy.

3.15 The case for abolishing illegitimacy as a status is in our view supported by the fact that such a change in the law would help to improve the position of children born out of wedlock in a way in which the mere removal of the remaining legal disabilities attaching to illegitimacy would not. No change in the law relating to legitimacy would help to improve the economic position of a child born out of wedlock in so far as he suffers from being the child of a 'one-parent family'; but an illegitimate child suffers a special disadvantage which does not affect the child of a widow or divorcee. He has a different *status*, even if the incidents of that status do not differ greatly from those attached to the status of a legitimate child; attention is thus focussed on the irrelevant fact of the parents' marital status. We believe that the law can help to lessen social prejudices by setting an example clearly based upon the principle that the parents' marital relationship is irrelevant to the child's legal position. Changes in the law cannot give the illegitimate child the benefits of a secure, caring, family background. They cannot even ensure that he does not suffer financially, since his father may not be in a position to support him. But they can at least remove the *additional* hardship of attaching an opprobrious description to him. . . .

3.16 If the law were changed so that there was no longer a legal distinction between the illegitimate child, it would also follow that in principle there would be no distinction between parents: both parents would have equal rights and duties unless and until a court otherwise ordered. . . . We have tentatively concluded that the advantages of removing the status of illegitimacy altogether from the law outweigh the disadvantages of giving all fathers parental rights.

The response of the National Council for One Parent Families, in *An Accident of Birth* (1980), supported the end but not the means:

In discussing the abolition of illegitimacy, we believe that it is necessary to draw a clear distinction between the rights of the child and the rights of the parents. We do not believe that the two models — that of abolishing the status of illegitimacy and that of preserving some distinction between the parental rights and duties of married and unmarried parents — are necessarily mutually exclusive. We believe that by giving all children equal rights, irrespective of the marital status of their parents, the status of illegitimacy is abolished. Any remaining difference in the custodial relationship of parents is a consequence of the status of marriage, of which we are not proposing the abolition. We recognise the need for reform in the area of parental rights, and would certainly support an increase in father's rights to encourage unmarried fathers to play a greater role in the upbringing of their children. However, we feel that there are strong arguments against giving all fathers *automatic* equal parental rights. . . .

  (*a*) In our experience, the majority of illegitimate children during early childhood are living with and being cared for by their mothers alone, and either have no contact, or very erratic contact, with their natural fathers. We believe that giving fathers automatic rights will remove the existing protection and security an unmarried mother has in bringing up her child alone, and will lead to increased pressure and distress, caused not only in the event of intervention by an estranged father, but also by the uncertainty of never knowing whether or not the father will exercise his rights, unless the issue is decided by the court.
  (*b*) If an unmarried father is to be given automatic parental rights, the question of establishing paternity takes on increased significance. We believe that many mothers will be deterred from entering the father's details on the birth certificate or will deny the identity of the father if automatic parental rights flow from paternity being established. This will act against the child's right to know the facts about his or her origins and will undermine the Law Commission's recommendation on this subject.

[However:] . . . There is a need to provide a procedure available to all unmarried parents, whether cohabiting or not, to make a *mutual declaration* of parentage and joint custody, and to register it with the court. Simple forms could be available at the Municipal Offices where births are registered, where such a declaration could be formalised. This would give full custody rights to unmarried fathers where the mother consents. Although we believe that such a consensual arrangement is the only one having a reasonable chance of success, it could be viewed as giving an unjustifiable veto to the mother. We therefore recommend that a further amendment should be made to the Guardianship of Minors Act 1971, to allow unmarried fathers to apply to the court for joint custody if the mother should not agree to a mutual declaration. In reaching its decision, the court would have to apply the cardinal principle of family law in regarding the welfare of the child as paramount.

[Finally:] We deplore the Law Commission's statement that 'One-parent families remain a major social problem'. The one-parent family is not problematic per se and it is not a deviation from the two-parent family. Despite the fact that one-parent families suffer both economic and social discrimination we believe that a one-parent family is a normal and viable family form in its own right and is able to carry out required family functions such as parenting. Given such negative attitudes it is not surprising that laws developed to suit a two-parent family fit so awkwardly on a one-parent family.

Residual social stigma affects the confidence of single women in their undoubted ability to provide a satisfactory upbringing for their children. Attitudes towards illegitimacy are part of wider social and moral codes affecting sexual behaviour and particularly attitudes towards women. The sense of shame, of feeling different and inferior, which has been the experience of so many illegitimate children in the past, is the result of society's punishing attitude towards the mother for contravening the moral code. In our concern to give equality to all children, we should not overlook that in the early childhood years, the fate of many children will be in the hands of one custodian only, usually the mother. The law must strike a balance which protects and respects her as custodian whilst at the same time keeping open the channels of access to the father.

Somewhat similar criticisms are voiced by Mary Hayes in her comment on the working paper (1980):

In accordance with their usual practice the Law Commission invite comment and criticism on the questions raised and the provisional conclusions drawn in their working paper. However, to limit comment and criticism to those questions summarised at the end of the paper would be to accept that the correct questions have been asked, and to accept that to work out the consequences of the abolition of illegitimacy in an impeccable legal way is what abolition of the status is all about. . . . One weakness of their paper is that only superficial attention is given to the practical implications of giving rights to fathers, while the emotional dimensions of implementing such a change are virtually ignored. Furthermore the effect of giving rights to fathers is not tested against the welfare principle; this means that the Law Commission fail to ask themselves some fundamental questions before they conclude, at an early stage, that abolishing illegitimacy promotes the welfare of the child.

The following questions incorporate some of those which she goes on to raise.

Questions

(i) The present law reflects the prima facie assumption that a husband and wife are living together with their child but that unmarried parents are not: is there anything in the evidence presented earlier to suggest that this prima facie assumption is incorrect?

(ii) Should an unmarried mother have to go to court to have the 'unmeritorious' or simply absent father excluded?

(iii) Would giving all fathers parental rights lead to an increase or a decrease in conflicts over custody and access?

(iv) Would the need to obtain or dispense with the father's agreement lead to delay in placing babies for adoption?

(v) Could an ex parte procedure for dispensing with the agreement of certain fathers be justified?

(vi) Is there even a risk that mothers would be deterred from placing their babies for adoption?

(vii) We have seen that a far higher proportion of illegitimate children are placed in local authority care at some time in their lives (and we shall see in Chapter 13 that they are more likely than most to stay there for long periods): should the father have the automatic right to remove his child from care without the mother's consent?

(viii) Should it be necessary for the local authority to assume the parental rights of both parents in order either to prevent an inappropriate discharge from care or to plan a permanent substitute home for the child?

(ix) It is possible to reconcile the Law Commission's liberal view on according automatic parental rights and duties to fathers with their restrictive view of the circumstances in which paternity should be recorded, registered and declared?

(x) Is it possible to abolish the status without giving automatic rights and/or duties to fathers? Might the Law Commission have considered any or all of the following additional models? (*a*) Abolition of the illegitimate child's exclusion from the lineage of his mother and his father, but maintaining the distinction as to the parental rights and duties in relation to his upbringing. (*b*) Abolition of those distinctions which deny rights to the child, whether in relation to his lineage or to his support, but keeping those which deny automatic rights over his upbringing to his father. (*c*) Abolition of the distinction by assimilating all children, not to the present position of the legitimate, but to the present position of the illegitimate: only mothers would then enjoy automatic parental rights and duties. (This last is not as ridiculous as it may sound: the Law Commission themselves suggested that a child's domicile of origin should *always* be that of the mother.)

(xi) Is the one parent family necessarily a social problem?

In their Report on *Illegitimacy* (1982), the Law Commission answer question (x) in the negative, but opt for a package of reforms corresponding to model (*b*):

4.44 . . . Some commentators expressed the view . . . that it would be perfectly possible to abolish the status of illegitimacy whilst preserving the existing rules whereby parental rights vest automatically only in married parents. We do not accept this view. The argument for 'abolishing illegitimacy' (rather than merely removing such legal consequences of that status as are adverse to the child) is essentially that the abolition of any legal distinction based on the parents' marital status would itself have an influence on opinion. The marital status of the child's parents would cease to be *legally* relevant, and thus the need to refer to the child's distinctive legal status would (in this view) disappear. This consequence could not follow if a distinction — albeit relating only to entitlement to parental rights — were to be preserved between children which would be based solely on their parent's status. There would remain two classes of children: first, those whose parents were married and thereby enjoyed parental rights; secondly, those whose parents were unmarried and whose fathers did not enjoy such rights. . . .

4.45 We believe, therefore, that it is impossible to avoid the stark choice between abolition of the status of illegitimacy and its retention (albeit coupled with a removal of the legal disadvantages of illegitimacy so far as they adversely affect the child).

4.49 In the result, we have come to the conclusion that the advantages of abolishing the status of illegitimacy are not sufficient to compensate for the possible dangers involved in an automatic extension of parental rights to fathers of non-marital children. . . .

4.50 Accordingly, . . . we can no longer adhere to the provisional proposal made in the Working Paper, that the status of illegitimacy be abolished. We are in no doubt that the law should be reformed so as to remove all the legal disadvantages of illegitimacy so far as they discriminate against the illegitimate child, but we do not think that parental rights should vest in the fathers of non-marital children without prior scrutiny of the child's interests by the courts. . . .

4.51 . . . whenever possible the terms 'legitimate' and 'illegitimate' should cease to be used as legal terms of art. The expressions which we favour in their stead . . . are 'marital' and 'non-marital', which avoid the connotations of unlawfulness and illegality which are implicit in the term 'illegitimate'.

The major specific reforms advocated thus remove the discrimination outlined in para. 2.10 of the Working Paper (p. 310, above), although with some reservations on points (iii) and (iv), and the procedural discrimination in para. 2.12. Some modification of the rights of fathers is also proposed, although some of the discrimination outlined in para. 2.11 of the Working Paper will remain. Thus:

Affiliation proceedings will be abolished, along with their time limits, corroboration requirement, restriction to mothers who are single women, and right of appeal to the Crown Court. Financial provision for all children will be obtainable under an amended Guardianship of Minors Act 1971, which will give the High Court and county courts power to make secured periodical payments orders, unlimited lump sum orders, and to require a parent to transfer or settle property for the benefit of the child. The father will be able to apply for an order against the mother, and orders will be possible without putting legal custody in issue, but will cease to have effect if the parents live together for six months or (for non-marital children) marry. There will be no discrimination against non-marital children in wardship or, if ever implemented, custodianship proceedings. Public authorities who provide for the child will be able to recover a contribution from the father in the usual way, subject to proof of paternity. Various incidental anomalies will also be removed and there will be a power under the 1971 Act to vary written maintenance agreements for children, but only where these contain an acknowledgment of paternity. The remaining differences in the law of succession will be removed, apart from those relating to titles of honour, but for the purposes of intestate succession it will be rebuttably presumed that a non-marital child has not been survived by his father or any person tracing relationship through the father; it will also be rebuttably presumed that a deceased left no relations traced through non-marital birth who might be entitled to a grant of probate or administration. In principle a non-marital child should be able to acquire citizenship through his father, in the same way as would a child born to married parents, but this is a United Kingdom matter upon which the English Law Commission cannot make definitive proposals.

In addition to his existing right to apply for legal custody or access (orders which cease if the parents cohabit for more than six months thereafter), the father will be able to apply for an order giving him either all the parental rights and duties or specified rights and duties other than actual custody, in each case either exclusively or jointly with the mother and irrespective of cohabitation between them. If he has been granted custody or any parental rights and duties (apart from simply access and/or financial provision), he will automatically gain the right to serve as guardian on the death of the mother, to appoint a testamentary guardian to serve after his own death, to object to a guardian appointed by the mother, to give or withhold agreement to the child's adoption or to a change in the child's surname, subject in each case to the courts' powers to override these rights. Only if he has been granted actual custody, however, will he gain the right to demand the child's return from voluntary care or to contest the assumption of parental rights by the local authority or to exercise the rights of a 'parent' under the Children and Young Persons Act 1969, although the last already applies to people who in fact have actual custody. Parents will be able to make agreements as to the exercise by them of any of the parental rights and duties, during any period when they are *not* living together in the same household, subject to the courts' power not to enforce agreements which will not benefit the child.

Questions

(i) Are you convinced by the Law Commission's argument on the parental rights point? Why is it not possible to abolish illegitimacy but to draw distinctions in various statutes dealing with parental rights between parents who are, or are not, married to one another?

(ii) Why should it not be possible for cohabiting parents to agree to share all parental rights and duties without having to go to court? Would not this have solved their main problem?

(iii) Suppose that a father, who does not live with the mother but has always taken a great interest in his child and contributed to their support, does not wish to claim full parental rights or to disturb the child's custody but would like to be recognised as the person entitled to assume both custody and guardianship should anything happen to the mother: will the court be able to grant him (*a*) automatic guardianship should the mother die; and (*b*) the automatic right to prevent the child's reception into care or the assumption of parental rights by the authority should death or some other misfortune strike her?

(iv) Should the Law Commission have kept to their original proposal?

6 What is a parent?

As a result of their provisional conclusion on illegitimacy, the Law Commission were obliged to stir up the hornets' nest of problems presented by artificial insemination using semen from a donor who is not the mother's husband. We can only touch upon the many issues here, and these have once more become the object of an official inquiry. We begin with the Law Commission working paper's consideration of the legitimacy of the A.I.D. child:

10.5 In order to put the matter in perspective, we first summarise the conditions under which A.I.D. is now performed with the approval of the Royal College of Obstetricians and Gynaecologists. The Royal College's guidelines provide that A.I.D. will only be performed on a married woman whose husband has given his consent in writing. The identity of the donor is not revealed to the patient or to her husband, and the donor is not told anything about the patient. Although as a matter of legal theory the donor may be made liable as the child's father to maintain the child (and could indeed apply for access or custody) the practical reality, if these guidelines are followed, is wholly different. Neither the child nor his mother will be able to trace the donor; hence they will not be able to enforce any liability to maintain. The donor will know nothing about the child and will not be in a position to seek access or custody. For the same reason it is unlikely that any intestate succession rights existing between donor and child will in practice take effect.

10.6 A doctor carrying out A.I.D. treatment in accordance with the Royal College's guidelines will seek to satisfy himself about the stability and maturity of the patient's relationship with her husband. Even if the relationship should subsequently break up, the husband would usually have nothing to gain in legal terms by putting the child's paternity in issue: he would have treated him as a child of the family and would thus effectively be under the same financial obligations to him as if the child were the husband's legitimate child. . . .

10.8 On one view, there is no need to make any special provision to deal with A.I.D. conceptions: the fact that an anonymous and untraceable donor would, in consequence of the proposed change in the law, have 'rights' which he would never be able to enforce does not (it may be said) justify interfering with the law, since this gives rise to no difficulty in practice. However, we do not find this argument convincing. Couples should not be put into a position, as they now are, where they are strongly tempted (and perhaps even advised) to make a false declaration on registering the birth; it brings the law into disrepute if it is believed that it can safely be defied. . . .

10.9 The policy of the legislation, we are at present inclined to think, should therefore be that where a married woman has received A.I.D. treatment with her husband's consent, the husband rather than the donor should, for all legal purposes, be regarded as the father of a child conceived as the result. . . .

10.11 The simplest way of implementing the policy which we have suggested would be a statutory provision deeming the husband to be the father of an A.I.D. child born to his wife; the only ground on which the husband could challenge the operation of this deeming provision would be that he had not consented to his wife receiving A.I.D. treatment. This approach seems to us to have the merit not only of simplicity, but also of giving effect to the likely feelings and wishes of the wife and husband. We note that statutory provision of the type we envisage has been made in several States of the USA. . . .

10.17 Although there are many advantages to such a statutory deeming provision, there are two main objections to it. The first involves a major point of policy: it could be said that the proposal involves a deliberate falsification of the birth register. The second objection is more theoretical: that the proposal would involve a transfer of legal rights from the donor to the husband, and that the law should accurately mirror that transfer.

A comment upon the first objection may be taken from a Ciba Foundation Symposium on the *Law and Ethics of A.I.D. and Embryo Transfer* (1973), from which our later interjections are also taken:

McLaren [geneticist]: Even though the genetic register which Canon Dunstan proposed might not be very useful, through being erroneous (owing to the possibility that occasionally the supposedly infertile husband fertilizes the egg), our present registry system is itself erroneous in all those cases where the husband is not actually the father of the child. Are there any statistics on how common this is? This is probably more frequent than the cases where a supposedly infertile husband was really the father of an A.I.D. child.

Philipp [consultant obstretrician and gynaecologist]: We blood-tested some patients in a town in south-east England, and found that 30% of the husbands could not have been the fathers of their children . . .

JH Edwards [geneticist]: There are various biases due to the social conditions which determine delivery in hospital rather than at home: these include primiparity, especially when conception precedes marriage. Analysis of some blood group data, making allowance for the fact that one could not detect all the illegitimacies, showed that in the 1950s in the West Isleworth area about 50% of premarital conceptions were not fathered by the apparent father. As the apparent fathers were questioned while visiting their wives immediately after the birth, most of them obviously thought they were the father. I think the group Mr Philipp referred to is also highly biased. In spite of much talk about artificial insemination by donor and all the difficulties with genetics and so on, natural insemination by donor is practised on quite a substantial scale on an amateur basis.

The Law Commission also consider one further problem raised by their basic approach:

10.25 A problem which would arise whichever method were used for dealing with A.I.D. is whether or not legal provision should be made so that the child would be entitled to ascertain the facts about his parentage. Under the present law and practice the truth about the child's genetic identity may well be concealed from him if he has been registered as the legitimate child of the mother and her husband; in any event it is up to his mother and her husband to decide whether or not to disclose the fact that he is an A.I.D. child. Even if they do decide to tell him what they know, they will not usually be able to tell him who the donor was.

10.26 The argument in favour of a procedure giving the child the right to know the facts about his conception is essentially that a person has the right to know the truth about his origins. This principle is now accepted in adoption law, and an adopted child is entitled to discover the recorded facts about his natural parentage on attaining his majority. It therefore seems logical that an A.I.D. child should have the same right. On the other hand, if the only fact which the child is able to discover is that he is not genetically the offspring of his mother's husband, but of a donor wholly unknown not only to him but to his mother and her husband, it is difficult to see that this would be of any real advantage to him. To go further, by giving the child the right to know the identity of the donor would involve a major, and probably unacceptable, change of policy and practice.

Graham [*child psychiatrist*]: As I understand it, the general practice in the UK now is that the A.I.D. child is not told about his origins. Professor Fried suggested that in the United States this was becoming a problem in various matrimonial and other related cases, where eventually the child came to know because of the judicial proceedings. Even if the secret of his origins is kept from the child for as long as possible, most likely the child will discover it in adolescence, during the sort of arguments that most healthy adolescents have with their parents, when they are concerned about themselves and their independence. I am concerned about children learning about their genetic origin at that particular time, when their identity is in a state of greater confusion than at practically any other time of their lives. At the moment, when the procedure is regarded as of doubtful ethical status, there may be special problems in telling the children, but I believe this is a strong argument in favour of clarifying the status of the procedure.

Academically, one can distinguish biological, genetic and social parentage; this is no problem. As far as the affected individual's perception of himself is concerned, the situation may be much more confused. It is all very well to say that the donor (that is, the genetic father) must not be involved but perhaps some donors are, despite themselves troubled by thoughts of children they may have fathered.

. . .

Himmelweit [*professor of psychology*]: The adopted child is told, 'you existed and I chose you'. The A.I.D. child would be told, 'I chose to make you with this raw material'. I agree with Fried that it is not a matter of eugenic planning; in A.I.D. a choice of parent exists which does not exist with the adopted child. At some stage, an A.I.D. child who derives in part from a mixed sperm bank may be told that he is such a child (many arguments favour telling him; previously it was thought that an adopted child should never be told the truth, but now we advise the opposite). Then the A.I.D. child might justifiably say 'I was made differently'. Such a person might also ask why mixed sperm from a bank was used, or 'why did the doctor, or you, not choose one special donor?' This problem of feeling that the mother chose badly is highly specific to the A.I.D. child. The idea of 'being made or manufactured' may be present. There was once a suggestion that the sperm of the most brilliant minds of the century should be banked. This seems a perfectly logical and socially sensible conclusion: I am not approving of it, but I believe it is a logical step which must be considered. The idea that A.I.D. will operate without eugenic planning is totally unrealistic; it might be bad eugenic planning but it will operate at some private level.

Kibrandon [*law lord*]: The parents could say to the child, 'we *did* choose the best — unfortunately Beethoven wasn't on offer'.

The Law Commission consider, and provisionally reject, two alternatives to 'statutory deeming': annotation of the birth register in order to preserve its integrity, and adoption, not only for that purpose but also to effect the legal transfer from donor to husband. However:

10.19 We doubt whether simply using the existing adoption procedure would be satisfactory, not least because no adoption order could be made before the child was some 4½ months old. We therefore consider two possible variants:

(i) **Accelerated adoption**

Under this proposal, a court would be obliged to make an adoption order if (*a*) the applicants were a married couple, (*b*) the child's conception followed A.I.D. treatment, and, (*c*) the husband had given his consent to the treatment. Under this proposal the court could make an order immediately after the birth, but not before.

(ii) **Adoption before and contingent upon birth**

Under this proposal, the court would (subject to the same conditions as in (i) above) make an adoption order during the pregnancy to take effect immediately on the birth of the child alive.

The main objection — apart from the possibility that the husband might already be the child's father — was this:

10.20 . . .

(*a*) The use of an adoption procedure would inevitably seem cumbrous and unreal to the husband and wife, who would no doubt see themselves, not as adopting someone else's child, but rather as legalizing the status of their own. Spouses do not use adoption to deal with the problem of A.I.D. at the moment, and we see no reason to suppose that they would wish to do so in the future.

Mention of adoption, however, leads us to ask whether the process of deliberately creating a child who is not the child of husband and wife, and who might otherwise never have been born, should not be subject to at least some of the controls which have been developed over the transfer of a child from one family to another:

Fielding [emeritus professor of moral theology]: How far is it possible to determine the obligations of a doctor in the procedure of A.I.D.? And if there is agreement on certain important issues, is there need to seek some further sanctions outside the profession? New provisions in the criminal code have been suggested but were not thought to be helpful, perhaps being even harmful. Could any statutory provisions support the ethics of the profession if there were sufficient agreement and public acceptance?

Not long ago I found myself on a panel organized by some social workers in a Canadian city. The purpose was to explore some of the problems presented to social workers by the practice of A.I.D. I based my opening remarks on the assumption, among others, that semen would be accepted only from a selected donor who had been carefully assessed at least with respect to the objective data of his medical and genetic history. A medical panelist seemed to feel that this assumption was a little naive on my part. His own practice, he said, was to ask one of his interns, who would bring the semen the next day and in exchange receive $25. At that time and place this appeared to be a perfectly acceptable practice. How much agreement is there about the proper medical procedure in selecting donors? If that question is important and if there is reasonable agreement, my next question is whether any statutory provision might help to support it. . . .

Mason [clinical assistant, infertility unit]: . . . We try to match the characteristics of the husband with those of the donor. Of course, this is not possible in great detail, but we try to match height and colour of hair, for example.

Himmelweit: I am surprised that the matching is primarily with regard to external appearance. Do you not attempt some genetic compatibility in much the same way as an adoption society carefully evaluates the characteristics of the true parents and attempts to match these with those of the adoptive parents?[6]

Mason: We do investigate. First, the donors must be perfectly fit and healthy. We now enquire about illnesses in their families among uncles, aunts, brothers, cousins, parents and grandparents. For example, before you marry, you do not ask your partner if his grandmother had diabetes, whereas if our potential donor's grandmother had diabetes, he would not be a donor. We also ask ourselves what sort of person the donor is. We require them to be above average in intelligence. I feel that I can give a more intelligent donor to a less intelligent patient, but not the other way round — perhaps I am wrong.

---

6. But see p. 494, below.

Since most of our donors are introduced by other donors, we know something about them beforehand and learn more over the period that they come in to deliver the samples. Having got to know him as a person, we do then have to make some judgment. Nobody can be God; but certainly if we believe that the donor is unsuitable, we reject him. As regards actually matching the donor to the couple we always consult the couples. A minority have extensive wishes such as musicality, athleticism etc., which we can often match. When we cannot we discuss the matter with the couples.

JH Edwards: . . . Adoption is not a useful precedent because the basis of adoption was established before it was clear that such hereditary diseases as exist in man are either extremely rare or chromosomal in nature (and detectable or recessive). . . .

Kibrandon: Most of us when we get married take our chance on genetic history. I see no reason why we should not do the same with A.I.D.

Stone [*reader in law*]: There is even less likelihood that this kind of enquiry into genetic history takes place before every act of sexual intercourse between persons who are not married to each other. Why should we worry that it is not done in this very small percentage of cases?

And if there is a problem with the selection of donors, there may also be a problem with the selection of mothers:

Stone: Many women seem to feel this great social pressure on them to have a child. A visitor to this country from the United States gave evidence in November 1972 to the Select Committee of the House of Lords on discrimination against women in employment. According to her the American experience has been that a large programme of education in contraception or abortion is not needed to reduce the birth rate. All that is needed is to reduce the social pressure on people to have children. This seems to be one reason for the recent rapid decline in the birth rate in the US. Is this whole phenomenon the result of pressures brought on women, namely that the one way in which a woman can justify her existence on this earth is by producing a child, preferably male?

Mason: I don't think so. The people who come to infertility clinics certainly do not come merely from pressure by other people. They are desperate to have babies. The social pressure is much less now. Since contraceptive advice has been available, I have seen the almost worrying change in attitudes of girls in this country: in complete contrast to the situation ten years ago, many girls say they do not want to have a family now or even ever.

Steptoe [*consultant obstetrician and gynaecologist*]: The woman who come to fertility or infertility clinics have thought very carefully. They will be responsible parents; probably much more so than many of the couples who have a high percentage of unplanned and unwanted pregnancies.

Stallworthy [*professor of obstetrics and gynaecology*]: The idea that the mother who has borne a child, whether through artificial or natural insemination or even embryo transfer, necessarily wants a child badly may be an oversimplification. Doctors know full well that some women, having conceived as a result of any method, then want to destroy the child by abortion. They have satisfied some inner desire to prove to themselves that they could conceive and having done so that is an end to the matter. This is a rare situation — but it does happen.

U.P.I. reported in 1980 that 'in two months time, 37-year-old Elizabeth Kane is due to give birth to a baby . . . someone else's baby. In March, Mrs Kane, a mother of three from Illinois, was artificially inseminated with the sperm of a husband whose wife could not have children. Mrs Kane (it is not her real name) is being paid 10,000 dollars by the couple, who came from Louisville, for her surrogate motherhood.' Lest it be thought that such things could never happen here, consider the following case:

A v C
(1978) 8 Fam Law 170, High Court, Family Division

In 1976 a bachelor of 27 years, a professional man, was living with a divorced woman five years older, the mother of two children, the younger of which, aged eight years, lived with them. They could have married but did not, as the man wanted a child of his own and the woman was unable to have another. They wanted his child before they married, to bring up themselves. The man was loathe to have sexual intercourse without feeling, and they decided to pay a prostitute £3,500 to have a child by artificial insemination for them. The woman approached a prostitute at Bow Street Magistrates' Court who declined, but offered to find someone for £500. The mother was produced, who was on the fringe of that world, and she accepted for a sum of £3,000. The donor and the mother went to a clinic where the insemination was done. There was no enquiry. A flat was provided for the mother, rent and rates paid. At the birth the mother had changed her mind, and the man and his future wife added further inducements which were refused.

The mother was granted care and control of the child in an interim order in wardship proceedings brought by the father, who originally asked for care and control. He was granted access, one hour twice a week. The mother and the Official Solicitor, as guardian ad litem, opposed the grant of access at the resumed hearing in front of Comyn J.

Comyn J: . . . The mother and the Official Solicitor favoured a complete break with the father, while the father said that despite the circumstances, he was the child's father, he wanted to contribute to the child's upbringing, and could, and the child ought to know and see his father. His Lordship did not lightly depart from the Official Solicitor's view, but controlled access would be given to the father. The judgment of Latey J in *M v M* [1973] 2 All ER 81 at 88 was referred to. The mother's care and control was not to be jeopardised, and the father was to understand that access was not to be used to win care and control, but to fulfil his duties to the child, plus the extra duties his behaviour had caused.

. . . The child would remain a ward of court until majority, with care and control to the mother, under a supervision order. The child's christian name was to be the mother's choice, and the surname as hers. Unless maintenance was agreed within 28 days, the mother was to be referred to the Department of Health and Social Security which would direct action to be taken. None of the parties was to disclose to the child the circumstances of his conception without leave of the court.

Until further order, or for two years from this day, the father and his wife would have access for two hours on a Saturday at the maternal grandmother's home, or alternatively any place agreed or fixed by the court. At the end of two years his Lordship hoped it would be possible for access to be agreed, if not, the parties were to come back to the court. His Lordship envisaged access at the father's and stepmother's home, and, further ahead, some limited form of staying access. If the father had the child's best interest at heart, and wished to keep continuing interest and restitution, he would consider regular deposits, in the child's name in some savings bank.

Question

What would have been the position if this man had not been the donor but the couple had agreed to 'buy' the baby?

This leads us to the possibility of embryo transfer, discussed by Olive Stone in her contribution to the symposium:

Embryo transfer
(*a*) As distinct from A.I.D. on which the first reported decision appears to be that of the court of Bordeaux in 1883, embryo transfer is so far only the subject of animal experiments. I understand that the work contemplated by Drs Edwards and Steptoe will be restricted to facilitating the birth of children genealogically descended from married couples, where the wife suffers from some maternal disability, such as tubal occlusion. In this procedure an unfertilized human embryo would be removed by laparoscopy, fertilized with the husband's sperm and grown on *in vitro* until the stage at which the embryo would normally enter the uterus. The embryo would then be surgically implanted in the mother's uterus, and normal gestation and birth would follow.

Such a procedure would give rise to no legal problems apart from the possibility of teratology, or induced foetal deformities, for which heavy damages might be recoverable.

Lord Kilbrandon has compared such a procedure to facilitating birth by Caesarian section. If successful it will result in the birth to the woman of a child of whom her husband is the biological father. Biological and legal relationship will coincide, as for the vast majority of births. Since

England has no statutory definition of a legitimate or an illegitimate child, drafting difficulties are unlikely to arise. Biological and mother will both be correctly registered as the parents of the child. . . .

(*b*) If the range of possible treatment were later to be extended to removal of an embryo from one woman and insertion after fertilization in the uterus of another woman, further questions might arise. It would be necessary to show that removal of the embryo was for the benefit of the woman from whom it was removed, as well as for the benefit of the recipient woman. The question of maternal rights as between the ovum mother and the uterine mother might present difficulty, but it is not thought that maternal rights are likely to inhere in the supplier of an unfertilized embryo. If partial parental rights were involved, a court order would be needed to terminate them, since they cannot be effectively renounced.

. . .

Andrejew [*professor of criminal law, Warsaw*]: Dr McLaren, what are the arguments against considering the woman A who has the child in her womb as the mother, rather than the donor woman B?

McLaren: This is a question of distinguishing the different types of motherhood: the genetic (or egg) mother, the uterine (or gestational) mother and the social mother who looks after the baby from birth onwards. From the woman's point of view the uterine, gestational aspect is important.

Andrejew: More important than the genetic mother?

McLaren: I don't think we have any grounds for saying that — I am speaking intuitively — but I definitely think it is important and should not be ignored.

Isaacs [*child psychiatrist*]: The movement of an infant inside the uterus has a profound psychological effect on the woman. I agree that identity is not only psychological, but since psychology is part of the social environment, psychological factors are important in identity.

Questions

(i) The Law Commission could see no relevant distinction between such a case and A.I.D., but do you suspect that ovum donation is a rather more complex matter than sperm donation?

(ii) If the uterine mother then decided to have an abortion, presumably the decision in *Paton v British Pregnancy Advisory Service Trustees* [1979] QB 276, [1978] 2 All ER 987, p. 49, above would apply a fortiori because the parties could not be married to one another?

(iii) Does the experience of abortion lead us to believe that it would be possible to control the activities of doctors in this field by means (*a*) of registration and/or (*b*) of the criminal law?

The Law Commission's eventual decision not to recommend the abolition of illegitimacy meant that the problem of the status of A.I.D. children was no longer urgent, but they repeated the above recommendations in their Report on *Illegitimacy* (1982). The Government seems, however, to have taken matters out of their hands by appointing a Committee under the chairmanship of Mrs Mary Warnock to:

consider recent and potential developments in medicine and science related to human fertilisation and embryology; to consider what policies and safeguards should be applied, including consideration of the social, ethical and legal implications of their development and to make recommendations.

No doubt all the issues raised above, along with many others, will be considered in the Committee's report.

CHAPTER 10

When parents part

Doreen: I feel very angry sometimes, that a man can literally decide that he wants to be free, free of responsibilities that *somebody* must take.. Somebody needs to when children are involved. But men can just walk off. I think because they know that the woman is going to be the strong one, that *she* will not . . . walk away.

Michael: The effects on my career have hurt. . . . The company begins to assess you a bit lower perhaps because your mind has family welfare as a higher priority than it should be. . . . I took Anne down to junior church as I always have done . . . but I'd never brushed her hair before or tied ribbons, and this was actually impossible to me.

These two lone parents, and others, talked about their lives to Catherine Itzin for her book on *Splitting Up* (1980). We cannot tell how many couples with dependent children separate each year, for the fact will not always be recorded by an administrator or a court. But the graphs overleaf show us the proportion of divorcing couples who have children and the numbers of children involved. These will have joined the ever-increasing ranks of lone-parent families, estimated by the Department of Health and Social Security at some 900,000 (*Social Trends 13* (1982)). Some of these will be children of unmarried mothers or widows, and some will be living with their fathers, but over half (Leete, 1978) will be living with their divorced or separated mothers. For many, however, this will be a transient state before their parents form new relationships: we shall consider what happens *after* the breach in the following chapter. This chapter is concerned with how it is decided where the children should live at the time when their parents part. For some, this is a matter of bitter contest: and as this is when lawyers are most likely to be involved, we must concentrate first upon them. The practice of the courts in such cases is also likely to affect the outcome in the far larger proportion of cases in which the parents determine for themselves who is to have care of the children. But for these we must consider whether the law has any part to play in monitoring or supervising their arrangements.

At the back of all these issues, however, lie the questions raised by Doreen and Michael. Is the law unfair to fathers who, like Michael, can learn to look after their children? Or is it unfair to mothers like Doreen, in assuming that they will shoulder the burden come what may? Or is the law simply following social realities and cultural expectations? Is it, in fact, doing its imperfect best to do what is best for the child? We shall deal first with the role of the courts in adjudicating according to the paramount consideration of the child's welfare. Next we examine the tension both in theory and in practice between the concepts of the 'status quo' and the alleged 'maternal preference'. The part played by the court welfare officer is then considered, both in relation to contested cases and as a prelude to the question of the role of the law in uncontested cases, with which we close.

Divorcing couples[1]: by number and age of children
England & Wales

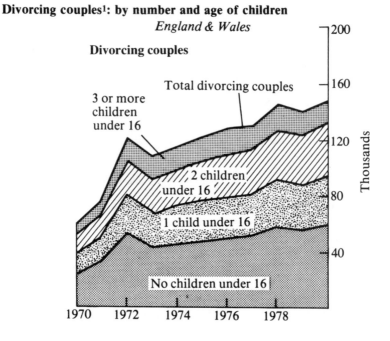

Divorcing couples

Total divorcing couples

3 or more children under 16

2 children under 16

1 child under 16

No children under 16

1970   1972   1974   1976   1978

[1]The *Divorce Reform Act 1969* came into effect in 1971

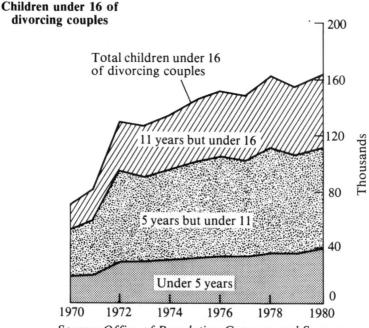

Children under 16 of divorcing couples

Total children under 16 of divorcing couples

11 years but under 16

5 years but under 11

Under 5 years

1970   1972   1974   1976   1978   1980

Source: Office of Population Censuses and Surveys

1 The role of the courts in custody disputes

In this chapter we are concerned solely with the decision as to who is to look after the child: the ways in which the parental powers and responsibilities may be shared or divided, between the parent who provides day-to-day care and the parent who does not, are considered in the next chapter. The issue may arise between mother and father (of a legitimate or illegitimate child) in proceedings for custody or access under s. 9 of the Guardianship of Minors Act 1971; or between surviving parent and the child's guardian, under ss. 10 or 11 of that Act; or between husband and wife (whether in relation to a child of their marriage or to any other child — other than one officially boarded-out with them — whom they have treated as a member of their family, see Chapter 1) in proceedings for financial support under the Domestic Proceedings and Magistrates' Courts Act 1978 or for a divorce, nullity, judicial separation or financial provision under the Matrimonial Causes Act 1973. It is also possible for any interested person to seek care and control of a child by making him a ward of the High Court. In all of these procedures the court has the option, in exceptional cases where it is happy with none of the contenders, of committing the child to the care of the local authority. In less extreme cases, it may see fit to make a supervision order.

Whatever the procedure used, however, the dispute itself is governed by a provision first passed in 1925 and now contained in the *Guardianship of Minors Act 1971*:

Principle on which questions relating to custody, upbringing etc. of minors are to be decided
1. Where in any proceedings before any court (whether or not a court as defined in section 15 of this Act) —
    (*a*) the legal custody or upbringing of a minor; or
    (*b*) the administration of any property belonging to or held on trust for a minor, or the
        application of the income thereof,
is in question, the court, in deciding that question, shall regard the welfare of the minor as the first and paramount consideration, and shall not take into consideration whether from any other point of view the claim of the father, [. . .] in respect of such legal custody, upbringing, administration or application is superior to that of the mother, or the claim of the mother is superior to that of the father.

The meaning of this, in law and in fact, is illustrated by the following case:

Re K (Minors) (Wardship: Care and Control)
[1977] Fam 179, [1979] 1 All ER 647, [1977] 2 WLR 33, 121 Sol Jo 84, Court of Appeal

The parents married in 1969. They had a son in 1971, who was now aged 5, and a daughter in 1974, who was now two and a half. The father was a Church of England clergyman. Through church activities, the mother met a young man named Martin in 1973. By March 1975, their friendship had become adulterous. The father wished the mother to give up her relationship with Martin and be reconciled. The mother wished to leave the father and set up home in a house to be bought jointly with Martin, but she was unwilling to go without the children. Accordingly, in May 1976 she applied to the local magistrates' court for their custody. The father halted those proceedings by applying to make the children wards of court. Reeve J granted care and control to the mother and the father appealed.

Stamp LJ: Before turning to the facts of the case, I would make some introductory observations. In the first place the law which is to be applied is not in doubt. It is that the welfare of the children is, in the words of the statute, the first and paramount consideration. It was stated with clarity and precision by Lord MacDermott in *J v C* [1970] AC 668, [1969] 1 All ER 788 in a passage in his speech which should be in the mind of every judge who tries an infant case, and which was indeed in the mind of Reeve J in the instant case. Lord MacDermott said:

'The second question of construction is as to the scope and meaning of the words ". . . shall regard the welfare of the infant as the first and paramount consideration". Reading these words in their ordinary significance, and relating them to the various classes of proceedings which the section has already mentioned, it seems to me that they must mean more than that the child's welfare is to be treated as the top item in a list of items relevant to the matter in question. I think they connote a process whereby, when all the relevant facts, relationships, claims and wishes of parents, risks, choices and other circumstances are taken into account and weighed, the course to be followed will be that which is most in the interests of the child's welfare as that term has now to be understood. That is the first consideration because it is of first importance and the paramount consideration because it rules on or determines the course to be followed.'

Applying the law so stated, this court in *S (BD) v S (DJ)* (*infants: care and consent*) [1977] Fam 109, [1977] 1 All ER 656 held that the earlier case of *Re L* (*infants*) [1962] 3 All ER 1, [1962] 1 WLR 886, where this court appears to have balanced the welfare of the child against the wishes of an unimpeachable parent or the justice of the case as between the parties, was no longer to be regarded as good law. I think it is a most unfortunate fact that *S (BD) v S (DJ)* (*infants: care and consent*) has never been reported in the Law Reports, as it should have been, with the result that we have more than once, notwithstanding that case, had *Re L* cited to us as being still of binding authority.

The second thing I would say at the outset is, I think, also implicit in the law as stated in *J v C* in the passage to which I have referred; it is that although one may of course be assisted by the wisdom of remarks made in earlier cases, the circumstances in infant cases and the personalities of the parties concerned being infinitely variable, the conclusions of the court as to the course which should be followed in one case are of little assistance in guiding one to the course which ought to be followed in another case.

Thirdly I would emphasise that where a judge has seen the parties concerned, has had the assistance of a good welfare officer's report and has correctly applied the law, an appellate court ought not to disturb his decision unless it appears that he has failed to take into account something which he ought to have taken into account or has taken into account something which he ought not to have taken into account, or the appellate court is satisfied that his decision was wrong; it is not enough that a judge of the appellate court should think, on reading the papers, that he himself would on the whole have come to a different conclusion. . . .

It is clear that, from the point of view of the children, nothing could be much worse than a continuation of the situation which the judge described, to which must be added the fact that the mother is, as I have indicated, continuing her intimate association with M and that one of them at least knows that something is wrong, and that both the children are, so it appears, fond of M, with whom they have become very well acquainted. As I have indicated, the father, because of his beliefs, will not divorce his wife, or consent to a divorce, so that the couple face for a period of five years during which they cannot marry, a situation which cannot I think continue from the point of view of any of the three adults concerned, or which could be tolerable for any lengthy period. To the extent that it does endure, the strains will become intolerable and the damage to the children incalculable.

The mother appears to have been somewhat ambivalent on the question whether if care and control were denied to her, she would stay in the home to look after the children, maintaining her liaison with M, or whether she would go and live with him. The judge thought that she could not contemplate the possibility of giving up either her children or M, but he considered that if care and control were given to the father, the greatest possibility was that she would go and live with M alone, but of course what she wants to do is to set up home with M and the children.

The arrangements which the father would make if he were to have care and control and the mother in fact went to live with M were summarised by the judge thus:

'Moreover, I bear this matter in mind. That the arrangements which the father can make — I refer to the roster which is exhibited to one of his affidavits — is on the face of it satisfactory in that these children will be cared for by worthy persons at all hours of the day, nevertheless it is not a satisfactory way, through no fault of the father's, in having children cared for. As has been pointed out, during the course of one week there may be five different persons who may be responsible for looking after these children. There will be some continuity in the care that the father can lavish on them. Nevertheless there would be a succession of other persons who would be assisting in that regard. That, as I say, is not the fault of the father, he is making the best arrangements that he can.'

Counsel for the father pointed out in the course of her submissions to this court that there was evidence not noticed by the judge that the father had made an arrangement under which he was to have three months off duty in order to resettle the children in their new way of life. I agree with the learned judge that the arrangements are far from satisfactory and that if the matter rested there it could hardly be doubted that it would be for the benefit of these children that effect should be given to the dictates of nature which make the mother the natural guardian, protector and comforter of the very young. But, as the judge pointed out in a judgment which shows the greatest possible sympathy with the father — a sympathy which I would emphasise that I share — in considering the welfare of the children one has to look also to their moral and spiritual welfare.

The father, who naturally holds his beliefs very strongly, not only wants to live according to his faith, but wants his children to be brought up in that faith, to hold the same beliefs as he does and to live their lives as he intends to live his life. I cannot do better than quote the words in which the learned judge put it; he said this:

'And he takes the view that if the care and control is committed to the mother this may do considerable harm, and he would put it a little higher perhaps, very considerable harm, to the children in that it would be hurtful to them spiritually. He does not attach so much importance to the difficulty which might exist in explaining to these children what it entails if their mother is living in sin, if one can use that old fashioned Victorian expression, with M. He does not attach any great importance to the difficulty that there no doubt will be in due course if the children are committed to the care and control of their mother of explaining to them how professed Christians can ignore one of the commandments, or any of them. But what he feels will do very considerable harm to these children is that they should be brought up in a home where their mother and another man are living together in blatant defiance of church doctrine and all that the father believes in. And as appears very clearly from their demeanour in the witness box where those two persons with whom the children would be living in those circumstances show no repentance.'

The judge remarked that there was considerable force in that argument.

But unfortunately, as the judge pointed out, if one yielded to that submission and committed the care of these children to the father, it would not in great measure protect them from the moral and spiritual harm which the father fears. The plain fact is that the children's mother intends to live with a young man who is not her husband. No one suggests that she should be denied access to the children and the judge thought, and I share that view, that it would have to be liberal access, including staying access. How could the children then fail to be aware, and constantly aware, that their mother was living with M in, to quote the judge's words 'blatant defiance of church doctrine and all that [the father] believes in'? And, if, as appears to be the case, the children are children who love their mother and are fond of M, to deprive them of her would, in my judgment, be as likely as not to cause a revolt against the very teaching that the father would have them imbibe and a revolt, so I would have thought, which in due course would be a revolt against the father himself. As the judge remarked, when the children start going to school they will come to meet children who are living in a home where the parents were not married. The situation of these children is, and will be, difficult enough with a mother living a life which is anathema to the father, and whatever course is taken with regard to their care and control, each parent will have to act with wisdom and restraint. If the children were faced with a future deprived of their mother's constant company, I venture to think that they would indeed revolt against the decision which had brought this about.

One cannot be sure that the relationship between the mother and M will remain a stable one; the judge said that that was possibly one of the most difficult aspects of the case on which to express a view with any degree of certainty. He said of it:

'That is possibly one of the most difficult aspects of this case on which to express a view with any degree of certainty. I know that they met in January 1975 [that was a slip for 1973], that their adulterous association has continued for about a year now and that at the moment there can be no question that they feel they are going to stay with each other and that the union between them, whether they are married or not, is going to be a permanent one. Moreover M has purchased a house which would be the "matrimonial home". I appreciate that there must be some question that this association between them may be no more than a temporary infatuation which will burn itself out when the glamour of what I suppose one could call their courtship over the last few months has gone. I face that danger. It is also submitted that if I took the children away from the home which the boy has known for over three years, and that is really the whole of his life which he can remember (and this is the only home that the girl has known) that that would cause a great upheaval in their lives. I attach no importance to that. These children would settle down perfectly well in any other environment if they are with their mother.'

M is, as I have said, well known to the children; he is, as the judge found, well liked by the children. The judge thought that it might well be that he had deliberately sought to worm his way into their affections in order to assist the mother's case when it came before the judge. The judge did not think he needed to decide whether that was the situation or not. He found as a fact that the children got on well with M; that he got on well with them, so that if care and control were committed to the mother, they were not going to a stranger.

I turn now to how the learned judge described the mother; at one point in his judgment he said this:

'But again I can appreciate the situation in which she now is. She is a desperately unhappy person. She cannot control her own emotions. She has the laudible and natural maternal instincts for her children. For that she can only be praised. But unfortunately — and the fact I criticise her for this is neither here nor there — she has equally strong emotions for M and those two emotions are so strong that she can write the notes to which I have referred but not in detail and are so strong that she cannot really see the wickedness of the step that she is taking in disrupting this family. And also she cannot see the very real goodness that there is in her husband both as a husband and as a father.'

The judge also says this of her earlier in his judgment:

'So far as their material welfare is concerned no sort of criticism has been made against the mother. As a mother she has been quite excellent. And there is no reason to suppose that in that regard she will change. These children will need for nothing if they are being fed, clothed and brought up in all those material particulars by their mother; they could not expect to have a better mother'

and it was at that point that the judge went on to point out that he also had to consider the children's spiritual and moral welfare. I would add this, that it is not suggested that the mother is in any degree lacking in the warmth which such very young children so much need.

The judge made it abundantly clear that if he were deciding the case by trying to do justice between the father and the mother, there could be only one way in which he could possibly decide it, and that was in favour of the father; but he correctly applied what was laid down in *J v C* and refused to set that consideration against the welfare of the children. The judgment, of which I have only quoted parts, is if I may say so, full, careful and thoughtful. In the course of it the judge said everything that could possibly be said in favour of the father's claim that the welfare of the children required that they should be in his care. In the end, he rejected it, concluding that the dictates of nature that the mother is the natural guardian, protector and comforter of very young children, and in particular of a very little girl, had not been displaced. He expressed himself towards the conclusion of his judgment in these terms:

'I propose to commit the care and control of these children to the mother. That has been obvious for some period during my judgment. Having thus stated my conclusion the mother is already feeling much happier. She will be able to act more naturally. She will be able to see the goodness in her husband that she has not been able to until this moment when she has heard my decision. I take the view that she is really a very nice person. It is a tragedy that her emotions have been such that she is blind to all advice and she really cannot control herself. But she is really a very nice person. Now that she has got what she wants, her children and her lover, I feel that she will be able to see that there is a lot of good in her husband, not only as a husband (though that is of no importance now because this marriage has irretrievably broken down whatever the father may think) but may also be able to see his goodness as a father. I have no fear in committing the care and control of these children to her that she will try and build up M as the father of these children. That last consideration is not the reason why I commit the care and control of these children to the mother. The real reason is this. Nothing that I have heard would induce me to take away a little girl who is not yet 2½ from a really good mother, and nobody has suggested that these children should be separated. It might cause untold harm to the little girl if she were taken away from her mother now.'

I can only say that I am quite unable to conclude that the judge came to a wrong conclusion; I agree with it and would dismiss this appeal.

Ormrod LJ: . . . For my part, I do not think that justice between parents in these cases is ever simple. On the contrary, it is a highly complex question which can very rarely be answered satisfactorily, and then only after exhaustive investigation. In the present case this aspect of it was, quite rightly, not pursued in any detail, because I do not think the welfare of the children required any such enquiry. So I prefer to keep an open mind as to where the justice of the case, as between the father and the mother, lies. It seems to me that all experience shows that, particularly serious-minded people such as the mother in this case, do not break up their marriages unless their relationship with their spouses has deteriorated very severely indeed. So I hesitate to make moral judgments in this class of case; I do not find it particularly helpful. . . .

Questions

(i) Do you consider that this decision was 'unfair' to the father?

(ii) If you do think it unfair, is that because: (*a*) the law requires the court to determine the case on the basis of the children's welfare and not upon the rights and wrongs of the marital dispute, or (*b*) the court gave effect to the 'dictates of nature which make the mother the natural guardian, protector and comforter of the very young'?

(iii) Following this case, is it ever relevant to a custody dispute that one of the parents is determined to break up the home whereas the other is anxious to hold it together?

(iv) What do you think was best for these two children?

In view of Lord Justice Stamp's remarks, we must beware of attaching too much importance to those decisions of the Court of Appeal which happen to appear in some published form. First instance examples of judges performing the exercise described by Lord MacDermott are, however, scarcely ever reported. The following appeal cases are therefore offered, not as authorities, but as illustrations of the range of problems encountered. In *Re K*, for example, the problem of disturbing the status quo was not serious, for the parents were still living under the same roof, under circumstances in which it might have been worse *not* to disturb matters. Nevertheless, even when the status quo is not clearly on his side, there may be cases in which a father can succeed:

S v S (Custody of Children)
(1978) 1 FLR 143, Court of Appeal

The parties married in 1971. They had two children, a girl who was now $7\frac{1}{2}$ and a boy of nearly 6. In April 1977, the mother began a lesbian relationship with a Mrs D. In August, her husband told her that she must choose between them, and she left, taking the children to the Ds' home. The children both subsequently returned to the matrimonial home, and in December the mother came back to care for them. She also resumed her relationship with Mrs D. Meanwhile, in August, the wife made an application for custody, and for an order that the husband vacate the home. This came first before the judge in September, when the wife and Mrs D denied their relationship. The judge refused the injunction and adjourned the custody hearing for a welfare officer's report. At the resumed hearing in May 1978, the judge granted custody to the father, with a supervision order, and the mother appealed.

Orr LJ: . . . The welfare officer, Mr Langley, refers in that report to the facts of the case and their effects upon the children. M considered for her age to be very perceptive and to have been aware for some time of the differences between her parents. She had expressed feelings of hurt to both her mother and her father but she had asked at the same time that the parents should be together. The welfare officer thought that during the last two months she had regained much of her lost confidence. The headmistress of her school thought that M seemed to know too much about her parents' differences and that she had always felt she should be with her mother. With regard to the boy the welfare officer reported that he had asked if his mother would stay with him for ever, but although he had shown some signs of insecurity at school he was, the welfare officer believed, less affected than his sister by the break up of the family. The conclusion of the welfare officer was that in his view as a layman the sexual identity of the two children was by now well established, but he recorded that they had both expressed a clearer wish to be with the mother than with the father. He considered the mother to be quite capable of caring for the material needs of the children whereas the father would be likely to have difficulties in this respect, and recommended that it would be best that the custody should be given to her, with a supervision order to the court welfare service, to be carried out by a man, and with reasonable access for the father, and he expressed the belief that it would be appropriate for the mother to remain a patient of a Dr Howells, whom she had consulted and to whom I shall shortly refer.

At the resumed hearing of the application for custody the husband produced a tape on which he had recorded a telephone call from the wife to him which quite clearly established what the wife had denied at the previous hearing, that she was well aware of the lesbian relationship that had subsisted between herself and Mrs D. The judge referred to that matter in his judgment and gave other reasons why he should approach with some caution the evidence of the wife and why, as regards some matters, he rejected it. There was evidence before the court of two psychiatric specialists: Dr Howells, whom the wife called and who is head of the Institute of Family Psychiatry at Ipswich Hospital, and Dr Klassnik, a consultant psychiatrist at Claybury Hospital, Woodford, called for the husband. It is true to say that Dr Klassnik had not seen either of the parties to this case before the hearing and he was not present on an earlier date when the wife's evidence was given. The conclusion of Dr Howells was that there was no danger in this case of the children being led into deviant sexual ways; and with that Dr Klassnik agreed but his concern was [as] to another matter, namely the social embarrassment and hurt which could be caused to the children in circumstances such as these if it became known in the locality that there was a lesbian relationship between the mother and Mrs D. He expressed anxiety as to that matter and thought it could be very harmful to the children, and for that reason he considered that it was right that the children in this case should be in the care of the father, although Dr Howells had recommended that in his view the mother was the more appropriate person to care for them.

These being in summary the facts of the case, the learned judge, in a careful judgment of which we have a transcript, having referred to the reasons he had for regarding the evidence of the mother with some suspicion, came to the conclusion that the father should have custody. He considered that there was no danger in this case of these children being turned into homosexuals but that there was the social danger to which Dr Klassnik had referred in his evidence. Considering the matter on the whole of the evidence, bearing in mind the recommendation made by the court welfare officer that the mother should have the care, and bearing in mind the evidence of Dr Howells, he came to the conclusion that it was in the interests of these children that they should be cared for by the father and not the mother. He quoted (and I need not repeat it) a passage from the judgment of Lord Wilberforce in *Re D (An Infant)* [1977] AC 602 at 629, and referred to the danger of children being exposed or introduced to ways of life of this kind and to the possibility that such exposure might scar them permanently.

Against that judgment this appeal is now brought, and the grounds of appeal are really two: first that the judge was wrong not to accept the recommendation of the court welfare officer and, second, that he was wrong to prefer the evidence of Dr Klassnik to that of Dr Howells. As far as the first ground is concerned it is clear that the judge rightly paid very great respect to the welfare report, but it was for him to decide whether or not, having heard the evidence, he agreed with the conclusion of the welfare officer; it seems to me impossible to base a ground of appeal in this case on his having decided otherwise than in accordance with that recommendation. As far as the doctors are concerned, the judge clearly bore in mind that Dr Klassnik had not seen the parties but nonetheless he preferred Dr Klassnik's evidence on the vital issue. This was essentially a matter for the learned judge, who had the advantage, which we have not had, of hearing the evidence, and it seems to me impossible to say he was wrong in preferring Dr Klassnik's evidence.

I can find no fault in the judgment of the learned judge, and in my judgment there is no basis upon which this appeal can succeed, and I would dismiss the appeal.

Stamp LJ: I agree. This must have been, as I think the judge in the court below recognized, a worrying case and a case which was far from easy for the learned judge to decide. My fears regarding the risks inherent in these particular children being brought up by this particular lesbian mother are not as great as those of the learned judge, and indeed different judges on very similar facts may legitimately take differing views as to where the interests of children lie. . . .

Questions

(i) What Lord Wilberforce said in *Re D (An Infant)* [1977] AC 602, [1977] 1 All ER 145, (in which a homosexual father's consent to the adoption of his son was dispensed with as unreasonably withheld) was this:

Whatever new attitudes Parliament, or public tolerance, may have chosen to take as regards the behaviour of consenting adults over 21 inter se, these should not entitle the courts to relax, in any degree, the vigilance and severity with which they should regard the risk of children at critical ages, being exposed or introduced to ways of life which, as this case illustrates, may lead to severance from normal society, to psychological stresses and unhappiness and possibly even to physical experiences which may scar them for life.

Do you agree?
(ii) Do you think a system is acceptable in which *by definition*, 'different judges on very similar facts may legitimately take differing views as to where the interests of children lie'?

In each of the following cases, however, the court was prepared to disturb a status quo which had existed for some time:

Re C (A Minor) (Custody of Child)
(1980) 2 FLR 163, Court of Appeal

The father, who was then in the army and living in barracks, and the mother, who was then married but separated from her husband, had an affair which lasted from 1973 to 1975. Their son was born in 1974 and was now nearly 6. After his parents' separation, he was out of contact with his father for some three years. Meanwhile the father got on in the world, married and had children. The mother remarried, but when her second marriage was in difficulties, in September 1978, she asked the father to look after their child. She then began her present relationship with a Mr D and in March 1979 she went down to Cornwall where the father lived, picked up the boy from school and brought him back to her home in London. The father began wardship proceedings almost immediately. The story is taken up by Ormrod LJ:

There was an interim order on 25 May 1979 giving care and control to the mother with access to the father and ordering a welfare report. Some access, including staying access, was given to the father. However, most unfortunately — and many times we have said this although I suppose it is unavoidable — there was a delay in getting the welfare report, which did not become available until 19 December 1979. Quite frankly, a delay like that in a case like this is quite unacceptable, and if one has to wait for the best part of nine months to obtain a welfare report, it is better to deal with the case without a welfare report because all this time goes by in the life of a child and the whole situation changes between the parents and the child so that when the case comes before a judge the facts are quite different from what they were when the case started. This is most undesirable because these matters should be dealt with as quickly as possible.

The case was heard by the judge in February 1980; he granted care and control to the father. The mother's appeal was heard in March.

Ormrod LJ: From that judgment it is perfectly plain that the judge arrived at the conclusion that he was much impressed by the father and his wife, as he said he was an intelligent and articulate man in a responsible job. On the other hand, he was not at all happy about the mother, because there was no doubt whatever that she has had, perhaps through no fault of her own, an extremely turbulent life so far. She is only 25 or 26 now and has had two marriages and two affairs.

It is not necessary to make moral judgments about people in these days, and no doubt she is behaving only as many of her contemporaries behave, but the problems that they create for themselves, the difficulties that they create for themselves by living this kind of life are appalling. One only has to look at the facts of this case to see what an absolute mess she has made of her life in the short period that she has been trying to live it.

So the judge was confronted with a situation where the father was able to offer this boy, whom he had made contact with again, and made quite a reasonable contact in 1979, so far as anyone could see, a stable, intelligent future, whereas, with the best will in the world, the mother's prospects could not be regarded as at all good. How long her relationship with Mr D will last no one can tell. Her past does not suggest that one could put much faith in it. Moreover he is proposing to return to Cumbria, where he comes from, and would like to go back to farming. She is a totally identified Londoner who would no doubt find the change to Cumbria almost unsupportable, but at any rate C would be miles and miles away from the father if that move took place. So the judge had a choice between a stable father who can offer, as far as one can see, a stable home life but without, of course, the mother to whom the child is unquestionably very attached and with whom he has lived, apart from the interval which I have mentioned, all his life, and the mother who cannot possibly, as I see it, offer, at the moment, the promise of a really stable background for this child.

It is purely speculative as to how she will cope in the future, and so the judge had to set off and balance one against the other — the much more favourable prospects which the father can offer, against the long established mother/child relationship which the mother had enjoyed over the years, apart from the break.

I dare say that if there had been no break, it would have been very difficult indeed for a judge to decide that it was in C's best interests to move from the mother to the father because we are all apprehensive about disturbing well-established bonds between children and one or other parent, and very disinclined to do it. But where the bonds have been broken as in this case by mother handing C over to the father, no matter what her difficulties were, from the point of view of the child that is what has happened.

So it is a much more open situation in this case than it usually is between two parents, and the judge had no hesitation in coming to the conclusion that the father was the parent of his choice. He said so in terms and said he was quite satisfied that the boy's welfare demanded that he should go to the father.

Appeal dividend.

L v L (Custody of Child)
(1980) 2 FLR 48, Court of Appeal

The parties married in 1975. Their daughter was born in 1976. In September 1978, the mother left the child with the father and went to live with another man. After a time that affair broke down. The mother attempted suicide, was an out-patient at hospital, took anti-depressants, moved from one address to another, squatting and 'living almost rough.' For about three weeks, when her husband began divorce proceedings, she drank heavily. She then applied for custody and it was common ground that if successful she would also obtain the tenancy of the former matrimonial home from the local authority. The judge granted her custody and the father appealed. The appeal was heard in February 1980.

Lord Denning MR: . . . The judge thought it was very evenly balanced: but he thought the right thing would be for the mother to have the custody of the child and return to the matrimonial home. He said that she would be able to look after the child full-time, including during the holidays, which the father would not be able to do.

I now refer to the welfare officer's report. It is quite plain the welfare officer thought that whoever had custody of the little girl there would be hazards. I will read two paragraphs from that report:

'With either parent having sole care and control [in] this case there appears to be the possibility of hazard for the child. The [mother] [is] a loving, and in a settled emotional state may well be quite a competent mother, but she remains a rather lost and unstable figure in her present situation. She may well have in mind a resumption of the relationship with Mr B but this is overtly denied. Her need for a supportive male is apparent and [the child's] interests might take second place.'

That is the welfare officer's assessment of the mother. As to the father, the welfare officer says:

'The [father] comes over as a conscientious parent who at present seems to have built his life around [the child]. However, the allegations that have been made about his over-severe chastisement are a source of anxiety as if founded they may indicate that his efforts to fill the roles of parent, housekeeper and breadwinner are causing him undue stress.'

I want to emphasize at the moment the allegation about 'over-severe chastisement.' There is evidence that Mrs W was very worried because of the bruises she found upon this little girl. She was so anxious about it that she took the little girl to the welfare officer and to a doctor. The doctor made a report which show that he found bruises on the buttocks of this little girl and also three finger marks. He drew a diagram showing where they were. He said:

'This child was examined today. [The child's] aunt was very concerned and saddened by the ill-treatment that this little girl had suffered. It is — according to her — not the first time that she discovered [the child] to be bruised'. [Then there is the diagram.] '. . . brought today by aunt Mrs W who is the child minder as well as [the child's] aunt on account of marked bruising she had discovered on the buttocks area. On examination there was swelling and 3 finger marks present'.

That is what the welfare officer was referring to when he or she referred to the 'over-severe chastisement.'

There is another worry in the case if the father continues to have this little girl. That is the relationship between Mrs W and the father. Mrs W gave evidence. It seems to me, reading that evidence, that it is not at all certain that the relationship between Mrs W and the father will continue for much longer. She said:

'I would like to continue to look after [the child] but I feel sometimes [the father] comes with something up his sleeve. And seems to have something against me — sometimes he does not speak to me. And I cannot manage financially. I would have [the child] to stay for a while with me if [the mother] had custody. I find it difficult to discuss matters with [father]. [The child] is a happy girl — not letting a lot bother her.'

What, to my mind, tends to turn the scale in this very evenly balanced case are these bruises — the alleged over-serious chastisement of the child by her father. He does not mean to do it. He is probably a strict disciplinarian. But there is an anxiety on that score. The other anxiety is how long Mrs W would be prepared to play the part of a second mother to this little girl when she is so suspicious of the father and tends not to get on with him. So that relationship may not continue. Those are the anxieties on that side.

There are also anxieties if the mother has the child. Will the mother continue to be lost and unstable? Will she take up the relationship again with Mr B? Will she start drinking again, or taking sleeping pills? Those are the anxieties on that side.

The judge seems to have thought that the right thing would be for the mother to go back to the matrimonial home and have care and control of the child: because the child ran with joy and delight when she met the mother. But she was a little more reserved with her father. At all events, it is as plain as can be that the child is exceedingly attached to the mother, as is the mother to her. Perhaps the right thing for the future — weighing the balance on each side — is as the judge found. He found that the mother and child — mother and daughter; that is always an important factor — should be together once more. The risk must be taken — because it is always a risk — that the mother will remain unstable: but in the hope that once they are together again, the mother will become stable. She will have her daughter with her in the home, and a competent relationship will grow between them.

I must say that one feels a great deal of sympathy for the father who, as far as one can see, has done nothing wrong whatsoever except perhaps in his character: being a little too severe, being a little too forthcoming, and being not quite open and helpful enough with Mrs W. Nothing else can be said against him. He is evidently a first-rate man in every way. Sad and disappointed as he must be at losing the case, I am afraid that, on balance, we must go by the judge's decision, and not overrule it unless we see good reason to do so. Now some things the judge did are very important. The judge made a supervision order: so that the welfare officer could keep continual watch on the position. He made careful provision for access. He retained the matter for himself so that he could make any necessary order about the matrimonial home. So that the position will be kept under continual review by the judge. That is the best that can be done. Having regard to all those arrangements, I do not think we should disturb his decision. I would dismiss the appeal accordingly.

Questions

(i) Would you conclude anything from the fact that a three-year-old girl ran to meet her mother, but was a little reserved with her father?

(ii) Do you think that either of these last two decisions is wrong? If so, which?

(iii) In one well-publicised case, a judge apparently told a father who had cared for his baby single-handed when his wife left that he should be at work and not drawing supplementary benefit in order to care for his child: do you agree?

(iv) How would you weigh the advantages of full-time parental care for a young child against the disadvantages of living on supplementary benefit?

The Court of Appeal has recently set out some views on the so-called 'maternal preference':

Re W (A Minor)
(1982) 126 Sol Jo 725, Court of Appeal

A little girl was born in May 1980 and cared for by her mother for nine months, until the mother left the matrimonial home in February 1981. She wished to take the baby, but the father would not agree. From February to July 1981, the baby was cared for by the father, with help from his family while he was at work. The father did everything for her while at home and formed a much closer relationship with her than 'most young fathers.' Since July 1981, the baby had largely been cared for by Mrs C, who became the father's cohabitant. Custody proceedings between the parents were first heard by magistrates in May 1981, when interim custody was awarded to the father, with daily access to the mother. In July, this was reduced to reasonable access, later fixed as weekly, with every other weekend spent at the mother's home. The case was transferred to the High Court, but not heard until July 1982, when Ewbank J awarded custody to the mother. The father appealed.

Cumming-Bruce LJ: . . . [Counsel for the father] submits that . . . the judge was weighing the scales too heavily against the father . . . [the judge] put it in this way:

'. . . the courts consider that a child of this age and a child considerably older than this too ought to be with the mother if other things are equal unless there is some strong ground for saying that the child's best interests will be away from her mother'.

I would not myself think it wise to make such a generalisation about the view of the courts. I would prefer to say that, as a matter of general experience, culled from the evidence that has been given in court, including the evidence of paediatricians, sociologists, social scientists, social workers and many varieties of educational people, is to this effect. First, the individual circumstances of every case vary so much that any generalisation has to be qualified in the light of a sensitive grasp of the realities of all the relationships between the child and the various grown-ups concerned. Secondly, the capacity of the grown-ups, who are put forward as claimants for care and control, is of immense importance in proving their capacity for forming affectionate, loving relationships with the child or children concerned.

Thirdly, if all such factors are nicely balanced, then probably it is right for a child of tender years to be brought up by his or her natural mother.

Fourthly, when, as a result of separation of the parents, the natural mother has been cut off for a significant period of continuous care for a small child, and the father and/or the father and another lady have stepped into the breach so that for months or years the child has been learning to place its security upon the father and/or the father's other lady, it becomes in each case a very delicate weighing exercise to decide whether it is now right, in the interests of the child, to take the risk of uprooting him or her in order that it may continue to be brought up by the natural mother. . . .

I would think it safer if one is trying to formulate the test, to substitute for the words 'unless there is some strong ground for saying that the child's best interests would be away from the mother', the words 'unless there is some ground for saying that the child's best interests would be away from the mother', though speaking for myself, the appreciation of the relevant factors varies so immensely in every single case that an attempt by a lawyer to grasp such a formulation is likely to be unhelpful. But in practical affairs, of course, particularly in the Law Courts, we have to try to formulate our criteria.

[Counsel for the father] submitted that, when this judgment is looked at fairly and squarely, the judge has expressed the test wrongly and applied the wrong test; that, if he had applied the right test, he would and should have come down the other way on these facts, because he should have appreciated that by July this little girl, who had lived for all her life in her father's home, had there had her rabbits and the rest of it, had her roots there and although it might be very sad for the mother to be the victim of circumstance, including the orders of earlier courts, the practical situation was that the little girl now was too deeply rooted and too emotionally bound up with her father and Mrs C, to make it right to take the risk of separating her from him. . . .

I am satisfied that the reasons for the learned judge's conclusions are these. He was perfectly clear that 'K's' roots had grown continuously in her father's home so that she was bound up more closely with her father and Mrs C than anybody else. I say that because the judge refers to the child's roots in the father's home again and again. He was not unaware of it — which is why he recognised that this was a difficult problem. But when one looks at the history, one finds that this is not one of those cases where the child has been cut off from the natural mother for a long period of time, because of access, first of all, after the first interval, seeing her baby every day and, when the court stopped that and substituted much less frequency, there was still such frequency that every week the mother was having some contact with her daughter. When staying access came into operation, every other week-end the child was spending a couple of nights with her mother. When the mother's evidence is considered, which the judge evidently did accept, the judge was satisfied on that evidence that the mother had managed to preserve a good relationship with the child. When she went on staying access, it was not one of those cases that we are familiar with of a child being dragged kicking and screaming from her home to the other parent. It was a totally different situation and the child apparently seemed to get on very well in her mother's home with the M children when they were there. Mr M [the mother's cohabitant] gave evidence and he comes through to me as a rather shadowy character, because his personal relationship with 'K' was not very deep. But there is no reason to suppose that, in that home, 'K' would not grow up in a stable, balanced household and so, when it came to the weighing exercise which the judge had to do, I am satisfied that he reached his conclusion because he was confident that the reality of the situation was that the child had in early life been in the care of her mother, who was ready and willing to go on bringing up her daughter, and with whom throughout she had preserved a relationship; that although the roots of the child were in her father and his home, the discontinuity of contact with the mother had not been such as to make it sensible to prevent the mother resuming the full time upbringing of her daughter. . . .

That being the judge's view, I am quite clear that it would not be right for this court to interfere. He has seen and heard the witnesses and his conclusion reflects his appreciation of the relationships in the case.

[Mrs Justice Butler-Sloss also delivered a judgment dismissing the appeal.]

Question

Counsel for the husband complained that the trial judge had not explained *why* it was in the child's long term interests to be brought up by her mother: do you think that the Court of Appeal provided a satisfactory answer?

The differences between custody disputes and other types of litigation and the inherent difficulties involved in knowing what the best solution will be, are spelled out by Robert H. Mnookin in *Child Custody Adjudication: Judicial Functions in the Face of Indeterminacy* (1975):

At the core of adjudication is the notion that government exercises authority through a process in which the persons affected can participate. Each party has an 'institutionally guaranteed . . . opportunity to present proofs and arguments for a decision in his favour.' A neutral judge resolves the dispute by ascertaining past events and evaluating those past events against articulated and described legal standards that are generally applicable. As part of this process, the judge is obliged to reconcile the rules used to evaluate these past events with those announced and applied in earlier disputes of the same sort. The parties then usually may ask some higher court to review the decision to determine whether the appropriate rules were applied and, to a limited extent, whether the past events were accurately ascertained. Child-custody disputes resolved under the broad best-interests-of-the-child principle differ from this model of adjudication in several closely interrelated ways.

1. 'Person-oriented' not 'act-oriented' determinations

The first and most striking difference relates to a distinction suggested by Lon Fuller: custody disputes under the best-interests principle require 'person-oriented,' not 'act-oriented,' determinations. Most legal rules require determination of some event and are thus 'act-oriented' (1971). A 'person-oriented' rule, on the other hand, requires an evaluation of the 'whole person viewed as a social being.' Several of the other important ways in which child-custody disputes differ from the paradigm of adjudication follow from this feature of person- rather than act-orientation. . . .

In deciding [ordinary] litigation, it will not be remotely relevant which disputant has more money, is more humane, works harder, gives more to charity, follows better religious practices, or takes better care of his house. The resolution will only be person-oriented to the extent that the judge must evaluate each as a social being in order to determine whether one should be considered more credible than the other.

Resolution of a custody dispute by the best-interests-of-the-child principle stands in sharp contrast to the foregoing. In a divorce custody fight, a court *must* evaluate the attitudes, dispositions, capacities, and shortcomings of each parent to apply the best-interest standard. Indeed, the inquiry centers on what kind of person each parent is, and what the child is like. That there is, however, nothing inherent in custody disputes requiring resolution by a person-oriented rule is shown by the nineteenth century examples of act-oriented rules for custody disputes between a child's parents.

2. Predictions not determinations of past acts

Adjudication usually requires the determination of *past* acts and facts, not a prediction of *future* events. Applying the best-interests standard requires an individualized prediction: with whom will this child be better off in the years to come? Proof of what happened in the past is relevant only insofar as it enables the court to decide what is likely to happen in the future. . . .

3. Interdependence of outcome-affecting factors

Because custody disputes involve *relationships* between people, a decision affecting any one of the parties will often necessarily have an effect on the others. The resolution of a custody dispute may permanently affect — or even end — the parties' legal relationship; but the social and psychological relationships will usually continue. The best-interests principle requires a prediction of what will happen in the future, which, of course, depends in part on the future behavior of the parties. Because these parties will often interact in the future, this probable interaction must be taken into account in deciding what the outcome is to be. For example, awarding custody to the mother may affect the father's behavior, which, in turn, can affect the mother's behavior and the child. The possibility of such feedback must be considered in applying the best-interests standard. Most disputes resolved by adjudication do not require predictions involving appraisals of future relationships where the 'loser's' future behavior can be an important ingredient.

4. Findings, precedent, and appellate review

A determination that is person-oriented and requires predictions necessarily involves an evaluation of the parties who have appeared in court. This has important consequences for the roles of both precedent and appellate review in custody cases. The result of an earlier case involving different people has limited relevance to a subsequent case requiring individualized evaluations of a particular child and the litigants. Prior reported cases now provide little basis for controlling or predicting the outcome of a particular case. Moreover, the trial court in custody disputes is often not required to make specific findings of fact, much less write an opinion about the case or reconcile what has been done in this case with what has happened before.

All of this makes the scope of appellate review extremely limited. Because the trial court's decision involves an assessment of the personality, character and relationship of people the judge has seen in court, appellate courts are extremely loath to upset the trial court's determination on the basis of a transcript. In the words of an English judge, 'So much may turn, consciously or unconsciously, on estimates of character which cannot be made by those who have not seen or heard the parties.' As Professor Fuller has written, 'It would be hard [for an appellate court to pass an intelligent judgment on the trial court's decision] unless it were prepared to summon the husband, wife and child before it and try the case over again.'

5. Participation by all affected parties

Normally, parties most obviously affected by a dispute have a right to participate in the adjudicatory process. *The* issue in a child-custody dispute is what will become of the child, but ordinarily the child is not a true participant in the process. While the best-interests principle requires that the primary focus be on the interests of the child, the child ordinarily does not define those interests himself, nor does he have representation in the ordinary sense. Even in states that allow for independent representation for the child in the dispute, the role of the child's advocate is different from that in normal adjudication. A lawyer usually looks to his client for instructions about the goals to be pursued. Except in the case of older children, a child's representative in a custody dispute must himself normally define the child's interests.

On the fourth point, the development of English law is explained by Ormrod LJ in *D v M (Minor: Custody Appeal)* [1982] 3 All ER 897, [1982] 3 WLR 891:

> The duties and powers of appellate courts in relation to appeals in cases relating to the custody of children have been very carefully considered in two cases in this court within the last ten years

or so, viz. *Re O (infants)* [1971] Ch 748, [1971] 2 All ER 744, and *Re F (a minor) (wardship: appeal)* [1976] Fam 238, [1976] 1 All ER 417. In these cases the court had to consider two schools of thought. One, of which Stamp LJ was the leading exponent, supported the view that in cases concerning the future well-being of children an appellate court should not interfere with the exercise of the discretion of the court of first instance, which had had the advantage of seeing and hearing the parties concerned, unless the decision of the court below was one which no reasonable court could have reached, or unless it could be shown that the court below had erred in law, or had taken into account any matter which should not have been taken into account, or failed to take into account any matter which ought to have been taken into account (see [1976] Fam 238 at 254, [1976] 1 All ER 417 at 430 per Stamp LJ). The other school took the view that was cogently expressed in the following passage in the judgment of Davies LJ in *Re O (infants)* [1971] Ch 748 at 755, [1971] 2 All ER 744 at 748–749.

> 'In my considered opinion the law now is that if an appellate court is satisfied that the decision of the court below is wrong, it is its duty to say so and to act accordingly. This applies whether the appeal is an interlocutory or a final appeal, whether it is an appeal from justices to a Chancery judge or from justices to a Divisional Court of the Divorce Division. Every court has a duty to do its best to arrive at a proper and just decision. And if an appellate court is satisfied that the decision of the court below is improper, unjust or wrong, then the decision must be set aside. I am quite unable to subscribe to the view that a decision must be treated as sacrosanct because it was made in the exercise of 'discretion': so to do might well perpetuate injustice.

In *Re O (infants)* this court decided that the school of thought represented by Davies LJ was correct in law. But the controversy continued and the views of the other school were frequently advanced by counsel in argument. Eventually the issue came to a head in *Re F (a minor) (wardship: appeal)*, and was resolved by the majority (Browne and Bridge LJJ, Stamp LJ dissenting) in favour of the opinion expressed by Davies LJ in *Re O (infants)*. This decision is binding on us but, perhaps because it was a majority decision, it is still not whole-heartedly accepted, as is clear from the judgments of the Divisional Court in the instant case.

We are clearly of the opinion that the very careful judgments of Browne and Bridge LJJ should be regarded as settling the question once and for all.

Question

Has Stamp LJ changed his mind? (Compare his remarks in *Re K*, p. 340, above, with those in *S v S*, p. 345, above.)

On Mnookin's fifth point, the Justice Report on *Parental Rights and Duties and Custody Suits* (1975) made the following recommendation:

89. . . .

> (*h*) The family court would include among its staff a new officer, having training in both law and applied social sciences. Among other things, his duty would be to act as overseer of children's interests in custody suits. We have referred to him already in our report as the 'Children's Ombudsman.'. . .

91. The role we envisage for the Children's Ombudsman includes that of a clearing agency, one branch at each family court. Everyone would know of his existence and would be expected to report to him. All relevant information would end up under one hand. He would have the power to request a welfare report whenever he thought it necessary. On behalf of a child the subject of a custody suit, he would act as the child's spokesman and would have the duty of instructing solicitors and counsel to represent the child's interests so that the interests of the child might be separately represented to the court independently of the adults and local or other authorities concerned. (He would have the power to do so in other legal proceedings as well.) As the child's spokesman, it would be his particular duty to ensure that the views of any child able to express them, verbally or otherwise, were ascertained in the absence of the parents or other adult 'custodian' and then made known to the tribunal. He would be responsible to the Lord Chancellor (the traditional delegate of the Crown as *parens patriae*).

92. We find unfortunate the decision in *H v H* [1974] 1 All ER 1145, [1974] 1 WLR 595 where the Court of Appeal held that judges cannot grant promises of confidentiality to children they meet in chambers. As the Field-Fisher Report [the 'Maria Colwell' report, see Chapter 13] indicates, children rarely have the opportunity to communicate privately with social service workers or other people in authority concerned about their welfare. Often, however, the child himself, even when quite young, can articulate what is in his own best interests; at least he can make it clear to a trained person where he believes he will be loved and secure. Foreign systems vary widely in their willingness to listen to the child. We will give a few examples. In Norway, children over 12 are interviewed 'as a rule'. In California, the judge's authority is purely discretionary. In West Germany, consideration is currently being given to a proposal giving the positive preference of a child over 14 full implementation, unless that preference is held to be against his own best interests. In Texas, a child over 14 is permitted to choose his own 'managing conservator' (a position similar to 'guardian') subject to court approval. Regardless, however, of whether the court actually hears the *child*, it is absolutely necessary that his *views* be ascertained and represented. The Children's Ombudsman would, of course, act as the link between the child on the one hand and his solicitor and counsel on the other hand.

Although divorce courts do have power to order that children be separately represented, only in wardship proceedings in the High Court is this at all common. A Family Division *Practice Direction* [1982] 1 All ER 319, [1982] 1 WLR 118, however, questions even this:

In the recent cases of *P v P* [1981] CA Bound Transcript 312 and *Re F (a minor) (adoption: parental consent)* [1982] 1 All ER 321, [1982] 1 WLR 102, the Court of Appeal drew attention to the increasing tendency of registrars in wardship and custody cases to join the children as parties and to invite the Official Solicitor to act as guardian ad litem. In many cases up to now the parties have asked the court to order the joinder by consent, without showing any special reason for it.

The Court of Appeal emphasised that in the great majority of cases such action was unnecessary and that it added considerably to the length and expense of a hearing, without any commensurate advantage in assisting the court. The Court of Appeal made it clear that only in special circumstances should the child be joined. In most cases the child's interest will be sufficiently protected by a welfare report. It is only in exceptional cases that the joinder of the child and his representation by the Official Solicitor is likely to be of assistance to the court. This is particularly the case where a child is not old enough to express a view as to his future.

It follows from these judgments of the Court of Appeal that such orders should not be made, even by consent, unless special reasons are shown for making them. The special reasons given by the judge or registrar should be noted by the associate or clerk together with any special directions for inquiries or investigation to be made in the case, and a copy of the note should be sent to the Official Solicitor for his guidance.

R L BAYNE-POWELL
8 December 1981   Senior Registrar.

Questions

(i) It is clear that constraints of cost will prevent the Justice recommendation being implemented, but do you (having regard to the discussion of welfare reports at pp. 364–370, below) regard the *Practice Direction* as an answer to the problem?
(ii) Bearing in mind that separate legal aid is to be made available to children and parents in care proceedings (see further in Chapter 14), and that the proportion of *contested* custody cases is small, might one solution be to allow the child to qualify for legal aid irrespective of his parents' income?
(iii) If you were the court, how much weight would you give to the wishes (*a*) of a five-year-old; (*b*) of a ten-year-old, and (*c*) of a 13-year-old?
(iv) Whatever the mechanism for doing so, should such wishes always be discovered?
(v) Might a friendly and private chat with the judge (or the magistrates) be the best way of doing this?
(vi) But would not that make the judge's role inquisitorial rather than adjudicative?
(vii) Would that matter?

Having concluded that child custody adjudication cannot fit the usual model of litigation, Mnookin goes on to consider whether it can fit a managerial model of rational decision-making:

Decision theorists have laid out the logic of rational choice with clarity and mathematical rigor for prototype decision problems. The decision-maker specifies alternative outcomes associated with different courses of action and then chooses that alternative that 'maximizes' his values, subject to whatever constraints the decision-maker faces. This involves two critical assumptions: first, that the decision-maker can specify alternative outcomes for each course of action; the second, that the decision-maker can assign to each outcome a 'utility' measure that integrates his values and allows comparisons among alternative outcomes. . . .

From the perspective of rational choice, the judge would wish to compare the expected utility for the child of living with his mother with that of living with his father. The judge would need considerable information and predictive ability to do this. The judge would also need some source for the values to measure utility for the child. All three are problematic.

a. The need for information: specifying possible outcomes
One can question how often, if ever, any judge will have the necessary information. In many instances, a judge lacks adequate information about even the most rudimentary aspects of a child's life with his parents and has still less information available about what either parent plans in the future. . . .

b. Predictions assessing the probability of alternative outcomes
Obviously, more than one outcome is possible for each course of judicial action, so the judge must assess the probability of various outcomes and evaluate the seriousness of possible benefits and harms associated with each. But even where a judge has substantial information about the child's past home life and the present alternatives, present-day knowledge about human behaviour provides no basis for the kind of individualized predictions required by the best-interests standard. There are numerous competing theories of human behavior, based on radically different conceptions of the nature of man, and no consensus exists that any one is correct. No theory at all is considered widely capable of generating reliable predictions about the psychological and behavioral consequences of alternative dispositions for a particular child.

While psychiatrists and psychoanalysts have at times been enthusiastic in claiming for themselves the largest possible role in custody proceedings, many have conceded that their theories provide no reliable guide for predictions about what is likely to happen to a particular child. Anna Freud, who has devoted her life to the study of the child and who plainly believes that theory can be a useful guide to treatment, has warned: 'In spite of . . . advances there remain factors which make clinical foresight, i.e. prediction, difficult and hazardous,' not the least of which is that 'environmental happenings in a child's life will always remain unpredictable since they are not governed by any known laws. . . .' (1958) . . .

c. Values to inform choice: assigning utilities to various outcomes
Even if the various outcomes could be specified and their probability estimated, a fundamental problem would remain unsolved. What set of values should a judge use to determine what is in a child's best interests? If a decision-maker must assign some measure of utility to each possible outcome, how is utility to be determined? . . .

Moreover, whether or not the judge looks to the child for some guidance, there remains the question whether best interests should be viewed from a long-term or a short-term perspective. The conditions that make a person happy at age 7 to 10 may have adverse consequences at age 30. Should the judge ask himself what decision will make the child happiest in the next year? Or at 30? Or at 70? Should the judge decide by thinking about what decision the child as an adult looking back would have wanted made? In this case, the preference problem is formidable, for how is the judge to compare 'happiness' at one age with 'happiness' at another age?

Deciding what is best for a child poses a question no less ultimate than the purposes and values of life itself. Should the judge be primarily concerned with the child's happiness? Or with the child's spiritual and religious training? Should the judge be concerned with the economic 'productivity' of the child when he grows up? Are the primary values of life in warm, inter-personal relationships, or in discipline and self-sacrifice? Is stability and security for a child more desirable than intellectual stimulation? These questions could be elaborated endlessly. And yet, where is the judge to look for the set of values that should inform the choice of what is best for the child? Normally, the custody statutes do not themselves give content or relative weights to the pertinent values. And if the judge looks to society at large, he finds neither a clear consensus as to the best child rearing strategies nor an appropriate hierarchy of ultimate values.

2 Maternal preference or status quo?

(a) THE ARGUMENTS

It should be clear from the previous section that judges and magistrates who determine custody are supposed, in theory, to consider all the circumstances in the particular case before them and be guided by no other vision than the ultimate welfare of the child. It is equally clear that judges, when questioned, will say that this is what they do (Dodds, 1981). In practice, however, faced with the uncertainties surrounding any attempt to discover where the child's true interests lie, judges may well be tempted to fall back on 'rules of thumb.' There is little doubt that a study of reported decisions will find judges falling back on the comforting proposition that 'mother is best' more often than not (even if it is as cautiously expressed as in *Re W* (1982), p. 348, above), and sometimes in circumstances where the decision seems hard to justify (Maidment, 1981). But although those decisions of the appellate courts which find their way into journals such as *Family Law* or *Current Law* may have some influence upon the behaviour of lower courts, at least in setting a trend, they are by no means a representative sample and can be highly misleading. Nevertheless, there are underlying factors which may well tempt judges in favour of maternal custody, some of which appear in this extract from an American study of *Child Custody Awards: Legal Standards and Empirical Patterns for Child, Custody, Support and Visitation after Divorce* (1979), by Lenore J. Weitzman and Ruth B. Dixon:

'The English tradition was that the father was the natural guardian of the children and controlled their education and religious training.' He had the primary right to his children's services and, in return, he was liable for their support and maintenance. It is therefore not surprising to find that if the parents separated, the father of a legitimate child, not the mother, had the right to and responsibility for child custody. As Blackstone stated the common law rule, the father had a natural right to the custody of his children, while the mother was not entitled to have any power over them; she was entitled only to their reverence and respect.

In the widely cited case of *R v De Manneville* (1804) 5 East 221, for example, Lord Ellenborough ordered a nursing infant returned to its French father, even though the man's cruelty had driven the mother and children from his home, because the father was 'entitled by law to custody of his child.'

'The common law preference for the father was secure,' as Foster and Freed note, 'as long as Feudalism flourished, but it disintegrated with the advent of the industrial revolution' (1978). As fathers moved off the farm into wage labor in factories and offices, women's maternal instincts were 'discovered,' and mothers became increasingly associated with child care. In 1839 the English Parliament modified the fathers' absolute right to custody by granting the mother the right to be awarded custody of children who were less than seven years old[1]. Thus, the 'tender years' presumption in favor of the mother was introduced into law.

'An absolute rule of paternal preference does not appear to have been generally applied in nineteenth century America' according to Professor Mnookin, 'and in many jurisdictions the courts were authorized to award custody to either parent as part of a divorce proceeding' (1975). American courts were more likely to look at the circumstances and facts of the particular case and to rely on fault as evidence of parental unfitness. Since social convention customarily led to the wife's filing for and being awarded the divorce as the innocent party, and since the fault-based custody standard assumed that children would be best taken care of by the innocent party, the courts' reliance on fault as evidence of parental unfitness was more likely to result in a larger proportion of maternal custody awards.

The twentieth century brought the establishment of a new legal presumption that *expressly* preferred mothers as the custodians of their children after divorce, particularly if the children were young. This new 'legal tradition' was established primarily through case law, rather than black letter law, for while most statutes continued to put the wife on an equal footing with the husband, and instructed the courts to award custody in the best interest of the child, the judiciary typically held that it was in the child's best interests not to be separated from the mother unless the mother was shown to be unfit.

---

1. In fact, this was a right to *apply* for custody, which the court might still refuse.

Thus the statutory standards of 'the child's best interest' and 'parental fitness' evolved into a judicially constructed presumption that the love and nurturance of a fit mother was always in the child's and society's best interest. The result was a consistent pattern of decisions which both justified and further reinforced the maternal presumption. For example, as one 1942 decision stated, the preference for the mother is 'not open to question, and indeed *it is universally recognized that the mother is the natural custodian of her young.* This view proceeds on the well known fact that *there is no satisfactory* substitute for a mother's love' (*Washburn v Washburn*, 49 Cal App 2d 581, 588, 122 P 2d 96, 100).

Eventually, the belief that the mother was the natural and proper custodian of her children became so widely assumed that it was rarely questioned and even more rarely challenged. As Roth recently observed, the rare rationales that were offered for the maternal preference had the ring of divine right theory (1976–77). For example, an Idaho court concluded that the preference for the mother 'needs no argument to support it because *it arises out of the very nature and instincts of motherhood; nature has ordained it'* (*Krieger v Krieger*, 59 Idaho 301, 81 P 2d 1081, 1083, 1938). Similarly, a 1958 New Jersey decision referred to the preference as the result of an 'inexorable natural force' (*Wojnarowicz v Wojnarowicz*, 48 NJ Super, 349, 353, 137 A 2d 618, 260), and a 1972 Maryland decision as a 'primordial' maternal tie (*Kirstukas v Kirstukas*, 14 Md App 190, 286, A 2d 535, 538).

In recent years some courts' justification for the maternal presumption seems to have shifted from the laws of nature to 'the wisdom of the ages,' as a 1973 appellate court phrased it (*Commonwealth ex rel. Lucas v Kreischer*, 450 Pa 352, 299, A 2d 243, 245). Along the same lines, a 1975 Utah decision affirmed the presumption in favor of the mother because it was grounded in the wisdom inherent in traditional patterns of thought (*Cox v Cox*, 532 P 2d 994, 996).

The wisdom of the maternal presumption was also supported by psychologists and child development specialists who emphasized the unique relationship between an infant and its mother. These professionals asserted that 'young children needed a mother in order to develop optimally' and that women were uniquely suited, biologically and psychologically, for the task of rearing children. The social science dogma was that men and women were 'biologically destined to play not only different but mutually exclusive roles as parents; that an inherent nurturing ability disposes women to be more interested in and able to care for children than are men; and that for their well-being, children need mothers in a way that they do not need fathers' (Levine, 1976).

For example, the noted psychologist, Dr Bruno Bettelheim (1956), cautioned against the unnaturalness of fathers raising children — even in cooperation with the mother:

'Male physiology and that part of his psychology based on it are not geared to infant care . . . infant care and child-rearing, unlike choice of work, are not activities in which who should do what can be decided independently of physiology. . . . The relationship between father and child never was and cannot now be built principally around child-caring experiences. It is built around a man's function in society: moral, economic, political.'

Surprisingly, even when the social science evidence which supported the maternal presumption was challenged, the presumption itself was considered wise because it avoided the 'social costs' of contested cases. In addition, even in recent years, when the passage of state Equal Rights Amendments would seem to require the elimination of the maternal preference doctrine, case law has continued to uphold it. Thus the judicially constructed preference appears to have operated as effectively as a statutory directive in upholding the mother's right to the post-divorce custody of her children.

The point about psychologists and child development specialists is particularly important. Judges profess to be sceptical of the evidence which they may give in custody cases: 'In the case of a happy and normal infant in no need of medical care and attention for any malady or condition who is sent to a psychiatrist or other medical practitioner for the sole purpose of calling the practitioner to give quite general evidence on the dangers of taking this, that or the other course . . . such evidence may be valuable if accepted but it can only be as an element to support the general knowledge and experience of the judge in infancy matters . . .' (Lord Upjohn in *J v C* [1970] AC 668, [1969] 1 All ER 788 discussed later in Chapter 13). Indeed, judges have frequently said that children must not be taken by one parent to see such practitioners without the consent of the other parent or the leave of the court (*Re S (An Infant)* [1967] 1 All ER 202, [1967] 1 WLR 396). Nevertheless, Michael King (1981) argues that it is not surprising that judges faced with difficult and emotionally charged decisions about children 'should search around for help both in making those decisions and in justifying them after they have been made. No more is it surprising that they should seek to give their decisions an aura of scientific respectability by making it appear that those whose advice they have accepted are indeed experts, and that the quality of their expertise is equated with that of a doctor over physical health or a scientist who makes discoveries and so advances our knowledge about the physical world.' Furthermore, judges seek to put into effect the values which they believe acceptable in society: 'Not so long ago, the judiciary perceived these social values as being based upon Christian morality. Today, however, given the decline of the Church and the growth of pluralism, the only universally accepted truths . . . appear to be those manufactured by scientists.'

It is therefore worth taking a brief look at some of the theories about child development which have both informed public opinion and formed the basis of much of the 'medical evidence' such as that given in *Re C (MA) (An Infant)* [1966] 1 All ER 838, [1966] 1 WLR 646, which is extensively quoted in the previous chapter (pp. 322–323, above). Prime amongst these was the work of John Bowlby, whose popular book *Child Care and the Growth of Love* was first published in 1953. The gist of his theory is stated at the outset:

> . . . What is believed to be essential for mental health is that an infant and young child should experience a warm, intimate, and continuous relationship with his mother (or permanent mother-substitute — one person who steadily 'mothers' him) in which both find satisfaction and enjoyment. It is this complex, rich and rewarding relationship with the mother in the early years, varied in countless ways by relations with the father and with the brothers and sisters, that child psychiatrists and many others now believe to underlie the development of character and of mental health.
>
> A state of affairs in which a child does not have this relationship is termed 'maternal deprivation'. This is a general term covering a number of different situations. Thus, a child is deprived even though living at home if his mother (or permanent mother-substitute) is unable to give him the loving care small children need. Again a child is deprived if for any reason he is removed from his mother's care. . . .
>
> The ill-effects of deprivation vary with its degree. Partial deprivation brings in its train anxiety, excessive need for love, powerful feelings of revenge, and, arising from these last, guilt and depression. A young child, still immature in mind and body, cannot cope with all these emotions and drives. The ways in which he responds to those disturbances of his inner life may in the end bring about nervous disorders and instability of character. . . .

Bowlby goes on to explain why the discussion in the book concentrates upon the mother and does not deal in detail with the father:

> The reason for this is that almost all the evidence concerns the child's relation to his mother, which is without doubt in ordinary circumstances by far his most important relationship during these years. It is she who feeds and cleans him, keeps him warm and comforts him. It is to his mother that he turns when in distress. In the young child's eyes father plays second fiddle and his value increases only as the child becomes more able to stand alone. Nevertheless, as the illegitimate child knows, fathers have their uses even in infancy. Not only do they provide for their wives to enable them to devote themselves unrestrictedly to the care of the infant and toddler, but, by providing love and companionship, they support the mother emotionally and help her maintain that harmonious contented mood in the atmosphere of which her infant thrives.

Question

It is noticeable that this paragraph is phrased, not in terms of how things necessarily *should* be, but of how they in fact are: do you think that his estimate of the respective roles of mother and father in caring for very young children generally holds good today?

It is scarcely surprising that those who do not accept the roles described should have attacked Bowlby's theories, although it is more surprising that his empirical base should have proved so vulnerable (Morgan, 1975). In *Maternal Deprivation Reassessed* (1972), Michael Rutter examines the components of the theory in the light of current research and concludes that various modifications are required. In particular:

A further point of departure from Bowlby's views concerns the supposedly special importance of the mother. He has argued that the child is innately monotropic and that the bond with the mother (or mother-surrogate) is different in kind from the bonds developed with others. The evidence on that point is unsatisfactory but what there is seems not to support that view. Two issues are involved. The first is whether or not the main bond differs from all others. It is suggested here that it does not. The chief bond is especially important because of its greater strength, but most children develop bonds with several people and it appears likely that these bonds are basically similar. The second concerns the assumption that the 'mother' or 'mother-surrogate' is the person to whom the child is necessarily most attached. Of course in most families the mother has most to do with the young child and as a consequence she is usually the person with whom the strongest bond is formed. But it should be appreciated that the chief bond need not be with the chief caretaker and it need not be with a female.

Furthermore, it seems to be incorrect to regard the person with whom there is the main bond as necessarily and generally the most important person in the child's life. That person will be most important for some things but not for others. For some aspects of development the same-sexed parent seems to have a special role, for some the person who plays and talks most with the child and for others the person who feeds the child. The father, the mother, brothers and sisters, friends, school-teachers and others all have an impact on development, but their influence and importance differs for different aspects of development. A less exclusive focus on the mother is required. Children also have fathers!

It is not, and could not be, our purpose to evaluate these competing views, but rather to demonstrate the influence which such views may have upon the development of the law. This is particularly so where a lawyer, a psycho-analyst and a psychiatrist collaborate in an attempt to use 'psychoanalytic theory to develop generally applicable guidelines to child placement.' That theory 'establishes, for example, as do developmental studies by students of other orientations, the need of every child for unbroken continuity of affectionate and stimulating experiences with an adult.' Thus in their influential book *Beyond the Best Interests of the Child* (1973), Joseph Goldstein, Anna Freud and Albert J. Solnit develop three basic concepts. The first is that of the relationship between a 'psychological parent' and a 'wanted child' whom they later define as follows:

A wanted child is one who receives affection and nourishment on a continuing basis from at least one adult and who feels that he or she is and continues to be valued by those who take care of him or her.

A psychological parent is one who, on a continuing, day-to-day basis, through interaction, companionship, interplay, and mutuality, fulfills the child's psychological needs for a parent, as well as the child's physical needs. The psychological parent may be a biological . . ., adoptive, foster, or common law . . . parent, or any other person. There is no presumption in favor of any of these after the initial assignment at birth. . . .

Secondly, they stress the need for continuity in this relationship:

Continuity of relationships, surroundings, and environmental influence are essential for a child's normal development. Since they do not play the same role in later life, their importance is often underrated by the adult world.

Physical, emotional, intellectual, social, and moral growth does not happen without causing the child inevitable internal difficulties. The instability of all mental processes during the period of development needs to be offset by stability and uninterrupted support from external sources. Smooth growth is arrested or disrupted when upheavals and changes in the external world are added to the internal ones.

Disruptions of continuity have different consequences for different ages:

In *infancy*, from birth to approximately 18 months, any change in routine leads to food refusals, digestive upsets, sleeping difficulties, and crying. Such reactions occur even if the infant's care is divided merely between mother and baby-sitter. They are all the more massive where the infant's day is divided between home and day care center; or where infants are displaced from the mother to an institution; from institutional to foster care; or from fostering to adoption. Every step of this kind inevitably brings with it changes in the ways the infant is handled, fed, put to bed, and comforted. Such moves from the familiar to the unfamiliar cause discomfort, distress, and delays in the infant's orientation and adaptation within his surroundings.

Change of the caretaking person for *infants and toddlers* further affects the course of their emotional development. Their attachments, at these ages, are as thoroughly upset by separations as they are effectively promoted by the constant, uninterrupted presence and attention of a familiar adult. When infants and young children find themselves abandoned by the parent, they not only suffer separation distress and anxiety but also setbacks in the quality of their next attachments, which will be less trustful. Where continuity of such relationships is interrupted more than once, as happens due to multiple placements in the early years, the children's emotional attachments become increasingly shallow and indiscriminate. They tend to grow up as persons who lack warmth in their contacts with fellow beings.

For *young children* under the age of 5 years, every disruption of continuity also affects those achievements which are rooted and develop in the intimate interchange with a stable parent figure, who is in the process of becoming the psychological parent. The more recently the achievement has been acquired, the easier it is for the child to lose it. Examples of this are cleanliness and speech. After separation from the familiar mother, young children are known to have breakdowns in toilet training and to lose or lessen their ability to communicate verbally.

For *school-age children*, the breaks in their relationships with their psychological parents affect above all those achievements which are based on identification with the parents' demands, prohibitions, and social ideals. Such identifications develop only where attachments are stable and tend to be abandoned by the child if he feels abandoned by the adults in question. Thus, where children are made to wander from one environment to another, they may cease to identify with any set of substitute parents. Resentment toward the adults who have disappointed them in the past makes them adopt the attitude of not caring for anybody; or of making the new parent the scapegoat for the shortcomings of the former one. In any case, multiple placement at these ages puts many children beyond the reach of educational influence, and becomes the direct cause of behavior which the schools experience as disrupting and the courts label as dissocial, delinquent, or even criminal.

With *adolescents*, the superficial observation of their behavior may convey the idea that what they desire is discontinuation of parental relationships rather than their preservation and stability. Nevertheless, this impression is misleading in this simple form. It is true that their revolt against any parental authority is normal developmentally since it is the adolescent's way toward establishing his own independent adult identity. But for a successful outcome it is important that the breaks and disruptions of attachment should come exclusively from his side and not be imposed on him by any form of abandonment or rejection on the psychological parents' part.

Adults who as children suffered from disruptions of continuity may themselves, in 'identifying' with their many 'parents,' treat their children as they themselves were treated — continuing a cycle costly for both a new generation of children as well as for society itself.

Thus, continuity is a guideline because emotional attachments are tenuous and vulnerable in early life and need stability of external arrangements for their development.

Thirdly, they discuss the child's sense of time:

A child's sense of time, as an integral part of the continuity concept, requires independent consideration. That interval of separation between parent and child which would constitute a break in continuity for an infant, for example, would be of no or little significance to a school-age youngster. The time it takes to break an old or to form a new attachment will depend upon the different meanings time has for children at each stage of their development.

Unlike adults, who have learned to anticipate the future and thus to manage delay, children have a built-in time sense based on the urgency of their instinctual and emotional needs. As an infant's memory begins to incorporate the way in which parents satisfy wishes and needs, as well as the experience of the reappearance of parents after their disappearance, a child gradually develops the capacity to delay gratification and to anticipate and plan for the future.

Emotionally and intellectually an infant and toddler cannot stretch his waiting more than a few days without feeling overwhelmed by the absence of parents. He cannot take care of himself physically, and his emotional and intellectual memory is not sufficiently matured to enable him to use thinking to hold on to the parent he has lost. During such an absence for the child under two years of age, the new adult who cares for the child's physical needs is latched onto 'quickly' as the potential psychological parent. The replacement, however ideal, may not be able to heal completely, without emotional scarring, the injury sustained by the loss.

For most children under the age of five years, an absence of parents for more than two months is equally beyond comprehension. For the younger school-age child, an absence of six months or more may be similarly experienced. More than one year of being without parents and without evidence that there are parental concerns and expectations is not likely to be understood by the older school-aged child and will carry with it the detrimental implications of the breaches in continuity we have already described. After adolescence is fully launched an individual's sense of time closely approaches that of most adults.

Finally, they point to the limits of the law's ability to supervise personal relationships and of knowledge to predict long-range outcomes:

While the law may claim to establish relationships, it can in fact do little more than give them recognition and provide an opportunity for them to develop. The law, so far as specific individual relationships are concerned, is a relatively crude instrument. It may be able to destroy human relationships; but it does not have the power to compel them to develop. It neither has the sensitivity nor the resources to maintain or supervise the ongoing day-to-day happenings between parent and child — and these are essential to meeting ever-changing demands and needs. Nor does it have the capacity to predict future events and needs, . . . [However] placement decisions can be based on certain generally applicable and useful predictions. We can, for example, identify who, among *presently available adults*, is or has the capacity to become a psychological parent and thus will enable a child to feel wanted. We can predict that the adult most likely suited for this role is the one, if there be one, with whom the child has already had and continues to have an affectionate bond rather than one of otherwise equal potential who is not yet in a primary relationship with the child. Further, we can predict that the younger the child and the more extended the period of uncertainty or separation, the more detrimental it will be to the child's well-being and the more urgent it becomes even without perfect knowledge to place the child permanently.

Beyond these, our capacity to predict is limited.

These concepts lead the authors to propose the following guidelines for all child placement decisions:

As an overall guideline for child placement we propose, instead of the 'in-the-best-interests-of-the-child' standard, 'the least detrimental available alternative for safeguarding the child's growth and development.' The new standard has as its major components the three guidelines which we have already described. The least detrimental alternative, then, is that specific placement and procedure for placement which maximizes, in accord with the child's sense of time and on the basis of short-term predictions given the limitations of knowledge, his or her opportunity for being wanted and for maintaining on a continuous basis a relationship with at least one adult who is or will become his psychological parent.

However, the reasoning behind this proposal also reveals how unhelpful it is in the normal custody dispute between parents:

To use 'detrimental' rather than 'best interest' should enable legislatures, courts, and child care agencies to acknowledge and respond to the inherent detriments in any procedure for child placement as well as in each child placement decision itself. It should serve to remind decision-makers that their task is to salvage as much as possible out of an unsatisfactory situation. It should reduce the likelihood of their becoming enmeshed in the hope and magic associated with 'best,' which often mistakenly leads them into believing that they have greater power for doing 'good' than 'bad'.

The concept of 'available alternatives' should press into focus how limited is the capacity of decisionmakers to make valid predictions and how limited are the choices generally open to them for helping a child in trouble. If the choice, as it may often be in separation and divorce proceedings, is between two psychological parents and if each parent is equally suitable in terms of the child's most immediate predictable developmental needs, the least detrimental standard would dictate a quick, final, and unconditional disposition to either of the competing parents.

It is difficult not to sympathise with the comment of Mnookin (1975):

I believe that psychologists and psychiatrists can rather consistently differentiate between a situation where an adult and a child have a substantial relationship of the sort we characterize as parent-child and that where there is no such relationship at all. But I do not think that existing psychological theories provide the basis to choose generally between two adults where the child has some relationship and psychological attachment to each. . . .

Often each parent will have a different sort of relationship with the child, with the child attached to each. One may be warm, easy-going, but incapable of discipline. The other may be fair, able to set limits, but unable to express affection. By what criteria is an expert to decide which is less detrimental? Moreover, even the proponents of psychological standards have acknowledged how problematic it is to evaluate relationships from a psychological perspective unless a highly trained person spends a considerable amount of time observing the parent and child interact or talking to the child. Superficial examinations by those without substantial training may be worse than nothing. And yet, that is surely a high risk. . . .

While the psychologists and psychiatrists have made substantial therapeutic contributions, they are not soothsayers capable of predicting with any degree of confidence how a child is likely to benefit from alternative placements. When the expert does express a preference, it too often is based on an unexpressed value preference. What is psychologically least detrimental will usually be no more determinate for expert and nonexpert alike than what is in a child's best interests; and to reframe the question in a way that invites predictions based on the use of labels and terminology developed for treatment is both demeaning to the expert and corrupting for the judicial process.

Questions

(i) Goldstein, Freud and Solnit's footnote to the last passage quoted from their book suggests that 'a judicially supervised drawing of lots between two equally acceptable psychological parents might be the most rational and least offensive process for resolving the hard choice.' Do you agree?

(ii) Might your view on question (i) be affected by the clear evidence from empirical studies that contested custody cases take much longer to reach final settlement?

(b) WHAT DO COURTS DO?

All the material above suggests that two 'rules of thumb' will weigh with the judiciary: a preference, in most cases, for maternal care, but a reluctance to disturb established ties. Two published studies of divorce court records in this country set out to discover what in fact usually happens to children whose parents divorce. In the 'Keele study', Susan Maidment analysed the records of one in five of all undefended divorce petitions involving children under 18 which were filed in a single north Midlands county court during 1973, a sample of 95 cases (*A Study in Child Custody* (1976)). The 'Oxford study' examined the records of decrees nisi involving children under 18 during 1974, one in twenty from each of nine provincial county courts in England and Wales, one in fifty from the principal divorce registry in London (a total sample of 652 cases), and one in thirty of all such cases in Scotland in 1975 (a sample of 203). Eekelaar has also studied 122 questionnaires returned by divorce court welfare officers relating to cases with which they were concerned during 1978 to 1980 (*Children in Divorce: Some Further Data* (1982)). All three studies covered both contested and uncontested cases. The extracts below come from the Oxford study, by John Eekelaar and Eric Clive, with Karen Clarke and Susan Raikes, published as *Custody After Divorce* (1977):

The legal outcome of the whole sample would at first sight support the suggestion of maternal preference:

England and Wales   **Final outcome of custody issue**
Scotland

Outcome	England and Wales		Scotland	
	No.	%	No.	%
Custody to husband	47	7.2	18	8.9
Custody to wife	496	76.0	160	78.8
Joint custody	22	3.4	0	0.0
Custody divided[2]	26	4.0	3	1.5
Custody to third party	1	0.2	1	0.5
Child committed to care	2	0.4	0	0.0
No order[3]	58	8.8	21	10.3
Totals	652	100.0	203	100.0

But this should be compared with the situation of the children at the time when the proceedings started:

England and Wales   **With whom children resident at time of petition**

With whom resident		Uncontested cases		Contested cases		All cases	
		No.	%	No.	%	No.	%
Wife	No.	461	76.0	17	37.7	478	73.3
Husband	No.	55	9.1	12	26.7	67	10.3
Both parents	No.	35	5.8	8	17.7	43	6.6
Split between parents	No.	18	2.7	6	13.3	24	3.7
In care	No.	8	1.3	0	0.0	8	1.2
Other	No.	29	4.8	2	4.4	31	4.8
Don't know	No.	1	0.2	0	0.0	1	0.2
Total		607		45		652	

The outcome should also be compared with the proposals for the children's future which have, under the Matrimonial Causes Rules, to accompany the petition:

13.7 Proposals of the parties

The vast majority of petitioners/pursuers simply sought the court's approval for the continuation of the existing state of affairs. In England and Wales only 4.8% of petitioners and in Scotland only 2.5% of pursuers proposed any substantial change in the child's residence, and those cases generally contained some abnormal feature (e.g. the children were in care or with third parties). . . . Since children generally lived with their mother, this meant that petitioners/pursuers generally wished this to continue. Indeed, it was relatively rare for a husband to challenge the continued care for his children by the mother. In England and Wales husbands expressed an initial intention to apply for custody of children currently in their wife's care only in 10.3% of such cases, whereas in 34.3% of cases where the children were living with the husband, the wife expressed an initial intention to seek custody herself. However, in only a few of these cases was the challenge pressed to a contest in the court. . . . In Scotland . . . as well as England and Wales . . . the evidence showed a very strong tendency on the part of mothers to claim custody of children in contrast to the fathers.

Earlier, the authors comment:

3.6 . . . Wives are more tenacious than husbands in their attempts to obtain possession of the children. In most cases the husbands are content to leave to the wife the task of bringing up the

---

2. Cases where the children were divided between different care-givers.
3. The legal effect of this is that mother and father retain equal parental rights but the authors comment that the court is unlikely deliberately to have chosen to make no order.

children. If they seek to do so themselves, they are far more likely to be challenged by the wife than is a wife who keeps the children. That the wife is seen as prima facie the proper person to have care of the children therefore appears as a factor of community opinion which is shared by the parties themselves. However, the very low success rate of wives where they did challenge their husbands' possession of the children shows that the courts do not necessarily share that assumption, or, if they do, they have regard to other factors in making their decisions.

This last point becomes clearer when the outcome of the small proportion of cases in which custody was contested is discussed:

6.1 Thirty-nine cases (6.0% of the sample) were classified as being contested on the custody issue at hearing and 6 more contested on access only. However, it is possible that a further 9 were contested on the custody issue and a further 3 on access alone. But only the clearly contested cases are analyzed in this chapter.

6.3 Well over half the contested cases were adjourned on decree nisi. . . . In nearly half of those adjourned, a welfare report was ordered, but in just over a third no steps are recorded in the documents, probably because further negotiations took place between the parties. . . . In all, welfare reports were available in 53% of contested cases. Because the total numbers are so small it is not easy to deduce any factor especially associated with the ordering of welfare reports in these cases, other than, perhaps, that a report is more likely to be ordered if the child is resident with the husband . . ., and if it is proposed the child should move. . . . Perhaps this indicates that the courts will look more seriously at proposals that a child should move from the husband than that it should move from the wife.

6.4 Of the 39 custody contests, custody was awarded to the husband in 4 cases, to the wife in 17, to the parties jointly in 5, and the children were divided in 4 cases. In one, custody was awarded to the husband's sister and in 7 others no order was made. In 3 of the 5 joint awards, care and control was given to the wife and in the other two to the husband. But in only 5 cases did the child's residential status quo change. Since this happened in only 13 instances in the whole sample, it is clear that, where a child's residence is to change, it is likely to be in the context of a custody dispute. . . .

6.5 In only two of the five cases . . . did the court order itself bring about a change of residential status quo, and, although they were both in favour of the wife, one of them also re-united separated siblings. Although, therefore, our study provided evidence of a certain judicial caution about allowing husbands to look after children, apart from these two cases, the principle in favour of the status quo prevailed even when contested by the wife. There were seven such cases, involving, in all, 1 boy and 1 girl under 4, 3 boys aged 5–11, and 4 girls in the same age bracket, and 2 boys and a girl between 12 and 15. In 6 of them, however, the court acted on the advice of a welfare officer's report. Furthermore, in all 4 cases where the children were divided between the parents, the court was maintaining the residential status quo. . . . Yet it is notable that, in the only two cases where the status quo was changed, in one the judge ignored the recommendation of the welfare report and in the other there was no report. . . . A similar observation was made in the context of uncontested cases.

The authors conclude:

13.29 Another striking finding emerged in the examination of the contested cases. This is that the courts did not favour either sex as the most suitable custodian (although they displayed more caution when the husband was the custodian), nor did they appear to operate in accordance with presumptions relating to the age or sex of the children. Instead, they followed the principle advocated by Goldstein, Freud and Solnit . . . of minimum disruption to the child's existing emotional ties.

These findings are highly comparable with those in the Keele study: custody was contested in only 12 of the 95 cases and the outcome in every case confirmed the status quo: in two cases, the children stayed in local authority care; in five cases, the children stayed with their mother; and in five they stayed with their father. Indeed, in only one of these originally contested cases was custody clearly awarded against the final wishes of the other parent. Eekelaar's later study (1982) confirmed the finding that mothers are more likely than fathers to dispute the other's custody, but he also found that at least one child was moved in no less than seven out of the 31 cases in which custody was disputed. Three were moved from mother to father and four from father to mother. The welfare officer was in favour of this in three cases, against it in two, and undecided in two. However, 'although when the father's sole custody was challenged by the mother he was less likely to retain them than when he challenged the mother's sole custody, a father is nevertheless more likely to retain custody than to lose it. If he loses custody this will usually have the approval of the welfare officer.' Fathers who want their children and are prepared to fight, therefore, would appear, statistically at least, to have a reasonable chance of success. The reasons why fathers do not fight, however, are likely to vary. Some are suggested by Martin Richards in his discussion of *Post Divorce Arrangements for Children: A Psychological Perspective* (1982), to which we shall return in the next chapter:

Mother or father?

Though the law itself does not favour mothers or fathers as potential custodial parents, if all else is equal and, especially if the children are young ('of tender years'), the mother is more likely to be granted custody in a dispute. Not all would concur with this point, but I think the weight of the evidence from reported cases and the surveys support a principle of a presumption that custody should be vested in the mother. Of course, I am not suggesting that the courts are entirely responsible for the fact that only in a small percentage of cases does a father have custody of his children after a divorce. In most cases the father has not sought custody and does not challenge his wife's claim. The main reason for this situation is that the general assumptions that are held about the sexual division of labour within marriage are extended to the post-divorce situation. Within most marriages, the prime responsibility for childcare falls on women and so it is after the marriage ends. A small and probably increasing proportion of men would like to have the custody and care and control of their children. In many of these cases it seems that they are so certain that this will not be granted to them that they do not bother to raise the issue with their solicitors. One man I interviewed recently thought that it was 'against the law' for men to have custody 'especially if they had daughters.' (He, incidentally, was looking after his children on his own and had consulted a solicitor. Later, after he received some counselling, he asked for and got the custody and care and control of his children.) In turn, solicitors are unlikely to suggest to their male clients that they might seek custody (or joint custody). If the client does bring it up the common advice seems to be that it is not worthwhile to proceed unless their partners will agree to the proposal. So [in] almost all cases where a man does get custody, it is because the spouses have agreed to this, or because the wife has left the matrimonial home and has not maintained contact with the children.

In recent years arguments have arisen from several quarters that have questioned the appropriateness of the presupposition of maternal competence and have suggested that it is not in the best interests of the children or adults. I do not want to go over this ground again, except to remind you that about one in seven of all single-parent families are headed by men and that the best evidence we have of the progress of these children is that there is precious little to choose between those looked after by men and those looked after by women.

One further reason for the reluctance to fight is suggested by the climax to Berthold Brecht's play, *The Caucasian Chalk Circle*:

Azdak: Plaintiff and defendant! The Court has listened to your case, and has come to no decision as to who the real mother of this child is. I as Judge have the duty of choosing a mother for the child. I'll make a test. Shauva, get a piece of chalk and draw a circle on the floor. *Shauva does so*. Now place the child in the centre. *Shauva puts Michael, who smiles at Grusha, in the centre of the circle*. Stand near the circle, both of you. *The Governor's wife and Grusha step up to the circle*. Now each of you take the child by a hand. The true mother is she who has the strength to pull the child out of the circle, towards herself.

The second lawyer (quickly): High Court of Justice, I protest! I object that the fate of the great Abashvili estates, which are bound up with the child as the heir, should be made dependent on such a doubtful wrestling match. Moreover, my client does not command the same physical strength as this person, who is accustomed to physical work.

Azdak: She looks pretty well fed to me. Pull!
The Governor's wife pulls the child out of the circle to her side. Grusha has let it go and stands aghast.
The first lawyer (congratulating the Governor's wife): What did I say! The bonds of blood!
Azdak (to Grusha): What's the matter with you? You didn't pull!
Grusha: I didn't hold on to him. *She runs to Azdak.* Your Worship, I take back everything I said against you. I ask your forgiveness. If I could just keep him until he can speak properly. He knows only a few words.
Azdak: Don't influence the Court! I bet you know only twenty yourself. All right, I'll do the test once more, to make certain.
The two women take up positions again.
Azdak: Pull!
Again Grusha lets go of the child.
Grusha (in despair): I've brought him up! Am I to tear him to pieces? I can't do it!
Azdak (rising): And in this manner the Court has established the true mother. *To Grusha*: Take your child and be off with it.

Questions

(i) Consider instead the way in which the English courts handled the case of the little boy in *Re C (A Minor) (Custody of Child)* (1980) 2 FLR 163, p. 345, above: was it an improvement?
(ii) In what circumstances would you advise a father to fight for custody?

3 The role of the welfare officer

The court welfare officer so frequently referred to earlier in this chapter is a probation officer, but in some centres, officers do no other work. Its origins lie with the 'police court missionaries' of the late nineteenth century, to whom magistrates turned for help, not only in dealing with some of their offenders, but also in trying to reconcile the couples who brought their matrimonial troubles to court. These couples came from the poorer sections of the community who would have little chance of seeking a divorce, and the missionaries' emphasis on 'marriage saving' is understandable. We shall discuss reconciliation procedures generally in Chapter 17, but it is clear that this aspect of the work has declined dramatically in recent decades (Manchester and Whetton, 1974). One reason for this is the equally dramatic decline in magistrates' matrimonial work generally. There is no long-standing tradition of 'marriage saving' in the divorce courts. In 1947, the Report of the Denning Committee on Procedure in Matrimonial Causes recommended that welfare officers should be appointed to give guidance to people contemplating divorce, but this was never implemented. A further recommendation, however, was that where the couple had dependent children, the court should have power, once the petition had been filed, to refer the case to a welfare officer for inquiry and report. The first welfare officer was attached to the Divorce Division for this purpose in 1950, and the practice was extended to other divorce towns in 1957. Magistrates were given power to call for reports in matrimonial cases in 1960, but had to wait until 1974 before they could do so in ordinary custody disputes. By then, the emphasis had clearly shifted from 'marriage saving' to 'child saving'. This was reinforced in 1958, when divorce courts were given power to order that the children be supervised. All courts exercising custody jurisdiction now have this power, but supervision may be carried out in some places by the local social services authority instead. Social services authorities may also be asked to prepare the reports for magistrates' courts, but not for divorce courts.

The Oxford study of *Custody After Divorce* (Eekelaar et al., 1977) found that welfare officers' reports were available in 53% of contested and 8.2% of uncontested cases (as to which we shall have more to say in the next section). The Keele figures were 50% for contested cases and 18% overall (Maidment, 1976), but it was difficult to be sure from the records alone how many cases had remained contested to the bitter end (cf. Eekelaar, 1982). Practice clearly varies in different parts of the country, but it appears rare for a case to reach the stage of a full-blown battle in court without a report being prepared. However, the other fact to emerge clearly from the Oxford study was the length of time from adjournment for a report until the case came back to court: in 45% of contested cases this took over six months. The responsibility for this delay does not lie in one quarter alone, but in the combination of the time taken to compile the report and the time then taken to get the case back into the lists for hearing. But it is scarcely surprising that in *Re C (A Minor) (Custody of Child)* (1980) 2 FLR 163 (p. 345, above) Ormrod LJ should question the value of adjourning for reports in such circumstances. It is also clear from cases such as *S v S (Custody of Children)* (1978) 1 FLR 143 (p. 343, above) that a judge is entitled to come to a different conclusion from the welfare officer. It has been said, however, that magistrates should not depart from a clear recommendation without making their reasons for doing so equally plain (*Re T (A Minor) (Welfare Report Recommendation)* (1977) 1 FLR 59).

It thus seems particularly important to try to discover what these reports are designed to achieve, and the best way of doing this is to study an example which has been used by probation officers themselves for training purposes. The characters are, of course, fictitious:

SPECIMEN WELFARE REPORT

BLANKSHIRE PROBATION & AFTER-CARE SERVICE

WOOD & WOOD

REPORT CONCERNING CUSTODY

Applicant:	Mrs Jean WOOD	— 22 years
Respondent:	Mr John WOOD	— 35 years
Child concerned:	Richard WOOD	— 5.5.77–3 years
Child:	Amanda FORBES	— 6 years
Respondent's co-habitee:	Janet SMITH	— 32 years
Children:	Mary SMITH	— 6 years
	Brian SMITH	— 5 years

1. ENQUIRIES:

I have read the Court file concerning this matter
I have had discussions with:
— the Applicant with Richard
— the Respondent and Co-habitee with Richard
— Richard by himself
I have had a telephone conversation with the Housing Department
I have had a telephone conversation with Dr Jones, the Respondent's Physician

2. BACKGROUND RELATING TO THE CHILD

I understand from both parties that initially their relationship was good though the Applicant claims the Respondent spent too much time with his mother. In March 1980 Mr Wood's father died and he invited his mother to live with him and his wife. The Applicant and her mother-in-law had never enjoyed a good relationship and there were immediate problems. Mrs Wood senior it is claimed assumed control of the family, gradually taking over responsibility for the housework and the care of both the Respondent and the child — Richard. There were constant quarrels and [in November 1980] following a violent disagreement, the Applicant left the matrimonial home on an impulse and stayed for a short period with a relative. Being without accommodation she did not feel it fair to Richard to take him with her at that time. Within three weeks she had found accommodation in a very small bedsitting room sharing a kitchen and bathroom with a family of five people; again a situation she felt unsuitable for Richard.

3. APPLICANT MOTHER

Mrs Jean WOOD — Mrs Wood, a full time housewife, impressed as a bright, outgoing young woman who is obviously deeply attached to her son. She told me she had found the situation in the former matrimonial home quite intolerable from the time her mother-in-law moved in. She claimed Mrs Wood senior had undermined her discipline of Richard and had tried to cause difficulties between her and the Respondent. She said that her reason for staying had been the fear that she might lose Richard and that she left only when she felt she could no longer cope with the situation. I understand that Richard's behaviour was untypically bad from the time she left home causing the Respondent to contact the family doctor. I am told the child's behaviour returned to normal once access was established [in December 1980]. Mrs Wood visits Richard twice weekly at the former matrimonial home. The Respondent has been quite adamant that he will not allow her to take the child away from the home. Until very recently, there were no difficulties concerning access. The Applicant feels, however, that the atmosphere has become tense since the Respondent's co-habitee moved into the home [in February 1980] [whereupon the grandmother left].

4. Of her own relationship with her co-habitee — Mr Forbes, the Applicant tells me she had known him some years ago and met him again soon after leaving her husband. She has lived with Mr Forbes since the beginning of January 1981 and has already formed an excellent relationship with his daughter — Amanda [who lives with them]. The Applicant and Mr Forbes plan to marry as soon as both are free to do so.

5. The Applicant Mother feels very strongly that she is the appropriate person to have the day to day care of Richard. She feels he has already been subjected to too many changes and that she can now offer him the stability he needs. She has made tentative enquiries concerning a play-school for Richard, but if granted custody would delay any decision until he was completely settled in his new home. Mrs Wood appears to fully appreciate the importance of the child having regular access with the Father and would have no objection to reasonable access which she suggests could be staying access on alternate weekends.

6. APPLICANT'S CO-HABITEE

Mr Michael FORBES — Mr Forbes presented as a pleasant, mature personality. He told me he had married very young, that his wife had had difficulty in managing on a low income and the resulting debts had caused difficulties between them. He told me that his wife left him 2 years ago and he has not heard from her since. He has made enquiries concerning her whereabouts as he is anxious now to petition for divorce. Mr Forbes has had the care of his daughter since his wife left and has coped admirably with the help of a neighbour. He is employed as a clerk and his salary is £60 per week. He tells me that because of the demands made on him in caring for his daughter, he has not been able to take advantage of promotion. However, now that the Applicant is caring for his daughter Amanda, he feels his employment prospects are excellent. Because the Respondent has refused to allow Richard to leave the home with his mother, Mr Forbes has not met the child. He is realistic about the possible difficulties should the Applicant be awarded custody but feels his experience with his own child will help.

7. APPLICANT'S HOME

The home is a 2-bedroomed flat which is adequately furnished and well kept. Mr Forbes expects to move to a 3-bedroomed maisonette in the near future having negotiated an exchange with another family. I have contacted the Housing Department who confirm that there are no objections to this transfer.

8. RESPONDENT

Mr John WOOD — Mr Wood is a quiet, introspective man. He tells me he was the youngest son in a large family. He has always enjoyed a very close relationship with his mother who did not approve of his relationship with the Applicant. Mr Wood tells me that his wife coped well with the home and the child until his mother moved in with them. He claims that the Applicant then became lazy and lost interest in the home, leaving everything to the grandmother. The Respondent is employed as a Sales Manager and his take-home pay is approximately £600 a month. In the course of his work he travels extensively, often away overnight and sometimes travels abroad. His co-habitee — Mrs Smith — has lived with him since mid January 1981 and although he has not known her for very long, the relationship appears to be sound and based on mutual interests. The Respondent told me that Richard has caused him some anxiety since Mrs Smith arrived and the grandmother left the home. He has again consulted the family doctor but feels that if a firm line is taken with Richard, he will quickly adapt to the new situation. The Respondent tells me that he is asking for custody of Richard as he does not wish to have another man involved in bringing up his son. He also feels he is in a better position to care for Richard's material needs than is the Applicant. He would have no objection to the present access arrangement being continued but would oppose staying access.

9. RESPONDENT'S CO-HABITEE

Mrs Janet SMITH — Mrs Smith is a quiet, intelligent woman who is studying for a degree with the Open University and would like a teaching career. She talked frankly about her own children saying that she was not very maternal and although she very much enjoys her children's monthly visits, she does not wish to see them more often. She expressed some reservations about bringing up Richard, especially with the Respondent being often away from home. She told me, however, that she is fond of Richard and is anxious to do whatever Mr Wood wishes.

10. RESPONDENT'S HOME

The home is a spacious, 4-bedroomed house where material standards are high. The property is owned by Mr Wood subject to a mortgage.

11. CHILD CONCERNED

Richard WOOD — Richard is a bright and lively child, obviously well cared for. I have seen him with the Applicant and also separately with the Respondent. When I saw Richard with the Respondent and Mrs Smith, he appeared to be anxious to do and say the right thing and was quieter and more subdued than when I interviewed him with the Applicant. With the Applicant, Richard was talkative and lively and very upset when the time came for her to leave. Although Richard is hardly 4, it appears that given the choice, he would wish to spend most of his time with his mother.

12. CONCLUSION

From my enquiries, it would appear that both parents care about Richard's welfare and either could offer him a good home. The Respondent is in a position to offer material advantages and wishes Richard to be privately educated. The Applicant Mother's means are more modest but the bond between mother and child is particularly close and the separation was of such short duration that it appears to have done no damage to the relationship. It has not been possible to see the Applicant's co-habitee with the child. On the other hand the child's relationship with the Respondent's co-habitee is not yet a close one. In fact, the child appears to be having some difficulty in relating to a third mother figure.

13. In view of the very close relationship between mother and child, it would appear to be in Richard's long-term best interests if legal custody was granted to the Mother.

14. Should this course of action be followed the Court may feel, in view of the Respondent's particular interest in Richard's education, that the parties should share joint responsibility for any major decision concerning Richard's education. It is clear that whichever parent has legal custody, Richard will experience problems in adjusting to the new step-parent. The Court may consider, therefore, that a short period of supervision would be of benefit to Richard in making this adjustment. In view of Richard's age, the Court may feel it appropriate for supervision to be undertaken by Social Services Department. However, during the enquiries a good working relationship has been established between the Welfare Officer, the parties, and more particularly Richard, which indicates that the Order may be more appropriately made to the Probation Service to allow continuity of contact.

February 1981   *Court Welfare Officer*

Questions

(i) If you were counsel for the mother in this case, what features of the report would you emphasise to the court?

(ii) If you were counsel for the father, would you advise him to settle the dispute along the lines suggested by the welfare officer?

(iii) If the father wished to fight the case, which features would you as counsel emphasise to the court?

(iv) As counsel for the father, how would you go about challenging the suggestion in para. 11 of the report that 'although Richard is hardly four, it appears that given the choice, he would wish to spend most of his time with his mother'?

(v) In *Re W* (1982), p. 348, above, the Court of Appeal was highly critical of a welfare officer who had not made it her business to observe the child and her relationships within each of the competing households: why are the welfare officer's observations of those relationships apparently as significant as the evidence given at the trial?

(vi) If you were the judge in the Wood case, and your impressions of the characters of the various people involved were broadly similar to those of the welfare officer, would you reach the same conclusion?

(vii) Why did the welfare officer reach 'conclusions' rather than make 'recommendations'?

In his study of divorcing parents, *Justice and Welfare in Divorce* (1980), to which we make several other references, Mervyn Murch makes several points about the role of welfare officers in contested cases:

Some claimed that their solicitors had told them that 'what the welfare officer says goes' and on the strength of this had been advised to settle out of court. Thus one father told us:
'The report was called for by both our solicitors before the custody. What they decided was rather than go to the expense of a custody hearing, get a welfare report and depending on its recommendations go from there. As a result of this I then dropped the case. That was the only reason I stopped the case.'
In another case a father, seeking the care of two school-age children, was not told the altered date of the court hearing by his solicitor. This is what he said happened:
'Well, he didn't even let me know. The next thing I knew was that I got a letter saying the children were to stay where they were with my former wife and I had joint custody. He [solicitor] told me later that even if I had been there I wouldn't have been able to do anything. It was all done on the welfare report and they do what the welfare man says. Apparently the two solicitors having seen the report had worked it all out together before the court. I was very annoyed about it I can tell you. The judge went on the written evidence and the welfare report. Whether this is usual I don't know. According to my solicitor it was. They don't necessarily interrogate the parties concerned.'
If this man's account is correct the practice of the solicitors concerned was grossly improper since the father had every right to be heard.
It is not possible to say how widespread is the practice of settling on the basis of the welfare officer's report. No doubt sometimes when it occurs it is perfectly acceptable to the parties. Yet, as in the two instances quoted above, there are occasions when the practice leaves at least one parent with an unsavoury taste of having been denied open justice. Injustice may be aggravated in other ways. First, the parents may be denied opportunity to see what was in the welfare officer's report. Secondly, they may not be present at the court hearing or present when solicitors reach settlement on their behalf. Thirdly, they may be deprived of the chance to cross-examine the welfare officer about the evidence because the officer in question did not attend court. Fourthly, delays may occur and things may have changed since the welfare officer wrote the report.

Nearly two-thirds of the 84 parents whom Murch had contacted through divorce court welfare officers had not been shown a copy of the report, and fewer than a quarter had been shown it by their solicitors. One reason may be that, although the Matrimonial Causes Rules 1977 provide that parents may see the reports, the actual document is stamped 'confidential.' The confusion should be cleared up by a recent *Practice Direction* [1982] 1 All ER 512, which provides:

The President has directed that the following wording should appear on all reports prepared by the court welfare officer at the Royal Courts of Justice:
    'It is a contempt of court, punishable by fine and/or imprisonment, to show or reveal the contents of this report to any person who is not either a party to the proceedings or the legal adviser to such a party. In addition, you may be liable for damages for libel or slander on the publication of its contents.'

R L BAYNE-POWELL
Senior Registrar

8 February 1982

Questions

(i) Do you think that welfare officers will be deterred from writing what they really think by the knowledge that the objects of their enquiry may see what they have written?

(ii) If your answer to question (i) is 'yes,' is that a good or a bad thing?

(iii) Even if it is a bad thing, can there be any justification for refusing to let parents see it if they wish to do so?

In a later chapter, Murch (1980) discusses the nature of the welfare officer's task. As to the primary reporting function, he comments thus upon the perception that 'what the welfare officer says goes':

Yet evidence suggests that at least where the care of children is disputed, it is rare for the courts to alter the existing status quo whether or not there is a welfare report. Of the 27 disputed custody cases studied by the Oxford research in which welfare reports were sought, only 2 involved a child changing residence as a result of the court's decision. In one of these the judge ignored the welfare officer's recommendation. Similarly, of the 24 custody disputed cases in the Bristol court welfare sample there was only one in which the court ordered that the care be changed. There were four others where change of care occurred but only as a result of a settlement between the parents (which may in part have been due to the welfare officer's intervention).

Nevertheless, he found that most parents accepted the need for an independent check upon the evidence, particularly in contested cases. A further suggestion (made, for example, in the Practice Direction appearing on p. 352, above) is that the welfare officer can assume the role of advocate for the child:

Cases are sometimes adjourned for welfare reports because the judge wants someone to interview the children informally in the familiar surroundings of their own home. It is not possible to tell how often this happens. When a judge asks for a welfare report the welfare officer is not usually present, and the judge's reason is not normally recorded. Even so, welfare officers nearly always do see the children, often individually without the parents being present.
    The evidence from this research suggests that most parents give a qualified approval to this practice. My impression is that parents realise it is a delicate and complex task and many of them view it apprehensively. The question that concerns them is not whether it should be done, but rather how it is done. I suspect that this holds good for the children too. In 1974 I conducted a small pilot interviewing programme with 15 children of divorced parents, all over the age of 8. Most indicated that they wouldn't mind being interviewed by a welfare officer provided it was someone they trusted, who would respect their feelings. The dangers of doing otherwise are obvious. For example, to ask children directly which parent they wish to live with (as evidently sometimes happens) may force children to commit themselves to one parent and be disloyal to the other. One 11 year-old girl who had experienced just such a question remarked:
    'I don't think they should ask you *which* parent you want to live with. They should just go round it. After all you love both parents, don't you?'

Yet for a welfare officer to dodge the issue which parent the child would be happiest to live with, when everyone concerned knows it is in question, can be seen by parents and children alike as unrealistic evasion. For my own part, I think this particular question can be safely approached once the officer has established trust with both the parents and the children, and has shown that he wishes to participate in the task of working out *with* them what is best for the children. But when insufficient time has been devoted to establishing the family's initial trust an interview with the children can create great anxiety.

A third possible role is conciliation, of which we have much more to say in the final chapter, but which means in this context 'exploring the common ground between the parties,' so that their dispute may be settled by agreement rather than adjudication:

A few parents had expectations that the welfare officer would attempt conciliation. In about a quarter of the sample the officer had evidently offered to do so. When it was attempted with the approval and consent of the parents, a number of successes were reported — sometimes much to the surprise of the parents concerned. Although it was not possible to say exactly how many times informal conciliation was attempted, it seemed to be more acceptable, and perhaps feasible, in disputes about access than where the care of children was in question. Even so, one of the cases in which conciliation seemed to have been most successful led to a child moving from one parent to the other. In some ways one could say that in the majority of cases an element of conciliation seemed to creep in, even though it may not have been specifically recognised as such by either the officer or the parents.

Where a welfare officer is used to further conciliation, *i.e.* to help the parents and children deal realistically with the consequences of the broken marriage, there is a strong case for earlier intervention. Three-quarters of the parents spoken to urged this, and not just because they felt their cases had been delayed by the welfare enquiry. They often took a more positive view. Because they had experienced the officer as helpful, they would have appreciated his influence in the case at a time when they may well have been facing greater difficulties and uncertainties. The Finer Committee endorsed the view expressed in both the Denning Report and in the report of the Royal Commission on Marriage and Divorce in 1956 that early referral to a conciliation agency was likely to increase the chances of a successful outcome, while long drawn-out conflicts often encourage parties to take up entrenched positions from which negotiated settlement of disputed matters becomes progressively more difficult. The evidence from this research suggests that the vast majority of parents would strongly agree.

Questions

(i) Eekelaar (1982) found that welfare officers almost invariably consulted the views of children once they had reached seven and that over a quarter of those aged five and six were also consulted: how many of these might have preferred a private chat with the judge who was to decide their future rather than to wait what might be many months for a sensitive discussion with a professional welfare officer?
(ii) Eekelaar also found that welfare officers saw themselves as 'making a significant contribution to the resolution of family conflict and thereby advancing the interests of children': do you see any dangers in their combining the roles of fact-gatherer for the court and mediator between the parties?

Murch also identifies other functions performed by the welfare officer, in addition to the formal reporting role, as 'cathartic listening,' 'family support,' and 'welfare rights advice.' All of these may also be relevant in uncontested cases, to which we now turn.

4 The court's role in uncontested cases

The central finding of the Oxford study (1977) was 'that the divorce process itself leaves the position of all but a fraction of children of divorce totally untouched.' In the vast majority of cases, the court ratifies the existing arrangements made by the parties. Why then are the courts involved at all? The reasons are explained in the *Report of the Royal Commission on Marriage and Divorce* (the Morton Report, 1956):

366. We received much evidence from our witnesses (many of whom held widely differing views on other topics) that the present procedure is not such as to ensure that in every instance the most suitable arrangements are being made for the future of the children. Concern was expressed on the following points in particular:
   (i) The court does not deal with the position of the children where no application is made for custody. It cannot be assumed that parents, influenced by strong feelings arising from divorce, are always likely to make the best arrangements for the children. There is at present no guarantee in such cases that the arrangements for the children have been maturely considered.
   (ii) Where an application for custody is unopposed it may be assumed that the court will grant the application. In the absence of any evidence to the contrary, it is indeed difficult to see on what grounds refusal could be justified. Yet the parent making the application may not always be the more suitable to have custody. There may, for instance, have been an understanding between husband and wife that if one of them will release the other by getting a divorce, the latter will allow the successful party to have the children. . . .
367. A large number of our witnesses, though not all of those who criticised the present arrangements, considered that the root of the trouble lay in the fact that there is at present no adequate means of ensuring that someone is specially charged to look after the children's interests. The solution which received most support was that the responsibility should be placed clearly upon the court, which should consider the arrangements for the children in every case, whether the question of custody was raised by either or both parties or not. The court could, however, effectively discharge this duty only if it had all relevant information about each case. That information, it was said, would be forthcoming only if the court always had before it an independent report about the circumstances of the home in which it was proposed that the children should live and any relevant information about the past and proposed future arrangements. A number of witnesses considered that to be effective such a system of reporting would require the setting-up of a service of court welfare officers, consisting of trained social workers, throughout the country. . . .
371. It is, however, important to keep the following considerations in mind. Whatever arrangements are devised for dealing with questions of custody of children, the decision must always be ultimately limited by the fact that the parents have separated and are living in separate establishments. The question in almost all cases is that of deciding which of the parents is to be responsible for the child's upbringing, and in which home the child is to live. However unsatisfactory some homes may appear to be, it is generally accepted that such conditions can often co-exist with strong ties of affection between parent and child. The alternative to leaving the child in the charge of the parent would be to try to find a suitable relative or friend who is willing to undertake the care of the child or, failing that, that the local authority should receive the child into care; and it is obvious that conditions would have to be really bad before one of these courses could be justified. Moreover, we consider that in the great majority of cases parents are the best judges of their children's welfare. Where they are agreed upon the arrangements for the children, very strong evidence indeed would be required to justify setting aside their proposals.
372. After a very careful examination of all aspects of the problem of children in divorce proceedings we have come to the conclusion that what is needed is a procedure which, firstly, will ensure that the parents themselves have given full consideration to the question of their children's future welfare, and secondly, will enable the control of the court over the welfare of the children to be made more effective. We think that these two aims are most likely to be achieved by a statutory provision that a divorce cannot be obtained until the court is satisfied as to the welfare of the children, and we are recommending accordingly. It will be seen that by 'divorce' we mean the decree absolute and not the decree nisi. We have considered whether it would be feasible to make the granting of a decree nisi dependent on suitable arrangements having been made for the children, but we have satisfied ourselves that such a requirement would be administratively impracticable, chiefly because of difficulties necessarily arising from the existence of the circuit system. . . .
376. We consider that the procedure which we propose would have the merit of ensuring that in every divorce case the interests of the children would be an issue before the court and that that issue would be recognised as one which is just as important as the question of divorce. In our view, the recognition of this principle was the underlying aim of the proposals put forward by our witnesses. Not only, however, would the issue of the children's welfare be before the court.

The fact that a divorce would not be obtained until there was a satisfactory solution of that issue would bring about a further positive and beneficial result. If the interests of the children were thus placed in the forefront the parents themselves would, we believe, be led increasingly to recognise their responsibility towards their children, and to appreciate that the fact of divorce, far from diminishing that responsibility, makes it all the more important that they should strive to make the best arrangements which they can devise for the children in the new situation created by the dissolution of the marriage.

377. It is this latter consideration — the desirability of bringing home to the parties to the divorce suit their continuing parental responsibility — that has primarily led us to reject the suggestion that investigation should be carried out by a court welfare officer in every case. If this were done, we foresee certain dangers. If a report were always to be required the procedure might in time deteriorate into a perfunctory and routine formality. The impression might be created in the minds of some parents that the decision about the future of their children was largely being taken out of their hands and that their views counted for less than the court welfare officer's report. Their sense of parental responsibility would be diminished, not strengthened. Where the parents were genuinely concerned to do the best for their children (and we believe the majority are) investigation by officials might only cause resentment and frustration, and would be counter to what is most desirable, namely, that the parents should themselves be encouraged to fulfil their responsibilities.

Questions

(i) Murch comments that 'It seems to me that the Royal Commission was here worried about the response of middle class parents . . . there is little doubt that such official intervention in family life would have offended their middle class values of privacy and freedom from state interference. . . . Yet once you take the view that all children from broken homes are potentially at risk the logical conclusion is that the court should investigate every case or find some other means to determine who are at risk.' Do you think that there should be an investigation in every case?

(ii) If your answer to question (i) is 'yes,' can you explain why this should be done in divorce cases, but not, for example, when cohabiting parents separate or when one parent dies?

(iii) If nevertheless you accept the case for some kind of check, is there any longer any good reason why it should not be done *before* the decree nisi? (The so-called 'special procedure' is described in Chapter 5.)

The present version of the duty recommended by the Royal Commission is contained in s. 41 of the *Matrimonial Causes Act 1973*:

41.—(1) The Court shall not make absolute a decree of divorce or of nullity of marriage, or grant a decree of judicial separation, unless the court, by order, has declared that it is satisfied —

(a) that for the purposes of this section there are no children of the family to whom this section applies; or

(b) that the only children who are or may be children of the family to whom this section applies are the children named in the order and that —

(i) arrangements for the welfare of every child so named have been made and are satisfactory or are the best that can be devised in the circumstances; or

(ii) it is impracticable for the party or parties appearing before the court to make any such arrangements; or

(c) that there are circumstances making it desirable that the decree should be made absolute or should be granted, as the case may be, without delay notwithstanding that there are or may be children of the family to whom this section applies and that the court is unable to make a declaration in accordance with paragraph (b) above.

(2) The court shall not make an order declaring that it is satisfied as mentioned in subsection 1(c) above unless it has obtained a satisfactory undertaking from either or both of the parties to bring the question of the arrangements for the children named in the order before the court within a specified time.

(3) If the court makes absolute a decree of divorce or of nullity of marriage, or grants a decree of judicial separation, without having made an order under subsection (1) above the decree shall be void but, if such an order was made, no person shall be entitled to challenge the validity of the decree on the ground that the conditions prescribed by subsections (1) and (2) above were not fulfilled.

(4) If the court refuses to make an order under subsection (1) above in any proceedings for divorce, nullity of marriage or judicial separation, it shall, on an application by either party to the proceedings, make an order declaring that it is not satisfied as mentioned in that subsection.

(5) This section applies to the following children of the family, that is to say —

(*a*) any minor child of the family who at the date of the order under subsection (1) above is —

(i) under the age of sixteen, or

(ii) receiving instruction at an educational establishment or undergoing training for a trade, profession or vocation, whether or not he is also in gainful employment; and

(*b*) any other child of the family to whom the court by an order under that subsection directs that this section shall apply;

and the court may give such a direction if it is of opinion that there are special circumstances which make it desirable in the interest of the child that this section should apply to him.

(6) In this section 'welfare', in relation to a child, includes the custody and education of the child and financial provision for him.

The petitioner is therefore required to file a statement of the arrangements proposed for such children, at the same time as filing the petition. Originally, these arrangements would be discussed during the divorce hearing itself, in the course of a series of leading questions between petitioner and her counsel (similar to the example given of an American uncontested divorce hearing on p. 176, above). An early study of the working of the procedure (Hall, 1968) reached the conclusion that 'perhaps the greatest weakness of the present procedure is that it sometimes gives the impression of superficiality.' While recognising the practical problems, some improvements in the system were suggested: most notably, perhaps, that hearings should take place in private, and in undefended divorces *before* the hearing of the divorce itself. The introduction of the special procedure and the withdrawal of legal aid from divorce hearings (see further in Chapter 5) gave the opportunity to transform the occasion from a formal question and answer session between counsel and client into a more informal discussion between parent and judge, although this still usually takes place on or after the day when the decree is formally granted. Even so, Murch (1980) expressed some doubts as to the propriety of this:

The children appointment has become another part of what seems to be evolving into an essentially inquisitorial system which enables the court itself to seek the facts. Further evidence for this proposition can be found in increased use of the court welfare service itself and in the burgeoning of a number of different schemes set up by local registrars to test the adequacy of information filed with the petition. In some courts, special questionnaires are now sent to divorcing couples before the judicial appointment to augment the information contained in the petition, the statement of arrangements and in the prayer for relief. Other courts are experimenting with the greater use of pre-trial directions hearings. All these measures amount to an inquisitorial approach, the purpose of which is to collect, scrutinise and test the information coming into the court machinery. The introduction of the special procedure has provided the opportunity for such developments . . .

Under the special procedure if judges are to engage in informal discussions of child welfare matters with parents there is a very real risk that some at least will find it difficult to restrain themselves from expressing, justifying and even imposing with the weight of judicial authority their own subjective value judgments. This problem may be compounded by the private nature of the encounter, particularly in the case of unrepresented parents, so that apart from court staff nobody else may know what goes on. All kinds of hobby-horses may be ridden by judges with absolutely no check.

Inquisitorial measures allowing wide measures of judicial discretion, if combined with a preventive child welfare approach, could make a powerful authoritarian paternalistic force, posing a real threat to the rights and liberties of ordinary citizens and their families. The problem arises because of the lack of accountability of both welfare and judicial authorities. One of the advantages of our traditional legalistic judicial attitude is that judges are likely to want to check and curb any misuse or abuse of welfare powers. Yet it can be argued that under the special procedure the judges themselves have effectively become welfare authorities . . .

Not only are judges sometimes performing a preventive child welfare task in their private appointments with divorcing parents, in some cases welfare officers are coming near to assuming a judicial role since there are courts that almost invariably follow their recommendations. In part this role confusion has been caused by the advent of the divorce court welfare service. . . .

Another problem is that of determining the point at which judicial inquisition should finish and standard adversarial procedures begin. Take for example a case where a judge has been actively enquiring at the children's appointment into the way a child is being provided for, and difficulties subsequently arise over custody or access. If that judge has already expressed opinions to one party about the child's circumstances and future welfare, can either parent be assured that the judge will remain impartial? Of course, there was risk of this even before the introduction of the special procedure, but it may be aggravated now that everything is heard in private and most parents are unrepresented. Even if that objection can be met, some judges may still have a problem in changing role from investigator to traditional adjudicator. Unless a wholescale revolution in modes of trial in family law is to be undertaken, some confusion and uncertainty is bound to arise from efforts to combine two such fundamentally different methods of adjudication. The time may have come to stop tinkering with the system and to think out the conduct of family litigation afresh. Ad hoc development of procedural law merely risks perpetuating ambiguity and uncertainty of purpose.

In my view, a firm distinction between adjudication and welfare must be maintained, and the responsibilities of judge and welfare officer clearly delineated.

Question

In this context, is it a cause for concern that the round figures of children in local authority care as a result of orders made under the Matrimonial Causes Act 1973 rose from 2,900 in 1977 to 4,200 in 1980?

Studies of how judges conduct children's appointments, by Davis, Macleod and Murch in Bristol (1981) and by Dodds in Manchester (1983), do not reveal rampant interventionism by the judges, but they do suggest other causes for concern. Dodds observed a total of nine judges conducting 402 appointments and his findings are highly comparable with those of the larger Bristol study. He reports them in *Children and Divorce* (1983):

. . . The first thing that was evident from the observed hearings was how little evidence most judges heard before granting satisfaction and the very limited number of reasons that prompted them not to do so. Most hearings were very short. Five of the nine judges took between four and five minutes on average while the other four took between six and eight minutes on average. . . .

In the majority of cases the time allowed for the hearing did not permit much to be said beyond the details that were already in the petition and the statement of arrangements. . . . In reality these forms provide little information. . . . However, the worst failing of the documentary evidence is that the statement of arrangements requires parents to describe 'proposed arrangements,' that is, what is going to happen to the children in a rather uncertain future. . . .

This makes what the parents say in the hearing all the more important. Unfortunately over 36% of parents did not attend, nearly 87% of them husbands, usually the non-custodial parent. . . . In only 28% of the hearings did the judge have the opportunity of hearing from both parties. In one court both parents were encouraged to come with the result that in 55% of cases both husband and wife were present. In the other three courts this was not done. Only the petitioner or the parent with custody was obliged to appear. . . .

The atmosphere of the hearings could be very formal. All the judges except two interviewed the parents in an empty court room as opposed to the judge's chambers. In many of the cases the judges were robed and four judges almost invariably required parents to swear the oath in the witness box. . . . The hearings in the judge's own room were much more relaxed. . . .

. . . There was a good deal of difference in the questions asked by individual judges. What was important to one judge was not inquired into by another and vice versa. One judge worried about the sleeping arrangements for the children but another asked few questions about this but was far more concerned with how the children got on with any person the custodial parent was living with. A third rarely asked about either subject but asked many more parents than his two fellow judges about whether there were friends or relatives nearby to help out if the custodial parent needed it. . . .

Some questions were asked frequently by all nine judges. These concerned frequency of access; whether the non-custodial parent maintained the children; where the custodial parent lived and who owned that accommodation; whether the custodial parent was having a relationship with any one; and whether the custodial parent was employed. Such questions checked what should have been in the documentary evidence already and often added little more in the way of evidence (the Bristol survey found that 31% of the parents they interviewed had negative feelings about the judges' questioning). These questions were also concerned more with the material and physical circumstances of the children.

Nevertheless, 76% of the judges who answered Dodds' questionnaire agreed that 'in most satisfaction cases a judge obtains all the information he wants in order to make a decision' and 77% agreed that 'a judge can usually spot when something is amiss in a case so that he can refer that case for a welfare report or supervision order.' Satisfaction was expressed without more ado in 91% of the cases, and welfare reports were ordered in only 4.9% (but nearly half of these by one judge). Only three supervision orders and five care orders were made in the total of 402 cases, and in the latter all the children were already in voluntary care. Most of the judges did think that the system was working well, but some critical comments were offered:

'Unless the other parent is present it is only the the judge's intuition that can detect if things are amiss — and that is an uncertain quality. It is only the honest, unintelligent or hapless parent who by her evidence or attitude leads one to suspect that all is not well and therefore to probe further. Generally this is the person who either needs advice and support at a much earlier stage than a satisfaction hearing.'

Another judge said that satisfaction hearings served little purpose. The sanction of withholding the decree absolute was in most cases 'derisory'. A third also criticised the idea of pretending that a divorce was dependent upon arrangements being made for the children when:

'(1) The decree is always made absolute eventually even if the parents take no steps to help their children; (2) the withholding of a divorce to parents is no comfort for an unhappy child; (3) the judge offers no help to the greater number of children whose parents do not seek a divorce.'

A further judge complained that he was being asked to do an impossible task. Unless every marriage was supervised until the children grow up, 'satisfaction' will be largely a matter of 'guess work and instinct'. A number of judges did not like being asked to act as social workers. The system was described as no more than a 'fig leaf' devised without real thought. A different judge added that what was satisfactory one day may not be in three weeks' time. Once a divorce had been obtained the courts had little control.

The Oxford study (Eekelaar et al., 1977), having noted that English courts were far more likely to seek further information than were the Scottish, commented:

13.23 . . .What is striking, however, is that despite this fairly marked contrast between the English and Scottish practice, the final outcome of these cases is the same in both jurisdictions. This is because it was so rare for courts in either jurisdiction to make an order which altered the child's residence. This was done in only 4 of the 607 uncontested cases in England and Wales (0.6%) and in one in Scotland. In three more of the uncontested English cases the child's residence was changed from where it was when the petition was filed, but this was by agreement between the parties, which the court accepted.

13.25 In uncontested cases, therefore, it is not clear what the courts achieve in practice by attempting to exercise the supervisory function. A 'satisfaction' report by a welfare officer, when sought, may indeed more fully inform the judge of the situation, but it is very unlikely to lead him to make an order which alters the existing situation. One obvious reason for this is the limited range of alternatives open to a judge. Even assuming the conditions in which the child is living are not very satisfactory, it would seldom be practicable or even sensible to transfer the child to the other parent (who may not want the child). If the proper solution lies in committing the child to the care of a local welfare authority, it is arguable that the jurisdiction to do this already exists under the child welfare law and that it is by no means clear that it is appropriate to move a child from his home environment under the divorce jurisdiction in circumstances where the requirements for such removal under child welfare law are not met.

13.26 In raising these questions about the exercise of the courts' supervisory jurisdiction in custody cases, we are not to be understood as opposing the policy that the children's interests are of vital concern in divorce proceedings. We are, however, concerned whether our social resources are employed to the best advantage under the existing procedure. There is evidence that one-parent families brought about by separation or divorce face greater financial hardship than other categories of single parent family and that they use the social services more. But those who require assistance do not in fact receive it because 'it would seem that the official services are not wholly geared to providing assistance to the one-parent family in dealing with the kinds of problems presented by the absence of the father or the mother.' Many such families were unaware of the services of which they had need. There would seem to be a case for the view that the needs of the children in families recently broken down through divorce would be better met by improving the awareness of the custodian parent of the available resources than by compiling reports to judges which rarely influence his actions.

13.27 . . . We think that it may be useful if consideration was given to devising a method whereby all adult parties to a divorce action who are caring for children be automatically advised, through the post (or by a clerk at the court), of the welfare rights available to single parent families. Further, it might be considered whether a screening mechanism could be devised which would identify those families to which a visit from a member of the welfare services would be advisable. The purpose of the visit would not be the compilation of a report for the use of the judge, but to see that the family is receiving proper social assistance and whether any further intervention is necessary in the children's interests.

Murch's interviews with parents involved led him to the following conclusions (1980):

This research has clearly demonstrated that most divorcing parents, when questioned, replied that they thought it right that the court should investigate their children's circumstances and those of other divorcees. But it has also shown that they were glad to have had the opportunity to discuss their various difficulties and plans for the future. They did not object to intervention save in a few cases. What was important was the style and manner in which it was done. What they clearly wanted was an open, even-handed approach which defined the limits of the welfare officer's intervention and did not infringe their basic legal rights if things went wrong. They valued most those welfare officers who helped the family as a whole adapt to the consequences of marriage breakdown. This was so whether the officer merely provided a sympathetic neutral ear or mediated when matters such as custody or access were in dispute. The divorce court welfare officer and the system he represents may be understood as facilitating the family's reorganisation. The weight of this research evidence suggests that this point should be acknowledged as the welfare officer's primary task. Such a task would seek to meet the main social and emotional needs of the families concerned and would be in line with much informal court welfare practice, if the testimony of the parents interviewed is to be believed. It also accords with the social casework of 'starting where the clients are' by considering their interests first. By contrast, as Platt (1969) and others have argued, the preventive child-welfare approach has at its root the need to protect community interest whether this be by preventing delinquency or other forms of deviant behaviour considered to disrupt the workings of society. One of the problems of paternalism claiming to act in other people's best interests is that it may arouse suspicion that it is not what it seems. Instead, other interests, including those of the practitioner, may be given preference. The mistrust and alienation that this may lead to may contribute to the very problems the preventive approach seeks to forestall. On the other hand, a participant approach to divorce court welfare practice, aimed at getting alongside families and working *with* them as they reorganise themselves after divorce would not only have more specific and realistically obtainable goals, it would help avoid the risk of consumer alienation and mistrust that sadly seems to have become a consequence of some of the most well-intentioned preventive social work. Paradoxically, this might well prove the correct way to be efficiently preventive.

Question

From the evidence and arguments presented here, which of the following would you favour: (a) more extensive monitoring, for example by a social worker visiting all children of divorce, as happens in Northern Ireland; (b) procedural improvements in the present system, for example by increasing the amount of information required by the court; (c) abolishing the 'satisfaction' system, but offering practical social work help to all who want it; (d) using the welfare officers' skills to help divorcing parents reach agreement with one another and come to terms with their changing lives?

CHAPTER 11

Family reorganisation: custodial and non-custodial parents and step-parents

For the great majority of children whose parents separate or divorce the vital question is not where and with whom they will live. It is, rather, how their parents will resolve what Murch (1980) has called the 'fundamental dilemma facing divorcing parents. This is how to disengage from the broken marriage while preserving a sense of being a parent with a part to play in the children's future. . . . Parenthood normally assumes a coalition between spouses. . . . These adjustments take time. They often proceed by painful trial and error before the family as a whole and its individual members can discover an acceptable equilibrium.' The law expects them to act in accordance with the best interests of their children, yet legal and expert and lay opinion remains divided about what sort of arrangements will be best. The basic choice at the time of separation or divorce is between a complete break with the past, some form of shared responsibility and control, or the most usual arrangement, which is full custody to one party with reasonable access to the other. We shall look first at the law governing this choice, then at the arguments about what is most in accordance with the children's needs, and conclude with the further adjustments needed should the custodial parent find a new partner. These include questions about whether or not step-parents of children who have lost a parent through death, divorce or illegitimacy should be allowed to adopt, and whether remarried custodial parents should be able to emigrate or change their children's surnames. Underlying it all is the problem of the balance to be struck between respect for the family of origin and respect for the family of nurture, questions which are also raised in the chapters on Illegitimacy and on Fostering and Adoption.

1 The law: custody, joint custody and access

(a) CUSTODY AND JOINT CUSTODY

The powers of the divorce courts have survived virtually unchanged through successive Matrimonial Causes Acts. They are contained at present in s. 42 of the *Matrimonial Causes Act 1973*:

Orders for custody and education of children in cases of divorce, etc., and for custody in cases of neglect
42.—(1) The court may make such order as it thinks fit for the custody and education of any child of the family who is under the age of eighteen —
    (*a*) in any proceedings for divorce, nullity of marriage or judicial separation, before or on granting a decree or at any time thereafter (whether, in the case of a decree of divorce or

nullity of marriage, before or after the decree is made absolute);

(b) where any such proceedings are dismissed after the beginning of the trial, either forthwith or within a reasonable period after the dismissal;

and in any case in which the court has power by virtue of this subsection to make an order in respect of a child it may instead, if it thinks fit, direct that proper proceedings be taken for making the child a ward of court.

(2) Where the court makes an order under section 27 above [see p. 96, above], the court shall also have power to make such order as it thinks fit with respect to the custody of any child of the family who is for the time being under the age of eighteen; but the power conferred by this subsection and any order made in exercise of that power shall have effect only as respects any period when an order is in force under that section and the child is under that age.

(3) Where the court grants or makes absolute a decree of divorce or grants a decree of judicial separation, it may include in the decree a declaration that either party to the marriage in question is unfit to have the custody of the children of the family.

(4) Where a decree of divorce or of judicial separation contains such a declaration as is mentioned in subsection (3) above, then, if the party to whom the declaration relates is a parent of any child of the family, that party shall not, on the death of the other parent, be entitled as of right to the custody or the guardianship of that child.

(5) Where an order in respect of a child is made under this section, the order shall not affect the rights over or with respect to the child of any person, other than a party to the marriage in question, unless the child is the child of one or both of the parties to that marriage and that person was a party to the proceedings on the application for an order under this section.

(6) The power of the court under subsection (1)(a) or (2) above to make an order with respect to a child shall be exercisable from time to time; and where the court makes an order under subsection (1)(b) above with respect to a child it may from time to time until that child attains the age of eighteen make a further order with respect to his custody and education.

(7) The court shall have power to vary or discharge an order made under this section or to suspend any provision thereof temporarily and to revive the operation of any provision so suspended.

Section 52(1) provides that 'custody', in relation to a child, includes access to the child. A difficult question, however, is what other parental powers and responsibilities may be included. Some discussion of the confusing array of terminology took place in the following case:

Hewer v Bryant
[1970] 1 QB 357, [1969] 3 All ER 578, [1969] 3 WLR 425, 113 Sol Jo 525, Court of Appeal

The point at issue was whether a 15-year-old boy who had been injured while working as an agricultural trainee was in the 'custody' of a parent for the purposes of the Limitation Act 1939 (for if he was, limitation would run from the date of the injury and not from the date of majority). In the course of holding that the boy was *not* in his father's custody for this purpose, the Court of Appeal reviewed the history of the term in other contexts:

Sachs LJ: . . . It is essential to note that amongst the various meanings of the word 'custody' there are two in common use in relation to infants which are relevant that need to be carefully distinguished. One is wide — the word being used in practice as almost the equivalent of guardianship; the other is limited and refers to the power physically to control the infant's movements. In its limited meaning it has that connotation of an ability to restrict the liberty of the person concerned to which Donaldson J referred in *Duncan's* case [1968] 1 QB 747 at 763. This power of physical control over an infant by a father *in his own right* qua guardian by nature and the similar power of a guardian of an infant's person by testamentary disposition was and is recognised at common law; but that strict power (which may be termed his 'personal power') in practice ceases on their reaching the years of discretion. When that age is reached habeas corpus will not normally issue against the wishes of the infant. Although children are thought to have matured far less quickly — compared with today — in the era when the common law first developed, that age of discretion which limits the father's *practical* authority (see the discussion and judgment in *R v Howes* (1860) 3 E & E 332) was originally fixed at 14 for boys and 16 for girls (cf., per Lindley LJ in *Thomasset v Thomasset* [1894] P 295 at 298).

This strict personal power of a parent or guardian physically to control infants, which is one part of the rights conferred by custody in its wider meaning, is something different to that power over an infant's liberty up to the age of 21 which has come to be exercised by the courts 'on behalf of the Crown as Parens Patriae', to use the phraseology at p. 68 of *A Century of Family Law* in the contribution by P. H. Pettitt, 'Parental Control and Guardianship.' It is true that in the second half of last century that power was so unquestioningly used in aid of the wishes of a father that it was referred to as if its resultant exercise was a right of the father. Indeed in the superbly Victorian judgments in *Re Agar-Ellis, Agar-Ellis v Lascelles* (1883) 24 Ch D 317 [p. 575, below], it seems thus to be treated: for the purpose, however, of the present issues it is sufficient to observe that if those judgments are to be interpreted as stating as a fact that fathers in practice personally had in 1883 strict and enforceable power physically to control their sons up to the age of 21, then — as Lord Denning MR has already indicated — they assert a state of affairs that simply does not obtain today. In truth any powers exercised by way of physical control in the later years of infancy were not the father's personal powers but the more extensive ones of the Crown (compare Lindley LJ, in *Thomasset v Thomasset* [1894] P 295 at 299), and hence the father's right was really no more than that of applying to the courts for the aid he required as guardian. The reason for emphasising the word *power* appears later in this judgment.

Similarly that personal power of a parent needs to be distinguished from those which may be conferred on him by courts exercising their jurisdiction under the Matrimonial Causes Acts.

In its wider meaning the word 'custody' is used as if it were almost the equivalent of 'guardianship' in the fullest sense — whether the guardianship is by nature, by nurture, by testamentary disposition, or by order of a court. (I use the words 'fullest sense' because guardianship may be limited to give control only over the person or only over the administration of the assets of an infant.) Adapting the convenient phraseology of counsel, such guardianship embraces a 'bundle of rights', or to be more exact, a 'bundle of powers', which continue until a male infant attains 21, or a female infant marries. These include power to control education, the choice of religion, and the administration of the infant's property. They include entitlement to veto the issue of a passport and to withhold consent to marriage. They include, also, both the personal power physically to control the infant until the years of discretion and the right (originally only if some property was concerned) to apply to the courts to exercise the powers of the Crown as parens patriae. It is thus clear that somewhat confusingly one of the powers conferred by custody in its wide meaning is custody in its limited meaning, i.e., such personal power of physical control as a parent or guardian may have.

The trouble is that whilst the legislature has distinguished between guardianship and custody, the courts have tended often to use the latter word as if it were substantially the equivalent of the former, thus leading to some confusion of thought. This confusion is abetted by the language of the Matrimonial Causes Acts and orders made under them. Whatever may have been the intention of the legislature when first using that word when in s. 35 of the Matrimonial Causes Act 1857 it referred to 'custody, maintenance, and education', the courts have come to give more than one meaning to it in orders. An unqualified order giving custody to a parent appears nowadays to be interpreted as having the wide meaning, but if at the same time 'care and control' is given to the other parent, then one of the powers, custody in the limited meaning of physical control, is taken out of 'custody' in the wide meaning. It would be a happier situation if by future legislation the courts were enabled to use the word 'guardianship' in orders in appropriate cases.

The practice of sharing or dividing 'custody' was developed in the days when the strong paternal preference had given way to a view that matrimonial guilt or innocence might determine the parents' claims. *Re A and B (Infants)* [1897] 1 Ch 786 was a simple custody dispute under the Guardianship of Infants Act 1886 between two equally 'guilty,' and probably equally unsatisfactory, parents: their children's time was divided equally between them, on condition that their governess went with them when they moved from one large household to the other. The divorce jurisdiction, however, was still based on the notion that one party was guilty and the other innocent (see further in Chapter 5). There may have been an aristocratic convention that husbands permitted themselves to be divorced by their wives, but an unimpeachable father who chose to do so could divorce his guilty wife and deny her even the right to see her children, until a new climate began to develop after the decision in *Mozley-Stark v Mozley-Stark and Hitchins* [1910] P 190. As divorce crept lower down the social scale, and domestic servants became less numerous, courts were driven to accept that an unimpeachable father might be unable to care for his very young children. An interim device, in which 'custody' was distinguished from 'care and control', was adopted. This is explained in the following case, which also discusses what should be done where both parents are thought 'unimpeachable.'

Jussa v Jussa
[1972] 2 All ER 600, [1972] 1 WLR 881, 136 JP 499, 116 Sol Jo 219, High Court, Family Division

The father, an Indian Moslem and a teacher by profession, married the mother, an English Christian, in 1964. They had three children, now aged nearly seven, five and two. The parents separated in 1971. In proceedings under the Guardianship of Minors Act 1971,[1] a magistrates' court granted custody to the wife, with reasonable access to the father. He appealed against the grant of sole custody to the mother, while admitting that she should have care and control.

Wrangham J: . . . . There is nothing in the circumstances of the parting which, in my view, should tell against either parent in the consideration of the matters in issue in these proceedings, and it is one of the happiest features of this case that each of the spouses admits freely and frankly that the other is an admirable parent. In her evidence the wife said that the children love their father and enjoy his visits. She made no suggestion against him as a father, but said that he took great care of them when he visited them. Equally, the husband had no word of criticism of the wife as a mother. It is therefore a case in which either party would be admirably qualified to look after the children, although it is conceded, in my view very rightly conceded, that the proper place for them now is with their mother. . . .

In these circumstances it becomes necessary to say something about the approach made by courts to the question of a split order, ie an order in which the responsibility for children is divided between spouses, either by a joint order for custody with care and control to one spouse, or, what must be the more normal form of split order, an order for custody to one spouse solely, with care and control to the other. The split order for separate custody is an order which appears to have been known for many years. There are references to its history in the decisions of the Court of Appeal in *Re W (JC) (An Infant)* [1964] Ch 202, [1963] 2 All ER 459 which was cited to us. The value of a split order of that kind was emphasised by Denning LJ in *Wakeham v Wakeham* [1954] 1 All ER 434 at 436 where he said:

'Cases often arise in the Divorce Court where a guilty wife deserts her husband and takes the children with her, but the father has no means of bringing them up himself. In such a situation the usual order is that the father, the innocent party, is given the custody of the child or children, but the care and control is left to the mother. That order is entirely realistic.'

It is plain that Denning LJ was attaching importance to the proposition that a wholly unimpeachable parent should not be cut out from having a voice in the future of his, or her, children.

The joint order for custody with care and control to one of the two parents is, perhaps, of rather more recent origin. When, in March 1964, an application was made to Karminski J (see *Clissold v Clissold* (1964) 108 Sol Jo 220) to sanction such a joint order for custody with care and control to the wife, he said that it was the first time that he had been asked to make such an order, and he was unwilling to do it on that occasion, first of all, because disputes might arise between the parents over questions relating to the child, in which case the matter would have to come back to the court, and, secondly, because it was, in his view, wholly inappropriate to the facts of that particular case. My own experience is that since 1964 the order which was then so exceptional has been made on many occasions, and I think it is not too much to say that the apprehensions expressed by Karminski J have not been fulfilled to their full extent. For my part, I recognise that a joint order for custody with care and control to one parent only is an order which should only be made where there is a reasonable prospect that the parties will co-operate. Where you have a case such as the present case, in which the father and the mother are both well qualified to give affection and wise guidance to the children for whom they are responsible, and where they appear to be of such calibre that they are likely to co-operate sensibly over the

---

1. As to the courts' present powers in such proceedings, see p. 383, below.

children for whom both of them feel such affection, where you have that kind of situation, it seems to me that there can be no real objection to an order for joint custody. Perhaps it is a little cynical (although it is the kind of cynicism which is difficult to avoid in this Division) to regard such a state of affairs as exceptional. It was regarded rather from that point of view, I think, by Cairns J in *S v S* (1965) 109 Sol Jo 289 decided about a year later than the case before Karminski J (*Clissold v Clissold*). There Cairns J said that he was satisfied that both parties had the welfare of their children at heart, and, in the exceptional circumstances, he would make the exceptional order asked for. But there was nothing apparently exceptional about that case, as reported, except for the fact that the children in question, two girls, were on good terms with both their parents, the bond of affection between the father and the younger girl being very close, and that both parents supported the proposal. In those circumstances, as it seems to me, it would be wrong to say that joint orders for custody should only be made in exceptional circumstances, unless by that is meant that the circumstances in which both parents can be expected to co-operate fully in making such an order work are themselves to be regarded as exceptional; and that, I hope, as I have said, is too pessimistic a conclusion. . . .

I now come to mention very shortly the actual arguments on the merits of the contention made by the husband that he should not be cut out altogether from a voice in his children's future; that he should be recognised still as their parent and their guardian. He is an unimpeachable parent. He has much, by reason of his career and training, to contribute to their welfare. And in this case there is perhaps an additional point to be made, that this was a mixed marriage between a man of Oriental origin and a woman of European origin. The children, therefore, have a mixed inheritance. For my part I would say this, that it is much in their interests to get the full value of that mixed inheritance. The husband can contribute to them something which no European could do; the wife can contribute something that no Oriental could do. I feel myself it would be a great advantage to them that they should retain the closest possible contact with their father while remaining, of course, in the care and control of their mother.

I am not so much impressed in this case as I might be in another with the argument that there must be somebody to decide, and that a multitude of counsels only brings complexity and difficulty. In my view, when one has two wholly unimpeachable parents of this character, who could, I think, be reasonably contemplated as capable of co-operating with each other in the interests of the children whom they both love, there can be no serious objection to an order for joint custody, and many advantages for the children from that order; and, of course, one comes back always to the point that it is the welfare of the children that is the paramount consideration.

The Court of Appeal has since gone further:

H v H

(1981) 11 June, (unreported) Court of Appeal

The father, an Englishman and a teacher by profession, married the mother, a Sikh, in 1969. They had one daughter, who was now aged seven and a half. They separated in 1979 and there was little contact between father and daughter until the father's application for custody and access was heard in late 1980. The judge awarded the parents joint custody, with care and control to the mother and reasonable access to the father. There were difficulties over access and the child did not want to see her father. The welfare officer thought that she was being affected by the feelings of the adults around her and that her father's influence and interest would be of greatest benefit to her when she approached the early-teen years. In May 1981, the judge continued the joint custody order, but made an agreed order that there should be no access by the father until further order or agreement between the parties; he also continued a supervision order. It was thus common ground that there should be no access at present, and the mother appealed against the joint custody order.

Waterhouse J: . . . The argument for the mother that was put before [the judge] was much the same as that put before us today and was, if I may say so, on conventional lines to the effect that the parties found it difficult to co-operate, and that, in particular, the mother did not wish to communicate with the father. On the other hand, on behalf of the father, the advantages to the child of continuing direct and informal links were stressed and emphasis was placed on the child's long term interests in the way that the welfare officer had explained them. . . .

It is, however, useful to cite what my Lord, Lord Justice Ormrod said in the case of *C v C* (1980) 17 April (unreported):

> 'The third point is that the learned judge, as many judges I think are, was influenced by the case of *Jussa v Jussa* [1972] 2 All ER 600, [1972] 1 WLR 881 . . . cited in *Rayden* for the proposition that joint orders for custody ought not to be made unless there is a reasonable prospect that the parties will co-operate together. No doubt in many cases that is a perfectly sensible proposition; but there are cases in which the party who has not got day-to-day control of the children is anxious to preserve as much of his or her contact with them as is possible in the new circumstances where the parties have separated, and there is a good deal to be said for recognising the responsibility and concern of the father in this case by making some order which shows that the court recognises that he is anxious to take an active part in their upbringing. Therefore, a joint custody order meets his problem as far as it can be met in the physical circumstances and should at least help him to get over the bitterness which he is bound to feel.'

I respectfully agree and, in my judgment, a joint custody order in this case is in the best interests of the child.

Questions

(i) What is the point of joint custody if the parent and child cannot meet?
(ii) The Oxford study (Eekelaar et al., 1977) found that joint custody was ordered in only 3.4% of cases in England and Wales, but more frequently in contested rather than uncontested cases: does this finding, together with the case of *H v H*, above, suggest that it may be used 'more as a compromise solution to a difficult problem than as a creative attempt to involve the absent parent with the child's future'?
(iii) Now that the Guardianship Act 1973 has provided that each parent of a legitimate child automatically enjoys parental rights and authority equally with the other, unless and until a court order is made, would it be preferable in some cases to make no order at all?

This apparent increase in enthusiasm for joint custody has been matched by a decrease in enthusiasm for the old type of 'split order'. This is understandable in view of the virtual abandonment of the concept of fault for the purposes of matrimonial relief, but has sometimes been couched in rather mysterious terms:

Dipper v Dipper
[1981] Fam 31, [1980] 2 All ER 722, [1980] 3 WLR 626, 124 Sol Jo 775, Court of Appeal

The parents married in 1967 and had three children, now aged ten, seven and nearly five. The marriage became unhappy in 1977 and both parties committed adultery. By agreement, they obtained cross decrees of divorce in 1979, but each applied for custody of the children. Wood J gave care and control to the mother, but sole custody to the father, so that the children could not be removed from their schools without the father being notified and having a say in their future upbringing. Both parties appealed, but on this point the appeal was settled on the basis that they should have joint custody, with care and control to the mother. The following statements were made by members of the Court of Appeal in the course of approving this settlement:

Ormrod LJ . . . It used to be considered that the parent having custody had the right to control the children's education, and in the past their religion. This is a misunderstanding. Neither parent has any pre-emptive right over the other. If there is no agreement as to the education of the children, or their religious upbringing or any other major matter in their lives, that disagreement has to be decided by the court. In day-to-day matters the parent with custody is naturally in control. To suggest that a parent with custody dominates the situation so far as education or any other serious matter is concerned is quite wrong. So the basis of the judge's order giving custody to the father and care and control to the mother was, in my view, unsound. In any event, these split orders are not really desirable. There are cases where they serve a useful purpose, but care has to be taken not to affront the parent carrying the burden day to day of looking after the child by giving custody to the absent parent. In this case a joint custody order seems to me entirely right because this is a case where the father has an intent to play an active part in his children's lives.

Cumming-Bruce LJ: . . . As Ormrod LJ has explained, the judge was there falling into error, it being a fallacy which continues to raise its ugly head that, on making a custody order, the custodial parent has a right to take all the decisions about the education of the children in spite of the disagreements of the other parent. That is quite wrong. The parent is always entitled, whatever his custodial status, to know and be consulted about the future education of the children and any other major matters. If he disagrees with the course proposed by the custodial parent he has the right to come to the court in order that the difference may be determined by the court. What is not practicable, when a judge is worried about the moral aspect of the parent who is going to have care and control, is to try to resolve the problem by giving the other parent an apparent right to interfere in the day-to-day matters or in the general way in which the parent with care and control intends to lead his or her life. If anxiety is such that it calls for an active control, the usual method is by making a supervision order.

Questions

(i) Were their lordships attempting to return to the 'narrow' meaning of custody as suggested by Sachs LJ in *Hewer v Bryant* [1970] 1 QB 357, [1969] 3 All ER 578 (p. 378, above)?
(ii) If they were, can this interpretation be reconciled with the provision in s. 52(1) of the Matrimonial Causes Act 1973 that 'custody' includes access?
(iii) Or were they simply pointing out that it is always open to the non-custodial parent to bring the case back to the divorce court if he is worried about any aspect of the child's upbringing?
(iv) Do you agree with Ormrod LJ that the old form of 'split order' is not 'really desirable'?

The effect of orders made in divorce courts may therefore be a little unclear, but the courts' powers under s. 42 of the Matrimonial Causes Act are relatively unfettered (as we shall see in Chapter 15, the powers of the High Court in wardship cases are almost completely so). In matrimonial proceedings in magistrates' courts and in custody cases under the Guardianship of Minors Act 1971, however, the Law Commission (1976) recommended a slightly different approach. The relevant parts of the *Domestic Proceedings and Magistrates, Courts Act 1978* provide as follows (and there is an equivalent provision in s. 11A of the Guardianship of Minors Act 1971):

8. . . . .
    (2) On an application for an order [for financial provision] under section 2, 6 or 7 of this Act the court, whether or not it makes an order under the said section 2, 6 or 7, shall have power to make such order regarding —
        (*a*) the legal custody of any child of the family who is under the age of eighteen, and
        (*b*) access to any such child by either of the parties to the marriage or any other person who is
           a parent of that child,
as the court thinks fit.
    . . . .
    (4) An order shall not be made under this section giving the legal custody of a child to more

than one person; but where the court makes an order giving the legal custody of a child to any person under this section, it may order that a party to the marriage in question who is not given the legal custody of the child shall retain all or such as the court may specify of the parental rights and duties comprised in legal custody (other than the right to the actual custody of the child) and shall have those rights and duties jointly with the person who is given the legal custody of the child.

Questions

(i) Does this approach seem preferable to awarding joint custody to both, with 'care and control' to one?

(ii) But what is the court to do if it wishes to grant a measure of parental authority to a party who has no automatic parental rights to 'retain,' such as a step-father (in matrimonial proceedings) or an illegitimate father (in Guardianship of Minors Act proceedings)?

The Law Commission were here both attempting to achieve greater clarity for the parties and to avoid affront to the person carrying the burden of day-to-day care. But it is still by no means clear exactly what 'the parental rights and duties' comprised in legal custody are. The *Children Act 1975* attempts to provide an 'explanation of concepts':

Parental rights and duties

85.—(1) In this Act, unless the context otherwise requires, 'the parental rights and duties' means as respects a particular child (whether legitimate or not), all the rights and duties which by law the mother and father have in relation to a legitimate child and his property; and references to a parental right or duty shall be construed accordingly and shall include a right of access and any other element included in a right or duty.

(2) Subject to section 1(2) of the Guardianship Act 1973 (which relates to separation agreements between husband and wife), a person cannot surrender or transfer to another any parental right or duty he has as respects a child.

(3) Where two or more persons have a parental right or duty jointly, any one of them may exercise or perform it in any manner without the other or others if the other or, as the case may be, one or more of the others have not signified disapproval of its exercise or performance in that manner.

(4) From the death of a person who has a parental right or duty jointly with one person, or jointly with two or more other persons, that other person has the right or duty exclusively or, as the case may be, those other persons have it jointly.

(5) Where subsection (4) does not apply on the death of a person who has a parental right or duty, that right or duty lapses, but without prejudice to its acquisition by another person at any time under any enactment.

(6) Subsections (4) and (5) apply in relation to the dissolution of a body corporate as they apply in relation to the death of an individual.

(7) Except as otherwise provided by or under any enactment, while the mother of an illegitimate child is living she has the parental rights and duties exclusively.

Legal custody

86. In this Act, unless the context otherwise requires, 'legal custody' means, as respects a child, so much of the parental rights and duties as relate to the person of the child (including the place and manner in which his time is spent); but a person shall not by virtue of having legal custody of a child be entitled to effect or arrange for his emigration from the United Kingdom unless he is a parent or guardian of the child.

Actual custody

87.—(1) A person has actual custody of a child if he has actual possession of his person, whether or not that possession is shared with one or more other persons.

(2) While a person not having legal custody of a child has actual custody of the child he has the like duties in relation to the child as a custodian would have by virtue of his legal custody.

(3) In this Act, unless the context otherwise requires, references to the person with whom a child has his home refer to the person who, disregarding absence of the child at a hospital or boarding school and any other temporary absence, has actual custody of the child.

Questions

(i) If (*a*) a divorce court, or (*b*) a magistrates' court, wished to make an order such as was made in the case of *Re A and B* (Infants) [1897] 1 Ch 786, (p. 379, above) could it do so?

(ii) Does a custody order made (*a*) by a divorce court, or (*b*) by a magistrates' court, include all or any of the following powers:

(*aa*) to decide whether or not a six-year-old should have his tonsils out;

(*bb*) to decide whether or not a 13-year-old should get a paper round, and if so how the money should be spent;

(*cc*) to decide whether a 16-year-old should stay on at school;

(*dd*) to enrol a five-year-old in Sunday school;

(*ee*) in the light of the decision of the European Court of Human Rights in the case of Re *Campbell and Cosans* (1982) 4 EHRR 293 (see later p. 597), to decide whether or not a child should be subject to corporal punishment at school?

(iii) Some decisions are both powers and duties: for example, a person having 'custody, charge or care' of a child under 16 commits a criminal offence if he 'wilfully assaults, ill-treats, neglects, abandons or exposes' the child 'in a manner likely to cause unnecessary suffering or injury to health' (Children and Young Persons Act 1933, s. 1(1)); and a person with actual custody of a child of compulsory school age is under the same duty as a parent to ensure that he attends school or is otherwise properly educated (Education Act 1944, ss. 36 and 114(1)). Does this mean that a person with 'actual' but not 'legal' custody, as defined by the Children Act 1975, has the power:

(*aa*) to decide whether a child should have urgently needed medical treatment;

(*bb*) to decide whether a child should have non-urgent, but therapeutically recommended medical treatment;

(*cc*) to decide which school to send the child to;

(*dd*) to decide whether a child should go on a field visit to Scotland?

It should be noted that the divorce rules are designed to prevent a unilateral change in the child's surname, and that there are special provisions available in all courts to prevent the child being taken abroad without consent. These are particularly relevant in the context of re-marriage (sections (5) and (6), below).

(b) ACCESS

Whatever the gap between theory and practice in the courts over joint custody, there has been such consistency on the question of access that in 1973, Eekelaar was inclined to describe it as one of the few remaining 'rights' of parenthood. Since then the courts have turned the terminology on its head, but without much effect upon the practice:

M v M (child: access)
[1973] 2 All ER 81, High Court, Family Division

The parents married in 1956 and adopted the child, a boy now aged seven, in 1966. The mother was not able to give him 'full maternal care' and in 1969 a supervision order was made. In 1970, the mother left both father and boy. Her matrimonial complaint to the local magistrates' court was unsuccessful and custody was awarded to the father, with reasonable access to the mother. Access did not run smoothly, because of the parties' extreme hostility to one another. Each began to commit adultery, but once the mother became pregnant, the father refused to allow her to see the boy. She applied for access to be defined; the father applied for it to be revoked. By the time of the hearing she had not seen the boy for a year. There was evidence that access had an extremely disturbing effect upon the boy and the justices revoked it. The mother appealed.

Wrangham J: [After reciting the facts, quotes from the magistrates' reasons:]
'In this case we felt the welfare of the child to be paramount. We considered that a secure, stable and emotionally satisfying environment had been provided by [the father] for [the child]. The child had already suffered several disturbances through adoption and through the breakdown of his first family and we felt that he must be given a chance to integrate and develop in his present family with a minimum of emotionally disturbing factors. In particular, he should no longer be the source of, or excuse for an emotional struggle between [the father and the mother].'
This decision is attacked by the learned counsel who put forward the mother's case with great care and persuasiveness, first on the very substantial ground that the justices, although they were referred to the well-known authority of *S v S and P* [1962] 2 All ER 1, [1962] 1 WLR 445, did not refer to that authority and, as was contended, acted in direct defiance of it. In *S v S and P*, which I think we must consider with a little care, a mother, who had left her children with the father, had gone off with another man, and against whom there were substantial grounds for criticism, applied to his Honour Judge Robson, sitting as Special Commissioner at Leicester, for access. That application was dismissed by the commissioner, who presumably saw the witnesses in the case, and then the matter was taken to the Court of Appeal. The Court of Appeal reversed his finding and made an order that access should be granted to the mother. Of course the facts of that case are not the same as the facts of this case but it is important to see the way in which the problem was approached by the learned Lords Justices on that occasion. In particular counsel for the mother relies on the judgment of Willmer LJ. I think I should quote some of what Willmer LJ says:
'Here the wife is asking for no more than periodical access to her own children. In the ordinary way that would be no more than the basic right of any parent. I agree with the view expressed by the commissioner that to deprive a mother altogether of access to her own children, particularly to two small daughters, is 'a very strong thing to do'. I should be disposed to go so far as to say that the court should not take that step unless satisfied that she is not a fit and proper person to be brought into contact with the children at all. [And then he gives an example.] Such a situation might arise, for instance, if she were a person with a criminal record, or one disposed to act with cruelty against children, or something of that sort. To say of a woman that she is a bad wife or mother may be an excellent reason for not giving her care and control, but, in my view, is not sufficient ground for depriving her of any kind of access.'
On the face of it, if one follows the words of Willmer LJ without regard to subsequent cases, there is a very strong argument to be made for the mother. No one has suggested that this mother is a woman who was not a fit and proper person to be brought into contact with the child at all, she has not got a criminal record, and there is not the smallest reason to suppose that she was disposed to act with cruelty towards this child. But since *S v S and P* was decided there have been other decisions of the Court of Appeal. One is *C v C*. The only report before me is the report in the Times newspaper of 28 May 1971. In that case Dunn J had refused access to a mother in the circumstances set out in that report. Again the facts do not bear the smallest resemblance to the facts in this case and are therefore of no importance here. But what is of importance is that Davies LJ in giving his judgment said:
'In such cases as the present the welfare of the children was the paramount consideration. Access, custody and care were not to be given as rewards for one parent or taken away as punishment for another.'
He adds that he agrees with the learned trial judge and emphasises that the children were living in a happy, secure and serene household.
He does not there deal with the argument which must have been put before the Court of Appeal based on the words of Willmer LJ in *S v S and P* [1962] 2 All ER 1, [1962] 1 WLR 445. *S v S and P* was in fact dealt with in *B v B* [1971] 3 All ER 682, [1971] 1 WLR 1486. That happens to have been an appeal from a case which I tried at first instance and once again the facts bear not the remotest resemblance to the facts in this case and I therefore do not refer to them. But Davies LJ comes to deal with the argument based on *S v S and P* and he recites the words of Willmer LJ,

that normally it is the basic right of every parent to have access to the child or children. He says: 'That of course is true. But there are exceptions to every rule . . .' The importance of the exception in this case was that on the finding that I had made at first instance there was no real criticism to be made of the father at all, merely a situation had been reached in which, as I then thought, no good could come to the child from companionship with his father, largely no doubt because of the attitude that the mother, who had care and control of the boy, had taken up during the years in which she had been looking after him. The Court of Appeal upheld the order that access should cease on the ground that even though there was no real criticism to be made of the father the paramount consideration was the welfare of the child, and the welfare of the child would not be promoted by access to the father.

It seems to me that the only way [in] which one can really reconcile *S v S and P* with the cases that followed, *C v C* and still more *B v B*, is to say that what Willmer LJ meant was that the companionship of a parent is in any ordinary circumstances of such immense value to the child that there is a basic right in him to such companionship. I for my part would prefer to call it a basic right in the child rather than a basic right in the parent. That only means this, that no court should deprive a child of access to either parent unless it is wholly satisfied that it is in the interests of that child that access should cease, and that is a conclusion at which a court should be extremely slow to arrive. It is not without significance that Edmund Davies LJ in *B v B* said:

'For a court to deprive a good parent completely of access to his child is to make a dreadful order. That is what has been done here, and the impact on both parent and child must have lifelong consequences. Very seldom can the court bring itself to make so Draconian an order, and rarely is it necessary.'

I should add that in that case the boy was in his teens, so that there was little prospect of making a change in the access arrangements later. The order cutting off access could only in the circumstances of that case be regarded as effectively final, whereas of course in many cases, and this is one, there would be no reason for supposing that the cessation of access need be final.

I think before parting with *B v B* one should also note that the members of the Court of Appeal criticised very strongly the mother who had had the care and control of this boy during the years in which he grew up and had used it to alienate him from his father. I cite the words of Edmund Davies LJ, who quoted the report of the Official Solicitor, who said he did not suggest that the mother had wilfully attempted to turn the boy against his father, but, because she honestly believed it was not in the interests of the boy for there to be access, she had done nothing towards creating an atmosphere in which the boy would willingly go to the father for access. Edmund Davies LJ's comment was this:

'In general, one parent who takes that attitude in relation to the other parent is undertaking a tremendous responsibility and discharging it thoroughly badly. Again speaking generally, it is the duty of parents, whatever their personal differences may be, to seek to inculcate in the child a proper attitude of respect for the other parent.'

For these reasons I do not think it can be said that the justices, in reaching the conclusion which they did, were acting contrary to the law as laid down by the Court of Appeal. Quite clearly they placed before themselves the rule that the welfare of the child is the paramount consideration; they say so in terms; and they came to their conclusion on the ground that the welfare of the child would not be promoted by the continuance of access and would be promoted by the cessation of access. . . .

Latey J: . . . Where one finds, as one does for example in *S v S and P* [1962] 2 All ER 1, [1962] 1 WLR 4452, a reference to the basic right of a parent to access to the child, I do not accept that the meaning conveyed is that a parent should have access to the child although such access is contrary to the child's interests, and when one reads *S v S and P* in conjunction with the more recent decisions of the Court of Appeal, to which Wrangham J has referred, I agree entirely, and as emphatically as I can, that what is meant is this: where the parents have separated and one has the care of the child, access by the other often results in some upset in the child. Those upsets are usually minor and superficial. They are heavily outweighed by the long term advantages to the child of keeping in touch with the parent concerned so that they do not become strangers, so that the child later in life does not resent the deprivation and turn against the parent who the child thinks, rightly or wrongly, has deprived him, and so that the deprived parent loses interest in the child and therefore does not make the material and emotional contribution to the child's development which that parent by its companionship and otherwise would make.

So viewed the cases which speak of the basic right to access of the non-custodian parent are to my mind, as Wrangham J has said, reconcilable and make sense. I do not believe that in modern times they were meant to convey any other meaning. They mean and are meant to mean not that a parent has any proprietorial right to access but that save in exceptional circumstances to deprive a parent of access is to deprive a child of an important contribution to his emotional and material growing up in the long term.

Appeal dismissed.

Questions

(i) How does one distinguish between upset to a child which is 'minor and superficial' and upset which is seriously damaging to the child?
(ii) Is the damage any less serious to the child even if the upset is caused by the attitude of the custodial parent?
(iii) How is the right of the child to the companionship of the non-custodial parent to be enforced if that parent does not wish to see him?

The problems of the law in attempting to enforce this 'right' against the wishes of the *custodial* parent are demonstrated in the following case:

V-P v V-P
(Access to Child) (1978) 1 FLR 336, 10 Fam Law 20, Court of Appeal

The parents married in 1971. The father came from Mauritius and was at that time working as a clerical officer in the civil service. The mother came from a Welsh farming family and was working in London as an assistant architect. They had one daughter, now aged six, but the father had an older son by an earlier relationship. They divorced in 1977 and custody of the daughter was awarded to the mother, but the mother strongly opposed access from the outset. In February 1978, the judge ordered that the father should have reasonable access, and made a supervision order. This order was unsuccessful and in May the judge ordered specified access. The mother permitted the first visit, but thereafter totally refused access and refused to co-operate with the welfare officer. The judge appointed the Official Solicitor to represent the child, but when the matter came before him in November, the mother was still opposed to access. The judge made no order as to access and the father appealed.

Ormrod LJ: [After reciting the facts:] That is the situation which led the learned judge to make the order which he did and far be it from me to criticize him for doing so. But the situation as it presents itself to my mind is this: the mother has put forward no real grounds at all for refusing access to the father. The evidence of the upset to this child is mimimal. It is totally uncorroborated in any way and it is in direct conflict with the impression that Mr Dunning, the supervising officer, obtained. He thought that the child was delighted to see her father and enjoyed it. Indeed the school mistress thought also that the child had benefited very much by seeing her father: she had come alive, as it were. So far as all the independent evidence is concerned, it is absolutely clear that there is nothing to suggest that F herself suffers in any way from seeing her father; in fact the suggestion is to the contrary.

That being so, a serious situation obviously arises. It is a difficult situation and one with which the court is not unfamiliar. An implacable opposition by one parent about access always means, of course, that it is nothing whatever to do with the child, but it is everything to do with the parents. What the background of the relationship between the father and mother is none of us knows. All we do know is that the mother seems to have been a very clever girl who got to London, got into higher education and started training as an architect. She has reached the stage of being an architectural assistant and is obviously, therefore, a person of great intelligence, who has retreated back into a very rural community, where it is reasonably obvious that her marriage to her husband is a matter of acute embarrassment to her and no doubt equally an acute embarrassment to her mother, because she has in fact, since her father's death, left her husband and gone back to her mother. . . .

Where this passionate opposition to access is coming from, whether it is really coming from the mother, who wants to put this mistaken marriage completely behind her, or whether it is coming from her mother, who totally disapproves of it, one does not know. But that the child is suffering as a consequence of this attitude of her mother and grandmother is abundantly plain and that she will certainly suffer in the future is even clearer.

In my judgment, this is a situation which cannot be accepted by any court which is responsible for making decisions as to what is in the best interests of this girl. Her best interests clearly involve keeping contact with her father. It may be, as I certainly thought at one stage during the argument, that the primary cause of embarrassment was the father turning up at Raglan, and that may be a factor. No doubt to both the mother and her mother his presence in the neighbourhood could well be a source of embarrassment. There is no reason, as far as I can see, why this child should not go and see her father, indeed stay with her father, at the former matrimonial home where the half brother R is. If ever there was a case which was a case for access it seems to me to be this one, although the difficulties in the way of organizing it are very great indeed, but in 99 families out of 100 there would be no problem.

It is difficult to know whether the mother appreciates what she is doing. I suppose that probably she does not see the full implications. No-one wants to make threats or to adopt a hostile, compulsive attitude in this kind of situation, but the court cannot possibly accept a situation like this unless the evidence leading to it is really conclusive. I have already said the evidence as to the upset of this child in respect of one period of access on May 23 is really much too slight to act upon. On the other hand, I fully appreciate the Official Solicitor's representative's view that head-on confrontations at this stage with mother and grandmother are not likely to be productive. But the court is dealing today with a woman who is highly educated, even if still perhaps rather unsophisticated. She must be a woman who has a sufficient moral sense to understand her duty to this child. She may be unable to deal with her own mother — I do not know whether that is so or not — but the responsibility that is resting upon her at this moment in refusing access to the father is very very great indeed. I hope that she at least will understand that, as a responsible member of society and a responsible mother, she has a duty to comply with orders made by courts in this regard. It should not be necessary when dealing with intelligent people for the court to be thinking in terms of sanctions. One only uses sanctions to compel the stupid to do things, or the obstinate. But if the court, having seriously considered the welfare of this child, comes to the conclusion that there should be access, the court is entitled to expect that the mother will seriously consider what this court says and will do her best to co-operate with it.

I have said that I do not want to issue threats, but the mother should, I think, realize this: the father has a home with the half brother in it, he is unemployed, he is available to look after both these children full time. The mother is fully occupied, so that the grandmother is playing a very important part in this child's life. The child is in a totally feminine environment at the present moment and one does not want a repetition of the situation where the mother has grown up under the domination of her mother. I would imagine the mother does not want to produce a situation in which, when this child is 12 or 13, she revolts against this feminine environment and goes to her father, which is a possibility.

That being so, it would be a mistake on the part of the mother, in my judgment, to assume that the order for custody in her favour is inevitable; it is not and if the situation goes on as it is at present then it may be necessary to reconsider the question of custody. I say no more, because no-one would willingly take this child away from her mother unless there were strong reasons for doing so, but there are what look to me like potentially strong reasons for taking that course if we are going to be confronted with a total non-cooperation on the part of the mother. I do not hold out any hopes for the father, it would be quite wrong that he should build any hopes on this, but in my view the right way to deal with this case is to make an order which demonstrates clearly to the mother and to her mother the view of the court.

The view of the court is that access to the father should take place. How it is to take place is another matter. I would allow the appeal and vary the order of the learned judge to this extent: I would order that there should be access as and when the supervising officer thinks right. I add to that, that does not mean that the father is to be badgering the supervising officer about it or worrying the supervising officer. The matter is to be left in the hands of the supervising officer with the clearest indication from the court that the court thinks that access is very much in this child's interest. So there is no order which is capable of being enforced and that is intentional. I think it would be right also, in order that there should be no misunderstanding on this matter, to make an order that the question of the custody of this child should be reviewed some time between October and November 1979. I do not mean by that that I am suggesting it should be changed, I am not, but I think it should come back to the court for review in order that there should be no misunderstanding on the part of the mother or the grandmother that they are at risk of losing this child if they maintain their present attitude.

I would therefore allow the appeal and make that order.

Questions

(i) If you were faced with a child's mother such as this, would you be inclined to do what one of the judges in Dodds' survey suggested (1981): 'Persuade. Threaten. Give Up.'?

(ii) Have you noticed how many of the cases in which the judiciary have emphasised the importance of retaining ties with both parents concern cross-cultural relationships? What effect, if any, do you think this may have had upon the result?

The law reports cannot reveal the other side of the coin, which may be a more common problem: if access is the 'right of the child,' how can the law enforce the corresponding duty of the non-custodial parent? In *Divorce and the Reluctant Father* (1980), Anne Heath-Jones gives a vivid account of the problem and her solution to it:

When my husband and I separated 12 years ago, we had two children who were then one and three years of age with long years of childhood ahead of them. . . .

James was never a doting father, which had been one of the problems of the marriage. In effect I had always been a single parent. The boys were very young and their awareness of, and attachment to, their remote father was slight. James was all set to vanish from our lives completely.

But somehow in all the mess, in all my own grief and loneliness, and in spite of all the bitterness I harboured against him, I knew that if I had strength to fight for anything it should be to maintain contact between the children and their father. . . .

In those early years the fact that he saw them at all was due to every imaginable ploy. Persuasion, appeal, anger and tears. I met him more than half-way on any arrangement that he was prepared to concede. I would deliver them to his flat and collect them. If he refused to have them to stay overnight then I settled for one day — or half a day. I felt anything was better than that they should lose touch and become strangers.

Meanwhile, I kept James informed of progress at nursery and later primary school. I made sure the boys remembered his birthday; I showed him school reports. I begged him (swallowing large hunks of indigestible pride) to attend school open days, birthday parties and Guy Fawkes parties. Most important of all I kept his image intact for his children. They never heard from me any criticism of his character, or knew of my deep hurt and resentment that their father needed so much coercion to see them or be involved in their lives.

For many years all the initiative for contact came from us. He never 'phoned or wrote or asked to see them. Then slowly, very slowly, the years of effort began to pay off. The boys and I moved from London into the country. James came down occasionally for the weekend and I would clear off and leave the cottage to them. After he re-married a more or less regular arrangement was worked out for the school holidays.

We were lucky in his choice of a new wife. She was friendly and accepted her two stepsons, and in time they formed an easy relationship with her. Christmases were now peopled with a whole new branch of extended family. Instead of moping alone with me (and some Christmases were very mopey) they had a welcome at their father's and his relations and even at the big family gatherings of his new wife. . . .

Now, 1967 seems a long time ago and their childhood is nearly over. The relationship with their father now is mutually warm, positive and spontaneous. At times the price to pay for nurturing that relationship has been high. If you idealise the absent parent you must be prepared for the consequences.

When life got tough for us, when the boys were unhappy with school or friends, or when they sobbed for the father whose contact I had so carefully preserved, the cry was 'I want to live with Dad.' It hurt of course because I had provided the years of love and security, it hurt because I knew their father wouldn't want them and it hurt because that was the last thing in the world that I could explain to the crying child.

In spite of the upheavals of those early years we have all survived. They now have a father they can respect and admire, a man they can talk to and learn from, and a model to emulate when they become husbands and fathers themselves.

One further point should be made on the law. Because of its broad power to do what it thinks fit, a divorce court or the High Court in wardship proceedings has always been able to order that the child should have access to (or even be cared for by) other significant adults in his life, such as grandparents, uncles and aunts. A power to award access to grandparents has now been granted to magistrates who make custody orders in matrimonial proceedings (Domestic Proceedings and Magistrates' Courts Act 1978, s. 14) and a similar power has been added to the *Guardianship of Minors Act 1971*. We quote the latter, because it also applies after one of the parents has died:

Access to minors by grandparents
14A.—(1) The court, on making an order under section 9(1) of this Act or at any time while such an order is in force, may on the application of a grandparent of the minor make such order requiring access to the minor to be given to the grandparents as the court thinks fit.

(2) Where one parent of a minor is dead, or both parents are dead, the court may, on an application made by a parent of a deceased parent of the minor, make such order requiring access to the minor to be given to the applicant as the court thinks fit.

(3) Section 11A(2) of this Act shall apply in relation to an order made under this section as it applies in relation to an order made under section 9(1), 10(1)(*a*), or 11(*a*) of this Act.

(4) The court shall not make an order under this section with respect to a minor who is for the purposes of Part III of the Child Care Act 1980 in the care of a local authority.

(5) Where the court has made an order under subsection (1) above requiring access to a minor to be given to a grandparent, the court may vary or discharge that order on an application made —
> (*a*) by that grandparent, or
> (*b*) by either parent of the minor, or
> (*c*) if the court has made an order under section 9(1)(*a*) of this Act giving the legal custody of the minor to a person other than one of the parents, by that person.

(6) Where the court has made an order under subsection (2) above requiring access to a minor to be given to a grandparent, the court may vary or discharge that order on an application made —
> (*a*) by the grandparent, or
> (*b*) by any surviving parent of the minor, or
> (*c*) by any guardian of the minor.

(7) Section 6 of the Guardianship Act 1973 [welfare officers' reports] shall apply in relation to an application under this section as it applies in relation to an application under section 5 or 9 of this Act, and any reference to a party to the proceedings in subsection (2) or (3) of the said section 6 shall include —
> (*a*) in the case of an application under subsection (1) or (2) above, a reference to the grandparent who has made an application under either of those subsections,
> (*b*) in the case of an application under subsection (5) or (6) above, a reference to the grandparent who has access to the minor under the order for the variation or discharge of which the application is made.

(8) Where, at any time after an order with respect to a minor has been made under subsection (1) above, no order is in force under section 9 of this Act with respect to that minor, the order made under subsection (1) above shall cease to have effect.

(9) A court may make an order under this section in favour of a grandparent of a minor notwithstanding that the minor is illegitimate.

Questions

(i) If the father runs away with the children and the mother does not apply for custody, why cannot the grandparents apply for access (except by making the children wards of court)?
(ii) If the father dies and the mother becomes a recluse, why cannot the mother's parents apply for access (except through wardship)?

2 What arrangements are best for the child?

There is ample evidence, particularly from studies of the 1950s and 1960s, of the problems that access can cause. These are recounted by Susan Maidment in *Access Conditions in Custody Orders* (1975):

The most noticeable fact in the writings of sociologists and psychiatrists on the subject of marriage breakdown is that access is always mentioned as a potential source of difficulty both for the parents and the child. It might be argued that their accounts are unrepresentative, that they focus on the abnormal, rather than the normal situation which, because it works, does not get mentioned. Yet it is believed here that access is a greater problem than is generally realised. Even where relations between the parents are good:

'(a)ccess, even at best, is unsettling. A child may appear to be coping with the emotional strain, but there are still the practical problems of too little time and of opportunities having to be missed. This is one of the hard facts about divorce. Parents can help by accepting it and showing restraint in the demands they make.' (Sanctuary and Whitehead, 1970)

However, access also provides the perfect opportunity for continuing the battle and bitterness between the couple. Thus Goode (1956) suggests that sometimes the children are actually used by the parents for their own ends:

'Whatever the custodial arrangements, these marriages usually continued after the divorce, through the lives of the children. . . . This relationship is often the only channel through which the other spouse can make legitimate demands upon the other: (*a*) the wife by support demands; (*b*) the husband by visitation demands. It may also offer the most convenient means for learning about the activities of the other spouse.

Further, this relationship contains the most important weapons in the conflict of wills between ex-spouses, both during the divorce conflict and afterwards. This exploitation of the parent-child relationship may, of course, be unconscious, since few parents can admit that they use their children as punitive instruments.'

The two main techniques for using the children are:

(*a*) threatening to withhold visits, or making them difficult; and (*b*) persuading the children to dislike or be suspicious of the other parent.

But even where the parents are not consciously or unconsciously using the children in this way, there is also the problem that the visits themselves will cause stress. Marsden (1969), writing about the problem of poverty as it affects the fatherless family, observed that:

'(t)ensions were most pronounced in the minority of families where the father had continued to visit frequently after separation or divorce. If the mother still had a lingering affection for him she fostered the children's loyalties and memories and supported his visits. But where, as usually happened, resentment built up between the parents, all too easily the father's visits or contacts with the children became a battle for their affections. Young children soon forgot even violence and neglect and were puzzled and distressed that the father could not stay. Happy visits when he was able to indulge their wants contrasted with the pinching and scraping and bad temper which were too often the result of the mother's financial position.'

Similar observations were made by Goode:

'The relationship between the usually absent parent and the child at such visits is nagged by the fact that the parent and child will separate once again; that the advice and corrections of the absent parent will be overruled; while the assurances of love must carry their own proof during his absence. Since it is a rare young child who sees any reason for his parents to divorce, the haunting suspicion of abandonment gnaws at the enjoyment of the visits.'

The net result of these problems associated with access seems to be that visits become less frequent and regular. Thus Marsden says:

'In the light of these difficulties it was easy to understand why only one of the fathers who now visited had been coming for as long as five years. The usual story appeared to be that visits which began well tailed off. . . . Repeated contacts with the father only served to dramatise and exacerbate the conflict of affection, and by active discouragement — or by an equally eloquent display of 'neutrality' when the child appealed to her for a decision about writing to or seeing the father — the mother worked to bring the relationship to an end.'

George and Wilding (1972) in a study of motherless families, reported similar findings:

'Our impression from the fathers' answers is that there is a tendency for visits to diminish in frequency and regularity with the passage of time. . . . (M)others, fathers, and children find that visits make demands on them all which generate stresses and conflicts that eventually tend to reduce the frequency of visits.'

This last perception is supported by the Oxford study of *Custody After Divorce* (Eekelaar et al., 1977):

England and Wales	Access by time from separation						
Whether access exercised	Time from separation in years						
	0–½	½–1	1–2	2–3	3–5	5–10	over 10
Access exercised %	66.6	59.0	50.6	49.6	48.6	33.3	18.1
Access not exercised %	28.3	33.7	37.7	37.6	38.9	56.1	54.5
Access infrequent[1] %	5.1	7.4	11.7	12.8	12.5	10.5	27.3
Total numbers of cases[2]	99	95	77	125	72	57	11

[1] Once or twice in previous year or since separation
[2] Excluding cases where exercise of access unknown

Murch's interviews with divorcing parents, reported in *Justice and Welfare in Divorce* (1980), present a more encouraging picture. It should be remembered, however, that in the petitioner sample only one parent, usually the one with custody, was interviewed; and that in the divorce court welfare officer sample, both were interviewed, but the case had obviously presented some difficulty which had caused the original referral to the welfare officer:

Satisfaction with access

	Petitioner Sample n = 102	DCWO Sample n = 82 Parents
	%	%
Having access — very satisfied	15.7	4.9
quite satisfied	19.6	25.6
the best in the circumstances	14.7	30.5
Sub total: those with access satisfied	50.0	61.0
Having access — not very satisfied	15.7	22.0
not at all satisfied	3.9	3.7
Sub total: those with access unsatisfied	19.6	25.7
No access — satisfied	26.5	6.1
not satisfied	3.9	2.4
Combined totals		
Satisfied with arrangements	74.4	67.0
Not satisfied with arrangements	22.5	28.0
Other	1.0	4.8

The findings of Murch's study and others are discussed by Martin Richards in *Post-Divorce Arrangements for Children: A Psychological Perspective* (1982), when he addresses the question 'why do non-custodial parents disappear?'

Almost all the evidence we have is about absent fathers so I will discuss this. However, there is no reason to think that male non-custodial parents disappear any more or less often than female ones, although the reasons may differ somewhat in the two cases. I will list some of the reasons that have been uncovered in the research studies.

(*a*) Some men believe that it is in their children's interests for them to disappear. They may feel that their visits will upset the children or that their continued presence makes it less likely that their ex-spouses will settle down with a new partner. Often, and especially in the early days after separation, a child's upset at what has happened is most likely to be apparent before and after a visit from the father. This may lead either parent to try to reduce or stop the visiting. It is hardly surprising that the child's feelings are most likely to be expressed at these times as they will be the most vivid reminders of what has happened. Indeed, it would be odd if any child accepted such a radical change in their lives without upset and in the long term it is probably much better that these feelings are expressed at the time. The real issue here is the capacity of the parents to accept the expression of such feelings at a time when they are likely to be feeling very vulnerable and upset themselves.

(*b*) It is often said, not least by mothers with custody that some fathers are uninterested in their children. Doubtless this is sometimes true but I suspect that this reason is often used to cover others.

(*c*) Some men believe, incorrectly of course, that if they do not see their children they will not be required to pay maintenance. More realistically, others assume that if they have no contact with their old families it will be hard for them to be traced and forced to pay maintenance. Others connect maintenance and access in another way so that they see the money they pay as an entitlement to visit. If they can only afford a little, they see themselves as having little entitlement to visit.

(*d*) Some men are prevented from seeing their children by their ex-spouse. Preventing contact with children is the most obvious weapon available to a custodial parent and some use it. After a long journey the father arrives to find the house empty. Or perhaps a child may always turn out to be 'ill' on access days. More bluntly, a father may simply be told at the doorstep that he cannot see his children. As I have mentioned above, the sanctions are few in such cases and without persistence and the ability to find the right kind of help the situation may seem hopeless.

(*e*) Some men feel that after a separation they want to move away and start again. Particularly if their spouse has a new partner, they may not want to live nearby. Distance may then create too many problems for the visiting arrangements to survive.

(*f*) A new partner may be very resentful of the contact with the children of the first marriage and bring pressure to try to end it. Not infrequently the custodial parent will attempt to argue for access orders which try to prevent the children having contact with a new partner. Although it is not hard to understand the feelings that give rise to such attempts, these are unrealistic and unreasonable from the point of view of both the adults and children and, in general, courts have not sanctioned them. But pressures from both the new and old spouse may effectively reduce access.

(*g*) Access visits may be so painful and upsetting that a father cannot bear to continue with them. This may be because the visits involve meeting the ex-spouse or because the father finds it very difficult to readjust to a new kind of relationship with his children. The latter is particularly likely if access visits are brief. Sometimes the conditions in an access order are such that it seems impossible that any parent could conform, e.g. two hours a month in the old matrimonial home in the presence of the ex-spouse (and often her new partner). If access is brief and the father's home is far away there is the problem of where to take the children. There is also the 'father Christmas syndrome' — where the father seems only able to relate to his children by giving gifts and treats. Anything more realistic and normal may seem threatening to his relationship with the children. As one might expect the problems of access are most acute at the beginning and they usually resolve over time provided, of course, that access continues.

(*h*) Last among the reasons I shall mention, but certainly not least, is the point made to me by many men I have interviewed — that all too often continued contact is not supported or encouraged by anyone. Indeed, I have been told of men being advised by a whole variety of professional people that access was a kind of selfish private indulgence they should give up as soon as possible. Very few had received any sensible advice or help — if they had it was usually from a court welfare officer, one of the few solicitors who specialise in family law or from another parent who had experienced a divorce. . . .

On the basis of current evidence it would be very difficult to give any indication of the frequency of the various reasons I have described. However, a recent study by Eekelaar (1982) does give some clues. This study concerns cases where there were disputes concerning children and relies on information provided by court welfare officers. Where access was infrequent or never occurred the officers gave the following explanations:

Reason	No. of cases
Lack of interest by absent parent	14
Consideration for the children	6
Consideration for other parent	2
'Legal advice'	1
Injunction against absent parent	5
Hostile attitude of other parent	5
Opposition by children	5
Practical difficulties	22
Unknown	3

Question

Eekelaar also found that children living with their fathers were less likely to retain a good relationship with their mothers than vice versa: why might that be?

Some would contend that the law already goes too far in trying to resolve these difficulties. Prime amongst these are Goldstein, Freud and Solnit, whose basic concepts of the parent-child relationship and the child's need for continuity have already been explained in Chapter 10. In *Beyond the Best Interests of the Child* (1973), they argue:

Children have difficulty in relating positively to, profiting from, and maintaining the contact with two psychological parents who are not in positive contact with each other. Loyalty conflicts are common and normal under such conditions and may have devastating consequences by destroying the child's positive relationships to both parents. A 'visiting' or 'visited' parent has little chance to serve as a true object for love, trust, and identification, since this role is based on his being available on an uninterrupted day-to-day basis.

Once it is determined who will be the custodial parent, it is that parent, not the court, who must decide under what conditions he or she wishes to raise the child. Thus, the noncustodial parent should have no legally enforceable right to visit the child, and the custodial parent should have the right to decide whether it is desirable for the child to have such visits. What we have said is designed to protect the security of an ongoing relationship — that between the child and the custodial parent. At the same time the state neither makes nor breaks the psychological relationship between the child and the noncustodial parent, which the adults involved may have jeopardized. It leaves to them what only they can ultimately resolve.

Richards (1982) argues for the contrary hypothesis — that continued contact is so much in the interests of the child that the system should try harder to encourage it. In discussing the needs of children, he first points to the lack of good direct evidence either way, and continues:

There are a couple of findings in the psychological studies which have turned up several times and are at least consistent with my hypothesis. The first is that some of the long-term disruptive effects on children whose parents divorce are most marked if the separation comes earlier (say before the age of five) rather than later (eg Douglas, 1970). Several explanations are possible but one of these is that the likelihood of losing contact with the non-custodial parent will increase over time and so is most likely to be lost after an earlier separation. A similar explanation can be given of the evidence that divorce is more upsetting for children who remain with their mothers if those mothers remarry (Douglas, 1970), as the presence of a step-father almost always reduces contact with the father (Furstenberg, 1981).

The nearest we get to a direct study of the question of continuing contact is an American one where groups of children spending varying amounts of time with each of their divorced or separated parents were compared (Keshet and Rosenthal, 1978). Here the children (and parents) who spent at least 25% of their time with each of their parents seem to adjust best. However, in this study we cannot be certain that factors other than the post-separation arrangements determined the outcome. For instance, it could be that parents who decide to share their time with their children after separation are also parents who prepare their children for the separation and support them before it occurs. However, this evidence is in the same direction as the hints which can be found in all the recent studies of children of divorced parents that continuing relations with both parents are desirable from the point of view of the children's adjustment (Weiss 1975, 1979; Wallerstein and Kelly, 1980). . . .

A continued relationship with the non-custodial parent would appear to offer many psychological advantages for children. One of the most obvious is that it offers a wider variety of experience; the experience of a relationship with a second parent. A child is not denied a close and continuing relationship with a parent of each gender. This may be of special value in the development of his or her own gender identity (which has been shown to be disturbed in some studies of children of divorce) (Hetherington, 1972). With two parents a child is given the opportunity of learning how to move from one relationship to another. Often this is seen in a rather negative sense as something a child must learn to cope with. But I think we should see it much more positively as a very necessary skill for adult life that allows us to live within a whole network of relationships of differing kinds and qualities. It might be argued that these aspects of development should be satisfied equally by any two (or more) adults, not just a child's parents. To some extent this may be true, but there are many indications that parental relations are usually very special and cannot be replaced by other adults in any easy way. To say this is not to evoke any concept of a blood tie but one of a psychological parent. The potency of a psychological parent lies in the continuity of the relationship with their child and their symbolic position as a parent. A separation that does not involve the loss of one parent is likely to be much less disturbing of a child's social connections outside the immediate family. Friends and relatives of the non-custodial parent are not lost to the child. The child has a much better chance of maintaining links with both sets of grandparents.

At a separation, it is usual that among the many feelings a child is likely to experience is anger (Wallerstein and Kelly 1980). This anger is associated with the wish or fantasy that the parents will come back together again and it is generally expressed towards the parent who spends most time looking after the child regardless of their role in the separation. If a child is able to maintain a relationship with both parents this anger gradually dissipates as the child begins to feel confident in the new kind of relationship that develops with both parents. The separation of the parents gradually ceases to be the total threat to the child's life it once had seemed. In a case where the child does not have contact with the non-custodial parent the resolution of the anger at the parents' separation may be much more complex and prolonged. The absent parent, just because he or she is absent, may be built up into a totally idealised figure while the custodial parent's role is seen as that of the person who has driven out the 'ideal' parent. Everything that goes wrong or frustrates the child may be laid at the door of the custodial parent. Under this emotional pressure even the strongest of parents begins to react so that the child may feel signs of rejection or anger in return. This in turn increases the child's anger and insecurity. Of course, not all children of divorce react in this way, but those who do are probably those who have lost contact with one parent.

It has been suggested that a continued relationship with both parents makes the acceptance of a step-parent much more difficult for a child. There is no evidence to support this idea, which is improbable in view of our understanding of a child's parental relations. The unlikely assumption here is that a child has the capacity for two parental relations and if both spaces are filled there will be no space for anybody else. In fact there is great variation in number and kind of relations that a child can maintain (Shaffer and Emerson, 1964). It seems much more likely that if children feel confident that they are going to lose neither of their parents despite the marital separation, that they will accept a new adult more easily. Certainly, we need to move beyond the simplistic notion of very fixed parental roles which can be occupied by anybody that a parent or a court chooses to place in that position.

At the social level there are several very powerful arguments that can be given for the maintenance of ties with both parents.

For many, if not most children, a marital separation is followed by a permanent or temporary period in a single-parent family. We have abundant evidence that these families suffer from many disadvantages (Ferri, 1976). Among these are the effects of a single person providing for all the children's needs day in and day out and the low incomes typical of such families. Both of these are likely to be reduced by continuing [contact] with the non-custodial parent. Such a parent not only provides the child with an alternative home but is also a relief for the custodial parent. These breaks allow the custodial parent to recharge emotional batteries and indulge in some adult life uninterrupted by the demands of childcare.

In principle, there is no connection between access and the payment of maintenance by non-custodial parents. However, this is not the way it is always seen by those involved. Parents who have regular contact with their children and maintain a close relationship are much more likely to want to pay maintenance and feel that it is fair and reasonable to do so. If the contact is maintained the needs of the children including financial ones will be more obvious and are likely to be more freely met.

One can also see the non-custodial parent as a kind of insurance policy for children. Lives of custodial parents cannot be predicted with certainty; changes may occur which make it very difficult or impossible for them to cope with children. If there is a disaster a second parent who is in close touch can often take the children and so avoid another major upheaval.

But what of the negative side — what arguments are there against the continuing involvement of both parents? There is a general belief, which is borne out by the research studies, that many difficulties are associated with access visits. However, the extent of these should not be exaggerated. Murch's study (1980), for instance, found a majority who are satisfied with their access arrangements and he also noted that initial difficulties often resolved in time. That difficulties occur around access visits is hardly surprising as this will often be the one point of contact between spouses. (Eekelaar, 1982) The remedy of cutting off the contact may be superficially attractive, but in the long term is unlikely to help the adults to resolve their difficulties, apart from its likely effects on the children.

Part of our ambivalence about access is expressed in the common attitude that, though access is desirable, it can easily be overdone and so it is necessary to limit visits in terms of both their duration and frequency. Over-long or frequent visits are held to lead to confusions of loyalty for the children and to undermine their security in their main home. Clearly, if two parents are determined to continue their battles via their children, heavy pressures can be brought to bear which, if long-lasting, could make life a misery for children. However, such battles are usually relatively short-lived. As the separated parents begin to rebuild their lives and acquire new concerns and interests the old battles begin to lose their fire. Also children are surprisingly resourceful in avoiding situations which cause them pain.

One of the feelings that most concerns children at a parental separation is the fear of loss of both parents. If one parent has chosen to leave home and live elsewhere, why should not the other one make the same decision at a future date? The only way in which these fears can be countered is by a demonstration that there is continuity in the new arrangements. But it is not always understood that a child's fears are best countered if continuity is demonstrated in *both* parental relationships. Part of the mistaken fear that access visits are disturbing rests on the assumption that they may unsettle the relationship with the custodial parent. However, unless the child has a reasonable amount of time with the non-custodial parent there is no chance to regain confidence in that relationship.

Perhaps the most common cause of difficulties in access is that visits are too brief. We are well-used to descriptions of the Sunday afternoon access visit spent in the park and cafe. Only a moment's reflection is required to see how difficult or impossible it would be to recreate a normal parental relationship on that kind of basis. What children and adults need is the chance to share some of the very ordinary and routine aspects of life. Access visits must be long enough to remove the sense that they are a special occasion. Excessive gifts and the provision of 'treats' are sure signs that an ordinary relationship has not been recreated. The matter was summed up very clearly by a man I interviewed who told me that it was only after he had first got angry with his children during a visit that he began to feel that they were getting back to a reasonable relationship.

Given the many factors that will influence a particular situation and the practical constraints in making visiting arrangements I feel it would be unwise to try to lay down norms for the length of visits. However, I think it is fairly obvious that difficulties will be more common if overnight stays are not possible.

Sometimes it is felt important that things like rules about bedtimes should be as similar as possible in the two homes. Children often make comparisons and talk about any differences they have noted. In general, I would take the ability to talk openly about such differences as evidence that they were coming to terms with the separateness of their parents. Children will, of course, also try to exploit differences between the homes, supposed and real, to get what they want from a parent. But it is simple enough to make it clear to them that rules between the homes may differ and the fact that they are allowed to do X in the other house is no reason why they should do it here. Far from seeing differences in rules and routines in the two homes as confusing for children, I think there are good reasons for viewing them as advantages. They are ways of seeing something of variety in life and learning that there is not always a single answer to a problem. If different activities are possible in the two homes, just as the two relationships with the two parents will each have its own characteristics, so much the better for the children.

Richards makes several suggestions about how we might encourage continued contact:

The awarding of custody to a single parent at divorce is a public acknowledgment and notice that the role of the non-custodial parent is expected to be reduced. My first suggestion is that we cease to give such notice in the majority of cases. Much more appropriate would be a public reaffirmation that, in spite of the adults' separation, parental duties persist. The most obvious way in which this could be done is by making joint custody the norm — courts could either automatically make such an order unless strong and specific arguments against it were brought forward or they could make no order as to custody in this situation so that the position existing before divorce could persist. There are many indications that more parents are pressing for joint custody and this trend needs every encouragement. Those who continue to believe that such orders always lead to trouble must be prepared to back their beliefs with some hard evidence.

The evidence needed to satisfy a court that appropriate arrangements have been made for the children should include information about the relationship with both parents. Access orders should not be allowed to go by default. If an access order is not asked of a court, the court needs to know why: . . .

When disputes arise over access, it is very common for a court to reduce the access frequency and/or duration. It would be much more logical in many of these cases to extend the time so that the non-custodial parent had a better opportunity to work out a more satisfactory relationship with the children. But, above all, access problems require conciliation. They are the one area in which we might expect most results from the work of court welfare officers and others involved in conciliation. In the turmoil and confusion of a separation, it is hardly surprising that the parents' own fears and desires may sometimes override a more reasoned approach to their children's needs. It is just such conflicts that conciliation is often able to sort out. Where it is done the success rate may be very high. . . . [see further, Chapter 17]

Given that much of what parents decide about their children is worked out with their solicitors and only reaches the court as a fait accompli, the way in which solicitors advise their clients is an important influence on the post-divorce arrangements for children. Much of what they advise is influenced by what they think the court will accept — bargaining in the shadow of the law — so that, if courts were to put much more emphasis on continuing links with children, this would be reflected in the advice of solicitors. But despite this there is plenty of room for individual differences in attitudes and approaches among solicitors which may be of considerable significance for their clients and their children. I am impressed in our studies by the ways in which many solicitors who specialise in matrimonial work use their knowledge, experience and skill to assist their clients in finding appropriate solutions to their problems. On the other hand, advice from those who do little of this work seems much more hit or miss. To a layman, there would seem to be a case both for better training and for a system that would allow a potential client to find a specialist.

My last point concerns other sorts of advice for those separating. As is clear from much of the sociological research on marital separation, one of the problems faced by those involved is that there is no widely accepted and readily discovered set of rules or conventions about what to do. (Hart, 1976) It is, for instance, a very different kind of experience from having a baby when there is a set of professional agencies, each with a well-known function and there are a whole series of public rituals and attitudes that guide the uninitiated. . . .

Given this relative absence of advice, I wonder if there is not a strong case for the production of a semi-official booklet (much, say, of the status of publications of the Health Education Council) which would describe the sorts of reactions children have to a separation and ways in which their needs can be best met. It could describe the common difficulties that arise over things like access. I know that some steps in this direction have been taken — for instance, the proposed visiting code produced by Justice (1975) — but the need is still there.

Question

In the course of your professional life, you will meet many divorcing parents who are convinced that continued contact with the other parent will be profoundly unsettling for the children. Will you: (*a*) advise them that it is their duty to afford access to the other parent, but that they may reasonably limit time and place to suit their own convenience; (*b*) reassure them that it is extremely unlikely that the other parent will want to go on visiting the children for very long (or as Jill Tweedie of the *Guardian* said, in 1979, 'give the father unlimited access and watch the cookie crumble'); (*c*) encourage them to encourage as much visiting as can possibly be arranged; or (*d*) hand them a copy of the Justice (1975) visiting code? This concludes:

Some important DON'TS for parents

(*a*) DON'T make standing arrangements inconvenient to any party so that there is a 'built-in' strain.

(*b*) DON'T be rigidly regular — always the same day and time each week can easily become a bind.

(*c*) DON'T forget the children's private lives — e.g. a favourite weekly 'telly' programme, other children's birthday parties, etc.

(*d*) DON'T have a pre-school child taken out of its usual home too frequently — visiting more frequently than weekly, if desired by the child, may well be better arranged at the child's home.

(*e*) DON'T carp or criticise before, during or after access visits — the child may be hurt.

(*f*) DON'T force the visiting parent to rely on tea-shops, the park and the cinema — this soon becomes trying for both parties and may lead the parent to bribe and promise pies in the sky.

(*g*) DON'T regularly arrange for the hand-over and return of the child to be undertaken by a third party, for example, a grandparent or other relative, or a universal aunt or solicitor's clerk. A civil and courteous exchange, even if very brief, between estranged, separated or divorced parents can be very valuable to the child, who needs to be able to love both parents without feeling guilty.

(*h*) DON'T send anybody as a bodyguard or spy on staying visits; this defeats the main object of the stay and injects dangerous tension into the visit. This is not to say that a person should not be present, if this be the wish of both parents — and the child.

(*j*) DON'T try to bribe the child with presents or promises; although they may accept them, children will usually see through the reason for them and no one will benefit.

ABOVE ALL, remember that access visits are for the good of the child and are not a parental right; that perceptible acrimony between parents may ruin the visit for the child, and that sensitive children may well feel humiliated at being apparently the cause of fights between the two people they love most.

3 Step-parenthood

As every child knows, there have always been step-parents, but their stereotype is the wicked step-mother who invades the family after their real mother is dead. Nowadays, however, the more appropriate stereotype would be the divorced father who has gradually faded out of his own children's lives, and has now married a woman who has children from a previous marriage or relationship. As Jacqueline Burgoyne and David Clark point out in *Reconstituted Families*, in *Families in Britain* (1982):

There is considerable evidence that the obligations and responsibilities of fatherhood are very diffusely defined in our own society; mothers are felt to be mainly responsible for the welfare and public behaviour of children (eg Newson, 1972); fatherless families are expected to manage on their own, albeit in reduced circumstances, although we do not have similar expectations of motherless families (see George and Wilding, 1972); fathers continue to play little or no part in the care of babies or toddlers in many families (eg Oakley, 1979). The obligations of fatherhood are most clearly articulated in terms of being a good provider, ensuring economic security for the mother who takes direct responsibility for the care of his children. . . . Therefore, even if divorced parents consciously desire to exercise a shared responsibility for the care of their children there are important informal pressures tending to undermine this intention especially where one or both of them has remarried.

Although there is insufficient data to draw very definite conclusions, it does seem from the limited evidence available that many non-custodial fathers lose contact with their children from their first marriage and may eventually become step-fathers to some-one else's children.

We have already seen how both marriage breakdown and illegitimacy have been increasing. The following table from *Social Trends 13* (1982) shows how remarriages form an increasing proportion of all marriages:

Marriages

Great Britain and United Kingdom						Thousands and percentages	
			Great Britain				United Kingdom
	1961	1966	1971	1976	1979	1980	1980
Marriages (thousands)							
First marriage for both partners	331	358	357	273	270	270	279
First marriage for one partner only							
Bachelor/divorced woman	11	14	21	30	33	33	33
Bachelor/widow	5	5	4	3	3	3	3
Spinster/divorced man	12	16	24	32	36	37	38
Spinster/widower	8	7	5	4	3	3	3
Second (or later) marriage for both partners							
Both divorced	5	9	17	34	43	45	45
Both widowed	10	10	10	9	8	8	8
Divorced man/widow	3	3	4	5	5	5	5
Divorced woman/widower	3	4	5	5	5	5	5
Total marriages	387	426	447	396	407	409	418
Remarriages as a percentage of all marriages	15	16	20	31	34	34	33

There has, however, been a tendency to assume that having dependent children is likely to reduce a woman's prospects of remarriage. The Finer Committee on One-Parent Families (1974) compared the remarriage rates of widowed mothers with those of all widows in the years 1968 and 1970 and found that those with children, whatever their age, were less likely to marry again than those without. The report concluded that 'it would be surprising if what is true for widows were not also true for divorced women'. Yet Richard Leete and Susan Anthony have studied the records of a sample of 1,000 divorces granted in 1973 (slightly under 1%) in order to discover who had remarried within five years: in 233 cases, neither husband nor wife had remarried, in 287 only the husband had remarried, in 212 only the wife, and in 268 they had both remarried. They also tabulated the percentage of women remarrying by their age at divorce and the number of their children, and reached the following conclusions, reported in *Divorce and Remarriage: A Record Linkage Study* (1979):

> . . . The hypothesis that women without children are more likely to remarry is not confirmed by the statistics; for all women in the sample the proportion who remarry is, in fact, slightly higher among those with children. It is only among women divorced after the age of 40, that those without children remarry more commonly than those with children. However, in neither case is the difference statistically significant and larger samples would be needed if definite conclusions had to be drawn. A factor which does seem to influence the proportion who remarry is the age of the youngest child at the time of divorce; women whose youngest child is under 10 years old remarry more commonly than those whose children are older, or those who have no children. It is possible that these differences may reflect the attitudes of children towards step-parents; if older children are more reluctant to accept them, this may affect the mother's attitude to remarriage.

Question

Would you expect widows to be more or less willing to remarry than divorced women?

The complexities of the step-relationship are explored from the point of view of a step-mother in Brenda Maddox' book *Step-parenting* (1980), from which we quote her comparison between step-parenthood and both adoption and natural parenthood:

What step-parenthood is not
Time and time again, people confuse step-parenthood with adoption. A typical comment was offered to me enthusiastically by a radio broadcaster sophisticated enough to know better:
> Step-parents — what a fascinating subject! My sister is a stepmother. She and her husband couldn't have any children of their own and then they got this Korean war orphan. That was fifteen years ago and now are they having their problems!
or, from a scientist:
> Being a step-parent must be just like adopting. Oh, all right, the motives may be different at the beginning. But after that, the feelings involved are the same as in adoption.
Adoption and step-parenthood, as a matter of fact, differ in almost every significant detail. The fact that many step-parents go to court and adopt their stepchildren (as I did) simply underlines the fact that they are two separate kinds of relationship and that adoption achieves certain legal objectives that step-parenthood does not begin to touch. Some of the emotional differences are glaring to anybody who has talked with both kinds of parent. Step-parents, by and large, think of their role as a duty. They may like it, they may hate it or feel inadequate, but they carry a sense of obligation about it and often refer to it as 'a job'. While the step-parent usually just wants to get married, adoptive parents (at least those who adopt strange children rather than the children of relatives) have put in long emotional preparation for a child. As one man who had adopted two children, as well as made a career as an expert in adoption, expressed it: 'I have never thought of adopting a child as a job. To me, it is self-fulfilment.' Not many step-parents would say that.

The difference between the two roles is so stark that I can illustrate it in two lists.

Adoption

1   Adoption involves a change in legal status.
2   It is permanent.
3   The adopting couple have a marriage of proven stability.
4   They both want a child.
5   They stand at the same distance from the child (unless they are adopting a child who is a relative).
6   They acquire an infant or young child with little memory of its parents.
7   They receive professional guidance on possible emotional problems ahead.
8   Their act is seen by society as kind and generous.

Step-parenthood

1   The step-parent has no legal rights over the stepchild.
2   The relationship usually dissolves with the marriage creating it.
3   Step-parenthood is simultaneous with the new marriage.
4   The fertility of the new marriage is usually untested.
5   The step-parent stands in opposite relation to the child and spouse, as one is the biological parent and the other a stranger.
6   The stepchild usually knows or remembers the parent whom the step-parent replaces.
7   There is virtually no professional guidance offered to the step-parent.
8   The step-parent is burdened with an ancient and unflattering myth. . . .

If families in which there is a step-parent differ from adoptive families, they differ far more from ordinary families. The reason is that the basic rules that govern family life are disturbed in families where the children are not the biological offspring of both the husband and wife in the household. These rules concern sex and money: who may have sexual relations with whom, who must support whom and who may inherit from whom. Father sleeps with a woman who is not his son's mother, and is therefore not explicitly forbidden to the son by the recognised incest taboo. The child sits at the table of the breadwinner of the household, but the child is actually supported by a father living somewhere else. Often children who ordinarily would expect to inherit from their father and mother find their parent's new spouse will take away some or all of what might have been their portion. Or, if there are children of the new marriage as well as of a former marriage, there often exists an uncomfortable situation in which there are two sets of children who live under the same roof, or who spend vacations together, but who have quite different financial expectations. One might be, say, the daughter of the late Aly Khan and the other of Orson Welles. . . .

Still, there is no model for how a step-parent should behave. The parent's obligations, by contrast, are clear. The anthropologist Bronislaw Malinowski has pointed out that 'the mother, besides feeling inclined to do all she does for her child, is none the less obliged to do it'. Step-parents often do not feel inclined to do anything for their step-children, yet they feel strong pressure from the community, and from their spouse, to do something. But what? For natural parents, not only the obligations but the ideals are clear. . . .

The social questions posed by the remarriage of parents have hardly been faced by a society that ostensibly accepts divorce as the right solution to an unhappy marriage. We have been told that the marriage bond is the structural keystone in our kinship system and that our identity depends entirely on the marriage unit (unless we come from old-established lineage like the Devonshires or the Rothschilds). Who we are depends entirely on two families — our family of origin and our family of procreation; we are the children of our parents and the parents of our children. But we are not told how to preserve our sense of identity if we have a mother in one family, a father in another, a son in a third, and a daughter in a fourth.

The problems of identity and confused responsibilities are critical for children and adults who live in families that are amalgams of other families, and begin to explain why step-parenthood is nothing like parenthood.

Burgoyne and Clark (1982) draw upon their research with step-families in Sheffield to reach the following conclusions:

We have tried to suggest that it is still often the case that step-families are reconstituted according to a normative blueprint which is based on the unbroken nuclear family. Those who marry again are, therefore, heavily reliant on criteria of success, failure and adequacy which are drawn from 'normal' family life. Consequently evaluations of stepfamily life are typically made according to criteria of 'ordinariness'. However it is clear that stepfamilies differ in the extent to which they consciously attempt to 'pass' as an unbroken nuclear family by, for example, taking a new job and moving to a new area. Naturally this may seem to be the most obvious strategy; it brings about the normalisation of family life and, in the case of young adults with small children where divorce and custody are uncontested, this may well prove to be both practical and expedient. However, this may be impossible for other families. Where legal aspects of custody, access and maintenance arrangements are disputed and where older children and non-custodial parents are in regular contact, then the stepfamily is less likely to succeed in attempts at normalisation. For these families two possible strategies are available. Some may, out of a sense of guilt, propriety or confusion, choose to fly in the face of the structural factors which make their existence as a stepfamily both visible and incontravertible. The pursuit of the goal of normal family life is inevitably frustrated, as subjective ideals clash continually with external and material constraints. Others, to the extent that they recognise the nature of these problems, may reject, either explicitly or implicitly, such a course. Members of these families, sensitised by media coverage of trends in divorce and remarriage, see themselves as pioneers of an alternative life. Having accepted their situation, they formulate an ideology and practice to match it. In marked contrast to some of the literature which emphasised the negative aspects of step-relationships, they are clear that their way of life may also represent a source of potential rewards and satisfactions of a type absent from more conventional nuclear families. Typically, these step-families emphasise the material and social benefits which stepsiblings derive from one another's presence in the family, the value and importance of additional parental figures, and the fulfillment which results from reconstituting a single family from its disparate elements.

4 Step-parents and the law: to adopt or not to adopt?

Until the mid-seventies, the common solution to the contradictions of the step-parent role was to adopt the children, but this practice came under increasing attack from, in particular, social workers who acted as guardian ad litem for the child in the proceedings. In 1970, a Departmental Committee on the Adoption of Children (then under the chairmanship of Sir William Houghton) published a *Working Paper* which made the following radical suggestion:

92. About half the adoptions by a natural parent and a step-parent are of legitimate children, the application being made jointly by one of the child's parents and a new spouse following divorce or death of the child's other parent. Adoptions of legitimate children by a parent on remarriage after divorce could well increase if there is an increase in the divorce rate. Family circumstances in these cases may be very varied. Although the consent of the first partner is required unless dispensed with by the court and although the consent of a minor child to his adoption is required in Scotland and the wishes of the infant are taken into consideration in England and Wales, such adoptions hold the serious implication of effectively cutting children off from one of their natural legitimate parents with whom they may have lived for a consider-able time; these are the adoptions most likely to involve older children. The child may not wish to lose contact with the other parent, for whom he may well have deep feelings and a sense of loyalty. He may not want to have his name changed. He may suffer from severance of contact not only with one parent, but with siblings (e.g. if the divorce court divided custody of the children between the two parents) and other relatives. He may lose rights of inheritance. Circumstances may indeed later arise in which his return to the other parent would be desirable, e.g. on the breakdown of the second marriage of the parent having his custody. Some, though not all, of these considerations apply on remarriage after death of the first spouse as well as after divorce.

93. Just as openness about adoption and illegitimacy is desirable, so is it desirable to recognise openly the fact and the consequences of divorce and of death. One of the consequences of divorce is that many children are living with a parent and a step-parent and retain contact with, or even live for part of the time with, their other parent, who may also have remarried. Such a situation may well be disturbing to the child, but it is not appropriate to use adoption in an attempt to ease the pain or to cover up these consequences of divorce. The legal extinguishment of a legitimate child's links with one half of his own family, which adoption entails in such circumstances, is inappropriate and may well be damaging. We consider therefore that adoption of a legitimate child by a natural parent and step-parent should no longer be possible.

94. We recognise that we are drawing a distinction between legitimate and illegitimate children in that a step-parent will be able to adopt his step-child only if the child is illegitimate. This distinction might be regarded as invidious, and it may be thought that adoption by a step-parent should be available in both cases or in neither. On the other hand the two situations are not truly analogous. An illegitimate child, by adoption, obtains a legal status and a family which he did not have before. A legitimate child does not gain a more favourable legal status; he exchanges one set of family relationships for another, and almost inevitable severs existing family links.

. . . What is required is a legal procedure which recognises the position and the responsibility of the step-parent with whom such a child is living, enabling the step-parent to act as guardian of the child jointly with his spouse. The extension of guardianship law to permit step-parents to apply to be appointed guardians would provide the requisite procedure, enabling questions of custody and access to be decided by the court from time to time in accordance with the welfare of the child.

Questions

(i) Do you consider either the fact (*a*) that adoption confers legitimacy, or (*b*) that a higher proportion of illegitimate children have had no prior relationship with their fathers, or (*c*) any other reason, sufficient to justify the distinction here proposed?

(ii) If not, would you have opted (*a*) for banning them all, (*b*) for leaving things as they were, or (*c*) for some form of discouragement?

The final *Report* of the Committee (now under the chairmanship of Judge FA Stockdale following Sir William's death) (1972) stated that:

108. The evidence we received was overwhelmingly opposed to our suggestion. Some witnesses pointed to the positive advantages of adoption to a legitimate child whose other parent is dead or where contact with that parent and his family is negligible or non-existent. Others were strongly opposed to the distinction between legitimate and illegitimate children, pointing out that a parent may have a legitimate and an illegitimate child and on the remarrriage of the parent the illegitimate child could be adopted by the step-parent but not the legitimate child.

Accordingly, the following provisions reflect the committee's conclusions:

Adoption Act 1976
14(3) If the married couple consist of a parent and step-parent of the child, the court shall dismiss the application if it considers the matter would be better dealt with under section 42 (orders for custody etc.) of the Matrimonial Causes Act 1973.

Adoption Act 1976
15(4) If the applicant is a step-parent of the child the court shall dismiss the application if it considers the matter would be better dealt with under section 42 (orders for custody etc.) of the Matrimonial Causes Act 1973.

Children Act 1975
37(1) Where on an application for an adoption order by a relative of the child or by the husband or wife of the mother or father of the child, whether alone or jointly with his or her spouse, the requirements of section 16 of the Adoption Act 1976 [see pp. 503–504, below] or, where the application is for a Convention adoption order, section 17(6) of that Act are satisfied, but the court is satisfied—
  (*a*) that the child's welfare would not be better safeguarded and promoted by the making of an adoption order in favour of the applicant, than it would be by the making of a custodianship order in his favour, and
  (*b*) that it would be appropriate to make a custodianship order in the applicant's favour,
the court shall direct the application to be treated as if it had been made by the applicant under section 33 [for an order vesting legal custody of the child in the applicant], but if the application was made jointly by the father or mother of the child and his or her spouse, the court shall direct the application to be treated as if made by the father's wife or the mother's husband alone.

Questions

(i) Can you describe the precise effect of the different working of these provisions?

(ii) Can you see any reason for imposing a different burden of proof as between step-parent adoptions of children whose parents have divorced, and children who are illegitimate or semi-orphaned?

However, the third of these provisions is not yet in force, because the custodianship procedure under s. 33 (which was proposed by the Committee primarily as an alternative to 'family' adoptions) is also not yet in force (see further in Chapter 13). As it is unlikely that there will be any problem with parental agreement, either to illegitimate or to post death adoptions, the only impediment in these cases is the court's general duty to safeguard and promote the welfare of the child throughout his childhood and to give due consideration to the child's own wishes (Adoption Act 1976, s. 6). If either parent is dead, the guardian ad litem appointed by the court to protect the child's interests has a special duty to inform the court of any relative of the deceased parent who wishes to be heard.

Questions

(i) For which of the following children do you consider that adoption will generally be the 'better' solution and why: (*a*) a legitimate boy of 7 whose parents divorced when he was 3, whose father sends birthday and Christmas presents but not sufficient maintenance to keep them above supplementary benefit level, and who sees his father two or three times a year; (*b*) an illegitimate girl of 6 who does not know who her father is; (*c*) a legitimate boy of 12 whose father was killed in a road accident two years ago?
(ii) If you consider that there are sound reasons against adoption in any of those cases, do you think that some means should be available for creating some legal relationship between the child and the mother's new husband?

The following chart from *Social Trends 13* (1982) shows a particularly dramatic drop in step-parent adoptions of legitimate children:

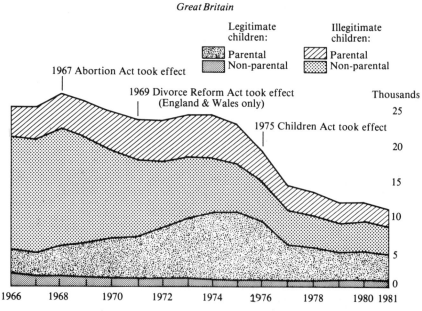

Annual number of adoptions

Great Britain

Source: *Office of Population Censuses and Surveys. General Register Office (Scotland)*

However, Judith Masson and Daphne Norbury have recently completed a study of the impact of these provisions in three different areas. Summarising their findings (1982), they report that the courts in each area were interpreting the new law in entirely different ways: in all areas, the number of applications, both for post-divorce and to a lesser extent for illegitimate children, fell; but in one area the success rate of post-divorce applications remained the same, at 96%, whereas in another it fell from 91% to 9%, and in the third, from 87% to 64%. The success rates for step-parent applications to adopt illegitimate children remained virtually the same in all three areas. Judges in the second area held strong views on step-parent adoptions, and would-be applicants were strongly discouraged by court staff, social workers and solicitors. This happened to some extent in the third area, while in the first, applicants encountered no such problems.

Re S (Infants) (Adoption by Parent)
[1977] Fam 173, [1977] 3 All ER 671, Court of Appeal

An adoption application for three boys aged from 11 to 6 was refused: the mother had herself refused their father's request to see them shortly before her remarriage and the adoption application was made only three months after the marriage; but the boys wanted to be adopted and the father had given his consent. In dismissing the appeal, Lord Justice Ormrod said this:

The effect of s. [14(3)], in our judgment, is to require the court, even in a case where adoption would safeguard and promote the welfare of the child, to consider the specific question whether, even so, the case might be 'better dealt with' under s. 42(1) of the Matrimonial Causes Act 1973, presumably by a joint custody order in favour of the natural parent and the step-parent, or by leaving the child in the custody of the natural parent. In cases like the present one the question becomes: 'will adoption safeguard and promote the welfare of the child better than either the existing arrangements or a joint custody order under s. 42?' . . . This will require considerably more investigation and information than in 'normal' adoption cases, in which a satisfactory report from the guardian ad litem is usually sufficient. In many cases it may be desirable that the judge should hear evidence from the other natural parent, even if his or her consent has been obtained, or at least have a detailed statement of his present attitud and of his past relationship with the child from the guardian ad litem. It will also be necessary to examine carefully the motives of each of the adopters, and in this respect the court many require assistance from the guardian ad litem, as the child's advocate, in the form of cross-examination. In fact, it will be the duty of the guardian ad litem, in this class of case, to draw the attention of the court to the disadvantages as well as the advantages of adoption.

Masson and Norbury in *Step-parent Adoption* (1982) uncovered a variety of procedures for putting this into effect:

In Area 1 no preliminary examinations of jurisdiction were held. In Area 2 the judges decided to review post divorce (and sometimes post death) cases at a 'hearing for directions' at which the applicants, their solicitor and the guardian ad litem were all present but the child was not. The judges explained the new law and why adoption was not appropriate in these cases. They then listed further enquiries which would have to be made before a full hearing. These included interviews with distant relatives and their attendance at the hearing even if they had not had recent contact with the child. As a result many applications were withdrawn.

Judges in Area 3 developed a variety of procedures. They tended to use the preliminary hearings to explain the new provisions and provide an opportunity for applicants to withdraw if they wished. A preliminary guardian ad litem's report was sometimes requested and in one court the original divorce file was obtained. . . .

Thus, in Areas 2 and 3, would-be applicants had to run the gauntlet of a discouraging interview with a court official, a social worker, their solicitor or even all three, a preliminary hearing and then the final hearing. In Area 1 they had no such problems.

One of the most comprehensive legal discussions of the advantages and disadvantages of step-parent adoptions comes from a county court case which was quoted by the Association of Child Care Officers in support of its argument for restricting them:

Re J (An Infant)
(1968) Child Care News No. 79, Edmonton County Court

The parents of a girl, now aged 5, were divorced. Her father had not been heard of for about two years and the judge would have been prepared to dispense with his agreement on the ground that he could not be found. The mother had remarried about a year ago. Her husband's son by a former marriage, now aged 6, also lived with them but there was no application to adopt him. The judge's discussion is addressed to whether adoption by the mother and step-father would be 'for the welfare of' the girl.

Judge HB Grant: . . . I am satisfied after considering the evidence and two meetings with the proposed adopters, that their motives in seeking an adoption are well intentioned and that there is nothing about them, their home or their upbringing of their respective step-children which exposes either to criticism. I accept that both want to do what they cosider right and best for the girl, but is adoption the right thing for her, bearing in mind that many of its objects can be achieved by alternative means not involving interference with the natural relationship between the child and its parents, which, it is generally agreed, is fundamental to the growth and health of human personality?

There is no advantage to the child in a case of this kind from the point of view of 'documentation.' Her birth certificate shows that she is legitimate; she is in fact legitimate. In these circumstances possession of the shortened form of birth certificate coupled with a certified copy of the appropriate entry in the Adopted Children Register are no gain to her.

But what about a change of name? — the desirability of the girl bearing her step-father's name is urged upon me; it is, I think, rightly said that the girl will want to bear the surname of the household in which she lives. I accept this, but adoption is not necessary for a change of the girl's surname. The step-father's name could become hers by repute, or, if desired, by deed poll as her natural father's disappearance dispenses with the need for his consent for her change of name (*Re T (otherwise H) (An Infant)* [1963] Ch 238, [1962] 3 All ER 970). The applicant's wish for the girl's change of name does not, therefore, require for its realisation an adoption order.

It is not that the child would obtain legal advantages by being adopted by her step-father which cannot be procured by other means. By accepting the girl as one of his family, he is henceforth in law liable to maintain her. It is true that the girl, unless adopted would not benefit on an intestacy on her step-father's death, or that she could not claim as a 'dependant' if she were unreasonably disinherited[2]. The answer is for the step-father to make a will and to include the girl amongst the beneficiaries. As I am told that he is a man of private means it would be sensible for him to make a will in any event.

Then it is said what about the girl's natural father? Can't he at any time, if he wants to, claim her or at least make a nuisance of himself by demanding access to the girl? Having regard to his disappearance and earlier history he seems very unlikely to do either. But assuming that, contrary to the probabilities, he were to attempt to assert claims to the girl as her natural father, the law provides ample machinery for defeating them. There is, therefore, as I see it, no real danger of interference by the father on the facts of this case and should he seek to interfere, his attempt will fail unless in the circumstances prevailing at the relevant time a court were to consider his proposals in the interest of the child.

Why then seek to adopt when there is no apparent need for it or resulting advantage for the girl? I think the real answer is the sense of insecurity and lack of confidence in the relationship

---

2. She could do so now as a 'child of the family,' under the Inheritance (Provision for Family and Dependants) Act 1975.

with their step-children which some step-fathers experience. This came out quite clearly during my meeting with the applicants when the step-father repeatedly expressed the wish that the girl should be 'his,' and agreed that it was fundamentally a 'psychological' matter. The truth of this is borne out by the fact that many step-fathers equally minded to do what is best for their step-children, refrain from adoption and that step-mothers, as illustrated by this case, in my experience, hardly ever seem to wish to do so.

I can fully understand the step-father's wish, but I do not believe that making the girl 'his' by adoption will help him to overcome this sense of insecurity, as this springs from the fact that the girl is not and never can be his natural child and not from any lack of legal or de facto control over her. Adoption, therefore, in my judgment is liable to prove an illusory step even from the step-father's pont of view and, in any event, I cannot see any direct or indirect benefit from it for the girl.

There are, no doubt, cases where a step-father's psychological difficulty is so severe that it threatens the stability of the marriage or prejudices his treatment of his step-child. It may be that adoption can help in such a situation although I doubt whether it can resolve it by itself without expert psychological treatment of the step-father.

This application is not that sort of case. I am quite satisfied on the evidence and having discussed with the step-father his wish for adoption that, regardless of the outcome of this application, he can and will treat the girl as an equal member of the family in exactly the same loving manner as he has done hitherto, just as his wife will always treat his son as if he was 'hers' without ever being his legal mother.

Questions

(i) Would it have been easier or more difficult to solve the practical problems in other ways if the child's father had not disappeared?

(ii) Given that those practical problems could be solved, how would you have balanced the 'psychological' advantages *for the child* of becoming 'his' against those of remaining the child of her absent father?

(iii) Why do you think that there was no application to adopt the step-father's son?

(iv) What do you think of the inquisitorial approach adopted by the judge in this case?

It would appear, however, that the Court of Appeal has had second thoughts on the matter:

Re D (Minors) (Adoption by Step-parent)
(1980) 2 FLR 102, 10 Fam Law 246, Court of Appeal

The parents of two girls, now aged 13 and $10\frac{1}{2}$, were divorced in 1973. In 1976 the mother married her present husband, who was also divorced and had the custody of the two children of his first marriage. The girls' name was changed to his by deed poll with the consent of their father. There was contact between the father and the eldest child until the end of 1977 and between him and the younger child until September 1978. In 1980 the mother and step-father applied to adopt the girls and the father consented. Both girls indicated to the guardian ad litem that they wished to be adopted. The family planned to emigrate to Australia. The guardian ad litem, after a thorough examination of the advantages and disadvantages, concluded that on balance the adoption order should not be made. The judge reached the same conclusion and the applicants appealed.

Ormrod LJ: . . . The difficulty in the case, of course, arises out of [s. 14(3) of the Adoption Act 1976], which has presented a considerable problem for the courts ever since it was passed. . . .

That provision was a new one in the 1975 Act and there is no doubt it was passed because, at the time, considerable anxiety was being caused by the multiplicity of adoption applications by step-parents. It is a matter of history that serious anxiety was aroused in many social workers' minds by this phenomenon, which was thought to be detrimental for a variety of reasons. It is not at all easy to know whether that anxiety was rightly based or not, but it is enough to say that Parliament accepted that this position required attention and so introduced this subsection.

It is, I think, important to note the terminology of the section. The section requires the court to dismiss an application for adoption if it considers that the matter would be *better* dealt with by means of a joint custody order. It is not a question of showing that an adoption order is itself better. The court has to consider whether or not the matter can be *better* dealt with by means of a joint custody order.

It is a very difficult decision to make because it is extremely difficult to know what criteria should be used in reaching the decision. The various financial provisions of the Matrimonial Causes Act 1973 and the Family Law Reform Act 1969 as well have now extended to the point when it is almost impossible to show any financial benefit from an adoption order. There may be some residual benefits which are of relevance in some cases but, in the vast majority of cases, it is impossible to show any material advantage to the children in an adoption order over and above custody. So the court has to consider very difficult psychological issues in coming to the conclusion that the matter can be better dealt with in one way or the other.

For my part, I find this an extremely difficult jurisdiction for the reason that I am by no means clear myself what are the appropriate criteria. Obviously an important factor in the matter, although by no means conclusive, is the fact that, under [s 6 of the 1976 Act], the court, in considering making an adoption order, is required by statute to ascertain, so far as practicable

'the wishes and feelings of the child regarding the decision and give due consideration to them . . .'

That, to my mind, must be an important consideration when dealing with children of the age of these children. They are fully old enough to understand, as I have said before, the broad implications of adoption and, if they actively wish to be adopted, even if they cannot give a very coherent reason for that wish, to refuse an adoption order in the face of that wish does require, as Brandon LJ said in the course of argument, some fairly clear reason. It does not appear from the learned judge's judgment that this point was in the forefront of his mind. It is, however, to me an important one.

I have mentioned other matters in this case which distinguish it from the run of these cases; and I think those can be summarized in a sentence by saying that the natural father of these children has dropped out of their lives both physically and psychologically to an extent which is much greater than one usually meets in this type of post-divorce situation. It is reasonable to infer that the children see themselves as members of the D family to a much, much greater extent than children of divorced parents normally do. There is no question of regarding Mr D as 'Uncle Tom' or whatever his name is. They clearly regard him as 'Dad'.

So it is a case in which, to my mind, all the indications are in favour of making an adoption order, more particularly as the family is about to emigrate to Australia. I can well understand the adults feeling that it would put their position in their new country much more clearly and explicitly if they go there with these two children as the adopted children of the family.

The points which troubled Mr White mainly seem to me to be, first, the fact that the children in this case had a full recollection of their natural father, and so it was not one of those cases such as *Re S* (1974) 5 Fam Law 88 where the children themselves have no recollection of their natural father and where the making of an adoption order gives legal effect to a situation which already exists in fact. But, to my mind, this is not a crucial distinction. The fact that they remember their natural father cannot be, in itself, a reason for not making an adoption order if the other indications suggest that it would be desirable. Of course these children remember their father.

Then it is said that the effect of an adoption order is to cut them off entirely from their father's family — to which, to my mind, the answer is that it may or may not do so. There is no magic in an adoption order. The fact that the child becomes a child of the new family does not, in itself, automatically cut off the children from the natural family. Of course it may do. An adoption order has that effect when the child is very young. I am always impressed by the differences in the considerations to be taken into account where one is concerned with the adoption of a small child, say up to two years, and an older child. The effect of adoption of a child up to two is to effect a complete severance with the natural family and, hopefully, a complete integration into the new family; but, once the child is older than that and has experience of a natural parent, adoption can never have that effect in fact. It may have in law that effect, but there is no reason why, if everyone is agreeable, children like these should not see their [paternal] grandparents should it be desirable. In fact, in this case we are told they are completely out of touch with the whole of the father's family, not only with the father himself. So that, with respect to Mr White and recognizing his extreme care in this case, I personally do not attach great significance to the fact that the children are fully aware of the existence of their natural father.

He was also troubled by what he thought would be the disturbing effect of the adoption order on the existing family unit. That I find hard to understand, because there seems to be no indication that an adoption order will materially alter anything in this new family except, if anything, to increas its cohesion and not diminish it. The judge was worried that, possibly, after an adoption order had been made, one of the children might turn on the adoptive father and challenge him as not being their own father. But, with respect, that point must apply with even more force to a situation where Mr D's position is simply that of a joint custodian under the Matrimonial Causes Act.

He also took the point — and one sees the force of it again — that there was a distinction here between the two children that we are dealing with and the two children of the husband because there was no suggestion of an application by the step-mother, Mrs D, for an adoption order in respect of them. We are told that the reason for that is that their mother, that is the first Mrs D, has so completely disappeared out of the children's lives that the proposed adopters in this case regarded proceedings for an adoption order in respect of those children as being quite super-fluous and unnecessary. If that is right — and it seems to me, on the face of it, reasonable to suppose that it is — then there does not seem to be any serious objection from that point of view. . . .

One can understand perfectly clearly the basis of the learned judge's decision but he does not seem to have asked himself what I think is the relevant question: can this matter be *better* dealth with by a custody order? If he had asked himself that question, he might have found it difficult to answer positively because, for my part, I can see no positive advantages in this case in dealing with the matter in that way.

In those circumstances, this court is, I think, entitled to review the exercise of the learned judge's discretion and, for my part, I can see no coherent objection to adoption, except possibly the theoretical objection against step-fathers, which has been advanced by some schools of thought. All the factual masterial in this case seems to me to point one way and I can see nothing pointing against adoption. I would be very hesitant, in a case where the natural father is consenting and the children wish to be adopted, to stand in the way of an adoption order being made. The children might well see this as 'an intrusion by authority' andan unnecessary one which they will not understand and will resent. I do not think it worthwhile to give hostages to fortune to teenage children of this age, at this time and in this period of history. They do not require much encour{}gement to be difficult about authority and this seems to me to be a way of making them resentful.

For those reasons I think all the indications in the case point towards an adoption order. I would, therefore, allow the appeal and make such order.

Emigration causes a lot of trouble. Under the Matrimonial Causes Rules 1977, r. 94, the divorce court usually prohibits the custodial parent from taking the children out of the country without the other parent's consent or the leave of the court. A holiday abroad is one thing, but how can the child's right to access be reconciled with emigration?

Barnes v Tyrrell
(1981) 3 FLR 240, Court of Appeal

The parents were married in 1967 and there were two children, a boy of 12 and a girl of 11. In 1976 the mother left the father and soon afterwards was granted the custody of both children. The father had liberal access to them and after decree absolute in 1977 he gave up his post as housemaster in a children's home and moved to another town in order to be near the children.

In 1977 the mother met an Australian. They began living together, a child was born in April 1979 and a month later they married. She applied for leave to take the two (elder) children out of the jurisdiction to Australia on the ground that her new husband considered that he had better prospects if he returned to Australia where all his family lived. On 31 March 1980, Balcombe J dismissed the mother's application because of evidence by the welfare officer that the boy in particular might be upset if he was taken to Australia and deprived of his regular contact with his father.

The mother's appeal against the judge's refusal was dismissed by the Court of Appeal on 8 May 1980. . . .

In June 1980 the mother obtained leave from Ewbank J for the children to go to Australia for a holiday. The evidence was that the holiday was a success. The boy had changed his mind about Australia and would like to live there and the girl was keen to go, although both children wished to keep contact with their father. The judge, because of what he called the children's 'marked change of view', made an order giving leave and providing for access to the father in this country annually for a holiday.

The father appealed, . . .

Dunn LJ: . . . In these cases one always has a great deal of sympathy for the parent who is, in effect, left beind. What is said in this appeal on behalf of the father is that the judge gave insufficient weight to the fact that these children had had very regular contact with the father, notwithstanding the breakdown of the marriage. It was not a case such as *P (LM) (otherwise E) v P (GE)* [1970] 3 All ER 659, where there was a very young child who hardly knew his father, but in this case the children obviously have a good relationship with their father and have been cared for by him for a period after the mother left.

Then it was said that these children of 11 and 12 would be uprooted from their schools, they would be sent to an entirely new system of education in Australia, and they would be taken away from what is nowadays called their 'extended' family, namely their grandparents, uncles and aunts and cousins, and would go to a strange country where they would only have their mother as a blood relation.

Speaking for myself it seems to me that all these matters were taken into account by the judge before he made the order. The principle which is followed by the court in these cases was stated by Sachs LJ in *P (LM) (otherwise E) v P (GE)* [1970] 3 All ER 659 at 662, where he said:

'When a marriage breaks up, a situation normally arises when the child of that marriage, instead of being in the joint custody of both parents, must of necessity become one who is in the custody of a single parent. Once that position has arisen and the custody is working well, this court should not lightly interfere with such reasonable way of life as is selected by that parent to whom custody has been rightly given. Any such interference may . . . produce considerable strains which would not only be unfair to the parent whose way of life is interfered with but also to any new marriage of that parent. In that way it might well in due course reflect on the welfare of the child. The way in which the parent who properly has custody of a child may choose in a reasonable manner to order his or her way of life is one of those things which the parent who has not been given custody may well have to bear, even though one has every sympathy with the latter on some of the results.'

The judge plainly had that passage in mind because he dealt at length with the arrangements for these children in Australia. He had the evidence not only of the mother and Mr B, but also of Mr B's father as to what the circumstances were in Australia. It appears from the evidence, which the judge accepted, that Mr B's financial prospects are better in Australia than they are in this country. He would be likely to command a better salary there than he does here. There is apparently a suitable house in a suburb of Sydney, where his parents live, and the judge had evidence from Mr B's father as to the schools available in Australia. The judge summed it up in this way:

'The prospect of the family, accordingly, is one of prosperity in Australia, or a very much more uncertain prospect in England. Mr B is very anxious to go back to his home. The baby is an Australian, and he would wish to bring her up in Australia.'

The judge came to the conclusion, accordingly, that the mother's wish to take the children to Australia was an entirely reasonable one and upon that basis he made the order.

5 What's in a name?

Most of the practical legal problems of step-parenthood can be solved in other ways than through adoption, but the most important psychological symbol of membership of a family group is the child's surname. Following the Guardianship Act of 1973, mother and father now have equal rights and authority over matters of custody and upbringing, so that the father's right to insist that his children bore his name has almost certainly gone. But once a surname has been assumed for the child, it is clear that neither parent may change it without the other's consent (*Y v Y (Child: Surname)* [1973] Fam 147, [1973] 2 All ER 574). Case law is reinforced by rule 92(8) of the *Matrimonial Causes Rules 1977*:

Unless otherwise directed, any order giving a parent custody or care and control of a child shall provide that no step (oter than the institution of proceedings in any court) be taken by that parent which would result in the cild being known by a new surname before he or she attains the age of 18 years or, being a female, marries below that age, except with the leave of a judge or the consent in writing of the other parent.

The problem is that fathers who are anxious to maintain their links with the children may be just as opposed to a change of surname as they are to an adoption: but whereas the courts have been most reluctant to override such a parent's objections to an adoption order (*Re D (Minors) (Adoption by Parent)* [1973] Fam 209, [1973] 3 All ER 1001; *Re B (A Minor) (Adoption by Parent)* [1975] Fam 127, [1975] 2 All ER 449) — unless they believe that contact with the parent will be positively harmful to the child (*Re D (An Infant) (Adoption: Parent's Consent)* [1977] AC 602, [1977] 2 All ER 145), they have experienced far more difficulty in deciding whether or not it is in the child's best interests to be known by another name:

R (BM) v R (DN)
[1978] 2 All ER 33, [1977] 1 WLR 1256, 121 Sol Jo 758, Court of Appeal

The case was a custody dispute about whether the youngest of four children, a boy now aged 6½, should continue to live with his father and new partner or should join the other children, who lived with their mother and her new partner, in army quarters at the rural camp where he was stationed. The trial judge gave custody to the mother and Stamp LJ described the father's appeal as 'hopeless.' One element in the father's objections to the transfer was the fact that the three older children were using the surname of their mother's new partner, Sergeant W, and it is on that point alone that their lordships are quoted.

Stamp LJ: . . . The judge was satisfied that Sergeant W would always be ready to remind the children that he was not their real father, but their real father was alive and well and very fond of them. The judge thought he would make it a point of honour to ensure that any of the children that were with him continued to remember and respect the father. . . . The point was made by counsel for the father in the course of his submissions in this court that the judge might not have been aware at that point or had it present to his mind at that point in his judgment that the three elder children, now in the camp where they are, are known officially by the surname of W, and it was suggested that this rather tended to counter the judge's findings that Sergeant W would always be ready to remind the child that he was not their real father. . . .

I think that too much attention is paid to these matters of names of children, the names by which they are known, on some occasions at least, and it must be most convenient that they should be known as W in the camp in which they are being brought up where Sergeant W is the head of the family.

Ormrod LJ: . . . It may be, I say no more than that, that r. 92(8) of the Matrimonial Causes [Rule 1977] has been drawn in a wider sense than the draftsman intended. I remember that at the time it was directed to preventing parents with custody or care and control orders changing children's names by deed poll or by some other formal means, but, unfortunately, it now seems to be causing a great deal of trouble and difficulty to school authorities and to children and the very last thing that any rule of this court is intended to do is to embarrass children. It should not be beyond our capacity as adults to cope with the problem of dealing with children who naturally do not want to be picked out and distinguished by their friends and known by a surname other than their mother's, if they are thinking about it at all. It is very embarrassing for school authorities and indeed to the court if efforts have to be made to stop a little girl signing her name 'W' when it really is 'R'. We are in danger of losing our sense of proportion. All one can say in this particular case is that one can understand the situation, which is not at all unusual, and I just hope that no one is going to make a point about this name business, in other words, to treat it as a symbol of something which it is not. There is nothing in this case that suggests that the mother or Sergeant W want to make a takeover bid for this family from the father and turn these children into their own children, nothing at all. Therefore, I hope that it can be treated as counsel in his exchanges with the learned judge below observed, 'This is a peripheral matter.' I would endorse that strongly.

Question

Did Ormrod LJ mean (*a*) that rule 92(8) does not apply to a purely informal change of name, or (*b*) that, if asked, he would have given leave under the rule for the name to be changed?

D v B (otherwise D) (Surname: Birth Registration)
[1979] Fam 38, [1979] 1 All ER 92, [1978] 3 WLR 573, 122 Sol Jo 486, 9 Fam Law 89, Court of Appeal

The mother became pregnant by her husband D, but left to live with B, and changed her name to his by deed poll, before the child was born. She registered D as the child's father, but gave B's name as 'the surname by which at the date of registration it is intended that the child shall be known.' The parents were divorced and the mother granted custody of the child, a boy now aged 2½. The father applied for access and for an order that the boy be known by the surname D. The trial judge ordered the mother to amend her deed poll and rectify the register, and forbade her to cause or permit the boy to be known by any other name than D without either D's consent or the leave of the court. The mother did not comply, and when faced in further proceedings with the threat of committal for contempt of court, appealed against the order. The Court of Appeal held (i) that she could not be ordered to amend the deed poll, as a deed poll was merely evidence of the name by which a person was generally known, which in her case was B, and (ii) that she could not rectify the register, because the information she had given was correct. The single judgment, with which Stamp LJ agreed, is quoted on the substantive issue of which surname the child should now use.

Ormrod LJ: . . . I am sure everyone understands that the question of the surname of a child is a matter of great emotional significance, particularly to fathers. If the name is lost, in a sense, the child is lost. That strong patrilineal feeling we all to some extent share. But this has to be kept within the bounds of common sense, in my judgment. It is not very realistic to be litigating over how a child of 2½ should be called, so far as its surname is concerned. A child at that age is quite unaware of its surname, even though it will acquire later on, fairly quickly perhaps, some idea of what his name or her name is. But what matters is whether the child identifies with the father in human terms. I suspect that children are much better at distinguishing between reality and formality than adults. If the child knows that D is his father, he may be confused later on if he is known by the name B, but I would doubt it. He is certain to be confused if everybody insists on calling him D when very nearly all the people he lives with are called B. But this is, as one appreciates all too clearly, a very sensitive issue. Fathers feel very sensitive about it. Mothers feel that it is a plague on a day-to-day basis: they have to explain to schools, people have to make special notes in records, and so on, about the name. The matter is one which, in my judgment, ought to be capable of being resolved by two sensible adults who bear in mind that they are dealing with a child, and a child who sooner or later, and probably sooner, will make some decisions for himself in the matter. Pressure, I would have thought, is more likely to produce unwanted results than anything else.

I cannot help reiterating the Official Solicitor's advice in this case,

'For [the child] to be known as [D] when his mother and [Mr B] are called [B] could cause him some embarrassment particularly when he attends school. The mother and [Mr B] might well have children of their own and this in itself could cause some distress insofar as [the child] will be the only one in the family unit with a different surname. In the circumstances, should the Court decide that the father should have access to [the child], and the Official Solicitor recommends that he should, the father might consider that it would be in [the child's] best interests for the future not to insist on his being known by his real surname of [D].'

If I may say so with great respect to the Official Solicitor, that passage seems to me the best statement of good sense that I have read in this context for a long time. It seems to me human, sensible and practical. Any other solution seems to me inhuman, impracticable and bound to lead to trouble.

Questions

(i) If a person's true surname in English law is 'that by which he is generally known,' why did the Official Solicitor describe D as the boy's 'real surname'?

(ii) By the same token, why did the judge (Mrs Justice Lane) assume throughout that the mother had *changed* the child's surname?

(iii) Did rule 92(8) apply to the case at all?

(iv) The facts of this case are quite different from those in *R (BM) v R (DN)* but the result reached on the substantial issue was the same: does this indicate that Stamp and Ormrod LJJ think that it will generally be better for children to adopt their step-parents' surnames?

W v A (Child: Surname)
[1981] Fam 14, [1981] 1 All ER 100, [1981] 2 WLR 124, 124 Sol Jo 726, 11 Fam Law 22, Court of Appeal

The parents separated in 1971 when their children were aged 3 and 1½. They were granted joint custody, with care and control to the mother and reasonable access, which was exercised, to the father. After divorce, both remarried; the mother married an Australian who wished to return with her and the children to his home country. The father agreed, provided that the mother undertook not to change the children's surname. The mother and both children, now aged 12 and 10, wished to use the step-father's name. The trial judge refused leave to change and the mother appealed. Bridge and Lawton LJJ both agreed with the single judgment dismissing the appeal.

Dunn LJ: . . . When the question of the change of name came before the judge, he was faced with the dilemma that there are two apparently conflicting lines of authority in this court on the question of changing children's surnames. The first is that the change of a child's surname is an important matter, not to be undertaken lightly. The second is that the change of a child's surname is a comparatively unimportant matter. The judge, faced with the choice between those two lines of authority, opted for the first. The primary grounds of this appeal is that in so doing he erred in law.

The first case to which he referred was *Re W G* (1976) 6 Fam Law 210. . . . Cairns LJ is reported as saying (6 Fam Law 210):

'It was, of course, important to bear in mind all the way through . . . that it was in the paramount interests of the child with which their Lordships were concerned. It had not been suggested on either side here that the court should approach a decision in the case from any other point of view. But his Lordship thought it important that it should be realised that the mere fact that there had been a divorce, that the mother had remarried and had custody of the child and had a name different from that of the child, was not sufficient reason for changing the child's surname . . . The courts recognise the importance of maintaining a link with the father, unless he had ceased to have an interest in the child or there were some grounds, having regard to his character and behaviour, which made it undesirable for him to have access to the child at all. It must greatly tend to create difficulties in the relations between a father and a child if the child ceased to bear the father's name.'

His lordship then referred to *R(BM) v R(DN)* and *D v B (otherwise D)*, pointing out that the first was a custody dispute and that in the second, the father had accepted that access rather than surname was the principal issue; he concluded that dicta on the change of the name were obiter; but if they were not, he did not agree; he then quoted from the decision of Latey J in *L v F* (1978) Times, 1 August:

'Until the two recent decisions expressed by Lord Justice Stamp and Lord Justice Ormrod the prevailing view, enunciated in *Re W G* and which had never been questioned, was that on the failure of a marriage a decision to change children's surnames should never be taken unilaterally and that unless parents were in agreement a decision about it should be approached by the court as a matter of real importance. [Pausing there for one moment, I agree with every word of that. The judge went on:] The fact that one approach had been evolved over many years and the other had only recently been expressed did not mean that either should automatically be accepted as correct. One had to make a fresh appraisal. His Lordship had reached the opinion that the approach expressed by Lord Justice Cairns in *Re W G* was the correct one. The court was concerned with cases where the parents were in disagreement. A marriage could be dissolved but not parenthood. The parents in most cases continued to play an important role in their children's emotional lives and development. From the point of view of the children's best interests it was essential that the parents' feelings should be taken very carefully, and anxiously into consideration. . . .'

'A very distinguished child psychiatrist had given evidence that, when they grew older, children were often greatly concerned with their biological origin. How then could one accept that a change of name was of little importance to the children? His Lordship could not. In one case a change might be of benefit to them. In another it might injure them. Surely it was an important decision?'

How then does the law stand with regard to the approach by courts in applications for change of a surname? As in all cases concerning the future of children whether they be custody, access, education or, as in this case, the change of a child's name, s. 1 of the Guardianship of Minors Act 1971 requires that the court shall regard 'the welfare of the [child] as the first and paramount consideration'. It is a matter for the discretion of the individual judge hearing the case, seeing the witnesses, seeing the parents, possibly seeing the children, to decide whether or not it is in the interests of the child in the particular circumstances of the case that his surname should or should not be changed; and the judge will take into account all the circumstances of the case, including no doubt where appropriate any embarrassment which may be caused to the child by not changing his name and, on the other hand, the long-term interests of the child, the importance of maintaining the child's links with his paternal family, and the stability or otherwise of the mother's remarriage. I only mention those as typical examples of the kinds of considerations which arise in these cases, but the judge will take into account all the relevant circumstances in the particular case before him. . . .

Speaking for myself, I think the judge was entirely right not to attach decisive importance to the views of two young children of 12 and 10 who were about to embark on the excitement of going to Australia with their mother and their new stepfather.

Other criticisms were made of the judge. It was said that there were positive advantages to these children in changing their surname. They were about to make a fresh start in a new country and it would be an advantage to them to go out as a united family. A change of name, it was said, would not make much difference to the father because the children would be at the other end of the world and he has two sons by his second marriage, so the name of A will survive in Gloucestershire. It is also said that, when they get older, if the children wished to change their name back to A they could always do so.

I have no doubt that the judge had all these matters in mind and there is nothing in his reasons, in his short judgment, which leads me to suppose that he did not. On the contrary, it seems to me that the judge approached this matter entirely rightly.

Questions

(i) Do you think that children of this age are any less entitled to a view on this point than they are on adoption?

(ii) Do you think that *either* of the opposing camps in the Court of Appeal is indeed putting the children's interests before those of the adults?

(iii) There are many cases in which a child's surname might be changed without resort to litigation — for example, if any of these fathers had consented, or if they were dead, or if the children had used their names despite being illegitimate — are the arguments against allowing this any less strong in such cases?

The empirical evidence in support of a child's 'right to know' has been collected in studies of children fostered or adopted by strangers and is therefore discussed in Chapter 13. But Wallerstein and Kelly's study of children and their parents in 60 divorced families in California can at least supply a foot-note to the present debate about step-parents. In *Surviving the Break-up* (1980) they discuss 'fathers versus step-fathers':

The child's relationship with stepfather and father, and the various ways in which this issue was resolved by the child and adults or continued as a source of open conflict, was of central importance in the psychological development and adjustment of the child within the remarried family. The extent to which the child was able to share in the benefits of the marriage depended in large measure on the satisfactory resolution of this conflict by the adults and the children.

Many children were able to maintain and enjoy both relationships. The father and the stepfather did not occupy the same slot in the child's feelings and the child did not confuse the relationship with the two men. Mostly, children enlarged their view of the family and made room for three major figures, all of whom were potentially and actually of major importance in shaping the child's psychological, social, and moral development and ultimately important life choices. . . .

The expectation of many people that the children would necessarily experience conflict as they turned from father to stepfather during their growing-up years was not borne out by our observations. Nor was the expectation that in the happily remarried family the biological father was likely to fade out of the children's lives. . . .

The stepfather's influence, in turn, was not undone by the child's continued visiting with the father. Neither divorce nor remarriage appeared to change substantially the importance or the emotional centrality of both biological parents for the growing child. At the same time, the stepfather's influence was enormous. He, clearly, could greatly enhance the child's development — broadening his or her intellectual horizons, strengthening moral development, and exercising a far-reaching, beneficial effect on every aspect of the child's character structure which was still in the process of formulation. Conversely, the stepfather could constrict the child's emotional life, narrow his or her vision of the world, increase unhappiness, or decrease self-esteem. But even with this major potential influence, the stepfather did not replace the departed father. Only when the child *voluntarily* rejected the father, or counter-rejected the father and voluntarily disidentified with the father and placed the stepfather in the father's role, did replacement occur. . . .

Most of the children in these remarried families made every effort to conceptualize stepfather, father, and mother together, and their efforts to make room for all of them were impressive.

Question

Ask yourself once more the questions posed on p. 404, above. Do you still reach the same conclusions?

CHAPTER 12

Children in care

In this chapter we are concerned with the child care service which local authorities provide for children who have no parents or whose parents are for some reason prevented from caring for them themselves. We shall see first how it evolved from the very different service provided under the Poor Law. Then we shall consider the concept of 'voluntary' reception into care, and the problems which this can create, for children, parents and social workers alike. The solution to those problems may sometimes be a decision of the local authority to assume the rights of the parents, and we must examine both the law relating to this controversial process and the arguments for its reform. We must also consider the accountability of local authorities, both to parents and to the courts, for the way in which they discharge their duty to look after the children in their care.

The fundamental question which underlies the material in this chapter — but also in the next three chapters (which are concerned with fostering and adoption, child abuse, parental autonomy and the rights of children) — is of the proper balance to be struck between the rights of parents to decide how their children shall be brought up and the claims of children to the upbringing they are thought by others to need. The 'welfare of the child' developed as a legal concept in private litigation between individuals — usually the child's mother and father — whose status in relation to the child and to one another could increasingly be seen as equal. Far more complex issues are raised in attempting to apply that concept between the child's own parents and the agencies of the state. Their flavour can best be summed up in Jean Packman's fear that some of our most recent developments in child care policy raise 'faint but ominous echoes of a more distant past, when deserving parents coped independently and undeserving parents lost their children to the Poor Law' (1981). Should the title of this chapter in fact have been: Back to the Poor Law?

1 Out of the Poor Law

In today's child centred world, it is worth remembering the evidence that attitudes in the past were very different, shown by Philippe Ariès in *Centuries of Childhood* (1960):

No one thought of keeping a picture of a child if that child had either lived to grow to manhood or had died in infancy. In the first case childhood was simply an unimportant phase of which there was no need to keep any record; in the second case, that of the dead child, it was thought that the little thing which had disappeared so soon in life was not worthy of remembrance: there were far too many children whose survival was problematical. The general feeling was, and for a long time remained that one had several children in order to keep just a few. As late as the seventeenth century, in *Le Caquet de l'accouchée*, we have a neighbour, standing at the bedside of a woman who has just given birth, the mother of five 'little brats', and calming her fears with these words: 'Before they are old enough to bother you, you will have lost half of them, or perhaps all of them.' A strange consolation! People could not allow themselves to become too attached to something that was regarded as a probable loss. . . .

The appearance of the portrait of the dead child in the sixteenth century accordingly marked a very important moment in the history of feelings.

Indeed, Edward Shorter in *The Making of the Modern Family* (1975) argues that the traditional indifference towards children lasted much longer among the ordinary people than amongst those who could afford portraits. His other addition to Aries is even more startling:

The high rate of infant loss is not a sufficient explanation for the traditional lack of maternal love *because precisely this lack of care was responsible for the high mortality*. At least in part. If children perished in great numbers, it wasn't owing to the intervention of some *deus ex machina* beyond the parents' control. It came about as a result of circumstances over which the parents had considerable influence: infant diet, age at weaning, cleanliness of bed linen, and the general hygienic circumstances that surrounded the child — to say nothing of less tangible factors in mothering, such as picking up the infant, talking and singing to it, giving it the feeling of being loved in a secure little universe. Now by the late eighteenth century, parents knew, at least in a sort of abstract way, that letting new-born children stew in their own excrement or feeding them pap from the second month onwards were harmful practices. For the network of medical personnel in Europe had by this time extended sufficiently to put interested mothers within earshot of sensible advice. The point is that these mothers did not *care*, and that is why their children vanished in the ghastly slaughter of the innocents that was traditional child-rearing. Custom and tradition and the frozen emotionality of ancien-régime life gripped with deathly force. When the surge of sentiment shattered this grip, infant mortality plunged, and maternal tenderness became part of the world we know so well.

If it be the case that many mothers were so indifferent to their children, we cannot expect any great degree of community concern. Jean Heywood explains the beginnings of the public service for the deprived child in her classic history of *Children in Care* (now 1978):

In pre-Reformation England the orphaned or illegitimate had a place in a feudal and employed community, though opportunities were open and found for human nature to exploit him. His safeguard, if it existed, lay in the communal nature of the society and its ethical canons, expressed — though not always observed — in the teaching against usury, on the duty of almsgiving, on the efficacy of the corporal works of mercy. In the fact that life was centred round the community rather than the family there lay the possibility of opportunity and protection for the unwanted child. In the community obligations of medieval society a way could be found to provide for him and the family setting was less vital to him than it is to us today. The medieval Church had exalted not the private family but rather the greater one, Christian society, endowing chastity, asceticism and celibacy with greater virtue than the sacrament of marriage. It was at the Reformation period when economic as well as religious changes were taking place, that men turned from the Church's teaching on celibacy, and as they found the social order crumbling away they discovered that in family life there could also be an opportunity to witness to the glory of God.

The ideal of the small home and personal family life could hardly be achieved until a middle class came into existence. The sixteenth century Tudor households of yeomen farmers, of small merchants and tradesmen provided the setting in which real family life became possible, and in a growing urban society, which was neither stable economically, nor ruled any longer by a philosophy on the good of a united community, the family became of major significance. Without it the individual was unsupported in society and became without identity.

The spread of destitution which followed the social and economic changes of the sixteenth century was the cause of the increasing legislation dealing with poor relief in the Tudor era. Vagrancy increased with unemployment, and everywhere the old order was breaking down and a new and as yet unstable society being formed.

The discharging of servants and apprentices increased the numbers of deprived children while the growth of poverty, vagrancy and unemployment made it more difficult for them to find a home or to be fitted in to the pattern of village life. Collections made for the poor in the parish churches were unable to meet the demand for alms. The dissolved houses of the monks and nuns were no longer able to provide out-relief, and the hospitals were falling into decay. In consequence laws were passed to make each parish responsible for providing a place where the sick, the old and the 'succourless poor child' could receive shelter and care. At this time, too, the right of destitute children to beg was recognised and they were given a licence.

. . . . In 1530, authority was first given for the compulsory apprenticing of vagrant children between the ages of five and fourteen, though sixteen years afterwards further legislation had to reduce the severity of apprenticeship regulations and give justices power to liberate children badly treated by master and mistress.

The crowds of vagrants and unemployed at this time (which included the child 'unapt to learning') were seen not only as a chronic nuisance but a serious danger to society, as social failures for whom the community was now legally and financially responsible. . . .

So many of the composite hospitals which were established at this time, at first by persuasive and finally by compulsory taxation, for the relief of the poor became also houses of correction and punishment for the idle, as well as technical schools for the young. The deprived child, in need of training, and old and sick people in need of care were accommodated together with vagrants sent for punishment. The degradation of the pauper had begun.

It was the Elizabethan statute, the Poor Relief Act of 1601, which set the pattern for our system of relief to the poor until 1948. Those responsible for the care of deprived children, the churchwardens and the parish overseers, were to take such measures as were necessary for setting them to work or binding them as apprentices. These bald embodiments of a constructive principle of care remained unaltered in our legislation for three hundred and forty-seven years, until the shadow of a grim farm-house fell across them, and darkened them for ever.

Question

Compare that Heywood says of the 'ideal of the small home and personal family life' with the historical material in Chapter 1: would other historians agree?

The responsibilities of the churchwardens and overseers later passed to the Boards of Guardians and relieving officers and later still to the public assistance committees and officers of local authorities, but their duty to care for the destitute was still expressed in the same terms. Section 15(1) of the *Poor Law Act* of 1930 imposed the following duties:

(*b*) to provide such relief as may be necessary for the lame, impotent, old, blind and such other persons as are poor and not able to work;

(*c*) to set to work or put out as apprentices all children whose parents are not, in the opinion of the Council, able to keep and maintain their children;

The 'grim farmhouse' to which Heywood refers was Bank Farm, Minsterley, in Shropshire, where Dennis O'Neill died on 9 January 1945. The bare facts of his death are recounted in Sir Walter Monckton's *Report* upon the scandal (1945):

2. . . . Dennis and Terence O'Neill were born respectively on the 2 March 1932, and the 13 December 1934, and were the children of Thomas John O'Neill, a labourer, of Newport, Monmouthshire, and Mabel Blonwyn O'Neill, his wife. On the 30 May 1940, Dennis and Terence were committed by the Newport Juvenile Court to the care or protection of the Newport County Borough Council, as a 'fit person' within the meaning of Sections 76 and 96 of the Children and Young Persons Act 1933, hereinafter referred to as the 1933 Act. Dennis was boarded out at Bank Farm, Minsterley, Shropshire, on the 28 June 1944. The foster-parents were Reginald Gough and Esther Gough, his wife. Terence joined Dennis at Bank Farm on the 5 July 1944. Dennis died there on the 9 January 1945. Terence was removed from Bank Farm to a place of safety on the 10 January 1945.

3. An inquest was held on the boy Dennis. The coroner's jury returned a verdict that his death was due to acute cardiac failure following violence applied to the front of the chest and back while in a state of under-nourishment due to neglect and added a rider that there had been a serious lack of supervision by the local authority. Reginald and Esther Gough were charged with

manslaughter. At Stafford Assizes on the 19 March 1945, Reginald Gough was found guilty of manslaughter and was sentenced to six years' penal servitude. Esther Gough was found not guilty of manslaughter but guilty of neglect and was sentenced to six months' imprisonment.

The Goughs had first taken Dennis in when another placement in Shropshire which the Newport authority had arranged fell through at the last moment and the school attendance officer who had been sent to escort the boys had to find somewhere for him that day: but thereafter, the placement continued without any adequate inquiry about the Goughs' suitability, the children were never medically examined, nor visited in accordance with the rules governing 'boarding out' and there were failures in communication and understanding between the Newport authority, the Shropshire education officers, and the Shropshire public assistance officers who were involved with other children at the farm during the same period. Sir Walter concluded, however, that little change in the law was needed:

54. . . . What is required is rather that the administrative machinery should be improved and informed by a more anxious and responsible spirit. I have indicated where I think improvement is needed. The boarding-out rules ought plainly to be obeyed in the letter and in the spirit. Their requirements should be treated as a minimum, not a barely attainable maximum. Greater attention should be paid to the careful selection of foster-homes and foster-parents. The personal relation in which the local authority, which has undertaken care and protection stands to the child should be more clearly recognized. The medical attention called for by the rules should be insisted upon. Adequate and regular supervision of the children in the foster-homes by competent persons should take place, and the responsible higher officials should satisfy themselves on this score. It may well be that, in order to ensure that those who supervise are competent for the purpose, some training or instruction should be required; but this is a question which would need fuller consideration. The duty to be sure in the care of children must not be put aside, however great may be the pressure of other burdens.

By that time, of course, plans were already afoot for the abolition of the Poor Law, and other influences were urging a different approach to the care of children:

WHOSE CHILDREN?
WARDS OF STATE OR CHARITY

To the Editor of *The Times*

Sir,

Thoughtful consideration is being given to many fundamental problems, but in reconstruction plans one section of the community has, so far, been entirely forgotten.

I write of those children who, because of their family misfortune, find themselves under the guardianship of a Government Department or one of the many charitable organisations. The public are, for the most part, unaware that many thousands of these children are being brought up under repressive conditions that are generations out of date and are unworthy of our traditional care for children. Many who are orphaned, destitute, or neglected, still live under the chilly stigma of 'charity'; too often they form groups isolated from the main stream of life and education, and few of them know the comfort and security of individual affection. A letter does not allow space for detailed evidence.

In many 'Homes', both charitable and public, the willing staff are, for the most part, overworked, underpaid, and untrained; indeed, there is no recognised system of training. Inspection, for which the Ministry of Health, the Homes Office, or the Board of Education may be nominally responsible, is totally inadequate, and few standards are established or expected. Because no one Government Department is fully responsible, the problem is the more difficult to tackle.

A public inquiry, with full Government support, is urgently needed to explore this largely uncivilised territory. Its mandate should be to ascertain whether the public and charitable organisations are, in fact, enabling these children to lead full and happy lives, and to make recommendations how the community can compensate them for the family life they have lost. In particular, the inquiry should investigate what arrangements can be made (by regional reception centres or in other ways) for the careful consideration of the individual children before they are finally placed with foster-parents or otherwise provided for; how the use of large residential homes can be avoided; how staff can be appropriately trained and ensured adequate salaries and suitable conditions of work, and how central administrative responsibility can best be secured so that standards can be set and can be maintained by adequate inspection.

The social upheaval caused by the war has not only increased this army of unhappy children, but presents the opportunity for transforming their conditions. The Education Bill and the White paper on the Health Services have alike ignored the problem and the opportunity.

Yours sincerely,
Marjory Allen of Hurtwood.

Hurtwood House, Albury, Guildford.

15 July 1944.

Accordingly, the Care of Children Committee was set up in March 1945 under the chairmanship of Miss Myra Curtis, in order to: 'inquire into existing methods of providing for children who from loss of parents or from any cause whatever are deprived of a normal home life with their own parents or relatives; and to consider what further measures should be taken to ensure that these children are brought up under conditions best calculated to compensate them for the lack of parental care.' This covered a large number of children — some 124,900 altogether — in a large number of separate administrative categories, as described in the Committee's *Report* (the 'Curtis Report,' 1946):

10. The children with whom we have concerned ourselves can be conveniently considered as falling within the following groups:

(*a*) children maintained by local authorities under the Acts and Regulations relating to the Poor Law;

(*b*) children found to be homeless on the winding up of the Government Evacuation Scheme;

(*c*) children brought before the Courts as delinquent or in need of care or protection and required by the Courts to live elsewher than in their own homes;

(*d*) healthy children maintained by local authorities under the Public Health Act;

(*e*) children cared for by voluntary organizations;

(*f*) children in the care of private persons who are not their parents or legal guardians whether or not with a view to legal adoption;

(*g*) children who by reason of physical or mental handicaps have to be placed for long periods in hospitals or other residential establishments;

(*h*) children orphaned by the way.

The largest group — some 57,000 — were in category (*a*) and 6,500 of these lived in 'public assistance institutions,' which is a polite word for work-houses. The Report paints a gloomy picture, even allowing for the disruption and austerity caused by the war:

138. The healthy children over the age of 3 to be found in workhouses should, under the present law, be limited to those received there temporarily or as an emergency measure. . . . We found however many older children who had been there for longer than the permitted six weeks. . . . It was clear that in some areas the workhouse served as a dumping ground for children who could not readily be disposed of elsewhere, and that in some districts where children's Homes provided insufficient accommodation, or boarding out had not been well developed, older children, for whom there had never been any properly planned accommodation, were looked after in the workhouse for a considerable length of time.

140. An example of this kind of motley collection was found in one century-old Poor Law institution providing accommodation for 170 adults, including ordinary workhouse accommo-dation, an infirmary for senile old people and a few men and women certified as either mentally defective or mentally disordered. In this institution there were twenty-seven children, aged 6 months to 15 years. Twelve infants up to the age of 18 months were the children of women in the institution, about half of them still being nursed by their mothers. In the same room in which these children were being cared for was a Mongol idiot, aged 4, of gross appearance, for whom there was apparently no accommodation elsewhere. A family of five normal children, aged about 6 to 15, who had been admitted on a relieving officer's order, had been in the institution for ten weeks. This family, including a boy of 10 and a girl of 15, were sleeping in the same room as a 3 year old hydrocephalic idiot, of very unsightly type, whose bed was screened off in the corner. The 15 year old girl had been employed in the day-time dusting the women's infirmary

ward. These children had been admitted in the middle of the night when their mother had left them under a hedge after eviction from their house. No plan appeared to have been made for them.

144. One nursery which was structurally linked to the Public Assistance Institution had sunk to the lowest level of child care which has come under our notice. . . . The healthy children were housed in the ground floor corrugated hutment which had been once the old union casual ward. The day room was large and bare and empty of all toys. The children fed, played and used their pots in this room. They ate from cracked enamel plates, using the same mug for milk and soup. They slept in another corrugated hutment in old broken black iron cots some of which had their sides tied up with cord. The mattresses were fouled and stained. On enquiry there did not appear to be any available stocks of clothes to draw on . . . The children wore ankle length calico or flanelette frocks and petticoats and had no knickers. Their clothes were not clean. Most of them had lost their shoes; . . . Their faces were clean; their bodies in some cases were unwashed and stained.

This nursery was an exception, and some were very good, but even for the 16,900 children who found their way into public assistance children's homes, conditions might not be much better:

171. . . . In another Single Home with accommodation for 18 boys there was 24 present at the time of our visit. They had only one small sitting room for meals, reading and play. The dormitories were tightly packed and there was no room for any provision in the way of lockers or other receptacles for the boys' own possessions, though they were said to be on order. Outside was a small asphalt yard.

It was attitudes, as much as organisation and resources, which were to blame:

154. . . . We do not mean to suggest that we found evidence of harshness for which the staff was responsible. Except in the one instance of the nursery unit described in paragraph 144 the ill-usage was of a negative rather than a positive kind and elsewhere sprang directly from unsuit-ability of buildings, lack of training and of appreciation of children's needs. Officials of local authorities suggested that the children suffered from the attitude of the public to children main-tained under the poor law. This attitude had affected some members of the Public Assistance Committees, some of whom had survived as Committee members from the days of the old Boards of Guardians and still held old-fashioned views about what was suitable for a destitute child.

This spilled over into other aspects of the children's lives:

193. . . . We gained the impression that many of the children in the Homes were educationally retarded. This may, of course, have been due to their unfortunate history rather than to the conditions of their lives, but it was surprising to find in some Homes that few of the children could tell the time, and that many of them did not know the date of their birthdays. The contact between the Home and the school was often unsatisfactory. There seemed to be a lack of co-operation. Some of us were concerned to notice a certain prejudice against 'Home' children in the schools. It was difficult to tell whether the fact that the majority of Homes had sent no children to Secondary or Technical Schools for a number of years was due to the poor quality of intelligence of children in the Homes or to the fact that their interest in school work or in future opportunities was not sufficiently encouraged; or to any other disadvantages which attached to their living in a Public Assistance Home. . . . [This] reflects in a serious way a failure to compensate the child deprived of a normal home life; not only because they are not getting the opportunities open to normal children, but because the lack of individual attention and of special teaching and stimulus in the infant and toddler stages may have directly contributed to their failure to reach the necessary standard.

The Committee also visited some of the 27,800 children who were boarded out, mainly by the Ministry of Health, but also in circumstances like the O'Neills':

370. . . . 'The contrast between the children in Homes and the boarded out children was most marked. The boarded out children suffered less from segregation, starvation for affection and lack of independence. They bore a different stamp of developing personality, and despite occasional misfits were manifestly more independent. For example, they were much more indifferent to visitors, were much better satisfied by their environment (by which we mean the

special features of security and love). There was, we thought, much greater happiness for the child integrated by boarding out into a family of normal size in a normal home.'

Question

Why was the fact that the children 'were much more indifferent to visitors' regarded as a good sign?

When it came to recommending solutions, the Committee assumed that most of the children would remain in public care for a long time. It was clear about what their substitute home *should* provide:

427. . . . If the substitute home is to give the child what he gets from a good normal home it must supply —
 (i) Affection and personal interest; understanding of his defects; care for his future; respect for his personality and regard for his self esteem.
 (ii) Stability; the feeling that he can expect to remain with those who will continue to care for him till he goes out into the world on his own feet.
 (iii) Opportunity of making the best of his ability and aptitudes, whatever they may be, as such opportunity is made available to the child in the normal home.
 (iv) A share in the common life of a small group of people in a homely environment.
Some at least of these needs are supplied by the child's own home even if it is not in all respects a good one; it is a very serious responsibility to make provision for him to be brought up elsewhere without assurance that they can be supplied by the environment to which he is removed.

Hence:

447. . . . Every effort should be made to keep the child in its home, or with its mother if it is illegitimate, provided that the home is or can be made reasonably satisfactory. The aim of the authority must be to find something better — indeed much better — if it takes the responsibility of providing a substitute home. The methods which should be available may be treated under three main heads of adoption, boarding out and residence in communities. We have placed these in the order in which, subject to the safeguards we propose and to consideration of the needs of the individual, they seem to us to secure the welfare and happiness of the child.

Nevertheless, boarding out did have its disadvantages:

461. . . . We should like at this point to deal briefly with the principle that (adoption apart) boarding out should be regarded as the ideal method of disposing of the children. We think this is true where the home is in every way satisfactory and suited to the particular child. The evidence is very strong that in the free conditions of ordinary family life with its opportunities for varied human contacts and experiences, the child's nature develops and his confidence in life and ease in society are established in a way that can hardly be achieved in a larger establishment living as it must a more strictly regulated existence. But as soon as the foster home falls below the entirely satisfactory standard, the institution — at all events the institution based on the small family group — begins to have advantages. Supervision of individual children placed in private houses is obviously much more difficult than supervision of groups under the care of employees of a local authority. If the foster parents are to any extent attracted by the payment made for the child and are themselves living on the verge of poverty the child may well suffer in bad times. There are also the various emotional dangers arising from changes of family circumstances — eg the return of a father from the Forces or the second marriage of a widow, or merely a change of mind in the foster mother towards the child. The primary requirements of the children for whom the substitute home must be provided are affection and stability. There is no doubt that these essentials have been secured in many foster homes, but we wish to say emphatically that no risk should be taken in this very serious matter. If there is a doubt about the home the child should not go there. . . .
 The O'Neill case supplies an example. It must be remembered that supervision and the possibility of removing the child from a bad or indifferent home are not a satisfactory safeguard, because the removal itself is bad for the child, who has already had at least one complete change of environment. Children undergoing several changes of foster parents are often worse off than if they had never been boarded out at all.

Therefore:

476. The difficulties in the way of boarding out, or arranging adoption for all the children for whom a home life must be provided are obviously very great, and we think that the need for institutional care must be faced, with the aim of making it as good a substitute for the private home as it can possible be. . . .
478. After very careful consideration we have come to the conclusion that this can best be accomplished in the institutional sphere by placing him at the earliest possible age in a small group of children of various ages under the care of a trained and sympathetic house mother or house mother and father. . . .

The Committee's main concern was with the fragmentation of responsibility amongst various different local authority and central government departments, which was so inimical to the 'anxious and responsible spirit' commended by the Monckton Report (p. 419, above). The *Curtis Report* was able to propose a more radical solution:

440. After carefully considering these arguments we favour the establishment of an ad hoc committee reporting direct to the council. . . . This Children's Committee would take the responsibilities that now fall to the council in respect of children not in their own homes under the Poor Law Act, the Public Health Act, the Children and Young Persons Act and the Adoption of Children Acts, and would become responsible for boarding out children where necessary. It would consider the needs of its area for residential accommodation for deprived children and make the necessary provision. It would manage the children's Homes, the approved schools and the remand homes provided by the authority. The combination of boarding out responsibility and the control of children's Homes under one committee is, we think, essential. Children may well be housed in the Homes in preparation for boarding out and should be under the same authority and supervision. The committee would also assume any additional responsibilities arising out of our recommendations for the extension of public responsibility. It would not be in a position, as the local authority is at present, to refuse to accept responsibility for children [found to be] in need of care and protection [by a court].

Above all, the Children's Committee should have:

441. . . . its own executive officer with the standing of an important administrative official of the council, in direct touch with the responsible committee. . . . We desire . . . to see the responsibility for the welfare of the deprived children definitely laid on a Children's Officer. This may indeed be said to be our solution of the problem referred to us. Throughout our investigation we have been increasingly impressed by the need for the personal element in the care of children, which Sir Walter Monckton emphasised in his report on the O'Neill case. No office staff dealing with them as case papers can do the work we want done — work which is in part administrative, but also in large part field work, involving many personal contacts and the solution of problems by direct methods . . .
443. . . . She (we use the feminine pronoun not with any aim of excluding men from these posts but because we think it may be found that the majority of persons suitable for the work are women) will of course work under the orders of her committee or board but she will be a specialist in child care as the Medical Officer of Health is a specialist in his own province and the Director of Education is in his; and she will have no other duties to distract her interests. She would represent the council in its parental functions. The committal of the child to the care of a council which takes over parental rights and duties is not without incongruity. To be properly exercised the responsibility must be delegated to an individual, and that individual one whose training has fitted her for child care and whose whole attention is given to it. Though committal by the Court to a 'fit person' should, in order to secure continuity and relieve the officer of an undue burden of liability, be still made to the authority, the Children's Officer would be the *person* to whom the child would look as guardian.

The major purpose of the Children Act 1948, therefore, was to create these new Children's Departments, with their motherly Children's Officers and a new breed of trained personnel to establish that 'personal relation' between authority and child.

Much, however, has changed since then, as Jean Packman recounts in her story of the development of child care policy since Curtis, *The Child's Generation* (now 1981). During the 1950s, for example, the initial enthusiasm for boarding out had to be revised in the light of bitter experience:

Gordon Trasler (1960) studied foster home breakdowns in Devon over a period of three years in the early 1950s. As a background to his study he gathered information from other children's committees in different parts of the country, which suggested an average failure rate of between one-third and two-fifths over all long-term placements. With more precision, Roy Parker (1966) looked at all long-term fosterings arranged in Kent in 1952 and 1953, five years after the placement began. In that particular sample, the failure rate was 48% and 'failure' in Parker's terms was rigorous and meant that the child had had to be removed from his foster home during the five-year period. Clearly the proportion of 'unsatisfactory' homes where breakdown might still occur, or where social workers were not entirely happy about the care given, would have been higher still. In Rachel Jenkins's (1965) study of placements made between 1958 and 1961 in three northern authorities, for instance, a third were reckoned by social workers, foster parents and/or the researcher as 'unsatisfactory' though the children were still in placement at the time. Nor did research provide evidence of improved techniques leading to fewer breakdowns, once children's departments got into their stride. Victor George (1970) looked at placements made in three Midland authorities between 1961 and 1963 and, using Parker's criterion of longevity for measuring 'success', he calculated that the failure rate was 59.8%. Unless there are wide regional variations in fostering failure rates (which is always possible, since most other indices of child care work vary a great deal) things appear to have got worse, rather than better. . . .

[Hence] . . . research and experience together helped to dampen the early enthusiasm for fostering, with which the service had set out. Gradually, the tone of the Home Office reports changes. The first Report, after the Children Act, draws attention to section 13, with its injunction to board out all children received into care, except 'where it is not practicable or desirable for the time being' to do so. By 1961, the same primary duty is spelled out, but the caveat is emphasized — 'a provision which recognises that boarding-out is not automatically and invariably the best course for all children'. By 1964, 'Boarding-out is not necessarily the best thing for every child . . . (and) . . . it is therefore not to be expected that the proportion of children boarded-out should continue to rise indefinitely.' . . . The proportion of children who were fostered not only ceased to rise, but took a marked downward turn and a complementary amendment in the legislation set the seal on the change. Section 49 of the Children and Young Persons Act, 1969, replaces section 13 of its 1948 predecessor, and local authorities are no longer bound to consider fostering as the preferred method of care, but may discharge their duty to provide accommodation and maintenance 'as they think fit'.

There was also the all-important effect of work such as John Bowlby's *Child Care and the Growth of Love,* first published in 1953 and expressly written for the new child care officers. Packman explains its impact thus:

Research studies of the period stressed the importance of the mother-child relationship and the damaging effects on a child's mental, emotional and even physical development, if the relationship were inadequate, disturbed or broken. Most studies examined the latter — deprivation by separation — the phenomenon in its most readily observable form. The emphasis therefore tended to rest on the temporary, or even irreversible damage caused to children by removing them from home. To these studies were added the observations of the child care workers themselves. Seeing, at first hand, the unhappiness and distress of many children in care, they were naturally spurred to seek ways of avoiding admissions. Depressingly, too, they saw that many deprived children themselves grew up to be inadequate parents whose children were, in turn, deprived. A 'cycle of deprivation' was acknowledged long before it became a political catchphrase.

To this central concern to avoid separating children from their parents, was added the complicating factor that some families were clearly incapable of providing even a minimum of physical or emotional care and stability for their children. Social workers were therefore faced with decisions about whether or not the deprivations suffered by a child within his family were worse and more hazardous than those he would suffer by removal from home. Such decisions were also affected by estimates of their own skills and the resources available to them, to intervene and *improve* the family situation, to the child's benefit; and by the standards of substitute care that might offset and compensate the child for the effects of separation.

Prevention thus came to be a two-pronged concept; prevention of admission to care; and prevention of neglect and cruelty in the family. A variety of methods of working towards each of these ends can be seen emerging, in response to the differing circumstances of the families concerned. With some families the work was clearly directed to their weaknesses, whether these were problems of poor home management and low standards of hygiene, or of disturbed and volatile relationships. . . .

In other situations more stress was laid on family and community strengths. Child care workers were aware that many children came into care at a time of family crisis, for lack of any alternative. It was their task to explore and encourage links with kin or with neighbours who could offer care for the children in a familiar environment. . . .

A third dimension to preventive work grew from the knowledge that some families collapsed through external pressures which were beyond their control, yet were within the power of children's departments to influence. A prime example lies in the field of housing. As early as 1951 concern was expressed at the effects on children, separated from their parents because of homelessness. . . .

Packman also quotes John Stroud's more cynical view from *The Shorn Lamb* (1960):

'When I first came galloping out of the University, in shining armour and with all pennants flying, it was to the Rescue of the Deprived Child. Light and air were going to be flooded into the dark places, all those miserable public waifs were going to have a new square deal. And indeed over the years this had happened, we had brought a measure of increased happiness to the children in care. What we hadn't stopped to consider was how they managed to get there in the first place. . . . But we'd only taken a few cautious steps in this direction when Whitehall seized upon the development with glee: here was an even better and even *cheaper* way of caring for children, so cheap it didn't cost anything! Don't care for them at all!'

Packman describes how local authorities developed various practices and policies aimed at prevention, but how there was a need for 'a clearer statement and demarcation of responsibilities.' That came in the Children and Young Persons Act 1963, which followed the Report of the Ingleby Committee on Children and Young Persons (1960). As Packman says:

Despite its shortcomings, the Ingleby Report did make some important observations which both reflected and amplified the debate on prevention. One was the link between child neglect and juvenile delinquency. The inclusion of the preventive clause in terms of reference that were concerned with delinquency and the juvenile court system assumed a connection between the two and Ingleby was the first of a whole series of reports and white papers in the 1960s, which explored this connection. . . .

A second significant thread in the Ingleby Report is its insistence on positive rather than negative prevention. 'Everything within reason must be done to ensure not only that children are not neglected but that they get the best upbringing possible. . . . It is the duty of the community to provide through its social and welfare services the advice and support which such parents and children need' and 'such help should always be directed towards building up the responsibility of the parents whenever this is at all possible'. This seems to imply a reaching out to a wide spectrum of families, and promotion of an optimum level of child care rather than the maintenance of a bare minimum; an extension, in fact, of Curtis standards for children living *away* from their parents to those living in the community *with* their parents.

The link which Ingleby and later reports drew between the 'depraved' and the 'deprived' child eventually led to the Children and Young Persons Act 1969: an account of this development appears in Chapter 14. For present purposes, however, its significance lies in the amalgamation of a service which was designed to offer a substitute home for children whose families were for some reason unable to provide for them, with a quite different system which was designed to contain and cure the juvenile offender. At the same time, following the Report of the Seebohm Committee on Local Authority and Allied Personal Social Services (1968), the children's departments were themselves amalgamated with the services provided by other local authority departments, for the old, the handicapped, the mentally disordered, and others, in new all-purpose social services departments. As Packman again explains:

Developments in prevention and work with delinquency not only strained, modified and redefined the original aims and methods of the child care service; they also contributed to its eventual demise. The pursuit of both policies increased the children's departments' involvement with and dependence upon other agencies and threw into relief their relationship with one another and the illogical and wasteful effects of the fragmented pattern of personal social services. As the two policies drew closer together, with prevention of neglect being seen more and more as a key means of forestalling delinquency, the pressure to change that pattern and to provide an integrated 'family service' in its place mounted.

Nevertheless, not everybody was delighted:

Oxfordshire's Children's Committee, in preparing its own evidence to Seebohm, said 'it would in our opinion, for instance, be damaging to the highly personal type of work done by the child care service to place it in such a large and general group of functions that the old pattern of the former Public Assistance Service might recur, with the disadvantages that would entail'. The spectre of the Poor Law still haunted the local councillors.

Question

How many women directors of social services are there? How many men are basic grade field-workers? How many men are Chairmen of Social Services Committees? Does it matter?

2 Voluntary reception into care

Local authorities' duty to care for children in need, originally contained in s. 1 of the Children Act 1948, has now been consolidated with their preventive duty, originally contained in s. 1 of the Children and Young Persons Act 1963, in the opening sections of the *Child Care Act 1980* (which also deals with how all children in care, whether received voluntarily under this power, or committed compulsorily by the courts, are to be looked after and treated):

General duty of local authorities to promote welfare of children
1.—(1) It shall be the duty of every local authority to make available such advice, guidance and assistance as may promote the welfare of children by diminishing the need to receive children into or keep them in care under this Act or to bring children before a juvenile court; and any provisions made by a local authority under this subsection may, if the local authority think fit, include provision for giving assistance in kind or, in exceptional circumstances, in cash.

(2) In carrying out their duty under subsection (1) above, a local authority may make arrangements with voluntary organisations or other persons for the provision by those organisations or other persons of such advice, guidance or assistance as is mentioned in that subsection.

(3) Where any provision which may be made by a local authority under section (1) above is made (whether by that or any other authority) under any other enactment, the local authority shall not be required to make the provision under this section but shall have power to do so.

(4) In this section 'child' means a person under the age of eighteen.

Duty of local authorities to assume care of orphans and deserted children etc.
2.—(1) Where it appears to a local authority with respect to a child in their area appearing to them to be under the age of seventeen —
(a) that he has neither parent nor guardian or has been and remains abandoned by his parents or guardian or is lost; or
(b) that his parents or guardian are, for the time being or permanently, prevented by reason of mental or bodily disease or infirmity or other incapacity or any other circumstances from providing for his proper accommodation, maintenance and upbringing; and
(c) in either case, that the intervention of the local authority under this section is necessary in the interests of the welfare of the child,
it shall be the duty of the local authority to receive the child into their care under this section.

(2) Where a local authority have received a child into their care under this section, it shall, subject to the provisions of this Part of this Act, be their duty to keep the child in their care so long as the welfare of the child appears to them to require it and the child has not attained the age of eighteen.

(3) Nothing in this section shall authorise a local authority to keep a child in their care under this section if any parent or guardian desires to take over the care of the child, and the local authority shall, in all cases where it appears to them consistent with the welfare of the child so to do, endeavour to secure that the care of the child is taken over either —

    (*a*) by a parent or guardian of his, or

    (*b*) by a relative or friend of his, being, where possible, a person of the same religious persuasion as the child or who gives an undertaking that the child will be brought up in that religious persuasion.

    . . .

    (6) Any reference in this section to the parents or guardian of a child shall be construed as a reference to all the persons who are parents of the child or who are guardians of the child.

    8. . . .

    (2) Where an order of any court is in force giving the custody of a child to any person, the foregoing provisions of this Part of this Act shall have effect in relation to the child as if for references to the parents or guardian of the child or to a parent or guardian of his there were substituted references to that person.

Question

You are an 18-year-old law student at Cambridge. Your parents and two sisters, aged 12 and 14, live in Manchester. During the Easter vacation, your parents are both killed in a car crash. You have no other close relatives. (*a*) Would you consider asking the local authority to receive the girls into care under section 2? (*b*) If not, why not? (*c*) If you would, and the local authority refused to accept responsibility for them, because they considered that you were old enough to do so yourself, would you (having carefully considered the cases of *Meade v Haringey London Borough Council* [1979] 2 All ER 1016, [1979] 1 WLR 637 and *Wyatt and Wyatt v Hillingdon London Borough Council* (1978) 76 LGR 727 in your Law library) take action against the authority? (*d*) On the other hand, if you wanted to set up home with your sisters in Cambridge, and the local authority thought that you were too young to do so, what could you do to prevent their receiving the girls into care? (Once again, you may need to consult s. 5 of the Guardianship of Minors Act 1971, pp. 441–442, below, to see whether it gives you any help.)

Some indication of the usual reasons for entering care under s. 2 may be gleaned from the DHSS. statistics of *Children in Care of Local Authorities* for the year ending 31 March 1980. DHSS evidence to the House of Commons Social Services Committee investigation into children in care (December 1982) did not give the 1981 figures, which at the time of writing were still provisional, but the total number of receptions was approximately 28,700 in England and a further 1,500 in Wales. The following table relates to all 'care episodes' which began during the 12 months ending on 31 March 1980, but to England only:

	All children	Boys	Girls
Short term illness of parent or guardian	8,365	4,490	3,873
Long term illness or incapacity	595	305	290
Confinement of mother	1,407	757	650
Family homeless	596	301	295
Parents dead, no guardian	213	109	104
Abandoned or lost	873	466	407
Death of one parent, other unable to provide	467	226	241
Deserted by one parent, other unable to provide[1]	3,327	1,827	1,500
Parent/guardian in prison	721	381	340
Unsatisfactory home conditions	5,429	2,819	2,610
Other reasons	8,019	4,297	3,722
Total (includes two unknown)	30,012	15,978	14,032

[1] This includes the former statistical category of 'child illegitimate, mother unable to provide.'

The total number of children actually in care at any one time is shown on p. 447, below which also shows how numbers have changed over the past two decades. DHSS evidence to the Social Services Committee (1982) estimated that some 80% of children in care have been there for a year or more, indicating a considerable number in long term care and a very rapid throughput of others coming in for the short term reasons indicated above. We shall return to the question of the children in long term care later in this chapter. The question of the relationship between ss. 1 and 2, and between reception into care and the problem of homelessness, has arisen in one case:

A-G ex rel Tilley v Wandsworth London Borough Council
[1981] 1 All ER 1162, 78 LGR 677; affd. [1981] 1 All ER 1162, [1981] 1 WLR 854, 125 Sol Jo 148, 79 LGR 406, 11 Fam Law 119, High Court and Court of Appeal

In July 1979, after a change of political control, the Wandsworth LBC passed a resolution to the effect that, if the housing department refused to accept responsibility for a family under the Housing (Homeless Persons) Act 1977 on the ground that its homelessness was intentional, the social services department should not provide accommodation by way of 'assistance' under s. 1 although consideration might be givn to receiving the children into care. When the former chairman of the social services committee challenged this resolution, the authority argued that s. 1 did not even permit the authority to provide accommodation. The High Court held that 'assistance' could include accommodation and further that the resolution was an invalid fetter upon the exercise of the authority's discretion to choose between ss. 1 and 2 of the Child Care Act as seemed best in individual cases.

Judge Mervyn Davies QC (sitting as a Deputy High Court judge) [After reviewing the authorities of *Associated Provincial Picture Houses Ltd v Wednesbury Corpn* [1948] 1 KB 223, [1947] 2 All ER 680; *Secretary of State for Education and Science v Tameside Metropolitan Borough Council* [1977] AC 1014, [1976] 3 All ER 665; and *Stringer v Minister of Housing and Local Government* [1971] 1 All ER 65, [1970] 1 WLR 1281]: . . . it seems to me that I may examine the resolution to see whether the local authority has thereby bound itself to make future decisions in individual cases under the 1963 Act without taking into account some of the considerations that under the Act ought to be taken into account. If the local authority has bound itself in that way the resolution is clearly bad. I think the local authority has so bound itself. I say that because when the local authority, acting by its social services committee or by its responsible social services officer, is considering a particular case of a child whose parents are prevented from providing for his proper accommodation the local authority have a duty under the [1980] Act to receive the child into care. At the same time the local authority must consider pursuant to the . . . Act whether any assistance given under that Act will promote the child's welfare by diminishing the need to receive him into care. Since assistance under the . . . Act includes the provision of accommodation it is plain that in every case where there is a family without a home for whatever reason, the local authority is obliged to consider whether the welfare of the child requires that some attempt be made to keep the family together. The local authority should on each occasion ask, should this child be taken from its homeless parents and received into care, or does his welfare require that, if some accommodation can be found for his family, that he remain with his parents? It may very well be, in many cases, that the interests of a child will be much better served by its being received into care. However, this question as to what is best to be done must, as I see it, be asked on every occasion when the local authority, acting by its responsible officer, is considering a receiving into care in respect of a child of homeless parents. The resolution dated 4 July 1979 means that consideration of the question I have mentioned will not be taken into account in respect of the children of the intentionally homeless. The resolution is therefore . . . invalid.

The Court of Appeal dismissed the local authority's appeal, Templeman LJ commending the judge's 'careful and lucid' judgment. But his lordship also said this:

Under [section 2 of the Child Care Act 1980] a child may be taken into care where it appears to a local authority, inter alia, that his parents through incapacity or any other circumstances, are prevented from providing for his proper accommodation, maintenance and upbringing. So in the case of a child, if his parents cannot provide him with proper accommodation, maintenance and upbringing the local authority can take that child into care; in other words, remove him from his parents and put him with foster parents or in a home. . . . The local authority must not take intentional homelessness into account for the purpose of punishing the child or punishing the parents of the child, but must take it into account in asking 'What is the best way, in the interests of the child, of exercising the powers which are given to us?' If, of course, there is a history of a parent who continually changes homes and causes great stress and worry to a child it may be that the local authority will say 'In those circumstances, we think we had better take the child into care.' On the other hand, if the intentional homelessness still enables the family to be brought up as a family under one roof, or does not require the child to be taken into care, the local authority may come to a different conclusion.

Questions

(i) Can Lord Justice Templeman's use of the word 'take' be reconciled with the so-called 'voluntary' principle, enshrined in s. 2(3) of the Child Care Act 1980 (p. 427, above) and in the decision of the House of Lords in the case of *Lewisham London Borough Council v Lewisham Juvenile Court Justices* [1980] AC 273, [1979] 2 All ER 297 (p. 443, below)?

(ii) But if the parents have no home and the local authority refuses to find them any accommodation, what choice have the parents got?

(iii) Is a parent who has wilfully neglected or ill-treated a child 'prevented . . . by reason of mental or bodily disease or infirmity or other incapacity or any other circumstances' from providing for him properly?

(iv) If s. 2 care is not available to a parent who *will* not (as opposed to *cannot*) look after his own child, may the child nevertheless be offered accommodation as 'assistance' under s. 1?

(v) But would such a child be 'in care' so that the local authority's powers and duties under Part III of the Act arise, and so that the parent may be obliged to contribute towards his maintenance under Part V?

(vi) If a child *can* be received under s. 2 in the circumstances outlined in question (iii), how voluntary is 'voluntary'?

(vii) In what circumstances is it lawful to receive a child under s. 2 without the parent's express consent?

Some idea of reception into care from the *parents'* point of view may be gained from the study of 40 cases reported by the National Council for One Parent Families in *Against Natural Justice* (1982): these cases are by no means representative, for 14 came from parents who had some contact with either One Parent Families or Family Rights Group, and a further 26 were contacted through four firms of solicitors operating in Great London. Their accounts are nonetheless indicative of what can happen:

Initial contact

The majority of the clients had referred themselves to social services departments. Four were referred by other agencies for support and guidance. A small number could not really remember who first made contact, but were agreed that family problems existed and that help was essential.

Three-quarters of the families were experiencing stressful home conditions. This phrase covers a multitude of practical and emotional problems. Many were in debt and could not manage on Supplementary Benefit, others had just left demoralising and painful relationships, others were living in overcrowded and intolerable conditions, and some found that a combination of all these factors had driven them to breaking point.

Ms Carter is a single mother aged 25. Her child is 5 years old. She referred herself to the social services department in 1980 because of extremely poor housing conditions and consequent illness of her child. After several meetings the social services department suggested that voluntary care would give her a break whilst she [sorted] out her practical and emotional problems.

Key figures in the community, like health visitors and community workers, often refer families to the social services department because either problems are already acute or because the worker forecasts difficulties ahead.

Miss Norton was 19 and her child 2 when the social services department made contact with her because of her complex family history. It is likely, but not certain, that the health visitor asked the workers to call round. Accommodation was bad and her relationship with a violent boyfriend was about to break down.

A number of parents came to the attention of social services for other reasons. Three were actually homeless and contacted social workers for help in getting rehoused. Two parents had very recently been bereaved and could not cope with their grief and the needs of the children. Finally, one mother was already in care herself and had been receiving social work support for many years.

Voluntary care

The request for reception into care or the suggestion of care by a social worker as a solution to the family's problems is unavoidably linked to the reason for the initial referral. For 23 parents the stress within the family became unbearable. Some found it impossible to cope emotionally after their marriage had collapsed. Others could no longer stand their bad housing. Family tension or poverty was unbearable for others and one or two could see no way out of their debts. Perhaps as a consequence of the above, a small number of parents asked for their children to be received into care. In our experience parents do place children in care in situations of trust with the expectations that the stay will be temporary and that they would get support to overcome their problems.

At the time of reception into care, three of the parents were actually homeless and a further six had been admitted to hospital and there was no alternative friend or relative able to care. Of the others, one child came into care because its parent was imprisoned, another because it was thought to be at risk, and a third to enable its grandparent to receive foster fees.

The other side of voluntary care, however, was poignantly revealed by Jane Rowe and Lydia Lambert, who in 1971 studied the 2,812 children under

11 who had been in the care of a selection of local authorities and voluntary agencies for at least six months. 1,891 of these had been admitted under s. 2 (as it now is) or its equivalent in Scotland (s. 15 of the Social Work (Scotland) Act 1968). Their report on *Children Who Wait* was published in 1973.

The growth of the illusion

Following the Children Act 1948 with its stress on the need to return children to their parents and the Children and Young Persons Act 1963 with its stress on prevention, the idea of bringing up children in care went very much out of fashion. Many social workers had become acutely aware of the problems of children who had been cut off from their families. They strove to emphasise plans for maintaining family ties and returning children home. There was therefore comparatively little interest in providing permanence or continuity or in the way an agency should carry out its parental role in relation to the children in its care. . . .

During the 1960s, reports on the work of local authority Children's Departments hardly mentioned long-term children or their needs. Much emphasis was laid on the high proportion of short-term cases, and the way in which Government statistics were presented created the impression that there was a constant turnover of children. It was impossible to deduce from the Home Office figures how long the children had been in care. They simply quoted roughly equal figures for admissions and discharges. The lack of any age breakdown for children over five (except over or under compulsory school age) also made it difficult to obtain a clear picture of what was going on with children in long term care.

A few warning notes were being sounded by the beginning of the 1970s. . . . In his 1971 National Children's Home Convocation Lecture, Professor R.A. Parker said: 'If it is widely assumed that speedy rehabilitation is not only desirable but also achievable, then the duration of a child's stay in care may be optimistically misjudge and a correspondingly lower priority given to planning responsibilities'. . . .

Thus, from a variety of sources, a general belief seems to have arisen that the era of the child in really long-term care is drawing satisfactorily to a close, that plans for rehabilitation usually work out and that hopes for preservation of family ties are being realised.

The findings of the study

The stark reality disclosed by this study is that if a pre-school or primary school age child has been in care for as long as six months, his chances of returning to his parents are slim. On the most liberal interpretation of the study figures little more than one child in four was expected to return to his family before he reached school leaving age. . . .

Estimated future time in care: all children in study

	All Agencies	Local Authorities England & Wales	Scotland	Voluntary Societies
Estimated future time in care	%	%	%	%
Impossible to assess	1	1	1	1
2 years or less	23	22	19	34
3–6 years	6	7	5	5
More than 6 years[1]	9	10	5	9
Until aged 18 years	61	60	70	51
	100	100	100	100
Number of children	2,812	1,815	606	391

[1] But not until aged eighteen years.

It is important to remember that the group expected to remain for six years and over included a number of youngsters who were already 8 to 10 years old and the group expected to stay less than two years included many of the 345 children for whom adoption was either definitely planned or at least was hoped for. This reduces to about one child in four the number thought likely to return to their parents before leaving school.

Social workers were asked to give the reasons which lay behind their estimates of the child's future stay in care. . . .

	Estimated future stay in care					
	Impossible to assess	2 years or less	3–6 years	More than 6 years	Until aged 18 years	All children in study
Factors on which estimates are based	%	%	%	%	%	%
Family problems	54	15	36	47	37	33
Lack of interest	—	*	2	19	43	28
Rehabilitation problems	35	38	46	14	1	14
Adoption problems	—	11	8	8	7	8
Child problems	4	1	6	10	11	8
Adoption planned	—	19	1	—	—	4
Rehabilitation planned	—	10	—	—	—	2
Other reasons (miscellaneous)	7	6	1	2	1	3
	100	100	100	100	100	100
Number of children	26	634	184	249	1,719	2,812

* Less than 1%

. . . The extraordinarily discouraging picture in regard to reuniting children with their families was borne out by their answers. In only sixty-two cases (2%) was 'rehabilitation planned' given as a reason for expecting a fairly rapid discharge, whereas 'rehabilitation problems' were mentioned in three hundred and eighty-two (14%) long-stay cases. 'Family problems' accounted for nine hundred and twenty-six (33%) of all the reasons behind the estimates, and almost as many children were expected to stay in care because of 'lack of parental interest' (28% of cases).

The other main findings of the study were equally disturbing:

Parental contact
The full extent to which children in care lose touch with their parents — if indeed they ever were in touch — is only too clearly demonstrated by the finding that out of 2,812 study children only 141 (5%) saw both parents 'frequently' (i.e. asoften as once a month).

Another 494 (18%) saw *either* mother *or* father at least once a month. 35% saw one or both parents occasionally, but there were 1,150 children (41%) recorded as never seeing either parent. In addition 19 were full orphans and in 15 cases it was not known whether there was any contact with either party. . . .

The extent to which parents visit their children is bound to be influenced by a variety of factors. These include their concern and affection for the child and their feelings of inadequacy, guilt and anger as well as practical problems of travel. The way they are received by foster parents or residential staff and the amount of support they receive from the social worker are important, but perhaps the most crucial factor is the response of the child himself — whether he is welcoming, hostile or indifferent. If, as one might suspect, indifference is hardest for parents to tolerate, it may be highly significant that so many of the children in the study had come into care too young to have any conscious memory of their parents or of life at home.

There was clear evidence that both age at admission and length of stay in care had a strong bearing on parental visiting. Only 14% of children who were less than 2 years old when admitted to care had frequent contact and 57% never saw their parents. The situation was reversed for children admitted over the age of 8 years. Of these 38% saw their parents frequently, and only 10% had no contact.

It seems that the longer children stay in care, the less often they see their parents. Over a third (37%) of the children who had been in care for less than two years had 'frequent' parental contact. In the group that had been in care for more than six years, this percentage had dwindled to 11% and by this time 58% had no contact at all.

Question

Compare this information with the data on visiting children after divorce and on the reasons there suggested for failure to visit (pp. 393–394, above): would you conclude from the fact that a parent was not in regular contact with a child: (*a*) that the parent was not interested in the child, or (*b*) that the child was not interested in the parent; or (c) might there be some other reason?

The other major finding from *Children Who Wait* may be succinctly stated:

The national picture
Over the country as a whole, there are probably at least 6,000 children of pre-school or primary school age who are in the care of social agencies and who need a substitute family. This estimate is based on the study finding that *626 children, or 22% of the total number surveyed, were thought by their social workers to need placement in a foster or adoptive home.*

Question

On the other figures — as to length of stay in care and extent of parental contact — do you think that the social workers are likely to have under- or over-estimated the numbers of children needing some form of permanent substitute family?

In 1972, the year before *Children Who Wait* was published, a Departmental Committee on the Adoption of Children, originally under the chairmanship of Sir William Houghton, had examined the other side of the coin: as they explain in their *Report* (1972):

139. At the time of our appointment concern had been expressed about a number of children who had been reclaimed by their natural parents after many years in foster homes, and we were asked to consider the position of long-term foster parents who wished to keep a child permanently, by adoption or otherwise, against the wish of the natural parent.

Nevertheless, studies done for the Committee revealed that in the year ending 31 March 1968, only 455 children had been reclaimed from voluntary care against the local authority's strong advice; only 66 of these had been in care for two years or more, and 16 of these appeared to have settled satisfactorily. As reported in an *Appendix* to the main Report:

4. The information given by the local authorities revealed some of the reasons why parents reclaimed their children, even after a considerable lapse of time. Sometimes a request to contribute financially to the child's maintenance may have precipitated the withdrawal. In a few cases, the child had reached working age. Sometimes an approach for consent to adoption seemed to precipitate the move. More often, however, the withdrawal of the child followed changes in circumstances in the natural family (often a solution of the original problem leading to the initial request for care), such as a marriage or remarriage, or rehousing. Some parents felt they could cope with their child once he was past babyhood. One authority commented that families with deep-seated problems often took five or six years to establish themselves; another, that some parents seemed to plan ahead consciously for the time when they would be in a position to have their child back.

Question

How many of these would you consider good reasons for removing a child from a long term foster home where he is happy? Would any factors other than the parents' motive influence your view?

The Committee took the following view:

148. . . . We start from the position that a child may be reclaimed by a parent who is a stranger, at short notice (or with no notice at all) without any opportunity for consideration of the position. This applies to all children in care and not just to those boarded out with foster parents. The sudden removal of a child from a children's home where he has established good relationships may be equally damaging. . . .

151. Good practice requires that, when a child is received into care, his needs should be explained to the parents, including the likelihood of his forming attachments with substitute parents which it might not be desirable to break, and which might have to be legally recognised if the parents fail to keep in touch with him. As an aid to good practice we recommend that an explanatory leaflet should be given, and explained orally wherever practicable, to the parents of every child coming into care, in the same way as a memorandum is given and explained to the parents of every child placed for adoption. The central departments might prepare a model explanatory leaflet covering the needs of the child and the rights and obligations of all concerned. We think that better communication of this sort, coupled with improvements in practice generally, would do much to prevent some of the more difficult tug-of-war situations arising.

152. At present the parents of a child received into local authority care may require his return at any time, irrespective of the length of time he has been in care, provided that parental rights have not been assumed. A sudden move, without preparation, can be damaging to the child and may have long-term repercussions. We therefore recommend that where the child has been in care for more than one year there should be a requirement to give 28 days notice of removal. Removal within the period of notice, without permission, would be prohibited in the same way as removal of a child subject to a care order. 28 days would be a maximum period of notice, which could be waived by the authority or voluntary society, who, in many cases, would be likely to agree to the child being returned in a much shorter period. This provision would help to prevent impulsive and temporary removals from care, and would give time for the child and parents to get to know each other again.

The second recommendation was given effect, modified in the light of *Children Who Wait*, in the Children Act 1975, now s. 13(2) of the *Child Care Act 1980*:

13 (2) Except in relation to an act done —
   (*a*) with the consent of the local authority or
   (*b*) by a parent or guardian of the child who has given the local authority not less than 28 days' notice of his intention to do it,
subsection (1) above shall apply to a child in the care of a local authority under section 2 of this Act (notwithstanding that no resolution is in force under section 3 of this Act with respect to the child) if he has been in the care of that local authority throughout the preceding six months; and for the purposes of the application of paragraph (*b*) of that subsection in such a case a parent or guardian of the child shall not be taken to have lawful authority to take him away.

Subsection (1) applies primarily to children over whom the authority has resolved to assume parental rights under s. 3 of the Act (see p. 442, below) and provides that an offence is committed by any person who:

   (*a*) knowingly assists or induces or persistently attempts to induce a child to whom this subsection applies to run away, or
   (*b*) without lawful authority takes away such a child, or
   (*c*) knowingly harbours or conceals such a child who has run away or who has been taken away or prevents him from returning.

The *DHSS Circular* (1976) giving guidance upon this and other 'time limit' provisions in the 1975 Act has this to say:

The provisions reinforce the concept that the all round development of the child is promoted by continuity of care and they restrict therefore sudden and unplanned removal from a home in which the child may have been well cared for long enough to have put down roots. They are designed to help ensure that the child's discharge has been carefully planned, and that the child has been adequately prepared for it and is returned to a home in which he or she is likely to thrive. . . . They are not intended to delay or prevent the child's discharge to loving and concerned parents who have kept in touch with their child to the best of their ability and whose home is ready and suitable. Many children in care may be longing to go back to their parents at the first possible opportunity. In most cases the welfare of the child and the rights of the parents will coincide and good social work practice should ensure that parents are continuously involved in planning for their child's future, and will resume his or her care as soon as practicable. Where there is a conflict of interests which cannot be resolved by social work support, the social worker will need to help parents to understand and if possible accept that the law requires that first consideration must be given to the welfare of the child.[1]

The same circular appends a model *leaflet to be given to parents of children who are likely to remain in care for longer than six months.* After giving details of how to contact the responsible social worker or an alternative, the leaflet continues:

Your child ___ has now been with us since ___ and seems likely to stay with us for more than 6 months.

If he is still in care on or after ___ you must give us 28 days' notice in writing[2] that you want to have him home. The law requires this because children may need a little time to get used to the idea of moving. People looking after your child also may need notice to prepare for these changes and to get his belongings together.

If you have been in constant touch with your child and with your social worker than it is very likely that your child will be able to return to you before the 28 days have passed, and in some cases almost immediately. At the latest, your child will return to you at the end of the 28 days unless there should be very special and particular circumstances.

If because of your own circumstances it seems that your child will not be able to go home in the near future, then you and your social worker must continue to talk about the best possible plans which should be made for your child's care. At regular intervals your social worker will consider your child's progress, your own circumstances and make plans and decisions for the child's future. Social workers have a duty to plan for children to return home as soon as this is in their best interests. You will be closely involved in discussion and in the making of plans and decisions.

Important points to remember

a. While your child is in our care we have a duty to give first consideration to his welfare and interests. If your child is old enough to understand, then we must find out his wishes and feelings about any plans.

b. For the sake of your child it is important for you to keep in touch with him and your social worker.

c. It is essential that we know where you are, so that we can get in touch with you at any time.

d. Wherever possible all decisions concerning your child will be made with your help and co-operation. If you have any problems or difficulties, we hope that you will ask your social worker to help you.

e. Your child wll not be moved to another address without previous discussion with you except in unforeseen circumstances. In such a case you would be given full information as soon as possible.

f. If your child has brothers and sisters or if you have other children in care, we shall do our best to keep them together or in touch with each other.

Protecting children in special circumstances

Unexpected difficulties can happen in everybody's life. After a great deal of thought some parents may even feel that they cannot have their child back to live with them. They may therefore make the painful decision that it would be best for the child to be permanently cared for by someone else. In that event the social worker will help parents to consider such a step very carefully and will explain what has to be done legally.

In rare cases children may need protection either from being taken out of care and being

---

1. Child Care Act 1980, s. 18(1), p. 436, below.
2. See Children Act 1975, s. 107(1), which is *not*, however, repeated in the Child Care Act 1980.

placed in a situation which is likely to be harmful, or from being suddenly removed from people who have cared for them for a long time and to whom they may have become attached.

[The procedure for assuming parental rights — see p. 442, below — is then explained briefly.]

When children have lived away from home for a long time

The longer children are away from home, the more attached they are likely to become to the people who are caring for them. What may seem a fairly short time to adults seems a very long time to children. The time may come when they want to remain with those who are looking after them. This does not necessarily mean that they have forgotten their own families. . . .

[The 'five year rule' relating to foster parent adoption is then explained briefly — see pp. 486–487 in Chapter 13, below]

Questions

(i) Does this document strike you as (*a*) a blatant encouragement to selfish or inadequate parents to dither about their children's future for as long as possible, or (*b*) a sinister attempt to gloss over the real dangers both of placing your child in care and of being unable to keep in regular touch with him, or (*c*) a fair and humane explanation of a complex and changing situation?

(ii) How would it affect your judgment in any fugure dispute about the child if all these beautiful promises were not kept?

Apart from the duty to rehabilitate, which derives from s. 2(3) of the *Child Care Act 1980* (see p. 427, above), the two other sections referred to in the Circular and Leaflet are:

9.—(1) The parent of a child who is in the care of a local authority under section 2 of this Act shall secure that the appropriate local authority are informed of the parent's address for the time being.

18.—(1) In reaching any decision relating to a child in their care, a local authority shall give first consideration to the need to safeguard and promote the welfare of the child throughout his childhood; and shall so far as practicable ascertain the wishes and feelings of the child regarding the decision and give due consideration to them, having regard to his age and understanding.

The choice of accommodation theoretically available to social workers is now set out in the *Child Care Act 1980*:

21.—(1) A local authority shall discharge their duty to provide accommodation and maintenance for a child in their care in such one of the following ways as they think fit, namely, —

(*a*) by boarding him out on such terms as to payment by the authority and otherwise as the authority may, subject to the provisions of this Act and regulations thereunder, determine; or

(*b*) by maintaining him in a community home or in any such home as is referred to in section 80 of this Act; or

(*c*) by maintaining him in a voluntary home (other than a community home) the managers of which are willing to receive him;

or by making such other arrangements as seem appropriate to the local authority.

(2) Without prejudice to the generality of subsection (1) above, a local authority may allow a child in their care, either for a fixed period or until the local authority otherwise determine, to be under the charge and control of a parent, guardian, relative or friend.

The DHSS statistics relating to the *Children in Care of Local Authorities in England* on 31 March 1980 reveal that children in care under s. 2 were accommodated thus:

Boarded-out

With a relative or friend	2,650
Already with relative	1,824
Others	18,015
Lodgings/residential employment	704
Community homes	
For observation or assessment	1,461
With education on premises	741
Hostel facilities	435
Residential nurseries	327
For less than 13	3,990
For more than 13	4,287
Voluntary homes and hostels	1,788
Special schools	941
Others	2,378
Under section 21(2)	1,641
	41,182

Question

Does this suggest anything to you?

The basic question remains: should the social workers be planning to reunite the family, or to find a new one? This issue is addressed by Margaret Adcock, in the course of discussing *Social Work Dilemmas* in a symposium on *Terminating Parental Contact: an exploration of the issues relating to children in care* (1980) — as to which specific problem, see both pp. 457–463 below, and pp. 467–474 in Chapter 13, below.

The importance of early decisions is clearly demonstrated by some of the research findings. For example:
- Social workers regard uncertainty about parental intentions as an obstacle to placing children in substitute family care.
- There is an association between the length of time in care and the number of placements for children who are in residential care.
- There is an association between the number of placements and disturbed behaviour.
- Disturbed behaviour and an increasing number of placements or breakdown then constitute child-centred obstacles to placing the child in a substitute family. . . .

In New York the court reveiws (Festinger, 1976) all children who have been in care for more than two years and determines whether they should be discharged to parents, remain in care, or be freed for adoption. Between 1972 and 1975 21.3% of children reviewed returned home and 34% were placed in adoptive homes. Of the 105 (44.7%) children still in care 37 were headed for adoption and 18 for discharge. Placing children for adoption does not necessarily involve a decision to terminate parental contact. Visiting tends to decrease anyway the longer children remain in care, so a considerable number of children will already have lost contact with their parents. . . .

The effects of social work intervention

Since frequency of parental contact and discharge from care have been found to be associated with social work contact, there is a great deal of controversy about which children could and should be helped to leave care. . . .

There is often a failure to provide the necessary resources to return a child from care or to keep a relationship viable by encouraging visiting rights at the beginning. Conversely, there are frequent attempts to keep together a family which never has been a family in any real sense of the word or to resolve long-standing severe emotional and personality problems in the parents. It is important to emphasise that there is no research evidence available to demonstrate that long entrenched personality problems or gross pathology can be altered by social work help.

Jones Neuman and Shyne (1976) evaluated the impact of intensive social work help to families at risk aimed at preventing or shortening placements in care. They conclude that successful outcomes were associated with the following factors:

- The parent's personal functioning was not a factor in the original need for placement.
- The emotional climate of the home was good — the child was loved and valued and the mother was thought to have a reasonable degree of emotional maturity.
- The most important problem was in the area of housing, financial need, or the marriage.
- The worker's predominant role was the arrangement of other services of an immediate practical nature which would relieve personal/relationship problems.

Cases likely to respond to help were thought to be young families coping with problems of recent origin and including an adult with some motivation to deal with the situation.

Is rehabilitation possible?

Further studies of the effectiveness of social work help are urgently needed but in the meantime decisions still have to be made about individual children. There is considerable evidence to show that the longer the child is separated from his parents, the more the effect of the separation experience itself on both parents and the children, militates against the resumption of care. The research findings suggest that the younger the child when he is separated from his parents, the less likely it is that parents will sustain visiting, and the more likely it is that the child will form strong bonds with his caretakers. Fanshel (Fanshel and Shinn, 1978) found that 50.3% of children who were under two at reception into care were still there five years later compared to 25.6% who had been between 9 and 12 years old at reception into care. . . .

These findings suggest that for a young child discharge from care must occur quickly since parental visiting does not have a high chance of being sustained. It may therefore be both harmful and unrealistic to encourage visiting, particularly where it is sporadic, after a child has been in care more than a short period of time unless there have been some realistic discussions with the parent about the child's long-term future.

The welfare of the child

In considering what plans to make for the child's future the following factors need to be considered:

- The history of the child including the previous experiences, and his age at separation.
- The history of the parent(s) and the problems which led to separation.
- The relationship between child and parent(s) before separation.
- The length of separation.
- The current relationship between parent and child including the visiting pattern.
- The availability of resources to remedy the problems and the length of time necessary for this.

The relevant information can be evaluated in the light of the overall need to provide a child with a permanent home of his own and reference to findings on situations in which children can be moved without undue long-term damage (Rutter, 1972; Rutter and Madge 1976). The important factors in the research seem to be:

- The child has not already experienced several previous separations.
- The child has not been unduly damaged before separation.
- The child has had a good experience in the foster home where the foster parents have had a clear understanding of their role.
- The transition back home is made as easy as possible.
- The parents can meet the child's needs on returning home, which may include understanding and dealing with his reactions to change.
- The child is not subsequently exposed to recurrent unhappy situations.
- The child is not returned to a home where there are many other stresses.

If a child has had many previous separations or been very damaged, his need for stability and continuity in his present home may outweigh all other considerations. If he has spent a lengthy period in a foster home and has come to regard the foster parents as his 'real parents' he may be overwhelmed by losing them. He may then be so difficult in his new home that the parents will not be able to meet his needs and he will provoke anger and rejection. Age is obviously a very important consideration. Young children quickly become attached to a person caring for them and become very distressed if these attachments are broken.

Finally, it is important to make an accurate assessment of the problems within the family. Some parents may be highly motivated to resume care of their children and yet clearly have many problems with which to contend. Rutter suggests that a child can develop satisfactorily in a home despite one chronic stress such as a mental illness of a parent. However, if there are two chronic problems the chances of the child developing a subsequent psychiatric disorder are quadrupled rather than doubled. Where there are more than two stress factors, for example, marital problems, bad housing, physical ill health or alcoholism, the risks are even greater.

(*Note*: Compare the findings reported here with those, especially, of Aidgate, p. 468, below.)

Questions

(i) Do you consider that it would be better for the courts, rather than social workers, to review the situation of children in care?

(ii) If you do, should they consider all children in care or only certain categories?

(iii) How often should such reviews be carried out?

(iv) What choices should be available to the court?

(v) How, if at all, can we reconcile the voluntary basis of reception into care under s. 2 with plans to provide a child with a substitute family?

It is to the present legal machinery for supplanting the rights of parents of children in care that we must now turn.

3 The power to assume parental rights

Section 13(2) of the Child Care Act 1980 (p. 434, above) is of no help, either to the child whose parent insists on discharging him from care when this is not in his best interests, or to the child whose social worker may be inhibited from making long-term plans for his future because of uncertainty surrounding his status. The difficulties were encountered both by the voluntary societies and the poor law authorities in the nineteenth century, as Jean Heywood relates in *Children in Care* (now 1978):

Rescue societies, had, however, no rights of custody over the children and were forced, under threat of a writ of habeas corpus to return children to parents, however neglectful, if they wished to have the child back. This, however, Barnardo consistently refused to do, thereby acting illegally, and at the same time openly admitting that, in the absence of any legal care of protection procedure, he abducted children from neglectful parents in order to give them the care and shelter of his Home. The position came to a head when the Crusade of Rescue, now more effectively organised to deal with its own children in need, attempted to reclaim from Barnardo the Roman Catholic children he had admitted in default of an organised denominational arrangement for their care. . . . Barnardo had received into care just such a child, Harry Gossage, whose cruel and drunken mother had sold him for a few shillings to a couple of foreign organ grinders who left him destitute in Folkestone. Brought by a police officer to London Barnardo admitted him, and then, after discovering the mother's whereabouts, wrote to her, seeking and obtaining her consent to the boy's entry. Barnardo then posted his standard form of agreement which, among other things, contained a clause granting him the right to arrange the child's emigration if suitable. These agreements, though formal, were not, however, legally binding on the parent.

Before this form was returned a Canadian gentleman called on Dr Barnardo wishing to take back to Canada one of the doctor's boys whom he proposed to educate in his own background. For this reason he made the condition that the boy should have no further contact with relatives and that he should be allowed to take the lad away without disclosing his future home. To these conditions Barnardo rashly agreed and as fate would have it Mr Norton's choice fell on Harry.

It had apparently never entered Barnardo's calculations that Harry's mother would wish to have him back. While the lad was on the high seas, however, the mother had taken the form of agreement to a priest for help in completion and Barnardo received a letter asking for the lad's immediate transfer to a Roman Catholic Home. As he did not comply the letter was followed by a writ for habeas corpus.

The litigation,[3] lasting ten months, which followed eventually led to an agreement between Dr Barnardo's Homes and the Roman Catholic Homes . . . But of greater administrative significance was the disclosure that all the great rescue organisations alike had no authority to protect

---

3. See *Barnardo v Ford, Gossage's Case* [1892] AC 326, 61 LJ QB 728.

children in care against even actively cruel parents who wished to reclaim them. . . . Accordingly, the House of Lords appointed a standing committee of three judges who eventually drafted a Bill which, known as the Barnardo Bill, received Royal Assent in 1891 as the Custody of Children Act. . . .

That Act is still in force:

3. Where a parent has —
    (*a*) abandoned or deserted his child; or
    (*b*) allowed his child to be brought up by another person at that person's expense, or by the
        guardians of a poor law union, for such a length of time and under such circumstances as
        to satisfy the Court that the parent was unmindful of his parental duties;
the Court shall not make an order for the delivery of the child to the parent, unless the parent has satisfied the Court that, having regard to the welfare of the child, he is a fit person to have the custody of the child.

Question

If Dr Barnardo's homes refused to return a child today and the mother either brought habeas corpus proceedings or made him a ward of court in order to recover him, would those proceedings be governed by this section or by s. 1 of the Guardianship of Minors Act 1971 (p. 339, above)? What difference would it make?

The Poor Law went further. Heywood earlier notes that the Report of the Committee on Parish Apprentices of 1815 stated that in London poor law relief was 'seldom bestowed without the parish claiming the exclusive right of disposing, at their pressure, of all the children of the person claiming relief.'

Question

When of the following do you think most likely to have motivated the parish claim: (*a*) a desire to protect the children from being uprooted from a happy home and returned to poverty and neglect; (*b*) the need to provide for the children as cheaply as possible, for example by apprenticing them to chimney sweeps; or (*c*) the hope of deterring parents from seeking parish relief at all?

Nevertheless, the parental right to custody emerged as a powerful factor in upper class litigation during the nineteenth century, while philanthropists developed a policy of rescuing deprived and pauper children from their supposedly corrupting environment. Hence, Heywood explains:

In all the planning of the various systems of care for the deprived child, the natural family, where it existed, remained a problem which, if it was not being treated, was certainly to be reckoned with. Separating the child and the unfit parent or relative of bad influence was a definite attempt to prevent pauperism reproducing itself in the next generation, but the policy was often difficult to effect even if it was considered ethically sound. The constructive work which the poor law attempted by providing a better environment for the child was frequently brought to nothing by what was described as the 'pernicious influence of the child's relations' particularly when the children passed out of the guardians' care at 16. Two solutions were found for coping with this problem: . . .
Boards of Guardians were empowered under the Poor Law Amendment Act of 1850 to emigrate orphan or deserted children under the age of 16 years, provided the child gave his consent. There were real opportunities, particularly in Canada where there was a shortage of labour and where food was cheap, and the guardians made use of these opportunities, though not to any great extent. In general voluntary organisations, such as Dr Barnardo's Homes or the

Roman Catholic Emigration Agency, were used as agents, the fittest and most promising of the eligible pauper children being chosen for his new life.

The more difficult problem of the child and the unfit parent was grappled with by Acts of 1889 and 1899. These gave the boards of guardians in England and Wales authority to assume complete rights and responsibilities of a parent over a child in care until he reached the age of 18. Such rights could be assumed only in respect of deserted children at first, but in 1899 their application was widened to include orphans and children of parents who were disabled or in prison, or unfit to have the care of them. This power to assume parental rights by the state was an expression of the public interest in the welfare of children and was intended to lay down a definite standard of parental care. . . .

The power to arrange emigration survives in s. 24 of the 1980 Act, essentially unchanged save that the Secretary of State must give his consent. It was hotly debated during the second reading of the Children Bill 1948 in the Commons, not only for the children's sake but also for the sake of a country which had recently lost so many young men in a world war. It is hardly, if ever, used today.

By contrast, the House of Commons had nothing to say about the power to assume parental rights, despite the fact that it remained in the law in the teeth of opposition from the *Curtis Report*:

425(ii) Orphans and children deserted by their parents
We consider that every orphan or deserted child coming within the range of public care should have a legal guardian to take the major decisions in his life and to feel full responsibility for his welfare. Apart from the cases where the Court commits a child to a local authority as a 'fit person', those in which the authority are managers of an approved school to which the child is committed and those in which the authority assumes guardianship under the Poor Law Act 1930, of a child maintained by it, there is no relation of legal guardianship between the authority and the child. We do not suggest that in every case the authority is the proper guardian, but we consider that the authority should be responsible for raising the question of guardianship in the cases where it takes responsibility for the child's welfare which, if our recommendations are approved, will be far more numerous than at present; and that failing a suitable relative, for whom inquiry should be made, or the Head of an approved voluntary Home which has the child under care, the authority itself should apply for appointment as guardian. The legal procedure by which guardians can be appointed appears to us to need revision. We do not favour the assumption of parental rights by a local authority under Section 52 of the Poor Law Act 1930, by mere resolution, without an initial application to a Court. We think it objectionable (even though in practice the Section may have worked satisfactorily or at any rate without criticism) that the rights of a parent or other guardian should be extinguished by a mere resolution of a Council. Even if extra publicity and work were involved in court proceedings, we are of opinion that they would be more than counterbalanced by the value of an impartial and detached judicial inquiry at the outset directed to the paramount welfare of the child. We understand that at present no statutory provisions exist in the Guardianship of Infants Acts 1886 and 1925, or elsewhere which confer on any Court the power to appoint a legal guardian (as opposed to making a custody order in certain cases) where a child is already without a natural or testamentary guardian; and that in such a case the only resort is to the inherent jurisdiction of the Chancery Division of the High Court. For reasons of expense and distances this is not practicable in regard to the children with whom we are concerned, or their relatives. We recommend that the statutory jurisdiction to appoint guardians should be extended (*a*) so as to enable a legal guardian to be appointed by a Court not merely where another is being removed or superseded under Section 6 of the Guardianship of Infants Act 1925, but also where a child has no natural or testamentary guardian at all; (*b*) so as to ensure that this extended statutory jurisdiction is exercisable by County Courts and Magistrates (Juvenile) Courts as well as by the High Court. If this simple procedure were available it might often make possible a stable relation short of adoption between a good foster parent and a child. The protection of the child against resumption of parental rights by undesirable parents would also be easier than under the Custody of Children Act 1891.

Section 5 of the *Guardianship of Minors Act 1971* now provides:

Power of court to appoint guardian for minor having no parent etc.
5.—(1) Where a minor has no parent, no guardian of the person, and no other person having parental rights with respect to him, the court, on the application of any person, may, if it thinks fit, appoint the applicant to be the guardian of the minor.

(2) A court may entertain an application under this section to appoint a guardian of a minor notwithstanding that, by virtue of a resolution under [section 3 of the Child Care Act 1980] a local authority have parental rights with respect to him; [. . .].

Question

When we come to consider the rights of foster parents in the next chapter, ask yourself why this section was only applied to orphans, and not to other 'deserted' children. What are the objections to doing so?

The power to assume parental rights by local authority resolution was originally contained in s. 2 of the Children Act 1948, and is now in s. 3 of the *Child Care Act 1980*:

3.—(1) Subject to the provisions of this Part of this Act, if it appears to a local authority in relation to any child who is in their care under section 2 of this Act —

(*a*) that his parents are dead and he has no guardian or custodian; or

(*b*) that a parent of his —

(i)   has abandoned him, or

(ii) suffers from some permanent disability rendering him incapable of caring for the child, or

(iii) while not falling within sub-paragraph (ii) of this paragraph, suffers from a mental disorder (within the meaning of the Mental Health Act 1959), which renders him unfit to have the care of the child,[4] or

(iv) is of such habits or mode of life as to be unfit to have the care of the child, or

(v)   has no consistently failed without reasonable cause to discharge the obligations of a parent as to be unfit to have the care of the child[4], or

(*c*) that a resolution under paragraph (*b*) of this subsection is in force in relation to one parent of the child who is, or is likely to become, a member of the household comprising the child and his other parent[5]; or

(*d*) that throughout the three years preceding the passing of the resolution the child has been in the care of a local authority under section 2 of this Act, or partly in the care of a local authority and partly in the care of a voluntary organisation,[5]

the local authority may resolve that there shall vest in them the parental rights and duties with respect to that child, and, if the rights and duties were vested in the parent on whose account the resolution was passed jointly with another person, they shall be vested in the local authority jointly with that other person.

(2) In the case of a resolution passed under paragraph (*b*), (*c*) or (*d*) of subsection (1) above, unless the person whose parental rights and duties have under the resolution vested in the local authority has consented in writing to the passing of the resolution, the local authority, if that person's whereabouts are known to them, shall forthwith after the passing of the resolution serve on him notice in writing of the passing thereof.

(3) Every notice served by a local authority under subsection (2) above shall inform the person on whom the notice is served of his right to object to the resolution and the effect of any objection made by him.

(4) If, not later than one month after notice is served on a person under subsection (2) above, he serves a counter-notice in writing on the local authority objecting to the resolution, the resolution shall, subject to the provisions of subsections (5) and (6) below, lapse on the expiry of fourteen days from the service of the counter-notice.

(5) Where a counter-notice has been served on a local authority under subsection (4) above, the authority may not later than fourteen days after the receipt by them of the counter-notice complain to a juvenile court having jurisdiction in the area of the authority, and in that event the resolution shall not lapse until the determination of the complaint.

(6) On hearing a complaint made under subsection (5) above the court may if it is satisfied —

(*a*) that the grounds mentioned in subsection (1) above on which the local authority purported to pass the resolution were made out, and

---

4. Grounds added to 1948 Act by Children and Young Persons Act 1963.

5. Grounds added to 1948 Act by Children Act 1975.

(*b*) that at the time of the hearing there continue to be grounds on which a resolution under that subsection could be founded, and

(*c*) that it is in the interests of the child to do so,

order that the resolution shall not lapse by reason of the service of the counter-notice.

(7) Any notice under this section (including a counter-notice) may be served by post, so however that a notice served by a local authority under subsection (2) above shall not be duly served by post unless it is sent by registered post or recorded delivery service.

(8) Where, after a child has been received into the care of a local authority under section 2 of this Act, the whereabouts of any parent of his have remained unknown for twelve months, then, for the purposes of this section, the parent shall be deemed to have abandoned the child.

(9) The Secretary of State may by order a draft of which has been approved by each House of Parliament amend subsection (1)(*d*) above by substituting a different period for the period mentioned in that paragraph (or the period which, by a previous order under this subsection, was substituted for that period).

(10) In this section —

'parent', except in subsection (1)(*a*), includes a guardian or custodian;

'parental rights and duties', in relation to a particular child, does not include —

(*a*) the right to consent or refuse to consent to the making of an application under section 18 of the Adoption Act 1976 (orders freeing a child for adoption in England and Wales) or section 18 of the Adoption (Scotland) Act 1978 (orders freeing a child for adoption in Scotland), and

(*b*) the right to agree or refuse to agree to the making of an adoption order or an order under section 55 of the Adoption Act 1976 (orders in England and Wales authorising adoption abroad) or section 49 of the Adoption (Scotland) Act 1978 (orders in Scotland authorising adoption abroad).

The first legal problem raised by this section is its relationship with the parental right to discharge the child from care (s. 2(3) of the Child Care Act 1980) and to the qualification to that right introduced by what is now s. 13(2) of the Act (respectively pp. 427 and 434, above). This has now been determined by the House of Lords. (*Note*: all references to the 1948 Act in this and other cases in this Chapter have been replaced with references to the 1980 Act.)

Lewisham London Borough Council v Lewisham Juvenile Court JJ
[1980] AC 273, [1979] 2 All ER 297, [1979] 2 WLR 513, 123 Sol Jo 270, 77 LGR 469, House of Lords

An illegitimate boy aged 18 months was placed in care by his mother and boarded out with foster parents. Eight months later his mother notified the local authority that she wished to have him back. Seven days after this, the authority passed a resolution assuming her parental rights. The mother objected and the local authority made a complaint to the juvenile court. The court ruled that it had no jurisdiction, being bound by the Court of Appeal's decision in *Johns v Jones* [1979] QB 411, [1978] 3 All ER 1222 to hold that once the mother had requested her child's return he was no longer 'in care under the foregoing section' (because of what is now s. 2(3)) and therefore no resolution could be passed. The authority sought mandamus to compel the justices to hear the case. The House of Lords ruled that mandamus should be granted and over-ruled the decision in *Johns v Jones*.

The Court of Appeal had reasoned that, as reception into care is at the parents' will and s. 2 gives the authority no right to retain the child once the parent desires to take over his care, a child cannot be 'in care' under that section once that desire has been expressed, even if he remains physically in local authority accommodation. One tempting method of avoiding such an inconvenient result would have been to deny that parents of children received under s. 2 had the right to reclaim them whatever the circumstances. However:

Lord Keith of Kinkel: . . . The first case in which the point presently in issue was the subject of direct decision is *Halvorsen v Hertfordshire County Council* (1974) 5 Family Law 79. A child had been received into care by the local authority under s. 2(1) of the 1980 Act, but was shortly afterwards removed to Norway by its mother, who had her origins in that country. Later the child was taken into care by the Norwegian child-care authority and Hertfordshire County Council, learning of this, arranged for the child to be returned to England and again received into their are, the whereabouts of the mother being then unknown. Two months later the local authority passed a parental rights resolution under s. 3(1). The mother, having reappeared, objection under s. 3(4) and the matter went before the juvenile court, which rejected her contention that the resolution was invalid. The mother appealed to the Divisional Court, and argued that her desire to resume care of the child had been intimated to the local authority when she took it to Norway, that that intimation was still operative, and accordingly that the child had ceased to be in the care of the local authority under s. 2 so that the necessary prerequisite for a resolution under s. 3(1) was missing. The court (Lord Widgery CJ, Milmo and Ackner JJ) rejected the argument. Lord Widgery CJ is reported as having said:

'The answer to that argument was that when s. 2(3) referred to a parent or guardian desiring to take over the care of the child, that must be a parent or guardian who was not disqualified by s. 2(1)(b) from being fit to take care of the child; the fact which brought about the intervention of the local authority was that the parent was incapable of looking after the child (s. 2(1)(b). It would be quite astonishing if, notwithstanding that the child had been taken into the care of the local authority, the parent could immediately demand its return. Indeed, there was authority to show that such a right could not exist. There would be no security of action if the parent, having surrendered the child under s. 2(1), could immediately claim it back under s. 2(3). In order to make sense of this section and give it a practical effect, the right in s. 2(3) to desire the return of the child was exercisable only by a parent who was not already disqualified from having the care of the child under the terms of s. 2(1)(b).'

. . .

The correct solution, in my opinion, involves a consideration of the intended interaction of ss. 2 and 3 of the 1980 Act. There can be no doubt that s. 2(1) does not contemplate any compulsory taking of a child into the care of a local authority. There is and has been since even before the Children and Young Persons Act 1933 other legislation to deal with situations where that may be necessary. The subsection deals with the case where a child is abandoned or lost, or where the parent or guardian is prevented, for some reason, from providing for the proper accommodation, maintenance and upbringing of the child. It says that where the requisite conditions are met it shall be the duty of the local authority to 'receive' the child into their care. The reception is regarded as voluntary from the point of view of any parent or guardian who is involved and who is capable of expressing any will in the matter. It is to be noted that nothing whatever is said about the case of a parent or guardian who is unfit, for any reason, to have the care of the child, that being a case which is contemplated by s. 3(1). . . .

Section 2(2) deals with the keeping of a child by the local authority, but sub-s (3) underlines the voluntary aspect of the reception into care, and lays down the policy of securing, wherever this is consistent with the welfare of the child, that its care is taken over by a parent, guardian, relative or friend. It seems to me that the first limb of the subsection is independent of and not coloured by the second limb. As sub-s (1) has not had in contemplation the case of an unfit parent or guardian, it appears to me not surprising that the first limb of sub-s (3) contains no proviso or qualification related to the situation where the parent or guardian appears unfit to have care of the child. If there had been any such proviso or qualification, there would have had to have been some provision for judicial review. The question of the unfitness of the parent or guardian could not properly have been left to the unfettered judgment of the local authority. So I conclude that the omission of any such proviso or qualification was deliberate, and that it cannot properly be implied. To that extent I consider that the reasoning of Lord Widgery CJ in *Halvorsen v Hertfordshire County Council* (1974) 5 Family Law 79 was wrong. . . .

Therefore I am of opinion that sub-s (3) does not permit the local authority to refuse to hand over a child received into care under sub-s (1) to a parent or guardian who demands its return, on the ground that the latter is unfit to have the care of the child. I agree with the Court of Appeal in *Bawden v Bawden* [1979] QB 419, [1978] 3 All ER 1216 that the subsection does not confer on the local authority any residual discretion in that respect. As to the expressions of opinion by Pennycuick J in *Re KR (an infant)* [1964] Ch 455, [1963] 3 All ER 337 and of Megaw LJ in *Krishnan v Sutton London Borough Council* [1970] Ch 181, [1969] 3 All ER 1367 to the effect that sub-s (3) imposes on the local authority no mandatory obligation to return the child, I consider these expressions of opinion to have been correct in the context in which they were uttered. In my opinion there may well be circumstances, such as a pending wardship application or a situation of practical impossibility, where no court could reasonably order the local authority to return the child. In that sense any such obligation is not mandatory. But that does not mean that the local authority have a general residual discretion as to whether or not the child should be returned.

All their lordships reaffirmed the basic principle that s. 2 gives the authority no right to retain a child against his parent's wishes. All similarly agreed that a resolution might nevertheless be passed after a parental request for the child's return. But their reasoning on this latter point differed slightly (although Lord Wilberforce made no speech, on the ground that they all agreed):

Viscount Dilhorne: . . . The keeping of a child in the case of a local authority in the performance of their duty under sub-s (2) does not end directly a parent desires to take over the care of his child. What the subsection says is that when such a desire is expressed, nothing in s. 2 shall authorise a local authority to keep a child in their care under the section. If it had been the intention that the keeping in care by the local authority should terminate immediately a parent desired to take over the care of the child and that the local authority must then hand the child over, that could easily have been expressed in clear and unambiguous language. All that the first part of the subsection provides, in my opinion, is that a local authority cannot, if such a desire is expressed, rely on s. 2 as authorising them to keep it. If they do not hand over the child, they must take steps under some other provision to entitle them to keep it. And s. 3 of the Act states a way in which that can be done. . . .

In *Wheatley v Waltham Forest London Borough Council (Note)* [1980] AC 311, [1979] 2 All ER 289 sitting in the Divisional Court of the Family Division on 15 June 1978 in the course of his judgment with which Sir George Baker agreed, Waterhouse J rejected the contention that as the parent had requested the return of her child before the resolution under s. 3 was passed, the child was not in the care of the local authority 'under the foregoing section' when the resolution was passed.

While I think that his actual conclusion was right for the reasons I have stated, I regard the grounds on which he based his conclusion as wrong. He said that s. 2(3) must be read with the new s. 13(2) and so read gave the authority 'a breathing space of 28 days in which to take the steps that it regards as appropriate'. There being, in my opinion, no ambiguity in sub-s (3), to use s. 13(2) as an aid to the construction of sub-s (3) was contrary to what was said to be permissible in *Kirkness (Inspector of Taxes) v John Hudson & Co Ltd* [1955] AC 696, [1955] 2 All ER 345. If sub-s (3) meant that the expression of the parent's desire terminated the keeping in care by the local authority (which in my opinion it does not), then s. 13(2) (which merely provided that the giving of at least 28 days' notice a parent could avoid liability for conduct which in the absence of such notice would be criminal), on his construction, was to be treated as amending sub-s (3) by delaying the termination of the keeping in the local authority's care for 28 days. This is my opinion s. 13(2) does not do, and while I appreciate the desire to try and make the Act workable if the expression of a desire to take over the child determined the local authority's keeping in care, no such strained construction is in my opinion either necessary or permissible.

Summarised my conclusions are as follows. (1) The desire of a parent to take over the care of his child does not terminate the keeping of the child in the care of the local authority. (2) That desire will, however, prevent the authority from relying on s. 2 as authorising the retention by them of the care of the child. (3) In all cases the authority must, where it appears consistent with the welfare of the child, endeavour to secure that the care of the child is taken over by a parent, guardian, relative or friend. (4) If the transfer of care to such a person would not be consistent with the infant's welfare, then, in order to be entitled to retain the child in their care, the local authority must either pass a resolution under s. 3 if the necessary conditions appear to them to be satisfied, or, it may be, institute other proceedings. (5) The insertion of the new s. 13(2) does not affect or amend the meaning of sub-s (3).

Lord Keith of Kinkel: . . . In my opinion this new subsection does not alter the meaning which was previously to be attributed to sub-s (3), nor is it to be regarded as clearing up an ambiguity in that subsection. I do not find that any ambiguity exists. So I consider that in *Wheatley v Waltham Forest London Borough Council (Note)* [1980] AC 311, [1979] 2 All ER 289 the Divisional Court attributed undue significance to the new subsection. . . . The child has been received into care under sub-s (1) and kept in care under sub-s (2), and in my opinion it continues to be in the care of the local authority until delivered up. In any case where some interval of time elapses between a parent expressing a desire to take over the care of the child and actually doing so, the local authority must continue to be under some duty as respects the care of the child, and that duty can only derive, in my view, from the provisions of s. 2. During any such period of time the child is, in accordance with the ordinary meaning of language, in the care of the local authority under s. 2. The contrary view rests, in my opinion, on an excessively technical and legalistic approach such as I do not consider likely to have been in the contemplation of the legislature, and which leads to an unreasonable and even a pernicious result.

Lord Scarman: . . . It does not follow that, because the subsection recognises the right of the parent to take over the care of the child, it has to be read as meaning that on the receipt of the parent's notice the local authority no longer have the care of the child under the section, for inevitably local authority care must continue until the parent in fact removes the child. In my judgment a child, who has been received and kept in care under the section, continues in care under the section until the parent removes him or a court makes an order transferring care to a parent or some other person in wardship or other proceedings. Indeed, I find no ambiguity in the subsection. Whatever a parent may say or do, it is not possible to be certain that he 'desires to take over the care of the child' until he does so or demands the child, indicating an instant will and readiness to take the child. The local authority, whose duty it is to act in the interests of the child, must, therefore, keep the child in care until the parent does take over the care.

If this be the correct interpretation of the subsection, s. 13(2) (introduced by the 1975 Act) falls neatly into the statutory pattern. Under sub-s (3) the local authority will have in most cases a brief opportunity to pass a parental rights resolution after the parent has communicated for (or his) desire to remove the child. Under s. 13(2) the child having been in care for six months (or such other period as may be ordered by the Minister), the local authority will have at least 28 days after the parent's notice to pass a parental rights resolution.

Lord Salmon: It would surely be shocking if the law does compel an authority to hand over a child in their care to a parent who is, for example, a violent alcoholic, likely to neglect, injure and do the child irreparable harm.

Such a parent might, however, go to the authority and demand that the child be handed over to her immediately. I am afraid the authority would then have no legal right to retain the child in their care under s. 2 of the Act unless the child had been in their care for six months or more (a point to which I shall return later). I think however that an authority might, if the child had been in their care for less than six months, well consider it to be their moral duty to keep the child long enough to have it made a ward of court. This is all they could do to save the child because once a parent presents herself to the authority and demands the immediate return of her child who has been in care of the authority for less than six months, the child ceases to be in the care of the authority under s. 2 and accordingly the authority have no power to pass a parental resolution under s. 3. . . .

S. 13(2) of the Act makes it illegal for a parent to take away a child who is and has been in the care of a local authority for six months or more unless the local authority consent or the parent has given the local authority at least 28 days' notice of his or her attention to do so. Accordingly, if a parent, without having obtained the authority's consent or given the notice required . . . were to come to the authority and take the child away or demand the immediate return of the child, this, in my view, would certainly not terminate the authority's care of the child under s. 2 of the Act, nor their right to pass a parental resolution under s. 3. Prior to s. 13(2), the parent could have taken the child away or demanded the immediate return of the child however long it had been in the authority's care, and this would automatically have taken the child out of the authority's care under s. 2 and destroyed the authority's right to pass any parental rights resolution under s. 3 of the Act.

The object of s. 13(2) is, I think, obviously to give the local authority ample time to make up their mind whether or not they consider it to be in a child's interest who has been in their care for six months or more to return the child to its parent; and, if they do, to prepare the child for the change and, if they do not, to pass a resolution under s. 3 of the Act vesting in themselves the parental rights and duties in respect of the child.

Questions

(i) In which of the following circumstances may a local authority pass a resolution: (*a*) child in care for seven months, parent gave written notice requesting return 30 days ago; (*b*) child in care for three months, in a telephone conversation with her social worker yesterday the mother said that she would like to have the child home; (*c*) child in care for five and a half months, the father is on the doorstep of the children's home demanding that the child be given to him immediately?

(ii) What difference would it make to the local authority's position in any of the above cases if the child were illegitimate?

(iii) What difference would it make to the local authority's position in any of the above cases if a court had awarded sole custody to the father? (See s. 8(2), p. 427, above.)

(iv) If, in the situation envisaged in question (iii), the mother then learned that her child was in care and wished to resume care herself, what steps should she take?

Official statistics do not reveal how many resolution are passed each year, although it is thought to be around 3,000; but they do show what proportion of children currently in care having been received under s. 2 of the 1980 Act are also subject to a s. 3 resolution:

England and Wales

Year	Children in voluntary care	Parental rights resolutions	Resolutions as % of all children in voluntary care
1963	43.3	9.5	22
1966	46.2	9.6	21
1969	46.4	11.2	24
1972	48.1	12.2	25
1973	49.0	12.4	25
1974	50.3	12.6	25
1975	50.6	13.2	26
1976	49.0	14.5	30
1977	47.6	16.3	34
1978	46.0	17.7	38
1979	45.0	18.4	40
1980	44.3	18.4	41
1981	42.0	18.1	43

DHSS statistics also reveal the distribution among the various grounds, for example, for the children subject to resolutions on 31 March 1981:

England

Parents dead, no guardian	1,200
Abandoned	2,000
Permanent disability of parent	200
Mental disorder	1,600
Parent's habits and mode of life	3,000
Failure to discharge parental obligation	6,500
Resolution already on one parent	100
Three years in care	2,600
Other	100

A right of appeal from the juvenile court to the High Court was first given in the Children Act 1975, but the only ground to have received much attention has been that of 'consistent failure' under what is now s. 3(1)(*b*)(v). The authorities to date were reviewed in the following case:

O'D v South Glamorgan County Council
(1980) 78 LGR 522, 10 Fam Law 215, High Court, Family Division

The mother, a divorced woman who had her 16 year old son living with her, gave birth to R, an illegitimate boy, on 26 April 1977. Although they boy was her fifth child the mother was singularly inept at caring for the infant and made frequent calls upon the council's social workers for assistance. At the request of the mother R spent several periods in the care of the council. Two of the periods were for a few days only. In April 1979 the mother again asked for help with the child. The child was once more taken into care. On 20 August 1979 the social services committee of the council passed a resolution assuming parental rights and duties in respect of the child on the ground . . .

that she had so consistently failed without reasonable cause to discharge the obligations of a parent as to be unfit to have care of the child. The mother objected to the resolution and the council made complaint to the juvenile court which upheld the resolution.

Sir John Arnold P: . . . In *Wheatley v Waltham Forest London Borough Council (Note)* [1980] AC 311 [1979] 2 All ER 289, Waterhouse J said at p. 316:

'Turning from the short statement of the justices' reasons to the wider aspects of the case, it is right to stress that a decision to divest a parent of her rights and duties is a very serious one. To justify it, the conduct of the parent must be culpable, and culpable to a high degree. The decision does not have the finality of an adoption order, because it can be rescinded; but, whilst it remains in force, its consequences in relation to both parent and child are drastic. For this reason, the guidance given by this court in relation to proceedings under the Adoption Act 1958 is helpful, provided that the difference in the objects of the two statutes is recognised.'

Sheldon J also adopted that principle in *M v Wigan Metropolitan Borough Council* [1980] Fam 36, 77 LGR 556. I quote from pp. 44 and 562:

'In my opinion, however, "the obligations of a parent" to which sub-paragraph (v) refers are not so limited and, in the words of Pennycuick J in *Re P (Infants)* [1962] 3 All ER 789, 794 [see p. 510, below] with reference to section 5(2) of the Adoption Act 958: "must include first the natural and moral duty of a parent to show affection, care and interest towards his child; and second, as well, the common law or statutory duty of a parent to maintain his child in the financial or economic sense". Whether or not the parent has failed, and has "so consistently failed", to discharge those obligations as to render him or her "unfit to have the care of the child" are questions of fact and degree depending upon the particular circumstances of the case. Clearly, in my view, to adopt the words of Sir George Baker P in *Re D (Minors) (Adoption by Parent)* [1973] Fam 209, 215, such failure "must be culpable and culpable to a high degree" or, as was said by Lord Denning MR in another case, quoting Diplock LJ "there must be some callous or self-indulgent indifference with regard to the welfare of the child". But I do not accept what I understood to have been Mr Sander's submissions that "consistently" has the same meaning as "persistently" (the word to be found in section 5(2) of the Adoption Act 1958 and, indeed, in section 2(1)(b)(v) of the Children Act 1948 after its amendment by section 48of the Children and Young Persons Act 1963 and before being substituted by section 57 of the Children Act 1975) and that such failure, to have been consistent, must have occurred throughout the whole or the greater part of the life of the child in question. In my opinion, the use of the adverb "consistently" in this context contemplates behaviour over a period which has constantly adhered to the pattern of which complaint is made (in this case, as it was put by Miss Bracewell on behalf of the local authority a "pattern of rejection"); but the length of the period will be a question of fact depending upon the nature of the behaviour under review. Apart from those comments, however, in my opinion, it is neither necessary nor desirable to attempt to define or to explain words of the section'.

It is plain from the authorities that the behaviour of the parent has to be callous, blameworthy, reprehensible, and that despite the absence of some such word in the section there must be an element of culpability if the requirement of having 'failed without reasonable cause' is to be justified. It is not for the mother to show that her behaviour was not culpable but for the local authority to establish that it was. The court must ask itself: was her behaviour culpable in the sense that that word is used in the cases? If it was so culpable then she has failed to discharge her obligation. If it was not culpable then there was no such failure.

On behalf of the local authority it has been submitted that if in a state of affairs something is not done which ought to be done and if that which should have been done is conducive to the welfare of the child then the not doing of that something is a culpable offence.

For the mother it was submitted that the omission to do something was not culpable unless there was an element of blameworthy conduct involving a departure from a proper standard of conduct which when subjectively considered could be regarded as morally reprehensible.

The latter interpretation is to be preferred. That interpretation is hallowed by derivation and usage. When considering whether a mother 'has so consistently failed without reasonable cause to discharge the obligation of a parent' there must be some blameworthiness, some self-indulgent indifference to the welfare of the child.

The mother was a woman with a substantial personality defect. When she saw the psychiatrist in August 1975 she complained of anxiety and mild depression. The psychiatrist saw her in February 1979 when her complaints were again of anxiety and mild unhappiness together with financial problems. The doctor last saw the mother on 1 August 1979. She then told him that the social services department had been responsible for R's frequent reception into care by suggesting that action when she felt under stress. The report goes on to state:

'I find it difficult to attach a diagnostic label to Mrs O'D. She undoubtedly finds it difficult to cope. She has always been anxious each time I have seen her. Furthermore, Mrs O'D plays down her difficulties in coping and tends to project the consequences of these difficulties on to other people and external agencies. Thus, she has blamed her first husband entirely for the breakdown of her first marriage; and has blamed the social services department for R's frequent reception into care when it has been her own request that he be taken into care. This projection in turn leads to a somewhat unrealistic attitude to the future (e.g. planning to leave her present husband if what she perceives as a bad patch occurs again) — this also underlines her difficulties in making interpersonal relationships and her tendency to see blame and responsibility totally detached from herself. These problems indicate an underlying immaturity of personality which is excessively difficult to treat with orthodox psychiatric methods; and this difficulty has been compounded by Mrs O'D's rather unreliable outpatient appearances. What has particularly concerned me about the health ofMrs O'D and of her son R is three things: — (i) R was conceived in a relationship which ended in acrimony: Mrs O'D's tendency to project faults could conceivably extend to the identification of R as the source of Mrs O'D's bitterness from her relationship with his father, (ii) Mrs O'D has twice been admitted to a psychiatric hospital shortly after R has been placed in care; this implies that her difficulties in coping escalate to "illness" proportions when she finds it difficult to cope with R.'

[His Lordship referred to the evidence of the social workers and continued.]

That evidence suggests to me that there was a total absence of callousness or self-indulgent indifference to the welfare of her child in the mother's dealing with the local authority when she called for their assistance. She recognised that she was an inadequate mother and that her inadequacy meant that the child would suffer ill-consequences. Her conduct has been reasonable throughout. Although her abrogation of the parental obligation to look after her child could be regarded as consistent it could not be regarded as culpable.

The appeal must be allowed.

Question

Are you relieved or horrified to learn that the child remains in care, at least for the time being, because the Court ordered him to be made a ward of court?

This case illustrates very well the problem of the 'yo-yo' child, within the context of a statutory scheme which is largely based on parental absence or unfitness. But there may also be difficulties where a child has been in care virtually since birth:

W v Sunderland Metropolitan Borough Council
[1980] 2 All ER 514, [1980] 1 WLR 1101, 124 Sol Jo 272, 78 LGR 487, 10 Fam Law 120, High Court, Family Division

An illegitimate girl was born in October 1977 to a mother who had a history of psychiatric problems, now cured. Because of these, the baby was looked after in the special care unit in the hospital, and as the mother felt unable to cope with her on leaving hospital, she was placed in care and fostered. Adoption was considered a possibility at that stage. The mother visited at most three times before August 1978 when she notified the authority of her desire to care for the baby. The authority passed a resolution on the 'consistent failure' ground. The mother objected and a court hearing was arranged for October. That hearing was adjourned indefinitely to see whether mother and child might be brought together. The mother began to visit regularly. In February 1979, she acquired a house which needed some putting to rights. The authority reviewed the position in May, by which time the mother's visits had fallen off slightly and the house was still not ready. It was decided that the rehabilitation plan should be abandoned, visiting reduced and long term fostering arranged. At the mother's instigation the court proceedings were reactivated. At a hearing in October 1979 the juvenile court confirmed the resolution. The mother appealed.

Sir John Arnold P: . . . There are in this case three matters which have to be decided. First of all, in order that the court should drect that the resolution should not lapse, it has, under s. 3(5), to be satisfied in the circumstances of this case that the mother had so consistently failed without reasonable cause to discharge the obligations of a parent as to be unfit to have the care of the child, on grounds which were already made out at the date of the passing of the resolution on 12 September 1978. Secondly, that there continued to be grounds on which that conclusion ought to be reached at the time of the hearing before the justices on 4 October 1979 and, finally, that it was in the interests of the child to direct that the resolution should not lapse.

. . . There is very little evidence as to exactly what it was which caused the contact between mother and child to be so minimal after 3 March 1978 up to the date in August 1978 when she asked for the child back, which undoubtedly took place. In the course of her evidence the mother suggested that access was refused, but certainly there is no indication that it was refused by the local authority; quite the reverse, they were offering to arrange it. And it seems to me, at any rate, that the justices were, on the material before them, fully entitled to take the view that that separation of mother and child for that long period of about six months was not explained in any way which should have led them to conclude that there was a reasonable cause for it.

The second matter relates to the period between the resolution of 12 September 1978 and the hearing a little over a year later on 4 October 1979. . . .

On 1 May it was decided that she had failed in her endeavour to bring about a state of things which would lead, or be likely to lead, to a reunion with her child. From that moment on that was abandoned. . . . So final was that departure that the justices did not consider it necessary at all to consider any question of whether there had been any failure in the duty indicated in s. [3(2)(*b*)(*v*)] of the 1980 Act at any time after 1 May 1979. . . .

The question that we have to consider under this head is whether the justices were entitled to regard the local authority as having discharged the onus, in respect of the period, theoretically between 12 September 1978 and 4 October 1979, practically, having regard to the way they set about their task, between 12 September 1978 and 1 May 1979, of demonstrating the failure concerned.

It has to be not only a consistent failure, but such a failure as to render the parent unfit to have the care of the child. Both those postulates have to be satisfied. The phrase is not the same as the phrase which is used in the adoption legislation [s. 16(2)(*c*) of the Adoption Act 1976, p. 504, below]. It is pointed out in the case to which our attention has been directed (*M v Wigan Metropolitan Borough Council* [1980] Fam 36, [1979] 2 All ER 958) that there is a distinction between the use of the word 'persistently' in s. 16(2)(*c*) of the 1976 Act and the word 'consistently' used in s. 3 of the 1980 Act, which is the section which we have under consideration. The difference which is relevant, so far as this case is concerned, is that the period for a persistent failure has to be a substantially longer period, whereas in the section we are considering the consistency has to be demonstrated only by reference to such period of time as is appropriate to the matters which arise in the particular case.

Two aspects of failure are put forward by the local authority on this appeal. One is (though faintly comprehending the period between the beginning of October 1978 and Christmas, more pertinently related to the period between Christmas and the end of April 1979) that there had been such gaps in the mother's visiting programme, such inadequacies of excuse, that the failure was made out in respect of that period on the basis, purely, of the failure to keep contact. The other is the failure between 19 February and 1 May 1979 to carry out expeditiously the maximum of three weeks' work, according to the foreman, which was required to render the house habitable so as to provide a place in which the mother could, if properly minded, discharge her duties to her child, by being able to take the child there if and when she had earned her right to do so by an effective reunion, by visiting the child. . . .

Having given the best consideration that I can to the present case, my conclusion is that there was not, between 12 September 1978 and 1 May 1979, or more relevantly between Christmas 1978 and 1 May 1979, material on which the justices could reasonably conclude that the failure had been made out in terms of s. 3(1)(*b*)(v) of the 1980 Act. In my judgment, therefore, this court ought to reverse the justices' decision and direct that the resolution should lapse.

Question

The law report does not reveal whether the local authority immediately made the child a ward of court: would this have been in her best interests?

Grounds (*c*) and (*d*) were added by the Children Act 1975, as a result of the following recommendations of the *Report of the Departmental Committee on the Adoption of Children* (1972):

156. We think it would be an advantage if . . . local authorities had a discretionary power to assume parental rights in respect of any child who had been in their care for a continuous period of three years. This would provide machinery for local authority intervention at a time when the parents, for whatever reason, have not been undertaking parental care for a considerable period, and at a stage in the history of a child in care where decisions as to his long-term future may be required. We think that to give local authorities this power after a shorter period, without the need to establish any other ground, would constitute an unwarranted threat to parents of children in care, while a period of more than three years would be too long in the life of a child. As at present, a parent would be able to challenge the local authority decision before the court, which should be required to consider not only whether the necessary three years period had elapsed, but also whether the continuation of the resolution would be for the long-term welfare of the child. It would need to be made clear that occasional visits to parents of short duration should not be treated as breaking a continuous period. Local authorities should still assume parental rights at an earlier stage where any of the existing grounds apply.

157. We consider that there should be power to retain in care a child in respect of whom parental rights can be assumed in regard to one parent only. We have in mind the situation where a mentally ill mother may not, on discharge from hospital, be sufficiently recovered to have the care of her child; she may even need further periods in hospital. Yet the father against whom parental rights cannot be taken may exercise his right to withdraw his child from care, thus returning him to the care of his wife despite her continuing incapacity. We recommend that where parental rights have been assumed in respect of one parent, the local authority should be empowered to retain a child in care so as to prevent his return to the care of a parent in respect of whom parental rights have been assumed.

But the wording of the three year ground has already caused some difficulty:

W v Nottinghamshire County Council
[1982] Fam 1, [1982] 1 All ER 1, [1981] 3 WLR 959, 125 Sol Jo 761, 80 LGR 217, 12 Fam Law 27, Court of Appeal

The facts of this cases were in all essentials the same as those in the *Sunderland* case, save that (i) as Sir John Arnold found, there was nothing 'in the smallest degree culpable' in the mother's behaviour between the resolution and the resumed hearing, for she had cooperated fully in a visiting programme which had been stopped because it upset the child; but (ii) by the time of the *resumed* hearing, the child had been in care for three years. The High Court held, however, that the local authority could not rely, for the purposes of s. 3(6)(*b*) on the three year ground in s. 3(1)(*d*), first because, once the resolution had been passed, the child was no longer in care under s. 2 but under a different form of care in s. 3, and secondly, because the ground relied upon for the purposes of s. 3(6)(*b*) had to be the same as that relied upon for the initial resolution. The local authority appealed.

Ormrod LJ: . . . On the first point, we are unable, . . . to accept the proposition . . . that the 1980 Act gives rise to two different forms of care: 'voluntary' care under s. 2 and some form of, presumably, involuntary care under s. 3. Counsel for the local authority has put forward an argument, based on other provisions of the 1980 Act, which seems to us to be conclusive against this proposition. First, s. 13(1) refers to a child 'in the care of a local authority under section 2 of this Act with respect to whom a resolution is in force under section 3 thereof . . .' Second, s. 17 provides that Part III of the Act relates to the powers and duties of local authorities 'in relation to children received by them into their care under section two of this Act . . .' Part III must, of course, apply to children with respect to whom a s. 3 resolution has been passed. They must, therefore, be children received into care under s. 2. Third, s. 15(1) of the Act states:
    'This section applies to a child — (*a*) who is in the care of a local authority under section 2 of this Act; and (*b*) with respect to whom there is in force a resolution under section 3 of this Act . . .'
Accordingly the phrase 'in the care of a local authority under the foregoing section' in s. 3(1)(*d*) must include children who have been subject to a resolution under this section at some time during the relevant three-year period.
    The other point is more difficult. . . .

We do not think that this proviso can be construed as meaning that the ground referred to in it must be the same ground as that relief on in the first place to found the resolution which is the subject matter of the proceedings before the court. Had that been the intended meaning it would have been easy to add a few words to proviso (*a*) and omit proviso (*b*) altogether. Furthermore, proviso (*b*) refers to *a* resolution and not *the* resolution. It requires the court to consider a hypothetical question, namely whether the facts were such at the time of the hearing that the local authority could lawfully have passed *a* s. 3(1) resolution, not necessarily a resolution founded on the same ground as the resolution under consideration.

What then is the point of the phrase 'there continued to be'? In other words, what is the element which is to be continued? We think that it means that, at the date of the hearing, the local authority must continue to be in a position to pass a valid resolution under the terms of s. 3(1). . . .

This construction avoids some surprising anomalies which would arise if the alternative construction is correct. We cite one of several examples given by counsel for the local authority in his able argument. Suppose that a resolution has been properly passed on the ground of consistent failure to discharge parental obligations without reasonable cause, so that proviso (*a*) is satisfied, and that, between that date and the time of the hearing, the mother has a mental breakdown within the meaning of ground (iii) of s. 3(1)(*b*). It might be held (we do not say that it would necessarily be correct) that ground (v) was no longer available because the local authority could not show that the failure was without reasonable cause. Ground (iii) could not be relief on to satisfy proviso (*b*) because it did not exist at the time when the resolution was passed, with the result that the resolution must be permitted to lapse, leaving as the only alternative wardship proceedings. Such an inconvenient, even perverse, result is to be avoided if it is possible to do so. We do not think that our construction puts an undue strain on the language of the proviso; it certainly gives effect to the obvious intention of the legislation.

Questions

(i) Do you think that any of the mothers in the *Glamorgan* (p. 447, above), *Sunderland* (p. 449, above) or *Nottinghamshire* cases should have been able to reclaim their children by the time the case got to the juvenile court?

(ii) Do you think that the social workers in this and the *Sunderland* cases are to be condemned or commended for endeavouring to reunite the mother and her child?

4 The case against s. 3

It is almost impossible to find anyone with a good word to say for the s. 3 procedure or its substance. The criticism of Goldstein, Freud and Solnit, in *Beyond the Best Interests of the Child* (1973) is revealed in their two versions of the following case:

Rothman v Jewish Child Care Association
(1971) 166 NY Law Journal 17, Supreme Court, New York County

Justice Nadel: In this proceeding, the natural mother seeks a judgment for the return of her 8-year-old daughter, Stacey. Petitioner gave her daughter to respondents for temporary care in December 1964, when she voluntarily entered a hospital for treatment of a mental illness. Petitioner left the hospital for a period of time and then was readmitted. In December 1969, the petitioner was released from the hospital and has not been hospitalized since. She is living with her parents, is employed as an executive secretary, and earns $140 per week.

The petitioner has never surrendered the child for adoption. The respondent, Jewish Child Care Association, opposes giving custody to the natural mother on the ground that she is unfit to care for the child by reason of her past mental illness. However, on the trial they failed to produce any evidence upon which the court could make a finding that the petitioner is unfit to have custody of the child. The burden is upon the non-parent respondent to prove that petitioner is unfit to care for her daughter, and that the child's well-being requires separation from her mother. The Court of Appeals has ruled that absent abandonment of the child, statutory surrender of the child or the established unfitness of the mother, a court is without power to deprive the mother of custody (*Spence-Chapin Adoption Service v Polk, N.Y.L.J.*, 27 Sept. 1971, p. 1, col. 1). At best, respondents have shown that the relationship between mother and daughter is not as good as it should be. That this is so, is primarily the fault of the Jewish Child Care Association. Its extrajudicial determination that the child should not be returned, its hindrance of visitation and its failure to encourage the parental relationship were, to a great extent, responsible for the lack of a better relationship. It has been established in the Family Court that the said Association failed to make any real efforts to encourage and strengthen the parental relationship. The petitioner had to commence court proceedings for visitation and custody of her child, which were denied her by the Association.

Not only have respondents failed to sustain their burden of proof, but the evidence submitted amply demonstrates petitioner's fitness to have custody of her child. It was in the interest of the welfare of her daughter that the petitioner gave respondents temporary custody when she was hospitalized and unable to care for the child.

In the period of nearly two years preceding this trial, petitioner has been gainfully employed and she has been active in community, charitable and religious affairs. During the trying period of her hospitalization and separation from her child, petitioner appears to have successfully rehabilitated herself.

The court has observed petitioner during the course of her testimony. After hearing and observing the petitioner, the court finds that she is sincere in her desire to care for her daughter, and that she is able to do so. Petitioner is residing with her parents, and they will be able to care for their grandchild in the interim between the child's return from school and the time when the petitioner comes home from work. Their presence adds two persons to aid petitioner in the care of her daughter.

The petitioner indicated that she realizes that the attitude of her daughter may require a transitional period before acquiring full custody. The parties shall, therefore, confer and shall submit in the judgment to be settled herein, a program for visitation and transfer of custody. Should the parties fail to agree, the court will determine such provisions, giving due consideration to their suggestions.

Question

Could an English local authority have assumed the mother's rights, (*a*) on the grounds originally enacted in the 1948 Act, (*b*) with the additions made in the 1963 Act, or (*c*) as they are now?

The authors' concepts of the 'psychological parent' and 'wanted child', of the child's need for continuity and of the child's sense of time (see pp. 357–359, above) have far more obvious implications in this context than in the context of parental divorce or separation. They persuade a fictional (and somewhat long-winded) Judge Baltimore to rewrite Judge Nadel's opinion in the light of their own guide-lines:

. . . The real question is: does Stacey need to have a parent assigned to her by the court? The petitioner's fitness could have become an issue only had it first been established that Stacey is currently an unwanted child in need of a parent. Not until then could the court admit evidence concerning the petitioner in order to determine who, among the available alternatives, would serve Stacey's interests by providing the least detrimental opportunity for meeting her needs.

What is strangely missing from the evidence is any material evidence on Stacey's needs. In the absence of such evidence the law must and does presume that Stacey is a wanted child, well settled in a reciprocal relationship with her custodians. The burden is on the petitioner to overcome the presumption that the adult or adults who currently are responsible for Stacey are fit to remain her parents. Another facet of these presumptions is that Stacey has been psychologically abandoned by her biological mother. Seven years have elapsed since their last contact. The burden then is on petitioner to establish that there is a necessarity for altering the long-standing ongoing relationship between Stacey and whoever may be her psychological parents. In short, petitioner must establish that Stacey is unwanted in her present family. If petitioner were to meet that burden, she would not then have to prove her fitness to be a parent. Rather, she would have to establish that among the available alternatives, her taking custody would be the least detrimental for Stacey's physical and psychological well-being.

Petitioner further argues that she never lost custody-in-law of Stacey. She established that she has always considered herself responsible for Stacey's care, that she had made 'temporary' arrangements for her with the respondent, that from the outset it was understood that they were to be temporary, and that she had always intended, once her health was restored, to care personally for Stacey. At no time during the last seven years, she asserts, has she abandoned Stacey; has she ever ceased being her 'mother.' If anyone is at fault, it is, she claims, the respondent Association. It has prevented her from maintaining or, at least, establishing a parental relationship with Stacey.

These arguments and the supporting facts reflect an understandable, but still mistaken notion. Abandonment of a child by an adult, at least for the purpose of determining who is parent, rests, not on the intentions of the adult, but rather on the impact such a leave-taking has on the child. Stacey, since the age of one year, has been deprived of continuous, affectionate, and otherwise nurturing contact with petitioner. In the absence of specific evidence to the contrary, for purposes of custody and care Stacey must be presumed in law to have been abandoned. If nothing else, from Stacey's vantage point, there has been a critical break in whatever psychological tie had begun to develop between herself and petitioner. Painful as it must be for this well-meaning woman, her intentions alone are not enough to prevent such psychological abandonment. Even if those intentions had been accompanied by a carefully designed program to maintain contact with the child, over the time elapsed petitioner could hardly have been the primary adult source for Stacey of affection, stimulation, and, most importantly, of a sense of continuity essential to securing healthy growth and development.

So far as Stacey's interests are concerned, it matters not that the implementation of those intentions may have actually been thwarted by the staff of the respondent Association or by anyone else, nor does it matter, for purposes of determining custody, whether petitioner's intentions were defeated through her misunderstanding, her illness, or her ignorance. Whatever the cause, whoever may feel responsible, the psychological fact, which the law must acknowledge, is that Stacey does not now recognize petitioner as a parent. . . .

Even if the Court decreed that Stacey be returned to her biological 'mother,' it would be wholly beyond its power to establish a psychological parent-child relationship between them. In addition, far from being benign, such a decree would inflict damage and pain on all parties, child as well as adults.

Though the status of parent is not easily lost in law, it can exist only so long as it is real in terms of the health and well-being of the child. It is a relationship from birth, whether legitimate or illegitimate, or from adoption, whether statutory or common-law, which requires a continuing interaction between adult and child to survive. It can be broken by the adult parent by 'chance,' by the establishment of a new adult-child relationship, which we call common-law adoption, or by 'choice,' through a more formal legal process we have come to call adoption. It is the real tie — the reality of an ongoing relationship — that is crucial to this court's decision and that demands the protection of the state through law. The court must not, despite its sympathetic concern for the petitioner, become a party to tearing Stacey away from the only affectionate parents she knows. Stacey must be presumed to be, in her present surroundings, a wanted child. . . .

Questions

(i) Which of the two Rothman decisions do you prefer?
(ii) But how would 'Judge Baltimore' have decided the *Glamorgan* case (p. 447, above)?

On the other hand, the National Council for One Parent Families has recently been gathering evidence of parents' dissatisfaction with the way in which they have been treated by social workers. One example of the 40 which they collected for *Against Natural Justice* (1982) may suffice to illustrate the criticisms which follow:

Ms David is a 17 year old single mother and she has one child aged 6 months. She was referred to the social services by the hospital when her child was born for support. She also had housing and financial problems. She was living in over-crowded conditions with her young brothers and sisters and her parents and was finding it impossible to cope with all these responsibilities. Ms David requested voluntary care to enable her to sort out her problems. However she was asked to sign voluntary care forms and parental rights resolution consent forms at the same time. She did not realise that she was signing away her parental rights. A resolution was passed several weeks later. Ms David was thought to be of such habits and modes of life as to be unfit to have the care of the child.[6] The child was then placed with foster parents. Later, Ms David contacted the social services department after access problems and was told that the resolution had been passed and that she had no right to object. She immediately contacted solicitors who applied for the order to be rescinded. The magistrate dismissed the resolution and her child was returned immediately. During that time she was able to resolve some of her practical problems.

Social work practice

The majority of the parents interviewed were poor, on Supplementary Benefit and under emotional stress. Voluntary care was often the only immediate solution to their prolems because other alternatives and resources did not exist. But the act of accepting this solution was often later interpreted as evidence of a parent's weakness and failure.

It is not the policy of local authorities to explain the limits of a social worker's power at the time of voluntary care. Consequently many were deeply shocked when resolutions were taken or access curtailed.

In one quarter of the cases examined, the parental rights resolution was applied for within days of the reception into care. Rehabilitation of the child with the parent was not therefore the main consideration of the social worker. This could be interpreted as against the spirit of the legislation. These resolutions were taken at a time when the parent was still under stress and therefore least able to resist and when their own case was certainly at its weakest.

It seems to be rare for social workers to involve parents in discussions about parental rights resolutions before the applications are actually made. Certainly written information was sent in virtually all cases, but for many parents this was not enough. Possibly some social workers themselves sent letters to avoid stressful personal visits.

A smaller number of parents were asked to consent to the resolution being passed by their social workers. No parent should be asked to do this without first taking legal advice. Our experience shows that parents are often ill-informed about their loss of rights at a time when they are depressed and in no fit state to make such a decision, and further are likely to be put under pressure by the social worker to sign the consent form.

The parents and solicitors contacted during this study may be amongst the best motivated. Nevertheless 17 parents received no legal advice at the time of the resolution so it is not surprising that only 1 of those objected to the procedure.

The choice and rationale of 'ground' to justify the passing of a parental rights resolution revealed worrying practice and differences of opinion. The ground, 'habits and mode of life' is open to moralistic judgment and a range of opinion and had a devastating effect on some of the parents. The use of the ground 'that the parent is dead' was used to exclude a relative from contesting the issue and was against all notions of justice.

In all but at most 2 cases, written notice of the resolution was sent to the parent. The letters reproduced however, were informal and cold and if they arrived without a social worker's explanation they were totally confusing.

No doubt many social workers would rightly protest, first, that this was a small and self-selected group of dissatisfied clients, secondly, that the study relied upon their unsubstantiated accounts of what happened, and thirdly that isolated examples of bad practice may occur even in the best regulated systems, but that there is no evidence to support allegations of wide-spread abuse. The Rowe and Lambert study which resulted in *Children Who Wait* (1973) also threw up some data on the use of s. 3 resolutions. Perhaps the most significant findings for our purposes were these, reported in *Children in Care and the Assumption of Parental Rights by Local Authorities* (1974):

Local authorities tend to assume parental rights over children who are expected to stay in care until they become 18 years old (76%). More than half of the children came into care before their second birthday and they generally have little or no contact with their natural parents. Many of the children are illegitimate. Parental rights are more likely to be taken over foster children than

---

6. Elsewhere in the text it is stated that: 'she was said to be irresponsible and on one occasion had left the child with a painter and decorator. In the event the painter and decorator turned out to be the father of her child.'

those in group care. As the original study did not provide information on when parental rights had been assumed it is impossible to know for sure from the study findings whether such resolutions generally precede efforts to place the child in a substitute family or whether they are used to secure an apparently successful placement. Although more Section [3] children were already placed in foster homes, there was no significant difference in the proportions of Section [2] and Section [3] children who were said to need family placement. . . .

There does not appear to be any general policy among local authorities of assuming parental rights if natural mothers and fathers lose touch and cease to fulfil any part of the parental role, since 35% of children still under Section [2] had no contact with their parents.

The overwhelming impression which emerges from the data is that although some overall trends can be observed, there is no well defined or generally accepted policy about which children need the protection of control of a court order or Section [3] resolution. Very similar children could be found in all groups.

Since then, it would seem that many local authorities have adopted a more 'aggressive' policy in order to feel freer to cater for the needs of the 'children who wait.' A study of all the resolutions passed by four local authorities between December 1978 and November 1980 had recently been completed by Margaret Adcock and Richard White. A summary of some of their findings (Adcock and White, 1982) indicates that 34% of the children were under 5; 54% of the resolutions were passed within 12 months of the child's current reception into care, 20% before the child had been in care for 3 months; of the 100 children (38%) for whom the resolution was taken within the first 6 months, 36 had had three or more receptions into care, 28 had had two, and 36 had had no previous reception. Of the characteristics of the parents, 67% seemed to fall into both the 'habits and mode of life' category and the 'consistent failure' category, 6% were wholly in the former, and 27% wholly in the latter. The authors conclude by quoting from Fanshel and Shinn (1978):

'We need to know more profoundly how individuals relate to their parental responsibilities. There are adults who are apparently intact emotionally and in their ability to function in many areas of their lives but who seem entirely undeveloped as parent figures. The case system is saturated with such parental types: the massive abandonment of children in care is a reflection of this. There is a very pressing need to determine whether undeveloped or damaged parental functioning as evidenced by the request for placement and early failure to visit is amenable to casework and other methods of treatment.'

Question

Why has there been so much research into how children grow up and so little into how parents react to their children?

Whatever conclusions may eventually be drawn from all this, *Against Natural Justice* (National Council for One Parent Families, 1982) is clear:

Natural justice
However, even if the powers were always used responsibly, that is as a last resort after attempts at rehabilitation had failed, the procedure would still remain fundamentally unjust. The reasons for this are fairly clear; the present system puts social workers in an invidious position in that they are forced to act for all parties during the procedure, reflected in the social workers' confusion over who they represented. Neither parent nor child has the right to appear before the committee or to have access to the social services department to put their point of view. In the study no parent had the opportunity to put their view to the committee. The committee members themselves have little training and most often act as a rubber stamp. They are advised by their own officers and act as judge and jury with those officers being the only witnesses. They are unlikely to call their professional advisers' judgment into question or risk losing their confidence.

It is against this background that the National Council for One Parent Families called in October 1981 for the abolition of parental rights resolutions and the substitution of Juvenile Court orders for these resolutions. The Child Care Bill which was introduced in the House of Commons by David Alton MP and in the House of Lords by Lord Avebury in April 1982 abolishes parental rights resolutions and places on the local authority the responsibility to take the parent to court if it wishes to obtain the care and control of the child already in its voluntary care. The decision would be made by the court in possession of all evidence and opinion. Both parent and child would be separately represented, although the parent can exercise the right not to contest the issue. If an order was made the Bill would give the parent leave to apply for access to the child. The final decision would be made by the Juvenile Court magistrates after hearing argument and evidence from all sides. The procedure is intended to be as consistent as possible with other legislation which affects care proceedings.

Under the *Child Care Bill 1982*, the following clause would have been substituted for the current s. 3:

3.—(1) Where a child is in the care of a local authority under section 2 of this Act, the local authority, if satisfied that one of the conditions in the following subsection is satisfied and that it is in the best interests of the child, may bring the parent or guardian of the child before a juvenile court.

(2) [Repeated the existing grounds but without the 'habits and mode of life' provision.]

(3) On an application by a local authority under subsection (1) of this section the court may make one of the following orders —

(i) a care order

(ii) a supervision order, subject to the conditions laid down in subsection (5) of this section.

(4) In determining whether or not to make a care order the court must be satisfied that one of the conditions in subsection (2) of this section exists at the time of the hearing and that the order is in the best interest of the child.

(5) Where the court is satisfied that condition (*c*) or (*d*) of subsection (2) of this section exist in relation to the child but the court decides not to make a care order, the court may make a supervision order if satisfied that such an order is in the best interest of the child.

(6) Before considering what are the best interests of the child the court must be satisfied that the local authority has fulfilled its duties under section 18 of this Act, and that the plans made by the local authority for the future care of the child are in accordance with the said section.

(7) Where, after a child has been received into the care of a local authority under section 2 of this Act, the whereabouts of any parent of his have remained unknown for 12 months, then, for the purposes of this section, the parent shall be deemed to have abandoned the child.

(8) In the circumstances of section [3](2)(*a*), [3](7) and any other circumstances where the parent does not take any part in the proceedings before the Court, a guardian ad litem under section 7 of this Act shall be appointed for the purposes of the proceedings.

(9) Where an application for a care order in respect of a child has been made by a local authority under this Act it shall be an offence, punishable under the Magistrates' Court Act 1980 section 33 to remove the child from the care and control of the local authority except with the authority of a Court, or under authority conferred by any enactment or on the arrest of the child.

Question

On 7 March 1983, the Government announced plans to amend the Health and Social Services and Social Security Adjudications Bill 'to provide that parents cannot sign away their rights to be informed when a local authority passes a resolution . . . , to object to the resolution and to get the matter referred to a court.' Which is the better solution?

5 Access and accountability

A resolution prevents the parent from reclaiming the child: but it must be obvious from what has gone before that whether the parent should be allowed to reclaim the child depends to a large extent upon what has happened *during* the child's stay in care. Whatever 'good practce' may be, the parent has no legal *right* to be consulted about, for example, whether the child lives in a children's home or with long term foster parents to whom he may become attached; or whether that placement is far away or nearby. Much the same applies to parental visiting:

Re Y (a minor) (child in care: access)
[1976] Fam 125, [1975] 3 All ER 348, [1975] 3 WLR 342, 119 Sol Jo 610, 73 LGR 495, 5 Fam Law 185, Court of Appeal

A child was made a ward of court by his father, but committed to the care of the local authority by the High Court under s. 7(2) of the Family Law Reform Act 1969. Such orders are governed by what is now s. 43 of the Matrimonial Causes Act 1973, sub-s. (5) of which provides that 'the exercise by the local authority of their powers under [ss. 18, 21 and 22 of the Child Care Act 1980] . . . shall be subject to any directions given by the court . . .'. The judge made an order for access to the child by his father and the local authority appealed.

Ormrod LJ: However, the learned judge, taking the view that no power to control access could be extracted from ss. 18, 21 and 22 or from s. 2 of the 1980 Act, went on to make the order which he did, 'filling up', as he thought, a gap in the local authority's powers.

I have not the slightest difficulty in understanding the anxiety of a local authority in relation to a decision which says in terms that in every case in which a child is in their care under s. 2 of the 1980 Act they have no power to control access. I can fully understand their anxiety and their desire to get that decision, if possible, reversed; clearly it would lead to chaos in the administration of their highly responsible duties under the various Children Acts. But the issue in this present case is a much narrower one. I think, with respect, that the learned judge was wrong to take the view, as I have indicated, that access was not in some way subsumed under ss. 18, 21 and 22 of the 1980 Act. Once one accepts that access is among the matters over which the court can direct a local authority under s. 43(5) of the 1973 Act all the local authority's real anxieties disappear. . . . I certainly would not wish anyone to think because of anything I have said that I have cast any doubt whatever on the powers of local authorities in ordinary cases under s. 2 of the 1980 Act to control access as part of their responsibility, but this is not an ordinary case under s. 2.

Appeal dismissed.

Question

Is this case authority for the proposition that a local authority may prevent a parent seeing a child who was received into care under s. 2 three months ago?

Such a parent might, of course, be in a position to remove her child at once (although in many cases this will not be so). The parent of a child who is subject either to a resolution or to a care order made by a court is in a much more difficult position, and might be tempted to ask the High Court for help:

A v Liverpool City Council
[1982] AC 363, [1981] 2 All ER 385, [1981] 2 WLR 948, 145 JP 318, 125 Sol Jo 396, 79 LGR 621, House of Lords

This was a 'leap-frog' appeal direct from the High Court to the House of Lords against the decision of Balcombe J that he was bound by authority to dismiss a mother's application to have her child made a ward of court without investigating the merits of her case.

Lord Roskill: . . . The relevant facts can be shortly stated. On 10 March 1980 the local authority obtained a care order pursuant to s. 1(2)(*a*) and (3) of the Children and Young Persons Act 1969 in respect of K. He was then placed with foster parents but the mother was allowed weekly access. That access continued until 16 June 1980 when the mother was told that henceforth only monthly supervised access would be allowed. That access was to take place at a day nursery and was to be limited to one hour. The local authority's stated reason was that 'rehabilitation' of the mother and K was not in K's best interest. Accordingly there was no point in maintaining regular access when no such 'rehabilitation' was still planned.

The local authority refused to reconsider its decision and it was with the intention of challenging that decision as 'wholly unreasonable' and 'arbitrary' that the present wardship proceedings were begun. The summons issued by the mother not only sought from the court an order for defined access but also care and control of K. The learned judge, rightly in my view, declined to express any view on the facts, being of the opinion as already stated that he was bound by authority to discharge the wardship proceedings. . . .

My Lords, I do not think it necessary to review the authorities on the interrelationship between prerogative and statutory powers. The basic principles were authoritatively determined by your Lordships' House in *A-G v De Keyser's Royal Hotel Ltd* [1920] AC 508: see especially the speech of Lord Summer ([1920] AC 508 at 561). My Lords, I do not doubt that the wardship jurisdiction of the court is not extinguished by the existence of the legislation regarding the care and control of deprived children, a phrase I use to include children whose parents have for some reason failed to discharge their parental duties towards them. I am not aware of any decision which suggests otherwise. It is helpful to examine the unsuccessful submissions in *Re A B* [1954] 2 QB 385 at 389–390 of J E Simon QC for the foster parents and the successful submission of R J Parker for the local authority. Mr Parker argued that 'the court's powers as parens patriae are limited by the Children Act 1948 by which Parliament has committed, in certain cases, the task and the right of the supervision of the welfare of children to local authorities'. It was this argument which Lord Goddard CJ was accepting (see [1954] 2 QB 385 at 398, [1954] 2 All ER 287 at 291). Indeed, Donovan J concurring on this point said ([1954] 2 QB 385 at 401, [1954] 2 All ER 287 at 293):

> 'Thus far, at any rate, Parliament has entrusted the welfare of the child to the local authority, and to that extent the prerogative right to secure the welfare of the child is, in my view, by necessary implication, restricted. Accordingly . . . the court cannot intervene simply because it differs from the local authority as to what is best for the child.'

It was this view which found favour with the Court of Appeal in *Re M*. Lord Evershed MR, with whom Upjohn and Pearson LJJ expressly concurred, stated his first two conclusions thus ([1961] Ch 328 at 345, [1961] 1 All ER 788 at 795):

> '(i) The prerogative right of the Queen as parens partriae in relation to infants within the realm is not for all purposes ousted or abrogated as the result of the exercise of the duties and powers by local authorities under the Children Act, 1948: in particular the power to make an infant a ward of court by invocation of s. 9 of the Act of 1949 is unaffected.
>
> (ii) But even where a child is made a ward of court by virtue of the Act of 1949, the judge in whom the prerogative power is vested will, acting on familiar principles, not exercise control in relation to duties or discretions clearly vested by statute in the local authority, and may, therefore, and in a case such as the present normally will, order that the child cease to be a ward of court.'

The statutory codes which existed in 1954 and in 1961 have been elaborated and extended and amended several times since these decisions as the social needs of our society have changed and, unhappily, the number of deprived children in the care of local authorities has tragically increased. It cannot possibly be said that the massive volume of legislation since 1961 culminating in the Child Care Act 1980, a consolidating Act which, though repealing the whole of the 1948 Act, left intact the early part of the 1969 Act has lessened the responsibilities of local authorities. This hardly suggests an intention by Parliament to restrict the scope of the statutory control by local authorities of child welfare in favour of the use by the courts of the prerogative wardship jurisdiction. On the contrary, the plain intention of this legislation is to secure the continued expansion of that statutory control.

I do not think that the language of s. 1 of the Guardianship of Infants Act 1925 and of its statutory successor in any way points in a contrary direction. The former statute, as its preamble shows, was largely designed to secure equality of rights as between father and mother in relation to their children and making the welfare of those children paramount in relation to those two henceforth equal interests. Nor do I think that the emphasis laid on that section in your Lordships' House in *J v C* [1970] AC 668, [1969] 1 All ER 788 [p. 474, below] casts any doubt on the correctness of the several earlier decisions to which I have already referred.

I am of the clear opinion that, while prerogative jurisdiction of the court in wardship cases remains, the exercise of that jurisdiction has been and must continue to be treated as circumscribed by the existence of the far-ranging statutory code which entrusts the care and control of deprived children to local authorities. It follows that the undoubted wardship jurisdiction must not be exercised so as to interfere with the day-to-day administration by local authorities of that statutory control.

My Lords, to say that is not to suggest that local authorities are immune from judicial control: in an appropiate case, as Lord Evershed MR himself said in *Re M*, the *Wednesbury* principle is available. The remedy of judicial review under RSC Ord 53 is also available in an appropriate case. Moreover, there are the specific, if limited, rights of appeal to which I have already drawn attention.

My Lords, I think this conclusion is strongly reinforced by the consideration that, though the law as laid down by the courts has been clear since 1961 when *Re M* was decided and though there have been many legislative changes since that date, noticeably in 1969 and again in 1975 when the new right of appeal to the High Court already mentioned was first created, no right of appeal or review such as the mother in effect now seeks to achieve by invocation of the wardship jurisdiction of the court has ever been accorded by Parliament. The inference that I would draw from that fact is that Parliament was satisfied with the restriction on the remedies available to a person aggrieved by a discretionary administrative decision of the local authority, declared by the cases to which I have referred, and decided to leave the law as thus laid down unaffected.

Much reliance on the mother's behalf was placed on the decision of the Court of Appeal affirming Balcombe J in *Re H (a minor) (wardship: jurisdiction)* [1978] Fam 65, [1978] 2 All ER 903, where that court, in agreement with the learned judge, exercised its wardship jurisdiction so as to enable the Pakistani parents of a child in respect of whom a care order had been made under s. 1 of the 1969 Act to remove that child from this country, notwithstanding the existence of that care order. . . .

The decision in *Re H* is, if I may respectfully say so, obviously sensible: whilst acknowledging the possibility of some risk to the child, this was the lesser of the only two possible courses which it was open to a court to take, the other being to leave the child behind in this country after its parents had returned to Pakistan.

I venture to think that the decision can perhaps be better supported on the ground that the wardship jurisdiction of the court could properly be invoked in addition to the statutory jurisdiction of the local authority because it was only in this way that the result which was best in the paramount interest of the child could be achieved, the local authority and juvenile court being unable within the limits of their powers to achieve that result.

Lane J in *Re B (a minor) (wardship: child in care)* [1975] Fam 36, [1974] 3 All ER 915 drew attention to the positive advantages which could flow from the invocation of wardship jurisdiction in cases of child abuse from the point of view of local authorities. Though the learned judge refused the grandmother's application for care and control of the child in the wardship proceedings which the grandmother had begun, she continued those proceedings so that if required the local authority could apply for an injunction restraining the child's undesirable stepfather from any contact or attempted contact with the child. A local authority may often be powerless to stop attempted interference by third parties. The exercise of wardship jurisdiction affords a simple method of attaining a result much to be desired in such cases. . . .

Appeal dismissed.

Questions

(i) *Re M* and *Re AB* were cases in which the local authority was trying to recover a child from foster parents who had signed the statutory undertaking (p. 465 in the following chapter) to return the child on demand: could the House have distinguished them on that basis?

(ii) If Parliament has passed legislation which defines and limits the powers of local authorities, is it an interference in the will of Parliament for the courts to use their inherent powers to assist local authorities to outstep those limits? (See further in Chapter 15).

(iii) On 7 March 1983, the Government announced plans to provide, in the Health and Social Services and Social Security Adjudications Bill, for 'parents who are refused any further access to their children in care to apply to the courts for an access order,' and for a Code of Practice to be laid before Parliament dealing with access to children in care: will these solve all the problems raised by the above case?

Jo Tunnard of the Family Rights Group contributed these thoughts on *A v Liverpool City Council* to a seminar on *Accountability in Child Care — Which Way Forward*? (1982):

A common feature in many of our cases is that local authority care is no longer being seen, or offered, as a supportive service to those families who have nowhere else to turn to for the help they need in caring for their children. Decisions about the permanent placing of children with substitute families are being pursued vigorously and systematically, not just to release children who have lingered too long away from their families but in many cases to sever family connections within a matter of weeks of children being admitted or committed to care.

The importance of making decisions has been properly highlighted in recent years but there's a real danger that decision-making is becoming inextricably linked to terminating a child's right to access to his or her family. The assumptions in documents and discussions about severing family links is that we all want to and will work towards rehabilitation and that we all know how to do that. But, if our casework is anything to go by, both these assumptions often prove to be false.

First, how real is the commitment to working towards keeping families together? One local authority has a new scheme of operations, called Child Care Career Planning (CCCP), designed to ensure that the future of every child in care or about to come into care is positively and decisively planned at the earliest and most useful time either before or after the commencement of the care episode. There are two study papers for social workers — 82 pages in total. They contain much sound advice about good social work practice, stressing the need for complete honesty, proper recording, keeping up-to-date with research material, making plans, setting goals and monitoring the work that is done. But I believe there's undue emphasis placed on the finding of substitute families, and there's barely a mention of prevention and rehabilitation. The longest reference to prevention is a short paragraph about daycare provision, one-quarter of the way through the document. . . .

And what of the second assumption, that social workers know how to work towards rehabilitation? There's plenty of research material that points to the need for proper planning of a child's return home, to the importance of maintaining clear links from the moment of separation, and for concrete departmental support for workers and families. A good starting point is the NCB's working party on caring for separated children (Parker, 1980). In that, reference is made to the DHSS Harvie Report on residential care for mentally subnormal children and its reminder that a child is more likely to be abandoned in care by its parents where the parents are effectively abandoned by the placing authority. I would say that that observation holds true of many other children in care today.

This is supported by Robert Holman, who said this when attacking the Children Bill in 1975, *In Defence of Parents*:

Perhaps the most severe criticism is that the government's child care legislation simply overlooks the link between child separation and poverty. Recent research has established that poverty is a major (though not the only) factor in causing children to leave their parents. Rosamund Thorpe concluded her study in February 1974: 'The evidence from this research points to the lamentable conclusion that poverty and deprivation are still closely associated with reception and committal to care.'

Poverty can lead to separation in two ways. Its grinding nature can affect its victims' behaviour. Their resulting apathy or aggression, and lowered child care standards, can mean their children are removed. This does not mean that the parents are subhuman. Studies suggest that their values, feelings and hopes are similar to most other people's. But as Harriett Wilson's research in the midlands concludes, 'Material shortages in the home and poor environmental conditions severely affect parental child-rearing methods. Life in the slum forces parents to adopt methods of child-rearing they do not approve of' . . . (1974). Alternatively, and more simply, separation occurs because parents cannot find adequate housing or day care. The total of 3,000 children received into care because of homelessness, underestimates the real situation. I have frequently found parents, particularly lone mothers, who after desperately seeking day care, reluctantly gave up their children.

The major child care need is thus to *provide the environmental facilities* which prevent family break-ups. Yet the Children Bill does nothing but encourage removals. It thus reinforces the belief that such natural parents are generally uncaring monsters who should be parted from their children.

The government has accepted at face value the common assertions that natural parents too easily and readily claim back their children, and that social workers are concerned above all else with reuniting families. Consequently, the Children Bill gives local authorities no extra resources or new duties to help bring the separated together again. Indeed, the new act will specifically be used to arrest any such work.

Yet what does research reveal of the practices of social workers? Professor Vic George's study (1970) found that contacts between natural parents and children are rarely encouraged, although lack of visiting was then taken as confirmation that the former did not care for the latter. My own research found that only 21% of parents regularly visited their children while 54% of the natural parents had not been seen at all by social workers in the previous twelve months. Thorpe's examination of fostering in the Midlands found that 61% of natural parents were not told where their children were; only 12% had regular contact; and in only 5% of cases was rehabilitation being considered. Yet this situation did not necessarily reflect the parents' wishes or abilities. 70% were already coping with other children, while nearly a half wanted their children back. Further, most parents felt they were not encouraged to maintain contact. They were 'tacitly, if not directly, excluded.' Lacking confidence, few parents would insist on seeing their children. The evidence suggests that cases of natural parents being needlessly kept from their children are *more numerous* than cases of parents wrongfully taking them back.

The tragedy is that research suggests that there is tremendous potential for rehabilitation — especially in the first year of removal, that is before the 'tug of love' situation develops.

6 A different way of doing things?

The following has been developed in the United States by Professor Sanford N. Katz:

MODEL ACT TO FREE CHILDREN FOR PERMANENT PLACEMENT

Section 1. Purposes of act; construction of provisions
(a) The general purposes of this Act are to:
    (1) provide prompt judicial procedures for freeing minor children from the custody and control of their parents, by terminating the parent-child relationship;
    (2) promote the placement of such minor children in a permanent home, preferably through adoption or by vesting their de facto parents with legal guardianship; and
    (3) ensure that the constitutional rights and interests of all parties are recognized and enforced in all proceedings and other activities pursuant to this Act.
(b) It is the policy of this State that:
    (1) whenever possible and appropriate, the birth family relationship shall be recognized, strengthened, and preserved through efforts and procedures as provided for under [state] statute(s);
    (2) removal of a child from his home shall occur only when the child cannot be adequately protected within the home;
    (3) if a child has been removed from his home for one year and cannot be returned home within a reasonable time thereafter, the state should promptly find an alternative arrangement to provide a stable, permanent home for him;
    (4) the interests of the child shall prevail if the child's interests and parental rights conflict; and
    (5) because termination of the parent-child relationship is so drastic, all non-judicial attempts by contractual arrangements, express or implied, for the surrender or relinquishment of children, are invalid unless approved by the court.
(c) This Act shall be liberally construed to promote the general purposes and policies stated in this section.

Section 3. Grounds for voluntary termination of the parent-child relationship
(a) If the court determines that termination of the parent-child relationship is in the best interest of the child, it may order such termination provided that:
    (1) a parent either directly or through an authorized agency voluntarily petitions for the termination of the parent-child relationship; or
    (2) a parent has executed an out-of-court notorized statement envincing to the court's satisfaction that the parent has voluntarily and knowingly relinquished the child to an authorized agency no earlier than 72 hours after the child's birth.

Section 4. Grounds for involuntary termination of the parent-child relationship
(a) An order of the court for involuntary termination of the parent-child relationship shall be made on the grounds that the termination is in the child's best interest, in light of the considerations in subsections (b) through (f), where one or more of the following conditions exist:
    (1) the child has been abandoned, [conclusively presumed if the child is found under such circumstances that the identity or whereabouts of the parent is unknown and has not

been assertained by diligent searching and the parent does not claim the child within two months after the child is found];

(2) the child has been adjudicated to have been abused or neglected in a prior proceeding;

(3) the child has been out of the custody of the parent for the period of one year and the court finds that:

    (i)   the conditions which led to the separation still persist, or similar conditions of a potentially harmful nature continue to exist;

    (ii) there is little likelihood that those conditions will be remedied at an early date so that the child can be returned to the parent in the near future; and

    (iii) the continuation of the parent-child relationship greatly diminishes the child's prospects for early integration into a stable and permanent home.

(*b*) When a child has been previously adjudicated abused or neglected, the court in determining whether or not to terminate the parent-child relationship shall consider, among other factors, the following continuing or serious conditions or acts of the parents:

(1) emotional illness, mental illness, mental deficiency, or use of alcohol or controlled substances rendering the parent consistently unable to care for the immediate and ongoing physical or psychological needs of the child for extended periods of time;

(2) acts of abuse or neglect toward any child in the family; and

(3) repeated or continuous failure by the parents, although physically and financially able, to provide the child with adequate food, clothing, shelter, and education as defined by law, or other care and control necessary for his physical, mental, or emotional health and development; but a parent or guardian who, legitimately practising his religious beliefs, does not provide specified medical treatment for a child, is not for that reason alone a negligent parent and the court is not precluded from ordering necessary medical services for the child according to existing state law.

(*c*) Whenever a child has been out of physical custody of the parent for more than one year, the court shall consider, pursuant to subsection (*a*)(3), among other factors, the following:

(1) the timeliness, nature and extent of services offered or provided by the agency to facilitate reunion of the child with the parent;

(2) the terms of any social service contract agreed to by an authorized agency and the parent and the extent to which all parties have fulfilled their obligations under such contract.

(*d*) When considering the parent-child relationship in the context of either subsections (*b*) or (*c*), the court shall also evaluate:

(1) the child's feelings and emotional ties with his birth parents; and

(2) the effort the parent has made to adjust his circumstances, conduct, or conditions to make it in the child's best interest to return him to his home in the foreseeable future, including:

    (i)   the extent to which the parent has maintained regular visitation or other contact with the child as part of a plan to reunite the child with the parent;

    (ii) the payment of a reasonable portion of substitute physical care and maintenance if financially able to do so; and

    (iii) the maintenance of regular contact or communication with the legal or other custodian of the child; and

    (iv) whether additional services would be likely to bring about lasting parental adjustment enabling a return of the child to the parent within an ascertainable period of time.

(*e*) The court may attach little or no weight to incidental visitations, communications, or contributions. It is irrelevant in a termination proceeding that the maintenance of the parent-child relationship may serve as an inducement for the parent's rehabilitation.

(*f*) If the parents are notified pursuant to Section 10(*a*) and fail to respond thereto, such failure shall constitute consent to termination on the part of the parent involved. The court may also, pursuant to Section 12(*c*), terminate the unknown father's relationship with the child.

As Shaw and Lebens (1978) point out: 'Many disputes which are on the face of it "technical" are probably thinly disguised disagreements on questions of value concerning the rights and needs of parents and children, the sanctity or utility of the family as an institution, and so on.' The two crucial values which inform both the model act quoted above and Margaret Adcock's discussion of rehabilitation (p. 437, above) are: (1) that the child's interests must prevail if the child's interests and parental rights conflict, and (2) that the child's interests are best served in a stable and permanent home of his own. These will again be crucial in the next chapter, where we consider the complexities of choosing and securing that 'stable and permanent home of his own', whether with natural parents, foster parents or adoptive parents.

CHAPTER 13

The tug of love: parents by birth, fostering and adoption

Former foster child A: It was only recently I was told that my natural parents could have removed me at any time if they wanted to. Even now when I think of it I shudder. . . . For me they would have been total strangers. Why remove me when I was so happy? I have met my natural mother recently and I see her from time to time. There is no bond between us. My 'mum' is my foster mum and my 'dad' is my foster dad. If I call my natural mother 'mum' when I meet her it is just for saving face. . . .

Former foster child D: I must have been 7 when I went to live with my foster parents. They were the second family I went to. The first family went abroad after promising to take me with them. They didn't and it broke my heart at the time. . . . The [foster parents] had two of their own and another foster child. Somehow I never felt I belonged there. We foster children did not fit in very well. I cannot say that I developed much attachment to them. My foster mother often threatened to send me back to the Corporation. Sometimes she would ring them but they would make her change her mind. I suppose I was difficult too, and I would hark back or argue. She would then smack me and send me to bed . . . I could be nasty and so could my foster mother . . . I left at 17 when our quarrels became worse, and I went to live in a hostel.

These two extracts from John Triseliotis' recent study of *Growing Up in Foster Care and After* (1980) can tell us a great deal about the problems of providing substitute family care for children separated from their families of birth. We have seen how the initial enthusiasm which followed the Curtis Report and the Children Act 1948 was cooled by the experience of many foster home breakdowns as well as the unhappy lives of many whose homes did not break down, like 'D' above (see p. 424, above). But we have also seen how Rowe and Lambert in *Children Who Wait* discovered that a large proportion of children in care had already spent the greater part of their lives there, that 61% were expected to remain there until 18, that 41% had no contact with either parent and a further 35% had only infrequent contact, but that only 22% were thought by their social workers to require placement in a foster or adoptive home (see p. 431, above). These findings, along with others, have not only led to an ever-increasing emphasis on positive planning for children in care but also to much more strenuous attempts to find substitute families, often on a more permanent basis than before. At the same time we have also seen how the supply of babies whose natural parents wish them to be adopted by another family has been diminishing (see p. 404, above). These developments have contributed to a significant and highly controversial reappraisal of the relative legal claims of natural parents, substitute parents and the children themselves, which it is the task of this chapter to examine.

One of the difficulties for lawyers in this field is that their involvement begins with the 'tug of love' where one family disputes with another the future of a hapless child. The considerations applicable, and the judgments appropriate, in that context may be quite different from those applicable at the point where the social worker begins, with a child who has just been separated, sometimes willingly but often unwillingly, from his natural family.

1 The dilemmas of fostering

At that point, of course, it may be quite clear that the child will only be in care for a short time and a short stay foster home may be found. The child usually has close links with his natural family and there is little confusion over the purpose of the foster home and the role to be adopted by the foster parents. The difficulty arises with those who are clearly going to stay longer than a few weeks, for no-one may know precisely how long that is likely to be, and still less how the foster parents should be expected to behave. The view taken following the 1948 Act is summed up by Jean Packman in *The Child's Generation* (now 1981):

Originally, fostering had frequently been seen as an *alternative* to parental care, when the latter had proved inadequate. Before children's departments existed many children who were fostered lost all contact with their natural families and the fostering became a 'de facto' adoption . . . The Children Act, moving away from this position, stipulated that children must be rehabilitated with their own families, when this was consistent with their welfare, and we have seen how the concept was increasingly applied. Though fostering was the favoured method of care, promising as it did a 'natural' upbringing and the warmth and intimate relationships that children need, it was now more often a short-term or impermanent arrangement, incorporating a far greater degree of sharing. If children were to be rehabilitated, they must be kept in close touch with their natural parents. . . . What was expected of foster parents became at once more subtle and more difficult. They must confer on the child all the benefits of loving family care, but should not seek to replace the parents in his affections. Their compassion and acceptance must be extended from the child himself, to his parents as well — even where the latter seemed 'to blame' for some of his past deprivations. They should act toward him as a good parent, yet give him up when the department judged the time to be ripe.

That expectation is summed up in the Form of Undertaking to be signed by foster parents who take a child for more than eight weeks, prescribed by the schedule to the *Boarding-Out of Children Regulations 1955*:

1. We will care for [the child] and bring him up as we would a child of our own.
2. He will be brought up in, and will be encouraged to practise, his religion.
3. We will look after his health and consult a doctor whenever he is ill and will allow him to be medically examined at such times and places as [the authority] may require.
4. We will inform [the authority] immediately of any serious occurrence affecting the child.
5. We will at all times permit any person so authorised by the Secretary of State or by [the authority] to see him and visit our home.
6. We will allow him to be removed from our home when so requested by a person authorised by [the authority].
7. If we decide to move, we will notify the new address to [the authority] before we go.

Question

Imagine that you have been asked to look after (*a*) a boy of 8 whose mother has just had a nervous breakdown and whose father works on an oil rig, (*b*) a handicapped toddler whose unmarried mother placed him in care when he was born and has visited him about six times since then, and (*c*) a girl of 9 who has no contact with her family, from whom she was removed at the age of 2, but whose former foster family had just emigrated. Could you sign the above undertaking in any or all of these cases?

(a) INCLUSIVE AND EXCLUSIVE FOSTERING: THE CONCEPT OF 'SHARED CARE'

The foster parents' undertaking to some extent reflects the concept of 'inclusive' fostering described by Robert Holman (who refers to his own work as 'Holman') in his seminal article on *The Place of Fostering in Social Work* (1975):

Inclusive fostering
. . . The inclusive concept is based on a readiness to draw the various components into the fostering situation. The foster parents can offer love without having to regard themselves as the real parents. Their attitude is that of the 36% identified by Holman (1973) who said 'I know he's not mine but I treat him the same'. A significant number did not wish to adopt, but this did not mean they lacked affection. The willingness to include others is further seen in the 31% of Holman's sample and 54% in Adamson's (1973) who considered that natural parents should see their children. Natural parents are regarded more positively, with a greater willingness that the children should possess full knowledge about them. The social workers are also included. Adamson records that over 50% of the foster mothers looked forward to visits from the social workers, and would immediately contact them if difficulties rose. Such foster parents, George (1970) pointed out, defined the social workers as official colleagues rather than informal friends. They were also more likely to regard themselves as possessing special skills which merited payment.
    Within the inclusive concept, emphasis is placed on the children's need to obtain a true sense of their present identity and past history within a framework of affection. It accords with Ruddock's (1972) model of a role tree in which realistic grasp of personal identity is necessary so that the person can integrate various parts into a coherent pattern which will both satisfy him internally and allow him to find satisfactory external roles. Moreover, it accepts that the inclusion of all the fostering participants — foster parents, children, natural parents and social workers — are needed in order to facilitate rehabilitation of the children if that is possible.

This he contrasts with a quite different type of fostering, the 'exclusive,' which he describes thus:

Exclusive fostering
Exclusive fostering may be so termed in that it attempts to contain the foster child within the foster family while excluding other connections. Thus Holman's study revealed that 63% of local authority foster parents regarded the children 'as their own' and would like to have adopted. Similarly, Adamson found that over half did not think of themselves as foster mothers. George records that 62.1% considered 'own parent' as the best description of their position. Seeing themselves as the parents, such foster parents want to exclude the natural parents. George established that 56% did not think the real parents had even a conditional right to visit. Of Holman's local authority foster mothers 35% thought natural parents should not be encouraged to visit while, in addition, a slightly smaller proportion thought it conditional upon suitable attitudes and intentions. Adamson confirmed that 46% thought it best if foster children did not see their own families. This negative attitude, Holman shows, is encapsulated in hostile opinions of the natural parents (such as 'She's disgusting', 'She doesn't deserve to have children') and is revealed in an unwillingness to accept or talk to the foster children about their background. It follows that if the children are regarded as natural ones then the social workers too cannot be fully accepted as having an official interest in them. Accordingly, George discovered that 48.6% of foster parents described their social workers only as 'friends', while 64.6% would not think it necessary to inform the social workers even if the foster children stole. Adamson also noted that a considerable number of foster parents felt unease about social workers' visits, while 34% would not have initiated contact with them even concerning a serious problem.
    The exclusive fostering concept appears to stem from a two-fold premise. Foster children need to be sheltered from the influence of, even knowledge about, natural parents. Further, the foster children and foster parents' greatest need is freedom from any fear that the fostering will be disturbed or even that the fact of fostering will be brought to their attention. In many ways, it is strikingly similar to the 'fresh start' which dominated much boarding out under the nineteenth century Poor Law.

He then quotes the following studies of foster children which suggest that they benefit from parental contact:

1. Weinstein (1960) established that regular natural parent contact was associated with the foster children achieving high scores on present and future 'well-being' scales.
2. Jenkins (1969) found that 57% of foster children aged over 1½ years at placement with no parental contact were 'disturbed' as against only 35% with regular contact. Similar findings were reported for those under 1½ years.
3. Holman (1973) observed that in general the less the contact the higher the incidence of certain emotional and physical symptoms such as soiling and ill-health.
4. Thorpe's (1974) recent work revealed a trend suggesting a relationship between satisfactory adjustment and contact (although it was not statistically significant except for 11- to 13-year-olds).

From these he concludes that:

In general, fostering success bears a closer relationship with the inclusive than with the exclusive type of fostering. The explanation, Holman suggests, is that foster parents of the exclusive kind in regarding themselves as natural parents create situations of role conflict or confusion. For at times their conception must be challenged by the reality of social workers' visits, natural parent contact, or questions from the children. The resultant anxiety and confusion can be conveyed to the whole family.

Nevertheless:

The association between fostering success and inclusive fosterings would be less noteworthy if they constituted the typical foster home. But a further implication [of the research studies quoted] is that a substantial number of long-term foster homes operate on the exclusive concept.

Furthermore:

The intensity of foster parent feeling has meant that social workers are also drawn into the fostering dilemma. The research suggests that most social workers hold the inclusive concept of fostering. They frequently work with foster parents who possess the opposite view, at a time of foster parent shortage. The social workers thus find themselves believing that foster children should be encouraged to know or know about their natural parents yet aware that to do so would endanger the fostering. . . . George's work suggests that generally the social workers collude with the foster parents. He found that only 3.8% of natural parents were encouraged to see their children . . . [he] concludes his study . . . by saying that social workers and foster parents 'by their active hostility or passive inaction towards natural parents have forced or have merely allowed natural parents to alienate themselves from their children. This alienation has in turn been used as evidence for the natural parents' lack of interest in their children and for their inability to care for them adequately.' . . . The studies concur in finding some workers so caught by the need not to disturb foster homes that they find themselves reinforcing the very concept of fostering with which they disagree.

Holman's call is for greater efforts among social workers to find foster parents who *can* accept the inclusive model and to make it work. However, there are certain assumptions underlying his whole argument which require closer examination. As Jane Rowe points out in her account of *Fostering in the 1970s* (1977):

Much of the social work writing about fostering has stressed the foster parents' difficulties in understanding their role, and their tendency to think of themselves as substitute parents when the agency wishes them to assume the role of caretaker or therapist. In reality a foster parent's role — like that of a residential worker — is always a combination of caretaker, therapist, compensatory parent and substitute parent, though the mix will vary according to the type of placement and age of the child, and may change from time to time during the child's stay in the foster home. . . .

Social workers are often more confused than foster parents about the appropriate division of role within the triangular fostering situation in which natural parents, foster parents and agency all carry some responsibility for the child. A foster parent's role must always depend upon which aspects of the parental role are still being exercised by the natural parents and which are being undertaken by the agency. The foster parent's difficult task is to fill in the gaps. . . .

The purpose of placement and the likely length of stay are crucial to role definition. . . . Divisions of responsibility which are satisfactory in the short term may become intolerable in the long term and, with young children in particular, caretakers quickly slip into a substitute parenting role unless natural parents remain closely involved.

On the likely length of stay, she observes:

Indefinite/medium-length foster homes are the text book homes used as part of the plan to rehabilitate families, though a great deal of private fostering also falls into this indefinite-length category. The placement may last a few months or a few years, but it is not intended to be permanent. In agency placements, the plan is usually to keep parents in touch. The therapeutic role of foster parents may be much to the fore. Some children and adolescents are consciously placed in a foster home as a means of solving their problems of behaviour and/or relationships. In other cases the main problem may lie in the parents' health or behaviour, homelessness or marital difficulties. Under these circumstances, foster parents may be expected to play an active part in work with natural parents and to help to re-establish the family. They are certainly not intended to take over the full parental role.

In social work literature, there is a generally held assumption that most foster homes nowadays are of this type and discussions about the foster parents' role are based on the expectation that the child will be going back to his family of origin. The fact is, however, that except for the fostering of teenagers, there are comparatively few medium-length fostering placements. *Children Who Wait* (Rowe and Lambert, 1973) and subsequent studies have shown that if children do not return home within a few months, they are likely to remain in care for a very long time and it is now only too clear that rehabilitation to parents is frequently difficult to achieve. Major findings from *Children Who Wait* were that 72% of the children needing foster home placements were thought to need a 'permanent home' and only half of those for whom a foster home for an indeterminate period was being sought were actually thought likely to return to their parents.

A detailed study of the foster children in one local authority by Shaw and Lebens (1976) showed that 88% were expected to remain in care until their eighteenth birthday, 54% of the children had already been in their foster homes for more than five years and a further 22% for between two to five years.

The discrepancy between social work theory and the fostering realities which these figures demonstrate is a serious threat to good practice. It goes a long way towards explaining the gap between social work emphasis on the need for foster parents to avoid possessiveness, and not become too emotionally involved with the child, and foster parents' persistence in considering themselves as substitute parents. It is clearly very difficult for foster parents to maintain a somewhat detached professional role for an extended period, but social workers often continue to apply expectations and policies that are out of keeping with the facts and with the psychological realities. It seems probable that this is due in part to social workers' very real difficulties over changing goals and plans. In part it may be due to reliance on imperfectly understood concepts of parent/child relationships, bonding and separation, and in part to failure to link knowledge of child development and the effects of the passage of time with departmental policies and plans for individual children.

Question

If you were trying to foster the handicapped toddler mentioned in the question on p. 465, above, which of the following would you find most difficult and which the most helpful: (*a*) the knowledge that you could return him if things became too much for you; (*b*) the possibility that the authority might consider a residential home better able to supply his needs; (*c*) answering his questions about mummies and daddies; (*d*) visits from a social worker every three months; (*e*) visits from his mother? Would your answers be the same if you were fostering either of the other children mentioned in that question?

The social worker's difficulties are compounded by the fact that her own attitudes and actions can have a very substantial effect upon the length of the child's stay in care. Jane Aldgate has studied the factors influencing the stay of children from around 200 families in Scotland in the early 1970s. Her results, reported in *Identification of Factors influencing Children's Length of Stay in Care* (1980), were:

Children seemed to have most chance of return when they were received into care from two-parent families who were living in stable accommodation, or from one-parent families headed by their mother following marital breakdown. Most at risk to long term care were young single-parent families and one-parent families headed by fathers following the desertion of the mother. The reason for care itself influenced the outcome. There was widespread poverty among the study families, so it was hardly surprising that eviction accounted for over one-third of receptions into care. Where the main cause of eviction was financial hardship, with practical support parents were able to find new accommodation and reunite the family. Children who had been received into care because of their mother's death, desertion or long-term psychiatric illness were far more vulnerable to lengthy separation.

. . . Parents' involvement with their children during the placement was a very significant factor in influencing return. This contact was in itself dependent on several other factors like the attitude of caretakers, the distance between the parental and substitute home, the reactions of children, and the encouragement given to parents by social workers early in the placement. Social work activity, whether in the form of general encouragement, practical support or more intensive problem-solving help with emotional difficulties had a significant effect on return from care. . . . A common feature among children in long-term care was the passive attitude of their social workers towards any plans for either rehabilitation or alternatives.

Finally, the length of time children were in care affected contact with their parents and their social workers, and influenced their chances of return. Contact declined substantially after two years in care: social workers became less enthusiastic about encouraging parents to maintain contact, while caretakers grew increasingly anxious to assimilate children into their own family. The result of this was that the longer children remained in care the less likely they were to return home.

Question

Be honest: do you think that families who are unable to house, feed and clothe their children on the resources available to them should be given more resources, whether in cash or in kind, or have their children taken away so that other people can be paid to bring them up?

(b) CONTACT AND CONTINUITY

Holman's argument also relies heavily on studies which associated the 'well-being' and 'adjustment' of foster children with contact with their natural families. Yet contact with, or at least knowledge of, the natural family is by no means the same thing as returning to live there. A more complex picture is suggested by Rosamund Thorpe in *The Experience of Children and Parents Living Apart* (1980). In 1971, she studied the psychological adjustment of all the children aged 5 to 17 years in the care of one English local authority who had been in their current foster home with non-relatives for at least one year. Her general finding reinforces some of the earlier doubts about the foster care preference, explored in the previous chapter:

Although foster home care is generally regarded as the best method of substitute care short of adoption, as many as 39% (almost two-fifths) of the sample foster children scored a seriously disturbed rating on the Rutter Behaviour Questionnaire. This compares with a proportion of 23% per cent of children in the general population . . . (Wolkind 1971). Additionally it appears that children in foster home care are as likely to be disturbed as children in residential care — which is not what one might reasonably expect, in view of the prevailing preference for fostering and the fact that the most disturbed children are more likely to be placed in residential rather than foster home care. . . . Recent research on residential care suggests that . . . residential care can be as successful as the natural family in providing an environment in which children can grow into successful and well-adjusted adults. (Wolins, 1969)

She then turns to the factors differentiating the seriously disturbed foster children from the rest:

With regard to the child's age at separation, those sample children who entered care at five years or older were significantly less disturbed than those who experienced separation during the first five years of their life. And within this latter group, those children who were placed in their current foster home before the age of two years were significantly less disturbed than those who were placed between the ages of 2 and 4 years. Clearly, early admission to care is related to greater disturbance, and children who enter care between 2 and 4 years are especially vulnerable. This may be explained in terms of the theory of attachment, (Bowlby, 1971) which suggests that it is likely that children placed before the age of 2 years make primary attachments to their foster parents in contrast with children who enter care after the age of 2 years who have already made primary attachments to their natural parents. Of these latter children the attachments made by those over 2 but under school age may not yet be sufficiently strong for them to handle the experience of separation very well, whereas those over 5 are better able to retain firm attachments to natural parents in their absence, and hence handle the experience of separation more positively. . . .

Apart from age at separation, the degree of damage resulting from separation is also influenced by the quality of care experienced prior to entry to care. In this study it was not possible to assess this retrospectively, but other research studies by Wolkind and Rutter (1973) suggest that this is an extremely important variable. This may well be the case, since in my study so few of the variables concerning the quality of care experienced after entry to care seemed to have a major effect on the adjustment of the sample foster children. There was, however, some evidence of factors which might reduce the risk of disturbance. For example, although not significant in a statistical sense, disturbance amongst the children clearly increased with the number of changes of placement they had experienced since entering care and was proportionately less where there had been pre-placement visits in preparation for the placement. Older, experienced foster mothers were associated with an absence of disturbance and, similarly, the presence of siblings in the same foster home appeared to have a beneficial effect. In addition, those children whose future was assured in the foster home were better adjusted, as were children who had clear and full knowledge and understanding of their situation, and those who were in contact with their natural parents and/or siblings living elsewhere. . . . It is important to emphasise the last three factors mentioned in relation to the adjustment of foster children — that is, self-knowledge, contact, and the existence of definite plans for the child's future — as these are the factors which in the interviews the children considered to be important to themselves.

The foster child's perception and experience of placement: the need for security

. . . 87% of the children were expected by their social workers to remain in the foster home until and beyond their discharge from local authority care at the age of 18 years; and 75% of the children identified with their foster parents and wanted to remain living with them. Despite the extent of expected permanence, concern with their security of tenure in the foster home nevertheless coloured the interview responses of several of the children. . . .

Thus the first and major conclusion must be that children in care need to know what is going to happen to them, whatever it is. Whilst, clearly, those children who have already spent a high proportion of their life in a foster home may need to be assured that they can remain there, for other children it may be necessary to plan and work more positively than hitherto for rehabilitation or a more appropriate placement. And for yet other children there will be a need for them to be aware when their future is uncertain. For knowledge of uncertainty is shared and thus bearable, whereas uncertainty of knowledge can be frightening, even disturbing, since in the absence of facts, fantasies and fears will run wild.

The need for a sense of identity

. . . Almost all of the children were concerned to know much more about their natural parents, and many were keen to retain or re-establish contact with them. For example, *Jane* (12 years), recently re-introduced to her natural mother, explained:

I saw Mum last week — the first time for five years. I was ever so pleased. She's nice; she talks nice and looks nice and dresses nice — but I don't know really because I don't live with her. She's not really as I imagined her. I thought she'd be all fussy sort of thing, but she weren't — only a little. It's a bit confusing. I'm very pleased to have seen her and if I don't see her it bothers me a bit in bed at night sometimes. I think it's best to see her once or twice. I don't really know why. I just think so. I want to see her again; I'd like to see her. I like staying here but I'd like to see my mum occasionally.

My dad, he's gone back to India. I've never seen him in my life. I would like to have seen him just once because I'd like to see my own dad instead of thinking someone else is my dad when they're not. It didn't bother me before when I was little, but I'd like to find out now that I'm bigger.

What Jane had to say highlights not only the need foster children have for a sense of genealogical roots in fixing the boundaries to a sense of self-identity, but also the way that, in the absence of facts, children will develop fantasies. Such fantasy pictures of natural parents may become extreme or bizarre, and this can lead to insecurity; this is further compounded by the fact that fantasies consume a great deal of emotional energy which cannot then be channelled into learning or making relationships. This in turn leads to the not unfamiliar picture of the child in care who is either under-achieving in school, or having difficulty in making relationships, or both. And this would account for the relationship between self-knowledge and emotional adjustment in foster children. . . .

The need for contact between foster child and natural parent

. . . There is a popular belief that children in foster homes experience a conflict of loyalties between their natural and their foster parents and feel 'different' because of this. However, this was not substantiated by my research. When the adults — natural and foster parents — accepted each other, the foster children appeared to experience no conflict of loyalties and accepted the foster situation with equanimity, understanding the reasons why it had to be this way for them. By contrast, when children could not identify with their natural parents, through a lack of knowledge or contact, they seemed to experience a sense of stigma in being fostered. *Robert* (15 years) is perhaps a good example:

> It is probably slightly harder being fostered just because you've got to fight this conscious fact of being fostered and not having parents of your own. For example, if you have the micky taken out of you at school — or fear they might find out and take the micky. It's just your fact and you have to put up with it. It's really just mostly a joke — they don't mean to hurt, they only think it's a game — but others may not.

This experience of stigma in being 'different' links in with the theoretical view that children often experience the separation from natural parents entailed in coming into care as rejection, and that their feelings of rejection may undermine their sense of personal worth. This was apparent in my research, in that those children who were in contact with their natural parents seemed reassured that they were loved, rather than rejected. They understood that the reasons for their being in care were not because they were bad, unlovable or 'no-good'; as a result they could tolerate the 'difference' implicit in being a foster child.

Bearing in mind how many foster children in fact remain in care until they are grown up, some light may be cast upon their needs by Triseliotis' study of 40 young adults who had each spent between 7 and 15 years in a single foster home. In *Growing Up in Foster Care and After* (1980), he classifies their fostering experience into four groups:

A. Mutually satisfying relationships (14 children):
Both foster parents and the young adults viewed the growing up period as one of enjoyment, or warm and caring relationships, of children being integrated into the family and with both foster parents playing an active parenting role. . . . An added characteristic of these foster parents was their predominantly positive feelings towards the families of origin and a general enjoyment of the children.

B. Possessive type relationships (8 children):
. . . used here to describe over-protective and largely 'exclusive' type relationships. These relationships contained considerable satisfactions but some of the former foster children made qualifications about the degree of possessiveness shown by the foster parents and their tendency to deny the child's status and family of origin. . . .

C. Professional[1] type relationships (9 children):
Though none of the foster parents in the previous two groups saw themselves or wanted to be seen as professionals doing a job, foster parents in this group accepted that their role developed into a kind of job, but they hoped they had not lost their caring qualities. The majority started as long-term foster parents with one or two children, but were persuaded to take on more than they originally intended. . . . The arrangement developed into a form of group foster care. . . . The foster mothers had mixed feelings about the change of their role . . . [they] were seen by the

---

1. The term 'professional' fostering can also refer to schemes in which foster parents are given training, intensive social work support, and higher rates of allowance, to help with the problems of particularly difficult children.

young adults as mostly caring people but 'there was not always enough to go round.' Compared with the young adults in the previous two groups, those in this group experienced the foster parents with less intensity, had less individual attention, were aware that they had to share them with a great number of others, and were critical of the ever-changing number of children in the family. More serious were the young adults' views about what happened to them after the statutory period of care was over . . . [they] had fewer contacts after leaving school; and only two continued to live in the foster parents' home, regarding it as their home.

D. Ambivalent type relationships (9 children):
Both parties in this group felt that the arrangement had not worked out well and that things went wrong somewhere. There was no agreement as to what went wrong. . . . The young adults claimed to have found their foster parents rather impatient, emotionally inaccessible, not understanding and often unpredictable. The foster parents in their turn complained mostly of difficult behaviour which they tended to explain in terms of the child's background and 'bad blood.' . . . Unlike the foster children in the first two groups, those in this group rarely referred to their foster parents as 'mum' or 'dad', and made few references about the foster home being 'home' or 'my family'. . . .

Twenty-four of the former foster children were coping well in adult life; of the six who were coping about half and half, five grew up in the 'professional type' relationship; the remaining ten who were doing 'less well' were mostly among those whose foster home relationships were described as 'ambivalent', ending up in disruption in mid or late teens. The author concludes:

The overall findings suggest that people who grow up in long-term foster homes, within which they are wanted and integrated as part of the family, generally do well. . . .
    The ten children who perceived their fostering as mostly negative and who were currently coping rather poorly, did not differ at placement from the other children in the sample. . . .
    Explanations for this outcome have to be sought mostly in the types of interaction that occurred between the children concerned and the foster parents, rather than in the children's background as such.

And on the issues relevant to the current debate:

In the early stages of placement children appear to retain their attachments to their natural families, but with the lapse of time, and particularly where parental visiting becomes too infrequent or ceases altogether, the children begin to transfer their loyalties to the people who care for them. A slow process of psychological bonding seems to develop that gradually cements itself to the point that the foster child becomes indistinguishable from other members of the caretaking family. Knowledge by the child about his family or origin and the circumstances of his fostering contributes to feelings of well-being and to better adjustment. Information and explanation about the family of origin helps the child to integrate it into his developing personality and base his identity on the concept of two families. Furthermore, it helps him to acknowledge feelings of loss and rejection surrounding the original parents, so that he can find his own peace.

(c) GUIDELINES FOR THE LAW?

It seems, then, that we may have to distinguish the long term foster child's need for security and continuity from his equally important need to know who he is and where he comes from. Goldstein, Freud and Solnit's influential but controversial work, *Beyond the Best Interests of the Child* (1973), has already been extensively quoted in Chapters 10 and 12. Their concepts of the 'psychological/wanted child' relationship, of the child's need for continuity, and perhaps above all of the child's sense of time have implications for children separated from their birth parents which are far more obvious and startling than those for children whose parents are divorced:

In foster or other less formal but temporary placements, the continuity guideline should prompt the development of procedures and opportunities in temporary placement for maintaining relationships between child and absent parent. Thus, unlike permanent placements, foster placements should be conditional. This does not mean that foster parents are to remain aloof and uninvolved. Nor does this mean that foster care is to be used as a means of keeping the child from establishing a positive tie with his 'temporary' adult custodians by constantly shifting him from one foster setting to another in order to protect an adult's right of reclaim. But once the prior tie has been broken, the foster or other temporary placements can no longer be considered temporary. They may develop into or substantially begin to become psychological parent-child relationships, which in accord with the continuity guideline deserve recognition as a common-law adoption.

. . . For the purposes of . . . acknowledging the existence of a common-law adoptive relationship, abandonment in law would have taken place by the time the parents' absence has caused the child to feel no longer wanted by them. It would be that time when the child, having felt helpless and abandoned, has reached out to establish a new relationship with an adult who is to become or has become his psychological parent.

. . . Such a statute would include a presumption that (barring extraordinary efforts to maintain the continuity of a 'temporarily interrupted' relationship) the younger the child, the shorter the period of relinquishment before a developing psychological tie is broken and a new relationship has begun.

Other aspects of their model child placement statute which are relevant are:

A child is presumed to be wanted in his or her current placement. If the child's placement is to be altered, the intervenor . . . must establish *both*

    (i)   that the child is unwanted, *and*

    (ii) that the child's current placement is not the least detrimental available alternative. . . .

All placements shall be unconditional and final, that is, the court shall not retain continuing jurisdiction over a parent-child relationship or establish or enforce such conditions as rights of visitation.

It is this last which is perhaps the most open to challenge from other psychiatrists. Arnon Bentovim, discussing the *Psychiatric Issues* involved in *Terminating Parental Contact: an exploration of the issues relating to children in care* (1980), having put the case for the 'least detrimental alternative,' continues:

Although it is important for a child's attachment to his current caretaking family to have primacy, it is also important for a child to have access to his own family of origin. Efforts should be made to maintain links with a child's biological family, even though the process might be painful and disturbing. Fanshel and Shinn (1978) in a longitudinal study of children in foster care in the United States found that children benefited from long-term relationships with their own parents. They maintain that 'this is a healthier state of affairs than that faced by the child who must reconcile questions about his own worth as a human being with the fact of parental abandonment. In the main, children are more able to accept additional concern and loving parental figures in their lives with all the confusions inherent in such a situation, than to accept the loss of meaningful figures.'

They also support the view that it is better for a child to have 'to cope with *real* parents who are obviously flawed in their parental behaviour, who bring a mixture of love and rejection, then to reckon with *fantasy* parents who play an undermining role on the deeper level of the child's subconscious'. They note that visiting by biological parents over a long period of time produces more overt disturbance than in children who are unvisited. They point out, however, that on a number of characteristics including IQ gains, emotional adjustment and positive assessments by teachers, visited children are better adjusted than those who remain unvisited. Despite these conclusions Solnit (in Fanshel and Shinn, 1978) argues that the foster parent with long-term parental responsibilities should have power and control to say whether or not that child is visited.

Fanshel and Shinn feel that for their best interests 'all children should be afforded permanency in their living arrangements'. Although they did not find any major deficiencies in long-term fostering, they felt that adoption did indicate for the child a full acceptance by the family and a real sense of belonging. To reconcile this with their view that there is advantage to these children to continue parental visiting, would need the introduction of more open adoption where parental contact does not have to cease completely. Such a notion seems a reasonable proposition for the children whom Fanshel and Shinn were investigating, that is, older children in long-term care.

The two viewpoints I have described can be seen as reflecting two basic orientations which are currently held in the field of psychiatry. They are views which I have experienced through training and practice. The concern to find the least detrimental alternative for the child derives from a psycho-analytic training and orientation which emphasises the needs of the individual child. The second, which relates to an orientation of an open system, family therapy approach, stresses the need to see the child as part of an extensive family network. His development relies on the meeting of both his needs as an individual and his need to find a place and an identity through the richness of his extended family.

Questions

(i) You will recall that 'In reaching any decision relating to a child in their care, a local authority shall give first consideration to the need to safeguard and promote the welfare of the child throughout his childhood; and shall so far as practicable ascertain the wishes and feelings of the child regarding the decision and give gue consideration to them, having regard to his age and understanding' (Child Care Act 1980, s. 18(1)). Would you now feel able to devise some sort of timetable of action for social workers when they receive a child into care and board him out with foster parents for a 'medium term' or 'indefinite' stay?

(ii) How do the problems of foster children differ from those of children whose parents have divorced (see Chapter 11)?

2 Foster parents — the legal battle

(a) WELFARE AND WARDSHIP

At present, the only means short of adoption whereby a foster parent may attempt to achieve some security in caring for the child is to make the child a ward of court. The principle to be applied in such cases was conclusively determined by the House of Lords in the following case:

J v C
[1970] AC 668, [1969] 1 All ER 788, [1969] 2 WLR 540, 113 Sol Jo 164, House of Lords

The facts of this case are discussed at length in the first instance judgment of Ungoed-Thomas J, reported at the same time as the speeches of the House of Lords, and by Lords Guest and Upjohn. It is almost impossible to summarise them dispassionately, but Lord Guest perhaps comes closest to doing so:

The story began in the autumn of 1957 when the infant's parents came to Britain from Madrid for the purpose of bettering their financial position by entering domestic service. The father was at that time a very lowly-paid worker living in poor housing conditions in Madrid. They are both of the Roman Catholic faith. They left behind a daughter then aged 4 who lived with the maternal grandmother. The mother became pregnant shortly after their arrival in Britain and the infant was born in hospital on 8 May 1958. As the mother was found to be suffering from tuberculosis and had to remain in hospital for some considerable time a home was found for the infant through the kind offices of a married couple who have been called the 'foster parents'. The infant was taken care of, from the age of four days, by them in their house in Northampton-shire while the mother remained in hospital. The foster parents had been both previously married and between them have four children by their previous marriages and now have two by their own marriage. The infant continued to remain with the foster parents until the mother was discharged from hospital in April 1959. The infant's father remained in employment near the foster parents' house and visited the infant from time to time. The infant thereafter rejoined his parents who had obtained employment in Surrey. The foster parents had also moved to Surrey. The infant remained with his parents at C for about ten months: the foster mother assisted the mother in looking after the infant and the parents kept in touch with the foster parents' family. In February 1960, the mother again became pregnant. As she was afraid of having another baby in this country she and her husband went back to Madrid taking the infant with them.

During the infant's stay in Madrid in the summer of 1960 his parents lived in what has been described as little better than a 'hovel'. The father was still a lowly-paid worker and the family lived in what were virtually slum conditions. In the summer heat of Madrid the infant's health rapidly deteriorated due to malnutrition and the local conditions which did not suit him. He only remained in Madrid with his parents for 17 months. In July 1961, he returned to Britain to stay with the foster parents. This move was made at the specific request of the parents who, through the intermediary of a Spanish maid of the foster parents, M, conveyed their request to the foster parents. This request was made on the ground of the infant's health. On his return to this country the infant's health rapidly improved and he has continued thereafter to enjoy good health. He has not lived with his parents since July 1961, and has continued to live with the foster parents ever since.

The parents were content at this time to leave the infant with the foster parents. There was some suggestion that the parents should return to England to take up domestic service, so that the infant could be with them, and the foster parents in fact made some arrangements to this end. But these arrangements came to nothing. In the winter of 1961 the parents went to Hamburg with the idea of further bettering their financial position in order to be able to obtain a house of their own in Madrid in more salubrious surroundings. They had left their elder daughter with the maternal grandmother in Madrid and they remained in Hamburg until the early part of 1963. In February 1963, the grandmother died and this necessitated the parents' return to Madrid, first the mother and latterly the father.

Up to this point of time the parents had evinced no wish to the foster parents to have the infant back with them in Madrid apart from a suggestion for a holiday. But in July 1963, the foster mother wrote to the mother what has been described as a tactless and most unfortunate letter. In this letter she described how the infant had become integrated with their family; he had gone to an English school and he had grown up an English boy with English habits, and that it would be most disturbing for him to have to return to live with his parents in Madrid. She also made critical remarks about the infant's father. This letter produced the not unexpected reaction from the mother who, after some previous correspondence, wrote on 25 September 1963, to the Surrey County Council, in whose official care the infant was, asking for the infant's return. The local authority did not act with conspicuous consistency or good sense. After appearing to agree to the mother's request they subsequently, after receipt of a letter from the foster parents expressing their point of view, resolved, on the advice of counsel, to apply to the Chancery Division to have the infant made a ward of court, which was done on 16 December 1963.

The proceedings took some considerable time to reach the judge and the parents were unfortunately led to believe by a letter from the Surrey County Council that they would be represented by counsel at the hearing who would state their case for them. For this reason the parents only lodged written representations which had been prepared for them by a Spanish lawyer. These, however, did express their wish for the infant's return. Affidavits were lodged by various other parties. After a hearing on 22 July 1965, Ungoed-Thomas J ordered that the infant remain a ward of court, that the care and control be committed to the foster parents, that the infant be brought up in the Roman Catholic faith and in the knowledge and recognition of his parents and in knowledge of the Spanish language.

Two years were to elapse before the final stage of the proceedings took place before the same judge. This stage had been initiated by the parents' summons — asking that they should have the care and control of the infant. This was made on 10 May 1967. An application was also made by the foster parents in January 1967, that the infant be brought up in the Protestant faith. This request for a change in the boy's religious upbringing was prompted by a desire on the foster parents' part that he should enter a choir school so as to avoid expense. The most convenient school was a Protestant school. The official solicitor also entered the proceedings, having been appointed next friend. On this occasion the judge heard evidence from all the parties and his judgment was given on 31 July 1967. No order was made on either application and his order was dated 20 September 1967. Owing to various delays, for which none of the parties is responsible, the Court of Appeal hearing did not take place until 5 July 1968, and the order of the Court of Appeal refusing leave to appeal was made on 30 July 1968.

In retrospect it is unfortunate that at the first hearing in 1963 before the judge the full facts were not before him. It is apparent that at that stage he was uncertain of the ability of the mother, on the ground of her health, to look after the child and he was not sure in his own mind that the parents genuinely desired the infant's return. It may be that if more expedition had been exercised by the parties in bringing the case to trial and the full facts had been known at the time, the judge's decision might well have been different in 1963. In 1963 when the parents first asked for the infant's return he was only 5 years old and he had only been parted from his parents for a matter of two years. Even in 1965 he was only 7 years old, but by the time of the second hearing he was 9½ and he is now 10½ years old. He has been at school in England since January 1963. He has not seen his parents since 1961 when he was 3, and apart from a matter of 27 months he has been living continually in the home of the foster parents with their family. There is no doubt, as the learned judge found, that the infant lives in happy surroundings in a united and well-integrated family. The mixed families have made it particularly easy for him to become integrated. He speaks English and only pidgin Spanish. He is especially friendly with P the child of the marriage of the foster parents who is only a little younger than him.

It is right at this stage to say that the house in which the parents now live in Madrid is entirely suitable for the reception of the infant. It contains three bedrooms and is in a modern block of flats in quite different surroundings from the previous home. The father is in good steady employment at a weekly wage of about £18 and the mother's health has been completely restored.

The reason which has impelled the judge to take the unusual step of taking the care and control from the parents and giving it to strangers is that, in his view, the risk of plunging this boy of 10½ years into a Spanish family, where he has not seen his parents since he was aged 3 and into a foreign country, would be too great to take and that the adjustment necessary might well permanently injure the infant's health at the impressionable age at which he has arrived. The judge has regarded the infant's welfare as the paramount consideration and he has decided that this demands that he should remain with his foster parents.

The account of the law which has been most frequently quoted in subsequent decisions is that of Lord MacDermott:

The course of the dispute and certain aspects of the evidence present a story which is involved and at times rather confused; but whether this needs to be traced in detail depends on the answer to be given to a question of law which stands on the threshold of the case and to which I turn at once. Counsel for the parents conceded that if the courts below had applied the right principles of law in reaching the decision appealed from he could not succeed in asking your Lordships to disturb that decision. The substance of his main argument may be stated shortly. All parties were agreed that the courts had jurisdiction and a duty to interfere with the natural right of parents to have the care, control and custody of their child if the welfare of the child required and the law permitted that course to be taken. But there agreement ended. For the parents it was submitted that the courts were in law bound to presume that the welfare of the child was best served by allowing him to live with his parents unless it was shown that it was not for his welfare to do so because of their conduct, character or station in life. Counsel for the infant and counsel for the foster parents submitted, on the other hand, that there was no such presumption of law, that the paramount and governing consideration was the welfare of the child and that the claim of natural parents, although often of great weight and cogency and often conclusive, had to be regarded in conjunction with all other relevant factors, and had to yield if, in the end, the welfare of the child so required.

The question of law under discussion is therefore whether there now is such a presumption as that contended for by the parents, or whether the correct process of adjudication is, instead, to consider all material aspects of the case, including the claims of the parents, and then to decide in the exercise of a judicial discretion what is best for the welfare of the child. I have already mentioned counsel for the parents' concession as to the position if his argument does not prevail. I may add here that if it does prevail the appeal, in my opinion, is bound to succeed since: (a) the evidence shows no defects of character or conduct on the part of the parents sufficient to disentitle them to custody; and (b) their position in life has so improved as to be no longer capable in itself of constituting an answer to their claim.

His lordship then reviews the developments in case law and statute before 1925 and continues:

I have referred to these Acts because, as in the case of the authorities, they record an increasing qualification of common law rights and the growing acceptance of the welfare of the infant as a criterion. In this way, and like the trend of the cases, they serve to introduce the enactment which has been so closely canvassed on the issue of law under discussion. It is s. 1 of the Guardianship of Infants Act 1925, [now re-enacted as s. 1 of the Guardianship of Minors Act 1971, see p. 339, above]. This section follows a preamble which runs thus:

'Whereas Parliament by the Sex Disqualification (Removal) Act 1919, and various other enactments, has sought to establish equality in law between the sexes, and it is expedient that this principle should obtain with respect to the guardianship of infants and the rights and responsibilities conferred thereby: . . .'

Section 1 itself reads:

'Where in any proceeding before any court (whether or not a court within the meaning of the Guardianship of Infants Act 1886) the custody or upbringing of an infant, or the administration of any property belonging to or held on trust for an infant, or the application of the income thereof, is in question, the court, in deciding that question, shall regard the welfare of the infant as the first and paramount consideration, and shall not take into consideration whether from any other point of view the claim of the father, or any right at common law possessed by the father, in respect of such custody, upbringing, administration or application is superior to that of the mother, or the claim of the mother is superior to that of the father.'

The part of this section referring to 'the first and paramount consideration' has been spoken of as declaratory of the existing law. See *Re Thain, Thain v Taylor* [1926] Ch 676, 95 LJ Ch 292 per Lord Hanworth MR (p. 689) and Sargant LJ (p. 691); and *McKee v McKee* [1951] AC 352 at 366 per Lord Simonds. There have been different views about this, but whether the proposition is wholly accurate or not, the true construction of the section itself has to be considered as a matter of prime importance.

Two questions arise here. First, is the section to be read as referring only to disputes between the parents of the child? In *Re Carroll (No. 2)* [1931] 1 KB 317, 100 LJ KB 113, Slesser LJ appears to have approved such an interpretation for he said (p. 355):

'This statute, however, in my view, has confined itself to questions as between the rights of father and mother which I have already outlined — factors which cannot arise in the case of an illegitimate child . . .'

Now, the latter part of the section is directed to equalising the legal rights or claims of the parents, and the preamble speaks only of achieving an equality between the sexes in relation to the guardianship of infants. But these considerations, do not, in my opinion, suffice to constrict the natural meaning of the first part of the section. The latter part beginning with the words 'shall not take into consideration . . .' does not call for or imply any such constriction for it does not necessarily apply to all the possible disputes which the earlier part is capable of embracing; and as for the preamble, it could only be used to restrict the applicability of the earlier part of the section if that part were ambiguous. See *A-G v HRH Prince Ernest Augustus of Hanover* [1957] AC 436 at 463 per Viscount Simonds. Having read the whole Act, I cannot find this important earlier part to be other than clear and unambiguous. On the contrary, its wording seems to be deliberately wide and general. It relates to *any* proceedings before *any* court, and as Eve J said in *Clarke-Jervoise v Scutt* [1920] 1 Ch 382 at 388: ' "Any" is a word with a very wide meaning, and prima facie the use of it excludes limitation.'

Thus read the section would apply to cases, such as the present, between parents and strangers. This construction finds further support in the following considerations. In the first place, since (as the Act and authorities already mentioned by way of background show) welfare was being regarded increasingly as a general criterion which was not limited to custody disputes between parents, it would be more than strange if the earlier part of s. 1 were meant to apply only to that single type of dispute. Secondly, the questions for decision which are expressly mentioned — custody, upbringing, administration of property belonging to or held in trust for the infant, and the application of the income thereof — are of a kind to suggest the involvement not only of parents but of others such as guardians or trustees. And thirdly, there is nothing in the rest of the Act to require a limited construction of s. 1. Section 6, indeed, would seem to point the other way for it provides for the settlement by the court of differences between joint guardians affecting the welfare of an infant and there is no apparent reason for confining this relief to differences between parents or for taking proceedings therefore out of the ambit of s. 1. For these reasons I would hold that the present proceedings are proceedings within that section.

The second question of construction is as to the scope and meaning of the words '. . . shall regard the welfare of the infant as the first and paramount consideration.' Reading these words in their ordinary significance, and relating them to the various classes of proceedings which the section has already mentioned, it seems to me that they must mean more than that the child's welfare is to be treated as the top item in a list of items relevant to the matter in question. I think they connote a process whereby, when all the relevant facts, relationships, claims and wishes of parents, risks, choices and other circumstances are taken into account and weighed, the course to be followed will be that which is most in the interests of the child's welfare as that term has now to be understood. That is the first consideration because it is of first importance and the paramount consideration because it rules on or determines the course to be followed. It remains to see how this 'first view', as I may call it, stands in the light of authority.

In *Re Thain* [1926] Ch 676, 95 LJ Ch 292 Eve J, had to determine, shortly after the Act of 1925 came into operation, the proper custody of a girl of 7. The father's wife had died soon after the child's birth and the father then accepted the offer of his wife's sister and her husband to take charge of the infant and bring her up with their own children. That was in 1919. In 1925 the father, having remarried and improved his position in life and obtained a suitable home, asked to have his daughter back but this request had been refused. Eve J awarded custody to the father and the Court of Appeal held that he had applied the correct principles of law and refused to interfere with the manner in which he had exercised his discretion. The headnote is so worded as to suggest that as the father was an unimpeachable parent his parental right stood first and an order had to be made in his favour. On its face this, if a true reflection of the ratio, is against the first view I have formed on the wording of s. 1. In my opinion, however, the headnote is misleading in this respect. The true ratio is contained in the last paragraph of Eve J's judgment, which reads thus (at p. 684):

'As I said at the commencement of my judgment, I am satisfied that the child will be as happy and well cared for in the one home as the other, and inasmuch as the rule laid down for my guidance in the exercise of this responsible jurisdiction does not state that the welfare of the infant is to be the sole consideration but the paramount consideration, it necessarily contemplates the existence of other conditions, and amongst these the wishes of an unimpeachable parent undoubtedly stand first. It is my duty therefore to order the delivery up of this child to her father.'

I appreciate that the reporter may have experienced some difficulty in epitomising this passage, but viewed in relation to the facts of the case I think there can be little doubt that Eve J was neither ignoring the welfare of the child nor the terms of s. 1 of the Act of 1925. He was not putting the wishes of the father above the welfare of the child. Having found that the child would be as happy and well cared for in one home as the other, he must have been satisfied that her welfare would be best provided for by respecting the wishes of the unimpeachable father and giving her custody to him. That was the view taken by the Court of Appeal and the view which has been generally accepted since. I therefore see nothing in *Re Thain . . .* to conflict with my first view of the meaning of s. 1.

His lordship then discusses the case of *Re Carroll (No. 2)* [1931] 1 KB 317, 100 LJ KB 113 which the House unanimously disapproved and continues:

The effect of s. 1 of the Act of 1925 was again considered in the Court of Appeal in *Re Adoption Application No 41/61* [1963] Ch 315, [1962] 3 All ER 553 and there Danckwerts LJ, had this to say on the subject (p. 329):

'. . . I would respectfully point out that there can only be one 'first and paramount consideration', and other considerations must be subordinate. The mere desire of a parent to have his child must be subordinate to the consideration of the welfare of the child, and can be effective only if it coincides with the welfare of the child. Consequently, it cannot be correct to talk of the pre-eminent position of parents, or their exclusive right to the custody of their children, when the future welfare of those children is being considered by the court.'

When that case went back to Wilberforce J he had to consider the import of the words from s. 7(1)(*b*) of the Adoption Act 1958 — 'that the order if made shall be for the welfare of the infant' — and what he said will be found in *Re Adoption Application No. 41/61 (No. 2)* [1964] Ch 48, [1963] 2 All ER 1082. The passage reads (p. 53):

'The section, apart from a particular direction given in sub-s. (2), does not prescribe what matters have to be considered in this connexion, so that it would seem to me that the court must take into account all the merits and demerits of the alternative proposals as they seem likely to bear on the child's welfare: not limiting itself to purely material factors, but considering, as they may bear on the welfare of the infant, such matters as the natural ties of blood and family relationship. The tie (if such is shown to exist) between the child and his natural father (or any other relative) may properly be regarded in this connexion, not on the basis that the person concerned has a claim which he has a right to have satisfied, but, only if, and to the extent that, the conclusion can be drawn that the child will benefit from the recognition of this tie.'

Now that passage was not directed to s. 1 of the Act of 1925, but it seems to me to be an apt description of the sort of process which s. 1 enjoins, for it too calls for an enquiry as to what will be for the infant's welfare. If such is the true nature of the enquiry, it goes far to confirm my first view of the construction to be placed on the words '. . . the court . . . shall regard the welfare of the infant as the first and paramount consideration'; and that means an end of any presumption of law respecting parental rights and wishes so far as the test of welfare is concerned.

Having then summarised and rejected the two subsidiary arguments of counsel for the parents (i) that the wardship jurisdiction ought not to be used so as to grant a de facto adoption against parental wishes, and (ii) that in the interests of 'comity' the court should not exercise its powers after united foreign parents had requested the return of a foreign child sent here temporarily, his lordship concludes:

For these reasons I conclude that my first view construction of s. 1 should stand, and that the parents' proposition of law is ill-founded and must fail. The consequences of this present little difficulty, but before coming to them I would add in summary form certain views and comments on the ground surveyed in the hope that they may serve to restrict misunderstanding in this difficult field. These may be enumerated as follows:

1. Section 1 of the Act of 1925 applies to disputes not only between parents, but between parents and strangers and strangers and strangers.

2. In applying s. 1, the rights and wishes of parents, whether unimpeachable or otherwise, must be assessed and weighed in their bearing on the welfare of the child in conjunction with all other factors relevant to that issue.

3. While there is now no rule of law that the rights and wishes of unimpeachable parents must prevail over other considerations, such rights and wishes, recognised as they are by nature and society, can be capable of ministering to the total welfare of the child in a special way, and must therefore preponderate in many cases. The parental rights, however, remain qualified and not absolute for the purposes of the investigation, the broad nature of which is still as described in the fourth of the principles enunciated by FitzGibbon LJ in *Re O'Hara* [1900] 2 IR 232 at 240.

[The court should act cautiously, and in opposition to the parent only when judicially satisfied that the welfare of the child requires it.]

4. Some of the authorities convey the impression that the upset caused to a child by a change of custody is transient and a matter of small importance. For all I know that may been true in the cases containing dicta to that effect. But I think a growing experience has shown that it is not always so and that serious harm even to young children may, on occasion, be caused by such a change. I do not suggest that the difficulties of this subject can be resolved by purely theoretical considerations, or that they need to be left entirely to expert opinion. But a child's future happiness and sense of security are always important factors and the effects of a change of custody will often be worthy of the close and anxious attention which they undoubtedly received in this case.

The conclusion I have reached on the parents' proposition of law make it unnecessary to enter on a review of the facts and circumstances which are material here. When the evidence and the judgments are examined the result is only to confirm the propriety of counsel for the parents' concession. The learned judge applied the appropriate principles of law and I can find no ground for interfering with the manner in which he exercised his discretion. On these grounds I am of opinion that the appeal fails and should be dismissed.

Their lordships all concurred in dismissing the appeal but on two points they are not quite unanimous. Lords Upjohn and Donovan state quite clearly that s. 1 of the 1925 Act changed the law. Lord MacDermott, as we have seen, expresses no definite view on the previous law, while Lord Guest concludes his review of the earlier authorities thus:

It is clear to me that even prior to the Act of 1925 the paramount consideration in regard to the custody of infants was the infant's welfare. The father's wishes were to be considered but only as one of the factors as bearing on the child's welfare. The father had no 'right' as such to the care and control of his infant children. The comparative absence of authority in the intervening years between 1900 and 1925 may have been due to the fact that the change in the climate of social conditions was taking place gradually and its influence on the courts was almost imperceptible and was taking place in the chambers of the Chancery Courts. But whatever may have been the state of the law prior to the Act of 1925, s. 1 of that Act set any doubts at rest and made it perfectly clear that the first and paramount consideration was the welfare of the infant. I do not agree with the parents' construction of s. 1. It is, in my view, of universal application and is not limited in its application to questions as between parents.

Lord Guest, like Lord MacDermott, goes on to quote with approval the words of Danckwerts LJ in *Re Adoption Application No. 41/61* [1963] Ch 315 at 329, whereas Lord Upjohn has this to say:

My Lords Eve J said that among other considerations the wishes of an unimpeachable parent undoubtedly stand first, and I believe, as I have said, that represents the law. In a jurisdiction which can only be exercised by the judge after full and anxious, but broad consideration of all the relevant facts I do not want to split hairs with other judges who have expressed it a little differently, but it seems to me that Danckwerts LJ in *Re Adoption Application No. 41/61* and Wilberforce J in *Re Adoption Application No. 41/61 (No. 2)* hardly did justice to the position of the natural parent(s). The natural parents have a strong claim to have their wishes considered; first and principally, no doubt, because normally it is part of the paramount consideration of the welfare of the infant that he should be with them but also because as the natural parents they have themselves a strong claim to have their wishes considered as normally the proper persons to have the upbringing of the child they have brought into the world. It is not, however, a question of the onus being on anyone to displace the wishes of the parents; it is a matter for the judge, bearing in mind the rule as laid down by Eve J.

Lord Donovan's short, sharp speech contains the following:

I think the section means just what it says — no more and no less; and although the claim of natural parents to the custody and upbringing of their own children is obviously a most weighty factor to be taken into consideration in deciding what is in the best interests of the infant, yet the legislature recognised that this might not always be the determining factor, whether the parents were unimpeachable or not.

Lord Pearson agrees with Lord MacDermott.

Questions

(i) If the governing criterion is what is best for the child, what weight would you attach to the following factors: (a) the foster father was a solicitor, though 'not well off,' while the natural father was a 'good workman,' but 'morose,' and had written letters to the foster parents which contained words too obscene for translation; (b) the foster parents planned to send the child to public school, whereas Spanish state education did not always continue even till 16; (c) the foster family was strongly pro-Spanish and often spoke in Spanish, but the child would answer in English and was the least pro-Spanish in the household; (d) the foster parents had brought the child up in the belief that his parents loved him and he had their photographs on his dressing table; (e) the child and his foster brother P were 'like twins;' (f) an eminent psychiatrist gave evidence that 'if the infant made a successful adjustment in Spain he would be integrated with his surroundings and the dichotomy of his present situation would be ended. But he was emphatic that the chances of that adjustment would be "very slim", and, if it were not achieved, there would be the gravest consequences for his future emotional stability and happiness. . . . The infant's symptoms, reported to him, of the last visit to Spain, were, he said, "symptoms of this maladjustment and not just physical illness. . . . The infant's prospects of proper adjustment and development were far better if his return to Spain came from the growth of his own natural inclination later on". . . .'; (g) the child's mother would have been sensitive to his problems of adjustment, but the father was not the kind of person who could 'cope with or even understand' them; (h) the natural parents had wanted him back since the summer of 1963, came from a culture which respected the 'sovereign right of the father', and now had a good home to offer?

(ii) But should such cases be governed by what is best for the child?

(iii) The local authority, says Lord Guest, 'did not act with conspicuous consistency or good sense.' Reminding yourself of the child care law contained in the previous chapter: (a) should they have received the child into care at all, either on the first occasion, or on the second? (b) Could they, as the law stood in 1963, have assumed the parents' rights? (c) Could they do so as the law now stands? (d) If they had assumed parental rights, might they nevertheless have decided to return the child to his parents? (e) If they had so decided, what (in the light of *Re M (An Infant)* [1961] Ch 328, [1961] 1 All ER 788 and *A v Liverpool City Council* [1982] AC 363, [1981] 2 All ER 385 p. 458, above) could the foster parents have done about it?

The last question emphasises two vital footnotes to the decision in *J v C*, which will rob it of much of its usefulness, even for those local authority foster parents who have the resources (of varying sorts) required to pursue a remedy in wardship. First, it is clear from *Re M (An Infant)* [1961] Ch 328, [1961] 1 All ER 788 and *A v Liverpool City Council* [1982] AC 363, [1981] 2 All ER 385 that the High Court should not permit the wardship jurisdiction to be used to challenge those decisions over which Parliament has ruled that local authorities should have control: one such decision is where the child should be accommodated during his stay in care (Child Care Act 1980, s. 21). The High Court will only intervene if, as here, the local authority has asked it to do so, or where the child is in voluntary care and the local authority's power to keep the child after a parental request for his discharge is limited (see *Re KR (An Infant)* [1964] Ch 455, [1963] 3 All ER 337 and *Re S (An Infant)* [1965] 1 All ER 865, [1965] 1 WLR 483). A foster parent who has the local authority on her side is unlikely to need to resort to wardship, and one who does not is unlikely to be able to do so.

A second footnote is that, at the time when the facts in *J v C* took place, notifying the local authority of an intention to apply to adopt the child was not sufficient to prevent the authority from removing him if they wished to do so. Under what is now s. 31(1) of the Adoption Act 1976, once such a notice has been received, the normal procedures for an agency to recover a child from prospective adopters under s. 30 apply: the agency may give notice requiring the child to be returned within seven days, unless an application has been made to the court, in which case such notice can only be given with leave of the court (nowadays, however, this must be read subject to the 'five year rule' contained in s. 28 of the 1976 Act — see further p. 486, below).

(b) THE MARIA COLWELL CASE

Fundamental though the principle decided in *J v C* may be, the most remarkable fact about the case is that it came to court at all. A far more common sequence of events was related in the *Report of the Committee of Inquiry into the Care and Supervision Provided in Relation to Maria Colwell*, published in 1974. The majority of the Committee (T.G. Field-Fisher QC and Alderman Mrs MR Davey) told the following story:

10. Maria Colwell was born on the 25 March 1965, so that when she died at the hands of her stepfather, William Kepple, on the night of the 6/7 January 1973 she was eleven weeks short of her eighth birthday. She was the fifth and youngest child of her mother's first marriage and within weeks of her birth her father had left her mother at Conway Street, in Hove, and within a further few weeks he had died on the 22 July 1965.

11. The only matter of note preceding her birth to which our attention was drawn was the origin of a feud between Maria's mother's family (the Testers) and that of her father (the Colwells) which we were frequently told came to affect Maria herself both directly and also indirectly through its influence upon decisions concerning her.

12. . . . Finding herself alone after the death of her husband with five young children to care for it is not altogether surprising that [Maria's mother] found it difficult to cope with the situation.

13. . . . She went completely to pieces. It is not perhaps necessary to go into further detail as to this save to say that there was ample evidence that Mrs Colwell's children were being consistently left alone, were neglected and dirty and that she was associating with numerous men. She was warned on several occasions about leaving the children alone, both by the NSPCC and the Hove Children's Department.

14. In August Mrs Colwell took Maria round to Mrs Cooper, her sister-in-law, who agreed to take her in and look after her. Mrs Cooper and her husband had by then brought up their own family and were living with an unmarried daughter. . . . This voluntary act by Mrs Colwell in

handing over Maria at the age of four months to a member of her late husband's family was to have deep and permanent repercussions upon all the personalities involved.

15. Maria continued to live with Mr and Mrs Cooper . . . until the 4 June 1966, when Mrs Colwell removed her, as of course she was perfectly entitled to do since the arrangement under which the Coopers had looked after since the previous August was an entirely private and voluntary one. This removal coincided apparently with her intention to set up house with her future husband Mr Kepple.

16. By the 11 June, only one week later, Mrs Colwell had run into severe difficulties over housing and had either been forced, or chose, to part with Maria again, not returning her to the Coopers as might perhaps have been expected but leaving her with another woman in circumstances and conditions which Inspector Curan of the NSPCC, who had knowledge of Maria's removal from the Coopers and also of the home in which Maria had been left, immediately recognised as requiring at once the obtaining of a place of safety order. Under the order Maria was returned by Inspector Curran to the Coopers as an interim measure. On the 17 August 1966 the Hove Juvenile Court made an order placing Maria in the care of the local authority [for care proceedings generally, see Chapter 14], in this case also the East Sussex County Council (hereinafter called 'East Sussex') who by now had all five of Mrs Colwell's children in their care. . . . After careful consideration, East Sussex decided that the proper course was to board Maria out with the Coopers as foster parents, placing great reliance upon the satisfactory way the Coopers had looked after her for the past year and also the undesirability of yet another move if it could possibly be avoided. Accordingly, the Coopers, who were devoted to the child, being willing and anxious to continue to look after her, were approved as her foster parents by the Children's Committee on the 29 October 1966, and at the time it was clearly explained to them that the long-term plan was for Maria to return to her mother.

17. The point was made to us by East Sussex that the Coopers were not 'ideal' foster parents . . . and it is indeed clear from the case notes that approval was given by the Children's Committee to them not in general terms as foster parents but limited in particular to Maria. In one respect we accept that they fell short of 'ideal' in that one of the qualities looked for in such foster parents is the willingness actually to encourage a transfer back to the natural parent when the time comes. This the Coopers, who were, after all, part of Maria's wider natural family, understandably found it impossible to do, although that is not to say that they obstructed the transfer. . . .

19. After the Coopers were approved as foster parents they continued to look after Maria with the devotion and care due to a child of their own and in those surroundings the little girl thrived and had a normal and satisfactory upbringing. . . .

24. On the 20 August 1969 Mrs Colwell applied to the Hove Juvenile Court asking for the care order relating to Maria to be varied so as to provide her with stated access to Maria and the Court, as it was obliged to do through lack of jurisdiction, had refused the application. Contact between Maria and her brothers and sister in their respective foster homes was, however, being occasionally maintained and she also saw her mother, who she was always told was her real mother, from time to time. . . .

28. [In July 1970, Maria's mother] Mrs Kepple informed Miss Lees [the social worker] of her hopes of an imminent move to a council house when she and Mr Kepple would get married and that she would go to the Court to get Maria back when she was in a position to do so. . . .

30. [In March 1971] Mrs Kepple was again consulting her solicitor about applying for revocation of the care order. By April she was anxious to know from Miss Lees whether she had to go to Court or whether Maria could go home on trial. As a result, a case discussion was held on the 26 April between Miss Lees, Mr Bennett her senior social worker and Miss Simpson, the assistant director of East Sussex social work services. . . .

36. The case discussion which lasted at least one and half hours was clearly a full review of the circumstances surrounding Maria as they appeared to those taking part and the prospects for her future with the Kepples or the Coopers were assessed taking into consideration the situation which had then developed. We were told that an accurate note of the discussion was taken, and because of its importance we set out below certain of the conclusions:

'It would seem that whatever the decision was taken concerning Maria it would involve stress and trauma for her at some time. On balance it was felt that future plans should be directed towards her eventual return to her mother. It was recognised that while she remains with the Coopers she would continue to be the centre of conflict. It is unlikely that the Coopers will be able to deal well with her feelings in adolescence concerning her natural parents [sic], and it is possible that at this age she would herself decide to return to her mother. It should be easier for her to build relationships with the Kepple family and to take her place within [it] at a younger age, particularly considering the good emotional grounding she has received from the Coopers.

It was seen that the best way to manage a situation of this type would be for Maria's visits to the Kepples to be gradually increased to include holidays, etc., and in this way to effect a gradual transferring of her roots from one family to the other. She would then go home on trial whilst still remaining in care and contact with the Coopers would gradually diminish until revocation of the Order could be supported. However, this type of management would not be possible in this case, because of the animosity between the Coopers and the Kepples, which is unlikely to diminish. Neither would be able to co-operate fully, and the tension for Maria would increase. On the other hand, her abrupt removal from the people she considers her own family to a household of which she knows relatively little would be extremely damaging.

It was felt that the best plan . . . was the gradual changeover up to the point when the stress for Maria appeared to be becoming too great, i.e. contact with the Kepple family should be encouraged and increased to give Maria the opportunity of knowing them better before her sudden transfer to them. With this in view, Mrs Kepple should be encouraged to delay her application for revocation and to go along with such a plan. If she insists on making such an application she should be opposed at this stage, but the long-term plan of Maria's return should be followed.'

There follows an upsetting account of Maria's visits to the Kepples' home over the next few months, of her protests at going and of her twice running away from them.

59. It is clear if one looks at the history of that summer and autumn as a whole that the laudable intention of East Sussex expressed in April to gain time was frustrated by the march of events. The increased visiting was producing increased resistance from and trauma for Maria, although the social workers comforted themselves with the belief, undoubtedly genuine and possibly justified, that she was building a satisfactory relationship with her mother and enjoyed the younger children. Mrs Kepple, apparently now pushed by Mr Kepple, was not prepared to hold off making her application to the Court any longer. . . .

62. The position had clearly been reached, as was anticipated in April, that the tension for Maria was approaching an unacceptable level. . . . That meant that a decision one way or the other had to be made, and by October it was known that Mrs Kepple's application would be heard in the near future. . . . East Sussex decided not to oppose. Their reasoning appeared to be that if Mrs Kepple did not succeed on this first occasion she would probably do so sooner or later and therefore it was better to accept the position and seek to control it.

Accordingly, Maria was transferred to her mother, technically 'on trial,' in October. She ran away a third time, but was returned, and on 17 November 1971, the care order was discharged and a supervision order substituted. It was common ground that that supervision was totally ineffective to prevent her subsequent neglect and ill-treatment until her eventual death 14 months later. On the transfer itself, the majority accepted the following basic proposition:

42. It is clear that the social workers considering the case in April did not consider themselves in a position to make an unfettered decision about Maria's future. They operated within a legal and social system in which when a child was taken into care the expectation was not that she would remain in care until the age of 18 but that she would return to her own family when their circumstances had improved. It was put to us and we accept that there was a strong presumption that the magistrates would return a child to the parent once the parent's fitness was proved unless it could clearly be shown not to be in the best interests of the child. In Maria's case the social workers concerned took the view that Mrs Kepple's application was likely to succeed within a short while given the improvement in her living conditions, her stable relationship with Mr Kepple and her apparent ability to cope with the children living with her. With this in mind consideration was given to the harm which would result from a court decision to return Maria to her mother before Maria had had sufficient opportunity to get to know the Kepples. The social services department therefore was seeking in April 1971 to control the timing of a move. This view of the inevitability of Maria's return to her mother underlay much of the thinking in 1971 and profoundly affected the decisions taken and the management of the case.

Nevertheless, they criticised the social workers: (*a*) for not investigating Mr Kepple's history and character at all; (*b*) for failing to interpret Mrs Kepple's 'physical and emotional condition;' (*c*) for assuming that it would be easier for Maria to return then, rather than later at her own wish; (*d*) for failing to draw up contingency plans in the event of the transfer's failure;

(*e*) for making no effort to obtain a medical opinion as to the depth and significance of Maria's protests between April and November; and (*f*) for not seeking to persuade the court to allow further time, and for 'seeking to appease Mrs Kepple', rather than placing the onus upon her to establish her present fitness.

The dissenting member was Miss Olive Stevenson, who would have been far more inclined to criticise the decision to place Maria with the Coopers when the care order was made than any of the subsequent decisions. The nub of her argument, after first reiterating the point made by the majority in paragraph 42, was as follows:

315. . . . There is much confusion, some of which was apparent in this inquiry, regarding social workers' attitude to the so-called 'blood tie'. . . . If that phrase means that an emotional relationship, which in some way takes precedence over others, exists simply because of consanguinity, then this is not generally accepted by social workers. . . . For those who work with children separated from their parents, the issue is seen much more in terms of the development in a child of a good self image and sound sense of identity. There are two elements in this; first, that a child shall know who his parents were; secondly, that his perception of them, coloured as it is by the adults who care for him, shall not be such as to make him feel he comes of 'bad stock'. It was the second matter which clearly concerned the East Sussex social workers and I have attempted in my analysis to show they had grounds for concern. It is partly for this reason that one finds references in their records to possible difficulties in adolescence, a time in which self doubt frequently leads to crises of identity.

The social workers had no wish to move Maria from the Coopers if Mrs Kepple were to remain uninterested. But, as her interest intensified, so did the tension between the 'two mothers', to Maria's detriment. As events rolled on through 1970 and 1971, it became clear that the conflicts were reaching a dangerously high level so far as Maria was concerned. I have referred earlier to the effect on the social workers of the legal climate. But even had that been different, I would concur with Miss Simpson's [assistant director of East Sussex social services] observation:

'I think foster parents always need to be able to allow a child to have the child's natural family to have a place in the child's life; whether that place is *merely in its thoughts and loyalties* (my italics) or whether a physical transfer as in this case obviously differs. . . .'

It is worth noting that what Miss Simpson is dealing with here are children's feelings, which no legal change or changes in social climate can change.

Questions

(i) Is Miss Stevenson here suggesting that even if the social workers had felt free to decide on the same principle as that adopted by the House of Lords in *J v C* (p. 474, above), they might still have reached the same conclusion?

(ii) Bearing in mind the positive views about the child's background which were apparently encouraged by the foster parents in *J v C*, might the social workers have been less worried about leaving him with them?

(iii) Does this mean that, of two sets of foster parents who have provided a loving and happy home for a child over a long period, those who have good reason for criticising the child's natural parents will be more likely to lose him than those who have nothing to criticise?

(iv) If the Coopers had been advised of the possibility of making Maria a ward of court, and had found the resources to do so, do you think that a High Court judge, applying the welfare principle, would have granted them care and control of her?

(v) However (bearing in mind *Re T (AJJ)* [1970] Ch 688, [1970] 2 All ER 865), might the Court have refused to hear the case on the ground that Parliament had invested the local authority with parental powers and duties and the Court should not interfere?

(vi) Do you think that the law should make any distinction between the claims of foster parents in the two types of case exemplified by *J v C* and the *Maria Colwell* case?

One footnote to this case (which had many other repercussions) is appropriate here: any person with whom the child has had his home for not less than six weeks, ending within the past six months, must be notified of any application in care proceedings; but the Magistrates' Courts (Children and Young Persons) Rules 1970 do not assign such a person any further role in the proceedings. Care proceedings generally are discussed in the next chapter.

(c) CUSTODIANSHIP AND ADOPTION

Two years before the Maria Colwell Report, the *Report of the Departmental Committee on the Adoption of Children* (the Houghton Report) had also discussed the rights of foster parents and other people caring for children:

116. There are many children who are not being brought up by their natural parents but are in the long-term care of foster parents or relatives. These people normally have no legal status in relation to the child, and the law provides no means by which they can obtain it without cutting his links with his natural family by adoption. They are faced with the choice of doing without the legal security, which may be damaging to the child, or applying for an adoption order. This is one reason why . . . adoption is frequently applied for in inappropriate circumstances, particularly by relatives.

120. We suggested in our working paper that the right to apply for custody under guardianship legislation should be made available to relatives and foster parents already caring for a child, subject to certain limitations. The evidence we received strongly supported this, particularly in the case of relatives.

121. There were more reservations about guardianship for foster parents, but we think there are some circumstances where guardianship by foster parents would be appropriate. We have in mind situations where the parents are out of the picture, and the foster parents and the child wish to legalise and secure their relationship and be independent of the local authority or child care agency, but the child is old enough to have a sense of identity and wishes to keep this and retain his own name. There are also a few cases where the parents are actively in touch with the child and the foster parents, and where this bond is secure, but the parents recognise that they will never be able to provide a home for the child. There are other cases in which for financial reasons the foster parents may feel unable to seek adoption but guardianship with financial assistance may be appropriate [but see p. 503, below].

122. There must be some restriction on the circumstances in which foster parents can apply for guardianship. While courts would not be likely to accede to an application by foster parents who had cared for a child for a short period, the natural parents ought not to be caused the anxiety of being involved in such proceedings. We therefore recommend that, as in the case of adoption [see now Adoption Act 1976 s. 13(2)] foster parents should not be allowed to apply for guardianship unless they have cared for the child for 12 months.

. . . .

125. Since a guardianship order can be reviewed by the court at any time, we do not propose any formal provisions for the giving of parental consent. The parents of the child should be notified of the application, as well as the local authority and any other interested person or body (including a local authority or voluntary society having care of the child), and they should all be parties to the application, with a right to attend and be heard.

126. We envisage that most guardianship orders would be made with the agreement of the natural parent, and that a natural parent who was unwilling to consent to the final severance of legal ties by an adoption order would sometimes be willing to consent to guardianship. But where a foster parent has cared for a child for five years, we consider that the position should be the same in respect of guardianship applications as with applications to adopt (see paragraph 164) and that the position should be frozen, so that, once an application had been made to the court, the child could not be removed without the leave of the court.

127. In deciding whether to make a guardianship order the court would be required to follow the principle in the existing guardianship law and regard the welfare of the child as the first and

paramount consideration. In deciding whether an order would be for the child's welfare, the court would be able to consider all the relevant factors, including the wishes of the child, where he was old enough to form a view; the wishes of his parents; and the suitability of the applicants.

. . . .

144. We suggested in our working paper that where foster parents had cared for a child for five years they should be able to apply to the court for adoption and the position should be frozen pending the court hearing even if the mother had not consented. . . .

. . . .

146. . . . There was a strong body of opinion, particularly from those experienced in the child care field, that the effect of our proposals would be to increase the number of 'tugs-of-war' between natural parents and foster parents in the courts; that the result would be a reduction in the number of children fostered and an increase in the number accommodated in children's homes, or kept by their mothers even if their situation was such that it was in the children's interest to be fostered; and thus changes in the law designed to further the welfare of some children might be harmful to the welfare of many others. It was argued that the number of cases in which children were reclaimed against their interests [see p. 433, above] did not justify putting at risk the whole fostering system. . . .

164. We adhere to our provisional proposition that foster parents who have cared for a child for five years or more should be entitled to apply to the court for adoption, in the knowledge that the position would be frozen until the application was heard, irrespective of the views of the natural parents or of any local authority or voluntary society in whose care the child may be. It would still be for the court to consider whether there were grounds for dispensing with the parent's consent, and whether an adoption order would be in the interests of the welfare of the child, bearing in mind the child's own wishes if he were old enough to form a view. Any local authority or voluntary society having care of the child would be a respondent to the application, with a right to be heard. We suggest that the position should be frozen from the time the foster parents notify their intention to apply to adopt, and the 'freezing' should lapse after three months if a formal application for an adoption order had not then been lodged.

All these proposals were enacted in the Children Act 1975, although the term 'custodianship' was used instead of 'guardianship' and the scheme was modified in two ways: (i) a relative (including the step-parent of an orphaned or illegitimate child) with whom the child has had his home for the past three months may apply, as may a foster parent with whom he has been for a total of twelve months including the past three, but only if the application has the consent of a person having legal custody of the child; but (ii) any person with whom the child has had his home for a total of three years including the past three months may apply without consent, and pending the hearing the child may not be removed. However, the custodianship provisions have not yet been brought into force and no timetable has been announced for doing so. One possible reason for this is criticism such as that of Robert Holman at the time of the Children Bill's passage through Parliament, *In Defence of Parents* (1975):

Despite the research findings, the government has decided on steps to encourage those fosterings where parental contact and knowledge is likely to be at a minimum. The new concept of custodianship will not only award legal custody of the children to the foster parents instead of the natural parents, it will also abolish the local authority's rights over the foster children (unless a court specifically orders otherwise). The consequent situation, with the foster parents able to exclude natural parents and social workers, is the very one which will lend itself to foster children being denied full understanding of their true position. Custodianship will blur the difference between fostering and adoption (both of which are valid forms of child care for certain children) and will maximise the children's confusion, while denying them the skilled help of social workers.

Lastly, the government, in choosing the focus of its child welfare legislation, has ignored the most vulnerable group of foster children — private foster children. The 11,000 private foster children are those placed by their parents through an informal arrangement with almost anyone who cares to take them. Although excellent private fosterings do occur, my research (1973) indicated that many were grossly unsatisfactory, that the emotional and physical deprivations were far more extensive than amongst local authority children and that local authorities, in practice, were powerless to intervene.[2] The social workers' lack of powers meant that frequently they saw no point in visiting private foster homes with the consequence that many were rarely if ever seen.

The study further revealed that frequently the parents, particularly deserted spouses and single mothers, placed their children only as a last resort after failing to find day care. I came across cases of parents now able to have their children back, but barred by the manipulations of private foster parents who had stopped them visiting until the child's affections were transferred. What does the Children Bill do for private fostering? The local authorities are not given one further power, not one extra penny, to control the trade in children. Indeed, as all the new powers to adopt and take custodianship also include private foster parents, the situation will grow worse. The prospect of legal custody will no doubt attract more into the trade, and offer extra incentives to keep natural parents at bay.

Question

Others might have said, why not allow all foster parents to apply for custody and trust the courts to apply the welfare principle sensibly?

Another reason why the custodianship provisions have not been implemented could be that (as we shall shortly see) adoption seems now to be adapting to cover many of the cases for which custodianship was originally devised. The 'five year rule' recommended in paragraph 164 of the Houghton Report is contained in s. 28 of the Adoption Act 1976. It does not, of course, remove the need for the applicant to persuade the court to dispense with the parent's agreement (see section 6, below). On the other hand, if the local authority has parental rights, whether under a s. 3 resolution (p. 442, above) or under a care order made by a court, the parent cannot remove the child in any event. If the local authority supports the application, therefore, it may be made long before the foster parents have had the child for five years.

3 Adoption past

For a summary of the extraordinary diversity shown by the institution of adoption, we may turn to *Adoption: A Second Chance* (1977), Barbara Tizard's account of her study comparing the adoption or rehabilitation of children in care:

The essence of adoption is that a child not born to you is incorporated into your family as though he were your own. This practice can be found in some form in most cultures — one of the best-known early adoptions was that of Moses. But just as the family, although a constant feature of all societies, has assumed many different forms and functions, so the characteristics of adoption have varied enormously during history. Today most people think of adoption as a process in which a young child, usually an infant, is permanently incorporated into a family into which he was not born. Typically, the adoptive parents and the biological parents are strangers, and the adoption is arranged through an agency or other third party. Great stress is laid on keeping the two sets of parents from meeting or even knowing each others' identity. All links between the adopted child and his natural parents are severed, and the adopted child has all the rights, and is treated in the same way, as a natural child of his new family. The primary purpose of the adoption is seen to be the satisfaction of the desire of a married couple to rear a child; at the same time, a home is provided for a child whose natural parents are unable to rear it. . . .

Perhaps the greatest contrast is with the custom of child exchange, or kinship fostering, formerly prevalent in Polynesia and parts of Africa. In these societies children were often not

---

2. The local authorities' legal powers are contained in the Foster Children Act 1980.

reared by their biological parents but sent to be raised by relatives, sometimes after weaning, sometimes from the age of 6 or 7. The exchange of children was arranged by the parents, who continued to maintain some contact with their biological child. It was believed that aunts, uncles and grandparents would bring children up and train them more effectively than their parents. This custom of child exchange seems to have been part of a system of mutual kinship obligations.

Adoption played a very different role in such ancient civilisations as the Babylonian, Chinese and Roman. There, its function was primarily to ensure the continuity of wealthy families by providing for the inheritance of property and the performance of ancestral worship. Roman law, for example, permitted adoption only in order to provide an heir to the childless, and laid down that the adopters must be past child-bearing age and the adoptee must be an adult. Until recently, the adoption laws of many European countries were influenced by Roman law; often adoptive parents had to be childless and over the age of 50.

Hindu law also recognised adoption as a method of securing an heir, both for religious purposes and for the inheritance of property. It specified, however, that the adopted child should be if possible a blood relative, and that the transaction must take place directly between the two sets of parents. For this reason, orphans could not be adopted. In most ancient civilisations adoption was only one among several possible ways of providing an heir, and often not the preferred one. In Islam, for example, divorce and remarriage, polygamy, and the legitimisation of children by maidservants were common practices, while adoption was not permitted.

In all these societies adoption was essentially concerned with preserving the property and the religious observances of the families of the ruling class. It was very much a service for the rich, and for men; it was men who wanted heirs, and for this purpose they wanted boys. The emotional needs of childless wives were not recognised; indeed if they did not produce an heir they were likely to be divorced or otherwise replaced. Nor was it a service for homeless children; the adoptees were often adult, or, if children, they were given to the adoptive parents by their biological parents in order to better their social status.

Indeed, adoption in Rome could serve a positive constitutional purpose, as Donald Dudley recounts in *Roman Society* (1970):

The problem of the Empire was to ensure that bad Emperors were not too frequent. Two of the five Julio-Claudians, Gaius and Nero, deserved the adjective 'bad', so did Domitian, the third of the Flavians and in the popular view by far the worst. The dynastic principle had failed, and after Domitian's death it was resolved to try something else. We have seen how the method of adoption had been used in the great republican families when there was no suitable heir: adoption of the 'best man' might solve the problem of succession to the Principate. And indeed it worked brilliantly in the sequence of five 'Good Emperors' from Nerva to Marcus Aurelius; their reigns, which stretched from A.D. 96 to 180, were traditionally the best years of the Empire. When Marcus Aurelius, the first of the five to have a son of his body, reverted to the dynastic principle in the choice of Commodus, the fortunes of Rome changed sharply for the worse.

Question

It may be easy to see why the modern idea of providing a home for an illegitimate and often pauper child found little favour in medieval England, but how do you account for the fact that the great English families did not wish to do as the Romans had done — so that, even now, an adopted child cannot succeed to a peerage or other hereditary title?

Tizard resumes her account thus:

It is only relatively recently that adoption has become a recognised practice in Western society. Before this time bastards were sometimes legitimised by the rich, but the orphans and illegitimate children of the poor were sent to the workhouse and contracted out as soon as possible to private employers for domestic service, or work in factories, mills or mines. Often, of course, the orphans of both rich and poor were cared for by relatives, but they were rarely accorded the same status as the biological children of the family. The position of illegitimate children was worse, because of the social and moral stigma attached to illegitimacy, coupled with a strong belief in the inheritance of moral qualities. Not only the unmarried mother but also her child were regarded as morally inferior. There was also a general belief that to care for the illegitimate child would condone or even encourage the immorality of his mother. People were reluctant even to admit illegitimate children into a household; it was thought that 'bad blood will out', and the sins of the mother would be visited on the child.

It was in the United States, where more egalitarian ideas prevailed, heredity was at a discount, and human labour was in short supply, that the modern practice of adoption began to evolve. The first modern adoption law was enacted in Massachusetts in 1851. But long before that time American homesteaders took homeless children and reared them, benefiting in exchange from their help on the farm. Often, these children were treated very much as second-class citizens. Indeed, for half a century after adoption was legitimised in the U.S.A. it continued to be seen as a charitable act, and the adopted child was expected to work harder than a natural child and repay his debt of gratitude. . . .

Adoption at this stage, then, was a way of giving a homeless child a more humane upbringing than he would have received in an institution, with the expectation of receiving services from the child in return. It was only gradually that adoption began to be seen as a way of giving infertile couples all the emotional satisfaction that they would have had from a biological child.

The English were still deeply suspicious. In 1921, the Hopkinson Committee reported in favour of providing for legal adoption, but its recommendations proved so controversial that a second Committee was appointed, under the chairmanship of Mr Justice Tomlin. The *Report of the Tomlin Committee* in 1925 is far from enthusiastic:

4. . . . There have no doubt always been some people who desire to bring up as their own the children of others but we have been unable to satisfy ourselves as to the extent of the effective demand for a legal system of adoption by persons who themselves have adopted children or who desire to do so. It may be doubted whether any such persons have been or would be deterred from adopting children by the absence of any recognition by the law of the status of adoption. The war led to an increase in the number of de facto adoptions but that increase has not been wholly maintained. The people wishing to get rid of children are far more numerous than those wishing to receive them and partly on this account the activities in recent years of societies arranging systematically for the adoption of children would appear to have given to adoption a prominence which is somewhat artificial and may not be in all respects wholesome. The problem of the unwanted child is a serious one; it may well be a question whether a legal system of adoption will do much to assist the solution of it.

9. [Nevertheless] . . . we think that there is a measure of genuine apprehension on the part of those who have in fact adopted other people's children, based on the possibility of interference at some future time by the natural parent. It may be that this apprehension has but a slight basis in fact notwithstanding the incapacity of the legal parent to divest himself of his parental rights and duties. The Courts have long recognised that any application by the natural parent to recover the custody of his child will be determined by reference to the child's welfare and by that consideration alone. The apprehension, therefore, in most cases has a theoretical rather than a practical basis. There is also a sentiment which deserves sympathy and respect, that the relation between adopter and adopted should be given some recognition by the community. We think, therefore, that a case is made out for an alteration in the law. . . .

Having reluctantly reached that conclusion, the Committee went on to consider how adoption should take place, and to what effect. Some of their arguments cast an interesting light upon more recent debates:

11. . . . some form of judicial sanction should be required. . . . The transaction is one which may affect the status of the child and have far-reaching consequences and from its nature is not one which, without judicial investigation, is likely to be any competent independent consideration of the matter from the point of view of the welfare of the child.

Inasmuch as many cases of adoption in fact have their origin in the social or economic pressure exercised by circumstances upon the mother of an illegitimate child, it is desirable that there should be some safeguard against the use of a legal system of adoption as an instrument by which advantage may be taken of the mother's situation to compel her to make a surrender of her child final in character though she may herself, if a free agent, desire nothing more than a temporary provision for it. Further, there are many who hold that a system of adoption so far as it tends to encourage or increase the separation of mother and child may of itself be an evil and should be therefore, if introduced, operated with caution. . . .

15. . . . Whichever be the tribunal selected it is important that the judicial sanction, which will

necessarily carry great weight, should be a real adjudication and should not become a mere method of registering the will of the parties respectively seeking to part with and take over the child. To avoid this result we think that in every case there should be appointed . . . some body or person to act as guardian ad litem of the child with the duty of protecting the interests of the child before the tribunal.

18. . . . No system of adoption, seeking as it does to reproduce artificially a natural relation, can hope to produce precisely the same result or to be otherwise than in many respects illogical, and this is made apparent in the diversity of provisions in relation to succession and marriage which appear in the adoption laws of other countries.

19. We think that in introducing into English law a new system it would be well to proceed with a measure of caution and at any rate in the first instance not to interfere with the law of succession . . . it does not require any profound knowledge of the law of succession to bring home to an enquirer (1) the impracticability of putting an adopted child in precisely the same position as a natural child in regard to succession, and (2) the grave difficulties which would arise if any alteration were to be made in the law of succession for the purpose of giving an adopted child more limited rights . . . but . . . the tribunal which sanctions the adoption should have power if it thinks fit, to require that some provision be made by the adopting parent for the child.

Question

What, if anything, was so different about the system of succession in classical Roman law that the complete absorption of the adopted child into his new family presented none of the difficulties apparently so obvious to English lawyers in 1925?

If these passages in the report betray (although they do not confess to) deep-seated attitudes about 'natural' and 'artificial' relationships, there is one point upon which the Committee's views have a decidedly modern ring:

28. . . . Certain of the Adoption Societies make this feature an essential part of their policy. They deliberately seek to fix a gulf between the child's past and future. This notion of secrecy has its origin partly in a fear (which a legalised system of adoption should go far to dispel) that the natural parents will seek to interfere with the adopter and partly in the belief that if the eyes can be closed to facts the facts themselves will cease to exist so that it will be an advantage to an illegitimate child who has been adopted if in fact his origin cannot be traced. Apart from the question whether it is desirable or even admissible deliberately to eliminate or obscure the traces of a child's origin . . . we think that this system of secrecy would be wholly unnecessary and objectionable in connection with a legalised system of adoption.

Thus the first cautious steps were taken in the Adoption of Children Act 1926 (a similar Act applicable to Scotland was passed in 1930). In 1927, just under 3,000 adoption orders were made in England and Wales (mainly by juvenile courts) and numbers rose steadily year by year, reaching just over 7,000 in 1940. During and after the second world war, numbers rose more sharply, reaching a peak of over 21,000 in 1946. There was then a decline to 12,700 in 1950 followed by a gradual recovery to an all-time peak of 24,800 in 1968, since when there has been a considerable fall. A graph tracing that fall appears on p. 404, above. During this time, the institution has changed its social and legal character quite dramatically, in line with equally dramatic changes in attitudes towards children and their families. The legal developments may be broadly classified under three headings: the arrangements for adoption, the effects of an adoption order, and the balance between parental wishes and the long term welfare of the child.

4 Today's 'traffic in children'

As Jean Heywood reports in *Children in Care* (now 1978):

The very popularity of adoption since it became legal in 1926 had led to an increase in the number of adoption societies and an extension of their activities, as well as an increase in the numbers of private individuals who arranged the placement of babies. Adoption work was entirely unsupervised and uncontrolled and the standard was naturally extremely variable and sometimes haphazard. . . . A committee of inquiry was set up in January 1936 under the chairmanship of Miss Florence Horsbrugh, MP whose recommendations were embodied in the Adoption of Children (Regulation) Act 1939. This legislation empowered the Secretary of State to make regulations about the way in which adoption societies conducted their work, and also laid certain duties with regard to them on the local authorities. Adoption societies must be registered as approved by the local authorities before they could place children for adoption; and the local authority was required to be notified seven days in advance of all children placed by private persons acting as third parties for adoption, and to supervise these placings until the adoption came to the court.

As the same author later comments, this reflected 'not only the growth of a personalised concern for the child to be adopted, but also the rise of a professionalised class of social workers with a recognised ethical code and a body of knowledge about the assessment of social and personal problems.' Something of what is expected of those social workers today can be seen from the current *Adoption Agencies Regulations 1976*:

8. No child shall be placed by or on behalf of an adoption agency in the actual custody of a person proposing to adopt the child until —

(*a*) the adoption agency has, so far as is reasonably practicable, ascertained the particulars set out in Schedule 4;

(*b*) the adoption agency has obtained a report by a fully registered medical practitioner as to the health of the child in the form set out in Schedule 5, or in a form to the like effect;

(*c*) the person proposing to adopt the child has been interviewed by or on behalf of the adoption panel;

(*d*) the agency has made an assessment of the personality of the person proposing to adopt the child and of that person's attitudes to matters which would have a bearing on the person's suitability to bring up that child;

(*e*) the agency has endeavoured to ascertain, where the persons proposing to adopt are a married couple, the state of the marriage, and, in particular, whether it has the stability which is likely to provide a sound basis for a secure parental relationship with an adopted child;

(*f*) an inspection has been made, on behalf of the agency, of any premises in Great Britain in which the person proposing to adopt the child intends that the child shall have his home;

(*g*) the agency has made enquiries to satisfy itself that there is no reason to believe that it would be detrimental to the child to be kept by that person in those premises. Where the agency is an approved adoption agency, the agency should make enquiries of the local authority in whose area those premises are situated so that that authority may properly inform the adoption agency that it has no reason to believe that the proposed adoption would be detrimental to the child;

(*h*) the adoption panel, in reaching a decision, has ascertained as far as practicable the wishes and feelings of the child regarding the decision and has given due consideration to them having regard to his age and understanding, and, after considering all the information obtained in pursuance of this regulation and having regard to all the circumstances (including, as far as is practicable, any wishes of the child's parents or guardian as to the religious upbringing of the child), first consideration being given to the need to safeguard and promote the welfare of the child throughout his childhood, has approved of the child being so placed.

Question

Who do *you* think would be more suitable to bring up a little girl of two, recently released for adoption by her mother, who had found it impossible to cater for either her physical or her psychological needs: (*a*) a childless couple in their 30s, who have turned to adoption in desperation after unsuccessful attempts to cure the wife's infertility, or (*b*) a couple in their 40s whose own three children are now aged 18, 15 and 10 and who have been acting as short-term foster parents but would prefer a permanent placement?

The increasing professionalism of adoption societies led to an increasing concern about the private placement of children for adoption, discussed in the *Report of the Departmental Committee on the Adoption of Children* (the 'Houghton Report') in 1972:

82. The statistical survey carried out in 1966 (Grey, 1971) covered a sample of some 3,400 adoption applications made in that year to 138 courts in Great Britain. These adoptions were arranged as follows:

	Per Cent	Per Cent
Adoptions arranged by voluntary societies . .	40	
Adoptions arranged by local authorities	19	
Total of agency adoptions		59
Adoptions by parents	29	
Direct placements with relatives	5	
Direct placements with non-relatives	3	
Adoptions arranged by third parties	4	
Total of independent adoptions		41
		100

83. The Hurst Committee estimated that in 1954 more than one-third of non-relative adoptions resulted from placements by third parties or by the natural parents. The 1966 survey figures given above show that the proportion was then very much less. Nevertheless there were some 1,500 children a year placed in this way. There are a number of reasons why people make independent arrangements without using agency services. One is the inaccessibility of agencies in some areas, which our recommendations [on p. 495, below] are designed to remedy. Others are people's dislike of the idea of enquiries by an agency, a desire to keep control of the situation themselves, or their trust in a person known to them, such as their family doctor. Some would-be adopters have been turned down by agencies, and others may seek independent placements because they realise that no adoption agency would consider them suitable.

84. Much concern has been expressed about these placements. The decision to place a child with a particular couple is the most important stage in the adoption process. Adoption law must give assurance of adequate safeguards for the welfare of the child at this stage, otherwise it is ineffective. This assurance rests mainly upon the skilled work of the adoption services, which includes preparation for adoptive parenthood. An independent adoption is one in which this assurance is lacking. We therefore suggested in our working paper that independent placements with non-relatives should no longer be allowed.

85. The evidence we received was divided. The main arguments against our proposal were that it was an interference with individual liberty, particularly in the case of direct placements by the mother; that there was no research evidence to prove that independent placements were any worse than agency placements, and that they should not be banned until agency work had improved; and that the investigation by the guardian ad litem and a court hearing were sufficient safeguards against adoption orders being made in respect of unsuitable placements.

86. Virtually no recent research has been done to compare the outcome of independent placements with that of agency placements, but there is no lack of evidence of unsatisfactory independent placements. Information received from the Church of England Board for Social Responsibility, which has contact with agencies working with unmarried mothers, revealed that in the course of a year a considerable number of highly unsatisfactory independent placements came to the notice of the social workers. Local authorities with experience of acting as guardians ad litem or carrying out welfare supervision of children placed for adoption have come across unsatisfactory independent placements which would not have been made by a reputable

adoption agency. This is confirmed by the written and oral evidence we have received and by the personal experience of some of our members.

87. . . . The greater imbalance between the numbers of couples wishing to adopt and the number of babies needing adoption could lead to an increase in third party activity in future. We have received no direct evidence of financial transactions in third party placements, but it is within the knowledge of some of our members that couples have alleged that they have paid an inflated fee for the investigation of infertility on the understanding that a child would be found for them to adopt, and that mothers have alleged that services, such as nursing home facilities, have been provided on the understanding that the child would be available for adoption.

88. Adoption is a matter of such vital importance to a child (who is usually too young to have any say in the matter) that society has a duty to ensure that the most satisfactory placements are made. Society manifestly does not do so while it is open to anybody to place a child for adoption. While the court hearing is intended as a final safeguard, safeguards are needed much earlier. Moreover courts are in difficulty about refusing to make an adoption order because there is no agency to which the child can be returned. Adoption agencies are increasingly staffed by social workers whose professional skills and knowledge are increasing. Agency practice has built-in safeguards through the Adoption Agencies Regulations and through general account-ability to the public. We therefore adhere to the view expressed in our working paper that independent placements should not be allowed once the new registration system for adoption agencies is in force, when these safeguards will be even greater. We include in this proposal direct placements by the parents, although, if they wished a particular placement to be made, the agency arranging the adoption should give this sympathetic consideration.

Questions

(i) What is so wrong about paying an unmarried mother to let you have her baby?

(ii) Can it be distinguished from paying a doctor to inseminate you with the semen of an unknown donor?

(iii) Or paying a woman to bear your child? (see p. 334, above).

(iv) Wait a moment — is not that what husbands do?

In *Growing Up Adopted* (1972), Jean Seglow, Mia Kellmer Pringle and Peter Wedge report upon a follow-up study of all the children born in a single week in 1958 who were adopted by non-parents: they were studied at birth, then again at seven, and further enquiries were made of their adoptive parents in 1967 and 1971. The lives of these children were subsequently compared with those of legitimate children and of illegitimate children who remained with their mothers, in *Children in Changing Families* (1980) by Lydia Lambert and Jane Streather, to which reference has already been made in Chapter 9. As Jane Rowe states in her foreword to the earlier book (1972):

The outstanding fact to emerge from this careful study is the power of the environment to affect children's development for good or ill. The adopted children are shown to have enjoyed a more favourable environment than the much larger group of illegitimate children who remained with their natural mothers. The illegitimate children were found to be vulnerable at birth. By the age of 7 years, the care, affection and material advantages provided by their new parents had enabled the adopted children to overcome their earlier handicaps and to compare very favour-ably with their peers in the general population. . . .

[Nevertheless] no-one reading this book carefully could spring to the conclusion that adoption is an easy solution to the problems of illegitimacy or childlessness. Not all the placements were happy and successful. Some of the agencies' work was evidently poor. Adoption is shown to have its own built in stresses. Many of the cherished theories of agency policy are once more challenged by the findings that factors such as age, health, social class and family composition are rather unimportant, while the authors demonstrate over and over again the importance of such intangible factors as attitudes, feelings and expectations.

Mia Kellmer Pringle takes up this last point in her concluding chapter:

... A recent 'Evaluation of adoption policy and practice' (Triseliotis, 1970) presents a depressing and alarming picture. 'To a large extent the general approach to the work was amateurish and aimed only at meeting legal and administrative requirements. . . . Many aspects of the practice . . . were a negation of basic social work principles . . . similarly, there was lack of conviction about the basic concepts of child welfare, such as the beneficial effect of environmental influences and the reversibility of certain experiences. In spite of reassurances in social work literature and in official documents that adoption is now practised mainly in the interests of the child, the study came across considerable evidence that . . . they were largely adoptive-parent orientated and seldom child-centred. . . . The work with natural parents, the child and adopters, bore little relation to the standards recommended by the social work profession.'

The author concluded that 'the greatest challenge facing adoption practice is the need for a change of those attitudes based on pre-conceived or out-dated beliefs and prejudices, and a shift away from amateurism and traditionalism so that adoption work may be brought into line with modern concepts of child welfare. Traditional attitudes, reflecting the desire to place "perfect babies", or match by socio-economic background, die hard, but the emerging need is for new policies and attitudes that can promote the needs of "hard-to-place children". . . .'

One of the greatest advantages of agency placement might be thought by lay people to be the enhanced opportunities it provides for suiting the child to the particular adopters, but Pringle has this to say:

'Matching' for similarities in physical appearance, temperament, intelligence, etc., is yet another myth which needs to be abandoned for a number of reasons. Being led to expect similarities between their adopted children and themselves, adoptive parents will feel cheated and justifiably resentful if their expectations are subsequently not fulfilled. Also, the younger the baby the more impractical it is to ensure any measure of success. Moreover, it increases the risk of playing into the hands of those adoptive parents who want to deny the reality of adoption.

But perhaps most important of all 'none of the evidence showed matching to be a favourable factor. The only associations, in fact, were in the opposite direction. Families in the "very high" match group on physical resemblance and ethnic background had more children in the problem groups at follow-up, and those in the "very low" match group had fewer children showing problems' (Ripple, 1968). In matching for intelligence it has been shown that children with a very unpromising background who are placed into adoptive homes of a much superior level tend to develop intellectual abilities more closely in keeping with those of their adoptive parents.

Perhaps, therefore, it is not surprising that in discussing the overall results of the study, Peter Wedge reports:

Agency versus private placement
Privately placed children accounted for some 21% of our sample. The remainder were placed by recognized adoption agencies. The former group of children did not differ significantly from children placed by an agency when their overall assessment of success in adoption was considered. The importance of this is not only that private placements seemed to be no less successful than agency placements, but that agency placements were no more successful than private placements. One would have expected that, where children were placed by agencies (presumably using specialist staff), then those children would have a more successful outcome than children placed privately, and so relatively haphazardly. If the practice of private placements justifies the criticism that has been frequently levelled at it, then now how necessary is it that the whole standard of adoption work among agencies should be raised above the level implied by this finding? Rather than banning independent arrangements, the first step must surely be to improve the alternative. . . .

In any event, it could well be that the prevalence of private placements is to a considerable extent dependent upon the effort made by other agencies in a particular locality. It would seem that where a local authority made real efforts to ensure that their own and other agencies' services were known, there were fewer private placements (Goodacre, 1966).

Nevertheless, the provision (which will become s. 11 of the Adoption Act 1976[3]) making most private placement a criminal offence came into force in

---

3. References have throughout been given to the consolidating Adoption Act 1976 although this will not be in force until all the changes made by the Children Act 1975 have been implemented.

February 1982. Sections 1 and 2, which are designed to provide a comprehensive agency service, have not yet been implemented. The latter result from the following recommendations of the *Houghton Report*:

33. . . . Over Great Britain as a whole, local authorities have made no systematic attempt to assess the needs of their areas and to develop services accordingly, and we have been told of areas which are ill-served. Moreover, where local authorities do provide a service, not all have integrated their adoption work with their other services for children and families.
34. These factors influence considerably the kinds of people, whether children, natural parents or prospective adopters, to whom a service is available and the quality of the service which is offered. What is needed is a service which is comprehensive in scope and available throughout the country.

The objectives and organisation of a comprehensive service
35. The service must meet the needs of children, persons wishing to adopt and natural parents. Local authority social services departments and voluntary organisations with a range of services for children should be able to offer a better and more comprehensive service for children than purely placement agencies, since they have a wider range of resources. This is particularly important where children with special needs are concerned . . . where more time is needed to find suitable homes, as well as good assessment facilities and highly developed casework skills.
36. If adoption is a child-centred service, aimed at providing homes for children, the service which an agency will offer to couples wishing to adopt will be ancillary to this central aim. . . .
38. What then should a comprehensive service cover? We consider that it should comprise a social work service to natural parents, whether married or unmarried, seeking placement for a child (which would include channels of communication with related community resources); skills and facilities for the assessment of the parents' emotional resources, and their personal and social situation; short-term accommodation for unsupported mothers; general child care resources, including short-term placement facilities for children pending adoption placement; assessment facilities; adoption placement services; after-care for natural parents who need it; counselling for adoptive families. In addition, it should have access to a range of specialised services, such as medical services (including genetic, psychiatric and psychological assessment services, arrangements for the examination of children and adoptive applicants, and a medical adviser) and legal advisory services.
. . . .
42. In order to ensure the provision of a service of the kind we have described, available to all those needing it in any part of the country, we propose that new responsibilities should be placed on local authorities. In the first place, local authorities should have a statutory duty to provide an adoption service as part of their general child care and family casework provision. A local authority social service cannot be considered comprehensive if adoption is not included. In the second place, it should be the duty of the local authority to ensure that a comprehensive service is available throughout their area. This will require an assessment, in co-operation with voluntary societies, of the needs of the area and of the resources available to meet them, and a co-ordinated plan for the provision of the service. In setting up their own service, the authority would take into account the services provided by voluntary agencies.

A precondition of this would be the transfer of the function of approving voluntary agencies from local to central government (ss. 3 to 5 and 8 to 10, which are in force) and to improve their standards. Improved standards in agencies would permit the rationalisation of two other social work functions in the adoption process (ss. 13, 22, 23 and 65, not yet in force):

Welfare supervision
237. We are in no doubt about the need for a settling-in period, and a period of supervision and help. This was introduced in 1949 and its value is well established. The Guide to Adoption Practice describes the aim of welfare supervision as being 'to offer a supporting service to adopters, help them to focus on the essential task of integrating the child into their family life, and look forward confidently to the future. The welfare supervisor . . . should concentrate on the particular needs of this period: the adoptive parents' pre-occupation with the physical care of the child, their adaptation to new family roles and changed relationships'. We are convinced that this kind of help can best be offered by the agency responsible for choosing the adoptive home and placing the child. The agency is in the best position to help the couple to adapt to their new role and to deal with any problems they may have. . . .

238. . . . We recommend therefore that in agency cases, once the new registration procedure is in force, welfare supervision by the local authority should not be required and the statutory responsibility for supervising the child in the adoptive home should rest with the placing agency throughout the period between the placement and the court hearing. The capacity of an agency to undertake this work would be among the factors considered when an agency applied for registration.

Information to the court
244. . . . We consider that the law ought to recognise the decisive part played by the agency in arranging the adoption by making the agency accountable to the court. The court will have to make judgments on assessments and decisions made by the agency. It ought to have a first hand account of them and the opportunity to question the agency about them. The agency should therefore make a comprehensive report to the court and should have the opportunity of explaining to the court the reasons for that particular placement.

The guardian ad litem — the present position
245. The present law requires the court to appoint a guardian ad litem in all adoption applications. The appointment is made soon after the adoption application has been lodged with the court. The guardian's primary duty is to safeguard the interests of the child before the court. In addition he has to investigate all circumstances relevant to the proposed adoption. This includes verifying the statements contained in the application, ascertaining that consents have been freely given, and helping to ensure that anyone who has a right to be heard has the opportunity. His duties are set out in considerable detail in the Court Rules in England and Wales and by Act of Sederunt in Scotland. His enquiries have to cover a number of matters of fact, as well as more intangible aspects of personality and understanding, to enable him to make an assessment as to whether adoption would be for the child's welfare.
. . . .
252. Our conclusion is that . . . the appointment of the guardian should be at the discretion of the court. Courts might regard some types of adoption application as requiring the automatic appointment of a guardian, for instance, where there is an application to dispense with consent. Agencies may often be able to advise the court about cases which might warrant the appointment of a guardian, thus reducing the risk of delay.
253. Where the court decides to appoint a guardian, it would be helpful if it would indicate the aspects of the case which give rise to concern or uncertainty and in respect of which it particularly needs help. We think it should be a matter of good practice for the guardian to make his enquiries of the agency or local authority in the first instance, so as to avoid unnecessary duplication of enquiries and to acquire an understanding of the background of the case.

Question

The Tomlin Committee thought a guardian ad litem essential so that there should be a real adjudication (see pp. 489–490, above): yet as judges almost invariably follow the guardian's advice, does it matter whether the court is advised by the agency or an independent person?

Behind these changes in policy and practice, however, lies a much more fundamental change in attitudes towards adoption, explained thus by Tizard in *Adoption: A Second Chance* (1977):

The fall in 'non-parent' adoptions since 1968 no doubt reflects the decline in the number of illegitimate births that took place during the period following the passing of the Abortion Act of 1968 — while the illegitimacy rate remained constant, the absolute number of illegitimate births fell by 10,000 between 1968 and 1973. It may also reflect the increased financial assistance available for single parents, and the widespread change of social attitudes, so that it is not only financially but also socially easier for the unmarried mother to bring up her child.
    The present 'famine' of babies must also represent an increase in the number of couples wanting to adopt. Unfortunately this figure is not anywhere available, but since the number of babies adopted by persons other than a parent was actually higher in 1973 than in 1958 it is clear that there is no shortage of babies by pre-1960s standards. . . . A much larger sector of society began to see adoption as an acceptable solution to infertility, or as an acceptable way of adding to their family. . . . For the first time, would be adoptive couples are faced with the choice of either waiting for years, often without success, for a healthy white infant, or adopting an infant with a physical or mental disability, whose mother feels unable to accept it, or a child well past infancy, often of a different race.

This situation is leading to a changing conception of adoption in our society. Since the twenties adoption had been seen primarily as a service for childless couples — a way of providing them with a substitute child to satisfy their emotional needs and cement their marriage.

The essence of the new view of adoption is that it is a form of child care, one among several possible ways of rearing children whose parents can't, or won't, look after them. At first sight this change in emphasis may seem to be only a verbal distinction, since adoption must necessarily provide a service to both adoptive parent and homeless child. The implications of the two viewpoints are, however, very different — different couples and different children are considered suitable for adoption, depending on whether adoption is seen primarily as a cure for infertility or as a form of care. According to the first viewpoint, which until recently prevailed, only infertile couples would be offered a child. Prolonged investigations into infertility were the rule, because it was assumed that if the couple subsequently had a child of their own they would reject the adopted child. The health, racial origins and family history of the infant were closely examined, because it would not be 'fair' to place with the couple a child dissimilar to the healthy infant who under optimal circumstances might have been born to them. Only healthy infants with a 'good' family history were offered.

Much social work went into 'matching' the physical characteristics and family background of the child and adoptive couple, with the object of ensuring that the adopted child could be assimilated into his new family as completely as possible. . . .

For the same reason only infants were offered for adoption, so as to approximate as closely as possible to the normal way of acquiring children. Because of the emphasis on meeting the needs of the parents, children with any visible imperfections or whose family history contained evidence of any abnormality were not considered suitable for adoption.

If, however, adoption is seen primarily as a way of providing care for a child outside his natural family, then any child in need can be considered for adoption, whatever his colour, family history, state of health or age. Adoptive parents for these children are selected not for their infertility but because of evidence (often from the rearing of their own children, or from the kind of work they have done) that they are likely to provide a loving, stable home for a child in need.

Question

What do you think makes it possible for one person to love and care for another person's child as if he were her own? Are you in any way surprised that it is possible? Why do you think that English policy-makers have found it so surprising until so very recently?

This 'child-centred' view of adoption is enshrined in the following section of the *Adoption Act 1976*:

6. Duty to promote welfare of child
In reaching any decision relating to the adoption of a child a court or adoption agency shall have regard to all the circumstances, first consideration being given to the need to safeguard and promote the welfare of the child throughout his childhood; and shall so far as practicable ascertain the wishes and feelings of the child regarding the decision and give due consideration to them, having regard to his age and understanding.

5 A legal transplant?

The next step after the first cautious moves in 1926 is described by Heywood in *Children in Care* (1978) thus:

The policy reflected in legislation for adoption . . . has moved on from providing legal *status*, for those who lacked this, to providing a legal *relationship* between adopted child and adopters as similar as possible to that which exists between a child and his natural parents. This principle was expressed in the Adoption of Children Act 1949, introduced as a private members' bill by Sir Basil Nield. The Act took great care to see, particularly by the safeguarding of consents, that the divestment of the natural family, and particularly the mother, should not be lightly undertaken, but that, where it was, the integration of the child with his new family should be complete and natural.

This was seen in the now compulsory provision of three months' supervision by the welfare authority of the placing immediately before the adoption order is made; by the fact that adopter and adopted child are now deemed to be within the prohibited degrees of consanguinity; that an adopted child can inherit as a member of his adoptive family and not of his natural family in case of intestacy (except in Scotland); and that application for an adoption order can now be made without the natural parents knowing the adopters' identity. . . .

The process was still not complete, as the *Houghton Report* (1972) explains:

Interpretation of wills and other instruments

326. The present law provides that for the purposes of inheritance (in Scotland, succession) and of the interpretation of dispositions made after an adoption order, an adopted person shall be treated as if he is a child born to the adopter in lawful wedlock and not the child of any other person. This means that an adopted child has the same rights on an intestacy occurring after the adoption order as a child born to the adopter in wedlock. In England and Wales an adopted person does not, however, benefit under a general gift to, say, grandchildren of the testator, where the disposition was made before the date of the adoption order unless it can be construed to include adopted children as such. (A will for this purpose is treated as having been made on the date of the death of the testator and not on the date the will was actually made.) For example, a man might leave part of his estate on trust to his wife for life, to be divided on her death among his grandchildren. A natural grandchild born after his death would benefit under this will, but a grandchild by adoption would not.

327. If adoption means the complete severance of the legal relationship between the child and his natural parents and the establishment of a new and irrevocable relationship, designed to make the child a full member of another family, it follows that that child should have exactly the same rights under wills and other instruments as a natural child of the adoptive family. We proposed that this should be the case and none of the evidence dissented from our proposition. It was pointed out to us that the passing of the Family Law Reform Act 1969 had placed illegitimate children in England and Wales in a better position than adopted children by providing, in section 15, that an illegitimate child may take under any disposition made after the Act came into force whether he was born before or after the disposition.

These recommendations were implemented in the Children Act 1975, so that there are now only three important exceptions to the principle that an adopted child is the same as a legitimately born child: he cannot succeed to peerages and similar dignities; the rules prohibiting marriages with certain relatives in his birth family remain and he is only debarred from marriage with his adoptive parent in the new family; and if he is adopted abroad he will not gain the same rights under nationality and immigration laws as would a child born abroad to United Kingdom parents or adopted here. Nevertheless, after the wholesale legal transplant, there remains the human problem which has received so much anxious attention in the context of long-term fostering. The following quotations come from the adopted adults who had sought their original birth certificates, as then permitted under Scottish but not English law, interviewed by John Triseliotis for his study of those *In Search of Origins* (1973):

'You look at yourself in the mirror and you can't compare it with anybody. You're a stranger because you don't know what your real mother looks like or what your father looks like. . . .'

'All through my life I had the feeling of unreality about myself; a feeling of not being real, something like an imitation antique . . . I have been told that I was born in the Poor House and that my birth mother was a bad lot. This has been haunting me. I tried desperately to avoid being like her but then who am I like? I feel I have nothing to pass on to my children. . . .'

'My parents were kind people but very isolated. We had few relatives calling and we had no habit of calling on others. My parents' relatives meant nothing to me and I must have meant nothing to them. . . . When I was 15 or 16 I was very curious to know "who I was" and especially to know about my natural parents and their families. With your adoptive family you can only go as far back as they are and not beyond. But with your natural ones you feel you want to go further back. . . .'

The *Houghton Report* summarised the results of his study and the arguments thus:

301. . . . . It seems that where an adopted person has been told of his adoption at an early age and his relationship with his adopters is good he is less likely to seek access to his original birth record. Two-thirds of those in the sample who sought this information came to know about their adoption when they were 11 or more years old, half of them being 16 or over and one as old as 40. Only two-fifths of those who applied had been told of their adoption by their adoptive parents, the others finding out by discovering documents or letters or from chance remarks by people outside the family, mainly other children. For many of them the late disclosure of their adoption came as a shock, and they had difficulty in coming to terms with it. It was also noticeable that two out of every five who sought this information had lost one or both adoptive parents by death, separation or divorce before they reached the age of 16, and in one-third of all the applications it was the death of an adoptive parent that triggered off the search for information about the natural parents. Two-thirds of those who sought this information had the immediate reaction that it was helpful or of some help to them, while one-third felt very upset by the information they had obtained. Some were unhappy to discover that they were illegitimate, while the few who were legitimate were equally sad to think that their parents, although married, had 'given them away'. When seen four months later, however, nine out of ten had no regrets about having taken steps to find out this information.

302. The other evidence we received was divided. . . . Some witnesses urged that the right of an adult adopted person to know the names of his natural parents was a basic human right. Others were concerned about the distress which might be caused as a result of widespread attempts by adopted children to seek out their original parents. The Scottish research showed that although 42 adopted persons, or 60% of the sample, sought to trace their natural parents, only four succeeded in doing so, although seven others were able to contact blood relations. The Deputy Registrar General for Scotland said that he could not recall any complaint made by natural relatives who had been traced through the Registrar General's records. The fear of being traced may therefore have been unduly magnified, particularly as all the indications are that the climate of opinion is changing and mothers are becoming less concerned to conceal the fact that they have had an illegitimate child. Research into the views of a sample of adoptive parents revealed that 63% considered that their adoptive children should be allowed free access to their original records.

303. The weight of the evidence as a whole was in favour of freer access to background information, and this accords with our wish to encourage greater openness about adoption. . . . We therefore recommend that all adopted adults in England and Wales, whenever adopted, should in future be permitted to obtain a copy of their original birth entry.

This probably provoked more public debate and controversy than all the other recommendations in the report. For example, on 10 October 1976, the *News of the World* declared:

Thousands of women are facing the fear that a secret shadow from the past may soon knock at their door and wreck their marriages. They are the mothers who have never told their husbands and their families that they had an illegitimate baby whom they gave for adoption.

Question

Whose needs do you think should be put first? Those of the adopted person or those of the birth parent and her present family?

As a compromise, all those adopted before 12 November 1975, when the Children Act 1975 was passed, were obliged to accept counselling before gaining access to their original birth certificate. In *Access to Birth Records* (1979), Cyril Day reports the generally reassuring results of his study of the first 500 interviews carried out at the General Register Office, for example:

9. There was compassionate understanding of the situation of the natural mother, both at the time of parting with her child, and as affected now by the retrospective legislation.

10. One reason for making application seemed to be the need, often long felt, to establish or complete a sense of true self-identity. This was assessed as the prime reason for 317 applicants. . . . Another 84 . . . appeared to be motivated by curiosity.
11. Locating a natural parent or relative was assessed as the prime reason in 46 cases. . . .
13. . . . 140 stated that they intended to try to trace a natural parent, 193 said they did not intend to trace and 167, at the time of interview, had reservations about seeking to arrange a face to face meeting. . . .
16. Applicants with an unhappy adoptive experience were much more likely to trace. 49 of the 113 with adverse factors intended to trace. . . .
18. Where the applicant intended to trace and meet a natural parent the possibility of precipitate, unwise or vindictive tracing gave counsellors 'cause for concern' in only 18 cases. . . .
22. Applicants felt that more 'openness' was needed in adoption. They thought that the new legislation would help to remove the secrecy, and even stigma, with which the subject had been clouded. . . .

However, one conclusion, which is similar to the Triseliotis findings, should give 'cause for concern':

6. Counselling experience has revealed that relatively few of those seen, less than 30%, had been well and helpfully told of their status by their adopters. Many had been inadequately informed, some not at all.

The *Adoption Agencies Regulations 1976* now provide:

14.—(1) The adoption agency shall, at the time the child is placed for adoption, provide the persons proposing to adopt the child with —
    (a) written information about the child's background, parentage, physical, mental and emotional development; and
    (b) a memorandum advising the adopters of the need to tell the child about his adoption and origins, and of the right of the child, on attaining the age of 18 in England and Wales or 17 in Scotland, to obtain a copy of his birth record, and of the provision of a counselling service for such adopted persons; and offering a counselling service on any problems relating to the adoption.

Questions

(i) Can you remember the period in your life when you dreamed that your real parents were not those who had brought you up, but royalty, media stars or the like?

(ii) If you had been adopted, would it have helped to know before or after that time?

(iii) Would you have instantly realised that if you were adopted, the likelihood was that your birth parents were unmarried?

(iv) If there is a stigma still attached to adoption, is it attached to the non-blood relationship as such or to the previous likely illegitimacy?

However, the more the 'total transplant' view of adoption took hold in law and practice, the more disquiet was felt about adoptions where this could not be achieved. On one category of these, the *Houghton Report* (1972) had little doubt:

97. . . . Adoption by relatives severs in law, but not in fact, an existing relationship of blood or of affinity, and creates an adoptive relationship in place of the natural relationship which in fact, though not in law, continues unchanged. In most cases the adopting relatives are already caring for the child and will continue to do so whether or not they adopt him; and adoption by relatives can be particularly harmful when it is used to conceal the natural relationship.

Yet even here, courts may see advantages which no order for legal custody (which is at present only available as a by-product of proceedings between the child's parents) could bring:

Re W (a minor) (adoption by grandparents)
(1980) 2 FLR 161, 10 Fam Law 190, Court of Appeal

The applicants appealed against the judge's refusal of an adoption order.

Ormrod LJ: This is a very unusual adoption case. It is an application by grandparents, now in their middle 60s, to adopt a grandchild, a boy aged 7, of whom they have had custody under the divorce proceedings which took place some years ago between the father and mother of this child — the mother being the daughter of the proposed adopters. She, the mother, has virtually disappeared out of their lives altogether. Nothing is known about her way of life, although she has signed the consent to the adoption and was eventually seen by the guardian ad litem and raised no objection. The father is a very undesirable person with a bad criminal record who has behaved wholly irresponsibly throughout this child's life, so all responsibility for the child has fallen on the grandparents.

The learned judge at the end of his judgment indicated that, had he thought that an adoption order was in the best interests of this little boy, he would have had no hesitation in dispensing with the father's consent as unreasonably withheld. Curiously, the learned judge decided that adoption was not in the best interests of this little boy. Having shortly set out the facts, he said this:

'The boy is being looked after admirably. I cannot see that the boy will be any better off if the custody order is turned into an adoption order. No one can see into the future. Anything may happen. Only one thing is certain; the grandparents are ageing. Variation of the custody order can be made from time to time. It may be that it will be wished to test this decision elsewhere. I encourage such a view. The main point is the disparity of age.'

Then he made it clear that he was refusing an adoption order purely on the basis that it was not in the child's best interests.

The grandfather in his affidavit sets out at length the reasons which led him and his wife to apply for this adoption order, although he did not actually in terms refer to what is clearly the most important aspect of the case, namely, the high desirability that they, as the persons responsible for this child, should be in a position after their deaths to make sensible provision for his care. In other words, they want to be in a position to appoint a testamentary guardian, which under a custody order they cannot do, but can under an adoption order.

The learned judge's suggestion that there could be a further application as to custody in divorce proceedings seems to be an extremely unsatisfactory, speculative and uncertain way of dealing with the future of a child of seven. Who is going to make the application? It would mean another intervention by an aunt or uncle or someone else. With respect to the learned judge, I do not think he can have realized the necessity that the grandparents, because they are ageing, should be in a position to control, so far as it is in their power, the future of this little boy. It is obviously in his interests that the future should be settled as far as possible now and should not be left to chance if the grandparents should die or become disabled.

In my judgment the learned judge did not grasp the essential point of the case. This court is therefore entitled to override the exercise of his discretion in the circumstances of this case. It is not very often that we can do so, but, having made it perfectly clear that he would not hesitate to dispense with the consent of the father, I think we should dispense with that consent, relying on the view of the learned judge, and make the adoption order. Plainly that is in the best interests of this child.

There is another group where similar problems might arise, and where the courts might also take a different view from that traditionally taken by social workers:

Re B (MF) (An Infant) Re D (SL) (An Infant)
[1972] 1 All ER 898, [1972] 1 WLR 102, Court of Appeal

Two brothers, then aged four and one, were removed from their parents as being in need of care. They were fostered with the appellants, with whom they 'made great strides' and were 'undoubtedly happy and extremely well cared for.' Their natural parents' home was 'nothing like as satisfactory,' they had three other young children and were in 'constant financial difficulties,' partly because of the father's psychiatric difficulties. After three years, the foster parents applied to adopt the boys and the natural parents both consented, but the county court judge refused to make the order. The foster parents appealed.

Salmon LJ: . . . The learned judge, in the exercise of his discretion, refused to make the order. Why he did so is not at all clear to me and certainly does not appear from his judgment or from the notes that he made of the proceedings before him.

I have assumed that he founded himself on the county council's report. Apparently the view which the county council take is that it would be better for the status quo to be preserved, that is to say for the children to remain as foster children with the appellants. It would have the advantage, so the county council think, of keeping the position fluid. There is no doubt that the position would remain fluid, but I am by no means persuaded that that fluidity could conceivably be in the interests of the children. Once an adoption order is made, then the children's position vis-à-vis the appellants is assured. The appellants would have the same legal obligation to the children as if they were their own natural children. I am not suggesting for a moment that they would not in any event continue to treat the children with the same affection and take the same interest in them and accept the same responsibility for them as they do now; and, of course, I know that the county council has no present intention of taking the children away from them. But the appellants feel — and indeed they feel rightly — that just as the children would have no legal rights against them unless an adoption order is made, so they would have no legal right to keep the children should the county council, in their wisdom, decide to remove the children in the future. I would have thought the insecurity which they not unnaturally feel would be just as unsatisfactory from the point of view of their relations with the children as it would be unsatisfactory for the children to have no security and no legal rights as against their adopters.

The only other point that I should deal with is the fact that the appellants take the view that Mr and Mrs D, for whom they have much sympathy, should from time to time visit the children, and particularly that these two boys should be kept in touch with their sister Pauline. It is quite true that in law Pauline will cease to be their sister after the adoption order is made, but Pauline will remain their natural sister and no order of any court can alter that fact.

As a rule, it is highly undesirable that after an adoption order is made there should be any contact between the child or children and their natural parents. This is the view which has been taken, and rightly taken, by adoption societies and local authorities as it has been by the courts in dealing with questions of adoption. There is, however, no hard and fast rule that if there is an adoption it can only be on the terms that there should be a complete divorce of the children from their natural parents. I refer to the case of *Re G (DM) (An Infant)* [1962] 2 All ER 546, [1962] 1 WLR 730, which in effect followed the dictum of Vaisey J in *Re A B (An Infant)* [1949] 1 All ER 709 at 710. Although the courts will pay great attention to the general principle to which I have referred, namely, that it is desirable in normal circumstances for there to be a complete break, each case has to be considered on its own particular facts.

The facts of this case are exceptional. Although it may be — I know not — that it would be a good plan if there were a complete break here between Mr and Mrs D and the two boys, the appellants (who I suspect know a good deal more about the situation than I do) consider that the occasional encounters between Mr and Mrs D and the boys and Pauline [are] for their good.

It is suggested that in the future the fact that the boys know the appellants as 'Mummy' and 'Daddy' and their parents as 'Daddy D' and 'Mummy D' may lead to stresses and strains. Mr and Mrs D are not prepared to have these children back. It is all they can do to cope with the three young ones they have at home now, and without any disrespect to Mr and Mrs D, through circumstances over which they have no control, it is obvious that it would be very much more in the interests of the two boys to stay where they have been so well cared for during the last three years.
Appeal allowed.

Questions

(i) Are the facts of this case indeed so exceptional?

(ii) Do you think that the Court of Appeal did the right thing?

(iii) If you do, how would your view be affected if the parents had refused to agree to the adoption, not because they wanted their children back, but because they wanted the right to go on seeing them?

(iv) Now compare your view on that last question with the material at pp. 508–513, below.

One last aspect of the blurring of distinctions between fostering and adoption is the implementation in 1982 of the following recommendation of the *Houghton Report* (1972):

Should adoption be subsidised?
93. We suggested in our working paper that consideration should be given to the possibility of guardians and adopters being paid regular subsidies in appropriate cases, and we said that we would welcome views on this. While there was considerable support for allowances for guardians . . ., many witnesses saw a clear distinction between adoption and guardianship and opposed the idea of any payments to adopters. Some took the view that payment would conflict with the principle that adoption should put the child in precisely the same position as a child born to the adopters. While some agreed with our suggestion that, if allowances were payable, more homes might be found for children with special needs, others said that it would be unfair to the parents of handicapped children if the adopters of these children could get an allowance which was not available to their natural parents. Some said that the law should not forbid agency payments to adopters but that there should be no national system of allowances.
94. We recognise the objection to singling out handicapped adopted children for special payments, and we do not advocate payments for adopters generally. However, we still think that there is a case for allowances in some circumstances, for example, where suitable adopters are available for a family of children who need to be kept together but, for financial reasons, adoption is not possible if an allowance cannot be paid. Although most witnesses were opposed to our suggestion, we should like to see a period of experiment during which evidence could be gathered. But at present even experiment is not possible, because it would contravene the law, and we recommend that the law should be amended so as to enable payments to be made by a few charitable bodies specially authorised by the Secretary of State for this purpose. There may be a number of difficulties, and we suggest pilot schemes which could be reviewed after, say, seven years, although the subsidy would have to be continued to those who had adopted on that basis for as long as they needed it.

Question

How many views about the 'deservingness' of foster parents are coloured by the fact that they receive an allowance, however inadequate, for their pains?

6 The parents' wishes and the child's best interests

At the heart of most of the dilemmas discussed in this chapter lies the weight to be given to the parents' wishes. As we have seen, the Tomlin Committee treated adoption as a 'transaction' between natural and adoptive parents, in which the court's task was to ensure that the private agreement did not prejudice the welfare of the child. Later developments placed more and more emphasis on the need for expert intermediaries who must now arrange and supervise the placement. Parents who want their child to be adopted can no longer choose who should have him; they cannot complain if they do not know his new parents' name; the only preference which agencies have any duty to respect is as to their religion (Adoption Act 1976, s. 7) — and why, indeed, should a minority practice be given even this degree of recognition when other preferences which could be just as important to some parents are given none?

Conversely, the Tomlin Committee assumed that parental consent would be required unless the parent had 'disappeared, abandoned the child, or become incapacitated from giving such consent.' Over the years, the circumstances in which the court has been empowered to grant an adoption without the parent's consent have varied. The present list is in s. 16 of the *Adoption Act 1976*:

16 (2) . . . that the parent or guardian —

(*a*) cannot be found or is incapable of giving agreement;

(*b*) is withholding his agreement unreasonably;

(*c*) has persistently failed without reasonable cause to discharge the parental duties in relation to the child;

(*d*) has abandoned or neglected the child;

(*e*) has persistently ill-treated the child;

(*f*) has seriously ill-treated the child (subject to subsection (5)).

. . .

(5) Subsection (2)(*f*) does not apply unless (because of the ill-treatment or for other reasons) the rehabilitation of the child within the household of the parent or guardian is unlikely.

Question

Compare these grounds with those for the less drastic deprivation of parental rights involved (*a*) in assuming parental rights by resolution under s. 3 of the Child Care Act 1980 (see p. 442, above) and (*b*) in making a care order under s. 1 of the Children and Young Persons Act 1969 (see p. 559, below). Do these grounds appear to you to be wider or narrower than either of those? Do the differences seem, at least at first sight, to be justified by the different circumstances in which the procedures are used?

In practice, dispensing with parental agreement to an adoption order arises in two quite different contexts: first, the parent who places her child for adoption and later changes her mind, and second, the parent who has never agreed to adoption.

(a) THE PARENT WHO CHANGES HER MIND

Re W (An Infant)
[1971] AC 682, [1971] 2 All ER 49, [1971] 2 WLR 1011, 115 Sol Jo 286, House of Lords

The mother was unmarried, in her early 20s. She was living in one room with her two little girls by an earlier relationship, now broken, when she found herself unintentionally pregnant again. She was a good mother to the girls but was doubtful of her ability to cope with a third child in that accommodation. Accordingly she made arrangements before the birth for the child to be adopted. She was offered better accommodation just before the birth, but still had doubts and so did not alter the arrangement. The child went to the applicants as temporary foster parents when he was 8 days old and had been there ever since. They began adoption proceedings when he was 10 months old, and the mother signed the consent form a few days later. She withdrew that consent the day before the hearing was first due to take place. She was now well settled with her two daughters and a cousin in her new flat, but she had had no contact at all with the child, who was 16 months old when the county court judge came to decide the case. He decided that she was withholding her consent unreasonably and made the order. Her appeal to the Court of Appeal was upheld, on the ground that her conduct had not been 'culpable' or 'blameworthy' ([1970] 2 QB 589, [1970] 3 All ER 990, CA) but a differently constituted Court of Appeal refused to follow this test in *Re B (CHO) (An Infant)* [1971] 1 QB 437, [1970] 3 All ER 1008, CA and the applicants in this case successfully appealed to the House of Lords.

Lord Hailsham of St Marylebone LC: . . . [Section 16(2)(*b*)] lays down a test of reasonableness. It does not lay down a test of culpability or of callous or self-indulgent indifference or of failure or probable failure of parental duty. . . . It is not for the courts to embellish, alter, subtract from, or add to words which, for once at least, Parliament has employed without any ambiguity at all. I must add that if the test had involved me in a criticism of the respondent involving culpability or callous or self-indulgent indifference, I might well have come to the same conclusion on the facts as did Sachs and Cross LJJ. But since the test imposed on me by the Act is reasonableness and not culpability I have come to the opposite conclusion.

The question then remains as to how to apply the correct test. The test is whether at the time of the hearing the consent is being withheld unreasonably. As Lord Denning MR said in *Re L (An Infant)* (1962) 106 Sol Jo 611:

'In considering the matter I quite agree that: (1) the question whether she is unreasonably withholding her consent is to be judged at the date of the hearing; and (2) the welfare of the child is not the sole consideration; and (3) the one question is whether she is unreasonably withholding her consent. But I must say that in considering whether she is reasonable or unreasonable we must take into account the welfare of the child. A reasonable mother surely gives great weight to what is better for the child. Her anguish of mind is quite understandable; but still it may be unreasonable for her to withhold consent. We must look and see whether it is reasonable or unreasonable according to what a reasonable woman in her place would do in all the circumstances of the case.'

This passage was quoted with approval by Davies LJ in *Re B (CHO) (An Infant)* by Lord Sorn in *A B and C B v X's Curator*, by Pearson LJ in *Re C* [1971] 1 QB 437, [1970] 3 All ER 1008, (*L*) [1965] 2 QB 449, [1964] 3 All ER 483 and by Winn LJ in *Re B (CHO)*. In my view, it may now be considered authoritative. In the words of Lord Sorn in *A B and C B v X's Curator*, 1963 SC 124 at 137–8:

'It appears from his note that the Sheriff-substitute envisaged two alternative ways of approaching the question; the first being to make the welfare of the child the sole, or primary, consideration; the second being to ignore the welfare of the child altogether. He chose the second alternative. . . . As I see it, neither of these alternative ways of approaching the question is right. The proper way to approach the question is to look at the matter from the point of view of the parent and, having regard to the whole circumstances, to ask whether the parent's decision to withhold consent was an unreasonable decision for the parent to have made.'

Lord Sorn then went on to quote Lord Denning MR in the passage from *Re L* which I have quoted above.

From this it is clear that the test is reasonableness and not anything else. It is not culpability. It is not indifference. It is not failure to discharge parental duties. It is reasonableness, and reasonableness in the context of the totality of the circumstances. But, although welfare per se is not the test, the fact that a reasonable parent does pay regard to the welfare of his child must enter into the question of reasonableness as a relevant factor. It is relevant in all cases if and to the extent that a reasonable parent would take it into account. It is decisive in those cases where a reasonable parent must so regard it. . . .

I only feel it necessary to add on this part of the case that I entirely agree with Russell LJ when he said in effect ([1970] 2 QB 589, [1970] 3 All ER 990) that it does not follow from the fact that the test is reasonableness that any court is entitled simply to substitute its own view for that of the parent. In my opinion, it should be extremely careful to guard against this error. Two reasonable parents can perfectly reasonably come to opposite conclusions on the same set of facts without forfeiting their title to be regarded as reasonable. The question in any given case is whether a parental veto comes within the band of possible reasonable decisions and not whether it is right or mistaken. Not every reasonable exercise of judgment is right, and not every mistaken exercise of judgment is unreasonable. There is a band of decisions within which no court should seek to replace the individual's judgment with his own.

Lord Denning's words in *Re L* were quoted with approval by every judge in the House of Lords, yet it is interesting to compare an actual decision of his which is almost contemporaneous with *Re W*:

Re P A (An Infant)
[1971] 3 All ER 522, [1971] 1 WLR 1530, 115 Sol Jo 586, Court of Appeal

An unmarried mother looked after her baby for some five weeks in her own mother's home before the baby was privately placed through the intervention of the mother's aunt. The mother signed the consent form but changed her mind three weeks after the adoption application had been lodged. The county court judge heard the case when the child was $10\frac{1}{2}$ months old and refused to dispense with the mother's consent. Other facts appear from the judgment in the Court of Appeal.

Lord Denning MR: . . . So, if Parliament had entrusted the entire welfare of the child to the courts, it may be that the right decision would be for the child to remain where she is. But that is not what Parliament has enacted. The natural mother is entitled to withhold her consent so long as she is not unreasonable in so doing. The question whether a mother is reasonable or unreasonable was considered recently by the House of Lords in *Re W (An Infant)*. That case shows that we are not to look solely at the welfare of the child. We are to see whether the unmarried mother is unreasonably withholding her consent. That is to be judged, not by her own feelings, but by what a reasonable mother in her place would do in all the circumstances of the case.

One circumstance which influenced the judge was that he thought the unmarried mother in her heart of hearts wanted to keep the child. She never at any time really wanted to have the infant adopted. Counsel for the applicants challenged that finding, but there was much evidence to support it. The unmarried mother was very reluctant to sign the form. The aunt pressed her on several occasions. Finally the grandmother's letter impressed the judge. His finding on this point cannot be upset. The other circumstance which influenced the judge is the fact that the unmarried mother is now engaged to be married. It is proposed that the baby should go to her mother and grandmother until the marriage, and then to the young married couple. The young man is entirely reliable.

Seeing that the unmarried mother is able to put forward such good prospects to the court, it cannot be said that she is unreasonably withholding her consent. She is withholding it reasonably in the hope and expectation that she herself will be able to form a secure home for the child.

I would add a further point. This baby is only just one year old. It may be somewhat upset by being moved to another home. But that upset will be only temporary. Soon she will benefit from the love and care of her natural mother, and later, if all goes according to plan, her foster father. She may perhaps be better off than she would have been with the adopting parents. In my opinion the judge's finding cannot be disturbed. The mother is not unreasonably withholding her consent.

Questions

(i) Given that the law is stated in virtually exactly the same terms in each of the above cases, how do you account for the difference in result? Was it, for example: (*a*) because the trial judge reached a result which the appeal courts felt unable to disturb; (*b*) because one was an agency placement (in a sense) and the other was directly arranged through the medium of the aunt; (*c*) because one mother was now engaged to an 'entirely reliable' young man, whereas the other's matrimonial chances were subject to the large question mark of two illegitimate children apart from the child under discussion; (*d*) because the judge in *Re W* took judicial notice of the damage likely to be caused by uprooting a 16-month-old child from the only home he had ever known (as to which, see pp. 357–359, above), whereas Lord Denning considered such an upset would be temporary; or (*e*) because the mother in *Re PA* 'never really wanted to have the infant adopted'?
(ii) How many of the above factors are relevant to deciding what an objectively reasonable mother would do in all the circumstances of the case?

Re H (Infants) (adoption: parental consent)
[1977] 2 All ER 339, [1977] 1 WLR 471, 121 Sol Jo 303, Court of Appeal

An unmarried mother of about 20 gave birth to twins in January. They were fostered until April when she signed a provisional form of consent to adoption and the children were placed with the applicants. In May she signed the formal consent forms but still had doubts. In July she indicated that she opposed the adoption. The hearing took place in December. The trial judge found that the children had formed a special attachment to the adoptive mother which it might be harmful to break and that the mother was immature and vacillating. He dispensed with her agreement and the mother appealed.

Ormrod LJ, delivering the first judgment at the invitation of Stamp LJ, stated the facts and said that it was impossible for the court to come to any other conclusion than that the judge's judgment must be upheld. His Lordship continued: The attitude of the court to the question of dispensing with consent, or holding that the consent is unreasonably withheld, has changed over the years, since adoption became possible in 1926. It has changed markedly since Lord Denning MR's judgment in *Re L (An Infant)* and perhaps even more markedly since the House of Lords' decision in *Re W (An Infant)* and probably it will change even more in consequence of the Children Act 1975, although, at the moment, this court has said that s. 3 [s. 6 of the Adoption Act 1976, p. 497 above] does not apply to this particular issue (*Re P (An Infant) (adoption: parental consent)* [1977] Fam 25, [1977] 1 All ER 182). However, it is safe to say this: the relative importance of the welfare of the children is increasing rather than diminishing in relation to dispensing with consent. That being so, it ought to be recognised by all concerned with adoption cases that once the formal consent has been given or perhaps once the child has been placed with the adopters, time begins to run against the mother and, as time goes on, it gets progressively more and more difficult for her to show that the withdrawal of her consent is reasonable.

I would respectfully suggest that those who are responsible for drafting the forms which are used in these cases should consider whether the forms in their present state really do make the position sufficiently clear or whether they have become, inadvertently, misleading. In the present climate of opinion, it is misleading to say to a mother, having signed the form of consent, 'You can always withdraw up to the last minute before the court hearing'. Of course she can withdraw, but she runs the risk, at this mother had done, of the court finding that her withdrawal was not reasonable. Therefore, the effect of the passage of time should somehow, I feel, be brought to the attention of the mothers in these adoption cases. I think there has been a sufficient shift in the attitude of the courts to call for a reconsideration of those parts of the forms which suggest rather forcibly that the mother is not committed until the date of the hearing. It is true, she is not legally committed, but I wish to emphasise that as time passes it get more and more difficult for her to justify the withdrawal of her consent.

Question

What is 'special' about the bond between psychological parent and wanted child?

The *Adoption Agencies Regulations 1976* require agencies to give parents an Explanatory Memorandum in a prescribed form. It has this to say about agreement:

Your agreement to the adoption
Before a court can make an adoption order, it has to be satisfied that you agree freely to the order being made, so you will be asked to sign a form of agreement to adoption which will be shown to the court. The proposed adopters will either be referred to on this form by a number or they may be named. If they are referred to by a number it will not be possible to tell you who they are but your social worker will be able to tell you something about them. You are not allowed by law to receive any money for giving your agreement. You will have the opportunity of making your views known to the court on the adoption application if you so wish, but where the proposed adopters are referred to by a number on the form of agreement, arrangements will be made for you to attend the court at a different time from them. The court will appoint a person called the guardian ad litem who will need to see you before the court makes the adoption order to make sure that you understand what the effect will be. The guardian ad litem has a duty to ensure that an adoption order will be in the interests of the child and the court must give first consideration to the welfare of the child. If you sign the form of agreement and then, before the adoption order is made, you wish to withdraw your agreement, you must inform your social

worker and the court. If you have signed your agreement and the proposed adopters have already sent the application papers to the court, the law does not allow you to remove the child unless you obtain the permission of the court. The court cannot make an order without your agreement unless it dispenses with your agreement on certain grounds. . . .

Question

How would you modify this statement to give effect to the views expressed by Ormrod LJ?

(b) THE PARENT WHO HAS NEVER AGREED

Re SMH and RAH
(1979) 14 February, (Unreported), Court of Appeal

In February 1975, a mother left her two young children with a neighbour and disappeared. The neighbour could only have them for a few weeks, and so the local authority obtained care orders under the Children and Young Persons Act 1969 and placed them with foster parents, who had cared for them ever since. On arrival, each child was in a highly vulnerable state, whereas by the date of the adoption hearing they had recovered their emotional security and physical health to a remarkable degree. In 1978, the mother applied for discharge of the care orders and when this was refused she appealed unsuccessfully to the Crown Court. The local authority and foster parents decided that an adoption application should be made. The county court judge dispensed with the mother's agreement on the ground that it was unreasonably withheld and the mother appealed.

Bridge LJ: . . . Before turning to the arguments of counsel in this matter it is right to see how the learned judge approached it. He put it in the forefront of his judgment that adoption was unquestionably the course which would most benefit these children. That is something he said at the outset. Having considered all the evidence which was before him he expressed his conclusion on the question of the unreasonable withholding of agreement to the adoption orders in this way: 'The only way in which I can say it is not reasonable is by firstly considering the totality of the evidence. I have done that, and am satisfied that for the welfare of the children it would be better for adoption to take place. The question is: would a reasonable parent consent to adoption? The only reason that this mother won't consent is that she wants to feel that they're hers. It seems to me that she's got very little thought for the children. The children are now secure and well looked after. It seems to me that any other course apart from adoption would not give sufficient security to the adoptive parents . . . I think she is withholding her consent for her own personal feelings, which I can well understand, but I think a reasonable parent, knowing all the facts and considering the children, would grant consent.' In the end, if one analyses it, the argument on behalf of the appellant natural mother in the case raises a very narrow issue. It is now conceded, and it was, indeed, before the learned judge, on behalf of the natural mother that it is unquestionably in the long-term interest of both these children that they should spend the rest of their childhood years in the care of the erstwhile foster-parents, now adoptive parents, as members of those parents' families. Having failed in her attempt to secure the discharge of the care orders in 1978 it is said, on the natural mother's behalf, that she recognises that as finally disposing of any possibility that she should, at any time in the future, recover the care of these children during the remainder of their childhood. It is even said, on her behalf, as to the length to which her concessions go, that she is willing to accept that she should have no access to the children other than such as should be decreed to be appropriate by a social welfare worker who had charge of the case. One of the difficulties which confronts the court, and which confronted the learned judge, and to which he referred, is to see how, if those concessions are made, and are rightly made, any legal machinery could be devised to give effect to those concessions in such a way as to ensure that the future position of these children as members of the foster parents' families should remain undisturbed short of the making of the adoption orders which the judge has made. . . .

So what is the other alternative, to look at the practical realities of this case? The other alternative is surely this, that the care orders under s. 1 of the 1969 Act should remain in force indefinitely. So long as that situation remains it would, no doubt, be the practical consequence, which the natural mother says she is prepared to accept, that access to the children by her would only be such as the supervising officer concerned with these children on behalf of the local authority was prepared to agree and arrange. It is said that the natural mother's concessions, and her assurances that those concessions will never be withdrawn, are a sufficient basis to provide for the future security of these children. But so long as the foster-parents remain, as they have been until the making of the orders under appeal, nothing more than foster parents, whose care of the children is strictly subject to the control and, indeed, technically, determination at any time by the local authority, their position must be precarious; and what is perhaps more important, because it is unthinkable that the local authority would want to interfere, at any time the natural mother would be in a position to change her mind and make a further attempt, it may be an unsuccessful attempt, but a further disturbing attempt to have the care order discharged. I emphasise the sentence in the judge's judgment: 'It seems to me that any other course apart from adoption would not give sufficient security to the adoptive parents.' That sentence seems to me only to express half of the story, although I have no doubt what the judge had in mind, and it has been very well put to us by counsel on behalf of the adoptive parents. Unless the adoptive parents are put in the legal position of being in the full sense parents of these little children they are never in the position, and never will be in the position, to give to the children the reassurance which the sense of security required by these children is surely going to need. The parents need to know that the children are full members of the family. The children need to know that they are fully the children of those parents and that nothing can happen to take them away. It is quite clear, if one looks at the whole of the material is this case, that the adoptive parents in each case represent the only security and the only stability which these two little children have known. If that security and stability is in any way put at risk, it will inevitably be to their detriment. It may be, although this is a matter on which it is unnecessary to pronounce a final judgment, that the very fact of continuing access to the children by the natural mother would be a disturbing factor. *Appeal dismissed.*

This case was quoted with approval by all three members of a differently constituted Court of Appeal in the very similar case of *Re F (A Minor) (adoption: parental consent)* [1982] 1 All ER 321, [1982] 1 WLR 102 in which Ormrod LJ remarked:

. . . in my judgment, in applying the objective test, the court must have regard to the practical consequences of making or refusing to make an adoption order. The factual situation in this case is quite different from what some people think of as a 'normal adoption', ie of a baby within weeks of birth. In such cases adoption means the grafting of the child into the adoptive family and its total elimination from the life of the mother; refusal means the return of the baby to the mother. In a case such as the present, the only difference *to the mother* is between dependence for access on a decision of the social workers (under the care order), or on the court (under wardship) or on Mr and Mrs S (under the adoption order). On the other hand, the difference to the child and to Mr and Mrs S, as Bridge LJ pointed out in the case referred to, is of great psychological significance.

In *Re H (A Child), Re W (A Child)* (1983) Times, 3 January, yet a third Court of Appeal, dealing with foster parents' applications to adopt children aged 10 and 11 who had been removed at an early age from unsatisfactory homes, stated that '. . . this court has moved towards a greater emphasis upon the welfare of the child as one of the factors to be considered when dealing with s. [16(2)(*b*)], but it is clear that short of amending legislation or further consideration in the House of Lords, there must be a limit to this shift.' After quoting from Lord Reid's speech in *O'Connor v A and B* [1971] 2 All ER 1230, [1971] 1 WLR 1227 that '. . . a reasonable parent or, indeed, any other reasonable person, would have in mind the interests or claims of all three parties concerned — the child whose adoption is in question, the natural parents, and the adopting family,' the court concluded that 'the chance of a successful reintroduction to, or continuance of contact with, the natural parent is a critical factor in assessing the reaction of the hypothetical reasonable parent . . .'.

Questions

(i) In *Re F*, Dunn LJ considered that no reasonable parent could have reached the conclusion that some contact with her child would be beneficial, because it was 'quite inconsistent with any objective view of the needs of the child.' But could a parent be reasonable in withholding agreement even if contact would not be beneficial?

(ii) On the other hand, is Ormrod LJ suggesting that a parent might be unreasonable even if contact would be beneficial?

(iii) Do you prefer the view of Gunn LJ, Ormrod LJ or the Court of Appeal in *Re H, Re W*?

(iv) Would it be unreasonable for a mother who placed her illegitimate baby in local authority care shortly after his birth to withhold her agreement to his adoption (by foster parents with whom he had lived for some two years) solely because she was a convinced Roman Catholic and did not trust the foster parents to bring him up in that religion?

(v) Why might a mother with a criminal and alcoholic past (*Re W*) be reasonable, while a homosexual father (*Re D*, p. 344, above) was not?

Ground (*c*) — the 'persistent failure' ground — was introduced in its modern form by the Adoption Act 1958, which used the term 'obligations of a parent' rather than 'parental duties.' In her contribution to *Growing Up Adopted* (1972), Mia Kellmer Pringle had this to say:

What then are the responsibilities or obligations of parenthood? Basically, they are twofold: first, to provide a loving, caring, dependable environment which gives the child optimal opportunities for physical, emotional, social and intellectual development; and to give this loving care unconditionally — irrespective of the child's sex, abilities, appearance or personality. Such acceptance is for better or for worse. It needs to be given without any expectation of or demand for gratitude.

It would seem that one court, at least, agreed:

Re P (Infants)
[1962] 3 All ER 789, [1962] 1 WLR 1296, 127 JP 8, 106 Sol Jo 630, 60 LGR 532, High Court

'Mrs' M left her husband and went to live with Mr M. In 1956, they had a son, J, whom Mrs M placed in care about two months after he was born. The local authority boarded him out with Mr and Mrs P, where he had been ever since, apart from four weeks in 1957 during which his mother removed him. In 1958 Mr and 'Mrs' M had another son, D. Shortly after his birth, 'Mrs' M agreed that both should be adopted by Mr and Mrs P and D was placed with them. From late 1958 onwards, 'Mrs' M expressed some wish to have the boys back, but took no active steps to that end. In 1961, Mr and Mrs P applied to adopt the boys and to dispense with 'Mrs' M's agreement on each of grounds then available. The judge rejected all but 'persistent failure.'

Pennycuick J: . . . . So far as [paragraph (*d*)] is concerned, the word 'abandoned' has been held in *Watson v Nikolaisen* [1955] 2 QB 286, [1955] 2 All ER 427 to connote conduct that would have rendered the parent liable under the criminal law. I am told that in the very recent, and so far unreported decision, of *Re W (Spinster) (An Infant)*, Plowman J has put a comparable meaning on the word 'neglected'. There is no suggestion that Mrs M has ill-treated the children. . . .

There remains [paragraph *c*] which seems to be the critical provision in the present case. . . . it seems to me that in this subsection the expression 'obligations of a parent' must include first the natural and moral duty of a parent to show affection, care and interest towards his child; and secondly, as well, the common law or statutory duty of a parent to maintain his child in the financial or economic sense. . . .

I have come to the conclusion that Mrs M has persistently and without reasonable cause failed to discharge her obligations as a parent towards each of the two children. First, as regards her natural and moral obligation, she parted with each child a few weeks after it was born. She had J back for less than four weeks in October and November 1957; but, with this exception, she has never had either child to live with her. Moreover, she never went to see J between August 1956, and October 1957, or made any inquiries with regard to him for the greater part of that time. Again she never went to see J between November 1957 and the birth of D in April 1958. She has only been to see the two children three times between April 1958, and June 1960, and not at all during the following year. Nor, it seems to me, was there any reasonable cause for this neglect. During the first period, after she placed J with the London County Council, she apparently never even troubled to inquire about his whereabouts for many months. Thereafter she could easily visit the children at Epping, which is only a short journey by bus or tube from London. At any rate from the autumn of 1958 she had accommodation where she could have had the children to live with her.

Second, as regards the financial obligations, throughout the period during which the children were with the Ps she sent the Ps £29 only towards their support. She may also have sent odd clothes and toys, but there is no evidence that these were of substantial value. Counsel for Mr and Mrs M relied on the payment of these sums amounting to £29 as representing all that Mr and Mrs M could reasonably have afforded. Now it becomes necessary to look shortly at the provisions of the Family Allowances Act 1945. . . .

The effect, then, of the allowances drawn and the payments made by Mr and Mrs M is this. Mr and Mrs M drew 18s. a week for two years — say £94, to which, because they had not performed the conditions in s. 3(2), they were not entitled. Mrs M paid over to the Ps £29. It seems to me that in no real sense can this be regarded as a discharge by Mrs M of her obligations towards the children. On the contrary, the substance of the matter is that Mr and Mrs M drew from the state money to which they were not entitled, paid over part to the Ps, and kept more than half for themselves.

I conclude therefore that Mrs M has in truth failed to discharge her financial obligation towards the children. Nor, it seems to me, has any reasonable cause for this failure been established. Mr M was throughout employed and in receipt of a wage of not less than £12 a week. At the very least there is no reason why Mrs M should not have contributed towards the maintenance of the children a sum at least equal to the amount of the allowances, which she in fact drew, and if she had so contributed could properly have drawn.

Question

Why did not the applicants in *Re SMH and RAH*, *Re F*, and *Re H*, *Re W* (pp. 508–509, above) rely upon grounds (*c*), (*d*), (*e*) or (*f*)?

(c) IS 'FREEING FOR ADOPTION' THE SOLUTION?

The *Houghton Report* recommended a new procedure which might help in solving both types of consent problem:

168. . . . There is considerable dissatisfaction with the timing and nature of the present consent procedure. Parental rights and obligations are not terminated at the time the parent signs the consent document. They continue until an adoption order is made some weeks or months later. The argument in favour of this system is that there is never a period when the child is not the legal responsibility of either natural or adoptive parents. But there is evidence that this procedure imposes unnecessary strain and confusion on the mother. Moreover, it may encourage indecisiveness on her part; and by maintaining her legal responsibility for the child until the adoption order is made, it may prevent her from facing the reality of her decision and planning her own future. This period of uncertainty can be considerably prolonged if there is a delay in the adoption arrangements.

169. The disadvantages for the adoptive parents are obvious. The welfare of the child is at risk while his future remains in doubt and there is a possibility that he may be moved. Even though this happens only in a small minority of cases, the knowledge that it is possible may give rise to

anxiety on the part of all prospective adopters, who may hesitate to give total commitment to a child whom they may not be allowed to keep.

170. We suggested in our working paper that in agency cases it should be possible for consent to become final before an adoption order was made. We outlined a system similar to that followed in some overseas countries, notably many states in the United States of America, which enables parents to take an irrevocable decision to give up their child for adoption, and to relinquish parental rights and obligations, before the child is placed. These rights and obligations are transferred by the court to an adoption agency, and in due course are transferred by the agency to the adopters when an adoption order is made. This enables the mother to give up parental rights and obligations before an adoption order is made, while providing for their exercise by the agency in the meantime . . .

. . . .

221. There is known to exist a sizeable number of children in the care of local authorities and voluntary societies for whom no permanent future can be arranged for a variety of reasons, for example, because the parents cannot bring themselves to make a plan, or do not want their child adopted but are unable to look after him themselves. Some of these children may have no contact with their parents and would benefit from adoption, but the parents will not agree to it. In other cases a parent may have her child received into care shortly after birth and then vacillate for months or even years over the question of adoption, thus depriving her child of the security of a settled family home life.

. . . .

223. In some of these cases a court might well consider that there were statutory grounds for dispensing with the parents' consent because they had persistently failed to discharge the obligations of a parent, or were withholding consent unreasonably. Under the present law there is no way of testing this without first placing the child with prospective adopters and awaiting a court decision after at least three months care and possession by them. If the court then decides that there are insufficient grounds for dispensing with the parents' consent the child must be returned to the agency. Moreover, unless the child is in the care of a local authority which has parental rights, or a care order has been made, the parents can frustrate the proceedings by removing the child before the court hearing. Agencies are therefore understandably reluctant to place these children for adoption.

224. We accept the principle that the natural family should be preserved wherever reasonably possible. But where a child is in care with no satisfactory long-term plan in mind, and lacking the possibility of long-term stable relationships, we think that it should be open to a local authority or a registered adoption agency to apply to a court for the parents' consent to be dispensed with on one of the statutory grounds, for parental rights to be transferred to the agency and the child thus freed for placement for adoption. The parents should not be permitted to remove the child from the agency's care without the leave of the court while the application is pending. This procedure would enable a decision to be taken without a child first being placed for adoption. The hearing would be in the nature of a relinquishment hearing but with the application made by the local authority or agency. Such an application would be made only where there was every prospect of a satisfactory placement for the child, and if it were granted the agency would have parental rights and obligations until an adoption order was made.

The resulting recommendations are shortly to be implemented in what will become sections 18 to 20 of the Adoption Act 1976:

18. Freeing child for adoption.

(1) Where, on an application by an adoption agency, an authorised court is satisfied in the case of each parent or guardian of the child that —

    (*a*) he freely, and with full understanding of what is involved, agrees generally and unconditionally to the making of an adoption order, or

    (*b*) his agreement to the making of an adoption order should be dispensed with on a ground specified in section 16(2),

the court shall make an order declaring the child free for adoption.

(2) No application shall be made under subsection (1) unless —

    (*a*) it is made with the consent of a parent or guardian of a child, or

    (*b*) the adoption agency is applying for dispensation under subsection (1)(*b*) of the agreement of each parent or guardian of the child, and the child is in the care of the adoption agency.

    (3) No agreement required under subsection (1)(*a*) shall be dispensed with under subsection (1)(*b*) unless the child is already placed for adoption or the court is satisfied that it is likely that the child will be placed for adoption.

. . . .

Questions

(i) Go back to question (iv) on p. 510, above; in those circumstances, could a local authority hope to succeed in a 'freeing' application?

(ii) Despite all these developments, the number of children adopted from local authority care was only 1,500 in 1979, 1,600 in 1980, and 1,700 in 1981 possible reasons include: (*a*) lack of specialist home-finding staff in local authorities; (*b*) compartmentalising adoptive and fostering placements so that the possibility of adoption is never raised between social worker and long-term foster parent; (*c*) failure to identify children for whom an adoptive placement could be found; (*d*) lack of suitable adoptive families for 'hard to place' children; (*e*) subsidised adoption is only in its infancy; (*f*) potential adopters are reluctant to take on a possible conflict in court if the parent does not give agreement; (*g*) despite what Ormrod LJ may say (p. 509, above), the outcome of such contests is still often in doubt. Can you think of any others?

(iii) Compare the procedure for freeing a child for adoption, including the grounds for dispensing with parental agreement, with the draft *Model Act to Free Children for Permanent Placement* (p. 462, above): which would provide some solution to more of the above difficulties?

(iv) Do you consider that solutions *should* be found?

7 A concluding case history

The following story is told by Barbara Tizard in *Adoption: A Second Chance* (1977):

The fifth set of foster parents, a comfortably-off middle-class couple in their 50s, had fostered children, mainly babies, for many years. Mrs E thought of 'David' as one of her own children. He had taken her name, and addressed her as 'Mummy'. There was, however, no possibility of adoption because his mother would not allow it.

She had placed David in care at the age of two months hoping to reclaim him in two years when she had finished her nursing training. Before this time however, she married, had another child and stopped visiting David. Since her husband didn't want to accept David, she planned to send him to her parents in Jamaica. The grandparents, however, had a large family of their own, and were reluctant to take him till he was 7. It was decided to keep him in the children's home, and hope that he would eventually be united with his family. His mother didn't visit him for two years, but when he was 4½ she reappeared, and talked of taking him and leaving her husband. Since she did not do so, David was eventually fostered with Mrs E at the age of 5. From this time, his only contact with his mother was via occasional telephone calls.

Foster mother 'He can't go back to her or even visit her, because the man she's married to just won't have him in the house. And she's got four children by this man. But she won't give David up — she feels that he's still her son, and she thinks that he might return to her when he's older, and stick up for her. But the thing is, he won't know her, he'll have no genuine feeling for her. He'll know that she's his mother, because she's black, but that's about all.'

Mrs E not only acted as a mother to David, but kept in close touch with his mother and gave her a lot of support.

Foster mother 'I'm the shoulder that she cries on. If things get on top of her, or she finds she's pregnant again she rings me up. My husband and I slip over occasionally, if I know that she's a bit down, and take some toys or clothes for her children. She usually sends David a pound at Xmas, and sometimes she writes to him but she doesn't see him.'

Mrs E tried to help David understand his position.

Foster mother 'I tell him that his Mummy just can't have him, because her husband doesn't want him living there. So he has to stay with us. He wanted to know who his Daddy was, and what he was like — how tall he was — how black he was —·where he came from — things like that. So I contacted his Mummy, and then I told him the basics. I've skimmed over the bad side of his father and given him a fair picture of him. One day, when I feel the time is right, I'll tell him his father left his mother in the lurch. I try to keep to the nicer side about his mother too, and make his family background sound as nice as possible. She rings me up and tells me about her parents and grandparents, and I pass it on to David. I think it's important he should have some background of his own.'

Partly because David is very black — both parents were West Indian — Mr E tried to foster a pride in his colour in him.

Foster mother 'Although he's been brought up white, I think he should never forget he's coloured, that he's got something to be proud of. He'll need this in a white community — He gets "Sambo" and "Nig-nog" at school already — if he's proud of himself it will be easier for him in the long run.'

Although Mrs E was 'only' a foster mother, she seemed to have the same deep commitment to David as if he were her own child.

Foster mother 'When he came to me he was a chronic asthma sufferer. He never ran — if he walked up the stairs he'd have to stop and get his breath back. Now he never sits still — he's out on a bike all day. He had his last attack 16 months ago — it was a very bad one. I never went to bed for three nights. The doctor wanted him to go to hospital, but I said I'd rather nurse him at home — if he were to get worse, then I'd go with him into hospital, I wouldn't leave him.'

. . . .

The issue of adoption did not arise, because Mrs E knew that David's mother would not consider it. Nevertheless, she felt quite secure in her relationship with David because she knew that there was no possibility of his developing a relationship with his mother. In this situation she was able to support his mother, whilst treating David as her own child.

Foster mother 'I think every mother if she's honest, has individual feelings for every child she's got. You feel differently about each of your children. I won't say I feel the same about David as the others — I feel differently about them all — but he's just like my own.'

. . . None of the foster parents saw this situation, however, as ideal — they would have preferred adoption.

Foster mother 'I'm a firm believer that the mother is the person to have a child. But as far as David is concerned, there could never be a very good relationship, because the man she's married to won't have him — and she's got the other children to look after. That sort of mother is no good to the child, is she?'

Questions

(i) Do you consider this (*a*) a perfect example of 'inclusive' fostering working to the benefit of all; or (*b*) a case in which the additional powers and responsibilities granted by an adoption order would benefit both child and adoptive parents?

(ii) If (*b*), would you advise either (*a*) Mrs E to apply to adopt and dispense with David's mother's agreement, or (*b*) the care authority to apply to free him for adoption?

(iii) With which of the following statements would you most agree: (*a*) 'the irrevocable commitment involved in adoption is the best guarantee both that the parent will provide what the child needs and the child will feel that he is truly wanted and belongs'; or (*b*) 'the consequences of adoption are far too drastic to impose upon David's mother when, with the right choice of foster parents and the right attitudes all round, David can have the best of both worlds'?

CHAPTER 14

Dangerous families

'I burned him later with the iron; I did it deliberately. I'd look at him, and think, oh you little bastard, you know? I just got hold of him and burned him on the back of the hand. I was so fed up! He'd been grizzling; he was tired out in the daytime because he didn't sleep at night. And of course *I* was tired too, and he wouldn't stop grizzling. I was ironing on the floor in the lounge because it was just something quick I wanted — I was kneeling down and he was sitting over by the window. I just got hold of his hand and I said, *that'll* make you sleep! It was all done in such a quick second, you know, that I didn't . . . it wasn't sort of premeditated; I just looked at him, had the iron in my hand, and did it.'

'I have had ten stitches, three stitches, five stitches, seven stitches, where he has cut me. . . .' 'I have had a knife stuck through my stomach; I have had a poker put through my face; I have no teeth where he knocked them all out; I have been burnt with red hot pokers; I have had red hot coals slung all over me; I have been sprayed with petrol and stood there while he has flicked lighted matches at me. . . .' These assaults did not just take place when he was drunk, but 'at any time; early in the morning; late at night; in the middle of the night he would drag me out of bed and start hitting me, he would do it in front of the children. He never bothered if the children were there. . . .' 'I have been to the police. I nicked my husband. He gave me ten stitches, and they held him in the nick over the weekend and he came out on Monday. He was bound over to keep the peace, that was all. On the Tuesday he gave me the hiding of my life'.

So said, respectively, the mother who told her story to Jean Renvoize for her investigation into *Children in Danger* (1974) and Mrs X who gave evidence to the House of Commons Select Committee on *Violence in Marriage* (1975). But an even more chilling illustration of the multifarious problems involved is provided in the dispassionate account of one family's story in the *Report of the Committee of Inquiry into the Provision and Co-ordination of Services to the Family of John George Auckland* (1975):

45. On 13 November 1965 Mr John Auckland married Miss Barbara Marsden, a local girl then 18 years old, whom he had been courting for some four months. His parents, Mr and Mrs George Auckland, were opposed to the marriage, partly on the grounds that it was taking place in such a rush, and Miss Marsden herself sought and obtained an assurance from Mr John Auckland that the reason for his wanting to marry her did not stem from [an] argument that he had had with his parents. After the marriage, Mr John Auckland and his wife moved into a small terrace house of their own at 11 Churchfield Avenue, Cudworth.

46. It soon became apparent that Mrs Barbara Auckland had no previous training whatsoever in domestic duties, and was incompetent at managing household finance. As she told us herself, she could not even peel potatoes. By 17 January 1966 things had reached such a pitch that both Mr and Mrs John Auckland sought the advice of Mr Tindall, the probation officer to whom Mr John Auckland was reporting, both agreeing that Mrs Barbara Auckland, who was working full-time, needed help and guidance with household management and cooking. Mr Tindall found Mrs Barbara Auckland to be at that time immature and not very capable, but willing to learn. He felt that, given time, she would develop more confidence in her own abilities and, to help with this process, he asked Mrs Mary Auckland to give her daughter-in-law some assistance. There is some evidence that Mrs Barbara Auckland was already being subjected to violence by her husband.

47. By February 1966 the marital situation seemed to be improving but it soon relapsed. Mrs Barbara Auckland left her husband at the beginning of March, and Mr John Auckland had

medical treatment, which he claims was for nervous upset occasioned by his wife's slovenly habits. The separation was not long-lasting but it set a pattern for the future. It is some evidence of Mrs Barbara Auckland's state of mind at this time that she was admitted to hospital in April 1966 having swallowed a quantity of a rubbing ointment in what appears to have been a suicidal gesture. . . .

49. Mrs Barbara Auckland became pregnant for the first time in 1967. Her husband welcomed this, as he had been anxious for some time to have a family. The baby girl, Marianne, was born on 9 April 1968. She was not premature but weighed only 4 1b 13 oz. . . .

54. The events of the night when Marianne died are recounted in a statement which Mr John Auckland made to the police seven hours after the event. In this statement he says that on the previous day he had ceased taking the 13 tablets prescribed for him by Dr Murray Park because he felt they were making him unwell. Instead he went out for some beer, and returned home at 9.30 p.m. with a headache, played cards for a while with his wife, ate some ham sandwiches, and drank some tea. The baby started crying upstairs, Mr John Auckland went up to quieten her, and then in his own words, 'this thing came over me like some evil, and I started banging her. Wife came upstairs and she tried to stop me, and I hit her as well'.

Before his trial for Marianne's murder, John Auckland was examined by several doctors:

57. . . . Dr Quinn's diagnosis is worth quoting for it reveals a pattern of behaviour on Mr John Auckland's part which we now know was to recur: '. . . I have formed the opinion that he (John Auckland) is an emotionally unstable individual, prone to alterations of mood. In the face of difficulties which he cannot readily reject or resolve, depression of mood reaches pathological intensity and renders him temporarily unable to evaluate and deal with his problems in a controlled and rational manner. The combination of constitutional factors and environmental pressures led over a number of months to the development of a depressive illness.'

58. At his trial at Leeds Assizes on 14–17 October 1968 Mr John Auckland was found guilty of manslaughter, by reason of diminished responsibility, and was sentenced to 18 months' imprisonment. After the verdict had been given, and before sentence was passed, Dr Orr was recalled by the Judge, Mr Justice Bridge, to give his prognosis and he then said that Mr John Auckland had all but recovered from his depressive illness and remained a person of average intelligence but of weak character. On being asked if there was a danger that if he were released in the near future he would commit a further offence Dr Orr replied that in his view the possibility was very remote indeed.

When John Auckland was released from prison, he was reunited with his wife. They moved from Cudworth to Shafton and had two more children, John Roy (born on 6 January 1971) and Mandy (born 17 March 1972). Then:

164. On 25 March 1973 Susan Auckland was born prematurely at Barnsley District General Hospital. Mrs Barbara Auckland was discharged home after 24 hours but the baby, only weighing 4 1b 1 oz, had to remain in the Special Care Baby Unit until 20 April. . . .

181. On Wednesday 27 March 1974, following an argument between herself and her husband, Mrs Barbara Auckland packed a few possessions into a carrier bag, put the baby Susan into a pram, and pushed the pram several miles to the home of her aunt, Mrs Doreen Nunn, who lived at Kendray. She arrived at Kendray about 11.40 p.m., and slept that night on the sofa. The next morning at about 9.00 or 10.00 a.m. Mrs Nunn telephoned Mr Martin Nurcombe, a social worker employed by the County Borough of Barnsley, to ask if the social services could help to find accommodation for Mrs Barbara Auckland and the child as she did not have room for them. Mr Nurcombe went to Mrs Nunn's home where he saw Mrs Barbara Auckland who said that she had left home and pushed the pram to Kendray because of her husband's cruelty to her, and because of the constant insinuations by his family that she was incapable of running a home. Mrs Barbara Auckland also told Mr Nurcombe that her husband was drinking heavily and beating her. She also told him that the family had been receiving help from Mr Jones of the Barnsley Division of the West Riding County Council Social Services Department, so Mr Nurcombe promised to contact Mr Jones and ask him to call and see her.

182. Meanwhile Mr John Auckland had informed the police of his wife's departure with Susan, and they had notified Mr Jones, who went to visit Mr John Auckland at his parents' home. Mr John Auckland had with him the two other children and he seems to have set out to prove himself to be the innocent husband and father who had been wronged by the deserting wife. . . .

183. On the same day, 28 March 1974, Mr Nurcombe tried unsuccessfully to contact Mr Jones to tell him where to find Mrs Barbara Auckland and Susan, but he was able to make contact early the following morning, and Mr Jones went straight to Mrs Nunn's home, where he arrived at about 9.30 a.m. Unfortunately, Mr Nurcombe did not tell Mr Jones that Mrs Barbara

Auckland had complained to him of being ill treated, but when he arrived at the house Mr Jones found her very distressed and complaining that her husband and his family 'picked on her'. She made some complaint of being maltreated and said at one point 'I have told you lies before, I have not told you what it is like', but Mr Jones did not invite her to explain further because he was mainly concerned with her intentions in relation to Susan. Mrs Barbara Auckland was proposing to go to her parents in London, whom she had not seen for seven years, and who lived in a school caretaker's flat where children were not allowed, so Mr Jones regarded her proposal to take Susan with her as misconceived. Furthermore, Susan was suffering from a bad 'nappy rash', of which Mrs Nunn rightly told Mr Jones, and which he later was able to observe for himself. Mr Jones persuaded Mrs Barbara Auckland to allow him to take Susan to her husband and other children who were at Mr and Mrs George Auckland's, and he summoned Mrs Angela Baines, a social work assistant, to act as escort for the journey. As they left Mrs Barbara Auckland, Mr Jones recalls her saying of the children, with an air of resignation, 'I suppose he will have them,' and she asked Mr Jones not to tell Mr John Auckland where she was, which, as Mr Jones appreciated, indicated that she was afraid of her husband. . . .

185. The two other children at Cudworth, John Roy and Mandy, were pleased to see their baby sister, and Mrs Mary Auckland was willing to accept responsibility for her so Mr Jones and Mrs Baines left her there. It does not seem to have occurred to either of them to go back to Mrs Barbara Auckland to tell her how Susan had been received, or to hear anything more she might want to say to them. . . .

194. On 5 April 1974 Mr Jones visited the Auckland children at their grandmother's and recorded that Mr John Auckland was 'still unsure of his future. He presumes that he will have a divorce but is presently looking for a "housekeeper". Prospects in this field seem poor. Mrs Auckland (senior) would like to go away for a fortnight. She asked if we could take Susan for a while'.

195. In response to Mrs Mary Auckland's request to be relieved of Susan for a time Mr Jones consulted Mr Carlson [the area officer] who agreed that she should be received temporarily into care, and placed in a foster home. The child was to go into care on 11 April 1974, and for that purpose certain forms had to be completed by Mr Jones which he signed on that day. The first form was a personal case record of the child (form CHN2) in which he entered as the reason for reception into care 'No suitable home — for a month'. Later in the form Mr Jones wrote:

'Mr Auckland is content to leave his children in the care of his mother. Indeed he has little choice at present. Mrs Auckland, Grandmother, is a capable woman, happy to look after the children, who are themselves happiest in their own company . . . Susan will be able to return to her Grandmother when the latter returns from her holiday. Her future then lies, at least in the near future, with her Grandmother, until Mr Auckland can sort out his home'.
(our underlining)

The committee underlined those last words because they were typed on a different machine and the committee thought that they had been added later. The Report does not accept that the social workers had ever contemplated that when Susan was discharged from care she might go, not to her grandmother in Cudworth, but to her father, and her brother and sister, in Shafton. Another reason for the committee's view was the following:

206. On 30 April 1974 Mr Jones received a letter from Mrs Barbara Auckland the material part of which read:
'Would you please be good enough to let me know how my three children are going on?'
The letter gave Mr Jones Mrs Barbara Auckland's London address, but he was asked to keep it to himself. . . . [And] on 1 May he replied to Mrs Barbara Auckland as follows:
'. . . your three children, staying with their Grandmother, are well. Susan has been staying for a month with a foster mother while Mrs Auckland has been on holiday.' . . .

214. [John Auckland] appeared at the social services department on Monday 6 May 1974, where he was seen by Mrs Baines. According to the note made by Mrs Baines, he claimed to have cleaned and decorated the home at Shafton, and to be having John Roy and Mandy back to live with him there on Wednesday or Thursday. He said that he would very much like Susan to join them. . . .

215. [Mrs Baines'] note reads:
'Advised him (John Auckland) Mr Jones was now on holiday but I would look into it sometime this week. Explained I would visit his mother to make sure adequate arrangements for care of children had been made. He was agreeable to this, he was also most anxious for me to visit his home in Shafton to see decorating he had done.' . . .

217. Then on Friday 10 May 1974 Mrs Baines visited Mrs Mary Auckland, and obtained confirmation that she and her daughters were prepared to give 'all the help and support that was

required.' John Roy and Mandy had returned to Shafton on the preceding day, so Mrs Baines went on to Shafton, where she found the family just finishing lunch and Mr John Auckland showing justifiable pride in his housekeeping. All seemed well, so Mrs Baines decided to return Susan that day. . . .

224. Mr Jones very soon learnt of Susan's return to her father, because she was returned on Friday 10 May 1974 and he was told what had happened on his return to work on the following Monday. On Tuesday 14 May 1974 he visited the family at Shafton. . . . [His note] reads:

'Visited Mr Auckland, who is now looking after all three children. He is coping well and receiving considerable support from his mother. Children all healthy — no apparent serious problems.'

226. . . . It goes on —

'Mrs Auckland has contacted me once by 'phone to enquire after the children's health. She has told me that she is taking legal advice towards a divorce.'

The wording does not suggest that the note was made on the same day as the telephone call, but Mr Jones told us that he did receive the telephone call on 14 May 1974, and that he told Mrs Barbara Auckland then of the return of the children to their father. Her attitude he said was one of resignation, reflecting her comment [in paragraph 183 earlier] when he had taken Susan from the house of Mrs Nunn. . . .

238. As to Mrs Barbara Auckland's activities during this period, on 25 June 1974, she telephoned Mr Jones to ask whether she could have her children to stay with her for a short period and he explained that this was impracticable but that arrangements could be made for her to see them if she came to Barnsley. Also on that day, she called to see Mr Douglas Drane, a social worker on duty in the Hounslow area of London. The following day, Mr Drane dictated a report of the visit which says that Mrs Barbara Auckland called for advice about housing so that she could have her three children in London with her. She recounted something of her history to Mr Drane,. . . .

241. On the night of 10 July 1974, Mr John Auckland left his three children in the care of Mr Michael Beaumont, his brother-in-law, and a neighbour, and went out for a drink, returning shortly after 10.00 p.m. Early the following morning he viciously assaulted his baby daughter so causing her death; the pathologist, Dr Alan Usher, on examining her body, found over a hundred marks of violence of different ages, the vast majority being soft tissue bruises which had been inflicted in the last ten to fourteen days of her life, many within the last thirty-six hours. To quote from his report —

'the injuries in this case though they fall short of the degree of violence required to break bones are far too numerous to be accounted for by a domestic accident or even a series of domestic accidents and I am in no doubt this child has been grossly physically abused by an adult.'

242. Mr John Auckland was subsequently charged with murder, tried at Sheffield Crown Court between 26–29 November 1974, and found guilty of manslaughter. He was sentenced to five years imprisonment which he is still serving. A charge that he had wilfully ill-treated his other daughter Mandy was not proceeded with, although there were three obvious marks of violence on her head and face at the time of Susan's death. Mr Jones failed to notice those marks when he went to the home after the killing, and he recorded that the surviving children were 'well'.

243. After the death of Susan, John Roy and Mandy were received into care and placed with foster-parents. Mrs Barbara Auckland subsequently took charge again of her two remaining children, and returned to live in Shafton; she was closely supervised by the social services and other agencies and to facilitate this, Barnsley Metropolitan Borough Council applied for a supervision order early in 1975, but were instead granted a care order which, even though the children remain with their mother, enables the local authority to remove them immediately should this prove necessary. Miss Ebo is currently supervising the family on behalf of the social services and we understand that the children are in good health and happy. Mrs Barbara Auckland is apparently coping well.

1 The search for explanations

Some impression of the huge research literature is given by Jenny Clifton in her account of *Factors Predisposing Family Members to Violence*, in the Scottish Social Work Services Group's collection of papers on *Violence in the Family* (1982):

The main perspectives from which researchers have attempted to explain the violence of family members are: the childhood experiences of violent individuals, pathological conditions, social stress and family interaction. These will be explored here, together with a brief mention of the victim's role as perceived by researchers. Each perspective will be explored in the context first of child abuse and then of wife battering.

Childhood experience

A number of researchers have found that the parent who abuses his or her child is likely to have been mistreated as a child. On this evidence it has been argued that a cycle of violence can occur whereby violent treatment of children is passed on from generation to generation (Ounsted and Lynch 1976; Court 1974). What this research fails to clarify is whether the important factor is violence to a child or neglect or rejection with which violence may be closely associated.

Two important studies which bear on this issue are those by Steele and Pollock (1968) and the NSPCC (1975), both of which emphasise the importance of early emotional experience. The mother's role as the attacker in both studies was attributed to her greater contact with the child and in Steele and Pollock's work the early emotional deprivation of both parents was felt to be of significance. The latter study describes parents who had experienced a lack of 'basic mothering', harsh discipline, conditional affection and high expectations of consistently good behaviour. The NSPCC study confirms the picture of poor emotional experience, actual physical abuse being less in evidence in the backgrounds of their mothers than severe disruptions and changes in caretaker. This study suggests that such emotional experiences seemed to be replicated in the following generation, the links being inadequate parental role models and the importance of a nurturing mother child relationship in the development of a healthy personality. The NSPCC study, however, admits to this being only a partial explanation and points out the unanswered questions. Why was the parental deprivation manifested in child abuse rather than some other form of disturbed behaviour? Why do not other parents with impoverished early lives batter their children? The study concludes that there remains 'little conception of the necessary or sufficient causes of child abuse' and that an emotionally deprived childhood is but one, albeit an important one. . . .

The interpretation of research into the impact of childhood experience of violence in the context of wife beating is complicated by lack of clarity about what counts as crucial violent history: whether it be the experience of violence or its observation and whether it is the wife's or the husband's experience which is more significant. The oft-quoted studies which investigate this are those of Gayford (1975) and Gelles (1972). The former was based on interviews with women at Chiswick Women's Aid refuge and has been severely criticised on methodological grounds (Wilson 1976). The findings clearly do need more careful testing. In a study likely to include the more extreme cases of battering, just 40% of wives said that their husbands had either been subjected to or had witnessed violence in childhood. Among the women themselves, 20% reported such experiences. Questions remain about the violent behaviour or victim status of the remainder. Gelles' study also leaves these unanswered questions. He concludes that those spouses who, whether as victims or witnesses, had experienced violence in childhood were more likely to be violent to their own spouse. Yet just as 50% of those in his sample who had witnessed violence engaged in it as adults, so the other half of that group did not become violent. Among those who had never experienced violence at the hands of their parents, 40% became violent to their spouse. As Marsden (1978) has said: 'It is not clear how much violence or what intensity, needs to be experienced as victim or witness in the family or via the media for it to be significantly associated with the later development of violent behaviour'. The value of Gelles' work to an understanding of this complex issue is his evidence on the widespread use of force in childhood socialisation which represents a general approval of violence. . . .

Pathology

Many attempts have been made to define the disturbed individual who is likely to batter his or her child. A wide range of psychiatric illnesses have been found to exist among battering parents, but there is no clear association between any of them and the phenomenon of child abuse. Frequently the only evidence claimed for the existence of a disturbed personality which is then said to be cause of violence, is the violence itself — a tautological argument at best. . . .

Some writers have attempted to delineate a particular personality type, independent of specific personality disorders and psychiatric illness, who might be violence-prone. Thus Steele and Pollock (1968) depict a type of person who has a very high expectation of the child's performance and a corresponding disregard for his needs and helplessness. Such a parent, feeling insecure and unloved, looks to the child for reassurance. Bad behaviour is interpreted as lack of such reassurance and violence can erupt. Steele and Pollock offer reasons for assaults on a particular child, such as sex or position in the family, and jealousy and compulsive behaviour figure in the pathology they propose. They quote a case:

> 'Kathy made this poignant statement: "I have never felt really loved all my life. When the baby was born, I thought he would love me, but when he cried all the time, it meant he

didn't love me, so I hit him''. Kenny, aged three weeks, was hospitalised with bilateral subdural haematomas'.

It is clear, however, that many of the families in the studies which attempt to describe a particular personality type face a range of stresses which might equally be used to explain their resort to violence.

As with parental abuse of children, it appears that some men who batter their wives are suffering from mental illness and that this plays the largest part in bringing about their violence. Studies such as those of Faulk (1974) and quoted by Scott (1974) indicate a high incidence of disturbance among battering men. However, much of this research has been based on highly selected, often criminal, populations. Erin Pizzey (1974) has spoken of battering men as psychopaths and cases of pathological jealousy are evidenced in the literature. Gelles (1972) quotes an example where a woman described her husband's harassment for her supposed infidelity:

'He would just keep it up until out of desperation I would admit anything in the world to get him to shut up. He would keep it up for five hours and not let me sleep. I would say, "Yes, I did, are you glad?" and then he would beat me.'

The instances quoted by Pizzey (1974) and by Dobash and colleagues (1978b) of frequent attacks when a wife is pregnant, may indicate pathological jealousy of the impending baby. . . .

There is not always a clear association between violence to a wife and violence to outsiders. While sub-culture theories and the idea that a man with a violent lifestyle or job will carry this behaviour into his family life and acquire an immunity to the effects of violence have been explored (Wolfgang and Ferracuti 1967; Westley 1970), it has not yet been substantiated that such men form the majority of battering husbands. Indeed it has been proposed that a more common situation may be that of the 'Jekyll and Hyde' marriage where the husband, while violent to his wife, is a perfectly respectable and pleasant person to everyone else (Marsden and Owens 1975). . . .

Some men, then, who beat their wives have personalities which lead them to be consistently violent and some are suffering from a range of psychiatric illnesses. The violence of some of these men will be exhibited more broadly than within marriage. However, it is unknown how many battering men fall into such categories and unclear how many 'ordinary' men engage in violence only to their wives and perhaps then only spasmodically. It is difficult too to reach any firm conclusions when the whole issue involves the contentious boundaries between pathology and normality.

Social stress

A number of writers on child abuse have noted the existence of a combination of stresses impinging on battering parents and often rely for their explanation of the violence on a stress-induced model. Writers have found poor housing, financial difficulties, social isolation, unemployment and illness among these parents. Gil (1973) argues that poverty is likely to be associated with abuse both because it weakens the parents' self-control and because there are distinct subcultural patterns of child rearing among poorer groups. The increased likelihood of the use of physical discipline may, it is suggested, spill over into violence of a more severe nature among poor working-class families where there are overcrowded living conditions and greater anxiety about adequate means of support. Steinmetz and Straus (1974) support this contention of the likelihood that violence will occur in association with stress factors, but argue against any simple assumption that child abuse is a working class phenomenon. They suggest that stress factors will press harder on poor families and increase the tendency for abuse to occur, so that stress rather than class is the important factor. The evidence is limited and it must be said that the apparent link between social stress and child abuse may well be due to the social class bias of the samples used in many studies. Most writers conclude that abused children come from all strata of society but that social deprivation and poor health are interacting factors which together increase the risk of violence. Whether the cause can be located in stress factors is perhaps less crucial to establish than the recognition that social deprivation enhances the likelihood of other problems or disorders associated with child abuse.

Stress as a factor in wife battering has been examined in a variety of ways. Some writers have suggested that such stress-inducing experiences as unemployment are associated with violence and have referred to the increased recorded incidence of violence in times of severe unemployment. In the present author's study of women who had used a refuge (Clifton, 1980) several women attributed the violence they had experienced to pressures and anxieties about money, the impact of which were sometimes increased when the husband had a drinking problem. Gelles (1972) argues that attacks by husbands on their wives can be seen as rational in the context of a response to stress which is translated into violence by means of a number of triggering factors such as alcohol. He maintains that alcohol is only indirectly related to violence through the release of inhibitions and that the use of alcohol may in itself be a response to stress. He feels that the link between violence and excessive drinking has been misrepresented and that drink may provide a rationalisation for violence. . . .

Family interaction
The quality of the marital relationship between the parents of the abused child has been considered by a number of authors but no single pattern of interaction is represented in the studies. Some have found considerable marital disharmony (Smith 1975) and others an extremely close and claustrophobic type of relationship (Ounsted and Lynch, 1976). Problems of lack of support for a young mother and unwanted pregnancies have been found to be common among abusing mothers and in a number of studies there is a high proportion of single parents (Smith, 1975; Gil 1973). The NSPCC studies (1975) have reflected upon the frequency of collusion in families of injured children. It may also be important to consider the impact of a father's lack of support in caring for the family when mother is under strain or is ill, as well as the pressures upon one partner not to seek advice although aware of his or her spouse's violence towards the child. In some instances both parents are emotionally vulnerable and there may be a complex chain of interaction whereby stress on one member may be felt by another whose response to the pressure is a violent one (Skinner and Castle 1969).

Another kind of stress has been posited as significant by those who seek for explanations in the arena of husband-wife interaction. O'Brien (1971) argues that status inconsistency in marriage may lead to violence. This may occur when a husband feels threatened by his wife's superior achievement or ascribed status, or where he is an under-achiever in the work setting. The likelihood of a particular individual perceiving this status inconsistency as a threat requires further explanation but it has been suggested by Pagelow (1977) that socialisation into and acceptance of the dominant role will vary in extent and that a man who has come to view male superiority as essential will be more likely to find such inconsistency stressful.

The role of the victim
There are indications in the research on child abuse that certain characteristics of the child may enhance the potential for abuse. Gelles (1973) has said that it is the very young child who is most at risk and that this ties in with unrealistic demands and expectations on the part of the parents. The premature baby is frequently over-represented in research samples (Skinner and Castle 1969; Lynch 1975). This has been explained in terms of the association of premature birth with lack of intimate contact between mother and child in the early weeks and the consequent prevention of bonding. Stress and ill-health in the mother and child may be common after premature birth, connecting prematurity and abuse in a different manner. A child who is particularly unresponsive or who cries excessively from birth may create unbearable stress for a parent and several studies have found innate variations between infants on a number of such behavioural factors (Schaffer & Emerson 1964; Birns et al 1969). Illegitimacy, the child's position in the family and his or her resemblance to another family member are all factors which have been considered significant (Allan 1978).

The consideration of the wife's role in cases of wife abuse has tended to focus less on passive factors and more on the question of provocation. Nagging, verbal aggression, even over-submission are all used in explanation and even justification in the literature (Storr 1974; Jobling 1974). It is hard, upon examining some of the case histories of battered women, to credit arguments that provoking words or actions could justify the type of torture and excessive beating inflicted upon them. Given the common acceptance of a husband's assumption of authority as head of the household, there is a wide range of behaviour which could be construed as challenging such dominance and which might lead to violence against the wife. In studying the evidence from their research the Dobashes (1980) concluded: 'The only pattern discernible in these lists (of provocative behaviour) is that the behaviour whatever it might be, represents some form of failure or refusal on the part of the woman to comply with or support her husband's wishes and authority'

Question

In *Meacher v Meacher* [1946] P 216, [1946] 2 All ER 307, Henn Collins J refused a divorce to a wife whose husband beat her because she refused to obey his orders not to visit her relatives: he thought that she 'had it in her own hands.' to prevent repetition of the attacks and so the court could not intervene even if her husband's orders were unreasonable. The Court of Appeal however found 'nothing in the legislation or authorities to justify the view that a wife who has suffered assaults cannot get a decree unless the assaults are likely to continue — nor is she disentitled to a decree because she has it in her power to put an end to the cruelty by obeying unreasonable orders from her husband.' Bromley in his textbook on *Family Law* (5th edn, 1976), however, used to argue that 'no spouse ought to be allowed to rely on the other's past conduct as a justification for living apart' where there is no probability of recurrence: (i) do you agree? and (ii) would that mean that a wife who can avoid recurrence of beating by obeying her husband's *reasonable* orders cannot get a divorce for his past behaviour? and (iii) can you think of some examples of orders so reasonable that disobedience merits a beating?

This points to an important argument which concentration on the personalities and motivations of individuals obscures. As Clifton herself points out:

While it is possible to examine the research into child abuse and wife battering within the same categories, there are several reasons for discussing the two forms of violence separately. Researchers have approached the two topics from different implicit theoretical standpoints and have asked different questions, making comparison difficult. The extent of overlap between different forms of violence in the same family is unclear but a link is not inevitable, and greater understanding may be gained from a focus on the differences in context between parent-child relationships and marital ones (Dobash and Dobash 1980). If the specific context of marital violence is fully considered, it proves possible to make sense of the direction of such violence — overwhelmingly from husband to wife (Lystad 1975) — by exploring attitudes to women rather than simply to violence.

And later

It has been argued . . . that such behaviour is best understood in terms of an extension of traditional male attitudes to female inferiority (Dobash and Dobash 1980). Such an approach, rather than concentrating attention upon individual men with disturbed personalities, focusses on the reasons why such pathology might be expressed in violence to a wife. This draws attention away from explanation based on deviant individuals and towards the normality of male dominance as an underlying feature of marital violence.

Even stronger support is provided by Michael Freeman in *Violence in the Home* (1979):

. . . Whitehurst has argued that the current move towards greater equality in marital roles may, in the short term, lead to an increase in marital violence. 'Men simply have no culturally approved ways of coping with "uppity" women who want to be really free'. (1974)

The ideology of superiority

Whitehurst's remarks lead conveniently to the final and most persuasive explanation as to why women are beaten by the men with whom they live. As the development of the Women's Movement has been a primary factor in sensitising our consciences to the plight of the battered woman, it is hardly surprising that theories as to the aetiology of male violence towards woman should have developed within the ideology of its liberation politics (Wilson, 1976). Nor is it surprising that the views of militant feminists should have created so little interest amongst government departments, the media or the general public. To them Erin Pizzey and Chiswick epitomise the problem and her definitions and solutions have become public property [the pathogical approach: see pp. 519–520, above]. The National Women's Aid Federation with a definition of the problem which indicts society is accorded little or no attention; its views, its solutions are too unpalatable for society to stomach.

The Women's Movement sees violence as a necessary concomitant of woman's generally oppressed position in the social structure. 'The challenge of Women's Aid', Weir writes, 'is that it demands a fundamental change in the way in which women are defined' (1977). The patriarchal bias endemic in culture and history and reflected in literature has been excellently documented by Millett (1969) and Bullough (1974). The view is thus propagated that the purpose of male violence is to control women. Male violence results from a Macho ideology which supports the male's use of violence to maintain his dominance over his mate.

Lest you consider such a suggestion extreme, it is worth recalling the words of John Stuart Mill in *The Subjection of Women* (1869):

The vilest malefactor has some wretched woman tied to him, against whom he can commit any atrocity except killing her, and, if tolerably cautious, can do that without much danger of the legal penalty. And how many thousands are there among the lowest classes in every country, who, without being in a legal sense malefactors in any other respect, because in every other quarter their aggressions meet with resistance, indulge the utmost habitual excesses of bodily violence towards the unhappy wife, who alone, at least of grown persons, can neither repel nor escape from their brutality; and towards whom the excess of dependence inspires their mean and savage natures, not with a generous forbearance, and a point of honour to behave well to one whose lot in life is trusted entirely to their kindness, but on the contrary with a notion that the law has delivered her to them as their thing, to be used at their pleasure, and that they are not expected to practise the consideration towards her which is required from them towards every-body else. The law, which till lately left even these atrocious extremes of domestic oppression practically unpunished, has within these few years made some feeble attempts to repress them. But its attempts have done little, and cannot be expected to do much, because it is contrary to reason and experience to suppose that there can be any real check to brutality, consistent with leaving the victim still in the power of the executioner.

Question

Do you think, as the magistrates (but not the Family Division) did in *Bergin v Bergin* [1983] 1 WLR 279, that a wife who accepted three black eyes 'as part of married life' can reasonably be expected to go on living with her husband when he next turns violent?

2 But is not violence a crime?

According to Erin Pizzey, in the book which first alerted the public to the modern realities of wife-beating, *Scream Quietly or the Neighbours will Hear* (1974):

The police attitude to wife-battering reveals an understandable but unacceptable schizophrenia in their approach to violence. Imagine that Constable Upright is on his beat one night and finds Mr Batter mugging a woman in the street. Mr Batter has already inflicted heavy bruises to the woman's face and is just putting the boot in when Constable Upright comes on the scene. The constable knows his duty and does it. He arrests Mr Batter, who is charged with causing grievous bodily harm and goes to prison for ten years.

Ten years later Constable Upright is on his beat when he is sent to investigate screaming which neighbours have reported coming from the home of the newly released Mr Batter. Mr Batter is mugging his wife. He's thrown boiling water at her, broken her nose, and now he's trying for her toes with a claw hammer. When Constable Upright arrives what does he do? Does he make an arrest? Of course not.

He knocks on the door and Mr Batter tells him to 'sod off'. He tells Mr Batter that the neighbours are complaining and he wishes to see his wife. Mr Batter says they have been having a minor row and he gets his wife who is looking bruised round the face and crying. The policeman will not arrest. In one case the husband even assaulted his wife in front of a policeman but still there was no arrest. All that he did was to advise her to go to the local magistrates' court the next morning and take out a summons against her husband, but he knew that she was unlikely to do this because she would have to live in the same house as her husband while she was taking him to court.

Much confirmation for what she says came from the evidence of various police bodies to the *House of Commons Select Committee on Violence in Marriage* (1975). Thus the Association of Chief Police Officers: '. . . Whilst such problems take up considerable Police time . . . in the majority of cases the role of the Police is a negative one. We are, after all dealing with persons "bound in marriage", and it is important, for a host of reasons, to maintain the unity of the spouses. Precipitate action by the Police could aggravate the position to such an extent as to create a worse situation than the one they were summoned to deal with. . . .'

Questions

(i) This is borne out by Jan Pahl's research (1982), which indicates that the police are far more likely to take action themselves if (*a*) the woman has already left for a refuge, or (*b*) although still under the same roof, the woman is not married to the man: can you list the 'host of reasons' why this might be?

(ii) How many of the reasons which might disincline a policeman to intervene appear to you to be valid?

(iii) What powers does Constable Upright have, if told to 'sod off' by a man who is apparently beating his wife inside the matrimonial home? (Consult *R v Thornley* (1980) 72 Cr App R 302.)

One problem is indicated by the evidence of the Metropolitan Police: 'whereas it is a general principle of police practice not to intervene in a situation . . . between a husband and wife in the course of which the wife had suffered some personal attack, any assault upon a wife by her husband, which amounted to physical injury of a serious nature is a criminal offence which it is the duty of the police to follow up and prosecute. Police will take positive action in every case of serious assault and will prosecute where there is sufficient evidence.'

Question

What is the distinction in law between a 'common assault' (for which the woman herself must prosecute privately) and an 'assault occasioning actual bodily harm' (for which the police could prosecute if they wished)? Is there a difference between 'actual bodily harm' under the Offences Against the Person Act 1861 and 'physical injury of a serious nature'?

Thus there may well be a difference between perceptions of seriousness in violence between husband and wife and those, for example, in violence between parent and child. But even if there were not, Mildred Dow puts her finger on the difficulty in *Police Involvement*, her contribution to *Violence in the Family* (edited by Marie Borland in 1976):

It has, however, been recognised in law for many centuries that the sanctity of marriage is something special. Until recent times a wife was seen as a chattel of her husband and had no real rights. In recent years it has become obvious to the writer, through years of police experience as a practical officer, that however often one says to a wife, 'Your rights are . . .' she will invariably be re-influenced by her husband and refuse to give the necessary evidence. Whether this is basically due to personal fear or to an essentially sexual attraction and influence, or to fear for the children of the union, it is difficult to determine. I only know how frustrating it is for a police officer who has taken much care and trouble in the preparation of the presentation of the case at court to be let down because his principal witness has had 'second thoughts'. If positive action is desirable when injury has been caused, quite often severe injury, we must overcome the problem of the wife who is unwilling to give evidence. Often her decision not to do so is made at the last minute, either as a result of reconciliation or perhaps through fear of retribution. From a practical viewpoint it would appear better to charge the husband and keep him in custody, rather than to follow the practice in some few police areas where the husband is reported for summons, thus giving him time to influence his wife. If some aggressive husbands are, by these means, kept away from the matrimonial home, more wives may be prepared to give the relevant evidence.

Question

A young constable is called to a 'domestic' dispute, in which (it turns out) the wife has suffered three cracked ribs and a dislocated collar bone in addition to numerous cuts and bruises. He arrests her husband, who is convicted of causing her grievous bodily harm and imprisoned. The constable later gives evidence in support of the wife's petition for divorce, which is granted. Three months after the husband is released from prison, the couple marry one another again. Has all his work been wasted?[1]

Hoskyn v Metropolitan Police Comr
[1979] AC 474, [1978] 2 All ER 136, [1978] 2 WLR 695, 122 Sol Jo 279, 67 Cr App Rep 88, House of Lords

The facts are taken from the speech of Lord Edmund Davies:

One evening in September 1975 a young woman, Janis Scrimshaw, was in a public house with her mother when she was called outside by the appellant, Edward William Hoskyn, with whom she had earlier in the year been on terms of friendship, but which she had later discontinued. Her mother remained inside, and shortly thereafter Janis suddenly fell through the door and into the bar, 'screaming and covered with blood'. When examined in a hospital casualty department, she was found to have sustained the following injuries inflicted by 'a sharp instrument': two stab wounds in the chest, penetrating the outer lining of the lung on each side; a 9 centimetre cut extending from the temple to her right ear; smaller cuts to her right lip and chin; and a 4½ centimetre cut to the left forearm.

She testified against the appellant before the examining justices and she named him as her assailant when submitting a claim to the Criminal Injuries Compensation Board. In February 1976 the appellant was committed for trial on a charge under s. 18 of the Offences against the Person Act 1861 of wounding Janis Scrimshaw with intent to cause her grievous bodily harm. On Friday, 1 October he was warned to attend for trial at the Central Criminal Court on the following Monday. On Saturday 2 October he married Janis Scrimshaw, and . . . on Tuesday 5 October his new bride was called for the prosecution and compelled to testify. . . . Following on his conviction and sentence to two years' imprisonment, Hoskyn unsuccessfully appealed to the Court of Appeal (Criminal Division) who, while refusing leave to appeal to this House, certified the following point of law involved as one of general public importance: 'Whether a wife is a compellable witness against her husband in a case of violence on her by him'.

Four of their lordships answered that question in the negative, overruling the decision of Court of Criminal Appeal in *R v Lapworth* [1931] 1 KB 117, 100 LJKB 52. Their reasons are summarised in the speech of Lord Wilberforce:

. . . A wife is in principle not a competent witness on a criminal charge against her husband. This is because of the identity of interest between husband and wife and because to allow her to give evidence would give rise to discord and to perjury and would be, to ordinary people, repugnant. Limited exceptions have been engrafted on this rule, of which the most important, and that now relevant, relates to cases of personal violence by the husband against her. This requires that, as she is normally the only witness and because otherwise a crime would go without sanction, she be permitted to give evidence against him. But does this permission, in the interest of the wife, carry the matter any further, or do the general considerations, arising from the fact of marriage and her status as a wife, continue to apply so as to negative compulsion? That argument was in just this form put to the House of Lords and in a general form answered in the affirmative [in *Leach v R* [1912] AC 305, 81 LJKB 616]. It was not faced in *R v Lapworth* at all.

But there was another point of view:

Lord Edmund-Davies: My Lords, when your Lordships' House is called on to determine a question of law regarding which there are no binding precedents and no authorities directly in

---

1. See the *Rideout* Case (the Oregonian marital rape) on p. 34, above.

point, and where it has accordingly to perform an act of law-making, I apprehend that the decision will largely turn on what is thought most likely to advance the public weal. . . . I have the misfortune to think that the law as your Lordships conceive it to be is inimical to the public weal, and particularly so at a time when disturbing disclosures of great violence between spouses are rife. Nor am I able to accept, as your Lordships have in fact said, that if spouses subjected to violence are to become compellable witnesses against their attackers it must be left to Parliament to say so. On the contrary, it is open to your Lordships to declare here and now that such is already the law, were you minded to do so.

His lordship then reviews the authorities and finds them balanced between the rule that, in general, a wife is neither a competent nor a compellable witness against her husband, and the rule that, in general, if a witness is competent, he is compellable. Accordingly, he concludes that their lordships are not bound to decide one way or the other, and continues:

The noble and learned Lord, Viscount Dilhorne, has spoken of the repugnance created by a wife being compelled '. . . to testify against her husband on a charge involving violence, no matter how trivial and no matter the consequences to her and to her family'. For my part I regard as extremely unlikely any prosecution based on trivial violence being persisted in where the injured spouse was known to be a reluctant witness. Much more to the point, as I think, are cases such as the present, as *Morgan*, and as others arising from serious physical maltreatment by one spouse of the other.

Such cases are too grave to depend simply on whether the injured spouse is, or is not, willing to testify against the attacker. Reluctance may spring from a variety of reasons and does not by any means necessarily denote that domestic harmony has been restored. A wife who has once been subjected to a 'carve up' may well have more reasons than one for being an unwilling witness against her husband. In such circumstances, it may well prove a positive boon [for] her to be directed by the court that she has no alternative but to testify. But, be that as it may, such incidents ought not to be regarded as having no importance extending beyond the domestic hearth. Their investigation and, where sufficiently weighty, their prosecution is a duty which the agencies of law enforcement cannot dutifully neglect.

Question

The Police and Criminal Evidence Bill (1982) implements the recommendations of the Criminal Law Revision Committee (pp. 54–55, above): 'repugnant' or a 'positive boon'?

Even if the problems of police and victim reluctance can be overcome, there remains the question of whether the criminal law is appropriate to the problem at all, or whether the various methods of 'diverting' such cases out of the criminal justice system present a better solution. One view is represented by Susan Maidment in her discussion of *The Relevance of the Criminal Law to Domestic Violence* (1980):

In this country police diversion occurs for all the wrong reasons. Police reluctance to prosecute arises from the fact that the wife often becomes subsequently a reluctant victim or witness, unwilling to give evidence against her husband; from a belief in victim precipitation; from a misplaced emphasis on a successful conviction rate as a measure of police efficiency; from an unwillingness to spend what is considered to be an exorbitant amount of time on relatively minor family disputes; from the dangers in the United States to the police if they get caught in the crossfire between husband and wife; and in general from what is considered to be a time-consuming distraction to the overall police effort, leading to job demoralisation, because it is incompatible with the obligations of a law-enforcement agency.

The reasons for police diversion may be considered to be wrong, but the fact of police diversion is further evidence of a general belief in society, as seen also in Parliament's provision of more and better civil remedies, that domestic violence should not be dealt with as a matter for the criminal law. As yet however police diversion has not been institutionalised, as it has for example in respect of juveniles in the juvenile liaison bureaux. . . .

Strong arguments can be put forward why the criminal law should be used in all cases of domestic violence. It would be a clear affirmation of social values, of condemnation by society, and a clear statement of the personal responsibility and accountability of the offender. We know that the criminal law can provide an effective and prompt protection for the victim. The criminal law can at least attempt to prevent an escalation of violence either through incarceration, or by making at the outset the strongest statement that society can make denouncing the act. The police are in any case often involved in emergency calls, and they may be the only agency with the authority and ability to cope with such volatile situations.

On the other side there are arguments against the use of the criminal law. It is a blunt tool. It misplaces emphasis on the offender, not the victim. There is no facility for treatment within the system, for example, for understanding and attempting to control aggression, except probation, but then the husband is still at large. No attempt is made to improve the marital relationship, to develop mutual respect between husband and wife. On a more technical level, there are problems of proof in criminal law, as compared with the easier standard of proof for an injunction. This may lead to some acquittals purely on technical grounds. For the wife however this means a lack of protection.

In more general terms a criminal conviction and sentence for the husband may be counter-productive for the wife in many ways. There may be financial disadvantage to the wife, emotional loss to the children. It may only escalate the problem because of the husband's anger and grudge against her; imprisonment is only a temporary respite (though this argument could equally apply to injunctions). It may not be what the wife really wants — she would like to have him treated. She may feel guilty and responsible for him being punished or locked away. Indeed her initial call to the police may not be a cry for criminal action at all; it is simply the only place she knows to turn to in an emergency.

Indeed the present operation of the criminal law, when it is invoked in these cases, makes a mockery of the criminal process, because of the derisory sentences that are passed, even for example where the charge is actual bodily harm (Select Committee, 1975; Pizzey, 1974). The basic problem to which the use of the criminal law gives rise has been well expressed in the following statement:

'Of all the areas in which an alternative to criminal treatment seems justified, the area of marital disputes is the most obvious. This is not to say that violence, theft or neglect between spouses should be ignored, but it does appear that these cases deserve different treatment than they are now given. Whether prosecution is decided upon or not, it would seem that beyond the point of immediate police response to danger, the criminal process is largely irrelevant in these cases. If anything, its very invocation may exacerbate poverty-related and/or psychological problems. The summary, rather shallow treatment given these complainants does not answer the need that they have expressed for help.' (Subin, 1966)

Nevertheless there are some cases where the criminal law has to be used. These cases should be restricted to those occasions when there is a need present for coercive prevention of violence in view of serious physical or emotional danger to the wife. It is all the other cases, where there is a choice between the civil and criminal remedy, which give rise to problems of decision-making. At present the choice of remedy is, as already described, haphazard. It depends partly on the wife's choice as to whether she goes to a solicitor or to the police, and on the police as to whether they are willing to prosecute. In practice the choice will effectively be made by the police since they will usually be involved in the very initial stages. But the fact is that the choice of remedy can and ought to be a professional principled decision. There are some clear issues to be considered, and serious arguments for and against the use of the criminal law as already described. A professional decision needs to be arrived at after full consideration of the alternative remedies available.

The other side of the argument is forcefully put from the other side of the Atlantic by Raymond I. Parnas, in *The Relevance of Criminal Law to Inter-Spousal Violence* (1978):

In the last ten years recognition of the peace-keeping role of the police and the exorbitant amount of criminal justice agency time spent on relatively minor family disputes has led to systematic attempts to deal with this problem. The efforts have primarily concentrated on crisis intervention training and techniques for the police, mediation centers, procedures for the prosecution and family court jurisdiction by the judiciary. The compassion and humanity of the social services has been increasingly interjected to effect more organized and 'knowledgeable' efforts at diversion, counseling, referral, mediation and treatment in much the same way that juveniles received the 'benefit' of such progressive thought by the creation of the quasi criminal juvenile courts and their behavioralist adjuncts at the turn of the century. . . .

The trouble with such a trend for inter spousal violence *now* is that the juvenile and adult processes, in the United States at least, confronted with intolerable rates of delinquency and criminality, have recently been discarding and rethinking the commendable, but still unproven, facets of models based on sickness, treatment and rehabilitation, and have been returning to the known entities of personal public accountability for bad acts, with appropriate and acknowledged punishment, enlightened and softened somewhat by prior experience with the social services. . . .

Incidents of inter-spousal violence, no matter how minimal, must remain subject to police intervention. For years a disproportionate number of disturbances, assaults, batteries, uses of deadly weapons, mayhems, and homicides have involved family members. Despite the resources necessary and the danger inherent in responding to such calls, no entity other than a police agency has the authority and ability to cope with such volatile situations. Central to the function of the police and the criminal law is the protection of life and limb.

The basic question is: what response, if any, should the legal system make after the dispute has been halted by police intervention? This is a crucial stage for another reason. It is at this point that an offender and a victim in a continuing volatile situation have been identified. All of the data showing the extent of inter-spousal violence and the experience of escalation from minimal to aggravated injury indicate that it would be irresponsible governmental action to drop the matter at this point. In fact, however, what we have been doing is to ignore the extremely important preventative, corrective, retributive, incapacitative, and deterrent implications of this early official knowledge of subsequent potential violence. At the very least, an adequate record keeping procedure must be implemented so that all those responding to subsequent incidents will know of the disputants' prior history so that an appropriate relevant additional response can be made. But even more important than our criminal law's traditional escalation of meaningless slaps on the wrist until too late, is recognition of the need for a breakthrough at the outset to the consciousness of the disputants as to the seriousness of their behavior and not later than the second time around at most.

In my judgment, only the coercive, authoritative harshness of the criminal process can do this. Efforts at therapy can, and I suppose should, be included in the process but should not be given undue emphasis, for there is simply no evidence that we know how to diagnose, much less treat, disputants' problems in a manner that will prevent repetition. Simply put, we must go with what we know. And we know that we cannot ignore or condone acts or threats of imminent violence. We know that the police are best equipped to protect others and themselves. We know how to punish, whether by fine, incapacitation, other denials of full liberty, embarrassment, inconvenience, *etc.* And we know punishment is a clear statement of the personal responsibility of the offender and the condemnation and retribution of society. We also know that where punishment is to be imposed, the criminal process provides the best safeguards that such punishment is imposed on the appropriate person under the most adequate circumstances. We know that incapacitation prevents repetition during the period of incarceration. Finally I submit that we are increasingly coming to believe that punishment, quickly, fairly, proportionately and appropriately imposed, may deter or reduce the quality and quantity of some kinds of bad conduct at least as well, if not better, than attempts at speculative therapy, and thus may serve the rehabilitation function even better from the perspective of non-repetition.

Questions

(i) Which of these two views is most likely to be held (*a*) by a person who subscribes to the individual pathology theory of causation (the 'Pizzey' view); (*b*) by a person who subscribes to the radical feminist theory (the 'National Women's Aid Federation' view); (*c*) by Constable Upright?

(ii) How many of these arguments apply with equal force to the prosecution of parents who ill-treat or neglect their children?

The arguments for and against the use of the criminal law against parents who abuse their children are well-rehearsed by Mrs C Somerhausen in her contribution to the Council of Europe's volume on the *Criminological Aspects of the Ill-treatment of Children in the Family* (1981):

Ill-treating a child may be an offence, however the facts are interpreted or explained, (Carter, 1977) and in many cases the first solution that suggests itself is punishment of the offenders and stiffening of the penalties. Even if one is convinced that the protection of the victim and prevention of further ill-treatment are equally — if not more — important, there is no escape from the law. But what do we want it to do? Most certainly, to punish a failure to abide by social values which are regarded as essential. Although a court case may solve nothing in itself, and do nothing to repair the damage to the victim, it does express violent reproof and a refusal to countenance behaviour beyond certain acceptable limits. 'If we do not punish parents who torment their children, are we not as good as saying that they have the right to torture them?' (Foulon, 1978) From this point of view the main justification for punishment is that it satisfies the social norm and reassures the community, by reaffirming the existence of rights and the obligation to respect them.

Punishment also has a positive effect in that it affords the victim immediate protection, by putting an instant stop to the ill-treatment and removing all opportunity for its perpetrator to do more harm.

In view of the growing number of cases reported it is permissible to ask, in this as in so many other fields, whether criminal punishment has much value as an example or deterrent; in this connection it is worth remembering that the father of Susan Auckland [pp. 515–518, above], who was responsible for her death, had previously been convicted of killing another of his children.

Even so, some people believe that a trial, or even the threat of prosecution, can bring pressure to bear upon an ill-treating parent, give him the jolt of a sudden encounter with reality and incite him to accept some other approach to the situation (Deltaglia, 1976). The risk remains that the parents will then affect ostensibly irreproachable behaviour while continuing the ill-treatment, but in some other, less easily perceptible form.

Punishment is one of the ways in which society strives to combat such situations and the criminal trial may settle the conflict between the offender and society, but it does nothing to improve the plight of the victim or solve the underlying problems, which can be analysed in the more complex terms of family dysfunction and the play of deviant interrelationships. The offender is the only target of the criminal case, which shows scant concern for the dialectics of the relationships uniting offender and victim or, in different terms, for the members of the family constellation.

Lastly, the clientele of the courts is the product of various selective processes, with the result that in practice, a degree of social discrimination is inherent in this extreme form of social response, and whatever operational value it might have becomes only relative.

Question

What does she mean by 'various selective processes'?

This point is important, because in the context of marital violence it is tempting to assume that those who seek explanations in the structure of society rather than in individual pathology will also be inclined to prefer the criminal to the therapeutic model for state intervention, not least because such theories are usually associated with objections to the all-curing 'therapeutic state.' Indeed, Freeman has voiced those objections in the context of child abuse (in his contribution to *Welfare Law and Policy* (1979), edited by Martin Partington and Jeffrey Jowell), but his views on prosecution for child abuse are clear and pragmatic: in *Violence in the Home* (1979) he says:

The criminal law as a mechanism to protect children from abuse is ineffective. It is often extremely difficult to obtain a conviction: there are problems of evidence and proof. An acquittal may be seen by the parent as a vindication of the legitimacy of his behaviour and this in turn makes therapeutic intervention impossible. Successful prosecutions, on the other hand, which are few and far between do not act as deterrents but tend instead to confirm the parent in his 'negative self-image'. There is also the danger that a parent who knows he may be prosecuted may neglect or delay to seek medical treatment for his injured child because of fear of the consequences. Furthermore, prosecutions may divide families. There is no doubt, though, that in really serious cases prosecutions must and do take place.

Question

Do you have any qualms about confirming the 'negative self image' of a parent who is guilty of neglecting or ill-treating his child?

Some of the special difficulties of allocating guilt in the traditional way may be illustrated by two cases, one of neglect and the other of ill-treatment, both of which raise broader issues of principle:

R v Sheppard
[1981] AC 394, [1980] 3 All ER 899, [1980] 3 WLR 960, 124 Sol Jo 864, 72 Cr App Rep 82, House of Lords

The facts are taken from the speech of Lord Edmund Davies:

My Lords, in November 1979 the appellants were convicted in the Crown Court at Northampton of cruelty to their son Martin between 1 July 1978 and 29 January 1979, contrary to s. 1(1) of the Children and Young Persons Act 1933. By leave of the single judge, they appealed to the Court of Appeal, Criminal Division, which dismissed their appeals and, in granting them leave to come to this House, certified the following to be a point of law of general importance:

'What is the proper direction to be given to a jury on a charge of wilful neglect of a child under s. 1 of the Children and Young Persons Act 1933 as to what constitutes the necessary mens rea of the offence?'

These are the relevant parts of s. 1:

'(1) If any person who has attained the age of 16 years and has the custody, charge, or care of any child or young person under that age, wilfully assaults, ill-treats, neglects, abandons, or exposes him . . . in a manner likely to cause him unnecessary suffering or injury to health . . . that person shall be guilty of a misdemeanour . . .

'(2) For the purposes of this section — (a) a parent or other person legally liable to maintain a child or young person shall be deemed to have neglected him in a manner likely to cause injury to his health if he has failed to provide adequate food, clothing, medical aid or lodging for him . . .'

Martin Sheppard, who died at the age of 16 months on 28 January 1979 of hypothermia associated with malnutrition, was the youngest of the appellants' three children. He had seemingly taken no solid food for about five days before death, and no milk for two days, and the complete absence of subcutaneous fat indicated that he had lacked sufficient food for a substantial period. For several days before death he had suffered from gastro-enteritis and this had rendered him incapable of ingesting nourishment. The home was poor and the main room lacked a power point. And the appellants had failed to keep three appointments made by the health visitor over a period of months for Martin to see a paediatrician. . . .

But the appellants seemed to be of low intelligence, and in summary form their case was (1) that, while they appreciated that Martin's physical development had been slow, this did not alarm them as so also had been his father's, (2) that, although they were aware that he had lately been vomiting back his food, they thought that this was due to no more than a passing upset which would soon disappear of itself, and (3) that they had accordingly not realised that he needed a doctor's attention. Directing the jury, the learned judge said:

'In addressing you [defence counsel] put forward this proposition. He said that if the defendants, either of them, do not know any better, how can they be guilty of neglect? If they do not know they are neglecting the child, how can they be guilty of neglect? I hope it is quite clear on what I have told you that in my judgment that is not the law . . . You ask yourself what a reasonable parent would have done in the circumstances. Would he or she have behaved in this way? Did the defendants or either of them fail to do that, for whatever reasons? If they did, it is objectively neglect by that parent, and the question remains; is it wilful? As I say, so far as "wilful" is concerned, there is *no* requirement that the parent who deliberately neglects should be found to have foreseen the consequences . . . The question is: is it deliberate?'

That direction was taken from the case of *R v Senior* [1899] 1 QB 283, 68 LJQB 175, in which the child's father knew of the risk to his child's physical health but failed to provide medical attention because his religion taught that this was sinful and against the interests of his child's spiritual welfare. All their lordships thought that *Senior* was right in its result, but the majority disagreed with the 'reasonable parent' direction. They supported Lord Diplock's answer to the certified question:

To 'neglect' a child is to omit to act, to fail to provide adequately for its needs, and, in the context of s. 1 of the 1933 Act, its physical needs rather than its spiritual, educational, moral or emotional needs. These are dealt with by other legislation. . . . The use of the verb 'neglect' cannot, in my view, of itself import into the criminal law the civil law concept of negligence. The actus reus in a case of wilful neglect is simply a failure, for whatever reason, to provide the child whenever it in fact needs medical aid with the medical aid it needs. Such a failure as it seems to me could not be properly described as 'wilful' unless the parent *either* (1) had directed his mind to the question whether there was some risk (though it might fall far short of a probability) that the child's health might suffer unless he were examined by a doctor and provided with such curative treatment as the examination might reveal as necessary, and had made a conscious decision for whatever reason, to refrain from arranging for such medical examination, *or* (2) had so refrained because he did not care whether the child might be in need of medical treatment or not. . . .

To give to s. 1(1) of the 1933 Act the meaning which I suggest it bears would not encourage parents to neglect their children nor would it reduce the deterrent to child neglect provided by the section. It would afford no defence to parents who do not bother to observe their children's health or, having done so, do not care whether their children are receiving the medical examination and treatment that they need or not; it would involve the acquittal of those parents only who through ignorance or lack of intelligence are genuinely unaware that their child's health may be at risk if it is not examined by a doctor to see if it needs medical treatment. And, in view of the abhorrence which magistrates and juries feel for cruelty to helpless children, I have every confidence that they would not readily be hoodwinked by false claims by parents that it did not occur to them that an evidently sick child might need medical care.

The minority, however, supported the *Senior* direction, for the reasons given by Lord Fraser thus:

The provisions of what is now s. 1 of the 1933 Act are intended by Parliament for the protection of children who are unable to look after themselves and are in the care of older people. There is nothing unreasonable in their being stringent and objective. If the offence required proof that the particular parents were aware of the probable consequences of neglect, then the difficulty of proof against stupid or feckless parents would certainly be increased and so I fear might the danger to their children. Such parents would not necessarily be unaffected by the existence of an absolute offence; they might not be able to appreciate when their child needed medical care whenever the child showed any signs of ill-health, even though the signs might seem to them to be trivial. I recognise that the climate of opinion has recently become less favourable than it once was to the recognition of absolute offences, but I do not think that such change of climate as has taken place justifies us in departing from a construction of this provision which has been consistently followed by the courts since 1899, and which is, at the very least, not manifestly wrong. Especially in these times when parental responsibility for children tends to be taken all too lightly, such a sharp change towards relaxation of the law on the subject seems to me appropriate only for the legislature and not for the courts.

Questions

(i) If you had been on the jury, and the 'right' direction had been given, what would have been your verdict?

(ii) Which is worse: failing to call the doctor out to a vomiting baby or caring for your child in such a way that he has a 'complete absence of subcutaneous fat'?

(iii) Do not let the fancy words fool you: this baby was 'starved' (in both senses of the word) to death: supposing that the parents had realised what was happening, do you consider them more or less blameworthy than John Auckland?

(iv) But if parents are so incompetent that they do not even realise that their child is starving, should they be allowed to have children at all? (But see *Re D (A Minor)(wardship: sterilisation)* [1976] Fam 185, [1976] 1 All ER 326, p. 577, below.)

(v) What would have been your verdict if Martin's father had said, 'the wife must have known that something was the matter, but of course I didn't; I left all that sort of thing to her; it's the mother's job to look after the kids . . .'?

(vi) And what if they had been a nice middle-class couple whose well-fed baby died after a night of vomiting during which they had agonised over whether to call the doctor but decided that it could not be serious enough to drag him out of bed at two o'clock in the morning?

R v Derriviere
(1969) 53 Cr App Rep 637, Court of Appeal

The Court upheld a sentence of six months' imprisonment in the following case, described in the judgment of Lord Widgery CJ:

The facts put forward by the prosecution were that on 27 August at about 5.30 p.m. the appellant was disturbed because his son, Cyril [aged 12] had not come home, and he went out to look for him. He found him, brought him home, reprimanded him for not having come in, and told him to apologise to his mother or explain to his mother why he had misbehaved. The child would not do this, and then it seems clear that the appellant struck him several blows. There was some dispute as to whether he struck him with his fist alone or whether he also banged his head against the wall, and it is perhaps more reliable to turn to the evidence of the doctor as to the consequence of the incident. The doctor who examined the boy found tenderness and swelling of recent origin below the right eye, swelling and tenderness of a similar character below the left eye, no sign of injury to the actual visual mechanism of either eye, the lower lip was swollen with bleeding lacerations on the internal aspect, there was also pain at the angle of the jaw on the right side. There was, however, no fracture or bony injury. It is that assault which gave rise to the present charge.

The appellant is thirty-three, he is from the West Indies, a married man with these two children, and there is nothing against him in his record except the offence of attacking his daughter to which I have already referred.

This case raises difficult issues which must be considered with care. It was said below, and no doubt with truth, that standards of parental correction are different in the West Indies from those which are acceptable in this country; and the Court fully accepts that immigrants coming to this country may find initially that our ideas are different from those upon which they have been brought up in regard to the methods and manner in which children are to be disciplined. There can be no doubt that once in this country, this country's laws must apply; and there can be no doubt that, according to the law of this country, the chastisement given to this boy was excessive and the assault complained of was proved.

Nevertheless, had this been a first offence, and had there been some real reason for thinking that the appellant either did not understand what the standards in this country were or was having difficulty in adjusting himself, the Court would no doubt have taken that into account and given it such consideration as it could. The really outstanding fact in this case is that this was not the first offence. There was, as I say, the earlier occasion in 1968 when his child was beaten very severely. As a result of the incident both her wrists were fractured, and that in itself tells its own tale. . . .

Notwithstanding that warning, within a few months he is found chastising this boy in a manner which is wholly unacceptable according to the law of England and in the face, as it seems to us, of the warning he had been given.

Questions

(i) *Lawful* chastisement is, of course, still a defence: suppose that instead of giving his son two black eyes and a cut lip Mr Derriviere had given him three strokes of a cane upon his bottom: would this have been 'wholly unacceptable according to the law of England'?

(ii) If your answer is 'no', does this mean that you may beat your child's bottom but not his head?

(iii) But if your answer is 'yes', what would you consider an appropriate sentence for (*a*) the headmaster of a state school, (*b*) the head boy of a public school, or (*c*) the officer in charge of a community home, each of whom administered similar punishment to a boy who stayed out late?

(iv) Do you accept that parents have a right to insist that children are on time for meals?

(v) If you do, what should parents do if their children are late?
(vi) How should the law react to the Asian father who beats his daughter for going out with boys?

One view on this issue has been succinctly put by Alec Samuels in *Never Hit a Child* (1977):

Violence begets violence. Violence is degrading. Violence solves nothing. A civilised society must abhor violence. The law should set clear and simple standards, and thus play its part, albeit a small and supporting part, in the education of our people. The proscription of parental violence by law would not in any way detract from the need for discipline of the child. But explanation, restraint, confinement to his room, deprivation of privileges, expression of displeasure, all these and many other proper methods could and should be used in order to attain a proper level of discipline. Spare the rod and spoil the child is a false aphorism because it assumes that only one of two extremes is possible, and that there is no middle ground. It may be objected that such a law would be broken and unenforceable. Such an argument has always been used against every good new law. The law cannot hope to eliminate social abuse. But it may be able to set people thinking to improve standards, to induce restraint, to reduce abuse, and to make the conviction of the abusers easier.

When George Bernard Shaw said: 'Never hit a child, except in anger,' he was rightly condemning premeditated abuse by the parent, and no doubt recognising the human frailty of the parent, who inevitably from time to time will lose his temper over the child. But the right-thinking parent recognises that he was wrong, and feels contrition. How much better for the law to say: 'Never hit a child.'

There is one further practical problem associated with prosecution, which is referred to by Robert Dingwall, John Eekelaar and Topsy Murray in their summary of the results of their recent research into decision-making in the care of children thought to have been abused or neglected, published in 1981 as *Care or Control?*

We offer no comments on the desirability or otherwise of such prosecutions, but do consider the effect of such prosecution on the decision respecting the pursuance of care proceedings regarding the children. We note that, despite the attempt by Home Office Circular to reduce the delays [which] prosecutions cause to the initiation of such proceedings, considerable delays can still occur, largely due to the time it takes the police to decide what course to take. During this period social services feel considerable reluctance in making long term plans for the child. Should the police decide not to prosecute, social services sometimes see this as an indication that care proceedings may fail.

Although some lawyers consider that care proceedings should never be brought while a prosecution was pending because this might prejudice the potential accused, other lawyers took a different view. We think that, unless the time taken for criminal proceedings to be concluded can be considerably shortened, care proceedings should take their course. In any case, communication between the police and social services while a decision about prosecution is awaited should be considerably improved.

But as with battered wives, it is one thing to question the utility of prosecution and quite another thing to deny the police a role in choosing the most appropriate response. The case for their involvement is put by the House of Commons Select Committee on Violence in the Family in its Report on *Violence to Children* (1977):

114. . . . While much of the tenor of our Report has been to suggest that early detection, and preventive and supportive work in the community provide hopeful means of dealing with non-accidental injury we do not wish to suggest that this is an area in which the criminal law should not operate. Throughout our enquiry we have had in mind recent shocking cases of violence to children which have greatly disturbed the public. We have stressed the need, the almost unlimited need, to find ways of helping parents of young children to cope and what we have suggested will, we hope, help to reduce the number of cases of non-accidental injury. But we recognise that there always will be cases of cold, calculated cruelty or extreme neglect, in which it is obvious that children must be removed speedily and probably permanently from their families. In such cases criminal prosecution of those who have had charge of the children may well be inevitable.

. . . .

116. In many areas there is good co-operation between the police and other agencies. Difficulties have however arisen over the extent to which police intervention may, in the view of other professionals, prejudice the chances of treating a family's total problem. On the other hand the point is sometimes made that because of their training the police are often more successful in finding evidence in the home and interviewing people to establish the truth than doctors and social workers, and also that it is unfair to everyone that the police should only be called in when the trail is cold. Nevertheless, involvement of the police need not, and usually does not, entail criminal prosecution.

117. We recognise the difficulties that the police face in dealing with non-accidental injury. But in a sense these difficulties reflect the dilemma the police in this country have always faced of being both law enforcement officers and, as one Chief Superintendent put it to us, 'the oldest social workers'. In this context we are pleased to note the obvious effort the police have put into 'community liaison' or 'community involvement'. We are confident that the police can and do contribute not only as those charged with the responsibility for prosecuting offenders, but also as those able to give information which will be of assistance in making decisions about families. They are, therefore, very much concerned with prevention. Too often in this field both the police and social workers are thought of as stereotypes. This does scant justice to the support and assistance that is given to children and their families by both. The difficult situations are those where it is suspected, on either side, that effective action, or the right action, will not be taken.

. . . .

119. We endorse the active cooperation and involvement of police in the management of non-accidental injury. Before this can become more general there must be confidence in the arrangements proposed by DHSS and the Home Office in their circular of November 1976. In particular we would stress the importance of communicating knowledge of any previous criminal record and other relevant information. There must be confidence that an invitation, as a matter of course, to attend case conferences will not result in any breach of confidentiality, that whenever possible the decisions of a case conference will be adhered to, and that there can be sufficient delegation from Chief Officers of Police to ensure that officers who attend can genuinely take part in the decisions made. We recommend that the police be fully involved in the management of non-accidental injury, and particularly that they be invited to all case conferences.[2]

Question

The following question is put by Mildred Dow, the Chief Superintendent of Police who contributed to *Violence in the Family* (1977): but contemplate what happened to Barbara Auckland and her children before answering it:

Why, I wonder, do many people feel we should back-pedal over cases of child abuse and that the parents responsible need help when they inflict what are sometimes dreadful injuries on their own children? Is this line of thought just fashionable at the moment? The same people feel that when a defenceless wife is battered, strong action should be taken by the police, the husband arrested and placed in the cells. Although the battered wife is capable of taking action in her own defence, both physically and later verbally, the battered child is often too young to speak, though cruelly injured beyond words. It is recognised that in the case of the child he can be removed from home under a place of safety order and, eventually, a care order. Many children, though, are returned home by both social workers and magistrates to face further atrocities. Have we got our priorities right?

---

2. Guidance from the DHSS issued in 1976 put these recommendations into effect.

3 The search for alternative protection for the battered woman

(a) THE DEVELOPMENT OF THE INJUNCTION

Mildred Dow may think that women can speak up for themselves, and certainly they may do so better than a tiny child, but many things may make her dumb. Much of what Mill (1869) had to say is surprisingly valid still:.

All causes, social and natural, combine to make it unlikely that women should be collectively rebellious to the power of men. They are so far in a position different from all other subject classes, that their masters require something more from them than actual service. Men do not want solely the obedience of women, they want their sentiments. All men, except the most brutish, desire to have, in the woman most nearly connected with them, not a forced slave, but a willing one, not a slave merely, but a favourite. They have therefore put everything in practice to enslave their minds. . . . All women are brought up from the very earliest years in the belief that their ideal of character is the very opposite to that of men. . . . All the moralities tell them that it is the duty of women, and all the current sentimentalities that it is their nature, to live for others; to make complete abnegation of themselves, and to have no life but in their affections. And by their affections are meant the only ones they are allowed to have — those to the men with whom they are connected, or to the children who constitute an additional and indefeasible tie between them and a man.

But surely women have their own means of getting their way?

I grant that a wife, if she cannot effectually resist, can at least retaliate; she, too, can make the man's life extremely uncomfortable, and by that power she is able to carry many points which she ought, and many which she ought not, to prevail in. But this instrument of self-protection — which may be called the power of the scold, or the shrewish sanction — has the fatal defect, that it avails most against the least tyrannical superiors, and in favour of the least deserving dependants. . . . The amiable cannot use such an instrument, the highminded disdain it.

Jenny Clifton's review of the literature (1982) suggests that such sentiments have survived into the days of legal equality:

It is important to view the battered wife in the context of a family network which may tacitly or explicitly support the husband's position. The problems of the wife who does not think she will be believed if she tells how her apparently normal husband is a batterer . . . represent a crucial component of the explanation for women remaining in a violent relationship. Women's own hopes and expectations of marriage and family life, added to the pressures from others to keep the family together, the very real hardships of life alone and the social disadvantages of divorced status offer plenty of scope for the explanation of women's apparent tolerance of a violent relationship without recourse to suppositions that women must need the violence in a pathological way (Holman 1970; Marsden 1978; Barker and Allen 1976; Hart 1976). This is not to say that conflict which may occasionally spill into violence does not sometimes become an integral part of a marital relationship (Cade 1978) but the consistent picture from research studies is that women who are beaten do not come to need or enjoy their victimisation (Dobash and Dobash 1980). Neither are conflict-ridden marriages and relationships which occasionally involve physical combat quite the same as marriages in which the wife is frequently and brutally subjected to physical force.

Human nature may not have changed, but the law has: Mill pointed out that 'it is contrary to reason and experience to suppose that there can be any real check to brutality, consistent with leaving the victim still in the power of the executioner.' The first step had therefore to be to improve and extend the procedures for releasing wives from their lifelong promise and legal duty to live with their husbands. But it is one thing to be told that you need no longer live with your husband, or even that you may find a new one, and another thing to pluck up the courage to live through the interim before the decree, and to find somewhere to live both then and thereafter. The courts recognised the first of these problems and developed the matrimonial injunction as a solution: its advantages and disadvantages are discussed by Susan Maidment in her valuable overview of *The Law's Response to Marital Violence in England and the USA* (1977):

Matrimonial injunctions, available in the High Court and county court, are of two kinds. The non-molestation injunction, i.e. an order to the offender not to molest, assault, pester or interfere in any way with the spouse (it thus covers lesser to graver situations including cases where there is not actually any physical violence), and the injunction to vacate the matrimonial home. The court may, instead of granting an injunction, accept an undertaking by the offender not to molest. The effect is the same for a breach of the injunction or undertaking and is a contempt of court, for which imprisonment can be the penalty. The contempt can be purged, i.e. a release from prison, by a promise of good behaviour in the future.

Procedurally injunctions are very flexible, indeed this is their greatest advantage. Normally two days' notice of the hearing to the offender is required to give him a chance to be heard in his own defence, and a full hearing is normally held seven days after the complaint. But in a case of emergency, an ex parte application can be made and an interim injunction granted in the absence of the offender. Solicitors have vied with each other in the race to see who can get the quickest injunction. One report claimed a record injunction to vacate served on the husband within four-and-a-half hours of having received the initial complaint from the wife (the speed was aided by the prior existence of an emergency legal aid application, and by not submitting written evidence to the court). . . .

The availability of injunctions is now helped by the judges in some areas, in particular London, being on a rota duty in the evenings and at weekends in case emergency injunctions are needed, and in other areas a judge will be contacted by a court officer by telephone where necessary. As a result of these new arrangements, injunction hearings can be held even at the judge's home, and on Sundays (even though as a general rule at common law judicial acts may not be done on a Sunday). . . .

Another advantage of the injunction is that the court can attach various subsidiary orders to it. e.g. an interim custody order to the wife or an order to the husband to return the child to the wife; an order that the husband be responsible for all outgoings; an order restraining the husband from parting with possession of the matrimonial home or its contents or damaging them, or interfering with the wife's rights of occupation; and an order for costs to be awarded against the respondent.

The ancillary nature of the injunction has been seen as its most serious flaw. The point has been made repeatedly that because a woman wants her husband to stop beating her it does not mean she wants a divorce. Marsden and Owens (1975) say: 'violence did not usually appear as a complete breakdown of relationships,' and in some cases it was seen as a 'baffling impediment to an otherwise loving relationship.' In fact it has already been pointed here that many a wife still wants her husband but just wishes he would stop being violent. Thus she wants a court order against him to 'stop it' and 'leave her alone,' in the hope that the enforced temporary separation, perhaps eventually in prison if he is in contempt, will create a breathing space and will force him to come to his senses and begin treating her well. In addition there is a lack of sympathy in the idea that a woman who needs emergency help desperately by way of an injunction is in a fit state to make a far-reaching decision about the future of her marriage. From a social policy point of view too it is irresponsible to force a person into legal action for a divorce where there is no inquiry into whether it is really what is wanted and no attempt to save the marriage where this is a possibility.

The second major problem with the law on injunctions is uncertainty over their availability after the divorce beyond the decree absolute, and over the principles on which injunctions to vacate will be granted. It would appear to be the law that a non-molestation injunction is available for the physical protection of the wife and children at any time before or after the divorce. Injunctions to vacate the matrimonial home are equally available before and after the divorce, so long as some substantive issue, e.g. financial provision or custody, still exists. They are also available it seems even when all issues are settled where necessary to protect the interests of children, or where it was 'imperative and necessary . . . for the protection of the health, physical or mental, of the wife or child.'[3]. . .

The third major problem in injunction law is its enforcement. The problem is one of preventing violence before the injunction is obtained, and after, and between breach and committal to prison. An injunction is an order from a civil court, breach of which is a civil contempt, so that its enforcement is undertaken by the civil law enforcers. The wife must first apply to court for a determination that the injunction has been breached, and if satisfied the

---

3. But now cf. *O'Malley v O'Malley* [1982] 2 All ER 112 with *Phillips v Phillips* [1973] 2 All ER 423.

court may order the husband to be imprisoned (for an unknown time), though this can be suspended, or fined. The court must then issue a warrant for his arrest, which will be carried out by the tipstaff in the High Court, and the registrar or bailiffs in the county court. As Erin Pizzey (1974) says so forcefully of tipstaffs and bailiffs: 'They are scarce, they finish at 5.30 and they don't work weekends.' . . .

Margeritte Russell, a barrister, gave many examples to the Select Committee of the problems involved, e.g. arrest not taking place until weeks after the court had committed the husband to prison for breaking the injunction. . . . The Metropolitan Police do not believe that there is an enforcement problem (Select Committee). If in the course of the breach of an injunction the husband commits a criminal offence or a breach of the peace, then they say adequate powers exist already to deal with him; otherwise the civil authorities should take the action. Two comments need to be made on this view. The first is that the police view is correct in theory, but the evidence of what actually happens in practice belies it, both at the time of the initial violence, and subsequent to the injunction. The police certainly do have adequate criminal powers, yet they have shown a considerable reluctance to use them in the battered wife context. The second is perhaps a more fundamental problem. It is the dichotomy between civil and criminal law, which in this context becomes somewhat artificial. The Metropolitan Police have said 'it would be wrong both constitutionally and practically to extend the criminal law to enable police to exercise powers to enforce orders made within the civil jurisdiction of the courts' (Select Committee). This is quite simply a blinkered and dogmatic view of the problem. The Select Committee was surely right to conclude:

'We recognise the arguments against involving the police in civil law but consider this is the only way to make enforcement effective and that the problem of battered women is exceptional enough to require an exceptional remedy'.

. . .

Divorce Court injunctions until the present time were only available to a married woman, dependent as they were on the activation of matrimonial proceedings. . . .

The only way a woman could protect herself against the man with whom she was living was by the use of criminal prosecution, or by bringing a claim for damages in tort (for assault or battery, or trespass to person or land) to which an application for an injunction could be ancillary. This method was the one advocated by women's groups. . . . But there is a strong principle that the claim for damages (in a county court) must be the substantial claim for damage done, and the injunction only ancillary to that. The battered cohabitee would have to admit that the injunction is her main remedy, and her claim for damages merely the vehicle for getting that.

Question

Married women do not usually rely on the law of tort either: but does Chapter 2 suggest to you a different reason from the one facing cohabitants?

One story from Erin Pizzey (1974) may be sufficient to illustrate the extent of the problems:

Joan took her husband before the High Court eleven times before she finally got him put in prison with a one-year sentence. The first time he broke in the police refused to come as they said there was nothing they could do on a High Court injunction. He beat her up and she came to Women's Aid. After that the poor woman yo-yoed back and forth with her three children using us as a refuge when her husband was around. Eventually she went back and tried to live in the home that the court said was hers when the divorce had been granted. He broke in, beat her up, punctured her ear-drum and raped her at the point of a knife. When she got him back into the High Court, the judge did not appear to have read the previous judges' notes and accepted the husband's story that he dropped in for some urgent papers at 3 a.m. and his wife had refused to let him have them. The judge gave him seven days and told him in effect that he was a naughty boy.

Part of Joan's problem was that whenever she took her husband to court they appeared in front of a different judge, and none of the judges bothered to read the file of her husband's atrocities, which was steadily getting thicker and thicker.

She gave up trying to live in 'her' home and moved in with us. Her husband broke our windows, screamed and raged outside the house, pestered the school and tried to snatch the children. We took him back to court and this time saw the same judge twice. He did read the case and was appalled enough to put him inside for a year. It was too late for Joan to claim her council house, though — the rent arrears had mounted up and the council had taken it back.

Erin Pizzey pioneered the idea of refuges for women like Joan, an idea quickly taken up by women's groups around the country:

NATIONAL WOMEN'S AID FEDERATION [NOW WOMEN'S AID FEDERATION ENGLAND and WELSH WOMEN'S AID]

NWAF began in March 1975 and has about 100 Womens Aid Groups affiliated who, between them run almost 150 Refuges in England and Wales. The Federation exists to co-ordinate activities of local Womens Aid groups and represent their interest at national and regional level.

The 5 aims of the Federation are:

1. To provide temporary refuge for women and their children who have suffered mental or physical harassment.
2. To encourage the women to determine their own futures and to help them effect their decisions whether this involves returning home or starting a new life elsewhere.
3. To recognise and care for the emotional and educational needs of the children involved.
4. To offer support, advice and help to any woman who asks for it whether or not she is a resident — also to offer support and after-care to any woman and child who has left the Refuge.
5. To educate and inform the public, the media, the police, the courts, social services and other authorities with respect to the battering of women, mindful of the fact that this is a result of the general position of women in our society.

Question

As the House of Commons Select Committee asked during its proceedings, why should we not create hostels to receive the battering husbands?

The Committee's conclusion (1975) was this:

21. The most insistent evidence we have received has been that specialised refuge facilities should be available very readily and rapidly for women who have been battered and who have decided to leave their husbands on this account. We accept the urgency of this constant plea and endorse it as a strong recommendation. However, we believe that refuges are not an entirely satisfactory solution to the problem. They are forced upon society by the short-term urgency of the situation. We believe that our other recommendations especially the legal ones, will have a significant effect for the future. It may be that ultimately housing provision for single men may be made easier, and women will be sufficiently protected by the law for the normal pattern of violent family breakup to be the departure of the man rather than the woman.

Questions

(i) How far does the definition of 'priority need' in s. 2(1) and (2) of the Housing (Homeless Persons) Act 1977 promote this pattern? (Space does not permit us to investigate the operation of that Act as a means of helping battered women, but see Binney, Harkell and Nixon, 1981.)
(ii) How far do the Domestic Violence and Matrimonial Proceedings Act 1976 and the Domestic Proceedings and Magistrates' Courts Act 1978 (see below) do so?

The *Domestic Violence and Matrimonial Proceedings Act 1976* was a private member's bill designed to remedy the defects in injunction procedure:

1.—(1) Without prejudice to the jurisdiction of the High Court, on an application by a party to a marriage a county court shall have jurisdiction to grant an injunction containing one or more of the following provisions, namely, —

(a) a provision restraining the other party to the marriage from molesting the applicant;
(b) a provision restraining the other party from molesting a child living with the applicant;
(c) a provision excluding the other party from the matrimonial home or a part of the matrimonial home or from a specified area in which the matrimonial home is included;
(d) a provision requiring the other party to permit the applicant to enter and remain in the matrimonial home or a part of the matrimonial home;

whether or not any other relief is sought in the proceedings.

(2) Subsection (1) above shall apply to a man and a woman who are living with each other in the same household as husband and wife as it applies to the parties to a marriage and any reference to the matrimonial home shall be construed accordingly.

2.—(1) Where, on an application by a party to a marriage, a judge grants an injunction containing a provision (in whatever terms) —

(a) restraining the other party to the marriage from using violence against the applicant, or

(b) restraining the other party from using violence against a child living with the applicant, or

(c) excluding the other party from the matrimonial home or from a specified area in which the matrimonial home is included,

the judge may, if he is satisfied that the other party has caused actual bodily harm to the applicant or, as the case may be, to the child concerned and considers that he is likely to do so again, attach a power of arrest to the injunction.

(2) References in subsection (1) above to the parties to a marriage include references to a man and a woman who are living with each other in the same household as husband and wife and any reference in that subsection to the matrimonial home shall be construed accordingly.

(3) If, by virtue of subsection (1) above, a power of arrest is attached to an injunction, a constable may arrest without warrant a person whom he has reasonable cause for suspecting of being in breach of such a provision of that injunction as falls within paragraphs (a) to (c) of subsection (1) above by reason of that person's use of violence or, as the case may be, of his entry into any premises or area.

(4) Where a power of arrest is attached to an injunction and a person to whom the injunction is addressed is arrested under subsection (3) above, —

(a) he shall be brought before a judge within the period of 24 hours beginning at the time of his arrest, and

(b) he shall not be released within that period except on the direction of the judge,

but nothing in this section shall authorise his detention at any time after the expiry of that period.

In reckoning for the purposes of this subsection any period of 24 hours, no account shall be taken of Christmas Day, Good Friday or any Sunday.

(5) Where, by virtue of a power of arrest, attached to an injunction, a constable arrests any person under subsection (3) above, the constable shall forthwith seek the directions —

(a) in a case where the injunction was granted by the High Court, of that court, and

(b) in any other case, of a county court,

as to the time and place at which that person is to be brought before a judge.[4]

(b) HOW SHOULD JUDGES EXERCISE THEIR DISCRETION TO GRANT INJUNCTIONS?

Consider the following two cases in which husbands appealed against county court orders that they be excluded from the matrimonial home:

Myers v Myers
[1982] 1 All ER 776, [1982] 1 WLR 247, 126 Sol Jo 48, Court of Appeal

Arnold P: . . . The judge excluded the husband from the house, subject to giving him permission to return thereto during weekday evenings, when the wife was doing her part-time job, to look after the child of the marriage, a little girl called Naomi who is 2 years old. The foundation of the judge's order was substantially that these two young people could not live together in the same premises, at any rate for the time being, because the wife had come to a conclusion that she would not do so, the court drawing the conclusion, as the judge said, that she really did mean that and it was not merely a passing whim. The wife said that she had reached that conclusion because she was scared.

When one looks at the history of the marriage, which had in fact endured for about two years although there had been a similar period of cohabitation previously, one finds that the basis of her fear was not very large, looking at it in the terms of her own evidence. She said that he had a tendency to violent outbursts (which I take to be verbal abuse) even prior to the marriage; over the last few months matters have deteriorated; she says he is continuing to drink very heavily and

---

4. Sections 3 and 4 — see pp. 43–45, above — permit the courts to regulate and restrict the rights of spouses to occupy the matrimonial home, whether it is in sole or joint names.

to take drugs (he says that is cannabis); that he goes out drinking twice a week, mainly at weekends, and when he returns home after his drinking sessions he very easily loses his temper and then becomes violent; except in so far as it is later particularised, there are no details about that. Then she says that he constantly abuses her, and indeed in a measure that is agreed by the husband. She says he is jealous and makes accusations of infidelity against her and related threats and that this is distressing to her and the marriage.

Then there are three specific allegations of violence. The first one which took place a fortnight before they were married was something which arose in the course of an argument in the street. The judge, rightly in my view, discounts that because it is so very shortly before the marriage.

Then there was an occasion a few months later, sometime in 1979 apparently, when the husband tipped the wife out of bed but no-one seems to have attached very much importance to that.

Then there was a substantial and most unhappy occasion of physical violence on 16 October 1981. There had been some disagreement between the parties at a dance to which they had gone, the husband resenting what he regarded as 'flighty behaviour' on the part of his wife, and in particular in one instance an impermissible approach by some man with whom she was dancing towards her. But the immediate occasion of the violence was that, when they got home, both of them being sensible of the desire for a reconciliation after the upsets of the evening, they went to bed and started to make love. At this time she was having some difficulty in this context of her marriage and at some late stage, so it is said by the husband, in the course of that contact she wished to terminate it and did so, much to the annoyance and frustration of the husband who gave her a 'thumping', as it is called. That the judge, in the face of a disputed piece of evidence, believed. The wife maintained before the judge, and here he did not believe her, that the marriage was all over. To quote the judge: 'She said consistently in the witness box that the marriage was at an end and that she cannot go back. I am not satisfied that is what in fact the future does hold.' Later on he says: 'I hope a reconciliation may still be possible', and then he said he thought 'it is more likely to occur if the parties are apart than if the wife is kept away or if they live under the same roof'.

The facts are that for something like three weeks after the occasion of violence on 16 October 1981 the parties continued under the same roof but, shortly before the case was presented on 5 November the wife moved away to her mother's where she was living in circumstances which the judge regarded as unsatisfactory and certainly appear to be those of overcrowding. . . .

What the judge never considered was whether there was any reasonable justification for this particular wife having come to the genuine conclusion that she could not go back. That is the point which is seized on by the husband in saying that the judge did not approach the exercise of this jurisdiction in a way shown by the cases to be the proper way. In support of that proposition the husband cites *Elsworth v Elsworth* (1978) 1 FLR 245, 9 Fam Law 21 in this court which was decided in June 1978. There is no doubt that the line of propriety in the exercise of the jurisdiction is there to be seen in the leading judgment with which the other two members of the court concurred, namely the judgment of Orr LJ in this way:

> 'The allegations of unreasonable behaviour made in the petition are not of a very serious character, as the judge himself recognized, and for my part I would not accept that the test to be applied in these cases is simply whether the wife has said she will not go back; the court has to consider whether there are reasonable grounds for her to be unwilling to do so, and in my judgment on the totality of the evidence in the present case it cannot be said that that test was satisfied.'

That was the basis of the decision of the court, so it was plainly part of the ratio. The other two judges agreed with that approach.

In the present case I think that the judge must be taken to have accepted on his findings, in the light of the evidence and the presentations, that what actuated the wife in her conclusion that she was unwilling to go back was fear, as she put in her evidence, fear of verbal abuse rather than actual violence. But what the judge never did was to examine the question whether the facts, as demonstrated before him, made that conclusion on the part of the wife a reasonable conclusion, a reasonable conclusion being, in my view, relevantly considered in relation to the personalities of both. But, of course, if the judge never did do that and if it is right that that is the method of exercising the discretion which is prescribed by *Elsworth v Elsworth*, then it does seem, unless one can demonstrate from the other decided cases that *Elsworth v Elsworth* is not the matter which regulates the exercise, that the judge erred in principle.

Both O'Connor LJ and Stephen Brown J agreed that the husband's appeal should be allowed.

Samson v Samson
[1982] 1 All ER 780, [1982] 1 WLR 252, 126 Sol Jo 155, Court of Appeal

Ormrod LJ: . . . The judge's judgment indicates considerable sympathy for the husband. He started it off by saying: 'This case causes me difficulty because of the sympathy which I cannot help but feel for the husband.' He went on to refer to the allegations in the wife's petition, which certainly are vague and far from 'strong'. The judge, having heard the wife in the witness box, noted and indeed commented on the fact that she could not actually state what her objections were to living with her husband, although he thought that she was an intelligent and articulate person. She could do no more than say 'I hate him', and so on. But the judge found at an early stage in his judgment, and this is one of the important findings in the case, that these two people cannot get on. He said that he thought the wife was 'relentless and unforgiving to her husband's faults and failings' but he accepted that she meant what she said when she said she could not bear to be in the same house as he. Note the language: 'could not bear to be in the same house as he.' The judge was satisfied that the wife would not return if the husband was living in the house. So he had to consider the resulting situation, which was that the wife and the two children, one aged not quite 5 and the other a year old, were living in grossly overcrowded conditions in the wife's mother's house. It meant that the 5-year-old child was sleeping on the floor and the mother and the two children were all in one room. That he thought was not at all a satisfactory arrangement for the children of a man earning a substantial income, as the husband in this case is. Having expressed considerable sympathy for the husband, he found himself constrained in the interests of the children to make the order which the wife sought.

Counsel, who has put forward a powerful argument on behalf of the husband, contends that the judge was wrong in making the order which he did because he did not follow a case called *Elsworth v Elsworth* (1978) 1 FLR 245, 9 Fam Law 21, which I think has only recently been resurrected and reported in the new set of Family Law Reports ([1980] 1 Fam L Rep 245). It is a case which was decided in this court as long ago as 1978. Things have changed quite a bit since 1978. It was referred to, and indeed followed, recently by this court in a case called *Myers v Myers* [1982] 1 All ER 776, [1982] 1 WLR 247. That case was heard on 4 December 1981 before Arnold P, O'Connor LJ and Stephen Brown J. Another case is referred to in the judgment of Arnold P called *Rennick v Rennick* [1978] 1 All ER 817, [1977] 1 WLR 1455, but there is no reference in the learned President's judgment to the cases which to my mind are the leading cases in this court on this topic; *Bassett v Bassett* [1975] Fam 76, [1975] 1 All ER 513 and, more particularly, *Walker v Walker* [1978] 3 All ER 141, [1978] 1 WLR 533.

Unfortunately *Elsworth* appears to reintroduce the old issue whether the wife was justified in leaving, and it recreates the situation where the court is trying to make assessments of the effect of conduct on what might be totally inadequate material. It also leads to the ignoring of the interests of the children which, to my mind, is very important. The fact that *Walker v Walker* was not referred to in *Myers v Myers* is a factor of considerable importance. I will not read the well-known passage in Geoffrey Lane LJ's judgment in the report of *Walker v Walker* [1978] 3 All ER 141 at 143, [1978] 1 WLR 533 at 536. That judgment follows very closely an earlier judgment of this court in *Bassett v Bassett* [1975] Fam 76, [1975] 1 All ER 513.

The upshot of those two cases is that the court must concentrate on the practical issues involved in the case and make as sensible an order as is possible in the circumstances, having regard to the interests of all the parties, father, mother and the children. The difficulty of counsel for the husband in this case is manifest because the first question one asks her is, 'What does your client propose to do if he succeeds on this appeal?' And the answer is, 'Well, my client's wife should come back', which, it is quite plain on the evidence and as the judge found, she will not. The next suggestion is that the children should come back to the matrimonial home and be looked after by him. But, as everybody knows, they will not be sent back by the wife unless there is an order of the court directing her to do so. There is no order and no attempt has been made by the husband to obtain one. As far as I can see from the way in which the case was conducted in the court below, there was no real issue before the learned judge as to which of these two parents should have the care of these small children. So the husband is driven into the position of saying that the children must remain in unsuitable circumstances in their grandmother's house, while he remains in the matrimonial home. Why? Because the wife cannot point to any conduct on his part to 'justify her leaving'.

I would refer briefly to one passage in my judgment in *Bassett v Bassett* [1975] Fam 76 at 83, [1975] 1 All ER 513 at 518, where I stated:

'In this case the wife says that she is frightened of her husband. He denies it and says that she has no reason to fear him. But, as I have already pointed out, he makes no alternative suggestion as to why she left. The case here might, of course, have been wholly different if there was some reason to think that perhaps the wife was associating with another man, or was so immature that she would run back to her mother at the slightest provocation. But in the absence of some such explanation, it is difficult to believe that any woman would put herself or her family to the discomfort that this lady has done without good reason. If there is good reason, prima facie she needs the protection of the court — not to save her from physical violence or of direct threat to herself but to enable her to have somewhere where she can make a home for her child.'

Those observations apply directly to this case. I take the point which counsel for the husband makes which is that any wife who takes her children and leaves the matrimonial home can force the court to make an order giving her the right to occupy the matrimonial home alone and make the husband move out. That may be the case, except that one has to remember that there are very few women in this world who will go to the length of moving themselves and the children out and breaking up the marriage simply for the satisfaction of turning the husband out of the matrimonial home. It is a very unreal view of life that that is how people may behave. Of course it is quite different if they have an ulterior motive for getting the husband out, either financial, sexual, or whatever, but here there is no suggestion whatever of lack of bona fides on the part of the wife. On the contrary it is suggested, and the judge has found in terms, that so far as she is concerned she has acted in what she believes to be the best interests of herself and the children. I do not think it is useful to draw dramatic pictures of the court being forced into making all kinds of unsuitable orders by women who choose to take a particular course of action. What is required, as Geoffrey Lane LJ and Cumming-Bruce J both said in *Bassett* and *Walker*, is to approach this matter on a strictly practical basis, looking first to the welfare of the children and being very largely guided by it. That is exactly what the learned judge did in this case. He arrived at the conclusion in their interests that there should be an order requiring the husband to leave, and I think that he was right. I would dismiss the appeal.

Dunn LJ and Heilbron J both agreed, Dunn LJ going so far as to regret that Elsworth had ever been reported.

Questions

(i) Is one possible explanation for the different approaches adopted in these two cases that Mrs Samson had already petitioned for divorce and was applying for an ancillary injunction, while Mrs Myers was applying under the 1976 Act?

(ii) Are you pleased that a differently constituted Court of Appeal, in *Richards v Richards* (1982) Times, 8 December, preferred the *Bassett, Walker* and *Samson* approach? Even though this meant that a wife who had left hoping to set up home with another man was able to oust her non-violent husband so that she and the children could live in the matrimonial home after her new relationship had failed?

(c) PRACTICAL PROBLEMS

PRACTICE NOTE

FAMILY DIVISION

To secure uniformity of practice, the President has issued the following note with the concurrence of the Lord Chancellor.

1. Section 1(1)(c) of the Domestic Violence and Matrimonial Proceedings Act 1976 empowers a county court to include in an injunction provisions excluding a party from the matrimonial home or a part of the matrimonial home or from a specified area in which the matrimonial home is included. Where a power of arrest under s. 2 of the 1976 Act is attached to any injunction containing such provisions, the respondent is liable to be arrested if he enters the matrimonial home or part thereof or specified area at any time while the injunction remains in force.

2. It is within the discretion of the court to decide whether an injunction should be granted and, if so, for how long it should operate. But whenever an injunction is granted excluding one of the parties from the matrimonial home (or a part thereof or specified area), consideration should be given to imposing a time limit on the operation of the injunction. In most cases a period of up to three months is likely to suffice, at least in the first instance. It will be open to the respondent in any event to apply for the discharge of the injunction before the expiry of the period fixed, for instance on the ground of reconciliation, and to the applicant to apply for an extension.

RL BAYNE-POWELL
21 July 1978   Senior Registrar

Question

What would you advise a battered wife to do once the three months are up if she is still very frightened of her husband, but does not want a divorce because of the various legal and other advantages to her of remaining married? (See p. 45, and p. 147, above for one idea which seems also to have occurred to others.)

Another problem is graphically illustrated by Erin Pizzey (1974):

Going to court is quite an ordeal. The High Court in the Strand is as awe-inspiring as it sounds. It is a massive crenellated building with white towers and spires outside and a huge arched hall inside. The place is honeycombed with narrow corridors that run off the central hall to the small courtrooms. Everywhere ant-like uniformed figures bustle around. Barristers stride along in their black flapping gowns and wrinkled white wigs, best-suited solicitors scurry in their wake, blue-suited ushers look officious. The people waiting in little knots look shabby and out of place in this impersonal palace of justice.

If the case is to be heard in the morning we have to be there by 10. Waiting to meet the solicitor is always an anxious time because if the husband has been told to attend the court too, it will be the first time that his wife has had to face him since she ran away.

If you manage to avoid meeting him before, you usually find him crouched on the hard little benches that line the ill-lit, crowded corridor outside the courtroom. There, knee to knee and face to face, the couple must wait, sometimes for hours, before they are called into court.

My first time was with Lesley. Pat had come along to hold her other hand and together we had to hold Lesley upright because she was in such a state of fear at the prospect of seeing her husband. He had a terrible reputation, and on the night she had left him, he'd gone to see her friends with a gang and broken into the house. The gang beat up the old couple upstairs and their two sons. It took ten policemen to get them out, and though he was charged he was released on bail. Now we were in court to ask for an injunction to give her custody of the three children, maintenance while her divorce petition went through and a non-molestation order to keep him from carrying out his threat to kill her.

Waiting to go into the courtroom, we were all frightened. The solicitor and the barrister were quite unperturbed, and the barrister gave the impression that Lesley was making an unnecessary fuss. We were due in court mid-morning, so we settled down on the little benches to wait, morosely contemplating the other silent people waiting, and gazing at the stained walls.

The tedium and the peace were disturbed by the arrival of Lesley's husband and his henchmen. Then began a cat-and-mouse shuffle as we moved round the narrow corridors trying to prevent him upsetting Lesley even more. By the time it was our turn Lesley was speechless with fright and we half carried her between us into the court.

The judge glanced at us all and seemed unimpressed. He looked at the affidavits on his desk, scowled, and then a rapid crossfire of conversation began between him and the two barristers. We were not any part of the proceedings. The longest argument was about the costs, with both barristers bobbing up and down and protesting volubly. We had no idea of the outcome until we got outside and our barrister said we had got everything we wanted. We were very pleased, but much more preoccupied with the problem of getting out of the building without the husband and his gang catching us. They lurked and we dodged, until after rushing into lavatories and dashing down long corridors, we slipped out of a back entrance and away.

Question

In what circumstances should a woman who alleges that she has been beaten be able to get an exclusion injunction ex parte (without giving notice to the person to be excluded)?

PRACTICE NOTE

FAMILY DIVISION

The President is greatly concerned by the increasing number of applications being made ex parte in the Royal Courts of Justice for injunctions, which could and should have been made (if at all) on two clear days' notice to the other side, as required by the rules.

An ex parte application should not be made, or granted, unless there is real immediate danger of serious injury or irreparable damage. A recent examination of ex parte applications shows that nearly 50% were unmeritorious, being made days, or even weeks, after the last incident of which complaint was made. This wastes time, causes needless expense, usually to the Legal Aid Fund, and is unjust to respondents.

Where notice of an application for an injunction is to be given and an early hearing date is sought, practitioners are reminded of the special arrangements which exist at the Royal Courts of Justice whereby the applicant's solicitor is able to select for the hearing any day on which the court is sitting. . . .

RL BAYNE-POWELL
Senior Registrar

26 June 1978

Questions

(i) If the relevant question is 'real immediate danger', is it obviously unmeritorious to apply 'days, or even weeks', after the last incident?

(ii) Which is the more unjust: making an alleged batterer leave the home for a short while before he has an opportunity of defending himself against the allegations, or making the alleged victim leave for a short while before she has an opportunity of putting her case before a court?

PRACTICE NOTE

FAMILY DIVISION

The police are holding some thousands of orders containing a power of arrest made under s. 1(1)(c) of the Domestic Violence and Matrimonial Proceedings Act 1976. Experience has shown that the police are rarely called on to take action on an injunction which is more than three months old, and the requirement that they should retain indefinitely the orders containing a power of arrest imposes an unnecessary burden upon them. . . .

To assist in easing the burdens of the police and in enabling them to concentrate on the cases where action may be required, judges should consider, at the time a power of arrest is attached to an injunction, for what period of time this sanction is likely to be required. Unless a judge is satisfied that a longer period is necessary in a particular case, the period should not exceed three months. In those few cases where danger to the applicant is still reasonably apprehended towards the expiry of three months, application may be made to the court to extend the duration of the injunction.

RL BAYNE-POWELL
Senior Registrar

22 December 1980

Questions

(i) Would a criminal court regard three months as an appropriate period for the suspension of a sentence of imprisonment for occasioning (a) actual or (b) grievous bodily harm?

(ii) The power of arrest is attached under s. 2 of the 1976 Act: why then does the Note refer specifically to s. 1(1)(c)?

(iii) Do these practice notes help us to understand why the WAFE study of women in refuges (Binney, Harkell and Nixon, 1981) found (a) that a power of arrest had little effect upon police willingness to arrest and prosecute; (b) that only 8% of the women left the refuges to return to live alone in their homes and only 4% were still there a year after the original interview; and (c) that the women had found refuges and self-help organisations more helpful than the official agencies?

(d) PERSONAL PROTECTION IN THE MAGISTRATES' COURTS

The *Domestic Proceedings and Magistrates' Court Act 1978* was passed as a result of the Law Commission's recommendations (1976) on the modernisation of magistrates' matrimonial jurisdiction following the reform of divorce law (see p. 94, above). Sections 16 to 18 replace the magistrates' old power to relieve a wife from the duty of living with her husband.

16.—(1) Either party to a marriage may, whether or not an application is made by that party for an order under section 2 of this Act, apply to a magistrates' court for an order under this section.

(2) Where on an application for an order under this section the court is satisfied that the respondent has used, or threatened to use, violence against the person of the applicant or a child of the family and that it is necessary for the protection of the applicant or a child of the family that an order should be made under this subsection, the court may make one or both of the following orders, that is to say —

    (*a*) an order that the respondent shall not use, or threaten to use, violence against the person of the applicant;

    (*b*) an order that the respondent shall not use, or threaten to use, violence against the person of a child of the family.

(3) Where on an application for an order under this section the court is satisfied —

    (*a*) that the respondent has used violence against the person of the applicant or a child of the family, or

    (*b*) that the respondent has threatened to use violence against the person of the applicant or a child of the family and has used violence against some other person, or

    (*c*) that the respondent has in contravention of an order made under subsection (2) above threatened to use violence against the person of the applicant or a child of the family,

and that the applicant or a child of the family is in danger of being physically injured by the respondent (or would be in such danger if the applicant or child were to enter the matrimonial home) the court may make one or both of the following orders, that is to say —

    (i)   an order requiring the respondent to leave the matrimonial home;

    (ii) an order prohibiting the respondent from entering the matrimonial home.

(4) Where the court makes an order under subsection (3) above, the court may, if it thinks fit, make a further order requiring the respondent to permit the applicant to enter and remain in the matrimonial home.

(5) Where on an application for an order under this section the court considers that it is essential that the application should be heard without delay, the court may hear the application notwithstanding —

    (*a*) that the court does not include both a man and a woman,

    (*b*) that any member of the court is not a member of a domestic court panel, or

    (*c*) that the proceedings on the application are not separated from the hearing and determination of proceedings which are not domestic proceedings.

(6) Where on an application for an order under this section the court is satisfied that there is imminent danger of physical injury to the applicant or a child of the family, the court may make an order under subsection (2) above notwithstanding —

    (*a*) that the summons has not been served on the respondent or has not been served on the respondent within a reasonable time before the hearing of the application, or

    (*b*) that the summons requires the respondent to appear at some other time or place,

and any order made by virtue of this subsection is in this section and in section 17 of this Act referred to as an 'expedited order'.

(7) The power of the court to make, by virtue of subsection (6) above, an expedited order under subsection (2) above may be exercised by a single justice.

(8) An expedited order shall not take effect until the date on which notice of the making of the order is served on the respondent in such manner as may be prescribed or, if the court specifies a later date as the date on which the order is to take effect, that later date, and an expedited order shall cease to have effect on whichever of the following dates occurs first, that is to say —

    (*a*) the date of the expiration of the period of 28 days beginning with the date of the making of the order; or

    (*b*) the date of the commencement of the hearing, in accordance with the provisions of Part II of the Magistrates' Courts Act 1980, of the application for an order under this section.

(9) An order under this section may be made subject to such exceptions or conditions as may be specified in the order and, subject in the case of an expedited order to subsection (8) above, may be made for such term as may be so specified.

(10) The court in making an order under subsection (2)(*a*) or (*b*) above may include provision that the respondent shall not incite or assist any other person to use, or threaten to use, violence against the person of the applicant or, as the case may be, the child of the family.[5]

---

5. Section 17 makes ancillary provisions, and section 18 provides for the addition of a power of arrest equivalent to that in other courts, save that magistrates must be satisfied that the respondent has 'physically injured' the applicant or child.

Questions

(i) Can you define 'violence'?
(ii) Why should a woman want to come to the magistrates' court rather than to the county or High Court?
(iii) Would either Mrs Myers or Mrs Samson be able to get either a personal protection order or an exclusion order from a magistrates' court?
(iv) Should they be able to do so?
(v) In *Davis v Johnson* [1979] AC 264, [1978] 1 All ER 1132, p. 272, above the man later sent some of his friends to remove all the furniture from the flat: if the couple had been married to one another, would an order under s. 16(10) have protected the woman from this?

(e) CRISIS CENTRES?

Despite its success with the law, one very important recommendation of the *House of Commons Select Committee* (1975) has not been implemented:

20. We recommend that each large urban area, say all towns and cities with a population over 50,000, should have a well-publicised family crisis centre open continuously to which wives, husbands and children can turn. DHSS told us that round the clock stand-by services were offered by local authority social service departments, accident and emergency departments and the police. We doubt, however, whether such services are generally available, and, even when they are, whether they are well-known to those most likely to need them. . . . The crisis centres should have three primary roles. Firstly, they should provide an emergency service, hence the 24-hour requirement. . . . Secondly they should be specially responsible for the co-ordination of the local arrangements already available to women and children in distress. . . . A battered wife needs the advice and help of a police officer, a doctor, a health visitor, a lawyer, a housing department officer, a social security officer, a clergyman, a probation officer, a marriage guidance counsellor, a citizens advice bureau worker and a social worker, just to name the most obvious. The third and non-emergency role we see for the family crisis centres is the development of specialist advisory services, education and publicity programmes, group support and meetings for women with similar problems.

But even this was not enough for Maidment; in her discussion of *The Law's Response to Marital Violence in England and the USA* (1977), she concludes:

The preference here is for a far more innovative role for the family crisis centres proposed by the Select Committee. Public salaried lawyers as professionals, expert and sympathetic to the persons and their problems, could make the vital decision to advise the woman to take criminal or civil proceedings. It may be difficult to give them the right to prosecute, rather than leaving it to the police as traditional prosecutors in this country, though there is a precedent in the right of the local authority to initiate care proceedings in the juvenile courts in respect of criminal offences, under the Children and Young Persons Act 1969. There is also the possibility of a system of public prosecutors, akin to the US or Scottish systems, to whom the family crisis centre lawyer could leave the decision. Whatever prosecution system exists however, if prosecution is not undertaken, it would be left to the family crisis centre lawyer to take the civil action. This action could be brought by the lawyer either as representative of the client, i.e. as a private lawyer-client relationship, or on behalf of the public agency.
The idea of a public agency bringing actions is traditionally a criminal notion, but a public agency bringing civil actions is not unknown as already mentioned, e.g. Race Relations Board, local authorities in care proceedings. There is no reason why a dogmatic distinction between criminal and civil notions must be maintained at all costs (as has already been said in the context of the police enforcing civil injunctions).
Family crisis centres would be ideally placed to provide the battered woman with accessible legal services. They would be open all day, every day, staffed by experts, with access to all the various services which might need to be called upon, including temporary refuges, marriage counselling, psychiatric and medical services, and housing advice, in addition to the legal remedies.

As far as the law itself is concerned, the changes now brought about by the Domestic Violence and Matrimonial Proceedings Act, making injunctions available in the county courts independently of matrimonial proceedings and regardless of marital status, and giving the police power to arrest for breach, are certainly necessary. But the whole question of the powers of the courts in granting an injunction has been ignored. The power of the judge to encourage the parties to undergo counselling or treatment, and order them to do so if they are at all willing, is essential. The courts must make a real attempt at problem solving.

'[The courts] are ill-suited to the task of permanently resolving such [domestic] disputes, and they know it. Furthermore, their traditional role offers scant room for improvement. The most successful response they can make is to insure that the disputes resulting in judicial attention are securely placed in the hands of resources capable of solving the problem' (Parnas, 1970).

Thus all along the line the law is seen as only one alternative method of dealing with the problem. It is important not to forget the psychological effect of an official invitation to attempt to save a marriage and/or behave better.

The final comment that needs to be made is a plea for realism. The law is a limited resource. Its effectiveness must not be over-estimated:

'Legal reforms cannot solve the problem of battered women, they can only alleviate it. No matter what legal changes are made, men will continue to batter women until there are profound changes in the structure of our society. In the meantime, the establishment of women's aid centres in every neighbourhood would provide a refuge and a source of moral support and practical assistance' (Gill and Coote, 1975).

Question

Imagine that when she left her husband (p. 516, above) Mrs Barbara Auckland had pushed Susan's pram, not to an aunt who had contacted the local social services department, but (*a*) to the local police station, or (*b*) to a battered woman's refuge in Barnsley. (i) What might the advice of each have been in 1974? (ii) What might it be in 1983? (Before you start concluding that either agency might have saved Susan's life, read the next section to see what the social workers *might* have done, then and now.)

4 'Managing' child abuse

(a) THE SOCIAL WORKERS' PERSPECTIVE

The most immediately striking thing about the deaths of Maria Colwell and of Susan Auckland, as well as all the other similar cases on which there have been official reports in recent years, is how well known the families already were to the social workers whose statutory duty it is to take action to protect children from harm (Children and Young Persons Act 1969, s. 2(1) and (2)). Thus even a small study of the factors which seem to influence their decisions must be of interest. Annette Lawson compared the files of ten children who had been separated from their families, whether voluntarily or compulsorily, with those of ten children who had not. She reports her results in *Taking the Decision to Remove a Child from his Family* (1980). She lists the categories of conditions affecting the social workers' concept of the child's need and leading to the decision to separate him from his parents thus:

CATEGORIES OF CONDITIONS AFFECTING CONCEPT OF CHILD'S NEED AND LEADING TO THE DECISION TO REMOVE FROM PARENT(S)

1. Signs of 'NEED'.
Social workers are more likely to believe child needs removal into care when the child

(*a*) shows signs of physical maltreatment — bruises, laceration.

(*b*) shows signs of neglect (physical and emotional) — too small, too pale, skin problems, dirty, badly clothed.

(*c*) shows signs of fear of parents — looks anxious/frightened, verbalises fear, clings to social workers, asks not to be taken home/to be taken away. Own wishes are expressed clearly.

2. Parental history and present condition

Social workers are more likely to believe child needs removal into care when, in the past, one or both parent(s)

(*a*) has been in care.

(*b*) experienced violence in childhood.

(*c*) is previously known to the department of social services and when in the present, one or both parent(s):

(*d*) is mentally ill.

(*e*) drinks heavily and/or is addicted to drugs.

(*f*) is in trouble with the police.

(*g*) is 'immature.'

3. General environment

Social workers are more likely to believe child needs removal into care when:

(*a*) the material standards of care are very low.

(*b*) there are frequent changes of address.

(*c*) parent(s) and/or child(ren) is illegitimate.

(*d*) other agencies, members (family, neighbours etc.) repeatedly express anxiety, repeatedly refer the case.

(*e*) there is a step-father or cohabitee.

4. Social worker's beliefs

Social workers are more likely to initiate care proceedings when they *believe*:

(*a*) there is *evidence* of maltreatment which will satisfy the court

(for example (i) police referral, police charge, finding of guilt

(ii) medical evidence — see 1(*a*) and (*b*) above).

(*b*) the essential 'bond of attachment' between parent and child is either absent or so fragile that it does not compensate for other difficulties.

(*c*) they can offer alternative care which is better.

(*d*) the parent(s) are unable to see their child(ren)'s needs as separate from their own.

(*e*) they cannot 'work' with the family to improve the situation, which is seen as lacking 'movement.'

But note that it is the last group which 'is important in influencing whether or not the child *will* be removed, either by court proceedings or admitted "voluntarily." The important factors I would suggest in determining which course of action is followed are the presence or absence of evidence to satisfy a court and the beliefs of social workers that they can or cannot continue to "work" with the family.' Later, she expands and exemplifies this:

4. Social worker's attitude

On the first reading of each case, I was struck by the way in which attention was paid during case conferences to whether or not sufficient *evidence* was available for care proceedings to succeed. The work of social services' departments is of necessity bounded by law and by court proceedings, by the kind of expert and other witnesses they can bring to bear which will demonstrate to the satisfaction of the magistrates that the child's welfare requires that he or she should be removed from the care of his/her 'natural' parent(s). Furthermore, social workers work with whole families, with the elderly, with children, with those classified as mentally ill and those found by courts because of infringements of the criminal codes to be in need of supervision. If a case does not succeed in the courts, the social services department as a whole and the social worker in particular is left having to continue to protect the child *within* the family, to support and work with the parent(s) against whom they have taken proceedings and have publicly voiced derogatory opinions of their parenting.

I therefore undertook a content analysis of the cases, searching for the use of the word 'evidence' or the precise expression of anxiety about whether proceedings were likely to succeed, or having been successfully taken, an application by the parent(s) for revocation of the care order would be likely to be successful in the face of evidence which the council could present.

There were only two 'care' cases where 'evidence' was *not* mentioned as a problem. In one of these the mother had been seen beating the child in a public place and had been removed by the police. (At a later date some anxiety about the removal of the new baby into care was expressed and, in the end, he was removed rather because he was being exposed to severe marital disharmony and violence than to personal maltreatment.) Similarly in the case of the child who was sexually assaulted, the father was prosecuted and, eventually, sent to prison so that the social services department was not concerned about its capacity to demonstrate the need for care. They were, however, continuing to 'monitor' the family which has younger children and there was some concern about whether they could be kept at home when the father came out of prison, and, in those circumstances, whether adequate evidence would be forthcoming, particularly as the father was very opposed to continuing social work.

The seriousness of the 'evidence problem' will be seen by a closer examination of one case. This case also shows the way in which voluntary care is used and compulsory measures pursued in the same case at different stages.

Darren H. Darren was born illegitimately on 26 February 1975. His mother, an adopted child, now aged 20, had been in care herself and was currently on probation. The maternal grandmother acted as a regular foster-parent for a voluntary society and had her daughter and grandson living with her.

On 28 August the grandmother referred the case complaining she didn't want to continue caring for her grandson and that her daughter was staying out late, wasn't capable of caring properly for the baby, and was liable to hit him when he woke for an early morning feed. At this stage, the social services department refused to take action, telling the grandmother to deal with her daughter's probation officer.

On 9 September the grandmother telephoned the probation officer to say she was 'putting her daughter and grandson out.' Apparently her daughter had hurt her quite badly in trying forcibly to put the baby back in the house. The police picked up both the mother and the baby, and after some discussion about a place of safety order, the mother was given time to make plans and the baby taken into care under section 2 (voluntarily). There then followed several days of to-ing and fro-ing with discussions between the social worker and the mother. It was noted that the baby was very well cared for and there were no bruises or marks at all. The mother was suspected of taking drugs and a good deal of argument ensued about the mother's right to see the baby, who was described as being quite upset at his foster-home. It was not until 16 September that the baby was brought to the office to see his mother. During this period, a great deal of anxiety is expressed in the notes about the presence or lack of adequate evidence. The mother was described on 10 September as 'seeming to be wanting a section [3] order' (that is, a resolution assuming parental rights in respect of a child already in section [2] care, under section [3] of the [1980] Act) and she was asking to be returned to Court for breach of probation. There was a long letter or report from the department for the solicitor's office, and it was reported they were 'waiting for a decision from County about Mrs H having Darren back.' By 15 September the grandmother seemed to be fully aware of the implications of her actions and was very upset. On 16 September there was a phone call with the county solicitor who said they could apply 'horworsen' [*sic*] since the grandmother's evidence was hearsay and not acceptable. Their case would be that the mother's habits and mode of life was unsuitable for the care of the baby. A further conversation with the solicitor's office was held on 17 September and on 23 September the baby was returned to his mother on the ground that there was insufficient evidence for section [3]. There then followed a period (by deliberate policy) of keeping very careful running records *in order to obtain evidence* of neglect which would lead to grounds for an Interim Care Order, which in the event was granted on 19 December and on 9 January 1976 a section 1(2) Care Order (CYPA 1969) was granted. Earlier, on 1 December a case conference meeting had decided 'there is doubt whether a court would grant a Care Order but may prefer to try a supervision order in the first place. . . . We should prefer to summons the mother to appear on an application to the Court under section 1.'

This preference was based on the fact that 'despite inadequate grounds on bruising,' the child had been left unattended at night while the mother worked at a bingo job which she had said she would give up. Darren had been found screaming, caught up in his pram straps. He was still sleeping in a pram although a cot had been provided and he had very bad nappy rash. Section 1 requires that the child's 'proper development is being avoidably prevented or his health is being avoidably impaired, or neglected, or he is being ill-treated.'

An example on the other side:

Jamie. . . . Jamie was born in October 1966 to a mother described as E.S.N. who had needed help from the special school after care service since she was 16. She referred herself for help on various occasions and when she married Ben in 1965 they sought help with housing.

The maternal grandmother of Jamie is described as very harsh but she did have the young parents and baby to live with her immediately after his birth. They were referred on various occasions with problems both practical and emotional. Although derogatory remarks appear in the case records in the descriptions of the father's personality he emerges repeatedly as charming, so that social workers and the other various welfare agencies again and again helped with money, and offers of accommodation. Nevertheless, early in the same month Jamie was born the social worker warned 'I am not at all sure that Vera and her husband will be able to cope with the care of a baby and running a home.'

As early as six weeks after the birth the senior child care officer noted that they were hoping to take the child into care on a Court Order as 'no other way could we give the child security.' The grandparents too decided in December the child should be in care. Jamie was admitted into care under section 1, 1948 on 12 December 1966, but this arrangement held only until 29 December when his father removed him.

Between then and October 1969, the history is one of rehabilitation, moves, practical help, and a long line of repeated referrals from the health visitors, NSPCC, police, neighbours and others for neglect.

But the case records also show the development of a very strong bond between the father and Jamie which seemed to account for his continuing healthy development despite their multiple problems. Even the anxious health visitor had to report in January 1968 'he looks well but is very dirty and badly clothed.'

In the same month the parents split up; the father wanted the child and the social worker arranged for him to collect Jamie warning him if he didn't do so, she would have to take Jamie into care since the mother 'cannot cope.'

A year later (January 1969) the child was again received into care voluntarily and boarded out with foster parents. The father kept visiting Jamie but on various occasions did not bring him back. This added to the picture being built of the father as both feckless and unreliable but also devoted to the child. At this time the department wanted to take a section [3] resolution but there were no *grounds* according to their own solicitor's advice. So Jamie was released again to the care of his father.

She concludes:

Social workers' beliefs
There are considerable differences between the 'care' and 'control' groups here which have been brought out in the discussion of cases above. They were elaborated in the interview and much material in the documents centred on the notion of 'bonding.' It was an idea used both to keep a child within the family and as a justification for removal, for denying or agreeing to access and for making provision for long-term care. I have pointed . . . to the influence the lack of adequate bonding is said to have on the aetiology of child abuse and it has entered the statutes with the emphasis in the 1975 Act on providing long-term security for children through fostering and adoption.

In the cases detailed above, the kinds of material which count as *evidence* for the social workers ranges from the 'hard' and physical, the 'measurable' injuries (we are, after all, dealing with children listed as being at risk of non-accidental injury), to the less easily discernible but crucial lack of 'bonding.' It includes the lack of consistency and stability (these two were the factors given in interview as essential children's needs) demonstrated by, for example, mental illness on the one hand, or repeated changes of address on the other. The duty placed on the social services to save life and limb requires an assessment of the risks they can take as professionals which in turn makes important their view of whether they can 'work' with the family, whether they can see 'movement' in it and have easy access to it.

Further, if the court refuses to make an order, they will continue to have responsibility for protecting the child, which has the practical effect of requiring continued visits from, usually, the same social worker who has given evidence against the parent(s). They will not therefore lightly take cases to court unless they believe they will succeed. This is one of the clearest ways in which the law can be seen as constraining. It can also be seen as enabling. In interview, social workers used examples of two cases where the mere threat of court proceedings allowed them access and a third case where, although they had been unable, as they saw it, to assess and 'get a measure' of the family adequately and did not, they said, know how seriously at risk the child was, they brought care proceedings in order to protect themselves from a possible accusation of neglect of duty.

I have suggested that these particular groups of factors take on the weight they do because the judicial process, the rules of evidence and the statutes themselves demand certain kinds of proof. . . .

Yet it was clear that, as Packman (now 1981) points out, these social workers were not merely acting as tools of the law, but positively contributing to its interpretation. In other words, they held general theories about the nature of children's needs and specific theories about the aetiology of child abuse. These were fed by the experience of dealing with the cases referred to them, by working within the social services, by professional constraints, by the possibility for alternative action *and* by the need to work within and through the law.

Some of Lawson's findings appear similar to those of the Dingwall, Eekelaar and Murray study of decision-making, basically in one English county but supplemented by smaller studies in another county and in a Metropolitan Borough. In their summary, *Care or Control?* (1981), they report:

We conclude Chapter Nine by considering what features will normally be necessary in a case to mark it for a decision in favour of legal intervention. We consider two factors to be of outstanding importance. The first is the perceived presence of 'parental incorrigibility'. By this we refer to a parent's repudiation of the legitimacy of concern about their parenting practices, for example, by failure to permit visits, attend appointments or accept advice. The voluntary relationship upon which the casework is based, the welfarist/libertarian compromise, has broken down. But so long as the appearance of co-operation can be maintained, the pressures for postponing legal intervention can be very strong and, in our view, lead to an indefinite perpetuation of conditions where children may be clearly suffering from their parents' inadequacy.

The eventual perception of parents as 'incorrigible' exposes the regulatory aspect of the social services' mandate. If the parent will not co-operate voluntarily, they may perhaps do so under pressure. Hence it is often (though not, of course, always) the case that care proceedings are initiated primarily with the purpose of gaining control over a family and not to remove the children from home. A care order gives the local authority power to remove the children at will, and this may be used as a lever in an attempt to secure compliance by the parents to social services' demands. However, the use of a care order in this manner is by no means uncontroversial and the matter will be returned to in the context of the disposition of care proceedings.

The second 'trigger' for legal intervention arises when there has been a failure to contain the case within the knowledge of a relatively small group of key personnel, usually in social services. When a case comes to the notice of other agents, proceedings may be initiated to defeat potential criticism of ineffectiveness of a voluntary programme. This may account for the prevalence of abuse over neglect cases which it is our impression reach the courts.

But they also make a point in support of Packman's observation that social workers are not as constrained by the legal requirements as (for example) was suggested by Olive Stevenson in her dissent from the majority view of Maria Colwell's return to her mother (see p. 484, above):

For social workers, court proceedings were characteristically seen as hazardous to a degree our data do not support. They lacked confidence in the status of their own evidence, an equally unjustified assumption but one which may be encouraged by lawyers' attitudes to it. Our explanation for the reluctance of social workers to pursue legal action is that it lies in the cultural and structural factors we have already discussed. The conflict between libertarian values and social regulation is compounded by a confusion over their role as social regulators and therapeutic agents.

(b) CASE CONFERENCES

Although social workers have the primary legal responsibility (under s. 2 of the Children and Young Persons Act 1969), there are, of course, numerous agencies of the welfare state which are involved in helping families with children. The Auckland family had been supported over the years by doctors and psychiatrists, health visitors, social workers, probation officers, social security, and the police, 'to such an extent that the family can almost be seen as a demonstration of how the welfare state operates.' (Report, 1975, para. 12). Yet even they had had little or no contact with local authority housing services, voluntary or religious organisations, education authorities or the NSPCC. The major concern of that report, as of most others, has been with the co-ordination of services, so that information is shared, risks properly identified, and action taken. This is a huge subject, and somewhat separate from the legal issues, but there are two aspects of officially approved methods of 'managing' child abuse which do raise issues of concern to lawyers. These are case conferences and registers of children at risk. The basic guidance to local social services authorities and health authorities is still that contained in the DHSS *Memorandum on Non-Accidental Injury to Children* (1974), the prime object of which was to set up area review committees at senior level to devise local systems for co-operation between the various services involved. Its advice on initial action in individual cases was this:

First action
3. When there is reasonable suspicion of non-accidental injury the child should at once be admitted to hospital, for diagnosis and for his own safety. Anything less would expose him to unacceptable risk. Area review committees should make it a priority task to secure the adoption of this policy in their areas. Referring doctors, health visitors and social workers should arrange for the admissions in accordance with procedures co-ordinated by the committees which should include considering the need to obtain a place of safety order[6]. . . . They should make every effort to establish a proper relationship between parents and officials and to secure the full understanding and co-operation of the parents or guardians who should if possible accompany the child to hospital and be encouraged to stay in close touch with him. In an emergency any child should always be taken to an accident and emergency department where he should be examined by a senior member of the medical staff preferably a paediatrician.
4. In cases where professional workers are suspicious but do not feel that their suspicions are firm enough to justify arranging for admission to hospital they should, in addition to consulting the family doctor, discuss the case with at least one colleague, either a senior colleague in the same profession or a colleague in another discipline who is working in the same area. This discussion should take place on the same day that suspicion is first aroused, or at latest next day. It should cover all aspects of the case, and particularly whether the risk of not arranging for immediate admission to hospital can be taken, and whether a case conference should be called.

Case conference
14. A case conference is recommended for every case involving suspected non-accidental injury to a child. In this way unilateral action will be minimized and all those who can provide information about the child and his family, have statutory responsibility for the safety of the child, or are responsible for providing services, will be brought together to reach a collective decision which takes into account the age of the child, nature of injuries and a medico-social assessment of the family and its circumstances.
15. A case conference should meet to consider a case as soon as possible and one person should always be made responsible for co-ordinating the agreed treatment. The co-ordinator should ensure that every member of a particular case conference is informed when a child leaves hospital, which should only occur after consultation with the Director of Social Services concerned. The case conference should retain overall concern for the management of the case and should be prepared to reconvene at each successive development in it or when any professional worker is particularly worried about the family.
16. A case conference should normally include:
  (*a*) persons having statutory responsibilities for the continuing care of the child eg the appropriate senior member of the social services department, the consultant in charge of the patient's medical care,
  (*b*) persons concerned with the provision of services likely to be relevant to the case eg area social worker, voluntary agency representatives, family doctor and health visitor, psychiatrist treating child or parents, day nursery matron;
  (*c*) persons with information regarding the child and his family eg family doctor and health

---

6. Place safety orders may be obtained from a magistrate at any time and by any person upon the grounds laid down either in s. 28(1) of the Children and Young Persons Act 1969 or in s. 40 of the same Act of 1933; the latter gives a police officer power to enter premises by force if need be, but the police have a more limited power to take and detain without any order, under s. 28(2) of the 1969 Act.

visitor (if not included under (b)), social workers including probation officers in previous and present contact, paediatrician and members of medical and nursing staff.

Others who may also be invited when appropriate include police surgeons, police officers, teachers and education welfare officers, representatives of housing departments, local authority legal staff, and any voluntary organisation working with the family (NSPCC, Family Welfare Association, National Council for One Parent Families, Family Service Units etc).

Subsequent· guidance has emphasised the importance of the police contribution (see p. 534, above) and of appointing a 'key worker' to ensure that decisions are implemented (DHSS 1976).

The Report of the House of Commons Select Committee on Violence in the Family, on *Violence to Children* (1977) was also enthusiastic:

Case conferences

93. We are convinced that the case conference is crucial to the effective management and treatment of child abuse. All the weight of professional evidence is in favour, despite certain doubts which have been expressed as to the numbers involved, the time taken and, in some cases, the failure to grasp the issues and make decisions. DHSS recommend a case conference for every case involving suspected non-accidental injury to a child, and that advice is reinforced by the report of the Somerset Area Review Committee for non-accidental injury on Wayne Brewer (1977) which stressed that case *discussions* should not be regarded as a substitute for the case conference.

95. Evidence from a variety of sources describes the task of the case conference. We feel that the objectives can be simply stated:
  (a) Diagnosis and assessment
  (b) A treatment plan
  (c) Implementation

In order to achieve this, information must be pooled not only about the family and its underlying problems, but also about the services available. . . .

99. . . . We do not believe that the case conference system need be inflexible. We have not stated in detail who should attend, preferring to rely on the common sense of those involved. We would stress, however, that it is obvious that if any of those taking part feel that their time is being wasted they should not hesitate to say so and thus encourage Area Review Committees to revise local procedures. It is also obvious that the case conference, which formalises the interdisciplinary approach to child abuse is only one part of that general approach. Co-operation must also be expressed in countless different practical ways. A well-run case conference system will, we are sure, encourage good working relationships between professionals, and give them a base from which to experiment confidently in new ways of handling non-accidental injury cases.

But as 'Mrs Jones', the mother who burned her child, says (Renvoize, 1974):

'You know, once you get the authorities in you never get them out. They look at everything you do. Never a week goes past without there's somebody in our flat checking up. They think you'll think it's just a social visit — but it's not, you know what they're looking for. Once you're on their books! They keep having case conferences about our family, I think it's appalling: *it's wrong!* They call them without you knowing, they hold them behind your back and so many outsiders go to them. People you've never met before know you. You go in and there's a new doctor, and when you give your name they say, Oh, *hello* Mrs Jones! — just like that — and you know they know all about you. I mind it, I really do mind it. All sorts of people who've got no reason to know about me get told all the details — they sit in on conferences about me, that I know nothing about, and *I'm* not told about them. I don't think it's right. I feel I've no privacy left at all'.

Questions

(i) Should parents have a right to know when a case conference is being held about them?

(ii) Should they have a right to expect professional people in whom they have confided to respect their confidence *even if* their children may thereby be endangered?

(iii) Should they have a right to attend, or at least make representations to, the case conference?

(iv) Or is that what the court hearing is for?

(v) If a councillor can see the files relating to children in care (*Birmingham City District Council v O* [1983] 1 All ER 497, [1983] 2 WLR 189), should not the parents be entitled to do so?

(c) REGISTERS OR REPORTING LAWS?

One reason for concern about case conferences is that they are charged with deciding whether a child's name should be included in, or removed from, the 'at risk' register. The Select Committee (1977) explained the functions of such registers thus:

Registers of children at risk

101. The register performs two important functions. It provides a safeguard for the child by aiding detection of a sequence of injuries and facilitating discovery of 'mobile families'. Secondly it provides a record for statistical purposes. More and better information is an aid in prevention of the problem of child abuse. None of those who have given evidence has attempted to persuade us that DHSS advice that registers should be set up is wrong in principle. It is clear to us that such registers are necessary in the interests of the child and that this should override all other considerations. Nevertheless we cannot ignore the problems which arise. . . .

Since then the DHSS has issued guidance to local social services authorities and health authorities on *Child Abuse: Central Register Systems* (1980). The criteria for registration represent a considerable broadening of scope from the original concentration on 'non-accidental injury':

CRITERIA FOR REGISTRATION

2.2 All authorities are asked to consider for registration children falling within the following criteria:

(a) Physical injury

All physically injured children under the age of 17 years where the nature of the injury is not consistent with the account of how it occurred or where there is definite knowledge, or a reasonable suspicion, that the injury was inflicted (or knowingly not prevented) by any person having custody, charge, or care of the child. This includes children to whom it is suspected poisonous substances have been administered. Diagnosis of child abuse will normally require both medical examination of the child and social assessment of the family background.

(b) Physical neglect

Children under the age of 17 years who have been persistently or severely neglected physically, for example, by exposure to dangers of different kinds, including cold and starvation.

(c) Failure to thrive and emotional abuse

Children under the age of 17 years
  (i) who have been medically diagnosed as suffering from severe non-organic failure to thrive; or
  (ii) whose behaviour and emotional development have been severely affected;
where medical and social assessments find evidence of either persistent or severe neglect or rejection.

(d) Children in the same household as a person previously involved in child abuse

Children under the age of 17 years who are in a household with or which is regularly visited by a parent or another person who has abused a child and are considered at risk of abuse.

The guidance goes on to prescribe the particulars which should be included. These relate to the child, his parents or care-takers, the whole household, the child's doctor, any school, nursery, play-group or child-minder, the date of registration and when next the case is to be monitored, the agencies involved and how the 'key worker' is to be found, the legal status of the child, a note of any enquiries to the register and of whether the parents have been informed that the child is on the register. But the key particulars are the 'nature of injury and by whom inflicted, reason for referral, and whether child abuse has been substantiated.' (Para. 2.3) It is suggested that the custodian of the register should initiate the reassessment of each case at least once every six months, by sending out forms to all the agencies involved. This is because:

Monitoring cases on the register
3.2 The inclusion of a child's name on the register is evidence of grave professional concern and the introduction of a system to facilitate regular monitoring of the case is recommended. Such a system should ensure regular reassessment of: —

(a) the child's family environment (including changes in adult members — eg cohabitees — and any recent or prospective births);
(b) the continued appropriateness and efficacy of the agreed plan of action and treatment.
(c) the continuing need for the inclusion of the child's name on the register;
(d) the accuracy of information held on the register.

But the crucial recommendations from the parents' point of view are these:

Registration
4.3 A decision to place a child's name on the register should only be taken at a case conference. Where it is decided at a case conference to include a child's name on the register, the details listed in paragraph 2.3 above should be forwarded by the convenor of the case conference to the custodian of the register in writing.

De-registration
4.4 A decision to remove a child's name from the register should only be made at a case conference, unless all agencies are agreed that an initial registration was made in error. The custodian should be told of the decision by the convenor of the case conference, who should then ensure that a note of the conference is circulated to all professionals known to be concerned with the child.
4.5 When a child's name is deleted, the custodian should remove the child's card from the register and, except where the original entry was made in error, retain it as inactive (ie not subject to monitoring) for a further 2 years or until a child attains the age of 5, whichever is the longer. . . .

Informing parents
4.6 When a decision has to be made whether or not to inform parents (or those caring for the child) that the child's name has been entered on the register, the child's best interests should be the chief consideration. In most cases parents should be made aware in the course of their contacts with professional workers that it is considered or suspected that their child has been abused and it is recommended that, unless in an individual case there are exceptional reasons for not doing so, parents should be informed that it has been decided to place their child's name on the register and should be given the opportunity to discuss and question the decision. When and by whom they are informed should be decided at the case conference. If a decision is taken not to inform the parents, a full record of the reasons for the decision should be included in the case conference minutes, so that it will be available in the case records of each agency concerned. Parents who have been informed of the registration of their child should also be informed when their child's name is removed from the register.

Confidentiality
4.10 As has been recommended in previous guidance, the register should be kept in conditions of strict security and the bona fides of all enquirers must be established by using a 'call back' system. There should be access to the register for all professionals to obtain information on families and children with whom they are working. Local guidelines should be agreed by the ARC. [Area Review Committee]

The Select Committee (1977) had expressed the view that 'the individual has a right to know what is being done. If this is the basis for "hardening up professional practice" so much the better.' (para. 110)

Question

Much of what happened in the Auckland case may have been conditioned by the fact that *one* of the files on the family contained the erroneous statement that Mrs Barbara Auckland had been in some way connected with Marianne's death: what safeguards would you propose to ensure that information on registers and in official files is accurate? Or can this not be done?

On the other hand, it can easily be argued that, by relying on administrative practice to solve the problem, English law does not go far enough. The following extracts are from Susan Maidment's article on *Some Legal Problems arising out of the Reporting of Child Abuse* (1978):

The existence of reporting laws internationally

Once the problem of child abuse had become a matter of public concern in the United States in 1962, a basic consensus emerged immediately about the need for reporting laws, though disagreements about detail inevitably existed. The result has been that at the present time child abuse reporting laws are in effect in every American state, in the District of Columbia, and in the Virgin Islands. In 47 of these reporting is mandatory. Since the laws were originally introduced in the mid-1960s, there has been a considerable redrafting of the legislative provisions in the light of experience of their operation. In particular there has been a trend towards the inclusion of professionals other than physicians required to report; a trend towards reporting to welfare agencies and away from police departments; and a trend towards providing penal sanctions for failure to report, so that today in over half the states such penalties exist.

The American example has been almost whole-heartedly approved. There has been an almost universal assumption throughout the English-speaking world over the past 15 years that child abuse reporting laws are a necessary and integral part of a protective child abuse legislative programme. Thus for example in Canada, eight out of ten Canadian provinces, and the Yukon territory have mandatory reporting laws, with Ontario leading the way in 1965 though making no provision for sanctions for not reporting. In Australia the three states of Tasmania, South Australia and New South Wales all have reporting laws. New Zealand is to my knowledge the only country which has made a deliberate choice not to enact a reporting law. In other countries commentators have noted the absence of a reporting law through default rather than design and called for its enactment.

The United Kingdom

. . . In the DHSS evidence to the House of Commons Select Committee on Violence in the Family: Violence to Children (1977), they agreed that compulsory reporting would

'ensure more extensive recording and exchange of information, but problems include the difficulty of deciding on action in cases of vague suspicion (and a possible reluctance to record such suspicion), of determining who has a duty to make such reports, and of enforcement.'

These problems were then spelt out in more detail:

'We have of course considered whether a system of compulsory notification would give greater protection to children but we think it would have the following disadvantages:

(*a*) So far from enabling cases to be picked up early, it may delay diagnosis, since the reporting of suspicion (which, rather than certainty, usually results from early signs) could not be compelled, and there might be a tendency to stick to the letter of the law and report only definite cases.

(*b*) It is not clear how firm suspicion would have to be before the legal obligation to make a report occurred.

(*c*) Any law which made notification mandatory would present difficulties of enforcement and detection. There would for example be difficulty in deciding retrospectively how firm such suspicions *were* at the time, if there were a question of proceeding against someone for not reporting a case.

(*d*) It is not clear how a distinction could be made between those who had a duty to make a report and those who did not. If everyone, e.g. neighbours, casual passers-by etc. had the duty in law, the problem of enforcement would be increased.

(*e*) The existence of a law making notification mandatory might make parents reluctant to seek help, and thereby increase the risk to children.

(f) There is a problem of definition which might focus on children physically injured as those are signs that can be seen whereas there are other equally serious and damaging forms of abuse.'

. . . In the discussion hardly any reference is made to the American experience, nor to any understanding of how that system has operated in practice. Moreover it will be argued here that many of the difficulties which were alleged to exist with a reporting law equally exist with the administrative machinery of case conferences and at risk registers which has evolved since 1974 instead in this country.

Question

Comparing the guidance which has since been issued (p. 554, above) with these objections, would you agree with Maidment that administrative machinery raises just the same difficulties?

Maidment reaches the following conclusion:

The argument will finally be made here that a local, administrative, post-reporting scheme is not adequate. First, the scheme curiously seems to lack its obvious, initial stage, i.e. how cases actually get reported, which then gives rise to the elaborate, local, administrative machinery. Secondly, voluntary administrative schemes have proved in this area notoriously difficult to organise and make effective. This is compounded by the third criticism, i.e. that the schemes being local do vary from one area to another. The creation of adequate local machineries, and then their harmonisation, has now become the main concern of the DHSS. . . .

In addition to the advantages of a legislative, compulsory, national machinery, one must add the argument that the legal and civil liberties issues raised by the machinery which clearly do exist, e.g. the parent's right to know, and the question of confidentiality and access to information, do not get adequately discussed when the system is set up through administrative reorganisation. For these issues a public debate, as occurs in the legislative process, is necessary, even if time consuming and controversial. But the issues do not go away because they are not discussed in the first place. That is why the arguments on these points are currently beginning to rear their heads, now that the impact of the new procedures has been fully understood.

Questions

(i) If we were to have a reporting law, who should be required to report?
(ii) When and what should they be required to report?
(iii) To whom should the report be made?
(iv) Should failure to report be a criminal offence?
(v) Would it, even now, be negligence if, for example, a doctor has strong grounds for suspecting non-accidental injury but takes no action?
(vi) But should any duty to report involve immunity from defamation for the reporter, whether or not he is malicious?

This raises the question of the part played by neighbours and the extended family. Here again the *Report* on the Auckland Case (1975) has some observations:

19. . . . Mrs Mary Auckland and her husband cared deeply for their only son John, and they did what they could to help him. They were not happy with his choice of wife, but took the trouble to visit her when she underwent domestic training in Cheshire. However, the loyalty of Mr and Mrs George Auckland to their son was such that for most of the time it amounted to blind prejudice, and their attitude was shared by their daughters. They knew their son to be violent and had themselves been assaulted by him, but their trust in him was boundless. Even today their criticisms are reserved for their daughter-in-law and others, so it follows that, as a protection for children who might be assaulted by their father, the extended family, although relied upon, were virtually useless.
. . . .
21. In an area such as Cudworth or Shafton the neighbours must have realised what, on occasions, went on in the Auckland's household and some of them told us in evidence what they knew. There is little evidence that they provided any support and we received the impression that Mr John Auckland, whose previous history was known, was not popular. Normally, it might be

expected that alarm signals would be raised by the neighbours if continued family violence was observed but nothing was ever reported, and neither the National Society for the Prevention of Cruelty to Children (NSPCC), nor any other agency, was ever alerted. Any neighbour who now feels tempted to criticise the services provided to the family or to castigate either Mr or Mrs John Auckland, should first take stock of what he or she did or could have done to avert the tragedy that eventually occurred.

D v National Society for Prevention of Cruelty to Children [1978] AC 171, [1977] 1 All ER 589, [1977] 2 WLR 201, 121 Sol Jo 119, 76 LGR 5, House of Lords

Lord Diplock: . . . In the afternoon of 13 December 1973 somebody told the NSPCC that the 14-month-old daughter of the respondent had been beaten and illtreated over the past six weeks. On receipt of this information an inspector of the NSPCC called on Mrs D at her home in order to see the condition of the child. The information turned out to be untrue. The child showed no signs of ill-treatment. She was healthy and well cared for.

The respondent was naturally very upset by this visit and to learn of the false accusation against her. As a result of this her health was affected. She wanted to know the name of the NSPCC's informant; but this was refused. After an unsuccessful attempt under RSC Ord 24, r 7A, to obtain discovery of documents from the NSPCC before commencing any proceedings, she issued a writ and statement of claim on 19 June 1974 claiming relief of two different kinds against the NSPCC: (*a*) damages for failure to exercise reasonable care in investigating the complaint that had been made about her child before repeating it to her; and (*b*) an order that the NSPCC disclose to her all documents in their custody, possession or power relating to the complaint and the identity of the complainant. . . .

At the present stage of the proceedings your Lordships are not concerned with the question whether the statement of claim discloses a good cause of action. . . .

On 26 September 1974 the NSPCC took out a summons under RSC Ord 24, r 2(5), for an order that there should be no discovery or inspection by the NSPCC of documents where such documents reveal or are capable of revealing the identity of the NSPCC's informant. . . .

Before this House the claim of the NSPCC to refuse discovery . . . was based squarely on the public interest in maintaining the confidentiality of information given to the society so that it may take steps to promote the welfare of a child, whether, as happens in the great majority of cases, by giving support, advice and guidance to the family of which the child is a member or, if this be necessary in the interest of the child, by instituting care proceedings in respect of him or prosecuting those who have committed offences against him.

. . . The uncontradicted evidence of the director of the NSPCC is that the work of the society is dependent upon its receiving prompt information of suspected child abuse and that, as might be expected, the principal sources of such information are neighbours of the child's family or doctors, school-teachers, health visitors and the like who will continue to be neighbours or to maintain the same relationship with the suspected person after the matter has been investigated and dealt with by the NSPCC. The evidence of the director is that without an effective promise of confidentiality neighbours and others would be very hesitant to pass on to the society information about suspected child abuse. There is an understandable reluctance to 'get involved' in something that is likely to arouse the resentment of the person whose suspected neglect or ill-treatment of a child has been reported. . . .

The fact that information has been communicated by one person to another in confidence, however, is not of itself a sufficient ground from protecting from disclosure in a court of law the nature of the information or the identity of the informant if either of these matters would assist the court to ascertain facts which are relevant to an issue on which it is adjudicating. . . . The private promise of confidentiality must yield to the general public interest that in the administration of justice truth will out, unless by reason of the character of the information or the relationship of the recipient . . . to the informant, a more important public interest is served by protecting the information or the identity of the informant from disclosure in a court of law. The public interest which the NSPCC relies on as obliging it to withhold from the respondent and from the court itself material that could disclose the identity of the society's informant is analagous to the public interest that is protected by the well-established rule of law that the identity of police informers may not be disclosed in a civil action, whether by the process of discovery or by oral evidence at the trial (*Marks v Beyfus* (1890) 25 QBD 494; 59 LJQB 479) . . . in *Rogers v Home Secretary* [1973] AC 388, [1972] 2 All ER 1057 this House did not hesitate to extend to persons from whom the Gaming Board received information for the purposes of the exercise of their statutory functions, under the Gaming Act 1968, immunity from disclosure of their identity analogous to that which the law had previously accorded to police informers. Your Lordships' sense of values might well be open to reproach if this House were to treat the confidentiality of information given to those who are authorised by statute to institute proceedings for the protection of neglected or ill-treated children as entitled to less favourable treatment in a court of law than information given to the Gaming Board so that gaming may be kept clean. . . .

Question

Should social workers be able to withhold their files (*a*) from a parent in juvenile court proceedings (see *R v Greenwich Juvenile Court, ex p Greenwich London Borough Council* (1977) Times, 11 May), or (*b*) from a child who alleges that the authority's negligence and breach of duty towards him while in care have caused injury to his mental health (see *Gaskin v Liverpool City Council* [1980] 1 WLR 1549, or (*c*) from councillors (see *Birmingham City District Council v O* [1983] 1 All ER 497, [1983] 2 WLR 189.

5 Care proceedings

(a) THE EVOLUTION OF THE PRESENT PROCEDURE

The main legal procedure for protecting children from their own families is set out in s. 1 of the *Children and Young Persons Act 1969*:

1.—(1) Any local authority, constable or authorised person [the NSPCC] who reasonably believes that there are grounds for making an order under this section in respect of a child or young person may, subject to section 2(3) and (8) of this Act, bring him before a juvenile court.

(2) If the court before which the child or young person is brought under this section is of the opinion that any of the following conditions is satisfied with respect to him, that is to say —

    (*a*) his proper development is being avoidably prevented or neglected or his health is being avoidably impaired or neglected or he is being ill-treated; or

    (*b*) it is probable that the condition set out in the preceding paragraph will be satisfied in his case, having regard to the fact that the court or another court has found that that condition is or was satisfied in the case of another child or young person who is or was a member of the household to which he belongs; or

    (*bb*) it is probable that the condition set out in paragraph (*a*) of this sub-section will be satisfied in his case, having regard to the fact that a person who has been convicted of an offence mentioned in Schedule 1 to the Act of 1933 is, or may become, a member of the same household as the child;

    (*c*) he is exposed to moral danger; or

    (*d*) he is beyond the control of his parent or guardian; or

    (*e*) he is of compulsory school age within the meaning of the Education Act 1944 and is not receiving efficient full-time education suitable to his age, ability and aptitude; or

    (*f*) he is guilty of an offence, excluding homicide,

and also that he is in need of care or control which he is unlikely to receive unless the court makes an order under this section in respect of him, then, subject to the following provisions of this section and sections 2 and 3 of this Act, the court may if it thinks fit make such an order.

(3) The order which a court may make under this section in respect of a child or young person is —

    (*a*) an order requiring his parent or guardian to enter into a recognisance to take proper care of him and exercise proper control over him; or

    (*b*) a supervision order; or

    (*c*) a care order; (other than an interim order); or

    (*d*) a hospital order within the meaning of Part V of the Mental Health Act 1959; or

    (*e*) a guardianship order within the meaning of that Act.

The curious route whereby three different problems were encompassed in one procedure is described by John Eekelaar, Robert Dingwall and Topsy Murray in *Victims or Threats? Children in Care Proceedings* (1982):

. . . A significant report published in 1816 by an unofficial Committee of the Society for Investigating the Causes of the Alarming Increase of Juvenile Delinquency in the Metropolis, attempted a radical assessment of the problem. Although it is sometimes thought that the significance of the home and community environment among the causative factors of delinquency is a modern realisation, this is not so. The 1816 Report numbered 'the improper conduct of parents, the want of education and the want of suitable employment' as the first of the five most significant causes of delinquency. Here is a recognition of human nature as being a product of environment, of behaviour being socially caused. The work of the reformatory movement was inspired by the same idea and it received statutory recognition in the Youthful Offenders Act 1854. But the scope of reform schools in combating juvenile delinquency was restricted by the major limitation that children were committed there only after having been convicted of an offence. . . .

[Nineteenth century reformers] maintained a distinction in classification between children who had committed offences and those who had not. They were to be kept in separate establishments. The industrial schools, which catered for the latter category, were a development of the 'ragged schools' of the eighteenth century which, as the Departmental Committee on Young Offenders of 1927 noted 'were an attempt to deal more radically with the problem of child welfare by providing education and industrial training for the class of children from whom delinquents were mainly drawn.' . . .

Yet it is clear that the children in industrial schools were there at least as much because they were thought of as being a *risk* to society as being at *risk* themselves and already by 1870 the Inspector of Industrial Schools reported that those schools had been assimilated to reformatories 'in their necessary arrangements and regulations and the main features of their management.' The children were sent there by warrant of a magistrate. The schools had become 'houses of detention for the young vagabond and petty misdemeanant.' There were thereafter many calls for the total assimilation of the two types of school because, as the Report of the Departmental Committee on Reformatory and Industrial Schools of 1913 observed 'it is often a mere accident whether a child happens to be convicted for begging or wandering.' Both types of school, it was said, were concerned to prevent children from falling into 'criminal courses. Otherwise, indeed, there would be no ground for the State contributing to their maintenance.' The 1927 Committee repeated the call for their assimilation, re-iterating the observation that

'there is little or no difference in character and needs between the neglected and the delinquent child. It is often a mere accident whether he is brought before the court because he is wandering or beyond control or because he has committed some offence. Neglect leads to delinquency and delinquency is often the direct outcome of neglect.'

As a result of the recommendations of this report, the Children and Young Persons Act 1932 (consolidated the following year as the Children and Young Persons Act 1933) abolished the distinction between reformatory and industrial schools, which together became 'approved schools.'

. . . The 1933 Act still maintained separate sections for juvenile offenders (s. 57) and children previously covered by the Industrial Schools legislation (ss. 61 and 62). The latter category were now grouped compendiously as children and young people who were 'in need of care and protection' and such a person was defined as one who '(a) . . . having no parent or guardian fit to exercise care and guardianship or not exercising proper care and guardianship, is either falling into bad associations or exposed to moral danger, or beyond control . . . (b) (has been the victim of certain offences).' Category (b) derives from another source and will be dealt with later. But the significant point is that both children falling under sections 57 and 61 could be committed to an approved school or into the care of a fit person (which now could include a local authority). As the Report of the (Ingleby) Committee on Children and Young Persons of 1960 stated with regard to proceedings under section 61: 'These are not criminal proceedings, and so there is no lower age limit, and no finding of guilt, yet the result may be what is regarded as the severest punishment for an offence, namely the sending of a child to an approved school.' We will return to the report of the Ingleby Committee later. We may observe, however, how by this stage the language of welfare rather than punishment is overtly being used to achieve the same ends as a penal regime: the protection of an existing social order by the containment and, at least theoretically, reform of potentially disruptive citizens. . . .

The third source which makes up the composition of section 1(2) of the 1969 Act had its origin in the Prevention of Cruelty to and Protection of Children Act 1889. The most significant provision of this Act created an offence if anyone over 16 who had custody, control or charge of a boy under 14 or a girl under 16 wilfully ill-treated, neglected or abandoned the child in a manner likely to cause unnecessary suffering or injury to health. On conviction of a parent for this offence, the court could commit the child to the charge of a relative or anyone else willing to have the care of the child who would have 'like control over the child as if he were its parent and shall be responsible for its maintenance, and the child shall continue under the control of such person, notwithstanding that it is claimed by its parents.'

The necessity of conviction of the parent is significant, for it reflects the basis of the justification for state intervention on which this provision rests. This is that the *parent's conduct* offends against the moral conception of society held by the Act's proponents. The purpose for the intervention was indeed, to protect children, but the method by which this was sought was morally to reform the parents. . . .

But in 1933 this category of children was included in the category of children formerly covered by the industrial schools legislation as being 'in need of care and protection.' This was a highly significant move for, as we have seen, children found to be in need of care and protection could be committed to approved schools as young offenders could be. It seems odd to find children who, even more clearly than the 'neglected' category, were in need of protection *from* adults, being dealt with under the very same statutory provisions, and indeed, court procedure, as children from whom the community sought to protect itself. It is revealing therefore to discover how this happened. The 1927 Committee was required 'to inquire into the treatment of young offenders and young people who, owing to bad associations or surroundings require protection and training.' They considered that their inquiry was concerned not only with the 'young offender' but also with 'the neglected boy or girl who has not yet committed offences but who, owing to want of parental control, bad associations or other reasons needs protection and training.' This, of course, reiterated the position of the 1913 Committee. However, the Committee went on to say: 'There are also young people who are the victims of cruelty or other offences committed by adults and whose natural guardianship having proved insufficient or unworthy of trust must be replaced.' We may note here what has been characteristic of all these investigations into the condition of children, that the concern has primarily been with the problem of troublesome children, and the question of child protection has been tagged on very much as a subsidiary and secondary question. . . .

There is no doubt that the result was to strengthen the provisions for protecting such children because local education authorities were now placed under a duty to inquire into such cases and bring them before a court and the courts were empowered to commit them into the care of local authorities. But these children had now become irredeemably intertwined with a group of children with entirely different problems and who were regarded by society as virtually inseparable from delinquent children.

In the meantime another significant development had been occurring in attitudes towards neglected and abused children. The evangelical movement had declined, but the growth of community health services provided an alternative model for intervention in family life. . . . The immediate impetus arose from the prosecution by the NSPCC of a blind couple for neglecting their children, and in 1952 the Children and Young Persons (Amendment) Act removed the requirement of prosecution of parents as a condition precedent for finding a child to be in need of care and protection within the 1933 Act. Henceforward it would be enough if the child had no parent or guardian or if his parent or guardian was 'unfit to exercise care of guardianship or (was) not exercising proper care and guardianship' and 'he was being ill-treated or neglected in a manner likely to cause him unnecessary suffering or injury to health.' Failure (for whatever cause) in the parenting function leading to a specified condition in the child became a ground for intervention. Although the approach is now overtly welfarist, the requirement that the child's condition should arise from parental failure still serves to maintain a distinction between this class of children and those from whom society sought to protect itself. The distinction was not to last for long.

The Ingleby Committee (1960) and the 1969 Act

. . . In dealing with the general issue of the circumstances in which the state may properly intervene in proceedings against parents for child neglect, the Committee states that 'difficulty has not arisen for several years over the reasonable requirements for nutrition, housing, clothing and schooling' although there had been some cases where parents had refused to give their children proper medical attention. No mention is made at all by the Committee of child abuse cases and the Committee proceeds, throughout the rest of the chapter, to consider the issue solely in terms of delinquency cases. By 1960, then, our society had become blind to potential conflicts between family autonomy and child protection. Apart from a few troublesome cases involving unconventional religious sects, the resolution of welfarist child protection and family autonomy was considered simple and unproblematic. In fact, it had been obscured by the overwhelming pre-occupation with delinquency. . . .

The two Government White Papers, *The Child, the Family and the Young Offender* and *Children in Trouble* (Home Office, 1965 and 1968) were, as their titles indicate, wholly concerned with the problem of juvenile delinquents. They set the basis for the policy of the 1969 Act. One cornerstone of that policy was that children should progressively cease to be prosecuted for offences and should, instead, be made subject to care proceedings under the Act. Accordingly, the grounds for bringing care proceedings were to be extended to include a ground that the child had committed an offence (excluding homicide). Child offenders were now to be treated under (almost) exactly the same process as troublesome children who were not offenders. And, as we have seen, child *victims* had by now been assimilated into this category. The logic of this assimilation compelled the abandonment, *for all categories of these children*, of any reference to parental inadequacy among the conditions precedent to bringing care proceedings. For, as the Home Office observed in its official guide to the Act, such a provision 'meant that proceedings inevitably appeared to cast blame for the child's situation or behaviour directly onto his parents or those looking after him' a fact which was quite irrelevant for the delinquent child (though, as will be argued below, crucially relevant in the case of the child victim). The Act, therefore, took the line originally proposed by the Ingleby Report and simply required that it be shown that the child was in need of 'care or control' which he would not receive if an order was not made.

The heart of care proceedings: children's rights and parents' rights
As is well known, the intentions behind the 1969 Act have never been fully realised. Criminal prosecution of children between 10 and 14 was to have been totally abolished and severely restricted for children under 17. The major vehicle for dealing with children and young people who had committed offences was to be by way of care proceedings under the 1969 Act. It is not surprising, therefore, that the structure of care proceedings take their shape from the type of situation which it was thought it was primarily designed to confront: *viz.* the child who, whether he had committed an offence or not, was a threat to the community. Yet the Conservative Government, elected in 1970, effectively reversed this policy so, while it is possible to use care proceedings for children who have committed offences, it is also possible to prosecute them. Since prosecution is preferred, the number of children made subject to care proceedings under the 'offence' condition is negligible. In 1978 there were only seven. By far the largest numbers of cases appear to fall within the class of cases where the object is to protect the child against abuse or neglect. (In 1978, out of 5756 orders made in care proceedings, 3330 were on grounds (*a*), (*b*) and (*bb*) of section 1(2). The next largest category, 1826 orders, were on the ground that the child was not receiving efficient full-time education.) So legislation and procedures designed primarily for one purpose are effectively being used for a wholly different purpose. The primarily criminal, or 'quasi-criminal' character of the procedures obscures, at every turn, the true nature of the issues in cases of child abuse and neglect.

(b) PROCEDURAL PROBLEMS

Numerous difficulties result from treating all three types of care proceeding as if they were a criminal prosecution against the child. On the one hand, local authorities have no right of appeal, either against the dismissal of the case or against the later discharge of a care order: we shall see in the next chapter how they have had to resort to the wardship procedure in the High Court to fill the gap. On the other hand, however, the procedures fail to distinguish properly between the interests of the child and those of his parents. When legal aid first became available in care proceedings, it may have been natural for lawyers to assume that the parents, and not the child, were their clients, for the parents would be first to consult the lawyer, and eligibility for legal aid would depend upon the parents' income. Certainly the actions of the solicitor in Maria Colwell's case (pp. 481–484, above) suggest that he regarded Maria's mother as his client. But partly as a result of that case, lawyers began to realise that this was not so: the difficulty is clearly explained in the *29th Report of the Lord Chancellor's Advisory Committee on Legal Aid* (1980):

Legal aid in proceedings relating to children
40. During the past year we have received a number of criticisms about the provision of legal aid and legal services in care proceedings before juvenile courts. A serious problem is that it is not possible for a parent to obtain legal aid in proceedings brought under section 1 of the Children and Young Persons Act 1969 because the child rather than the parent is regarded as a party to the proceedings. Difficulty arises in those cases where the local authority brings proceedings because of some alleged inadequacy of the parent. Here the interest of the parent and child may be in conflict. Consequently a solicitor representing a child may not be able to accept instructions from the parent as well.

41. This situation has attracted the attention of the courts. The Lord Chief Justice in *R v Worthing Justices ex p Stevenson* [1976] 2 All ER 194 pointed out that 'in proceedings of this kind the real issue is nearly always between the local authority and the parents, and one will expect therefore to find machinery whereby the parents become entitled to legal aid for the purpose of the proceedings'. Parliament has tried to deal with this problem in the Children Act

1975. Section 64 empowered the court to order that parents should not be treated as representing their child where there appears to be a conflict of interest between parent and child and section 65 extends the power of the court to grant legal aid to parents or guardians for the purpose of taking part in the proceedings.

42. To date sections 64 and 65 have not been implemented where parents are in dispute with the local authority. In *R v Welwyn Justices ex p S* (1978) Times, 30 November and *R v Milton Keynes Justices, ex p R* [1979] 1 WLR 1062 the courts, while recognising the parents' right to participate in the proceedings by defending themselves against allegations or cross examining the local authority's witnesses and giving evidence, were compelled to hold that they were not entitled to legal aid. In particular they held that they were not entitled to representation under section 2(4) of the Legal Aid Act 1974 because they were not parties to the proceedings.

43. We cannot help expressing our very considerable concern at the present unsatisfactory state of affairs. It cannot be right that parents should be denied full opportunity to put their side of the case where their capacity to discharge their parental responsibilities is in question and where the court has power to sever their relationship with their child. Local authorities instituting such proceedings are invariably represented by solicitors and produce technical evidence from social workers and other child care specialists. It is hard to see how justice can be seen to be done when the parents are denied legal representation to test the evidence supporting the allegations against them. We also believe that the present position is contrary to the best interests of the children involved. In some cases solicitors may unwittingly fail to represent the best interests of the child through attempting to represent both the parents and the child. In other cases the solicitor representing the child may pay insufficient attention to the parents' view of past events and future prospects. We have no doubt that local authorities always act in what they consider to be the best interests of the child, but it seems unduly sanguine to assume that their view is always right.

In fact, ss. 64 and 65 *had* been implemented, but only for the 'Maria Colwell' type of case — where an application for the discharge of a care or supervision order was unopposed (although it also covers, for example, the case of a teenage truant whose supervisor no longer thinks the order necessary). A further obstacle to putting matters right, however, was that full implementation would involve *two* more items on the public bill. This is because s. 64 of the Children Act 1975 added two new sections to the Children and Young Persons Act 1969: s. 32A provides for the separation of interests of parent and child, and s. 32B provides for the appointment of a guardian ad litem for the child, to be drawn from a panel of experienced social workers set up under s. 103 of the 1975 Act. Nevertheless, pressure mounted from all sides — the judiciary, the Law Society, and the family pressure groups — and a compromise solution was announced in July 1982. The compromise, and the problems which may still remain, are clearly explained in the following leading article from the *Legal Action Group Bulletin* (1982):

First ss. 64 and 65 confer a considerable discretion on magistrates. Magistrates *may* grant legal aid to parents only *if* they, in their discretion, consider that there *appears* to be a conflict of interest between parent and child. How will they decide this? What guidance will be offered by new rules of court? How can magistrates find out whether or not there is or might be a conflict unless there is a lawyer representing the parent and able to address the court on this very point? How can they refuse separate representation without investigating the very issues which form the reason for bringing the care proceedings in the first place? The only workable solution is for the rules to provide that a conflict shall be presumed to exist if one of the parties concerned — child, parent or local authority — alleges it.

The second problem is the role of parents in care proceedings. They are not parties — that status is conferred only on the child and the local authority. Under rule 14B of the Magistrates' Courts (Children and Young Persons) Rules 1970 a parent is entitled:

'(*a*) to meet any allegations made against him in the course of the proceedings by calling or giving evidence; and

(*b*) where the court has made an order under s. 32A of the Act of 1969, to make representations to the court.'

Different courts interpret these provisions in different ways. Can the parents cross examine local authority witnesses? It has been held that the court has a *discretion* to allow this (in *R v Milton Keynes Justices, ex p R* [1979] 1 WLR 1062). There is no judicial guidance on the precise meaning of 'making representations' or on what issues parents can make representations. Can parents raise objections to the way the local authority presents its case? In the recent case of *R v Wood Green Crown Court, ex p P* (1982) Times, 23 March, it was held that they could, at least, object to the introduction of hearsay evidence. Can parents appeal or apply to revoke a care order on behalf of their children when the latter are separately represented? This question has been given conflicting answers. At the moment it seems that they can despite any objection by the children's solicitors. This is a desirable result even if it has been reached by somewhat illogical reasoning. In a recent Divisional Court case a magistrates' court had refused to allow a parent what would appear to be the elementary right to be legally represented in care proceedings on the ground that only parties had a right to be represented. The Divisional Court was able to reverse this decision only by resorting to the notion that the court had an inherent jurisdiction to conduct its own proceedings and should allow representation where the interests of justice required it. (*R v Gravesham Juvenile Court, ex p B* (1982) Times, 18 June.)

The problems revealed in these cases all arise from a single source — the denial of party status to parents in care proceedings.

DHSS officials may argue that if the new regulations conferred party status on parents they would be *ultra vires* and that the change requires primary legislation. The legal position on this is unclear. What is clear, however, is that it would be perfectly possible for the regulations to provide that the parent *shall be treated* as a party whenever the court makes an order under s. 32A. There is a precedent for such a formula and it would go a long way towards solving the problem. . . .

Finally, what about the child? Section 32B provides that where the court makes an order for separate representation under s. 32A the court shall appoint a guardian ad litem for the child 'unless satisfied that to do so is not necessary . . .'.

This section will not be brought into force as it will add greatly to the cost of care proceedings. The DHSS has for long accepted that it is legally feasible to introduce s. 32A and s. 65 without introducing s. 32B. It may be feasible for solicitors to represent children without having a guardian ad litem from whom to take instructions but is it desirable? Although there are obvious benefits in having a guardian ad litem, the system provided for in the Children Act has serious defects. First the guardians would have to be chosen from a panel consisting largely of social workers from neighbouring local authorities. This gives rise to fears that the neighbouring social worker acting as guardian might not be sufficiently independent or critical of local authority practices in general or those of a neighbouring authority in particular. Second, it is not in any case clear from the existing rules (1970 Rules, r 14(A)(6)) what the guardian's role is. Is the guardian simply meant to take the place of an instructing parent, be an expert witness, an adviser to the court or a 'reviewer' of what the local authority proposes for the child? A solicitor who wants expert social work advice when preparing or presenting a case on behalf of a child already has the option of employing a social worker as an expert witness and it is possible that this is preferable to the introduction of the system of panels of guardians ad litem as envisaged in s. 32B of the Act. Everyone will welcome the introduction of legal aid for parents but it is vital to the interests of all the parties involved that the right decisions are made on the content and scope of the regulations. Otherwise even more problems and injustices will be introduced into an area of the law already seriously defective.

Questions

(i) It was announced on 7 March 1983 that the Government intends, after all, to implement both s. 32A and s. 32B: which is better — a lawyer who may decide to employ an independent social worker, or a social worker who may decide to employ a lawyer?

(ii) If you were a lawyer acting for a child in care proceedings, what would your approach be if the child were of an age to tell you that he did not want to be taken into care?

The present position in English law is obviously the result of the history explained earlier by Eekelaar, Dingwall and Murray (p. 559, above). But do we all assume that justice requires that parents and children should be separately represented as often as possible? There is, it seems, another point of view, expressed by Joseph Goldstein in *Psychoanalysis and a Jurisprudence of Child Placement — with special emphasis on the role of legal counsel for children* (1978):

I propose that the state restrict its *provision* of legal counsel for children to requests by parents who cannot obtain such assistance; and its *imposition* of such services without regard to parental wishes, to the disposition stage after an adjudication of at least one ground for modifying or terminating of parent-child relationships or, before such an adjudication during an emergency placement. Contrary to the current practice, there would be no justification for the imposition of a child advocate at the invocation stage when a charge of neglect, abuse, or delinquency is made. To deprive parents at that point of their right to represent their child either through counsel of their own choice or without counsel and to appoint counsel for a child without parental consent would be to presume on the basis of an unproven — an unadjudicated — ground that parents are incompetent to serve the interests of their family and consequently the interests of their child. This would deprive a child, without due process, of his right to be represented by his parents before the law.

On the other hand, not to appoint legal counsel for a child *following* an adjudication of a ground for modifying or terminating the child's relationship to the parents and *before* the *disposition* is determined would be to expose the child, uninsulated by an adult, to the state's authority. At that point (the disposition stage) — as well as during emergency placements prior to adjudication when a child is outside of parental care and control — a child requires a legal representative who will assure that the process of placement and the placement itself will make the child's interests paramount and provide the child with the least detrimental alternative.

The House of Commons Select Committee's report on *Violence to Children* had little doubt of the proper solution:

173. . . . More pertinently, we consider that there is a strong argument for making the parent a full party to the proceedings. We do not believe that a wholly new legal principle would be involved since we note that section 58 of the 1975 Act enables a child to be made a party in proceedings between a parent and a local authority [relating to parental rights resolutions]. The child may thus be represented by a guardian (when implemented) as a full party. The parent may be prevented in care and related proceedings from putting forward the precise case which led to the application, on the child's behalf. When separate representation of the child is extended to opposed proceedings this will be of even greater relevance. If the parents' view cannot be adequately presented to the court, a sense of grievance will hinder any continued contact with social workers that may be necessary.

Questions

(i) How attracted are you by the contrary arguments (*a*) that it would be difficult for magistrates to adjust to a three-party rather than a two-party proceeding; (*b*) that it would unnecessarily protract procedure in the majority of cases in order to deal with the minority; (*c*) that the whole procedure is quite misconceived and should be transferred either to the magistrates' domestic court or to the county court?

(ii) If there were to be a family court (see Chapter 17), should care proceedings be included?

(c) THE GROUNDS

The great majority of child abuse cases are brought under s. 1(2)(*a*), as to which Dingwall, Eekelaar and Murray observe in *Care or Control?* (1981):

We note that, apart from one feature, local authority lawyers had experienced few difficulties in bringing cases within the wording of the Act. The exception concerned the framing of the condition of the child in the present tense. This is a real difficulty, both in strict legal interpretation and in practice. The issue does raise an important point of principle, *viz.* whether magistrates should have power to remove children from their families on the basis of apprehended future injury, as a recently published study alleges has been happening . . . we record our dissatisfaction with the fact that if injury is only apprehended, the only method of legal intervention is by wardship proceedings.[7] We consider it unsatisfactory that a local authority may, in care proceedings, acquire the power of total separation of mother and child on establishing a relatively minor injury but cannot use those proceedings to obtain any control over the situation where a child's life might be in danger.

The point arose in the following case:

Essex County Council v TLR and KBR (Minors)
(1978) 9 Fam Law 15, Queen's Bench, Divisional Court

The father of two children, a serving soldier, was granted custody of them in divorce proceedings. In March 1974 the children were put into the care of the county council voluntarily and went to live with foster parents already known to them because the father was posted to Hong Kong. In March 1976 the father, then stationed in Northern Ireland informed the foster parents that he was going to Hong Kong to marry a Chinese wife and would be returned to Northern Ireland via London and would wish to take the children to Northern Ireland with him to live. The county council took the view that this would not be beneficial to the children who were settled with the foster parents and sought a care order in the juvenile court. The [court] refused to give the wording of s. 1(2)(a) of the Children and Young Persons Act 1969 any wider meaning than that their proper development was 'being unavoidably prevented or neglected' to cover the present case where there was no evidence of the existence of circumstances whereby the condition could be satisfied and dismissed the suggestion.

Held on appeal that the section of the Act was only concerned with presently existing events and not with future events no matter how imminent those events might be. The construction of the section . . . was the only possible [one] having regard to its context. However advisable it might be for a juvenile court to have a wider discretion, it was the duty of the present court to give effect to the words of the statute. The application of the county council would be refused.

Question

But *is* it desirable for the authorities to be able to intervene *before* anything happens and even if neither of the conditions (*b*) or (*bb*) is satisfied?

On the other hand, could condition (*a*) be too wide?

F v Suffolk County Council
(1981) 79 LGR 554, 125 Sol Jo 307; Queen's Bench Division

The mother gave birth to an illegitimate boy F on 20 November 1979. A health visitor and a social worker, both of whom knew the mother already and doubted her ability as an adequate mother, frequently visited her and the child. The putative father, who had previously been convicted of assaulting another child of his, was sent to prison and his relationship with F's mother having terminated she formed an association with another man. On his release from prison in August 1980 the putative father forced his way back into the house which he had formerly shared with the mother and child, and the county council obtained a place of safety order for the child on 5 September 1980.[8] The mother was allowed by the county council to retain the child on condition that she stayed at a hostel, but she left with the child within a few days. Following a request from the mother to the county council for short-term help in caring for the child, the juvenile court made an interim care order. The child was placed with foster-parents and thereafter he made a satisfactory bond with his foster-mother. On 24 September 1980 the county council applied to the juvenile court for a care order under section 1 of the Children and Young Persons Act 1969 on the [grounds set out in section 1(2)(a) and (bb); the justices did not think that the putative father might become a member of the household and so rejected (bb); but they were of the opinion that mental development was a proper consideration under (a) and so made a care order, The mother appealed.]

---

7. See Chapter 15, above.
8. Under s. 28 of the Children and Young Persons Act 1969.

McNeill J: . . . In my view, the word 'development' is not confined to physical development and can properly be extended to mental development and, if it be different, emotional development. The proper development of a child must include both physical and mental characteristics.

Then, said Miss Hallon [counsel for the mother], if the court is to consider mental development it should do so only if there is professional evidence, and in particular evidence of a psychiatrist or someone qualified in like manner to assess mental development or the neglect or prevention of it, and that in the absence of professional evidence there was not sufficient evidence to justify the juvenile court in coming to the conclusion which it did.

I do not accept that that sort of evidence is necessary. There are two reasons. One is that the juvenile court has great experience of these matters and its members are picked to sit in that capacity because of their experience on the one hand and their common sense on the other. Secondly, they have the assistance of two very experienced officers, Mrs Roberts (the social worker) and Miss Bawden (the health visitor) to whom I have already referred.

Of course it is open to justices, if they think fit in a particular case, to require other evidence, but here there was plenty of material from which the juvenile court could find as it did that there had been a prevention or neglect of the child's proper mental development.

The next point which was made by Miss Hallon was that on Mrs Roberts' evidence the only effect on the child's development was something which was to be in the future and not a present effect on development. She submitted that the extent of the evidence of Mrs Roberts was that she feared, as I have said, for his future development if he were to go back to his mother.

In that connection I was referred to a decision of this court in *Essex County Council v TLR and KBR* (1978) 9 Fam Law 15. Robert Goff J giving the judgment in that case is recorded as having held that an appeal under the same section as that here was only concerned with presently existing events and not with future events no matter how imminent those events might be. It was held: 'However advisable it might be for a juvenile court to have a wider discretion, it was the duty of the court to give effect to the words of the statute.'

The facts of the *Essex County Council* case (*supra*) were very far removed from those of the present case. . . . It was a sort of quia timet situation and the local authority applied for a care order. The court, if I may say so, inevitably held that that was quite the wrong procedure in those circumstances.

What the court has to consider, as I see it, is this: is there present avoidable neglect or prevention? That is the present tense application to these words. Is [there] something which is happening now, or it may be has happened, with the result that the proper development of the child is affected in those ways? The proper development of the child is a continuing process, past, present, and future, and what the court has to look at, in my view, is the present conduct and its effect on the development of the child in the past, at the present time and at any rate in the foreseeable future. Development being a continuing matter, I do not think this section is intended to rule out of consideration either mental development or development in its broadest and continuing sense.

The criticisms which Miss Hallon made of the evidence were cogently put in this sense that this is a case in which there is no material evidence of physical ill-treatment or injury. It is true that there were occasions when the social worker or health visitor found that there was neglect in the form of nappy rash and there were two incidents of scorching. But the whole picture which the justices had was of a mother whose general conduct in relation to this child was to take him out in his push-chair at the beginning of the day and to push him round the streets until quite late at night, day in and day out, when she had him in her sole charge. That, the justices thought, with if I may say so good sense, was a reason why the child was reacting against his push-chair with the foster-parents.

The justices also had this material before them that the child was forming a satisfactory bond with his foster-mother. 'Before he went to foster-parents he seemed prepared to spend time with anybody' said Mrs Roberts 'but now he seems only to want to be with the foster-parents.' The justices were fully entitled to take the view that he had developed an emotional attachment to his foster-mother, an attachment which had been lacking in his relationship with his natural mother.

Appeal dismissed.

Questions

(i) Do you think that the local authority would have founded its case on the comparative amounts of love offered by mother and foster parents had it not been for the facts (*a*) that the putative father had a recent conviction for injuring another child of his; or (*b*) that both the health visitor and the social worker knew the mother already and doubted her ability as an adequate mother?

(ii) Leave out those two facts: of how many families might a social worker honestly say, 'The child is apparently physically normal for his age, but I fear for his future development if he were to go back to his mother — as much or more for his mental and emotional side than the physical . . .'?

(iii) Who is to set the standard for a child's 'proper' mental and emotional development — health visitors, social workers, or justices or public opinion?

(iv) Does 'proper' mean 'optimum for that particular child' or 'good enough for that particular child'?

The other condition which may be relevant to 'children as victims' (although there is little doubt that it is more often used for children whose precocious promiscuity is seen as a threat) is condition 1(2)(*c*). A vivid illustration of the problems of sexual abuse of children is provided by Anna Raeburn's article on p. 18, above. The only reported case on this condition raises questions which are relevant throughout child abuse:

Mohamed v Knott
[1969] 1 QB 1, [1968] 2 All ER 563, [1968] 2 WLR 1446, 132 JP 349, 112 Sol Jo 332, Queen's Bench Divisional Court

The appellant was a 26-year-old Nigerian Moslem studying medicine in England. He married a 13-year-old Nigerian Moslem girl (Rabi) in Nigeria according to the Nigerian Moslem law. That marriage was valid by the law of Nigeria where both were domiciled, but it was potentially polygamous. It was held to be valid by English law because both parties were domiciled in Nigeria at the time of the marriage. The appellant brought his wife to this country and took her to a doctor to be fitted with a contraceptive. The doctor took the view that she was extremely young and reported the matter to the local authority, which brought care proceedings. The magistrates made a care order for the following reasons:

'Here is a girl, aged thirteen or possibly less, unable to speak English, living in London with a man twice her age to whom she has been married by Moslem law. He admits having had sexual intercourse with her at a time when according to the medical evidence the development of puberty had almost certainly not begun. He intends to resume intercourse as soon as he is satisfied that she is adequately protected by contraceptives from the risk of pregnancy. He admits that before the marriage he had intercourse with a woman by whom he has three illegitimate children. He further admits that since the marriage, which took place as recently as January of this year, he has had sexual relations with a prostitute in Nigeria from whom he contracted venereal disease. In our opinion a continuance of such an association notwithstanding the marriage, would be repugnant to any decent minded English man or woman. Our decision reflects that repugnance.'

Lord Parker CJ: . . . I would never dream of suggesting that a decision by this bench of magistrates with this very experienced chairman, could ever be termed perverse; but having read that, I am convinced that they have misdirected themselves. When they say that 'a continuance of such an association notwithstanding the marriage, would be repugnant to any decent minded Englishman or woman', they are, I think, and can only be, considering the view of an English man or woman in relation to an English girl and our western way of life. I cannot myself think that decent minded English men or women, realising the way of life in which Rabi was brought up, and the appellant for that matter, would inevitably say that this is repugnant. It is certainly natural for a girl to marry at that age. They develop sooner, and there is nothing abhorrent in their way of life for a girl of thirteen to marry a man of twenty-five. Incidentally it was not until 1929 that, in this country, an age limit was put on marriage. Granted that the appellant may be said to be a bad lot, that he has done things in the past which perhaps nobody would approve of, it does not follow from that that the wife, happily married to the appellant, is under any moral danger by associating and living with him. For my part, as it seems to me, it could only be said that she was in moral danger if one was considering somebody brought up in and living in, our way of life, and to hold that she is in moral danger in the circumstances of this case can only be arrived at, as it seems to me, by ignoring the way of life in which she was brought up, and the appellant was brought up.

Question

Why is it right to consider the way of life in which this girl and her husband were brought up but wrong to consider the way of life in which young Derriviere and his father (p. 532, above) were brought up?

In 1980, Goldstein, Freud and Solnit published a second book, *Before the Best Interests of the Child*, in which they examine the justifications for state intervention in the child's relationship with his parents. Their argument rests on two simple premises:

First, we believe that a child's need for continuity of care by autonomous parents requires acknowledging that parents should generally be entitled to raise their children as they think best, free of state interference. This conviction finds expression in our preference for *minimum state intervention* and prompts restraint in defining justifications for coercively intruding on family relationships. Second, we believe that the child's well-being — not the parents', the family's, or the child care agency's — must be determinative once justification for state intervention has been established. Whether the protective shell of the family is already broken before the state intrudes, or breaks as a result of it, the goal of intervention must be to create or recreate a family for the child as quickly as possible. That conviction is expressed in our preference for *making a child's interests paramount* once his care has become a legitimate matter for the state to decide.

So long as a child is a member of a functioning family, his paramount interest lies in the preservation of his family. Thus, our preference for making a child's interests paramount is not to be construed as a justification in and of itself for intrusion.

Questions

(i) Are you inclined to agree so far? Is not that what the grounds for care proceedings are designed to do?
(ii) However, apart from parental requests for the state to place the child and the existence of familial bonds between children and their longtime care-takers who are not their parents, the only circumstances which the authors see as justifying intervention are:
(*a*) The death or disappearance of both parents, the only parent or the custodial parent — when coupled with their failure to make provision for their child's custody and care: but what if that provision is inadequate?
(*b*) Conviction, or acquittal by reason of insanity, of a sexual offense against one's child: but what about an offence against another child?
(*c*) Serious bodily injury inflicted by parents upon their child, an attempt to inflict such injury, or the repeated failure of parents to prevent their child from suffering such injury: but when does neglect become an injury?
(*d*) Refusal by parents to authorise lifesaving medical care when (1) medical experts agree that treatment is non-experimental and appropriate for the child, and (2) denial of that treatment could result in death, and (3) the anticipated result of treatment is what society would want for every child — a chance for normal healthy growth or a life worth living: but see Chapter 15. Are all these covered by the grounds for care proceedings? Do those grounds go further? If they do, which do you prefer?

These questions raise the problem of the proper balance to be struck between family autonomy and the paternalism of the state, to which we shall return in the next chapter.

(c) OUTCOME

The structure of s. 1 of the 1969 Act, combined with the Magistrates' Courts (Children and Young Persons) Rules 1970, suggests that there should be three elements in the magistrates' decision. First, has one or more of the 'primary conditions' (*a*) to (*f*) been established? Second, is the child in need of care or control which he is unlikely to receive unless the court makes an order? The answer to the second may not necessarily follow from the answer to the first. In *Re S* (*A Minor*)(*Care Order: Education*) [1978] QB 120, [1977] 3 All ER 582, the Crown Court allowed an appeal against a care order imposed by magistrates upon a boy who had not been to school for almost a whole school year, on the ground that as an otherwise well-brought-up and well-cared-for youngster, he was not 'in need of care or control.' The order was eventually restored in the Court of Appeal. Lord Denning MR said this: 'If a child was not being sent to school or receiving a proper education then he was in need of care. He was in need of care in respect of his own education. "Care" applies not only to the physical well-being of a child, his meals and comfort at home, but also to his proper education.' However, the third question is whether, if the first two elements are proved, the court should make an order, and if so which. In *Re S*, the Crown Court had thought that to stay at home without education was better for the boy's welfare than living in a children's home, which was the only way of ensuring that he went to school. The Court of Appeal disagreed, but the case does demonstrate that, in theory at least, the applicant in care proceedings should be able to demonstrate that an order will be better for the child than leaving things as they are.

Question

Consider the example of sexual abuse, as described in Anna Raeburn's article on p. 18, above; consider also the advantages and disadvantages of placing a teenage or pre-teenage girl in residential care: what course should the court take in such cases?

Dingwall, Eekelaar and Murray in *Care or Control?* (1981) summarise what normally happened in the care proceedings which they studied thus:

We then describe what we hold to be the central issues in care proceedings: that is, the matters which tend to be primarily in contention before the court. The first is the condition of the child. However, we observe that allegations concerning a child's physical condition are not often contested in court: medical evidence on this matter is rarely challenged. This evidence is seen as being of a factual nature. However, medical evidence often extended to surmises of the causes of the child's condition and, although the parents might dispute this in abuse cases, it seems rare for this to be done by the production of opposing evidence, perhaps due to the difficulty of persuading one doctor to testify against another in matters of this kind. In neglect cases it seems unlikely that medical evidence on causation will be strongly challenged at all. We suggest that written medical evidence of this nature should be admissible if all parties agree. We were also struck by the lack of resort to expert testimony when the emotional condition of the child was in question. The reason may lie in lawyers' distrust of psychiatric evidence, but is more likely to be found, in our view, in the readiness of lay people to resort to their common sense notions of normality in making these assessments. This attitude is taken further when attempts are made to assess the effects on a child of its environment. Fieldworkers and courts are prepared to use such concepts in determining the degree of deviance in parental behaviour (and, accordingly, the child's upbringing) and to impute from that consequences for the child. . . .

This leads us to consider the central issue in care proceedings as being assessment of parental competence. We build our discussion of this around a particular case (Leonard). . . . The main point in dispute was whether a burn had been deliberately inflicted on the child. Nevertheless, as we show, the character of the child's parents was examined from a multitude of facets and the picture revealed was crucial to the outcome of the case. We also show how significant, in this and in other cases, is the issue of the preparedness of the parent to co-operate with social services and to accept the legitimacy of their concern. All these matters are as crucial in court as they are in the earlier stages of the process: they amount, in effect, to the construction of a case against the parent, which the parent is obliged to 'answer'.

We argue next that a third major issue in care proceedings relates to the plans regarding the child and the family held by the authority should they establish their case. However, the technical division of care proceedings into two stages (based on the criminal model), if strictly applied, would relegate this matter to consideration after the finding had been made that a ground for making an order had been established. Insistence on the two-stage procedure seemed to vary and to depend heavily on the view of its appropriateness held by the local authority lawyers in the area. Our data suggested that the division was, in practice, difficult, if not impossible, to maintain, and indeed its observation might be inconsistent with the 'care or control' test. However, we saw no attempts to distinguish evidence presented to establish one of the 'grounds', and evidence directed at the 'care or control' test.

. . . We revert to our contention that the purpose of seeking care proceedings may frequently have as its prime object the acquisition of greater control over family functioning, and that care orders are frequently used for this purpose. We consider the propriety of using care orders in this way and conclude by referring to the very limited opportunities, in the available methods of disposition, for making orders which specify with any degree of refinement or precision, the measures that may be taken concerning the child.

Questions

(i) What do you think should be done for a child who is shown to be 'in need of care or control' under this section?

(ii) Who should decide *exactly* what is to be done — the court or the professionals charged with helping the family?

Before we assume that all such children should be permanently removed from their parents and adopted, it is as well to consider the findings of those who first alerted the world to the 'battered baby syndrome.' Ruth S. Kempe and C. Henry Kempe discuss the treatment of abusive parents in *Child Abuse* (1978):

What can be done to prevent the appalling waste of happiness, health, even life that results from child abuse? Before we go on to discuss this we should explain that talk of treatment only applies to what might be called the norm among abusive parents. There is a group, amounting to about 10% of the total, who are very seriously mentally ill — too seriously, in fact, for any treatment to be possible. For these there is only one alternative — to end the care-giving relationship by placing the child with relatives or in permanent foster care, or by formally terminating parental rights, to be followed by adoption.

This 10% is made up of four groups. The first is that 1 or 2% of abusive parents who suffer from a delusional psychosis of which their abused child has been made part. Some of these may even believe, 'God is telling me to kill my child.' More usually the delusion involves the mother seeing her child as an extension of herself, with no identity of her own at all. For example, we have known a mother to say, 'no, I'm sure the baby doesn't need to be fed yet; I'm not hungry yet.' . . .

Another 2 or 3% of abusive parents are aggressive sociopaths; that is, individuals with such low boiling points that they communicate only by bashing. They bash their friends, their wives, and their children indiscriminately. . . .

A further 1 or 2% of untreatable abusive parents are individuals who are frankly 'cruel': they torture their children in a premeditated, prolonged, repetitive, and often self-righteous way for such infractions as bed-wetting or slight delays in obedience. . . .

The final 2 or 3% who are seriously mentally ill are the 'fanatics'. This group includes a great variety of people who use religious or other terms to justify beliefs and approaches to child-rearing that to the rest of the world seem clearly and wholly irrational . . . (such as a couple who believed their baby should live only on carrot juice, since all other food was poisonous).

Aside from the parents in these groups, there are others to whom we cannot recommend returning children who have had to be hospitalised. First are the parents so addicted to alcohol or drugs that they cannot provide even minimum care for their babies. . . .

Second are the families when the parents are too retarded or the mothers simply too young to raise children. This is a complicated evaluation. . . . But, in general, parents with IQs under sixty and mothers under fifteen years old seem to warrant a judicial review to determine whether termination of parental rights is indeed required.

Third are the families where other children have already been seriously injured, and where there may have been one or more unexplained deaths. . . .

These groups, seven in all, represent about ten per cent of the families with hospitalised abused children. . . . We also seek termination of parental rights for the ten per cent of abused children whose families, after six or nine months of treatment, show little or no improvement. There is another groups of parents, unable to accept any kind of help within a reasonable time framework of six months to a year, who remain adamant about their right to treat their children as they see fit or who continue a life style so chaotic and lacking in fixed relationships that they have little to offer their children. . . . Also, we often seek termination successfully in cases of abandonment where an earnest effort has been made to locate the parents and they, in turn, have failed to communicate with their child or his care-giver for more than six months (or in some jurisdictions, a full year). . . .

. . . after subtracting that further 10% for whom treatment is tried but fails, we are left, in Colorado, with an overall success rate of 80%. These families are reunited within nine months and without further reinjury. . . . For abusive parents there are two kinds of treatment: the life-saving telephone line or crisis nursery and the long-term therapy designed to help them overcome their own depressing or devastating past histories in order to be able to love and care for their own children. . . .

Questions

(i) Does that seem improbably utopian to you or a sound argument *against* social workers' reluctance to intervene in cases where they find it only too easy to understand the pressures upon the family?

(ii) On p. 483, above appears the view of the committee which enquired into the case of Maria Colwell, to the effect that social workers in the early 1970s assumed that magistrates would return a child to the natural family once the parent appeared fit to resume care. Section 21(2A) of the 1969 Act now provides that courts must not discharge care orders in respect of children who are still in need of care or control, unless satisfied that they will receive that care or control after the order is discharged. Why cannot the law simply provide that such applications be governed by the paramount consideration of the child's current welfare?

(iii) Do the orders available to the court, coupled with the possibilities of placement discussed in the previous two chapters, seem to provide a sufficient legal framework for carrying out these aims?

(iv) Or would you favour a more comprehensive approach, along the lines of the *Model Act to Free Children for Permanent Placement* (see p. 462, above)?

CHAPTER 15

Wardship, parental autonomy and the rights of children

Thus the *European Convention of Human Rights* seeks to achieve a free and plural society through, among other things, a proper balance between family privacy and the right to learn. Two aspects of the tension between family privacy and State intervention are of particular concern to the family lawyer. One is the 'marriage-saving' activities of agencies of the State, which may hinder both the satisfactory protection of individuals and the satisfactory resolution of disputes. We shall deal with the latter in the final chapter. The other aspect is the 'child-saving' efforts of the State, which may constitute an unwarranted intrusion into the rights of parents to bring up their children as they see fit. In this chapter, we shall deal first with the particular problem posed by the modern development of the Crown's ancient jurisdiction over wards of court, then with some recent discussions of the problem in the United States, where very similar provisions to those above are embodied in the Constitution, and finally with the emerging concept of children's rights.

1 Parental rights and the development of wardship

The concept of parental 'rights' achieved its legal prominence in the nineteenth century. An example of eighteenth century thinking is Sir William Blackstone in the first volume of his *Commentaries on the Laws of England* (1765):

1. And, first, the duties of parents to legitimate children: which principally consist in three particulars; their maintenance, their protection, and their education.

The duty of parents to provide for the *maintenance* of their children is a principle of natural law; an obligation, says Puffendorf, laid on them not only by nature herself, but by their own proper act, in bringing them into the world: for they would be in the highest manner injurious to their issue, if they only gave the children life, that they might afterwards see them perish. By begetting them therefore they have entered into a voluntary obligation, to endeavour, as far as in them lies, that the life which they have bestowed shall be supported and preserved. And thus the children will have a perfect *right* of receiving maintenance from their parents. And the president Montesquieu has a very just observation upon this head: that the establishment of marriage in all civilized states is built on this natural obligation of the father to provide for his children; for that ascertains and makes known the person who is bound to fulfil this obligation: whereas, in promiscuous and illicit conjunctions, the father is unknown; and the mother finds a thousand obstacles in her way; — shame, remorse, the constraint of her sex, and the rigor of laws; — that stifle her inclinations to perform this duty: and besides, she generally wants ability.

The municipal laws of all well-regulated states have taken care to enforce this duty: though providence has done it more effectually than any laws, by implanting in the breast of every parent that natural ςοργη, or insuperable degree of affection, which not even the deformity of person or mind, not even the wickedness, ingratitude, and rebellion of children, can totally suppress or extinguish.

After discussing the relevant provisions of English Law, including its deficiencies in the matter of education, he continues:

2. The *power* of parents over their children is derived from the former consideration, their duty; this authority being given them, partly to enable the parent more effectually to perform his duty, and partly as a recompence for his care and trouble in the faithful discharge of it. And upon this score the municipal laws of some nations have given a much larger authority to the parents, than others. The ancient Roman laws gave the father a power of life and death over his children; upon this principle, that he who gave had also the power of taking away. . . .

The power of a parent by our English laws is much more moderate; but still sufficient to keep the child in order and obedience. He may lawfully correct his child, being under age, in a reasonable manner; for this is for the benefit of his education. The consent or concurrence of the parent to the marriage of his child under age, was also *directed* by our ancient law to be obtained: but now it is absolutely *necessary*; for without it the contract is void. And this also is another means, which the law has put into the parent's hands, in order the better to discharge his duty; first, of protecting his children from the snares of artful and designing persons; and, next of settling them properly in life, by preventing the ill consequences of too early and precipitate marriages. A father has no other power over his sons *estate*, than as his trustee or guardian; for, though he may receive the profits during the child's minority, yet he must account for them when he comes of age. He may indeed have the benefit of his children's labour while they live with him, and are maintained by him: but this is no more than he is entitled to from his apprentices or servants. The legal power of a father (for a mother, as such, is entitled to no power, but only to reverence and respect) the power of a father, I say, over the persons of his children ceases at the age of twenty one: for they are then enfranchised by arriving at years of discretion, or that point which the law has established (as some must necessarily be established) when the empire of the father, or other guardian, gives place to the empire of reason. Yet, till that age arrives, this empire of the father continues even after his death; for he may by his will appoint a guardian to his children. He may also delegate part of his parental authority, during his life, to the tutor or schoolmaster of his child; who is then *in loco parentis*, and has such a portion of the power of the parent committed to his charge, viz. that of restraint and correction, as may be necessary to answer the purposes for which he is employed.

3. The *duties* of children to their parents arise from a principle of natural justice and retribution. For to those, who gave us existence, we naturally owe subjection and obedience during our minority, and honour and reverence ever after; they, who protected the weakness of our infancy, are entitled to our protection in the infirmity of their age; they who by sustenance and education have enabled their offspring to prosper, ought in return to be supported by that

offspring, in case they stand in need of assistance. Upon this principle proceed all the duties of children to their parents, which are enjoined by positive laws.

Questions

(i) How much of this represents the modern law?
(ii) Do you think that Blackstone's account of the rationale underlying parental power could equally well be applied today?

In the nineteenth century, these parental powers were translated by the courts into enforceable legal rights (see Pettitt, 1957). The zenith, or nadir, came in a case which Lord Upjohn, in the course of *J v C* [1970] AC 668, [1969] 1 All ER 788 could 'only describe as dreadful:'

Re Agar-Ellis Agar-Ellis v Lascelles
(1883) 24 Ch D 317, 53 LJ Ch 10, 50 LT 161, 32 WRI, Court of Appeal

A Protestant father agreed at his marriage that any children would be brought up Roman Catholics, but at the birth of the first child he changed his mind. The mother, however, taught the children Roman Catholicism and eventually they refused to go to a Protestant church. The father made them wards of court and the court (see (1878) LR 10 Ch D 49, 48 LJ Ch 1) restrained the mother from taking them to confession or to a Roman Catholic church and left the father to do what he thought fit for their spiritual welfare. He therefore took the children from their mother and placed them with other people, allowing her to visit only once a month and censoring her letters. In 1883, the second daughter, then aged 16, wrote to the judge begging to be allowed the free exercise of her religion and to live with her mother. The father agreed to the former but not the latter. Accordingly, she and her mother petitioned the court to allow them a two-month holiday together and freedom of correspondence and access. The father opposed this because he feared that the mother would alienate his child's affections. Pearson J dismissed the petition on the ground that the court had no jurisdiction to interfere with the father's legal right to control the custody and education of his children, in the absence of any fault on his part. The petitioners appealed.

Brett MR: . . . But the law of *England* has recognised the natural rights of a father, not as guardian of his children but as the father, because he is the father. The rights of a father as guardian, if they could be limited to his rights as guardian, would probably be the same as the rights of a testamentary guardian; but the father has greater rights than those which a testamentary guardian, or any other guardian, can have. A testamentary guardian is not called on to feel affection for his ward; he is not called upon to forgive the ward; he is not called upon to treat the ward with tenderness. The law recognises the rights of the father because it recognises the natural duties of the father. Now the natural duties of a father are to treat his child with the utmost affection and with infinite tenderness, to forgive his child without stint and under all circumstances. None of those duties are expected of a testamentary guardian, but they are the natural duties of a father, which, if he breaks, he breaks from all that nature calls upon him to do; and if he breaks from these duties, the law may not be able to insist upon their full performance. The law cannot inquire in every case how fathers have fulfilled their duties. The law does not interfere because of the great trust and faith it has in the natural affection of the father to perform his duties, and therefore gives him corresponding rights. . . .

But there are limits to the forbearance and patience of the law in particular cases, which have been already referred to in argument. If, for instance, a father by his immoral conduct has become a person who really is unfit in the eyes of everybody to perform his duties to his child, and, therefore, to claim the rights of a father towards his child, the Court then will interfere. That is, if the child be a ward of Court; for unless the child be a ward of Court, the Court has no greater jurisdiction as between the father and child than it has between any other persons. But if the child be a ward of Court, and if the father has been guilty of that amount of immorality which convinces the Court that he is not fit to claim his rights as a father, the Court will, at the instance of the ward, interfere. And so, if the father has allowed certain things to be done, and then, out of mere caprice, has counter-ordered them, so as, in the eyes of everybody, to cause an injury to the child, then the Court will not allow the capricious change of mind, although if the thing had been done originally the Court could not have interfered. I am not prepared to say that the patience of the Court, in the case of its ward, might not be exhausted by any other conduct of the father — by cruelty to a great extent, or pitiless spitefulness to a great extent. I am not prepared to say the Court would not interfere in such a case, although no Court has yet decided it, but the Court could not interfere on such grounds as that except in the utmost need and in the most extreme case. . . .

The rights of a father are sacred rights because his duties are sacred duties. . . .

Bowen LJ: . . . This is a case in which, if we were not in a Court of Law, but in a court of critics capable of being moved by feelings of favour or disfavour, we might be tempted to comment, with more or less severity, upon the way in which, so far as we have heard the story, the father has exercised his parental right. But it seems to me the Court must not allow itself to drift out of the proper course; the Court must not be tempted to interfere with the natural order and course of family life, the very basis of which is the authority of the father, except it be in those special cases in which the state is called upon, for reasons of urgency, to set aside the parental authority and to intervene for itself. I for one should deeply regret the day, if it ever came, when Courts of Law or Equity thought themselves justified in interfering more than is strictly necessary with the private affairs of the people of this country. Both as regards the conduct of private affairs, and of domestic life, the rule is that Courts of Law should not intervene except upon occasion. It is far better that people should be left free, and I do not believe that a Court of Law can bring up a child as successfully as a father, even if the father was exercising his discretion as regards the child in a way which critics might condemn. . . .

. . . Judicial machinery is quite inadequate to the task of educating children in this country. It can correct abuses and it can interfere to redress the parental caprice, and it does interfere when the natural guardian of the child ceases to be the natural guardian, and shews by his conduct that he has become an unnatural guardian, but to interfere further would be to ignore the one principle which is the most fundamental of all in the history of mankind, and owing to the full play of which man has become what he is.

Now the Court must never forget, and will never forget, first of all, the rights of family life, which are sacred. I think all that could be said on that subject has been said far better than I could repeat it by Vice-Chancellor *Kindersley* in the case of *Re Curtis* [see p. 577, below], and the cases to which he there refers. Those are as to the rights of family life. Then we must regard the benefit of the infant; but then it must be remembered that if the words 'benefit of the infant' are used in any but the accurate sense it would be a fallacious test to apply to the way the Court exercises its jurisdiction over the infant by way of interference with the father. It is not the benefit to the infant as conceived by the Court, but it must be the benefit to the infant having regard to the natural law which points out that the father knows far better as a rule what is good for his children than a Court of Justice can.

As soon as it becomes obvious that the rights of the family are being abused to the detriment of the interests of the infant, then the father shews that he is no longer the natural guardian — that he has become an unnatural guardian — that he has perverted the ties of nature for the purpose of injustice and cruelty. When that case arrives the Court will not stay its hand; but until that case arrives it is not mere disagreement with the view taken by the father of his rights and the interests of his infant that can justify the Court in interfering. If that were not so we might be interfering all day and with every family. I have no doubt that there are very few families in the country in which fathers do not, at some time or other, make mistakes, and there are very few families in which a wiser person than the father might not do something better for that child than is being done by the father, who however has an authority which never ought to be slighted.

Questions

(i) Take out the sex discrimination and apply these arguments to a couple's decision: (*a*) that their child shall not go on the school trip to France; (*b*) that their child shall go to Sunday school every week; (*c*) that their child shall not

be vaccinated against whooping cough; or (*d*) that their child should not receive sex education in school. Should the law interfere?
(ii) How relevant to your view of the *Agar-Ellis* decision was it (*a*) that mother and father disagreed with one another, and (*b*) that the child was, by the hearing, aged 17?

In the case of *Re Curtis* (1859) 28 LJ Ch 458, 34 LT(OS) 10, quoted with such approval by Bowen LJ, Kindersley VC said this:

If it be the case, as I believe has been suggested, that the Judge of the Court for Divorce and Matrimonial Causes, when he decrees a judicial separation is armed with the authority to determine what the custody of the children of the marriage shall be, simply with reference to what is most for their interests, I can only say that there is no such jurisdiction in this Court. This Court has not the right simply to consider that. This Court does not exercise the jurisdiction in merely considering whether it would be for the benefit of the children that their custody should be with the father or with the mother, or with some other relative, or with strangers, simply because, upon the whole, it would be most for the benefit of the children that there should be that custody. I repudiate all such jurisdiction as belonging to this Court. If such a jurisdiction existed, I suspect that the peace of half the families in this country would be disturbed by applications shewing, or attempting to shew, what, I am afraid, might be shewn in a great many cases, that it was most for the interest of the children that they should be removed from the custody both of the father and of the mother; but happily there is no such jurisdiction.

Yet, since then the law has adopted a principle of equal rights for mothers and fathers, and of the paramountcy of the child's welfare (see p. 339, above), and has applied the latter principle to disputes between parents and 'strangers' in the case of *J v C* [1970] AC 668, [1969] 1 All ER 788 (p. 474, above). Owing to the continued existence of the wardship jurisdiction of the High Court, which is now governed by that principle and open to all, the result which those nineteenth century judges so much feared has all but come to pass. Four recent cases, out of many, should be sufficient to demonstrate this:

Re D (A Minor)(wardship: sterilisation)
[1976] Fam 185, [1976] 1 All ER 326, [1976] 2 WLR 279, 119 Sol Jo 696, High Court, Family Division

D, now aged 11, was born with 'Sotos syndrome', the symptoms of which included epilepsy, clumsiness, an unusual facial appearance, behavioural problems, and some impairment of intelligence. Her mother was convinced that she was seriously mentally handicapped and would be unable to care either for herself or a child of her own. The paediatrician who had taken an interest in her case from an early stage took a similar view. When she reached puberty, therefore, mother and paediatrician arranged with a gynaecologist that she should be sterilised immediately, because they were afraid that she might be seduced and bear an abnormal child. The people responsible for her education, however, thought that it would be wrong to perform an irreversible and permanent operation upon her; her behaviour and social skills were improving steadily; she was of dull normal intelligence and it was common ground that she had sufficient intellectual capacity to marry in due course. The educational psychologist therefore made her a ward of court and applied for an order continuing the wardship in order to delay or prevent the proposed operation. It was not proposed that D should be removed from the care and control of her widowed mother, who had looked after her 'splendidly.'

Heilbron J: . . .

Is wardship appropriate?

I have first of all to decide whether this is an appropriate case in which to exercise the court's wardship jurisdiction. Wardship is a very special and ancient jurisdiction. Its origin was the sovereign's feudal obligation as parens patriae to protect the person and property of his subjects, and particularly those unable to look after themselves, including infants. This obligation, delegated to the chancellor, passed to the Chancery Court, and in 1970 to this division of the High Court.

The jurisdiction in wardship is very wide, but there are limitations. It is not in every case that it is appropriate to make a child a ward, and counsel for Mrs B has argued with his usual skill and powers of persuasion that, as this case raises a matter of principle of wide public importance, and is a matter which affects many people, continuation of wardship would be inappropriate.

In his powerful argument, counsel for the Official Solicitor, on the other hand, submitted that the court in wardship had a wide jurisdiction which should be extended to encompass this novel situation, because it is just the type of problem which this court is best suited to determine when exercising its protective functions in regard to minors. As Lord Eldon LC said many years ago in *Wellesley v Duke of Beaufort* (1827) 2 Russ 1, 5 LJOS Ch 85:

> 'This jurisdiction is founded on the obvious necessity that the law should place somewhere the care of individuals who cannot take care of themselves, particularly in cases where it is clear that some care should be thrown around them.'

It is apparent from the recent decision of the Court of Appeal in *Re X (A Minor)* [1975] Fam 47, [1975] 1 All ER 697 that the jurisdiction to do what is considered necessary for the protection of an infant is to be exercised carefully and within limits, but the court has, from time to time over the years, extended the sphere in the exercise of this jurisdiction.

The type of operation proposed is one which involves the deprivation of a basic human right, namely the right of a woman to reproduce, and therefore it would, if performed on a woman for non-therapeutic reasons and without her consent, be a violation of such right. . . . As the evidence showed, and I accept it, D could not possibly have given an informed consent. What the evidence did, however, make clear was that she would almost certainly understand the implications of such an operation by the time she reached 18.

This operation could, if necessary, be delayed or prevented if the child were to remain a ward of court, and as Lord Eldon LC, so vividly expressed it in *Wellesley's* case: 'It has always been the principle of this Court, not to risk the incurring of damage to children which it cannot repair, but rather to prevent the damage being done.'

I think that is the very type of case where this court should 'throw some care around this child', and I propose to continue her wardship which, in my judgment, is appropriate in this case.

The operation — should it be performed?

In considering this vital matter, I want to make it quite clear that I have well in mind the natural feelings of a parent's heart, and though in wardship proceedings parents' rights can be superseded, the court will not do so lightly, and only in pursuance of well-known principles laid down over the years. The exercise of the court's jurisdiction is paternal, and it must be exercised judicially, and the judge must act, as far as humanly possible, on the evidence, as a wise parent would act. As Lord Upjohn pointed out in *J v C* [1970] AC 668, [1969] 1 All ER 788 the law and practice in relation to infants —

> 'have developed, are developing and must, and no doubt will, continue to develop by reflecting and adopting the changing views, as the years go by, of reasonable men and women, the parents of children, on the proper treatment and methods of bringing up children; for after all that is the model which the judge must emulate for . . . he must act as the judicial reasonable parent.'

It is of course beyond dispute that the welfare of this child is the paramount consideration, and the court must act in her best interests.

The judge then reviews some of the evidence and arguments, including the facts that D had as yet shown no interest in the opposite sex, and had virtually no opportunities for promiscuity; that other methods of contraception or even abortion would be available should the need arise; and that there was no therapeutic reason for performing the operation now. She continues:

Dr Gordon, however, maintained that, provided the parent or parents consented, the decision was one made pursuant to the exercise of his clinical judgment, and that no interference could be tolerated in his clinical freedom.

The other consultants did not agree. Their opinion was that a decision to sterilise a child was not entirely within a doctor's clinical judgment, save only when sterilisation was the treatment of choice for some disease, as, for instance, when in order to treat a child and to ensure her direct physical well-being, it might be necessary to perform a hysterectomy to remove a malignant uterus. Whilst the side effect of such an operation would be to sterilise, the operation would be performed solely for therapeutic purposes. I entirely accept their opinions. I cannot believe, and the evidence does not warrant the view, that a decision to carry out an operation of this nature performed for non-therapeutic purposes on a minor, can be held to be within the doctor's sole clinical judgment.

It is quite clear that once a child is a ward of court, no important step in the life of that child can be taken without the consent of the court, and I cannot conceive of a more important step than that which was proposed in this case.

A review of the whole of the evidence leads me to the conclusion that in a case of a child of 11 years of age, where the evidence shows that her mental and physical condition and attainments have already improved, and where her future prospects are as yet unpredictable, where the evidence also shows that she is unable as yet to understand and appreciate the implications of this operation and could not give a valid or informed consent, but the likelihood is that in later years she will be able to make her own choice, where, I believe, the frustration and resentment of realising (as she would one day) what had happened could be devastating, an operation of this nature is, in my view, contra-indicated.

For these, and for the other reasons to which I have adverted, I have come to the conclusion that this operation is neither medically indicated nor necessary, and that it would not be in D's best interests for it to be performed.

Questions

(i) If the proceedings had not been brought and the operation had gone ahead as planned, would the gynaecologist have committed a battery upon D?

(ii) What difference, if any, would it have made: (*a*) to question (i) above, or (*b*) to the result of the wardship case, if D had been 15 and able to understand the consequences of the operation?

(iii) What difference, if any, would it have made if the operation, although controversial, had been therapeutically indicated: for example, an abortion?

In *Re P (A Minor)* (1981) 80 LGR 301, Butler-Sloss J did indeed balance the arguments for and against a 15-year-old girl having an abortion. This was an example of the more common problem, where medical opinion (and indeed the girl herself) was in favour of an operation to which the parent was opposed. The judge did not discuss whether the girl's own consent would have been sufficient had she not been made a ward of court, but had little difficulty in concluding that the abortion was in her best interests. Nor were the parents' views strictly crucial, as the local authority had parental powers by virtue of a care order. A more extreme example is the following:

Re B (A Minor)(wardship: medical treatment)
[1981] 1 WLR 1421, 125 Sol Jo 608, Court of Appeal

B was born with Down's syndrome and an intestinal blockage from which she would die in a few days unless operated upon. Her parents refused to consent to the operation. The doctors contacted the local authority who made the child a ward of court and asked the judge to give care and control to the authority and to authorise the authority to have the operation carried out. The judge did so, but when B was moved to a different hospital for the operation to be performed, the surgeon declined to operate in the face of the parents' objections. The local authority therefore came back to the judge.

Other surgeons were prepared to carry out the operation. Ewbank J refused to order it to be carried out and the local authority appealed.

Templeman LJ: . . . The question which this court has to determine is whether it is in the interests of this child to be allowed to die within the next week or to have the operation in which case, if she lives, she will be a mongoloid child, but no can say to what extent her mental or physical defects will be apparent. No one can say whether she will suffer or whether she will be happy in part. On the one hand the probability is that she will not be a cabbage as it is called when people's faculties are entirely destroyed. On the other hand it is certain that she will be very severely mentally and physically handicapped.

On behalf of the parents Mr Gray has submitted very movingly, if I may say so, that this is a case where nature has made its own arrangements to terminate a life which would not be fruitful and nature should not be interfered with. He has also submitted that in this kind of decision the views of responsible and caring parents, as these are, should be respected, and that their decision that it is better for the child to be allowed to die should be respected. Fortunately or unfortunately, in this particular case the decision does not and cannot lie either with the parents or with the doctors, but lies with the court. It is a decision which of course must be made in the light of the evidence and views expressed by the parents and the doctors, but at the end of the day it devolves on this court in this particular instance to decide whether the life of this child is demonstrably going to be so awful that in effect the child must be condemned to die, or whether the life of this child is still so imponderable that it would be wrong for her to be condemned to die. There may be cases, I know not, of severe proved damage where the future is so certain and where the life of the child is so bound to be full of pain and suffering that the court might be driven to a different conclusion, but in the present case the choice which lies before the court is this: whether to allow an operation to take place which may result in the child living for 20 or 30 years as a mongoloid or whether (and I think this must be brutally the result) to terminate the life of a mongoloid child because she also has an intestinal complaint. Faced with that choice I have no doubt that it is the duty of this court to decide that the child must live. The judge was much affected by the reasons given by the parents and came to the conclusion that their wishes ought to be respected. In my judgment he erred in that the duty of the court is to decide whether it is in the interests of the child that an operation should take place. The evidence in this case only goes to show that if the operation takes place and is successful then the child may live the normal span of a mongoloid child with the handicaps and defects and life of a mongol child, and it is not for this court to say that life of that description ought to be extinguished.

Accordingly the appeal must be allowed and the local authority must be authorised themselves to authorise and direct the operation to be carried out on the little girl.

Questions

(i) Is it indeed a question to be governed by the 'best interests of the child' when the choice is between life and death? Could this be reconciled with the criminal liability of parents (and others) who wilfully fail to secure adequate medical aid for children (see p. 530, above)?

(ii) But how far does 'adequate medical aid' extend? Ian Kennedy, in *The Karen Quinlan Case: Problems and Proposals* (1976) supports the view of a *doctor's* obligations to his patient, put forward in 1957 by Pope Pius XII: 'Doctors, he said, were obliged to continue with "ordinary" measures but were not obliged to carry out "extraordinary" measures. The latter he defined not in terms of what a doctor would regard as extraordinary or non-standard procedures, a definition which would change as developments occurred, but rather as whatever "cannot be obtained or secured without excessive expense, pain or other inconvenience for the patient or for others, or which, if used, would not offer a reasonable hope of benefit to the patient" '. Does this strike you also as a reasonable definition of the limits of a parent's duty to secure adequate medical aid for his child?

(iii) But even if the matter of life and death may be governed by slightly different criteria, is the principle of the 'best interests of the child' appropriate to medical problems which are not immediately life-threatening? Should the court, for example, be able to decide whether a child (*a*) should have complicated and risky surgery to alleviate a gross congenital deformity of the face, or (*b*) should have relatively simple surgery to correct a cleft palate and hair lip?

The courts in the United States of America have found these issues difficult, complicated as they are by constitutional protection both for family privacy and for the free exercise of religion (as to which see articles 8 and 9 of the European Convention of Human Rights, p. 573, above). Although a New York court did intervene to allow surgery in case (*a*) in question (iii) above (*Re Sampson*, 29 NY2d 686, 278 NE2d 918, 1972), another New York court refused to do so in case (*b*), albeit partly because the child himself, aged 14, was opposed (*Re Seiforth*, 309 NY 80, 127 NE2d 820, 1955). A Pennsylvania court in *Re Ricky Ricardo Green*, 448 Pa 338, 292 A2d 387, 52 ALR 3d 1106 (1972) refused to find a 16-year-old a 'neglected child' when he required surgery for a collapsed spine; his mother objected to this because it might involve a blood transfusion, contrary to her beliefs as a Jehovah's witness; but the court did remand the case to discover what the boy's own views were, as his interests were directly affected. And a California court in *Re Phillip B*, 156 Cal Rptr 48 (1979) refused a petition to have an 11-year-old Down's syndrome boy declared a dependant of the court so that he could have heart surgery to which his parents objected, even though their concern was not based on religious objections and the child had always lived away from home in residential care. But in all these cases, the condition was not immediately 'life-threatening.' In *Re Custody of a Minor*, 379 NE2d 1053, 97 ALR 3d 401 (1978), the Supreme Judicial Court of Massachussetts held that the State might intervene where parents declined to continue chemotherapy for a child suffering from leukemia, where the evidence indicated that treatment could save his life. And although Karen Quinlan was 21 and thus not a child, it is noteworthy that the New Jersey court refused her adoptive parents' request to disconnect her life support machine, even though she was in a 'persistent vegetative state' but with residual brain activity in one small sector (355 A2d 647, 1976).

In *Before the Best Interests of the Child* (1980), Goldstein, Freud and Solnit suggest the following criteria for over-turning the parents' decisions as to the medical treatment:

The state would overcome the presumption of parental autonomy if it could establish: (*a*) that the medical profession is in agreement about what nonexperimental medical treatment is appropriate for the child; (*b*) that the denial of the treatment would mean death for the child; and (*c*) that the expected outcome of that treatment is what society agrees to be right for any child — a chance for normal healthy growth or a life worth living. . . .

This ground does not justify coercive intrusion by the state in those life-or-death situations in which (*a*) there is no proven medical procedure; *or* (*b*) there is conflicting medical advice about which, if any, treatment procedure to follow; *or* (*c*) there is less than a high probability that the nonexperimental treatment will enable the child to have either a life worth living or a life of relatively normal healthy growth, even if the medical experts agree about treatment.

Questions

(i) Would these authors (*a*) have allowed B, p. 579, above, to die; or (*b*) have allowed D, p. 577, above, to be sterilised, if they adhered strictly to these criteria?

(ii) Or, given that the United States Supreme Court in *Planned Parenthood of Missouri v Danforth*, 428 US 52 (1976) (see p. 50, above) have ruled unconstitutional a statute giving a parent the absolute right of veto over a

minor child's decision to have an abortion, might it be argued that a woman's control over her own fertility is in a different category?
(iii) Why, in both the D and the B cases earlier, did the local authority not bring care proceedings on the ground that the child's 'proper development is being avoidably prevented or neglected or his health is being avoidably impaired or neglected . . .' (s. 1(2)(*a*) of the Children and Young Persons Act 1969)?
(iv) Why, in the P case quoted on p. 579, above, did the local authority not authorise the abortion themselves, as they had parental powers by virtue of a care order?

Mention of local authorities brings us to another problem posed by the wardship procedure. The cases above all concerned a single, albeit vital, question in the child's upbringing. There was no dispute about where the child should live or about who would normally be in charge of the daily decisions which bringing up a child involves. But where the State wishes to challenge the parents' right to bring up their child at all, the normal procedure has been laid down by statute and circumscribed in the ways already discussed in Chapters 12 and 14. We have already seen how the courts refuse to interfere at the request of parents and foster parents if the decision is one which Parliament has said that the local authority may take (see p. 458, above). But what if the local authority themselves wish to use wardship because the limits of the statutory procedures do not enable them to act in what they believe to be the best interests of the child? Here again, two cases, out of many, may suffice as illustration:

Re C (A Minor)(justices' decision: review)
(1979) 2 FLR 62, 10 Fam Law 84, Court of Appeal

C was born in November 1977. In July 1978, the local authority obtained a place of safety order under s. 28 of the Children and Young Persons Act 1969 over him and then began care proceedings. A series of interim orders was made until the full hearing, which took place in November 1978. Both mother and child were represented at that hearing. The juvenile court decided that the authority had not proved its case (under s. 1(2)(*a*) of the Children and Young Persons Act 1969). The local authority immediately made the child a ward of court. The mother applied to the High Court to decline jurisdiction on the ground that wardship proceedings were being used in effect as an appeal against the decision of the juvenile court. Purchas J refused the mother's application and the mother appealed.

Ormrod LJ: . . . the basic cause of the difficulties which arise in cases of this kind is the absence of any satisfactory appeal procedure under the 1969 Act. It is not surprising that both parents and local authorities regard the present arrangements as unsatisfactory and feel that they ought to have an opportunity of obtaining a review of findings which have such serious consequences, for the child, for the parents and for the local authority, yet no such opportunity for review is provided. Such an opportunity is particularly important in cases concerning children, where there is always scope for a considerable difference of opinion between sensible and responsible experienced people about what is best for a child. Speaking for myself, I think it is a pity — a great pity — that no improvement has been made in the appeal procedure in these cases.

In this case the learned judge was faced, as I see it, with the position that a responsible local authority, who had had this child in their care for nearly six months at the time when the case came before the juvenile court (that is nearly half the child's life) felt sufficiently strongly about the decision of the juvenile court to issue an originating summons that same day to protect, as they see it, the child. That very fact, in my judgment, if I were the judge of first instance, would strongly influence me to proceed at the least to investigate the facts. It would be a very strong thing indeed for a judge to reject the originating summons without any investigation when it had been taken out in such circumstances. Therefore I broadly agree with the approach of Dunn J in the case of *Re D (A Minor)(Justices' Decision: Review)* [1977 Fam 158, [1977 3 All ER 481. I think he was right in saying that the approach by the juvenile court is necessarily different in some respects from the approach of the Family Division judge in wardship proceedings. The terms of section 1(2) of the Children and Young Persons Act 1969 do require the juvenile court actually to find certain facts in order to give it jurisdiction to exercise the wide powers which it undoubtedly has. When the necessary facts have been found the court, of course, acts in accordance with the universal rule that its decision must be governed by the paramount interests of the child.

It is at the preliminary stage that juvenile court proceedings may fail, because of the difficulties of proof. One has only got to postulate such a situation as this: evidence that the child in July was very much underweight and in a generally poor state of health; some evidence of bruising; a very young mother living under very awkward and difficult conditions; the child taken into care because it is crucially important to protect children at risk before any further damage takes place; then, when the case is heard, five or six months later, for one reason or another the local authority's evidence is not sufficient to convince the juvenile court that the child's proper development, whatever that may mean, was being avoidably prevented or neglected, or his health was being avoidably impaired or neglected, or he was being ill-treated. All these alternatives in fact, even if not strictly in law, carry a flavour of fault or guilt and look as though they involve a finding against the parent and so create an apparent adversary situation which may sometimes inhibit juvenile courts with the result, in the hypothetical case I have taken, that after six months or thereabouts the local authority, having failed to obtain a care order, have no longer any authority to keep the child. They are legally obliged, unless they take wardship proceedings, to hand the child over to the parent, quite regardless of his or her arrangements or of how he or she is going to look after the child, whether there is accommodation or equipment, or anything else for the child. The local authority's powers end instantly.

On the other hand, if the matter is being dealt with under the wardship jurisdiction, fault of course has to be taken into account, but it is not in the forefront of the case. The child's interest is in the forefront of the case from beginning to end. The court is then concerned to assess risk, not to attribute blame. According to its assessment of risk, so it will make its order. Moreover wardship continues indefinitely; supervision orders can be made or discharged, and so on. So, it is right to say that the approach in these cases is significantly different in the two jurisdictions and that the High Court has power to act over a much wider area and with much less restriction than the juvenile court.

In any case, where a local authority is faced with this dilemma, it seems to me that it would be wrong to refuse to entertain their originating summons when they decide to issue one. Given a less hurried time schedule, the local authority would I am sure have filed a short affidavit giving their reasons for taking wardship proceedings in this case.

In my judgment, the primary test to be applied, as in the cases involving conflict with the jurisdiction of overseas courts is whether the interests of the child prima facie require the High Court to intervene. In domestic cases this will usually involve something special to the particular case but the issue is not whether the reasons for initiating wardship proceedings are 'special' but whether the interests of the 'child in the particular circumstances justify the wardship proceedings.

Question

Would the High Court have been prepared to take the case if the local authority could instead have appealed to the Crown Court? If it is acceptable to use wardship to make good the *procedural* defects in the statutory schemes devised by Parliament, is it acceptable to use wardship to make good their *substantive* limitations?

Re CB (A Minor)
[1981 1 All ER 16, [1981 1 WLR 379, 125 Sol Jo 219, 79 LGR 153, Court of Appeal

C was born in January 1977, the illegitimate daughter of a 17-year-old girl. In October 1977, C was left with her maternal grandmother, who asked for her to be taken into local authority care. The mother agreed and C was boarded out with Mrs R, one of the authority's short-term foster parents. The mother visited occasionally. In April 1978 she married a man who was not C's father and indicated that she wanted C back. To oppose this, the local authority made C a ward of court and asked for care and control. Interim care and control was granted in June. From August 1978 until June 1979 the local authority social workers were on strike and no further steps were taken. The mother visited C twice. When the strike ended, it was decided that C needed long-term foster care but that Mrs R, for various reasons, could not provide it. In September, therefore, C was transferred to her present foster parents, where she had settled down very well. Meanwhile, the mother had re-established her relationship with C's father. The full hearing took place before Bush J in May 1980, at which the local authority were plaintiffs and the mother and Mrs R were first and second respondents. Bush J awarded care and control to the mother. The local authority appealed and C's present foster parents were added as second and third plaintiffs.

Ormrod LJ [On the local authority's original decision to make C a ward of court:] . . . So in those circumstances, faced with the difficulties which local authorities have to contend with in this area of their duties, owing to the difficulties of the legislation which they have to operate, it was decided that the right thing, in the interests of Claire, was to make the child a ward of court. The object of doing that is to fill a serious gap in the local authorities' powers where children are concerned, when a period of voluntary care looks as if it is going to be brought to an end by the withdrawal of the consent of the relevant parent. This produces a situation of great difficulty for the local authorities; they have obviously a very important and serious duty to the child in such cases, and it is all too easy to see how the interests of the child may clash with the wishes of the parent.

So the local authority's social workers in this case, and we all should recognise this, are in an invidious position: great responsibility, great moral responsibility but, as some would say, inadequate legal powers, to discharge those responsibilities. And so it has become customary, or perhaps not 'customary' but quite frequent, for the local authorities nowadays to resort to the ward of court procedure to help them over their difficulties. This court has never said, and I hope never will say, anything to discourage that practice. It has always seemed to me that when a serious dispute arises about the welfare of a child it is asking too much for the social workers to be made to be judges as well as social workers in these cases, and that it is to the advantage of all parties, including the local authority, to resort to the court in order that a judge may take the responsibility for the decision. . . .

Now on the facts of the case, the position is quite simple. Stated baldly, they are these. This child has known one stable home up to September 1979, and only one stable home and that is with Mrs R. The mother is a virtual stranger to her; the father is a total stranger to her. But since September 1979 she has begun to make, and it appears from all the evidence, particularly the welfare report and the short affidavit which has been filed today by the foster parents, is making, a successful relationship with her present foster parents. There she is alone with no other children; they are described as eminently suitable foster parents. It is obvious from reading their brief affidavits that they are sensitive and responsible and reliable people, and from the evidence (such as it is and it is strong from the welfare officer and from the present foster parents themselves) that the child is extremely well placed with them and is forming a secure relationship with them.

So the judge, in practice, had three possible alternative solutions to this problem: one was to leave the child where she is with the present foster parents: another to send her back to her pseudo-mother, her mother substitute, Mrs R; and the third was to hand her over to her own mother.

The indications for the first, that is leaving the child where she is with the present foster parents, are first, that she has settled down with them; second, that they are in a position to offer her the very highest standard of care; and, third, that any further changes in this child's life are bound to add to her intense insecurity and are bound to be very upsetting to her, if not in the short-term then in the long-term. There are all sorts of psychological problems which might or might not arise from sending her back or moving her away from the present foster parents.

The attraction of Mrs R, of course, is that the child is going back to an environment with which she is familiar and where she might feel equally secure. But against that, the court has to bear in mind the views of the social workers concerned that this arrangement was not going to be viable in the long-term and might have to be changed later, but it was clearly an alternative which was a practical alternative.

The third proposition that Claire should be handed over to her own mother and father, although emotionally attractive, in my judgment has very little to support it. It is absolutely vital in these cases that we look at it through the eyes of the child. It is clear that the child would be grossly disturbed by being handed over to yet a third couple and a third couple with whom she has had no contact at all, although she may have some vague memory of her mother. So it would require, I think, a very, very strong case to justify taking this child of three and handing her over to total strangers simply because they are her blood mother and blood father.

Now the judge did not, as I see it, approach the case in the way in which I have just indicated. In his judgment, having set out very fairly the facts, he said:

'This decision does not turn on the relative merits of John and Margaret [the present foster parents] and the mother in the ideal parents stakes. No doubt the mother would come off second best, particularly as she has not been given a chance to show what she can do with Claire. The question turns on whether the local authority has shown that it is undesirable that the child should be or continue to be under the care of either of her parents. The court must look at the totality of the circumstances, bearing in mind that Parliament intended that children should remain with their parents if at all possible, and bearing in mind also, that the welfare of a child is the paramount consideration.'

With respect to the judge I think he was wrong and misdirected himself there in that passage because the decision *does* turn on what he called 'the relative merits of John and Margaret and the mother in the ideal parents stakes'.

It may be that the judge was confused by the form of the relief which was sought by the originating summons. In it the local authority asked, first, that the child should remain a ward of court during her minority or until further order, and, second, that the care and control of the minor should be committed to them. As I have already said, the registrar made an order for interim care and control to the local authority. It seems to have got into the mind of the judge that the whole case was dominated and controlled by s. 7(2) of the Family Law Reform Act 1969. That subsection, which is in identical terms with the corresponding provision in the Matrimonial Causes Act 1973, s. 43(1), reads:

'Where it appears to the court that there are exceptional circumstances making it impracticable or undesirable for a ward of court to be, or continue to be, under the care of either of his parents or of any other individual the court may, if it thinks fit, make an order committing the care of the ward to a local authority; and thereupon Part [III] of the [Child Care Act 1980] (which relates to the treatment of children in the care of a local authority) shall, subject to the next following subsection, apply as if the child had been received by the local authority into their care under section [2] of that Act.'

That is the section which the judge treated as controlling the whole of the case. So, instead of considering who was going to look after this child and considering, as he ought to have done, what the welfare of the child as the paramount consideration required, he was led to consider whether or not there were exceptional circumstances making it 'impracticable or undesirable' for the ward to be under the care of either of her parents.

He treated the matter as one of law. He felt that he had to find first that the circumstances were exceptional and second he had to decide whether it was impracticable or undesirable for the ward to continue to be in the care of either of her parents or any other individual. In fact, of course, s. 7(2) of the 1969 Act never applied at all in this case because at all times the proposal of the local authority was that the child should remain in the care of the present foster parents that is 'another individual' within s. 7(2). Nor is it at all difficult, in a case like this, to find exceptional circumstances. No one, I venture to think, would dream of making an order committing the care of a ward to a local authority unless the circumstances were exceptional. Nor would they contemplate doing it unless it was the only practical solution open to the court at the time.

It was a mistake to treat this case as if it was an s. 7(2) case because the local authority were the plaintiffs. This is the first point to be made so far as the wardship jurisdiction is concerned. It is an unfettered jurisdiction to place the ward in the care and control of any person who can best look after him or her.

Ever since *J v C* [1970] AC 668, [1969] 1 All ER 788 [p. 474, above], the principles are absolutely clear: the court in its discretion must decide what the paramount interests of the child require. It is not concerned with allocating blame or adjusting rival claims. It has to make a decision sufficiently difficult in all conscience, but the decision it has to make is what is in the best interests of this child at this stage. . . .

The judge unfortunately did not approach the matter, I think, in the right way. He was sidetracked by considering whether he had the necessary jurisdiction under s. 7(2) of the 1969 Act. But in this case the local authority were themselves the plaintiffs in the originating summons asking for 'care and control', not for an order under s. 7(2). Had he had the present foster parents before him as parties, I do not think that this error would have crept in. The result is that, with respect to the judge, the conclusion is inescapable that he exercised his discretion on an entirely wrong basis. He did not, at any stage, compare the mother's proposals with the present foster parents' proposals for the child. He did not weigh one against the other and make an assessment of the advantages to the child in regard to one course or the other, in the short-term or the long-term. He was almost wholly concerned with deciding whether the local authority had made out their case under s. 7(2), but, as I have already said, if a local authority takes the initiative of making a child a ward I do not think that s. 7(2) comes into the case at all. Section 7(2) was passed to give the court power in proceedings between parents, or between a parent and a third party, to make an order committing the child to the care of the local authority, or to make it clear that the court, in wardship proceedings, had the same powers as it has under the Matrimonial Causes Act 1973.

Questions

(i) Why did the local authority not assume the mother's rights by a resolution under s. 3 of the Child Care Act 1980 (p. 442, above)?
(ii) What might the result have been if the proceedings had not been so long delayed?
(iii) Why were they so long delayed?
(iv) Should the answer to question (iii) have any bearing on the outcome for the child?

The case also gives rise to technical difficulties. For example, if care and control is committed to foster parents in wardship proceedings, the child will no longer be in the care of the local authority, and the authority will no longer have power to pay a boarding out allowance (see *Lewisham London Borough v M* [1981] 3 All ER 307, [1981] 1 WLR 1248). Similarly, if simple 'care and control' of the child is given to the local authority, instead of a care order under s. 7(2), can the child be 'in care' for the purposes of the 1980 Act? But if the court makes an order under s. 7(2), does the child remain under the guardianship of the court? The court has power to give directions to the local authority as to the exercise of its functions under ss. 18, 21 and 22 of the Child Care Act 1980 (see s. 43(5) of the Matrimonial Causes Act 1973, which governs such orders both in wardship and in matrimonial causes), but is this the same as the right to be consulted about every major decision in the child's life, which is the normal consequence of wardship? It seems that the Court does normally continue the wardship, and may well direct the local authority to work towards either the rehabilitation of the child with his natural family or his establishment in a new one. But in *Surrey County Council v W (A Minor)* (1982) Times, 16 January, Lord Justice Ormrod stressed that this direction should only be exercised 'in a broad way,' and not so as to place the local authority in an impossible position in attempting to implement the court's desires.

There remains a serious question of principle. *In Victims or Threats? Children in Care Proceedings* (1982) (already extensively quoted in Chapter 14), Eekelaar, Dingwall and Murray have this to say about the first two paragraphs which we have quoted from the judgment of Lord Justice Ormrod in *Re CB* (above):

They raise issues of the profoundest kind concerning the basis of state intervention in the relationship between parent and child and the role of social workers and the courts in cases involving the protection of children against parental abuse and neglect. For they represent a claim by judges of the Family Division of the High Court to a jurisdiction to intervene in that relationship and to remove a child from the control of his parents and into that of a state agency bounded only by the judges' assessment that such a course is in the child's best interests. The apparent restriction upon the jurisdiction of the High Court to commit children into local authority care in wardship proceedings contained in section 7(2) of the Family Law Reform Act 1969 was effectively neutralised.

Both Ormrod and Bridge LJJ stated that, where the authority planned that the child should reside with foster parents such a person was an 'other individual' within the provision and hence no question of committing the ward to the authority arose. Ormrod LJ declared that the subsection was not intended to apply if the local authority had taken the initiative and made the child a ward. The effect of these arguments is that, while the court would not commit the child into care *under that subsection*, it may nevertheless commit the child into the *care and control* of the authority, a distinction which, from the point of view of the child/parent relationship, is insubstantial. Furthermore, Ormrod LJ's observation that it was not at all difficult, in a case like this, to find 'exceptional circumstances' suggests that a court will have no difficulty in committing a child under the subsection because, ex hypothesi, the circumstances will always be exceptional.

Whatever the merits of these arguments, their implications are of the first importance. It is well established that the criterion by which a judge decides on the final disposition of a wardship case is that of the 'best interests of the child.' No guidelines assist as to the manner in which the judgment about these interests is to be reached. If the judge, on a broad view of the evidence, considers that it would be better for the child to be committed to care rather than remain with his parents, he may commit the child. In *Re CB* Bridge LJ went as far as to say that 's. 7(2) indicates no parliamentary a priori preference for giving the care of a child to natural parents as against giving it to anyone else. The paramount consideration in a case like this, and the sole consideration, is what will best serve the welfare of the child.' The rules of evidence are greatly relaxed in wardship proceedings; decisions may be made on the basis of affidavits; the hearsay rule does not apply. An order can even be made on the basis of *apprehended* rather than actual detriment to the child. In contrast to the width of this broad, discretionary jurisdiction, child welfare law operates within more precisely defined limits. The grounds upon which a local authority may pass a resolution vesting in itself parental rights over a child currently in its care are set out in section 3 of the Child Care Act 1980. If the child is not in local authority care, section 1(2) of the Children and Young Persons Act requires a juvenile court to be satisfied that specific grounds exist before it may commit the child into local authority care.

Hence a consequence of the expansion of the wardship jurisdiction into the territory of these statutes is that state agencies will be licensed to relieve parents of their responsibility to bring up their children as a result of the assessment by a judge that it would be better for the child that this be so. It will not be necessary to point to specific conditions concerning either the child or the parents in order to justify such intervention. That an indeterminate basis of intervention should exist in exceptional cases is one thing; that it should become 'frequent' is another. Such a development marks a decisive shift in the balance between family autonomy and state intervention.

Questions

(i) Are you inclined to favour this shift?

(ii) If you have doubts about it, are these in any way assuaged by the knowledge that wardship is a relatively complicated and expensive proceeding, which most local authorities would probably not engage in unless they had serious cause for concern?

(iii) Even so, why are some children entitled to the 'Rolls Royce' protection of a High Court judge, sometimes with the assistance of the Official Solicitor to act for the child, whereas others must make do with the lay magistrates and ordinary social workers?

(iv) Should it be possible, as happened in the case of *Re C* (p. 582, above), for a local authority to keep a baby from his mother for seven months without any court finding that they had good grounds for doing so?

(v) What would be the implications (as canvassed by the Lord Chancellor's Department in 1983) of allowing circuit judges to deal with wardship in the county courts?

2 Arguments for parental autonomy

In *Beyond the Best Interests of the Child* (1973), Goldstein, Freud and Solnit produced a powerful argument for legal standards which would secure the continuity and stability of relationships between a child and his psychological parents, even if this conflicted with the claims of his family of birth. In a second book, *Before the Best Interests of the Child* (1980), the same authors employ the same concepts of a child's development to support their argument for severe limitations upon the State's power to intervene between parent and child:

. . . Constantly ongoing interactions between parents and children become for each child the starting point for an all-important line of development that leads toward adult functioning. What begins as the experience of physical contentment or pleasure that accompanies bodily care develops into a primary attachment to the person who provides it. This again changes into the wish for a parent's constant presence irrespective of physical wants. Helplessness requires total care and over time is transformed into the need or wish for approval and love. It fosters the desire to please by compliance with a parent's wishes. It provides a developmental base upon which the child's responsiveness to educational efforts rests. Love for the parents leads to identification with them, a fact without which impulse control and socialization would be deficient. Finally, after the years of childhood comes the prolonged and in many ways painful adolescent struggle to attain a separate identity with physical, emotional, and moral self-reliance.

These complex and vital developments require the privacy of family life under guardianship by parents who are autonomous. The younger the child, the greater is his need for them. When family integrity is broken or weakened by state intrusion, his needs are thwarted and his belief that his parents are omniscient and all-powerful is shaken prematurely. The effect on the child's developmental progress is invariably detrimental.[1] The child's need for safety within the confines of the family must be met by law through its recognition of family privacy as the barrier to state intrusion upon parental autonomy in child rearing. These rights — parental autonomy, a child's entitlement to autonomous parents, and privacy — are essential ingredients of 'family integrity.' 'And the integrity of that life is something so fundamental that it has been found to draw to its protection the principles of more than one explicitly granted Constitutional right.'

Two purposes underlie the parents' right to be free of state intrusion. The first is to provide parents with an uninterrupted *opportunity* to meet the developing physical and emotional needs of their child so as to establish the familial bonds critical to every child's healthy growth and development. The second purpose, and the one on which the parental right must ultimately rest, is to safeguard the *continuing maintenance* of these family ties — of psychological parent-child relationships — once they have been established. . . .

Put somewhat differently, two stages in the parent-child relationship generally define the right of family integrity that deserves recognition and protection from interruption by the state. The first is the stage at which the *opportunity* for the development of psychological ties between parent and child exists; the right usually comes about through a child's being placed with natural parents at birth, or through legally sanctioned adoption. These opportunities merit protection from state intrusion because it is only through continuous nurture of the child within the privacy of the family that the second stage can be reached. At that stage, primary psychological ties between parent and child have been established and require for their *maintenance* continuous nurture free of state intrusion. The liberty interest in these familial bonds, including bonds established between children and longtime fostering adults who are not their parents, has not yet been clearly perceived or firmly established in law. It is as deserving of recognition and protection as is the first stage, normally associated with biological reproduction or with adoption.

---

1. The authors' footnote here refers to Rutter (1972), Clarke and Clarke (1976), Tizard (1977), Kearsley, Zelazo, Kagan and Hartmann (1975) and Kagan, Kearsley and Zelazo (1978), but suggests that these authors' 'reliance on the resilience of cognitive function as evidence of the child's well-being is simplistic,' whereas their own 'psychoanalytic theory, along with Piaget's work on cognitive development, recognizes that maturational capacities and social environmental experiences are dynamically involved in the child's developmental capabilities and progression.' (Eg Piaget, 1937; Freud and Burlingham, 1944; Bowlby, 1969.)

Beyond these biological and psychological justifications for protecting parent-child relationships and promoting each child's entitlement to a permanent place in a family of his own, there is a further justification for a policy of minimum state intervention. It is that the law does not have the capacity to supervise the fragile, complex interpersonal bonds between child and parent. As *parens patriae* the state is too crude an instrument to become an adequate substitute for flesh and blood parents. The legal system has neither the resources nor the sensitivity to respond to a growing child's ever-changing needs and demands. It does not have the capacity to deal on an individual basis with the consequences of its decisions, or to act with the deliberate speed that is required by a child's sense of time. Similarly, the child lacks the capacity to respond to the rulings of an impersonal court or social service agencies as he responds to the demands of personal parental figures. Parental expectations, implicit and explicit, become the child's own. However, the process by which a child converts external expectations, guidance, commands, and prohibitions into the capacity for self-regulation and self-direction does not function adequately in the absence of emotional ties to his caretakers.

A policy of minimum coercive intervention by the state thus accords not only with our firm belief as citizens in individual freedom and human dignity, but also with our professional understanding of the intricate developmental processes of childhood.

The authors therefore distinguish between two forms of legislation which curtail parental autonomy:

The first has been to set relatively precise limits on parental judgment concerning matters about which there is a clear societal consensus. For example, parents are not free to send their children into the labor market or to refuse to let them attend school or be immunized against certain contagious diseases. Legislative enactments like those concerned with child labor, compulsory education, and immunization are infringements upon parental autonomy which give parents fair warning of what constitutes a breach of their child care responsibilities and provide advance notice of the extent of the state's power to intervene. In thus defining the authority to intrude in precise terms, legislatures also restrict the power of administrative agencies and courts to breach the state's general commitment to family privacy and parental autonomy. . . .

This second form of legislation, unlike the first form, invests judges and state agency personnel as *parens patriae* with almost limitless discretion in areas generally under the exclusive control of parents. Such legislation is used to justify the *ad hoc* creation of standards of intervention in case-by-case determinations to investigate, supervise, and supervene parental judgments. It invites the exploitation of parents and children by state officials. Acting in accord with their own personal child-rearing preferences, officials have been led to discriminate against poor, minority, and other disfavored families.

Question

Is there a 'clear societal consensus' in this country in favour of vaccination against whooping cough?

The precise limits which these authors propose should be placed upon state intervention of the second variety have been set out on p. 569. It is obviously possible to disagree with these while accepting the basic argument. Another reason for accepting it is the obvious fact that many children who grow up in public care are at a serious disadvantage compared with those who do not (see Chapters 12 and 13). It might be possible to overcome this disadvantage if we were prepared to arrange a permanent substitute home as soon as it became clear that early rehabilitation was not a practicable proposition (see, for example, Tizard, 1977). The draft *Model Act to Free Children for Permanent Placement*, quoted on p. 462, above, is designed to balance the competing interests along these lines; but it does raise the spectre feared by Packman (1981) and others, of the deserving poor coping independently while the undeserving poor lose their children to the Poor Law.

Meanwhile, there is also the question of the role of the State where parent and child are at odds with one another — where parents seek to 'put away' their children, whether because they are too handicapped for the parents to be able to cope, or because their behaviour is such that the parents cannot, or will not, control them. This issue has arisen in the United States in connection with the right of parents to 'volunteer' their children for treatment in a psychiatric hospital. The following anonymous discussion of the *Mental Hospitalisation of Children and the Limits of Parental Authority* (1978) provides a summary of the arguments:

Five justifications are most often advanced to support parental authority. They may for convenience be termed *social pluralism, social order, parental privilege, family autonomy* and *child's welfare*. Once each of these proffered justifications has been considered, the constitutional limits on a parent's power to admit his child to a mental hospital will emerge.

A. Social pluralism
It is a 'fixed star in our constitutional constellation,' especially with respect to the education of children, that the state shall not impose an orthodoxy 'in politics, nationalism, religion, or other matters of opinion.' And, especially in matters that relate to families and childrearing, the Constitution also disfavors state practices that threaten to impose on all a single conception of a worthwhile way of life. The institution of parental authority, by fragmenting decisions about the goals and methods of childrearing, serves to militate against such an orthodoxy. This, historically, has been part of its rationale and is today one reason for treating parental authority, when asserted against the state, as a constitutional right. It is therefore not surprising that the Supreme Court has acted more readily to protect parental authority against state intrusion when the threat to social pluralism has been acute.[2]
. . . Yet where, as here, the conflict under consideration is between parents and their children, the social pluralism rationale offers little direct guidance. Although a rule favoring parents over the state will always be a bulwark against a state-imposed orthodoxy of social values, a rule favoring parents over their children may or may not have that effect. The goal of social pluralism might just as well be advanced by allowing children to decide for themselves. . . .

B. Social order
Historically, the law recognized society's interest in having children reared so that as adults they would be economically self-sufficient and would conform their conduct to society's norms. Parents, according to one court, were ordinarily entrusted with this task 'because it [could] seldom be put into better hands,' but they were subject to state supersession if they failed. Parents are still, to some extent, viewed as child-socialization agents of the state. . . .
To the extent that parents actually do admit their children to mental hospitals as a method of social control, they are acting in their role of child-socialization agents of the state and are, therefore, subject to the same constitutional constraints as would apply if the state had acted directly. . . .

C. Parental privilege
It is not uncommon for parents to seek to express their own personalities through their children. This interest of parents may serve as the basis for the claim they advance to have 'the power to dictate their [children's] training, prescribe their education and form their religious opinions.' To the extent that the law protects this claim of parents, it creates a *parental privilege* — that is, a

---

2. The author's footnote reads: Compare *Wisconsin v Yoder*, 406 US 205 (1972) (invalidating state compulsory education law as applied to Amish children) and *Pierce v Society of Sisters*, 268 US 510 (1925) (invalidating state law requiring parents to send their children only to public schools) with *Prince v Massachusetts*, 321 US 158 (1944) (upholding statute prohibiting street solicitation by children as applied to Jehovah's Witness distributing religious literature). The Court in *Yoder* noted especially that the statute as applied 'substantially interfer[ed] with the religious development of the Amish child and his integration into the way of life of the Amish faith community' and 'carrie[d] with it a very real threat of undermining the Amish community and religious practice.' 406 US at 218. Enforcement of the statute in *Prince*, however, posed no such threat to the Jehovah's Witnesses' way of life; the Court in *Prince* took pains to note that its holding left parents free to accomplish the religious training and indoctrination of their children by all means 'except the public proclaiming of religion [by their children] in the streets.' 321 US at 171. More importantly, in *Yoder* and *Pierce* but not in *Prince* the effect of a holding in favor of the state would have been to compel children to confront daily a set of religious and social values antagonistic to those that their parents sought to foster.

prerogative of a parent to rear his child to be a person whose conduct, character, and belief conform to standards of the parent's choosing. There can be no doubt that this interest of parents, when asserted against the state, is within the scope of liberty protected by the Constitution. But in situations in which a parent's choice conflicts not with the state but with the preferences of his own child, parental privilege as a justification for parental authority is less deserving of support. . . .

It is regarded by many as unjust for one adult to impose his conception of the good life on another and as demeaning to another's dignity not to respect his choice of his own life plan. Psychological studies show that at adolescence, children of normal intellect are in this respect substantially like adults: they have the basic cognitive capacities to choose intelligently among competing values and to formulate their own life plans. So, as applied to adolescents, parental privilege — the prerogative of parents to impose on their children values and styles of life that best express the *parents'* personalities — is especially hard to justify on moral grounds. These moral considerations derive implicit legal sanction from those court decisions that permit an adolescent to act on his own values over the objection of his parent. . . .

D. Family autonomy
The state's interest in preserving the family unit is often cited to justify state sanction of parental authority. But protecting the family from outside interference is quite distinct from fortifying the family's power over one of its members. . . .

When a parent, in his role of family governor, exercises authority over the child, his action has a moral basis that the exercise of bare parental privilege lacks. But there are other criteria for the moral assessment of social institutions — whether an institution that makes claims against some provides some reciprocal benefit for each of those whose liberty it restricts, or whether it makes an equal relative contribution to the good life of each of its participants. Although family life may often require that some good of one individual be foregone for the well-being of the family as a whole, a family that excessively derogates the interests of one for the sake of the others undermines its own moral basis.

These moral considerations suggest a legal norm. The state need not intervene in every family dispute, but if it does, it must treat each family member affected as having a distinguishable interest, which is equally entitled to the protection of the state. And, in particular, where parents solicit or simply avail themselves of the sanction of law to augment their controls over family life, the child's own individual interest must be taken into account. Therefore, if it is based on the family autonomy rationale, the legitimacy of state sanction of parental authority with respect to a certain class of decisions depends on the consequences of those decisions for family well-being, on what the child is being asked to sacrifice for the sake of his family, and on what he ultimately stands to gain.

E. Child's welfare
The last of the proffered justifications of parental authority is that it serves the child's welfare. It has been suggested that allowing parents to be the supreme arbiters of their child's fate is justified because it is conducive to the child's long term psychological health. More commonly, parental authority is defended on the ground that someone must choose for children since they lack the capacity to choose for themselves; parents are assigned this role because they are presumed to be better able to perform the task than anyone else.

The legitimacy of parental authority based on the child's welfare rationale depends primarily on the child's capacity to choose for himself. This capacity will vary with age. Parental authority over preadolescents is justified because the assumption that children are not competent to make their own choices is, as applied to them, generally correct. Since, however, parents under this rationale are presumed to act as guardians of the child's interests, parental authority would lose its underlying legitimacy if exercised for purposes unrelated to the child's welfare or in ways that create for the child a substantial risk of harm. . . .

For the adolescent, the situation is more complex. Psychologists agree that about the time of adolescence a major transformation occurs in the quality of a child's thought. As a consequence of a shift to what is called formal operational thought, the youngster is capable of abstract, logical, and scientific thinking, which enables him to see the practical possibilities of real-life situations and to anticipate and evaluate the consequences of his own conduct. Simultaneously, or perhaps as a consequence of the same underlying process, the individual acquires an appreciation for the social ramifications of individual conduct, and a capacity to formulate his own personal and social ideals.

When a person makes choices after having identified the likely consequences for himself and others and having evaluated those alternatives in light of an overall life plan, he has chosen intelligently, even if unwisely from someone else's point of view. By this criterion, the psychological evidence shows that the typical adolescent will have acquired a basic capacity for intelligent choice by about fourteen years old.

Question

It is easy to conclude how the author would approach the question of a 15-year-old boy 'volunteered' against his will for psychiatric treatment, or a 15-year-old girl whose parents refused to consent to the abortion she desired, but to what extent would the same arguments apply (*a*) to the case of D on p. 577, above, or (*b*) to the case of F on p. 566, above (of each of which, we may be relatively sure, the authors of *Before the Best Interests of the Child* would disapprove)?

Eventually, the issue of hospitalisation reached the United States Supreme Court: the legal argument, of course, was not simply for or against the autonomy of parents — the State's laws could only be declared unconstitutional if they invaded the liberty of the child without such due process of law as was required by the circumstances of the invasion.

Parham v JL and JR
444 US 584, (1979) United States Supreme Court

JL was admitted to hospital at the request of his mother when he was 6 years old. He had been expelled from school as uncontrollable, was extremely aggressive and diagnosed as having a 'hyperkinetic reaction to childhood.' His parents were divorced and his mother had remarried. He had had two months' treatment as an outpatient before his mother requested indefinite admission. Further attempts were made at re-integration but the parents found that they could not control him. Four years after his admission, they voluntarily relinquished their parental rights.

JR was removed from his family of birth because of their neglect when he was three months old. He experienced seven different foster placements before being admitted to hospital at the age of seven. His last foster placement had broken down because of his behaviour. He had also proved disruptive and incorrigible at school. The diagnosis was borderline mental handicap with an 'unsocialised, aggressive reaction to childhood.'

The laws of the State of Georgia permitted children to be admitted to state mental hospitals on the application of their parents to the hospital superintendant; the superintendant could admit for observation and diagnosis and had then to decide whether the child was mentally ill and suitable for treatment. It was submitted that the invasion of these children's liberty was such that a full adversary hearing was required prior to commitment.

Mr Chief Justice Burger delivered the opinion of the Court: [It was not disputed that a child had a substantial liberty interest in not being confined unnecessarily for medical treatment; but this interest was inextricably linked with the parents' interest in and obligation for the welfare and health of their child, so that the private interest at stake was a combination of the child's and parents' concerns. As to the latter:] Our jurisprudence historically has reflected Western Civilization concepts of the family as a unit with broad parental authority over minor children. Our cases have consistently followed that course; our constitutional system long ago rejected any notion that a child is 'the mere creature of the State' and, on the contrary, asserted that parents generally 'have the right, coupled with the high duty, to recognize and prepare [their children] for additional obligations.' *Pierce v Society of Sisters*. 268 US 510, 535 (1924). See also *Wisconsin v Yoder*, 406 US 205, 213 (1972); *Prince v Massachusetts*, 321 US 158, 166 (1944); *Meyer v Nebraska*, 262 US 390, 400 (1923). Surely, this includes a 'high duty' to recognize symptoms of illness and to seek and follow medical advice. The law's concept of the family rests on a presumption that parents possess what a child lacks in maturity, experience, and capacity for judgment required for making life's difficult decisions. More important, historically it has recognized that natural bonds of affection lead parents to act in the best interests of their children. . . .

As with so many other legal presumptions, experience and reality may rebut what the law accepts as a starting point; the incidence of child neglect and abuse cases attests to this. That some parents 'may at times be acting against the interests of their child' as was stated in *Bartley v Kremens*, 402 F Supp 1039, 1047–1048 (ED Pa 1975), vacated, 431 US 119 (1977), creates a basis for caution, but is hardly a reason to discard wholesale those pages of human experience that teach that parents generally do act in the child's best interests. See Rolfe & MacClintock 348–349. The statist notion that governmental power should supersede parental authority in *all* cases because *some* parents abuse and neglect children is repugnant to American tradition.

Nonetheless, we have recognized that a state is not without constitutional control over parental discretion in dealing with children when their physical or mental health is jeopardized. See *Wisconsin v Yoder, supra*, at 230; *Prince v Massachusetts, supra*, at 166. Moreover, the Court recently declared unconstitutional a state statute that granted parents an absolute veto over a minor child's decision to have an abortion: *Planned Parenthood of Missouri v Danforth*, 428 US 52 (1976). Appellees urge that these precedents limiting the traditional rights of parents, if viewed in the context of the liberty interest of the child and the likelihood of parental abuse, require us to hold that the parents' decision to have a child admitted to a mental hospital must be subjected to an exacting constitutional scrutiny, including a formal, adversary, pre-admission hearing.

Appellees' argument, however, sweeps too broadly. Simply because the decision of a parent is not agreeable to a child or because it involves risks does not automatically transfer the power to make that decision from the parents to some agency or officer of the state. The same characterizations can be made for a tonsillectomy, appendectomy or other medical procedure. Most children, even in adolescence, simply are not able to make sound judgments concerning many decisions, including their need for medical care or treatment. Parents can and must make those judgments. Here there is no finding by the District Court of even a single instance of bad faith by any parent of any member of appellees' class. . . .

In defining the respective rights and prerogatives of the child and parent in the voluntary commitment setting, we conclude that our precedents permit the parents to retain a substantial, if not the dominant, role in the decision, absent a finding of neglect or abuse, and that the traditional presumption that the parents act in the best interests of their child should apply. We also conclude, however, that the child's rights and the nature of the commitment decision are such that parents cannot always have absolute and unreviewable discretion to decide whether to have a child institutionalized. They, of course, retain plenary authority to seek such care for their children, subject to a physician's independent examination and medical judgment.

[The court went on to hold that procedures in Georgia were sufficient to meet this standard. It also held that, although there was no natural affection to guide their action, there was a statutory presumption that the State acted in the best interests of those children (including JR) who were wards of the State, and thus that no further safeguards were needed in that case. There was a dissent from Mr Justice Brennan and two other justices on the degree of due process required, particularly in relation to wards of the State.]

Questions

(i) Does this opinion remind you of anything?

(ii) Do you accept that children have 'liberty interests' which should be safeguarded against State intrusion by due process of law?

(iii) If so, does that interest arise (*a*) at birth, (*b*) at ten years of age, or (*c*) at 16, or (*d*) at some other age?

(iv) Can you work out which provisions of English law caused us to suggest (*b*) and (*c*) in question (iii)?

(v) If children of whatever age have 'liberty interests' to be safeguarded, which of the following should count as an interference with their liberty: (*a*) committal to care for failure to attend school; (*b*) committal to care for being in moral danger; (*c*) admission to an NHS hospital for treatment for physical disorder; (*d*) admission to an NHS hospital for treatment for mental disorder; (*e*) reception into care because of parental inability to care; (*f*) reception into care because of parental ill-treatment or neglect; or (*g*) committal to care because of parental ill-treatment or neglect?

(vi) Does the parental agreement involved in (*f*) constitute a rational ground for distinguishing between (*f*) and (*g*) in question (v)?

(vii) If children have 'liberty interests' to be protected against State intrusion, should those interests also be protected against parental intrusion?

3 Children's rights

The introduction of the American 'due process' problem into the debate about parental autonomy and family integrity serves to remind us that the interests of children are of two kinds and that the State performs a different role in relation to each. Where the 'liberty interest' of the child is at stake, the State's actions will be in opposition to that 'liberty interest' and our present procedures for both care and criminal proceedings in juvenile courts acknowledge this. Where the other interest of the child — in being properly nurtured until old enough to care for himself — is at stake, the State's actions will be in support of the child but against those upon whom the law has placed the duty of providing that nurture. But as we have already seen in the previous chapter, our present procedures in care proceedings do not acknowledge this crucial distinction. In their conclusion to *Victims or Threats? Children in Care Proceedings* (1982), in which Eekelaar, Dingwall and Murray explain how this arose, the authors provide us with an interesting analysis of the latter question in terms of 'rights':

. . . The primarily criminal, or 'quasi-criminal' character of the procedures obscures, at every turn, the true nature of the issues in cases of child abuse and neglect. What is the true nature of those issues?

In order adequately to answer this question, it is necessary first to attempt to understand how the controlling legislation attributes rights, recognisable by the law, to both parents and children. The language of children's rights is often used in promoting claims regarding what policies towards children should be followed. The 'rights' claimed for children may be as varied as the policies preferred. Arguments that children have rights to education, physical nurture, emotional stability and so on are but strong forms of assertions of what the priorities of social policy should be. In the same way, claims that children have rights to be treated as adults advance libertarian opinions of varying strength about how we should treat children. [See Freeman, p. 596, below.] It is not proposed to approach the question of children's and parents' rights in this fashion. The intention, rather, is to examine how far the language of 'rights' can help us to understand more clearly the relationships between parents, children and state *presently ascribed by law*, as currently interpreted and implemented.

To do this, it is first necessary to clarify what we understand to be the necessary implication of the statement that 'X has a right.' The issue is by no means unproblematic in jurisprudence. The classic formulation is that of Hohfeld, who considered that a right *stricto sensu* (often called a 'claim-right') could be said to be held by X if and only if Y is under duty to perform the act to which X has the right. The refinement proposed by Hart that the right holder should be in a position to waive, extinguish, enforce or leave unenforced the other's obligation would create insuperable difficulties in formulating coherent concepts of children's (MacCormick 1976) and parents' rights, and is accordingly rejected.

Apart from the general duties (enforced, normally, by the criminal law) which we all owe to children, as to all persons, to respect their physical integrity, it is clear that *additional* duties are placed upon those who are in a peculiarly strong position to affect a child's life. This can take the form of the application of criminal sanctions against anyone in charge of a child who fails to take certain safety precautions. More important, from our point of view, are the provisions of section 1(2) of the Children and Young Persons Act 1969. Here the law empowers care proceedings to be taken on the establishment of certain conditions relating to the child. The difference between these provisions and the criminal offences mentioned earlier is that they do not expressly impose duties upon specific persons. How, then, are we to explain either of these situations in terms of children's rights?

While we accept, for the purposes of our analysis, the proposition that a right can only exist if someone owes a correlative duty to the rightholder, it does not follow that a right always exists where a person is under a duty. At this point a social dimension is added to the analytic tool of 'rights-talk.' For in order to use the language of rights usefully, it is necessary to locate with reasonable exactness who the beneficiary of the duty is. Our duty correctly to complete our tax returns cannot, without strain, be said to constitute the confirmatory element in a 'right' of (the Inland Revenue? the Crown? the Community?) to receive correct ones. We find it difficult to consider duties not to inflict cruelty on animals as constituent elements of the rights of animals to freedom from cruelty. This is not for any analytic reasons concerning the nature of rights, but because of uncertainty whether the interests protected are perceived to be those of the animals, of people who may become distressed or the perpetrators of the cruelty, who are deemed corrupted by it. Hence it is that MacCormick (1976) argues that, in the case of children, the duties are imposed *because* children have rights. This conclusion is essentially an empirical one for it has to do with the way people think about their obligations and it is reasonable to suppose that people now regard the interests of children themselves as the primary, or even the sole, objects protected by these duties.

This may provide a satisfactory explanation for children's rights in cases where duties are expressly placed on their caretakers. But, as has been seen, this is not done by the 1969 Act. The historical explanation for this lies in the fact that the antecedents of these provisions of the Act are to be found in legislation which sought to protect society against children. They were intermingled with provisions enabling curative action to be taken against children who had committed offences. Attribution of rights and duties must be very obscure in such a situation. Can the children themselves be considered to be placed under duties in the same way as adults are not to commit offences, fall into moral danger or drift beyond parental control? But these provisions must not be seen in isolation. They must be read in the context of a legal and social system which attributes certain rights to parents respecting their children. Such rights, as is well known, have a far longer history of articulation than children's rights. The concept of parents' rights should not be seen as standing in opposition to ideas that children have rights: rather, it can help us to formulate a coherent notion of children's rights. This is not the place to attempt an elaboration of what rights parents have. It is enough to say that it is central to the ideology of family life in our society that it is the parents of a child who have the right to care for and socialise the child. This is expressed in the legal rule that a child's parents are its natural guardians, and this tenet is firmly rooted in our society and is reflected in the practices of the agencies with responsibilities for child protection. These rights can be conceptualised as rights in the sense used here insofar as third parties, whether in the form of individuals or state agencies, may not, except in legally defined situations, exercise these functions in place of the parents. But there is a dimension to these functions in which they differ significantly, from, say, a property owner's rights against third parties to enjoy his property. The parent has to exercise these functions to the child's benefit. Hence it is equally appropriate to talk about parental 'responsibilities.' There is no inconsistency in regarding parental functions as holding characteristics which pertain both to the concept of rights and also of duties. So long as a parent has his child in his care, he is not free to abandon or waive the proper exercise of his rights.

The significance of the provisions of section 1 of the Children and Young Persons Act 1969 in this context is that, by specifying certain goals in the upbringing of children in objective terms, the parents' exercise of their rights to bring up their children is made subject to these objectives. The goals are broadly drawn. The child's health and proper development shall not be avoidably prevented or neglected and he should not be ill-treated or exposed to moral danger. If the exercise by the parents of their functions is failing to achieve these objectives, it is the duty of the local authority to intervene. It is thus possible to conceptualise these goals in terms of the rights of children. Whatever other 'rights' children should have, these rights at least children can indubitably be said to possess under our law.

How then, does one analyse the interaction between the rights of the parents and those of the children? Perhaps the most useful conceptual model to have been advanced is that of the trust (Beck and others, 1978). Trustees have legal rights over trust property which they may assert against the world, but must use them for the benefit of the beneficiaries. Failure to do this, whether due to wilfulness or incompetence, allows remedies to be used on behalf of the beneficiaries. Trustees must use their powers to promote the purposes of the trust. In the case of parents, the purposes of their powers can readily be seen to be the promotion of the welfare of their children. The scrutiny of the exercise of these functions in care proceedings is analogous to an action on behalf of beneficiaries for failure of trustees properly to exercise their duties.

This analysis seems to characterise well the social perceptions of the provisions of the 1969 Act relevant to child protection. The fact that these provisions refer to the condition of the child is significant. It allows us to perceive the intervention not primarily as a punishment of the parents but as a realisation of children's rights. Hence magistrates and clerks often tell parents that they are 'here to do what is best for (the child)' and try to avoid creating the impression that they are punishing the parents. Yet, and this is of fundamental importance, the issues invariably involve judgments about the parents' competence. But this is an inseparable part of the process of safeguarding the children's rights; for these are rights to have the discharge of the responsibilities of their parents properly scrutinised. Indeed, if there has been no failure of competence by a parent, the justification for intervention, on this analysis, collapses.

The conclusion that can be drawn, therefore, about the nature of care proceedings is that they are essentially civil in nature; that the local authority is, on behalf of the child, calling the parents to account for the discharge of their trust. This perception entails the attribution to the local authority of the role of guardian of children's rights. The legitimacy of this role must be recognised if those rights are to be adequately safeguarded. The judgment the authority must make is twofold: is the child in such a condition that a right ascribed to him by the legislation is violated? Is this attributable to a failure in the functioning of a parent? The true defendant in the case is therefore the parent. It is nonsense (on this analysis) to set up, as the present structure does, the local authority in artificial opposition to the child. It is equally nonsense that the parents are not parties to the case. This is the criminal model, not our model. The present structure of care proceedings is thus fundamentally flawed and, until the model is changed, anomalies and injustices will remain. But neither is the model one of paternalist power based on furthering the best interests of children, as judicially conceived. Nor, is it, in essence, an inquisitorial model. The local authority presents the evidence upon which it bases its judgment: the parents, if they wish, contest it. The court decides whether the local authority has discharged its functions as guardians of the child's rights by establishing its 'case' in accordance with the statutory provisions.

This model, it is contended, represents the underlying reality of cases of child abuse and neglect presently brought in juvenile courts. The procedure governing those cases in those courts should therefore be brought into line with this reality. The model represented by wardship proceedings is a different one. It co-exists uneasily alongside the juvenile court system and its role, in relation to that system, is uncertain. Yet it is a matter of great consequence for our conception of parents' and children's rights and therefore demands careful, but urgent, assessment and appraisal.

Questions

(i) Do you find this analysis attractive?

(ii) What changes would be required in the structure of care proceedings to give effect to it?

(iii) How would you accommodate the child who is (*a*) in moral danger, or (*b*) beyond parental control, in your revised structure?

(iv) What would you do with wardship?

All this is far too tame for some of the proponents of 'children's rights' — Eekelaar, Dingwall and Murray may reject 'paternalist power' in the State, but they certainly accept that *some-one* should be paternal. An alternative view-point is described, and refuted, by Michael Freeman in *The Rights of Children in the International Year of the Child* (1980):

There is a distinction between two approaches to children's rights. Rogers and Wrightsman distinguish the 'nurturance orientation' and the 'self-determination orientation.' (1978) The former 'stresses the provision by society of supposedly beneficial objects, environments, services, experiences, etc. for the child'; the latter 'stresses those potential rights which would allow children to exercise control over their environments, to make decisions about what they want, to have autonomous control over various facets of their lives.' They continue: 'The nurturance orientation may be simplistically considered as "giving children what's good for them," while the self-determination orientation may be thought of as "giving children the right (*sic*) to decide what's good for themselves." ' The distinction is not unlike that made by Richard Farson, a leading liberationist thinker, in *Birthrights*, who distinguishes between protecting children and protecting children's rights. Put in this way, it can be seen that the first orientation adopts a paternalistic view of children and fits in closely with the child-saving ethos; whereas the second approach would grant a measure of autonomy to children, in matters felt to affect them most directly. So-called rights of self-determination are, of course, more meaningful the older the child is: a young child denied the protection of nurturance rights may never reach the stage of being in a position to assert or exercise the sort of autonomy envisaged by the liberationists. . . .

More generally, the question must be considered as to whether rights bestowed on children should be the same as those conferred on adults, or whether those same rights should be specifically tailored to meet the different requirements of children or should, indeed, be rights special to children. The different orientations and positions already referred to take different stances here too. The liberationist school would argue that the legal status of children should not in any way be dependent on the age factor. Just as the civil rights movement and women's movement have argued that a person's legal status should not be made dependent upon race or sex, unless there is a highly cogent justification for so doing, the same considerations are asserted in the case of children. But it should be obvious that age is a relevant differentiating factor: small children are dependent on adults. The assertion of the irrelevance of age does not square with either our knowledge of biology or economics. . . .

Crucial to an understanding of children's rights is that, so far from having self-determination, children are often not in a position to assert interests at all. . . . If children cannot assert rights, the obligation on others, particularly parents, to act in particular ways to further children's interests assumes paramount importance. Advocating that parents and society generally should act in the best interests of children may seem a slippery path to take. After all many of the most punitive measures in, for example, the area of juvenile delinquency, have been taken with this supposed end in view. This is why I find Brian Barry's discussion of this idea in *Political Argument* so forceful.

He argues that we are acting in another's interests if we help him to get what he wants (1965). He argues further that, unless we inculcate the kinds of habits that will be useful in satisfying the wants that children may assert when they mature, we are not justified in frustrating any of their present wants, as we are not justified in trying to alter their character. Children must be so treated that their true capacities are advanced. . . . Rawls states that decisions made in the interests of the child ought always to be guided by whatever 'settled preferences' the child has defined, as long as they are not irrational. 'We try to get for him the things he presumably wants whatever else he wants. We must be able to argue that with the development . . . of his rational powers the individual in question will accept our decision on his behalf and agree with us that we did the best thing for him.' (1972) The importance is thus stressed again of the child being given the opportunity to develop his rational powers.

Question

'Is it not almost a self-evident axiom that the State should require and compel the education, up to a certain standard, of every human being who is born its citizen?' (Mill, 1859)

In practice, however, although the authors of *Before the Best Interests of the Child* (1980) (see pp. 588–589, above) appear to regard compulsory education as unproblematic, this can be a most difficult area in which to reconcile the rights of the child with the values of a free and plural society. In *Wisconsin v Yoder*, 406 US 205 (1972), the United States Supreme Court invalidated a state compulsory education law insofar as it compelled Amish children to stay at school beyond the age (14) at which their parents believed it might prejudice their upbringing in the Amish way of life. The European Convention of Human Rights deals with the matter in Article 2 of Protocol No. 1 (see p. 573, above), the interpretation of which was discussed in the following case:

Campbell and Cosans
European Court of Human Rights, Strasbourg, 25 February 1982

Mrs Campbell's son, Gordon, attended a primary school in Scotland at which corporal punishment was used for disciplinary purposes, although in fact Gordon was never so punished while he was at that school. Mrs Cosans' son, Jeffrey, attended a secondary school where corporal punishment was also used. On his father's advice, Jeffrey refused to accept corporal punishment for trying to take a prohibited short cut on his way home from school. As a result, he was suspended from school until such time as he was willing to accept the punishment. He remained suspended from September to the following May, when he ceased to be of compulsory school age. Each mother claimed a violation of the second sentence of Article 2, Protocol No. 1, and Mrs Cosans claimed that Jeffrey's suspension violated his right to education under the first sentence of that Article. (They also claimed breach of the prohibition of 'torture' or 'inhuman or degrading treatment or punishment' in Article 3 of the Convention, but the Court found that no such treatment had taken place.)

Judgment of the court: . . . in the submission of the Government, the obligation to respect philosophical convictions arises only in relation to the content of, and mode of conveying, information and knowledge and not in relation to all aspects of school administration.

As the Government pointed out, the *Kjeldsen, Busk Madsen and Pedersen* judgment states:
'The second sentence of Article 2 implies . . . that the State, in fulfilling the functions assumed by it in regard to education and teaching, must take care that information or knowledge included in the curriculum is conveyed in an objective, critical and pluralistic manner. The State is forbidden to pursue an aim of indoctrination that might be considered as not respecting parents' religious and philosophical convictions. That is the limit that must not be exceeded.'

However, that case concerned the content of instruction, whereas the second sentence of Article 2 has a broader scope, as is shown by the generality of its wording. This was confirmed by the Court in the same judgment when it held that the said sentence is binding upon the Contracting States in the exercise, inter alia, of the function 'consisting of the organisation and financing of public education'. . . .

The Government also contested the conclusion of the majority of the [European Commission of Human Rights] that the applicants' views on the use of corporal punishment amounted to 'philosophical convictions', arguing, inter alia, that the expression did not extend to opinions on internal school administration, such as discipline, and that, if the majority were correct, there was no reason why objections to other methods of discipline, or simply to discipline in general, should not also amount to 'philosophical convictions'. . . .

Having regard to the Convention as a whole . . . the expression 'philosophical convictions' in the present context denotes, in the Court's opinion, such convictions as are worthy of respect in a 'democratic society' . . . and are not incompatible with human dignity; in addition, they must not conflict with the fundamental right of the child to education, the whole of Article 2 being dominated by its first sentence. . . .

The applicants' views relate to a weighty and substantial aspect of human life and behaviour, namely the integrity of the person, the propriety or otherwise of the infliction of corporal punishment and the exclusion of the distress which the risk of such punishment entails. They are views which satisfy the various criteria listed above; it is this that distinguishes them from opinions that might be held on other methods of discipline or on discipline in general. . . .

Mrs Campbell and Mrs Cosans have accordingly been victims of a violation of the second sentence of Article 2 of Protocol No. 1. . . .

The right to education guaranteed by the first sentence of Article 2 by its very nature calls for regulation by the State, but such regulation must never injure the substance of the right nor conflict with other rights enshrined in the Convention or its Protocols. . . .

The suspension of Jeffrey Cosans — which remained in force for nearly a whole school year — was motivated by his and his parents' refusal to accept that he receive or be liable to corporal punishment. . . . His return to school could have been secured only if his parents had acted contrary to their convictions, convictions which the United Kingdom is obliged to respect under the second sentence of Article 2. . . . A condition of access to an educational establishment that conflicts in this way with another right enshrined in Protocol No. 1 cannot be described as reasonable and in any event falls outside the State's power of regulation under Article 2.

There has accordingly also been, as regards Jeffrey Cosans, breach of the first sentence of that Article.

Questions

(i) In the *Kejeldsen, Busk Madsen and Pedersen* case (7 December 1976, Series A no. 23) the Court held that compulsory sex education in state schools was *not* a contravention of the duty to respect the parents' religious and philosophical convictions: can you explain why?

(ii) What would have been the position if Jeffrey Cosans had wanted to exercise his right to education, but his parents had prevented him?

The case also raises the question of the State's obligation to provide for the needs of children whose parents have insufficient resources to do so. It is to the provision by the State of financial support for families that we must now turn.

CHAPTER 16

State support for families

1 The private law obligation and the State — maintenance and supplementary benefits

> The law of pensions and supplementary benefits requires as much expertise and demands as much study from practitioners as any other branch of family law, of which it is, essentially, a part.

> In the absence of an explicit government family policy, the interrelationship between social security and the family is likely to be haphazard, contradictory and at times negative. Social security often walks the tightrope between its wishes to support the family and its fear lest the help it provides undermines either the very family virtues it wants to foster or other social values that override family considerations. . . .
> In brief, then, while society supports the stability of the family and the welfare of children, it also supports other values related to work, self-support and individualism with the result that social security provision for the family is half hearted, conditional and at times even negative.

The point which is made both by Finer J in *Reiterbund v Reiterbund* [1974] 2 All ER 455, [1974] 1 WLR 788, and by Victor George (1973), can be illustrated through an examination of the cases where a husband has left his wife to form a new liaison with some other person, and his wife applies for maintenance. The husband is treated in law as a 'liable relative' under s. 17(1) of the Supplementary Benefits Act 1976. Yet the state also has an obligation to provide support to the wife through supplementary benefits in the case of need. Can the husband morally argue that his new responsibility is with his new liaison, leaving the state to provide support for his wife?

It is this question which lies at the heart of the *Report of the Committee on One-Parent Families*, the Finer Report (1974):

The dilemma of liable relatives
4.179 At this stage, it will be helpful to create the characters in an everyday drama. John, let it be supposed, contracted a marriage by which there are children of school age, or younger. He earns an average wage in a semi-skilled occupation. His marriage has broken down, and he has left home. He may or may not be divorced. Mary is John's former or deserted wife. Her lack of training, or the demands of the children, or both, prevent her from taking employment, or, at any rate, from earning more than a small amount in part-time work, insufficient for the needs of herself and the children. John is living with his second wife, or with his mistress. She and John have children of their own, or, it may be, she has children by a former marriage or association whom John looks after as his own. This woman also earns little or nothing.
4.180 In the postulated circumstances, there are two families in being for the purposes of supplementary benefits: Mary's family, consisting of herself and her children; and John's family, consisting of himself, his second wife or his mistress, and the children of their household. Mary, being unemployed or in part-time work only, is eligible for supplementary benefit, the amount of which will depend upon the calculation of the requirements and resources of her family. If John falls out of work, he will be entitled to benefit, the amount of which will depend upon the calculation of the requirements and resources of his family; but if he is in full-time work, then no member of his family is eligible for benefit. . . .
4.181 If John is still married to Mary he has a statutory obligation to support Mary's family under section [17(1) Supplementary Benefits Act 1976], that is to say, he is a 'liable relative'.

Further, whether still married to Mary or not, John may be under an obligation to maintain Mary's family under a maintenance order made by the magistrates or in the divorce jurisdiction. Given John's earning capacity, however, it is clear that he cannot, when in work, earn enough money to maintain both the families. If he elects to do his duty by Mary's family, he will to that extent relieve the Supplementary Benefits Commission from paying money to Mary, but the inevitable effect will be to deprive the family of which he is a current member of the means of subsistence in circumstances where, since he is in work, they will not themselves be eligible for benefit. If, on the other hand, he elects to maintain the latter family, then, with equal inevitability, he has to break his obligations towards Mary's family. But she, in that case, can claim supplementary benefit; in such circumstances neither family starves.

4.182 When a man is put in such a dilemma the solution he will lean towards is tolerably clear. He will feed, clothe and house those with whom he is living, knowing that the State will provide for the others. It is the almost inescapable consequence of the principles on which the supplementary benefits scheme is founded that wherever there is not enough money for the husband to support two women, it is the one with whom he is not living who has to resort to the Supplementary Benefits Commission. This was recognised, with blunt realism, by the Commission's predecessor, the National Assistance Board, in their annual report for 1953.

'If (the husband's earnings) or other resources are not enough to maintain, besides himself, both his wife (with her children, if any) and the paramour (with her children, if any) the defect has got to be met at one point or other by assistance. The Board are then faced with the delicate problem of deciding whether the assistance is to be given to the wife or to the paramour. Respect for the marriage tie suggests that it is the legal wife whose maintenance should be the prior charge on the husband's income . . . but important practical considerations, not least the avoidance of unnecessary expenditure of public monies, lead inescapably to the other view. . . . Extracting money from husbands to maintain wives from whom they are separated is at best an uncertain business; it is easier to enforce the maintenance of those with whom the man is living than of those from whom he is parted.'

4.183 Moreover, the Supplementary Benefits Commission's defence of the cohabitation rule [in its report *Cohabitation* (1971)] suggests, at least implicitly, that this solution of the dilemma is right as well as inevitable. The Commission argue:

'A man who is entitled to supplementary benefit living with a woman not his wife is entitled to benefit for her, and for their children, when he is sick or unemployed; it would be manifestly unreasonable if, while he is at work, his partner could claim supplementary benefit . . . in her own right. . . . (This would be) to treat the women who have the support of a partner both as if they had not such support and better than if they were married. It would not be right, and we believe that public opinion would not accept, that the unmarried "wife" should be able to claim benefit denied to a married woman because her husband was in full-time work.

It has been suggested that it is morally wrong to infer that because a man and woman are living together as man and wife, the man is in fact supporting the woman and her children especially where these are from a former union. But to leave the choice to pay or not to pay to the man, and to make no effort to get him to maintain the woman would be inconsistent with the Act and *repugnant to the general view of family responsibility.*'

Ashley v Ashley
[1968] P 582, [1965] 3 All ER 554, [1965] 3 WLR 1194, 130 JPI, 110 Sol Jo 13, High Court, Probate Divorce and Admiralty Division

On appeal from a maintenance order made by magistrates, the divisional court had to consider whether it was relevant that a deserted wife was entitled to state support. The husband's counsel argued that it was entirely proper to be aware that in a case where the husband had relatively small earnings (as in this case) the benefit of payments will in practice be received ultimately by the National Assistance Board (under the present scheme, the National Assistance Board has been replaced first by the Supplementary Benefits Commission, and since 1980, by the Secretary of State).

Cumming Bruce J: . . . The order of the court in favour of the wife for herself and the children should be such that the husband's contribution to their support will not have the effect of reducing his income below the subsistence level; the subsistence level is the appropriate level for consideration when the problem of a small income such as this falls to be considered. In spite of the argument of Mrs Puxon [counsel for the husband], I understand the justices to state that they regarded material factors to be both the wife's receipt of national assistance and the fact that she would not receive the benefit of any payments ordered to be made by the husband. I am satisfied that both the factors referred to in that sentence of their reasons did materially affect the amount that they ordered the husband to pay. I have come to the conclusion, in spite of Mrs Puxon's argument, that the fact that the wife would not receive the benefit of any payments ordered by the court was irrelevant for the purpose of the matters which the justices had to consider. Justices under the statute have to have regard to all the circumstances of the case but as has been said again and again, those words have to be construed as meaning all the relevant circumstances of the case and it is for this court to give guidance where necessary as to what circumstances are relevant and what are irrelevant. For my part I am satisfied that for the purposes of the exercise of the jurisdiction of justices to make permanent orders for periodical payments under the Act of 1960, the fact that the result of an order of the court in favour of a wife is likely to be that the National Assistance Board will ultimately receive the benefit and not the wife at all, is wholly irrelevant to the question of what amount the justices should order the husband to pay.

Sir Jocelyn Simon P: I agree. Where cohabitation has been disrupted by a matrimonial offence on the part of a husband, the wife should be awarded maintenance at such a rate as would give her and the children in her custody a standard of living appropriate to the husband's income, having regard always to the fact that his income now has to support two households in place of one where household expenses were shared. Therefore, in general the standard of living of the wife and children, although it may now have to be lower than if the parties were still living together, should not be significantly lower than that which the husband enjoys. See *Kershaw v Kershaw* [1966] P 13, [1964] 3 All ER 653. . . . The matrimonial court should consider all circumstances of the case, including, certainly, the fact that national assistance is available and may be required, but it should not, as the conclusion of the adjudication, allow the husband to enjoy a substantially higher standard of living than the wife, or shift his responsibilities for his wife and children on to the community generally through the National Assistance Board. On the other hand the matrimonial court must remember that the National Assistance Board does not supplement wages. They must therefore not make such an order as would bring the husband below subsistence level. If the order so limited leaves the wife and children still below subsistence level, the National Assistance Board may properly be looked to to supplement their income. Both parties and the children will then unhappily be at no better than subsistence level, but the result will be just as between the husband and his wife and children on the one hand, and between the husband and the general community as symbolised by the National Assistance Board on the other.

The wife was awarded an order for herself by the magistrates of 15s a week towards her own maintenance, and 7s 6d each towards the maintenance of her two children (aged seven and four years). The Divisional Court substituted for that order, the order that the husband pay his wife the sum of £2 a week, and for each of the two children the sum of 30s a week.

Question

Would there have been a material difference, in the result of this case before the Divisional Court, if the husband had disclosed that he was now living with another woman who had no work and who had to stay at home to look after their child?

Barnes v Barnes
[1972] 3 All ER 872, [1972] 1 WLR 1381, 116 Sol Jo 801, Court of Appeal

The parties were married in 1960. They had four children — aged eleven, ten, eight and seven. In March 1971, the wife obtained a decree nisi of divorce, the decree being made absolute in June 1971. In July 1971, the husband remarried. The second child, Peter, remained with his father until May 1971, then went to his mother, returned for a short time to his father, and at the time of the appeal in this case was in a residential home.

The other children remained with their mother. In March 1971, the county court judge made an order in favour of each of the three children who were with their mother in the sum of £2.50 per week. He made no order for the wife. By the order of 30 June 1971, the judge reduced the weekly payments to the three children to £2.00 each and made an order with respect to Peter for £2.00. He made a nominal order of 5p per annum in respect of the wife. On 13 March 1972, the judge ordered that the husband should pay only £1.50 for each of the children and the payment of 5p for the wife should continue. The wife appealed against the orders of 30 June 1971 and 13 March 1972 on the ground that the judge erred in making only nominal orders for periodical payments for herself.

Edmund Davies LJ [referred to the order made on 30 June 1971 and continued]: That order has been criticised by Mr Tyrell, for the wife, on a number of grounds, basically, and principally, that it was wrong to make nothing more than a nominal order in her favour. Certain figures have been agreed between the parties as to the financial position at the time material to the making of that order. It appears from the affidavit of the husband, dated 28 June 1971, that he was then in receipt of a sum which, in terms of decimal currency, amounted to roughly £24.75. Taking from that figure items in respect of accommodation, food, electricity, gas and bus fares to work, there was a net figure of £14.50 left. The submission made by Mr Tyrell on behalf of the wife is that in those circumstances the figure of £8, which had been ordered by the judge was, as he put it, 'too low, although not a lot too low,' and his submission was that there should have been an award to the wife of something in the order of £3 and for each of the children £1.75, making a total sum of £10.

The first question that arises is: has it been demonstrated that the judge went wrong in arriving at that conclusion? One matter that has emerged perfectly clearly is that, as far as the evidence goes, any variation by way of reduction in the totality of the sums ordered to the wife and the children of the marriage would be reflected by adjustment of the social security benefits that the family would receive. There is evidence showing that on a later occasion when, pursuant to the second order [ie of 13 March 1972] to which we must presently turn, there was a reduction in the order made against the husband, the wife was not one penny the worse off because there was a corresponding increase in the social security benefit; and one of the two interesting questions that have arisen in the course of this case has been: what regard, if any, should the court have to the fact that social security benefit is available in cases of need?

In my judgment, the problem is not an easy one. It is submitted by Miss Gillespie, for the husband, that such benefit is to be regarded as coming within section 5 (1) (*a*) of the Matrimonial Proceedings and Property Act 1970, as being comprised within the 'other financial resources which each of the parties to the marriage has or is likely to have in the foreseeable future.' I find it difficult to regard such state benefits as coming within such a frame, and I repeat that I do not regard the problem as easy. . . .

But some assistance is to be gained from a decision of the Probate, Divorce and Admiralty Division, which relates not to a social security benefit but to national assistance. In *Ashley v Ashley* [1968] P 582, [1965] 3 All ER 554, the court held that in cases such as the one there involved:

'. . . where the husband's income was small, the order of the court in favour of the wife for herself and the children should not be such as to have the effect of reducing the husband's income below the subsistence level, . . . for if the order so limited left the wife and children still below subsistence level, the National Assistance Board could properly be invoked to supplement their income and both parties and the children would then be at no better than subsistence level, but the result would be just as between the husband and his wife and children on the one hand, and between the husband and the general community as symbolised by the National Assistance Board on the other.'

Having heard the submissions of counsel, the conclusion to which I have come is that in the first place when the court is seeking to arrive at what would be a proper order, it is desirable that regard should not be had to social security benefits but that one should, looking at all the features of the case, which are adverted to and set out in section 5, seek to arrive at a fair figure. But if the case is one in which the income of the parties is of modest proportions, and if the total available resources of both parties are so modest that an adjustment of that totality would result in the husband's being left with a sum quite inadequate to enable him to meet his own financial commitments, then the court may have regard to the fact that in proper cases social security benefits will be available to the wife and the children of the marriage. Having such regard, the court is enabled to avoid making such an order as would be financially crippling to the husband if it considered only the combined income earning capacity and property of the parties. It would be, I am persuaded, unrealistic to take any other course, . . .

Having made those general observations, I ask myself whether it has been demonstrated that Judge Lee clearly went wrong in making the order of 30 June. When one looks at what the husband had as disposable income — something in the region of £14.50 after deduction of the items to which I have already made reference — for my part I do not think it has been established that in awarding the children of his first marriage and his wife a totality of £8, he misdirected himself. . . .

Now as to the second order, which had the effect of reducing by £2 the amount being paid to the wife and the four children. The order that the same judge made was that each of the four children was to receive £1.50, and the nominal order of 5p per annum in respect of the wife remained unvaried. So, as I have said, there was a reduction of £2. It is said that Judge Lee was wrong in failing to increase the wife's nominal order to one of realistic proportions, and in reducing the children's maintenance from the £2 awarded in June 1971 to £1.50 per week.

The figures that we are presently concerned with are these: from the wife's affidavit of January 1972 it appeared that she was receiving the £8 from the husband, £2.90 family allowance and £7.60 social security. That made £18.50. Then, as a part-time barmaid, she was earning £2 per week, that being a sum which would not affect the amount of the social security benefits that she would be receiving. So in all her income was £20.50. As against that she was paying rent of £5.72, £2.10 a month for some hire-purchase charges, £1 a week for electricity and 50p per week in respect of gas.

Now what of the husband? His gross income was £32.27; his net income, after deduction of the same items as those to which I have referred in relation to the first order, was, taking it in round figures, £20. It was said on behalf of the wife that she is now paying some £5 rent which she was not previously paying when she was living with her parents, and that the husband is earning more money. The submission made by Mr Tyrell, on behalf of the wife, was that an order in the region of the total sum of £11 should have been made against the husband, made up of £3 for the wife and £2 for each of the four children. If that be adopted, the husband would be left with something like £9 for himself and his wife. Before the order was made, he was left with £20, out of which he had to pay £6 to his wife, leaving the sum of £14. Would it be just, in all the circumstances of this case, to vary the order of March 1972 to the extent urged by Mr Tyrell, increasing the amount from £6 to £11, leaving the husband with, as I may say, a mere £9 for himself and his wife? In my judgment, while variation to a degree is called for, Mr Tyrell goes much too far on behalf of his client. I think the time has come when the wife should have an order made in her favour. How much better off she is going to be is extremely open to doubt; nevertheless, I would be for allowing the appeal against this second order to this extent and to this extent only: while leaving the four children to have the sum of £1.50 a week each, I would be in favour of ordering that the wife receive the sum of £2, making a totality of £8. That would mean that the husband would have something in the region of £12 weekly for himself and his wife. I hope and believe that that would meet the justice of the case; beyond that I would not be prepared to go. To that extent I would allow the appeal against the second order.

Russell LJ: I agree. I too would not interfere with the June 1971 order that was left alone for so long. I wish to add only a few words with regard to the impact on these matters of social security benefits.

What should be the proper approach? Prima facie a husband, or former husband, ought to support his wife and children — subject, of course, to any independent income or earnings of the wife — and he ought to support them to a proper standard. But in the lower income groups, this is frequently not possible out of the earnings of the husband, consistently with the husband being able to maintain himself to a proper standard and having regard also to any new responsibility he undertakes, as by law he is entitled to undertake, in the shape of a second wife and perhaps a second family. It is at this stage that the social security benefits to the first wife come into the picture.

The existence of such benefits enables the court in effect to deal with a larger purse than would otherwise be available; but it would be quite wrong to say (and indeed it is not said) that the existence of those social security benefits either enables, or entitles, a husband to throw on to social security the burden which he ought himself to bear, consistently with being left himself with a proper standard. In my view the approach should in general be that the husband may be left with a proper standard, though his contribution to the wife and children is as a result inadequate to provide by itself a proper standard for the first wife and children, bearing in mind that social security benefits will provide sufficient addition to his contribution to the wife and children, producing a proper standard for them.

Questions

(i) Can you think of *any* advantages from the point of view of the wife for obtaining a court order in her favour in a case such as *Barnes v Barnes* [1972] 3 All ER 872, [1972] 1 WLR 1381?

(ii) As a tax payer, can you see any justification for the legal aid fund being used in this case on behalf of the wife's applications?

The *Finer Report* also discusses the practice of the supplementary benefit authorities in relation to private support claims:

The allegations of pressure
4.193 Several of the organisations which gave evidence showed concern that women who are reluctant to institute legal proceedings for maintenance against liable relatives are, or at least feel themselves to be, subjected to pressure from officials to do so. We quote from some of the representations we have received:

'. . . health visitors have noted with concern the distress of some deserted or unmarried mothers when social security officers insist that legal proceedings be instituted . . . undue pressure is sometimes brought to bear at a time when the mother is already under considerable stress (Health Visitors' Association).

While the Department of Health and Social Security deny that pressure is ever brought on women to apply for court orders against liable relatives, we have knowledge of many cases in which the woman had been given the definite impression that her supplementary benefits would cease if she omitted to take such action. Women in this situation frequently sue their husbands for a matrimonial offence when in fact they have no case and as a result have a very humiliating and embarrassing experience in court. We have known cases of women who have left their husbands by mutual agreement but have, as a result of this misunderstanding, sued them for desertion . . . (Women's National Commission).

Pressure by the Department of Health and Social Security is often the cause of such (maintenance) proceedings where it might not otherwise be taken (NSPCC).

Mothers of illegitimate children are currently sometimes required to agree to take out an affiliation order against their child's putative father when they apply to receive supplementary benefit (NEC of the Labour Party).

If a woman eligible for supplementary benefits applies for and obtains a maintenance order in her favour which is less than the full rate of her benefit entitlement, she may authorise the magistrates' clerk to divert any payments which are received to the DHSS:

4.207 . . . When such a transfer is effected, the wife receives an order book entitling her to supplementary benefit (calculated on the basis that there is no maintenance order) which she can cash at the post office: and the clerk of the court transmits to the Department whatever is paid in to the collecting office under the maintenance order. (The procedure is also available in the much rarer case where the amount of the maintenance order exceeds the supplementary benefit entitlement; but here no invitation to transfer the maintenance order is made until the circumstances, such as repeated failure to pay on the order, show this to be desirable.) The effect is that the wife receives her full entitlement regularly, whether the maintenance order is paid in full, intermittently or not at all. She is relieved of the anxiety of irregular payments and the harassment and indignity of commuting between different officials and different procedures.

(This 'diversion' procedure is, of course, only available where the order is either made or registered in the magistrates' court, so that payment is not made direct to the recipient but through the magistrates' clerk.)

The *Finer Report* itself makes it clear that the Commission (now the Supplementary Benefits Officers) would on many occasions accept an offer of payment from a liable relative. If the husband makes an offer which is less than the amount of supplementary benefit it will nonetheless be accepted if he provides evidence to show that his offer is reasonable:

4.188 We understand that, subject always to the discretion to make any adjustments considered appropriate in the individual case, the Supplementary Benefits Commission have established guidelines to help their officers decide whether an offer is reasonable. The requirements of the liable relative are normally taken to be the supplementary benefit scale rates for himself and any dependants with whom he is living, plus an allowance to meet the rent in full (or, in the case of boarders, the appropriate supplementary benefit rate) plus the sum of £5, or a quarter of his net earnings (his take-home pay after deduction of national insurance contributions and income tax), whichever is the higher. Any income in excess of this will be regarded as being available to meet the liable relative's obligation under section 22 of the Act of 1966. An offer by the liable relative to pay an amount approximate to that arrived at under the formula will normally be regarded as reasonable, and will be accepted by the Commission.

4.189 A practical example of the application of the formula would be as follows. Suppose that John earns £38 gross. His family consists of himself, his second wife or his mistress, and two children, so that there are also family allowances of 90p a week. After income tax and insurance contributions his family's net income would be £31.35. His net housing costs, after rent allowance or rebate, are £5.25 a week. The Supplementary Benefits Commission would ordinarily consider an offer of approximately £2.75 a week for the maintenance of Mary's family as reasonable, that sum being calculated as follows:

Requirements of John's family (as from October 1973):	£
Supplementary benefit scale rates —	
— for self and second wife	11.65
— for two children (under 5)	4.10
actual housing costs	5.25
one quarter of net earnings	7.60
Total	28.60
Balance of net income available to meet liability under section 22	2.75
Total net income of John's family	31.35

But if Mary were to apply to the court for maintenance, perhaps only after John had refused to pay the sum of £2.75 to the authorities in fulfilment of his liability, would the court make an order for £2.75 — or does the court take account of other factors? This question has arisen in several cases:

Shallow v Shallow
[1979] Fam 1, [1978] 2 All ER 483, [1978] 2 WLR 583, 121 Sol Jo 830, Court of Appeal

The Registrar had made an order in favour of a former wife for £12 per week, orders in favour of the two children for £5 per week, and directed the former husband to continue to pay the mortgage and rates totalling £8.50 per week on the former matrimonial home. The former husband appealed against these orders on two grounds which are relevant for our present purposes: first, that the judge was wrong in law in failing to have regard to the guide-lines issued to the officers of the Supplementary Benefits Commission, and secondly that the judge was wrong in law in making an order which would depress the husband below subsistence level.

Ormrod LJ: In a written note of his reasons for dismissing the appeal the judge said that the wife clearly needed the amount ordered by the registrar and that although the husband was left with less than the 'supplementary benefit scale,' he could afford the amount and that the order accordingly should stand. The first ground of appeal is therefore unsustainable because the judge did have 'regard to' the so-called supplementary benefit scale but decided not to adopt it in this particular case.

On the figures, which have been agreed by counsel in this court (they differ appreciably from those used by the judge), the position is that the husband has a gross annual income of £3,960 a year which after tax and allowances, leaves him with a net weekly income of £62.44. The order in the aggregate amounts to £30.50, leaving the husband, who is a single man, with £31.94 to live on. Since this is rather more than the wife has on which to keep herself and two children, it is absurd to suggest that the husband has been reduced below the subsistence level, unless that phrase has acquired some purely technical meaning. The other ground of appeal therefore appears equally unsustainable. Mr Inskip, who appeared for the husband in this court, was, as he recognised, in great difficulty, but he has developed his client's case as well as it could be put. His argument, for which the court is grateful, really amounts to saying that the court ought to adopt the practice which the Supplementary Benefits Commission use to determine the liability of the 'liable relative' to contribute to the support of his dependants, and he based his submission on a decision of the Divisional Court earlier this year in *Smethurst v Smethurst* [1978] Fam 52, [1977] 3 All ER 110. But for some observations of Sir George Baker P in that case, Mr Inskip conceded that the appeal would have been unarguable.

The matter arose originally from the Report of the Committee on One-Parent Families, which is conveniently referred to as the Finer Report. That report called attention to the differences between the practice of the courts and of the Supplementary Benefits Commission in assessing the liability of husbands and ex-husbands for the support of their families, and suggested, expressly or by implication, that the courts might bring their practice more into line with that of the commission. In paragraph 4.189, the Finer Report disclosed for the first time to the public the existence of a formula used by the Supplementary Benefits Commission for their own purposes in such cases. This formula contains three factors: (1) husband's rent: (2) amount which would be payable in supplementary benefits to him if he had not other resources for himself and dependants (if any); (3) one quarter of his net income (i.e. gross income less tax and national insurance contributions).

For certain purposes only (which are referred to in more detail later) the Supplementary Benefits Commission consider that the husband should be permitted to retain an amount equal to the aggregate of these sums for his own use and so limit their claim for contribution to the remainder of his income. . . .

Smethurst v Smethurst [1978] Fam 52, [1977] 3 All ER 1110 is the first case in which reference has been made to it. In the course of giving judgment in that case (which raised a number of quite different issues) Sir George Baker P said, at p. 477:

> 'Another way of looking at this matter is to consider whether, and if so how far, the husband is on or above subsistence level. If the Supplementary Benefits Commission were seeking a contribution from this man, they would apply the formula, which is to be found in the Report of the Committee on One-Parent Families — The Finer Report (1974) (Cmnd. 5629), vol. 1, pp. 136–138. As stated in paragraph 4.190, "Nothing could exceed the confusion created by three modes of assessment of a liability, all different from each other, and two of them employed in courts of law acting in ignorance of the third mode which the Supplementary Benefits Commission use in making decisions which affect the very same group of people." "I am not aware," the President went on, "of this approach having been used before in the courts, but I see no reason why it should not be, and to my knowledge justices are considering it." '

. . . .

The significant part of those observations is the first sentence, in which the President appears to be equating the figure which was produced by the formula with 'subsistence level,' a phrase which at once calls to mind the line of authority, beginning with *Kershaw v Kershaw* [1966] P 13, [1964] 3 All ER 653 and *Ashley v Ashley* [1968] P 582, [1965] 3 All ER 554 in which it was said that, except in unusual circumstances, orders for maintenance or periodical payments should not reduce the husband below 'subsistence level.' Sir Jocelyn Simon at pp. 590–591 related 'subsistence level' closely to the amount which would be payable in supplementary benefits *to* the husband, if he had no other resources for the support of himself and his dependants, if any. Those cases were approved in principle in more general terms by this court in *Barnes (RM) v Barnes (GW)* [1972] 3 All ER 872, [1972] 1 WLR 1381 [p. 601, above]. If, therefore, the product of the formula is now to be equated with 'subsistence level,' and the principle of *Ashley* applied to it, something very like 'protected earnings' will be imported into the process of assessing liability for maintenance and periodical payments. . . . The formula has nothing to do with subsistence levels. It produces, in fact, nothing more than a negotiating figure for the use of the commission's officers when seeking contributions from 'liable relatives.' If a liable relative makes an offer which is more or less consistent with the product of the formula, the officers can accept it as reasonable and one which, experience shows, is more likely to be paid regularly than a higher sum imposed on the liable relative. If, on the other hand, the commission itself undertakes to enforce an order for periodical payments or maintenance made by a court, it seeks enforcement of the full amount of the order.

The subsistence level, in the language of *Ashley v Ashley*, therefore remains what it was, namely, approximately the current amount of supplementary benefit appropriate to a single man or a man with dependants, as the case may be. These amounts are prescribed by the government from time to time and are available in the form of a statutory instrument.

Ormrod LJ continued by comparing the use of the one-third formula and the liable relative formula on the basis of the figures which were agreed in this case:

On the one-third basis the husband's gross weekly income is approximately £75 per week, from which national insurance contribution is to be deducted (£228 per annum or £4.25 per week) together with something for travelling and other expenses of earning his income leaving, say, £68. The wife has no income except £3 per week child benefit. The aggregate is therefore £71, one third of which is £24, from which £3 is to be deducted, leaving £21 as the starting point for the wife's own order. This is close to the registrar's figure for £20.50 (made up as to £12 plus £8.50 mortgage repayments and rates) for the wife herself.

On the Supplementary Benefits Commission formula the calculation is

Rent	£9.50	
Supplementary benefit (rate for single man)	£12.70	£22.20
¼ net income (¼ of £62)	£15.50	
	£37.70	

This leaves a balance of £24.30 (£62 minus £37.70) as the figure which the commission would be content to collect from a 'liable relative.' The position looks rather different from the wife's point of view. On current scales her so-called 'subsistence level' is:

Rent	£8.50	
Supplementary benefit for herself	£12.70	
Supplementary benefit for each child (£4.35 × 2)	£8.70	
	£29.90	(of which £3 per week is payable as child benefit)

On the one-third basis the husband has half his net income for himself while maintaining the wife and two children on the other half at a few pence above their so-called subsistence level, while he himself is between £9 and £10 a week above his 'subsistence level.'

On the formula, the husband is about £15 a week above his 'subsistence level' and the wife and children about £2 a week below theirs. This can scarcely be regarded as an equitable or reasonable division of the available income. Moreover, it would have the effect of transferring part of his liability to the taxpayer since the wife would be entitled to receive supplementary benefit at the rate of about £2 per week. (Her total income, out of which she would have to pay mortgage instalments and rates, would be £24.30 from the husband plus child benefit at £3 a week; that is, £27.30 as against a 'subsistence level' of £29.90). It is, therefore, obviously impossible to contend that in the instant case the formula produces a more equitable result than the one third approach. On other sets of facts and figures the position may be reversed, particularly where the husband's income is lower or his liabilities higher than in the present case, but this can only be determined by making both calculations and relating the results to the facts of the case. The judge was clearly right in the present case to reject the result of the formula.

Mr Inskip advanced three general arguments in support of the formula. Echoing the Finer Report, he urged the advantages of uniformity of approach. But this proves largely illusory because former husbands are not 'liable relatives,' so that the Supplementary Benefits Commission cannot recover contributions from them and consequently do not have occasion to use the formula in cases where the parties are divorced. Secondly, he urged that men are more likely to keep their payments up to date if their orders are smaller. That may or may not be so as a general proposition. Thirdly, he suggested that it is desirable to provide an incentive to men to continue in work. In the present case the probability of the husband giving up his job and a net income (after payment of the amount due under the order) of about £31 per week for supplementary benefit at the rate of £22 per week, seems remote.

In these circumstances this appeal must inevitably be dismissed on all grounds, with the result that the registrar's order, which was plainly a reasonable and proper one, stands.

In *Shallow v Shallow*, the former husband was living on his own. In the next case, the former husband left his first wife to live with another woman and her children:

Tovey v Tovey
(1978) 8 Family Law 80, Court of Appeal

Ormrod LJ: The question then was should he be able literally to off-load the whole of his obligation to his wife and his three children on to the State, simply by taking over another woman with two children? It seemed to his Lordship, even in these days, a startling proposition that a man who was in regular work should be required to make no contribution at all to the maintenance of his own children. It was true that it could be argued that he had taken two children off social security by going to live with this lady, and that from the tax-payers' point of view was a benefit. But at the same time, as a pure matter of public policy it was very undesirable indeed that a man should not, even in a purely formal sense, continue to contribute to the children who were his primary liability. It was very unfortunate that the liability was blurred by considerations such as the supplementary benefits regulations; they blurred that responsibility, which was very unfortunate.

In *Tovey v Tovey* the husband was ordered to pay £1.00 per week for each child. Only a nominal order was made for the wife. This award nonetheless reduced the husband to an income level below the supplementary benefit rates then applicable to himself and his new dependants.

In the cases cited above, the husbands had employment. Had they themselves been on supplementary benefits, it has been emphasised in the High Court that only nominal orders are appropriate (*Williams v Williams* [1974] Fam 55, [1974] 3 All ER 377; *Chase v Chase* (1982) Times, 23 October).

Question

Do you think that such an order as in *Tovey v Tovey* is justified so as to impress upon fathers that their primary obligation is to their legitimate children? (Reread the observations in the Finer Report, p. 600, above.)

Ormrod LJ's view about the undesirability from a public policy view of permitting a man to 'offload' his responsibility on to the State appears in an even starker form in a decision of a court not normally concerned with family matters:

Hulley v Thompson
[1981] 1 All ER 1128, [1981] 1 WLR 159, 125 Sol Jo 47, High Court, Queen's Bench Division

The father of two children was divorced from the mother. At the time of the divorce a consent order was made that the father should not pay any maintenance to the mother, but should transfer to the mother his half-share in the matrimonial home (worth £12,500). It was agreed also that no maintenance should be paid to the children. The Supplementary Benefits Commission paid benefit to the wife for the children.

The Commission brought a complaint against the father, who was earning between £55 and £70 per week, seeking to recover from him such sums in respect of the benefit paid as the court considered appropriate. The magistrates came to the conclusion that they had a discretion whether or not to make an order. In the light of the consent order made in the divorce proceedings, they declined to make any order and the Commission appealed. The father submitted that the transfer of the house had been made in lieu of his liability to maintain the children.

Waller LJ: . . . In my judgment the liability of both wife and husband is unambiguously set out in s. 17(1) of the 1976 Act. That indicates that each of them is liable for the maintenance of their children and while there may be cases where, as between husband and wife, other arrangements might be made, in the case of children it is difficult to see how a consent arrangement can avoid the husband's or wife's liability to maintain the children.

In this case the Supplementary Benefits Commission have paid benefit to the wife in respect of the children. It follows from that that the wife herself must have been entitled to benefit for the children. In those circumstances the question must arise what is the father doing in respect of his liability, because prima facie he would be responsible for all that which the wife was unable herself to provide. Counsel for the respondent submits that the respondent has provided for that liability by the capital sum of half his share in the house which he transferred to the wife.

In my judgment it is quite impossible to take that simplistic view. The justices should have been considering how much the husband could pay towards the maintenance of the children. Prima facie he should be paying the balance of that which the wife was unable to pay. But it may well be that on consideration some deduction should be made in the circumstances of the case, which would take into consideration the whole of the terms of the consent order in the county court.

In my judgment the justices came to the wrong conclusion in exercising the discretion which they did, and this case must go back to be reconsidered. They should reconsider this case on the basis that the respondent is liable to maintain these two children. Prima facie the amount he is earning, £55 to £70 per week, does include resources sufficient to enable him to meet his responsibility to maintain these children. Is there something in the light of the order made in the county court which would reduce that responsibility in any way? It may be that they could come to either conclusion: either there is nothing to reduce it or there is something to reduce it. That would be a matter for them. I would send this case back with that indication.

Questions

(i) Is your first impression of this decision that it is right?
(ii) Now go back to Chapter 6 and study the recent approach of the divorce courts to the settlement of the matrimonial home after divorce and to the doctrine of the 'clean break': if the couple in this case had not reached agreement, might the court nevertheless have made a similar order?
(iii) If the divorce court had deliberately made such an order, would it have been right for the magistrates or the Queen's Bench Division to undermine it in this way?

2 Poverty and the one-parent family

In her chapter on *Income Maintenance for Families with Children*, in *Families in Britain* (1982), Ruth Lister, the Director of the Child Poverty Action Group, describes the basic framework of the present system of State support:

The basic framework for today's income maintenance provisions was laid down in the Beveridge Report of 1942. The Beveridge Plan envisaged a comprehensive 'scheme of social insurance against interruption and destruction of earning power' combined with a 'general system of children's allowances, sufficient to meet the subsistence needs' of children. Family allowances (for all children but the first) and contributory national insurance benefits (such as unemployment and widows' benefits) were introduced after the war. The Beveridge Plan also included the safety-net of a means-tested national assistance scheme designed to protect the minority who fell through the meshes of the insurance scheme. It was intended that this safety-net would wither away until it was catering for only a tiny minority. Instead, because of the failure to pay adequate national insurance benefits, as recommended by Beveridge, the numbers claiming means-tested assistance (renamed supplementary benefit in 1966) trebled from one to three million between 1948 and 1978. Further, governments have attempted to bolster up inadequate income maintenance provisions for both those in and out of work through the introduction of a range of means-tested benefits, which have been much criticised. A classic example was the introduction, in 1971, of Family Income Supplement for poor working families, as an alternative to fulfilling an election pledge to increase family allowances. The failure to pay high enough national insurance benefits and family allowances was one reason for the growing dependence on means-tested benefits. The other was the exclusion from the Beveridge Plan of people such as the congenitally disabled who could not meet the contribution conditions attached to the insurance benefits. During the 1970s a number of non-contributory benefits were, therefore, introduced to help the disabled and those at home to care for disabled relatives.

The overall picture today is, thus, one of a confusing patchwork of contributory, non-contributory and means-tested benefits. Much of this patchwork has grown up in isolation from the other main element in our income maintenance provisions: the tax system. . . . The system of personal tax allowances was supposed to ensure that 'there should be no income tax levied upon any income which is insufficient to provide the owner with what he requires for subsistence' (Royal Commission on the Taxation of Profits and Income, 1954). I use the past tense advisedly for the personal tax allowances patently no longer perform this function. The value of the tax allowances has been so eroded since the war that people can now start to pay tax at incomes which are below the poverty line. . . . When you take the growing dependence on means-tested benefits and add to it the growing numbers of low income working families drawn into the tax net, the result is one of the more ludicrous aspects of the income maintenance scheme: 'the poverty trap'. The 'poverty trap' is a term 'used to describe the situation in which a family loses more in terms of extra tax paid and reduced benefits received than it gains from a pay increase which brought them about' (Pond, 1978). It is families with children who are most vulnerable to the poverty trap.

The most recent development in income maintenance provision for families has been the introduction of the child benefit scheme. This represented the fusion of two hitherto separate strands of financial support for children: family allowances and child tax allowances.

One particularly large group for whom the 'safety net' is a way of life are one-parent families, other than those headed by widows (for whom national insurance benefits are provided) or by men (most of whom manage to remain in employment). Sir William Beveridge's *Report on Social Insurance and Allied Services* (1942) had this to say of the divorced and separated:

347. End of marriage otherwise than by widowhood
Divorce, legal separation, desertion and voluntary separation may cause needs similar to those caused by widowhood. They differ from widowhood in two respects: that they may occur through the fault or with the consent of the wife, and that except where they occur through the fault of the wife they leave the husband's liability for maintenance unchanged. If they are regarded from the point of view of the husband, they may not appear to be insurable risks; a man cannot insure against events which occur only through his fault or with his consent, and if they occur through the fault or with the consent of the wife she should not have a claim to benefit. But from the point of view of the woman, loss of her maintenance as housewife without her consent and not through her fault is one of the risks of marriage against which she should be insured; she should not depend on assistance. Recognition of housewives as a distinct insurance class, performing necessary service not for pay, implies that, if the marriage ends otherwise than by widowhood, she is entitled to the same provision as for widowhood, unless the marriage maintenance has ended through her fault or voluntary action without just cause. That is to say, subject to the practical considerations mentioned in the note below she should get temporary separation benefit (on the same lines as widow's benefit), and guardian or training benefit where appropriate.

NOTE.—The principle that a married woman who without fault of her own loses the maintenance to which she is entitled from her husband should get benefit is clear. It is obvious, however, that except where the maintenance has ended through divorce or other form of legal separation establishing that the default is not that of the wife, considerable practical difficulties may arise in determining whether a claim to benefit, as distinct from assistance, has arisen. There will often be difficulty in determining responsibility for the break-up of the marriage. There will in cases of desertion be difficulty in establishing the fact or the permanence of desertion. There will in all cases be the problem of alternative remedies open to the wife. The point to which the principle of compensating a housewife for the loss of her maintenance otherwise than by widowhood can be carried in practice calls for further examination. It may for practical reasons be found necessary to limit the widow's insurance benefit to cases of formal separation, while making it clear that she can in all cases at need get assistance and that the Ministry of Social Security will then proceed against the husband for recoupment of its expenditure.

The proposal was not adopted. A major reason why the idea did not meet with approval may lie in the need to reconcile the collective security involved in an insurance scheme with the concept of individual responsibility. In a welfare state, the moral virtue of contributing to a scheme which will provide relief against, for example, sickness and unemployment — both your own and your neighbours — is, one hopes, self-evident. Contributing to a scheme which provides relief for the wives in other people's broken marriages, however, is not so easy to justify. Another problem, even assuming that the philosophical difficulty could be overcome, would be the difficulties inherent in asking civil servants to allocate blame for a marriage breakdown.

Questions

(i) The Beveridge proposal was not confined to cases where separated women were faced with the task of bringing up children on their own: was this a defect?
(ii) Why did Beveridge limit his proposal to women who were not at fault?

In contrast with Beveridge, the Finer Report was concerned to alleviate the monetary hardship of *all* one-parent *families*. The numbers and different types of such families in Great Britain in 1971 and 1979 are shown by the following diagrams (published by the National Council for One-Parent Families):

Number of one-parent families by marital status, in Great Britain

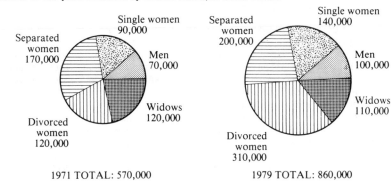

1971 TOTAL: 570,000   1979 TOTAL: 860,000

Source: Office of Population Censuses and Surveys

In a written answer to the House of Commons (29 June 1982), the Minister concerned disclosed the provisional estimates based on the 1981 census figures of the percentage of families with dependent children aged under 25 which were one-parent families. For *England*, this figure was 14% as a proportion of all households with dependent children, and 5% as a proportion of all households. The National Council for One-Parent Families' information sheet on *Key Facts and Figures* (1983) summarises their financial circumstances in this way:

Income and spending
In 1980, the average disposable income of a one-parent family was £76.08 a week (£82.56 gross). For a comparable two-parent family it was £146.52 (£179.28 gross). The average expenditure of a one-parent family was £79.59 a week and of a comparable two-parent family £33.77.

Supplementary Benefit

One-parent families make up 49.6% of families with children on Supplementary Benefit. There were 392,000 lone parents with 660,000 children on Benefit in December 1981. Of these 374,000 were women and 18,000 were men. Among the women 124,000 were divorced, 122,000 were separated wives, 116,000 were single, 8,000 were widowed and 4,000 were prisoners' wives. The average payment to one-parent families was £43.57 a week, of which £15.71 was for housing costs.

One Parent Benefit

In December 1981, 471,000 one-parent families were receiving One Parent Benefit (formerly Child Benefit Increase), the addition to Child Benefit. But about 158,000 did not gain by claiming because they received Supplementary Benefit from which One Parent Benefit is deducted. The take-up among those who would gain remains low at 60%. About 140,000 parents who would have gained by claiming One Parent Benefit were not claiming it.

Family Income Supplement

44% of families on Family Income Supplement (FIS) are one-parent families. At the end of September 1982, 70,000 lone parents were receiving FIS and their average payment was £10.70 a week.

There were 88,000 two-parent families receiving FIS, and their average payment was £8.80.

Poverty trap

In July 1981, a working single mother with two children aged 4 and 6 and earning £50 a week would have had a net weekly spending power of £50.90 after tax and taking account of all relevant benefits. A pay increase of £24 would leave her *worse off* by £3.96 a week as she would have to pay extra tax and would become ineligible for some benefits.

Employment

In 1977–79, 22% of lone mothers worked full-time and 24% part-time compared with 15% and 37% respectively for married women. Around 80% of lone fathers rely on earnings as their main source of income.

Thus a substantial proportion of one-parent families are living at the officially defined subsistence level, and as Ruth Lister (1982) points out:

> There is a growing body of evidence which shows that the supplementary benefit scale rates fail to provide a 'defence against poverty' as defined by the SBC. This is particularly the case with respect to the children's scale rates. Research done in other countries suggests that they seriously underestimate the costs of children relative to adults (Lister, 1977, 1979). More recently, a study of the costs of children by David Piachaud (1979) concluded that 'the supplementary benefit scale rates for children need to be increased by about one half if they are to provide genuinely for even the minimum requirements for a child'. Given that these scale rates are used as a benchmark against which to measure the extent of poverty in the population as a whole, the implication is that official figures could be seriously underestimating the extent of child poverty in this country.

Question

Do you consider that the state has a responsibility to ensure that children do not spend most of their childhood living at the officially-defined subsistence level? If you do, do you consider that the child with only one parent is deserving of greater help than, for example, the child of a two-parent family where the bread-winner is unemployed for a long period?

The Finer Committee looked for an alternative benefit to resolve the lone parent's problems, and opted for a 'guaranteed maintenance allowance' (GMA). There were, for the committee, six 'ideal' requirements or principles upon which such a benefit should be based. These are summarised and discussed by John Eekelaar in *Public Law and Private Rights: The Finer Proposals* (1976):

The six principles
(i) GMA should be 'a replacement, so far as the recipient is concerned, for maintenance payments, so that lone mothers should be freed from the worry and distress which the inadequacy and uncertainty of these payments now produce.'

It follows from this principle that the benefit becomes payable without regard as to whether the mother seeks or obtains a maintenance order on her own account. Her support becomes entirely a matter of public law. The administering authority is, in its turn, free to recoup what it may from the liable relative, but that, too, is a matter of public law. The rights between the adults are irrelevant because the benefit is for the child, for whom the liable relative retains liability irrespective of the equities between the parents. Hence the Report recommends that the authority administering GMA should be able to make an 'administrative order,' immediately binding on the liable relative, based on disclosed principles of assessment. . . .

Yet although the Committee sought to achieve 'a rational relationship between State support for one-parent families and the private obligation to maintain' it is precisely concerning this relationship where the Report is at its weakest. If the right of the administering authority against the liable relative is a right of the public deriving from its support for the parties' children, the authority must surely be entitled to ascertain the relevant information about the liable relative from the recipient. Yet all the Report says is that the mother would be 'asked' to give information initially to enable the authority to identify and communicate with the liable relative. There is certainly no reason to suppose the information will be readily forthcoming, especially in the case of unmarried mothers. Yet the Report says nothing about what should happen if the mother refuses to disclose the father's identity. It may even be that the Committee contemplated that the whole recoupment process should depend on the voluntary co-operation of the recipient, for they say, in connection with a similar proposal for recoupment by the SBC of supplementary benefit, that the SBC should be enabled to make its 'administrative order' against the liable relative 'if the lone mother wishes it.' . . .

But this is not all. Impressed by the prospective efficiency of the 'administrative order' system, the Committee recommends that the authority administering GMA should be free to assess the liable relative to pay an amount exceeding the sums which it is paying the recipient by way of GMA. No longer would the authority be acting as a public agency recouping payments from public funds, but it would be an agent of the recipient, enforcing her private rights against the liable relative. It is not clear whether the recipient must expressly authorise this. The Committee recognises that, to the extent by which the assessment is in excess of the GMA payments, the liable relative should be entitled to raise any defences (*e.g.* conduct) he may have against the other party. But as the administering authority's assessment would become immediately binding (like a tax assessment), the onus would clearly lie with the liable relative to contest the matter in court. The harnessing of bureaucratic power on the side of one party in a dispute over private rights could be severely oppressive to the liable relative.

(ii) GMA should be 'large enough to offer the lone parent a genuine choice about whether or not to work'; and

(iii) 'designed to provide effective help for those with part-time or low full-time earnings.'

The case for a special benefit for one-parent families rests on two propositions. One is that these families suffer special deprivation. The other is that they have special needs. Both propositions are amply supported by the Report. The main source of income for 40% of all fatherless families is supplementary benefit. Nearly one-half receive it for periods exceeding two years. Those not in receipt of supplementary benefit are characterised by an exceedingly low level of general earnings due, largely, to the low earnings of lone mothers. Yet 'the expenses of running a home do not change greatly because there is one adult less'. Household costs (fuel, rates, rent) remain the same. If the parent works, there is less time to economise and greater dependence on prepared foods. Child-minding may add to the expense. It is therefore concluded that GMA should be above supplementary benefit level. But the Report goes further in accepting the principle that it should be sufficient to provide a genuine choice whether or not to work. '. . . a woman should not be obliged by financial pressures to go out to work when she feels it is in the best interests of her children for her to be at home.' At the same time, lone mothers who wish to work should not be discouraged from doing so. One of the Committee's major criticisms of the supplementary benefits scheme is that the earnings disregards are so low that this discourages part-time working. As for full-time employment (when supplementary benefit ceases to be available), the earnings of women are so low that they will often be better off on supplementary benefit.

To meet these points, GMA, though structured like supplementary benefit, is pitched higher. . . .

The benefit departs radically from supplementary benefit, however, by being payable whether or not the recipient is in full-time work. So as not to discourage employment, the 'adult' portion of GMA would only cease to be payable when the recipient earnings reached about the level of average *male* earnings. After an initial disregard, GMA would taper off until the earnings reached that level. But the 'child' additions would remain payable. The principle upon which these recommendations is based is surely sound. That the community should regard the mother's basic needs while caring for her child as the child's needs is surely right . . .

(iv) GMA should be 'of universal application; that is, it should be available to all kinds of one-parent families, without discrimination, since all are at a disadvantage.'

This principle is a logical corollary of seeing the benefit as a benefit for the child. It would be available equally to widows as to unmarried mothers, though in the case of the former their national insurance benefits would be taken into account in assessing their income . . .

(v) GMA should be 'simple to claim, avoiding face to face interviews, searching inquiries and constant reporting of changes.'

This principle seeks to meet the constant stream of criticism levelled against the supplementary benefits administration where, it is alleged, claims are often made in humiliating conditions, there is constant prying into claimants' affairs . . .

(vi) GMA should be 'equitable, in the sense that it should not tip the scales too far in favour of one-parent families as compared with low income two-parent families.' . . .

The Committee's sixth principle holds good, not as an inducement for parties to remain married, but because the justification for the benefit is (i) that the recipient unit is a one-parent family and (ii) such units suffer special deprivation. If the unit suffers no such deprivation, justification for payment ceases. For this reason the benefit is means-tested. For the same reason the cohabitation rule must apply. The reason for the rule is not the enforcement of 'conventional' morality, nor the expectation that the cohabiting man must support his mistress's children. It is that, insofar as the fact of cohabitation has made more funds available for the mother, she must look to those funds and no longer to the public for support during child-care.

The ten main features of the proposed benefit are summarised in the *Finer Report*:

(1) The allowance would normally, in the hands of the lone parent, be a substitute for maintenance payments; maintenance payments would be assessed and collected by the authority administering the allowance; they would be offset against the allowance paid and any excess paid to the mother; the need for lone mothers to go to court to sue for maintenance awards would be largely eliminated;

(2) the level of the benefit would be fixed in relation to supplementary benefit payments, and, like them, would be reviewed regularly, so that, taken in conjunction with whatever family support was generally available (family allowances or tax credits) it would normally be sufficient to bring one-parent families off supplementary benefit even if they had no earnings;

(3) all one-parent families would be eligible for the benefit, including motherless families;

(4) the benefit would be non-contributory;

(5) the benefit would consist of a child-care allowance for the adult and a separate allowance for each child;

(6) the benefit would not be adjusted to the particular needs of individual families, except in so far as it would reflect the size of the family;

(7) for lone parents who are working or have other income the benefit would be tapered, after an initial disregard, so that it fell by considerably less than the amount by which income increased;

(8) the adult benefit would be extinguished by the time income reached about the level of average male earnings, but the child benefit would continue to be payable to all lone parents, whatever their income;

(9) once awarded, benefit would be fixed at that level for three months at a time, without in the normal way being affected by changes in circumstances. There would thus normally be no need for changes, including the beginning of a cohabitation, to be reported, until a fresh claim to benefit was made. Taken in conjunction with subparagraph (6) above this should much reduce the need for detailed enquiries;

(10) the benefit would be administered by post, on the lines of the family income supplements scheme.

Questions

(i) The Finer proposals have not been adopted: besides the obvious economic reasons, why do you think the Conservative and the Labour parties, for their differing reasons, have both been slow to support the scheme?

(ii) Do you think that public opinion in the 1980s would object to a *contributory* scheme for one-parent families?

It is noteworthy that only a very small proportion of one-parent families headed by widows are obliged to rely upon supplementary benefit. This is because widowed mothers are entitled to a widowed mother's allowance if the deceased husband has paid the necessary contributions (and the contribution conditions are not very severe). The parent is entitled to a flat-rate benefit and an addition for each child. There is no reduction for earnings, or indeed for any other income, such as a pension from her deceased husband's occupational pension scheme, or from life insurance.

Question

Are there any arguments against extending this benefit to include unmarried, divorced and separated mothers? Or separated fathers?

A scheme along these lines was presented to the Finer Committee by the National Council for the Unmarried Mother and her Child (which has since become the National Council for One-Parent Families). The *Finer Report* describes the scheme, referred to as CHAID, thus:

5.81 The CHAID scheme consists of two parts: a national insurance benefit and a discretionary scheme. In their evidence the NCUMC said, 'Under the national insurance part of our scheme, we recommend the introduction of a Children's Aid Allowance, made up of two elements — Child's Allowance and a Child Care Allowance. . . . The benefits we propose should be payable in respect of all children residing in a family with only one parent, with the exception of children living with widowed mothers who obtain more generous benefits under the existing provisions for widows.' The allowance would be set at the same level as short-term national insurance benefits. In terms of the rates current in October 1973, this would be £2.30 for the first child, £1.40 for the second child and £1.30 for the third and subsequent children, with a child care allowance of £7.35. These allowances would be taxable.

5.82 The NCUMC place great stress on the importance of an insurance-based benefit: 'We have attached the CHAID allowances to the insurance principle, because we believe they must be available as of right; this means there must be some contribution element.' Their recommendation is that national insurance provision should be extended to ensure maintenance of all children in one-parent families. 'This does not mean the "insurance" of a marriage or coverage for mothers. The benefits that we recommend would be wholly *for* the child and for the child's care. It is possible to extend the insurance principle to the child because the child cannot contribute to his status as the child of a one-parent family. It is desirable to extend the insurance principle to this group because the number of children concerned is now quite significant. In the early twentieth century the death of one or other parent was a major cause of child deprivation and was recognised as an insurable risk; now it is the separation or divorce of his parents which puts the child at risk and a refusal to recognise this fact in the social security provisions is to deny the social changes which have occurred in marriage and the status of women.' The contribution conditions under which CHAID would be paid could be satisfied on the contribution record of either the mother or the father, or, if necessary, both. The qualifying period of payment of contributions should be as short as possible, and contributions paid by a woman before marriage should count even after a lapse of years.

5.83 Like widowed mother's allowance, national insurance CHAID would be free of any earnings rule: the NCUMC see as one of the most important factors in CHAID that it would supplement the earnings of lone mothers and thus enable those who wished to work and support themselves without recourse to supplementary benefit to do so. CHAID would also follow widowed mother's allowance in that it would cease on remarriage or cohabitation.

5.84 The NCUMC recognise that a benefit awarded on the basis of contributions as set out in paragraph 5.82 above would not be available for all one-parent families: there would be bound to be some, and in particular the very young, who could not satisfy contribution conditions, however limited these might be. They therefore propose that, in addition to the national insurance CHAID, a CHAID allowance should be introduced and administered by the Supplementary Benefits Commission for children of lone mothers on the following grounds:

    (1) in the case of unmarried mothers, that the mother was less than 17 years and 9 months of age when the child was born; or

    (2) that a mother who had not qualified for the national insurance CHAID should be able to transfer from present supplementary benefit payments to supplementary benefit CHAID if she wished to enter regular employment and the wage which she could earn in such employment was less than the national average wage.

A mother who paid the necessary national insurance contributions by taking up employment after being awarded supplementary benefit CHAID would have the right to transfer to national insurance CHAID. The amount of allowance paid would be the same but one would be of right whereas the other would have a discretionary element.

5.85 The NCUMC state as a cardinal principle that 'the position of the family within our society should not be undermined and fathers should continue to be responsible for maintaining their wives and children.' They describe the basis on which contributions from fathers should be assessed as follows: 'These contributions should be intended to cover about 80% of the cash payments made for the child's maintenance. . . . His contributions should, however, be on a scale approved by Parliament, which would take fully into account his income and other family responsibilities. The family with which the father is living should receive priority. This would mean that relatively few fathers would be paying the full amount. . . .' The contributions would be collected by the State and the NCUMC suggest that it might be possible to collect them through the PAYE system by taking away child allowances and earned income relief from the father. They estimate that some 30% of the total cost of the scheme might be recovered from fathers.

5.86 Mothers would retain their present rights to go to court and sue for maintenance, but courts would have regard to the national scheme in deciding on any extra financial provision needed. The NCUMC estimate that men with incomes up to one and one third times national average earnings would have their maintenance payments covered by the CHAID scheme. Only men with higher incomes than this would be likely to have orders for additional payments made against them by courts.

The National Council for One-Parent Families is still advocating a similar scheme, as Paul Lewis explains (1979): 'A non-means tested, non-contributory social security benefit at the rate of widowed mothers' allowance would lift over 95% of one-parent families off supplementary benefit and restore to all one-parent families the freedom to work and the dignity and status of an independent income . . . it would cut family poverty in half.'

Question

If you consider that *something* should be done to improve the financial lot of the one-parent family, which of the following would you recommend:

    (*a*) go back to the Beveridge proposal;

    (*b*) press for the introduction of GMA;

    (*c*) introduce CHAID, at least for the divorced and separated mothers; or

    (*d*) persuade the Secretary of State to pursue 'liable relatives' more strenuously?

It may help in answering the question above to consider the figures given by the Secretary of State for Social Services in a written answer in the House of Commons on 10 May 1982. Mr Howell MP asked for information showing the net weekly spending power of lone parents in and out of work, and working part-time. Before giving the statistical information requested, the Secretary of State made a number of observations on the hypothetical circumstances the Member of Parliament had chosen.

One of the assumptions he asked to be made was that work expenses were £15 a week. This is very high compared with the Department's assumption of work expenses of £4.40 a week, which represents the average cost of fares to work to heads of households using public transport.

Tables 1 and 2 show the net weekly spending power, with ordinary and long-term supplementary benefit rates respectively, at the levels of part-time earnings specified by my hon. Friend. Supplementary benefit would be payable only if the lone parent were working fewer than 30 hours a week.

Tables 3 and 4 show the full-time earnings required to give the same net weekly spending power. In these examples, family income supplement (FIS) could be awarded only if the lone parent were working at least 24 hours a week.

In all the tables it is assumed that the family has no capital or income except as shown.

Table 1
Net weekly spending power (£) of a lone parent with two children aged 4 and 6; receiving supplementary allowance (ordinary rate) at various levels of earnings

Supplementary allowance	Child benefit	Net earnings	Rent	Rates	Free school meals	Free welfare milk	Net weekly spending power
43.45	13.80	4.00	12.10	4.45	2.25	1.30	48.25
42.45	13.80	6.00	12.10	4.45	2.25	1.30	49.25
41.45	13.80	8.00	12.10	4.45	2.25	1.30	50.25
40.45	13.80	10.00	12.10	4.45	2.25	1.30	51.25
39.45	13.80	12.00	12.10	4.45	2.25	1.30	52.25
38.45	13.80	14.00	12.10	4.45	2.25	1.30	53.25
37.45	13.80	16.00	12.10	4.45	2.25	1.30	54.25
35.45	13.80	20.00	12.10	4.45	2.25	1.30	56.25
30.45	13.80	25.00	12.10	4.45	2.25	1.30	56.25

Table 2
Net weekly spending power (£) of a lone parent with two children aged 4 and 6; receiving supplementary allowance (long-term rate) at various levels of earnings

Supplementary allowance	Child benefit	Net earnings	Rent	Rates	Free school meals	Free welfare milk	Net weekly spending power
49.80	13.80	4.00	12.10	4.45	2.25	1.30	54.60
48.80	13.80	6.00	12.10	4.45	2.25	1.30	55.60
47.80	13.80	8.00	12.10	4.45	2.25	1.30	56.60
46.80	13.80	10.00	12.10	4.45	2.25	1.30	57.60
45.80	13.80	12.00	12.10	4.45	2.25	1.30	58.60
44.80	13.80	14.00	12.10	4.45	2.25	1.30	59.60
43.80	13.80	16.00	12.10	4.45	2.25	1.30	60.60
41.80	13.80	20.00	12.10	4.45	2.25	1.30	62.60
36.80	13.80	25.00	12.10	4.45	2.25	1.30	62.60

Note on tables 1 and 2
The supplementary allowance figures shown are the amounts by which the family's income falls short of their requirements. In these examples, it is calculated by adding together the appropriate scale rates, the heating addition for a child under 5 and the sum of the rent and rates payable; from this total is deducted child benefit and net earnings after allowing the appropriate disregard.

Table 3: Gross earnings needed to provide net weekly spending power equivalent to that available with supplementary allowance at ordinary rate, as in table 1

Gross earnings	Tax	National insurance contribu- tion	Child benefit	Family income supple- ment	Rent rebate	Rates rebate	Fares	Free school meals	Free welfare milk	Net weekly spending power
£	£	£	£	£	£	£	£	£	£	£
28.08	—	2.18	13.80	20.00	12.10	4.45	15.00	2.25	1.30	48.25*
29.16	—	2.26	13.80	20.00	12.10	4.45	15.00	2.25	1.30	49.25*
30.24	—	2.34	13.80	20.00	12.10	4.45	15.00	2.25	1.30	50.25*
31.33	—	2.43	13.80	20.00	12.10	4.45	15.00	2.25	1.30	51.25*
32.41	—	2.51	13.80	20.00	12.10	4.45	15.00	2.25	1.30	52.25*
33.50	—	2.60	13.80	20.00	12.10	4.45	15.00	2.25	1.30	53.25*
34.58	—	2.68	13.80	20.00	12.10	4.45	15.00	2.25	1.30	54.25*
36.87	—	2.86	13.80	20.00	12.10	4.34	15.00	2.25	1.30	56.25*
36.87	—	2.86	13.80	20.00	12.10	4.34	15.00	2.25	1.30	56.25*

* If working fewer than 30 hours a week could qualify for a supplementary allowance.

Table 4: Gross earnings needed to provide net weekly spending power equivalent to that available with supplementary allowance at long-term rate, as in table 2

Gross earnings	Tax	National insurance contribu- tion	Child benefit	Family income supple- ment	Rent rebate	Rates rebate	Fares	Free school meals	Free welfare milk	Net weekly spend- ing power
£	£	£	£	£	£	£	£	£	£	£
34.96	—	2.71	13.80	20.00	12.10	4.45	15.00	2.25	1.30	54.60
36.10	—	2.80	13.80	20.00	12.10	4.40	15.00	2.25	1.30	55.60
37.28	—	2.89	13.80	20.00	12.10	4.31	15.00	2.25	1.30	56.60
38.49	—	2.98	13.80	20.00	12.08	4.21	15.00	2.25	1.30	57.60
40.17	—	3.11	13.80	20.00	11.66	4.08	15.00	2.25	1.30	58.60
88.97	14.32	6.90	13.80	—	5.35	2.00	15.00	*2.25	—	59.60
91.48	15.07	7.09	13.80	—	4.93	1.85	15.00	*2.25	—	60.60
96.58	16.60	7.48	13.80	—	4.06	1.54	15.00	*2.25	—	62.60
96.58	16.60	7.48	13.80	—	4.06	1.54	15.00	*2.25	—	62.60

* Mandatory provision of free school meals ceases when title to FIS ceases, but local education authorities have discretion to allow free or cheap meals to other children and this table illustrates the case where an authority continues to apply the November 1979 conditions for entitlement.

Questions

(i) If child benefit (including the extra one-parent benefit for the first child) were to be increased to an amount which was broadly within the proposed guide-lines for the child element of G.M.A., would some of the financial problems of the lone parent be solved? As a guide, you might take the level of child support provided for long-term national insurance beneficiaries, which on 1981/82 figures was £12.95 for each dependent child; but remember that child benefit is taken into account in full in calculating entitlement to means-tested benefits — both supplementary benefit for those who are not in 'full-time' work and family income supplement for those who are.

(ii) Do you think that Mr Howell meant 'fares' when he asked the Government to assume that work expenses were £15 per week?

(iii) Does it cost a lone parent more to go out to work than it does the 'bread-winner' in a two-parent family?

(iv) Why does not the supplementary benefits scheme do as both the family income supplements scheme and the tax threshholds do, and treat a one-parent family the same as a two-parent one?

3 Support for two-parent families

Any discussion of one-parent families must take account of the financial resources of two-parent families. The following two tables were supplied in written answers on 20 July 1982 and 7 April 1982 respectively:

Table 1: Families not receiving Supplementary Benefit Great Britain 1979 Average

Employment category	Below supplementary benefit level		Above supplementary benefit level but within 10 per cent of it		Above supplementary benefit level but within 20 per cent of it		Above supplementary benefit level but within 40 per cent of it		Total below supplementary benefit and above supplementary benefit level but within 90 per cent of it (Thousand)	
Families with	Families	Children	Families	Children	Families	Children	Families	Children	Families	Children
In full time work or self-employed										
One parent	[*]	[*]	[*]	[10]	[*]	[10]	[10]	[10]	[10]	[10]
Two parents	90	180	[40]	[100]	120	320	390	960	480	1,140
One and two parents	90	180	[50]	[110]	130	330	400	970	490	1,150
Sick or disabled for more than three months										
One and two parents	[*]	[*]	[10]	[10]	[20]	[40]	[40]	[90]	[40]	[90]
Unemployed for more than three months										
One and two parents	[10]	[30]	[10]	[20]	[20]	[30]	[30]	[40]	[40]	[70]
Others										
One parent	[†]	[†]	[†]	[†]	[†]	[†]	[†]	[†]	90	[50]
Two parents	[†]	[†]	[†]	[+]	[†]	[†]	[†]	[†]	[20]	[20]
One and two parents	[50]	[70]	[10]	[10]	[10]	[30]	[50]	[100]	100	170
Total numbers of families and children										
One parent	[40]	[60]	[10]	[20]	[20]	[60]	70	130	110	190
Two parents	110	220	60	130	150	370	450	1,070	570	1,290
One and two parents	160	290	70	150	180	430	520	1,190	680	1,480

Notes:

* Indicates that the number in the group is below 10,000;

† Indicates that the sample is too small for a reliable estimate to be made.

The figures shown in square brackets are subject to very considerable proportionate statistical error.

Table 2: Families receiving Supplementary Benefit
Great Britain — 1979 average

Thousands

Employment category	One-parent families		Two-parent families		One and two-parent families	
	Families	Children	Families	Children	Families	Children
Sick or disabled for more than three months	[*]	[*]	[10]	[20]	[10]	[20]
Unemployed for more than three months	[*]	[10]	110	280	120	280
Others	310	570	[*]	[10]	320	580
Totals	320	580	130	310	450	880

Notes:
* indicates that the number in the group is below 10,000.
The figures shown in square brackets are subject to very considerable proportionate statistical error.

During the last decade there has been an attempt to allocate resources towards families with children. From 1945, there was in existence a system of family allowances. The philosophy behind this scheme was that the State should not meet the whole cost of the needs of children. The amount of the allowance therefore was based on the estimates of the cost of meeting physical needs only, for example, for food, clothing and housing. There was no notional account taken of items such as toys or books.

In particular, allowances were not payable for the first child of the family. Family allowances were subject to a tax 'claw-back'. But, under a child tax allowance scheme, tax payers could obtain exemption from a certain amount of their income from taxation for each dependent child. Tax allowances of course only benefited those subject to tax, and would hardly be of any value to those categories of persons who fall within or close to the poverty trap. Child benefit was phased in as from 1977, and provides a merger of CTA and family allowances. Child benefit is an universal, non-means tested and tax-free cash benefit for all children. The benefit was seen by politicians from all parties as a way 'to put cash into the hands of mothers and to give a measure of independence to mothers' (Patrick Jenkin MP on 9 February 1977, in a debate on the Child Benefit Scheme in the House of Commons). In the same debate the then Minister, Mr Stan Orme MP said:

Child Benefit is non-means tested and non-taxable. The scheme has two big advantages over the present method of family support which relies on child tax allowances and family allowances. The child benefit will be paid to the mother, as it is typically the mother who is responsible for the house keeping in raising the children. This contrasts with the child tax allowances, which typically go to the father. Thus, income is transferred within the family from father to mother. Wage earners who earn under the tax threshold do not get the benefit of the child tax allowances, but they will get the child benefit.

However, another MP present during this debate, Mr John Ovenden MP said:

Successive Governments have a pretty shameful record of support for families. They have an even worse record if we attempt to make international comparisons. There are few European and non-European countries with which we stand any comparison in this league. That is why it is important to talk about the whole level of family support and why we should commit ourselves to policies aimed at relieving the problem of family poverty.

His point is made very clear by the following table:

Child support in the EEC
(Monthly rates in £ at October 1, 1976)

Position of child in family

	1st	2nd	3rd	4th	5th & subsequent
Belgium	20.62	37.72	44.81	45.70	46.03
Denmark	14.06	14.06	14.06	14.06	14.06
France	—	18.48	31.07	31.07	27.71
Germany	12.16	17.02	29.18	29.18	29.18
Irish Republic	2.30	3.60	4.35	4.35	4.35
Italy	7.02	7.02	7.02	7.02	7.02
Luxembourg	15.74	15.74	42.54	42.54	42.54
Netherlands	12.80	22.88	22.88	30.52	30.52
U.K.	4.66	6.50	6.50	6.50	6.50

Source: Hansard, 28th February, 1977

Family benefits in cash as a percentage of average industrial earnings 1974

Number of children

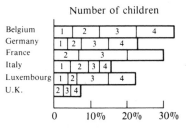

Percentage of average industrial earnings

Excluding FIS in U.K. and Allocation de Salaire Unique in France.

Very little has changed. In May 1982, the Secretary of State admitted in the House of Commons that there are about 1.5 million children in families whose income is below the tax threshold (there are about 10.4 million in families whose income is subject to tax at the basic rate). Family Income Supplement was introduced in 1970 to provide some assistance for families with children where the wage earner was on a low salary. The wage earner must be working 30 hours a week if part of a two-parent family, and 24 hours if a single parent. The number of families with children who were receiving family income supplement (FIS) fell from about 89,000 in December 1977 to an average of about 77,000 in 1979. From 1979, there was a marked increase, and on 29 December 1981, the number of families on FIS had increased to 132,000. Extra resources were allocated to FIS in the November 1980 uprating, but only 10,000 new awards were attributable to the uprating. It is probable that the substantial increase in take-up is a result of more effective publicity. The details of calculating FIS are outside the scope of this book; in brief, the income of the family is set against prescribed limits — the family will then be entitled to half the difference between its income and the prescribed limit. These limits vary with the number of children, but not with the number of adults. Entitlement to FIS, like entitlement to supplementary benefit, acts as a passport to a range of other benefits — for example, free prescriptions, dental treatment and glasses, free welfare milk for children under school age and expectant mothers, and free school meals.

Question

Might FIS be a 'palliative'? Why do we not (*a*) introduce a national minimum wage, and/or (*b*) allow employer and employee to negotiate a true maket wage?

Part of the answer to that last question is indicated by Ruth Lister in *Income Maintenance for Families with Children* (1982) when putting the argument for family benefits:

A family with children requires a larger income than a single person or childless couple to achieve the same standard of living as the latter. The wages system cannot accommodate these differences in family needs and therefore it is seen as the role of the State to provide some support for those with children either through the tax or cash benefit systems or both. It is not, however, always a very popular role, for the attitude 'they choose to have them, they should pay for them' is not uncommon. (This view often goes hand in hand with the view that benefits for children encourage large families and that it is large families that cause poverty. There is no evidence to support the former view and the latter does not tally with the facts: although it is true that the risk of poverty is greater among large families, half the children living below the poverty line are in families with one or two children ('Hansard', 31 January 1980).)

The case for the community as a whole sharing responsibility for the financial support for children rests on two powerful arguments. The first was put by Sir John Walley (1972) in the following terms: 'A nation's compassion may be shown in its care for the disabled and those past work, but for evidence of its concern for its future (which also includes its capacity to exercise this compassion) we can only look at its care for children.' As Margaret Wynn has pointed out (1972), 'most of the time, trouble, and money expended on rearing the next generation falls on the shoulders of a minority of the present generation. Is there not a case therefore for the community as a whole helping to ease the burden slightly from the shoulders of that minority?'

The second argument stems from the fact that, although at any one point in time only a small minority of households are caring for children, many more households have the care of children at some point in their lives. Community financial support for children helps 'to reduce the difference between living standards at different stages of a person's life' (Report of the Committee on Family Policy, 1972) by redistributing resources to the childrearing years when help is needed most. This introduces the concept of the family life-cycle, to which I shall return later. There are also strong economic arguments for providing families with adequate financial support. The alternative for families with inadequate incomes can be the reception of a child into care, which costs the community considerably more money than decent child benefits. The same argument applies to adequate support for those caring for disabled and infirm relatives at home.

Later she considers some policy options:

As Melanie Phillips (1978) observed: 'Child Benefit will no doubt be seen as a watershed when the history of family policy comes to be written.' But there are a number of issues concerning child benefits which still need to be resolved and child benefits are not themselves the be all and end all of income maintenance for families with children. With regard to the child benefit scheme itself, the eventual level of the benefit still has to be settled. There appears to be a fairly wide consensus that the immediate goal should be to raise the benefit to the same level as the child additions paid with unemployment and sickness benefit. After that, some would argue that the benefit should eventually be high enough to subsume all the social security additions for children. Perhaps one of the most crucial requirements is that child benefit should be index-linked. In the absence of a statutory duty to uprate them annually, such as exists for national insurance benefits, there is a distinct danger that child benefits will repeat the history of the family allowance and end up virtually worthless.

Thought also needs to be given to whether the benefit should continue to be flat rate. For instance, should larger families get more help, as in some other European countries? Some countries also provide more help for older children to take account of their higher cost. Certainly it appears absurd to some people to pay the same for a one-year-old as a fifteen-year-old. Moreover cutbacks in the education budget, which have meant the withdrawal of free school meals from many children and the abolition of the duty to provide subsidised school meals suitable as the main meal of the day, have added to the costs of schoolchildren for parents. There is also the question of whether there should be special help for children who stay on at school after school-leaving age. At present, such help is only given at the discretion of local education authorities and is usually totally inadequate.

The only benefits for children that are age-related at present are the supplementary benefit scale rates. As I have already suggested, these are too low to meet even the minimum cost of maintaining children. There is a very strong case for a thorough-going review of the supplementary benefit scale rates which determine the living standards of over a million children. Even the Supplementary Benefits Commission has been forced to admit that the evidence collected by the DHSS 'strongly suggests that the supplementary benefits scheme provides, particularly for families with children, incomes that are barely adequate to meet their needs at a level that is consistent with normal participation in the life of the relatively wealthy society in which they live' (DHSS/SBC, 1977). Unfortunately, as the SBC (1979) points out elsewhere, because of a preoccupation with 'work incentives', 'until the incomes of low paid workers with children are improved there will be insurmountable political obstacles to securing better rates of benefit for families living on supplementary benefit. . . . Higher child benefits offer the best means of removing these obstacles.' This serves to underline again the importance of the child benefit scheme, even though improvements in child benefits do not directly help those on social security. (This is because an increase in child benefit is offset by a reduction in social security benefits.)

Preoccupation with the need to improve the child benefit scheme has helped to divert attention from the question of whether the community should provide more support for those with the care of children as well as meet the needs of the children themselves. One proposal that has emerged in recent years has been for a home responsibility payment. This proposal has taken various forms. Some have suggested that such a payment should be made only to those who stay at home to care for children or other dependants. The Meade Committee on the other hand recommended that a home responsibility payment should be paid regardless of whether the parent or carer stayed at home. As it would be taxable, it would in any case be of more value to a family where the person in receipt of it did not go out to work. A home responsibility payment could provide a mechanism for providing extra help for parents with pre-school children for it could either be confined to these parents or could be paid at a higher rate to them. It could also subsume the invalid care allowance, which currently is paid only to carers who stay at home to care for severely disabled people. Married women are denied entitlement on the grounds that 'they might be at home in any event' (Social Security Provision for Chronically Sick and Disabled People, 1974).

A home responsibility payment that was confined solely to those who stayed at home to care for dependants would create a number of practical problems including the creation of a severe 'poverty trap' when the carer wished to re-enter the labour market. More fundamentally, it raises the question of whether income maintenance policies should be designed to encourage the traditional division of family responsibilities or whether they should recognise the changes that have been taking place and facilitate them. In Sweden, one of the few countries with a coherent family policy, it has been one of the explicit aims of this policy to give men and women equal opportunities for combining gainful employment with the care of their children. Under a parental insurance scheme, parents are allowed nine months leave at 90% of normal earnings after the birth of a child. This leave can be divided up between the two parents. In Sweden and also Hungary, Norway, the DDR and the Federal Republic of Germany, parents are allowed paid leave to care for a sick child. Policies such as this are not even on the political agenda at present in Britain. Maternity provisions and help with the cost of maternity lag behind those in many other countries. Child care provision is also important in this context. As the EOC . . . has pointed out, 'It is clear that the shortage of adequate child care facilities prevents a considerable number of women from making a much-needed contribution to the household income.' A number of surveys have found that many mothers would return to work sooner if adequate child-care facilities were available.

Adequate child care facilities (for school age as well as pre-school children) are particularly crucial for one-parent families. . . .

The case for special help for lone parents is a strong one. But it is important also that lone parents are not treated as a group in isolation from other parents and other mothers in particular. Many of their problems are the problems that all parents face but writ large, and, as the Finer Report itself pointed out, advance for lone working mothers depends upon improving the position of all working mothers. Higher child benefit, improved child care facilities, a home responsibility benefit would benefit one-parent as well as two-parent families. In fact, a home responsibility benefit could provide the framework for a one-parent family benefit as it could be paid at a higher rate to one-parent than two-parent families.

Most would agree that the solution to the poverty trap for families with children would be to try somehow to increase child benefits. This increase would have to be paid for. One suggestion is to abolish the married man's tax allowance (discussed in Chapter 2) and to use the income saved to fund increases in child benefits. The *Equal Opportunities Commission's response to the Government's Green Paper on the Taxation of Husband and Wife* (1981) comments upon this proposal thus:

The Finer Report (1974) noted that 'until the eve of the second world war, all but a small proportion of women stopped work when they got married' (para 2.5); many women in the professions were debarred from paid employment upon marriage. In those circumstances the MMA had some social and economic justification. It is now conceded on all sides that the historical basis for the MMA has been almost completely eroded. If the basis of the MMA was that it enabled the male breadwinner to carry the burden of a dependent wife, the proper question in present day circumstances is: what is the legitimate and objective burden of dependency which affects the earning capacity and therefore the taxable capacity of individuals which should be recognised by the tax system? The largest class of dependants consists of children, although the burden of caring for other dependants, mainly elderly relatives, is also important as it falls mainly upon women.

In considering the possible deployment of the savings resulting from the abolition of the MMA the Commission has concentrated first on the consequences and implications of increasing child benefit. The Commission is not apprehensive, as is the Green Paper, of 'the major shift in the tax burden between different family units which would be produced by a system of mandatory independent taxation' (para 55). The Commission sees no justification for treating a family unit or individual with no dependants in exactly the same way as one with dependants to care for. The Commission recognises that the abolition of the MMA at a stroke might cause hardship for many married couples, and it has considered the possibility of phasing out the MMA over a period of, say, five years. This has the attraction of enabling those who would be affected by the measure to adjust gradually to the change. However, the main attraction of abolishing the MMA (apart from the considerations set out above) is that it enables the savings to the revenue to be deployed in increased child benefit, and the effect of phasing out the MMA gradually will inevitably be that the increase in child benefit will also have to be phased in gradually. This will undoubtedly cause administrative difficulties as well as increasing the uncertainty about the entitlement to child benefit during the phasing-in period. For these reasons the Commission on balance recommends the abolition rather than the phasing out of the MMA.

Question

Can you see any arguments against these proposals?

CHAPTER 17

Adjudication and conciliation

'Time and again,' observes Eekelaar at the end of his monograph on *Family Law and Social Policy* (1978), 'it has been evident that, in family law, legal procedures are as important as, or even more significant than, the law which is actually applied.' Like him, therefore, we propose to conclude with a discussion of the structure of the courts adjudicating in family matters, and then to broaden that discussion into the very nature of the courts' role, and that of other agencies of the State, in the resolution of conflict in the family.

1 Family courts past and present

At the beginning of Chapter 14 appears the story of one woman with a desperate problem who may also serve to illustrate our present subject. Married to a dangerous but plausible man who has already killed their first child, having now three children under school age, apparently herself inadequate to cope with the role of wife and mother, one night she leaves her home and pushes the baby for several miles in the pram in order to seek shelter with an aunt. In the true story, a social worker is called and the mother is persuaded to let him take the baby back to the father while the mother goes to stay with her own parents. But what might have happened had she gone to a solicitor instead? He would have had to advise her of all the legal procedures which might have been relevant to her case, and then seek her instructions as to which, if any, should be pursued (notes overleaf):

Remedy under:	Parties	Court(s)	Appeal
Child protection procedures			
CYPA 1933, s. 40	A v C	J	None
CYPA 1969, s. 28	A or P v C	J	None
CYPA 1969, s. 1	LA, P or NSPCC v C	JC	CrC
CCA 1980, ss. 2 and 3	LA v M and F	JC	FD
Wardship	A v M and F	HC	CA
Custody, etc. procedures			
Wardship	M v F	HC	CA
GMA 1971, s. 9	M v F	MC, CC or HC	FD, CA, CA
Domestic violence procedures			
DVMPA 1976, s. 1	W v H	CC	CA
DPMCA 1978, s. 16	W v H	MC	FD
Matrimonial home procedures			
MHA 1967, s. 1	W v H	CC	CA
DVMPA 1976, s. 4	W v H	CC	CA
MWPA 1882, s. 17	W v H	CC or HC	CA
Support procedures			
DPMCA 1978, ss. 1, 6 and 7	W v H	MC	FD
MCA 1973, s. 27	W v H	CC(D) or HC	CA
Divorce, judicial separation and ancillary relief			
MCA 1973, ss. 1 and 17	W v H	CC(D) or HC	CA

Note

The table omits those remedies in the ordinary law of tort or property which are available, for example, to solve problems of violence or the occupation and ownership of property, to all persons irrespective of family relationship.

Abbreviations

CYPA: Children and Young Persons Act
CCA: Child Care Act
GMA: Guardianship of Minors Act
DVMPA: Domestic Violence and Matrimonial Proceedings Act
DPMCA: Domestic Proceedings and Magistrates' Courts Act
MHA: Matrimonial Homes Act
MWPA: Married Women's Property Act
MCA: Matrimonial Causes Act

A: Anyone
C: Child
P: Police
LA: Local authority
M: Mother
F: Father
W: Wife
H: Husband

J: Single Justice
JC: Juvenile court
HC: High Court
MC: Magistrates' court
CC: County court
CC(D): Divorce county court
Cr C: Crown Court
FD: High Court, Family Divisional Court
CA: Court of Appeal

Question

What modifications and additions to the table would be required if the couple had not been married to one another?

The criticisms are most trenchantly put in a working paper on *The Family Court*, published by the Law Reform Commission of Canada in 1974:

Despair, confusion and frustration

The most distressing effect of the present state of affairs is the despair, confusion and frustration it causes to the participants. It should not be necessary nor even feasible to apply to one court for maintenance upon desertion, another for custody, a third for wardship or adoption, and yet another for divorce. As far as the general public is concerned there appears to be no reason why all legal matters arising from a matrimonial or family dispute should not be dealt with by a single court. Public expectations of a family court may far exceed the realistic potential of any court of law since there is no legal process which can solve all of the problems arising from marriage or family breakdown, but to circumvent the existing maze of jurisdictions seems a step in the right direction.

Overlapping jurisdiction

. . . 'Forum-shopping' can also develop from the existing situation. Certain parties may prefer a court bound by formal rules and procedures to an informal, conciliatory chamber. This may affect the outcome of hearings and lead to results that are not in the best interests of all parties. There have been instances where actions commenced in a family court have been barred by the opposing party taking the same issue to a higher court.

Cost

Present systems cause duplication of effort by judges, lawyers, witnesses, court administrators and the parties themselves and this naturally leads to increased costs. Consolidation of family law jurisdiction in a single court would reduce the cost of legal services to the individuals, although an effective system of family courts with access to support services would not necessarily reduce the financial cost to the state.

Inability of courts to deal with the total problem

By forcing parties to go to different courts in relation to different facets of a single problem, the process denies any one court the opportunity to view the problem as a whole. As a result no one person sees all the evidence, and remedies may be granted which are not the best.

We consider that family conflicts require special procedures, designed to help individuals to reconcile or settle their differences and where necessary to obtain assistance. Therefore, the resolution of family conflicts, particularly those involving children, require some modification of the traditional adversary process. To leave reconciliation and settlement of issues exclusively in the hands of the lawyers is inadequate.

Lack of respect for the courts and the law
A system of law that prevents parties from finding simple, dignified means of solving their problems within a reasonable time, often while they are under very great emotional strain, encourages distrust of the legal process as a means of solving family problems.

Although the concept of a 'family court' had become a commonplace elsewhere it did not gain currency in English public debate until the 1960s. *The Legal Background to the Family Court* was described thus by Neville Brown in 1966 (significantly, in the British Journal of Criminology):

The first programme of the newly-created Law Commissioners for England includes this item:
'An examination of the jurisdiction of the courts dealing with family matters (including wardship and guardianship); in particular as to how such jurisdiction should be allocated between the courts, and whether or not any new courts should be constituted to deal with such matters.'
In this article it is proposed to outline the legal background to current thinking about family courts, whether it be the truncated version suggested in the White Paper *The Child, the Family and the Young Offender* or the more ambitious species hinted at by the Law Commission. . . .

Use and Abuse of the Term 'Family Court'
Whether or not we like it, English society seems destined to develop on the American pattern, though with the time-lag of a decade or two. In the United States the case for family courts was being argued from the end of the First World War, and by the late 1940s several such courts had been brought into being in various States of the Union. For example, in Ohio the Family Court of Toledo was set up as long ago as 1925 and has since proved a fertile mother of similar courts both within that State and beyond. Another landmark was the study promoted by the New York Bar in 1954 and published as *Children and Families in the Courts of New York City*, in which the case for a family court was fully argued, and which led to implementing legislation in 1961. . . .

It is significant that the American family court grew out of the juvenile court. The first specialised court to handle juvenile delinquents was established in Chicago in 1899, and in the next few years the movement spread across the whole United States. The Americans had a short lead over the corresponding movement here initiated by our Children Act 1908. Roscoe Pound . . . has claimed the juvenile court as the most significant advance in the administration of justice since Magna Carta. Certainly, the juvenile court demonstrated how legal institutions, with the help of the social sciences, could successfully resolve social problems in an intelligent and constructive way; that is, that 'courts and the law may serve to help people in trouble, as well as to vindicate rights, redress wrongs and mete out punishment'. . . .

From juvenile court to family court is a natural transition for it is a commonplace that for successful treatment of the child in trouble it may be essential to work with the whole family and that delinquency, child neglect, and matrimonial difficulties may be simply different facets of a larger family problem. It is this concept of the family as a social unit that underlies the American family court. For, in the words of one of its most influential advocates: 'Treating the family situation as a series of single separate controversies may often not do justice to the whole or to the several separate parts. The several parts are likely to be distorted in considering them apart from the whole, and the whole may be left undetermined in a series of adjudications of the parts' (Pound, 1959).

In its 'classical' form, such as at Toledo, a family court indicates an integrated and unified jurisdiction in a single court with competence over all aspects of family stress. . . . It includes therefore: juvenile delinquency (hence family court absorbs juvenile court); divorce, nullity and separation (hence family court absorbs divorce court); guardianship and custody disputes; maintenance; matrimonial property disputes; domestic assaults; child neglect and cruelty; adoption; affiliation. Instead of jurisdiction over such matters being fragmented between several courts, it is consolidated in a single court, although there may need to be specialised divisions or sections within that one court. Such a family court is not only a children's court or a parents' court: it is also a court for husbands and wives. . . .

Nor is this a merely American phenomenon: family courts on the American pattern have spread to Canada and Japan and are currently attracting interest in the Federal German Republic. . . .

Having surveyed the jurisdictional tangle as it existed at that time, he continues:

The reasons for the present disarray are partly historical. At the time of the last great tidying up operation of our court structure — the Victorian Judicature Acts of 1873–1875 — neither the matrimonial nor the juvenile jurisdiction of the magistrates was in existence. Moreover, the county courts were still relative newcomers and concerned almost exclusively with small debt actions. The collectivist or welfare role of the county courts was to come later. For instance, the protection of employees dated from the Workmen's Compensation Act 1897; tenant protection began with the Rent Acts following the 1914–18 war; consumer protection stems from the Hire-Purchase Act 1938; and in child protection the extensive, although not exclusive, jurisdiction of the county courts under the guardianship and adoption statutes is subsequent to the Judicature Acts.

History is not the only explanation of the jurisdictional jungle. It is also the result of that empirical approach characteristic of the pragmatical English. . . .

He then puts forward a skeleton scheme for a unified family court, but asks, as we must still ask, whether it should be a court at all:

This proposal for a unified family court is built upon the premiss that the courts are the appropriate agency for settling legal problems, whether juvenile or matrimonial, that arise from the family under stress. But it may be asked (and has been in some quarters) 'Why *courts* at all?' or 'Why *only* courts?' Some fifteen years ago the case was urged by an eminent Queen's Counsel for substituting a simple procedure of registration for the rigmarole of the undefended divorce suit (Harvey, 1953) and more recently there have been suggestions for entrusting the delinquent child or one in need of care, protection or control into the hands of a 'Family Panel' (as the Kilbrandon Report (1964) termed its version of the Swedish 'Child Welfare Boards') or a 'Family Council' (as put forward in the White Paper), with powers, overt or disguised, for dealing with the child as they think fit.

The notion of shifting the resolution of family conflicts and disorder into social or administrative agencies has made little headway in the United States. There it has foundered upon the rock of the Constitution with its entrenched requirement of 'Due Process of Law.' Indeed, even the relaxed procedural safeguards in some American juvenile courts have aroused criticism that due process was being undermined. Witness such emotive titles to articles as 'Juveniles being denied basic rights'; 'Fairness to the juvenile offender'; 'Juvenile justice: due process or travesty?'

In this country we have no constitutional guarantee of due process in the sense of a right to a court adjudication on matters touching our life, liberty or property. On the other hand, there does exist an ingrained public conviction in favour of judicial process. As Dr Jackson (1964) puts it in the fourth edition of his classic, *The Machinery of Justice in England*: 'My own feeling is that it would be better to adopt a committee system at least for the younger children, but it is not worth canvassing. English opinion, as shown in the evidence of all kinds of organisations, political, social, professional, specialist or general, appears to be overwhelmingly in favour of retaining judicial process. The argument is that compulsory powers may have to be used; the personal liberty of the child and the rights of parents are involved, and such matters should be decided by a court. So juvenile courts will continue'. . . .

. . . Thus, most lawyers would brave a charge of self-interest to voice their instinctive misgivings at a further encroachment of the State within the family circle; nor would they blindly accept the professional social worker as a new priesthood sent to lead us to the promised land. To leave in the discretion of an official, however well intentioned, however well qualified, the right to decide what social medicine is good for us (or for our children) as well as the power to make us drink it, is viewed as a danger both to judicial process and to other fundamental values of our society — individual freedom, the privacy of the family, and parental responsibility.

Having said that, however, the author (writing before the sweeping reform of divorce law which took place in 1971) had this to say of the *substantive* task of such a court:

Finally, Americans preach that the procedure of the family court must be therapeutic (Alexander, 1949; *cf.* Rheinstein, 1956). This means no more (but no less) than that, just as the juvenile court seeks to do what is best for the child, so the family court should approach its wider jurisdiction inspired by a similar philosophy. In every case it would seek to diagnose and cure the underlying cause of the family disorder. Thus, in divorce it would think first of marriage-mending before marriage-ending. For this remedial function it would need to be buttressed with adequate expert assistance, whether within the court or in the local community. Where, however, cure proved impossible, the family court would perform its legal operation (such as divorce) with the least traumatic effect on the personalities involved.

Questions

(i) Is the attempt to 'cure' a family problem any less of a danger to those 'fundamental values of our society' if it is performed by a judge rather than a social worker?
(ii) Is it proper to treat juvenile delinquency in the same court and in the same manner as the breakdown of a marriage?
(iii) Is it proper for a court to which the parties go for a divorce to think 'first of marriage-mending before marriage-ending'?

It is in these vital matters of principle that the debate about courts and procedures in family disputes has moved furthest away from this starting point in the sixties: for about the need for such a court there has been remarkably little disagreement.

2 Finer and after

In the event, the Law Commission abandoned its inquiry into family courts when it became apparent that the *Report of the Committee on One-Parent Families*, the Finer Report (1974), would devote a whole section to the subject. The Report deals first with general principles:

CRITERIA

4.282 Our approach owes little to American experience or writings, or to any preconceived attachment to the notions of a 'family court'. We have been guided pragmatically by specific considerations emerging from our study of the matrimonial law and courts in this country, which has established for us the need for and the character of the institution we have in mind. We have, in the first place, traced the personal and social mischiefs to which the dual system of matrimonial jurisdiction gives rise. We have also shown how this system offers financial provision to wives, mothers and their children by means of orders which in many cases are not honoured by those whose obligation to maintain their dependants has been affirmed by the courts. To ensure that these women and children survive, the social security authorities provide the subsistence which the law promises. The contribution of the private obligation to maintain is interstitial; that of social security is fundamental. We therefore conclude that only an institution which is shaped by the recognition of these facts can adequately serve the needs of broken families. The second major point is that members of families which have collapsed come to court at a stage when critical decisions will have to be taken about issues, other than those directly affecting matrimonial relief or finance, around which conflicts are likely to develop. There may be disputes over the custody of the children, or the ownership or occupation of the matrimonial home. Such practical matters have to be settled or determined at some time, and the presence of the parties in court provides the best opportunity that may ever occur for discussion and decision. Thus, we have come to think of the family court as an institution which will improve on our inherited system by eliminating the overlap, the contradictions and the other weaknesses and defects of the legal jurisdictions we have exposed earlier in this Part of the Report, and which at the same time will also improve the machinery and services which are available to deal realistically with the practical problems resulting from marriage breakdown.
4.283. In the light of the foregoing considerations, we set out the six major criteria which a family court must in principle satisfy:

(1) the family court must be an impartial judicial institution, regulating the rights of citizens and settling their disputes according to law;

(2) the family court will be a unified institution in a system of family law which applies a uniform set of legal rules, derived from a single moral standard and applicable to all citizens;

(3) the family court will organise its work in such a way as to provide the best possible facilities for conciliation between parties in matrimonial disputes;

(4) the family court will have professionally trained staff to assist both the court and the parties appearing before it in all matters requiring social work services and advice;

(5) the family court will work in close relationship with the social security authorities in the assessment both of need and of liability in cases involving financial provision;

(6) the family court will organise its procedure, sittings and administrative services and arrangements with a view to gaining the confidence and maximising the convenience of the citizens who appear before it.

The first two criteria are elaborated thus:

THE FAMILY COURT AS A JUDICIAL INSTITUTION

4.285 The fundamental principle which must govern the family court is that it shall be a judicial institution which, in dealing with family matters, does justice according to law. This may seem to be so obvious a point as hardly to be worth mentioning; but the need to emphasise it arises from the nature of a jurisdiction which aims to do good as well as to do right. To promote welfare is an unusual function for a court of law. To some extent, the courts which deal with matrimonial disputes and with children are already familiar with that function through references in the statutes to reconciliation in husband and wife disputes, and through the statutory obligation in many forms of proceedings which involve children to have first and paramount regard, in any decision the court may reach, to their welfare. But the deliberate attempt to expand and systematise the welfare function, which is an essential part of the family court concept, carries risks, as well as potential advantages, which can be eliminated only by clear thinking and firm practice regarding boundaries and priorities. The court must remain, and must be seen to remain, impartial. This is of particular importance now that local authorities and governmental agencies of various kinds have powers and duties imposed on them which bring them into the proceedings, either as interested parties or as advisers to the court. The object of achieving welfare must not be permitted to weaken or short cut the normal safeguards of the judicial process — the dispassionate examination of evidence properly adduced to the court, regular procedures which promote an orderly and fair hearing, and the allowance of legal representation. The court must not see the men, women and children with whom it is concerned as 'clients', and still less as 'patients' for whom the court process is one form of, or a preliminary to, 'treatment'. Professional staff serving the court, including any who are responsible for assisting the court to reach sound conclusions on welfare issues, must be answerable to the court for what they do and how they do it. The aim must be to make adjudication and welfare march hand in hand, but there should be no blurring of the edges, either in principle or in administration. Through the family court it should be possible to make a new and highly beneficial synthesis between law and social welfare, and the respective skills, experience and efforts of lawyers and social workers; but the individual in the family court must in the last resort remain the subject of rights, not the object of assistance.

THE FAMILY COURT IN A UNIFORM SYSTEM OF LAW

4.286 The poor are not denied access to the divorce court today as they were in the past. But the magistrates' court remains the resort almost exclusively of the poor. Social and cultural habits originally established among poor people in the days when poverty did bar their access to the High Court have proved remarkably persistent among the poorest stratum of the population. Associated with this is the fact that the social agencies which deal with the poor habitually steer them in their matrimonial troubles to the magistrates' jurisdiction. . . .

Points (3) and (4) will be expanded later in this chapter, for they are crucial to the direction in which reform is now moving. As to point (5):

RELATIONS BETWEEN THE FAMILY COURT AND SOCIAL SECURITY AUTHORITIES

4.337 Throughout this Report we stress that for the bulk of the casualties of broken homes, family law and the law of social security are different sides of the same coin. Nevertheless, the separate institutional structures — the courts and the social security authorities — which are concerned with these casualties are ill-acquainted with each other. Indeed, each has taken pains to define and maintain an isolated identity. Realism and reason alike require that the courts and the social security authorities be brought, not into any sort of merger, but into an intimate working relationship. At this point we do no more than state the principle of co-operation, which we regard as one of the most powerful of all of the keys that are needed to unlock the problems of one-parent families.

The Report goes on to discuss the structure and organisation of the court in accordance with point (6):

Materials
4.347 In seeking to bring structural order out of this confusion there can be no question of starting afresh with brand new materials. There has to be a new model court, but it can only be established by use of the components that are, or are likely to come, to hand. . . .

The role of the magistrate
4.348 We desire to emphasise that the inclusion of the magistrates in the family court would for us be a matter of choice even if it were not a matter of necessity. The criticisms we have made of the matrimonial jurisdiction of the magistrates are not intended to spill over to the magistracy, whose fate it has been to try to make that jurisdiction work. It is probable, indeed, that only the care which so many magistrates have devoted to this task has saved the jurisdiction from foundering long ago under the weight of its inherent defects. . . . The family court will have a continuing need for the services of the lay magistracy, not only as a source of manpower, but as an equally indispensable source of lay experience and outlook which is a traditional feature in the administration of family law in England and Wales. In our view, it should be a continuing and expanding feature. One of the advantages of the family court is that it will allow greater flexibility in the association of professional and lay judges in the work of the court, and through such association give the magistrates the possibility of sharing in the disposal of more interesting and difficult cases than are apt to come their way at present.

Local jurisdiction
4.349 It will be essential, also, for the family court to provide, as the county courts and the magistrates now do, facilities for the local determination of cases as quickly and as cheaply as the nature of the case permits. . . .

The shape of the family court
4.352 The family court will be an institution to which the whole of the business of family law now dealt with in the Family Division of the High Court, the county courts and the magistrates' courts, will be assigned. It will be a civil court, conducting its business in accordance with the procedures, terminology and spirit of the civil law. It will be linked to the High Court and to the system of second or final appeals through the Family Division, but, subject to that link, the family court will be a unitary structure, operating to a large extent at the local level, and providing internally for the first appeal. It will make full use of existing resources of judicial manpower, professional and lay, and of court staff. . . . Within the unified structure, the anomalies and confusion caused by overlapping and competing jurisdictions will be eliminated.

One remedy, one court
4.353 It follows from this last point, and we emphasise its importance, that the structure of the family court will not allow for the options which exist within the present system for litigants to select the court from which to ask for a remedy that more than one court provides. Any legal system has the need to service problems of different orders of complexity at different levels. The family court will, like any other, have to devise rules for the efficient distribution of business, and this may well involve cases which fall within the same general category of description being dealt with in different tiers because of the presence of some special factor, such as length or difficulty of the investigation. But this does not breach the principle of eliminating options. There will be no duplication of remedies in the family court, and no possibility of choosing between tiers otherwise than as may be determined by rules which the court itself has established for the proper allocation of its business. The effect will be not only to terminate a state of disorder which does no credit to a judicial system, but, more particularly, to terminate arrangements which, whatever the theory may be, now ostentatiously cater on a second-class basis for poor people seeking matrimonial relief short of divorce. . . .
4.355 The focus of the family court at the local level should be the county court judge, and the work of the court should be carried on at the county court building. . . . In selecting the county court judge as the central judicial figure in the first or local tier of the court we have in mind that

much matrimonial work is already done in the county court, and that it is desirable that responsibility for local organisation and administration be placed upon a professional judge, although, no doubt, he will be working with local committees upon which the lay bench will be represented. Principally, however, we wish to mould the first tier of the family court so far as possible round a core taken from the county court because of the importance of eliminating from the new jurisdiction all those elements in the summary matrimonial jurisdiction that we have found to be inefficient or unsuitable for the conduct of a matrimonial court. The first tier of the family court, even although it ought and will have to make use of existing resources, must not be permitted to become a second version, under another title, of the existing magisterial jurisdiction. For this reason, although it may be necessary for reasons of manpower economy to include the stipendiary magistrate in the court's muster, we would prefer it if this could in the longer run be avoided, save in the case of the stipendiary who was prepared to specialise in matrimonial work.

And on jurisdiction:

4.362 Within the family court, once it has been established, we should prefer to see the exercise of nothing but a civil jurisdiction. We have spoken of family courts elsewhere which deal with crime, especially juvenile crime, whenever that seems to bear some prescribed relationship to the family situation, but we consider that the arguments of principle for an undiluted civil jurisdiction outweigh the advantages (such as they may be) of permitting it to spill over into penal law.

4.363 However, one difficulty arises in connection with care proceedings under the Children and Young Persons Act 1969. These are at present dealt with in the juvenile court. The conditions which the court has to find present before it can make any order frequently arise in connection with matrimonial troubles and family breakdown. It would thus far seem at least logical for a family court to take over this jurisdiction. On the other hand, one of the alternatives in the conditions is that the child or young person should have been guilty of an offence, so that the transfer of care proceedings to the family court would, at least in such cases, involve it in investigation and findings of criminal or delinquent behaviour. We can find no neat solution for this problem, which will merit careful attention at the time when the details of the family court's jurisdiction are being considered. We are certain, however, that no proceedings other than care proceedings which may involve investigation into criminal conduct should be considered for inclusion in the family court jurisdiction.

And finally on procedure:

4.404 We are impressed by the unanimity of the commentators in favour of greater informality in family matters. But we are impressed, too, by the lack of studies of the effect of legal ritual upon citizens who use the courts. We do not know how representative a figure is the trade union leader who observed of the Industrial Relations Court that, if his members are to be sent to prison for contempt of court, he desires it to be done by a judge properly robed in scarlet and ermine. On these aspects of court procedure, we think that decisions should be delayed until they can be based on knowledge of what will best satisfy the citizen user's desire for fairness and dignity in the determination of matrimonial cases.

4.405 Another much canvassed procedural question is how far the hearings in the family court should be inquisitorial rather than adversary in nature. In the accusatorial or adversary form of procedure, as it characterises our civil litigation, the parties not only choose the issues which form the subject matter of the dispute, but also determine what evidence shall be brought before the court. The court has no right and no means to act as its own fact-gatherer. In the inquisitorial form of procedure, the court is not confined to acting as a referee, but may, so far as it has the means, take steps of its own to inform itself of the facts and circumstances it considers it ought to know in order to make a just determination. But the two forms of procedure are not, in truth, mutually exclusive. In the divorce jurisdiction, the court has always been charged with the duty of being 'satisfied' that it can grant relief, which must involve, in appropriate cases, a duty to enquire into matters as to which the parties themselves may not be in dispute. So again, in matters affecting custody of and access to children the court has to have regard to the child's paramount interests, which is a matter which the views of the parties, even to the extent that they coincide, do not determine. The proper balance of the two forms of procedure in the family court should, in our view, be determined by the following considerations. It is desirable that the court itself should not come into the arena. To the extent that the court requires assistance by way of investigation or expert assessment of circumstances which it considers material, this function should be discharged by ancillary services which are attached to or can be called upon by the court, but whose personnel are not themselves members of the court. The bench of the family court is to consist only of judges, professional or lay, and experts or assessors should not be constituents. On the other hand, the bench as so constituted should, in every aspect of its jurisdiction, be able to call upon the aid of a competent person to make social and welfare enquiries and reports.

And the Report concludes the discussion thus:

Respect for the family court
4.424 The aim of all our recommendations in this Section and the last is to establish a family court and a family law which will command the confidence and respect of the whole community. We have been compelled to the conclusion that the summary jurisdiction in its present form does not achieve this object. This failure cannot be explained merely in terms of its inherent weaknesses. Those who mostly resort to the jurisdiction are drawn from the sections of the community who have the least confidence in any part of the legal administration and who need the most help in learning how to use it for their advantage. But there is a recent lesson to demonstrate in this very field how the law can rapidly win confidence for itself by remedying its own deficiencies. The post-war history of the divorce courts until 1969 shows widespread and increasing mistrust and disapprobation for a jurisdiction that was being driven into what was often a virtual disregard of the law it was supposed to apply in order to serve personal and social needs which most of those who used it regarded as legitimate. Yet the reforms of 1969–1970 produced an almost instantaneous reversal of public attitudes. We know of no serious criticism which is now directed to the divorce jurisdiction other than in such matters as the costs of litigation, which affect the administration of the law as a whole. There is no branch of legal administration for which the respect of the community is more important than the administration of family law, and in the ultimate resort, the case for a family court is that it is the institution through which respect for the law can be fully achieved.

Questions

(i) Could we not achieve a family court by the simple expedient of abolishing the domestic jurisdiction of magistrates?
(ii) What are the objections to doing that?

Manifestly, much of the Finer Committee's view was coloured by the deficiencies which they perceived in the domestic jurisdiction of magistrates. These stemmed partly from the outdated substantive law which was then applicable in matrimonial proceedings and partly from a general impression of dissatisfaction with their organisation, atmosphere and service. The main evidence for the latter came from *Separated Spouses* (1970), a study by OR McGregor, L Blom-Cooper and C Gibson, for Professor McGregor was also a member of the committee. Predictably, therefore, the main voices raised against the proposals came from the magistrates and their clerks, who could assert, with some justice, that the evidence was itself out of date and that much had since been done to improve matters. The Law Commission then recommended changes in the substantive law which took some of the steam out of the 'one law for the rich and another for the poor' argument. Significantly, however, the Law Commission were not called upon to consider whether there was any longer any need for such a jurisdiction. Indeed, one consequence of the Domestic Proceedings and Magistrates' Courts Act 1978 has been the setting up of specialist domestic panels of magistrates to try family cases, similar to the juvenile panels which have manned the juvenile courts for so long. Nor is the jurisdiction quite as unpopular as the Judicial Statistics would suggest: in 1979/80, the last full year before legal aid was replaced with 'assistance by way of representation' in such cases, a total of over 50,000 legal aid certificates were issued to litigants (most to complainants but some to respondents) in the magistrates' civil family jurisdiction. Some 21,800 of these were to complainants in matrimonial matters, some 7,500 to complainants in affiliation, and some 10,500 to complainants in other types of case, for example under the Guardianship of Minors Act 1971.

Question

How many of these complainants could have used an equivalent remedy in the county court? Might the legal aid authorities have required them to use the cheapest?

It soon became clear that the Government had no intention of implementing the Finer proposals, despite the fact that they had found favour with many commentators. In most essential respects, they agreed with the suggestions made earlier by Judge Jean Graham-Hall (1971), and later by the Justice Report on Parental Rights and Duties and Custody Suits (1975), the Society of Conservative Lawyers (1979), and the Family Law Sub-Committee of the Law Society in *A Better Way Out* (1979; see also 1982, where the same proposals are reiterated). This last document strongly refutes the Government case against the proposals, in the course of making some additional suggestions, for example on accommodation:

142. It is obvious from Government statements on the Finer Committee's recommendations that the problem of accommodation is seen as a major obstacle to the setting up of a Family Court, indeed an insuperable one for some time to come. This approach is based on a fundamental misconception, for it confuses the function of a court, which can very well be exercised under the proverbial palm tree, with the building in which it is now traditional that a court should be housed. During the House of Commons debate on the Finer Report (Hansard 20 October 1975) the Secretary of State for Social Services, Mrs Castle, said that the Government saw 'no prospect of accepting the recommendations for family courts' because of the cost of the new buildings which would be needed. It was 'out of the question to contemplate building new courts throughout the country. On any reckoning, therefore, family jurisdiction would have to go on being exercised in our existing courtrooms' (cols. 59–60).

144. The House of Lords debate on One-Parent Families (Hansard 19 January 1977) revealed the same inability to distinguish between the function and forum of a court. Lord Wells-Pestell, the Government spokesman, said 'I think the Noble and Learned Lord would agree with me that there has to be a special kind of environment. There has to be a special kind of setting if one has to have a family court'. He did not explain what kind of environment or setting but it seems that he envisaged a traditional courtroom as he also observed: 'You cannot take a room in the town hall and make it into a family court and then move it all out the next day'.

145. We do not see why you cannot. . . .

147. . . . We feel that it is essential that a Family Court should operate informally, avoiding the ritual which characterises the procedure of other English courts with their formal and distant atmosphere. Many of its proceedings would involve private and often painful aspects of the intimate relationships of those involved who would often be in a state of distress and confusion. The Family Court would operate more effectively in a reassuring and accessible atmosphere. It is undesirable that Family Court proceedings should be held in a formal courtroom. Any reasonable sized room could be used, of the kind in which industrial tribunals, the Commissioners or Special Commissioners of Inland Revenue, rent assessment committees and juvenile courts operate. A wide range of such accommodation exists even though a single room would not be sufficient where more than one case was to be heard. A waiting room and one or more interviewing rooms would be needed except perhaps in places where the Court sat only occasionally. Lord Wells-Pestell's town halls and also school buildings, for example, can usually provide these facilities.

148. We believe, therefore, that once the question of the Family Court's accommodation is approached without preconceptions about the setting its title demands, the answer is relatively easy. Simplicity and suitability may well coincide.

And on procedure:

153. Under the present system, the various elements of a divorce case are dealt with separately. The petition for divorce or dissolution itself is either heard in open court by a judge or, where Special Procedure is used, investigated in chambers and the judgment pronounced in open court. Applications for maintenance and other forms of financial relief are heard by a registrar in chambers and applications relating to custody of children by a judge in chambers. The reasons for this fragmentation are largely historical. Formerly, great significance was attached to the actual dissolution of marriage and custody and financial matters were treated rather as incidental details. The decree itself was therefore heard by a judge, whereas financial arrangements were left to the registrar. The custody of children fell between the two in the scale of importance and was dealt with by a judge, though not in court. Though contemporary needs have led to a reversal in the relevant significance of the dissolution of the marriage and the making of consequential arrangements, the form of the current system still reflects old attitudes. Though the decree itself is still granted by the judge, the actual dissolution of marriage is now rarely even the subject of dispute — in 1977, only about 1.6% of divorces were defended . . . whereas arrangements about money, which are left to a registrar, are frequently extremely important to the parties' future. One disadvantage of the system of fragmented hearings of cases is the increased cost, both directly in money and indirectly because of the increased time, not all of which is immediately obvious. How much a hearing costs can be appreciated when it is considered how many people are typically involved: a judge or registrar, the two spouses, their legal advisers, and perhaps witnesses and children as well. Furthermore, the preparation through each stage requires expenditure of time in getting the case ready for 'trial' and some part of each actual hearing itself is taken up in re-acquainting the court with the facts of the case and informing it of the results of earlier proceedings. In some parts of the country, the distance which the parties and their legal advisers may have to travel to reach the court may be an appreciable factor in the cost of the case. The more often attendance at court is required, the greater is the likelihood of time being wasted in waiting because of slippage in court time tables. This last factor may not seem very significant to an outsider but anyone with experience of litigation will know that waiting time can contribute noticeably to legal costs.

154. A reduction in the number of separate hearings in divorce proceedings would, we think, bring about material savings in costs both to public and private funds.

Both of these features, besides their intrinsic advantages in helping both the efficiency and the quality of adjudication, would, the Sub-Committee thought, result in substantial savings of cost, so that the only features which would actually add to the total expenditure would be the new counselling services (of which more later) and the judiciary. Nevertheless, it remains unlikely that any such radical change will be contemplated, and Mervyn Murch offers an intriguing explanation for this resistance in *Justice and Welfare in Divorce* (1980):

In my view, at present, because the notion of a family court is still relatively ill-defined, the arguments against it on the basis of cost and administrative inconvenience have not been properly advanced nor are they the main stumbling blocks. One has to look into the workings of the existing system itself to understand why major reform has seemed so elusive. There may be two main reasons. First, because the system contains many deep philosophical contradictions. Its ambiguity and confusion allows all kinds of conflicting interests to be served — at the cost of consumer satisfaction. Secondly, the system by its traditional caution offers practitioners within it, and also in a sense the parties, and officials, for example, registrars and judges, a high degree of emotional security. Practitioners seem to need this in order to deal with the problems arising from matrimonial and family conflicts which may provoke within them deep anxiety. In short, the existing system functions as a kind of institutional defence against anxiety, and attempts to change the system are perceived as threats to this emotional defence mechanism. This may to some extent account for the inertia which seems such a powerful force in resisting change. . . .

Family conflict and marriage breakdown generates considerable anxiety not only in the family members concerned but in practitioners like doctors, lawyers, judges and social workers who are called on to deal with the consequences. Marriage breakdown and the whole process of family reorganisation that follows in certain respects challenge firmly held traditional beliefs in the value of marriage and the integrity of the nuclear family unit. Most people have fantasies built up since early childhood both about the nature of 'good secure happy relationships' and 'bad aggressive' forces which can damage and destroy individual relationships and family integrity. The breakdown and stress in other people's family relationships can easily, through a process of projective identification, activate the practitioner's own inner fantasy world and arouse stress and anxiety. Most adults will have experienced rejection and the powerful grief and depression that follows broken emotional attachments. The need therefore to differentiate their inner fantasies and feelings from the objective reality of the case being dealt with, can make heavy demands on the maturity and experience of the practitioner. It is only too easy for a practitioner to project his own fantasies into his current work so that he becomes uneasy and anxious because he experiences external situations and events as a mixture of objective reality and fantasy. I think this goes some way to explaining the frequently observed phenomenon of practitioners who make powerful identification with, and assumptions about, the position of the children of a breaking marriage. The more sensitive the practitioner the greater the risk of his being overwhelmed by intense and unmanageable anxiety. It is perhaps not surprising therefore that individual practitioners, their organisations and the wider social systems within which they work, develop techniques, practices and procedures which help the individual contain and modify that anxiety. Nor is it surprising that they should seek to preserve these defences when change is threatened.

[This] hypothesis and its application to the practice of family law may help explain many of the practices that consumers of the system complain of, such as procedures which depersonalise, create delays and which fragment the handling of their affairs by parcelling them up so that different parts are dealt with by different people in different places, at different times. The hypothesis also probably goes some way to explain the manifest resistance to major reform. When the rational case for reform of the system is so strong, obstruction tends to take the form of inertia, or prevarication. It is only to be expected, therefore, that a failing social system contains many members who cling to the familiar even when the familiar has obviously ceased to be appropriate or relevant.

Questions

(i) Would it make sense, as canvassed by the Lord Chancellor's Department (1983) to combine the jurisdictions of the Family Division of the High Court and of county courts into a single, multi-tier Family Court along the lines of the Crown Court?

(ii) The Lord Chancellor's Department suggested that High Court judges, circuit judges and registrars would all sit in such a court. To whom would you allocate the following business: (*a*) wardship, (*b*) financial provision and property adjustment, (*c*) approval of post-divorce arrangements for children, (*d*) defended and undefended divorce, (*e*) ouster injunctions?

(iii) Would such a system be any solution to the problems of over-lapping remedies and separate hearings?

3 Reconciliation and conciliation

The *Finer Report* begins its discussion thus:

4.288 In the discussion which follows we shall be using the terms 'reconciliation' and 'conciliation' to denote two different concepts. By 'reconciliation' we mean the reuniting of the spouses. By 'conciliation' we mean assisting the parties to deal with the consequences of the established breakdown of their marriage, whether resulting in a divorce or a separation, by reaching agreements or giving consents or reducing the area of conflict upon custody, support, access to and education of the children, financial provision, the disposition of the matrimonial home, lawyers' fees, and every other matter arising from the breakdown which calls for a decision on future arrangements.
4.289 The distinction between reconciliation and conciliation, and the influence which the family court may bring to bear in promoting either of them, is of cardinal importance in the consideration of any proposal for a family court. We have therefore in the first instance to examine the development and current status within the two branches of the matrimonial jurisdiction of these aspects of the court's work. We shall find that the law concentrates almost exclusively on reconciliation.

Explicit in Professor Brown's conception of a family court was a prior commitment to 'marriage-mending' — a court-based attempt to reunite the parties. An extreme example of such attempts is the Los Angeles Court of Conciliation: the procedure, its advantages and disadvantages are wittily revealed in an imaginary discussion (also quoted extensively in Chapter 5) between a judge, a bishop, a professor and a doctor, who are American delegates to the 'First International Interdisciplinary Congress on Family Stability and the Rights of Children,' in Foote, Levy and Sander, *Cases and Materials on Family Law* (1976):

Judge: . . . When a divorce case is filed, but before there is any action on the divorce petition itself, we send the couple to a trained marriage counselor.

Bishop: This is the first sensible suggestion I've heard from any of you tonight. Does it work?

Judge: It certainly does. I have had no satisfaction in my career comparable to that represented by the marriages our court has saved. I guess I'm just sentimental, but when I meet a couple on the street strolling along arm in arm and they say, 'Hello, Judge, do you remember us?' and they tell me they're one of our reconciliations, I get a real glow. Why, the very day I left for this conference I got a letter which is typical. It said, in effect: today is the second anniversary of our signing the conciliation contract in your office, and we just want to let you know that we are happier together all the time and eternally grateful to you.

Bishop: What is a conciliation contract?

Judge: That's really the secret of our success. After the parties have worked things through with a marriage counselor and decided on a reconciliation, we get very formal and have them make a contract with each other and the court. It's a real contract and violation of it constitutes contempt of court.

Doctor: I don't understand.

Judge: The contract is a long, detailed document covering more than 30 pages which evolved out of the court's experience. The parties agree to reconciliation, may agree to accept long-term counseling from some agency, agree to look forward and forget the past —

Doctor: That would be some achievement.

Judge: And the contract covers all the matters which we have found to have caused difficulties — how to handle money, the division of responsibility in the home and in the family, mutual friends, in-laws, methods of speaking to each other, not bearing grudges, avoidance of late hours, sex, and so forth. We also have special clauses to insert where appropriate, such as an agreement by one spouse to attend Alcoholics Anonymous.

Doctor: Could you be a little more specific? For example, you mentioned sex.

Judge: The contract points out the importance of mutual respect in sexual intercourse and the importance of achieving a mean between excessive demands on the one hand and reluctance or uncooperativeness on the other. The parties also agree not to ignore the important phase of leisurely love-making as a prelude to intercourse, with the husband agreeing to take his time and the wife agreeing to respond to his attentions.*

Doctor: So that if someone tries to have intercourse without the prelude he goes to jail for contempt of court?

Judge: Go ahead and ridicule us, Doctor. We're used to having fun poked at us, although I hardly expected it from you. You have no idea how often the couples use this agreement. They tell us they read it over and over. It gives them an anchor to windward, a standard to which they can hew. The agreement concludes, incidentally, with a family prayer, because we recognize that God's help is needed if reconciliation is to be achieved. Of course the contempt of court provision is largely a psychological weapon, although we have used it in extreme situations. That isn't the heart of the matter, however. What we have done is to prove that reconciliation works and that most of these marriages can be saved. Just come to my court someday and I'll let you read the mail received in a single week. That will prove it to you.

Professor: I presume you hear only from those who reconcile and stay reconciled. What is your over-all success rate?

Bishop: Here we go again! Don't let them sidetrack you with statistical sleight of hand, Judge. You're obviously doing great work. Just keep it up.

Judge: Never fear, Bishop, I'm ready for them. I'll send you copies of our annual reports. In round figures, 60% of the cases that come to our court are reconciled and 75% of those reconciliations last.

---

* E.g., from the Los Angeles husband-wife agreement: 'The wife agrees to respond to the husband's efforts in lovemaking and not to act like a patient undergoing a physical examination. For the husband to acquire proficiency in making intercourse pleasurable to the wife, he must learn to relax physically and to take his time.'

Doctor: Psychiatrists are always being criticized for drawing generally applicable conclusions from the small unrepresentative sample of patients they see. Do you mean to tell me that 60% of all divorce actions in your city are being reconciled?

Judge: No, I said 60% of the cases in our Conciliation Court.

Professor: And the cases that come to your court come on petition of one of the parties, is that it?

Judge: Mainly, yes. It would be a physical impossibility for us to handle all the cases, or even just all those cases in which children are involved. We have inadequate facilities as it is, or our success rate would be even higher.

Doctor: So you deal with a self-selected and not a representative sample, just the way I do.

Professor: Judge, are you aware that about 30% of all divorce cases filed in the United States are dismissed voluntarily by the parties or by the court for want of prosecution? The most probable hypothesis is that most of these 30% are reconciled without outside intervention and there is some evidence that this is so.

Judge: It proves what I've always maintained — that it is never too late to try reconciliation.

Professor: It also may show that your success rate, as you call it, is meaningless as a purported justification of your elaborate and expensive court apparatus. These cases that give you such a glow may well be the very ones that would have reconciled themselves anyway.

Note: Do not forget the professor's remarks when you consider the evidence about our own very different conciliation schemes later in this chapter.)

Doctor: What happens if the unwilling spouse refuses to be counseled?

Judge: Then we can issue a subpoena.

Doctor: There is something about that that really repels me. I'm not only a psychiatrist; I also happen to be a citizen of a democratic state who believes that the right to privacy is an important attribute of liberty. If someone wants help with the neurotic problems in his marriage and comes to me, I'll try to help him, but you can't force therapy. If a man and a woman decide they want a divorce, as far as I'm concerned they should get it and I don't care what their reasons are. I'm willing to delay a little, to make sure they're not acting on temporary impulse. I'm affirmatively anxious to make available counseling facilities, although I don't think they should be attached to the court.

Professor: What about a procedure whereby a party merely files a notice of intention to seek a divorce and the parties are then told where they can get free counseling services during the waiting period before any further steps are taken on the divorce action? It would be a kind of 'cooling off' period, buttressed by the availability of counseling help.

Judge: I repeat that in that way we'll miss the important cases. We get cases referred to us long before that when one spouse goes to a social agency for marriage counseling but the other spouse refuses to come in. Then they refer the case to us because we can use compulsion.

Professor: Let's withhold judgment on that until we see how successful your procedures are with that particular kind of case.

Doctor: I reject that kind of compulsion no matter what the results are. Damn it, marriage is a private affair. When I think of the Judge's court issuing orders telling people not to speak harshly to one another or how often to go to bed together or what technique to use in making love — well, it sickens me. It must be unconstitutional. Isn't there some amendment that prohibits that sort of prying into the intimacy of one's private life?

Professor: Judging by the Supreme Court's decision in the Connecticut birth control case, there are a lot of constitutional provisions protecting family privacy. What really disturbs me about this current craze for counseling, however, is its motive. I have no objection to making counseling available, or even to the use of the minimal amount of compulsion employed in the Judge's court. But it is ridiculous to expect counseling to have much effect on divorce or dissolution rates. It is significant that in the Judge's city the regular courts are still open side by side with the Conciliation Court, and so long as the requirement for conciliation is not universal, people who want to avoid it will flock to the easy courts, just as they have always done. This process is what Rheinstein has called the application of Gresham's law to divorce. But more important, even if you could overcome this problem of evasion, the implicit premise of the counseling approach seems to be that it is individual failure which causes our high breakdown rate. That is really the same basic error as that into which I feel the Bishop has fallen, the only difference being that the Bishop's root cause is immorality and the Judge's is psychopathology.

Doctor: I couldn't agree more. It is destructive social forces in our society and not individual

psychopathology which threaten the family. It seems obvious to me that psychiatry can't roll a ball uphill when everything else in society is conspiring to roll it down. The real danger I see in both the Judge's and the Bishop's approaches is that by their emphasis on false issues they keep us from tackling the basic problems of family life in modern society.
Bishop: Gentlemen, the time has come to agree to disagree.

Note: The Bishop's words are prophetic — see pp. 651–653, below.)

The English experience of reconciliation provisions is recounted in the *Finer Report* (1974):

Reconciliation in the divorce jurisdiction
4.290 In 1946, the Lord Chancellor, Viscount Jowitt, appointed a committee under the chairmanship of Lord Denning (then Mr Justice Denning):
> 'to examine the present system governing the administration of the law of divorce and nullity of marriage in England and Wales; and, on the assumption that the grounds upon which marriages may now be dissolved remain unchanged, to consider and report upon which procedural reforms ought to be introduced . . . in particular whether any (and if so, what) machinery should be made available for the purpose of attempting a reconciliation between the parties, either before or after proceedings have been commenced.'

The report laid great stress on the importance of preserving the marriage tie and attempting reconciliation in every case where there was a prospect of success. It examined the role of the Service Departments during the then recently ended war in effecting reconciliation between serving men and their wives, and the part played by voluntary organisations such as the Marriage Guidance Council. The principal conclusion in this area was:
> 'There should be a Marriage Welfare Service to afford help and guidance both in preparation for marriage and also in difficulties after marriage. It should be sponsored by the State but should not be a State institution. It should evolve gradually from the existing services and societies just as the probation system evolved from the Court Missionaries and the Child Guidance Service from the children's clinics. It should not be combined with the judicial procedure for divorce but should function quite separately from it.'

It was also recommended that welfare officers should be appointed to give guidance to parties who resorted to the divorce court or contemplated doing so, and that where there were dependent children the court should at any time after the petition had been filed be entitled to refer the case to the court welfare officer for enquiry and report. The recommendation for a marriage welfare service fell by the wayside, but the report did foreshadow arrangements under which welfare officers (the first of whom was appointed in 1950) became attached to the divorce jurisdiction to investigate and report, when requested, on matters arising in matrimonial proceedings which concern the welfare of a child.

The work of the divorce court welfare officers in this respect is dealt with in Chapter 10, where their origins in the nineteenth century 'police court missionaries' are also explained. Between the wars, this led them into a great deal of 'marriage-saving' among litigants in magistrates' courts, a role which has recently declined dramatically. The *Finer Report* continues:

The English experience of reconciliation through the courts
4.298 It may, indeed, be said to be the virtually unanimous opinion of those who have the relevant experience that there is little room for optimism when the court to which the parties have presented themselves to formalise or regulate the breakdown of the marriage seeks to use that occasion for mending it. The Denning Report concluded on the evidence it received:
> 'The prospects of reconciliation are much more favourable in the early stages of marital disharmony than in the later stages. At that stage both parties are likely to be willing to co-operate in an effort to save the marriage; but if the conflict has become so chronic that one or both of the parties has lost the power or desire to co-operate further, the prospects sharply diminish. By the time the conflict reaches a hearing in the divorce court, the prospects are as a rule very small. It is important therefore that the general public should be brought to realise the importance of seeking competent advice, without delay, when tensions occur in marriage.'

4.299 The Morton Commission, which took a good deal of evidence on this subject, recorded:
'If matters are allowed to develop into a condition of chronic disharmony one or perhaps both of the spouses will probably have lost the ability or desire to make any attempt to restore the marriage, and by the time steps have been taken to institute divorce proceedings the prospects of bringing husband and wife together again are greatly reduced. This view won a wide measure of support from our witnesses.'

4.300 The Law Commission considered that reconciliation procedures started after the filing of the petition achieve little success and 'have tended to become pointless and troublesome formalities'.

Despite these views, expressed in *Reform of the Grounds of Divorce: The Field of Choice* (1966), the Law Commission recommended two provisions, now embodied in the *Matrimonial Causes Act 1973*:

Attempts at reconciliation of parties to marriage

6.—(1) Provision shall be made by rules of court for requiring the solicitor acting for a petitioner for divorce to certify whether he has discussed with the petitioner the possibility of a reconciliation and given him the names and addresses of persons qualified to help effect a reconciliation between parties to a marriage who have become estranged.

(2) If at any stage of proceedings for divorce it appears to the court that there is a reasonable possibility of a reconciliation between the parties to the marriage, the court may adjourn the proceedings for such period as it thinks fit to enable attempts to be made to effect such a reconciliation.

The power conferred by the foregoing provision is additional to any other power of the court to adjourn proceedings.

The second power was supported, 'so long as the power is sparingly exercised,' because 'the saving of even a very small number of marriages is worthwhile, provided that it is not accompanied by a disproportionate waste of time and effort in a great many others.' In matrimonial proceedings before magistrates, where it may be thought that the prospects of reconciliation are greater, the *Domestic Proceedings and Magistrates Courts Act 1978* provides:

26.—(1) Where an application is made for an order under section 2 of this Act the court, before deciding whether to exercise its powers under that section, shall consider whether there is any possibility of reconciliation between the parties to the marriage in question; and if at any stage of the proceedings on that application it appears to the court that there is a reasonable possibility of such a reconciliation, the court may adjourn the proceedings for such period as it thinks fit to enable attempts to be made to effect a reconciliation.

(2) Where the court adjourns any proceedings under subsection (1) above, it may request a probation officer or any other person to attempt to effect a reconciliation between the parties to the marriage, and where any such request is made, the probation officer or that other person shall report in writing to the court whether the attempt has been successful or not, but shall not include in that report any other information.

Question

Do you think that these provisions are: (*a*) too little and too late, or (*b*) an unwarranted restraint on the litigant's right to a speedy determination of his or her claim to relief? Why do you think that the Law Commission (1976) did not suggest that the duty and power should apply to applications for personal protection and exclusion orders?

The solicitor's duty under s. 6(1) of the Matrimonial Causes Act 1973 has, if anything, proved even less effective than the courts' powers: there is nothing to prevent his certifying to the court that he has *not* discussed reconciliation and that he has *not* given his client the list of names and addresses. Some reasons for this are suggested by Nicholas Tyndall, Chief

Officer of the National Marriage Guidance Council, in a short article on *Helping Troubled Marriages* (1982):

This Act envisaged a partnership between solicitors and marriage counsellors for the benefit of clients. In practice that partnership did not develop. The referrals of clients were few, joint work on behalf of clients even less. Solicitors with a concern for marriage continued to serve on marriage guidance councils. But where there was no will, contact remained negligible.

There are three main reasons for this failure to respond to the opportunities presented in the 1969 Act. First, solicitors and counsellors have radically different understandings and work settings. Solicitors primarily search for facts. They know what the law says and they are trained in an adversarial approach with one spouse as their client. Counsellors explore feelings, assisting changes in relationships, encouraging people away from fixed positions, explaining the grey areas rather than the black and white, with the couple as the client. Counsellors fear that solicitors may draw them into the legal arena and challenge their confidentiality. Solicitors fear that conciliation attempts by counsellors may weaken their clients' position vis-à-vis their spouses.

Secondly, the process of referral which the Divorce Reform Act advocated is not easy. Advising anyone to go to consult a third party may arouse suspicion, fear of the unknown, even hostility, or may risk the response, 'If I'd wanted to go to marriage guidance I'd have gone there in the first place!' Any attempt at referral is only likely to be successful when motivated by a sincere regard for the client based on a close knowledge of the client and of the Marriage Guidance Council (MGC). Even then it requires experience to spot who and when to refer. Many clients approach solicitors driven by a determination to take action out of their unhappiness, angry and bitter with their spouse or having abandoned hope. How hard for any helper to listen to that anguish and also to hear underneath where there is a wish still to maintain the marriage if only the relationship can be improved.

And, thirdly, co-operation is impeded by lack of knowledge of the work of each other's profession. How can a solicitor know what can be achieved by a counsellor with these potential referrals unless they talk together? Ideally he needs some feedback from the counsellor, for otherwise he will have to rely on impressions related by his clients, and that will probably be feedback from clients who were least helped by counselling.

Questions

(i) Why do you think that Tyndall uses the word 'conciliation' rather than 'reconciliation'?

(ii) Should the law make some attempt to encourage couples who 'do it themselves' in divorce proceedings to see a counsellor?

Tyndall might have added that, perhaps because the Act uses the word 'reconciliation,' solicitors have failed to grasp that marriage guidance agencies of all types have altered their objectives quite dramatically in recent years. The change is described in *Marriage Matters* (1979), a consultative document issued by a working party on marriage guidance set up by the Home Office in consultation with the DHSS:

1.12 The pioneers of the marriage councils were as clear in their avowed aims as they were prudent, able and persuasive in the pursuit of them, and in their first selection and training of counsellors. They were out to save marriages — to 'mend' them, not to 'end' them. The aim appealed to intelligent and compassionate people everywhere, particularly among those with an educated understanding of the problem, and sufficient leisure to offer their services for its remedy. It appealed to the churches because it was wholly consistent with their theological understanding of marriage as a lifelong and exclusive relationship. It appealed to the growing profession of social work, particularly those branches of it concerned with children whose welfare was jeopardized by broken homes. It appealed to the State, because the aiding of divorce litigation was expensive, as was the social and material care of children and others disadvantaged by divorce. People unhappy in their marriages were to be helped, then, towards reconciliation, to live again within the institution of marriage. . . .

A gradual change of objective

1.15 The avowed objective of 'marriage guidance' work, to mend marriages, changed under the influence of a number of factors. There were changes in the public attitude towards marriage and divorce, and in the divorce law itself. Legal aid, social and economic factors, including a wider liberty for women to support themselves by working outside the home, contributed to a growing resort to divorce — though not necessarily to a growing incidence of marital breakdown. These and other changes reduced the pressure to 'keep couples together'. The practice of marital counselling itself was a powerful contributor to change. The training of counsellors, specialist and lay, disseminated to a wider public some of the insights into the dynamics of human behaviour, including marital behaviour, derived from psycho-analysis. Methods of 'case-work' were developed: for a generation they were the staple of practice and training in social work. They were designed to enable the client to understand more of himself and his problems, and, in understanding, to help himself. Out of this grew 'marital counselling' rather than 'marriage guidance' — a change of name denoting a sensitive shift of method and intent.

1.16 Labels can limit and distort concepts and skills to which they are attached. Even worse, they can become slogans, heraldic emblems around which warriors rally for fight. We shall avoid, therefore, the temptation to simplify our present task by labelling these methods and passing on. It is relevant to our task, however, to observe that, in a long-established moral and pastoral tradition, the 'counsel' has denoted some fairly clearly directed course of action, stronger than 'advice', which the recipient was told to pursue for his good. Early social work, and perhaps early marriage guidance work, stood in, or in the penumbra of, this tradition. Some persons may still need it and profit from it; and some ready helpers are willing to give it. But the giver seldom knows the meaning of the advice to the receiver or how he will distort it; and the very giving of advice may entrench the giver in an unhelpful relationship. So it is only the most skilled and sensitive counsellor who may safely offer it. By and large, 'counselling' is now by another way: the counsellor offers the client a relationship in which he may discover himself and find resources within himself — and within his marriage — by which to help himself and find his own way; in short, to enlarge his area of freedom and to move within it. The outcome may be in a marriage mended — renewed ability and will to continue and improve the matrimonial life; or it may be a marriage ended, though with less hurt, perhaps less insult to the emotional and spiritual relationship, than otherwise there might have been.

1.17 This approach has a firm place in the tradition of Christian spiritual direction, shown for example in a prayer of St Ailred, abbot of the Cistercian monastery of Rievaulx in Yorkshire from 1147 to 1157:

> 'So teach me, gracious Lord, to admonish the unruly, to strengthen the faint-hearted, to support the weak; and to adapt myself to each one according to his nature, his way of life, disposition, capacity or simpleness, and according to place and time, as would seem to thee good . . .'

For the modern counsellor, as for the medieval pastor, the critical point lies in the phrase 'to adapt *myself* to each one'. Wise counsellors know how wide is the spectrum of possible relationships, and how dangerous it is to invest any method with some ideological or absolute authority which does not belong to it. The test is practically how people are helped best.

A later section of *Marriage Matters* describes how the earlier Finer Report had drawn a clear distinction between *reconciliation* and *conciliation*:

Reconciliation and conciliation

7.4 The Finer Committee proposed the creation of a new family court, and considered reconciliation and conciliation in connection with it. By 'reconciliation' they meant, as we do, the re-uniting of the spouses. By 'conciliation' they meant:

> 'assisting the parties to deal with the consequences of the established breakdown of their marriage, whether resulting in a divorce or in a separation, by reaching agreements or giving consents or reducing the area of conflict upon custody, support, access to and education of the children, financial provision, the disposition of the matrimonial home, lawyers' fees, and every other matter arising from the breakdown which calls for a decision on future arrangements.'

We have suggested in paragraph 4.84 a more general meaning of 'conciliation' as the moderation of bitterness and the reduction of areas of disagreement, and the Finer definition incorporates a statement of those matters upon which disagreements may exist precedent to or consequent upon a divorce or upon a separation. Sir George Baker, President of the Family Division of the High Court, has recently said: '. . . the expressed opinion from many judges is, alas, that the fight, albeit in chambers over children and money, is now more bitter and fiercer than ever before' (1977).

7.5 After reviewing the English and overseas experience of reconciliation through the courts, the Finer Committee reached the conclusions — first, that reconciliation procedures conducted through the court at the stage where parties are presenting themselves for decrees that will formalise their marriage breakdown have small chance of success; and, secondly, that conciliation procedures conducted through the court at this same stage have substantial success in civilising the consequences of the breakdown. Neither our experience nor the evidence given to us leads us to any different conclusion. . . .

The idea of a court conciliation service

7.8 As we have described in earlier chapters, the probation service and the social services departments over recent years have become increasingly involved in the work of the domestic courts, providing reports about the future of children and where necessary supervising them under court orders. How these children cope with the break up of their families depends very much upon the relationship between their separated parents. Therefore conciliation is often of the essence of this complicated and time consuming work.

7.9 With its recommendation for the establishment of a family court, the Finer Report coupled a family court welfare service. The functions of the latter would include the provision of a service specifically concerned with conciliation. The Attorney General announced in 1976 that the government had reluctantly decided that there was no prospect of implementing the recommendation for the establishment of a family court. However, the provision of a court conciliation service is not dependent on the establishment of a family court. Although the existing division of jurisdiction is to remain, a service could be established to serve the divorce court and the magistrates' domestic court; but because additional work would be created, additional resources would be required, whether the task be undertaken by an existing service or by a new service.

7.10 The conciliation service we envisage would be on lines similar to that proposed in the Finer Report and would exist side by side with the legal structure. Whereas the function of the courts is judicial, the main purpose of the conciliation service would be to help individuals and couples to sort out their views, attitudes and feelings, make decisions which are most beneficial to the mental and emotional health of themselves, their spouses and their children, and begin to adapt themselves to the implications of those decisions. The court assumes that people are clear what they want and adjudicates when there is a clash of interest between spouses. However, many people experiencing marital breakdown who go through legal process for divorce or separation have conflicting feelings at various stages or indeed throughout. Sometimes this ambivalence may be apparent at the point of their first consulting a solicitor; sometimes it may surface as legal action is taking place and uncertainty about the future mode of life highlights the forgotten positive aspects of the relationship that is being terminated; sometimes the permission to divorce, perhaps at the granting of the decree nisi, provides such a shift in the marital relationship that the old marriage can be resumed on a new basis.

7.11 The divorce process is thus often accompanied by feelings of uncertainty, sadness, panic, bitterness or regret or even reluctance; individuals or couples can benefit from talking these through with a counsellor or welfare officer experienced in conciliation. In particular it is important for time to be available for each parent to talk about his or her feelings about the children, and about the future plans for the children's welfare, including arrangements for continuing the relationship with the parent who will then be absent from them. The continuing role of parent, after both parents are no longer cohabiting is fraught with difficulty. Often some supervision of the children will be necessary for some time, either to help with any bitterness transmitted into the post-divorce relationships with children or to safeguard access arrangements. These are all matters of fundamental importance with which the law as a judicial agent is not well placed to help. It is not a question of either legal process or a conciliation service. Many couples have need of both, and both have a complementary role to fulfil. From our viewpoint, an undue share of time, skill and finance goes into the execution of the law, and we think more resources of all sorts should be diverted to the process of conciliation in the wide sense we have used it here.

It is noteworthy that some encouragement to court-based conciliation through the court welfare officers was provided in a *Practice Direction* issued shortly after the Divorce Reform Act 1969 took effect:

Parliament, by enacting s. 3 of the Divorce Reform Act 1969 [now s. 6 of the Matrimonial Causes Act 1973], has once more shown its concern that the possibility of reconciliation between spouses who are contemplating or engaging in matrimonial litigation should be explored, in order to ascertain whether this might not be more conducive to the happiness of the spouses and their children than the forensic prosecution of their dispute. Experience has shown that reconciliation is more likely to be achieved and to be permanent if expert help is made available to the parties with this object.

Moreover, even if complete reconciliation cannot be achieved, expert help will often enable the parties to resolve, with the minimum possible anxiety and harm to themselves or their children, many of the issues liable to be ancillary to the breakdown of a marriage. Short of this, it should at least identify the issues on which the parties remain seriously at variance and on which in consequence they require adjudication of the court.

Accordingly, with the co-operation of the various organisations concerned with marriage reconciliation and welfare it has been decided to make generally available in the High Court and in divorce county courts the machinery set up experimentally and locally . . .

The machinery will operate as follows:

(*a*) Where the court considers that there is a reasonable possibility of reconciliation or that there are ancillary proceedings in which conciliation might serve a useful purpose, the court may refer the case, or any particular matter or matters in dispute therein, to the court welfare officer.

(*b*) The court welfare officer will, after discussion with the parties, decide whether there is any reasonable prospect of reconciliation (experience having shown that reconciliation is unlikely to be successful in the absence of readiness to co-operate on the part of the spouses) or that conciliation might assist the parties to resolve their disputes or any part of them by agreement.

(*c*) If the court welfare officer decides that there is not such reasonable prospect, he should report accordingly to the court.

(*d*) If the court welfare officer decides that there is some reasonable prospect of reconciliation, or that conciliation might assist the parties to resolve their disputes or any part of them by agreement, he will, unless he continues to deal with the case himself, refer the parties to either (i) a probation officer, or (ii) a fully qualified marriage guidance counsellor recommended by the branch of the appropriate organisation concerned with marriage guidance and welfare; or (iii) some other appropriate person or body indicated by the special circumstances (eg denominational) of the case.

(*e*) The person to whom the parties have been referred will report back to the court welfare officer, who in turn will report to the court. These reports will be limited to a statement whether or not reconciliation has been effective, or to what extent (if at all) the parties have been assisted by conciliation to resolve their disputes or any part of them by agreement.

Direction issued by the President with the concurrence of the Lord Chancellor.

D NEWTON

27 January 1971   Registrar

However, referrals to the divorce court welfare service for reconciliation have always been remarkably few: in 1974, there were 637, and in 1976, 549 (Murch, 1980). More recently, however, there have been much more vigorous attempts to develop services which expressly reject the old association with reconciliation and concentrate instead on conciliation. As yet, these have been locally-based enterprises, but an inter-departmental committee is currently investigating the possibilities of developing the concept more generally.

The main question for policy makers — apart from the basic question of whether further conciliation schemes should be promoted and supported from public funds — is what would be the best form for such schemes? In *Conciliation or Litigation*? (1982) Gwynn Davis offers some preliminary thoughts on the alternatives:

Independent Conciliation Services

Independent services will tend to be used at an early stage of divorce, often before a petition has been filed. This may provide a quick relief of tension for parents and children. Underlying resistances can be fully explored and the parties' emotional state taken into account. Conciliation early in the divorce may also offer a means whereby contact between the parties can be re-established and reasonableness shown. If this is achieved before entrenched positions are taken up, it may set the pattern for future negotiations.

In terms of savings to the legal aid fund, the value of conciliation at a pre-litigation stage is difficult to measure and therefore may be underestimated. First, there may be fewer problems to resolve when the parties eventually consult solicitors or approach the court. Secondly, the effect of conciliation may be to lighten the atmosphere generally. This is not measurable, but it is possible that there will be a 'carry over' effect to other issues.

The principal limitation of independent schemes is that it is difficult to see how they can be developed on a national scale. Independent services rely, almost by definition, on local initiatives. They are likely to be organised in different ways, enjoy varying levels of support from the courts and legal profession, and offer markedly differing services in many respects. This suggests that independent services cannot provide a uniform framework for a settlement seeking approach. However, they could provide a 'second tier' conciliation to which Registrars and Judges could refer.

Conciliation by the Divorce Court Welfare Service

A number of Divorce Court Welfare Services are seeking to expand their traditional role in order to include conciliation. However, there is doubt as to whether conciliation is fully compatible with the other responsibilities and values underlying divorce court welfare officers' work. First, welfare officers have to prepare reports for the court. Negotiations cannot be 'privileged' if the mediator also has a reporting function. Second, the focus of mediation is conflict resolution, whereas the divorce court welfare service is concerned predominantly with child welfare. Whilst the two values are not necessarily incompatible, a preoccupation with the welfare of the child may blur considerations of justice between the parties.

Such considerations may be offset by the obvious advantages attached to conciliation being undertaken by officers of the court. Furthermore, welfare officers may be aware of these limitations and be determined to offset them, as is the case with the Conciliation Bureau (Beckenham and Bromley) which is under the auspices of the South East London Probation and After-Care Service, but is run as a completely separate entity.

Mediation by Judge or Registrar

This normally involves the settling of specific legal issues usually within a single appointment. This mediation is likely to attract the confidence of lawyers and will also be viewed by the parties as carrying a measure of authority. It is said that conciliation comparatively late in the day concentrates the mind because the next stage would be a court hearing. It may also focus more efficiently on those matters which cannot be resolved by other means.

The main limitations of Registrar or Judge mediation are lack of time; the fact that some options may already have been foreclosed; and the likelihood that not all Registrars or Judges will be interested in, or skilled at, the task. If 'conciliation' is undertaken abruptly by a Judge or Registrar who is impatient or fearful of negotiating with the parties then it is unlikely to be of much value.

Mediation is not part of the traditional judicial role; it may also appear a suspiciously 'lightweight' procedure. On the other hand, it should always be regarded as a first, not a last resort. Furthermore, any method of dispute resolution involves the compromise of some values, whether these be of openness, proper rules of evidence, privacy for the parties, or responsiveness on the part of the court. It is important not to be too purist in our definition of the court's role so that we mimic a procedure better suited to other fields of litigation. The extent of the unresolved conflict encountered in interviews with divorcing parents suggests that many people 'give up' on disputes. In other words, the expense and cumbersome nature of court procedure acts as a rationing device.

Gwynn Davis has been conducting research into conciliation in Bristol where two schemes, which incorporate all three types mentioned above, are currently in operation. We turn to them in the next section.

Question

At this stage, which of the methods of conciliation put forward by Davis seems to you to be the best? Or do we need all three?

4 The Bristol schemes

Bristol is by no means the only place in the country to have set up a conciliation scheme, but its efforts are by far the best documented. In fact, there are two schemes, quite independent of but complementary to one another — the Bristol Courts Family Conciliation Service (BCFCS) and the 'in-court' conciliation procedure practised in the Bristol divorce court. The initiative for BCFCS came from local lawyers, social workers and others, who wished to put the Finer Report's recommendations on conciliation into practice. It is quite independent of the courts and was originally funded by a grant from the Nuffield Foundation, supplemented by contributions from the legal aid fund (for legally aided clients) and sometimes from the clients themselves. There is a co-ordinator, a secretary and a team of conciliators who are trained and experienced in marital and family work. The aims of the service were summed up by its co-ordinator, Lisa Parkinson, and one of the local solicitors involved, John Westcott, thus (1980):

> The Bristol courts family conciliation service is a pioneer scheme to help separating and divorcing couples to deal with the consequences of marriage breakdown. It provides a quick and informal means of clarifying confused situations and reducing conflict by mediating between the parties before formal proceedings are started. The aims of the service are to resolve actual or incipient disputes, especially where children are involved (eg over custody and access), and to promote parental co-operation, while helping the couple concerned to disengage from a broken marriage without undue bitterness and hostility.

In the *Bristol Courts Family Conciliation Service* (1982), Lisa Parkinson provides an account of their experience since the scheme was first launched in February 1978:

> We have found in Bristol that the four main factors influencing the use of the Conciliation Service are:
> (1) a clear definition of the meaning and objectives of conciliation;
> (2) the involvement of experienced legal practitioners in the planning and development of the scheme;
> (3) early availability and easy accessibility before contested court proceedings are embarked on;
> (4) independence of statutory welfare authority and of the stigma which may be associated with the exercise of that authority.

> **Definition**
> A precise definition of conciliation is important because it seems to have become a fashionable portmanteau word. Previously familiar in the context of industrial and commercial disputes it is now being applied not only to the resolution of matrimonial disputes but also more generally and ambiguously to the counselling of divorcing individuals. This is confusing both to professionals and non-professionals and makes the evaluation of conciliation even more difficult.
> We define conciliation as helping separating or divorcing couples to resolve disputes and reach agreed decisions on matters arising from the breakdown of their marriage (or established relationship), especially matters involving children. This definition adheres closely to the Finer Committee's definition . . . and is also very similar to definitions used in other countries. . . .
> Conciliation is not synonymous with divorce counselling because counselling may involve only one party and because counselling may take place on the periphery of the legal process, without addressing legal issues. Furthermore, counselling may continue over a long period, with abstract rather than practical objectives. Conciliation, in contrast, is concerned with helping both parties to reach consensual decisions on specific issues, in the short term. These decisions usually have major legal and financial implications and consequences. Therefore, it must be clearly understood that conciliation offers an alternative to contested court proceedings, not a substitute for legal advice and assistance. Conciliators work within a legal frame of reference because 'divorcing parents do not bargain in a vacuum . . . they bargain in the shadow on the law' (Mnookin, 1979).
> Conciliation should be distinguished from reconciliation (reuniting the parties), but conciliation does not exclude possibilities of reconciliation and a number of cases referred to BCFCS have led to reconciliation. In other cases, non-acquiescing respondents have come to terms with the irretrievable breakdown of their marriage. In our experience it is most important to define conciliation in terms that are acceptable to those seeking divorce and to those inclined to defend the divorce.

Relation to solicitors

We have found that, contrary to the popular image of the gladiatorial divorce advocate, many solicitors are very willing to adopt a conciliatory, agreement-seeking approach, rather than one which fragments the family by concentrating on such questions as, 'How much can I get?' Research by Davis at Bristol University has shown that experienced matrimonial solicitors in Bristol accept the need for a neutral intermediary and value this function, especially in relation to children. Maintaining parental ties and responsibilities, while disengaging from an irretrievably broken marriage, is an extremely complex and difficult task, especially as marriage breakdown is so often accompanied by failed communication — or very negative communication — between the spouses concerned. The conciliator quite frequently uncovers profound misunderstandings and distortions. The correction of these misunderstandings modifies the perceptions and attitudes of each spouse and consequently their presentation of the situation to their solicitor, and, by extension, the advice which the solicitor then gives.

It may not be possible to isolate disputes involving children from the related issues of the matrimonial home and ancillary relief. These interrelated issues produce a combination of social, emotional, legal and financial problems, which may need different kinds of professional advice and help. Parties to a dispute have a conflict of interests as individuals as well as a mutual interest in reaching settlement. A single neutral adviser is insufficient because the neutrality of one person may be, or become, suspect and may not adequately safeguard the individual rights and interests of the weaker party. Nor is it adequate, or even responsible, to rely solely on a system of separate legal advice and representation because in this system, the victims of the dispute, i.e. children, are not necessarily represented and insufficient priority may be given to them.

Conciliation provides a model which holds the balance between competing individual and family concerns and between the legal and non-legal aspects of the situation. The different professional standpoints and expertise of solicitors and conciliators complement each other, without duplication. Clients can have the advantage of both, and can opt either for a negotiated settlement, with continuing advice from their solicitor, or for trial of the issue by the court.

Agreements can be worked out in conjunction with separate legal advice to each party and with liaison between conciliators and solicitors. Applications to the court can then be made with consent. . . .

Early availability

Solicitors are frequently consulted on matrimonial matters long before a divorce petition is filed. We have found a particular need for conciliation at this early stage, especially during the critical period of separation, when long-term decisions are often taken hastily and under stress. Decisions taken at this time generally form the basis of the status quo which, later on, the court can do little other than approve. As the previous Lord Chancellor acknowledged, 'Inevitably, it is very difficult for the Judge to do more than approve whatever arrangements the petitioner proposes' (*Hansard*, 15 June 1976). There is great value, both for parents and children, in separating or separated parents discussing their options with regard to custody and access so that the Statement of Arrangements which is eventually submitted to the court is based on decisions to which both parties are likely to adhere.

The sudden, unexplained departure of one parent from the matrimonial home causes deep shock and distress to children. Some children become depressed and lose ground at school; others may act out their feelings in some form of delinquency. A recently published American study of 131 children, over a 5-year period, contrasts the grief and anger of children who felt abandoned by one parent, with the stability and contentment of children who maintained a loving relationship with both their parents, despite their separation (Wallerstein and Kelly, 1980).

Access arrangements need to be worked out at the time of separation. If there are difficulties, conciliation should be the first resort, not a last-ditch attempt. Long-standing access disputes are much harder to resolve if a pattern of rejection and counter-rejection has become established. The ultimate enforcement of an access order presents the court with severe problems.

Early conciliation can have both immediate and long-term benefits. Eekelaar and Clive's research on custody disputes stressed that 'there is room for adapting our procedures to the urgency of these situations in recognition of the importance of their resolution in the interests of the children concerned' (1977). Another research study carried out at Sheffield City Polytechnic by Burgoyne and Clarke [see also pp. 399–402, above] found that, in nearly every case studied, disputes arising at the time of separation had profound and long-term consequences, both for children and for the adults concerned, when they remarried.

Many separating couples need short-term help with a focus on the present and future needs of the family, rather than on recriminations about the failure of the marriage. We have observed that angry reactions to a punitively worded divorce petition may find expression in disputes over ancillary matters. Our experience supports Eekelaar's finding that the choice of 'fact' may have important repercussions on issues concerning children. Early conciliation can influence both the timing and the content of applications to the court and can avoid the court's time being wasted on unnecessary applications.

Quick accessibility
Marital breakdown often leads to a crisis, especially at the time of separation. There may be physical violence, and the risk of further violence. The risks of suicide and depressive illness are also much higher for separated individuals than for those in stable marriages (Morgan, 1979). Solicitors recognize the urgency of many of the situations on which their advice is sought, and need access to a service which can provide help without delay. In our experience, this service also needs to be directly accessible to the public. From one to five new cases may be referred in one day (many of them via the Citizens' Advice Bureau) and the Service has a carefully organized intake system which provides quick reception of appropriate referrals and the booking of appointments within a week of referral, or even on the same day. If the parties have not sought legal advice, we encourage them to do so, in conjunction with conciliation. Our simultaneous approach to them both may offer them a safety-valve for the release of pent-up emotion and anxiety. Their response indicates that this kind of safety-valve is greatly needed. It should be stressed, however, that conciliation involves considerable pressures; it is not suitable for inexperienced volunteers, however well-meaning. Conciliators need professional training and experience of marital and family work and a sound grasp of the legal process and of the legal frame of reference in which decisions are being taken. . . .

Acceptance of conciliation
The first requirement for effective conciliation is the voluntary participation of both parties. We find that this is considerably affected by the manner in which the offer of conciliation is made. A brusque or officious approach would act as a deterrent. Letters need to be carefully worded, explaining the purpose of conciliation and making it clear that the Service seeks to promote consensual decisions between the parties, not preconceived aims of its own. Clients seem to appreciate the fact that conciliators are not arbitrators and that they have no power to impose decisions, nor to make assessments which may influence a judicial decision. The distinction between conciliation, which takes place without prejudice to court proceedings, and welfare inquiries, which are reported to the court, is important for many people. They may have irrational fears about statutory powers to take children into care, or they may associate welfare agencies with criminality or social failure. An independent conciliation service, operating with the blessing of the courts, but not under their direction, encourages the parties to take responsibility for their own family arrangements. By doing so, it may also increase their capacity to work on their problems and to restore the self-esteem which is often damaged by the experience of marriage breakdown.

As mentioned, Gwynn Davis has been monitoring the scheme, and he reports some results in *Conciliation or Litigation*? (1982)

I have undertaken two separate studies of BCFCS. The first of these was designed to monitor the work of the service in its first year of full-scale operation and involved the study of all cases referred from 1 June to 30 November 1979. I also interviewed 40 Bristol solicitors whose clients had used the service. The second research was conducted from September 1980 to August 1981 and was aimed at measuring BCFCS' impact, if any, on the number and cost of applications for legal aid.

Outcome of conciliation through BCFCS
The first survey showed that the parties reached an agreement on all contested issues in 35% of cases in which both were seen; partial agreement, or agreement on some issues but not others, was achieved in 43%; and no agreements were reached in 21%. The overall level of agreements reached was slightly higher in the second study, with 40% of cases in which both parties were seen resulting in total agreement.

Both studies showed that BCFCS achieves a high level of agreement in disputes over the dissolution of marriage and on custody issues, with 54% and 58% complete agreement respectively. The outcome of conciliation on access tends to be less clear-cut (complete agreement in 43%, but partial agreement or an uncertain outcome in a further 34%).

Measuring outcome is often difficult. In some cases parties moved from previously entrenched positions, but without reaching firm agreement in the course of conciliation. In other cases there was an initial agreement, but this subsequently broke down. Conciliation may therefore be viewed as one factor in a very complex scene.

Solicitors' opinions of conciliation

The majority of cases in which conciliation took place were referred by solicitors, but self-referral has increased considerably as BCFCS has become better known. Of the 40 Bristol solicitors interviewed, 75% had referred cases to the service — a high proportion compared with Bristol solicitors as a whole.

These solicitors' attitudes to BCFCS were, for the most part, favourable and encouraging. The service was valued because it was non-partisan; because it could devote time to each case; and because it gave couples an opportunity to modify previously entrenched attitudes. The conciliator was also in a position to take into account each partner's emotional state and the needs of the whole family. Whilst most solicitors claimed to adopt a conciliatory approach, it was generally felt that BCFCS offered an important additional dimension.

A few solicitors were uneasy about the effect of a conciliation service on the solicitor/client relationship. There was also concern that clients might feel abandoned if referred to another agency. A minority felt that a conciliatory approach on the part of both solicitors was sufficient, without having recourse to a specialist service.

There was general agreement that matters of detail (notably in access arrangements) could best be tackled through a mediator, but some solicitors adopted a different approach with regard to custody or the matrimonial home, which were seen to affect the future of the family fundamentally. Financial or property disputes were on the whole regarded as inappropriate for conciliation.

There was no fear that BCFCS would be regarded as an alternative source of legal advice. There was, on the other hand, a general awareness of the shortcomings of the adversarial system in this field. This, coupled with the withdrawal of legal aid from the decree proceedings in undefended divorce, has led solicitors to find a separate conciliation service broadly acceptable.

The *Bristol In-Court Conciliation Procedure* was established in 1977, following an initiative from the presiding High Court judge and the setting-up of a specialist divorce court welfare service in Avon. It is described from the court's point of view by GM Parmiter, a registrar at Bristol county court (1981):

The 'In-Court' Conciliation Scheme

The scheme — at first, affecting only defended decree proceedings, but since extended to applications for custody and/or access — works as follows: first, the registrar identifies those cases in which there is no urgency and which are likely to be capable of settlement by solicitors without any intervention. These cases are then excluded . . . only to be caught up by the scheme at a later date if the registrar's initial assessment has proved to be incorrect.

In the remaining cases the court, of its own motion, gives an appointment for directions (to be known locally as a 'conciliation appointment'). This appointment calls for the attendance of the parties as well as their advisers (if any). Part of the success of the scheme depends upon the involvement of the parties in the court procedures in their litigation; part depends upon their presence to take part in the conciliation procedure.

Both parties attend with their solicitors, and frequently, the mere presence of all at the same time in the waiting area before the appointment without intervention enables constructive negotiations to take place for the first time, and a successful outcome to be arrived at. . . . The second stage is to go before the registrar. If the issue is more of law or fact, rather than involving the emotions, the registrar can assist by pointing the way towards possible resolution. . . . The real issues between the parties are often complex involving ancillary matters as well as the decree issues, and are often not apparent from the pleadings. Litigants in person often have difficulties in direct discussion with the other party's solicitor and attendance in the registrar's chambers helps to ensure confidence in the litigant in person. If the issues are emotional or involve children, the parties withdraw to the interview rooms with the duty welfare officer, [see further below] who adopts a combination of conciliatory investigatory techniques, as necessary. It should be recalled that the *Finer Report on One-Parent Families*, para 4.312 quoted with approval a paper by LV Harvey, who emphasised the 'considerable and important differences between a counsellor who is therapeutically involved with a client and the person who uses the same interviewing methods in order to assess the client's marriage' . . . 'In the second case, the interviewer is making judgments and assessments about the client. He will communicate these to others who will make decisions about the client.'

There has been much talk of the extent to which inquisitorial rather than adversary procedures should be used in divorce (*Finer Report*, para 4.405): it will be recognised that the investigation by the registrar is necessarily inquisitorial. This does not offend current court procedure as it does not result in his making a judicial determination on contested issues, merely consent orders.

If consent is not forthcoming, he reverts to treating the appointment as a normal directions appointment. The remarkable effectiveness and its humane appeal must in part lie in the use of the inquisitorial procedure, but also in its being used so early in the court procedure.

This procedure led to a dramatic reduction in defended divorce and was partially extended to disputes about custody and access. A similar procedure was introduced for contested custody and access cases in the Principal Registry of the Family Division in January 1983. Parmiter concludes his discussion of the Bristol scheme thus:

First, the experiments show conclusively the validity of the proposals set out in the *Finer Report* for conciliation as part of the family court process. Secondly, there are very clear benefits to the litigants arising from much speedier resolution of their problems as well as the elimination of bitterness. Thirdly, there are very clear and substantial benefits to the litigants and their children. Fourthly, there are very clear advantages to solicitors and savings to the legal aid fund. . . . Fifthly, there are substantial savings to the welfare service which are desperately needed if present delays in welfare officer reporting are to be contained. Although at Bristol there is a specialist divorce court welfare service, this is not necessary for the implementation of the procedure. All probation officers are trained in matrimonial matters.

Whilst there seems to be no possible reason for continuing to deprive litigants, solicitors and the state of their respective benefits achievable from the national adoption of these procedures (it requires no legislation, at most simple changes of the Matrimonial Causes Rules), there is a need for research. It is far from certain which scheme — either of those in Bristol, a combination of them or something completely different — is best.

This touches upon the problem of the relationship of welfare officers' conciliation work with their more traditional investigation on behalf of the court. The subject is taken up in the account of the same scheme given by the chief divorce court welfare officer, David Fraser, in *Divorce Avon style — The Work of a Specialist Welfare Team* (1980): he prefaces this extract by a reference to studies of *Custody after Divorce*, by Eekelaar and Clive, already discussed in Chapter 10:

If, generally speaking, the decision of the court is to leave the children where they are, then the role of the welfare officer can be seen more primarily as providing counselling and an opportunity for conciliation to help the parties adjust to the situation, rather than providing information to the judge per se.

If then, what we actually do is to provide a conciliation service, then is the format of the traditional divorce court report the best way to carry this out?

The experience of the specialist team over the past two years suggests clearly that often it is not. In fact there are indications that writing traditional divorce court welfare reports can be sometimes counterproductive of a true 'conciliation' effort. What seems to happen when the judge requests a traditional welfare report, is that the parties often perceive the judge as saying that he is going to ask the welfare officer to help him decide 'who is the better parent'.

Thus, the conflicts and bitterness which we see acted out in the worst possible way in the judicial arena, can become infused into the preparation of the welfare report. Each parent pushes into the welfare officer his and her anxieties, resentments and other conflicts. The reports can become, in effect, another arena in which the fight between the parents is to be managed. This is one of the reasons why welfare reports have tended to be very long [there is the shortest example we could find on p. 365, above], and why they are experienced by the inquiring officer as such emotionally charged exercises. Such an atmosphere often militates strongly against any true conciliation effort which an enterprising welfare officer might try to create.

In an effort to increase the effectiveness of the welfare officer's conciliation approach, a new form of intervention has been operated at the Bristol county court as a result of consultation and close cooperation between the welfare officers and the office of the registrar. This practice has involved the registrar in identifying an increasing number of cases for conciliation, instead of referring them for traditional divorce court reports.

The method is based on the attendance of the parties and their solicitors at directions hearings before the registrar, with a welfare officer in attendance. At these hearings the registrar asks how the solicitors have progressed in dealing with whatever issues are still being fought over. The emphasis of the hearing is to encourage the parties to conciliate with each other over the issues to be decided, and that it is in the interests of their children that further disputes should be avoided.

The registrar often adjourns the hearing to enable the welfare officer to discuss the problems with the parties. Some 'on the spot' conciliation work then takes place. In this situation the parties perceive the court as saying, 'we would like you to go away and work on this problem with the welfare officer.' This is very different from the perceived message when the court orders a traditional divorce court welfare report.

The welfare officers have found that this 'at the door of the court' setting has often been a very enabling one for them and the parties concerned. In many cases in two hours, or often less, the welfare officer has been able to identify some of the more poignant feelings which underlie the issues being fought over. These feelings are then worked with, and the parties helped to acknowledge them. This has often resulted in the parents being able to see the need for them to make some sensible plan concerning their children, and other issues which might affect them. Not all cases end so happily. But many do, with couples often expressing immense relief that an alternative method to fighting their way through their divorce has been offered to them.

In a good proportion of the cases worked with, parents have been helped by the welfare officer to reach agreement on a plan concerning their children and divorce, and thus have been constructively diverted from carrying on their fight by means of expensive defended hearings. This has resulted in an improved atmosphere and environment for the children, and in many cases has reduced the pressure that was bearing directly upon them. In this way the small specialist team of welfare officers has brought about considerable savings in money as a result of cases not being listed for further defended hearings. These have been costed out with some care, and the combined savings in legal aid, litigant and court fees for the first two years of operation now stands at £21,000. This sum is the result of 147 cases worked with successfully.

It is much easier to measure the cost savings of a scheme such as this than it is with a pre-litigation scheme such as BCFCS, for as Davis points out in the article quoted earlier, one can never be sure what would have happened had conciliation not taken place. These may be the cases (as the American quadrilogue suggested) which would have settled in any event; on the other hand, the impression of the BCFCS itself is that solicitors tend to refer the more difficult cases which they are unable to settle themselves (Parkinson, 1982).

Questions

(i) Are you convinced of the case for spending public money on conciliation services?
(ii) Which method (of those outlined by Davis on p. 644, above) now appeals to you the most?

5 The role of the courts

These procedural issues lead us into the fundamental question of the role of legal institutions in family breakdown. One view is that proposed by Mervyn Murch in *Justice and Welfare in Divorce* (1980), in which he puts forward a scheme for what he terms 'participant justice.' The basic principles of the scheme are described thus:

(i) Primary task
The participant model defines the primary task of legal and welfare processes in a new way. It starts from the assumption that there is a common objective about which all parties could reach agreement, even though they may differ as to the means of reaching that objective. This common objective is that of arriving at a fair and reasonable basis upon which the family can reconstitute itself following divorce, paying due regard to the interests of the children. In other words, the primary task of divorce machinery is to find a way of providing for the interests and welfare of family members after divorce. I doubt very much whether more than a small minority of divorcing parents would not subscribe to this objective, likewise few lawyers or welfare officers would dissent fundamentally.

(ii) Membership of the conflict-resolving system

Once it is accepted that there is a common objective, all the actors within the machinery of justice — judges, members of the Bar, solicitors, welfare officers and the family members themselves, who have temporarily become part of the system — can be perceived as being bound together in a common pursuit of an agreed objective. This becomes the task, and each actor within the system has a responsibility to work towards the common goal. To a large extent therefore the task of working towards the common goal becomes itself an authority from which the actors derive their responsibility and by which their roles are defined and differentiated.

This way of thinking perceives the courts, its welfare officers and the legal representatives combining together with family members to form a group or small organisation with the purpose of changing the divorcing couple's status, resolving conflict, and safeguarding according to law the welfare of the children. . . .

Two points must be kept in mind; first the notion that all the actors in the drama of divorce proceedings may be perceived as forming a temporary social system. By including the family members themselves within the boundary of the system, instead of seeing them as external to it, it becomes possible to see them as having an important contribution to make to the decision-making process itself. This is realistic because their perceptions and circumstances must be taken into full account. By their control of information which they may give or withhold to their solicitors, to the welfare officer, or to the judicial officers, they influence the decisions which the court can make. The participant model thus becomes a system which is dependent for its effective function on the collaboration of all its members. Their collaboration depends on trust. That is fostered by procedures based on openness, and by the frank recognition of the value of each member of the system.

Once the actors recognise that they are members of a system they more easily recognise their relatedness to each other. By contrast, more authoritarian approaches, particularly those based on the inquisitorial justice model or a preventive child welfare approach, start from the presumption that the family is to be regarded only as a social system distinct from the decision-making system. In a sense the family becomes an object to be processed. We have essentially two systems, the family and the legal machinery, confronting each other. This results in the reinforcement of all the attitudes that go with confrontation — mistrust, secret procedures, reluctant communication and so on.

The second point concerns the notion of a common primary task, and the assumption that members of the participant system can share a sense of commitment to a common purpose however elusive it may appear to them at times. But this means that the definition of the task by the actors within the system becomes a crucially important issue, since in order to pursue it they have to agree what it is. At present it seems the actors are frequently at cross-purposes. Judges, welfare officers and solicitors individually often define their tasks in different ways. Is it any wonder that parents and their children may feel confused and helpless? Such confusion arises from the interaction of competing philosophies, value systems and perceptions at work within a system that has developed pragmatically and rapidly within the last quarter century, in the absence of a clear policy.

The realities of divorce as they affect modern families are forcing the actors, whatever the nature of their assumptions, to acknowledge the most important issues — namely that a large and growing number of children are now affected every year by their parents' marriage breakdown; that the State cannot possibly assume more than a brief responsibility for their future welfare without enormous expense; that most parents wish to do the best they can in the circumstances for their children, and that it therefore makes sense to try to mobilise their resources and strengths in the pursuit of that objective; that when marriages break up some division of responsibility in relation to the future care of children and the family property has to be made. Decisions about all these matters must in the last resort be reasonably acceptable to the family members themselves if they are to stick and be made to work, and if the risks of future emotional conflict and litigation are to be minimised. Today no-one dissents from the Law Commission's view (1966) that one of the purposes of a good divorce law should be that:

> '. . . when regrettably a marriage has irretrievably broken down (the law should) enable the empty legal shell to be destroyed with the maximum fairness and the minimum bitterness, distress and humiliation.'

> . . . .

> 'Given the increasing acceptance by practitioners of objectives such as these, one must ask which strategies and tactics are most likely to contribute to a fair and civilised reorganisation of the family after divorce and what kind of machinery is needed to give effect to them. As I have already argued, the basic choice of strategies is between seeking to do things *to* and *for* families, or, by encouraging their participation, seeking to work *with* them towards agreed objectives.'

Questions

(i) Can you remember what the Law Commission thought the *first* objective of a good divorce law should be?

(ii) Murch based his proposals on his research evidence that 'there seemed to be a remarkable consensus about the kind of legal machinery that the majority of divorcing parents felt to be necessary.' Do you think that the *population as a whole* is ready to accept that the object of divorce machinery should be to enable couples to work together for the 'happy ending' of their marriage?

(iii) What do you think that the American bishop would have thought of this?

The actual scheme which Murch envisages involves a three stage process. In the first, the parties and their solicitors identify the issues, settle those which they can and refer others to a Bristol-type pre-litigation conciliation scheme. In the second, a new 'family tribunal' would perform four tasks — it would sift the documentary evidence in order to ascertain whether those matters in which the State has an interest were adequately made out (such as the breakdown of the marriage or the interests of the children), it would seek further information if the evidence were insufficient, it would grant orders by consent, and finally it would promote the settlement of any remaining disputes in a manner similar to the Bristol 'in-court' scheme. The third stage would be a 'family court' to adjudicate in a traditional manner upon matters which were still in dispute.

In *Towards a More Humane System of Divorce* (1981), Michael Freeman offers a criticism of Murch's scheme which is rather different from that implied by the questions posed above:

But is there a 'common objective' and, if so, who defines it? I suspect that an 'objective' is imposed *ex cathedra* and that it is not common at all. This, to use the author's own words, would 'cast the decision-maker in an elevated or superior position and the recipient in a dependent submissive role'. Murch's assumptions continue equally suspiciously: 'once it is accepted that there is a common objective, all of the actors within the machinery of justice . . . can be perceived as being bound together in a common pursuit of an agreed objective'. . . . This is to impute a consensus of goal and rationality of purpose to participants with different roles and ideologies. I do not believe in 'common pursuits' or 'agreed objectives' nor do I think that evidence adduced by Murch himself as to the way the different participants actually operate vindicates his own faith in their existence. Indeed, only a matter of pages later he tells us that the 'actors are frequently at cross-purposes. Judges, welfare officers and solicitors individually often define their tasks in different ways. . . . [There are] competing philosophies, value systems and perceptions at work within a system that has developed pragmatically and rapidly within the last quarter century in the absence of a clear policy'. . . . This is a lesson familiar to those who have watched the Children and Young Persons Act 1969 founder.

The trouble with participation, and Murch's blueprint does not, I think, overcome this, is that it can easily become a cloak to enable yet another group of professionals to take over. This has been the Scottish experience with their children's hearings system (see e.g., Brown and Bloomfield, 1979). I suspect also the introduction of an element of public participation is often geared towards making life easier for the decision-maker.

As to the scheme itself, Freeman sees scope for participant justice in the first stage, but even here he has a reservation:

The first is geared towards the promotion of informal settlement in the pre-litigation phase. [Murch] notes 'when people take their matrimonial problems initially to solicitors, the matter is essentially private to themselves and their legal representatives. It is only later, when it reaches court, that it becomes public'. . . . I doubt whether this distinction is tenable. As Mnookin has put it 'divorcing parents do not bargain . . . in a vacuum. Instead, they bargain in the shadow of the law'. . . . Public considerations inevitably intrude into the divorce process at all stages.

And of the tasks of the proposed 'family tribunal' Freeman is even more sceptical:

There is nothing revolutionary about the first three of these tasks which are currently accomplished by registrars or under the pursuance of a county court Judge or in the clerks' office of magistrates' courts. The fourth task is relatively innovative but the question must be asked as to whether it would enable the tribunal to become 'the forum for . . . participant powers'; even if these are limited to the investigation of evidence, [it] does not strike me as one likely to succeed in a goal of facilitating settlements. Murch wants a legal chairman: he wants (and would clearly get whether he wanted it or not) formal rules of evidence to apply. He does not want complete informality but he expects a 'friendly' and 'relaxed' atmosphere. But surely the point is, as Aubert has shown (1963 and 1967) that once a lawyer is brought in in an arbitral capacity compromise is well-nigh impossible, the problem is objectivized and the parties' freedom is restricted. Murch does nothing to indicate to me that this would not happen to his system. Tribunals deal in norms not interests; the past and not the future. I doubt if there is much scope for participant justice in stage two: a fortiori in stage three which raises once again the promise of a family court. This is to be 'a conventional body' . . ., hearing disputes 'in the traditional way'.

Finally

I, too, favour a family court concept but do not think the implications of the family court have been properly thought through. The concept is not as unproblematic as Murch, and others who urge its adoption, have assumed. Rather than seeing it as something new we ought to place it and demands for it into the historical context of the therapeutic state. Could it be that moves away from formal adjudication, of which the family court idea forms an essential part, are moves towards an intensification of control? Murch, to his credit, is concerned with rights and justice rather than treatment and therapy. But could the latter inevitably take over once the ideal was established? What is crucial is that 'experts' are controlled. That is why participant justice is so important and why I am disappointed that Murch's scheme, though purporting to focus on it, in reality gives it little scope.

Questions

(i) What do you understand by the term 'therapeutic state'? Do you feel threatened by it?

(ii) Even if you do not, did it occur to you to wonder why — if couples were to be allowed, even encouraged, to make their own arrangements — such an expensive and elaborate machine would be necessary?

These questions lead us to Professor RH Mnookin, whose article *Bargaining in the Shadow of the Law — The Case of Divorce* (1979) has been mentioned in several extracts. He begins:

I wish to suggest a new way of thinking about the role of law at the time of divorce. It is concerned primarily with the impact of the legal system on negotiations and bargaining that occurs *outside* of court. Rather than regard order as imposed from above, I see the primary function of contemporary divorce law as providing a framework for divorcing couples themselves to determine their respective rights and responsibilities after dissolution. This process, by which parties to a marriage are empowered to create their own legally enforceable commitments, I shall call '*private ordering*.'

The main part of the article consists of an examination of how couples might be expected to behave in their bargaining. Of the impact of substantive law he has this to say:

Divorcing parents do not bargain over the division of family wealth and custodial prerogatives in a vacuum. Instead, they bargain in the shadow of the law. The legal rules governing alimony, child support, marital property and custody give each parent certain claims based on what each would get if he or she simply went to court and had the court impose some allocation. In other words, the outcome that the law would impose if no agreement is reached gives each parent certain bargaining chips — an 'endowment' of sorts.

A simplified example might be illustrative. Assume that in disputed custody cases the law flatly provided that mothers had the right to custody of minor children and that fathers, on the other hand, only had the right to visitation two weekends a month. Absent some contrary agreement acceptable to both parents, a court will order this arrangement. Assume further that the legal rules relating to marital property, alimony, and child support gave the mother some determinant share of the family's economic resources — say one-third.

In the negotiations between divorcing spouses under this regime, neither would consent to a division that left him or her worse off than if he or she insisted in a court proceeding upon their legal entitlement. It might be fairly assumed that the mother would consider only alternative allocations of child time and money that made her at least as well off as this outcome. Her well-being would of course be measured by her own preferences. Similarly, the father would accept no negotiated outcome unless it made him better off by his preferences. Thus, the range of negotiated outcomes is limited to those that leave both parents as well off as they would be in the absence of a bargain.

It is of critical importance to understand that, if private ordering is allowed, we should not expect couples necessarily to split custody and money the way a judge would if they fail to agree. Through negotiations the father might well end up with more child-time and the mother with less. This result might occur for two different kinds of reasons. First, the father might make the mother better off by giving her more dollars to compensate her for accepting less child time. Alternatively, if the mother found custody burdensome, she might consider herself better off with less custody. Indeed, she might even agree to accept fewer dollars (or pay the father) if he agreed to relieve her of some child-rearing responsibilities. In all events, because the parents' tastes with regard to the trade-offs between money and child-time may differ, it will often be possible for the parties to negotiate some outcome that makes both better off than they would be if they simply accepted the result a court would impose. Any negotiated outcome will obviously be influenced by the preferences of the divorcing spouses. Moreover, differences in preferences concerning alternative outcomes will often create negotiating opportunities for the spouses.

Mnookin goes on to note that the process is complicated by the indeterminacy and discretion which the law currently favours in both child custody and property disputes, for not only will the outcome of litigation be more difficult to predict — the bargain will also be affected by the parties' relative willingness to take risks in pursuit of their respective desires.

Questions

(i) Does this not mean that the party who possesses a high 'bargaining endowment' (for example, the wife in a custody dispute) is bound to have an unfair advantage over one who does not?[1]

(ii) Should the law seek to be as neutral as possible in order to facilitate the bargain which suits the particular parties best?

(iii) But if it does that, how can the law define a criterion for adjudicating on those cases in which the parties cannot reach agreement?

Supposing, however, that the parties have reached agreement, Mnookin goes on to examine why it should be necessary for them to submit that agreement to a court at all. He examines four possible justifications for a judicial proceeding:

1. Ceremonial function
A judicial proceeding might be thought to serve a ceremonial function that re-confirms, both for the divorcing parties and the general public, the seriousness with which the state takes marriage and divorce. Rituals are important, and the court proceeding can be seen as a socially imposed divorce ritual. But as a ritual, the court proceeding for uncontested divorces, seems peculiar. . . .

---

1. How, for example, is it possible for a couple to reach sensible conclusions about the practical consequences of a divorce when one of them does not want to split up and the law permits him to delay matters for so long?

2. Review ensures fair outcomes: fairness between the spouses
The requirement of judicial approval of post-marital agreements might be justified on the ground that the state has an interest in ensuring that the results of the bargaining process are fair, as between the spouses. A judicial proceeding might protect people from their own ignorance, and might also be thought to prevent unfair results arising from unequal bargaining capacity between the spouses. These arguments have a plausible air, but the reality of the present day system might suggest that they mean very little in practice. Courts typically rubber stamp an agreement reached between the parties. Moreover, there are reasons to doubt that the requirement of judicial review is very often necessary for these purposes. There may well be cases where one spouse (presumably the husband) is highly sophisticated in business matters, while the other spouse (the wife) is an innocent lamb being led to the slaughter. But typically married couples generally have similar educational and cultural backgrounds. Moreover, most individuals perceive very well their own financial interests and needs at the time of divorce.

3. Effects on out-of-court settlements
It might be thought that the requirement that undisputed cases go to court, improves the private settlement process outside of court. Knowing that they will have to display their agreement to a judge, the parties (and their attorneys) may deal with each other in a fairer way and be more likely to reach an agreement reflecting the appropriate social norms. Behavioural scientists have suggested that the presence of an 'audience' can affect bargaining. With respect to out-of-court negotiations, the judge represents both an 'actual' audience and 'abstract' audience. He is an actual audience in that parties know that eventually they may have to explain their agreement to a judge. This may mitigate extreme claims. The judge also represents an abstract audience as well, which symbolically represents the social interests in the child and various notions of honour, reputation, and history.

It is extremely difficult to evaluate this argument, and to know how the requirement of judicial proceedings in undisputed cases affects negotiations in such cases. A requirement that disputed cases alone would go before a court might be sufficient to bring the 'audience' benefits to the process of negotiation. Moreover, it is possible that the requirement of judicial approval makes dispute settlement more not less difficult. For one thing, the requirement probably means that lawyers are more often involved in the process than would otherwise be the case. As earlier noted, it at least seems an open question whether having lawyers in the process facilitates dispute resolution in those cases where the parties might otherwise reach agreement anyway. Moreover, there is always the possibility that in the occasional case where the judge does upset the agreement reached by the parties, the eventual outcome may on balance be no more desirable (or even less desirable) than would otherwise be the case.

Mnookin's fourth possible justification is child protection and his arguments on this point are the same as those canvassed in the course of our discussion of s. 41 of the Matrimonial Causes Act 1973 in Chapter 10. His conclusion, however, brings us straight back to the conciliation debate:

If one accepts the proposition that disputes settlement should be the primary goal of the legal system, the analysis does not imply that the state should simply withdraw all resources from the process, and leave it to the divorcing spouses to work things out on their own, unassisted by any professional help. Instead, this inquiry should underline the desirability of learning more about how alternative procedural mechanisms might facilitate dispute resolution during a typically difficult and painful time in the lives of parents and children alike.

Question

We are, of course, civilised people: go back for a moment to the case of Barbara Auckland, with which we started this chapter, and ask yourself what sort of a legal system would best have catered for her family's needs?

Index